10,000
VITAL RECORDS OF
EASTERN NEW YORK

1777–1834

10,000
VITAL RECORDS OF
EASTERN NEW YORK

1777–1834

Fred Q. Bowman

Second printing, 1989
Third printing, 1999
Fourth printing, 2008
Library of Congress Catalogue Card Number 86-81711
ISBN 978-0-8063-1165-4
Made in the United States of America

VITAL RECORDS OF EASTERN NEW YORK, 1777-1834

(5192 marriages; 4920 deaths)

1.   ____, Isaac m 1/3/04 Charlotte Traver, dau of Jacob P., all of
        Clinton (Dut. Co.); Rev. Dodge (8-1/17)
2.   ____, John m 8/24/07 Pamelia Ward, dau of Col. Joshua of Pleasant
        Valley; Rev. John Cornwall (8-8/26)
3.   ____, Michael of Clinton (Dut. Co.) m 3/16/11 Polly Germond of
        Washington (Dut. Co.) (8-3/20)
4.   ____, Rebecca, 22, wf of B (name blurred) and dau of Capt. John Denny
        of Albany, d 2/22/31 in Louisville, KY (1-3/15)
5.   ____, Samuel, "a coloured man aged one hundred and five years", d 9/18/27
        in Hyde Park (was a family servant of late David Johnston) (8-11/21)
6.   ____, Thomas, Esq., attorney, of Palmyra m 10/8/18 Mrs. Eleanor Cuyler
        in Phelps; Rev. Townsend (8-10/28)
7.   ____, W. C., "nearly 8",s of late Capt. Alexander ____, drowned
        9/2/08 in Hudson (6-9/6)
8.   ____ay, Samuel m 6/22/23 Olive Grenell in Galway; Rev. Nott. All of
        Galway. (2-6/24)
9.   ____idge, Thomas Atwood,Esq., surrogate of Albany Co., m 9/1/24 Sarah
        Rivington, dau of James, in Albany; Rev. William B. Thomas (8-9/8)
10.   ____nds, Robert Esq., "an aged inhabitant of Rhinebeck", d in Rhinebeck
        (8-3/23/25)
11.   Abbatt, Elizabeth H., 23, wf of Daniel and only sister of George
        Chittenden, d 3/11/07 in Kinderhook (6-3/17)
12.   Abbatt, Robert, 74, formerly of Pleasant Valley, d 8/9/26 in NYC (8-8/16)
13.   Abbatt, William, 2nd son of Robert of Pleasant Valley, d 5/29/12 (8-6/3)
14.   Abbe, Joshua "of the District of Maine", merchant, m 8/20/15 Marcia
        Grosvenor at the home of E. Williams Esq. in Hudson; Rev. Chester
        (6-8/29)
15.   Abbey, Dorrephus m 1/8/16 Catharine M. Clark of Mount Pleasant, PA
        (9-1/9)
16.   Abbot, Jonas m 11/27/14 Harriet St. John, both of Brunswick; Rev. Coe
        (9-11/29)
17.   Abbot, Matthias m 7/15/07 Eve McChesney, both of Brunswick; Rev. Coe
        (9-7/21)
18.   Abbott, Caroline Frances, 18, oldest dau of James Esq. of Detroit, Mich.
        Terr., d 9/4/31 at the home of James Hands in Sandwich, Upper Canada
        (had gone to Canadain an attempt to escape scarlet fever then prevalent
        in Detroit) (1-9/16)
19.   Abbott, Esther, 55, wf of Daniel, d 12/9/07 in New Lebanon (6-12/22)
20.   Abbott, Jud m 1/19/06 Elizabeth Way; Rev. Coe? (9-1/21)
21.   Abeel, Garret, 72, formerly first judge of Greene Co., d 10/23/29 in
        Catskill (1-10/31)
22.   Abeel, Garret B., 61, d 12/21/29 in NYC (1-12/24)
23.   Abel, Daniel, merchant, of Cincinnati, OH m 6/17/30 Julia Goodman, dau of
        Simeon Esq. of Delhi, NY, in D; Rev. E. K. Maxwell (1-6/28)
24.   Abel, Ebenezer m 1/19/29 Esther Bailey, both of Sharon, CT, in Amenia, NY;
        Rev. C. P. Wilson (8-2/4)
25.   Ableman, Stephen Van Rensselaer of Albany m 5/4/31 Elizabeth B. Jarvis, dau
        of John Esq. of NYC, in NYC; Rev. T. Brientall (1-5/7)
26.   Abrams, Joseph m 5/9/25 Mrs. Lucy Ellis in Saratoga Springs (2-5/24)
27.   Ackerman, Gerloyn of Fishkill m 2/27/12 Martha Collins of Beekman; Rev.
        C. C. Cuyler (8-3/11)
28.   Ackerman, Isaac m 11/13/16 Maria Van Voorhis in Fishkill (8-11/20)
29.   Ackerman, Teunis m 12/22/30 Jane Thorn, dau of late Dr. James; Rev. M. W.
        Dwight. All of La Grange. (8-12/29)
30.   Ackert, Henry, 80, d 3/19/34 in Poughkeepsie (8-4/2)
31.   Ackert, William H. m 9/20/26 Margaret Bartley; Rev. C. C. Cuyler (8-10/18)
32.   Ackley, Calvin, 25, d 8/4/14 in Milford (3-8/11)
33.   Ackley, M. m 2/7/11 Betsey Richmond, both of Hudson (6-2/15)

1

34. Ackley, Thomas m Mehitable Becraft in Hudson (6-2/17/07)
35. Adam, Samuel F. of Canaan, CT m 4/17/05 Mary Sampson, dau of Rev. Ezra of Hudson (6-4/23)
36. Adams, Abigail, 74, consort of late Pres. Adams, d 10/28/18 in Quincy, MA (8-11/4)
37. Adams, Abner of Lisle (Broome Co.) m 11/22/28 Betsey Pennoyer, dau of Jonathan of Northeast; Rev. C. P. Wilson (8-12/3)
38. Adams, Alida, 55, wf of Elisha, d 9/6/10 in Brunswick (9-9/18)
39. Adams, Alson m 10/30/24 Sally Glen, both of Milton, in Galway; Rev. Samuel Nott (2-11/30)
40. Adams, Barent of Troy m 5/21/14 Maria Berry of Bloomfield; Rev. Coe (9-5/31)
41. Adams, Betsey, 35, consort of Capt. Nathaniel, d 8/18/07 in Troy (9-8/25)
42. Adams, Charles, Esq., 2nd son of the U.S. Pres., d 11/30/00 in NYC (8-12/16/00 and 3-12/18/00)
43. Adams, Charles, one of the proprietors of the Republican Herald, m 10/19/11 Cordelia Delavan, both of Poughkeepsie: Rev. Cuyler (8-10/23)
44. Adams, Charles, Esq., youngest son of the late President, m "Miss Brooks" in Boston (state not given) (8-9/9/29)
45. Adams, Charles, Esq., attorney, m Mary Ann Barrell in Burlington, VT; Rev. Ingersoll (7-1/4/34)
46. Adams, Charles C., proprietor of the Republican Herald, d 4/6/14 in Poughkeepsie ("pulmonary complaint") (8-4/13)
47. Adams, Chauncey m 10/9/23 Mary Benedict in Columbia (Herk. Co.); Rev. Huse (3-10/27)
48. Adams, Daniel, 102, d 2/28/11 in Cambidge (9-3/12)
49. Adams, Daniel, Jr. of Jaffrey, NH m 10/24/28 Betsey Holmes of Peterborough, NH in Troy, NY; Rev. Willis (double ceremony; see marr of Samuel Holmes) (9-10/28)
50. Adams, Daniel P., late editor and proprietor of the People's Press, m 12/17/29 Maria Seaver in Batavia; Rev. Lucius Smith (1-12/23)
51. Adams, David m 11/23/04 Sally Stephens, both of Carmel; Rev. Dodd (8-12/18)
52. Adams, Elizabeth (Mrs.), 91, d 5/2/07 in Plattsburgh (9-5/19)
53. Adams, Grace, 25, consort of Herman of Troy, d 12/29/22 (surv by husband "and three infant children") (9-12/31)
54. Adams, Henry of the firm of Boardman and Adams (printers and publishers of the Huntsville Alabama Republican) m 8/20/21 Mary Susan Fairchild of Troy, NY in T; Rev. Dr. Coe (9-8/21)
55. Adams, Hiram (Rev.), pastor of the Episcopal Church in Watertown, m 1/11/31 Harriet Brown, dau of Maj. S. Brown of Brownsville (Jeff. Co.) in B; Rev. Dorr (1-1/22)
56. Adams, Isaac (Lt.) of the U.S. Army and commander of the Arsenal in Baton Rouge, La, d 10/19/29 (yellow fever) (1-11/20)
57. Adams, James (Dr.) m 11/25/97 Susan Morrison, dau of Malcom Esq. formerly of Dutchess Co., in Schenectady; Rev. Dr. Smith (8-12/12)
58. Adams, James J. m 11/13/28 Hetty Ann Winne in Brunswick; Rev. Beman (9-11/18)
59. Adams, John of Milford m 4/3/23 Sarah Lane of Hartwick in H (3-4/7)
60. Adams, John, Esq., principal of Phillips Academy in Andover, MA, m Mrs. Mabel Burritt of Troy; Rev. Beman (1-9/10/31)
61. Adams, John m 11/10/31 Charlotte Turner; Elder Welch (1-11/15)
62. Adams, John R. m 10/3/30 Abigail Baker in Albany; Rev. Welch. All of Albany. (1-10/5)
63. Adams, Joseph m 10/28/15 Tinby Vanderheyden, both of Brunswick; Rev. Coe (9-10/31)
64. Adams, Leonard of Wilton m 12/12/28 Elizabeth Lansing, oldest dau of Richard of Saratoga, in S; Dr. Priestly (9-12/19)
65. Adams, Mary, 43, wf of Benjamin B., d 9/20/20 in Amenia (8-10/4)
66. Adams, Mary C., 2nd dau of Dr. Elijah late of Geneva and formerly of Fishkill, d 12/24/31 in Catlin "at the head of Seneca Lake"(8-1/18/32)
67. Adams, Moses of Sharon m 7/13/26 Almira Smith in Springfield; Rev. Andrew Oliver (3-7/24)
68. Adams, Nathaniel m 4/9/08 Clarissa Converse, both of Troy; Rev. Butler (9-4/12)
69. Adams, Nathaniel (Col.) d 3/9/23 in Troy (funeral from his late home "near the nail factory") (9-3/11)

70. Adams, Norman H. of Unadilla m 9/28/31 Caroline Frisbee of Rensselaerville
    at Trinity Church in R; Rev. Samuel Fuller (1-10/3)
71. Adams, Samuel A., Esq., 81, late governor of Mass., d 10/2/03 (8-10/18)
72. Adams, Schuyler, age blurred, d 12/13/30 in Albany (funeral from the
    home of his brothers, John R. and Nathaniel) (1-12/15)
73. Adams, Stephen G., Esq., of Buffalo, NY m 10/1/29 Lavina Hurd, dau of
    Jonas, Esq., of Middle Haddam, CT, in M. H.; Rev. Bently (1-10/19)
74. Adams, William (Dr.), 103, formerly of Schenectady, NY, d in Annapolis,
    MD "where he had gone to spend the winter with his granddaughter"
    (1-2/12/30)
75. Adancourt, Francis, editor of the Farmers Register, m 8/1/10 Lucinda
    Buckley of Athens, NY in A (9-8/7)
76. Addison, Robert (Rev.), 72, d 10/6/29 at his home, Lake Ledge, near
    Niagara (was for 38 yrs pastor of the Episcopal Church in Niagara)
    (1-10/17)
77. Addoms, Elizabeth (Mrs.), 91, d 6/2/07 in Plattsburgh (3-6/4)
78. Addoms, John (Maj.), 86, formerly of NYC, d 6/8/23 at his home at
    Cumberland Head (near Plattsburgh) (funeral sermon by Elder Bromley)
    (deceased had settled near Plattsburgh from Rockland Co. about 1793;
    member of Meth. Episc. Church from 1808 until death) (7-6/14)
79. Addoms, John Young, 3, half-son of Rev. John T. of Plattsburgh, d 9/17/18
    (7-9/19)
80. Adee, Hannah, 37, wf of Samuel H., d 12/6/32 in Pleasant Valley (8-12/12)
81. Adema, Jane, 46, wf of John G., d in NYC (9-1/2/27)
82. Adgate, Asa (Hon.), 64, d 2/16/32 in Keeseville (one of the oldest
    settlers there; former judge of Essex County Common Pleas; state
    assemblyman; and a Congressman in 1815-16) (4 [Keeseville Herald]-2/21)
83. Adgate, Charles m 8/31/31 Caroline Myrick in Birmingham; Rev. Lyman
    (double ceremony; see marr of Samuel S. Hickock) (4[Keeseville Herald]9/6)
84. Adgate, Harry of Chesterfield m 9/29/21 Lydia Olcott, dau of Phineas
    of Peru, in P; Horace Beach, Esq. (7-10/6)
85. Adgate, Luther of Chesterfield (Essex Co.) m 10/29/12 Nancy Lord, dau of
    Maj. Lord of Canaan, in C (9-11/10)
86. Adgate, Martin of Peru, "missing about 4 wks.", d "by accidental drowning"
    (per coronor's inquest) (his body found "in the river opposite the
    ship yard") (7-12/18/24)
87. Adgate, Matthew, Esq., 83, d 3/1/18 in Peru (served on the Committee of
    Safety during the Rev. War; was a delegate to the first state consti-
    tutional convention; state assemblyman; judge of the court of common
    pleas both in Albany Co. before its division and afterwards in Columbia
    Co. before moving to Clinton Co.) (7-3/7)
88. Adriance, Abraham, Esq., 59, formerly one of the judges of common pleas
    of Dutchess Co., d 9/30/25 in Poughkeepsie (8-10/5)
89. Adriance, Abraham of Fishkill m Mary Klapp, dau of Isaac B. of Union-Vale;
    Rev. M. Buttolph (8-10/8/34)
90. Adriance, Charles, d 9/16/32 in Poughkeepsie (8-9/19)
91. Adriance, George B. m 12/15/30 Sarah Thorn, dau of late Samuel, in
    Fishkill; Rev. Dwight. All of Fishkill (8-12/22)
92. Adriance, George C., hatter, (only brother of Capt. Cornelius of Troy),
    d 4/1/22 (consumption) (9-4/9)
93. Adriance, Hannah T., dau of Garret Esq., d 1/12/34 in Pleasant Valley
    (8-1/15)
94. Adriance, Helena, wid of late Theodorus, d 6/24/32 in Stormville (8-6/27)
95. Adriance, Jacob of Fishkill m 9/22/05 Polly Brill of Beekman; Rev.
    De Witt (8-10/1)
96. Adriance, John, 4, s of Garrett, Esq., d 5/6/12 (8-6/3)
97. Adriance, Maria (Miss) d 1/18/34 in Poughkeepsie (8-1/22)
98. Adriance, Richard Parmelee, 8 mo, s of John, d 2/18/34 in Poughkeepsie
    (8-3/12)
99. Adriance, Theodorus (Maj.), an aged inhabitant of Fishkill, d 5/14/17
    at his home in Fishkill (8-5/21)
100. Adriance, Thomas Edward d 2/17/32 in Richmond, VA. Also Harriet
     Newell Adriance d 2/20 (both of scarlet fever; both are children of
     Charles P. Adriance, formerly of Fishkill, NY)(8-2/29)
101. Adsett, Hiram of Pleasant Valley m 8/21/28 Phebe Barton of Stamford;
     Isaac Sutherland, Esq. (8-8/27)

3

102. Adsit, Samuel, 83, d 4/11/06 in Stanford (Dut. Co.) (8-4/22)
103. Agan, James, "over 70", d 9/15/27 in Brunswick (9-9/18)
104. Agur, William m 12/14/17 Mrs. Fanny Ingals, widow of late Erastus W. and
     dau of Peter Goodsell, in Burlington (Otsego Co.); Rev. Taylor (3-12/22)
105. Aiken, Aaron Burr of Greenbush m 4/6/30 Caroline C. Williamson of NYC
     in NYC; Rev. Thomas De Witt (1-4/10)
106. Aiken, Benjamin, 21, d 10/19/08 at the home of William Terny in
     Washington (Dut. Co.) (8-11/2)
107. Aiken, Benjamin, Sr. d "recently" in Greenbush (1-12/16/31)
108. Aiken, Edward, inf s of John, Esq. of Poughkeepsie (late one of the
     proprietors of the Poughkeepsie Journal),d 1/1/06 in Poughkeepsie
     (8-1/7)
109. Aiken, Isaac of Albany m 12/23/30 Hester Ann Ackerman, dau of James;
     Rev. M. W. Dwight (8-12/29)
110. Aiken?, John, Esq. m 1/4/03 Belephame? Cooke, dau of John, merchant, of
     Poughkeepsie; Rev. Chase (8-1/11)
111. Aiken, John, 3 yrs, youngest s of James, d 10/21/29 in Albany (1-10/22)
112. Aikens, William Sager, 6 mo., s of James, d 1/6/29 in Albany (1-1/8)
113. Aimes, Robert m 11/30/11 Amelia Doughty, both of Clinton (Dut. Co.)
     (8-1/15)
114. Aitken, Alexander m 6/22/31 Caroline Dusenberry, dau of late Richard Esq.
     of Albany, in NYC (1-6/30)
115. Akin, Daniel D. m 3/25/24 Sally Howard in Pawling (8-4/21)
116. Akin, John, Esq. of Troy, former editor of the Poughkeepsie Journal,
     d 11/22/08 at the home of Philip Hart in Washington (Dut. Co.)
     (surv by wf and 2 small ch.) (8-11/30)
117. Albert, Pierre Antonie, 40, (rector of the French Protestant Church
     du St. Esprit) d 7/19/06 in NYC (6-7/29)
118. Albertson, John B. of Hyde Park m 2/12/31 Dorotha Schryver of Clinton
     (Dut. Co.); Levi Van Vliet, Esq. of Clinton (8-2/23)
119. Albertson, Lucretia, 12, d 9/11/26 in Poughkeepsie (8-9/13)
120. Albertson, Richard T. m 6/7/27 Emeline F. Lamb; Rev. Howard. All of
     Troy. (9-6/12)
121. Albro, John A. of Troy m 8/20/22 Eliza Atwood of Lansingburgh (9-8/27)
122. Aldrich, Nicholas m 10/27/07 Cynthia Swift, dau of John, in Hudson
     (6-11/10)
123. Aldridge, Martha, 36, wf of Stephen, Jr., d 12/6/19 in Pittstown (9-12/14)
124. Aldridge, William m 2/26/24 Armenia Maxwell in Ballston; Rev. Reuben
     Smith (2-3/9)
125. Alerton, Archibald M. m 12/3/03 Rebecca Chamberlain, both of Amenia;
     Rev. Hernet (8-12/13)
126. Alexander, Joseph m 4/23/18 Rebecca Jacket, both of Lansingburgh; Rev.
     Luckey (9-5/5)
127. Alexander, Moses, 95, m 4/11/31 Mrs. Frances Tompkins, 105, in Bath
     (Steub. Co.); Rev. D. Smith (1-4/28)
128. Alger, W. F. (Dr.) m 9/16/33 E. Cochran in Plattsburgh; Rev. Heman
     Garlick. All of Peru. (7-9/21)
129. Allcott, Amos, late of the firm of Allcott and Langworthy of Ballston
     Spa, d 2/25/24 in Rochester (2-3/2)
130. Alld (sic), Samuel of Peterborough, NH m 12/31/23 Lydia Perry of Troy
     in T; Rev. Griffin (9-1/6/24)
131. Allen, Abraham of Clinton (Dut. Co.) m 12/18/16 Susan Ward of Poughkeepsie,
     dau of John I.; Rev. Jewitt (8-12/25/16)
132. Allen, Adelaide (Miss), 19, oldest dau of William, Esq. of Hyde Park,
     d 5/20/25 in NYC (8-5/25)
133. Allen, Amos m 9/3/17 Betsey Wilson, both of Troy; Rev. Dr. Coe (9-9/9)
134. Allen, Benjamin, Jr. m 8/2/12 Harriot(sic) Swift, dau of Capt. John, in
     Hudson (6-8/10)
135. Allen, Benjamin, L.L.D., of Hyde Park m 10/21/29 Sarah Starr of NYC at
     St. James Church in NYC; Rev. Dr. Milner (1-10/28 and 9-11/4)
136. Allen, Charles of Albany m (perhaps 1/20/20) Phila Webster of Canaan
     (possibly a double ceremony - see marr of Chester Burrows) (9-2/8)
137. Allen, Charles N., 23, d 1/29/28 in Amenia (consumption) (8-3/12)
138. Allen, Christopher, 27, d 3/13/13 in Cherry Valley (3-3/20)
139. Allen, Clinton m 7/16/18 Zilpha Winchel, dau of Martin, in Plattsburgh;
     Rev. Frederick Halsey (7-7/18)

4

140. Allen, Cyrus, 33, d in Otsego (3-11/28/25)
141. Allen, Daniel B. of Springfield, MA m 10/29/21 Elizabeth Cornell of Peru,
    NY, in Essex; Henry A. Hawley, Esq. (7-11/5)
142. Allen, David, attorney, of Huntington, CT m 5/23/99 Eliza Lansing, oldest
    dau of Cornelius, Esq. of Lansingburgh, NY (9-5/28)
143. Allen, Deborah, 62, wid of Thomas, d 2/6/22 in Plattsburgh (7-2/16)
144. Allen, Dorcas, 39, wf of Capt. Ebenezer, d 9/23/04 in Washington (Dut. Co.)
    (surv by husband and 8 small ch.) (8-10/9)
145. Allen, Ebenezer, 48, d 7/16/05 in Washington (Dut. Co.) (8-7/23)
146. Allen, Elizabeth L. H., wf of Hon. Heman, late minister of the U.S. to
    the Court of Chili, d 5/1/34 at Grass Mount, Burlington, VT (7-5/10)
147. Allen, Ethan B., Esq. m 7/26/12 Harriot (sic) Eliza Seymour, both of
    Hillsdale, in H; Rev. Somers (6-8/3)
148. Allen, Ethan R., oldest s of Capt. Ebenezer late of Washington (Dut. Co.),
    d 3/10/12 in Charleston, SC (8-6/10)
149. Allen, Ethan Z. m 7/20/26 Lydia Marsh, dau of Joseph C., in Chazy (7-7/29)
150. Allen, George m 9/19/13 Almira Olds, dau of Horace, in Plattsburgh
    (7-9/25)
151. Allen, George P., publisher of the Northern Spectator, m 1/14/34 Clarinda
    H. Hyde, oldest dau of Samuel, Esq. of Malone, at the Baptist Church
    in Malone; Rev. J. Howland Coit, rector of Trinity Ch., Plattsburgh
    (4 [Keeseville Herald]- 1/21)
152. Allen, Gideon, Esq. of Washington (Dut. Co.) d 3/29/18 (8-4/8)
153. Allen, Haywood T. m 11/3/32 Freelove Wilber; Daniel H. Schultz, Esq.
    All of Clinton (Dut. Co.) (8-11/14)
154. Allen, Hepsabeth, 40?, d in Hudson (6-12/12/20)
155. Allen, Horatio, Esq. of Hyde Park m 11/27/34 Mary M. Simons, dau of late
    Rev. J. Dewar Simons, in Charleston, SC; Rev. Christopher Gadsden
    (8-12/17)
156. Allen, Hosmer, 25, late teller of the Central Bank in Cherry Valley,
    d 10/16/24 in Winfield (3-10/25)
157. Allen, Isaac of NYC, 30, s of William of Pleasant Valley, d 12/12/28 in
    P.V. (surv by wf and "three infant children") (8-12/17)
158. Allen, Isaac M., Esq., one of the proprietors of the Cayuga Patriot
    (pub. in Auburn) m 8/18/31 Susan Mott of Skaneateles in S; Rev. Bruce
    (1-8/27)
159. Allen, Jacob of Clinton (Dut. Co.) m 11/11/18 Eliza Newcomb, dau of
    Christian of Poughkeepsie; Rev. Clark (8-11/18)
160. Allen, James, printer, late of NYC and formerly editor of the Chillicothe
    (OH) Times, d 3/8/31 in New Orleans, LA (1-4/9)
161. Allen, James H. m 4/23/28 Ann Eliza Frear, dau of Jacobus; Rev. Welton.
    All of Poughkeepsie (8-4/30)
162. Allen, John, Esq. of Red Hook d in NYC (8-1/25/09)
163. Allen, John, Jr. d 11/28/10 in Stanford (Dut. Co.) (8-12/5)
164. Allen, John, teacher and son of Capt. George, d 8/19/14 in Troy (9-8/23)
165. Allen, John, 33, recently from West Springfield, MA, d 5/30 near Catskill
    (was dragged by his team of horses after his fall from a load of logs
    on his wagon) (3-6/13/16)
166. Allen, Joseph m 1/8/29 "Mrs. Striker" of Washington (Dut. Co.) in
    Poughkeepsie; Rev. Welton (8-1/14)
167. Allen, Keziah, consort of Joseph, d 3/12/28 in Poughkeepsie (8-3/19)
168. Allen, Louisa (Miss), about 15, dau of John, d 5/9/23 in Plattsburgh
    (7-5/10)
169. Allen, Lovena, consort of Joseph, Jr. of Hudson, d 11/20/20 (6-11/28)
170. Allen, Lydia (Mrs.), 55, mother of late "Lt. Comandant" W. H. Allen of
    the U.S. Navy, d 1/7/23 in Hudson (7-1/25)
171. Allen, Maria C., wf of William, Esq., d 2/2/25 in Hyde Park (8-2/9)
172. Allen, Martha C., 15, dau of Asa K., d 6/18/29 in Rochester "by the
    rupture of a blood vessel" (1-6/23)
173. Allen, Mary, relict of John, Esq., "formerly of Philadelphia, deceased",
    d 7/22/02 in Red. Hook (Mary the oldest dau of David Johnston, Esq.
    of Dutchess Co.) (8-8/3)
174. Allen, Mary, 79, relict of late Benjamin, d 5/23/10 in Providence, RI
    (6-6/22)
175. Allen, Mary, 50, wf of Dr. Benjamin of Hyde Park, d 11/11/28 (8-11/12)
176. Allen, Nancy, 14, d 7/14/05 in Pittsfield, MA (6-7/30)

5

177. Allen, Richard m 3/9/25 Phebe Lamoree, dau of Timothy, all of Pleasant Valley (8-3/16)
178. Allen Richard (Rev.), First Bishop of the African Meth. Episc. Church, d 3/26/31 in Philadelphia, PA (1-4/5)
179. Allen, Ruth, 3, dau of Anson H. and Mary, d 9/12/31 in Keeseville (4 (Keeseville Herald)-9/13)
180. Allen, Sidney, merchant, of Rochester m 9/6/31 Lucinda A. Sheldon, dau of Aaron, Esq. of Rupert, VT, in Troy, NY; Rev. Beman (1-9/10)
181. Allen, Squire, 53, d 12/19/08 in Hudson (6-12/27)
182. Allen, Stephen (Dr.) m 11/24/08 Sarah Clement at the Friends Brick Meeting House (place not given) (8-12/7)
183. Allen, Submit, 87, relict of late Jabez, d 1/1/26 in Peru, NY ("one of the first settlers in this country") (7-1/7)
184. Allen, Thomas, Jr., Esq. of Pittsfield, MA m 9/15/04 Sally Ingersoll, dau of Jonathan, in Stockbridge, MA; Rev. West (6-10/2)
185. Allen, Thomas, Jr., Esq. of Pittsfield, MA d in Boston (state not given) (6-4/8/06)
186. Allen, Thomas (Rev.), 67, d 2/12/10 in Pittsfield (state not given; prob. MA) (6-2/22)
187. Allen, Whiteley, late of Plattsburgh, d 10/2/16 in Canandaigua (7-1/18/17)
188. Allen, William of Cazenovia d 6/25/00 (a tree he was cutting fell on him; he died instantly) (surv by wf and one ch) (3-7/17)
189. Allen, William, 18, m Betsey Kells, 11, in Granger (Col. Co.); Rev. Cobel (6-7/20/10)
190. Allen, William (Capt.), 56, d 10/16/14 in Cherry Valley (3-10/20)
191. Allen, William m 10/22/17 Sarah Beebe in Chatham; Rev. Joel T. Benedict. All of Chatham (6-10/28)
192. Allen, William H. (Dr.) of Providence (state not given) m Sarah Sanger, late of Burlington, VT and dau of late Rev. Dr. Sanger of Bridgewater, MA (7-11/16/33)
193. Allen, Zenas, Esq., 46, d 3/27/11 in Plattsburgh (had just moved from Vermont "and was getting into a profitable line of business") (buried with Masonic honors) (7-4/20)
194. Allen, Zimri E., 21, d 8/22/13 in Colchester (7-9/18)
195. Allendorph, Philip C. of Dutchess Co. m Cornelia T. Wiley of NYC in NYC; Rev. Dr. McElroy (8-11/9/31)
196. Allerton, Melton B., merchant, of Amenia m 1/20/25 Eliza Belden, youngest dau of Joseph of Amenia, in Washington (Dut. Co.); Rev. Willson (8-2/2)
197. Allyn, William G. of the firm of Allyn and Joslin m 5/13/29 Jerusha Brigs, oldest dau of Noah; Rev. S. C. Aiken. All of Utica (1-5/29)
198. Alston, Joseph, Esq. of South Carolina m 2/2/01 Theodosia Burr, only child of Hon. Aaron, Esq., in Albany, NY; Rev. John B. Johnson (9-2/10 and 3-2/12)
199. Alvord, Thomas G., Esq. m 2/15/33 Amelia Ann Kellogg, dau of A. Kellogg, Esq. (cashier of the Bank of Salina), in Salina; Rev. J. W. Adams (4 [Keeseville Herald]-2/26)
200. Ames, Benjamin m 10/30/03 Sarah Titus, both of Beekmantown; Samuel A. Barker, Esq. (8-11/22)
201. Ames, David m 12/14/17 Louisa Gordon in Poughkeepsie (7-12/20)
202. Ames, James m 3/21/29 Maria Van Zandt; Rev. Welch. All of Albany (1-3/25)
203. Ames, James m Sally Doughty in Washington (Dut. Co.); Rev. A. Bronson (8-2/23/31)
204. Ames, Robert N. of NYC m Mary Eliza Sands, dau of Griffith, Esq. of Locust Grove, L.I., NY, in Locust Grove; Rev. Clarke (1-9/7/30)
205. Amidon, Phillip m 10/8/22 Sally Child, both formerly of Sand Lake, in Batavia (9-10/22)
206. Ammerman, Peter, merchant, of NYC m 5/25/29 Mary W. Farrington of Newburgh in N; Rev. McCarrell (1-5/30)
207. Amsden, Abigail, 32, consort of Maj. Joel, d 5/19/12 in Malone (surv by husband and 2 small ch) (7-5/29)
208. Amsden, Manly, Esq. of Waterford, NY m 8/30/31 Sarah Amsden of Lebanon, NH in Lebanon (1-9/8)
209. Anderson, Augustus A., druggist, m 10/3/16 Sally Hathaway, both of New Berlin, in Norwich (3-10/10)
210. Anderson, Dominick m 12/24/20 "Miss Le Bar" (7-1/6/21)
211. Anderson, Henry James m 8/3/31 Frances dal Ponte, dau of Lorenzo, at St. Thomas' Church in NYC; Rev. Dr. Upfold. All of NYC (1-8/5)
212. Anderson, James m 10/29/28 Lorinda Hutchinson; Rev. C. P. Wilson. All of Northeast (8-11/12)

6

213. Anderson, John, 63, d 3/31/16 in Claverack (6-4/2)
214. Anderson, Joseph m 8/16/04 Elizabeth Stacy, dau of Isaac, in Cooperstown;
    Rev. Isaac Lewis. All of Cooperstown (3-8/23)
215. Andrew, Job m 4/27/22 Maria Andrew, both of Pittstown; James Mosher, Esq.
    (9-5/7)
216. Andrews, Aretus m Judith Folger, both of Hudson (6-8/19/06)
217. Andrews, Frederick, Esq., attorney, of Quebec, Canada m 7/21/30 Julian E.
    W. Whale, dau of Thomas of NYC, at St. John's Church in NYC; Rev. Dr.
    Onderdonk (1-7/26)
218. Andrews, George B. (Rev.), rector of the church at Sharon, Kent, and New
    Preston (all in CT), m 10/15/23 Sarah Newcomb Hitchcock of Amenia,NY at
    Christ Church in Sharon, CT; Right Rev. Bishop Brownell (8-10/22)
219. Andrews, Henry d 3/10/22 in Saratoga Springs (2-3/13)
220. Andrews, Loring, late one of the editors of the Charleston Courier and
    formerly of the Albany Centinel (sic), d 10/19/05 in Charleston, SC
    (9-11/12)
221. Andrews, Margaret, 50, wf of Thomas, d 6/4/32 in Union Vale (8-6/6)
222. Andrews, Mary (Widow), 89, d 6/12/24 in Milton (cancer) (deceased formerly
    of Ware, MA) (2-7/6)
223. Andrews, Mary Jenks, wf of Dr. Michael and dau of Ezra Coates of Milton,
    MA, d 7/31/20 in Berthier, Lower Canada (surv by husband, 2 small
    children, and numerous relatives and friends "in Massachusetts and
    New York" (7-8/19)
224. Andrews, Thomas, Esq. m 2/23/06 Margaret Cline, both of Beekman; Rev.
    Johnson (8-3/4)
225. Andrews, Cone, 46, a judge in Franklin Co., d 12/10/21 in Malone (8-12/15)
226. Andus, Stephen R. of Canada m 9/11/28 Amanda Melvina Andus of Troy in T;
    Rev. Samuel Merwin (9-9/16)
227. Angel, Amanda (Miss), 24, dau of Benjamin, d 11/3/23 in Burlington (Ots.
    Co.) (3-11/10)
228. Angel, Emily, 33, wf of William G., Esq., d 5/12/23 in Burlington (Ots.
    Co.) (3-5/19)
229. Angel, Ephraim m 10/5/11 Mary Thorne, both of Clinton (Dut. Co.); Rev.
    C. C. Cuyler (8-10/9)
230. Angel, Henry S. of Providence, RI m 4/29/32 Phebe Hopkins of Poughkeepsie,
    NY; Rev. Dr. Reed of Poughkeepsie (8-5/2)
231. Angel, Ira S. m 1/3/22 Lucy Angel on Angel Hill in Exeter; Rev. Dan Barnes
    "in the presence of nearly thirty Angels" (3-1/14)
232. Angel, Jeremy R., 14, s of Caleb of Exeter, d 9/27/11 in Cooperstown
    (3-9/28)
233. Angel, John B. m 3/31/18 Martha Tiffany, both of Burlington (Ots. Co.);
    Rev. Nash (3-4/6)
234. Angel, William of Milford m 9/13/20 Eunice Fairchild of Hartwick in
    Milford; Rev. Bowen (3-9/25)
235. Angell, Sally, 27, dau of Asa, d 9/21/26 at her father's home in New Berlin
    (3-10/16)
236. Angevine, Henry, Esq. of Poughkeepsie m 10/23/28 Caroline Jones, dau of
    Nathan of Pleasant Valley; Rev. Clark (8-10/29)
237. Angevine, Joshua C. of Poughkeepsie m 1/23/25 Sarah Ferris, 2nd dau of
    Solomon of New Paltz, in N.P.; Rev. Ostrom (8-1/26)
238. Angle, Katherine, 56, wf of Nicholas W., Esq., d 9/7/29 in Moreau
    (1-9/24)
239. Angle, Peter m 11/27/22 Almira Clark, both of Charlton, in C; Rev. Joseph
    Sweetman (2-12/10)
240. Annable, Joseph d "recently" near Whitehall (the funeral service appears
    to have been conducted in Albany) (1-9/26/31)
241. Annan, George Theodorus of Fishkill m 2/13/34 Lucy Myrick, dau of Samuel
    of Carmel, in C; Rev. Eli (8-2/19)
242. Anson, Ebenezer of Clinton (Dut. Co.) m 7/24/31 Mary Rinds of Washington
    (Dut. Co.) in W; Howard Tripp, Esq. (8-8/3)
243. Anthon, Henry (Rev.) m 5/27/19 Amelia A. Corre, dau of Joseph, at St.
    Paul's Church in Red Hook; Right Rev. Bishop Hobart (8-6/2)
244. Anthon, John, 72, d 3/12/34 in Fishkill (8-3/19)
245. Anthony, Nicholas of Fishkill m 11/27/28 Maria Klapp, dau of Col. David
    of Putnam Co.; Rev. Dewing (8-12/10)

246. Aplin, Betsey, consort of William and dau of Abner Pier late deceased,
     d 1/10/11 in Cooperstown ("within ... seven weeks four members of this
     family have fallen victims to the typhus fever") (3-1/12)
247. Aplin, Samuel m 10/21/24 Joanna Chase in Hartwick; Elder Bostwick
     (3-10/25)
248. Aplin, Thankful, 72, relict of late James, Esq., d 2/25/24 in Hartwick
     (3-3/1)
249. Arbottle, John m 5/10/06 Sophia Vassar, dau of James; Rev. Phillips.
     All of Poughkeepsie (8-5/13)
250. Archer, _____, 3, child of Richard, d 8/14/06 in Hudson (6-8/19)
251. Archer, Richard, 1, s of Richard, d 4/12/07 in Hudson (6-4/28)
252. Archibald, John m 12/31/23 Elizabeth Butcher; Rev. Beman (9-1/13/24)
253. Arden, John d 11/3/16 in Poughkeepsie (cancer) (8-11/6)
254. Arden, Thomas S., bookseller, of NYC d in Westchester (9-9/24/05)
255. Armington, Henry m 1/20/25 Aurelia Gates in Ballston; Rev. Anson (2-2/1)
256. Armisted, George G., Esq. m 11/7/31 Alice Virginia Fontaine, youngest
     dau of late Carter Fontaine, Esq. of Prince William, VA in Aldie,
     Loudoun Co., VA; Rev. Cutler (1-11/16)
257. Arms, J. Lyman, 41, d in Glens Falls (9-12/23/28)
258. Armstrong, Aaron m 7/7/10 Catherine Hoffman, both of Poughkeepsie; Rev.
     Covel (8-7/11)
259. Armstrong, Aaron, 39, formerly of Poughkeepsie, d 6/1/29 in Steuben Co.
     (consumption) (8-6/11)
260. Armstrong, Abigail (Widow), 85, of Hudson d 9/14/05 (6-10/1)
261. Armstrong, Alida, 60, wf of Gen. Armstrong of Red Hook, d 12/25/22
     "at the family mansion" in Red Hook (8-1/8/23)
262. Armstrong, Asahel, 82, d 4/3/25 in Hyde Park (8-4/6)
263. Armstrong, Betsey, dau of Moses, Esq., d 9/28/23 in Poughkeepsie (8-10/1)
264. Armstrong, Charles m 10/10/30 Phebe Smith, dau of William C.; Rev.
     Jewett (8-10/13)
265. Armstrong, George of Poughkeepsie m 3/12/34 Phebe Ann Hermans of Fishkill
     in Poughkeepsie; Rev. George Coles (8-3/19)
266. Armstrong, James, about 21, s of Robert of Lansingburgh, drowned 6/28/00
     "in crossing the creek ... about six miles below Albany ... "tried to
     swim ashore from a boat." (9-7/8)
267. Armstrong, Moses, Esq. d 1/10/27 in Poughkeepsie (8-1/17)
268. Armstrong, Richard, 99, d 4/26/23 in Ballston (2-4/29)
269. Armstrong, Thomas, "interpreter of the Seneca Mission, m 12/14/20 Rebecca
     Hemferman at the home of James Young near the Seneca village (double
     ceremony - see marr of Jonathan Jacket) (T. Armstrong and R. Hemferman
     are both white persons who were taken at the close of the Revolution
     "from the cradles of their parents") (Rev. Stephen N. Rowan, Pres. of
     the N.Y. Missionary Society, and Rev. Paschal N. Strong, corresponding
     secretary of the Society, witnessed this marriage) (9-1/2/21)
270. Armstrong, William m Chloe Paine, both of Amenia (8-12/11/16)
271. Armstrong, William of the firm of Matthew and William Armstrong of NYC
     m 4/7/28 Martha Ann Buckley, dau of William of Pine Grove, in Pine Grove
     (8-4/9)
272. Arnold, Alexander A. (son of Joseph, Esq. of Pawling, NY and member of
     the senior class in Yale College) d in New Haven, CT (8-1/11/26)
273. Arnold, Anson m 9/24/12 Sally Gardner, both of Troy; Rev. Coe (9-9/29)
274. Arnold, Archibald H. R. m 12/16/29 Catharine M. E. Saultz, dau of John
     F., all of Clinton (Dut. Co.); Isaac Sutherland, Esq. of Stanford
     (8-12/23)
275. Arnold, Ashley of Peru, NY m 10/7/33 Sarah A. Walker of Chesterfield;
     E. Williams, Esq. (4 [Keeseville Herald]-10/15)
276. Arnold, Benedict (Brig. Gen.), "notorious thro'out the world", d in England
     (9-8/11/01)
277. Arnold, David, Esq., 62, d 9/19/31 in Pawling (8-9/21)
278. Arnold, Ezekiel W. m 2/12/25 Mary B. Swan in Ballston Spa; Rev. Babcock.
     All of Ballston Spa. (2-2/15)
279. Arnold, Fluvia (Miss), 22, d 1/17/22 in Laurens (3-2/11)
280. Arnold, Fluvia, 5, dau of Rodney, d 3/17/25 in Milford (3-4/4)
281. Arnold, Freeborn Garretson, s of Rev. Smith Arnold, d 12/19/30 in Union
     Vale (8-12/22)
282. Arnold, Helen Maria McKeen, 34, wf of Benjamin, Esq., d 8/22/31 in
     Arnoldton on the Wallkill (Ulster Co.) (funeral from Friends Mtg. Hse.,
     Poughkeepsie) (8-8/24)

283. Arnold, Jacob m 10/18/31 Mrs. Betsy Peckham, both of Pawling, in
     Washington (Dut. Co.); Howard Tripp, Esq. (8-10/26)
284. Arnold, Jacob, 17, s of Joseph of Poughkeepsie, d 10/21/31 in NYC
     (8-10/26 and 1-10/24)
285. Arnold, James of Pawling m 10/28/31 Marcy E. Turrill of Pleasant Valley
     in P.V.; Rev. Dr. Reed (8-11/2)
286. Arnold, Lydia, 69, wf of Levi, d 2/2/31 in Poughkeepsie (8-2/9)
287. Arnold, Nathan, merchant, of Poughkeepsie d 10/9/09 (typhus) ("a young
     man") (8-10/18)
288. Arnold, Smith W. of Union Vale m 5/8/29 Maria Cross of Rhinebeck in R;
     Rev. Benedict (8-5/28)
289. Arnold, Susanna, 92, relict of Jacob, d 5/25/32 in Pawling (8-5/30)
290. Arnold, Thomas R., 24, d 9/11/26 in Hyde Park (8-9/13)
291. Arnold, Welcome, son of Ahab, Esq. of Clinton, m 10/24/05 Mary Row, dau
     of Bas____ Row of Northeast (8-11/12)
292. Artcher, Edward, merchant, of Albany m 10/7/29 Ann Whipple, dau of
     Malachi of Bern,in B; Rev. Van Wagoner (1-10/8)
293. Arthur, John D., merchant, of Catskill m 11/18/29 Dorinda H. Nelson,
     oldest dau of William, Esq. of Peekskill in P; Rev. Leggett (8-11/25 and
     1-11/23)
294. Arthur, Richard D.m2/20/30 Minerva Durming in Ticonderoga; B. Tomlinson,
     Esq. (1-3/24)
295. Ashby, James m 12/15/05 Polly Raiment, both of Fishkill; Rev. Barrit
     (8-1/7/06)
296. Ashby, James of Beekman m 11/24/31 Sarah Van Benschoten of La Grange in
     L.G.; Rev. P.P. Sandford (8-11/30)
297. Ashley, Henry (Hon.) d in Catskill (an early settler in that village)
     (1-1/27/29)
298. Ashley, James, 47, d in Middlefield (3-2/16/24)
299. Aspinwall, Gilbert, Esq., merchant, of NYC d 9/18/19 in Jamaica, L.I., NY
     (yellow fever) (8-9/22)
300. Aspinwall, Lewis of Albany m 5/9/31 Maria Murfey of Colchester, CT in C;
     Rev. Strong (1-5/16)
301. Atherton, Charles of New Marlborough m 12/12/32 Cynthia Maria Bennett
     of Poughkeepsie; Rev. Dr. Cuyler (8-12/19)
302. Atkinson, Kesiah (Mrs.), dau of James Vassar, d 4/27/34 in Poughkeepsie
     (funeral from the Baptist Meeting House) (8-4/30)
303. Atkinson, William B., a native of England but lately of Poughkeepsie,
     NY, d 10/3/25 in "Carracas, South America" (8-1/11/26)
304. Atwater, Caleb (Rev.) m 4/24/06 Diana Lawrence, dau of Col. Bigelow
     Lawrence, in Marcellus. All of M (6-5/13)
305. Atwater, Diana, wf of Rev. Caleb and dau of Col. Bigelow Lawrence of
     Marcellus, d 3/24/07 (along with her infant son) in Marcellus (she died
     "of a pleurisy") (6-5/26)
306. Atwood, Sarah (Mrs.), 30, dau of Abraham I. Myers of Fishkill, d 11/15/21
     in Newburgh (8-11/21)
307. Auchincloss, Arthur m Clarinda C. Thorne in NYC (6-3/29/03)
308. Austin, Alice, 29, wf of Seth, d 9/12/07 in Hudson (6-9/15)
309. Austin, John M., printer, m 10/4/28 Sarah Ann Somendyke, both of Troy, in
     NYC; Rev. Patton (9-10/7/28)
310. Austin, Jonathan, Esq. of Fort Edward m 10/20/30 Maria Reynolds, dau of G.
     Reynolds, Esq. of Moreau (Sara. Co.) in M; Rev. J. A. Clayton (1-11/2)
311. Austin, Oliver m Mary Slawson in Pittstown; Michael S. V. D. Cook, Esq.
     (9-12/15/07)
312. Averell, Horatio, merchant, m 3/3/23 Jane H. Webb, youngest dau of late
     Gen. Samuel B. of Claverack, in Cooperstown; Rev. Tiffany (3-3/10)
313. Averill, ____, 11 mo., ch of Nathan, d 4/11/19 (7-4/17)
314. Averill, Clinton Walworth, 6, s of J. K., Esq., editor of the Democratic
     Press, d 9/19/33 in Plattsburgh (7-9/21)
315. Averill, Emily Eliza, 4, dau of C. K., Esq., d 3/10/31 at Rouse's Point
     (7-3/22)
316. Averill, Henry, Esq. of Cooperstown m 8/5/30 Jane A. M. Russell of
     Claverack in C; Rev. F. Y. Tinney (1-8/12)
317. Averill, Henry K., Esq. m 5/29/24 Elizabeth Platt at Cumberland Head near
     Plattsburgh; Rev. Halsey. All of Plattsburgh (7-6/19)
318. Averill, James, Sr., 84, d in Cooperstown (3-11/15/19)

9

319. Averill, Joseph, about 14, s of Wyman Averill of Peru, NY, d 9/5/12 (fell under the wagon on which he was drawing rails) (7-9/11)
320. Averill, Rosannah, wf of Nathan, Sr., d "some days since" in Plattsburgh (7-1/8)
321. Averill, Stephen m 4/4/12 Susannah Moor, dau of Joel F., in Plattsburgh; Noah Broadwell, Esq. All of Plattsburgh (7-4/17)
322. Avery, Albert of Eaton (Mad. Co.) m 3/6/Orpah Ransom of Middlefield in M; Rev. Hazelius (3-3/10)
323. Avery, Humphrey J., 23, s of John H. of Owego, NY, d 7/21/31 in Petersburg, VA (1-8/13)
324. Avery, John m 12/23/23 Caroline Osborn; Rev. Tiffany (3-12/29)
325. Avery, Lewis m 3/4/24 Sally Black in Ballston; Rev. Reuben Smith (2-3/9)
326. Avery, Solomon, 25, d 6/20/08 in Hudson (6-6/28)
327. Axtell, _____, age 5, and Axtell, _____, age 3, d 1/26/21 "in the evening in the flames (when) the house of their father, a Mr. Axtell" in Pierpont (St. Law. Co.) burned (copied from the Potsdam Gazette) (7-2/3)
328. Axtell, Henry of Lawrenceville, NJ m Juliet Lay, dau of John, Esq. of Clinton (Oneida Co.), NY, in Clinton; Rev. D. C. Axtell (1-9/18/30)
329. Axtell, Phebe, 89, relict of late Maj. Henry and mother of Rev. Henry of Geneva, NY, d 7/6/29 near Morristown, NJ (1-7/21)
330. Aylsworth, Asahel m Sylvia Olmstead in Canaan (6-2/9/13)
331. Aylsworth, Sylvia, 21, wf of Asahel and dau of Nathaniel Olmsted of Canaan, d 4/13/14 in De Ruyter (Mad. Co.) (6-5/10)
332. Aylsworth, William D., 52, d 3/18/13 in Canaan (6-4/6)
333. Aylwin, John Cushing (Lt,) of U.S. Navy d 1/28/13 at sea on board the frigate "Constitution" (mortally wounded in the battle with the "Java")(3-3/13)
334. Ayres, Isaac of Troy m 12/30/22 Nancy Brown of Brunswick; Rev. Griffin (9-1/7/23)
335. Babbet, William, 17, s of Rev. James, d 3/5/31 in Jay (7-3/29)
336. Babbit, Christopher, 76, d 11/15/05 in Cooperstown (3-11/28)
337. Babcock, _____, 40, wf of Gardner, d 10/4/25 in Sherburne (Chen. Co.) (3-10/10)
338. Babcock, Cyrus, 20, d 6/30/21 in Westford (3-7/9)
339. Babcock, Daniel, 34, d 4/12/14 in New Canaan (state not given) (6-4/26)
340. Babcock, Edward m 12/9/28 Armina Eldridge in Troy; Rev. Mark Tucker. All of Troy (9-12/12)
341. Babcock, Enoch m 9/7/25 Betsey Prevost in Westford (3-9/19)
342. Babcock, Euphemia Augusta, 14, dau of late Frederick, Esq. of NYC, d 5/5/33 (8-5/8)
343. Babcock, Frederick, Esq. m Euphemia Hoffman, dau of late Anthony, Esq. of Poughkeepsie,in NYC (8-10/29/17)
344. Babcock, Gersham, 62, d 2/17/15 in Canaan (6-3/21)
345. Babcock, J. M. m Lydia Jackson in Rensselaerville; Rev. Henry Stead (1-9/29/29)
346. Babcock, John W., Jr. of Harpersfield m 10/13/31 Mary A. Lusk, dau of William, Esq. of Lisle,in Spencertown (Col. Co.); Rev. Joel Osborn (1-10-24)
347. Babcock, Josiah m 3/17/24 Lorinda Chapin, both of Broadalbin, in B; Elder Groom (2-3/23)
348. Babcock, Mary (Miss), dau of Christopher, d 5/25/30 at Coeymans Landing (1-6/3)
349. Babcock, Nichols H. of NYC m 11/29/31 Martha M. Hamlin of Beekman; Rev. Buttolph (8-12/7/31)
350. Babcock, Robert, 78, d 12/27/31 in Albany (funeral from 41 Maiden Lane) (his son-in-law Robert Holden [prob. of the Albany area] is mentioned) (1-12/28)
351. Babcock, Rufus, Jr. (Rev.) of Poughkeepsie m 5/11/24 Olivia Bicknell Smith, dau of Nathaniel, Esq., in Barrington, RI (8-6/2)
352. Babcock, Timothy m 1/30/28 Julia R. Purdy; Rev. Butler. All of Troy (9-2/1)
353. Bachelor, Elijah (Rev.), 49, minister of the Methodist Church, d in Homer (3-1/21/22)
354. Bachus, John, Esq., about 34, sheriff of Franklin Co., d 8/9/30 in Plattsburgh (1-8/26)

10

355. Backus, Asel (Rev. Dr.) Pres. of Hamilton College, d 12/29/16 at his home
at the college (born in Conn.; educated at Yale Col.; earned his B.A.
in 1787; ordained at Bethlehem, CT (6-1/7/17, 8-1/8/17, and 3-1/9/17)
356. Backus, Whiting of Hudson m 9/19/02 Lydia Parker of Loonenburgh (Athens,
NY) in L (6-9/28)
357. Bacon, Alonzo C., merchant, m Angeline Squires, youngest dau of Lewis, in
Binghamton; Rev. Marks. All of Binghamton (1-10/26/30)
358. Bacon, Cyrus m Melinda Guernsey, both of Ballston, in B; Rev. Sweetman
(2-5/8/22)
359. Bacon, Elijah C., 26, lately of Simsbury, CT, d 10/3/27 in New Paltz
(8-10/17)
360. Bacon, Hermitton, 2, s of William C., d 11/14/31 in Peru, NY (4 (Keeseville Herald)-12/6)
361. Bacon, Jesse, Esq., attorney, of Troy d 6/8/03 in Troy (9-6/14)
362. Bacon, Miriam, 74, consort of Benjamin, d in Canaan (6-11/15/14)
363. Bacon, Rufus, Esq. of Hamilton m 2/17/29 Eliza Bartholomew, a teacher
at Troy Female Seminary, at the Troy Female Seminary; Rev. Howard
(1-2/18)
364. Baden, Darius m 9/27/21 Elizabeth Field, both of Troy (9-10/2)
365. Badger, Ebenezer, 77, d 9/10/24 in Poughkeepsie (born in Cheshire, CT;
"early in life" became a member of the Episcopal Church)(8-9/15)
366. Badger, James, Esq., formerly of Poughkeepsie, m 1/9/07 Eliza Franklin
of Cayuga in C; Rev. David Higgins (8-1/27)
367. Badger, William, senior publisher of the American Traveller, m Sophia
Ann Cross in Boston, MA (1-7/23/30)
368. Badgley, Joshua, 28, s of Joseph, Esq., formerly of Saratoga Co., d 9/13/29
in Albany (1-9/16)
369. Bailey, Altie, 66, consort of late Col. John of Poughkeepsie, d 11/9/07
(8-11/11)
370. Bailey, Charles, 73, d 9/8/26 in Otsego. In the same entry: Sarah
Bailey, 72, d 9/13/26 in Otsego (relationship of these two not stated)
(3-9/25)
371. Bailey, Constant m 10/31/02 Lanenta Byington in Branford, CT (6-11/2)
372. Bailey, Eli W. of NYC m 6/21/34 Esther A. Whitney of Philadelphia, PA
in Philadelphia; Rev. T. G. Allen (8-6/25)
373. Bailey, Eli W. A., formerly of Poughkeepsie, d 8/1/24 in NYC (consumpt.)
(8-8/4)
374. Bailey, Eli William Augustus m 10/31/11 Alathea Power, both of Poughkeepsie;
Rev. Lossing (8-11/13)
375. Bailey, Elizabeth, 13, dau of John, d 12/4/33 in Fishkill (8-2/12/34)
376. Bailey, Henry A., 19, d 6/2/32 in Poughkeepsie (consumpt.) (8-6/13)
377. Bailey, James, Sr., 44?, d 6/1/18 in Plattsburgh (buried with Masonic
honors) (7-6/6)
378. Bailey, James, 62, of the firm of Bailey and Holmes of NYC d in Plattsburgh (8-8/8/32)
379. Bailey, John m 1/10/07 Sarah Waldry, both lately from Ireland; Rev. Coe
(9-1/13)
380. Bailey, John N., merchant, of Poughkeepsie m 9/18/02 Betsey Du Bois, dau
of Christian of Fishkill; Rev. Van Vranken (8-9/28)
381. Bailey, Joseph T. of Philadelphia, PA m Mary Potter, dau of late Sheldon
of Poughkeepsie, in Philadelphia (state not given); Rev. Bishop
Onderdonk (8-6/25/34)
382. Bailey, Lemuel (Capt.), 67, d 12/1/08 in Hudson (6-12/6)
383. Bailey, Louisa, dau of Dr. Rowland Bailey of Frederickstown, d 1/23/08
(funeral sermon by Rev. Dodd) (8-2/10)
384. Bailey, Nathaniel (Col.) m 12/31/05 Ann Willcox, both of Troy; Rev. Coe
(9-1/14/06)
385. Bailey, Rebecca, 26, consort of Gen. Theodorus and dau of Col. James
Tallmadge, d 8/28/07 in Poughkeepsie (surv by husband "and three infant
children") (8-9/2)
386. Bailey, Robert (s of Gen. Bailey, postmaster of NYC) d 1C/20/21 in NYC
(8-10/24)
387. Bailey, Samuel d 1/1/13 in Chazy (7-1/8)

388. Bailey, Tallmadge S. (possibly I.), 21, s of Gen. Bailey of Plattsburgh
     and grandson of Col. James Tallmadge of Poughkeepsie, d 4/29/19 on
     board the ship "Chauncey" lying at the Fejee (sic) Island (about 1816
     the deceased had commenced the study of medicine under Dr. Hosack; with
     a lung complaint he had sailed to Rio De Janeiro where the ship was
     seized and he for several days confined in a damp prison cell) (8-2/23/20)
389. Bailey, Theodorus (Gen.), "almost 70", postmaster of NYC, d 9/6/28 in
     NYC (8-9/10)
390. Bailey, Theodosius (Lt.) of U.S. Navy m 6/23/30 Sarah Ann Platt of NYC;
     Rev. Dr. Brownlie (1-6/28)
391. Bailey, Titus of Greenfield m 2/18/23 Isabella Canada of Marcellus in
     Galway; Rev. Reuben Smith (2-2/25)
392. Bailey, William, Jr., 22, s of Judge Bailey of Plattsburgh, d 10/16/24 in
     NYC (funeral sermon by Rev. Samuel W. Whelpley) (7-10/23)
393. Baily, Henry H. m 1/30/30 Rebecca S. Baker; Rev. Welch. All of Albany
     (1-2/3)
394. Baily, Samuel (Brig. Gen.), 60, d 5/25 in Greenfield (funeral sermon by
     Rev. Jacob St. John) (2-5/29)
395. Bain, Peter, 54, d 5/27/14 in Taghkanick (6-6/7)
396. Bainbridge, Mahlon of Romulus m 6/16/29 Roenna Burnett, dau of late
     Gen. Burnett of Phelps, in P; Rev. A. D. Lane (1-6/29)
397. Baker, _____, 2, only child of George, d 9/5/18 (killed when run down by
     a horse which had broken loose on Market Street in Poughkeepsie (8-9/9)
398. Baker, _____ (Mrs.) d 9/13/19 in Beekmantown (7-9/18)
399. Baker, _____, wf of Eddy Baker, d 11/1/22 in Malta, NY (2-11/12)
400. Baker, _____, wid of late Valentine Baker, d 11/29/26 in Poughkeepsie
     (8-12/13)
401. Baker, Abel d 6/8/19 in Hudson (buried with Masonic honors) (6-6/15)
402. Baker, Albert, Esq., 74, d 12/1/05 at Sandy Hill (Wash. Co.) (9-12/17)
403. Baker, Cenia(?), about 10, dau of Ozias and granddau of Daniel Baker,
     Esq. of Plattsburgh, drowned 7/10/26 in Plattsburgh (7-7/15)
404. Baker, Ebenezer C. m 1/9/29 Martha H. Spafford, dau of Dr. Spafford of
     Lansingburgh, in L; Rev. McIlvaine (1-1/15)
405. Baker, Edmund (Capt.), 88, (a Rev. officer) d 2/14/19 in Kinderhook
     (6-2/23)
406. Baker, George m 9/23/15 Jane Owen, both of Poughkeepsie; Rev. Smith
     (8-9/27)
407. Baker, George of Stillwater (Sara. Co.) m 1/11/24 Jemima K. Baker of
     Pleasant Valley; Alfred Raymond, Esq. (double ceremony - see marr of
     Valentine Baker) (8-3/17)
408. Baker, Jacob, 24, d 10/13/18 (in Poughkeepsie?) (8-10/21)
409. Baker, Jane, 19, wf of Capt. Samuel of U.S. Army and dau of Henry Barnes,
     d 3/22/15 in Poughkeepsie (surv by husband and a son 13 days old)
     (8-3/29)
410. Baker, John, merchant, of Albany m Eliza Chace of Lansingburgh in L
     (9-2/10/01)
411. Baker, John m 11/10/08 Betty Madough, both of Fishkill; Rev. Dr. Covel
     (8-11/16)
412. Baker, John d 12/7/16 in Plattsburgh (consumption) (7-12/21)
413. Baker, John of Poughkeepsie m 11/11/19 Sarah Hinckley of NYC in NYC;
     Rev. Dr. Clark (8-11/17)
414. Baker, John m 1/28/29 Mary Ann Schryver, dau of Peter A., Esq., all of
     Hyde Park; Rev. Dr. Cuyler (8-2/4)
415. Baker, Johnson m 10/14/29 Elizabeth Hulette in Clinton (Dut. Co.);
     Rev. Welton (8-10/28)
416. Baker, Joseph (Capt.), 31, d 9/25/02 in Lansingburgh (9-9/29)
417. Baker, Joseph W. d 7/18/20 in Plattsburgh (buried with Masonic honors)
     (7-7/22)
418. Baker, Leonard m 1/4/03 Abby Ranney, both of Lansingburgh; Rev. Close
     (9-1/11)
419. Baker, Lewis of Hyde Park m 9/1/30 Adeline Worden of Pleasant Valley;
     Rev. Wile (8-9/15)
420. Baker, Mariah, consort of Nehemiah and dau of Mr. Belina Buck of Troy,
     d 8/3/22 (9-8/13)
421. Baker, Mary (Miss), 20, dau of late Valentine Baker, d 9/27/19 (in
     Poughkeepsie?) (8-9/29)

12

422. Baker, Nehemiah of Plattsburgh m "a few days since" Maria Buck, dau of
     Bilinia Buck of Troy, in Troy (7-11/25/20)
423. Baker, Peter m 1/18/12 Jane Ann Tompkins, both of Poughkeepsie; Rev.
     Clark (8-1/22)
424. Baker, Peter, s of Valentine, d 9/28/24 in Poughkeepsie (8-10/13)
425. Baker, Samuel, Esq., atty, m 12/7/16 Ann De La Vergne, dau of Dr. Isaac,
     all of Pleasant Valley, at the home of John De La Vergne in Fishkill;
     Rev. C. C. Cuyler (8-12/11)
426. Baker, Valentine of Stillwater (Sara. Co.) m 1/11/24 Sylvia Baker of
     Pleasant Valley; Alfred Raymond, Esq. (double ceremony - see marr of
     George Baker) (8-3/17)
427. Baker, William, Esq. of Springfield m Bianca Crane, dau of Dr. Rufus of
     Warren (Herk. Co.) in W; Rev. Aaron Putnam (3-3/6/26)
428. Baker, William Edwin, 2, s of Solomon, printer, d 12/30/28 in Albany
     (1-1/1/29)
429. Balch, Benjamin m 4/24/19 Ann Van Benthuysen, both of Troy, in Lansing-
     burgh; Rev. Dr. Blatchford (9-5/4)
430. Balding, ____, relict of Isaac, deceased, d 3/7/14 (8-3/16)
431. Balding, Isaac d 10/4/11 at his home in Staatsburgh (8-10/9)
432. Balding, Isaac I. of Poughkeepsie m 5/13/25 Mrs. Sarah Budd of Fishkill;
     Rev. Thomas De Witt (8-5/18)
433. Balding, Theophilus (Capt.) d 3/13/18 (in Poughkeepsie?) (8-3/18)
434. Baldwin, Abiah, 51, wf of Ebenezer of Poughkeepsie, d 8/1/03 (8-8/2)
435. Baldwin, Clarissa Ann Elizabeth, 1 yr, dau of Charles, Esq., d 12/28/08
     (8-1/4/09)
436. Baldwin, Ebenezer, 53, d 7/6/08 in Poughkeepsie (8-7/20)
437. Baldwin, Ebenezer m 10/3/21 Thusday (sic) Murray, both of Whitehall;
     Rev. (surname blurred) (9-11/6)
438. Baldwin, Frederick of Catskill m 2/5/04 Lucretia Goodrich of Claverack
     in C; Rev. Gephard (6-2/14)
439. Baldwin, James M. (Midshipman), 22, of U.S. Navy d 7/30/15 (death the
     result of a wound received 9/11/14 on Lake Champlain)(7-8/5)
440. Baldwin, Johnson of Butternuts m 9/9/22 Mary Baldwin of Cooperstown in C;
     Rev. Smith (3-9/16)
441. Baldwin, Johnson G., merchant, m 6/17/24 Jane Broadwell of Newark, NJ at
     the Sans Souci Hotel in Ballston Spa, NY (2-6/22)
442. Baldwin, Joseph of Hudson m Polly Mandell, dau of Ephraim of Harpersfield
     (6-8/30/08)
443. Baldwin, Lora, 15, 2nd dau of Joseph, d 9/10/13 in Cooperstown (3-9/11)
444. Baldwin, N. A. of Oakland, Mich. Terr. m 5/30/30 Margaret Roseburgh, dau
     of James, Esq. of Groveland (Liv. Co.) in G; Rev. Bull (1-6/15)
445. Baldwin, Normand, 20, d 1/25/25 in Pleasant Valley (born in New Milford,
     CT; member of Bapt. Ch.; had lived in P.V. for only "the past 9 months")
     (8-2/2)
446. Balis?, Smith m 4/20/34 Emeline Darling; Rev. Low. All of Amenia (8-5/7)
447. Ball, Charles. See, possibly, Bill, Charles.
     Ball, Heman (Rev.), D.D., 56, d in Rutland, VT (3-1/21/22)
448. Ball, Hiram m 11/3/28 Eliza Ann Bush; Rev. Richardson (8-11/19)
449. Ball, Martha (Mrs.), 56, d 11/26/87 in New Hackensack (8-12/5)
450. Ball, Stephen (Dr.) m 9/27/31 Caroline Chase, dau of "Mr. Maria Chase",
     in Auburn; Rev. Josiah Hopkins. All of Auburn (1-10/1)
451. Bancroft, Edward of Becket, MA m 1/16/06 Amanda Lewis of Troy, NY; Rev.
     Coe? (9-1/21)
452. Bancroft, Thaddeus F. of Albany m 2/28/29 Evolinah Bancroft of Geddes
     (Onon. Co.) in G; Rev. Bibbens (1-12/23)
453. Banker, Ezra m 5/27/32 Eliza Whitney in Peru, NY; Rev. Heman Garlick
     (7-6/2)
454. Banker, John, Sr., 87, d 2/14/21 in Plattsburgh (7-2/21)
455. Banker, Nehemiah of Plattsburgh m 10/29/20 Maria Buck, dau of B. Buck
     of Troy (9-10/31)
456. Banker, Platt N. m 12/30/21 Thankful Marshal in Plattsburgh; Rev. Halsey
     (7-1/5/22)
457. Banker, Thomas H., 1 yr, s of John, d 3/10/18 in Plattsburgh (7-3/21)
458. Banks, Edmund P., 24, late editor of the Belvidere (NJ) Apollo, d
     "recently" in Easton, MD ("He took an effective leave of his readers
     some months since in an article entitled "The Last Paragraph", his
     having burst a blood vessel which rendered his recovery helpless
     (1-6/19/30)

13

459 _____ (This was an erroneous posting now deleted)
460. Banks, William m 6/16/21 Mary Vanorder, both of Troy (9-6/19)
461. Bantam, William m 7/10/31 Marion Jones; Rev. Dr. Ludlow. All of
     Albany (1-7/15)
462. Banyar, Goldsborough, Jr., Esq. m 4/22/01 Maria Jay, oldest dau of Gov.
     Jay, in Albany; Rev. Thomas Ellison (9-4/28)
463. Banyer, Goldsbrow, Esq. d 11/19/25 in Albany (9-11/21)
464. Barber, _____, wf of Amos, d 9/23/20 in Beekmantown (7-9/30)
465. Barber, Amos m 12/2/21 Clarissa Orton in Plattsburgh; Rev. Whelpley (7-12/8)
466. Barber, Elliot m 6/2/24 Eliza S. Stevens, both of Poughkeepsie, in P;
     Rev. Babcock (8-6/9)
467. Barber, Gideon m 12/31/12 Priscilla Taylor, both of Greenbush (9-1/5/13)
468. Barber, John, publisher of the Albany Register, d in Albany (6-7/19/08)
469. Barber, John, 50, "printer to the state", d 7/12/08 in Albany (8-7/20)
470. Barber, Ralph m 9/8/04 Sally Coffin in Loonenburgh (Athens) (6-9/11)
471. Barber (possibly intended for Barker), Robert, 26, s of Jacob of NYC,
     d 12/24/30 on board the ship "Mobile" "on her passage from New York for
     Buenos Ayres" (1-3/23/31)
472. Barber, Simeon, 23, d 4/15/11 in Peru, NY (small pox) (7-4/26)
473. Barclay, Thomas (Col.), 77, late British Consul to the U.S., d 4/21/30
     in NYC (8-4/28)
474. Barculo, Seward, attorney, of Poughkeepsie m 5/12/34 Cornelia Tallman, dau
     of John H. of NYC, in NYC (8-5/14)
475. Bard, Mary, 74, d 5/24/21. Her husband, Dr. Samuel Bard, d 5/25/21.
     Both died at their home in Hyde Park. "Mrs. Barton", age 90, d 5/28/21
     at the home of Dr. Bard in Hyde Park (8-5/30)
476. Bard, Susan Mary, dau of late John, d 10/28/31 in Hyde Park (1-11/3 and
     8-11/9)
477. Bard, William, Esq., s of Dr. Samuel of Hyde Park, m 10/7/02 Catharine
     Cruger, dau of late Nicholas of NYC, in NYC (8-10/12)
478. Baremore, James, 71, of Pleasant Valley d 5/9/32 (8-6/6)
479. Bargy, Polly, wf of Peter of Schuyler, d "instantly" while attending a
     ball at Schuyler (7-1/16/19)
480. Baright, Stephen of Ithaca m 5/7/31 Julia Ann Swartwout, youngest dau of
     Robert, Esq. of Perryville, in P; Rev. John Carle (1-5/30)
481. Barker, Caleb of the firm of Barker and Lockwood, merchants, of Pough-
     keepsie m 9/29/19 Rachel W. Sands, dau of Benjamin of Marlborough, at
     the Friends Meeting House in Marlborough (8-10/6)
482. Barker, Edward of Clinton (Dut. Co.) m 2/5/31 Eliza Lee of Poughkeepsie;
     Rev. Jewett (8-2/9)
483. Barker, Esther (Mrs.), 87, mother of Samuel Augustus, Esq., d 10/31/14 in
     Beekman (8-11/9)
484. Barker, George m 8/24/23 Maria Peck, dau of Nathaniel, in Amenia; Rev.
     C. I. Wilson (8-8/27)
485. Barker, James m 4/29/21 Areta Roberts, both of Plattsburgh, in P; Rev.
     Frederick Halsey (7-5/5)
486. Barker, Margaret, consort of Caleb, d 1/28/18 in Poughkeepsie (surv by
     husband "and little children")
487. Barker, Peter B. m 7/4/30 Sarah Jenkins, dau of Thomas, Esq.,(all of
     Hudson) in Troy; Rev. Stebbins (1-7/10)
488. Barker, Pierre Augustus, merchant, of Philadelphia (state not given),
     son of Gen. Samuel A., m 7/18/12 Ann Livingston of Dover, NY; Rev. Clark
     (8-7/22)
489. Barker, Richard (Capt.) m Catharine Rabine in Hudson (6-9/11/04)
     Barker, Robert. See, possibly, Barber, Robert.
490. Barker, Samuel Augustus (Gen.) m 12/15/99 Meredith Collins, dau of
     Hezekiah, Esq., all of Beekman. (8-12/17)
491. Barker, Samuel Augustus (Gen.), 63, d 11/19/19 at his home in Beekman
     (fought in the Rev. War; served repeatedly in the state legislature)
     (8-11/24)
492. Barker, Samuel S. m 12/8/31 Mary Ann Eggleston in Palmyra; Rev. E.
     Blakesley (1-12/20)
493. Barker, William J. of Canada m Caroline Cornell, dau of William of
     Clinton (Dut. Co.) , at the Friends Meeting House in Clinton (8-3/12/34)

14

494. Barlow, John Charles, 14 mo, s of Lemuel, d 8/14/18 in Plattsburgh (7-8/22)
495. Barlow, Lemuel d 3/17/22 in New Orleans, LA (7-5/22)
496. Barlow, Mansfield, printer, m 3/4/27 Eliza M. Daniels in Troy; Rev. Howard. All of Troy (9-3/6)
497. Barnard, Abishai (Capt.), 63, d 6/28/15 in Hudson (a long-term resident there) (6-7/11)
498. Barnard, Abner (Dr.) of Lockport m Harriet Jane Hepburn of Perinton in Pittsford; Rev. A. Mahan (1-6/16/29)
499. Barnard, Charles E. of Cooperstown m 12/8/16 Lorinda Osborn, dau of Elnathan of Middlefield, in M; Rev. John Smith (3-12/12)
500. Barnard, Christopher m 12/13/10 Betsy R. Little (6-12/28)
501. Barnard, Frederick J. m 2/28/20 Emmeline White, dau of Dr. Samuel, in Hudson; Rev. Stanton. All of Hudson (6-2/29)
502. Barnard, James m 9/27/28 Mary Kirkpatrick; Rev. Samuel Merwin. All of Troy (9-9/30)
503. Barnard, Love, 32, wf of Capt. Enoch of Hudson, d 7/10 in Claverack (6-7/22/06)
504. Barnard, Mary, 73, wid of late Capt. Joseph, d in Hudson (6-1/21/06)
505. Barnard, Mary, 70, relict of late Capt. John, d 5/10/16 in Hudson (6-5/14)
506. Barnard, O. F. H. m Susan Ransom, dau of Col. Asa, in Ransom Grove (Erie Co.); Rev. Shelton (1-12/3/30)
507. Barnard, Sarah W., consort of Hon. D. D., member of Congress from NYC, and dau of late Henry Gilbert Livingston, Esq. of NYC, d 3/2/29 in Washington City, Dist of Columbia (1-3/8)
508. Barnegl (sic), ____ (Mr.) d 10/12/15 at Cumberland Head near Plattsburgh (surv by "a large dependent family") (7-10/14)
509. Barnes, Alexander F., 4, s of Dr. John, d 11/22/31 (8-12/7)
510. Barnes, David Henry, inf s of David, d 9/4/27 (8-9/12)
511. Barnes, Enos (Dr.) m 6/22/14 Rebecca Wickes, dau of Silas; Rev. Clark. All of Clinton (Dut. Co.) (8-6/24)
512. Barnes, Horace m 1/18/24 Phebe Parsons, an adopted dau of Elias Woodruff, in Plattsburgh; Rev. Whelpley (7-1/24)
513. Barnes, James N. of New Milford m 11/21/27 Charity Ives of Kent in Amenia; Rev. A. Bronson (8-12/12 and 8-12/19)
514. Barnes, John m 3/31/14 Maria Harris, both of Poughkeepsie; Rev. Cuyler (8-4/6)
515. Barnes, Noah, about 2, s of Jeremiah, d 7/9/18 in Plattsburgh (7-7/11)
516. Barnes, Phebe, wf of Jeremiah, d in Beekmantown (7-2/17/27)
517. Barnes, William m 11/25/32 Jane Ann McLean, both of Poughkeepsie; Rev. Dr. Cuyler (8-11/28)
518. Barnes, William, 39, formerly of Fishkill Landing, d 3/5/34 in NYC (8-3/12)
519. Barnet, Caleb D. m Caroline Clark, dau of Douglas, Esq.; Rev. T. Winter. All of Northeast (8-3/19/34)
520. Barnet, John, Jr. m 12/11/12 Pamelia Knapp; Rev. John Barnet. All of Amenia (8-12/16)
521. Barney, John of Troy m 4/23/18 Ann Griswould of Nassau. NY; Rev. Dr. Coe (9-4/28)
522. Barney, John m 5/23/20 Thankful Low in Middlefield; Elder John Sawin. All of Middlefield (3-5/29)
523. Barney, Lewis, 105, d 1/16/13 in Champlain (7-1/29)
524. Barnham, Minerva, 11, 2nd dau of Caleb, d 12/9/03 in Meredith (6-12/20)
525. Barns, Hellen, 16, dau of Richard, Esq., d 1/27/12 in Chatham (6-2/3)
526. Barns, Moses d 7/2/14 in Cooperstown (buried with Masonic honors in the Presbyterian burying ground)(3-7/7)
527. Barns, William, Jr. m Susan Fowler, both of Pittstown, in Schaghticoke (9-9/3/05)
528. Barnum, Ephraim P. of Amenia m 12/14/23 Rebecca Ward of Washington (Dut. Co.); Rev. Silliman (8-12/24)
529. Barnum, Moses, Jr., 25, d in Stockbridge (crushed by a saw-mill log) (6-2/2/13)
530. Barnum, Philo B., publisher of the Gospel Messenger, m 9/2/30 Augusta Foster of Auburn in A; Rev. Dr. Rudd (1-9/11)
531. Barnum, Thomas B. of Newtown, CT m 9/16/24 Harriet Rose of Amenia, NY in A; Rev. C. P. Willson (8-9/22)
532. Baron, Charles Samuel Swartwout of Belmont, OH m 4/22/30 Mary Wilhelmine ... Zieglar of Marietta, OH in M; Silas Cook, Esq. (8-5/9)

15

533. Barr, Martha (Miss)d 12/14/24 in Amenia (small pox) (for many years a member of the Methodist church)(8-12/22)
534. Barratt, Ezra m Diana Blin in Canaan; Rev. Morse (6-1/19/13)
535. Barritt, James C. m 5/1/22 Maria Strang, both of Fishkill; Rev. Barrett (8-5/29)
536. Barron, Jonathan, merchant, m Louisa Smith, dau of Ella (sic) Smith, Esq., in Le Roy; Rev. Beckwith (1-10/12/31)
537. Barrow, Thomas J., merchant, of NYC m 3/10/31 Mary W. Brown, dau of Henry C., Esq., in Pittsfield, MA; Rev. Tappan (1-3/19)
538. Barrows, E. S. (Rev.) of Pompey m 5/7/22 Catherine C. Fuller, dau of Dr. Thomas, in Cooperstown; Rev. Putnam (3-5/13)
539. Barry, Ann (Mrs.) (age blurred), d 7/2/31 in Albany (funeral from the home of "Mrs. Cochran" on North Pearl St.) (1-7/4)
540. Barstow, Samuel, merchant, m 6/27/29 Mary Tyler Blossom, dau of late Elisha, Esq.; Rev. Shaeffer. All of NYC (1-7/1)
541. Bartholomew, _____ (Mrs.) d "recently" in Albany (funeral from her late home, corner N. Market and Lumber Sts.)(mentioned are Andrew Bartholomew [possibly her husband] and her son-in-law, Andrew Kirk) (1-10/11/31)
542. Bartholomew, Mary, wf of Capt. Andrew d 10/9/31 in Albany (funeral from her late residence, corner N. Market and Lumber Sts.) (1-10/10). See Entry 541 above.
543. Bartlet, Charles, 20, d 12/7/19 in Hudson (6-12/14)
544. Bartlett, Dudley m 7/28/24 Mabell Otis, dau of Perez, Esq., in Galway; Rev. Nott. All of Galway (2-8/3)
545. Bartlett, Henry W. m 1/3/24 Lydia Parks, dau of David, Esq.; Isaac Sutherland, Esq. All of Stanford (Dut. Co.)(8-1/7)
546. Bartlett, Hiram m 1/4/19 Mary Ann Fisher in Hartwick; Elder Bostwick. All of Hartwick (3-1/11)
547. Bartlett, John S. of the firm of A. Fitch and Co. m 7/28/30 Sarah A. Dibble in Auburn; Rev. Dr. Richards. All of Auburn (1-8/6)
548. Bartlett, Joseph, 43, d 6/21/08 in Hudson (consumption) (6-6/28)
549. Bartlett, Joseph of Charlton m 9/9/25 Mary Ann Otis of Galway in G; Rev. S. Nott (2-9/20)
550. Bartlett, Joseph of Stanford (Dut. Co.) m 1/1/29 Eliza Swift of Washington (Dut. Co.); Isaac Sutherland, Esq. (8-1/7)
551. Bartlett, Joshua B., 62, d 10/29/33 in Jay, NY("Printers in Vermont and New Hampshire will please notice the death") (deceased is survived by "several children")(4 [Keeseville Herald]-11/5)
552. Bartlett, Laura, 46, wf of Dr. J. B. Bartlett, d 10/12/32 in Jay Lower Vil. (4 [Keeseville Herald]-11/13)
553. Bartlett, Samuel Lathrop of NYC, 24, d at the home of Mrs. Thurston near Hudson (6-9/6/14)
554. Barton, Amos A., 63, d 7/8/25 in Stanford (Dut. Co.) (8-8/10)
555. Barton, Cyrus, Esq., editor of the New Hampshire Patriot, m Hannah Hale in Keene, NH; Rev. Sullivan (1-7/13/29)
556. Barton, Ebenezer C., Esq., sheriff-elect of Rensselaer Co., m 11/21/31 Harriet Cone, dau of Dr. Timothy, in NYC. All of Lansingburgh (1-12/1)
557. Barton, Francis m 7/21/27 Susan Homes, both of Troy; Rev. Howard (9-7/31)
558. Barton, Henry W. of Kingston m 9/15/27 Jane Ann Law of Poughkeepsie; Rev. C. C. Cuyler (8-10/3)
559. Barton, Hiram m 2/15/27 Laura Sherman, dau of William, in Stanford (Dut. Co.); Rev. Wilson (8-2/21)
560. Barton, James m 3/8/27 Elizabeth Smith; Rev. Howard. All of Troy (9-3/13)
561. Barton, Johnson m 3/12/26 Sally Tompkins in Smithfield; Rev. R. G. Armstrong (8-3/22)
562. Barton, Martha, wid. of late Roger, d 10/7/18 in Fishkill (8-10/14)
563. Barton, Michael H., editor of Something New, m 7/18/30 Sarah French of Tewksbury, MA in Charlestown, MA (8-8/4)
564. Barton, Peter m 3/11/28 Henrietta Wilson; Rev. Willis. All of Troy (9-3/14)
565. Bartow, William A. of NYC m 4/15/26 Jane Hasbrook, dau of Tunis, Esq. of Fishkill, in F; Rev. De Witt (8-4/26)
566. Bascom, Ashel m 5/27/32 Mary Anne Gould in Leedsville; Rev. W. Hutchinson of Amenia (8-6/6)
567. Bassett, Eleanor, 69, relict of Capt. John of NYC and mother of Rev. Dr. Bassett, d 7/25/05 in Albany (funeral sermon by Rev. Dr. Miller at the Boght) (9-7/30)

16

568. Bassett, Joseph m 3/22/27 Elmira Rose in Amenia; Rev. Bronson (8-4/4)
569. Bates, _____ (Rev.) of Keeseville m 4/26/33 Minerva Reid, dau of William,
    Esq. of Amsterdam, NY, in A; Rev. Wood (4 [Keeseville Herald]-5/7)
570. Bates, Augustus S. of Troy m 7/8/27 Eliza McCradle of NYC in NYC; Rev.
    Monteith (9-7/13)
571. Bates, Benoni m Susan Wires in Hartwick (3-3/28/25)
572. Bates, Chloe, 66, wf of John, Esq. formerly of Granville, MA, d in
    New Hartford, NY (6-12/5/09)
573. Bates, Daniel m 7/9/17 Harriet Patterson, both of Troy; Rev. Dr. Coe
    (9-7/15)
574. Bates, Isaac of Coventry (Chen. Co.) m 8/17/23 Mahitable Cunningham of
    Hartwick in Laurens; John Blood, Jr., Esq. (3-8/25)
575. Bates, Merritt (Rev.) of Burlington, VT m 7/16/34 Mrs. Eliza Ann Woodward
    in Plattsburgh; Rev. S. D. Ferguson (7-7/26)
576. Bates, Phineas, 80, d 11/15/29 in Canandaigua (settled there in 1789)
    (1-11/30)
577. Bates, Simeon, 86, d 10/9/24 in Milford ("Thirteen grandchildren followed
    him to the grave.") (3-11/1)
578. Bates, William m 12/30/21 Clarissa Sampson in Plattsburgh; Rev. Halsey
    (7-1/5/22)
579. Battel, Martha, wf of Joseph of Durham (Greene Co.) and sister of Josiah
    Sherman of Albany, d 10/30/29 at the home of her son, Minott Mitchell,
    Esq. of White Plains (perhaps Minott is her son-in-law?)
580. Battey, Robert, merchant, of Peru, NY m 11/2/12 Susan Ketchum of Platts-
    burgh in P; Rev. W. R. Weeks (7-11/20)
581. Battey, Robert, 2, s of Robert, d 1/17/21 in Peru, NY (7-1/20)
582. Bauman, Sebastian (Col.), 64, postmaster of NYC, d 10/19/03 in NYC
    (8-10/25)
583. Baxter, Carline P., 2, dau of Jotham and Ann, d 4/28/34 in Chazy (7-5/10)
584. Baxter, Jotham m 1/16/26 Ann McFarland in Chazy; Rev. Byington. All of
    Chazy (7-2/18)
585. Bay, Harman, Esq., 46, d 12/7/31 in Claverack (1-12/10)
586. Bay, Mary (Miss), 37, dau of John, Esq., d 11/26/08 in Claverack (6-12/6)
587. Bay, Thomas, inf s of Thomas, Esq., d in Hudson (6-12/12/20)
588. Bayeux, Cynthia, 19, dau of Henry B., d 1/10/15 in Troy (9-1/17)
589. Bayeux, Henry F. (Capt.) m 6/26/23 Martha Louisa Vail, both of Troy;
    Rev. Beman (9-7/1)
590. Bayeux, Thomas (Capt.) of the firm of Rogers and Bayeux m 5/11/31 Sarah
    Ann Topping; Rev. Welch. All of Albany (1-5/13)
591. Baylies, Francis (Hon.) of Taunton, MA m 6/23/22 Elizabeth Deming, dau of
    Howard of Troy, in Nassau, NY; Rev. James Romeyn (9-7/9)
592. Beach, Aaron, 95, (a Rev. soldier) d in Chittenden, VT (b Wallingford, CT
    in 1725; served under Gen. Pepperell at the taking of Louisburg)
    (7-7/6/22)
593. Beach, Edward, merchant, m 9/9/34 Louisa Van Kleeck, dau of late Teunis;
    Rev. Samuel A. Van Vechten. All of Poughkeepsie (8-9/10)
594. Beach, Miles, merchant, m 4/18/07 Cynthia Warren in Ballston; Elder Elias
    Lee (9-5/19)
595. Beach, Samuel (Dr.) m 6/24/17 Susan Maria Jervis, niece of John W.
    Bloomfield, Esq., in Constantia; Rev. John Dunlap. All of Constantia
    (3-7/10)
596. Beadle, Clarence, 7 mo., s of Daniel W., d 5/6/30 in Poughkeepsie (8-5/9)
597. Beadle, Clarence D., 1 yr., s of Daniel W., d 7/28/34 in Poughkeepsie
    (8-7/30)
598. Beadle, Daniel W. m 9/3/17 Clara Power, both of Poughkeepsie (8-9/4)
599. Beadle, Edward L. (Dr.) of Hyde Park m 10/14/32 Adeline Bogert, dau of
    James, Jr., Esq. of NYC, in Hyde Park; Rev. William Cahoone (8-10/17)
600. Beadle, James d 3/2/16 in Cooperstown (3-3/7)
601. Beadle, Richard, 21, only surviving s of Timothy, d 3/22/05 at the home of
    his father in Clinton (consumption) (deceased is surv by two small daus,
    eight children having died previously) (8-4/2)
602. Beadle, Timothy, Jr., s of Timothy of Clinton (Dut. Co.) d 2/27/01 (8-3/3)
603. Beadle, William, farmer, of Beekman (Dut. Co.) d 11-29/04 (8-12/4)
604. Beal, Horace of Hillsdale m 10/30/13 Sally Shaw, dau of Noah of Chatham,
    in C; Rev. Waters (6-11/9)

17

605. Beal, Louisa, 2, dau of Lewis and Permela, d 7/14/16 in Hudson (6-7/23)
606. Beale, Lewis of Hudson m 6/4/08 Permela Frisbee, dau of Col. Philip of
    Canaan; Rev. John Waters of New Concord (6-6/14)
607. Beale, Timothy, an old inhabitant of Washington (Dut. Co.) d 8/2/11
    (8-8/7)
608. Beall, Samuel W., Esq. of Marlborough, MD m 5/24/29 Elizabeth Fenimore
    Cooper, dau of late Isaac, Esq., in Cooperstown, NY; Rev. F. T. Tiffany
    (1-6/2)
609. Beam, Jeremiah m 1/16/34 Catharine Wagar, both of Red Hook; Rev. William
    J. Eyer (8-1/22)
610. Beam, John of Rhinebeck m 12/6/26 Anna Hawver (possibly Hawven) of Clinton
    (Dut. Co.); Tilley Crouse, Esq. (8-12/13)
611. Beard, Stephen, 30, d 7/2/02 in Packersfield, NH (hydrophobia from a dog
    bite) (6-7/20)
612. Beardslee, Augustus M. (Hon.) of Manheim, NY m 5/20/29 Elizabeth Frey,
    only dau of Henry I., Esq., in Palatine, NY; Rev. Van Olinda (1-5/25)
613. Beardslee, Jonathan H. m 1/8/14 Rhoda Boice, both of Poughkeepsie; Rev.
    Leonard (8-1/12)
614. Beardsley, _____, 32, wf of Amos, d 12/3/25 in Richfield (3-12/12)
615. Beardsley, Asher, merchant, of Peru, NY m 11/24/33 Susan H. Macumber in
    Chesterfield; Thomas D. Gilson, Esq. (4 [Keeseville Herald]-11/26)
616. Beardsley, Edwin, 1 yr, s of Jabez, d 8/5/07 in Hudson (6-8/11)
617. Beardsley, Evans (Rev.), 59, d in Sangerfield (1-1/8/31)
618. Beardsley, Jonathan H., 55, d 2/19/34 in Poughkeepsie (8-3/5)
619. Beardsley, M. L. of Canandaigua m 2/11/30 Sarah M. Williams (of Cherry
    Valley?) in Cherry Valley; Rev. Tiffany (1-2/13)
620. Beardsley, Morgan Lewis, Esq., 26, late teller of the Utica Branch Bank
    in Canandaigua, d 9/9/31 in Cherry Valley (consumption) (surv by wf
    and an inf s) (1-9/15)
621. Beardsley, Myron m 2/10/24 Sally Schriver, dau of Peter, all of Hyde Park;
    Rev. Clark (8-3/3)
622. Beardsley, Seth W., s of Obadiah, Esq. of Richfield, m 11/29/22 Mary
    Egbert Davoue, dau of late Frederick of NYC, at Trinity Church, NYC;
    Right Rev. Bishop Hobart (3-12/9)
623. Beare, Maria, wf of William H. and dau of William Seaman, d 2/4/31 in NYC
    (1-2/8)
624. Beaumont, A. L., Esq. m 8/24/29 Clarissa G. Holley, 2nd dau of Myron,
    Esq. of Lyons, in Geneva; Rev. L. Hubbell (1-8/29)
625. Beaumont, Samuel, 32, d 12/10/13 in Plattsburgh ("pleuritic complaint")
    (7-12/11)
626. Beaumont, Samuel of Plattsburgh m 8/31/20 Charlotte Taylor of Amboy, NJ
    in A; Rev. Chapman (7-9/30)
627. Beaumont, William (Dr.) of U.S. Army m 8/31/21 Mrs. Deborah Platt of
    Plattsburgh; Rev. Halsey (7-9/1)
628. Bebee, Samuel of Marlborough m 6/29/29 Eliza Slater of Poughkeepsie; Rev.
    Cuyler (8-7/2)
629. Bebee, Selden m 2/22/15 Ophelia Speary, both of Troy; Rev. D. Butler
    (9-2/28)
630. Beck, Nicholas F., Esq., 33, Adjutant General of the State of NY, d 6/30/30
    in Albany (funeral from his late home on Columbia St.) (1-7/2)
631. Becker, Henry W., 26, s of William, d 8/7/07 in Claverack (6-8/25)
632. Becker, Henry (Capt.), 83, (a Rev. patriot who defended the Schoharie area
    in that war) d 12/28/29 at Schohariekill (funeral sermon by Rev. Henry
    B. Stimson; his ch, gr.ch., and great gr.ch, about 80 in number,
    "followed his bier as mourners") (he had been a member of the Dutch Ref.
    Church in Schoharieville) (1-1/20/30)
633. Becker, Peter m 10/31/26 Sally Shute in Hartwick; Rev. John Smith (3-11/6)
634. Beckwith, Daniel m 1/7/14 Huldah Buck in Plattsburgh (7-1/15)
634A 635.* Beckwith, Jacob m 1/2/23 Hannah Bradford, both of Plattsburgh (7-1/4)
636. Beckwith, Josiah Gale (Dr.) m 2/1/31 Jane Maria Seymour, youngest dau of
    late Moses, Jr., Esq., in Litchfield, CT; Rev. Lucas (8-2/16)
637. Becraft, William, 100, d 7/18/25 in Schoharie (b in Suffield, CT; "settled
    in Schoharie about 80 years ago where he has lived ever since") (8-8/3)
638. Beddoe, Lynham James of Geneva m 9/6/31 Eleanor Cuyler Cost, dau of Col.
    Elias of Phelps, in P; Rev. Bruce (1-9/10)
* 634A. Beckwith, Isaac m Amy Horton, both of Stanford; John Osborn, Esq. (8-3/17/13)

18

639. Bedell, Gregory T. (Rev.) m 10/30/16 Penelope Thurston, both of Hudson, at Christ's Church in Hudson; Right. Rev. Bishop Hobart (6-11/5)
640. Bedell, Israel, 81, father of Rev. T. Bedell of Philadelphia, long a resident of NYC, d in Elizabethtown, NY (1-9/9/30)
641. Bedford, _____ of Fishkill m 8/26/07 Mrs. Eleanor Smith, wid of late Stephen of NYC, in NYC; Rev. Kuypers (8-9/2)
642. Bedford, Gunning S. (Dr.) of Baltimore, MD m Jane Maria Van Solingen of NYC in NYC; Rev. Dr. Kuypers (1-9/19/29)
643. Bedford, Jonathan m 1/9/02 Sally Peters, both of Clinton (Dut. Co.) (8-1/19)
644. Bedford, Maria, 21, dau of John, d 8/17/15 in Fishkill (8-8/23)
645. Bedford, Nehemiah, 23, shoemaker, d 1/29/11 in Hudson (born in NJ and "until recently" lived in NYC) (6-2/1)
646. Bedford, Stephen m 3/9/24 Fanny Street in Fishkill; Rev. William B. Thomas (8-3/17)
647. Beebe, John, 40, d 2/12/13 in Chatham (6-2/23)
648. Beebe, Patience, 61, consort of Hosea, Esq., d 3/13/13 in Chatham (6-3/23)
649. Beebe, William m 9/16/29 Maria Van Zandt, dau of Benjamin of Bethlehem, in B; Rev. Ferris (1-9/18)
650. Beebee, Joseph (Deacon), 78, d 12/15/03 in Danbury, CT (6-1/3/04)
651. Beecher, Calvin of Waterbury, CT m 10/7/29 Adeline Benton, dau of Joel, Esq. of Amenia; Rev. Armstrong (8-11/25)
652. Beecraft, Jonathan, 58, d 8/2/10 in Hudson (buried with Masonic honors) (6-8/10)
653. Beekman, Catharine, 20, consort of Dr. John P., d 5/1/15 in Kinderhook (6-5/9)
654. Beekman, Fletcher of NYC m 10/31/05 Phebe Hathaway, dau of Capt. John of Hudson, in H (6-11/5)
655. Beekman, Maria, wf of Dr. Stephen D. and last surviving child of late Vice Pres. George Clinton, d 4/17/29 in NYC (8-4/22)
656. Beekman, Henry m 9/7/23 Sally Crapo of Ballston in B; Rev. Smith (2-9/16)
657. Beers, Ebenezer of New Milford m Sally Osburn of Pawling (8-3/15/03)
658. Beers, Lewis m 4/24/23 Polly Holmes; Tilley Crouse, Esq. All of Clinton. (8-5/14)
659. Beers, William P., Esq., clerk of the city and county of Albany, d 9/13/10 in Fairfield, CT (7-9/21 and 8-9/26)
660. Belden, Ann, 22, wf of Ebenezer, publisher of the Commercial Advertiser, d 7/30/03 in NYC (6-8/9)
661. Belden, Charles, 15, s of John of Washington (Dut, Co.),d 3/26/24 (fell from a cart with the wheels running over him) (8-4/7)
662. Belden, Lawrence m 4/15/23 Louisa Gregory in Dover; Rev. C. P. Willson (8-4/16)
663. Belden, Louisa, dau of Capt. William T., d 7/11/28 (8-7/16)
664. Belden, Samuel, 17, s of William T. of Poughkeepsie, d 5/2/16 in Newburgh (buried in the Episcopal Church cemetery in Poughkeepsie) (8-5/8)
665. Belden, Samuel (Dr.), 84, formerly a resident of PleasantValley, d 6/4/30 in NYC (8-6/9)
666. Belden, Silas T. m 4/21/24 Cornelia Ann Northrup, dau of late William; Rev. C. P. Wilson. All of Washington (Dut. Co.) (8-4/28)
667. Belden, Thomas of Hartford, CT m 5/4/22 Margaret Case, dau of late Rev. Wheeler Case of Pleasant Valley; Rev. C. C. Cuyler (8-5/8)
668. Belden, William I. (Dr.), s of Capt. William T. of Poughkeepsie, d 4/27/25 in NYC (8-5/4)
669. Belding, George of Dover m 5/29/32 Harriet A. Northrop of Washington (Dut. Co.) in W; Rev. W. Hutchinson of Amenia (8-6/6)
670. Belding, Silas, Esq. of Washington (Dut. Co.) m 1/14/19 Jane Gregory of Sand Lake (Renss. Co.); Elder Job Foss (8-1/27)
671. Belding, Uriah, 12, s of Silas, d 6/1/32 in Amenia (8-6/6)
672. Belding, Wells m 3/23/20 Eliza Steele, both of Troy; Rev. Sommers (9-3/28)
673. Belknap, Abel, 73, d 10/17/09 in Westford (3-10/21)
674. Belknap, David of Westford m 6/6/19 Harriet Birge of Litchfield, CT in L (3-6/14)
675. Belknap, Royal, 17, m Fanny Sprague, 15, in Randolph, VT (8-2/14/27)
676. Belknap, William, 80, (a Rev. patriot) d 7/26/31 in Newburgh, NY (born in Charlestown, MA 2/21/1751)(1-7/30)

19

677. Bell, Anna (Miss), 18, d 5/11/07 in Whitesborough(?)(looks like "Whittesburgh") (8-5/20)
678. Bell, Electa, 52, wf of William, Esq. late of Troy, d 4/27/14 in Trenton, NY (9-5/3)
679. Bell, Hiram, 27, 2nd s of Capt. David ("a student of medicine"), d 11/25/30 at his father's home in Schodack (1-12/21)
680. Bell, John of Hyde Park m 12/18/23 Sally Heermans of Clinton in C; Rev. Babcock (8-12/24)
681. Bell, John, 77, d 5/11/26 in New Lisbon (3-5/29)
682. Beman, Samuel, 91, d 7/20/21 in Plattsburgh (7-8/4)
683. Beman, Sarah, 56 or 36? (posting blurred), wf of Samuel, d 12/19/20 in Chazy (7-12/23)
684. Bement, Caleb N., merchant, of Albany m 11/6/14 Harriet Holmes of Saratoga Springs in S.S. (6-11/22)
685. Bement, Deborah, 36, consort of William, d 5/5/12 in Hudson (6-5/11)
686. Bement, Jonathan, "a young man from Suffield, Conn.", d 2/21/16 in Hudson (6-2/27)
687. Bement, Lucy (Wid.), 62, d 7/9/09 in Red Hook (6-8/15)
688. Bemis, Calvin (Dr.), 40, d 4/10/24 in Cooperstown (3-4/12)
689. Bemis, John, 65, (a Rev. soldier) d 9/8/29 in Saratoga Springs ("born on the farm comprising Bemis Heights then owned by his father, deceased; lived there until recent years") (1-9/19)
690. Benaway, Garrit m 6/18/03 Linah Rinaus, both of Poughkeepsie; Rev. Chase (8-6/28)
691. Benedict, Alexander, 30, d 5/12/24 in Ballston (2-5/18)
692. Benedict, Charles J. (Capt.) of Philadelphia, PA m 3/24/31 Susan Y. Burr, dau of late Gen. Gershom of Philadelphia, in NYC; Rev. Baldwin (1-3/29)
693. Benedict, David d 3/7/26 in Maryland, NY ("Printers in Fairfield Co., Conn. are requested to notice the above") (3-3/27)
694. Benedict, Ebenezer of Pawling m Molly Stewart of Franklin (8-3/15/03)
695. Benedict, Edwin C. m 1/17/27 Eliza Halsey in Plattsburgh; Rev. Halsey (7-1/22)
696. Benedict, Hart, 16, only s of Trowbridge Benedict, d 10/30/18 in Sherburne (Chen. Co.) (had lain down in a rut in a burning coalpit. Coroner's jury's report: death by suffocation of smoke from the pit) (3-12/14)
697. Benedict, John (Rev.), D.D., 72, d in Plainfield (state not given) (9-2/27/16)
698. Benedict, Joshua, 72, formerly of Danbury, CT, d 3/10/25 in Poughkeepsie (8-3/16)
699. Benedict, William Marvin, 5, s of Lewis, d 5/5/31 in Albany (funeral from the corner of Spring Street and the Park) (1-5/7)
700. Bingham, Catharine, 20, wf of James formerly of Troy, d 1/26/15 in Albany (9-1/31)
701. Benjamin, Bela E., 32, d 10/9/03 in Amenia (surv by wf and 3 ch.) (8-10/25)
702. Benjamin, Cyrus, Esq., merchant, of Fishkill d 7/19/17 (8-7/23)
703. Benjamin, Daniel, Esq. m 1/22/14 Nancy Mead, both of Amenia; Rev. Birch (8-2/2)
704. Benjamin, David C., merchant, m 11/19/14 Susan Budd, dau of U. Budd, Esq., all of Fishkill; Rev. Price (8-11/23)
705. Benjamin, Elijah P., merchant, of Geneva, NY m 5/28/27 Margaretta L. Crooks, dau of John of Poughkeepsie; Rev. Dr. Reed (8-5/30)
706. Benjamin, Elizabeth, 54, wf of Capt. J. Benjamin, d 9/5/29 in NYC (8-9/9)
707. Benjamin, George W., merchant of Burlington, VT m 8/20/33 Adeline Powell, dau of Horatio of Malone/ in M; Rev. A. Parmelee (7-8/24)
708. Benjamin, John (Capt.), 84, brother of Capt. Caleb, d 7/5/06 in NYC (9-7/15)
709. Benjamin, Joseph (Maj.), 38, d 4/27/03 in Egremont, MA (surv by wf and 6 ch) (6-5/3)
710. Benjamin, Miles (Capt.), formerly of Troy, m 2/19/23 Elizabeth Cooper in Cooperstowm; Rev. Tiffany (3-3/10 and 9-3/18)
711. Benjamin, Nathan, 44, (b in Berkshire, MA) d at his home in Catskill (6-4/27)
712. Benner, Hendrick, 58, of Red Hook d 6/3/17 in Red Hook (dropsey) (surv by wf and children) (6-6/10 and 8-6/11)
713. Bennet, _____, 5, dau of R. O. K. Bennet, d in Troy (9-2/13/16)
714. Bennet, Alva, principal of Johnstown Academy, m 4/27/29 Euphemia McArthur, dau of John, all of Johnstown, in J; Rev. Whipple (1-5/1)

715. Bennet, Isaac m 3/6/03 Ann Losee, both of Washington (Dut. Co.); Rev. Clark (8-3/15)
716. Bennet, John m 8/9/13 Hannah Baker; Rev. Birch. All of Stanford (Dut. Co.) (8-8/25)
717. Bennet, John m 12/5/23 Hester Huddlestone, both of Amenia; Rev. Rider (8-12/10)
718. Bennet, Jonathan m 6/22/16 Abigail Veley, both of Poughkeepsie (8-6/26)
719. Bennet, Lewis of Fredericktown (Dut. Co.) m 12/12/02 Catharine Smith of Franklin (8-1/4/03)
720. Bennet, Nathan of Springfield d 5/22/97 (suicide by hanging) (3-5/25)
721. Bennet, Philip m 10/7/30 Hannah Potter, dau of William R., both of Union Vale; Rev. Richardson (8-10/13)
722. Bennet, Robert O. K. m Cornelia Ostrander in Albany (6-5/13/06)
723. Bennett, Moses B. m Olive Moore in Burlington, VT; Rev. G. G. Ingersol (7-7/26/34)
724. Bennett, Russel of Camillus m Polly Bennett of Ballston in B; Rev. Smith (2-9/16/23)
725. Bennett, Thomas m 2/25/01 Becka Wilber in Amenia (8-3/3)
726. Bennitt, Beverly, 23, son of Capt. Increase Bennitt, was accidentally killed a few days since by the accidental discharge of a musket which was lying in the bow of a canoe (6-10/18/03)
727. Benson, David m 12/29/28 Maria Pruyn, dau of Francis C.; Rev. Dr. Ludlow. All of Albany (1-1/1/29)
728. Benson, Frederick, Esq., postmaster of Jordan, NY, m 7/26/31 Frances Baker, dau of Erastus, Esq. of La Fayette (Onon. Co.) in L. F.; Rev. A. Corning (double ceremony - see marr of Charles H. Drake)
729. Benson, Henry (Capt.),"formerly well known in Poughkeepsie",d "last week" on Long Island (8-8/27/23)
730. Benson, James of Marbletown m 10/14/30 Eliza Tompkins, dau of Michael, in Hyde Park; Rev. Welton (8-10/20)
731. Bentley, Caleb, Esq., 84, (a Rev. officer) d 3/5/27 in Berlin, NY (had fought first in the French War) (9-3/9)
732. Bentley, Darius m 7/24/14 Hannah Allen, both of Berlin, NY, in Troy; Rev. Jonas Coe (9-7/26)
733. Bentley, Phebe was murdered "recently" in Rensselaer County by her husband (surv by her brother Barnabas Paine (8-11/12/99)
734. Bentley, Richard, s of Richard W., d 10/10/19 in Livingston (6-10/12)
735. Bently, John, an aged ... inhabitant of Milton" (Sara. Co.) d 7/20/30 in Milton (1-7/31)
736. Benton, Albert, merchant, of Unadilla m 7/1/24 Mary Albright of Annapolis, MD in A (3-7/26)
737. Benton, Albert S., Esq. m 8/6/23 Emily Jackson in Goshen; Rev. Fish. All of Goshen (8-8/20)
738. Benton, Caleb, 67, d 7/28/25 in Catskill (3-8/15)
739. Benton, Caleb, 89, d 12/25/31 at his home in Amenia (8-1/4/32)
740. Benton, Orlando, Esq., attorney, formerly of Unadilla, NY, d in East Haven, CT (3-8/21/31)
741. Benton, William m 6/7/26 Betsey Reed, dau of Ezra; C. P. Wilson. All of Amenia (8-6/14)
742. Berger, J. (Rev.), A.M., (pastor of Christ's Church in Ghent and St. Luke's Church in Millville) m 12/23/30 Catharine Miller, dau of Hon. John J., in Claverack; Rev. A. Wackerhagen (1-1/1/31)
743. Bergh, John C. of NYC m 6/15/31 Frances L. Satterlee, dau of Edward R., Esq. of Albany; Rev. Ferris (1-6/17)
744. Bergh, Tunis, 63, of NYC d 8/5/28 in Syracuse (while travelling to Niagara with his family) (1-8/13)
745. Berrien, Rebecca S., wf of John M., attorney general of the U.S., d in Baltimore (1-9/7/30)
746. Berry, _____, 10, s of Enoch, earlier bitten by a cat, d 6/20/00 in "Scarborough" (state or country not specified) of "canine madness" (8-8/5)
747. Berry, Arelur(?) (perhaps intended for Arthur?) m 2/23/21 Waldimall(?) (sole name listed for the bride) of Clinton (Dut. Co.) (8-3/7)
748. Berry, Luke (Rev.), pastor of St. Mary's Church, d 12/7/31 in NYC (1-12/13)

21

749. Berryman, Robert m 3/17/25 Matilda Hunter ("A son and daughter of Erin's land"); Rev. Whelpley (7-3/26)
750. Besley, William of Fishkill m 1/17/32 Jenett Monell, dau of James of Poughkeepsie; Rev. Jewett (8-1/25)
751. Bessac, Henry W. m 10/17/20 Maritta Hammond, dau of Abner, Esq. of Claverack; Rev. Gephart (6-10/24)
752. Besse, Silas of the firm of Scott and Besse of Waterford d 6/15/01 in W (9-6/16)
753. Betts, Andrew m 9/22/24 Rebecca Oliver in Broadalbin (2-10/12)
754. Betts, Edward m 10/23/19 Rachel McChesney, both of Brunswick (9-10/26)
755. Betts, Harvey of Troy m 10/13/14 Ruah Brown of Brunswick; Rev. Coe (9-10/18)
756. Betts, John, printer, m 10/19/06 Fanny Baldwin, both of Hudson; Rev. Gebherd (6-10/21)
757. Betts, Peter J. of Bainbridge m 8/23/29 Mary Ann Noble of Unadilla at St. Matthew's Church in Unadilla; Rev. Norman H. Adams (double ceremony - see marr of A. D. Williams)
758. Betts, Polly, wf of Burwell Betts, d 2/3/06 (9-2/4)
759. Beutner, Anthon A., Esq. of the"Island of Curaccoa"d 4/27/19 "on his passage to New York" (8-6/9)
760. Bevier, John H. (Rev.) of Wawarsing m 9/21/31 Margaret C. Van Wyck, dau of Cornelius C., Esq. of Fishkill, in F; Rev. G. Fisher (9-9/28, 1-9/30, and 1-10-24)
761. Bicknell, Elijah, 65, d 7/15/30 at his home in Albany (1-7/17)
762. Biddle, Truman of Tolland, MA m Eveline Doughty of Sharon, CT in Amenia, NY; Rev. Asahel Bronson (8-10/8/28)
763. Bidwell, Adonijah S., 36, d 12/10/30 in Hillsdale ("his death the consequence of an Anarism upon his thigh occasioned by the accidental stab of a penknife about 17 years since ... had just had the artery taken up Nov. 24") (1/1/21/31)
764. Bierce, Joseph, 74, d 1/8/16 in Cornwall, CT (8-1/17)
765. Bigden, Robert late of Poole, Dorsetshire, England m "Monday before Christmas" Amy Mary Dennis of Buffalo, NY in St. Paul's Church (in Buffalo?); Rev. Addison Searle (1-1/8/29)
766. Bigelow, Gregory m 9/29/16 Henrietta Barney, both of Worcester, in W (3-10/10)
767. Bigelow, Palmer m 2/14/07 Deborah Connell, both of Cambridge; Rev. Coe (9-2/24)
768. Bigelow, Timothy (Hon.), 55, d at his home in Medford, MA (For a long period was Speaker of the House of Representatives from Mass.)
769. Bignall, Harriet Eliza, 12 mo, dau of John "of the Albany Theatre", d 12/10/31 in Albany (1-12/12)
770. Bigsby, William of Hillsdale m 7/18/19 Christina Esselstyne of Claverack in C; Rev. Gephard (6-7/27)
771. Bill (or Ball), Charles m 9/23/04 Susan Clark in Hudson; Rev. Sears (6-9/25)
772. Bill, James, Esq., 73, formerly of Catskill, d 3/27/30 in Oswego (1-4/5)
773. Billings, ____, wf of Perez, d 3/16/22 in Milton (2-3/20)
774. Billings, Andrew (Maj.), 64, d 4/28/08 in Poughkeepsie (interred in the Episcopal burying ground) (member of Solomon's Lodge [Masonic] and of the Mechanic Society) (8-5/3)
775. Billings, Benjamin of "Dickison, St. Lawrence Co." (probably intended for Dickinson which today lies in Franklin Co. on the St. Law. Co. line) m 1/22/34 Mrs. Rachel Duke of Ausable Forks in Peru, NY; E. Williams, Esq. (4 [Keeseville Herald]-2/4 and 7-2/1)
776. Billings, Cornelia (Mrs.), 67, d 11/18/20 in Poughkeepsie (8-11/22)
777. Billings, Daniel m 3/11/15 Elizabeth Vermillion(?), both of Fishkill; Rev. Smith (8-3/15)
778. Billings, Dolly, 30, wf of Jabez S. and dau of Widow Durkee of Burlington (VT?), d 5/25/31 in Keeseville (4 [Keeseville Herald]-5/31)
779. Billings, Jesse L., Esq. of Salem, NY m 9/15/19 Eliza Smith in Rutland, (VT?) (7-10/9)
780. Billings, John S. of Rochester m Sophronia Brown of Batavia in B; Rev. Lucius Smith (1-7/26/31)

781. Bindon, Joseph, Esq., 86, d 5/29/32 at Rouse's Point (after living in
     Montreal, Can., he settled in Philadelphia, PA where he remained until
     coming to Rouse's Point in 1805 with his home within 1½ miles from the
     Canadian border) (7-6/9)
782. Bingham, Daniel, Jr., 16, d 10/3/07 in Hudson (6-10/6)
783. Bingham, David of Cooperstown m 8/29/27 Catharine Romain, dau of
     Benjamin, in Poughkeepsie; Rev. A. Welton (8-9/5)
784. Bingham, Fanny, 23, consort of Flavel and dau of Daniel White of Coventry,
     CT, d 7/11/04 (in Utica?) (6-7/24)
785. Bingham, Flavel, 28, (late consort of Fanny who d 7/11 of typhus)
     d 8/13/04 in Utica (typhus) (6-8/28)
786. Bingham, Hannah, 58, wid of Caleb, Esq. late of Boston (state not given),
     d 10/16/20 (in Hudson, NY?) (6-10/24)
787. Bingham, Julia, 20, wf of Chester and dau of Stephen Andres, Esq.,
     d 4/4/15 in Troy ("she left an infant seven days old") (9-4/11)
788. Bingham, Luther of the firm of Livingston and Bingham m 2/25/12 Sally
     Jenkins, both of Hudson, NY, in Salisbury, CT (6-3/2)
789. Bingham, Thomas m 9/22/27 Emeline Selleck, both of Troy, in T (9-9/25)
790. Binney, Mary (Mrs.), 61, d in Tyringham, MA (6-7/2/01)
791. Bird, John, Esq., 37, attorney, d 2/2/06 in Troy (9-2/4 and 6-2/11)
792. Bird, Milo (Col.), 38, d 10/12/30 at his home in Manlius (1-10/19)
793. Bird, Sally, 35, relict of John Bird, Esq., d 8/4/15 in Litchfield, CT
     (9-8/22)
794. Bird, Seth (Dr.), 73, "a physician of great celebrity" and father of J.
     Bird, Esq. of Troy, NY, d at South Farms, CT (9-10/15/05)
795. Bird, William of Salisbury m 10/18/12 Charlotte Bull of Northeast; Rev.
     Alerton (8-11/4)
796. Birdsall, Anna, 51, wf of Maurice, Esq., d 6/12/29 in Greene (Chen. Co.)
     (1-6/20)
797. Birdsall, Orison m 10/14/30 Sarah Ann Carman, youngest dau of John V., all
     of Poughkeepsie; Rev. Dr. Cuyler (8-10/20)
798. Bisby, Hiram of Albany m Caroline Blood of Schenectady in S; Rev. Goodsell
     (1-6/12/29)
799. Bishop, Deborah, 67, wf of Deacon David, d 8/16/25 in Paris, NY (3-8/29)
800. Bishop, Earl H. m 6/14/34 Belinda Sleight in Stanford (Dut. Co.); Henry
     Tallmadge, Esq. (8-6/18)
801. Bishop, Jacob m 12/17/05 Deborah Roberts, both of Troy; Rev. Butler
     (9-12/24)
802. Bishop, James D. m 2/17/31 Eliza G. Hoffman, both of Poughkeepsie; Rev.
     Dr. Cuyler (8-2/23)
803. Bishop, Votney, 19, formerly of Clinton (Dut. Co.), d 8/3/17 in Hudson
     (8-8/13)
804. Bissell, Isaac, 75, d 6/19/23 in Hartwick (consumption) (3-6/23)
805. Bissell, Josiah, Jr. of Rochester d 4/5/31 in Seneca Falls where he was
     then erecting a large flour mill (had been in poor health) (founder of
     the pioneer line of stages between Albany and Buffalo) (buried in
     Rochester) (1-4/16 and 4 [Keeseville Herald]-4/26)
806. Bixbee, William, 49, d 5/25/31 in Marion (Wayne Co.) (thrown from a wagon,
     Sunday [5/22], while riding to church)(1-6/1)
807. Bixby,   (Miss), about 17, d 7/24/22 (7-7/27)
808. Blackall, Edward B. m 5/27/30 Isabella Busher Sturges in Albany; Rev.
     Green (1-5/29)
809. Blackman, Homer of the firm of Davis and Blackman m 12/19/31 Emmeline Hall,
     dau of Green Hall; Rev. Campbell (1-12/22)
810. Blackman, James m 3/20/23 Mary Ann Washbon, dau of Zebah, in Butternuts;
     Rev. Wheeler (3-4/7)
811. Blackmun, Andrew (Deacon), 77, m 12/25/16 Relief Alvord (Widow), 71;
     Rev. Johnson of Potsdam (7-12/28)
812. Blair, Ammon of Galway m 3/18/24 Maria Starkweather of Broadalbin in B;
     Rev. Nott (2-3/23)
813. Blair, Eli, 40, and his wife, Abby, d 9/27/31 in Lyons ("both were taken
     sick the same day - with the same disease - and died within seven hours
     of each other") (1-10/21)
814. Blake, Elisha of Canaan m Marilla Crane of Northeast in N (8-12/4/11)
815. Blake, Francis (Hon.), 43, attorney, d 2/23/17 in Worcester, MA (7-3/15)

23

816. Blake, James m 11/1/07 Susannah Traverse, both of Brunswick, in B;
William McManus, Esq. (9-11/3)
817. Blake, Joseph R. (Lt.) of the U.S. Navy d in Washington City (D.C.)
(1-5/16/31)
818. Blake, William m 9/21/34 Harriet Trickey in Napanoch; Rev. Switz. All of
Napanoch (8-10/8)
819. Blakeman, Amos Y. m 5/14/22 Adaline Gibson "both of this city" (whether
the city of reference is Albany or Troy is left unclear) (9-5/21)
820. Blakeslee, Hannah, 25, consort of Amaziah of Poughkeepsie, d 11/2/07
(8-11/4)
821. Blakeslee, Nathaniel m 10/31/25 Catharine Van Bunschoten, both of
Poughkeepsie; Rev. Dr. Reed (8-11/16)
822. Blanchard, ____, 40, wf of Capt. John, d 10/1/06 in Burlington (Ots. Co.)
(died of "childbirth fever"; surv by husband and 9 children, "the
youngest not yet 2 weeks old") (3-10/16)
823. Blanchard, Alonzo L. m 9/16/21 Mariah Everton, both of Albany; Rev.
Sommers (9-10/2)
824. Blanchard, Reuben I. m 10/29/29 Ann Maria Parsons, both of Albany, in A;
Rev. Welch (1-10/31)
825. Blatchford, John of Stillwater m 5/18/25 Frances Wickes in Jamaica, Long
Island, NY (2-5/31)
826. Bleecker, ____, child of G. V. S. Bleecker, d "recently" in Albany
(funeral from the father's home, 87 Pearl St.) (1-12/28/30)
827. Bleecker, ____, wf of Barent, d "recently" in Albany (funeral from
her late residence, 317 North Market St.) (1-10/12/31)
828. Bleecker, ____, wf of Nicholas, d "recently" in Albany (funeral from her
late residence, 288 North Market St.) (1-12/6/31)
829. Bleecker, Anna Josepha, 13, dau of James, d 3/2/31 in NYC (1-3/10)
830. Bleecker, Anthony J. of NYC m 11/24/24 Cornelia Van Benthuysen, dau of
late John, Esq. of Poughkeepsie; Rev. Dr. Reed (8-12/11)
831. Bleecker, Gerret V. S., Esq. m 2/8/29 Jane Sheperd, 2nd dau of late Thomas,
all of Albany; Rev. Ferris (1-2/10)
832. Bleecker, Phebe, wf of Maj. John, d 7/31/19 in Plattsburgh (7-7/31)
833. Bleecker, Rutger, 30, only s of John H., Esq., d 3/17/31 in Albany
(1-3/18)
834. Bleecker, Rutger, Esq. d 3/17/31 in Albany (funeral from the home of his
father, John R., 334 North Market St.) (1-3/19)
835. Bleeker, Anthony, 20, s of Maj. John, d 6/10/24 in Plattsburgh (funeral
sermon by Rev. Whelpley) (7-6/12)
836. Bliss, Alexander, Esq., attorney, of Boston, MA and partner of the Hon.
D. Webster, d 7/30/27 in Plymouth, MA (8-8/1)
837. Bliss, Chester S. m 1/8/32 Susan Elizabeth Marsh; Rev. Hard (7-1/14)
838. Bliss, Chester S., 32, d 10/7/34 in Plattsburgh (7-10/11)
839. Bliss, Harriet, oldest dau of William M., Esq. of Troy, d 9/22/23 (9-9/23)
840. Bliss, Harry of Albany m 11/3/16 Albertine Van Buren of Schodack at
Schodack Landing; Rev. Van Buren (6-11/12)
841. Bliss, John of New Orleans, LA m 9/30/30 Abbey Williams of Canaan Centre
in C. C.; Rev. Hutchins Taylor (1-10/7)
842. Bliss, Maria A., wf of Dr. James C. and dau of late John P. Mumford, Esq.,
d 3/2/31 (1-3/10)
843. Bliss, Pelethia, 33, one of the proprietors of the Troy Post, d 10/1/18
in Troy (9-10/6 and 8-10/21)
844. Bliss, Sidney m 1/26/34 Maria Bradford, both of Jay; E. Williams, Esq.
(7-2/1 and 4 [Keeseville Herald]-2/4)
845. Blois, Samuel (Dr.) m 8/12/30 Sarah S. Bergh, dau of late Tunis, Esq.,
in NYC; Rev. Dr. Lyell. All of NYC (8-8/18)
846. Bloodgood, Abraham d in Albany (9-3/3/07)
847. Bloodgood, Daniel m 6/27/22 Olive Whipple; Rev. John Clark. All of
Pleasant Valley (8-7/3)
848. Bloodgood, Francis, Esq. of Albany, NY m Mrs. Anna Morris in Philadelphia,
PA; Right Rev. Bishop White (3-11/17/23)
849. Bloodgood, John, Esq. of Mobile, AL m 11/24/29 Catharine Mary Hildreth,
dau of late Matthias, Esq. of Johnstown (Mont. Co.), in NYC; Rev.
Schroeder (1-11/27)
850. Bloodgood, John, Esq., 53, d 12/19/30 in NYC (1-12/22)

851. Bloom, George, Esq. of Poughkeepsie m 9/3/18 Eliza Murray of Coldenham
     in C; Rev. Phinny (8-9/9)
852. Bloom, George, Esq., attorney, d 11/28/24 in Pleasant Valley (8-12/1)
853. Bloom, George C., 22, s of late George, Esq. of Dutchess Co., d 7/28/32
     in Lansing, NY (cholera) (8-8/8)
854. Bloom, Henry (Brig, Gen.) died (no further info. given) (source credited
     to the Albany Register) (7-10/3/18)
855. Bloom, Isaac (Hon.) of Cliton (Dut. Co.) d 4/26/03 in Clinton (was first
     a judge of the court of common pleas in Dutchess Co. and subsequently
     a Congressman - elected in fall, 1802) (8-5/3 and 9-5/10 and 3-5/19)
856. Bloom, James m 9/5/22 Jane Gay of Pleasant Valley; Rev. Clark (8-9/11)
857. Bloom, John M. of Dutchess Co., NY m 12/1/04 Frances D. Jaques of
     Burlington Co., NJ (8-12/18)
858. Bloom, Jonathan, Esq. m 2/21/19 Sally Rowland, both of Clinton (Dut. Co.);
     Rev. Clark (8-2/24)
859. Bloom, Mary, inf dau of George, Esq. of Poughkeepsie, d 7/6/14 in
     Poughkeepsie (8-7/13)
860. Bloom, Mary, 34, wf of Jonathan, d 3/8/18 in Clinton (Dut. Co.) (8-3/11)
861. Bloom, Richard Hart, inf s of John M., d 3/16/14 in Clinton (Dut. Co.)
     (8-3/23)
862. Bloom, Sarah, wf of Jonathan, late of Dutchess Co., d in NYC (8-12/26)
863. Bloomer, Benjamin D. m 4/26/30 Susan Mills in Poughkeepsie; Rev. Welton
     (8-5/5)
864. Bloomfield, Daniel m 9/2/34 Helen Van Valen; Rev. Dr. Reed (8-9/10)
865. Bloomfield, William m 10/18/32 Pamilia Pine, both of Poughkeepsie; Rev.
     Dr. Reed (8-10/24)
866. Bloss, Samuel (Dr.) m 10/11/25 Lydia Southwick, dau of Zadoc; Rev. C. C.
     Cuyler (8-10/19)
867. Blossom, Abigal M., 19, (dau of late Ezra of Blandford, MA and niece of
     Col. William Blossom of Canandaigua, NY) d 7/5/30 (consumption) (1-7/13)
868. Boadman (sic), Mary (Mrs.), 99, formerly of Coeymans, d 10/22/31 at the
     home of Col. Ira Jenkins in Jordan (Onon. Co.) (1-11/7)
869. Boardman, ____, wf of Elisha, d 4/29/22 in South Hero, VT (7-5/25)
870. Boardman, Elijah (Hon.) of Connecticut d "lately" in Ohio "whither he
     had gone on business"(3-9/8/23)
871. Boardman, Horace, s of Capt. Boardman of Middlebury, VT, m 3/28/21 Harriet
     Addoms, dau of John, Esq. of Plattsburgh, NY, in P; Rev. John T. Addoms
     (7-3/31)
872. Boardman, John d 6/4/13 in Troy (9-6/8)
873. Boardman, John m 8/18/28 Helen Delong, both of Poughkeepsie; Rev. Dr.
     Cuyler (8-8/27)
874. Boardman, Lucia A. (Miss), 23, dau of H., Esq., d in Colchester, VT
     (7-9/27/34)
     Boardman, Mary (Mrs.), formerly of Coeymans, ... See, possibly,
       Boadman, Mary (Mrs.), ...
875. Boardman, Mary James (sic), dau of Capt. E., d 10/20/17 at the cantonment
     near Plattsburgh village (7-10/25/17)
876. Bockee, Abraham, Esq. m 3/4/09 Patty Oakley in Poughkeepsie; Rev. Cuyler
     (8-3/8)
877. Bockee, Alexander Phoenix of Northeast, "late of the detached milita of
     Harlaem", d 12/1/14 in Poughkeepsie (8-12/7)
878. Bockee, Jacob, Jr., 22, d 11/24/10 at the home of his father in Amenia
     ("last winter the deceased had commenced the study of medicine with Dr.
     Bradhead") (8-11/28)
879. Bodden, William m 2/15/34 Elizabeth Wilson in Springfield (near Poughkeepsie);
     Rev. Price of Hughsonville (8-2/19)
880. Bodley, John R., for many years clerk of the state prison, d 12/7/31 in
     Auburn (1-12/24)
881. Boerome, Jacob m 10/16/00 Catharine Polmantier, both of Poughkeepsie
     (8-10/21)
882. Boerum, ____, consort of Jacob of Poughkeepsie, d 3/10/14 (8-3/16)
883. Boerum, David, merchant, m 10/26/31 Amelia Green, dau of William; Rev. Dr.
     Cuyler. All of Poughkeepsie (8-11/2)
884. Boerum, Garrit m 5/13/03 Sally Schoonmaker, dau of Maj. Henry of
     Poughkeepsie; Rev. Brouwer (8-5/17)

25

885. *Boerum, Hannah, 61, (wid. of late Jacob of Boerum and Wynkoop, merchants, of NYC) d 3/24/27 in Poughkeepsie (8-3/28)
886. *Boerum, Jacob, 44, merchant, of NYC d "last week" in NYC (8-6/25/05)
887. *Boerum, Jacob m 2/11/15 Betsey Free, both of Poughkeepsie; Rev. L. Leonard (8-2/15/15)
888. Bogardus, Anna Louise, (age blurred), consort of William W., Esq., d 10/25/16 in Poughkeepsie (8-11/6)
889. Bogardus, Cornelius (Rev.), pastor of the Dutch Reformed Church in Schenectady, m 11/8/10 Elizabeth Shear of Hopewell in H; Rev. C. C. Cuyler (8-11/14)
890. Bogardus, Francis S., 26, formerly of Fishkill, NY, d 9/27/34 in Peoria, IL (8-10/29)
891. Bogardus, Jacob, Esq. ("an aged inhabitant") d 9/21/29 in Greenville (Greene Co.) (1-9/26)
892. Bogardus, Jacob E. m 1/29/18 Fanny Fosdick, dau of Judah, in Hudson; Rev. Pickering (6-2/3)
893. Bogardus, James m 11/13/16 Elsey Wiltse, both of Fishkill (8-11/20)
894. Bogardus, Richard m 1/31/ 18 Gertrude Van Deusen in Claverack; Rev. Sluyter (double ceremony - see marr of Daniel Humphrey) (6-2/10)
895. Bogardus, Richard m 9/10/20 Ruth Barton, both of Hudson, in Claverack; Rev. John C. Gebhard (6-9/12)
896. Bogardus, Stephen H. of the firm of Lent and Bogardus m 8/31/30 Sophia Ann Trivett, both of Poughkeepsie; Rev. Welton (8-9/1)
897. Bogardus, William W., Esq., about 60, attorney, formerly of Poughkeepsie, d in Marlborough (8-1/31/27)
898. Bogart, _____, s of Nicholas, merchant, of NYC, d "a few days ago" ("inhumanly killed by the enemy in New Jersey"(5-10/1/78)
899. Bogart, Alexander J. of the firm of E. and A.J. Bogart m 6/19/29 Olivia Howland, youngest dau of Reuben, all of NYC, in NYC; Rev. William A. Clark (1-6/24)
900. Bogart, Alwin (Dr.) m 9/1/29 Elizabeth Donly Walker, dau of late Dr. Richard L., in NYC; Rev. D. S. Bogart. All of NYC (1-9/4)
901. Bogert, Nicholas, Esq., 88, d 1/28/14 in Beekman (8-2/2)
902. Boggs, Rachel, wf of Capt. William of Lansingburgh, d 9/18/01 (9-9/22)
903. Bogue, Horace P. (Rev.) of Butternuts m 2/27/23 Grace C. Brown of Bridge-water in B; Rev. Alpha Miller (3-3/5)
904. Bolles, John A., Esq. of Boston, MA m Catharine A. Dix of Boscawen, NH, sister of John A. Dix, Esq., Secretary of State of NY (8-11/26/34)
905. Bolles, Joshua, 67, d 8/18/12 in Franklin (Dela. Co.) (6-9/14)
906. Bolles, Sally (Miss), dau of Richard, d 11/18/15 in Hudson (6-11/21)
907. Bolles, Samuel, 1 yr, s of John R., d in Hudson (6-5/10/08)
908. Bolt, David m 11/30/03 Kesiah Covel, both of Franklin; Rev. Joseph Tresdall (8-12/13)
909. Bolt, William, one of the first settlers in Milton, d 6/28/24 in M (2-7/6)
910. Bolton, _____, consort of Rev. Bolton of Burlington (Ots. Co.) d 12/25/09 in B (3-12/30)
911. Bolton, Daniel (Elder), 69, d 6/8/20 in New Lisbon (3-6/19)
912. Bomford, Louisa Sophia, wf of George, d 1/10/15 (8-1/18)
913. Bonaparte, Jerome, youngest brother of the Full Consul of the French Republic, m 12/31/03 Elizabeth Patterson, oldest dau of William, merchant, of Baltimore, in B; Rev. Bishop Carroll (8-1/10/04)
914. Bond, Joshua, Esq., Consul of the U.S. for "Montevelde" m 11/7/28 Mary C. Hawkins, dau of late Col. Samuel of NYC, at the home of S. Sherwood, Esq. in Delhi, NY (8-11/19)
915. Bond, William M. (Col.) of Lockport, NY m 9/3/31 Nancy L. Bond of Keene, NH in Lockport ; Rev. Clark (this is a remarriage of this couple late in life, their having been previously divorced from each other; their many children attended this ceremony of 9/3) (1-9/13 and 8-9/21)
916. Bonesteel, Nicholas, 80, d 1/10/34 in Red Hook (8-1/15)
917. Bonesteel, Philip I., merchant, of NYC m 11/27/34 Phebe Ann Tripp of Clinton (Dut. Co.); Rev. P. F. Wilde of Pleasant Valley (8-12/3)
918. Bonney, Luke d in June in Catharine (Broome Co.) (3-8/13/07)
919. Bontecou, Peter m 4/30/23 Semanthe Brockway, dau of Reed Brockway, Esq. of Troy; Rev. Griffen (9-5/6)
*For Boerum, Richard see Boorum, Richard

26

920. Booge, Ebenezer, 13 mo, youngest and 4th s of Ebenezer, Esq., d 8/27/27 in Stephentown (9-9/18)
921. Bookee, Jacob, farmer, 63, d 10/19/19 at the home of Isaac Smith, Esq. in Washington (Dut. Co.) where he was visiting (had served in the NY legislature) (8-10/27)
922. Boone, Thomas m 6/9/22 Polly T. Rhodes, both of Berlin, NY; Rev. Satterly (9-6/18)
923. Boorn, Francis, "an aged citizen", d 2/15/27 in Plattsburgh (7/2/17)
924. Boorum, Richard m 11/21/98 Mary Brinckerhoff, dau of late John, all of Fishkill; Rev. Van Vranken (8-11/27)
925. Booth, Abigal, 82, consort of Hezekiah, d 12/10/17 in Claverack (6-12/16)
926. Booth, George of Poughkeepsie m "last week" Mary Armstrong of Clinton (Dut. Co.) (8-1/4/03)
927. Booth, Helen M. (Miss), 20, dau of George, d 9/16/30 in Poughkeepsie (8-9/22)
928. Booth, Hezekiah, 38, formerly of Newtown, CT, d 6/4/18 in Claverack (6-6/9)
929. Booth, Mary, wf of George of Poughkeepsie, d 4/27/04 (8-5/1)
930. Booth, George m 4/28/06 Maria Vassar, dau of James; Rev. Williams. All of Poughkeepsie (8-5/6)
931. Borgeast, W.T., 26, "the celebrated balance master and circus rider" d "about two weeks ago" in Otsego Co., NY (1-6/19/30)
932. Borland, John of the firm of Borland and Abbott of Boston (state not given) m 7/17/16 Rebecca Nelson Woolsey, dau of Gen. Melancton L. of Cumberland Head (near Plattsburgh); Rev. Hewlet (7-7/20)
933. Bortle, Jacob m 11/27/08 Alberta Philip in Claverack; Rev. Gebhard (6-11/29)
934. Boss, John, "an aged citizen", d 8/26/16 in Poughkeepsie (8-8/28)
935. Boston, John m 1/22/26 Eliza Stewart; Rev. C. P. Wilson. All of Amenia (8-1/25)
936. Bostwick, _____, wf of Solomon, d "a few days since" in Champlain (8-7/27/22)
937. Bostwick, David of Hartwick m Fanny Mather in New Lisbon (3-9/19/25)
938. Bostwick, Henry d 9/19/00 "at Oaks creek" (fell between two waterwheels at Mudge's Mills and was drowned) (surv by wf and 6 small ch) (3-9/25)
939. Bostwick, Mary, 22, (wf of R. W. of the firm of Fyler, Dibble and Co., merchants), d 9/20/17 in Pine Plains (8-9/24 and 6-9/30)
940. Bostwick, Polly (Mrs.), 65, d 4/6/29 at the home of Dr. Robert Noxon (8-4/8)
941. Bostwick, Reuben, merchant, of Dutchess Co. m 7/24/16 Mary Pratt, late of Troy, in Greenbush; Rev. De Witt (8-7/31)
942. Bosworth, Jabez, 73, formerly of Poughkeepsie, d 3/29/26 in Pike, PA (8-5/3)
943. Bosworth, John T., 21, late acting surgeon's mate at the New York Navy Yard, d 2/18/27 in Poughkeepsie (8-2/21)
944. Bosworth, Julia, dau of Jabish, d 2/8/21 in Poughkeepsie (8-2/21)
945. Bosworth, Mindwell, 67, relict of David late of Lenox, MA, d 7/23/16 in Cooperstown, NY (3-7/25)
946. Bosworth, Stewart (Dr.), 29, a native of Poughkeepsie, NY, d 6/28/25 in Smithfield, NC (8-7/13)
947. Bosworth, Susan, dau of late Josiah, Esq. of Poughkeepsie, d 11/7/30 on the brig "Laurel" on her passage to St. Barta (was en route there for her health) (8-12/8)
948. Bosworth, William, 15, s of James, Esq., d 7/26/15 in Poughkeepsie (8-8/2)
949. Botsford, _____, wf of Caleb P., d 2/22/15 in Troy (9-2/28)
950. Botsford, Charles G. of Hartwick m 9/4/22 Harriet Andrews of Cherry Valley in C. V.; Rev. Fitch (3-9/9)
951. Bouck, Maria, 43, consort of Harmanus, Esq., d 9/15/29 in Schoharie (1-9/18)
952. Boudinot, Elias of the Cherokee Nation of Indians m Harriet R. Gold, dau of Deacon Benjamin R. Gold, in Cornwall, CT (8-4/26 and 3-5/1/26)
953. Boughton, John m 10/30/28 Sarah Ann Broas, both of Poughkeepsie; Rev. Dr. Cuyler (8-11/4)
954. Boughton, R. H. of Youngstown,NY m 7/17/29 Maria Barton, dau of Benjamin, Esq. of Lewiston, in L; Rev. Green of Niagara (1-7/31)

27

955. Bounticou, Susan (Mrs.), 69, d in New Haven, CT (6-12/3/05)
956. Bourke, James (Capt.), 68, of Hudson d 10/11/02 (6-10/12)
957. Bourn, Russel (Lt.) m 10/23/23 Maria Tanner in Otsego; Rev. Smith (3-10/27)
958. Boutell, James, Jr. m 2/19/26 Polly Wheaton, dau of John, in Burlington
     (Ots. Co.); A. Sheldon, Esq. (3-2/27)
959. Bouton, Abbey, 64, wf of Nathan, d 10/5/27 in Troy (9-10/9)
960. Bouton, Josiah, merch.,m 3/15/27 Emeline Parker; Rev. Butler. All of
     Troy (9-3/20)
961. Bow, Daniel, 27, d 3/12/15 in Cooperstown (3-3/16)
962. Bow, Oliver m 11/28/21 Eliza Hitchcock, both of Troy; Rev. Dr. Coe
     (9-12/11)
963. Bow, Oliver of Hartwick m 9/28/26 Thurzy Eaton in New Lisbon; Rev. Stone
     (3-10/2)
964. Bowen, Romeo m 4/13/26 "Miss La Fayette Loop" in Cooperstown; Rev. John
     Smith (3-4/17)
965. Bowen, Sylvester of White Creek m 1/16/22 Julian Ann Cross of Shaftsbury,
     VT in S; Rev. Tinkham (9-2/26)
966. Bowers, Henry, Esq. d 2/6/00 in NYC (3-2/20)
967. Bowles, Dickinson, 20, s of William, d 5/8/19 in Plattsburgh (consumption)
     (7-5/15)
968. Bowles, Pierce m 9/29/22 Olive Alvira Knappen of Beekmantown in B; Halloch
     Brumley, Esq. (7-10/5)
969. Bowman, _____, inf s of Nathaniel, d 7/23/14 in Hudson (6-8/2)
970. Bowman, _____, wid of late Joseph, d 8/12/23 in Poughkeepsie (8-8/20)
971. Bowman, Charles Henry, 2 yrs, s of Nathaniel, d 6/26/20 in Hudson (6-6/27)
972. Bowman, George, 24, of Poughkeepsie d 9/8/10 (8-9/12)
973. Bowman, Godfrey m 5/20/10 Catherine Van Kleeck, both of Poughkeepsie; Rev.
     Cuyler (8-5/23)
974. Bowman, Godfrey, 40, printer, of Poughkeepsie d 3/1/22 (8-3/6)
975. Bowman, Horace m 5/8/10 Eunice Folger in Hudson; Rev. Cooper (double
     ceremony - see marr of Reuben C. Folger)
976. Bowne, Henry (Capt.), 78, (a Rev. patriot), formerly of Albany, d 12/25/29
     in Charlton (1-12/30)
977. Bowne, James, merchant, of Poughkeepsie m 9/9/23 Phebe Conklin, dau of Maj.
     Nathan of Amenia; Rev. Armstrong (8-9/17)
978. Bowne, Richard M., druggist, of NYC m 7/26/04 Penelope Hull of Stanford
     (Dut. Co.) (8-8/14)
979. Bowne, Robert L., 56, late of Butternuts, d 6/8/21 in Cooperstown (3-6/11)
980. Bowne, Samuel of Butternuts m Cordelia Shove in New Lisbon (3-3/19/21)
981. Bowne, Samuel m 4/3/23 Phebe Rapalje; Rev. Westbrook. All of Fishkill
     (8-4/9)
982. Boyce, Peter, 77, of Poughkeepsie d "recently" (8-12/6/03)
983. Boyd, David m 9/27/31 Hannah Thorn; Rev. Campbell. All of Albany (1-9/30)
984. Boyd, Hugh (Rev.) m Mary Dorr, dau of Dr. Jonathan, in Cambridge; Rev.
     McLaren (3-6/17/22)
985. Boyd, James of Laurens m 10/14/20 Abigail Thorp of Butternuts in B
     (3-10/23)
986. Boyd, Jane (Mrs.), 79, d 4/11/31 in Albany (funeral from the home of her
     husband whose given name appears to be James but this is not clearly
     signified) (her "sons" are mentioned but not by given names) (1-4/13)
987. Boyd, John (a clerk in the Registers office in Philadelphia, PA) d 9/19/98
     in Philadelphia (yellow fever) ("Printers in Albany are requested to
     publish this") (8-10/9)
988. Boyd, John, Esq., attorney, of Hamilton (St. Law. Co.) m 2/6/12 Elizabeth
     Livingston, oldest dau of late Robert N., Esq. of Poughkeepsie; Rev.
     Cuyler (8-2/12)
989. Boyd, John H., Esq., attorney, m Lucretia Adams in Whitehall; Rev. Kennedy.
     All of Whitehall (1-2/18/30)
990. Boyd, Samuel, Jr. (Dr.) of NYC m 10/27/29 Sophia E. Keyser, dau of Samuel,
     Esq. of Baltimore, in B; Rev. Duncan (1-10/31)
991. Boyington, Joseph m 1/17/22 Clarissa Haskins, dau of Azariah, merchant,
     all of Pittstown (9-1/22)
992. Boynton, Abel (Col.) of Troy d 9/2/14 in Williamsville near Buffalo
     (9-9/27)
993. Boynton, B. A. (Lt.), 2nd Regiment, U.S. Infantry, m 3/15/18 Eleanor
     Sailly, dau of Peter, Esq., in Plattsburgh; Rev. Halsey (7-3/21)

994. Boynton, Charles B. m 5/7/28 Margaret Day; Rev. Beman (9-5/9)
995. Boynton, Clirenda, 42, wf of Jedediah of Hinesburgh, VT, d 9/27/22(7-10/19)
996. Brackenbury, Joseph H.,"a Mormon preacher" , d 3/7/32 in Pomfret, VT
      ("recently emigrated from Ohio accompanied by one or two Society members")
      (4 [Keeseville Herald]-4/3)
997. Brackett, Ichabod, 55, d 12/2/31 in Salina (1-12/17)
998. Bradbury, Samuel m 3/10/17 Rebecca Campbell; Rev. Cuyler. All of
      Poughkeepsie (8-3/12)
999. Bradford, Cornelius, Esq., American Consul at Lyons, France, formerly of
      NYC, d 8/2/30 in Jerusalem, Palestine (1-12/28/30)
1000. Bradford, George W. of Cooperstown m 3/13/18 Mary Ann Walker of Middle-
      field in M; Rev. John Smith (3-3/22)
1001. Bradford, Helen Maria, 1 yr, dau of George W. of Cooperstown, d 9/2/19
      (3-9/6)
1002. Bradford, John M. (Rev.) m Mary Lush, dau of Stephen, Esq. of Albany;
      Rev. Dr. Linn (6-12/15/07)
1003. Bradford, Mary, 82, d 8/6/30 in Hebron (Wash. Co.) (one of the first
      settlers of that town) (1-8/20)
1004. Bradford, Sally, consort of Perez, d 3/25/07 in Hartwick (surv by
      "a large family") (3-4/2)
1005. Bradley, Anson, 26, s of the Widow Helen of Ballston Spa, d 2/22/23 in
      B. S. (funeral sermon by Rev. William A. Clark) (buried with Masonic
      honors) (2-2/25)
1006. Bradley, James of Marbletown m 5/9/32 Hannah Hirst of Poughkeepsie;
      Rev. Dr. Reed) (8-5/16)
1007. Bradley, Joel (Rev.), 54, d in Orville (Onon. Co.) (formerly served as
      pastor of the Presbyterian Church in Ballston) (2-8/12/23)
1008. Bradley, Lemuel m 4/12/19 Mary Covell, dau of Benjamin, merchant, of
      Troy; Rev. Dr. Coe (9-4/20)
1009. Bradley, Ogden m 11/4/34 Cornelia Tappen, youngest dau of Gen. Tappen, in
      Ulster Co.; Rev. Henry Ostrander (8-11/11)
1010. Bradley, Thomas, 20, only s of Daniel of Salisbury, CT, d 8/30/01 (killed
      by the kick of a horse) (6-9/3)
1011. Bradner, Alonzo of Danville m Jane Clark of Watertown in W; Rev. George
      S. Boardman (8-5/28/34)
1012. Bradt, James F. of Albany m Jane Van Aps of Rotterdam, NY in Schenectady;
      Rev. J. Boyd (1-1/15/30)
1013. Bragau, Samuel m 5/2/16 Ann Covenhoven, both of Poughkeepsie; Rev. Cuyler
      (8-5/15)
1014. Bragaw, Isaac m 1/24/22 Catharine Yerry, both of Poughkeepsie; Rev.
      Cuyler (8-1/30)
1015. Brainard, Edwin m "Thanksgiving Day" Lucy Whitmore in East Haddam (state
      not given - probably CT) (double ceremony - see marr of Halsey Brewer)
      (8-12/28/31)
1016. Brainard, Lawrence, merchant, m Phidelia B. Gudcomb, both of Troy
      (9-1/19/19)
1017. Brainard, Leonard W. (Capt.) m 8/8/29 Sarah Ann Kenyon, both of Albany,
      in Bethlehem; Rev. Bois (1-8/11)
1018. Braman, Daniel m Jemima Wood in Easthampton ("The groom has become the
      grand-son of his father and the son of his brother. The bride has become
      the daughter of her grandfather and the sister of her father. The father
      is older than the grandfather.") (8-1/16/28)
1019. Braman, Samuel m 5/16/32 Helen Van Vliet, dau of Cornelius, Jr; Rev.
      William Cahoone. All of Hyde Park (8-5/23)
1020. Brand, Rebecca (Miss), 15, d 1/13/24 in Plattsburgh (7-1/24)
1021. Brandel, _____ of Schenectady drowned 11/6/01 when knocked overboard (by
      the boom) from a Newburgh sloop en route to NYC (6-11/19)
1022. Brandt, Mary, 36, wf of Philip, d 6/24/22 in Troy (9-7/9)
1023. Brannack, George S. of Troy m 11/23/28 Jane Wadsworth, dau of Joseph, Esq.
      of Pittstown, in P; Rev. Kinet of Hoosick (9-12/2)
1024. Brant, Joseph (Capt.), "a celebrated Indian chief",d 12/24/07 "at his seat
      at the head of Lake Ontario" (6-12/29)
1025. Bratt, John of Troy m 1/28/24 Lenchy Reeve, dau of John, Esq. of Berlin,
      NY, in B; Rev. Hull (9-3/2)
1026. Braun, Anthony Theodore (Rev.), 60, pastor of Evangelical Lutheran Churches
      of Brunswick and Greenbush, d 3/19/13 (funeral sermon by Rev. David of
      Troy (9-3/30)

1027. Brayton, Milton, merchant, of Utica m 5/19/30 Eleanor McKnight, dau of
       John, Esq. of Reading, PA, in R; Rev. Hemon Norton (1-6/7)
1028. Brazle, Nicholas m 11/14/11 Loretta Eggleston, both of Tockhomack; Rev.
       Millerton (8-12/4)
1029. Breck, Moses (Capt.), 47, d in Kinderhook (6-9/15/07)
1030. Breck, Sally (Miss), 17, dau of Capt. Moses, d 4/9/04 in Kinderhook
       (surv by parents and 3 sisters) (6-4/24)
1031. Brecklehasset(?), Herman, Esq., attorney, m 1/23/31 Sarah W. McKinnen,
       both of NYC; Rev. Archibald McClay (1-1/31/31)
1032. Breese, Catherine, 33, wf of Arthur, Esq., d 8/24/08 in Utica (8-8/31)
1033. Breese, David of Milford m Ruth Baker of Hartwick in H (3-2/24/23)
1034. Breeze, Arthur of Whitestown m 11/3/93 Caty Livingston, dau of Henry,
       Jr., Esq. of Poughkeepsie; Rev. Spierin (8-11/6)
1035. Brett, Henry of Charleston, SC m 9/27/20 Maria Louisa Lawrence, dau of
       Thomas, Esq. of Fishkill Landing; C. D. Westbrook (8-10/4)
1036. Brewer, Halsey of Chatham m "Thanksgiving Day" Louisa Whitmore in East
       Haddam (the first-named town perhaps and the second-named town
       probably in Connecticut) (double ceremony - see marr of Edwin Brainard)
       (Louisa and Lucy are daus of Joseph who "has 13 daughters 6 of whom are
       married") (8-12/28/31)
1037. Brewer, John m 8/7/23 Hannah Fitch in Cooperstown; Rev. Tiffany (3-8/11)
1038. Brewer, Phillip C. m 10/25/28 Sarah Lawless in Poughkeepsie; Rev. Welton
       (8-11/4)
1039. Brewerton, Cornelius V., Esq., 26, late of Salem (Wash. Co.), d 8/29/01
       in NYC (9-9/8)
1040. Brewerton, Henry, Esq., 35, from NYC d 9/5/03 in Cocksackie (surv by
       wf and 3 small ch) (6-9/13)
1041. Brewster, Bela (Dr.) of Rensselaerville m 10/3/21 Harriet E. Platt of
       Waterford; Rev. Dr. Coe (9-10/9)
1042. Brewster, Charles of Little Falls m 10/21/24 Mary Platner of Cooperstown
       in C; Rev. Smith (3-10/25)
1043. Brewster, Sanford, 26, d 10/6/30 at his father's home in Poughkeepsie
       (8-10/13)
1044. Brewster, William R., merchant, of Canandaigua m 5/12/29 Elizabeth B. Mott,
       dau of Samuel of NYC, in NYC "by His Honor the Mayor" (1-5/16)
1045. Briant, David m 11/14/05 Eleanor Herrington, both of Hebron (9-11/26)
1046. Briard, William A., Esq. of Portsmouth, NH m 7/19/21 Elizabeth G. Frith
       of Poughkeepsie, NY in P; Rev. Reed (8-8/1/21)
1047. Brick, Eliza (Miss), 21, dau of Capt. Moses, d 2/24/07 in Kinderhook
       (surv by her parents and 2 sisters) (6-3/17)
1048. *Bridge, James m 6/12/27 Mary Baily, both of Troy; Rev. Howard (9-7/10)
1049. Bridgen, Thomas, Esq. d in Albany (3-9/4/26)
1050. Brig, John m 6/17/07 Bethiah Dogherty, both of Clinton; Rev. D. Dodge
       (8-7/22)
1051. Briggs, Abner m Sally Russell, both of Easton, in E (9-3/15/03)
1052. Briggs, Avery (Rev.) of Hudson m Mary Winsor of Providence, RI in P;
       Rev. Dr. Gano (6-1/13/18)
1053. Briggs, Benjamin m 9/6/23 Elizabeth Montross; Tilley Crouse, Esq. All
       of Clinton (8-9/10) (Clinton in Dutchess Co.)
1054. Briggs, Cornight d 9/14/03 in Catskill (6-9/20)
1055. Briggs, Isaac m 3/21/29 Mary Ann Leech, both of Poughkeepsie; Rev. Dr.
       Reed (8-3/25)
1056. Briggs, Lot m 2/27/23 Sally Potter, both of New Lisbon, in Hartwick; Rev.
       Huse (3-3/3)
1057. Briggs, Peter m Mahetable Eliza Mosher, dau of Isaac, Esq., all of Hyde
       Park; Henry Tallmadge, Esq. (8-10/29/34)
1058. Briggs, Rufus, merchant, of Red Hook d in R.H. (6-10/1/16)
1059. Briggs, Silas m 11/1/21 Lydia Hodgeman in Ballston; Rev. R. Smith (2-11/7)
1060. Briggs, Stephen, Jr. m 12/14/31 Phebe Hewlett, dau of late Samuel, in Hyde
       Park; John S. Van Wagner, Esq. All of Hyde Park (8-12/21)
1062. Briggs, Tibbits m 5/11/30 Sarah Smith, dau of Hon. Munson, in Schaghticoke;
       Rev. David Butler of Troy (1-5/15)
1063. Brigham, Bela Brewster (Capt.) of Lobo, Upper Canada m 1/30/23 Abigail
       Whitney, dau of Nathan of Richfield, NY, in R; Rev. Huse (3-2/24)
1064. Brigham, Elijah (Hon.) d 2/22/16 in Washington City (Congressman from
       Mass.) (9-3/5)
* For Bridge family addendum see
  footnote (1048A), next page.   30

1065. Brill, Daniel m Meribeth Doughty, both of Beekman; Rev. Pell (8-10/27/13)
1066. Brill, Peter, Jr. m 9/15/10 Catharine Carman, both of Beekman; Ebenezer
     Cary, Esq. (8-9/19)
1067. Brimmer, Martin, Esq. of Boston, MA m 1/15/29 Harriet Wadsworth, dau of
     James, Esq., in Genesee, NY; Martin Brimmer, Esq. (1-1/31)
1068. Brinckerhoff, A. D., Esq. of Plattsburgh m 1/14/24 Matilda L. Moore, dau
     of late Judge Moore of champlain, in C; Rev. Labaree (7-1/24)
1069. Brinckerhoff, Abraham, Jr. m 3/16/99 Maria Platt, dau of Judge Platt of
     Poughkeepsie; Rev. Baldwin (8-3/19)
1070. Brinckerhoff, Derick A., Esq., late sheriff of Dutchess Co., d 2/13/15
     at his home in Fishkill (8-2/15)
1071. Brinckerhoff, Dirck, son of Abraham, Esq. of Fishkill, m 8/1/94 Caty
     Hoffman, dau of Robert, Esq. of Poughkeepsie; Rev. Van Vranken (8-8/6)
1072. Brinckerhoff, George, an aged inhabitant of fishkill, d 7/10/34 in
     Hopewell (8-7/16)
1073. Brinckerhoff, George C. (Capt.), 68, d 4/26/12 in Fishkill (surv by wf)
     (8-5/6)
1074. Brinckerhoff, Margaret Platt, wf of Stephen J., Esq. of Red Hook and
     oldest dau of Hon. Isaac Smith of Washington (Dut. Co.) d 3/18/18
1075. Brinckerhoff, Maria, 37, wf of Tunis, d 12/8/31 in Fishkill (8-12/21)
1076. Brinckerhoof, Derick A., Esq. m 8/26/10 Catherine Van Vrankin, both of
     Fishkill; Rev. Westbrook (8-8/29)
1077. Brinckerhoof, Margaret Platt, 17, wf of Stephen I. of Red Hook and oldest
     dau of Isaac Smith, Esq. of Washington (Dut. Co.) d 3/18/18 (8-3/25)
1078. Brinker, Dinah, 44, wf of Timothy, d 1/24/04 in Loonenburgh (Athens, NY)
     (6-1/31)
1079. Brinkerhoff, George T., 36, d 11/26/20 at his home in Fishkill (surv by
     wf and 6 ch)
1080. Brinkerhoff, Isaac, 61, merchant, of Troy d 12/29/22 (surv by a wife,
     "in feeble condition and a large family of children") (9-12/31)
1081. Brinkerhoff, Roelef, 82, father of Gen. H. R. of Owasco (Cay. Co.)
     d 12/28/#0 in Auburn (1-1/10/31)
1082. Brinkerhoff, Sophia, eife of late Isaac, d 3/2/23 (9-3/11)
1083. Brisban, Mary (Mrs.), about 100, wid of James, d "during the last week"
     at the poor house in Poughkeepsie (Her husband, James, who died several
     years before Mary, was the youngest son of a Protestant clergyman in the
     north of Ireland. He married Mary soon after his arrival in NY) (8-5/24
     and 5/31/20)
1084. Brisbin, John, 20, of Saratoga Co., "a member of the medical class",
     d 1/8/31 in Fairfield, Herkimer Co. (lung disease) (1-1/20)
1085. Bristol, Abel, about 66, d 1/19/20 at the Cumberland Hotel (this hotel
     probably in Plattsburgh) (7-1/22)
1086. Bristol, Abigail (Miss), 26, d in Canaan (6-12/13/03)
1087. Bristol, Asa M. m 4/2/28 Maria Bowers in Sand Lake; Rev. Samuel Amy. All
     of S.L. (9-4/8)
1088. Bristow, Henry of London (presumably in England), 2nd s of John of London,
     m 8/13/29 Rebeckah Pope (dau of late Thomas Pope, Esq., architect, of NYC)
     in Catskill; Rev. Joseph Prentiss (1-8/22)
1089. Britton, Seabry W. m 7/10/27 Lucy Holbridge, both of Watervliet, in
     Gibbonsville; Rev. Howard (9-7/17)
1090. Britton, Sebre W. of Troy m 11/818/28 Mary Ann Robinson of Albany in A;
     Rev. Lessis(?) (9-11/28)
1091. Broadhead, James O. (Col.) m 2/10/29 Caroline Wackenhagen, dau of Rev. Dr.
     Wackenhagen, in Clermont; Rev. Dr. A. Wackenhagen (1-2/25)
1092. Broadhead, Seth C., merchant, of Red Hook m 11/14/21 Mary Ann Earl
     (of NYC?); Rev. McMurray (8-11/21)
1093. Broadhead, Thomas (Dr.), 66, d 11/6/30 at his home in Clermont (was a
     practicing physician for more than 40 yrs and had served as pres. of
     the Medical Soc. of Columbia Co.) (8-11/17)
1094. Broadwell, Charles P. m 12/26/20 Jane Cuyler in Willsboro (7-1/6/21)
1095. Broadwell, Jared L. m 11/13/25 Mary Atherton of Jericho, VT in
     Plattsburgh, NY (7-11/19)
1096. Broadwell, John S. m 7/24/26 "Miss Reynolds", dau of Reuben, Esq. of
     Essex Co., in Plattsburgh (7-7/29)
1097. Broadwell, Noah, Esq., 53, d 5/2/26 in Plattsburgh (7-5/6)
1048A from pg. 30: Bridegroom's surname in Entry 9, pg. 1, should read Bridge.

31

1098. Broadwell, Rhoda, 38, wf of Noah, Esq., d 3/15/14 in Plattsburgh (7-3/19)
1099. Broadwell, Rhoda, 4 mo., d 6/29/14 in Plattsburgh (7-7/2)
1100. Broas, John m 11/30/11 _____ Griswold, both of Poughkeepsie; Rev. Covel
      (8-12/4)
1101. Broas, Sarah Ellen, 21, wf of Smith Broas, d 11/10/28 (funeral at the
      Reformed Dutch Church in Poughkeepsie)(8-11/12)
1102. Broas, Smith m 3/8/28 Sarah Ellen Lawson, both of Poughkeepsie; Rev.
      Cuyler (8-3/12)
1103. Broas, William m 8/26/20 Catharine Field, both of Poughkeepsie; Rev.
      Reed (8-8/30)
1104. Brock, John M. m 8/17/28 Margarett Reckord, both of Grafton; Jonathan
      Reed, Esq. of Pittstown (9-8/29)
1105. Brock, Stuart m 3/24/30 Phebe B. Skinner, dau of Joseph formerly of
      Plattsburgh, in Hawksbury, Upper Canada (1-4/22)
1106. Brockway, _____, inf s of Reed Brockway, d 3/10/21 in Troy (9-3/20)
1107. Brockway, Daniel m 2/6/23 Diana Thomas; Rev. Griffin (9-2/11)
1108. Brockway, Hannah, 49, wf of Levi, d 10/9/25 in Otsego (3-10/17)
1109. Brockway, Hiram S. m 1/1/22 Betsey Graves, both of Chazy, in C; Rev.
      Joel Byington (7-1/5)
1110. Brockway, Lathrop of Clinton (Oneida Co.) m Merilla Ticknor of Springfield
      in S; Rev. Putnam (3-1/27/23)
1111. Brockway, Marilla, 26, wf of Lathrop, d 12/16/23 in Clinton (Oneida Co.)
      (3-12/29)
1112. Brodhead, Thomas, M.D., 66, d at his home in Clermont (1-11/17/30)
1113. Brodrick, John S., merchant, m 3/23/23 Sarah Donnelly in Milford; Rev.
      John smith (3-4/7)
1114. Bromley, Anna Maria, 1 yr, dau of Daniel W. and Mary B., d 8/26/34 in
      Plattsburgh (7-8/30)
1115. Bromley, Sarah, wf of Elder Daniel, d 7/17/34 in Beekmantown (near
      Plattsburgh) (7-7/26)
1116. Bronson, Asael (Rev.) m 2/22/15 Mary Tompkins, both of Clinton (Dut. Co.);
      Rev. Cuyler (8-3/1)
1117. Bronson, Josiah W. m 2/5/31 Sarah Ann Voorhees, youngest dau of Ralph;
      Rev. Buttolph. All of La Grange (8-2/9)
1118. Brook, James m 5/23/15 Mrs. Mary Hillequist, both of Poughkeepsie; Rev.
      Leonard (8-5/31)
1119. Brooks, Alexander S. (Maj.) of the "Regiment of Light Artillery" m Sarah
      Turner in Boston (state not given); Rev. Holley (7-6/21/17)
1120. Brooks, Amos of Sand Lake m 8/7/19 Pamelia Pease of Troy; Rev. Sommers
      (9-8/10)
1121. Brooks, Bela m 3/30/23 Alice Botsford, dau of Capt. Vine Botsford, at Zion
      Church in Butternuts; Rev. Wheeler (3-4/7)
1122. Brooks, Benjamin F. of the firm of Blackwood and Brooks of Herkimer
      m 3/4/29 Sarah Griswold, dau of late Hon. Gaylord Griswold of Herkimer,
      in H; Rev. Henry Snyder (1-3/7)
1123. Brooks, Daniel H. of the firm of Henry Brooks and Co. m 11/16/31 Catharine
      Ann Reynolds, youngest dau of Nathaniel, in NYC, all of Albany; Rev.
      Hawks (1-11/21)
1124. Brooks, Daniel N., Esq. of Poughkeepsie, attorney, d 8/28/21 (8-9/5)
1125. Brooks, David (Lt.) of the 2nd Regt. of Infantry m 1/10/22 Frances S.
      Morris of Utica in U; Rev. Anthon (8-1/23)
1126. Brooks, David (Lt.) of the 2nd Infantry, U.S. Army, son of Hon. David
      Brooks formerly of Dutchess Co., NY, d 5/16/27 at Fortress Mackinac, MI
      (8-6/20)
1127. Brooks, Henry of the firm of H. Brooks and Co. m Cornelia Holmes, youngest
      dau of Eldad, Esq.; Rev. William Parkinson. All of NYC (1-12/13/30)
1128. Brooks, Isaac, 30, of Poughkeepsie d 5/6/93 (consumption) (surv by wf and
      3 small ch) (8-5/15)
1129. Brooks, James G., Esq. m 1/23/29 Elizabeth Aiken, dau of late John, Esq.
      of Dutchess Co., in NYC; Rev. Upfold (1-1/28)
1130. Brooks, John m 10/29/14 Ann Grimshaw of Poughkeepsie; Rev. Leonard
      (8-11/2)
1131. Brooks, John E. of Rhinebeck m 7/14/23 Orpha M. Bugbee, late of Troy, in
      Chatham; Rev. Theodorius Clark (9-7/22)
1132. Brooks, Jonathan, 90, d 4/3/29 in Albany (funeral from his late home,
      15 Plain St.) (1-4/6)

1133. Brooks, Marietta (Miss), 16, formerly of Middle Haddam, CT, d in Hudson, NY (6-1/25/11)
1134. Brooks, Peter, 53, d 5/11/30 in Albany (funeral from his late home, 100 Hudson St.)(1-5/12)
1135. Broom, William, Esq., 62, of "Cromelbo" (Crum Elbow) (Dut. Co.) d 1/9/30 in Albany (Jacob Mancius is mentioned as a friend or relative) (funeral from 20 Montgomery St., Albany) (1-1/10)
1136. Broome, John (Hon.), Lt. Governor of NY, m 7/9/06 "Mrs. Hunter", wid of Robert, Esq. of NYC; Rev. Dr. Rodgers (9-7/15)
1137. Broome, John (Hon.), 72, Lt. Gov. of NY, d 8/7/10 in NYC (6-8/10 and 8-8/15)
1138. Brother, Valentine, Esq., state assemblyman from Ontario Co., d 1/9/20 in Seneca (3-1/17)
1139. Brotherson, Philip of Schenectady m 1/2/25 Alice Odell, wid of late Maj. Odell, in Ballston Spa; Rev. Babcock (2-2/8)
1140. Brower, John W., 15, s of William, drowned 6/17/10 (along with the three named below) "while bathing in the Hudson River a little below the city of Albany": Isaac Rue Halenbake, 13, s of Isaac B.; William Kidney, 12, s of Jonathan; and Peter Clapper, 16, an apprentice of Mr. Kidney and s of the late "Mr. Clapper" of Bethlehem (6-6/22)
1141. Brown, A. E. of Albany m 5/20/29 Elizabeth S. Nixson, dau of W. E. of NYC, in NYC; Rev. Dr. Knox (1-5/28)
1142. Brown, Abner m 2/17/31 Sally Winchell, dau of Philo M., in Northeast; Rev. Thomas Winter (8-3/9)
1143. Brown, Abraham m 10/8/26 Rachel Bates, both of Fishkill, in F; Rev. Pierce (8-10/11)
1144. Brown, Alfred H., about 28, merchant, of the firm of Brown and Heart of Troy d "recently" (was drowned when his carriage, through milling oxen, was forced off a ferry boat about three miles above Norwich, CT on the Shetucket River while he was en route to Boston by way of Providence (9-8/18/07)
1145. Brown, Amelia Caroline, dau of Dr. Christopher B. Brown, d 5/3/30 in Greenfield (a bean passed into her windpipe) (1-5/13)
1146. Brown, Amos m 2/17/25 Perris Chase in Maryland, NY; Rev. Caldwell (3-2/28)
1147. Brown, Andrew, merchant, of Albany d 2/16/07 in Albany (9-3/3)
1148. Brown, Benjamin, Jr. of Troy m 6/20/21 Roxanny Ranney of Gibbonsville; Rev. Dr. Yates of Schenectady (9-6/26)
1149. Brown, Betsy (Miss), 30, only dau of Joseph, Esq., d 2/3/22 at the home of her father in Charlton (2-2/13)
1150. Brown, Caleb, 58, d 9/29/15 in Plainfield, NY (3-10/5)
1151. Brown, Calvin H. m 12/30/27 Phebe Godfrey; Calvin P. Vary, Esq. All of Berlin (9-1/15/28)
1152. Brown, Charles of Loonenburgh (Athens, NY) m 9/11/04 Sally Hatch of New Canaan (state not given) in New Canaan (6-9/25)
1153. Brown, Charles, 74, for many yrs a deacon in the Baptist Church, d 6/5/17 in Hudson (6-6/10)
1154. Brown, Charlotte Maria, inf dau of Rev. David, d 1/15/31 (1-1/17)
1155. Brown, David (Rev.), rector of St. James Church in Hyde Park m 6/7/21 Mary B. Cruttenden, oldest dau of L. Cruttenden of Albany, at St. Peter's Church, Albany; Rev. Lacey (8-6/13)
1156. Brown, David of Troy m 12/24/23 Caroline Dwelley of Lansingburgh in St. Paul's Church; Rev. Butler (9-12/30)
1157. Brown, Deborah, 77, wf of late Francis of Nantucket/ d 2/22/07 in Hudson (state not given) (6-3/3)
1158. Brown, Edward, 6 mo, s of Henry, d 2/13/31 in Albany (1-2/16)
1159. Brown, Elizabeth, 8 or 3 (blurred), dau of Stephen C., d 2/17/27 (8-2/28)
1160. Brown, Ephraim (Dr.), 29, d in Batavia, NY (3-5/22/26)
1161. Brown, Frederick W. m 6/21/34 Mary Valentine, oldest dau of Isaac of Poughkeepsie; Rev. Dr. Reed (8-6/25)
1162. Brown, George lately from NYC drowned 7/30/96 near or in Catskill (sail boat upset) (3-8/11)
1163. Brown, George (Col.) m 9/13/26 Hannah Hopkins, dau of Judge Enos; Rev. Winter. All of Northeast (8-9/20)
1164. Brown, Henry, Esq. of Springfield m 3/18/17 Clarissa Starr of Cooperstown; Rev. John Smith (3-3/27)

33

1165. Brown, Hester, 37, (relict of Charles, lately deceased) d 6/21/17 in
      Hudson (6-6/24)
1166. Brown, Hiram m 10/3/25 Julia Bird, dau of Moore Bird, in Amenia; Rev.
      Willson (8-10/12)
1167. Brown, Isaac, merchant, of Albany m 5/27/30 Isabella Brown, 2nd dau of
      late Henry, Esq. of Knox, in K; Rev. Williams (2-5/29)
1168. Brown, Jacob (Lt.), quartermaster, of the 6th U.S. Infantry m 1/24/19
      Sarah Smith of Montgomery Co. at the cantonment in Plattsburgh; Rev.
      Whelpley (7-1/30)
1169. Brown, James of Cincinnati, OH m 11/24/30 Maria C. Page of Unadilla at
      St. Matthew's Church in Unadilla; Rev. N. H. Adams (1-12/4)
1170. Brown, James, Esq. of the firm of Brown Bros. and Co. of NYC m 9/14/31
      Eliza M. Coe, dau of late Dr. Jonas Coe of Troy, in Watervliet; Rev.
      Dr. Nott (1-9/16)
1171. Brown, James m 10/27/31 Mahettable Flanders; Richard D. Arthur, Esq.
      All of Ticonderoga (1-11/4)
1172. Brown, James W., 4, s of Capt. Joseph, d 8/29/21 in Pittstown (funeral
      service conducted by Rev. Dr. Coe and Rev. Younglove) (9-9/4)
1173. Brown, Jane, 23, dau of Widow Martha, d 3/14/29 in Albany (consumption)
      (1-3/16)
1174. Brown, John (Rev.), rector of St. George's Church in Newburgh, m 11/22/19
      Frances Elizabeth Ludlow, youngest dau of late Robert, Esq. of Newburgh,
      at St. George's Church in Newburgh; Right Rev. Bishop Hobart (8-11/24)
1175. Brown, John, 66, late flour inspector of NYC, d 10/20/30 in NYC (1-10/26)
1176. Brown, John, late of Plattsburgh, d in Willsborough (7-7/26/34)
1177. Brown, Jonas of Troy m 3/30/23 Lois Choat of Lansingburgh in L; Rev.
      Leland Howard (9-4/8)
1178. Brown, Jonathan, m 3/17/25 Ursula Jackson in Burlington (Ots. Co.); Rev.
      Nash (3-3/21)
1179. Brown, Josiah m 5/22/31 Maria Clark in Keeseville; Rev. Chamberlin
      (4 [Keeseville Herald]-5/24)
1180. Brown, Malachi W. m 8/5/27 Eliza Dunlap, both of Lansingburgh; Rev.
      Howard (9-8/7)
1181. Brown, Mary (Mrs.), about 29,(formerly of Windsor, VT), consort of Jonas,
      d 8/20/22 in Troy, NY. Their infant dau d 8/30. (9-9/3)
1182. Brown, Mary Caroline, dau of late Charles Bruckden Brown, d 3/11/30 in
      Philadelphia (1-3/17)
1183. Brown,Mathew, Jr. m 1/4/29 Mary Ann Burnham of Black Rock in B. R.; Rev.
      Addison Searle (1-1/8)
1184. Brown, Matilda, 3, youngest dau of Edmund, d 3/4/30 in Albany (funeral
      from her father's home on North Market St.) (1-3/6)
1185. Brown, Matthew, Sr., 90, (a Rev. patriot) d 3/25/31 in Rochester (was
      an early settler there) (1-4/5)
1186. Brown, Nancy (Mrs.), 21, d 10/29/09 in Athens, NY (6-11/7)
1187. Brown, Nehemiah m 7/7/01 Sally Byington in Hudson (6-7/9)
1188. Brown, Orlando of Ogden (Genesee Co.) m 11/9/25 Maria Allen of
      Burlington (Ots. Co.) in B; A. Sheldon, Esq. (3-11/14)
1189. Brown, Pamela, 26, wf of Nehemiah, Jr., d 3/5/31 in Rye, NY (1-3/7)
1190. Brown, Reuben m Marcia Griggs, both of Troy; Rev. Coe (9-3/17/07)
1191. Brown, Samuel, 27, d 11/28/02 in Lansingburgh, NY (lately from Spittal,
      Lincolnshire, England - landed at NYC "about seven weeks since and it
      is believed had no connections in this country" - further information
      available from Mr. Archibald Campbell of Lansingburgh) (9-11/30)
1192. Brown, Thomas m 12/22/03 Polly White, both of Northeast (8-1/10/04)
1193. Brown, Timothy of Hartford, CT m 6/1/04 Phebe Hensdel in Canaan, NY
      (6-6/11)
1194. Brown, William B. (Dr.) of Falmouth, MA m 11/8/27 Beulah W. Purinton, dau
      of Abijah of Troy, at the Friends Meeting house (town not given)
      (9-11/13)
1195. Brown, William J. of Beekman m 11/22/20 Maria Skidmore, dau of Walter of
      Clinton (Dut. Co.), in C; Rev. Clark (8-11/29)
1196. Brown, William W. of Freedom m 12/30/21 Freelove Davis of Pleasant Valley;
      Rev. C. C. Cuyler (8-1/2/22)
1197. Brownal, Thomas C., professor of chemistry at Union College, Schenectady,
      m 8/6/11 Charlotte Dickerson of Lansingburgh in L; Rev. David Butler
      (9-8/13)

34

1198. Brownejohn, Ann, 59, wid of late Samuel, Esq., d 12/20/16 (8-12/25)
1199. Brownell, Benjamin of Sand Lake m 1031/15 Clarissa Richy of Troy; Rev.
Coe (9-11/7)
1200. Brownell,Mary, 66, wid of Aaron, Esq. formerly of Beekman, d 7/29/31 in
Poughkeepsie (8-8/3)
1201. Brownell, Russell m 4/21/25 Mary Rockwell; Rev. Smith (3-4/25)
1202. Browning, Aaron, "an aged inhabitant of Freedom", d 5/31/22 at his home
in Freedom (8-6/5)
1203. Brownson, Allen, 39, d 7/22/29 at the home of Dyer Ames in Plainfield,
NY (he had claimed to have been born in East Windsor [state not given]
and to have left a wife and three children living in Middleborough, MA)
(he had further requested that his death be published in papers of New
London and Hartford, CT, in the Albany Argus, and papers in Syracuse, NY
as well as New Bedford, MA) (1-8/21)
1204. Brownson, Rumina, 2 yrs, d "last week" in Plattsburgh (7-4/9/13)
1205. Bruce, James m 2/12/29 Mary Hillson, both of Albany, in Troy; Rev. Tucker
(1-2/19)
1206. Bruen, M. (Rev.) m Mary Ann Davenport in NYC (3-1/20/23)
1207. Bruen, Matthias (Rev.), pastor of the Bleecker Street Presbyterian Church
in NYC, d 9/6/29 in NYC (1-9/9 and 8-9/9)
1208. Brugiere, Juliet, 15, dau of Charles, Esq., d 5/15/30 in NYC (1-5/19)
1209. Brumfield, Stephen G. m 6/6/29 Martha Smith, both of Fishkill; Rev.
Cornelius D. Westbrook (8-6/17)
1210. Brumley, _____, 4, s of Hallock Brumley, d "last week" in Beekmantown
(Clinton Co.) (7-10/16/19)
1211. Brumley, Fanny, 3, dau of Hallock, d 5/9/23 in Beekmantown (Clinton Co.)
(7-5/24)
1212. Brundage, Stephen m 1/26/06 Polly Reynolds, wid of Zadock Reynolds and
dau of Jonathan Reynolds (perhaps in Salem, NY); Rev. Ely (8-2/11)
1213. Brunson, Josiah m 8/15/02 Abigail Bearding in Franklin (6-8/24)
1214. Brush, Edmond, Esq., attorney, m 4/12/12 Fanny Holden, both of
Poughkeepsie; Rev. Cuyler (8-4/15)
1215. Brush, Eliza Treat, 45, wf of Platt Brush, Esq., d 11/18/28 in
Chillicothe, OH (8-12/10)
1216. Brush, Hannah (Mrs.) d "recently" in Albany (mentioned are her brother,
John Stone, and her brothers-in-law, Ezra Bugbee and Jesse G. Brush
(funeral at the home of Ezra Bugbee, corner Swan and State Sts.)
(1-10/3/31)
1217. Brush, Lemuel, 85, d 2/2/31 in Amenia (8-2/9)
1218. Brush, Valentine, oldest s of Gen. Brush, d 8/18/24 in Poughkeepsie
(8-8/25)
1219. Brush, William (Col.), 80, (a Rev. officer) d 5/18/30 in Norwich (1-6/10)
1220. Bruyn, Cornelius, merchant, of Shawangunk m 1/22/29 Sarah Bevier,
youngest dau of Philip, deceased, in Rochester (Ulster Co.); Rev.
Westfall (1-2/9)
1221. Bryan, Calvin H., Esq., attorney, m 2/11/22 Nancy Angel, both of
Burlington, in B; Rev. Daniel Nash (3-2/25)
1222. Bryan, Henry, Esq., attorney, of Olean m Clarissa L. Forbes (or Fobes)
of Canandaigua in C; Rev. A. D. Eddy (1-1/26 and 1-1/31)
1223. Bryan, Pernelley, 34, wf of James, Esq., d 8/28/13 in Hillsdale (6-9/7)
1224. Bryan, Richard S. (Dr.) of NYC m 6/1/29 Mary Elizabeth Richards, dau of
Rufus of Troy, in Troy; Rev. Butler (1-6/10)
1225. Bryan, Sarah, 91 (wid of Ezra, deceased) d 11/19/29 in Northeast (8-12/2)
1226. Bryan., William Nelson of Schaghticoke m 10/8/28 Elizabeth Fort, dau of
Col. Fort of Saratoga, in S; Rev. Francis Whayling (9-10/14)
1227. Bryant, _____ (Capt.) of the 10th U.S. Infantry d 11/28/13 in Plattsburgh (7-12/4)
1228. Bryant, Laura (Miss), 25, dau of Amos of Northeast, d 5/20/31 (8-5/25)
1229. Bryant, Schuyler m Nancy Matteson (in Laurens?); Rev. King (1-9/3/29)
1230. Buck, _____, consort of Belina of Troy, d 4/20/22 (9-4/23)
1231. Buck, Ephraim m 3/7/13 Mary Baker; Rev. Halsey. All of Plattsburgh.
(7-3/12)
1232. Buck, Israel of Washington (Dut. Co.) m 11/14/28 Jane Eliza Green of
Stanford (Dut. Co.); Isaac Sutherland, Esq. (8-11/26)
1233. Buck, John, "an aged inhsbitant of Milton", d 9/10/25 in Milton (2-9/13)

35

1234. Buck, Ruth, 32, consort of Belina, d 4/20/22 in Troy (7-5/11)
1235. Buck, Uphema, 6, dau of B. Buck, Esq. of Troy, d 3/26/23 (9-4/1)
1236. Buckbee, Enos m 12/29/30 Eliza Badgley; Rev. Green. All of Albany
       (1-12/31)
1237. Buckingham, C. R. (Lt.) of the U.S. Army m 7/5/30 Mary E. Gird in
       Litchfield; Rev. Goodyear (1-7/23)
1238. Buckingham, Gideon m 1/14/13 Maria Josephine Crowley, both of Troy
       (9-1/19)
1239. Buckley, George, 18, step-son of Francis Adancourt, d 1/28/27 in Troy
       (9-1/30)
1240. Buckminster, Jane (Mrs.), 68, d 10/21/33 in Keeseville (4 [Keeseville
       Herald]-10/29)
1241. Budd, Underhill, Esq., formerly of Fishkill, d 6/20/31 in Schodack,
       Rensselaer Co. (8-7/6)
1242. Buel, Anson of Ballston Spa m 12/27/21 Mary Wakeman of Ballston in B; Rev.
       Reuben Smith (2-1/2/22)
1243. Buel, Caroline C. (Miss), 18, d 8/21/13 (probably in Burlington, VT)
       (7-9/4)
1244. Buel, David, Jr., Esq. of Troy m 5/22/14 Harriet Hillhouse, dau of late
       John G., Esq. of Montville (CT?) in Norwich, CT; Rev. Dr. Strong
       (9-5/31)
1245. Buel, Elam, Esq. of Troy m 1/11/28 Frances Huntington of Hinsdale, MA;
       Rev. Beman (9-1/15)
1246. Buel, Elias (Maj.) (a Rev. veteran), father of Jesse, Esq. late editor of
       the Albany Argus, d 6/1/24 (7-6/5)
1247. Buel, Hannah, 51, wf of Elam, d 4/23/27 in Troy (9-5/1)
1248. Buel, Horace m 10/21/18 Sally Decamp, both of Troy, in Lansingburgh;
       Rev. Dr. Blatchford (9-10/27)
1249. Buel, Josiah, Jr., 46, d 11/21/20 in Easton (Wash. Co.) (9-11/28)
1250. Buel, Olive (Miss), 16, d 9/27/12 in Hudson (formerly of Fairhaven, VT)
       (dau of late William of Fairhaven) (6-10/5)
1251. Buel, Samuel, 25, s of David of Troy, d 1/28/15 in Charleston, SC
       (consumption) (9-2/28)
1252. Buel, Samuel T. of Plattsburgh m 7/17/34 Jane Briggs of Rochester, VT
       in R; Rev. Fuller (7-7/26)
1253. Buel, William (Deacon), 89, d 11/27/95 in Marlborough (state not given)
       (surv by 4th wf and 3 children out of 11 total) (3-12/10)
1254. Buel, William of Essex, VT m 3/8/23 Loucy (sic) Flagg of Plattsburgh in
       P; Rev. Frederick Halsey (7-3/15)
1255. Buell, Ezra (Maj.), 90, (a Rev. officer) d 10/28/33 in Stillwater (7-11/16)
1256. Buell, Horatio, Esq., formerly first judge of Warren Co., d 3/9/33 in
       Ballston (4-[Keeseville Herald]-3/12)
1257. Buell, Oliver of Middlefield m 4/26/20 Betsey Granger of Cherry Valley
       in C.V.; John Gault, Esq. (3-5/1)
1258. Bugbey, Eliza, wf of Dr. Abel, d 8/5/05 in Lansingburgh (9-8/13)
1259. Bugby, Abiel, 42, d 7/15/30 in Albany (funeral from his late home on
       Quackenbush St.) (1-7/17)
1260. Bulkley, Ellen, about 58, wf of Joseph, Esq., d 1/16/19 in Poughkeepsie
       (8-1/20)
1261. Bulkley, Horace W. m 11/3/15 Margaret Clendening, dau of John, Esq., in
       NYC (9-11/14)
1262. Bulkley, Silas Butler, 10, s of Chester, d 5/9/31 in Albany (funeral from
       the home of Keous(?), 65 Hudson St.) (1-5/20)
1263. Bulkley, William, "woolen Manufacturer", of Pleasant Valley d 12/19/31 in
       P. V. (8-12/21)
1264. Bull, Archibald, Esq. m 12/27/27 Mary Ann Bigelow, both of Troy; Rev.
       Howard (9-1/1/28)
1265. Bull, Jasper of Chesterfield m 3/12/33 Elizabeth Coffrin of Saranac in
       Peru, NY; Ezra Williams, Esq. (4 [Keeseville Herald]-3/19)
1266. Bull, John L., 23, a native of Sacketts Harbor, NY d 9/22 in Washington
       (no indication as to which Washington in the report) (1-10/1)
1267. Bull, Nathaniel of Morristown, NJ m 10/20/18 Rebecca Jenison of Troy; Rev.
       Dr. Coe (9-10/27)
1268. Bull, William H. (Maj.) m 9/20/29 Sarah Whiting, dau of Col. John, at the
       Methodist Church in Bath (Steuben Co.); Rev. William Bostwick (1-9/26)

36

1269. Bullen, Jeduthan (Capt.), 35, d 12/6/19 in Peru, NY (died from injuries sustained "in the flight of a span of horses") (7-12/11)
1270. Bullions, Alexander (Rev.) of Cambridge m 2/24/31 Mary McClellan of Hebron in H; Rev. Irvine (1-3/7)
1271. Bullis, Charles m 11/21/33 Rachel Breyman, both of Peru, NY; Ahaz Hays, Esq. (4 [Keeseville Herald]-11/26)
1272. Bullmore, William B., 22, formerly of Poughkeepsie, m 1/2/15 Mrs. Easther Hall, 55, of Amenia; John Jewett, Esq. (8-2/1)
1273. Bullock, Joseph H. m 11/26/29 Mary Ann Jones, dau of William of Bethlehem, in B; Rev. Kissam (1-11/28)
1274. Bulmore, Edy (Mrs.), 68, widow, d 11/26/21 in Poughkeepsie (member of Baptist ch.) (8-11/28)
1275. Bumstead, Thomas m 10/21/21 Eleanor Van Arnum, both of Troy; Rev. Griffin (9-11/6)
1276. Bunce, William of Egremont, MA m Sally Sturges in Kinderhook, NY; Rev. Sickles (6-11/9/13)
1277. Bunker, Alexander, Esq. of Athens, NY m Almira Bushnell of Baltimore (MD?) in Troy; Rev. Griffen (9-2/18/23)
1278. Bunker, Edward, 2, s of Capt. George, d 7/5/08 in Hudson (6-7/19)
1279. Bunker, Elizabeth, 20, d in Hudson (she was the 2nd child and the first female born "after the settlement of Hudson") (6-1/22/05)
1280. Bunker, Harzillia, 76, formerly of NYC and a member of the Society of Friends, d 7/25/30 in Hudson (1-7/31)
1281. Bunker, Jeremiah B. of Plattsburgh m 8/16/21 Elizabeth Scribner of Beekmantown (near Plattsburgh); Rev. Halsey (7-9/1)
1282. Bunker, Judith (Miss), 19, dau of Capt. Solomon, d 7/8/02 in Hudson (6-7/13)
1283. Bunker, Mary, 24, wf of Capt. George, d 8/28/08 in Hudson (6-8/30)
1284. Bunker, Nancy, 21, wf of Timothy, d 5/6/07 in Hudson (6-5/12)
1285. Bunker, Peleg, 78, d 3/29/06 in Hudson (6-4/1)
1286. Bunker, William, 18, s of Capt. Elijah of Hudson, d in NYC ("fell from aloft on the deck of a ship and fractured his skull") (6-11/15/08)
1287. Bunker, William (Capt.), formerly of Hudson, d in Athens, NY (6-4/12/14)
1288. Bunton, Elisha S. (Dr.) of Albany m 1/13/30 Elizabeth Eddy, oldest dau of late Col. Tisdale Eddy, deceased, of Pittstown (Renss. Co.); Rev. H. R. Weed (1-1/15)
1289. Burbanks, Abraham m 7/4/19 Margaret Mackoll, both of Sandy Hill (Wash. Co.); Rev. Sommers (9-7/6)
1290. Burch, George, Esq., 69, d 2/9/14 in Hudson (6-2/15)
1291. Burdett, Wigglesworth (Mr.), 45, d 5/21/20 in Cooperstown (3-5/22)
1292. Burdick, Abraham, 23, d 10/30/34 in Poughkeepsie (8-11/5)
1293. Burdick, David m 11/3/25 Olive Tanner, both of Edmeston; Rev. Cone (3-11/21)
1294. Burdick, Ira m 2/14/24 Polly Wilcox; Rev. Saterlee (9-3/2)
1295. Burdick, Phineas H. (Dr.) m 5/17/29 Sally Dyer, dau of John of Scott, in Cortland Co.; Rev. L. Lyons (1-6/11)
1296. Burge, Sarah (Miss), 41, d 11/6/04 in Cooperstown (breast cancer) (3-11/15)
1297. Burge, Seneca, supposed formerly to have lived in Waterville, d 8/30/30 at the home of Charles Scrafford in Guilderland ("had been a clerk in a store that burned "last spring" in Waterville (1-9/2)
1298. Burgert, George (Capt.), 34, d 11/25/04 in Kinderhook (surv by wf and 5 small ch) (6-12/4)
1299. Burgess, Thomas, formerly a sergeant in Capt. Spencer's Co., 29th U.S. Infantry, d 1/17/18 at Fort Covington (7-2/14)
1300. Burget, Lambert (Capt.), 81, d 4/18/17 in Kinderhook (6-4/22)
1301. Burghdoorf, Philip m 1/5/03 Tamer Hedden (8-3/1)
1302. Burknap, Cyrus m 10/24/20 Eunis Harris of Northeast; Rev. R. G. Armstrong (8-11/15)
1303. Burlingham, Ezekiel of Hartwick d 9/4/13 in Albany (3-9/11)
1304. Burnham, Jonathan C. of Sullivan (Mad. Co.) m 8/29/18 Harriet Tucker of Schenectady; Rev. Butler (9-9/1)
1305. Burnett, Thomas B. d 9/4/22 in Ballston (kicked by a horse) (funeral sermon by Rev. Clark) (buried with Masonic honors in the town of Malta) (2-9/10)
1306. Burnham, Asa A., Esq., attorney, 40, d at his home in Union Square (consumption) (1-6/29/30)

1307. Burnham, Asa N. d 6/15/30 at Union Springs (Cay. Co.) (1-6/22)
1308. Burnham, Dyer, Esq., attorney, m 8/31/31 Sophia E. Goodell, dau of late
Hon. Richard. All of Adams (Jeff. Co.) (1-10/29)
1309. Burnham, Goerge, Esq. of Burlington, VT m 5/9/21 A. P. Buel of Champlain
in C; Rev. Labaree (7-5/12)
1310. Burnham, Gordon of Meriden, CT m 6/19/31 Ann G. Ives of Utica, NY at
Trinity Ch. in Utica; Rev. Benjamin Dorr (1-6/23)
1311. Burnham, Henry (Dr.), 24 (2nd s of Michael, Esq., senior editor of the
Evening Post) d 2/15/30 in NYC (deceased was resident physician "in the
Hospital attached to the Penitentiary and Alms House" in NYC) (1-2/18)
1312. Burnham, Hiram, merchant, m 12/14/22 Minerva Chittenden of Williston in
W; Mr. Clark (7-12/21)
1313. Burnham, Samuel W., merchant, m Betsey Inslee, dau of Joseph, in
Canandaigua. All of Bath (Steuben Co.) (6-3/31/07)
1314. Burnham, William E. m 11/7/18 Ann Mariah Kittle, dau of Capt. S., at Union
Village; Elder Barber. All of Union Village (9-11/24)
1315. Burnit, Aaron of Freedom m 10/4/21 Allicia Hambleton of Pleasant Valley;
Rev. Clark (8-10/10)
1316. Burnitt, James of Washington (Dut. Co.) m 5/30/22 Jane Christian of
Freedom; John Clapp, Esq. (8-6/5)
1317. Burnley, John m Mrs. Maria Green in Fishkill; Rev. Thomas (8-4/7/24)
1318. Burns, Frederick, printer, of Poughkeepsie m 2/7/22 Eliza Garrison of
Newburgh;Patrick B. Collins, Esq. (8-2/13)
1319. Burnside, John of Maryland, NY m 12/22/13 Patty Johnson of Kortright
in K; Elder Lake (3-1/8/14)
1320. Burr, Hulda, 61, wf of John, d 10/30/22 in Malta, NY (2-11/12)
1321. Burr, Isaac, 69, d 7/6/29 in NYC (8-7/8)
1322. Burr, James S. of the house of Burr and Seaman and son of late Isaac,
d 2/26/31 in Pensacola (presumably in Florida) (8-4/6)
1323. Burr, Jonathan, merchant, of Lansingburgh m 4/8/99 Sally Dickinson, dau
of Tertullus, Esq. of Westchester Co. (9-4/23)
1324. Burr, Nathan m 1/31/03 Mrs. Grace Terry, both of Pawling; Job Crawford,
Esq. (8-3/1)
1325. Burr, William H. m 11/16/34 Chloe C. Pearce; Elder Nehemiah Johnson.
All of Pawling (8-11/9)
1326. Burrall, ____, consort of Thomas D., Esq., d 4/5/31 in Geneva (8-4/20)
1327. Burrall, Charlotte, wf of Thomas D., Esq. of Poughkeepsie and dau of
William Davies, Esq. of Poughkeepsie, d 9/14/20 (in Geneva, NY?)
(data from a lengthy obit. from the Geneva Gazette as reflected in
the Poughkeepsie paper of reference, namely: 8-9/27)
1328. Burrall, Thomas D., Esq. of Geneva, NY m 1/24/22 Sarah I. Mann of Hudson
in H; Rev. Reed (8-1/30)
1329. Burrell, Addin of Middlefield m 3/27/22 Betsey Gilliland of Westford
in W; Rev. Sawin (3-4/1)
1330. Burrell, Andrew W. m 4/28/14 Hannah Graves in Cooperstown (3-4/30)
1331. Burrell, John, 45, s of Jonathan, both of Cooperstown, d 4/13/11 (3-4/20)
1332. Burrit, Curtis R., 16, s of Dr. Eli of Troy, d 2/9/15 (consumption)
(9-2/28)
1333. Burritt, Ely (Dr.), 50, d 2/1/23 in Troy (9-2/9)
1334. Burroughs, Ezekiel, printer, m 8/25/22 Maria Applebye; Rev. Reed. All of
Poughkeepsie (8-8/28)
1335. Burroughs, George (Dr.) m "lately" Ann Collins, dau of Hezekiah, Esq., all
of Beekman; Rev. Barculoo (8-10/28/07)
1336. Burroughs, Mary, consort of Capt. Elijah, d 1/8/26 in Irasburgh (state not
given - - probably Vermont) (7-1/28)
1337. Burroughs, Thomas, 74, of Fishkill d 3/22/13 in Poughkeepsie (8-4/7)
1338. Burrows, Charles E. (Dr.) of Troy m 3/24/27 Sarah Ann Gager of Pleasant
Valley in P. V.; Rev. Pierce (9-3/30)
1339. Burrows, Chester m 1/20/20 Visa Webster, both of Canaan (possibly a
double ceremony - see marr of Charles Allen to Phila Webster) (9-2/8)
1340. Burrows, John m 6/27/27 Maria Giles; Rev. S. Arnold. All of Fishkill
(8-7/4)
1341. Burrows, Lorenzo (of the firm of R. S. and I. Burrows of Albion (Orl. Co.)
m 5/11/30 Louisa Lord of Groton in G (1-6/1)
1342. Burrows, Mary Van, 29, wf of Silas E., d 1/30/31 in NYC (1-2/4)

1343. Burrows, Thomas m 11/29/18 Ann Warren, both of Fishkill, in Poughkeepsie;
      Rev. Dr. Covel (8-12/2)
1344. Burt, Adolphus m 8/7/19 Deborah Barker in Plattsburgh (7-8/14)
1345. Burt, David, Esq., merchant, of Buffalo m 9/8/30 Harriet R. Whiting at
      the home of Joel Northrop, Esq. in Utica; Rev. S. C. Aiken (double
      ceremony - see marr of Henry H. Sizer) (1-9/17)
1346. Burt, Raney, 65, wf of Col. Abram, d 8/21/31 in Watervliet (1-9/3)
1347. Burt, Thomas M. of Warwick m 5/21/29 Lydia Butts of South Hadley, MA in
      Brattleboro, VT (1-6/2)
1348. Burtch, Frederick F., manufacturer, of the firm of Turner and Burtch of
      Pine Plains, m 10/8/34 Susanna Smith, dau of Wright Smith of Stanford
      (Dut. Co.); Henry Tallmadge, Esq. (8-10/15)
1349. Burtis, John m 1/22/24 Betsey Eycleshimer; Samuel S. Hide, Esq. All of
      Pittstown (Renss. Co.) (9-2/3)
1350. Burtis, Thomas of La Grange m Anny Haight of Clinton at the Friends
      Meeting House in Clinton (Dut. Co.) (8-9/3/34)
1351. Burton, Abraham of amenia m 9/7/23 Selia Sayrs of Washington (Dut. Co.);
      Rev. Willson (8-9/17)
1352. Burton, Barney K. of Amenia m 1/25/25 Clarinda Leet of Stanford (Dut. Co.)
      in S; Rev. Willson (8-2/2)
1353. Burton, Daniel M. of Amenia m 2/15/26 Caroline V. Rowe of Stanford (Dut.
      Co.); Rev. C. P. Wilson (8-2/22)
1354. Burton(?), Fosbert(?) (name blurred), 31, formerly of Poughkeepsie but
      late of NYC, d 6/19/26 in Poughkeepsie (8-6/21)
1355. Burton, John I., Esq., attorney, m 11/6/30 Ann Augusta Parks, both of
      Albany; Rev. Dr. Ludlow (1-11/9)
1356. Bush, Alva C., merchant, m 9/22/30 Ellen Bigelow, both of Bainbridge,
      in B; Rev. N. H. Adams (1-9/29)
1357. Bush, Conradt, 101, "one of the poor of Troy", d 5/15/02 in Troy (9-5/19)
1358. Bush, George Macartney (Dr.) of NYC (Professor of Anatomy and Physiology)
      m 4/13/29 Elizabeth Noel, dau of late Joseph, Esq., in Edinburgh
      (sara. Co.) (1-6/12)
1359. Bush, James m 1/11/26 Sally Hesley, dau of James; Rev. M. Clark. All of
      Pleasant Valley (8-1/18)
1360. Bush, Jason(?) (name blurred), 71, d 2/14/26 (was born in Germany but had
      lived many years until his death in Poughkeepsie, NY) (8-2/15)
1361. Bushnell, Alvah, formerly of Salisbury, CT, m 4/10/19 Malinda Lapham, dau
      of Solon, Esq. of Stanford (Dut. Co.), in S; Elder Birch (8-4/14)
1362. Bushnell, Campbell, Esq., attorney, of Hudson m 2/28/19 Catherine Van
      Valkenburgh of Schodack in S; Rev. Van Buren (6-3/2)
1363. Bushnell, Henry, Esq. m 4/17/19 Eliza Stewart, dau of Col. Henry, in
      Stanford (Dut. Co.) (8-4/21)
1364. Bussy, John, 22, s of Enos of Poughkeepsie, d 12/2/26 in NYC (8-12/6)
1365. Butler, _____ "who lives in the mountains on the road to Fredericksburgh"
      was shot fatally by mountain thieves (he was "a good whig and leaves
      a small family of children") (5-4/26/81)
1366. Butler, Benjamin F., Esq. of Albany m 5/11/18 Harriet Allen of Hudson in
      H; Rev. Stanton (6-5/12)
1367. Butler, Elias (Gen.), 41, d 11/24/04 in Walton (Dela. Co.) (6-12/4)
1368. Butler, Elias m 6/3/30 Mary A. Hicks, dau of Oliver H., all of NYC, at
      St. Thomas Church in NYC; Rev. Upham (1-6/7)
1369. Butler, Ezekiel, Jr., merchant, of Hudson, NY m 2/25/29 Lois Bartlett of
      North Guilford, CT in N. G.; Rev. Whetmore (1-2/25)
1370. Butler, George, Esq., 31, 3rd s of Rev. David Butler, rector of St. Paul's
      Church in Troy, d 8/27/31 at the home of Maj. Popham in White Plains
      (1-9/2)
1371. Butler, Hannah, 49, wf of William, d 10/6/29 in Hudson (1-10/10)
1372. Butler, Henry of NYC m 9/30/31 Sarah M. Morgan of Albany; Rev. Dr.
      Matthews (1-10/7)
1373. Butler, Joseph was executed 10/26/89 for burglary. Also Joseph Butler,
      William Parin, Michael Gainer and William Kearney were executed for
      robbery. Finally Charles Berry was executed for forgery) (place of death
      not stated - probably Poughkeepsie) (8-10/27)
1374. Butler, Mary, 58, wf of Charles of Poughkeepsie, d 11/30/31 (8-12/7)
1375. Butler, Samuel, merchant, m 10/11/23 Sarah Valentine in Poughkeepsie; Rev.
      Babcock (8-10/15)

1376. Butler, Susan Vanderport, 9 mo, dau of Hon. Benjamin F., d 1/11/34 in Washington (Dut. Co.) (8-1/22)
1377. Butler, William (Maj.) of the U. S. Infantry d in New Orleans, LA (9-10/31/15)
1378. Butman, Benjamin m 10/5/18 Anna Loop in Cooperstown; Rev. Paddock. All of Cooperstown (3-10/12)
1379. Butterfield, James (Maj.), 64, (a Rev. officer) d 10/31/18 in Hartwick (he was a prisoner of the Indians for many years) (3-11/9)
1380. Butterworth, John F. of NYC m 6/1/29 Mary McLean Ross, dau of Hon. William of Newburgh, at St. John's Church in NYC; Rev. Onderdonk (1-6/3)
1381. Button, Elias of Brookfield (Mad. Co.), age 105, d 12/28/23 (3-1/5/24)
1382. Button, Elisha, Esq. m 4/5/32 Lovicy B. Averill; Rev. H. Garlick (7-4/7)
1383. Butts, Daniel B. (Rev.) of Rome, NY m Julia Morris of Binhamton in B; Rev. Lockwood (1-10/28/29)
1384. Butts, Eveline, 31, wf of Joseph formerly of Poughkeepsie, d 10/1/29 in Kent, CT (8-10/7)
1385. Butts, George W. m 11/17/31 Jane A. Rysdorph in Greenbush; Rev. Ostrander. All of Greenbush (1-11/22)
1386. Butts, Mulford m 4/10/19 Polly Mulliner of Washington (Dut. Co.) "after a tedious courtship of one night"; Milton Barlow, Esq. (8-4/14)
1387. Butts, William m 12/1/31 Ann Van Valkenburgh in Bloomingdale (Renss. Co.); Rev. Ostrander. All of Bloomingdale (1-12/6)
1388. Byington, Joel (Rev.) of Chazy m 12/2/19 Delia Storrs, dau of Col. Storrs of Middlebury, VT; Rev. Merrill (7-12/11)
1389. Byrnes, Joseph T. of Fishkill m 1/11/32 Martha Clementine Newbold of Glen Brook in G. B. (8-1/25)
1390. Byvank, Evert, Sr., 75, d 5/1/81 at Little Falls, NJ (5-5/24)
1391. C____ (surname blurred), John H. (surname possibly Cavanaugh) m 1/10/34 Mrs. Catharine Cunningham; Rev. Armstrong. All of Fishkill (8-1/29)
1392. Cable, Baltus m 6/17/15 Clarissa Losee, both of Poughkeepsie; Rev. L. Leonard (8-6/21)
1393. Cable(?), James m 4/2/31 Hannah Jacocks; Rev. Welton (8-4/6)
1394. Cable, John M. m 3/26/25 Elida Dubois, both of Poughkeepsie; Rev. Young (8-3/30)
1395. Cable, Robert Barclay, 4 mo, s of Charles, d 1/11/34 in Poughkeepsie (8-1/15)
1396. Cadmus, Amanda, 14 mo, dau of Thomas, d 4/22/30 in Albany (1-4/24)
1397. Cadwell, Edward (Dr.) of Rome, NY m 8/23/31 Esther H. Sherrill, 2nd dau of Jacob, Esq. of New Hartford, in New Hartford; Rev. Goodrich (1-9/2)
1398. Cadwell, Hiram m 12/26/21 Harriet Rawson, both of Lansingburgh; Rev. Griffin (9-1/1/22)
1399. Cady, Benjamin, 46, d in Hudson (lived there for many years) (6-5/11/13)
1400. Cady, Daniel B., Esq., attorney, of Chittenango m 11/3/31 Mary J. Fay, dau of Dr. Jonas of Utica, in U; Rev. Aiken (1-11/17)
1401. Cady, Heman of Plattsburgh m 1/28/13 Maria Platt, dau of Theodorus, deceased, in Peru, NY (7-1/29)
1402. Cady, Oliver, Sr., 72, d 10/25/13 in Canaan (6-11/2)
1403. Cahoone, William (Rev.) of Hyde Park m 5/2/32 Sarah Ann Storm, dau of Jacob of Stormville (Dut. Co.) in S; Rev. Charles Whitehead (8-5/9)
1404. Cain, Henry, 84, m Mrs. Maxwell, 96, in Glasgow (state or country not defined) (this was his sixth and her ninth marriage) (9-1/31/15)
1405. Calder, Francis, 14 mo, only s of J. D. W. Calder, d 7/23/28 in Troy (9-8/8)
1406. Caldwell, Belinda E. (Miss), 18, d 1/26/20 in Poughkeepsie (8-2/2)
1407. Caldwell, George of the firm of Lieber and Caldwell of Canajoharie m 12/7/30 Eleanor Janetta Read, dau of Joshua, Esq. of Palatine (Mont. Co.) in P; Rev. Ransford Wells (1-12/16)
1408. Caldwell, James d 2/1/29 "at an advanced age" in Albany (funeral from the home of James Gourlay on Washington St.) (1-2/3)
1409. Caldwell, Mathew m "last week" Betsey Demott of Poughkeepsie (8-5/29/93)
1410. Calkin, William H. of the firm of Parmelee, Van Keuren and Co., merchants, m 6/23/30 Catharine Parmelee, dau of Joseph, all of Poughkeepsie, in P; Rev. Dr. Cuyler (8-6/30 and 6-7/3)

40

1411. Callahan, James m 9/11/23 Lucy Jennings of Charlton in C; Rev. Smith (double ceremony - see marr of Samuel Jennings) (2-9/16)
1412. Calligan, James m 12/22/10 Amelia Leroy, both of Poughkeepsie; Rev. Dr. Covel (8-1/9/11)
1413. Calwell, Elenor (Widow), 62, d 9/24/20 in Hudson (6-9/26)
1414. Camel, Robert, 32, d 8/19/27 in Plattsburgh (buried with Masonic honors) (7-8/25)
1415. Cameron, Alexander, merchant, of Syracuse m 2/5/30 Nancy Fuller of Buffalo in B; Rev. Eaton (1-2/20)
1416. Cameron, Duncan, about 45, d 11/9/28 at his home in Washington Co. (7-12/6)
1417. Cameron, John of Albany m 7/29/29 Soproma Rowell of Troy in T; Rev. Beman (1-7/30)
1418. Campbell, Elisha, Esq. of Sacketts Harbor m Sophia Hale, dau of late Col. George of Catskill, in C; Rev. Porter (6-5/3/11)
1419. Camp, George T. (Col.), merchant, of Mayville (Chaut. Co.) m 5/13/29 Martha E. Gilbert of Middletown, CT in M; Rev. Crookson (1-6/11)
1420. Camp, John m 1/25/19 Peggy Brown, dau of Peter; Rev. McMurry. All of Rhinebeck (8-2/3)
1421. Camp, Nancy, 47, consort of Talcott Camp, d 8/31/06 in Utica (6-9/16)
1422. Campbell, Alfred E. (Rev.) of Worcester m "Miss Shepherd" of Paris (Oneida Co.) in P (3-8/2/24)
1423. Campbell, Alonzo m 11/16/26 Amy Dunham in Middlefield; Rev. John Smith (3-11/20)
1424. Campbell, Archibald, Esq., about 65, d 11/27/30 in Richmond, VA (a long-time resident there but formerly of NYC (deceased was a brother to the poet Campbell) (1-12/8)
1425. Campbell, Edward (Dr.) d 5/11/22 in NYC (2-5/15)
1426. Campbell, Frederic m 12/7/05 Polly Noxon Stit, only dau of Mrs. Margaret Stit; Rev. Brouwer. All of Poughkeepsie (8-12/10)
1427. Campbell, James, Esq. m "lately" Mrs. Sally Moore, formerly widow of St. John Honeywood, Esq., in Augusta, Upper Canada (9-10/15/05)
1428. Campbell, James, merchant, m 12/10/28 Mary L. Platt, dau of Hon. Levi; Rev. Halsey. All of Plattsburgh (7-12/13)
1429. Campbell, James Mason, Esq. of Baltimore (MD?) m 5/27/34 Anna Arnold Taney, dau of Hon. R. B., in Washington City; Rev. McCullum (8-6/4)
1430. Campbell, Jane, 6, dau of Robert, Esq., 6/20/23 in Cooperstown (3-6/23)
1431. Campbell, John m 4/29/20 Ann G. Rice, both of Gibbonsville; Rev. Sommers (9-5/16)
1432. Campbell, John of the firm of J. and S. Campbell m 10/18/31 Sarah P. Smith, dau of John Augustine Smith, in NYC; Right Rev. Bishop Onderdonk (1-10/20)
1433. Campbell, Major (given name is "Major") m 12/12/14 Philinda Church in Canaan; Rev. Churchill (6-1/10/15)
1434. Campbell, Robert C. m 9/16/30 Margaret Bain, both of Argyle, at the home of Peter Bain; Rev. P. Bullions (1-9/17)
1435. Campbell, Sabrina, 52, wf of Dr. William, d 2/1/30 in Cherry Valley (1-2/4)
1436. Campbell, Sarah, inf dau of Capt. Alexander, d 2/2/29 in Albany (funeral from the home of Capt. Campbell's brother-in-law, Dr. P. Van O'Linda, corner of Green and Hamilton Sts.) (1-2/3)
1437. Campbell, William, 59, d 9/13/31 in Albany (funeral from his late home, "Webb's row in Maiden Lane") (1-9/15)
1438. Campbell, Zurial, d 3/13/26 in Plainfield, NY (3-3/20)
1439. Candy, David M., 16, d 5/28/21 in Pleasant Valley (born in Somersetshire, England) (surv by his parents and a brother) (8-5/30)
1440. Canfield, Alvah T., 31, d 2/17/21 in Poughkeepsie (8-2/21)
1441. Canfield, George of Catskill m 9/14/30 Hannah Smith of Poughkeepsie; Rev. Dr. Cuyler (8-9/22)
1442. Canfield, Samuel, 70, d 11/19/15 in Middlefield (3-11.23)
1443. Canfield, Samuel L. of NYC m 11/14/31 Jane Starr, oldest dau of Packard Starr of Albany; Rev. Lucky (1-11/15)
1444. Caniff, Jeremiah m 10/24/18 Mary Weeks, both of Catskill (9-10/27)
1445. Canniff, William drowned 6/15/03 while fishing with friends "on a mill pond near Carpenter's Mills"(8-7/12)

41

1446. Cannon, James (Col.), 78, (a Rev. officer) d 9/12/29 in Cherry Valley (he was the first surrogate in Otsego Co.) (1-9/18)
1447. Canon, Le Grand of Norwalk, CT m 8/17/14 Esther Bouton of Troy at St. Paul's Church in Troy; Rev. David Butler (9-8/23)
1448. Canovan, Thomas of Albany m 12/1/29 Elizabeth Rude, dau of Nathan of Weedsport, in W; Rev. J. S. Hough (1-12/8)
1449. Cantine, Cornelia, 30, dau of Peter, Esq., d 1/27/20 in Poughkeepsie (8-2/2)
1450. Cantine, Eleanor, relict of late Judge C., d 11/28/20 in Poughkeepsie (funeral from her late home on Mill Street) (8-11/29)
1451. Cantine, John M. of Ithaca m 10/25/30 Eliza Caroline King, dau of Henry, Esq. of Morristown, NJ, in M; Rev. J. Potts (1-11/1)
1452. Cantine, Julia Radcliff, dau of late Gen. Moses, d 6/13/30 in Albany (funeral from the home of her sisters at 9 Columbia St.) (1-6/15)
1453. Cantine, Margaret, 21, dau of Peter, Esq., d 12/28/16 at Red Hook Landing (8-1/1/17)
1454. Cantine, Matthew, Esq., 38, d 1/15/21 in Poughkeepsie (8-1/17)
1455. Cantine, Moses I., Esq. of Catskill m 10/27/01 Christina Witbeck of Lansingburgh (9-11/11)
1456. Cantine, Moses I., Esq., 40 or 50 (blurred), senior editor of the Argus, d 1/24/23 in Albany (reportedly, his death resulted from his drinking "Noyeau imbued with Prussic acid") (2-1/28; 7-2/1; 3-2/3)
1457. Cantine, Peter William, 19, youngest s of late Peter, d 9/5/22 in Poughkeepsie (pulmonary complaint) (8-9/11)
1458. Carbine, Horace of Montrose, PA m 2/7/20 Betsey Stephens, dau of Josiah of Cooperstown, NY, in Montrose (3-2/21)
1459. Card, Stephen, 41, d 6/15/06 in Gallatin (surv by wf and 5 ch) (8-7/1)
1460. Card, Walter, Esq. m 11/4/23 Harriet Russell, dau of Ely; Rev. John Buttolph. All of Northeast (8-11/12)
1461. Carey, Ebenezer (Dr.), 70, d 5/18/15 (8-5/24)
1462. Carey, Egbert m 10/24/13 Tamer Flagler, dau of Solomon of Beekman; Rev. Price (8-11/10)
1463. Carey, James R. m 12/16/20 Rhoda Rebecca Potter, both of Beekman; Rev. Cuyler (8-12/20)
1464. Carhart, William, 15, m 9/21/10 Clara Crandall, 14, both of Dover; John Jewlet, Esq. (8-10/3)
1465. Carl, William m 9/5/16 Margaret Clark, both of Poughkeepsie; Rev. Dr. Covel (8-9/11)
1466. Carle, Andrew m 2/26/29 Susan Carter in Freedom; Rev. Welton (8-3/4)
1467. Carlton, Al-- m 10/20/19 Eluzai Gorton; Artemos Osgood, Esq. All of Troy (9-10/26)
1468. Carlton, William, 33, a printer of the Salem Register, d in Salem (6-8/6/05)
1469. Carman, Baltus, 39, d 6/20/18 in Poughkeepsie (8-6/24)
1470. Carman, Catharine, 28, consort of Thomas of Poughkeepsie, d 5/15/15 (8-5/17)
1471. Carman, Charles m 8/26/24 Catharine Adriance, dau of Abraham, Esq., all of Poughkeepsie; Rev. Cuyler (8-9/1)
1472. Carman, Jacoba, 76, widow of Joshua, d 11/7/27 (8-11/14)
1473. Carman, Morris, 79, d 3/13/30 at his home in Stanford (Dut. Co.) (member of the Society of Friends) (8-3/24)
1474. Carman, Nancy, 49, wf of Aaron, d 2/11/22 in Poughkeepsie (8-2/27)
1475. Carman, Samuel m 4/28/31 Angelina Merritt in Hyde Park; Rev. William Cahoone. All of H. P. (8-5/4)
1476. Carman, Thomas m 5/5/04 Catharine Sypher, both of Poughkeepsie; Rev. Clark (8-5/8)
1477. Carmichael, Maria, 38 or 58 (blurred), wf of John and youngest dau of late Stephen Mack, Esq., d 9/22/29 in Owego (1-10/6)
1478. Carmichael, William M. (Rev.) of Albany, NY m 12/31/29 Harriet S. Glentworth, oldest dau of Dr. P. F. of Trenton, NJ, in T (1-1/20/30)
1479. Carpenter, ____, dau of William, d "recently" (funeral from her parents' home, 71 Hudson St., Albany) (1-5/12/29)
1480. Carpenter, Benjamin, "late of the Flats near Albany", m 7/23/07 Charlotte B. Alden, step-dau of Rev. Woodruff, in Aurora (Cay. Co.); Rev. Hezekiah Woodruff (6-8/11)

42

1481. Carpenter, C. C., Esq. of Henderson m 1/17/31 Cynthia M. Swain, dau of
       Rev. Calven H. of Adamsville (Wash. Co.), in A; Rev. Dillaway (1-2/12)
1482. Carpenter, Caleb, 90, d 12/26/26 at his home in Pleasant Valley (8-1/17/27)
1483. Carpenter, Catharine, 63, wf of Gen. Matthew, d 10/19/30 in Elmira (had
       lived there many years) (1-11/13 and 11/30)
1484. Carpenter, David, 77, d 3/4/25 in Poughkeepsie (member of Dutch Reformed
       Church for many years) (8-3/9)
1485. Carpenter, Edmund T. m 2/13/23 Ann Maria Harris, dau of William; Rev.
       John Clark. All of Pleasant Valley (8-2/19)
1486. Carpenter, Gardner M., 26, d 10/10/19 in Pittsfield (Ots. Co.) (3-10/25)
1487. Carpenter, George W., 27, s of Daniel of Troy, d 7/15/06 (of scurvy) on
       the ship "Print" on his homeward-bound passage from Menola, South Sea
       to Boston (9-9/30)
1488. Carpenter, George Washington of Pittstown m 4/2/23 Eliza Jane Lester of
       Troy; Rev. Griffen (9-4/8)
1489. Carpenter, Gilbert m 3/20/28 Lucinda Brown, both of Hoosick; Rev. Keach
       (9-3/28)
1490. Carpenter, Harry T., Esq. d 4/30/25 in Hadley (2-5/17)
1491. Carpenter, John m 11/1/27 Laura Numan; Rev. Beman. All of Troy (9-11/9)
1492. Carpenter, Leonard m 1/16/27 Philipina Fields; Rev. Welton (8-1/17)
1493. Carpenter, Margaret, nearly 30, wf of Gilbert, d 4/19/27 in Hoosick
       (consumption) (9-4/27)
1494. Carpenter, Mary, wife of David of Poughkeepsie, d 11/22/93 in P (8-11/27
       and 8-12/4)
1495. Carpenter, Zeno, Jr., formerly of Dutchess Co., m 2/20/13 Ellen Turney,
       dau of Abel of Fairfield, CT; Rev. Williams (8-3/10)
1496. Carpenter, Zeno, about 37, of the firm of Carpenter and Bishop, ship
       carpenters, of NYC d in Darien, CT (cholera) (8-8/1/32)
1497. Carr, Ephraim m 1/7/16 Sally Todd in Hartwick; Rev. Smith (3-1/11)
1498. Carr, Peter G. m 7/5/26 Mary Durkee in Plattsburgh; Rev. Quinlan (7-7/15)
1499. Carrier, Cynthia, 49, formerly of Burlington, VT, wf of Capt. Cyrus (he
       one of the proprietors of the <u>Michigan Sentinel</u>) d 9/15/34 in Monroe,
       MI (cholera) (7-10/4)
1500. Carrington, Samuel (Dr.) of Utica m Nancy Dimond of Lenox, MA in L
       (6-3/16/02)
1501. Carroll, Charles, 6, only s of Hon. Charles H., d in Groveland (Liv. Co.)
       (1-1/30/30)
1502. Carson, Samuel P. (Hon.), congressman from North Carolina, m 5/10/31 S.
       Catharine Wilson, dau of James, Esq. of Tennessee, in Rutherford Co.
       (state not given) (1-6/11)
1503. Carter, Abijah, 49, d 11/11/33 in Keeseville ("Printers in New Hampshire
       and Massachusetts are requested to note the above") (4 [<u>Keeseville</u>
       <u>Herald</u>]-11/12)
1504. Carter, Asa (wife possibly "Huldah") drowned about 3 weeks prior to
       5/29/02 in the Hudson River "opposite Poughkeepsie" (identities
       of above names based on papers found in his pockets) (8-6/1)
1505. Carter, Desire, consort of Jirah, d 10/19/05 at Fly Creek (surv by
       several young children) (3-10/24)
1506. Carter, Elizabeth, 75, wf of late "Mr. Carter", d 3/11/08 in Hudson
       (6-3/22)
1507. Carter, Enoch, Esq., about 75, (father of Harvey, Esq. of New Sweden)
       d 5/17/31 in Jackson (Wash. Co.) (4 [<u>Keeseville Herald</u>]-5/31)
1508. Carter, John (Hon.), congressman from SC m 2/12/29 Ellen Marbury, dau of
       Capt. William of Georgetown (state not given) (1-2/23)
1509. Carter, John C. (Lt.) of the U.S. Navy m 6/28/31 Elizabeth S. Phelps
       (dau of R. B., Esq. of NYC and sister of Charles S.) in Poughkeepsie;
       Rev. Dr. Cuyler (double ceremony - see marr of Charles S. Phelps)
       (8-7/6 and 1-7/7)
1510. Carter, John C., late of Keeseville, m Elizabeth Fredensburgh of Hoosick
       Falls in H. F.; Rev. Blodget (4 [<u>Keeseville Herald</u>]-9/10/33)
1511. Carter, Luther, about 36, d 2/18/20 in Plattsburgh (7-2/19)
1512. Carter, Nathaniel, Esq. of NYC, editor of the <u>Statesman</u>, d 1/2/30 in
       Marseilles, France (1-2/24)
1513. Carter, Samuel, Jr. (Capt.) of Plattsburgh m 2/28/27 Charlotte Lynde,
       youngest dau of Jonathan, Esq. of Willsboro, in W (7-3/3)

43

1514. Carter, William, merchant, of Albany m 7/23/29 Frances Huntington of Hudson in H; Rev. Chester (1-7/31)
1515. Carver, Caleb, widower, 18, m Augusta Copeland, 34, in Leeds (8-9/12/27)
1516. Cary, Betsey (Miss), 22, d 8/22/25 in Springfield (3-8/29)
1517. Cary, Jeremiah E., Esq. m 10/26/29 Mary Elizabeth Brackett, dau of James, Esq. of Cherry Valley, in C. V.; Rev. Tiffany (1-10/29)
1518. Cary, Lucius, printer, d 2/23/04 in Canandaigua (8-3/13)
1519. Cary, Phebe Maria, 2, youngest dau of Sturges Cary, d 11/19/31 in Beekman (8-12/7)
1520. Caryl, Leonard of Stockbridge, VT m 10/5/24 Mary Crippen, dau of Silas, Esq., in Worcester; Rev. Alfred E. Campbell (3-10/18)
1521. Case, _____ (Mrs.), wf of Rev. Wheeler Case, d 11/4/90 in Pleasant Valley (8-11/6)
1522. Case, Covill of Saratoga m 1/21/30 Minerva Sackett of Stanford (Dut. Co.); Rev. Armstrong (8-2/10)
1523. Case, Noah O. m 1/19/03 Lucretia Treadwell in Franklin (6-2/8)
1524. Case, Roger m Betsy Bostwick in Meredith (6-11/23/02)
1525. Case, Roger, Esq. of Franklin, late sheriff of Delaware Co., m 8/28/26 Permelia Ward of Delhi in D; Rev. E. R. Maxwell (3-9/4)
1526. Case, Van Rensselaer m 3/5/32 Charity Cropser, both of Clinton (Dut. Co.); Daniel H. Schultz, Esq. (8-4/11)
1527. Case, Wheeler (Rev.), pastor of the church in Pleasant Valley, d 8/31/91 in P. V. (8-9/8)
1528. Case, Wheeler, Esq., attorney, of Goshen m 10/30/17 Betsy Wilkin, dau of Hon. James W., congressman from Orange Co., NY (8-11/12)
1529. Casey, Elizabeth, 76, wid of late Thomas, d 8/25/30 in Poughkeepsie (8-9/1)
1530. Casey, Silas (Lt.) of the U.S. Infantry m Abby Pearce, dau of Hon. Dutee J., in Newport; Rev. Wheaton (1-7/23/30)
1531. Cash, Joseph m 10/7/27 Phebe Bugbee; Isaac Sutherland, Esq. All of Stanford (Dut. Co.) (8-10/10)
1532. Cash, Smith, 19, m 7/16/13 Charlotte Waters, 28, both of Stanford (Dut. Co.); J. Sacket, Esq. (8-7/28)
1533. Casley, Elvira, 19, wf of Peter, d 12/20/33 in Keeseville (4 [Keeseville Herald]-12/24)
1534. Cassady, Thomas, merchant, m 2/15/01 Susan Spencer, both of Pittstown, in P (9-2/17)
1535. Cassidy, James, 18, of Albany d 4/23/30 in Newburgh (killed "by an explosion of the boiler of the Chief Justice Marshall") (1-4/27)
1536. Cassidy, James, 25, d 8/19/31 in Albany (funeral from the home of his mother, "Mrs. Cassidy", at 47 Maiden Lane)(1-8/20)
1537. Cassidy, John d "recently" in Albany (1-4/24/30)
1538. Castine, Jane, 119, "a colored woman", d 6/1/30 at the poor house in Erie Co. (born at Nine Partners, Dutchess Co.) (1-6/12)
1539. Castle, _____, about 6, dau of Amos, d "last week" at Salmon River (South Plattsburgh) (death resulted from her clothes "taking fire") (7-9/18/13)
1540. Castle, Miles B., 20, s of Capt. Elijah late of Ballston, d 5/14/25 in Albany (was a student at Union College, Schenectady) (2-5/17)
1541. Castle, Moses m 2/10/13 Mary James, both of Amenia; Rev. Allerton (8-3/17)
1542. Caswell, George Philander, 16, nephew of John, d 12/29/28 in Poughkeepsie (8-12/31)
1543. Caswell, Hiram m 11/7/24 Catharine Earles in Ballston; Elder Elias Lee (2-11/9)
1544. Caswell, John, merchant, m 10/30/17 Clara M. Van Vliet, dau of Cornelius, in Clinton (Dut. Co.); Rev. Wynkoop (8-11/5)
1545. Caswell, John, 45, of the firm of Caswell and Barnes, merchants, of Poughkeepsie d 11/3/34 (8-11/5)
1546. Cathcart, John A., merchant, of Rochester m Sarah Fairman of Butternuts in B; Rev. Russell Wheeler (3-4/29/22)
1547. Catkameir(?), John H. of Fishkill m 8/17/26 Susan Mulliner of Poughkeepsie; Rev. Marseillus (8-8/23)
1548. Catlin, Charles T. of NYC m 6/10/30 Lucy Ann Derby, dau of late Gen. E. H., in Boston (state not given); Rev. Palfrey (1-6/15)
1549. Catlin, Witt, 33, s of Asa, d 7/16/29 in Kingsbury (1-7/25)
1550. Cauldwell, Charles m 2/20/15 Rachel Ralph, both of Beekman; Rev. L. Leonard (8-2/22)

44

1551. Caulking, Ebenezer, Esq. of Sullivan m Sally Noyes, dau of Nathan, Esq. of Canaan, in Sullivan; Rev. Sylvanus Palmer (6-5/7/05)
1552. Caulkins, Abel (Lt.), 62, formerly of Lisbon, CT, d 12/20/13 in Hartwick (3-1/8/14)
    Cavanaugh, John H. See, possibly, C ? , John H. (Entry 1391)
1553. Caywood, Thomas W. m 1/8/31 Susan Kronk, both of Poughkeepsie; Rev. Dr. Reed (8-1/12)
1554. Center, A. H., Esq., merchant, of Albany m 5/24/24 Maria Bellows of Walpole, NH in W (3-6/7)
1555. Center, Abbey (Miss), 24, late of Sheffield, MA, d in Albany, NY (6-9/21/10)
1556. Center, Joab (Capt.) of Hartford (state not given) m Eunice Jenkins of Hudson, dau of late Capt. Benjamin, in Hudson; Rev. Sears (6-8/11/07)
1557. Center, Stephen Keyes, 6 mo, s of Robert, Esq., d in Hudson (6-7/13/10)
1558. Center, Stephen Keyes, 1 yr, s of Robert, Esq., d 4/21/12 in Hudson (6-4/27)
1559. Chadwick, Holland W. of Brockport m 7/6/29 (name blurred), dau of Hezekiah ? , Esq. of Skaneateles, in S; Rev. Hollister (1-7/14)
1560. Chaffee, Chauncy of Amenia m 12/6/26 Mary Ann Ketcham of Poughkeepsie; Rev. Cushman (8-12/13)
1561. Chaffee, Elmore of the firm of Dundee and Chaffee d 8/10/34 in Pough-keepsie (buried in Sharon, CT) (8-8/13)
1562. Chamberlain, Eleazar m 12/5/27 Polly Doughty in Amenia; Rev. Bronson (8-12/12)
1563. Chamberlain, James m Hannah Smith in Hudson; Rev. Wigton. All of Hudson (6-12/2/06)
1564. Chamberlain, John, (Hon.) (one of the judges of the court of common pleas in Seneca Co.) d 7/26/31 in Waterloo (1-8/8)
1565. Chamberlaine, Richard H. of the firm of Brett and Co. in Norfolk, VA, m 11/27/31 Mary E. Wilson, dau of William, Esq. of NYC; Rev. Dr. Snodgrass (1-12/1)
1566. Chamberlin, Catharine, 59, widow of late Col. Colbert Chamberlin, d 5/25/08 in Amenia. Also Conrad Winegar, 78, father of the deceased, d 5/26 (both lived in the same house and both were buried at the same time)(8-6/15)
1567. Chamberlin, Hannah (Mrs.), 75, d 12/13/20 in Plattsburgh (7-12/23)
1568. Chamberlin, Mercy, 41, d 12/1/23 in Stanford (Dut. Co.) (surv by her husband and 7 young children) (8-12/10)
1569. Chambers, David d "recently" in Albany (funeral from his late home at 11 North Market Street)(1-4/21/30)
1570. Chambers, George, a recent emigrant from Scotland, d 12/21/31 at the home of Levi Heron on Bass Street in Albany (1-12/22)
1571. Chambers, James A. (Dr.) of Ogdensburgh m 8/29/31 Eliza A. M. S. Breaken-ridge, dau of late James of Elizabeth township, Upper Canada, in Charlotte, VT; Rev. Calvin Yale (1-9/12)
1572. Chambers, William (Dr.), "celebrated for his cure of Intemperance", d 7/22/27 in NYC (8-7/25)
1573. Champlain, Josiah m 10/29/26 Fanny Talbot, both of Brookfield, in B; Rev. Coon (3-11/6)
1574. Champlin, Penelope, wid of John T., Esq., d 11/18/30 in NYC (1-11/20)
1575. Champlin, Robert of Walton m 4/16/23 Gertrude Fisher, dau of William of Hartwick, in H; Rev. Tiffany (3-4/21)
1576. Chandler, Solomon, merchant, of Amenia m 1/10/93 Mrs. Alethea Pennoyer, wid of John, Jr. of Sharon (8-1/23)
1577. Chapin, Allen of western Massachusetts m 11/26/20 Laura Barber of Troy; Rev. Dr. Coe (9-11/28)
1578. Chapin, David, Esq., 50, d 2/5/22 in Edmeston (3-2/18)
1579. Chapin, Nabby, 38, consort of Gad, d 8/1/06 in Burlington (Ots. Co.) (surv by her husband and 5 children) (3-8/21)
1580. Chapin, Theodore of Rochester, NY m 2/2/29 Mary A. Chapin, only dau of Deacon Enoch of South Hadley, MA, at South Hadley Canal; Rev. E. Griswold (1-2/25)
1581. Chapin, Volney of Ogdensburgh m 10/27/29 Chloe Sloan of Rochester in R (1-11/2)

1582. Chapine, Augustus L. (Rev.) of Walton (Dela. Co.) m 5/12/31 Abby Hays, dau of Col. Stephen of Newark, NJ, in N; Rev. Baxter Dickinson (1-5/16)
1583. Chapman, Amas m 3/16/25 Priscilla Cooper, both of Sharon, CT, in Amenia, NY; Rev. C. P. Wilson (8-3/30)
1584. Chapman, Elijah (Rev.), 73, (a Rev. soldier) d in Tolland, CT (3-1/2/26)
1585. Chapman, George L. of Troy m 3/23/28 Margaret E. Taylor of Greenbush; Rev. Ludlow (9-3/28)
1586. Chapman, Mason W. m 7/31/28 Jane Nagus in Albia; Rev. Beman (9-8/5)
1587. Chapman, Richard m 10/14/34 Sarah Wheeler; Rev. E. Perkins. All of Dover (8-10/22)
1588. Chapman, Rodman m 12/13/19 Cleora Fillmore, both of Middlebury, VT, in M (7-12/25)
1589. Chapman, William E. of Oxford, one of the editors of the Chenango Republican, m 9/10/29 Harriet Sellick in Ulysses (Tompkins Co.); Rev. Peck (1-9/22)
1590. Chappel, James C. d 8/16/23 in Plattsburgh (7-8/23)
1591. Charles, Ann (Mrs.) d "recently" (funeral from the home of her son, George Charles, corner of Lumber and North Market Streets, Albany) (1-4/16/29)
1592. Charlot, Aaron, late of Hudson, was accidentally drowned 6/7/16 or earlier (his body was found "on the beach below the cold spring") (6-6/11)
1593. Charlot, Sally, 57, d 2/25/08 in Hudson (6-3/1)
1594. Charlot, William, 62, d 7/26/01 in Hudson (6-7/30)
1595. Charlott, Enoch of Hudson m Rachael Starr of Catskill in C (6-2/7/09)
1596. Charruraud, John of the West Indies m Eliza Ballentine of NYC; Rev. Reed (8-8/31/14)
1597. Chace, Ira A. m 2/23/12 Polly Shaw in Hillsdale; Rev. Somers (6-3/9)
1598. Chase, Ebenezer, a member of the Universalist Society in Hoosick, d 2/23/13 in Hoosick (surv by wf and children) (9-3/30)
1599. Chase, Josiah, 65, d 8/2/13 in Maryland (Ots. Co.) ("Printers in the western district are requested to give the above an insertion") (3-8/28)
1600. Chase, Moses (Rev.) m 10/15/27 Mrs. Esther Whitcomb, both of Plattsburgh; Rev. F. Halsey (7-11/3)
1601. Chase, Tallman m Sally Wallace, both of Hoosick, in H; S. Persons, Esq. (9-3/23/24)
1602. Chatterton, Abraham m 7/20/22 Elizabeth Swartwout, dau of John B.; Rev. Cuyler. All of Poughkeepsie (8-7/24)
1603. Chattington, George of New Marlborough (Ulster Co.) m 5/4/22 Mary Ann Carson, dau of John of Poughkeepsie; Rev. Arnold (8-5/8)
1604. Chauncey, Anna, 87, mother of Commodore Chauncey, d 7/26/29 at the Navy Yard in Brooklyn (1-7/30)
1605. Chessebrough, Peleg, merchant and farmer, d "last week" at his home in Fishkill (8-11/6/93)
1606. Cheeseman, Joshua of Hyde Park m 6/8/31 Mrs. Mary Pine of Clinton in C; Rev. William Cahoone (8-6/15)
1607. Cheetham, Aaron A. m Charlotte Bennett, both of Hudson; Rev. Bedell (6-2/3/18)
1608. Cheetham, James, 38, editor and proprietor of the American Citizen and Republican Watch-Tower, d 9/19/10 at Bloomingdale near NYC (surv by his wife, 3 sons, and 2 daus) (8-9/26; 6-9/28; and 3-9/29)
1609. Cheever, William D., about 37, d 8/12/20 in Saratoga (9-8/15)
1610. Cheles, Melissa (Miss), about 18, dau of John, d 1/17/19 in Middlefield (3-1/25)
1611. Chelles, Nathaniel m 12/24/07 Louise Howe, both of Troy; Rev. Coe (9-1/5/08)
1612. Cheney, Wales (Col.), a tutor in Middlebury Academy, m 3/27/30 Esther Stanton, dau of Gen. Phineas, in Middlebury (Genesee Co.); Rev. Eli S. Hunter (1-4/24)
1613. Chesebrough, Daniel of Lansingburgh m 11/15/21 Mary Fowler of Brunswick; Rev. Sommers (9-12/11)
1614. Chester, _____ (Mrs.), 76, d 1/19/23 in Poughkeepsie (8-1/22)
1615. Chevalier, James, editor of the Mercantile Advertiser in NYC, d 8/23/99 in NYC (yellow fever) (8-8/27 and 9-9/3)
1616. Chever, Betsey, 27, consort of W. D., merchant, d 10/12/05 in Troy (9-10/15)

46

1617. Child, Caleb, 70, d 2/1/30 in Albany (his sons, Edmund B. and Caleb, Jr., are mentioned; funeral from 16 Orange St.) (1-2/3)
1618. Child, Ephraim (Dr.) of Stillwater d 6/10/30 in Providence (Sara. Co.) (deceased was one of the oldest physicians in Saratoga Co.) (1-6/21)
1619. Child, Olive, wf of Salmon, Esq., late first judge of Saratoga Co., d 5/2/25 in Greenfield (2-6/10)
1620. Childs, Frances, 13, dau of late David W., Esq. of Utica, d 9/16/31 in Pittsfield, MA (consumption) (1-9/24)
1621. Childs, Lewis, 47, d 5/14/29 in NYC (1-5/20)
1622. Childs, Parker m Sabina Robinson in Exeter; Rev. Duncan (3-3/22/24)
1623. Childs, Philander m Mary Ann Preston in Clay (9-12/23/28)
1624. Childs, Timothy (Hon.), Congressman from NYC m Mrs. Louisa Dickinson of NYC in Norfolk (state not given); Rev. M. L. Chevers of Hampton (Note: The towns of Norfolk and Hampton exist in both NY and VA - they are far apart in NY and close together in VA) (1-1/6/31)
1625. Chisholm, George m 1/19/22 Isabella Roberts, both of Poughkeepsie; Rev. C. C. Cuyler (8-1/30)
1626. Chittenden, Alonzo of Schoharie m 12/10/28 Lucy M. Plant, dau of David of Little Falls, in L. F. (9-12/19)
1627. Chittenden, Robert m 11/28/29 Rebecca Beebe in Stuyvesant; Rev. Sturges. All of Stuyvesant (1-12/5)
1628. Choate, Sally, 20, oldest dau of Francis, d 11/6/02 in Lansingburgh (9-11/9)
1629. Cholwell, Voltair, 35, d 5/12/34 in Red Hook (8-5/21)
1630. Chotwell, Voltsien(?) m 2/27/23 Sally Smith, dau of Arthur, Esq. of Red Hook; Rev. Andrew N. Kittle (8-3/12)
1631. Christian, Antoine, about 30 or 50 (blurred), a Canadian, d 9/12/19 in Plattsburgh (surv by his wife and a large family of children) (7-9/18)
1632. Christian, James m 12/31/22 Jozette Savage; Rev. Frederick Halsey (7-1/4/23)
1633. Christie, John (Col.) of the regular army d lately at Fort George (9-8/17/13)
1634. Christie, Robert m 11/14/15 Lucy Stoughton, both of Troy; Rev. Coe (9-11/21)
1635. Chrystie, Thomas (Maj.) of the U.S. Army d 10/18/15 in NYC (9-10/31)
1636. Chrystler, Sylvester of Bern m Ellen Matilda Vanalstine of Knox in K (1-1/25/30)
1637. Chubb, Simon M. m 10/17/43 Lydia Neilson, both of Stillwater (Sara. Co.); Rev. Isaac Westcott (Washington County newspaper, unidentified but dated 10/26/43)
1638. Church, _____ (Dr.) m Phebe R. Barton; Josiah Sutherland, Esq. All of Stanford (Dut. Co.) (8-1/30/22)
1639. Church, Angelica, 57, wf of John B., Esq. and dau of late Gen. Philip Schuyler of Albany, d 3/13/14 in NYC (8-3/16)
1640. Church, Charles of Barrington, MA (perhaps intended for Great Barrington) m 2/5/20 Eliza Kellogg of Claverack, NY in C; Rev. Sluyter (6-2/15)
1641. Church, James (Dr.) "inventor and vendor of Church's famous Cough Drops &c.",d 10/2/01 (in NYC or in Hudson - not clearly indicated in the report) (9-10/14 and 6-10/15)
1642. Church, John of Montpelier, VT m Martha A. Harrington of Middlesex, VT in Waterbury, VT (7-10/18/34)
1643. Church, John B. of Angelica, NY m 10/4/31 Maria Turnbull Silliman, dau of Benjamin, Esq. of New Haven, CT, in New Haven; Rev. Dr. Taylor (1-10/10)
1644, Church, Julius m 10/29/17 Charlott Moor; Rev. Dr. Coe (9-11/4)
1645 Churchill, Alfred m 12/23/24 Emma Darbyshire in Hartwick; Rev. Dr. Hazelius (3-12/27)
1646. Churchill, Ezekiel, merchant, m 1/9/32 Mary Ann Graves in Champlain; Rev. Byington (7-1/14)
1647. Churchill, John, farmer, of Fishkill d 6/5/02 (fell from his barn) (8-6/8)
1648. Churchill, Mary Ann, about 25, wf of Ezekiel, d 7/19/34 in Chazy (7-7/26)
1649. Clapp, Henry of Freedom m 9/14/29 Nancy Grant of Dover in D; Rev. Asahel Bronson (8-9/16)
1650. Clapp, Jesse I., "an aged farmer" of Freedom d 10/27/28 in Freedom (9-11/4)
1651. Clapp, John m 6/23/29 Lydia Strong in Norwich; Rev. Edward Andrews (1-7/4)

1652. Clapp, John S. (Sgt.), 24, of the U. S. Artillery, late a printer in
      Windsor, VT, d 1/16/14 in Plattsburgh, NY (7-1/29)
1653. Clapp, Leonard H., 35, merchant, of Pittsford d 10/5/31 in NYC (1-10/10)
1654. Clapp, Susan (consort of Jesse I., farmer, of Beekman) d 11/7/18 in
      Beekman (8-11/18)
1655. Clapp, William of Westchester m 1/28/03 (possibly 2/28/03 - blurred)
      Elizabeth Arthur of Pawling (8-3/1)
1656. Clarge (sic), Arthur, inf s of George, Esq., d in Hyde (Springfield)
      (3-11/20/26)
1657. Clark, ____, 9, s of Cyrus of Cooperstown,drowned 6/21/06 in Cooperstown
      when he fell from a canoe containing his brother, age 7, and an
      apprentice of their father (3-6/26 and 6-7/8)
1658. Clark, ____, inf s of George, d in Hudson (6-12/12/20)
1659. Clark, Abel H. of the firm of Stowel and Clark, merchants, m 9/22/30
      Mary Elizabeth Ernst, dau of John F., in Cooperstown; Rev. Tiffany
      (1-9/28)
1660. Clark, Alma, 25, consort of Lester, d 6/12/12 in Amenia (surv by her
      husband and their two-day-old child as well as her parents and her
      brothers and sisters) (8-7/8)
1661. Clark, Alva, merchant, of Penn Yan m 4/28/31 Charlotte E. Whitney of
      Troy in Troy; Rev. Tucker (1-4/30)
1662. Clark, Ama, consort of Capt. Jerome of Hartwick, d 3/3/07 (surv by her
      husband and "a family of promising children") (3-3/12)
1663. Clark, Ann, 77, relict of late Alexander, d 8/21/30 in Albany (born in
      Scotland but had lived in Albany more than 50 yrs) (1-8/26)
1664. Clark, Arthur Fitch, 9 mo, s of Asahel, engraver, of Albany, d 4/14/31
      (croup) (funeral from his father's home, 11 Daniels St.) (1-4/16)
1665. Clark, Asahel of Albany m 10/21/24 Sarina A. Loomis of Otsego in O;
      Rev. Smith (3-10/25)
1666. Clark, Aurilla, 38, wf of Benedict and dau of Stephen Gillet, Esq. of
      Kingsborough, d 5/13/22 in Milton (surv by husband and"several young
      children") (2-5/15 and 2-6/12)
1667. Clark, Benjamin m 11/15/07 Olive Parker, both of Hartford, NY, in H;
      Rev. Lyman Hall (9-11/24)
1668. Clark, Betsey, 17, dau of Abel, d 1/10/19 in Cooperstown (3-1/25)
1669. Clark, Catherine (Miss), dau of Allen, d 2/10/23 in Poughkeepsie
      (8-2/12)
1670. Clark, Charles L., Esq. of Albion m 6/7/31 Mehetibel E. Ward, dau of
      Levi, Jr., Esq. of Rochester; Rev. Joseph Penney (1-6/13)
1671. Clark, Charles P., about 19, d 2/9/13 in Burlington (VT?) (7-2/12)
1672. Clark, Charles V. (Capt.), merchant, of Sharon, CT m Maria Russell, dau
      of Isaac of Northeast, NY, in N; Rev. John Buttolph (8-9/8/24)
1673. Clark, Cyrus, Esq., 50, d 5/10/22 (3-5/13)
1674. Clark, Cyrus, merchant, of Brookfield m 1/20/29 Catherine E. Jacobs in
      Catskill; Rev. Loomis of Hudson (1-2/14)
1675. Clark, Daniel A., 17, s of Abel of Pierstown and clerk to James McNamee,
      d 2/14/15 in Cooperstown (funeral sermon by "Rev. Smith") (3-2/23)
1676. Clark, Edward m 9/17/33 Mrs. Elizabeth Green; Thomas D. Gibson, Esq.
      (4 [Keeseville Herald]-10/13)
1677. Clark, Edwin m Sarah S. Hasbrouck of Ogdensburgh in O; Rev. Todd
      (1-8/22/29)
1678. Clark, Erastus, Esq., 57, d 11/6/25 in Utica (3-11/14)
1679. Clark, Erskine Grenville (Dr.) of Sandy Hill (Wash. Co.) m Jane Maria
      McDonald, dau of William, Esq. of Glens Falls, in G. F.; Rev. Clark
      of Waterford (1-4/4/31)
1680. Clark, Ezekiel, 65, d 6/22/25 in Pompey, NY (3-7/18)
1681. Clark, Franklin, merchant, of Penfield m 5/29/31 Jane A. Fellows,
      formerly of Lenox, MA, at St. Stephen's Church in NYC; Rev. Francis L.
      Hawks (1-6/2)
1682. Clark, George m 6/4/19 Polina Heath, both of Hudson, in Claverack; Rev.
      Gephard (6-7/20)
1683. Clark, George m 4/10/24 Sally Burlingham, both of Poughkeepsie; Rev.
      Babcock (8-4/14)
1684. Clark, George L. m 2/6/08 Rezina Bogert in Fishkill; Rev. Buckley
      (8-2/10/08)

48

1685. Clark, Harriet Phebe, 21, (wf of Thomas S., merchant, and dau of Capt. Ira Ford of the steamboat "Chief Justice Marshall") d 6/8/29 in Troy (1-6/17)
1686. Clark, Henry (Dr.) of Plainfield (Ots. Co.) m 7/14/21 Lucy Clark, dau of Henry, Jr., Esq. of Brookfield (Ots. Co.) at the Baptist Church in Brookfield; Rev. Henry Clark (3-8/6)
1687. Clark, Henry (Lt.), 28, of the 5th Regiment, U.S. Infantry d 10/18/30 "at his lodgings in the Arcade, Rochester" (had been at the recruiting station in R about 2 mo) (deceased is son of late John of New Haven, CT)(1-10/19)
1688. Clark Isaac (Gen.), 72, (a Rev. officer) d in Castleton, VT (3-3/4/22)
1689. Clark, James, 14, s of Henry, d 9/13/08 in Hudson (6-9/20)
1690. Clark, Jared m 3/19/12 Mercy Williams, both of Cooperstown; Rev. John Smith (3-3/28)
1691. Clark, John (Rev.) m Sarah M. Foot, dau of Capt. Elisha, in Northampton (2-1/28/23)
1692. Clark, John m 12/15/28 Elizabeth White Brayan, dau of William, in NYC; Rev. Berrian (9-12/19)
1693. Clark, John, Pioneer agent, of Geneva, NY m 9/10/29 Mary Lee, dau of Francis of Benton, in B; Rev. Eddy of PennYan (1-9/19)
1694. Clark, John, attorney, m 10/5/30 Elizabeth Smith, dau of William, Esq., in Watertown; "Mr. Boardman" (1-10/16)
1695. Clark, Jonathan m 5/3/07 Betsy Philips in Hudson; Rev. Hopkins (6-5/5)
1696. Clark, Jonathan (age blurred) d 8/26/08 in Hudson (6-8/9)
1697. Clark, Jonathan, 93, d 11/28/31 at his home in La Grange (blind for many years) (member of the Society of Friends) (8-12/7)
1698. Clark, Joseph W., 28, s of James, d 10/21/30 in Albany (funeral from his late home, 23 Montgomery St.) (1-10/22)
1699. Clark, Julius H., one of the editors of the Syracuse Argus, m 12/15/31 Cornelia Morse; Rev. P. Dyer. All of Syracuse (1-12/24)
1700. Clark, Justin m 8/13/15 Lucy Williams of Pierstown in P; Rev. Nathaniel Stacy (3-8/17)
1701. Clark, Justin, 27, late of Montrose, PA, d 5/6/22 in Otsego (3-5/13)
1702. Clark, Luther (Rev.) of Hector m Rachel Aurelia Clark, dau of Rev. John of Pleasant Valley (8-10/6/24)
1703. Clark, Luther of New Haven, NY m 4/14/31 "John Pain's wife of Scriba" in Scriba; Norman Roe, Esq. (8-5/25)
1704. Clark, Martha, consort of Lewis, d 10/31/31 in Albany (funeral from Lewis' home, corner Patroon and Orchard Sts.) (1-11/1)
1705. Clark, Mary, 35, wf of George T., d 1/15/31 in Albany (funeral from her husband's home, 46 Hudson St. (1-1/17)
1706. Clark, Nathan S. (Dr.) of Clintonville m 9/12/33 Mrs. Eliza Davis in Peru, NY; Rev. Lyman (7-9/21)
1707. Clark, Oliver, 24, d 4/17/25 in Poughkeepsie (8-4/20)
1708. Clark, Orasmus B., editor of the Seneca Falls Jounal, m Prudence Darrow in Seneca Falls (1-2/8/30)
1709. Clark, Patrick, 32, d 4/29/31 in Albany (funeral from his late home, corner Lydius and Lark Sts.) (1-4/30)
1710. Clark, Paul, Esq., 66, d 3/28/31 in Albany (funeral from his late home, corner Lydius and Lock (sic) Sts. (1-3/30)-(See address in Entry 1709)
1711. Clark, Perry m 2/19/29 Caroline Winchell, dau of Philo M., all of Northeast; Rev. Thomas Winter (8-3/4)
1712. Clark, Ralph of the firm of Clark, Williams and Co. m 4/26/31 Abigail Anna Bogert, dau of James, Jr., in NYC; Rev. Dr. Knox. All of NYC (1-4/29)
1713. Clark, Robert, 83, d 10/20/23 in Hartwick (3-10/27)
1714. Clark, Rodman d 5/10/26 in Plattsburgh (7-5/13)
1715. Clark, Roswell m 1/19/25 Elizabeth Clancy, oldest dau of William, in Kingsborough; Rev. Clancy. All of Kingsborough. (2-2/1)
1716. Clark, Rufus, papermaker, m 11/9/06 "Miss Eddy Vosburgh" in Kinderhook; Rev. Sickles (6-11/18)
1717. Clark, Samuel (Maj. Gen.), 82, one of the first settlers in Saratoga Co., d 2/17/23 in Malta, NY (formerly a state assemblyman and "a Judge of the Court") (2-2/25)
1718. Clark, Samuel W., printer, m 9/28/06 Rebecca Davis, dau of Jacob, in Hudson; Rev. Judd. All of Hudson (6-9/30)

49

1719. Clark, Samuel W., about 25, d 5/8/22 in Plattsburgh (consumption) (7-5/11)
1720. Clark, Silas, merchant, of Watertown m 10/14/31 Sarah E. Ely, oldest dau
of Horace, Esq. of Lyme, CT, in L; Rev. Hawes (1-10/29)
1721. Clark, Solomon, 40, d 10/14/14 in Cooperstown (3-10/20)
1722. Clark, Stephen m 5/5/25 Polly Clark in Sherburne; Rev. Fulton (3-5/9)
1723. Clark, Thomas of Greene Co., NY d at sea "on his passage from St. Croix
to Providence"(6-8/19/06)
1724. Clark, Thomas, 75, d 9/7/27 in Troy (9-6/18)
1725. Clark, Thomas Brown (Dr.) of Detroit, Mich. Terr., m 10/9/27 Deborah
Brown Hill of Troy; Rev. Butler (9-10/12)
1726. Clark, Thomas S. m 1/31/27 Harriet P. Ford, dau of Ira, Esq.; Rev. Butler
(9-2/2)
1727. Clark, Willard, about 40, d 2/8/16 in Troy (9-2/13)
1728. Clark, William, 31, d 1/5/10 in NYC (surv by wf and 2 small ch) (8-1/24)
1729. Clark, William, 42, d 2/13/32 in Ballston Spa (4 [Keeseville Herald]-2/21)
1730. Clark, William Dana, 23, preacher of the gospel, d 3/6/13 in Jay
("Printers in Windsor, Vt. are requested to insert the above") (7-4/30)
1731. Clarke, Alfred of the firm of Wemple and Clarke m 3/3/30 Catharine S.
Andrews, dau of Henry, Esq. (all of NYC), in NYC; Rev. Dr. Seedgrass
(1-3/8)
1732. Clarke, Alvet of Plainfield m 10/25/26 Sally Davis of Brookfield in B;
Rev. Maxon (3-11/6)
1733. Clarke, G. B., Esq. (of Chesterton Lodge, Oxfordshire, England), youngest
s of G. Clarke, Esq. of Hyde Hall, Cheshire, and of Hyde Hall, Otsego
Lake, NY, m 7/9/30 Elizabeth Byron, oldest dau of late Rev. H. Byron,
at St. Martin's (state or country not given) (1-9/1)
1734. Clarke, George Hyde, Esq., 80, of Hyde "in the county of Cheshire" d 7/4/24
at his home on Grafton Street in London, England (grandson of George
Clarke, Esq., formerly Lt. Gov. of NY, and father of George Clarke, Esq.
of Hyde, Springfield, Otsego Co., NY (3-8/30)
1735. Clarke, James, merchant, of Medina m 7/20/30 Adeline R. Coffin, dau of
Ralph, Esq. of Batavia, in B; Rev. Smith, rector of St. James Church
(1-7/28)
1736. Clarke, John m 12/9/10 Hester Everitt, both of Poughkeepsie; Rev. Covel
(8-12/12)
1737. Clarke, Jonathan (Lt.) m Mrs. Betsey Priet in Nottingham, NH (groom is the
father of 13 ch by one wife and the bride is mother of 14 ch by one
husband) (8-10/17/27)
1738. Clarke, Luther m 12/9/19 Mary Rogers, both of Hyde Park; Rev. P. S.
Wynkoop (8-12/15)
1739. Clarke, Martha, 53,d 8/9/07 in Half Moon (Sara. Co.) (8-9/9)
1740. Clarkson, Charles m Mary Cunningham, both of Beekman; Cyrus Benjamin, Esq.
(8-8/2/03)
1741. Clarkson, Matthew (Gen.), 67. (a Rev. patriot) d 4/24/25 in NYC (3-5/2)
1742. Clarkson, Samuel G. (Dr.) of the U.S. Navy d 5/16/29 on board the U.S.
schooner "Grampus" (1-6/17)
1743. Clary, Joseph, attorney, of Buffalo m 2/1/30 Maria Theresa Rathbone, dau
of Samuel, Esq. of NYC, in NYC; Rev. A. Maclay (1-2/4)
1744. Clary, Samuel m 7/21/99 Tine Ben, both of Amenia; Jesse Thompson, Esq.
(double ceremony - see marr of Gideon Coffin) (8-7/30)
1745. Clayton, John G., Esq., editor of the Northern Spectator, of Malone
m 6/9/31 Catharine Hicks of New York (City?); Rev. Dubois (1-6/13)
1746. Clearwater, Jeremiah m 1/9/30 Welthy Farrington, dau of Timothy, all of
Pleasant Valley; Oliver D. Collins, Esq. (8-1/20)
1747. Cleavland, Eliphaz (Mr.), about 30, of Claverack d 11/30/20 (had fallen
from a shed a few days previous to his death) (6-12/5)
1748. Clement, Jonathan m 10/22/07 Deborah Allen, both of Washington, Dutchess
Co., at the Friends Meeting House in Nine Partners (8-10/28)
1749. Clement, Moses (Dr.) d 12/3/31 in Coeymans (for many years a physician
there) (1-12/28)
1750. Clements, Egbert m 12/9/24 Patty Baker; Stoddard Judd, Esq. All of
Beekman (8-12/22)
1751. Clench, Johnson, Esq., s of late Col. Clench of Niagara, Upper Canada,
m 10/27/31 Eliza Whissler, dau of Maj. Whissler of the U.S. Army,
Commander of Fort Niagara, at F. N.; Rev. Thomas Green (1-11/7)

1752. Clendener, Mary, wf of P., d 12/12/28 in NYC (9-12/16)
1753. Clerc, Laurent of La Balme, France m 5/3/19 Eliza C. Boardman of Whitesboro at the home of Benjamin Prescott, Esq. in Cohoesville near
Waterford; Rev. Butler (both deaf and dumb; Mr. C.is a principal
instructor and Miss B. a pupil in the asylum for the deaf and dumb in
Hartford, CT) (3-3-5/17 and 8-5/19)
1754. Same as Entry 1753 above except that the groom's name is listed as
Laurent Clero. (9-5/11/19)
1755. Cleveland, James, 59, d 12/18/27 in Brunswick (9-12/25)
1756. Cleveland, Lemuel, 46, d 9/26/07 in Hartwick (surv by wf and 9 ch)
(3-10/4)
1757. Cleveland, Salter of Cazenovia m 2/15/24 Lydia Ann Chapin of Edmeston
in E; Rev. Daniel Nash (3-3/1)
1758. Cleveland, Solomon d 12/13/28 in Rochester (died "of a quincy")
1759. Cleveland, Stephen, Esq., attorney, of Poughkeepsie m 7/25/19 Deborah
R. Vaughan of Essex in E; Rev. Ira Manly (7-7/31 and 8-8/11)
1760. Cliff, Charles m 7/6/05 Jane Anthony, 2nd dau of Capt. Anthony of
Southeast; Sheldon Monger, Esq. (8-7/23)
1761. Clinton, De Witt (His Excellency), Gov. of NY, m 4/21/19 Catharine Jones,
dau of late Dr. Thomas of NYC, in NYC; Rev. Arthur J. Stansbury
(9-4/27; 8-4/28; and 7-5/8)
1762. Clinton, George W., Esq. m 5/15/32 Laura Catharine Spencer, dau of Hon.
John C., at St. John's Church in Canandaigua; Rev. Kearney (8-5/23)
1763. Clinton, James (Gen.), 75, d 12/22/12 at his home in Orange Co. (was an
officer in 1760 in the French War and also in the Rev. War) (8-1/6/13)
1764. Clinton, James m 4/27/16 Mary Ann Lockyear, both of Patterson; Rev. Ca_?__
(surname blurred) (8-5/5)
1765. Clinton, Maria, wf of Gov. Clinton, d 7/30/18 at Mount Vernon near NYC
(9-8/4; 3-8/10; 8-8/12; and 7-8/15)
1766. Clinton, Mary, 57, consort of John of Cooperstown, d 12/16/05 (funeral
sermon by Rev. Daniel Nash) (3-12/26)
1767. Close, John T. d "recently' in Waterford (8-3/1/20)
1768. Cloud, Caleb W. (Dr.), 24, assistant surgeon in the U.S. Navy, d 9/10/31
on board the U.S. ship "Vincennes" at Port Royal, Island of Jamaica
(yellow fever) (1-9/30)
1769. Clowes, Hiram, formerly of Troy, NY, d 12/12/13 at Chestnut Hill near
Philadelphia, PA (9-12/28)
1770. Clowes, Mary Ellen, 7 weeks, dau of Thomas, d 11/15/21 in Troy (9-11/20)
1771. Clowes, Thomas Jefferson, 2, s or Thomas, Esq., d 1/9/22 in Troy (9-1/22)
1772. Cluett, John W. m 5/12/29 Mary Ann Meadon; Rev. Williams. All of Albany
(1-5/14)
1773. Cluett, Peter R. of Schenectady m 6/2/30 Elizabeth Kidney, youngest dau
of Jonathan of Albany; Rev. Dr. Ludlow (1-6/4)
1774. Clute, Henry m 10/30/32 Mrs. Hannah Carpenter in Plattsburgh; St. John
B. L. Skinner, Esq. (7-11/2)
1775. Clute, Jeremiah m 9/22/18 Alenda Clute, both of Waterford; Rev. Sommers
(9-9/29)
1776. Clute, John (Sgt.), 6th U.S. Infantry, m 2/2/19 Laura Caster of Swanton,
VT in Plattsburgh (7-2/6)
1777. Clute, William m 10/11/15 Susan Ensign, both of Watervliet; Rev.
Blatchford of Lansingburgh (9-10/31)
1778. Clyde, George C. of the firm of Angel and Clyde of Burlington (Ots. Co.)
m 6/4/29 Catharine V. S. Dorr, dau of late Dr. Russell Dorr of Chatham,
in Ghent (Col. Co.) (1-6/16)
1779. Clyde, Louisa, 22, dau of Col. Joseph, d 5/23/29 in Cherry Valley (1-5/28)
1780. Coan, Charles, 32, formerly of Cooperstown, d 6/7/22 in Johnstown (3-6/10)
1781. Coates, Charles, Esq. of Albany m 8/13/30 Catharine Falconer of NYC in NYC;
Rev. Dr. Cox (1-8/16)
1782. Cochran, John of Peru, NY m 2/28/19 Remma Bedel of Plattsburgh (7-3/13)
1783. Cochran, Noah m "Miss Brown, both of Peru, NY, in P; Elder Garlick
(7-12/30/15)
1784. Cochran, Robert (Col.), 73, d 7/3/12 in Kingsbury (born in Mass.; fought
in the French War (Fort Edward, Ticonderoga, Crown Point) with Rogers
Rangers. In 1764 went to Arcade and Nova Scotia with the New England
emigrants. Was a Rev. officer in the NY Line (9-7/28)

1785. Cochrane, _____, wf of Walter, Esq. and dau of Hon. Peter Smith, d in Albany (3-10/3/25)
1786. Cocks, Albert, merchant, of Poughkeepsie m 9/6/21 Mary Dodge, dau of William of NYC, in NYC (8-9/12)
1787. Coe, _____ (Rev. Mr.), "minister of the Presbyterian Church in Troy", d "a few days since" in T (7-7/27/22)
1788. Coe, Charity (Miss), 20, dau of William of Plattsburgh, d 8/9/19 at Cumberland Head (near Plattsburgh) (7-8/14)
1789. Coe, John (Rev.), s of Rev. Dr. Coe of Troy, d 9/30/23 at Whitehall Landing (he was pastor of "an infant church" in Whitehall) (9-10/7)
1790. Coe, John A., s of William of Plattsburgh, d 12/31/19 in Buffalo (7-1/22/20)
1791. Coe, John R. (Rev.), 23, 2nd s of late Rev. Dr. Coe of Plattsburgh, d 10/7/23 in Whitehall (born in Troy and graduated from Union College at age 16; attended the Seminary at Princeton, NJ; was licensed to preach in 1820; was ordained as pastor of the Presbyterian Church in Whitehall in July 1822 shortly before his father's death (7-10/11)
1792. Coe, Jonas (Rev.), D.D., 64, pastor of the Presbyterian Church in Troy, d 7/21/22 in Troy (9-7/23; 8-7/24; and 3-7/29)
1793. Coe, Mary Rebecca (Miss) about 24, d 4/17/28 in Plattsburgh (7-4/26)
1794. Coe, Sarah M., dau of Benjamin, Esq., d 12/24/18 at her father's home in Haverstraw (Rock. Co.) (9-1/19/19)
1795. Coffin, Albert I. of Middlefield m 6/5/17 Jane Lee of Cooperstown in C; Rev. Smith (3-6/12)
1796. Coffin, Caleb, 50, d 6/4/29 in Athens, Greene Co. (1-6/13)
1797. Coffin, Edward, 2 yrs, s of Salmon, d 12/27/06 in Hudson (6-12/30)
1798. Coffin, Frederick, Esq., attorney, m 8/17/11 Charlotte Green in Somers (West. Co.) (6-9/6)
1799. Coffin, Gideon m 7/21/99 Sally Clary, both of Amenia; Jesse Thomson, Esq. (double ceremony - see marr of Samuel Clary) (8-7/30)
1800. Coffin, Hezekiah R. of Washington (Dut. Co.) m 3/22/32 Myra Barlow, dau of Thomas, Esq. of Amenia; Rev. Andrews (8-4/4)
1801. Coffin, Jemima (Mrs.), 70, formerly of Nantucket, d 2/2/09 in Hudson, NY (6-2/7)
1802. Coffin, Lydia, wf of Alexander J. of Poughkeepsie,d 3/24/32 (8-3/28)
1803. Coffin, Noah, 63, d 7/3/25 in Cooperstown (formerly of Nantucket and a member of the society of Friends) ("Nantucket and Hudson papers are requested to publish the above")(3-7/11)
1804. Coffin, Sally, wf of Capt. Gorham Coffin and dau of James Nixon, Esq. of Hudson, d in NYC (6-2/24/12)
1805. Coffin, Shubael, 77, d 2/23/17 in Clinton (member of the Society of Friends) (8-3/19)
1806. Coffin, Silvanus, 18, late of Hudson, NY, d in Kingston, Jamaica (yellow fever) (6-3/2/02)
1807. Coffin, Uriel (Capt.), 64, formerly of Nantucket, MA, d 2/21/31 at his home in Chatham (state not given) (1-3/7)
1808. Coffin, William (Capt.) of Hudson, master of the ship "Syren", d in the East Indies (6-5/30/09)
1809. Coggswell, _____, inf s of Smith Coggswell, d 3/12/21 in Troy (9-3/20)
1810. Cogswell, Francis (Lt.), 24, 11th Regiment, U.S. Infantry, d 12/8/12 in Plattsburgh (4th s of late Hon. Thomas, Esq. of Gilmantown, NH; "received the honours of Dartmouth College in August, 1810"; was a preceptor of an academy in Alexandria, VA) (7-12/18)
1811. Cogswell, Horace m 6/18/21 Catherine De Camp, both of Troy; Rev. Dr. Coe (9-6/19)
1812. Coit, Thomas C. of Natchez, Mississippi m 8/3/29 Mary Ann Morgan, dau of late Elias of Hartford, CT, in H (1-8/14)
1813. Colden, Cadwallader D., 64, attorney, d 2/7/34 in Jersey City, NJ (was 2 years mayor of NYC, a member of congress, a state assemblyman, and a state senator) (8-2/12)
1814. Colder, Joseph m 5/23/25 Helen Keeling, both of Cherry Valley, at Christ Church in Cooperstown; Rev. Tiffany (3-5/30)
1815. Cole, Albert m 10/28/19 Harriet Niles, both of Austerlitz, in A; Rev. Somers (6-11/9)
1816. Cole, Benjamin of Schaghticoke m 7/21/11 Abigail Fanning of Troy; Rev. Coe (9-7/23)

52

1817. Cole, Betsey, 28, wf of Peter, d 8/6/07 in Hudson (6-8/11)
1818. Cole, Caroline, inf dau of Philo K., d 8/3/31 in Albany (1-8/8)
1819. Cole, Daniel m 2/13/23 Polly Talmage, both of Milton, in Ballston; Rev.
      Reuben Smith (2-3/4)
1820. Cole, Daniel W. (Dr.) of Oswego m 12/25/26 Philura Bostwick, dau of late
      William of Auburn, at St. Peter's Church in Auburn; Rev. Dr. Ludd
      (9-1/2/27)
1821. Cole, Eleanor, 36, wf of John O., Esq., d 6/5/30 in Albany (funeral
      from her husband's home, 88 South Pearl St.) (1-6/7)
1822. Cole, Isaac, 103, d 4/28/14 in Plattsburgh (moved from Dutchess Co. to
      Plattsburgh with his son-in-law,Jacob Ferris, in 1786; later moved
      with this same family to La Chine [state or country not
      given - probably in Quebec, Canada] where he lived several
      years) (7-4/30)
1823. Cole, John H. (Dr.), formerly of Hudson, m 12/16/30 Esther P. Cooke, dau
      of Palmer, Esq. of Red Hook, in R. H.; Rev. Augustus Wackerhagen
      (8-12/22 and 1-12/28)
1824. Cole, John O., Esq., police magistrate, m 6/20/31 Adelaide Dougherty,
      oldest dau of W. W., Esq; Rev. E. N. Kirk. All of Albany (1-6/21)
1825. Cole, Peter m 2/18/03 Eliza Hamilton, dau of Dr. Joseph of Hudson, in H
      (6-2/22)
1826. Cole, Peter, merchant, m 8/19/08 Maria Hamilton, dau of late Dr. Hamilton;
      Rev. Sears (6-9/9)
1827. Cole, Philo K. m 12/3/29 Frances Caroline Parmele; Rev. Dr. Sprague. All
      of Albany (1-12/5)
1828. Cole, Romelia, 4, dau of Peter, d 11/22/08 in Hudson (6-11/29)
1829. Cole, Sally Maria, 15 mo., dau of Peter, d 8/23/07 in Hudson (6-8/25)
1830. Cole, William, Esq. of Franklinville m 2/2/34 Priscilla Burnett, dau of
      William, Esq. late of Ednamville (sic) in Hackensack, NY; Rev. C. L.
      Cleef (8-2/5)
1831. Coleman, Hannah, 80, wid of Dr. Noah, deceased, d 3/15/24 in Otsego (3-3/29)
1832. Coleman, Horace of Otsego m 4/23/12 Sally Cone, dau of Joseph O., Esq.;
      Rev. Daniel Nash (3-4/25)
1833. Coleman, Horace m 2/10/25 Malvina Van Benschoten; Rev. Wadsworth (3-2/14)
1834. Coleman, James of Troy m 2/15/06 Betsey Bugbee of Greenbush in G; Rev.
      Baker (9-3/18)
1835. Coleman, William of Hudson m 4/10/08 Mrs. Hannah Bemington of Stanford
      (Dut. Co.); William Bell, Esq. (8-4/27)
1836. Coleman, William H., 33, only s of late William, Esq., d 7/25/30 in NYC
      (1-7/28 and 8-8/4)
1837. Coles, Dennis, printer, m 5/15/02 Caty Van Duerson, dau of William, all
      of Newburgh (8-5/25)
1838. Colgrove, Asa of Richfield m Electa Mack (in Warren?); Rev. Wadsworth
      (3-2/14/25)
1839. Coller, Isaac H. m 1/13/31 Rebecca Dubois, both of Poughkeepsie; Rev. Dr.
      Reed (8-1/19)
1840. Coller, John of Pleasant Valley, Ulster Co., m 9/21/11 Sarah Southwick of
      Poughkeepsie; Daniel Hebard, Esq. (8-9/25)
1841. Collier, Benjamin, 44, d 4/3/13 in Troy (9-4/6)
1842. Collier, Elizabeth, 68, wf of Thomas, Sr., editor of the Broome Republican,
      d 9/15/29 in Binghamtom (1-9/23)
1843. Collier, Harriet, inf child of John A., Esq. of Binghamton, d 8/9/29 in
      Utica (1-8/18)
1844. Collier, Lydia Ann, 20, wf of John A., Esq. of Chenango Point, NY,
      d 10/2/29 in Norwich, CT (where she had gone for her health)
      (Her remains, attended by her husband and friends, were brought to
      Albany, NY Oct. 6 by the steamboat "Constitution" on their way to
      Chenango Point) (1-10/7)
1845. Collins, _____, wf of Isaac, bookseller, of NYC, d in Westchester
      (9-9/24/05)
1846. Collins, Benjamin, 44, d 4/3/13 in Troy (3-4/17)
1847. Collins, George of Beekman, NY m 11/17/13 Eliza Borden of Troy, MA
      at St. John's Church; Right Rev. Bishop Hobart (Note: Fall River, Mass.
      was called Troy from 6/18/1804 to 2/12/1834) (8-11/24)

53

1848. Collins, Gilbert of Beekman m 2/17/14 Susan Bogart of Fishkill; Rev.
       Price (8-3/9)
1849. Collins, Hezekiah, Esq., 88, d 4/12/28 at his home in Freedom (8-4/23)
1850. Collins, Levi (Rev.), preceptor of Hartwick Academy, 44, m 3/5/18 Allice
       Allen, 15, in Exeter, NY; Rev. Donalson (3-3/9)
1851. Collins, Lyman (Dr.), formerly of Le Roy, NY, m Harriet Whittlesey, dau of
       Hon. Elisha of Canfield, OH, in C; Rev. Stratton (1-8/10/30)
1852. Collins, Martin of Clinton m 3/6/13 Nancy Forman, dau of Isaac of
       Poughkeepsie; Minard Velie, Esq. (8-3/17)
1853. Collins, Oliver D. m 8/9/04 Sally Ward, dau of John, all of Clinton;
       Rev. Clark (8-8/14)
1854. Collins, Phebe Eliza, 6, dau of George and Eliza of Union Vale, d 11/8/30
       (8-11/17)
1855. Collins, Rhoda, wf of Hezekiah, Esq., d 3/31/26 in Freedom (8-4/5)
1856. Collins, Ricketson, 55, d 6/24/34 in Union Vale (8-7/16)
1857. Collins, Shuball m 6/23/36 Olive Lovake in Jay; _____ Vanderwarker, Esq.
       (4 [Keeseville Herald]-7/13)
1858. Collins, William S. of NYC m 3/31/31 Sophia Jackson of Blandford, MA in
       Albany, NY; Dr. William B. Sprague (8-4/6)
1859. Colon, Margaret, 15, dau of David of Hudson, d 1/9/08 (6-1/19)
1860. Colt, Joseph, about 65, brother of Gen. S. Colt of Geneva, d 2/4/31 in
       Palmyra (1-2/14)
1861. Colt, Joseph S., Esq. of Palmyra m Henrietta L. Peckham of Albany at
       St. Peter's Church, Albany; Rev. Dr. Lacy (1-10/1/30)
1862. Colter, Phineas (Rev.), 56, formerly of Vermont, d 9/30/34 in Livonia, NY
       (8-10/29)
1863. Colvard, Asa, Esq., 64, high sheriff of Albany Co., d 10/5/31 at his home
       in Rensselaerville (1-10/6)
1864. Colver, Dorius S. m 5/31/18 Mary Bennett, both of Hudson; Rev. Colver
       (6-6/2)
1865. Colver, Laura (Mrs.), 39, d 4/22/23 in Sharon, CT (8-4/30)
1866. Colvin, Catharine Louisa, 4, dau of James, d 12/25/29 in Albany (croup)
       (1-12/28)
1867. Colvin, David S. (Dr.) m 12/31/27 Harriet Eliza Morgan, dau of late Peter
       B. of Poughkeepsie, in Syracuse; Rev. Barlow (8-1/9/28)
1868. Colwell, _____, 8, dau of John, d 9/29/06 in Hudson (6-10/7)
1869. Colwell, Charles of Poughkeepsie m 10/2/31 Mrs. Ann Sanford, dau of William
       Tidd of Somers, in NYC; Rev. McClane (8-10/5)
1870. Colwell, Joseph C. of Freedom m Cynthia Noxon of Washington (Dut. Co.)
       in W; Rev. Luman Birch (8-10/14/29)
1871. Colwill, Joseph, 64, of Fredericktown d 5/14/04 (8-5/29)
1872. Combe, Michael (Col.) [of the Ex-Imperial Guards and Officer of the
       Legion of Honour], s of Col. Chevalier Sebastian Combe, a native of
       France, m 7/17/23 Eliza Walker, only dau of late Col. Benjamin of Utica,
       NY, in New Utrecht; Rev. Baiety (3-7/28)
1873. Combs, Jacob, merchant, of Hartford, CT m 4/24/28 Mary Merchant of Troy,
       NY in T; Rev. Howard (9-4/25)
1874. Comstock, Cyrus, 21, d 6/22/26 in Middlefield (3-6/26)
1875. Comstock, Edith (Miss), about 18, dau of Matthew, d 2/15/16 in Washington
       (Dut. Co.) (8-2/21)
1876. Comstock, Elizabeth, 60, consort of Capt. Calvin, d 5/11/13 (3-6/12)
1877. Comstock, Lewis, 7, s of Capt. Miles, d 5/4/26 in Cooperstown (3-5/8)
1878. Comstock, Lucy, 72, d 6/14/17 in Burlington (Ots. Co.) (Of her 14 children
       13 died of consumption) (3-6/19)
1879. Comstock, Mary, 84, relict of late Capt. Daniel, d 5/4/28 in Shelburne, VT
       (7-5/17)
1880. Comstock, Matthew, 64, farmer, of Washington (Dut. Co.) d 2/27/31 (8-3/9)
1881. Comstock, O. C., Jr. (Dr.) m 2/4/29 Hannah H. Halsey, oldest dau of N.
       Halsey, in Halseyville (Tompkins Co.); Rev. John H. Carle (1-2/16)
1882. Comstock, Paris W. of Berlin, NY m 7/4/27 Roxsina Hiscox of Petersburgh
       in P; Rev. Thomas (9-7/13)
1883. Comstock, Sally, consort of Joseph B., d 6/30/24 in Lansingburgh (2-7/6)
1884. Comstock, Samuel, merchant, of Lansingburgh m 4/6/03 Sally B. Comstock of
       Providence, RI (9-4/26)
1885. Comstock, Thomas, 79, d 3/11/11 in Hudson (member, Society of Friends
       in Hudson) (6-3/15)

1886. Comyn, Thomas, merchant, of Johnstown m 3/28/29 Lydia Ann Van Buren of Glen (Mont. Co.) in G; Rev. Morris (1-4/3)

1887. Conant, Samuel S. (editor of the late National Advocate "which was afterwards united with the Statesman under the title of the New York Morning Herald")d in Brandon, VT (1-12/8/30)

1888. Concklin, Catharine, wid of late Isaac of Hyde Park, d 5/24/29 "at an advanced age" in Fishkill (8-5/27)

1889. Concklin, Jacob Van Benschoten m 4/2/29 Nelly Shute at the home of Jacob Van Benschoten, Esq.; Rev. Dwight. All of Fishkill (8-4/8)

1890. Conde, Patty Ann, 6, dau of Jonathan, Esq., d 5/6/23 in Charlton (2-5/20)

1891. Condit, Catherine, 22, wf of Silas H., d in Hudson (6-4/24/04)

1892. Cone, John, 35, d 5/17/09 in Hebron, CT (fatally injured in the improper firing of a field piece) (3-6/10)

1893. Congdon, Caleb, merchant, of Providence, RI m 12/23/23 Olivia Rudd in Poughkeepsie; Rev. Dr. Reed (8-12/24)

1894. Congdon, James, Jr. m 4/28/22 Eliza Dubois, dau of Koert, Esq., at the Friends Meeting house in Crom Elbow (8-5/8)

1895. Conger, Sarah, 34, wf of Stephen M., d 9/11/05 "together with her infant child"(9-9/17)

1896. Conger, Stephen M. of Troy m 11/17/05 Rachel Hitchcock; Rev. Jonas Coe (9-11/19)

1897. Coningham, Grove, a European, m 5/11/99 Eliza Baldwin of Southeast, dau of late Squire Baldwin of Southeast; Rev. Dodge (8-6/4)

1898. Conklin, Charles, s of Charles, Sr., d "recently" in Albany (funeral from his father's home on Westerlo St. (1-1/14/30)

1899. Conklin, Charles E. of Peekskill m 1/4/26 Mary Ann Van Evert of Poughkeepsie; Rev. Dr. Reed (8-1/11)

1900. Conklin, F. Garretson of Freedom m 9/29/24 Margart G. Newcomb, dau of Dr. Zacheus Newcomb of Pleasant Valley; Rev. Clark (8-10/6)

1901. Conklin, Harvey m 1/14/22 Louisa Woolbridge, both of Staatsburgh; Rev. Wynkoop (8-1/23)

1902. Conklin, Henry, merchant, of Poughkeepsie m 5/26/18 Mary Ann Hewitt, dau of Thomas of NYC, in NYC; Rev. John Williams (8-6/3)

1903. Conklin, Jeremiah M., 35, merchant, of Poughkeepsie d 6/19/21 (8-6/27)

1904. Conklin, Joel of the firm of Raynor and Conklin, m 7/26/29 Mary Ann King, dau of late William, Esq. of NYC, in NYC; Rev. Thomas Brienthal (1-8/3)

1905. Conklin, John, 98, d 11/20/23 in Pleasant Valley (8-11/26)

1906. Conklin, John B. m 2/4/29 Comfort Wood, granddau of Isaac, all of Hyde Park; Rev. Clark (8-2/11)

1907. Conklin, Mathew m 1/17/22 Ellen Goulder, both of Staatsburgh; Rev. Wynkoop (8-1/23)

1908. Conklin, Matthias B. of Pine Plains m 1/24/28 Amanda Stone, dau of Nathaniel of Lenox, MA; Rev. Samuel Shepherd (8-1/30)

1909. Conklin, Nathan, 68, d 4/23/27 at his home in Northeast (8-5/2)

1910. Conklin, Nehemiah, merchant, of Poughkeepsie d 4/22/31 in Poughkeepsie (8-4/27 and 1-5/5)

1911. Conklin, Solomon Goodrich (Lt.), 22, of the U.S. Army d 8/9/10 at Fort Henry in Baltimore (son of Capt. Benjamin Conklin of Amenia, NY (8-8/29)

1912. Conkling, Theodore Herring, inf s of Jonas, d 8/23/30 in Albany (1-8/25)

1913. Conkling, William of Hudson m 8/12/24 Maria Mott of Poughkeepsie; Rev. C. C. Cuyler (8-8/18)

1914. Connolly, John (Right Rev.), Bishop of the Roman Catholic Church in NYC, d 2/16/25 in NYC (7-2/19)

1915. Connolly, John m 4/26/29 Emily Berault, dau of John M., Esq., in NYC; Rev. Dr. Powers. All of NYC (1-4/30)

1916. Conrad, Christian m 12/11/30 Betsey Fisk in Albany; C. H. Shear. All of Albany (1-12/13)

1917. Constable, John of Schenectady m 2/17/11 Susan Maria Livingston, dau of Gilbert R. of Red Hook, in R. H.; Rev. Kittle (6-2/22 and 8-2/27)

1918. Constable, Susan, 37, wf of John, d 5/9/30 in Schenectady (1-5/13)

1919. Constant, Joseph A., Esq. m 12/20/31 Eliza Sands Sinclair, dau of William J. of the U.S. Navy, at Grace Church, NYC; Rev. Dr. Wainwright (1-12/24)

1920. Conteright, John W. m 2/23/11 Sally Thomas, both of Poughkeepsie; Rev. Clark (8-2/27)
1921. Converse, Elam m 1/30/18 Susan Salisbury; Rev. Sommers. All of Troy (9-2/3)
1922. Converse, Eliza, 35, consort of John of Troy, NY, d 11/5/15 in Norwich, CT (9-11/14)
1923. Converse, Howard m 12/11/06 Rosanna Weeks, both of Troy, in T (9-12/16)
1924. Converse, J., Esq. of Troy m 7/7/23 Caroline Davis, dau of Richard, Esq. of Waterford, in W; Rev. Dorr (9-7/15)
1925. Converse, John, merchant, d 12/10/31 in Troy (1-12/15)
1926. Converse, Julia Sarah, 22, wf of Alexander B., Esq. and dau of Stephen Ross, Esq., d 11/27/21 in Troy (9-12/4)
1927. Converse, Sherman, Esq., editor of the Connecticut Journal, m 6/28/24 Eliza Bruen Nott, dau of Rev. Samuel, in Franklin, CT (3-7/12)
1928. Cook, ____, age 8 or 9, s of George, drowned 12/29/17 in Capt. Harris' Mill Pond (fell through the ice; the two or three physicians called to his aid were unable to save his life) (8-12/31)
1929. Cook, Abner, Jr., Esq., attorney, m 9/21/30 Catharine Nichols, dau of William, all of Cooperstown, in C; Rev. John Smith (1-9/29)
1930. Cook, Adam m in March Elizabeth Farrington, both of Milford (3-4/2/07)
1931. Cook, Alanson, 24, d 2/23/15 (in Troy?) (9-2/28)
1932. Cook, Asaph, Jr. m Polly Steward in Granville; Rev. Hall. All of G (9-3/15/03)
1933. Cook, B. Thomas, Jr., editor of the Anti-Masonic Telegraph, m 9/22/31 Mary Ann Clark, both of Norwich, in N; Rev. Rexford (1-10/1)
1934. Cook, Benjamin C., Esq. of Cohocton (Steuben Co.) m 8/6/26 Harriet Todd of Worcester in W; Rev. Cole (3-8/14)
1935. Cook, Cyrenus d 9/15/20 in Middlefield (3-9/25)
1936. Cook, Daniel, 47, merchant, of Geneva d 11/28/31 in Hartford, CT (1-12/11)
1937. Cook, Harry, formerly of Hartford, CT but for the last 20 years a resident of Poughkeepsie, NY, d 4/13/30 in Poughkeepsie (8-4/14)
1938. Cook, Henry B. of the firm of William and H. B. Cook, merchants, of Albany and formerly of Cooperstown, d 5/26/25 in Albany (3-5/30)
1939. Cook, Hiram D. m 1/27/27 Ann Green, both of Watervliet, in Gibbonsville; Rev. Howard (9-1/30)
1940. Cook, James M. (Maj.) m 8/30/29 Elizabeth Harnum in Ballston; Rev. Babcock. All of Ballston (1-9/4)
1941. Cook, Jannitzie, about 104, d 6/7/30 in Bethlehem (she lived with her father in Saratoga when it was "burned by the savages" in the French War [she was then about age 14]; she lived with her husband, Adam, upwards of 70 years. Adam d "about 10 years ago", age 96) (1-6/9)
1942. Cook, John, 59, "vender of mineral waters", d 8/20/23 in Albany (2-8/26)
1943. Cook, John, "well known for many years as the proprietor of the Albany Reading Room", d in Albany (8-8/27/23)
1944. Cook, Jonathan (Capt.) m 10/27/31 Mary Sanborn in Provincetown, MA (deceased, age 78 at time of death, was father of 10 ch, 52 grandch, and 32 great-grandch) (1-11/17)
1945. Cook, Joshua, 59, d 9/3/23 in Hartwick (consumption) (3-9/8)
1946. Cook, Lewis m 9/9/03 Hannah Darling, both of Amenia (8-9/27)
1947. Cook, M.S.V.D. (Maj.) m 12/14/06 Sally Eddy, both of Pittstown, in P (9-12/16)
1948. Cook, O. R., bookseller, of Plattsburgh m 1/28/34 Elizabeth M. Severance, dau of C., Esq. of Burlington, VT, in B; Rev. K. Converse (4 [Keeseville Herald]-2/4 and 7-2/1)
1949. Cook, Phineas P. (Lt.) m 10/11/30 Mary B. Pratt, dau of Henry, Esq., in Rochester; Rev. Jones (or Rev. James?). All of Rochester (1-10/19)
1950. Cook, Phinehas, Esq., 52, d 3/22/26 in Otego (pulmonary complaint) (surv by wf and 9 ch) (3-4/10)
1951. Cook, Rice of Rutland, VT m 9/1/02 Ann Bacon of Stillwater, NY in S; Rev. Paige (9-11/3)
1952. Cook, Seth, merchant, of Cooperstown m 3/10/12 Lucy Crafts of Hartwick; Rev. John Smith (3-3/14)
1953. Cook, Seth, merchant, 37, d 2/8/19 in Cooperstown (3-2/15)
1954. Cook, Stephen, Jr. m 2/10/19 Jennet Wy-- in Malone; Rev. Asahel Parmelee (7-2/20)

1955. Cook, Timothy of Sharon m 12/27/24 Elizabeth Wescott of Milford in M;
       Rev. Soul (3-1/10/25)
1956. Cook, Zebediah F., 70, d 11/19/15 in Hartwick (3-11/23)
1957. Cooke, Henry T. of Poughkeepsie m 11/4/12 Nancy Penniman of Lansingburgh
       in L (8-11/18)
1958. Cooke, John, Esq., district attorney of Allegany Co., d 9/9/30 in Angelica
       (1-9/17)
1959. Cooke, Joseph Pratt m 1/26/31 Sophia Ferris Wolden, 2nd dau of Jacob T.,
       Esq., in Walden (Orange Co.); Rev. William H. Hart (1-2/1 and 1-2/4)
1960. Cooke, Juliana (Miss), 32, d 12/5/22 (8-12/18)
1961. Cooke, Oliver D., Jr., 35, s of Oliver D., Sr. of Hartford, CT, d 10/31/31
       in East Windsor, CT (1-11/3 and 8-11/9)
1962. Cooke, Samuel (Dr.), about 45, d 5/26/83 in Poughkeepsie (funeral
       sermon by Rev. Wheeler Case) (buried 5/28 at the Dutch Church in Pough-
       keepsie) (5-6/12)
1963. Cookingham, Andrew m 1/18/27 Lucy Ann Lambert, dau of Col. George, all of
       Rhinebeck; Rev. William J. Byer (8-1/24)
1964. Cookingham, Elizabeth, 35, wf of Philip, d 3/1/24 in Clinton (8-3/10)
1965. Cooley, Richard m 11/22/21 Angelina Grace in Cooperstown; Rev. Tiffany
       (3-11/26)
1966. Coolidge, Catharine Ann (Mrs.), 45, d 8/25/34 in Poughkeepsie (8-9/3)
1967. Coolidge, Daniel, 50, formerly of Poughkeepsie, d 10/14/31 in NYC (8-10/19)
1968. Cooly, Lydia (Mrs.), about 81, d 8/20/22 in Benson, VT (9-9/3)
1969. Coon (or Cook?), Jesse, 73, d 3/27/30 at his home in Duanesburgh (1-4/3)
1970. Cooney, Michael m 5/4/30 Mary Ann Doris, both of Albany; Rev. Charles
       Smith (1-5/7)
1971. Coonhoven, Jacob of Poughkeepsie m 12/15/15 Penelope Van Kleeck of Fishkill;
       Rev. Leonard (8-12/20)
1972. Coonly, John m 12/16/17 Catharine Rykert, both of Stanford; Isaac Sherrill,
       Esq. (8-2/19)
1973. Coonrod, Henry m 8/9/11 Belinda Tappin in Stamford (Dela. Co.) (6-8/23)
1974. Coons, Nicholas m 1/12/13 Hannah Finch, both of Greenbush; Rev. Jonas Coe
       (9-1/19)
1975. Coop, David, 66, brewer, d 6/11/05 in Hudson (6-6/18)
1976. Cooper, ____, consort of William of Poughkeepsie, d 9/4/08 (8-9/7)
1977. Cooper, Apollos, Esq. m 2/1/31 Mrs. Elizabeth Griffin in Utica; Rev.
       Aiken. All of Utica (1-2/18)
1978. Cooper, Benjamin m 10/4/01 Phebe Folger; Rev. Dr. Gano (6-10/8)
1979. Cooper, Benjamin, 3, s of Benjamin, d 7/9/07 in Hudson (6-7/14)
1980. Cooper, Benjamin Franklin, Esq. of Utica, NY m Mary Ann Brantley, oldest
       dau of Rev. W. T. of Philadelphia, PA in P; Rev. John L. Dagg (1-10/12/29)
1981. Cooper, Charles D. (Dr.), 60, d 1/30/31 in Albany (1-2/1)
1982. Cooper, Christian H. m 9/20/27 Phebe Saunders in Albia; Rev. Beaman
       (9-10/2)
1983. Cooper, Elizabeth, dau of R. F., Esq. of Cooperstown, d 9/30/11 in Albany
       (her clothing caught fire from a candle) (3-10/5)
1984. Cooper, Elizabeth, oldest dau of James of Cooperstown, d 7/3/13 (3-7/17)
1985. Cooper, Fayette, s of Ananias, Esq., was baptized in Rhinebeck by Rev.
       Stephen Van Voorhis (this child was named to honor "the illustrious
       General the Marquis de la Fayette") (5-10/17/82)
1986. Cooper, Fenimore, 1, only s of James Cooper, Esq., d 8/5/23 in NYC (3-8/11)
1987. Cooper, Grenville C. of the U.S. Navy m 6/15/29 Jane Agnes Shedden of
       Washington City (Dist of Columbia) (1-6/20)
1988. Cooper, Hannah (Miss), oldest dau of William, Esq. of Cooperstown,
       d 9/10/00 in Butternuts when thrown from her horse (had set out with
       her brother, Richard F., Esq., on a visit withGeneral Morris of Butter-
       nuts) (funeral sermon by Rev. Daniel Nash) (3-9/18)
1989. Cooper, Hannah, 15, dau of Richard F., Esq., d 12/3/17 in Cooperstown
       (3-12/11)
1990. Cooper, Isaac m 12/24/04 Mary Ann Morris, oldest dau of Gen. Jacob of
       Butternuts; Rev. Daniel Nash (3-12/27)
1991. Cooper, Isaac, Esq., 36, d 12/30/17 in Cooperstown (interred in the
       family burying ground) (3-1/5/18)
1992. Cooper, James, about 60, d 2/15/11 in Fishkill (8-2/27)
1993. Cooper, John, 26, d 10/26/02 in Canaan (consumption) (6-11/2)

1994. Cooper, John of Paulus Hook, NJ m 1/5/06 Louiza Haxton, dau of Benjamin of Beekman, NY, in B (8-1/7)
1995. Cooper, John (Dr.) of Poughkeepsie m 7/6/14 Rebecca Hardenbrook, dau of William A., Esq. of Little Bloomingdale, in L. B.; Rev. William Harris (8-7/13)
1996. Cooper, John (Rev.), 60, pastor of the Baptist church in Preston Hollow, d 10/9/29 in Rensselaerville (1-10/15)
1997. Cooper, John I., merchant, of Clinton (Dut. Co.) m 11/12/14 Abbey Ham of Washington (Dut. Co.); Rev. Jenks (8-11/16)
1998. Cooper, Julia H., 13, dau of John and Rebecca, d 9/9/34 in Poughkeepsie (funeral from her father's home on Main St.) (8-9/10)
1999. Cooper, Peter of Poughkeepsie m 12/31/11 Anne Degraff of Fishkill; Rev. Covel (8-1/8/12)
2000. Cooper, Phebe, 17, sister of Benjamin, d 4/11/07 in Hudson (6-4/14)
2001. Cooper, Richard, attorney, m Mary Storrs, dau of Amariah of Hudson, in Claverack; Rev. Sluyter (1-6/2/31)
2002. Cooper, Richard F., Esq. d 3/5/13 in Albany (buried in Cooperstown 3/9) (3-3/13)
2003. Cooper, Samuel m 4/2/12 in Cooperstown; Rev. John Smith (3-4/11)
2004. Cooper, William, brewer, of Hudson m Eliza Julia Ann Mills, dau of John, Esq. of Claverack; Rev. Judd (6-2/14/04) (See, possibly, Entry 2008)
2005. Cooper, William, Esq., 55, of Cooperstown d 12/22/09 in Albany (interred in the Episcopal burying ground in Cooperstown) (funeral service by Rev. Daniel Nash and Rev. William C. Schenck) (surv by wf and several ch) (3-12/30/09; 8-1/3/10; and 6-1/18/10)
2006. Cooper, William, Esq., 33, s of late William, Esq., d 10/19/19 in Cooperstown (3-10/25)
2007. Cooper, William of NYC m 8/5/29 Mary M. Wilson, oldest dau of E. Wilson, Jr., Esq. of Troy, NY, at St. Thomas' Church in Taunton, MA (1-8/11)
2008. Cope?, William from England m 2/15/04 Mary Ann Julia Mills of Claverack in Hudson (8-2/21) (See, possibly, Entry 2004)
2009. Copeland, J. W., editor of the National Standard, m 7/14/30 Georgiana Croswell in Middlebury, VT; Prof. Fowler (1-8/10)
2010. Copelin, _____ (Capt.) of the 10th U.S. Infantry d 11/30/13 in Plattsburgh (7-12/4)
2011. Copeman, Jacob of Poughkeepsie d 12/10/16 (8-12/11)
2012. Copeman, John, 67, d 8/5/05 in Poughkeepsie (surv by wf and children) (8-8/13)
2013. Copp, William, printer, one of the proprietors of the Rising Sun at Kingston, d in NYC (8-9/18/98)
2014. Corbin, Alpha of Champlain d 8/17/27 in Plattsburgh (7-8/18)
2015. Corbin, Lyman, formerly of Otsego Co., m 2/6/25 Lydia Bryant of Newark (Wayne Co.) in N; Rev. Pomeroy of Palmyra (3-2/21)
2016. Corey, Mary, 83,(relict of Capt. Oliver formerly of Charlestown, NH, deceased) d 11/10/13 in Rockingham, VT ("printers in the state of New York are requested to insert the above for the information of friends") (7-11/27)
2017. Corkran, Elanor (Miss), 18, d in NYC (9-1/2/27)
2018. Corlies, Joseph, 46, merchant, d 3/15/31 in NYC (1-3/22)
2019. Cornelius, John m 6/19/22 Cornelia Swartwout, both of Clinton (Dut. Co.); Stephen Thorn, Esq. (8-6/26)
2020. Cornell, Cornelius m 1/6/30 Mary Brinkerhoff, both of Freedom; Rev. Dr. Cuyler (8-1/13)
2021. Cornell, Douw, farmer, of Poughkeepsie d 7/6/03 (8-7/12)
2022. Cornell, James d 4/6/17 in Poughkeepsie (8-4/9)
2023. Cornell, Martha Jane, dau of Stephen, d 6/15/32 in Poughkeepsie (8-6/27)
2024. Cornell, Russell of NYC m Maria W. Cornell of Troy in T; Rev. Howard (9-12/12/28)
2025. Cornell, Samuel M. of the firm of Foster, Nostrand and Co. of NYC m 11/7/31 Eveline J. Howland, dau of James, 2nd, of New Bedford (state not given) in N.B.; Rev. Dewey (1-11/15)
2026. Cornell, Thomas F., Esq., attorney, of Florida m Sarah T. Munn, dau of Stephen, Esq. of NYC; Rev. Dr. Broadhead (1-11/23/29)
2027. Cornell, Walter, Esq., an assemblyman from Washington Co., d 3/6/33 in Albany (4 [Keeseville Herald]-3/12)

2028. Corney, George m 5/24/24 Ann Jones, both of Poughkeepsie; Rev. Seney (8-5/26
2029. Corning, Elisha, s of Elisha, Sr., d in Burlington (Ots. Co.) (3-7/10)
2030. Corning, Elizabeth, 24, wf of Edward, d 11/16/31 in NYC (1-11/19)
2031. Corning, Erastus of Albany m 3/9/19 Harriet Weld, dau of Joseph of Troy; Rev. Coe (9-3/16)
2032. Corning, Gurdon, merchant, of Troy m 11/8/06 Arabella Cornell of Flushing in F (9-11/25)
2033. Corning, Joseph Weld, 17 mo, s of Erastus, d 8/15/30 in Albany (1-8/17)
2034. Corning, Nathan of Chatham m 10/23/11 Clarissa Smith "of Canaan (Chatham Society)" in Canaan (Chatham Society);Rev. Walters (6-11/4)
2035. Cornwall, Henry m 11/14/13 Sally Van Hoesen in Athens, NY (6-11/16)
2036. Cornwall, Josiah, Esq. of Stanford (Dut. Co.) m 2/27/13 Clarissa Chatman of Kent, CT; Rev. Perry (8-3/17)
2037. Cornwall, Nathan, Jr., 18, oldest s of Nathan of Danbury, CT, d "lately" in New Milford, CT (small pox) (3-4/16/01)
2038. Cornwell, Aspinwal m 3/9/14 Mrs. Abigail Gifford; Abraham D. Van Wyck, Esq. (bride and groom both of Fishkill) (8-3/16)
2039. Cornwell, Eliza, 29, wf of William d 4/1/31 in Poughkeepsie (8-4/6)
2040. Cornwell, John Eden of Stanford (Dut. Co.) m 11/22/26 Bebe ___?___ of Sharon, CT; Rev. Robert G. Armstrong (8-12/27)
2041. Cornwell, Morris m 9/4/28 Laura M. Earl; Rev. Tucker. All of Troy (9-9/5)
2042. Cory, Henry m 1/1/12 Julia Clark; Rev. Smith. All of Cooperstown (3-1/4)
2043. Cory, Holder of Cooperstown m 10/4/24 Etna Maria Grace of Troy in T; Rev. Butler (3-10/11)
2044. Cory, Jemima (Mrs.), 72, mother of David of Ballston Spa, d 5/19/25 in B. S. (2-5/24)
2045. Cory, William, about 10, s of Ellery Cory, d 10/4/26 in Cooperstown (3-10/16)
2046. Cossaert, Staley (sic) m 9/19/24 Mrs. Anna Gilliland, wid of late David, in Westford; James Birge, Jr., Esq. (3-9/27)
2047. Cossit, Rufus, Esq. of Onondaga m 1/13/23 Eliza Van Kleeck of Poughkeepsie; Rev. C. C. Cuyler (8-1/15)
2048. Coster, Gerard H. m 6/9/31 Matilda Prime, dau of N., Esq., "at Hurlgate"; Rev. Dr. Wainwright (1-6/13)
2049. Cotes, Evan of Springfield m Laurina Hawskins (sic) of Danube (Herk. Co.) in D (3-7/14/23)
2050. Cotes, Mary, 25, wf of Evan, d 6/17/21 in Springfield (3-6/25)
2051. Cotting, John m 5/10/27 Julia Ann Traver, both of Rhinebeck; Rev. William J. Eyer (8-5/16)
2052. Cotton, Experience, 33, wf of Owen and dau of Jonas ___?___, Esq. of Marcellus, d in Attica (consumption) (1-6/21/30)
2053. Cottrel, Samuel m 5/18/22 Rebecca Westervelt; Rev. C. C. Cuyler (8-5/22)
2054. Couch, Lydia, wf of Dr. John W. of Northeast, d 8/15/25 in Northeast (8-8/17)
2055. Coughtry, Margaret Curby(?), youngest dau of Andrew H., d 10/16/29 in Albany (1-10/20)
2056. Covel, Jonathan (Deacon) of Salem m Mrs. Patience Mercer of Troy; Rev. Ogilvie (9-7/29/17)
2057. Covel, Napoleon B. m 12/15/31 Charlotte Smith in Keeseville; Horace Beach, Esq. (4 [Keeseville Herald]-12/20)
2058. Covell, Lemuel (Rev.) of Cheshire, MA d in Clinton, Upper Canada "while on a missionary tour among the Indians and frontier settlements" (deceased was of the Shaftsbury Baptist Association; until shortly before death he was "the settled preacher of the First Baptist Church in Pittstown, NY")(9-1/13/07)
2059. Coventry, Alexander (Dr.), 69, d 12/9/31 in Utica (was the oldest physician "in that place") (1-12/14)
2060. Coventry, Charles B. (Dr.) of Utica m 4/23/29 Clarissa Butler, oldest dau of Hon. Medad of Stuyvesant (Col. Co.), in S; Rev. J. Sickles (1-5/2)
2061. Covert, Elisha, 70, d 8/29/17 in Lexington (6-9/2)
2062. Covill, Alanson L. (Rev.) of Addison, VT m Sarah J. Woods, dau of Rev. Abel Woods of Essex, in E; Rev. J. H. Dwyer (7-2/16/28)
2063. Cowdry, Christiana, 55, wf of Col. John, d 4/26/30 in Waterloo (1-5/6)

2064. Cowen, Elizabeth, 61, wf of Hector, d 2/21/31 in Stamford (Dela. Co.) (1-3/10)
2065. Cowing, James, 81, m 7/18/21 Mrs. Editha Fullington, 73, both of the town of Seneca; Richard Hogarth, Esq. (groom's fourth and bride's fifth marr) (8-8/1)
2066. Cowins, Elizabeth (Mrs.), 103, d in Schenectady ("read without spectacles until her death and but two years ago she ... razed grass with a scythe") (8-10/7/07)
2067. Cowles, Berah, 4, only dau of John, d 5/26/30 in Poughkeepsie (8-6/2)
2068. Cowles, Dolly, 16, 2nd dau of Zenas and Polly, d 9/21/03 in Farmington, CT (6-10/18)
2069. Cowles, Henry, 9, s of Truman, d 1/19/11 (6-1/25)
2070. Cowles, John, merchant, of Poughkeepsie m 10/30/27 Julia Ann Haight, dau of Samuel, Esq. of Milan, in M; Stephen Thorn, Esq. (8-11/7)
2071. Cowles, Welthy Diana (Miss), 20, d 8/9/30 (8-8/11)
2072. Cox, Edward B. m Arvilla Brace in Centerville; Rev. Shedd (7-3/29/31)
2073. Cox, James (Dr.) of Philadelphia (state not given), brother of Rev. Dr. Cox and of Dr. A. L. Cox of Albany, NY, d 12/21/31 in Philadelphia (consumption) (1-12/31)
2074. Cox, John d 7/26/07 in Troy ((9-7/28)
2075. Coye, Lucinda, 41, wf of Jason, d 9/10/12 in De Ruyter (3-10/10)
2076. Cozine, John (Hon.), one of the state supreme court judges, d 9/14/98 (place of death not given) (8-9/18)
2077. Crafts, James A. of Hartwick m Maria Low of Milford; Elder Crane (3-11/21)
2078. Crafts, Royal, 51, d 6/12/21 in Cooperstown (3-6/25)
2079. Crafts, Willard, Esq., attorney, of Bridgewater (Oneida Co.) m Jane Anne Baker of Cairo (Greene Co.) in C (3-6/30/23)
2080. Crafts, William, editor of the Charleston Courier, d in Lebanon Springs, NY (3-10/2/26)
2081. Craig, John m 12/14/26 Elizabeth Kent, both of Plattsburgh, in P; Rev. Frederick Halsey (7-12/16)
2082. Craig, Matthew m 1/5/25 Anne Clough, both of Pleasant Valley, in Poughkeepsie; Rev. Babcock (8-1/12)
2083. Cramer, Abraham of Poughkeepsie m 10/19/22 Carmella Losee of Freedom; Rev. Clark (8-10/23)
2084. Cramer, James m 1/15/23 Catharine Richardson, both of Saratoga, in S; Rev. Duryee (2-1/21)
2085. Cramer, John m 1/19/02 Sarah Van Wagenen, both of Rhinebeck; Rev. Romayn (8-2/2)
2086. Crandal, Chauncey m 6/19/25 Laura Tuttle, both of Butternuts, in B (3-6/27)
2087. Crandal, E. B., editor of the Watch Tower, m 11/11/19 Mary Todd; Rev. Smith. All of Cooperstown (3-11/15)
2088. Crandal, Enos of Columbus m 12/4/25 Armylla Bardwell of Burlington (Ots. Co.) in B; Artemas Sheldon, Esq. (3-12/12)
2089. Crandall, Luther m 10/22/19 Sarah Willmarth, both of Albia; Rev. Sommers (9-10/26)
2090. Crandell, Reynolds m 1/26/06 Margaret Sincebox, both of Beekman; James De Long, Esq. (8-2/11)
2091. Crane, Aner, 47, wf of Joseph, Esq., d 5/7/07 in Southeast (consumption) (surv by husband and children) (8-5/20)
2092. Crane, Ezra d 4/3/03 in Hudson (6-4/5)
2093. Crane, Hiram of Havana (Tioga Co.) m 11/25/30 Emeline Demcrest of Catskill in C; Rev. Wyckoff (1-12/13)
2094. Crane, Ira m 11/9/09 Hannah hopkins, both of Carmel; Rev. Dodd (8-11/22)
2095. Crane, John, Esq., 84, d 6/9/27 at his home in Carmel ("In the struggle for Independence Judge Crane was an ardent Whig") (8-7/11)
2096. Crane, Polly, 67, wf of Ezra, d 2/11/26 in Otsego (3-2/13)
2097. Crane, Robert, Esq., 40, d 4/27/30 in Patterson, Put. Co.) (8-5/5)
2098. Crane, Tamar, 76, consort of Judge John, d 5/19/23 in Carmel (surv by an aged husband, 9 children, 54 grandchildren, and 33 great grandchildren) (interred in the family burying ground) (8-6/4)
2099. Crane, Thomas of Elizabethtown, NJ m 6/29/26 Elizabeth Price of Wappingers Creek, NY; Rev. Price (8-7/12)
2100. Crane, Timothy B. m Sally Teller in Poughkeepsie; Rev. Baldwin (8-3/6/98)
2101. Crane, William C. (Col.) m 6/18/26 Persis Narina Tunnicliff in Warren (Herk. Co.); Rev. George Sawin (3-6/26)

2102. Crapser, George m 8/24/13 Nancy Johnston, dau of William; Rev. Clark. All of Clinton (Dut. Co.) (8-9/1)
2103. Crary, Archibald, 19, s of Hon. John of Salem (Wash. Co.) d 12/6/29 in NYC (1-12/11)
2104. Crary, Edward C. of Liverpool, England m 6/21/31 Cornelia Livingston Fulton, dau of late Robert, in NYC; Rev. Dr. Spring (1-6/23)
2105. Crary, Elizabeth (Miss), 46, dau of late Col. Crary of Newport, RI, d at the home of Hon. James Emott (8-2/29/32)
2106. Crary, Laura Maria (Miss), dau of late Col. Crary of Newport, RI, d 5/31/18 at the home of her mother in Poughkeepsie (8-6/10)
2107. Crassour, Ferdinand of NYC m Sarah Jane Corwin, oldest dau of Elisha, Esq. of Haverstraw, in Mount Pleasant; Rev. Clark,   (1-9/28/30)
2108. Crausman, Elijah (Dr.) m 4/20/06 "Mrs. Wilson", wid of Alexander, in Hoosick (9-4/29)
2109. Craven, Thomas Tingey (Lt.) of the U.S. Navy m 10/5/31 Virginia Ann Wingate, dau of Hon. Joseph F., in Bath, ME; Rev. Seneca White (1-10/17)
2110. Crawford, Cinthia, 21, wf of Ammi, d 3/10/24 in Saratoga Springs (2-3/16)
2111. Crawford, Elizabeth, 42, wf of George, d 4/9/08 in Hudson (6-4/12)
2112. Crawford, George, merchant, of Hudson m 8/23/08 Mary I. Wilson Livingston, dau of late Hon. Peter R. of the Manor of Livingston; Rev. H. Veeder of the Manor of Livingston (6-8/9)
2113. Crawford, John, merchant, of Hudson m 2/18/13 Margaret Livingston, dau of Col. Walter T. of the Manor of Livingston, at that place; Rev. Vedder (6-2/23)
2114. Crawford, Ruth, 58, consort of Job, Esq., d 9/20/13 in Pawling (8-10/6)
2115. Crawter, Robert m Ruth Harman, both of Hillsdale; Rev. Morse (6-1/19/13)
2116. Crehan, John of Troy m 8/22/15 Sally Weaver of Poughkeepsie in Fishkill; Rev. John Brown (9-9/5)
2117. Creighton, John Orde (Capt.) of the U.S. Navy m Harriet Halsey, dau of T. I., Esq., in Providence, RI (9-3/28/15)
2118. Crippen, Silas m 1/1/24 Catherine Barney in Maryland, NY; Elder Wright (3-1/5)
2119. Crippen, Silas, 74, (a Rev. Soldier) d 3/7/31 in Worcester (Ots. Co.) (1-3/14 and 1-3/15)
2120. Critchley, Charles m 7/3/31 Mary Ann Green, both of Fishkill, in Newburgh; Rev. John Brown (8-7/20)
2121. Crittenton, Alonzo, principal of the Albany Female Academy, m 8/5/29 Mary W. Warner, dau of Elias, all of Albany; Rev. Weed (1-8/6)
2122. Crocker, L. B. of the firm of Marshall, Bronson and Co. in Oswego, m 1/12/31 Ann E. Pardee, dau of Luther, Esq. of East Canada Creek (Herk. Co.), in E. C. C.; Rev. Ketchum (1-1/20)
2123. Croes(?), Robert B. (Rev.) of Troy, NY m 5/10/30 Helen Robertson, dau of James Esq. of Richmond, VA, in R; Right Rev. Bishop Moore (1-5/19)
2124. Crofts, Alexander, merchant, of the firm of Mullany and Crofts of NYC m 2/23/09 Mary Livingston, dau of Col. Robert T. of the Livingston Manor, in the Manor House; Rev. Vedder (6-3/7)
2125. Crofut, Jesse m 11/29/07 Elizabeth Bailey, both of Troy; Rev. Coe (9-12/1)
2126. Croghan, _____ (Lt. Col.) m Serena Livingston, dau of John R., Esq., in NYC; Right Rev. Bishop Hobart (7-5/24/17)
2127. Croghan, _____ (Lt. Col.) m Levina Livingston, dau of John R., Esq., in NYC (6-5/27)
2128. Crolius, Clarkson, Jr. m 11/27/31 Elizabeth H. Seaman, dau of late David, Esq. of NYC; Rev. Hawks (1-12/1)
2129. Cronck, Solomon d "a short time since" in Cambridge (died from an infected wound in his hand caused by a scythe cut) (9-11/21/15)
2130. Cronk, Samuel W. m 7/19/29 Catharine Swartwout, dau of John B., in Poughkeepsie; Rev. Welton (8-7/22 and 1-7/25)
2131. Cronke, Solomn d "recently" from an infected cut from a scythe (3-11/23/15). See Entry 2129.
2132. Cronkhite, Jeremiah of Richfield m 4/19/24 Emelina Jones in Cooperstown; Rev. F. T. Tiffany (3-4/26)
2133. Cronkite, William W. m 10/6/11 Nancy Pine, both of Fort Ann in Fort Ann; Rev. Harrington (7-10/25)
2134. Crook, Hannah, 67, wf of James, d 6/18/34 in Beekmantown (7-6/21)
2135. Crook, John Welton, 2nd s of Samuel W. and Catharine of Danbury, CT, d 2/21/34 in Poughkeepsie, NY (8-2/26)

61

2136. Crook, Thomas m Hannah Delong of Plattsburgh in Beekmantown; Rev. Kingsley (7-3/31/21)
2137. Crookshank, Nathaniel m 2/24/03 _?_ _?_ (her name is blurred but her surname probably ends in "mew"); Lemuel Conklin, Esq. All of Dutchess Co. (8-3/8)
2138. Crosby, Cyrenus (Dr.), about 70, formerly of Poughkeepsie, d 12/21/31 in Amenia (8-1/4/32)
2139. Crosby, Platt H., Esq., formerly of Poughkeepsie, m "Mrs. Holliday" in NYC (8-11/27/16)
2140. Cross, Ellena (Miss), 26, dau of Edward, d in Middlesex (Yates Co.) (1-9/29/29)
2141. Cross, Laura M. (Miss), 22, d 6/4/34 in Fairfax, VT (7-6/21)
2142. Crossen, Daniel m 2/13/23 _?_ Beckwith; Rev. Frederick Halsey (7-2/15)
2143. Crosset, Edward m Hannah Carter, dau of Jacob, in Claverack; Rev. Gebhard (6-8/30/08)
2144. Crossett, Lydia, 28, d 7/7/23 in Plattsburgh (7-7/19)
2145. Crossett, Samuel (Dr.) of Aurelius, NY m 6/15/05 Sally Polhemus of Flemington, NJ; Rev. Oliver W. Hunt (6-7/2)
2146. Crossman, John m 11/10/27 Sylvia Chase; Clark Baker, Esq. All of Hoosick (9-11/23)
2147. Croswell, Betsey, wf of Mackay Croswell, editor of the Western Constellation, d 9/22/03 in Catskill (surv by her mother, husband, and 3 young children) (6-9/27)
2148. Croswell, Caleb, Jr. of Catskill, NY m 9/30/01 Mary Phelps of Litchfield, CT in L (6-10/8)
2149. Croswell, Caleb, Jr., 27, of Catskill d 9/23/03 in Litchfield, CT (6-10/4)
2150. Croswell, Caleb d 10/1/06 in Blenheim, NY "at an advanced age" (6-10/7)
2151. Croswell, Edwin, Esq., editor of the Albany Argus, m 9/15/24 Catharine Adams, dau of John, Esq. of Catskill, in C; Rev. Prentiss (3-9/27 and 7-10/9)
2152. Croswell, Hannah, 89, relict of late Capt. Caleb and grandmother of the editor of the Argus, d 4/9/29 in Gilboa (Schoharie Co.) (she was born in Hartford, CT, youngest and last surviving of the children of Jacob Kellogg) (1-4/16)
2153. Croswell, James m 12/1/20 Eliza Manney, both of Poughkeepsie; Rev. Cuyler (8-12/6)
2154. Croswell, Jennet, 16 mo, dau of Harry, d 9/22/08 in Hudson (6-9/27)
2155. Crouse, Adam D. m 10/25/21 Eunice Brownell, dau of Aaron, Esq., all of Beekman; Rev. De Witt (8-11/28)
2156. Crouse, Tilly, Esq. of Clinton (Dut. Co.) m 10/21/23 Martha Schryver, dau of Capt. Peter A. of Hyde Park; Rev. Cuyler (8-10/29)
2157. Crouse, William m 9/4/28 Rosetta Sleight, both of Clinton; Rev. William J. Eyre (8-9/10)
2158. Crowninshield, Benjamin V., 21, oldest s of Hon. B. W., d in Salem (1-2/6/29)
2159. Crowninshield, Jacob, Esq. of Salem, MA m 5/12/31 Mary M. Schuyler, oldest dau of Arent, Esq. of Bloomingdale, NY, in NYC; Rev. Dr. Wainwright (1-5/16)
2160. Cruger, Hannah, 40, wf of Gen. Damiel, d 12/14/31 in Syracuse (1-12/17)
2161. Cruger, Jefferson m 12/17/31 Mary Sherwood, both of Poughkeepsie; Rev. Dr. Cuyler (8-12/28)
2162. Cruger, John C., attorney, m 6/2/31 Frances Ann Jones, dau of late Joshua, Esq. All of NYC (1-6/6)
2163. Crupin, Henry m 2/26/20 Hester Davis, both of Clinton (Dut. Co.) (8/3/1)
2164. Cruttenden, Fortiscue m 9/23/29 Caroline Merrill, dau of Capt. Nathaniel, in Geneva; Rev. Strong (1-10/10)
2165. Crysler, Ralph M. of Niagara, Upper Canada m 7/21/30 Elsie Gansevoort, dau of Leonard, Jr., Esq.; Rev. Dr. Ludlow (1-7/23)
2166. Cullen, Edward, 25, merchant, d 4/25/06 in Troy (9-4/25)
2167. Culver, _____, 61, wf of Francis, d 6/9/24 in Beekmantown (7-6/12)
2168. Culver, Adrietta, 63, wid of James, d 8/12/24 in Hyde Park (8-8/25)
2169. Culver, Allen J. m 1/6/31 Pamela Ostrom, oldest dau. of John H.; Rev. Wile. All of Pleasant Valley (8-1/12)
2170. Culver, Marshall m 1/25/26 Mary I. Ostrom, both of Hyde Park; Rev. Clark (8-2/1)

2171. Culver, Oliver m 12/24/15 Abigail Gale, dau of Abraham, in Beekmantown (Clinton Co.); R. H. Walworth, Esq. All of Plattsburgh (double ceremony - see marr of Joshua Smith) (7-12/30)
2172. Cumming, Francis H. (Rev.) of St. Luke's Church, Rochester, m Caroline A. Hulbert, dau of Hon. John W. of Auburn, at St. Peter's Church in Auburn (3-2/25/22)
2173. Cumming, Francis H. m Charlotte Hart at St. Luke's Church in Rochester; Rev. Dr. Rudd of Auburn (1-4/13/31)
2174. Cumming, Hooper (Rev.), D.D., late of Albany, d 12/15/25 in Charleston, SC (3-1/2?26)
2175. Cummings, Daniel of Washington (Dut. Co.) m 9/14/21 Sally Oliver late of Ireland; Rev. Ryder (8-10/10)
2176. Cummings, David of Washington (Dut. Co.) m 1/23/22 Sally Maxfield of Stanford (Dut. Co.) in S; Abner Wilcox, Esq. (8-1/30)
2177. Cummings, Jasper, 15, late of Burlington (Ots. Co.), d 5/28/24 in a building collapse in Attleborough, MA (3-6/14)
2178. Cummings, Prudence, 13, d 11/21/15 in Cooperstown (fell into a fire "a fortnight since" when seized by a fit) (3-11/30)
2179. Cummings, William, 29, d 11/17/29 in Albany (1-11/20)
2180. Cumpston, Edward (Maj.), 72, late of Esperance, d 8/22/25 in Auburn (3-9/5)
2181. Cunningham, _____, consort of Garwood H., d 1/3/11 in Poughkeepsie (8-1/9)
2182. Cunningham, Frederick of Poughkeepsie, NY d 7/27/20 in Greensville Springs, KY (8-8/16)
2183. Cunningham, Garwood m 3/4/09 Helen Myers (in Poughkeepsie?) (8-3/8)
2184. Cunningham, Garwood H. (Maj.), formerly of Poughkeepsie, d about 10/1/13 at Fort George (8-10/13)
2185. Cunningham, George, Esq., 22, formerly of Poughkeepsie, NY, d 7/24/14 in Haysborough, TN (8-8/10)
2186. Cunningham, Henry Davis, 7 mo, s of Walter, d 8/20/22 in Poughkeepsie (8-8/21)
2187. Cunningham, Maria (Miss) d 2/4/23 in Poughkeepsie (pulmonary complaint) (8-2/12)
2188. Cunningham, Rachael (Miss), 34, d 12/19/32 in Beekman (Dut. Co.) (8-12/26)
2189. Cunningham, Samuel m 7/26/20 Elizabeth Ellis, both of Gibbonsville; Rev. Sommers (9-8/8)
2190. Cunningham, Walter, merchant, m 10/14/19 Elizabeth Davis, dau of Henry, Esq., at the Episcopal Church in Poughkeepsie (8-10/20)
2191. Cure, Statirah, 22, wf of Elias, d 3/8/03 in Kortright (surv by her husband, a child, and her parents)(6-4/5)
2192. Curran, Patrick, 23, recently from Brooklyn, NY, d 8/9/29 in Newark, NJ ("by falling into a kettle of hot soup in a manufactory where he was at work") (1-8/13)
2193. Curren, Michael m 1/15/25 Jane Traver; Tilly Crouse, Esq. (8-1/19)
2194. Currier, Samuel (Capt.) m Mary Archer (Mary is his 7th wife, "the sixth having been buried just three weeks before") (3-11/14/25)
2195. Curry, Samuel, 58, of Poughkeepsie d 1/10/02 (from a fall from his wagon) (8-1/12)
2196. Curtenius, Peter (Maj. Gen.) of the First Brigade, NY Artillery, d 3/26/17 in NYC (buried with military honors) (6-4/1)
2197. Curtis, Andrew, 23, of Ballston d 6/13/22 in Ballston (2-6/18)
2198. Curtis, Benjamin of NYC m 9/2/30 Rebecca T. Edwards, oldest dau of Col. William of Greene Co., NY, at the Hotel of the American Ambassador in Paris, France; Rev. Henry H. Lascombe, vice chaplain of the British Embassy (1-10/8)
2199. Curtis, David of Malone m 11/30/23 Sibra Broadwell, dau of Aaron of Mooers, in M (7-12/6)
2200. Curtis, Elijah W., Esq., attorney, m 12/31/29 Amanda Terrey, dau of Erastus, all of Geddes (Onon. Co.); Rev. Cloud (1-1/10/30)
2201. Curtis, John, merchant, of Middlebury, VT m 6/9/00 Polly Palmer of Lansingburgh, NY; Rev. Coe (9-6/17)
2202. Curtis, John, 60, late from Connecticut, m 6/16/05 Mrs. Anna Schultz, 38, "after a courtship of ten days" (6-7/2)
2203. Curtis, Moses S., Esq. of Salem m Susan Rathbun of Lansingburgh; Rev. Roe (9-2/1/03)
2204. Curtis, Susan, wid of late Samuel formerly of Union Vale, d 12/11/31 "at an advanced age" in Poughkeepsie (8-12/14)

2205. Curtiss, Erastus (Dr.) m 9/25/23 Mary Metcalf, dau of Arunah, Esq., in Otsego; Rev. Smith (3-9/29)
2206. Curtiss, Hastings, Esq., 36, sheriff of Oswego Co., d 7/26/31 at his home in Central Square (settled in the C. S. region in 1815 when it was part of Oneida Co.) (1-8/12)
2207. Curtiss, Isaac (Capt.) m 10/7/22 Lydia Boothe in Ballston; Rev. Smith. All of Ballston (2-10/22
2208. Curtiss, Mary, 28, wf of Dr. Erastus and dau of Arunah Metcalf, Esq., d 7/18/29 at the home of Dr. Lay near Cooperstown (1-7/21)
2209. Curtiss, Stephen (Rev.) of Springfield m 10/11/26 "the Widow St. John" of Warren in W; Elder G. Sawin (3-10/16)
2210. Curtiss, Zachariah m 1/13/25 Sally Ann Whitford, both of Saratoga Springs, in Ballston Spa; Thomas Palmer, Esq. (2-1/18)
2211. Cushing, Zatia(?), first judge of Chautauqua Co., m 6/1/17 Eunice Elderkin, dau of Rodolphus of Cooperstown, in Burlington (Ots. Co.) (3-6/5)
2212. Cushman, Hetta, 25, wf of David, d 2/21/24 in Exeter (surv by her husband, children, and her parents) (3-3/1)
2213. Cushman, R. W. (Rev.), pastor of the Baptist Church in Poughkeepsie m 9/14/26 Lucy Sprague of Duxbury, MA in D (8-10/11)
2214. Cushman, Ralph (Rev.), late pastor of the Presbyterian Church in Manlius, d 8/27/31 in Worcester, OH ("billious fever") (1-9/17)
2215. Cushman, Rufus (Rev.), pastor since 1806 of the Congregational Church in Fairhaven, VT, d 2/4/29 in Fairhaven (father of Calvin of the Choctaw Mission and of the Rev. Ralph of Manlius, NY (1-2/21)
2216. Cushney, Richard H. m 3/11/29 Mary Henry, only dau of Henry B. Henry, all of Johnstown in J; Rev. Dr. Hossack (1-3/20)
2217. Cuthbert, Lemuel, editor and printer of the Schoharie Republican, m 5/18/22 Louisa Topping, dau of Henry "of this city" (probably Schenectady, based on other data); Rev. Proal (9-5/21)
2218. Cuthbert, Lemuel, 27, late proprietor of the Schoharie Republican, d 8/23/29 (surv by his wf and 2 ch) (1-8/18)
2219. Cutler, Alpheus, about 30, unmarried, formerly of Guilford, VT, d 8/6/12 at Cape Vincent, NY (recently of Adams, NY from which place he was recently drafted into Capt. McNitt's Company [Lt. Col. William Stone's Regiment]) (was accidentally shot while on duty by "Soldier Jacob Weaver")(funeral sermon by Rev. Nathaniel Smith of Windsor, VT) (3-8/29)
2220. Cutler, Stephen m 1/3/07 Sally Fitch, dau of John, all of Washington (Dut. Co.); Ebenezer Haight, Esq. (8-1/13)
2221. Cutter, Smith, Jr. m 5/20/31 Sarah Jane Swan, dau of William, at the Middle Brick Church in NYC; Rev. Dr. Brownlee (1-5/22)
2222. Cutting, William, Esq., attorney, m 7/6/98 Gitty Livingston, dau of Walter, deceased, in "Tivot Dale";Rev. Romeyne (8-7/17)
2223. Cuyler, _____ (Lt. Col. of his Majesty's 3rd Regiment and oldest s of late Henry Cuyler, Jr. of Greenbush, NY, d in Alderney (an island in the British Channel) (9-10/29/05)
2224. Cuyler, C. C. (Rev.), pastor of the Reformed Dutch Church in Poughkeepsie, m 2/16/09 Eleanor De Graff, dau of Isaac, Esq. of Schenectady, in S; Rev. Bogardus (8-2/22)
2225. Cuyler, Dorothy, 49, wid of Tobias V., d 9/26/31 (funeral from her late home, 650 South Market St.) (1-9/27)
2226. Cuyler, Henry, Esq. d 2/5/03 in Greenbush (9-2/15)
2227. Cuyler, Jacob C., 62, brother of Rev. C. C. Cuyler of Poughkeepsie, d 10/25/28 in Albany (8-10/29)
2228. Cuyler, Jacob I., merchant, of Otego m 8/24/08 Polly Soul of Schoharie in S; Augustus Wachenhagen (3-8/27)
2229. Cuyler, Jane, 65, wid of late Cornelius and mother of Rev. Cornelius C. Cuyler, d 1/15/13 (member of Dutch Reformed Church about 40 yrs) (her husband died 18 years earlier and the sole care of her children fell on her shoulders) (8-1/20)
2230. Cuyler, John De Graff, 1 yr, s of Rev. Dr. Cuyler, d 8/29/30 (8-9/1)
2231. Cuyler, Maria, 3, dau of Rev. C. C. Cuyler, d 6/8/18 in Poughkeepsie (8-6/10)
2232. Cypher, Lodwick m 9/25/11 Maria Frear, both of Poughkeepsie; Rev. Cuyler (8-10/2)

2233. Daken, Homer of Northeast m 10/21/11 Susan Chane of New Milford; Rev.
Andrew Elliott (8-12/4)
2234. Dakin, Albert, 21, s of Ebenezer K., d 8/16/22 in Poughkeepsie (typhus)
(8-8/21)
2235. Dakin, Caleb, 71, d 10/2/18 in Amenia (8-11/18)
2236. Dakin, George, s of Ebenezer K. of Poughkeepsie, d 3/12/25 (8-3/16)
2237. Dakin, Henry m 10/20/11 Henrietta Jenkins in Hudson; Rev. Chester
(6-10/28)
2238. Dakin, Theodore m 7/23/22 Dorothy Staples of Poughkeepsie; Rev. Cuyler
(8-7/31)
2239. Dallas, Alexander J., Esq., late Secretary of the Treasury,d 1/18/17 in
Philadelphia (7-2/8)
2240. Dalliba, James, the anti-masonic candidate "for elector from this
district", d 10/9/32 in Moriah (4 [Essex Republican]-10/13 and
4 [Keeseville Herald]-10/16)
2241. Dan, Selick, about 56, d 5/23/30 in Madison (Greene Co.) (kicked by a
horse on 5/21) (1-6/2)
2242. Dan, Thaddeus, 25, schoolmaster, m 5/10/00 Caty Chase, "aged 11 yrs. and
6 months", both of Frederickstown; Daniel Ketcham, Esq. of Northeast
(8-5/21)
2243. Dana, Cyrus, Esq., attorney, m 9/20/27 Elizabeth C. Stockwell in
Binghamton; Rev. Lockwood (9-10/12)
2244. Dana, Joseph (Rev.), D.D., 84, senior pastor of the 2nd Congregational
Church in Ipswich, MA, d 11/16/27 in Ipswich (9-11/23)
2245. Danforth, Azel m 11/8/21 Polly Stickles of Ballston in B; Rev. R. Smith
(2-11/21)
2246. Danforth, George, Esq., 41, of Middleburgh, NY d 8/16/31 in Savannah, GA
(had left Middleburgh the previous Nov. intending to travel to St.
Augustine, Florida (had consumption) but in a weakened condition had
terminated his trip at Jacksonville; en route north "he reached only
Savannah where death overtook him") (1-9/2)
2247. Danforth, George W. m 9/14/28 Mrs. Patience B. Davis, both of Watervliet,
in West Troy; Rev. Howard (9-9/16)
2248. Danforth, Henry of Ballstown m 11/5/29 Fidelia Barron of Albany in A; Rev.
Weed (1-11/7)
2249. Danforth, Jackson, 15 mo., only ch of John Jay Jackson, Esq., d 6/6/30 in
Amsterdam, NY (1-6/8)
2250. Danforth, John Jay, Esq., 32, attorney, d 7/16/30 at his home in Amsterdam,
NY (consumption) (had spent the previous winter in St. Augustine, FL)
(surv by wf and 2 children) (1-7/22)
2251. Danforth, Jonathan, Esq., 54, one of the judges of the court of common
pleas, d 2/5/07 in Schoharie (6-3/3)
2252. Danforth, Simon m 10/3/26 Lucy B. Bridges in Milford; Rev. Edward
Fairchild (3-10/9)
2253. Daniels, David S. m 8/1/22 Harriet Roblee, both of Chazy, in C (7-8/10)
2254. Danielson, Lucretia, 27, d 3/6/25 in Butternuts (3-3/14)
2255. Dann, Bailey m 9/19/27 Semantha B. Deming of Troy; Rev. Beman (9-9/21)
2256. Dann, Frederick of Danbury, CT m 10/25/30 Sarah Ann Boerum, dau of Jacob
of Poughkeepsie; Rev. Dr. Cuyler (8-10/27)
2257. Danvers, Matthew D., Esq., formerly clerk of Washington County, d 2/6/31
in Fort Edward (1-3/1)
2258. Dare, E. B. (Rev.) of Batavia m 9/22/30 Mrs. Margaret B. Congdon, dau of
Nathaniel Bennett, Esq. of Williamsville (Erie Co.), in W; Rev. James
M. Smith (1-10/7)
2259. Dare, John Goodland m 6/27/22 Elizabeth Mackay; Rev. C. C. Cuyler (8-7/3)
2260. Darling, Bradford m 11/6/28 Harriet Row, dau of Andrus; Rev. C. P. Wilson.
All of Northeast (8-11/12)
2261. Darling, William, Esq. of Troy m 6/28/31 Ann Russell, dau of Thomas, Esq.
of Albany; Rev. Dr. Sprague (1-6/30)
2262. Darrah, David (Dr.), 28, dentist, d in Trenton, NJ (9-12/26/15)
2263. Darrah, Henry T. of Sussex, NJ m 8/20/29 Mary Ogden Haines, dau of late
Elias, Esq. of NYC, in Auburn, NY; Rev. Dr. Rudd (1-9/2)
2264. Darrah, James of Maunyunk, PA m 4/22/30 Helena Whit(?), dau of Dr.
Barton Whit(?), in Fishkill; Rev. Dr. Westbrook (double ceremony -
see marr of Thomas S. Newlin) (8-5/12)

65

2265. Darrow, John, Esq., 59, d in Chatham (6-3/30/13)
2266. Darrow, John F. m 6/5/11 Eliza Stebbins, both of Catskill, in C
      (6-6/14)
2267. Darrow, Samuel K. of Poughkeepsie m 9/20/34 Sarah M. Deniston, dau of
      Archibald, Esq. of Fallsburgh, in F; Rev. Cyrus Stillman (8-9/24)
2268. Dart, Philander Camp, formerly of Erie, PA,m Rhoda Waterbury in
      Saratoga Springs, NY (4[Keeseville Herald]-7/25/31)
2269. Dater(?), Eliza (Miss), 21, dau of Abraham, d 10/12/28 in Poughkeepsie
      (8-11/12)
2270. Dater, Jacob m 5/6/19 Mary Roberts, both of Troy; Rev. Butler (9-5/11)
2271. Dater, Philip m 12/17/21 Caroline Read, dau of Capt. Leonard of Troy;
      Rev. Griffen (9-1/1/22)
2272. Dates, Anna, 61, of Fishkill d 3/23/08 (8-3/30)
2273. Dates, James of Poughkeepsie m 12/18/31 Hannah Maria Van Dyne of La Grange
      in L. G.; Rev. Dwight (8-1/25/32)
2274. Daton, Catharine Elizabeth, 1 yr, dau of Jacob, d 12/30/26 in Troy
      (9-1/5)
2275. Dauchy, Henry B., merchant, of Troy d 3/5/33 in Troy (4 [Keeseville Herald]
      -3/12)
2276. Dauchy, Jesse B., 31, of the firm of Messrs. H. B. Dauchy and Co.,
      merchants, of Troy d 5/21/28 (9-5/23)
2277. Davenport, David m 2/12/23 Julia Hamlin, both of Schenectady, in Ballston;
      Rev. Reuben Smith (2-3/4)
2278. Davenport, Hiram, 16, d in Williamson (suicide by hanging) (2-2/8/25)
2279. David, Peter A., drum major of the 6th U.S. Infantry, m 11/6/17 Sally White
      "of this station" in Plattsburgh (7-11/8)
2280. Davidson, George I. m 7/10/28 Eliza Van Every; Rev. Richardson. All of
      Poughkeepsie (8-7/16)
2281. Davidson, John of Hartwick m 11/22/19 Mrs. Matilda Spalding of Cooperstown
      in C; Rev. Smith (3-11/29)
2282. Davidson, Matthew of Hopkinton m 6/22/26 Catharine Allen of Peru, NY; Rev.
      Heman Garlick (7-7/1)
2283. Davidson, Ph?(entry torn) , wf of John, d 2/28/17 in Hartwick (surv by
      husband and children) (3-3/6)
2284. Davies, D. m 7/1/29 Phebe Hart, oldest dau of John I., all of NYC; Rev.
      P. A. Hart (1-7/7)
2285. Davies, Eliza, 15, dau of William, Esq., d 2/4/15 in Poughkeepsie (8-2/8)
2286. Davies, Polly, consort of William, d 7/23/14 in Poughkeepsie (8-7/27)
2287. Davies, Susan Mary, 9 mo, only child of Gen. Thomas L. of Poughkeepsie,
      d 3/21/30 (8-3/24)
2288. Davies, William, Esq. m 12/31/14 Mrs. Maria Foote (wid of late
      Justin, Esq.) "at Governor Smith's in Sharon; Rev. Perry
      (bride and groom are both of Poughkeepsie, NY; the town of Sharon
      may be in Connecticut) (8-1/4/15)
2289. Davies, William, Esq. of Poughkeepsie m 4/5/18 Alice Antle of Coldenham
      (Orange Co.) at the home of Judge Colden in C; Rev. Reed (8-4/8)
2290. Davis, ____ (Mrs.), "a lady who recently came to Poughkeepsie from
      England", d 2/4/20 in Poughkeepsie (8-2/9)
2291. Davis, Abraham m 4/3/17 Catherine Hobes, both of Poughkeepsie; Rev.
      James Covel (8-4/9)
2292. Davis, Ann, 39, wf of James, d 9/14/18 in Washington (Dut. Co.) (8-9/16)
2293. Davis, Anna, 49, consort of Henry, d 7/23/17 in Red Hook (funeral sermon
      by Rev. Fox) (8-8/6)
2294. Davis, Benjamin of Bergen, NY m Mary Ann Kingman of Worthington, MA; Rev.
      Howard (9-5/20/28)
2295. Davis, Calvin d 4/16/31 in Peru, NY (4 [Keeseville Herald]-4/19)
2296. Davis, Charles T. m 12/6/27 Eleanor Crawford, both of Watervliet, in
      Gibbonsville;Rev. Howard (9-12/11)
2297. Davis, David R. m 6/20/32 Catharine Snedecer, both of Fishkill; Rev.
      Buttolph (8-6/27)
2298. Davis, Edmund Romney m 12/20/29 Julia Ann Wilcox, dau of Silvester; Rev.
      W. B. Lacey. All of Albany (1-12/23)
2299. Davis, Edward (Rev.) m 10/15/26 Belinda Emott, dau of James, at Christ
      Church in Poughkeepsie (8-10/18)
2300. Davis, Elijah of Homer m 12/25/06 Lorain Peirce of Albany; Rev. Roe
      (9-12/30)

66

2301. Davis, Elizabeth (Mrs.), 77, formerly of Poughkeepsie, d 4/17/28 in Albany
(8-4/23)
2302. Davis, George m 9/6/31 Mary Ann Meacham, dau of Horace(?); Rev. Kirk.
All of Albany (1-9/8)
2303. Davis, Grace, 38, wf of Col. Thomas, d 11/29/13 in Troy (9-11/30)
2304. Davis, Henry B., Esq., attorney, of Albany d 11/14/24 at the home of his
father in Poughkeepsie (8-11/24)
2305. Davis, Ichabod, 42, d 5/29/26 at his home in Butternuts (3-6/12)
2306. Davis, John, an old inhabitant of Poughkeepsie, d 6/19/15 (8-6/21)
2307. Davis, John H., Esq. m 12/24/27 Caroline Williams, dau of Josiah; Rev.
Richardson. All of Poughkeepsie (8-12/26)
2308. Davis, John H., Esq., 33, of Poughkeepsie d 12/4/31 (8-12/7)
2309. Davis, John Henry, 5, s of John H., Esq., d 6/28/34 in Poughkeepsie
(8-7/2)
2310. Davis, Jonathan m 12/13/18 Sally Smith in Middlefield; Elder Benjamin Sawin.
All of Middlefield (3-12/14)
2311. Davis, Louisa M. (Miss), 18, d 4/29/24 in Poughkeepsie (pulmonary
complaint) (8-5/5)
2312. Davis, Margaret, consort of Richard, Esq. of Poughkeepsie, d 1/21/00
(funeral sermon by Rev. Chase) (interred in the Episcopal Church burying
ground) (8-1/28)
2313. Davis, Nicholas m 11/20/22 Almira Wilcox in Saratoga; James Mott, Esq.
(2-11/26)
2314. Davis, R. (Dr.) of Chillicothe, OH m 11/20/06 Elizabeth Hudson, dau of
Judge Hudson, at Cherry Valley; Rev. Nash (3-11/27)
2315. Davis, Raushe(?), wid of John formerly of Poughkeepsie, d 12/15/26 in Hyde
Park (8-12/20)
2316. Davis, Richard, one of the oldest inhabitants of Poughkeepsie, d 7/24/14
in P (8-7/27)
2317. Davis, Richard m 2/4/15 Mary Crapsey, both of Clinton (Dut. Co.); John F.
Schultz, Esq. (8-2/8)
2318. Davis, Samuel, merchant, of Freehold m 1/19/09 Eyfa Cooper of Madison,
"Greene County", in Madison; Rev. Reed (6-2/7)
2319. Davis, Sarah M. (Mrs.), 27, dau of Samuel Murdock of Essex (he sheriff of
Essex Co.) d 12/1/34 at Crown Point (consumption) (7-12/20)
2320. Davis, Sheldon of Fishkill m 11/29/27 Mahala Palmer of Washington (Dut.
Co.) (8-12/5)
2321. Davis, Silas of Troy m 1/1/23 Sally Shrimpton of Gibbonsville; Rev.
Griffin (9-1/7)
2322. Davis, Thomas, 78, d in Barnstable, MA (had lived 70 years with his mother
who died at age 98 and the last seven with his sister [not named])
(after his father's death in 1752 he never shaved, never spoke to his
minister, and never sought a physician's aid in sickness) (6-10/9/04)
2323. Davis, Thomas (Col.) of Troy m 3/22/20 Ann Hinman of New London, CT;
Rev. David Butler (9-4/11)
2324. Davis, Thomas (Col.), 47, d 4/21/23 in Troy (9-4/22)
2325. Davis, Thomas L., Esq. m 9/4/26 Jane C. E. Reed, dau of Rev. Dr. John
Reed. All of Poughkeepsie (8-9/6)
2326. Davis, William R. of NYC m 6/6/31 Jane Elizabeth Coughtry, dau of Henry
of Albany; Rev. Dr. Sprague (1-6/7)
2327. Davis, William S., preceptor of the Lancaster School in Poughkeepsie, m
10/8/20 Amanda Spring of Hyde Park; Rev. Leonard (8-10/18)
2328. Davis, William W. (Dr.), 25, of Amsterdam, NY, a recent graduate of Union
College, d a short time since" in Newark, NJ (1-7/31/30)
2329. Davison, Clark (Capt.) of Hartwick m 11/1/21 Abigail Tracy of Cooperstown;
Rev. Hazelius (3-11/5)
2330. Davison, Nathan, Esq., 64, d 5/10/21 in Hartwick (3-5/14)
2331. Davison, Peter m 3/8/15 Polly Colwell, both of Beekman; Rev. John Clark
(8-3/15)
2332. Davitt, John m 5/12/07 Anne Manley, both of Brunswick; Rev. Coe (9-5/19)
2333. Dawes, William m 5/16/11 Cornelia Van Zandt, both of NYC; Rev. Coe (9-5/21)
2334. Day, Benjamin F., 24, one of the editors of the Ontario Messenger, d 8/2/31
in Cambridge (1-8/15)
2335. Day, Betsey, 22, dau of Amos, d 1/13/22 in Peru, NY (7-1/19)

2336. Day, Cornelia (wf of Rodman G., merchant, and dau of Thomas Hoag, Esq. of Nassau, NY) d 10/22/31 in Nassau (consumption) (1-11/7)
2337. Day, Darius, 2, s of Rufus, d 10/17/24 in Peru, NY (7-10/23)
2338. Day, Edward of Hudson m Alice Rogers of Hartford, CT in H (6-5/25/13)
2339. Day, Horace m 11/12/18 Milison Hildreth, both of Hudson, in H; Rev. Avery Briggs (6-11/17)
2340. Day, Ralph, printer, d 1/11/15 (consumption) (9-1/17)
2341. Day, William W. of Greenfield, NY m 12/18/27 Mary N. Horton of Norton, MA; Rev. B. W. Horr (9-12/25)
2342. Dayks, Peter of Poughkeepsie m 11/12/28 Cynthia Wyckoff of Freedom; Rev. M. W. Dwight (8-11/26)
2343. Dayton, _____ (Mrs.), about 60, wf of Robert, d 12/5/21 in Plattsburgh (7-12/15)
2344. Dayton, Hezekiah, 62, d at his residence in Butternuts ("Printers generally are requested to publish the above") (3-12/14/18)
2345. Dayton, John W., merchant, m 4/30/07 Polly Trowbridge in Hudson; Rev. Wigton (6-5/5)
2346. Dayton, Ruth, 49, wf of Hezekiah of Hudson, d 7/11/01 (6-7/16)
2347. Dayton, Selden (Capt.), 38, commander of the schooner "Richard" and s of Robert of Plattsburgh, d in early October in "Havanna" (state or country not given) (yellow fever - so probably Havana, Cuba intended) (Letter from his brother reads: 'He has left a truly distressed family - his poor wife, bereft of her reason, and two little children.... His father is dead also...and my mother constantly confused.") (7-10/19/22)
2348. Dean, Aaron m 4/27/30 Mary Martin, both of Poughkeepsie; Rev. Dr. Reed (8-5/5)
2349. Dean, Amos m Rhoda Mead, both of Carmel (8-8/31/02)
2350. Dean, Arthur, 25, s of Israel formerly of Plasant Valley, d 8/24/29 at the Indian Springs, GA (8-9/16)
2351. Dean, Clarissa, 45, wf of Charles B., d 3/2/31 in Albany (1-3/5)
2352. Dean, David, 37, of Pleasant Valley d 8/9/31 in Stanford (Dut. Co.) (8-8/17)
2353. Dean, Erastus, 46, d 9/29/23 at his home in Laurens (3-10/6)
2354. Dean, Isaac of Coxsackie m 11/3/06 Rebecca Porter of Hillsdale in H; Rev. Williams (6-11/18)
2355. Dean, Jonathan M. of Pleasant Valley m 9/28/25 Helen Maria Barker of Freedom; John Klapp, Esq. (8-10/12)
2356. Dean, Joseph L. of Beekman m 12/4/13 Ann Palmer of Fishkill; Rev. Dewitt (8-12/22)
2357. Dean, Mary, wf of John of Frederickstown, d 1/27/02 (8-3/30)
2358. Dean, Minard of Beekman m 10/21/15 Catharine Hustead of Poughkeepsie; Rev. Leonard (8-10/25)
2359. Dean, Myron (Col.) of Northeast m 2/5/34 Lucy M. Canfield of Stanford (Dut. Co.) in S; Rev. Birch (8-2/13)
2360. Dean, William Willis, Esq., merchant, of Otsego Co. m 7/5/31 Eliza Ophelia Sergeant, dau of Col. A. Sergeant of NYC, at St. John's Chapel in NYC; Right Rev. Bishop Onderdonk (1-7/7)
2361. De Angelis, Severin E. (Capt.) s of Hon. Paschel C. L. De Angelis of Trenton, NY, m 5/12/22 Celestia Burr, dau of John of Whitesboro, in W (3-5/27)
2362. Dearborn, Henry (Gen.), 78, (a Rev. patriot) d 6/6/29 at the home of his son (not named) in Roxbury, NY (1-6/12 and 8-6/17)
2363. Dearin, Henry W. of Dutchess Co. m 10/21/34 Maria P. Armstrong of NYC; Rev. Stratton (8-10/29)
2364. Dearin, James, Jr., merchant, m 6/10/13 Lucy Drake, dau of John, Jr., Esq., both of Hamburg, Wappings Creek (Dut. Co.); Rev. Eliphalet Price (8-6/16)
2365. Dearin, William I. m 10/26/11 Jane Luckey; Rev. Backulo (8-11/13)
2366. Dearing, John m 1/6/14 Jane Wright, dau of Gilbert; Rev. Price. All of Fishkill (8-1/12)
2367. De Bono, Johannis, 75, one of the early settlers of Beekman (Dut. Co.), d 1/6/04 in B (8-1/17)
2368. De Bresson, Katharine L. (Madame), wf of Charles Joseph and oldest dau of Hon. Smith Thompson, d 1/28/24 in Wshington City, D.C. (8-2/4)
2369. Decaix, Eugine of Paris, France m 2/12/27 Julia Frances Curtis, dau of Capt. Z. of Troy, NY; Rev. McGilligan (9-2/16)

2370. De Cantillon, Mary, wid of late Richard, Esq., d 8/29/08 in Hyde Park
      (8-8/31)
2371. D'Cantillon, Richard, Esq., 60, of Clinton (Dut. Co.) d 2/18/06 (8-2/25)
2372. D'Cantillon, Richard of Clinton (Dut. Co.) m "a few weeks since"
      Rebecca Teller, dau of Col. Henry R. of Schenectady, in S (8-9/25/11)
2373. Decantillon, Thomas S., Esq. m 5/3/10 Sarah B. Lee, both of Clinton
      (Dut. Co.); Rev. Clark (8-5/9)
2374. De Chamont, Charles Le Roy of England m Elizabeth Pearl Harris, dau of
      late Charles of Philadelphia (state not given),in P (1-6/8/31)
2375. Decker, James m 3/20/28 Azuba Ann Betts, both of Brunswick; Rev. Martin-
      dale (9-3/28)
2376. Dederick, John of Clinton (Dut. Co.) m 9/10/31 Hannah Dederick, dau of
      late William of Claverack, in C; Rev. J. Berger (8-9/21)
2377. Dedrick, Jacob m 1/21/02 Catharine Cramer, both of Rhinebeck (8-2/2)
2378. De Forest, Alpheus of NYC m 11/15/31 Jennett R. Hatfield, dau of late
      Edmund of Albany, in A; Rev. Dr. Ludlow (1-11/17)
2379. De Forest, Harry m 1/30/12 Sally Howard, both of New Berlin, in N. B.;
      Rev. Knight (3-2/8)
2380. De Forest, Isaac, 32, d 11/11/02 in Hudson (6-11/16)
2381. De Forest, Mary (Miss), only dau of Samuel, Esq., d 1/23/25 in Ballston
      (2-1/25)
2382. De Forest, Susan, 23, oldest dau of Abel, Esq., d 6/12/15 in Edmeston
      (3-6/22)
2383. De Freest, Daniel P., 23, s of Peter, Esq., d 3/13/21 in Greenbush
      (9-3/20)
2384. De Freest, John m 12/10/14 Tanica Vanalstine, both of Greenbush; Rev.
      Coe (9-12/20)
2385. De Freest, John P. m 1/14/13 Nancy Membert, both of Greenbush (9-1/19)
2386. De Freest, John R. m 9/17/14 Cornelia De Freest, both of Greenbush
      (9-9/27)
2387. De Freest, Philip L. m 10/27/13 Susan De Freest, both of Greenbush
      (9-11/30)
2388. De Freest, Sarah Ann, 6, 2nd dau of Jacob F., d 6/19/31 in Bath, NY
      (1-6/28)
2389. De Gourlay, Armand J. A. of Paris, France m 2/3/31 Maria Laight of NYC
      in Paris, France (1-4/21)
2390. De Graff, Abraham, 62, of Hyde Park d 1/2/32 (8-1/4)
2391. Degraff, Amos Thorne m 10/4/21 Harriet Sleight, both of Freedom; Rev.
      C. C. Cuyler (8-10/10)
2392. De Graff, Emanuel, merchant, m Diana Hagerman, dau of John; Rev. Wood.
      All of Amsterdam, NY (1-9/29/31)
2393. Degraff, Jacob m 1/15/22 Harriet Eliza Gay, both of Hyde Park; Rev.
      Wynkoop (8-1/23)
2394. De Graff, Jesse D., Esq. of Albany m 8/10/30 Gazena Catharine Visscher,
      dau of late Herman, Esq. of Johnstown, in J; Rev. Dr. Cuyler (1-8/14
      and 8-8/18)
2395. De Graff, Joel m 2/4/29 Charlotte Wilbur, dau of James, in Hyde Park; Rev.
      A. Welton (8-2/11)
2396. De Graff, Joel, 25, d 3/3/29 in Hyde Park (married just one month at
      time of his death) (funeral sermon by Rev. Welton) (8-3/11)
2397. Degraff, John m 6/10/23 Eliza Tompkins, both of Freedom; Rev. Cuyler
      (8-6/25)
2398. De Graff, Joshua m "a few days since" Sally Beyeaux, dau of Thomas. All
      of Poughkeepsie (8-3/13/04)
2399. Degraff, Oliver Green of Albany m 1/7/24 Maria Frear, dau of Jacobus, Esq.
      of Poughkeepsie; Rev. C. C. Cuyler (8-1/14)
2400. De Graff, Simeon m 7/10/96 Mrs. Nelson, both of Fishkill (8-7/13)
2401. Degraff, Simeon of Freedom m 5/15/22 Mrs. Leah Wood of Pleasant Valley;
      Rev. C. C. Cuyler (8-5/22)
2402. De Graff, Susan (Mrs.), 68, d 3/14/29 in Schenectady (mother of Hon. John
      I. De Graff, congressman from Schenectady-Schoharie District, and
      mother-in-law of Rev. Dr. Cuyler of Poughkeepsie) (8-3/18)
2403. De Graff, Susanna, 67, consort of Isaac, Esq. and mother of Hon. John I.,
      late congressman from Schenectady, d 3/14/29 in Schenectady (1-3/18)
2404. Degraff, William T. of Poughkeepsie m Cornelia A. L. Gale, dau of Jeremiah, Esq.
      of Monticello (Sull. Co.), in M; Rev. Fowler (8-11/14/32)

69

2405. De Graw, Abraham (Capt.), 45, late master of the steamboat "Seven",
d 7/28/32 in New Brunswick, NJ (cholera) (8-8/1)
2406. Degroat, Peter m 8/15/27 Mary Ann Miller, both of Troy; Rev. Howard
(9-8/21)
2407. Degroff, Abram m 9/6/14 Sally Maria Lansing, dau of Garrett P., in
Hyde Park; Rev. Welton (8-9/14)
2408. De Groff, Stephen m 7/7/23 Sally Low, both of Lansingburgh; Rev. Noah
Bigelow (9-7/15)
2409. De Hart, Cyrus (Capt.), 73, (a Rev. officer) d 9/7/31 at his home in
Elizabethtown, NJ (1-9/16)
2410. Deitz, Adam (Maj.), 75, d 9/29/30 in Bern (1-10/7)
2411. De Kay, J. E. (Dr.) m "Miss Eckford", dau of Henry, Esq., in NYC (3-8/6/21)
2412. De La Cadena,Mariano Velasquez m 8/13/30 Catharine Ann Livingston,
youngest dau of John W., Esq.; Rev. Dr. Berrien. All of NYC (1-8/24)
2413. Delamater, Claudius D., d in Hudson (6-12/5/09)
2414. Delamater, Claudius I., Esq., 64, d 7/14/16 in Albany (6-8/6)
2415. Delamater, Conrad, 46, d 9/1/25 in Rhinebeck Flats (8-9/7)
2416. Delamater, Edward, about 21, d 6/22/29 in Hyde Park (8-6/24)
2417. Delamater, Edwin, about 21, d 6/22/29 in Hyde Park (1-6/26)
2418. Delamatter, Jacob I. (Dr.), late of Albany, d in Florida (Mont. Co.)
(6-11/15/14)
2419. Delameter, Phebe, about 18, d "recently" in Champlain (7-1/8/13)
2420. De Lancey, Warren, formerly of Fishkill, m Elizabeth Hoxie, dau of John,
Esq., in Brookfield (Mad. Co.) (8-12/20/20)
2421. Delano, Huldah, 72, wf of Stephen, d 4/19/28 in Sharon, CT (8-4/30)
2422. Delano, Mortimer F., Esq. m 1/31/31 Sarah C. Guernsey, dau of James R.,
Esq., all of Pittsford, in P; Rev. Asa Mahan (1-2/7)
2423. Delav___, George of Freedom m 3/17/24 Polly Yates, dau of John of Fishkill;
Rev. De Witt (8-3/24)
2424. Delavan, _____, s of Edward C., d "recently" in Albany (1-4/1/31)
2425. Delavan, Charles, s of Edward C., d 3/30/31 in Albany (funeral from
32 La Fayette St.) (1-3/31)
2426. Delavan, Mary O., dau of Gen. Daniel, d in Mount Pleasant (1-5/29/29)
2427. De Lavan, Nathan, 37, of North Salem d 5/7/93 while plowing a field -
his two young sons being with him at the time (8-5/15)
2428. Delavergne, Alonzo m Jerusha Davis of Long Island in Clinton (Dut. Co.);
Rev. Clark (8-8/31/08)
2429. De La Vergne, Edwin m 3/18/29 Antoinette Hughson, dau of Stephen, Esq.,
all of Fishkill; Rev. Dwight (8-3/25)
2430. De Lavergne, Isaac m 2/13/02 Sally Beadle, dau of Timothy; Rev. Van
Vranken (8-2/16)
2431. Delavergne, Lewis m 11/1/28 Almira Stebbins, both of Amenia; Rev.
C. P. Wilson (8-11/12)
2432. Delavergne, Nicholas m 3/15/23 Mrs. Susan Remington in Stanford (Dut. Co.);
Isaac Sutherland, Esq. (8-3/19)
2433. De La Vergne, Peter m 2/9/25 Ann Yates, dau of John; Rev. De Witt. All
of Fishkill (8-3/16)
2434. Delavan, Benjamin K., merchant, m 12/23/24 Theresa Stephens, oldest dau
of Ebenezer; Rev. C. P. Wilson. All of Dover (8-12/29)
2435. De Long, David m 2/4/34 Adriannah Low, dau of late John A. of Poughkeepsie,
in Poughauag (Beekman); Rev. Barber (bride and groom both of
Poughkeepsie) (8-2/12)
2436. De Long, Egbert m 10/16/25 Sarah Crandell, both of Beekman; Rev. Smith
Arnold (8-11/23)
2437. Delong, Israel V., 22, formerly of Poughkeepsie, d 5/2/29 in Fishkill
(8-5/7)
2438. Delong, Simon of Freedom m 6/28/29 Jane Westervelt, dau of Daniel, in
Poughkeepsie; Isaac Sutherland, Esq. (8-7/2)
2439. Delord, Henry (Hon.), "an old resident of Plattsburgh", d 3/28/25
(funeral attended by members of Clinton Lodge (7-4/2)
2440. De Mentar, George H. of Williamstown m 12/4/03 Catharine McCartar of
Amenia; Ebenezer Mott, Esq. (8-12/13)
2441. Deming, Asa, 49, d 9/11/07 in Kinderhook (6-9/29)
2442. Deming, David D, of Dorset, VT m 9/2/12 Betsey Moulton of Troy; Rev. Coe
(9-9/8)

2443. Deming, David D., Esq., merchant, formerly of Troy, NY but lately of NYC, d 11/6/20 in Charleston, SC (consumption). (His son, William B., 6, died 10/3/20) (9-11/28)
2444. Deming, Dwight C. m 9/19/27 Maria F. Sharpe, both of Troy; Rev. Beman (9-9/21)
2445. Deming, Eli of Edmeston m 4/2/26 Clarissa Birdwell of Burlington in B; Rev. Rexford (3-4/10)
2446. Deming, Elias, 7 mo, s of John C., d in Hudson (6-4/26)
2447. Deming, Henry R. m 5/7/15 Mary P. Lathrop, both of Red Hook, in R. H.; Rev. Andrew N. Kittle (6-5/23)
2448. Deming, Miranda, 37, wf of John, d 6/8/30 in Albany (funeral from her late home, 558 South Market St. opposite Church St.)(1-6/9)
2449. Deming, Walter H. of NYC m 7/15/29 Sarah Ann Walter, dau of late William of Boston, in Philadelphia; Rev. Dr. Delancey (1-7/20)
2450. Deneyse, Garrit drowned at New Utrecht, L.I., NY (6-7/23/01)
2451. Denison, James m 10/29/20 Esther Green; Rev. William Satterlee. All of Berlin, NY (9-11/7)
2452. Denne, Anthony m 3/30/27 Hester Woolsey; Rev. Martindale. All of Troy (9-4/3)
2453. Dennis, ?hephen A. m 9/10/28 Maria Allen of Troy; Rev. Tucker (9-9/12)
2454. Dennis, Cyrus C. of the firm of Coffin and Dennis in Ithaca, m 2/24/30 Eunice Wood, dau of James of aurora (1-3/9)
2455. Dennis, Isaac m 10/12/31 Mary Underwood, dau of Weeden, Esq.; Rev. Cahoone. All of Hyde Park (8-10/19)
2456. Denniston, David, printer, d in Newburgh (6-12/27/03)
2457. Denny, Thomas m 11/17/23 Eliza Barton; _____ Judd, Esq. All of Beekman (8-11/26)
2458. De Normandie, John Abraham (Dr.), formerly of Bristol, PA, d 9/22/05 (age 84) at Bellfield, the home of John Johnson, Esq. near Poughkeepsie (8-10/1)
2459. Denton, Benjamin, 38, of Amenia d 2/13/02 (8-3/2)
2460. Denton, Benjamin of Amenia m 10/26/24 Sally Burden of Northeast in N; Rev. Wilson (8-11/10)
2461. Denton, Benjamin m 1/29/28 Elida Manney, dau of Richard; Rev. C. C. Cuyler. All of Poughkeepsie (8-1/30)
2462. Denton, Joel, 75, (a Rev. soldier), father of Joel, Jr., d 6/15/34 in Northeast (8-7/9)
2463. De Patchin, Aaron (Dr.) of Hoosick m 1/31/02 Sally Royce of Lanesborough (state not given - probably Massachusetts) (9-2/17/02)
2464. De Pew, Peter, 88(?), d 5/24/29 at the home of his son (not named) in Poughkeepsie (8-5/27)
2465. Depew, William m 12/12/15 Helen Roe, both of Fishkill (8-12/20)
2466. De Peyster, Pierre G., 61, of NYC d 11/22/07 at the home of J. Rutsen Van Rensselaer, Esq. in Claverack (6-12/1)
2467. Depuy, Samuel m 2/13/22 Nancy Hughson; Rev. Wynkoop. All of Hyde Park (8-2/20)
2468. Derby, Charles m 10/20/33 Harriet C. Hitchcock of Vergennes, VT in Whitehall, NY; Rev. A. Flemming (7-10/26)
2469. Derby, John m 6/4/19 Catherine Winslow, both of Hudson, in H; Rev. Briggs (6-7/20)
2470. Derby, Moses of Hudson m 10/14/14 Lavena Tompkins of Greenville, Greene Co.; Elder Stewart (6-10/25)
2471. De Reimer, Peter, 75, d 10/2/14 in Hyde Park (8-10/12)
2472. Derick, John S. of Brunswick m 10/9/23 Phebe Eliza Granger of "Glens-Ville"; Rev. Marrs (9-11/4)
2473. De Riemer, Elsie, 74, relict of late Peter of Hyde Park, d 10/19/18 in Poughkeepsie (8-10/21 and 8-10/28)
2474. Dermick, Nehemiah W. m 12/4/25 Catharine Snow, both of Poughkeepsie; Rev. C. C. Cuyler (8-12/28)
2475. Derry, Charles m 11/11/33 Harriet C. Hitchcock of Vergennes, VT in Whitehall, NY; Rev. A. Flemming (4 [Essex County Times]-11/14)
2476. Derry, Owen m 6/26/30 Jane Armstrong, both of West Post; Rev. Welton (8-6/30)
2477. Derthick, John (Capt.) m 2/22/23 Harriet Jaques in Richfield; Rev. Huse (3-3/3)

2478. De Russy, R. (Capt.) of the U.S. Corps of Engineers, m 12/21/16 Eliza T. Brown, dau of Jackson Brown, Esq., deceased, in Brooklyn; Rev. Henshaw (7-1/4/17)
2479. Deshous, Christiana (Mrs.), about 22, d 10/26/23 in Plattsburgh (7-11/1)
2480. Deuel, Content, 72, relict of late Jonathan, d 7/6/34 in Washington (Dut. Co.) (8-7/16)
2481. Deuel, Melinda, 38, d 1/23/27 in Stillwater (funeral sermon by Rev. Wallis of Troy)(9-2/2)
2482. Deuel, Walinda, 38, formerly of Stanford (Wash. Co.), wf of Stephen, d 1/22/27 in Stillwater (Sara. Co.) (surv by husband and 7 ch) (8-2/7)
2483. Deusenbury, Joseph of Brunswick m 1/6/20 Catharine Miller of Troy; Rev. Sommers (9-1/11)
2484. De Varney, _____ (Mr.), 67, m Widow Susan Emery, 16, in New Orleans, LA (8-12/15/24)
2485. Deveaux, Ann Maria, relict of late Col. Andrew, d 5/28/16 in Poughkeepsie (8-5/29)
2486. Devo, John of Washington (Dut. Co.) m Rachel Anson of Stanford (Dut. Co.); Jehial Sacket, Esq. (8-1/26/14)
2487. De Voe, David m 7/4/12 Ann Wheeler, both of Clinton (Dut. Co.); Rev. Cuyler (8-7/15)
2488. Dewel, David m 2/12/25 Harriet Bates, both of Washington (Dut. Co.; Isaac Sutherland, Esq. (8-2/16)
2489. Dewel, David A., 25, s of Benjamin, d 11/25/21 in Peru, NY (7-12/8)
2490. Dewey, Chester, Esq., professor of mathematics and natural philosophy in Williams College, m 5/18/25 Olivia Pomeroy, dau of Lemuel, in Pittsfield, MA; Rev. Bailey (3-5/30)
2491. Dewey, Cythiana Melissa, 3 mo, only child of Royal Dewey, merchant, d 11/17/26 in Peru, NY (7-11/18)
2492. Dewey, Eliphalet, Esq., 37, late sheriff of Chautauqua Co. and formerly of Hartwick, d 12/15/22 in Fredonia (3-12/30)
2493. Dewey, Joshua Hyde (Col.) m 8/20/29 Susan Margaret Swackhammer in Hartwick; Rev. Dr. Hazelius (1-8/27)
2494. Dewey, Loan m 10/19/18 Eliza Fitch in Hartwick; Rev. Smith (3-11/2)
2495. Dewey, Martha, dau of Eliphalet, Esq. of Hartwick, d 3/24/13 (3-4/3)
2496. Dewey, Rollin C. Esq. in 6/16/14 Rebeckah Dillingham in Hudson; Rev. Chester (6-6/21)
2497. Dewhurst, John d 6/2/01 in NYC (6-6/11)
2498. De Wint, John, Esq. d 9/22/02 at his home at Fishkill Landing (formerly a merchant in NYC) (8-9/28)
2499. De Witt, Andrew m 12/17/29 Mary Eddy (in Poughkeepsie?); Rev. Welton (8-12/23)
2500. De Witt, Andrew H., 22, of Binghamton, only s of Col. De Witt, d 8/28/31 in Binghamton (1-8/30)
2501. De Witt, Catharine, 48, wf of John, Esq. late of Dutchess Co. but now of Albany, d "a few days since" on Long Island (8-10/9/04)
2502. De Witt, Henry, Jr. (Maj.) 39, merchant, of Hudson d 10/28/08 (6-11/1)
2503. De Witt, John (Rev.), Professor of Belles Lettres in Rutgers College at New Brunswick, NJ, d in N. B. (8-10/19/31)
2504. De Witt, Rachel, 70, widow of Peter, d 7/20/94 in Clinton (Dut. Co.) (8-7/23)
2505. De Witt, Richard Varick, Esq. m 5/18/31 Sarah Walsh, dau of late Dudley Walsh; Rev. Lacey. All of Albany (1-5/19)
2506. De Witt, William H. of the firm of E. and W. H. De Witt, merchants, of Albany m 10/22/28 Ann Covenhoven of Troy in T; Rev. Ludlow (9-10/24)
2507. De Wolf, Hepzebah, 50, wf of Daniel, dropped dead instantly 5/18/30 in Lenox (Mass.?) while with her husband she watched with Napthah Webb (father of John, Esq.) who was sick. N. Webb, 77, died 5/19/30. (1-5/28)
2508. Dexter, Andrew, Esq., 65, only brother of late Hon. Samuel of Boston (state not given), d 11/12/16 in Athens, NY (6-11/19)
2509. Dexter, Charlotte (wf of Andrew, Esq. of New Phila, Alabama Terr. and dau of Hon. Perez Morton of Boston (state not given), d 8/16/19 in New Phila [Phila may be the intended abbreviation of Philadelphia] (6-9/21)
2510. Dexter, Daniel, 67, (a Rev. soldier) d in NYC (8-6/6/21)
2511. Dexter, Eliza P., 20, wf of John B. of Hudson and dau of late Capt. Lemuel W. Jenkins, d 9/2/18 (6-9/8)

2512. Dexter, John B., Esq. m 6/4/18 Eliza P. Jenkins, both of Hudson (6-6/9)
2513. Dexter, Simon Newton, Esq. m 10/24/11 Laura Northrop, both of Athens, NY, in A; Rev. Prentice (6-10/28)
2514. Deyo, Sarah, wf of Nathan formerly of Kinderhook "but now of Harlaem", d 7/30/21 in Hyde Park (8-8/1)
2515. Deyoe, Jonathan of Easton m 2/4/24 Abigal Buckly of Schaghticoke in S; David Tallmadge, Esq. (9-2/24)
2516. Dibble, Christopher, 68, d 5/27/04 (8-6/5)
2517. Dibble, Daniel D. T. m 9/7/30 Ann Hall, dau of John, at Christ's Church in Poughkeepsie. All of Stanford (Dut. Co.); Rev. Dr. Reed (8-9/8 and 1-9/11)
2518. Dibble, Ebenezer, Esq. d 2/13/26 at his home in Pine Plains (8-2/15)
2519. Dibble, Edgar C., Esq., attorney, m 9/13/30 Eliza Bianca Jones in Batavia; Rev. Whiting. All of Batavia (1-9/18)
2520. Dibble, Eli L. m 2/28/21 Eunice Alley, both of Troy (9-3/6)
2521. Dibble, Elizabeth, 69, d 12/8/03 in Stanford (Dut. Co.) (surv by husband and children)(8-12/13)
2522. Dibble, Isaiah, 68, d 12/1/27 in Pine Plains (8-12/12)
2523. Dibble, O. B., merchant, of Schuylerville m 10/31/21 Cornelia Livingston of Stillwater; Rev. Dr. Coe (9-11/6)
2524. Dibble, William A., merchant, m 9/30/34 Charlotte I. Winchell, dau of Aaron E., merchant, of Pine Plains, in P. P.; Rev. William N. Sayre (8-10/8)
2525. Dibblee, Frederick Ebenezer, 2, s of Henry, d 9/26/15 in Hudson (6-10/3)
2526. Dibblee, Fyler, merchant, of Dutchess Co. m 10/8/09 Frances Wilson, dau of Hon. Judge Wilson of Clermont, in C; Rev. Kittle (6-10/10 and 8-10/18)
2527. Dibblee, Henry of Hudson m 10/31/04 Huldah Reed, dau of Ezra, Esq. of Coxsackie, in C; Rev. Ostrander (6-11/6)
2528. Dibblee , Sally (Miss), 70, only surviving sister of late Ebenezer Dibblee, d 3/17/27 "suddenly" in Catskill (8-3/28)
2529. Dick, Peter (born in Holland) d 5/1/34 in Poughkeepsie, NY ("member of the Poughkeepsie Beneficial Society of Journeymen Cordwainers") (8-5/7)
2530. Dickens, Sarah (Mrs.), 104, d 10/19/99 in North Salem ("Dutchess County") (lived with her husband 66 yrs [he d age 95] and lived to see her 5th generation) (funeral sermon by Rev. Solomon Meed) (8-10/29 and 9-11/19)
2531. Dickerson, James m 4/7/28 Abigail Clark in Troy; Rev. Willis (9-4/11)
2532. Dickinson, John L. of the firm of Wood and Dickinson m 9/15/29 Olive Dewey, dau of David, in Richland (Oswego Co.); Rev. T. R. Smith (1-9/23)
2533. Dickinson, Philemon (Gen.), 69, (a Rev. officer) d near Trenton, NJ (6-2/14/09)
2534. Dickson, James, Esq. of Blackheath, England m 6/20/31 Mary Sullivan Parsons of Hartford, CT in Brooklyn, NY; Rev. Joel Parker (1-6/24)
2535. Dickson, John, 39, d 1/15/30 in Albany (1-1/18)
2536. Dickson, William, printer, editor of the Lancaster Intelligencer for more than 24 years, d 1/18/23 in Lancaster, PA (8-1/22)
2537. Diefendorf, Abraham (Dr.), 39, d 9/9/31 in Ithaca (1-9/19)
2538. Diell, Mary, relict of late John, formerly a merchant of Cherry Valley, d 3/19/19 in C. V. (3-3/29)
2539. Dietz, John, s of James, m 5/21/09 Mary Walley, dau of Garret, in Milford; Rev. Toll (3-6/10)
2540. Digert, Seffrenus, about 66, "a wealthy farmer", d 5/15/31 in Canajoharie; his wife, "Mrs. O. Digert", about 62, d 5/25; his son, Warner, about 32, d 5/27; and his dau, Catharine Digert, 26, d 6/4. (1-6/14)
2541. Dill, John B. m 5/14/29 Mary Ann Warden at St. Peter's Church in Auburn; Rev. Dr. Rudd (double ceremony - see marr of George H. Wood) (1-5/25)
2542. Dillingham, Charles K., merchant, of Philadelphia (state not given) m 10/14/34 Mary E. Raymond, dau of A., Esq. of Poughkeepsie; Rev. A. Perkins (8-10/22)
2543. Dimock, Ward, 26, s of Timothy, d 4/9/21 in Burlington (Ots. Co.) (2-4/16)
2544. Dinge, Charlotte, 34, dau of Mabe (sic) of Pawling, d 8/30/34 in Poughkeepsie (8-9/3)
2545. Disbrow, ____, 10, dau of Elias, drowned 9/20/23 in the cistern at her parents' home (9-9/23)

73

2546. Disturnell, John of Troy m 3/21/27 Mary Eliza St. Claire, formerly of NYC, in Lansingburgh; Rev. Blatchford (9-3/27)
2547. Dix, Joshua G. of the firm of J. G&P. Dix, merchants, of Albany, NY m 3/10/30 E. R. Fisher, oldest dau of Paul, Esq., in Dedham, MA; Rev. Lampson (1-3/25)
2548. Dix, Perry of the firm of J. G. and P. Dix, merchants, m 12/30/30 Harriet Smith, dau of the widow S. S. Fuller; Rev. Dr. Sprague. All of Albany (1-1/1/31)
2549. Dixon, Elizabeth (Mrs.), 46, d in Hudson (6-11/24/07)
2550. Dixon, George C., Esq. m Henrietta C. C. Gourgas in Geneva (7-9/21/33)
2551. Doane, George Washington (Rev.), assistant pastor of Trinity Church in NYC, m 9/19/29 Eliza Green Perkins at Christ Church in NYC; Rev. Dr. Gardner (1-9/22)
2552. Dobb, Martin of Pleasant Valley m 11/3/24 Ann Albertson of Poughkeepsie; Rev. Babcock (8-11/10)
2553. Dobbs, Dorcas (Widow), 73, d in Hudson (6-11/20/04)
2554. Dobbs, Jacob m Betsey Jones, dau of late Seth (6-8/9/08)
2555. Dockum, Thomas m 11/10/25 Lucinda Jan_?____ in Beekmantown; Rev. Haley (7-11/19)
2556. Dodds, George m 6/9/32 Elizabeth Chappell, both of Plattsburgh, in P; Rev. Chase (7-7/21)
2557. Dodge, Ann S., 37, wf of Col. Richard, merchant, d 5/23/08 in Johnstown (8-6/1)
2558. Dodge, Edwin, Esq., attorney, of Gouverneur m Jerusha Sterling of Watertown in W (1-1/7/30)
2559. Dodge, Eleazer, 22, s of Elijah, d in Hudson (6-4/10/04)
2560. Dodge, Ezekiel of NYC m 5/20/06 Jane Power, dau of Nicholas of Poughkeepsie; Rev. Phillips (8-5/27)
2561. Dodge, Helenah, 80, wid of Samuel, Esq., d 3/14/17 in Poughkeepsie (8-4/2)
2562. Dodge, Henry (Capt.), 64, d 2/19/20 in Poughkeepsie (enlisted at age 17 among the first from Dutchess Co. at the outbreak of the Rev. War; has been a m ember of the NY state legislature; in 1810 became a member of the Baptist Church in Poughkeepsie; in 1816 became deacon of that church (8-12/20 and 8-12/27)
2563. Dodge, James (Dr.) of NYC m "last week" Susan Kelsey, dau of Jonas of Poughkeepsie; Rev. Brouwer (8-12/16/95)
2564. Dodge, James, s of Henry, Esq. of Poughkeepsie, m 1/5/14 Electa Seward, dau of William, Esq. of Fishkill; Rev. De Witt (8-1/12)
2565. Dodge, John R. (Rev.), pastor of the First Baptist Church in Brockport, m 6/4/29 Harriet M. Winchester, author of "Hesselrigge", etc, in Batavia; Rev. Joseph Elliot (1-6/11 and 1-6/20)
2566. Dodge, M. Samuel, 72, d 10/4/07 in Poughkeepsie (8-10/7)
2567. Dodge, Nathan C. m 12/4/28 Sally Wait; Rev. Frederick Halsey. All of Plattsburgh (7-12/6)
2568. Dodge, Noah, 66, d 5/14/29 at his home in Montgomery Co. (1-5/19)
2569. Dodge, Rachel, 68, wf of Newel Dodge, d 2/6/07 in Pawling (8-2/25)
2570. Dodge, Sarah, 66, relict of late Henry, Esq., d 4/23/23 in Poughkeepsie (8-4/30)
2571. Dodge, William H. of NYC m 4/9/32 Catharine De La Vergne, only dau of La Grange; Rev. Dwight (8-4/18)
2572. Dole, Almira, 39, wf of James, Esq. of Troy, d 10/20/03 in Troy (6-11/8)
2573. Dole, Charlotte Elizabeth, 8, dau of Lewis G., d 1/17/24 in Troy (9-1/20)
2574. Dole, James, Esq. of Troy m 9/20/06 JaneMcCready of Albany; Rev. Coe (9-9/23)
2575. Dole, Jane, wf of James, d 4/2/08 in Troy (9-4/5)
2576. Dole, Sidney, Esq. (formerly of Troy, NY and lately a member of the legislative council of Michigan) d "recently" in Pontiac, Mich. Terr. (9-8/5/28)
2577. Dolsom, Jacob m 10/31/12 Jane Coe; Rev. C. C. Cuyler (8-11/4)
2578. Dominy, Henry, about 70, d 1/22/17 in Plattsburgh (7-1/25)
2579. Dominy, Henry, Esq., under-sheriff of Clinton Co., d 9/7/34 in Beekmantown (7-9/13)
2580. Dominy, John, Jr., 25, d 1/31/14 in Plattsburgh (7-2/12)
2581. Donaldson, Sovereign B., 30, d 3/9/31 in Poughkeepsie ["His remains were accompanied to the grave by Capt. Pine's Corps of Artiller of which (he) was a member"] (8-3/16)

2582. Done, Truman m 11/22/23 Eliza Emmerson, both of Amenia; Rev. Willson (8-12/10)
2583. Doney, George of Geneva m 8/25/31 Sarah Maria Frisbie, dau of Dr. Frisbie of Vienna, NY, in V (1-9/10)
2584. Donnelly, James m Ann Walworth in Milford (3-2/2/24)
2585. Donnelly, Terence, 18 mo, youngest s of John M., d 9/5/30 in Catskill (1-9/11)
2586. Doolittle, _____ m Eliza Lamb in Granville; Rev. Hall. All of Granville (9-3/15/03)
2587. Doolittle, _____, child of Calvin, d "recently" in Albany (funeral from the home of her father, 116 South Pearl St.) (1-8/13/29)
2588. Doolittle, Calista, dau of Calvin, d 12/15/29 (funeral from the home of her father, 116 South Pearl St.) (1-12/18)
2589. Doolittle, Charles W., merchant, m 6/29/29 Abigail P. Obear, dau of Capt. Oliver; Rev. Aiken. All of Utica (1-7/2)
2590. Dorchester, Walter of Northeast m 2/1/21 Polly Sutherland of Stanford (Dut. Co.); Rev. Birch (8-2/21)
2591. Dorland, John m 2/1/07 Phila Potter, both of Beekman; Smuel A. Barker, Esq. (8-2/3)
2592. Dorland, Phebe, about 45, wf of Philip of Beekman, d 4/1/32 (8-4/11)
2593. Dorland, Samuel G. of Fishkill m 12/9/24 Paulina Christie of Freedom; J. Klapp, Esq. (8-12/15)
2594. Dorlon, Benjamin, 79, d 11/17/29 in Pleasant Valley (8-11/25)
2595. Dorr, Benjamin (Rev.) of Lansingburgh, NY m 7/12/27 Esther K. Odin, dau of John, Esq. of Boston (state not given), in Boston; Rev. Potter of St. Paul's Church (8-8/1)
2596. Dorr, Russell (Dr.), 52, d 3/29 (3-4/12/24)
2597. Dorris, John m 2/6/23 Eliza Osburn; Rev. Griffin (9-2/11)
2598. Doty, Adam m Anna Overacker, both of Schaghticoke, in S; Rev. Paige (9-3/15/03)
2599. Doty, David m 2/6/22 Sarah Van Wagoner, dau of John of Pleasant Valley; Rev. Clark (8-2/13)
2600. Doty, Elias m 9/1/21 Mercy George, both of Plattsburgh, in P; St. J. B. L. Skinner, Esq. (7-9/1)
2601. Doty, Horace of Amenia m 2/1/27 Trena Maxim; Rev. C. P. Wilson (8-2/28)
2602. Doty, Prudence, 53, wf of Elias, d 12/15/18 in Plattsburgh (7-12/18)
2603. Doty, Rensselaer (s of Capt. Joseph W.)late of the U.S. Army and apprentice to William Twogood m 9/14/23 Lydia Baker, step-dau of Michael Morton, in Hoosick; Clark Baker, Esq. All of Pittstown (9-9/23)
2604. Doty, Samuel, 27, d 11/19/31 at his home in Clinton (Dut. Co.) (8-11/23)
2605. Doty, Simeon m 8/19/28 Eliza Lacy; Rev. C. P. Wilson. All of Amenia (8-8/27)
2606. Doty, Thomas S. m 1/12/32 Maria Wing of Clinton (Dut. Co.); Isaac Sutherland, Esq. (8-1/18)
2607. Doubleday, Elisha m 11/12/23 Eunice Williams in Otsego (3-11/17)
2608. Doubleday, Mercy, relict of Abner, d 12/20/17 in Cooperstown (3-1/5/18)
2609. Doubleday, Sally, 18, d 7/23/10 in Cooperstown (3-7/28)
2610. Doubleday, William H. m 1/1/29 Emeline Sherrill, dau of Dr. Nathaniel, all of New Hartford, NY, in Rome, NY; Rev. Gillet (1-1/14)
2611. Dougery, James m 3/9/06 Clarissa Bontecou in Lansingburgh; Rev. Daniel Butler (9-3/11)
2612. Dougherty, John of Keeseville m 1/1/33 Ann Taggard of Clintonville in Keeseville; Rev. James Francis Raftery (sic) (4 [Keeseville Herald]-1/15)
2613. Doughty, David S., 37, s of Joseph of Beekman, d 8/17/22 in NYC (yellow fever) (8-8/21)
2614. Doughty, Hull, 19, s of Joseph of Beekman, NY, d "in August last" on his passage to the West Indies (8-6/10/18)
2615. Doughty, Isaac T. m 8/23/18 Eliza Merkel, dau of George; Rev. C. C. Cuyler. All of Poughkeepsie (8-9/2)
2616. Doughty, John, printer, of NYC (formerly of Poughkeepsie) m 7/9/16 Sally Armstrong, dau of Jacob of Clinton (Dut. Co.) (8-7/17)
2617. Doughty, Joseph C. of Beekman m 9/30/34 Mary Wilkinson, dau of John of Union Vale; Rev. M. Buttolph (8-10/8)
2618. Doughty, Mary (Miss), 29, dau of Joseph, d 12/30/16 in Poughkeepsie (consumption) (8-1/1/17)

2619. Doughty, Nehemiah, merchant, m 8/16/03 Catharine Dennis, both of Beekmantown; Rev. Van Vranken (8-8/23) (probably Beekmantown is intended for Beekman [Dut. Co.])
2620. Doughty, Phebe (Mrs.), consort of Joseph, d 11/8/12 in Poughkeepsie (8-11/11)
2621. Doughty, Timothy of Staatsburg m 9/16/98 Margaret Kidney of Poughkeepsie; Rev. Brower (8-9/18)
2622. Douglas, Alanson, Esq., attorney, of Lansingburgh m 6/12/03 Ann Sutherland, oldest dau of late Hon. Solomon of Poughkeepsie, in Stanford (Dut. Co.); Rev. Wood (9-6/21)
2623. Douglas, David D. m 2/14/13 Nancy Douglas in Plattsburgh (7-2/19)
2624. Douglass, E. W. of Lower Canada m Delilah Weeks of Champlain in Chazy; Rev. J. Byington (7-1/8/25)
2625. Douglass, Hannah, 70, relict of late Thomas, d 1/30/31 in Albany (funeral from the home of Mrs. Isabella Thayer , 62 Ferry St.) (1-1/31)
2626. Douglass, Nathaniel, 66, d in Sherrington, Lower Canada (7-10/13/21)
2627. Douglass, Sutherland (Rev.) s of Alanson, Esq. of Troy, d 5/4/31 in London, England "from an attack of fever" (he had sailed for England a few months earlier hoping through travels in Europe to improve his health) (1-6/18)
2628. Douglass, Thomas W. of NYC m 9/2/34 Almira S. Woodworth of Hyde Park, dau of William, Esq.; Rev. Quinn (8-9/10)
2629. Dougrey, James, Jr. of Lansingburgh m 10/4/31 Frances E. Moulton, dau of H. Moulton of Troy; Rev. Butler (1-10/6)
2630. Dow, Jonathan G., 23, formerly of Vermont, d 4/25/34 in St. Catherine's, Upper Canada ("Printers in this state [NY] are requested to publish the above for the information of a brother of the deceased who is supposed to reside within its limits") (7-6/28)
2631. Dow, Josiah L. of Milton m 8/21/28 Frances Belinda Yelverton of Poughkeepsie; Rev. Dr. Reed (8-8/27)
2632. Dow, Lorenzo, "a well-known Itinerant Preacher", d 2/2/34 in Georgetown, Dist. of Columbia (b in Coventry, CT; was a preacher for more than 30 yrs.) (8-2/12)
2633. Dow, Samuel, 31, d in Otsego (3011/17/23)
2634. Down, James (Dr.) of Clinton (Dut. Co.) m 2/25/03 Sally Gould, dau of David of Sharon (8-3/8)
2635. Downer, Dana m 12/21/30 Cynthia Munger in New Lisbon (3-1/1/31)
2636. Downes, Charles (Midshipman) of the frigate "Gurriere", brother of Capt. John of the U.S. Navy, d "in the Mediterranean")9-12/5/15)
2637. Downes, Daniel D. m 12/8/21 Elizabeth Wolf, both of Troy (9-12/11)
2638. Downes, John (Capt.) of the U.S. Navy m 10/30/21 Maria Gertrude Hoffman, dau of Herman, Esq. of Red Hook, NY; Rev. Kittle (8-11/7 and 3-11/12)
2639. Downie, George, Esq., "a post captain in the Royal B. Navy", d 9/11/1811 (data taken from a gravestone erected in Plattsburgh, NY "by his affectionate Sister-in-law, Mary Downie") (8-9/9/18)
2640. Downing, Daniel, merchant, 31, d 1/24/07 in Hudson (6-1/27)
2641. Downing, James m 10/23/28 Meyry Phillips, both of Fishkill; Rev. M. W. Dwight (8-11/26)
2642. Downing, Obadiah I. m 2/15/27 Lydia H. Titus; John Klapp, Esq. All of Freedom (8-2/21)
2643. Downs, J. Milton of NYC m 12/19/30 Phebe Ann Albertson, dau of Samuel of Hyde Park, in H. P.; John Van Waggoner, Esq. (8-1-5/31)
2644. Downs, John m 10/25/21 Nancy Lee, dau of Daniel, in Milford; Ezra Adams, Esq. (3-10/29)
2645. Downs, John (Dr.), 43, brother of Dr. James Downs of Pleasant Valley, d 7/23/25 in Greenbush (8-8/3)
2646. Dows, John of the firm of J. Dows and Cary m 3/12/29 Adrianna Maria Cook, dau of late John; Rev. W. B. Lacy. All of Albany (1-3/13)
2647. Dowse, William, 88, d 5/30/08 in Cooperstown (born in England 12/25/1719; came to America in 1762) (3-6/4)
2648. Dowse, William, Esq., 42, congressman-elect from the 15th District, d 2/11/13 in Cooperstown (surv by wf and children) (3-2/20)
2649. Dox, George Talcott, 3, youngest s of Gerrit L., d 3/14/30 in Albany (funeral at the home of his father on Howard St.) (1-3/15)

2650. Dox, Myndert M., 42, late collector of the port of Buffalo, d 9/8/30 in Buffalo ("during the last war [was] a captain in the U.S. Army") (buried with military honors) (1-9/15)

2651. Dox, Peter, 89, ("a native and for the greater part of his life a resident of Albany") d 11/27/31 in Benton (Yates Co.) (prior to the Rev. War he was a skipper on the north River between Albany and NYC) (1-12/5)

2652. Dox, Peter B., Esq., postmaster of Albany and late sheriff of Albany Co., d 11/21/15 in Albany (9-12/5)

2653. Drake, Catharine, 4 yrs, dau of William, d 7/10/29 (funeral from her father's home, corner of State and Capitol Sts) (1-7/11)

2654. Drake, Charles H., merchant, of Jordan m 7/26/31 Betsey Baker, dau of Erastus, Esq. of La Fayette (Onon. Co.), in L. F.; Rev. A. Corning (double ceremony - see marr of Frederick Benson, Esq.) (1-8/2)

2655. Drake, Cornelia, 60, wf of John, Jr., Esq., d 6/12/30 in New Hamburgh (Poughkeepsie area) (8-7/14)

2656. Drake, Francis m 1/6/30 Rachel Luckey, both of Poughkeepsie; Rev. Dwight (8-1/13)

2657. Drake, Jonas Williams of the firm of Bush and Drake m 6/1/29 Susan Betts, 2nd dau of Samuel, Esq., in NYC; Right Rev. Bishop Hobart (1-6/4)

2658. Drake, Leonard, 27, d 5/10/21 in Westford (3-5/21)

2659. Drake, Mary, 14, dau of Dr. S. Drake, d 3/27/27 in Troy (9-3/30)

2660. Draper, Lydia Ann Elizabeth, inf dau of John C., d 10/3/30 in Albany (1-10/5)

2661. Draper, Philip N. (Dr.) m 5/14/23 Sila Ann Post, dau of Dr. James Post of White Creek, in W. C.;Rev. Samuel Draper of White Creek (2-5/27)

2662. Draper, Richard (Capt.), 81, d 8/24/30 in Poughkeepsie (8-8/25 and 1-8/27)

2663. Draper, Rufus d 1/19/22 in Maryland (Ots. Co.) (3-1/28)

2664. Draper, Samuel (Rev.) of Whitehall, about 50, d 7/7/24 at the home of Peter Power in Amenia (typhus) (8-7/14)

2665. Dresser, Horace, Esq. m 3/24/30 Lucy Knapp, dau of Dr. Colbey Knapp, in Guilford (Chen. Co.); Rev. Asa Donaldson (1-3/31)

2666. Drinkwater, Brooks m Temperance Pond in NYC ("a cold water match") (8-6/9/30)

2667. Drum, Simeon m 9/9/32 Sarah Place; Samuel C. Allen, Esq. (8-9/19)

2668. Drury, _____ m 12/4/28 Mahala Barns in Alexandria; Rev. Filmore (9-12/19)

2669. Dryer, Alanson m 11/13/19 Harriet Gillispie, both of Albany, in A; Rev. Hooper Cumming (6-11/23)

2670. Duane, Mary (Mrs.), 85, d in NYC ("her remains were taken to Duanesburgh and deposited in the family vault") (3-5/14/21)

2671. Duane, William m Mrs. Margaret Hartman Bache in Philadelphia (state not given) (3-7/17/00)

2672. Duboice, Cornelius m 9/2/13 Catharine Sharp of Greenbush; Rev. Coe (9-9/7)

2673. Duboice, Henry m 11/16/28 Mary Winslow; Rev. Richardson (8-11/19)

2674. Dubois, Charles L. m 2/25/24 Catharine Hasbrook, dau of Tunis, Esq., all of Fishkill; Rev. De Witt (8-3/3)

2675. Dubois, Cornelius of Pleasant Valley m 5/9/27 Julia Moore, dau of William A., Esq. of Fort Ann, in F. A. (8-5/16)

2676. Du Bois, Elias, s of Gen. Du Bois of Poughkeepsie Precinct,m 5/10/87 _____ Van Benschoten, dau of Col. Van Benschoten of Poughkeepsie Precinct (8-5/16)

2677. Dubois, Elias of Plattekill m 12/2/20 Mrs. Maria Gay, widow of Barnet, of Poughkeepsie; Rev. Cuyler (8-12/6)

2678. Dubois, Helanah, 81, relict of late Christian, d 3/4/26 in Fishkill (8-3/15)

2679. Du Bois, Henry A. m 6/9/30 Evelina Dusch, dau of John, Esq.; Rev. E. Holmes. All of Livingston (Col. Co.) (8-6/30)

2680. Dubois, Hiram m 12/18/30 Helen Elmira Meddaugh, both of La Grange; Rev. Buttolph (8-12/29)

2681. Dubois, Jeremiah m 7/19/17 Matilda Palen, both of Poughkeepsie; Rev. Dr. Covel (8-7/30)

2682. Dubois, John, merchant, of Red. Hook m 6/23/11 G. Brodhead, oldest dau of Dr. Thomas Brodhead of Clermont, in C; Rev. Kittle (6-7/5)

2683. Du Bois, John, Esq., 43, of Red Hook d 1/8/28 at the home of Dr. Thomas Broadhead in Clermont (8-1/23)
2684. Dubois, John B. m 2/17/26 Helen Kidney, both of Poughkeepsie, at the Episcopal Church in Poughkeepsie; Rev. Dr. Reed (8-2/22)
2685. Dubois, Koert, 66, farmer, of Pleasant Valley d 4/25/31 (8-4/27)
2686. Du Bois, Lewis (Gen.), 80, (a Rev. officer) d 3/4/24 in Poughkeepsie (8-3/10)
2687. Dubois, Nathan, 81, d 10/8/21 in Poughkeepsie (8-10/10)
2688. Dubois, Oliver m 8/1/16 Almira Pease; Rev. Lewis Leonard of Poughkeepsie (8-8/7)
2689. Dubois, Peter F. m 1/1/30 Caroline Newcomb Dean, dau of Gilbert, all of Pleasant Valley, in P. V.; Rev. Wilder (8-1/6)
2690. Du Bois, Peter K. m 11/18/17 Sally Lattin, both of Clinton; Rev. Leonard (8-11/19)
2691. Dubois, Philip m Esther Freer, dau of Zacharias of New Paltz (9-9/5/15)
2692. Du Bois, Robert K. of Pleasant Valley m 3/8/27 Mary Conklin, dau of Benjamin, Esq. of Freedom; Rev. John Clark (8-4/4)
2693. Dubois, Thomas K., 36, d 6/7/29 in Pleasant Valley (8-6/25)
2694. Dubois, Uriah (Maj.), 47, formerly of Poughkeepsie, d 1/10/29 in Burlington, VT (8-1/28)
2695. Dubois, William, 18, s of -oert (perhaps intended for Koert), d 2/16/26 in Rhinebeck (8-2/22)
2696. Duboise, George (Rev.) of NYC m 3/30/25 Caroline Maison of Poughkeepsie; Rev. Dr. Reed (8-4/6)
2697. Dudley, Stoddard of New Berlin m 12/29/16 Laura Banks of Pittsfield in P; Rev. William B. Lacy (3-1/2/17)
2698. Dudly, Harry d 5/3/18 "about three miles east of the village of Whitehall" (had stopped at a house there 4/31, at times deranged, reporting that he had fallen down a flight of stairs apparently the cause of his death; said he had a brother "in the western country") (9-5/5)
2699. Duel, Benjamin m 2/2/25 Lydia Segar in Warren; Rev. Stone (3-2/14)
2700. Duels, Ephraim of Washington (Dut. Co.) m 1/17/22 Phebe Sanford of Amenia; Rev. Robert G. Armstrong (8-2/20)
2701. Duer, Edward A., 16, 2nd s of Hon. Judge Duer, President of Columbia College, d 12/15/31 in NYC (1-12/19 and 1-12/21)
2702. Duffee, Daniel, 65, d 3/22/05 in Poughkeepsie (8-3/29)
2703. Duffee, Mary Ann, "a young lady", d 6/28/30 in Skaneateles "having mistaken a poisonous preparation for spirits to relieve a tooth ache" (1-7/3)
2704. Duffee, Barnard m 12/18/06 Lucretia Prescott, both of Troy; William McManus, Esq. (9-12/23)
2705. Dumond, Solomon W. m 2/19/31 Harriet Lake, both of New Paltz, in Washington (Dut. Co.); Rev. A. Bronson (8-2/23)
2706. Dumont, William m 10/4/31 Georgiana Depeyster, dau of George, Esq., at St. Luke's Church in NYC; Rev. Bishop Ives. All of NYC (1-10/7)
2707. Dunbar, James, Esq. of Cork, Ireland m 5/10/32 Elizabeth Handy, 2nd dau of late Dr. William Handy, in NYC by Rev. Dr. Levine "and afterwards by the Right Rev. Bishop Onderdonk"(8-5/30)
2708. Duncan, David, merchant, d 8/31/99 in Dover (town of Pawling) (yellow fever) (had just returned from NYC) (8-9/3)
2709. Duncan, James, Esq., 78, (formerly a merchant in NYC and more recently a justice of the peace in Fishkill) d 7/20/82 in Fishkill (5-7/25)
2710. Duncan, Rebecca of Pleasant Valley m 1/15/24 Maria Manning of Hyde Park; Alfred Raymond, Esq. (8-1/21)
2711. Dunham, ____, about 2, a child of Guy Dunham, d 9/27/21 in Plattsburgh (7-9/29)
2712. Dunham, Abner, Esq. m 10/28/15 Gratis Griffin, dau of Samuel, Esq., in Middlefield; Rev. Smith (3-11/2)
2713. Dunham, Abner (Col.), 48, d 2/16/22 in Middlefield (3-2/18)
2714. Dunham, Guy m 7/11/11 Emily Everst of Plattsburgh in P; Reuben H. Walworth, Esq. (7-7/19)
2715. Dunham, Jacob, printer, m Fanny Morgan (6-8/6/01)
2716. Dunham, John C. m 2/9/31 Emily Bicknell, both of Morrisville, in M; Prof. Sears of Hamilton (1-2/18)
2717. Dunham, Mary (Miss), 19, d in Athens, NY (6-11/21/09)

78

2718. Dunham, Obadiah, 83, d 2/10/13 in Middlefield (one of the first settlers there) (3-2/20)
2719. Dunlap, James A. (Col.), U.S. District Attorney for the Middle District of Florida, d 11/6/31 in NYC (1-11/9)
2720. Dunlap, Robert of the late firm of Diell and Dunlap, merchants, m 9/8/13 Hannah Burgess, step-dau of Jesse Johnson of Cherry Valley, in C. V.; Rev. Cooley (3-9/11)
2721. Dunlap, Robert, 62, d 4/4/24 in Ballston Spa (2-4/6)
2722. Dunn, Elizabeth (Mrs.) of Poughkeepsie d 1/22/94 (8-1/29)
2723. Dunn, Hannah, relict of late Christopher, d 12/6/31 at the home of her sister in Fishkill (1-12/17)
2724. Dunn, James , 32, of the firm of Douglas and Dunn d 10/20/29 in NYC where he had gone for his health (funeral from his late home, 57 South Pearl St.) (buried near his father's home in Guilderland)(1-10/22)
2725. Dunn, John m 11/18/13 Amity Price, both of Hartwick, in H; Elder Wier (3-11/27)
2726. Dunn, Margaret,94, relict of late Richard, d 12/17/31 in Albany (funeral from her late home, 43 Maiden Lane) (mentioned are her son, Edward, and her dau, Margaret McCabe, both probably of the Albany area) (1-12/26)
2727. Dunning,_____ (Mr.) and his wife (not named) d "recently" in Plattsburgh (both buried in one grave) (7-1/8/13)
2728. Dunning, Clarissa, 16, dau of Gen. John, d 1/21/23 in Ballston Spa (2-1/21)
2729. Dunning, Philo (Dr.) of Rhinebeck m 9/6/22 Sarah Resler of NYC in Hudson; Rev. Cyrus Stebbins (8-10/2)
2730. Duplessis, Carmer Lanoblet, N. P., Lower Canada m 12/23/27 Mary Ann Porter,dau of Dr. Porter of Plattsburgh; Rev. Frederick Halsey (7-1/19/28)
2731. Durand, Marinus Frances (sic) (Col.), 68, of Plattsburgh d 1/26/34 at the home of his dau at River du Loup, Lower Canada (7-2/1)
2732. Durando, Peter, formerly of Dutchess Co., m 7/19/17 Martha Mider of NYC in NYC; Rev. Labagh (8-8/20)
2733. Durham, Lois (Mrs.), 42, d in Jefferson (Schoharie Co.) (6-2/22/10)
2734. Durkee, Jireh of Burlington, VT m Anne Van Ness, dau of late Gen. David, in Rhinebeck; Rev. Gosman(8-10/11/26)
2735. Durkee, Joseph of Plattsburgh, NY m 1/29/32 Lucy Hodgkins, dau of William, in South Hero, VT; S. Addoms, Esq. (7-2/4)
2736. Durland, Enoch, about 78, d 8/31/34 in La Grange (8-9/3)
2737. Durrall, Thomas D., attorney, of Geneva m 8/25/13 Charlotte Davies, dau of William of Poughkeepsie; Rev. Reed (8-9/1)
2738. Duryee, Abraham, farmer, of Fishkill d "some time since"(8-8/8/02)
2739. Dusenberry, Gabriel m Lydia Power, dau of Thomas, in Hudson; Rev. Chester (bride and groom both of Hudson) (6-3/29/14)
2740. Dusenberry, Isaac m 6/1/17 Clarissa Marsh, both of Poughkeepsie; Rev. Clark (8-6/4)
2741. Dusenberry, John m 7/27/15 Sarah Balding, both of Poughkeepsie; Rev. C. C. Cuyler (8-8/2)
2742. Dusenberry, Sarah, 72, d 5/27/29 in Peekskill (1-6/19)
2743. Dusenbury, Jervis of Brunswick m 10/10/12 Hannah Winne of Lansingburgh (9-10/13)
2744. Dusenbury, Stephen d 9/27/16 in Poughkeepsie (8-10/2)
2745. Dutcher,_____, wf of David, d 5/30/04 (consumption) (8-6/5)
2746. Dutcher, David m 3/14/16 Elizabeth Vanderwater, both of Fishkill; Rev. Lewis Leonard (8-3/27)
2747. Dutcher, Harriet Maria, about 11 months and only dau of John W., d 3/19/29 in Albany (funeral from 30 South Pearl St.) (1-3/20)
2748. Dutcher, Jacob m 10/1/12 Peggy Smith, both of Stanford (Dut. Co.); Rev. Birch (8-10/21)
2749. Dutcher, John D. m 5/11/28 Hannah Cobb, both of Troy; Rev. Howard (9-5/20)
2750. Dutcher, John W., printer, m 12/17/18 Harriet F. Shepard, dau of Noah, in Hudson. All of Hudson; Rev. Briggs (6-12/22 and 9-12/29)
2751. Dutcher, Luther S. (Capt.) m 12/1/32 Adelia Giddings, dau of Buel Giddings, Esq.; Leonard Vincent, Esq. All of Dover (8-12/12)

2752. Dutcher, Silas m 11/12/28 Laura Boothe, oldest dau of John; Thomas Hammond, Esq. (Bride and groom both of Washington [Dut. Co.])(8-11/19)
2753. Duton, Susanna (Miss), 24, dau of George W. of Boston, MA, d 12/13/27 in Plattsburgh (7-12/22)
2754. Dutton, Matthew Rice, 42, professor of mathematics and natural philosophy at Yale College, d 7/17/25 in New Haven, CT (3-8/1)
2755. Dutton, Samuel B. m 10/18/20 Catherine Vandeburgh, both of Clinton (Dut. Co.); Rev. Leonard (8-10/25)
2756. Duval, J. (Capt.) of Sag Harbor, L.I., NY "was killed (7/4/01) at Savannah by the accidental discharge of a cannon" (6-7/30)
2757. Duvall, Joseph W. (Dr.) m 8/19/30 Eliza Ann Ogden, youngest dau of late Benjamin, in NYC; Rev. F. E. Schaeffer. All of NYC (1-8/23)
2758. Duyckinck, Gerardus, Esq., 59, d 1/12/14 at his home in Poughkeepsie ("held a commission among the first troops embroiled in the city of New York at the commencement of the late revolution") (8-1/19)
2759. Dwight, Henry E., 47, d 5/20/25 in Cooperstown (3-5/23)
2760. Dwight, Nathaniel (Rev.), 62, M.D., of Norwich, CT d in Oswego, NY (10th child and 6th son of Timothy Dwight of Northampton (state not given) and a brother of late President Dwight of Yale College (1-7/11/31)
2761. Dwyer, William d "recently" while imprisoned at the NYC penitentiary after having "pleaded guilty" (charge against him not stated) (hanged himself in his cell) (1-9/26/31)
2762. Dyckman, Harriet d 10/27/31 in NYC (wf of William, merchant, of NYC and niece of John A. Thompson, Esq. of Catskill) (recently her mother and "a gifted brother" died) (1-11/7)
2763. Dyer, Abraham m 12/13/21 Maria Conklin, both of Gibbonsville; Rev. Sommers (9-1/1/22)
2764. Dyer, Edward G. (Dr.) of Manlius m Ann Eliza Morse, dau of William of Trenton (state not given), in T; Rev. Isaac Pearce (1-2/18/31)
2765. Eames, Orlando m 10/9/18 Sylvia Seaward in New Hartford; Rev. Coe (3-10/19)
2766. Earl, Christopher of Providence, NY m 3/18/24 Mary McClelland of Galway in Providence; Rev. Mairs (2-3/23)
2767. Earl, Susan, 22, wf of John and dau of John B. Swartwout of Hyde Park, d 5/31/32 in NYC (8-6/6)
2768. Earl, Ralph, 50, portrait painter (a pupil of Sir Joshua Reynolds), d 8/16/01 in Bolton, CT (9-9/1)
2769. Earle, Sylvester Z. (Dr.) of St. John's, New Brunswick m 12/9/13 Maria Hughson, dau of William, Esq. of Fishkill; Rev. Price (8-12/22)
2770. Earle, William of Burlington, VT m 11/23/05 Sally Pease of Troy, NY in T; Rev. Jonas Coe (9-11/26)
2771. Eastburn, Edward B., s of late James of NYC, d 11/7/30 "on the passage from Liverpool to Charleston, S. C." (1-11/22)
2772. Easton, Charity (Miss), 23, d 11/10/24 in Columbia (Herk. Co.) (3-12/6)
2773. Eaton, Amos, Esq., attorney, of Livingstonville (Schoharie Co.) m 9/16/03 Sally Cady of New Concord (Col. Co.); Rev. John Wartrous (6-9/20)
2774. Eaton, Calvin of Burlington, VT drowned 9/30/20 in the Onion River "in passing from the shore to an island a little below the falls on horseback which he had frequently done before" (7-9/30)
2775. Eaton, Chloe, aged 116, "a coloured woman", d in Goshen, CT (had been a slave in the family of Rev. Eaton, the first settled minister in Goshen "about a century ago") (1-12/26/31)
2776. Eaton, D. C., merchant, of the firm of Doughty, Robertson and Co. of NYC m 12/27/30 Harriet Eliza Cady, dau of Daniel, Esq. of Johnstown; Rev. Dr. Hosack (1-12/31)
2777. Eaton, Elizabeth, 65, wid of late Gen. William, d 5/20/31 at the home of her son-in-law, David Hayden, Jr., in Auburn (1-6/3)
2778. Eaton, John H. m 1/1/29 Mrs. Margaret Timberlake, wid of late J. Timberlake of the U.S. Navy, in Washington City, D.C.; Rev. Ryland (1-1/8)
2779. Eaton, Polly, 20, consort of Amos, Esq., d 9/12/02 in New Concord, NY (6-9/21)
2780. Eaton, Theophilus, printer, late of Albany, d 5/6/20 in Bethlehem, NY (3-5/22)
2781. Eaton, William (Gen.), "the hero of Derne", d in Brimfield, MA (9-6/25/11)

2782. Echols, Philip Henry, Esq. of Monticello, GA m 7/13/31 Margaret L. M. Berrien, dau of J. Mcpherson Berrien, Esq. of Georgia; Rev. Johns (1-7/22)
2783. Ecker, Theodore M. of Ithaca m 6/7/31 Harriet Frances Thompson, dau of Hon. William A. of Thompsonville (Sull. Co.) in T; Rev. Fowler (8-6/1 and 1-6/4)
2784. Ecker, William, Esq., 46, state assemblyman from Orange Co., d 7/20/27 in Newburgh (8-7/25)
2785. Eckert, William, 75, m 5/2/26 Elizabeth Linsenbigler, 17, both of Montgomery Co., in Philadelphia (state not given); Rev. J. W. Dechant (8-5/31)
2786. Eddy, Devotion (Mr.), 78, d 6/8/13 in Pittstown (9-6/15)
2787. Eddy, Nancy (Miss), 25, dau of Capt. Willard, d 6/28/22 in Richfield (3-7/1)
2788. Eddy, Samuel, 32, d 3/3/27 in Troy (9-3/6)
2789. Eddy, Sherman, 64, of Pittstown d 6/30/29 in Brunswick (broke his neck in a fall while climbing a fence) (1-7/4)
2790. Eddy, Tisdale m 1/16/06 Betsy Button, both of Pittstown, in P (9-1/28)
2791. Edgar, John (Gen.), 90, of New Jersey (a Rev. officer) mEliza Stephens, 14, in Williamsburg, IL (9-2/3/24)
2792. Edgerton, Bela m 3/24/11 Phebe Ketchum, both of Plattsburgh; Rev. Halsey (7-4/20)
2793. Edgerton, Harry K., 16 mo, s of Bela of Chazy, d 10/20/21 in Chazy (7-11/5)
2794. Edgerton, Jabez of Coventry, CT m 6/8/13 Eliza Bradley in Hudson; Rev. Chester (6-6/22)
2795. Edget, Isaiah, merchant, m 6/30/02 Bashaba Asite, both of Stanford (Dut. Co.); Rev. Bullock (8-7/6)
2796. Edmonds, John W., Esq. m 8/7/20 Sarah Barker, dau of Mark, in Hudson; Rev. Sampson (6-8/8)
2797. Edmonds, Samuel (Gen.), 66, d 3/15/26 in Hudson (a Rev. soldier and paymaster general of the state of NY in the War of 1812) (3-3/27)
2798. Edmonds, Samuel H., 18, s of Gen. Edmonds, d 7/29/19 (6-8/3)
2799. Edmund, Erastus m 11/30/26 Betsey Preston; Thomas Hammond, Esq. All of Dover (8-12/6)
2800. Edson, Dean, Esq., attorney, of Essex, NY m "not long since" Emily Coates of Boston, MA in B (7-5/1/12)
2801. Edson, Emily Jenks, 2, only dau of Dean Edson, Esq., d 4/15/22 in Essex (7-4/27)
2802. Edson, Jacob, merchant, m 6/16/19 Saphronia Bowen, both of Milford, in M (3-6/28)
2803. Edson, Uriah C., 18, s of Oliver, d 10/1/24 in Ballston Spa (2-10/5)
2804. Edson, Willis (Dr.) m Sally Noble, dau of Elnathan, Esq., in New Lisbon; Rev. D. Nash (3-11/12/08)
2805. Edson, Wyllis (Dr.), 40, d 8/31/23 in Unadilla (3-9/8)
2806. Edwards, Alfred of the firm of Arthur Tappan and Co. of NYC m Sophia Matilda Lewis, 2nd dau of Z., Esq. of Brooklyn Heights; Rev. J. B. Waterman (1-6/24/31)
2807. Edwards, Ansel of Albany, NY m 12/21/31 Rowena Darling of Chesterfield, MA (1-12/24)
2808. Edwards, Benjamin, 22, member of the senior class at Yale College, d 8/10/29 at the home of his father in Brookhaven, L.I., NY (1-8/22)
2809. Edwards, Charles m 2/19/24 Eliza Skinner in Ballston; Rev. Reuben Smith (2-3/9)
2810. Edwards, D. B., surgeon in the U.S. Navy m 11/23/30 Harriet Eliza Henry, youngest dau of late William, Esq. of NYC, in Brooklyn; Rev. Carroll (1-11/26)
2811. Edwards, Harriet, wf of Hon. Ogden and oldest dau of Daniel Penfield, Esq., d 1/10/29 in NYC (1-1/14)
2812. Edwards, John d 9/3/31 (a Saturday) in Newburgh (On the previous Friday his child had died and on the Tuesday following his death the only remaining family member, his wife, also died) (1-9/10)
2813. Edwards, Jonathan (Rev.), D.D., President of Union College, d 8/1/01 in Schenectady (9-8/4 and 3-8/13)
2814. Edwards, Jonathan W., attorney, s of late Pres. Edwards of Union College, d 4/3/31 in Hartford, CT (1-4/9)

2815. Edwards, Lewis B., printer, m 9/15/23 Marsha Starr in Milton; Rev.
      Ambler (2-9/16)
2816. Edwards, Pierpont (Hon.), 76, district judge of the U.S. for Connecticut,
      d in Bridgeport, CT (3-4/17/26)
2817. Edwards, Richard, Esq. d 1/1/07 in Cooperstown ("asthmatic disorder")
      (member of the Masonic Order) (surv by wf and several young children)
      (3-1/8)
2818. Efner, Abram m 10/14/29 Helen Shaw; Rev. John C. Green. All of Albany.
      (1-10/16)
2819. Egerton, Edward, 28, d 7/25/30 in Albany (1-7/27)
2820. Eggleston, John M. of Port Kent m 2/9/34 Elizabeth F. Derby of Keeseville
      in K; Rev. Lyman (7-3/1)
2821. Eights, Catharine, 80, wid of late Abraham, d 6/9/29 (funeral from her
      late home, 28 Dean St., Albany)
2822. El--ot, Andrew of Mason, NH m 1/16/16 Lydia Wilson of Troy, NY; Rev. Dr.
      Coe (9-1/23) (Groom's surname could be Elliot but not necessarily so)
2823. Elder, George m 4/3/31 Margaret Maria Roff, both of Albany, in Gibbonsville;
      Philip Lennebacker, Esq. (1-4/7)
2824. Eldred, Elisha of Hartwick m 2/27/21 Sarah Ann Higby of Otsego in O;
      Rev. Tiffany (3-3/5?)
2825. Eldred, Elisha, 69, of Hartwick, NY d 10/16/25 in Detroit, Mich. Terr.
      ("while on a visit to his relatives") (3-12/5)
2826. Eldred, Julius of Hartwick m 12/25/11 __?__ Higby of Otsego; Rev. Nash
      (3-1/4/12)
2827. Eldred, Stephen, Esq. m 2/22/22 Cynthia Briggs of Adams, MA in Hoosick,
      NY (9-2/26)
2828. Eldridge, Charles M., Esq. of Redford m 3/10/33 Mary Durkee of Burlington,
      VT in Redford, NY (7-3/23)
2829. Elias, Henry, 24, d 12/1/09 in Hudson (6-12/12)
2830. Elias, Rachael (Miss), 25, d 8/20/04 in Hudson (6-8/28)
2831. Ellickson, Peter m 5/3/25 Sarah Bell; Rev. Dr. Reed (8-5/11)
2832. Elliot, Andrew. See, possibly, Entry 2822
2833. Elliot, Ethalinda, 65, wf of Dr. William, d 8/14/29 in Goshen, Orange Co.
      (1-8/17)
2834. Elliot, William H. (Dr.) of NYC m 12/8/31 Elizabeth E. Lummis, dau of Dr.
      William N. of Maxwell (Wayne Co.) at Christ Church (town or city of
      the church's location not given); Rev. John A. Clark (1-12/13)
2835. Elliott, Henry H. m 11/9/29 Elmira Whittemore, dau of Samuel, Esq., at
      St. John's Church, NYC; Right Rev. Bishop Hobart (1-11/11)
2836. Elliott, John B. W. of Dover m 10/25/12 Maria Wilkinson of Stanford
      (Dut. Co.); Leonard Barton, Esq. (8-11/4)
2837. Elliott, William (Dr.), "an old inhabitant of Goshen", d 9/2/29 in G
      (1-9/12)
2838. Ellis, David of West Troy m 12/23/30 Jane Maria Low of Poughkeepsie;
      Rev. Dr. Cuyler (8-12/29)
2839. Ellis, Henry, 88, (a Rev. soldier) d 11/12/34 in Poughkeepsie (8-11/19)
2840. Ellis, Humphrey d 11/28/11 in Hudson (6-12/2)
2841. Ellis, Powhatan, congressman from Mississippi, m 2/28/31 Eliza Winn, dau
      of Timothy of Albany, NY, in Washington City, D.C. (1-3/10)
2842. Ellis, Robert, 54, d 4/10/22 in Saratoga Springs (surv by wf and two
      small ch) (2-4/17)
2843. Ellison, Elizabeth (Widow), 78, d 1/9/31 in Albany (funeral from her late
      home, 19 Water St.) (1-1/12)
2844. Ellison, Gabriel, 88, a native of England and for many years a teacher in
      Poughkeepsie, d 2/19/25 (8-2/23)
2845. Ellison, John m 11/1/12 Gitty Van Vliet; Rev. Cuyler (8-11/4)
2846. Ellison, Smith m 11/27/31 Maria Barnes, both of Clinton (Dut. Co.); Daniel
      H. Schultz, Esq. (8-12/7)
2847. Ellison, Tripp of Northeast m 10/30/23 Mary Ann Arnold of Pine Plains;
      Peter Fish, Esq. (8-12/3)
2848. Ellison, William, 77, d 9/23/18 in Cooperstown (was a long-term resident
      there) (3-9/28)
2849. Ellsworth, Lewis of Troy m 12/1/28 Chloe M. Skinner of New Lebanon in
      N. L.; Rev. Churchill (9-12/9)
2850. Ellsworth, Oliver (Hon.), 63, d in Windsor, CT (6-12/8/07)

2851. Ellsworth, William, merchant, of Staatsburgh m 11/14/21 Ruth Bramin in
Bellgrove near Hyde Park; Rev. Peter S. Wyncoop (8-11/21)
2852. Elmendorf, Cornelius Edmund m 5/13/29 Ann Maria Pitcher in Red Hook; Rev.
Andrew N. Kittle (8-5/20)
2853. Elmendorf, Garetta, 47, consort of Jacob C., Esq., d in Red Hook (surv by
her husband and 8 children) (8-12/31/28 and 1-1/3/29)
2854. Elmendorf, John S., 26, s of Edmund, d 3/27/31 at Red Hook Landing (1-3/30)
2855. Elmendorph, _____, consort of Col. Cornelius of Red Hook, d 12/21/12 in
Red. Hook (6-12/29 and 8-12/30)
2856. Elmendorph, Cornelius m 12/15/13 Polly Van Deusen, both of Claverack, in
C; Rev. Gebhard (6-12/21)
2857. Elmendorph, Jacob of Claverack m 8/17/06 Christina Van Deusen of Hudson
in Claverack; Rev. Gebhard (6-9/9)
2858. Elmore, Asa, Esq., about 49, d 2/27/22 in Peru, NY (consumption)
(buried with Masonic honors) (7-3/2)
2859. Elmore, James m 1/14/26 Fanny Bragg in Peru, NY; Nathan Taylor, Esq.
All of Peru (7-2/18)
2860. Elmore, Lott, merchant, of Peru, NY d 8/2/18 in Quebec, Canada (he was
there delivering a raft of lumber) (7-8/8)
2861. Elmore, Ora m 1/4/19 Ann Mercy Wilmarth, both of Troy; Rev. Sommers
(9-1/19)
2862. Elmore, Washington, attorney, m 5/18/25 Ann Powers, dau of Henry, merchant,
of Plattsburgh, in P; Rev. Halsey (7-5/21)
2863. Elmore, Washington, dau d 4/9/31 in Peru, NY (4 [Keeseville Herald]-4/12)
2864. Elsbery, Garshom m 11/14/12 Tamer Jane Smith; Silas Woodle, Esq. All of
Washington (Dut. Co.) (8-12/16)
2865. Elsworth, James m 8/26/27 Sarah Sands, both of Poughkeepsie; John S. Myers,
Esq. (8-8/29)
2866. Elsworth, John m 9/15/30 Margaret Pawling in Hyde Park; Rev. Hardenburgh
of Rhinebeck (8-10/6)
2867. Elting, Catharine, 75, wid of late Henry of Kingston, d 2/3/31 at the home
of Zachariah Hoffman, Esq. in Red Hook (8-2/9)
2868. Elting, George m 2/19/31 Almira Ransom, both of New Paltz, in Washington
(Dut. Co.); Rev. A. Bronson (8-2/23)
2869. Elton, Rhesa of Calverack m 8/3/07 Maria Wey Murray of Red Hook in R. H.
"after a courtship of seven years"; Rev. Kittle (6-8/11)
2870. Elwood, Daniel (Capt.), 30, d 8/10/24 in Otsego (typhus) (3-8/23)
2871. Elwood, Richard, 74, (a Rev. patriot) d 9/24/25 in Springfield (Stewart's
Patent) (3-10/3)
2872. Ely, Samuel M. m 8/27/08 Rebecca Smith, dau of Jacob, in Clinton; Rev.
Clark (8-8/31)
2873. Ely, Stephen, merchant, d "lately" in Pleasant Valley (8-2/2/14)
2874. Emeigh, Jervis(?) m 1/20/26 Mary Ann Devine, dau of William, all of
Washington (Dut. Co.); Rev. Clark (8-2/1)
2875. Emerson, Charles m 12/28/24 Betsey Curliss in Warren; Rev. Swan. All of
Warren (3-1/17/25)
2876. Emes, Henry, Esq. m 10/4/10 Rachel Schruyver, both of Clinton (Dut. Co.),
in Hyde Park; Rev. Clark (8-10/10)
2877. Emes, Jesse (Capt.), 89, d 5/7/29 in Staatsburgh (8-5/27)
2878. Emigh, Daniel m 1/23/22 Rhoda Manny, both of Beekman; Rev. De Witt (8-2/6)
2879. Emigh, Eve (Widow), 100, d 4/14/25 in Beekman (8-5/11)
2880. Emmons, Roxey Ann, 19, an only dau, d 10/26/21 at the house of her deceased
father, Maj. Asa (surv by her mother) (3-10/29)
2881. Emmons, Uri of NYC m 5/21/31 Phebe Carman of Hyde Park in Poughkeepsie;
Rev. Dr. Reed (8-5/25)
2882. Emott, _____, consort of Hon. James, d 11/28/17 in Poughkeepsie (8-12/3)
2883. Emott, Celia, 68, consort of William, Esq. of Poughkeepsie, d 12/31/15
(8-1/3/16)
2884. Emott, Melissa, consort of Hon. James, d 2/3/20 in Poughkeepsie (8-2/9)
2885. Emott, William, Esq. m 7/6/25 in Poughkeepsie (born in New Jersey but
lived in Poughkeepsie "for about half a century") (8-7/13)
2886. Eno, Olive, wf of Stephen, Esq., d 2/8/18 in Northeastern (8-2/11)
2887. Ensign, Anson m 12/31/28 Julia Rhodes. All of Amenia; Rev. Armstrong
(8-1/21/29)
2888. Ensign, Lewis (Capt.) of Albany m 12/11/29 Elizabeth Dumbleton of NYC in
Brooklyn; Rev. Covil (1-1/28/30)

83

2889. Ensign, William (Capt.), 39, formerly of Albany, d 2/19/30 in NYC (1-2/24)
2890. Ensworth, Lucy (Mrs.), 60, relict of late Jedediah, d 12/28/22 in Mansfield, CT (3-1/20/23)
2891. Epps, Henry of Watervliet d 10/7/31 "in the Lunatic Asylum, Hudson" (1-10/11)
2892. Ernst, John Frederick, Jr. of Cooperstown m 8/18/02 Catherine Bidelman, youngest dau of Valentine, Esq. of Sussex Co., NJ; Rev. John Frederick Ernst of Cooperstown, NY (6-8/31)
2893. Ernst, John Frederick (Rev.), Lutheran minister of the church in Manheim, NY, d 10/24/05 in M (surv by several ch) (6-11/12 and 1-11/21)
2894. Ernst, William G. (Rev.) of Marietta (state not given - perhaps intended for the village in Onondaga Co., NY) m 3/28/15 Elizabeth McCammon in Lancaster, PA (bridegroom the brother of John F. Ernst of Cooperstown, NY; bride the dau of John McCammon, Esq. of Middletown [state not given]) (3-4/20)
2895. Erwin, David (Gen.), 74, d 12/9/31 in Westville(pioneer settler there) (4 [Keeseville Herald]-1/3/32)
2896. Esble?, Eber m 4/29/04 Susannah Jacobs, both of Rhinebeck; Rev. Quitman (8-5/8)
2897. Esmond, Joseph m 2/18/13 Chloe Hathaway, both of Hillsdale, in H (6-2/23)
2898. Esselstyn, Richard M. m 7/24/03 Charity Van Hoesen, both of Hudson; Rev. Judd (6-7/26)
2899. Estill, Wallace (Capt.), 72, (a Rev. officer) m 4/27/30 Miss Mary Braim, 54, both of Franklin Co. (1-5/19)
2900. Eustace, John Skey, 45, d 8/31/05 (probably near Newburgh) (fought in the French Revolution as a Major General) (6-9/3)
2901. Evans, Alfred of Broome Co. m 7/22/29 Lucinda Williams, dau of Judge Williams of Berkshire, Tioga Co., in Berkshire; Rev. Bush (8/4)
2902. Evans, Thomas G. (Dr.), about 40, d 8/515/29 in Goshen (1-8/17)
2903. Evens, Roger m 10/20/03 Elizabeth Backus in Claverack; Rev. Gephard (6-10/25)
2904. Ever, William I. (Rev.) (Lutheran minister at Rhinebeck and Wittenberg, [Dut. Co.]) m 5/7/29 Charlotte Havemeyer, oldest dau of Frederick of NYC, in St. Matthew's Church; Rev. S. Geissenheimer, Jr. (1-5/13)
2905. Everest, Deborah, wf of James of Lansingburgh, d 12/21/02 (9-12/28)
2906. Everest, James m 10/1/02 Deborah Green, both of Lansingburgh; Elder Caleb Green (9-10/6)
2907. Everett, Abigail, 48, wf of Jesse formerly of Albany, d 2/6/29 in NYC (1-2/25)
2908. Everett, Jediah (Mrs.), 66, d 11/7/27 in Warren, CT ("She was thrown from a wagon on her return from public worship") (9-11/16)
2909. Everett, Jesse of Stephentown m 12/28/05 Mary Morey of Lansingburgh (9-1/7/06)
2910. Everhard, Joseph from Germany m 12/31/20 Ellen Margaret Sluiterman, late of Amsterdam (country or state not given), in Plattsburgh, NY (7-1/13/21)
2911. Everingham, Gilbert, 73, d 4/21/31 in NYC (1-4/28)
2912. Everitt, Abigail, wid of Richard, Esq., d 12/19/26 in Poughkeepsie (8-12/20)
2913. Everitt, Benjamin, Esq., 79, d 1/22/18 at his home in Fishkill (8-1/28)
2914. Everitt, Harvey E. m 1/23/22 Arietta Maria Luyster; Rev. De Witt. All of Fishkill. (8-2/6)
2915. Everitt, Helen Maria, 7 mo, dau of John, d 5/17/06 in Poughkeepsie (8-5/20)
2916. Everitt, John d 11/7/17 in Poughkeepsie (8-11/12)
2917. Everitt, John d 6/23/32 at his home in New Hackensack (Dut. Co.) (8-6/27)
2918. Everitt, Mary, 25, consort of John, d 2/27/11 (surv by her husband and her parents [not named]) (8-3/6)
2919. Everitt, Philip, 15, s of late Richard of Poughkeepsie, d 12/1/25 in Poughkeepsie (8-12/7)
2920. Everitt, R. John, Esq., attorney, of Poughkeepsie m 6/16/30 Elizabeth Reynolds, dau of Philip, Esq. of Johnstown (Mont. Co.), in NYC; Rev. W. Berrian (1-6/19 and 8-6/23)
2921. Everitt, Richard, Esq., 75, d 9/21/24 in Poughkeepsie (buried with Masonic honors) (8-10/6)
2922. Everitt, Samuel S., about 25, d 10/13/27 in Poughkeepsie (8-10/17)

84

2923. Everitt, William H., formerly of Poughkeepsie, m 6/8/27 Susan Braverse of NYC in Bloomingdale; Rev. Gunn (8-6/13)
2924. Everson, Cornelia, consort of George B., d 1/29/08 in Poughkeepsie (8-2/3)
2925. Everson, Jacob R., 25, s of Jacob of Pleasant Valley, d 2/2/03 in the West Indies (8-3/29/03)
2926. Everson, Margaret, 63, wid of Jacob, Esq., d 11/18/07 in Newburgh (buried in Pleasant Valley, "her late residence") (8-11/25)
2927. Everts, Charles of Plattsburgh m Anna Carpenter of Middlebury, VT in M; Rev. Cheney (7-3/11/20)
2928. Everts, John, 49, d 7/22/12 ("when thrown from his wagon descending Beecraft mountain near Hudson with a load of stone") (6-8/3)
2929. Everts, Stephen, 69, (a Rev. soldier) d in Stanford (Dut. Co.) (8-1/27/30)
2930. Evertsen, John d "recently" in Albany (funeral from his late home, 65 Fox St.) (1-11/18/31)
2931. Evertson, Alida, 51, wf of John, d 7/8/29 in Albany (funeral from 65 Fox St.) (1-7/11)
2932. Evertson, George B., Esq., formerly of Poughkeepsie, d 8/12/29 in Ithaca (8-8/19)
2933. Evertson, Jacob, Jr. m 2/5/29 Elizabeth Cluett, oldest dau of late Garret, all of Albany; Rev. Dr. John Ludlow (1-2/7)
2934. Evertson, Jacob, 61, d 7/12/29 in Albany (funeral from his late home, 22 Fox St.) (1-7/14)
2935. Evertson, Walter, Esq. of Poughkeepsie m 10/22/07 Elizar Rosevelt, dau of C. C., Esq. of NYC, in NYC; Rev. Dr. Livingston (8-10/28)
2936. Evitts, Submit (Mrs.), 85, d in Salisbury, CT (6-1/26/02)
2937. Eyer, William I. (Rev.), Lutheran minister in Rhinebeck and Wittenberg, m Charlotte Havemeyer, oldest dau of Frederick of NYC, at St. Mathew's Church in NYC; Rev. Geissenheimer, Jr. (8-5/13/29)
2938. Fairbanks, Charles L. m 9/16/30 Sarah Ann Gilmore, dau of Robert of New Milford, in New Milford; Rev. Adams (1-9/25)
2939. Fairchild, Benjamin, 36, d 12/18/01 in Hudson (6-12/24)
2940. Fairchild, Gabriel, 41, d 3/10/26 in Milfordville (3-3/20)
2941. Fairchild, Isaac (Capt.) m 10/24/31 Elizabeth Martin, both of Bethlehem; Rev. Campbell of Albany (1-11/19)
2942. Fairchild, James, 77, of Patterson (Put. Co.) d 11/12/15 in Hudson (6-11/21)
2943. Fairchild, John F., printer and stationer, m 6/8/07 Flavia Merrill in Sherburne; Joel Thompson, Esq. All of Sherburne (3-6/25)
2944. Fairchild, Lucy, 34, wf of William, d 5/12/22 in Unadilla (3-5/20)
2945. Fairchild, William m 1/4/04 Lucy Higby, both of Cooperstown; Rev. Daniel Nash (3-1/5)
2946. Fairlee, Louisa, dau of late James of NYC, d 9/17/31 in Bristol, PA (1-9/23)
2947. Fairman, Elizur m 10/12/20 Emmeline Beebe, oldest dau of Levi, Esq., in Hartwick; Rev. Henry Chapman (3-10/16)
2948. Fairman, Richard, 33, engraver, d 12/1/21 in Philadelphia (state not given) (3-12/17)
2949. Fake, _____ (Mr.) d 2/22/16 in Pittstown (fatally injured when thrown from a wagon while returning from Lansingburgh) (9-2/27)
2950. Falk, Lawrence, Jr., merchant, m 10/20/29 Lucinda Phelps, dau of Col. Darius Phelps of Broome (Schoharie Co.), in B; Rev. Spoore (1-11/11)
2951. Falls, Hiram of the firm of Veltman and Falls,Newburgh, m 12/11/28 Deborah Birdsall of Newburgh in NYC; Rev. John Johnston (9-12/16)
2952. Fancher, John G., Jr. m 8/1/33 Ann Johnson, both of Essex, in E; Rev. B. Hitchcock (7-8/10)
2953. Fancher, Matilda, 39, wf of Samuel N., Esq., d 2/15/34 in Poughkeepsie (member of Methodist Episcopal Ch.) ("Her funeral and that of her twin babes a few days old were attended on the 16th inst.") (8-2/19)
2954. Fanning, Annah Dorothy, inf dau of Hiram, d 9/19/31 (funeral from the home of her father, 279 North Market St.) (1-9/20)
2955. Fanning, Frederick, about 40, d 8/16/08 in Preston, CT (6-8/30)
2956. Fanning, Maria Angelica, 25, wf of Hiram, d 10/25/31 in Albany (funeral from 279 North Market St.) (1-10/26)
2957. Fanning, Patrick, merchant, m 11/5/15 Susan A. Thurston; Rev. Gregory T. Bedell. All of Hudson (6-11/7)
2958. Fanning, Robert Walter, 6, s of Robert B., d 11/22/29 in Poughkeepsie (8-11/25)

2959. Fanning, Thomas, Jr. m 9/21/11 Mary Mills, both of Poughkeepsie; Rev. Cuyler (8-9/25)
2960. Fanning, William J., 4 mo, s of Robert B. of Poughkeepsie, d 2/8/32 (8-2/15)
2961. Fardon, Sachariah m 4/23/08 Mary Giddings, both of Dover; John Jewitt, Esq. (8-5/4)
2962. Faribault, J. N., Esq., about 35, d 8/17/27 in Plattsburgh (born in Canada; was an advocate of the Court of the King's Bench, Montreal, Can.)(funeral sermon by Rev. Quinlan) (7-8/25)
2963. Farley, Alice McKeen (consort of William J., Esq. and dau of late Dr. Joseph McKeen, first Pres. of Bowdoin College) d in Thomastown, ME (8-5/23/27)
2964. Farlin, James Warren, s of Dudley of Warrensburgh, m 2/15/31 Adeline Morgan, adopted dau of Hon. Roswell Weston of Sandy Hill, in Schroon (1-2/24)
2965. Farling, Sally, 30, consort of Andrew, d 11/4/02 in Cooperstown (3-11/11)
2966. Farling, William H. m 6/13/27 Hannah Vanhoesen, both of Troy; Rev. Martindale (9-6/15)
2967. Farnam, Frederick W., Esq., cashier of the Bank of Newburgh, d 5/3/30 in Newburgh (1-5/11 and 8-5/12)
2968. Farnham, David L., Esq. of Enosburgh, VT m 6/12/29 Hannah Collin, dau of David, in Hillsdale, Col. Co., NY; Rev. Timothy Woodbridge (1-6/17)
2969. Farnsworth, M. L. (Rev.) m 6/22/30 Joanne B. Gosman, dau of Jonathan B., Esq., in Danby (Tompkins Co.); Rev. Putnam. All of Danby (1-7/5)
2970. Farnsworth, Reuben, 62, d 8/19/13 in Burlington, VT (7-9/4)
2971. Farnum, John of Berlin m 5/15/15 Mary M. Staples of Troy at the Friends Meeting House in Troy (9-5/16)
2972. Farnum, Samuel J. of the firm of Southwick and Farnum, Newburgh, m 3/23/29 Sally Ann Swartwout, dau of late Benardus of Poughkeepsie; Rev. Dr. Cuyler (8-3/25)
2973. Farquhar, James, Esq., 88, d 10/21/31 in NYC (1-10/24)
2974. Farrington, Daniel of Poughkeepsie m 2/5/12 Jane Dates of Fishkill; Rev. Cuyler (8-2/12)
2975. Fasset, John V. of Troy m 9/15/28 Ann Maria Robinson of Bennington, VT in B; Rev. Daniel A. Clark (9-9/19)
2976. Fasset, Olive, 33, wf of Amos J., d 4/23/30 in Champlain (7-5/22)
2977. Favor, John (Capt.) of Rochester m 9/17/29 Sarah R. Bond, dau of Col. William M. of Lockport, in L; Rev. Castle (1-9/29)
2978. Fay, E., Esq., principal of Dutchess Academy, m 4/20/29 Mary Lee, dau of Samuel of Poughkeepsie, on board the steamer, "North America"; Rev. Dr. Reed (8-4/22)
2979. Fayer, Isaac I., 67, d 4/16/31 in Albany (son-in-law, Charles Smyth of 77 North Market St., Albany, is mentioned) (1-5/12)
2980. Fearing, Daniel B. of the firm of Hoyt and Co. of NYC, m 7/26/30 Harriet Richmond, dau of Samuel N. of Providence (state not given), in P; Rev. Dr. Crocker (1-7/31)
2981. Featherstonehaugh, George William, Esq., late of Duanesburgh, NY, m 1/28/31 Charlotte Williams Carter, youngest dau of Bernard M. Carter, Esq. of Virginia, in Philadelphia, PA; Rev. Dr. Abercrombie (1-9/12)
2982. Featherstonehaugh, Sarah G., 8, d in Duanesburgh (3-4/4/25)
2983. Feeter, _____ (Mrs.), 60, wf of Col. William, d 8/19/31 at Little Falls (1-9/6)
2984. Felie, Maria Ann, consort of Joseph, d 2/12/19 in Beekman (8-3/24)
2985. Fellows, Abraham m 3/9/15 Harriet Chichester; Rev. Coe. All of Troy (9-3/14)
2986. Fellows, Lewis of NYC m 3/4/28 Emily Schell of Rhinebeck in R; Rev. G. W. Bethune (8-3/12)
2987. Fellows, Lucy, 30, wf of Joshua, d 5/5/07 in Hudson (6-5/12)
2988. Fellows, Samuel, 21, private, 8th Regiment, NY Detached Militia (in Ensign Edwards' Company), d 12-10/12 in Chazy (7-12/18)
2989. Felyhousen, Barent W., 28, formerly of Albany, d 5/17/31 in Schenectady (1-5/24)
2990. Fenner, J. P., Esq. m 10/4/19 Frances D. Gardner, both of Washington City (D.C.); Rev. Hawley (8-10/13)

2991. Fenner, Thomas, Esq. of Poughkeepsie m 107/06 Mrs. Dorothy Alder of NYC
in NYC (8-1021)
2992. Fenner, Thomas, 66, d 1/17/15 in Poughkeepsie (born in Canterbury, England;
lived for many years in Poughkeepsie, NY) (8-1/18)
2993. Fenner, Thomas, 25, formerly of Poughkeepsie, d 10/4/20 in Mount Vernon,
IN (8-11/22)
2994. Fenno, Edward (Capt.) d before 11/10/23 in New Orleans. LA (3-12/22)
2995. Fenno, George, Esq., 43, d 4/18/29 in Mount Upton (Ots. Co.) (1-4/28)
2996. Fenno, John W., 23, bookseller, formerly proprietor and editor of the
Gazette of the United States, d in NYC (6-3/16/02)
2997. Fenton, Horace m Rheuma Abbot in Rutland, VT (9-2/9/27)
2998. Fenton, Mary (Widow), 80, d 12/628 in Boston (state not given) (9-12/19)
2999. Fenton, Richard F. of Burlington (Ots. Co.) m 9/3/23 Sally Tew of Otsego
in O; Rev. Smith (3-9/8)
3000. Fergerson, George D., Esq. of Johnstown (Mont. Co.) m 2/18/29 Elizabeth
Easton of Troy in T; Rev. Mark Tucker (1-2/27)
3001. Ferguson, Robert m 9/16/32 Luretta Fisher in Essex; William Smith, Esq.
(double ceremony - see marr of Jerome Fisher) (4 [Essex Republican]-
9/29)
3002. Ferguson, William (Capt.) of Poughkeepsie m 8/21/34 Susan Matholf, dau of
Capt. James of NYC; Rev. Dunbar (double ceremony - see marr of Edwin
Lockwood, Esq.) (8-9/3)
3003. Ferris, Benjamin, Esq., 65, d 7/25/29 in Westchester (formerly a state
assemblyman from Westchester Co.) (1-7/30)
3004. Ferris, Benjamin G., Esq. m 5/10/30 Cornelia Woodcock, oldest dau of Hon.
David, in Ithaca; Rev. Keep (1-5/17)
3005. Ferris, Embres m 9/17/25 Phebe Worden, both of Pawling; Rev. Johnson
(8-9/28)
3006. Ferris, Marian (Miss), 18, dau of Solomon, d 3/11/30 at her father's home
in New Paltz (8-3/17)
3007. Ferris, Nathan m 3/25/15 Jerusha Maps, both of Ancram; James Lester, Esq.
(6-4/18)
3008. Ferris, Nathaniel, merchant, formerly of Poughkeepsie, m 12/20/21 Mary D.
Warne, dau of Elbert P. of NYC, in NYC (8-12/26)
3009. Ferris, Reed, farmer, of Pawling d 3/18/04 (8-4/3)
3010. Ferris, Samuel C., 15, s of Solomon, d at his father's home in New Paltz
(consumption) (8-6/2/30)
3011. Fessenden, William, 36, editor and printer of the Brattleborough Reporter,
d 1/20/15 at South Hampton (presumably on Long Island, NY) (9-1/31)
3012. Fetridge, Edward m 2/17/19 Catharine Eager, both of Troy; Rev. Dr. Coe
(9-2/23)
3013. Fidler, Elizabeth, 16, dau of Robert, d 9/4/06 in Hudson (6-9/9)
3014. Fidler, Lancelot of Hudson m 4/4/11 Mary Taylor, dau of John, merchant,
of Albany, in A; Rev. Ostrander (6-4/12)
3015. Field, Arthur (Rev.) d 7/14/24 in New Berlin (3-7/26)
3016. Field, Fanny (Mrs.), dau of S. Kellogg Field of Troy, d 3/21/29 in
Montreal, Mass. (sic) (1-4/2)
3017. Field, Henry, 25, s of Joseph C., Esq., sheriff of Dutchess County,
d 10/21/11 (consumption) (8-10/23)
3018. Field, Joseph C., Esq., formerly sheriff of Dutchess County, d 7/24/13
in NYC (8-7/28)
3019. Field, Martha (Mrs.), widow of late John, d 4/24/28 in Poughkeepsie
(8-4/30)
3020. Field, Reuben of Troy m 11/5/19 Martha McQueen of Waterford; Rev. Sommers
(9-11/7)
3021. Fields, Hiram m 11/25/27 Elizabeth Wheeler, both of Troy; Rev. Howard
(9-11/30)
3022. Fields, John of Poughkeepsie m "a few days since" Martha Hughson of
Fishkill (8-9/11/98)
3023. Fields, William C., merchant, m Evelina Dean in Laurens; Rev. King
(1-9/3/29)
3024. Fifield, Daniel m 12/25/21 Sally McFarland in Beekmantown (Clinton Co.);
Rev. Joel Byington (7-12/29)
3025. Fifield, Moses m 11/21/31 Juliette A. Howard; Rev. Welch. All of Albany
(1-11/24)

3026. Filkins, Henry of Troy m 5/21/21 Martha Dyer of Watervliet; Rev. Dr. Coe
       (9-5/29)
3027. Filkins, Henry of New Paltz m 4/17/31 Eliza Worden of Pleasant Valley in
       Union Vale; Rev. Bronson (8-4/27)
3028. Filkins, Thomas of Pittstown m 3/20/08 Mary Storer of Troy (9-3/22)
3029. Fillmore, De La Fayette, 20, master's mate of U.S. ship "Peacock" and
       son of Lavius of Middlebury, VT, d at Gosport Navy Yard (in VA)
       (7-10/2/19)
3030. Fillmore, P. P., Esq. of Middlebury, VT m 3/13/34 Mildred Cooper of
       Champlain, NY "in Champlain (Lower Village)"; Rev. Kenney (7-3/22)
3031. Fillmore, Phebe, 49, consort of Nathaniel, Eq. of Aurora (Erie Co.), NY
       d 4/2/31 in Aurora (deceased is mother of "Mr. Fillmore"of the NY state
       assembly) (1-4/13)
3032. Finch, Golbert, 24, d 12/31/15 in Canaan (while tending a coal pit)
       (6-1/2/16)
3033. Finch, James m 9/1/11 Catherine Platt in Plattsburgh; Rev. Halsey
       (7-9/6)
3034. Finch, James m 8/15/27 Elizabeth McDonald, both of NYC; Rev. Dr. Reed
       (8-8/22)
3035. Finch, James M. m 8/21/31 Lucretia Ames at the Baptist Church in Keeseville;
       Rev. Bryant (4 [Keeseville Herald]-9/6)
3036. Finch, Samuel d 2/27/23 in Ballston Spa (buried with Masonic honors)
       (2-3/4)
3037. Fink, Elias of the firm of Fink and Gray m 7/7/30 Martha Newman, dau of
       Henry, Esq., in Albany; Rev. Mayer (1-7/8)
3038. Finkle, William m 7/7/11 Maria Highdecker, both of Gallatin; John W.
       Reichter, Esq. (6-8/2)
3039. Finnay, Nathaniel, 31, d 3/10/11 (6-3/15)
3040. Fish, John m 11/6/19 Sarah Wickoff in Otsego (3-11/15)
3041. Fish, William L., editor of the Waterford Reporter, m 11/20/23 Ruth Dow
       of Waterford in W (2-12/2)
3042. Fisher, Amy Kendall, 40, wf of John N., d 11/12/31 in Albany (funeral
       from her husband's home, 215 North Market St.) (1-11/15)
3043. Fisher, Betsey, 51, consort of Thomas, d in Keene, NH (6-12/2/06)
3044. Fisher, Fairlee m 3/29/27 Malona Delong in Beekmantown (Clinton Co.)
       (7-3/31)
3045. Fisher, Henry, only s of Rufus, Esq., m 9/22/29 Mary C. Hedges, only dau
       of William, Esq., in Lansingburgh; Rev. McIlvaine. All of Lansingburgh
       (1-9/24)
3046. Fisher, James C. (Dr.) m 5/9/31 Eliza Sparks, dau of late Samuel of
       Philadelphia (PA?), in Paterson, NY; Rev. Samuel Fisher (1-5/14)
3047. Fisher, Jerome m 9/16/32 Eliza Winslow in Essex; William Smith, Esq.
       (double ceremony - see marr of Robert Ferguson) (4[Essex Republican]-
       9/29)
3048. Fisk, Benjamin m 10/14/19 Minerva Allen, both of Plattsburgh; Rev. Halsey
       (7-10/16)
3049. Fisk, Harvey (Rev.) of New Jersey m Anna Maria Plumb in Lodi; Rev. E. M.
       Spencer (1-2/28/29)
3050. Fisk, Jared, 46, d 2/22/19 (6-3/2)
3051. Fisk, Jonathan, Esq. of Newburgh m Mrs. Sally Onderdonk of Poughkeepsie;
       Rev. Chase (8-1/19/02)
3052. Fitch, Aaron, 39, innkeeper, d 7/12/26 in Cooperstown (3-7/17)
3053. Fitch, Benjamin, 48, d 4/4/16 in Salem (died of a fractured skull
       "given by Mr. John Gitty of Hebron, the latter committed to gaol for
       trial") (3-4/11)
3054. Fitch, Caleb M. m Temperance Davis in Chatham (6-10/8/01)
3055. Fitch, Charles (Rev.) of Cherry Valley, NY m Sarah Hamilton of Princeton,
       NJ in P (3-6/17/22)
3056. Fitch, Cypran (Capt.), 59, d 2/28/13 in Canaan (6-3/9)
3057. Fitch, George of Troy m 5/11/28 Susan Denslow of New Haven (state not
       given) in New Haven; Rev. Merwin (9-5/30)
3058. Fitch, Jabez, Esq., 77, (a Rev. officer) d 1/5/29 at his home in
       Saratoga Springs (1-1/15)
3059. Fitch, John, one of the editors of the Middlebury Mercury, m Charlotte
       Mosely in Middlebury, VT (6-10/9/04)

88

3060. Fitch, Nathaniel of Pawlet, VT d 7/28/14 in Troy, NY (9-8/2)
3061. Fitch, Nehemiah (Deacon), 80, d 4/7/22 in Plainfield (Ots. Co.) (3-4/15)
3062. Fitch, Samuel m 11/14/02 Naomy Sumner in Franklin (6-11/23)
3063. Fitch, Timothy, Esq., attorney, of Batavia m Mary Eliza Beecher of
      Westfield in W; Rev. Samuel Orton (1-7/26/31)
3064. Fitzhugh, William W., 45, formerly of Alexandria, VA, d 6/26/31 in
      Frederick, VA (1-7/13)
3065. Flacler, Isaac m 9/30/13 Jane B. Ward, dau of Col. Joshua; Rev. Clark.
      All of Clinton (Dut. Co.) (8-10/27)
3066. Flagg, Artemas m B ? Squires, both of Richmond, VT in R (7-10/11/17)
3067. Flagg, Hezekiah, Esq., attorney, late of Cooperstown, NY d in Charleston,
      SC (3-7/23/21)
3068. Flagg, Keziah (Miss), 23, d 11/17/21 in Essex, VT (typhus) (7-12/1)
3069. Flagler, ____, consort of Thomas, merchant, of New Hamburgh, d 7/18/17
      in New Hamburgh (8-7/23)
3070. Flagler, Alvah m 10/24/27 Margaret Adriance of Pleasant Valley in P.V.;
      Rev. Welton (8-10/31)
3071. Flagler, Henry, merchant, m 5/26/25 Maria Adriance, dau of G. Adriance,
      Esq.; Rev. Clark. All of Pleasant Valley (8-6/1)
3072. Flagler, John O. (Dr.) m 10/4/31 Christina Van Vleck in Kinderhook; Rev.
      Jacob Sickles (1-10/8)
3073. Flagler, Lewis, merchant, of Pleasant Valley m 11/27/14 Maria Vanderburgh,
      dau of Henry, Esq. of Clinton (Dut. Co.) (8-11/30)
3074. Flagler, Maria, 32, wf of Henry, Esq. and dau of Garret Adriance, Esq.,
      d 12/11/34 in Pleasant Valley (surv by husband and 3 small ch) (8-12?24)
3075. Flagler, Martha, wf of Solomon, d 7/23/27 in Pleasant Valley (8-7/25)
3076. Flagler, Peter m 3/30/19 Mrs. Catharine Myers, wid of late Samuel of
      Poughkeepsie; Rev. Cuyler (8-4/7)
3077. Flagler, Zachariah, 85, of Clinton (Dut. Co.) d 7/27/07 (8-9/9)
3078. Flanagan, Christopher, bookseller, of NYC d in Bedford (West. Co.)
      (9-9/24/05)
3079. Fleming, Margaret (Mrs.), 82, d 5/24/31 in NYC (8-6/1)
3080. Flint, Daniel, about 53, d 7/3/20 in Plattsburgh (buried with Masonic
      honors) (7-7/8)
3081. Flint, Hannah, 28, wf of Moses H., d 9/2/13 in Cooperstown (left 5 young
      children) (3-9/4)
3082. Flint, Hiram, merchant, m 3/2/31 Eliza Campbell, dau of Matthew, in
      Cherry Valley; Rev. Cowan. All of C. V. (1-3/10)
3083. Flint, Samuel m 5/4/17 Ann Dominy in Plattsburgh (7-5/10)
3084. Flower, Richard, Esq., 68, "a distinguished emigrant from England",
      d 9/2/29 at his home, Park House, in Albion, IL (1-10/1)
3085. Flowers, Lorenzo m 10/31/26 Cornelia Becker in Hartwick (3-11/6)
3086. Floyd, Benjamin (Col.), 80, (a Rev. officer) d in Suffolk County (8-6/6/21)
3087. Floyd, William (Gen.) (a Rev. officer) d 8/4/21 at his home in Western
      (Oneida Co.)(one of the signers of the Declaration of Independence -
      only three other signers still alive at time of his death: John Adams,
      Thomas Jefferson, and Charles Carrol) (surv by wf, children, and grand
      children) (3-8/6 and 8-8/15)
3088. Folger, ____ (Mrs.), 73, d 3/3/19 in Athens, NY (6-3/23)
3089. Folger, Abishai, 70, d 3/7/14 in Hudson (6-3/15)
3090. Folger, Elisha m 9/3/15 Amy Sanford in Queensbury; William Robards, Esq.
      All of Queensbury (9-9/12)
3091. Folger, George L., 25, s of Benjamin F. of Hudson, NY, d 9/7/18 in New
      Orleans, LA (yellow fever) (6-10/27)
3092. Folger, John m 9/8/03 Maria Van Loan, both of Loonenburg (Athens), NY,
      in L (6-9/13)
3093. Folger, Laban (Capt.), formerly of Hudson, NY, d "lately" in Montreal,
      Canada (6-5/4/10)
3094. Folger, Lydia, 16, dau of Widow Deborah, d 8/26/10 in Athens, NY (6-8/31)
3095. Folger, Nathan (Capt.), 66, d 8/17/03 in hudson (6-8/23)
3096. Folger, Obed. W. m Mary Fitch of Chatham in C (6-12/24/01)
3097. Folger, Reuben C. m 5/8/10 Nancy Bates in Hudson; Rev. Cooper (double
      ceremony - see Horace Bowman) (6-5/18)
3098. Folger, Reuben W. m 2/29/12 Frances Sampson, both of Hudson (6-3/9)
3099. Folger, William, 20, s of late Abraham, d in Hudson (6-10/14/06)

3100. Follet, William, 62, d 3/10/08 in Pittstown (surv by wf, 8 children, and his father) (9-3/22)
3101. Follett, Mary, 3 mo, dau of F. M. and Susan Follett, d 7/11/31 in Albany (1-7/13)
3102. Follett, Nancy, 28, wf of Oran, one of the editors of the Buffalo Journal, d 3/16/30 in Buffalo (1-3/23)
3103. Folts, Melchert, Esq., 83, (a Rev. patriot) d 5/2/29 in Herkimer ("he kept a regular history...in the German language in a plain manner with his left hand" his having suffered [in 1802] a paralytic stroke which left him unable to speak") (1-5/18)
3104. Fonda, Abraham L. (Capt.) d 2/8/31 in Claverack (born there and always lived there) (surv by wf and children) (1-2/14 and 8-2/16)
3105. Fonda, David, 48, merchant, of Albany d 8/3/05 in Ballston Springs (9-8/13)
3106. Fonda, Douw I., Esq., formerly sheriff of Saratoga Co., d "a short time since" in Albany (9-1/13/07)
3108. Fonda, Eliza, 24, wf of Maj. John L., d 3/24/12 in Poughkeepsie (8-4/1)
3109. Fonda, James H. of Poughkeepsie m 8/16/32 Aminta K. Wood, dau of John A., Esq. of Pleasant Valley; Rev. Dr. Reed (8-8/22)
3110. Fonda, Jelles, 72, d 5/4/30 in Schenectady (1-5/7)
3111. Fonda, Jesse (Rev.), 40, (pastor of the Reformed Dutch Church in Montgomery (Orange Co.),d in M (8-5/16/27)
3112. Fonda, John m 8/21/14 Patty Baringer, both of Brunswick; Rev. Coe (9-8/23)
3113. Fonda, John L. m 2/5/15 Helen Kelsey, both of Poughkeepsie; Rev. Reed (8-2/8)
3114. Fonda, Richard J.,merchant, m 3/23/25 Amy Pine, dau of Samuel, all of Poughkeepsie; Rev. Dr. Reed (8-3/30)
3115. Fonda, Ryckman G., 13 mo, s of James H., d 9/24/34 in Poughkeepsie (8-10/1)
3116. Fonda, Thomas H. of Rhinebeck m 1/10/28 Elizabeth Allen of Poughkeepsie; Rev. Dr. Reed (8-1/16)
3117. Foot, Charles A. (Hon.), attorney and late congressman, d 8/1/28 in Delhi, NY (pulmonary complaint) (9-8/5)
3118. Foot, Ebenezer, Esq., attorney, d 7/21/14 in Albany (9-7/26 and 9-7/28)
3119. Foot, Henry Smith, 4, s of Dr. Lyman Foot, surgeon, U.S. Army, d 3/24/27 in Plattsburgh (7-3/31)
3120. Foot, Isaac, 32, d 12/25/21 in Plattsburgh (surv by wf and 1 child) (7-12/29)
3121. Foot, John m 1/5/30 Hannah Bishop, both of Poughkeepsie; Rev. Dr. Cuyler (8-1/13)
3122. Foot, Lucius of Burlington (Ots. Co.) m Electa Harwood in Winfield; Rev. Hovey (3-5/3/24)
3123. Foot, Lyman (Dr.) of the U.S. Army m 8/26/21 Ann T. Platt, dau of Isaac C. of Plattsburgh; Rev. Halsey (7-9/21)
3124. Foote, Ebenezer (Hon.), 74, (a Rev. patriot) d 12/28/29 at Arbor Hill in Delhi, NY (for many years first judge of Delaware Co.) (1-1/4/30)
3125. Foote, Ebenezer, 74, (a Rev. soldier), for many years one of the judges of Delaware Co., d 1/4/30 at Arbor Hill in the town of Poughkeepsie (8-1/6/30)
3126. Foote, Elisha, Esq. of Cooperstown, NY m P. Blague of Saybrook, CT in S (3-11/12/31)
3127. Foote, Eliza J., 35, wf of Elisha, Esq., d 6/28/29 in Cooperstown (1-7/7)
3128. Foote, Levi B. of Burlington, VT m 10/29/22 Caroline Ferris of Peru, NY in P (7-11/9)
3129. Foote, Mary, 31, wf of Elisha, Esq., d 9/28/20 in Cooperstown (consumption) (3-10/2)
3130. Foquet, Douglass L. m 2/2/23 Rhoda Sperry, both of Plattsburgh, in P; Rev. Halsey (7-2/8)
3131. Forbes, Abner, 56, first assistant judge of Windsor Co. and president of the Bank of Windsor, d in Windsor, VT (1-1/13/29)
3132. Forbes, Polly, 18, dau of Elisha, d 10/17/12 at Sandy Hill (Wash. Co.) (9-11/3)
3133. Forbus, Benjamin (Capt.), 40, d 10/29/25 (consumption) ("Affectionate as a son and a brother ...") (8-11/2)

3134. Forbus, John, 70, d 10/24/27 in Poughkeepsie (lived there many years)
(8-10/31)
3135. Forbus, Martha, 60, consort of John, d 5/25/18 in Poughkeepsie (member of
Baptist Ch.) (surv by husband and children) (8-5/27)
3136. Forbus, Mary (Miss), dau of John, Esq.,d 9/30/25 in Poughkeepsie (8-10/5)
3137. Forby, William m 4/10/31 Catharine Jane Sickles, dau of James; Rev. Green.
All of Albany (1-4/25)
3138. Force, David m 8/26/04 Hannah Reynolds; William D. Williams, Esq. All of
Beekman (8-9/4)
3139. Ford, Charles H. L., merchant, of Lawrenceville m 6/24/30 Eliza M. Cruger,
youngest dau of Daniel, Esq. of Syracuse, in S; Rev. Dyer (1-6/26)
3140. Ford, Horace, 26, d 1/1/27 in Plattsburgh (funeral sermon by Rev. T.
Addams)(7-1/8)
3141. Ford, Lauren, Esq. of Herkimer, NY m 10/9/16 Mary Kingman of Bridgewater,
MA in B; Rev. Flint (6-10/22)
3142. Ford, Nathan, 65, d 3/29/29 at his home near Ogdensburgh (in 1797,
locating himself at the "Old Barracks", he founded the village of
Ogdensburgh) (1-4/6)
3143. Fordham, Thomas S. m 12/20/21 Sally Roberts; Rev. Halsey (7-12/29)
3144. Forman, Frederick, 13 mo, s of Hon Joshua, Esq., first judge of Onondaga
Co., d 8/29/13 in Hudson "while passing through ... on a journey with
his parents" (6-8/31)
3145. Forman, Isaac of Poughkeepsie m 1/15/20 Elthera Elliot of New Paltz; Rev.
Cuyler (8-1/26)
3146. Forman, Isaac, Jr. m 3/4/29 Mary Beadle, dau of Elisha, in Pleasant Valley;
Rev. Welton (8-3/11)
3147. Forman, Mary, wf of Aaron, d 4/2/00 in Poughkeepsie (8-4/8)
3148. Forman, E., Esq. of Paris m 11/5/29 Louisa Antoinette Bolsaubin, dau of
Vincent, Esq. of Morristown, NJ, at St. Peter's Church in NYC; Rev.
Dr. Power (1-11/9)
3149. Forsyth, Julia Frances, oldest dau of Hon. John, d 4/7/31 near Augusta
(1-5/6)
3150. Forsyth, Robert, Esq., 44. of Keeseville d 9/6/34 in Plattsburgh (7-9/13)
3151. Forsyth, Russell (Dr.) m 1/24/02 Sally Seymour, dau of Daniel of Lansingburgh; Rev. Coe (9-1/27)
3152. Fort, Abraham, 72, an old resident of Poughkeepsie,d 8/9/22 in Poughkeepsie
(surv by "an aged partner and a large family of children)(8-8/14)
3153. Fort?, Catharine, youngest dau of late Maj. Abraham, d 5/19/30 in Poughkeepsie (8-5/26)
3154. Fort, Gilbert, s of Capt. John "of the old village in Schaghticoke",
d 1/24/03 "at the old village" (9-2/15)
3155. Fort, Lewis, 22, d 11/2/05 in Cambridge (Rev. Frelich, Rev. Dunlap, and
Rev. Chapman participated in the funeral service) (9-11/12)
3156. Foster, Alfred M. m 11/17/31 Mary Ann Frear, dau of late John B., all of
Poughkeepsie; Rev. Dr. Cuyler (8-11/23)
3157. Foster, Amos (Col.) of Salisbury (Herk. Co.) m 11/4/30 Lucinda Todd, dau
of Samuel, in Fairfield (Herk. Co.); Rev. Messenger (1-11/16)
3158. Foster, Dwight (Hon.), 65, d in Brookfield, MA (3-5/19/23)
3159. Foster, Elizabeth, 74, wid of late Benjamin, one of the earliest
settlers in Westerlo, d (date and place not given) (1-10/27/31)
3160. Foster, James (Capt.) of NYC m 5/1/10 Ann Colson of Athens, NY in A;
Rev. Joseph Prentice (6-5/4)
3161. Foster, John m 12/14/05 Susan Gillespie, both of Lansingburgh; Rev. Coe
(9-12/24)
3162. Foster, Jonah m 6/14/14 Martha T. Nile, both of Cooperstown, in Milford
(3-6/22)
3163. Foster, Nathaniel, Esq., 56, magistrate and church officer, d 4/15/87
in Southeast Precinct (deceased was a Rev. soldier) (8-5/16)
3164. Fouquet, John Louis, 55, d 8/26/27 in Plattsburgh (in his youth
accompanied some of the first settlers in this region) (funeral
sermon by Rev. Chase) (7-9/1)
3165. Fouquet, Merin? m 1/9/28 Cynthia Gilman, both of Plattsburgh; Rev.
Frederick Halsey (7-1/19)
3166. Fournier, John m 8/15/27 Esther Marcaud in Plattsburgh; St. John B. I.
Skinner, Esq. (7-8/18)

91

3167. Fowler, Daniel, 81, formerly of Massachusetts, d in Hudson, NY (6-11/21/09)
3168. Fowler, George William m 3/16/27 Sally Coon; Rev. Butler. All of Troy (9-3/20)
3169. Fowler, Hubbard of Beekman m 3/17/11 Tina Miller of Schodack (8-3/20)
3170. Fowler, Isaac m 1/25/27 Carolin F. Dorlon, both of Troy; Rev. Butler (9-1/30)
3171. Fowler, Jacob, merchant, m 11/14/10 Ruth Clapp, both of Beekman; Rev. Cuyler (8-11/21)
3172. Fowler, John, 16, m 10/5/32 Nancy Buck, 15, (probably in Peru, NY); N. Rice, Esq. (4 [Keeseville Herald]-10/16)
3173. Fowler, Jonathan B. m 12/30/19 Philena Perry, both of White Creek, in W. C.; Rev. Daniel Finkum (9-1/11/20)
3174. Fowler, Martha E., 27, formerly of Pleasant Valley (Dut. Co.), d 5/12/34 in NYC (8-5/14)
3175. Fowler, Samuel S. of Albany m 2/23/29 Julia F. Gregory, dau of Abraham V. P. of Sand Lake, in S. L.; Rev. Justus Gregory (1-2/25)
3176. Fowler, Temperance, 77, wf of Daniel, d 4/14/07 in Hudson (6-4/28)
3177. Fox, Alanson, 42, one of the judges of Warren Co., d 7/13/29 in NYC. His body was brought to the vault "of the Hon. Mr. Lansing-burgh later to be interred in the Fox burying ground at the home of the deceased in Chester, Warren Co.". (1-7/24)
3178. Fox, Jabez, Esq., 35, clerk of Herkimer Co., d in Herkimer (3-2/7/25)
3179. Fox, Jacob M. (Col.), 83, (a Rev. officer) d 11/27/24 in Decatur (buried with Masonic honors) (3-12/6)
3180. Fox, Jonas of Ephratah d "recently". Dr. L. Doty testified ("death by intoxification") at the inquest. (1-6/30/29)
3181. Fox, Leander m Jane Ann Wigg(?), both of Poughkeepsie (8-11/14/32)
3182. Fox, Sarah, 35, (formerly of Otsego Co., NY), consort of Rev. James A. of Pinckneyville, Mississippi and sister of J. A. Otis, Esq. of Otsego Co., NY, d 6/24/26 "on her passage from New Orleans to New York" (3-8/14)
3183. Fraiser, Edward A. of Whitesboro m 11/3/31 Louisa A. Newell of Albany; Rev. B. T. Welch (1-11/4)
3184. Franchot, Pascal of Otsego Co. m 8/28/06 Catharine Hansen of Albany; Rev. Dr. Linn (3-9/11)
3185. Franchot, Paschal, Esq., late sheriff of Otsego Co., m 11/4/20 Deborah Hansen in Schenectady; Rev. Monteith (3-11/13)
3186. Franchuve, Samuel m 11/7/13 Matilda Lewis, both of Patterson; Rev. Dagget (8-12/8)
3187. Francis, John W. m 11/16/29 Maria Eliza Cutler in NYC; Rev. Cutler of Quincy (1-11/18)
3188. Francis, Joseph m 8/17/24 Risbie(?) Tankard in Plattsburgh; Rev. Whelpley (7-8/21)
3189. Francisco, Henry, 134 yrs old, d 10/25/20 near Whitehall, NY (born in England; "emigrated to this country about 80 or 90 years ago") (3-11/13)
3190. Francisco, Isaac m 12/20/23 Almira Coon in Pittstown; Rev. Griffin (9-1/6/24)
3191. Frank, Daniel, 44, drowned 9/26/09 "at the lower ferry" in Poughkeepsie (8-10/14)
3192. Frank, James m 10/13/27 Elizabeth Smalley; Rev. De Freest. All of Troy. (9-10/16)
3193. Franklin, Thomas, 67, register of NYC, d 4/30/39 in NYC (1-5/3)
3194. Frary, Cornelia, 4, youngest child of Giles, d 11/28/07 in Chatham (buried in Hudson) (6-12/1)
3195. Frary, Giles (Capt.), 41, d 2/16/03 (6-2/22)
3196. Frary, Harriet, 8, dau of Giles, d 1/12/06 in Chatham (6-1/21)
3197. Frary, Harry Croswell, 2, s of Jonathan, d 2/8/14 in Hudson (6-2/15)
3198. Frary, Jonathan of Albany m 2/6/10 Achsah Fowler of Hudson in H
3199. Fraser, Alexander, Sr., 74, d 4/6/19 in Athens, NY (6-4/13)
3200. Fraser, Daniel M. of Troy m 12/27/19 Sarah Numan of Cortright, Delaware Co., in Sand Lake; Rev. Dr. Coe (9-1/4/20)
3201. Fraser, Mary E., wf of William and only dau of Benjamin Haxton, Esq. of Catskill, d 8/15/32 in Athens, NY (her husband pre-deceased her by just a few hours) (8-8/22)

3202. Frats, Elias m 2/16/08 Nancy Van Derheyden, both of Troy; Rev. Coe (9-2/23)
3203. Frazer, Mary, 58, consort of James of Johnstown (Mont. Co.), d 7/18/30 (1-7/22)
3204. Frear, Baltus m 2/25/24 Lavina Westervelt, both of Poughkeepsie; Rev. C. C. Cuyler (8-3/10)
3205. Frear, Elizabeth, 25, consort of John B., d 8/10/16 in Poughkeepsie (8-8/14)
3206. Frear, Hannah, wf of Col. John, d "a few days since (in Poughkeepsie) at an advanced age" (8-5/21/00)
3207. Frear, Henry m 8/6/17 Dorcas Humphry, both of Troy; Rev. Dr. Coe (9-8/12)
3208. Frear, Jacobus, 70, farmer, of Poughkeepsie d 11/6/05 (8-11/12)
3209. Frear, John (Col.) m 4/3/92 Mrs. Hannah Snedeker, both of Poughkeepsie; Rev. Gray (8-4/5)
3210. Frear, John B. of Poughkeepsie m 12/15/12 Elizabeth Hagaman of Fishkill; Rev. Thomas Dewitt (8-12/30)
3211. Frear, Maria, wf of James B. of Poughkeepsie, d 1/17/31 (8-1/19)
3212. Frear, Mary, 73, wid of Simeon, d 7/22/27 in Poughkeepsie (8-7/25)
3213. Frear, Matilda, 26, wf of James B., d 8/15/25 in Poughkeepsie (8-8/17)
3214. Frear. Mindert m 2/21/20 Eliza Churchill; Rev. Leonard (8-12/27)
3215. Frear, Mynard, 33, d 6/26/30 in Poughkeepsie (8-6/30)
3216. Frear, Simeon I. (Capt.) of Poughkeepsie, father of John S., Esq. of Poughkeepsie, d 12/22/17 (8-12/31)
3217. Fredenburgh, Elizabeth, 6, dau of Dr. Benjamin B., d 12/3/30 in Coeymans (1-12/18)
3218. Free, Alva H. m 11/23/31 Rebecca Bennet, dau of Thomas, Esq. of Syracuse, in Troy; Rev. Tucker (8-11/30)
3219. Free, Deborah, 58, wf of John I., 69, d 8/21/32 in Poughkeepsie (8-9/5)
3220. Free, James B. m 1/2/28 Jane Ketcham, dau of Israel, all of Poughkeepsie; Rev. Welton (8-1/9)
3221. Freeland, Anna Eliza, 3, d in Claverack (her clothing caught fire) (6-11/9/10)
3222. Freeman, George of Albany m 8/23/15 Lydia V. Burr, formerly of Troy, in Albany; Rev. De Witt (9-8/29)
3223. Freeman, Nathan m Mrs. Elsie Whipple in New Brunswick, NJ (8-2/4/29)
3224. Freeman, P. G. m 10/26/27 Helen Harris of Poughkeepsie; Rev. Welton (8-10/31)
3225. Freeman, Phineas G., 25, d 1/23/29 in Poughkeepsie ("the artillery company of which he was a member attended his funeral"; Rev. Welton preached the funeral sermon in the Presbyterian Church) (8-1/28)
3226. Freeman, Robert of Clintonville m Elizabeth Roberts of Glens Falls; Rev. Fox (4 [Keeseville Herald]-10/16/32)
3227. Freligh, Daniel of Clinton m 10/3/11 Ann Bragaw of Poughkeepsie; Rev. C. C. Cuyler (8-10/9)
3228. Freligh, John G. m 9/20/12 Margaret Savage, both of Plattsburgh, in P (7-9/25)
3229. Frelot, Gilbert, inf s of Dr. I. W. Frelot, d 9/26/27 inTroy (9-10/2)
3230. French, C. m 2/14/11 Eliza Power, dau of Nicholas, all of Poughkeepsie; Rev. Wayland (8-2/27)
3231. French, Daniel of NYC m 5/19/27 Ann Maria Chapman of Troy; Rev. Butler (9-5/22)
3232. French, David B. m 9/16/23 Elizabeth Bain in Argyle; Rev. F. Bullion (9-9/23)
3233. French, Ebenezer (Capt.) d 9/25/23 in Milton (2-9/30)
3234. French, Eliza (Mrs.), 28, dau of Nicholas Power formerly of Poughkeepsie, d 9/21/20 in Trenton, NJ (8-9/27)
3235. French, Jane (Miss), 21, dau of Bronson French, d 2/6/30 in Poughkeepsie (8-2/10)
3236. French, Joel K. m 10/10/32 Mary Jane Putnam in Lewis; Rev. E. Benedict (4 [Essex Republican]-10/13)
3237. French, John m 10/28/17 Polly Maria Chatfield, both of Bedford, CT; Rev. Dr. Covel (8-11/5)
3238. French, Maynard of the firm of Gill, French, and Webster of Albany m 1/21/29 Julia Ann Eames, granddaughter of Judge Sanger of New Hartford, in New Hartford; Rev. Treadway (1-1/28)

3239. French, S. A., 21, s of John, sheriff of Montgomery Co., d 8/22/30 in Canajoharie (1-8/26)
3240. French, Wheeler m 4/26/15 Mary Webb, both of Poughkeepsie; Rev. Leonard (8-5/13)
3241. French, William, formerly of Cooperstown, d 2/8/13 in NYC ("spotted fever") (deceased had been a sutler to the troops in New Jersey) (3-2/20)
3242. Frey, Henry I., Esq., attorney, of Palatine (Mont. Co.) m 5/7/07 Elizabeth Van Schaik, dau of Hon. Peter, Esq. of Kinderhook, in K; Rev. Judd (6-5/14)
3243. Frey, Henry J. S., 21, of Palatine Bridge d 1/7/30 in St. Augustine, East Florida where he had gone for his health ("pulmonary affliction") (1-2/12)
3244. Frink, Maria W. (Miss), 28, d 5/9/29 in Kinderhook (1-5/16)
3245. Frisbee, Philip (Col.), 73, d 3/11/13 in Canaan (6-3/23)
3246. Frisbee, William S. (Dr.), 32, formerly of Duanesburgh, d 8/15/30 in Lockport (graduated at Pittsfield, MA and started medical practice in Canajoharie, NY (1-8/28)
3247. Frisbie, Huldah, 48, wf of Gideon, Esq., d 12/21/04 in Delhi (Dela. Co.) (6-1/15/05)
3248. Frisbie, Joseph of Clinton (Dut. Co.) m 8/1/12 Ann Manly of NYC in Rhinebeck; Rev. William McMurry (8-8/19)
3249. Frisbie, Joseph, 26, d 8/14/14 at Rhinebeck Flats (typhus) (surv by wf and inf s) (8-8/24)
3250. Frisby, Pierpont, merchant, m 5/13/29 Mrs. Betsey Pugsley, both of Poughkeepsie, in Sing Sing, NY (8-5/21)
3251. Frith, Euphemia (Mrs.), 55, d 9/2/20 at the home of Col. Henry A. Livingston in Poughkeepsie (had recently arrived from the West Indies "on a trip to her relatives and friends") (8-9/6)
3252. Frost, Aaron m 9/27/27 Lydia H. Arnold, both of Poughkeepsie, at the Friends Meeting in Poughkeepsie (8-10/3)
3253. Frost, Abner of Clinton (Dut. Co.) m 10/8/23 Elizabeth Merritt of Hyde Park; Tilley Crouse, Esq. (8-10/15)
3254. Frost, Edmund W., 18, printer, d in Geneseo (7-9/21/33)
3255. Frost, Electa, wf of Samuel of Lansingburgh, d 10/14/02 (9-10/27)
3256. Frost, Eliza, 13, dau of Solomon V. of Poughkeepsie, d 7/19/30 (8-7/21)
3257. Frost, George P. m 9/2/20 Eliza Benjamin, dau of Joseph, Esq., in Ithaca; Rev. Wisner. All of Ithaca (3-9/18)
3258. Frost, Leonard of Ulster Co. m 2/11/12 Sophia Downs of Fishkill; Rev. C. C. Cuyler (8-2/26)
3259. Frost, Stephen, merchant, of the firm of Frost and Gadley m 4/24/28 Mary Williamson, dau of Griffin, at the Friends Meeting House in Poughkeepsie (8-4/30)
3260. Frost, William of the firm of N. V. Frost and Co. m 1/6/31 Susan H. Woolley, both of Poughkeepsie (8-1/12)
3261. Frothingham, Thomas, Jr., 20, d 2/25/02 in Hudson (6-3/2)
3262. Fry, Benjamin m 3/4/32 Lydia M. Baker, both of Amenia; Samuel Allen, Esq. (8-3/14)
3263. Fry, William G. (Capt.) m 5/7/29 Sarah S. Southwick, dau of Wilmarth Southwick and niece of Solomon Southwick, Esq.; Rev. Ferris. All of Albany (1-5/9)
3264. Frye, Daniel M., Esq., attorney, of Montgomery, NY m 2/1/17 Ann Butler of Poughkeepsie; Rev. C. C. Cuyler (8-2/5)
3265. Fuller, _____, wf of Thomas, d in Ballston (2-11/12/22)
3266. Fuller, _____, wf of Stephen, d 8/31/23 in Saratoga Springs (2-9/2)
3267. Fuller, Amos (Lt.), 82, formerly of Frederickstown (Put. Co.), NY, d 2/19/13 in Warren, CT (8-3/10)
3268. Fuller, Anson of Hartwick m 10/27/07 Lydia Warren of Cooperstown in Pierstown (3-10/31)
3269. Fuller, Benjamin d 4/2/12 in Poughkeepsie (8-4/8)
3270. Fuller, Benjamin of Clinton (Dut. Co.) m 5/31/15 Ann Maria Wainwright of Washington (Dut. Co.); Rev. L. Leonard (8-6/7)
3271. Fuller, Dayton Hewitt m 12/1/28 Lydia Ann Judd; Rev. Beman. All of Troy (9-12/9)
3272. Fuller, Edward m 6/9/29 Catharine Lossing, both of Union Vale; Stephen Force(?), Esq. (8-6/17)

3273. Fuller, Harriet S., 6, dau of Elijah, d 4/6/26 in Columbus (Chen. Co.)
(3-5/8)
3274. Fuller, Leonard (Capt.), 45, of Constantia d 8/18/29 at Fort Brewerton
(1-8/25)
3275. Fuller, Mercey (Mrs.), 88, d 2/8/16 in Warren, CT (8-2/21)
3276. Fuller, Nathaniel, 67, older brother of Dr. Thomas of Cooperstown, NY,
d 8/30/25 in Ohio "while on a visit from Massachusetts"(3-9/26)
3277. Fuller, Samuel of Rensselaerville m Flora Backus, dau of late Col.
Electus, at Trinity Church in Athens, NY; Rev. Prentice (6-10/4/14)
3278. Fulton, Robert, Esq., 42, the celebrated boat inventor, d 2/23/15 in
NYC (9-2/28 and 8-3/1)
3279. Fulton, Robert of Chesterfield m 8/2/21 Eleanor Starks, dau of Stephen
of Peru, NY, in P; Horace Beach, Esq. (7-8/4)
3280. Fulton, William, about 4 yrs old, d 5/24/11 in Plattsburgh (7-5/24)
3281. Furdus(?), Abraham W. m 3/5/22 Catharine Taylor, both of Barnegatt
(state not given but perhaps intended for NJ); Rev. Cuyler (8-3/13)
3282. Furman, Aaron of Clinton (Dut. Co.) m 5/25/15 Eliza Webb of Poughkeepsie;
Rev. Leonard (8-5/31)
3283. Furman, Charles Edwin (Rev.) of Clarkson m 1/19/31 Harriet Emeline Jane
Johnson, dau of Joseph, Esq. of Rochester; Rev. Charles G. Finney
(1-1/28)
3284. Furman, Ezekiel m 2/23/30 Eliza Filkins, both of Hyde Park, in H. P.;
John S. Van Wagner, Esq. (8-3/3)
3285. Furman, Philip m 2/20/23 Polly Cogswell, both of Schenectady, in Ballston;
Rev. Reuben Smith (2-3/4)
3286. Furnham, Dudley of Albany m 6/18/20 Emily Brush of Troy; Rev. Dr. Coe
(9-6/20)
3287. Gabaudan, Hamilton Brown, inf s of John of Pleasant Valley, d 10/16/21 in
P. V. (8-10/31)
3288. Gabaudan, Pamela, 31, wf of John and dau of Col. Joshua Ward, d 3/17/21
in Pleasant Valley (member of Presbyterian Church there for many years)
(8-3/21)
3289. Gabaudon, John m 8-24/07 Pamelia Ward, dau of Col. Joshua of Pleasant
Valley; Rev. John Cornwall (8-8/26)
3290. Gadsden, Christopher (Capt.), 31, of the U.S. brig "Vivian" d 8/28/12
(7-9/25)
3291. Gaedike, Helmuth I. (Midshipman), 33, of the U.S. Navy d in NYC (1-12/19/29)
3292. Gage, Alden S., merchant, m 11/9/30 Malina Loomis, dau of Thaddeus, in
Salisbury (Herk. Co.); Rev. W. Judd (1-11/16)
3293. Gage, George, 65, (a Rev. soldier) d 5/11/06 in Pittstown (9-5/13)
3294. Gager, Reuben, 24, s of John. Esq., d 11/22/15 in Clinton (Dut. Co.)
(8-11/29)
3295. Geggett, Thomas of Pittstown m "the week before last" Nancy Banker of
Troy; Rev. Griffen (9-3/4/25)
3296. Gagnon, C. E., Esq. of Riviere du Loup(Lower Canada) m 6/20/26 Jane J.
Durand, dau of Col. M. F. of Plattsburgh, NY, in Lacoule, Lower
Canada; Rev. J. B. Paquin (7-7/8)
3297. Gaine, Hugh, 80, printer, d 4/25/07 in NYC (9-5/5 and 6-5/12)
3298. Gaines, George, Esq., 53, attorney and formerly "Reporter of the
Supreme Court of this state", d 7/10/25 in Catskill, NY (3-7/25)
3299. Gale, Adam H. m 1/25/31 R. W. Slack of NYC; Rev. Manton Eastburn (1-1/31)
3300. Gale, Ann Eliza, 19, consort of John Jr., d 2/7/23 in Plattsburgh
(her father John Stephenson is mentioned but not further defined)
(7-2/8)
3301. Gale, Betsey, 44, wf of John, d 4/20/25 in Plattsburgh (7-4/23)
3302. Gale, George W. (Rev.) of Adams m 9/21/20 Harriet Selden of Troy in T; Rev.
Tucker (9-9/26)
3303. Gale, John m 12/31/20 Eliza Stevenson in Plattsburgh (7-1/6/21)
3304. Gale, Josiah, Esq. a Dutchess County farmer, d 11/22/98 (8-12/19)
3305. Gale, Samuel (Dr.) of Troy m 9/15/11 Mary Thompson, dau of Ezra, Jr. of
Poughkeepsie; Rev. C. C. Cuyler (8-9/18)
3306. Gale, William (Dr.) d 9/2/99 at the home of Judge Radcliff (had recently
returned from Savannah, GA where he had gone for his health) (8-9/3)
3307. Gale, William, 30, of the firm of S. and W. Gale d 3/3/13 in Troy (9-3/9)
3308. Gallaher, John L. m 1/9/22 Sarah Bates of Troy; Rev. Dr. Coe (9-1/15)

95

3309. Gallimore, George, a native of England, d 10/7/24 in Poughkeepsie, NY
(8-10/13)
3310. Gallow, Joseph, 66, d 8/30/05 in Poughkeepsie (8-9/3)
3311. Gallt, Orlando of the firm of Gallt and Lobdell m 9/14/31 Ann Finck, dau
of J. C., Esq., in Weedsport; Rev. D. C. Hopkins (1-9/17)
3312. Galpin, Horace (Rev.) of Geneseo m 6/9/27 Sarah Cropsie of Fishkill;
Rev. U. Dwight (8-6/13)
3313. Galpin, Hulda, relict of late David, d 12/1/19 in Waterford ("Printers
throughout the United States are requested to notice the above")
(3-1/3/20)
3314. Galusha, Nancy, 67, 4th wf of Gov. Galusha, d in Shaftsbury, VT (1-8/12/31)
3315. Gamage, Eliza and Cornelia, aged 7 and 4 respectively, d 11/23/09 in
Hudson (both are daughters of Samuel) (6-11/28)
3316. Gansevoort, _____ (Gen.) d 7/2/12 in Albany (9-7/7)
3317. Gansevoort, Ann, wf of John and dau of late John C. Cuyler of Albany,
d 11/29/30 at her home in Watervliet (1-12/1)
3318. Gansevoort, Catharine, 78, relict of late Gen. Peter, Jr., d 12/30/30 in
Albany (funeral from her late home, 316 North Market St.) (her son
Peter Gansevoort is mentioned) (1-12/31/30 and 1-1/1/31)
3319. Gansevoort, Henry, Esq., 30, d 6/9/31 in Monmouth Co., NJ (1-6/4)
3320. Gansevoort, Leonard H., Esq., 38, late sheriff of Albany Co., d in Albany
(7-12/29/21)
3321. Gansevoort, Leonard, Esq., 80, d 12/16/34 in Albany (7-12/20)
3322. Gansevoort, Peter, Jr. (Brig. Gen.), 62, of Albany d 7/2/12 (7-7/10)
3323. Gansevoort, Peter C., 34, s of Conrad of Albany, d 6/7/19 in Bath (1-6/12)
3324. Gardenier, Henry H., 78, d 11/21/05 in the eastern part of Troy (was an
early resident there) (9-11/26)
3325. Gardiner, _____, wf of Gayer Gerdiner, d in Hudson (6-10/22/05)
3326. Gardiner, Addison (Hon.), judge of the 8th circuit, m 6/7/31 Mary S.
Selkrig in Rochester; Rev. Penney (1-6/13)
3327. Gardiner, Augustus, Esq. m 10/12/26 Pamila Shankland in Cooperstown; Rev
Smith (3-10/16)
3328. Gardiner, Charles, merchant, of Manlius m 7/18/15 Abby P. Center, dau of
Robert, Esq. of Hudson, in H; Rev. John Carter (6-8/1)
3329. Gardiner, Robert C., Esq. of South Kingston, RI m Julia Day, dau of Stephen,
Esq., in Catskill; Rev. Porter (6-3/27/04)
3330. Gardiner, William (Col.), 74, of Manlius, father of Hon. Addison of
Rochester, d 9/6/31 in Avon (1-9/12)
3331. Gardinier, Barent, attorney, d 1/10/22 in NYC (3-1/21)
3332. Gardner, Abby, wf of Charles of New Orleans, LA and dau of Robert Center,
Esq. of NYC, d 8/31/20 (6-9/5)
3333. Gardner, Asa, merchant, of Troy m 12/31/05 Helen Ann Townsend of Bath; Rev.
John M. Bradford (9-1/7/06)
3334. Gardner, Asa, about 51, d 11/26/21 in Brunswick (9-12/4)
3335. Gardner, Asa m Lydia Lasell at St. Paul's Church in Troy; Rev. Butler.
All of Troy (1-2/1/30)
3336. Gardner, Elisha, 58, d in Hudson (6-12/4/04)
3337. Gardner, Gayer, merchant, m 1/19/09 Lydia Collins in Hudson; Rev. Wigton
(6-2/7)
3338. Gardner, George Esq. of Newburgh d 2/15/23 in Newburgh ("Judge Gardner
had been on business in the westward and on his return in Sullivan
County became chilled with cold ...") (8-3/5)
3339. Gardner, John F., about 34, d 3/14/29 in Ipswich, MA (1-3/27)
3340. Gardner, Josiah m Amelia Thorp in Hudson (6-12/18/04)
3341. Gardner, Laban (Capt.) of Nantucket m 5/16/03 Phebe Vail of Troy, NY
in T (6-5/31)
3342. Gardner, Ruth, 75, wf of Paul, d 1/4/22 in Burlington (Ots. Co.)
(lived with her husband 57 yrs; mother of 15, gr-mother of 95, great-
gr-mother of 72) (3-1/21)
3343. Gardner, Sarah, 28, wf of Augustus, d in Middlefield (consumption)
(3-7/2/21)
3344. Gardner, William m Polly Ackley in Cooperstown (3-12/9/02)
3345. Gareau, Leon m 5/24/28 Flavina Hill, both of Troy; Rev. Howard (9-5/27)
3346. Garland, Richard, 65, member of Parliament on the Island of Antigua,
d 8/8/ in Albany (funeral "at the Misses Carter, 91 North Pearl St.)
(1-8/9)

3347. Garlay, Ward M., editor of the Index, m Elizabeth Carter of
      Newburgh in N; Rev. John Johnson (3-7/15/22)
3348. Garlic, Eliphalet m Betsey Lawrence of Lisbon, CT; Rev. Reed (8-5/19/13)
3349. Garlock, _____, 6 mo, s of Rev. Heman Garlock, d 9/2/19 in Peru, NY
      (7-9/4)
3350. Garner, Joshua of Wappingers Creek m June Doughty, dau of Thomas of
      Beekman, in B (8-3/5/17)
3351. Garnet, John, about 110, (a Rev. soldier) d "a few weeks since" in the
      Goshen Poor House" (born in Scotland) (8-4/7/30 and 1-4/10/30)
3352. Garnryck, Theophilus m 10/13/20 Elizabeth Vanarnum, both of Brunswick
      (9-10/19)
3353. Garnsey, David, Esq., 50, supervisor of Clifton Park, d 8/#0/31 at his
      home in Clifton Park (1-9/8)
3354. Garretson, Freeborn, Jr., Esq. of Rhinebeck m 9/26/23 Elizabeth H. Waters,
      dau of Hon. Francis H., in Somerset, MD (8-10/8)
3355. Garrettson, Freeborn (Rev.), 75, of Rhinebeck ("a preacher of the Methodist
      confession") d 9/26/27 at the home of George Suckley, Esq. in NYC
      (8-10/3)
3356. Garrison, John, Esq., 66, d 1/22/31 in Brooklyn (1-1/27)
3357. Gary, George (Rev.) m 1/30/17 Laura Trall in Hartwick; Rev. Charles Giles
      (3-2/6)
3358. Gary, John m 10/19/05 Eliza Pettice, both of Poughkeepsie; Rev. Brouwer
      (8-10/22)
3359. Gary, Joseph of Troy m 10/26/15 Lucretia Storms of Schaghticoke in S; Rev.
      David Butler (9-10/31)
3360. Gaskin, Abigail, 36, wf of John, d 8/7/25 in Guilderland (Albany Co.)
      (3-8/15)
3361. Gasley, Ward M., Esq., editor of the Political Index, m 6/13/22 Elizabeth
      Carter of Newburgh in N (8-6/26)
3362. Gates, George Washington, 3, 5th s of Horatio, Esq., d 1/22/29 in Montreal,
      Canada (1-1/26)
3363. Gates, Horatio, Esq. of Lockport m 9/6/30 Ann Edmonds of Rochester in R;
      Rev. Whitehouse (1-9/13)
3364. Gates, Horatio, "an eminent merchant of the house of Horatio Gates and
      Co.", d in Montreal, Canada (8-4/23/34)
3365. Gates, Lydia, 59, relict of late Maj. Lemuel, d 4/26/22 at the home of
      Col. Learned on Paca Street in Baltimore, MD (7-5/18)
3366. Gates, Michael Eldridge, 9, s of Horatio, d 12/7/29 in Albany
3367. Gates, Silas, 20, s of Capt. John, d 11/8/13 in St. Albans, VT (Had
      studied at Harvard U; was apparently A.W.O.L. from the militia and was
      fatally shot by a militiaman when he [Gates] jumped out a window to
      escape) (the militiaman who fired the shot was to be tried for "wilful
      murder") (deceased was surv by his parents and their adopted dau)
      (8-12/8)
3368. Gates, Theron m Laura Fisher, both of Burlington (Ots. Co.), in Exeter;
      Rev. J. C. Hulbert (3-5/2/25)
3369. Gaudren, Richard m 8/1/18 Laura Abigail Stewart, dau of Solomon W., in
      Hudson; Rev. Sampson (6-8/4)
3370. Gaul, Conrad m Polly Waltenmire, dau of Michael, in Claverack; Rev.
      Gepherd (6-6/18/05)
3371. Gaul, David of Claverack m Catharine Kittle of Kinderhook in K; Rev.
      Sickels (6-1/30/16)
3372. Gaul Jacob, 70, d 5/4/15 in Claverack "after an infirmity of 21 years...")
      (6-5/9)
3373. Gaul, Jacob, 16, d 6/22/15 in Claverack (my notes for this entry read
      "surv by wf and 5 children" but this seems incongruous for a young
      man age 16. Perhaps I have his age wrong although he could have
      married, shortly prior to his death, a widow with children, etc.)
      (6-6/27)
3374. Gauntley, _____, merchant, of NYC m 8/2/15 Maria Hosmer, dau of Prosper
      Hosmer of Hudson, in H; Rev. Chester (6-8/8)
3375. Gay, George W. m 8/17/31 Catharine B. Enders, both of Albany; Rev. Burch
      (1-8/18)
3376. Gay, Henry, s of Amos, d "recently" in Albany (funeral from the South
      Ferry) (1-10/20/31)

97

3377. Gay, Jane, 38, consort of Barnet, d 3/25/06 (8-4/8)
3378. Gay, Luther, 65, d 3/30/32 at his home in Washington (Dut. Co.) (8-4/11)
3379. Gay, William B. of Troy m 11/8/27 Eliza Ann Gregory of Clinton (Oneida Co.); Rev. Howard (9-11/13)
3380. Gaylord, Josiah, 46, d 10/16/06 in Catskill (typhus) (6-10/28)
3381. Gazlay, Stephen m 1/20/18 Ann Harris; both of Clinton (8-1/21)
3382. Gear, Ezekiel G. (Rev.), rector of Zion Church in Palmyra,m 5/13/29 Mary Y. How at St. Peter's Church in Auburn; Rev. Dr. Rudd (1-5/25)
3383. Gear, Milton, 20, d 9/2/11 in Plattsburgh (7-9/6)
3384. Gearey, Lucy (Mrs.), 84, d 10/11/16 in Hudson (6-10/15)
3385. Gebhard, Anna Maria, 72, relict of late Rev. John, d 11/12/29 in Claverack (1-11/21)
3386. Gebhard, Philip, Esq., attorney, "of Delaware" m 8/3/01 Eleanor Demerest of Catskill; Rev. Labagh (6-8/6)
3387. Gebherd, Margaret, wf of Dr. J. G., d 9/11/13 in Troy (9-9/14)
3388. Geddes, Mary, 19, dau of James, Esq., d 7/18/21 in Onondaga (3-8/6)
3389. Geer, John of Troy m 2/3/21 Susanna Winne of Lansingburgh; Rev. Sommers (9-2/6)
3390. Geer, John B. m 9/21/22 Lydia Barker of Troy; Rev. Griffin (9-9/24)
3391. Geer, Shubael m 11/10/21 Maria Miller, both of Troy; Rev. Sommers (9-11/13)
3392. Gelston, Cotton, 58, d 10/3/16 in Hudson (6-10/8)
3393. Genet, Cornelia Tappen, 34, consort of E. C., Esq. and 2nd dau of George Clinton, Esq., Vice Pres. of U.S., d 3/23/10 in Greenbush (6-4/5)
3394. Gere, Almira, 49, wf of Luther, Esq., d 8/20/31 in Ithaca (1-8/29)
3395. Germand, Lewis of Salisbury, CT m 8/9/23 Eve Wilsey of Pine Plains, NY in Amenia; Rev. C. I. Wilson (8-8/27)
3396. Germond, James, Jr. of Clinton (Dut. Co.) m 11/7/12 __?__ Cronkite of Poughkeepsie; Rev. Cuyler (8-11/18)
3397. Germond, James m 1/5/32 Laura Anson, both of Washington (Dut. Co.); Isaac Sutherland, Esq. (8-1/11)
3398. Germond, James P., 64, d 7/27/17 at his home in Clinton (Dut. Co.) (8-7/30)
3399. Germond, Jane, 29, consort of Peter P., d 2/7/11 (consumption) (8-3/6)
3400. Germond, Peter m 11/20/32 Martha Davis, both of Washington (Dut. Co.); Rev. Buttolph (8-11/28)
3401. Germond, Phebe, 43, wf of Peter P., farmer, of Clinton (Dut. Co.) d 2/28/02 (8-3/9)
3402. Germond, Silas of Clinton (Dut. Co.) m 6/19/13 Helen Cary, dau of Dr. Cary of Beekman; Rev. Price (8-7/7)
3403. Germond, William, 58, d 7/1/32 in Poughkeepsie (8-7/4)
3404. Gevekoht (?), Charles Theodore of the firm of Gloysford and Gevekoht of Bremen (Germany?) m 10/25/30 Catharine Marshall, dau of late Anthony of NYC, at St. Peter's Church in NYC; Rev. Quarter (1-10/27)
3405. Gibbs, Alfred of the firm of Gibbs and Van Deusen, merchants, of Hudson, NY m 10/8/15 Hannah Nye of Wareham, Ma in W (6-10/17)
3406. Gibbs, Betsey, 48, relict of late Dr. Leonard Gibbs, d in Granville (1-9/8/29)
3407. Gibbs, Joseph, 19, m 12/20/05 Miss Rachel Baden, 49, in Pittstown (9-1/28/06)
3408. Gibbs, William C., gov. of RI, m 6/2/22 Mary Kane, dau of Elias, Esq. of Albany, in A; Rev. Dr. Chester (6-6/12)
3409. Gibson, Colin, 70, m 10/15/07 Peggy Miller, 18, both of Cambridge, in C; Jesse Fairchild, Esq. (9-11/3)
3410. Gibson, Isaac, s of late Wood Gibson, Esq. of Liverpool (Eng.?) m 7/27/29 Magdalen R. Post of Liverpool (Eng.?) in NYC; Rev. Dr. Wainright (1-7/30)
3411. Gibson, Isabella, 18 mo, dau of John, d 8/21/31 in Albany (1-8/22)
3412. Gibson, John m 9/13/34 Mary Ann Thomas in Clintonville; E. Williams, Esq. All of Peru, NY (7-9/27)
3413. Gibson, Lewis, Esq. of the firm of Bridges and Gibson, merchants, in Augusta, GA, m 7/28/30 Almira Brooks Clarke, dau of Lot, Esq. of Lockport, NY, in L; Rev. Smith (1-8/3)
3414. Gidley, Ricketson of Poughkeepsie m 12/22/25 Harriet Sleght, dau of Col. James of Freedom; Rev. C. C. Cuyler (8-12/28)

3415. Gidley, Townsend E. of the firm of Frost and Gidley, merchants, m 9/27/30 Emily Power in Poughkeepsie; Rev. Perkins. All of Poughkeepsie (1- 9/29 and 1-10/1)
3416. Gifford, Benjamin m 4/16/03 Maria Quinlan, dau of Dr. Quinlan, all of Beekman; Rev. Peter Mariarty (8-4/26)
3417. Gifford, Benjamin m 12/26/11 Hansy Birge of Chatham in C; Rev. Waters (6-1/6/12)
3418. Gifford, Elisha, 83, m Mrs. Mary Washburn, 28, in Carmel (Put. Co.) (8-6/2/30)
3419. Gifford, Elizabeth, 45, consort of Humphrey, d 6/15/05 (6-6/18)
3420. Gifford, Ellery m 2/15/03 Bythena Snyder, both of Schaghticoke, in S; Edward Ostrander, Esq. (9-2/22)
3421. Gifford, Gideon m Elizabeth Griffin, both of Schaghticoke, in Pittstown (9-9/3/05)
3422. Gifford, John of Lee, MA m 3/11/07 Ursula Barnard of Troy; Rev. Coe (9-3/17)
3423. Gifford, John, 73, d in Stanford (Dut. Co.) (8-2/9/31)
3424. Gifford, Nathan m 4/24/24 Lydia Carson in Poughkeepsie; Moses Armstrong, Esq. (8-4/28)
3425. Gifford, Ruby, 17, only ch of John of Greenfield, d 1/5/22 in Greenfield (2-1/16)
3426. Gifford, Samuel m 10/24/11 Maria Dutcher; Rev. Chester (6-10/28)
3427. Gilbert, Abigail, 70, wf of Butler Gilbert, d in Laurens (3-2/3/23)
3428. Gilbert, Anna, 65, wf of Asahel, d 4/15/27 in Troy (9-4/17)
3429. Gilbert, Clark m 3/10/16 Martha White, both of Troy; Rev. Dr. Coe (9-3/12)
3430. Gilbert, Eleazer, 27, d 6/29/03 in Albany ("had occasionally resided in this village [Lansingburgh] and left here [on the day he died] on his way to Albany from a visit to his friends in Saratoga") (9-7/5)
3431. Gilbert, John C. of Troy m 10/8/29 Maria Thompson of Poughkeepsie; Rev. Dr. Cuyler (8-10/14 and 1-10/16)
3432. Gilbert, Lucien M. m 11/22/30 Elizabeth Erwin, dau of John; Rev. Campbell. All of Albany (1-11/24)
3433. Gilbert, Luther m 3/1/27 Lucetta Sormberger, dau of John S., in North ? (town name blurred); Rev. C. P. Wilson (8-3/21)
3434. Gilbert, Marcellus m 8/23/30 GertrudeMargaret Brooks, youngest dau of Peter, Jr., Esq; Rev. Dr. Hosack. All of Johnstown (1-8/26)
3435. Gilbert, Newman, about 35, d 1/26/30 in Goshen (his residence place not known - said he had worked in albany "last summer" and had a niece in Troy) (1-1/30)
3436. Gilbert, Wheeler (Dr.) m 5/24/14 Martha Rogers, both of Beekman; Rev. Lewis (8-6/8)
3437. Gilchrist, Mary, wf of Capt. Daniel, d 9/16/24 in Springfield (3-9/27)
3438. Gilchrist, Mary, wid of late William, d in Springfield (3-10/3/25)
3439. Gildersleeve, John m 12/11/28 Catharine De Long, both of Washington (Dut. Co.); Rev.Clark (8-12/17)
3440. Gildersleeve, Romulus (Col.) of Cayuga Co. m 10/26/30 Emeline Peck, dau of Judge Peck of Benton, in B; Rev. Tooker (1-11/13)
3441. Gilderslieve, Edmond m 10/6/24 Dency Ostrom, dau of Daniel, Esq.; Rev. Clark. All of Pleasant Valley (8-10/13)
3442. Giles, Gilbert, 44, (alderman of the 1st ward) d 1/4/24 in Troy (9-1/13)
3443. Giles, John m 9/15/07 Betsey Kip, both of Poughkeepsie; Rev. Brouwer (8-9/23)
3444. Gill, Caroline Watson, 14 mo, dau of Bennington Gill, d 11/7/29 in Albany (1-11/9)
3445. Gill, Charles W., printer, m 12/17/29 Miranda Holmes of Cooperstown in C; Rev. Job Potter (1-1/8/30)
3446. Gill, Theodore Paul, 5, s of Bennington Gill, d 11/4/29 in Albany (funeral from his father's home on North Pearl Street (1-11/6)
3447. Gillender, Theophilus of NYC m 6/4/34 Jane Ann Schell, dau of William, Esq. of Rhinebeck, in R; Rev. Hardenburgh (8-6/11)
3448. Gillens, James of Rhinebeck m 10/2/20 Sarah Weaver of Poughkeepsie; Rev. Reed (8-10/4)
     Gillette, David. See, possibly, Jillett, David
3449. Gillies, James m 8/5/18 Margaret Uhl, dau of Capt. Frederick of Staatsburgh; Rev. William McMurry of Rhinebeck (8-9/16)

99

3450. Gillies, James (Capt.), 36, d 2/10/29 in Camillus (surv by wf and 3 young children) (8-3/11)
3451. Gilliland, Mary E., 7, dau of William, Esq., d 1/31/27 in Plattsburgh (7-2/3)
3452. Gilliland, William m 8/8/11 Nancy Staats, both of Plattsburgh, in Peru, NY (7-8/16)
3453. Gillingham, Jacob, 16, d 12/18/29 in Bristol, PA. Matthias, 28, d 12/19 in Rocklesstown (sic), NJ. "It is about five weeks since we had to recordthe decease of Moses Gillingham, the father of these young men." (1-1/1/30)
3454. Gillins, James m 11/1/32 Gitty Donalsson; Rev. Dr. Reed. All of Poughkeepsie (8-11/7)
3455. Gillmore, James, Jr. m 3/11/23 Mary Green, both of Cambridge; Rev. Alexander Bullion (9-3/25)
3456. Gilman, Rufus A. m 4/21/27 A. Mooers, youngest dau of Maj. Gen. Benjamin of Plattsburgh, in P; Rev. Frederick Halsey (7-4/28)
3457. Gils, Gilbert of Sharon(Scho. Co.) m 9/11/29 Margaret Hewson, dau of Thomas of Albany; Rev. Ludlow (1-9/16)
3458. Gilson, James m 9/13/12 Diantha Worden, both of Union Village, in U. V.; Rev. Edward Barber (9-9/29)
3459. Gilson, Thomas Warren, 2, youngest s of Thomas D. and Elizabeth, d 12/1/33 in Peru, NY (4 [Keeseville Herald]- 12/10)
3460. Gittman, Uriah m 9/12/22 Azubah Coats at Le Roy in the town of Otsego; Rev. Huse (3-9/16)
3461. Givan, Robert, Esq. (father of John of Pleasant Valley) d 10/5/30 in Westchester (born in Scotland; emigrated to the U.S. in 1795) (8-10/13)
3462. Given, William of Fishkill, 20, d 5/2/26 in Charleston, S.C. (had spent the winter in St. Augustine, East Florida for his health - died of a "pulmonary disease") (deceased was s of James of Fishkill) (8-5/17)
3463. Glad, David m 10/2/06 Susan Thacker, both of Poughkeepsie; Rev. Brouwer (8-10/7)
3464. Gladd, Erick, merchant, d 2/17/10 (in Poughkeepsie?) (buried with Masonic honors) (8-2/21)
3465. Gladding, _____,d "recently" at the parents' home on Quackenbush Street, Albany (1-9/10/30)
3466. Gladding, Stephen m 12/24/31 AnnCassidy; Rev. Dr. Smith. All of Albany (1-12/26)
3467. Glean, Anthony B., 29, of Saratoga Springs d 5/27/27 (9-6/1)
3468. Glen, Henry, Esq. d in Schenectady (8-2/2/14)
3469. Glen, John V., 55, d 6/19/31 in Schenectady (formerly of U.S. Army and was aide-de-camp to Gen. Wilkinson)(1-6/23 and 4 [Keeseville Argus]-6/28)
3470. Glover, Alphena, wf of Hon. James, d 9/17/30 in Oswego (1-9/28)
3471. Glover, Mabel, 56, wf of Benjamin, d 12/22/22 in Butternuts ("Printers in New England are requested to publish this death)(3-1/6/23)
3472. Godfry, David (Capt.) of New Hamburgh m 3/26/26 Betsy Hunt of Dover; Rev. Job F_____ (surname blurred) (8-4/5)
3473. Goelet, Eliza, 45, wf of Thomas B. of Fishkill, d 4/1/32 (8-4/4)
3474. Goertner, J. P. (Rev.) d 2/27/29 in Canajoharie (consumption) (1-3/5)
3475. Goes, Catherine, 87, wid of late Isaac, Esq., d 1/30/13 in Kinderhook (surv by 5 ch) (6-2/9)
3476. Goes, Henrietta, consort of Richard J. of Kinderhook, d 8/3/05 (6-8/13)
3477. Goewey, Ann, 31, wf of Jacob, d 8/20/29 in Albany (funeral from her late residence, 51 Fayette St.)
3478. Goewey, Daniel m 7/12/17 Elizabeth Rouse, both of Brunswick (9-7/15)
3479. Goff, Nathan, Esq., 86, d 3/23/10 in Burlington (Ots. Co.) (surv by his wf "with whom he had lived nearly 64 years") (3-4/7)
3480. Goheen, Zaccheus of Albany m 11/10/05 Catherine Wray of Troy (9-11/12)
3481. Golder, Abraham of Clinton (Dut. Co.) m 2/8/24 Maria Aiken, dau of late Benjamin, in Greenbush; Rev. J. Walker (8-2/12)
3482. Golder, William m Phebe Hewitt in Hyde Park (8-7/21/24)
3483. Goldsborough, Lewis M. of the U.S. Navy m 11/1/31 Elizabeth Gamble Wirt, 2nd dau of Hon. William, in Washington (Dut. Co.); Rev. Nevins (1-11/9 and 8-11/16)
3484. Goldsmith, John, about 22, s of Thomas, d 3/7/19 in Chazy (7-3/13)
3485. Gonse, John m 2/21/11 Betsey Platt, dau of Zephaniah, in Fishkill; Rev. Clark (8-2/27)

100

3486. Good, Joseph C., 20, (son of late William of Demerara), late a student in Poughkeepsie, d 5/15/19 at the home of William Radcliff in Rhinebeck (pulmonary complaint) (8-6/2)
3487. Good, William W., 30, d 8/25/26 in Poughkeepsie (8-8/30)
3488. Goodale, Eleanor (Widow), 82, d 6/13/31 at the home of her son, Dr. R. Goodale,in Watertown (1-6/18)
3489. Goodale, William m 11/1/06 Hannah Castle, both of Greenbush, in G; William McManus, Esq. (9-11/4)
3490. Goodenow, Eli m 4/23/11 Ann Roberts; R. H. Walworth, Esq. (7-4/26)
3491. Goodman, Eldad W., late of the Theological Seminary at Princeton, NJ, m 9/29/23 Nancy Wakeman of Ballston in B (2-10/14)
3492. Goodman, Henry T., 13, s of Titus, Jr. of York (Liv. Co.) d 8/5/30 in Pittsfield, MA (1-9/1)
3493. Goodrich, Arabella Marsh, wf of Chauncy, d 11/29/34 in Burlington, VT (7-12/6)
3494. Goodrich, Charles Sidney Jones (Dr.) m 6/14/29 Mary Gardner, dau of George, Esq., in St. Paul's Church, Troy; Rev. Butler. All of Troy (1-6/17)
3495. Goodrich, Elihu Chauncey, Esq. of Claverack d 8/20/02 in Niagara (6-9/14)
3496. Goodrich, George m 4/21/31 Julia Colwell in Poughkeepsie; Rev.Welton (8-4/27)
3497. Goodrich, Josiah B. m 9/17/14 Mary Dater, both of Brunswick (9-9/27)
3498. Goodrich, Walstien of Amenia m 10/3/22 Caroline Tibbits of Salisbury, CT; Rev. Perry (8-10/9)
3499. Goodrich, William, Jr. of Hoosick m10/31/21 Maranda Williams of Dover; Elder Job Foss (8-11/7)
3500. Goodrich, Zenas, Esq., 62, d 9/10/29 in Auburn (1-9/19)
3501. Goodsell, Deborah, 45, relict of late Lewis, d 4/12/21 in Cooperstown (3-4/16)
3502. Goodsell, Elizabeth R., 41, consort of Peter of Cooperstown, d 2/26/13 in C (3-2/27)
3503. Goodsell, Lewis, 43, d 2/19/13 in Cooperstown (3-2/20)
3504. Goodsell, Nathan of Kent, CT m 10/24/34 Phebe Welch of Beekman, NY; Lucas Baker, Esq. (8-10/29)
3505. Goodwin, Benjamin of the firm of Center and Goodwin of Hudson d in Havana (NY?) (6-7/20/19)
3506. Goodwin, Charles, 20, oldest s of "Mr. Goodwin" of Hudson, d 1/24/12 in H (6-2/3)
3507. Goodwin, Sarah, 61, consort of Samuel of Clinton, d 9/22/02 (dau of Ebenezer Townsend of New Haven, CT) (8-10/12)
3508. Gookins, Seymour, A.B., principal of Franklin Academy m 3/31/31 Fidelia Loomis, dau of Gamaliel, Esq., in Prattsburgh; Rev. Rudd. All of P (1-4/13)
3509. Gorden, James Clinton, 20, a native of Newburgh, NY, d 11/29/31 in Charleston, S.C. (1-12/10)
3510. Gordon, James, s of William, d in Hudson (6-8/16/15)
3511. Gordon, Lucy, wf of William I. of Hudson, d 9/23/18 in Hingham, MA (6-10/6)
3512. Gordon, Samuel, Esq., attorney, of Delhi m 10/16/31 Frances M. Leet, dau of Martin, Esq. of Meredith, in M; Rev. Tuttle (1-10/22)
3513. Gordon, William I., about 30, d 10/1/20 in Hudson (6-10/3)
3514. Gordon, Zephus, Esq. of Troy m 7/8/29 Caroline Sergeant, dau of James of NYC, in NYC; Rev. Summers (1-7/13)
3515. Gorton, Ethan m 3/15/27 Mary Sagges, both of Stanford; Rev. C. P. Wilson (8-3/21)
3516. Gorton, James m 1/2/12 Hannah Ferris, both of Stanford; John Thompson, Esq. (8-1/15)
3517. Gorton, Phebe, wf of William, d 2/20/01 in Washington (Dut. Co.) (8-3/3)
3518. Gorton, William of Washington (Dut. Co.) m 1/18/02 Mrs. Lois Hall of East Haddam, CT (8-2/9)
3519. Goslin, Simmons m 10/19/11 Charlotte Garret in Clinton (Dut. Co.); Rev. Dr. Dodge (8-10/23)
3520. Gosmond, John (Rev.) m Mary Hay of Cambridge in C (9-5/19/07)
3521. Gott, Sarah, 43, consort of Nathaniel of Cooperstown, d 12/30/97 (3-1/4/98)
3522. Gould, Ann, 26, wf of Abraham, d 4/16/30 in Albany (funeral from 35 Fox St.) (1-4/17)

101

3523. Gould, Anthony of the firm of W. and A. Gould & Co., law booksellers, m 12/22/31 Martha Jenett Bellows, adopted dau of Christian H. Shear, Esq.; Rev. Kirk. All of Albany (1-12/24)
3524. Gould, Charles, about 16, s of "Mr. Gould" of Rutland, VT., d 5/13/31 at the home of his brother-in-law, Selencia Elmore, in Peru, NY (4 [Keeseville Herald]-5/17)
3525. Gould, James of Westerlo m 9/14/31 Mrs. Mary Evans of Greenville in Rensselaerville; Judge Moore (1-9/17)
3526. Gould, James R., Esq., 27, attorney, d 10/10/30 in Augusta, Ga (son of Hon. James Gould of Litchfield (state not given) (Graduated from Yale College in 1824) (1-11/17)
3527. Gould, Pliny of Stephentown m 4/5/21 Pamela Cox of Nassau, NY in Troy; Rev. Ross (9-4/10)
3528. Goundry, Margaret, 33, consort of Gen. George, d 4/16/30 in Greenbush (1-4/24)
3529. Gourley, Susannah (Widow), 55, d 8/13/30 in Goshen (1-8/26)
3530. Gouverneur, Samuel Lawrence, Esq. of NYC m 3/16/20 Maria Hester Monroe, youngest dau of James Monroe, Pres. of U.S., in Washington City; Rev. Hawley (6-3/21 and 2/27)
3531. Gove, Elizabeth (Miss) d 7/26/30 in Albany (funeral from the home of her brother-in-law, John C. Draper of Park Place) (1-7/27)
3532. Grace,Henry m 1/19/06 Nancy Criscy; Rev. Coe(?) (9-1/21)
3533. Gracie, Susan Hude, wf of Robert and dau of William Neilson, d 4/7/31 in NYC (1-4/11)
3534. Graham, Abigail, wf of Alexander and dau of John Drake, Jr., d 12/2/15 in Fishkill (pleurisy) (surv by husband, four small children, and her parents) (8-12/6)
3535. Graham, Alexander, Esq. m 11/30/22 Margaret Sebring, dau of Isaac, in Fishkill; Rev. Price (8-12/4)
3536. Graham, Ann (Miss), 26, dau of Adam, d 7/7/26 in Poughkeepsie (8-7/12)
3537. Graham, Curtiss m 6/25/07 Sally Charlott, both of Hudson (6-6/30)
3538. Graham, David m 4/29/09 Eliza Beyeaux, both of Poughkeepsie (8-5/3)
3539. Graham, David A. of Poughkeepsie m 4/22/30 Phebe Underhill of La Grange; Rev. Dr. Cuyler (8-5/5)
3540. Graham, Davis m 5/4/31 Catharine Barns in Chesterfield; Rev. Lyman (4 [Keeseville Herald]-5/10)
3541. Graham, Duncan m "last week" "Mrs. Cooper", both of Fishkill (8-3/6/98)
3542. Graham, Duncan, Jr. of Fishkill m 11/9/24 Juliana Ward of Freedom; Rev. Cuyler (8-11/17)
3543. Graham, Hester, 38, consort of Joseph, d 10/1/19 in NYC (yellow fever) (6-10/5 and 7-10/16)
3544. Graham, James M., merchant, of Poughkeepsie m 12/12/27 Emeline Cordelia Jenks, dau of late Nathaniel, Esq.of NYC, in NYC; Rev. Lyell (8-12/19)
3545. Graham, Joseph, merchant, of Catskill, NY m 8/2/01 Hepzibah Washburn, dau of Noah of Hartford, CT, in Catskill; "Mr. Sampson" (6-8/6)
3546. Graham, Mary Elizabeth, 5, dau of Capt. James M., d 3/5/34 in Poughkeepsie (8-3/12)
3547. Graham, Theodorus V. W., Esq., 63, attorney, d 7/6/22 in Albany (3-7/15)
3548. Graham, William m 2/23/20 Mary Blair, both of Middlefield, in M (3-2/28)
3549. Graham, William m Sarah Ann Aiken, both of Poughkeepsie; Rev. C. C. Cuyler (8-5/1/22)
3550. Graham, Wines M., 20, s of Aclam, d 7/18/26 in Poughkeepsie (8-7/26)
3551. Grange, William, cutler, m 7/12/30 Jane N. Dunn in Albany; Rev. Keys. All of Albany (1-7/13)
3552. Granger, _____, 39, wf of Harvey, Esq. of Saratoga, d 5/21/27 (member of Reformed Dutch Church in Saratoga for 7 yrs prior to her death) (9-6/1)
3553. Granger, Erastus, Esq., 62, among the first settlers of Buffalo, d 12/21/26 in B (Had served as Indian agent, collector of the port of Buffalo Creek, postmaster, and judge of the Niagara County Court of Common Pleas) (9-1/2/27)
3554. Granger, Gideon, 55, late Postmaster General of U.S., d in Canandaigua, NY (2-1/28/23)
3555. Granger, Harvey, merchant, of Northumberland m 1/6/08 Rebecca Low of Troy; Rev. Butler (9-1/12)

3556. Granger, Harvey, Esq. of Saratoga m 11/14/29 Maria Fort, dau of late Maj. Abraham, in Poughkeepsie' Rev. Dr. Cuyler (8-11/18)
3557. Granger, Henry F. of Keeseville m 10/31/31 in NYC Jane A. Nelson of Poughkeepsie (8-11/23)
3558. Granger, John A. m 4/23/29 Harriet Jackson, dau of late Amasa, Esq. of NYC, in Canandaigua; Rev. A. D. Cady (1-5/5)
3559. Granger, Ralph, Esq. of Ohio m 4/16/21 Catherine Van Ness, dau of Hon. William W., in Claverack; Rev. D. Gebhard (3-4/23)
3560. Granger, Roswel m 11/28/05 Charlotte Slason, both of Troy; Rev. Coe (9-12/10)
3561. Grant, Alexander H. of Dover m 12/1/30 Lucy Hatch of Danbury, CT in D (8-12/8)
3562. Grant, James m 6/30/29 Mary Oakley, dau of John W.; Rev. Dr. Reed. All of Poughkeepsie (Two of the reports define the groom as James Grant, Jr.) (8-7/1; 1-7/2; and 1-7/4)
3563. Grant, James A. (Capt.) of Bainbridge m Abigail G. Platt of Franklin (Dela. Co.) in F; Rev. Waterbury (1-3/10/31)
3564. Grant, Josephine of Troy m 1/4/27 Miranda Clark of Champlain in C; Rev. Byington (7-1/13)
3565. Grant, Joshua, 72, d 1/30/26 in New Berlin (Chen. Co.) (3-2/13)
3566. Grant, Richard, Jr., 30, "secretary to the general republican committee of young men and secretary in the Tammany Society", d 9/17/29 in NYC (1-9/21)
3567. Grant, William, member of senior class at Yale College and s of James, Esq. of Dover, NY, d 12/8/30 at sea on his way from NYC to Charleston, S.C. (8-1/5/31)
3568. Grants, Henry m 7/20/17 Katharine Orendorff, both of Columbia (Herk. Co.), in C (3-7/24)
3569. Grapser(?), Jacob m 7/1/26 Mrs. Elizabeth Sleight, late widow of James S. Sleight, in Leicester (Liv. Co.). All of Pine Plains (8-8/2)
3570. Graves, Abner, Jr. m 9/12/22 Eva Platner in Cooperstown; Rev. Stewart (3-9/16)
3571. Graves, Ashbel m 5/29/08 Aroxey Hamlin in Burlington (Ots. Co.); Hon. Elijah H. Metcalf, Esq. All of Burlington (3-6/4)
3572. Graves, Benjamin, Esq. m 8/7/18 Mrs. Lucretia Hubbard, both of Champlain, in C (7-8/15)
3573. Graves, Frances Rebecca, dau of Calvin, d 7/4/26 in Cooperstown (3-7/17)
3574. Graves, George m 12/5/13 Louisa Ransom, both of Chazy, in C (7-12/11)
3575. Graves, Huldah, about 36, wf of Benjamin, Esq., d 10/18/16 in Champlain (7-11/9)
3576. Graves, Jeremiah m Laura Marvin in Plattsburgh; Rev. Hewit (7-4/6/16)
3577. Graves, Jesse of Cooperstowm m 5/1/17 Nancy Fairchild of Hartwick in H; Rev. John Smith (3-5/8)
3578. Graves, Myron, s of Benjamin, Esq., m 6/26/25 Frances White in Champlain (7-7/9)
3579. Graves, Richard m 12/2/30 Rebecca Warner, both of Canaan; Rev. Taylor (1-12/20)
3580. Graves, Roxana, 31, wf of Ashbel, d 5/2/21 in Cooperstown (3-5/7)
3581. Graves, Susan, 49, consort of Recompense, d 3/18/13 in Cooperstown (3-3/27)
3582. Graves, Zerriah, 62, wf of Ezra, d 11/23/21 in Chazy (7-12/8)
3583. Gray, John W. m 8/14/31 Sarah Ann Howard; Rev. Welch. All of Albany (1-8/17)
3584. Gray, Kelson, 52, d in Montpelier, VT "a victim of the Thompsonian system of quackery ... under the operation of Lobelia" (1-11/17/30)
3585. Gray, Moses of Harpersfield m 3/29/25 Ann Elisa Anson of Amenia; Rev. Clark (8-4/13)
3586. Gray,Richard of Northeast m 7/11/13 Agnes Cantly of Amenia; Jesse Thompson, Esq. (8-7/28)
3587. Gray, S. H. (Rev.) of NYC m 9/22/29 Mary N. Arnett of Auburn in A; Rev. William Johnson (1-10/6)
3588. Gray, William (Hon.), 74, d 11/4/25 in Boston (state not given) (3-11/14)
3589. Gray, William B., Esq., 48, s of late Hon. William Gray, d 7/29/31 in Boston (state not given) (1-8/4)
3590. Green, _____, 14 mo, child of Thomas, d 8/30 in Plattsburgh (7-9/1)

103

3591. Green, Bartholomew of Fishkill m 12/3/06 Deborah Dodge, dau of Henry of Poughkeepsie; Rev. Barcalaw (8-12/9)
3592. Green, Charles B. of NYC m 9/11/27 Mary Green, dau of Oliver of Freedom, in F; Rev. Dwight (8-9/19)
3593. Green, Daniel m 1/20/25 Rosannah Rhodes, both of Bridgewater, in B (3-1/31)
3594. Green, Daniel M. m 8/21/28 Elizabeth R. Hill, both of Pittstown; Jonathan Reed, Esq. of Pittstown (9-8/29)
3595. Green, Elisha m 7/23/22 AnnTabor in Broadalbin; Rev. Groom. All of B (2-8/13)
3596. Green, Gertrude, 49, wf of Joseph I., d 5/30/24 in Plattsburgh (7-6/4)
3597. Green, Henry, Esq. m 3/22/31 Emily Augusta Ewing, dau of Hon. Charles, chief justice of the state of NJ, in Trenton, NJ; Rev. Alexander (1-4/1)
3598. Green, Ira m 10/12/23 Phebe Reynolds, dau of John F. of Fort Edward (Wash. Co.); Saunders Lansing, Esq. (9-11/4)
3599. Green, Isaac, 57, d 10/16/14 in Middlefield (3-10/20)
3600. Green, Isaiah, 81, late of Poughkeepsie, d 2/20/31 in New Paltz (8-2/23)
3601. Green, Israel m 2/24/03 Eve Hunt, both of Schaghticoke, in S; Rev. Paige (9-3/1)
3602. Green, Israel, 89, d 7/20/31 in Plattsburgh (8-8/3)
3603. Green, Jacob m 11/6/19 Harriet Fields, dau of John; Rev. John Reed. All of Puoghkeepsie. (8-11/10)
3604. Green, James of Cambridge m 12/4/23 Betsey Coulter of Jackson; Rev. Alexander Bullions (9-12/16)
3605. Green, Jesse m 9/29/21 Nancy Palmer, both of Washington (Dut. Co.); Rev. Brayton (8-10/10)
3606. Green, John, 3, s of John, Sr., d 6/25/30 (8-6/30)
3607. Green, John B., merchant, m 3/14/31 Elizabeth Simmons, dau of Capt. Abraham, in Phelps; Rev. Strong (1-3/29)
3608. Green, Joseph I., Esq. m 4/11/32 Mrs. Abigale Elkins (7-4/14)
3609. Green, Lowery m 12/28/30 Jane Eliza Doughty, dau of Cornell; Rev. Robertson. All of Beekman (8-1/12/31)
3610. Green, Oliver m 4/6/00 Jemimah Van Bunschoten, both of Fishkill; Rev. Van Vranken (8-4/8)
3611. Green, P. P. m 1/25/32 Celia M. Morgan of Burlington, VT; George Robinson, Esq. (7-3/17)
3612. Green, Peter m 5/11/20 Cena Bailey in Cherry Valley; Elder Benjamin Sawin (3-5/22)
3613. Green, Samuel, about 20, s of William, d 8/25/34 in Poughkeepsie (8-9/3)
3614. Green, Seth m 12/31/15 Cleory Dorset, both of Troy; Rev. Dr. Coe (9-1/9/16)
3615. Green, Stephen B., printer, of Albany m 7/10/25 Harriet E. Lee of Saratoga Springs; Rev. Lee (2-7/19)
3616. Green, Theodorus m Lucinda Pinney of Galway in G; Rev. William Chester (2-1/9/22)
3617. Green, Thomas m 2/4/13 Betsey Platt, dau of Theodorus; Rev. Halsey. All of Plattsburgh (7-2/5)
3618. Green, Thomas, 60, d 4/20/25 in New Haven, CT (his ancestors had been printers - for many years he was proprietor of the Connecticut Journal) (3-5/9)
3619. Green, William (Gen.) (a Rev. soldier) d in Somers (West. Co.) (3-9?8/23)
3620. Green, William m 8/25/34 Sarah Martin; Rev. George Coles. All of Poughkeepsie (8-9/3)
3621. Greenbrech(?), Ann Eliza, wf of John and youngest dau of Hon. John C. Fredinrch(?) d 12/22/30 in Albany (both surnames blurred, hence uncertain) (1-12/24)
3622. Greene, Benjamin, nearly 70, newscarrier for past 13 years, d 3/13/07 in Granville (a native of RI and brother of lateGen. Greene (9-3/24)
3623. Greene, John, 23, "a foreigner", d 8/31/19 in Red Hook (buried with Masonic honors) (6-9/7)
3624. Greene, John C. of NYC m 6/26/29 Louisa Charlotte Adelphine Martin Cornet, dau of late Gen. Cornet of Paris (country or state not given), in Paris (1-8/27)
3625. Greene, Joseph H., merchant, of Albany m 2/28/22 Sarah Haswell of Watervliet; Rev. Dr. Coe (9-3/5)

3626. Greene, Mary Haswell, 2, dau of Joseph H., d 9/14/31 in Albany (funeral from her father's home on Patroon St.) (1-9/16)
3627. Greene, Nathaniel, Esq., 67, formerly judge of the court of common pleas of Columbia Co., d 4/29/06 in Hudson (6-5/6)
3628. Greene, William A., Esq., attorney, of Sacket's Harbor m 10/6/30 Rebecca Pierce of Watertown; "Mr. Boardman" (1-10/16)
3629. Greenland, Joseph of NYC m 9/3/29 Delia Philo of Albany in A; Rev. J. J. Matthias (1-9/5)
3630. Greenleaf, Thomas, editor and printer of the Argus of NYC and the Patriotic Register, a Country Paper, d 9/14/98 (8-9/18)
3631. Greenman, William L., 3, s of Josiah, d 5/19/06 in Greenbush (9-5/27)
3632. Gregory, Albert of the firm of Gregory and Seaman m 2/20/28 Jane Low, dau of John A. of Poughkeepsie; Rev. C. C. Cuyler (8-2/27/28)
3633. Gregory, Ann (Miss), 19, d in Butternuts (3-3/14/25)
3634. Gregory, B. d in Albany (funeral from his late home, 8 Orange St)(1-3/5/31)
3635. Gregory, Benjamin, 15, of Richfield m 1/16/17 Martha Churchill, 11, dau of Capt. Edward; Abner Wilcox, Esq. (8-1/29)
3636. Gregory, Delos, inf s of Stephen, d in Cooperstown (3-5/20/22)
3637. Gregory, Ebenezer of New Lebanon m 9/8/25 Ruth Lanard of Hartwick in H; Elder Bostwick (3-9/26)
3638. Gregory, Enos, Jr. d 6/14/24 in Milton (2-6/15)
3639. Gregory, Henry of Owasco Flats m 9/10/30 Elizabeth Post of Geneva at Trinity Church in Geneva; Rev. Dr. Mason (1-9/18)
3640. Gregory, Stephen B. of the firm of Gregory, Bain and Co. m 11/23/30 Harriet Stafford, dau of Spencer, Esq. of Albany; Rev. Benjamin C. Taylor (1-11/25)
3641. Gregory, Theodorus, Esq. of Sand Lake m 4/9/26 Charlotte Hammond of Dover; Rev. C. P. Wilson (8-4/19)
3642. Gregory, William M. of the firm of Marvin and Gregory m 12/14/29 Catharine W, Trowbridge, only dau of Henry; Rev. Dr. Lacey. All of Albany (1-12/15)
3643. Greig, Benjamin of Rochester m 7/13/29 Guliaelma Carpenter of Macedon in M; Rev. Campbell (1-7/15)
3644. Grenebach, Lucy Ann, 18, wf of George E. of NYC and dau of Stephen Pardee of Poughkeepsie, d 2/4/29 in Poughkeepsie (8-12/9)
3645. Grenekback, George E. of NYC m 11/3/28 Lucy Ann Pardee, dau of Stephen of Poughkeepsie; Rev. Dr. Reed (8-11/12)
3646. Grensbach, George E. of NYC m 1/3/31 Sarah M. Pardee of Poughkeepsie in P; Rev. Dr. Reed (1-1/8). See also 3648.
3647. Grenzebach, John of NYC m 12/20/25 Hannah Nelson of Poughkeepsie; Rev. Dr. Reed (8-12/28)
3648. Grenzeback, George E. of NYC, merchant, m 1/3/31 Sally Maria Pardee, dau of Stephen of Poughkeepsie; Rev. Dr. Reed (8-1/5). See also 3646.
3649. Grey, Richard T. m 12/3/31 Louise Hammond; Amos Bryan, Esq. All of Northeast (8-12/14)
3650. Gridley, Sally, 2, dau of Noah, d in Hudson (6-12/12/09)
3651. Grier, Thomas (Rev.), 55, d 5/19/34 in Cold Spring (8-5/28)
3652. Grieve, John, 30, s of late Gen. Walter of Geneva, NY, d 8/21/29 in Carlisle, NY (1-8/31)
3653. Grieve, Walter, Esq., 53, (Brig. Gen.) of the 4th Brigade, NYS Artillery d 12/21/26 in Geneva (9-1/2/27)
3654. Griffen, Isaiah m 8/8/12 Waite Butler, both of Hudson (6-8/10)
3655. Griffin, B. B. m 4/27/31 Sarah M. Hunting, both of Albany, in Troy; Rev. Hill (1-4/29)
3656. Griffin, Bartholomew m 10/7/10 Sally Filken, both of Washington (Dut. Co.); Rev. Clark (8-10/10)
3657. Griffin, Harriet d 2/27/15 in Cooperstown (3-3/2)
3658. Griffin, Isaiah m Pamelia Oliver, both of Stanford (Dut. Co.), in Amenia; Joel Barton, Esq. (8-11/17/19)
3659. Griffin, Jacob m 2/5/03 Deborah Doughty, dau of Samuel, in Washington (Dut. Co.); Rev. Clark (8-2/15)
3660. Griffin, Kirtland, Esq., 77, (a Rev. Soldier) d 4/9/30 in "Saxouit(?), Paris" (b in Guilford, CT) (8-4/28)
3661. Griffin, Samuel, Jr., Esq., 32, attorney, (late of Otsego Co., NY) d 7/31/20 in Home's Ville, Mississippi, near New Orleans (3-9/11)
3662. Griffin, Timothy S. of Union Vale m 11/10/32 Mary Ann Leroy of La Grange; Rev. Fisher (8-11/14)

105

3663. Griffin, Ward, 40, d 6/29/25 in Cooperstown (3-7/4)
3664. Griffin, William, Esq., 48, sheriff of Dutchess County,d 5/20/23 (buried
    in Fishkill with Masonic honors) (8-5/28)
3665. Griffing, Jared, Esq. of Little Falls m 10/23/30 Elizabeth Glover of
    Sag Harbor, L.I., NY in Sag Harbor; Rev. Miller (1-11/16)
3666. Griffith, Daniel, 87, d 3/11/14 in Laurens (asthma) (3-3/19)
3667. Griffith, Edmund D. (Rev.), (age blurred), d 8/31/30 in NYC (blurred age
    could be a 25 or a 95) (1-9/3)
3668. Griffith, Hugh m 11/13/24 Margaret Griffith, both of Freedom; Rev. Cuyler
    (8-11/17)
3669. Griffith, John (Capt.) d 2/29/20 in West Stockbridge, MA (death resulted
    from a fall from a horse) (6-3/7)
3670. Griffith, Samuel (Capt.), 49, brother of Nijah Griffith, Esq. of Laurens,
    NY, d 7/5/15 "at the Missouri" (deceased had lived in Louisiana more
    than 20 years) (3-3/21/16)
3671. Griffith, Walter S. of Rochester m 8/1/31 Elizabeth S. Norton, dau of Col.
    Heman of NYC, in NYC; Rev. Erskin Mason (1-8/4)
3672. Griggs, Ichabod of Troy m 3/12/07 Roxy Oldiman of Watervliet; Rev. Coe
    (9-3/17)
3673. Griggs, Ichabod, Jr. of Springfield m Sally Abbott of Bethlehem in
    Albany; Rev. Weed (3-2/3/23)
3674. Griggs, Julia Sophia, inf dau of William C., d 8/22/31 in Catskill
    (1-8/27)
3675. Griggs, William C. of the firm of Cooke, Wilson, and Griggs m 9/1/29 Helen
    McKinstry, only dau of Henry, Esq., in Catskill; Rev. Dr. Porter. All
    of Catskill (1-9/5)
3676. Griswold, _____ (Mr.) of the firm of Doud and Griswold, merchants, d
    "recently" in Hudson (6-9/6/03)
3677. Griswold, Chester m 6/23/13 Abigail Moulton, both of Troy; Rev. Coe
    (9-6/29)
3678. Griswold, Elizur Horace, 19, 3rd s of Chester, Esq., d 3/3/30 in Utica'
    (fifth child to die in this family within the past five years)
    (1-3/13)
3679. Griswold, George, 63, d 11/30/28 in Moreau (9-12/19)
3680. Griswold, Hiram F., merchant, of the firm of H. M. Griswold and Co. of
    Burlington, VT m 2/20/34 Harriette R. Lamport of Port Kent in P.K.;
    Rev. Truman Seymour of Keeseville (7-3/1)
3681. Griswold, Josiah m 5/23/01 Nancy Charlott in Hudson; "Mr. Sampson"
    (6-5/28)
3682. Griswold, Landin m 2/4/27 Patience Barber; Rev. Satterlee. All of
    Berlin, NY (9-2/27)
3683. Griswold, Martha, about 40, wf of Col. Amos, d 12/5/28 in Salisbury
    (9-12/19)
3684. Griswold, Samuel B., 35, of the U.S. Army d 8/24/30 at the home of his
    father in Redhook, L.I., NY (1-8/27)
3685. Griswold, William A. (Hon.) of Burlington, VT m 12/19/33 Permelia Adams
    in Waterbury, VT; Rev. Warren (7-12/25)
3686. Griswould, Henry m 3/22/23 Alma Hill, both of Troy; Rev. Griffen (9-3/25)
3687. Groesbeck, _____, s of John, d "recently" in Albany (funeral from John's
    home, 5 Fox St.) (1-10/29/31)
3688. Groesbeck, Jane, 42, wf of Cornelius W., d 1/22/30 in Albany (funeral
    from her husband's home on Water St.) (1-1/23)
3689. Groesbeck, Lucretia, 4, youngest dau of David W., d 11/10/29 (1-11/12)
3690. Groesbeck, Maria, 56, dau of late William of Albany, d 11/18/31 at Little
    Falls (1-12/5)
3691. Groesbeck, Sybrent of Troy m 7/8/29 Eliza Wintringham, dau of John of
    NYC (in NYC?); Rev. Jacob H. Brouner (1-7/13)
3692. Groesbeeck, Deborah, 61, wf of Gerrit I., d 12/10/30 in Bethlehem
    (1-12/13)
3693. Groom, William, 92, d 4/18/12 in Catskill (6-4/27)
3694. Groome, Anna (Mrs.), 83, d in Athens, NY (6-8/15/09)
3695. Grosvenor, Aaron P. m 2/20/23 Hannah Stone in Milford; Rev. Henry
    Chapman (3-2/24)
3696. Grosvenor, Abel M., about 30, merchant, of Buffalo d 1/3/13 in Durham
    (Greene Co.) (en route to visit friends in Hudson to escape the
    "fever" in Buffalo) (surv by wf and 2 infant sons) (6-1/5)

3697. Grosvenor, Abigail, 65 (relict of Capt. Seth formerly of Pomfret, CT and mother of Hon. Thomas P.) d at the home of Frederick Stanley, Esq. in New Hartford (Oneida Co.), NY (6-8/13/16)
3698. Grosvenor, Joseph m 6/23/16 Sally Forbes, both of Middlefield, in M; Elder Benjamin Sawin (3-6/27)
3699. Grosvenor, Seth (Capt.), formerly of Pomfret, CT, d 1/14/08 in Windsor, MA (6-1/19)
3700. Grosvenor, Stephen K., merchant, of Buffalo m 2/29/16 Lucretia S. Stanley, "adoptive daughter of D. W. Lewis, Esq.", in Geneva; Rev. Clark (6-3/19)
3701. Grosvenor, Thomas P. (Hon.), congressman "from this district" (Hudson, NY area) m 3/16/15 Mary Ann Hanson at the home of W. Hanson, Esq. near Baltimore, MD; Right Rev. Bishop Kemp (6-3/28)
3702. Gue(?), John of New Paltz m 6/7/20 Mary Minerva Booth, dau of James of Poughkeepsie, in Fishkill; Rev. Crane (8-6/14)
3703. Guernsey, Mary Ann (wf of Dr. Peter B. and dau of Stephen Thorn, Esq.) d 11/18/34 in Poughkeepsie (typhus) (8-11/26)
3704. Guest, Elizabeth, wf of Edward, was killed by lightning 9/14/02 in Hudson (9-9/29)
3705. Guey, Louis Joseph, 31, d 11/2/09 in Hudson (6-11/7)
3706. Guild, Israel, 68, of Cooperstown m 3/1/98 Mrs. Anna Butts, 61 (3-3/8)
3707. Guild, Israel, 74, d 10/18/01 in Cooperstown (an early settler there) (3-10/22)
3708. Guiteau, Francis W. (s of Dr. Francis Guiteau, deceased, of Oneida Co.) d 12/20/29 in Bloomingdale (1-12/24)
3709. Gullen, William m 1/11/06 Catharine Plue, both of Poughkeepsie; Rev. Phillips (8-1/14)
3710. Gulliver, George m 10/20/21 Margaret Briggs, both of Rhinebeck; Rev. David Parker (8-11/28)
3711. Gulnac, Gitty, 53, wf of Jacob, d 2/28/07 in Hudson (6-3/10)
3712. Gunion, Peter m 11/1/25 Mary Bockus; Tilly Crouse, Esq. All of Clinton (8-11/6)
3713. Gunn, Alexander (Rev.), D.D., d 10/1/29 in Bloomingdale (apparently in NYC?) (Deceased was "a pastor in the Reformed Dutch Church") (1-10/5)
3714. Gunn, Isaac, formerly of Poughkeepsie, d 10/9/21 in Bellnemus, VA (8-10/24) (Addendum: Isaac age 22 at time of death)
3715. Gunn, Joseph m 11/9/28 Margaret Roberts, both of Poughkeepsie; Rev. Dr. Reed (8-11/12)
3716. Gunn, Maria, wf of Joseph, d 8/22/25 in Poughkeepsie (8-8/24)
3717. Gunn, Mary, 62, wf of John, d 8/30/18 in Hudson (6-9/15)
3718. Gunn, Stephen of the firm of Gunn and Sampson of Hudson m 7/25/18 Gertrude Van Ness, dau of W., Esq. of Claverack, in C; Rev. Gebberd (6-8/4)
3719. Gurley, Ephraim of the firm of Starbuck and Gurley, for many years a mechanic in Troy, d 2/7/29 in Troy (1-2/11)
3720. Gurnee, William m 1/1/22 Isabel Peck in Mayfield; Elder Simmons (2-1/16)
3721. Gurney, Henry B. of Albany m 10/6/29 Mary Clark of Coeymans; Rev. Kissam (1-10/10)
3722. Gurst, Edward m Betsey Phinney, dau of Jabez, in Hudson; Rev. Judd. All of Hudson (3-1/26/04)
3723. Guthrie, Lauren L., 24, s of Joseph, Esq. of Sherburne (Chen. Co.) d 6/15/29 in Tompkins (Dela. Co.) (died from "a fall from the piazza of a building ... fractured his scull") (1-6/20)
3724. Gwynne, T. F. (Lt.) of the U.S. Army m 11/8/30 Mildred Ann Perkins Brown, dau of Elisha, Esq. of Albemarle, VA, in Detroit, MI; Rev. Bury (1-12/3)
3725. Hackett, Charlotte, 17, youngest dau of Allen Hackett, d 4/22/14 in South Hero, VT (7-4/30)
3726. Hadley,Maryann L., 19 mo, only dau of Samuel W., d 10/2/19 in Plattsburgh (7-10/9)
3727. Haff, Peter, 47, d 2/23/22 in Troy (9-2/26)
3728. Hagadon, Harriet Jane, 10 mo, only dau of John and Harriet, d 2/18/34 in Poughkeepsie (8-2/26)
3729. Hagadorn, _____, wf of Peter, d "recently" in Albany (funeral from the home of her husband, 203 South Pearl St. (1-11/11/30)
3730. Hagadorn, Julia Ann, 4, youngest dau of Capt. Jacob, d 8/20/20 in Hudson (6-8/29)

3731. Hagadorne, Jacob, 42, d in Churchtown (Claverack area) (6-6/21/14)
3732. Hagaman, Cornelius, 66, of Beekman d 1/29/06 (8-2/11)
3733. Hagaman, John A., 58, farmer, of Fishkill d 1/12/13 (8-1/20)
3734. Hagar, Luther m 8/24/13 Sally Adams in Middlebury (state not given -
      perhaps intended for Vermont) (7-9/4)
3735. Hageman, Cornelius "who for many years kept a ... boarding house at
      Coenties Slip" (in NYC?) d in NYC (8-9/20/03)
3736. Hageman, Henry, Esq., late of Poughkeepsie, d 1/19/94 in NYC (8-1/29)
3737. Hageman, John, 18, oldest s of John, d 3/22/34 in NYC (8-3/26)
3738. Hageman, Margaret T., 8, only dau of Mrs. Eliza D., d 6/10/32 in
      Pleasant Valley (8-6/13)
3739. Hagley, William, merchant, of Albany m 11/3/29 Elizabeth B. Boardman,
      2nd dau of late Rev. William; Rev. J. Sandford of Philadelphia (state
      not given) (1-11/6)
3740. Haight, _____, wf of Robert, d 10/19/21 in Poughkeepsie (pulmonary
      complaint) (8-10/24)
3741. Haight, Ann Maria, 25, consort of Thomas, d 7/12/31 in Poughkeepsie
      (funeral at the home of her husband [not named] on Main St.)
      (8-7/13)
3742. Haight, Burling m 11/9/31 Polly Jones, both of Rensselaerville, in Bern;
      Judge Moore (1-11/11)
3743. Haight, Caleb d 5/4/23 (died from a wound received in the accidental
      discharge of a gun four days earlier) (8-5/7)
3744. Haight, Ebenezer, Esq., 52, d 3/8/21 in Poughkeepsie (8-3/14)
3745. Haight, F. M., Esq. m 9/25/29 Mary Ann Brown, dau of Dr. M. Brown, Jr.,
      in Rochester; Rev. James (1-10/1)
3746. Haight, George m 10/16/29 Sarah R. Wheeler in Washington (Dut. Co.);
      Rev. Armstrong (8-11/25)
3747. Haight, Jacob of Clinton (Dut. Co.) m 3/16/14 Catharine S. Ketcham of
      Poughkeepsie; Rev. John Clark (8-3/30)
3748. Haight, Jacob (Hon.) of Catskill m 4/30/25 Mrs. Maria H. Seckel of Athens,
      NY in A; Rev. Preston (3-5/9)
3749. Haight, Jonathan, Esq. d 12/11/32 in Stamford (8-12/19)
3750. Haight, Morris m 10/11/21 Eliza Myrick, both of Washimgton (Dut. Co.)
      (8-10/17)
3751. Haight, Rachel, dau of Ebenezer, Esq., d 8/24/27 in Poughkeepsie (8-8/29)
3752. Haight, Richard m 10/10/07 Hannah Lapham, both of Washington (Dut. Co.)
      (8-10/21)
3753. Haight, Richard of Poughkeepsie d 4/18/27 (8-4/25)
3754. Haight, Samuel, 52, d 11/9/17 in Athens, NY (6-11/11)
3755. Haight, Samuel B. of Troy m 2/3/27 Maria Koon, dau of Judge Koon of
      Greenbush, in G; Rev. Willis (9-2/6)
3756. Haight, Sarah, 53, wf of Gen. Samuel S. formerly of Bath, d 11/10/30 in
      Angelica (1-11/24 and 1-11/30)
3757. Haight, Silas, "an aged member of the Society of Friends", d 11/20/29 at
      his home in Washington (Dut. Co.) (8-11/25)
3758. Haight, Silas R. of Washington (Dut. Co.) m 10/22/23 Lydia W. Congdon of
      Freedom at the Friends Meeting House in Freedom (8-10/29)
3759. Haight, Thomas m 9/20/26 Ann Maria Parsons, both of Poughkeepsie; Rev. Dr.
      Reed (8-9/27)
3760. Haight, William of the firm of Haight and Williamson of NYC m 1/20/17
      Lydia Jenkins, dau of Thomas of Hudson; Rev. Prentice (6-1/28)
3761. Haight, William, 22, oldest s of Hon. Jacob of Catskill, d 5/12/29 in
      Catskill (1-5/23)
3762. Haightman, Abraham of Milan m 9/27/34 Mary Wirehouse of Pine Plains;
      Rev. William N. Sayre (8-10/8)
3763. Haile, John James, inf s of W. F. Haile, d 2/4/24 in Plattsburgh (7-2/7)
3764. Haimer, George m 11/29/27 Margaret Fellers, dau of Hon. Andrew; Rev. Gooden.
      All of Sand Lake (9-11/30)
3765. Haines, Charles G., Esq., 32, attorney and Adjutant General of NY, d 7/3/25
      in NYC (3-7/11 and 1-7/12)
3766. Haines, Sidney P. m 3/9/30 Diadamia Austin, dau of late Alanson, Esq. of
      Warwick, in W; Rev. J. J. Christie (1-3/22)
3767. Hake, Samuel m 8/24/05 Eliza M. C. De Peyster, only dau of James W., Esq.
      of NYC; Rev. Kuyper (8-9/10)

3768. Halbert, Enos S. m 7/4/22 Elizabeth Ann Cotton in Gilbert's Ville (Butter-
      nuts); Rev. Bogue (3-7/15)
3769. Hale, _____, relict of late Daniel, Esq. of Albany, d 3/3/29 in NYC
      (1-3/13)
3770. Hale, George (Col.), 44, d 8/15/03 in Catskill (funeral sermon by Rev.
      Porter) (6-8/23)
3771. Hale, James of Waterford m Azuba Adams of Brunswick; Rev. Coe (9-1/9/16)
3772. Hale, James Carleton, Esq. m Jane Amelia Yoe, dau of Charles, Esq. of
      Mount Pleasant, in Mount Pleasant; Rev. Crosby (1-9/29/29)
3773. Hale, W. F. (Capt.) of the U.S. Army m 4/15/22 Ann B. Kirtland, dau of
      John, Esq., in Granville (7-5/4 and 3-5/27)
3774. Halenbake, Dolly d "recently' in Albany (funeral at the home of
      Alexander McHarg on Ross St.) (1-4/3/30)
3775. Hall, Ann, 70, consort of Thomas, d 1/20/08 in Hartwick (funeral service
      by Elder Bostwick) (3-1/30)
3776. Hall, Benjamin m 8/28/03 Lucretia Warner in Canaan; Rev. Bogue (6-9/6)
3777. Hall, Cyrus m "Miss Chloe Hall, widow of John Hall", in Whitehall;
      Nathaniel Hall, Esq. All of W (7-9/28/16)
3778. Hall, Daniel, Esq. of Troy m 4/19/19 Anjinette Fitch of NYC in NYC; Rev.
      Whelpley (9-4/27)
3779. Hall, Ephraim of Utica m 11/16/25 Caroline Huntley, dau of Calvin, Esq.
      of Exeter in E; Rev. Giles (3-11/21)
3780. Hall, Ira of Hope m Eliza Shepherd of Broadalbin (2-10/12/24)
3781. Hall, Israel B. m 4/1/29 Eliza Palen, dau of Capt. Peter G., all of
      Poughkeepsie; Rev. Richardson (8-4/8)
3782. Hall, John, merchant, m 10/24/20 Louisa(?) Gardner, both of Troy
      (9-10/31)
3783. Hall, John A., merchant, of Troy m "a few days since" Henrietta St.
      John of Norwalk, CT in N (9-10/12/13)
3784. Hall, Jonathan, 26, d 9/17/00 in Cooperstown (surv by wf and 1 child)
      (3-9/25)
3785. Hall, Joshua (Rev.), 72, d 8/2/23 in Otsego (a Baptist minister) (3-8/11)
3786. Hall, Leonard, 1, s of Israel B., d 3/6/34 in Poughkeepsie (8-3/12)
3787. Hall, Luke (Capt.) of the ship "America" d "at quarentine", NYC (born in
      Duxbury, MA; lived for a time in Athens, NY) (6-7/11/15)
3788. Hall, Lyman, merchant, m 5/4/01 Electa Day, dau of Hon. Stephen, Esq.,
      in Catskill; "Mr. Sampson (6-5/21)
3789. Hall, N. N. of the U.S. Army m Margaret E. Bloodgood in Newark, NJ
      (7-7/18/18)
3790. Hall, Philo B. m 6/1/26 Ann M. Balis (or Balie?), dau of William, Esq.,
      in Amenia; Rev. C. P. Wilson (8-6/14)
3791. Hall, Ransom E. m 1/20/30 Sarah Allen, both of Geneva, in G; Rev. Eliakim
      Phelps (1-1/30)
3792. Hall, Thomas, 71, d 6/17/08 in Hartwick (5 children survive him) (3-7/30)
3793. Hall, William C., 27, of the firm of Hotchkiss and Hall, merchants, of
      New Haven, CT and son-in-law of Mr. G. W. Stanton of Albany, d 2/16/29
      in Charleston, SC (1-3/3)
3794. Hall, William T. of Kingston, NY m 3/27/30 Lucy West, dau of John of
      Burlington County, NJ; Rev. John Seger (1-4/6)
3795. Halland, Henry m 2/6/11 Phebe Race in Hudson; Rev. Chester (6-2/15)
3796. Hallaway, Ransom m 11/30/20 Rebecca Dodge, dau of Joseph, all of Pawling;
      Rev. Johnson (8-12/13)
3797. Hallenbeck, _____, dau of Lawrence, d "recently" in Albany (funeral from
      her father's home, 108 Washington St.) (1-11/1/30)
3798. Hallenbeck, _____, wf of Lawrence, d "recently" in Albany (funeral from
      her husband's home, 108 Washington St. (1-10/14/31)
3799. Hallenbeck, George (Capt.) m 1/20/29 Christina Hallenbeck in Hudson; Rev.
      Chester (1-2/14)
3800. Hallenbeck, Jeremiah m 11/13/13 Magdelene Evertson in Coxsackie (6-11/16)
3801. Hallock, Anna, 100, (member of the Society of Friends) d 1/7/32 in Peru,
      NY (4 [Keeseville Herald]-2/21)
3802. Hallock, Edward T., 4 mo, only s of James, d 12/16/34 in Utica (8-12/31/34
3803. Hallock, George m 11/26/34 Mrs. Mary Gifford, both of Peru, in P; L.
      Stetson, Esq. (7-11/29)
3804. Hallock, Mehitabel, 25, consort of Israel, d 8/9/11 in Poughkeepsie

109

3805. Hallock, Peter m 11/7/02 Levinah Vail, both of Clinton (Dut. Co.); Rev.
Clark (8-11/30)
3806. Hallock, Robert m 11/28/27 Amelia Barret, dau of Abraham of Milton, at
the Friends Meeting house in Milton (Ulster Co.) (8-12/5)
3807. Hallock, Samuel Titus of NYC m 12/4/34 Sarah C. Bailey of Deerfield, MA
in D (8-12/24)
3808. Hallock, William A. (Rev.), secretary of the American Tract Society of
NYC, m 9/1/29 Fanny Leffingwell Lathrop, dau of Charles, Esq. of Norwich,
CT, in N (1-9/7)
3809. Hallowell, George m 12/4/30 Julia Simmons, both of Poughkeepsie; Rev.
Welton (8-12/8)
3810. Halsey, Abraham (Dr.) of Fishkill m 5/1/06 Lucretia Green of NYC in NYC;
Rev. Dr. Miller (8-5/20)
3811. Halsey, Abraham (Dr.), for many years a physician in Hopewell, d 5/8/22
at his home in Hopewell (8-5/15)
3812. Halsey, Benjamin, Esq., druggist, m 6/11/29 Cornelia Evertson, dau of
G. B., Esq., in Ithaca; Rev. William Wisner (1-6/16)
3813. Halsey, David S. of Long Island m 1/16/19 Almira Mulford of Poughkeepsie
(8-1/20)
3814. Halsey, Frederick of Plattsburgh m 9/15/16 Hannah Rogers of Poughkeepsie;
Rev. Cuyler (8-9/18)
3815. Halsey, Frederick (Rev.) of Plattsburgh m 9/28/16 Maria Livingston, about
16, dau of James of Plattsburgh (7-9/28)
3816. Halsey, Frederick (Rev.) m 10/31/27 Mrs. Maria Mann, both of Plattsburgh;
Rev. Moses Chase (7-11/3)
3817. Halsey, Hannah, about 56, wf of Rev. Frederick of Plattsburgh, d 3/10/22
in Plattsburgh (7-3/16)
3818. Halsey, Isaac, 9, s of Rev. Frederick, d 2/12/20 in Plattsburgh (7-2/19)
3819. Halsey, Latitia, about 36, wf of Frederick Halsey and dau of Judge Charles
Platt, Esq., d 1/22/14 in Plattsburgh (7-1/29)
3820. Halsey, Mary, 35, wf of Dr. Gains Halsey, d 7/26/30 in Kortright (1-8/16)
3821. Halsey, Samuel B., Esq. of Fishkill m 9/5/21 Sarah D. Jackson, dau of
Col. Jackson of Rockaway, NJ, in R (8-9/12)
3822. Halsey, William of Troy m 12/7/28 Mary Ann Sickles of NYC; Rev. Patten
(9-12/12)
3823. Halstead, Michael, 19, s of Capt. Reuben, d 1/9/16 in Pittstown (9-1/16)
3824. Halsted, Thomas, 71, d 4/7/06 in Pittstown (9-4/15)
3826. Halsted, William m 3/22/20 Martha Haskins, both of Pittstown; Rev. Sommers
(9-3/28)
3827. Ham, Casper of Washington (Dut. Co.) m 6/16/19 Polly Hallett of
Poughkeepsie; Rev. Clark (8-6/23)
3828. Ham, Frederick, Jr. m 1/21/18 Eliza Ann Gazlay, dau of Joseph, all of
Clinton (8-1/28)
3829. Ham, Frederick C. of Washington (Dut. Co.) m 5/6/29 Sarah B. Snedeker of
Union Vale; Rev. S. Arnold (8-5/13)
3830. Ham, George of Washington (Dut. Co.) m 12/2/24 Catharine Marshall, dau of
James of Clinton (Dut. Co.); Rev. John Clark (8-12/15)
3831. *Ham, George of Washington (Dut. Co.) m 1/19/25 Ruthetta Clark*(8-1/26)
3832. Ham, Henry m 3/15/21 Elizabeth Thorne, both of Washington (Dut. Co.); Rev.
Clark (8-3/21)
3833. Ham, Jacob m 11/18/02 Margaret Ham, both of Clinton; Rev. Clark
3834. Ham, John W., merchant, m 10/21/17 G. Heermance, dau of late Andrew G.,
in Red Hook; Rev. Kittle. All of Red Hook (8-10/29)
3835. Hamblin, Eli of Amenia m 11/30/16 Lydia Stickles of Northeast (8-12/11)
3836. Hamblin, Hiram of Amenia m 11/30/16 Charity Tripp of Ancram (8-12/11)
3837. Hamblin, Hiram (Col.), 35, d 6/16/31 in Pine Plains (8-6/22)
3838. Hamersley, William James of the firm of Hamersley and Hyde m 11/11/29
Laura Sophia Cooke, oldest dau of Oliver D., Esq. of Hartford, CT,in
H; Rev. Hawes (1-11/20)
3839. Hamilton, _____, wf of Dr. Joseph, d 2/27/02 in Hudson (6-3/2)
3840. Hamilton, Abigail d 1/29/31 in Greenville, Greene Co. (paralytic
affection) (1-2/3)
3841. Hamilton, Catharine Louisa, 21, dau of Isaac, d 5/9/31 in Albany
(funeral from the home of James Gourlay, Esq. on Washington St.)(1-5/11)
3842. Hamilton, Clinton, Esq., about 28, d 11/27/20 in Athens, NY (6-11/28)
*(3831 addendum: Ruthetta is dau of Rev. Clark of Pleasant Valley)
110

3843. Hamilton, George C., Esq., attorney, of Athens m 10/16/11 AnnB. Malcolm, dau of Dr. Malcolm of Hudson, in H; Rev. Prentice (6-10/21)
3844. Hamilton, James, Esq. "of the woodlands near Philadelphia"(state not given) d 7/20/17 in Poughkeepsie, NY (8-7/23)
3845. Hamilton, John, about 67, d 1/24/21 in Plattsburgh (born in Scotland; was a soldier in the British artillery at the "siege of Gibralter") (7-2/3)
3846. Hamilton, John (Capt.) m Mrs. Rebecca Colby in Wiscasset (state not given). The bride, not yet age 20, "has now a third husband and has lived a widow for the last six weeks") (8-12/22/30)
3847. Hamilton, Joseph, M.D., 66, "for several years an eminent Physician" (in Hudson) d 3/4/05 (6-3/12)
3848. Hamilton, Sally, 21, 2nd dau of Samuel of Athens, NY, d 9/4/13 in Athens (inquest jurors' verdict: "wilful murder by the hands of some person or persons unknown") (7-9/11)
3849. Hammill, William Henry, 32, late a lieutenant in the U.S. Infantry, d 10/16/15 in NYC (9-10/31)
3850. Hammond, Ethan m 1/1/32 Mary Stow in Plattsburgh; Rev. Frederick Halsey (7-1/14)
3851. Hammond, Hannah (Widow), 89, d 12/16/26 in Plattsburgh (7-12/23)
3852. Hammond, Isaac, 68, m 9/16/26 Helenor Cedar, 70, both of Pleasant Valley; William Stevenson, Esq. (8-9/27)
3853. Hammond, John, 3, oldest s of Abijah, d in Hudson (6-12/5/09)
3854. Hammond, Miranda, 42, wf of Jabez D., d 8/28/31 in Albany (funeral from 107 Washington St.) (1-8/29)
3855. Hampton, Henry H., 23, d 10/17/30 in Albany (funeral at the home of James B. and Zalmon Hampton [brothers of the deceased] at the corner of Bass and Dalius Sts.) (1-10/18)
3856. Hanabergh, Ann (Mrs.), 30, d 10/28/25 "under her parental roof" (surv by husband and 2 ch) (8-11/23)
3857. Hanabergh, Peter, merchant, m 2/14/22 Ann Shultz, dau of Jacob, Esq. of Rhinebeck (8-2/20)
3858. Hancy, Alexander R. m 9/12/31 Almira Brown, both of Albany, in Syracuse; Rev. Gilbert (1-9/20)
3859. Hand, Aaron A. m 12/1/30 Maria Furman, dau of Garrit, Esq., in NYC; Rev. Dr. William McMurray (1-12/6)
3860. Haner, Elizabeth, 39, consort of Capt. Philip, d 11/8/15 in Claverack (6-11/14)
3861. Hanes, Benjamin m 10/11/18 Sally Powel, both of Hudson, in Claverack; Rev. Gebhard (6-10/27)
3862. Hanford, Apollos B., 34, d 1/21/30 in Monticello, NY (1-2/1)
3863. Hanford, John of Cleveland, OH m 6/12/24 Eliza Noble of Unadilla, NY at Zion Church in Butternuts, NY (3-6/21)
3864. Hanley, John, pvt. in Capt. McGlashin's Co., 6th Regt. of U. S. Infantry, d 3/9/18 at the Plattsburgh cantonment (a veteran of the War of 1812) (7-3/14)
3865. Hansen, Tunis, auctioneer, m Polly Johnson, dau of Capt. Walter, in Hudson; Rev. Cooper (6-11/15/08)
3866. Hanson, Abraham of Williamstown m 3/18/24 Catharine Van Cott of Troy; Rev. Howard (9-3/30)
3867. Harcourt, Nathaniel m Gitty Likes, both of Red Hook, in Hudson; Rev. Chester (6-5/3/11)
3868. Harcy(?), Samuel, 54, d 10/12/30 in Albany (1-10/14)
3869. Hard, John Landon, 7, s of Peter N., formerly of Clinton, d 2/17/16 in Troy (8-3/13)
3870. Hardaway, Herman m 4/25/27 Roda Sage, both of Troy; Rev. Howard (9-4/27)
3871. Hardaway, More m 1/11/27 Lucretia Van Ranst, both of Troy; Rev. Howard (see also the marr. of Peleg More, same evening by the same clergyman) (9-1/23)
3872. Hardcastle, Thomas W., merchant, of Dayton, OH m 9/13/31 Adelaide Josephine Humphrey, oldest dau of Dr. Gideon, "at the village green near Philadelphia" (state not gvien); Rev. Stephen Rider (1-9/17)
3873. Hardeck, Cornelia, 8 mo, dau of Peter F., d 12/8/07 in Hudson (6-12/15)
3874. Hardenburgh, Helen Mary, wf of Cornelius, Esq. of New Brunswick (state not given) and dau of John Crooke of Poughkeepsie, NY, d 4/27/25 in P (8-5/4)

111

3875. Harder, Wilhelmus m 3/1/11 "Miss Gardenier", both of Kinderhook, in Hudson; Rev. Chester (6-3/15)
3876. Hardick, Abraham, 65, d in Hudson (6-8/1/09)
3877. Hardick, Peter F. m 5/25/06 Mariam Bunker, dau of Capt. David, in Hudson. All of Hudson (6-5/27)
3878. Hare, Almira, about 18, dau of David, d 3/4/27 in Plattsburgh (7-3/10)
3879. Hare, Daniel of Plattsburgh m 7/22/19 Susan Winch, dau of Nathaniel of Jay, in J (7-7/31)
3880. Hare, David m 1/1/23 Nancy Winch (7-1/4)
3881. Hare(?), George Emlen (Rev.) m 6/22/30 Elizabeth Catherine Hobart, dau of Right Rev. Bishop Hobart,at St. John's Chapel in NYC; Rev. Dr. Berrian (1-6/25)
3882. Hare, Joseph of Plattsburgh m 8/31/26 Elsey Irish of Peru, NY in P (7-9/2)
3883. Hargraves, John m 11/10/32 Alice Ashworth in Burmingham (state not given); Rev. Bates (4 [Keeseville Herald]-11/13)
3884. Haring, John S. of the firm of Hart, Haring, and Rider, m 9/15/31 Mary Clark, dau of William, in NYC; Rev. Dr. McMurray (1-9/17)
3885. Haring, Samuel (Capt.), 53 or 58?, formerly of the U.S. Army, d 7/12/30 at his home in Albany (1-7/13)
3886. Harkins, Jonah (Mr.), 54, d 1/29/16 in Amenia (8-2/21)
3887. Harkness, Asa of Peru, NY m 2/2/27 Sarah Heszeltan of Mooers at No. 5 in Mooers; Joshua Palmer, Esq. (7-12/8)
3888. Harkness, Nehemiah (Capt.) m Deborah Everitt in Peru, NY; Hon. E. Williams (4 [Keeseville Herald]-1/28/34)
3889. Harley, Isaac, Esq., late of South Carolina, d 12/14/28 in NYC (9-12/19)
3890. Harlow, Isaac, Esq., 72, "one of the first settlers in the northern country", d 1/11/29 in Whitehall (1-1/31)
3891. Harlow, John of the firm of Harlow and Hullen of New Orleans, LA, m 8/5/31 Maria Skilbern, dau of late Joseph of NYC; Rev. Dr. McCartee (1-8/12)
3892. Harlow, Josiah W. m 9/19/32 Maria Warren, both of Westport, in W; William Smith, Esq. (4 [Essex Republican]-9/29)
3893. Harmance, Andrew (Col.), 71, d 8/15/18 in Troy (6-8/18)
3894. Harmon, _____, a child of Dr. E. D. Harmon, d 8/21/13 (probably in Burlington, VT) (7-9/4)
3895. Harper, Benjamin m 1/9/23 Nancy Angell, both of Schuylerville, in S; Rev. Philip Duryee (2-1/21)
3896. Harper, Elizabeth, 34, consort of James, d 4/13/90 in Cooperstown (3-4/14)
3897. Harper, James, 60, d 9/14/21 in Cooperstown (3-9/17)
3898. Harper, James, cashier of the U.S. Bank, d 10/25/31 in Lexington, KY (1-11/11)
3899. Harper, Robert Goodloe, Esq. m 5/8/01 "Miss Carroll", dau of Charles Carroll, Esq. of Carrolton in C; Right Rev. Bishop Carroll (6-5/21 and 3-5/28)
3900. Harral, George E. (Dr.) of Utica m Julia Ann Neafus of Rochester in R (9-1/19/27)
3901. Harrington, Andrew A. m 10/12/30 Priscilla P. Ferris, both of Poughkeepsie; Rev. Dr. Reed (8-10/13)
3902. Harrington, Benjamin (Deacon), an early settler of Burlington (Ots. Co.) d 3/3/26 in Burlington (born inPownal, VT) (3-3/13)(addendum: died at age 58)
3903. Harrington, Elisha, about 35, d 7/31/22 in Plattsburgh (7-8/3)
3904. Harris, Abigail, consort of Asa, d 3/15/07 at Stewart's Patent (in the town of Cooperstown) (surv by husband and several adopted children) (she was from Connecticut and her maiden surname was Davenport) (3-3/19)
3905. Harris, Asa, 70, of Otsego m Mrs. Alice Dowe, 50, of Coventry, CT in C; John Spier, Esq. (within past 3 yrs and 3 mos Asa had been the husband of three different wives, this one his fourth) (3-9/3/07)
3906. Harris, Caroline, 22, youngest dau of Ezekiel of Bedford, Westchester Co., NY d 12/15/28 in Natchez, Mississippi (1-3/4)
3907. Harris, David of Newburgh m 10/23/27 Margaret Pells, dau of John A. of Poughkeepsie; Rev. C. C. Cuyler (8-10/31)
3908. Harris, George W. m 11/23/30 Lucinda Morgan, wid of late Capt. William, in Batavia; Hon. Simeon Cummings (1-12/2)

3909. Harris, Isaac of Poughkeepsie d 8/1/25 in Utica ("His remains were conveyed to the grave by the Journeymen Cordwainers' Society by whose liberality he was supported during his illness") (8-8/17)
3910. Harris, Jacob C. m 5/5/25 Jane Phillips; Rev. C. C. Cuyler. All of Poughkeepsie (8-5/11)
3911. Harris, James of NYC m 7/16/29 Rebecca Martha Maverick, dau of Samuel of NYC, at St. John's Church in Johnstown (Mont. Co.); Rev. Alva Bennett (1-7/24)
3912. Harris, John m "Mrs. Miles" (7-5/15/19)
3913. Harris, Joseph m 9/9/98 Hannah Overrocker, both of Beekmantown (possibly intended for Beekman in Dut. Co.) (8-9/18)
3914. Harris, Mary L., 26, wf of Edward, Esq. of Moorestown, NJ and dau of John Lang, Esq. of NYC, d about 2/7/30 in Pisa, Italy (1-2/23)
3915. Harris(?), Richard m 9/11/93 Maria Deyo, both of Poughkeepsie; Rev. Gray (8-9/18)
3916. Harris, Seth as well as Freeman Cobb, Jonathan Hammond, "Mr. Merrill", Capt. Enos Wood, and Willis Wood, all family heads, were lost in the sinking of the schooner, "Atlas", on Lake Ontario (copied from a Palmyra, NY newspaper [title not given] and printed in 8-1/16/22)
3917. Harris, Silas of Northeast m 4/11/21 Maria Pugsley, dau of Edward of Stanford; Rev. Armstrong (8-4/18)
3918. Harris, William (Rev.), D.D., 64, Pres. of Columbia College, d 10/18/29 (1-10/21)
3919. Harris, William H. m 9/28/28 Hannah Simmons, both of Troy; Rev. Howard (9-10/7)
3920. Harrison, _____, about 5, s of Frederick of Hudson, d 1/14/06 ("mortally wounded by the accidental discharge of a musket in a neighboring store") (6-1/28)
3921. Harrison, Charles A. of Troy m 9/8/23 Hannah Miller "of New Ark" in New Ark; Rev. Hay (9-9/16)
3922. Harrison, George of Waterville, VT m 8/1/31 Lydia P. Hines of Sandy Hill (Wash. Co., NY) (at Sandy Hill?); Rev. Seney or Sevey? (1-8/8)
3923. Harrison, Hiram m 10/1/29 Malvina Tibbits, both of Troy; Rev. Whittemore (1-10/7)
3924. Harrison, John, editor of the Weekly Museum, d "last week" in NYC (8-8/21/04)
3925. Harrison, John m 1/1/22 Jane Allen, both of Troy; Rev. Griffen (9-1/22)
3926. Harrison, John Cleves Symmes, Esq., 32, oldest s of Gen. William H., d 10/30/30 at North Bend, OH (1-11/16)
3927. Harrison, Richard, Esq., 80, "the Patriarch of the N.Y. Bar", d 12/7/29 in NYC (8-12/9)
3928. Harrison, William H., Esq. m 6/7/31 GertrudeWaddington Ogden, dau of Thomas Waddington, Esq., in NYC; Right Rev. Bishop Onderdonk (1-6/10)
3929. Harrison, Zillah, 48, wf of Frederick of Poughkeepsie, d 4/22/29 (8-4/29)
3930. Hart, _____ (Deacon), 70, d 8/3/27 in Hamden, CT (stung by a bumble bee and died in less than one hour) (9-8/21)
3931. Hart, Alonzo O. (Capt.) of Hartford (Cort. Co.) m Eveline Maria Tobey, dau of Nathaniel of Caroline (Tompkins Co.) in C; Rev. Riggs (1-2/28/29)
3932. Hart, Benjamin, merchant, of Washington (Dut. Co.) m Maria Gidley of Poughkeepsie; Rev. John Clark (8-5/19/13)
3933. Hart, Borden m 1/14/24 Celestia Foot, both of Kingsborough (Mont. Co.), in Salisbury (Herk. Co.); Rev. Whipple (8-1/28)
3934. Hart, Delia Maria, 27, consort of Richard of Cambridge and dau of James Dole, Esq. of Troy, d 7/2/05 in Troy (consumption) (married "scarcely five months") (9-7/9; 6-7/16; and 8-7/23)
3935. Hart, Edmund (Capt.) d 12/24/30 in St. Augustine, FL (had been an engineer on the Hudson River in NY [steamboat "Victory"] but, ill with consumption, moved to Florida "a few months since") (1-1/15/31)
3936. Hart, Elihu, 53, d in Catskill (6-9/9/06)
3937. Hart, Ephraim, Esq. of Utica, NY m 5/1/21 Martha Seymour of Hartford, CT in H; Rev. Dr. Flint (3-5/14)
3938. Hart, Jacob A., merchant, of Troy m 1/7/13 Anna Maria Moore, dau of Maj. Benjamin of Coxsackie, in Albany; Rev. David Butler (9-1/12)

113

3939. Hart, John m 9/21/Laura Augusta Smith (dau of Counsellor J. H. Smith
       and gr-dau of Judge Smith, Kings Co. Chief Justice before the Rev. War)
       at Trinity Church, NYC; Rev. Dr. Berrian (1-9/29)
3940. Hart, Mary Ann (Miss), 4th dau of Elisha, Esq., d 10/30/30 in Saybrook,
       CT (1-11/5)
3941. Hart, Norman m 11/29/31 Eliza Oakey in Albany; Rev. Luckey. All of
       Albany (1-12/1)
3942. Hart, Phebe Bloom, 12, dau of Richard P. of Troy, d 2/26/13 in Troy
       (8-3/10)
3943. Hart, Richard, s of Philip pf Washington (Dut. Co.) m Phoebe Bloom, dau
       of Judge Bloom of Clinton (Dut. Co.) (8-1/28/00)
3944. Hart, Richard P., merchant, of Cambridge m Delia Maria Dole, dau of James,
       Esq., in Troy (6-2/19/05)
3945. Hart, Richard P. of Troy m 2/8/16 Betsey Amelia Howard, dau of William of
       NYC, in NYC; Rev. Dr. Romeyn (9-2/13)
3946. Hart, Seth C., Esq., attorney, m 2/9/31 Mary Oathout of Lockport in L;
       Rev. W. F. Curey (1-2/24)
3947. Harshorn, Polly, 19, d 5/17/17 in Otsego (death "occasioned by her taking
       Corrosive sublimate which was dealt out to her by her physician
       instead of Tartar Emetic") (3-5/22)
3948. Hartwel, Niles m 9/30/19 Mary Winchell, dau of Philo M., all of Northeast;
       Rev. John Buttolph (8-10/13)
3949. Hartwell, Abraham, 45, d 2/2/18 in Cooperstown (3-2/9)
3950. Hartwell, Luther of Cooperstown m 1/29/17 Harriet Benjamin of Poughkeepsie;
       Rev. John Reed (8-2/5)
3951. Harvey. Asahel, one of the publishers of the Ontario Repository, m 6/30/31
       Eveline Hall, dau of John formerly of Canandaigua, in Zanesville, OH
       (1-7/11)
3952. Harvey, Charles, 18, youngest s of Maj. James, d in Salem (Wash. Co.)
       (1-9/5/29)
3953. Harvey, James H., an officer of the Dutchess Co. Bank and late of Harvey's
       Neck, NC, d 1/8/34 in Poughkeepsie (8-1/15)
3954. Harvey, James Henry, Esq. of Edenton, NC m 8/15/24 Anne Caroline Crary of
       Poughkeepsie at Christ's Church in Poughkeepsie; Rev. Dr. Reed (8-8/18)
3955. Harvey, Thomas S. of Petersburgh m 9/7/19 Mary Hatch of Troy; Rev. Dr. Coe
       (9-9/14)
3956. Hasbrook, Abraham, formerly of Fishkill, NY, d 1/29/34 in Louisville, KY
       (8-3/12)
3957. Hasbrook, Janette, wf of Benjamin of NYC and dau ofMaj. A. Hatch of
       Poughkeepsie, d 11/23/32 in NYC (buried in Poughkeepsie) (8-11/28)
3958. Hasbrook, John A. m 4/15/15 Mary Vail, both of Fishkill; Rev. Price
       (8-4/26)
3959. Hasbrouck, Abraham Bruyn, Esq. of Kingston m 9/12/19Julia Frances Ludlum
       of New Jersey at the home of Robert Morris, Esq. in Claverack (6-9/21)
3960. Hascall, Hannah, about 16, dau of late Ralph, d 5/22/24 in Malone
       (7-6/4)
3961. Hascall, Ralph, about 45, d 7/6/23 in Saratoga Springs (7-7/19)
3962. Hascall, Ralph, Esq., 47, of Essex Co., NY, formerly a state senator,
       d in "Balston" (3-8/4/23)   (addendum: deceased was an attorney)
3963. Haserodt, Henry I. m 7/30/26 Rebecca Shultz of Pine Plains; Rev. R. G.
       Armstrong (8-8/2)
3964. Haskell, Abigail, wf of Zebulon and only surviving sister of John Swift
       of Hudson, d in Middleborough, MA (6-8/16/11)
3965. Haskell, Sarah Ann, only dau of Roger formerly of Cooperstown, d in Geneva
       (3-8/28/20)
3966. Haskill, Joseph m 8/30/18 Clarissa Pier; Rev. Lee. All of Troy (9-9/8)
3967. Haskins, David, Esq. m 7/25/13 Harriet Elsbury, both of Washington
       (Dut. Co.); Jahul Sacket, Esq. (8-7/28)
3968. Hastings, Elijah of Amherst, MA m 2/8/27 Adaline Weston, dau of Ephraim
       of Hoosick, in H; Rev. May (9-3/2)
3969. Hastings, Truman, Esq. of Geneseo m 8/10/28 Elizabeth Vail of Troy;
       Rev. Beman (9-8/15)
3970. Haswell, Anthony, Esq., 61, editor of the Green Mountain Farmer and one
       of the earliest printers in Vermont, d 5/23/16 in Bennington, VT
       (3-6/6 and 7-6/8)

114

3971. Hatch, Daniel L., 30, d "in August last" in Shippensport, KY; also, in this same release is the record of the death (2/23/26) of Samuel Hatch, 28, who died in Columbia (Herk. Co.), NY (3-3/13/26)
3972. Hatch, George W. of NYC m 10/14/29 Mary Ann Daniels, dau of Warner, Esq. of Albany; Rev. Dr. Lacey (1-10/16)
3973. Hatch, Isaac, merchant, of Sherman, CT m 9/18/30 Eliza Tomlinson of La Grange; Rev. Arnold (8-9/22)
3974. Hatch, Menzo, 11 mo, s of Capt. Dorus Hatch, d 12/6/26 in Richfield (3-12/8)
3975. Hatch, Oliver m 10/21/21 Elizabeth Forrester, both of Schenectady; Rev. Griffin (9-11/6)
3976. Hatch, "Mrs. Seers" d 1/25/13 in Troy (9-2/2)
3977. Hathaway, _____, inf child of Capt. Baley Hathaway of Hudson, d in NYC (6-10/25/08)
3978. Hathaway, Bailey (Capt.), 60, d 8/18/31 ("very suddenly from drinking ice water") in Hudson (1-8/24)
3979. Hathaway, Ezra m 10/21/23 Amy Cass; James Hyde, Jr., Esq. (3-11/3)
3980. Hathaway, John (Capt.) "an old inhabitant of Hudson" d 3/10/18 (6-3/10)
3981. Hathaway, John B. of Hudson, NY m 8/30/29 Lucy G. Crofut of Danbury, CT in Ridgebury, CT; Rev. G. Benedict (1-9/7)
3982. Hathaway, Robert, 41, d in Hudson (6-3/25/41)
3983. Hathaway, Sally, consort of Capt. Nicholas, d 7/22/14 in Hudson (6-8/2)
3984. Haven, Samuel (Rev.), D.D., 79, d 3/3/06 and his wife Margaret, 60, d 3/6/06 in Portsmouth, NH (6-3/25)
3985. Havener, Peter m 12/14/20 Gitty Butler in Ghent; Rev. Sluyter (6-12/19)
3986. Havens, Byram, 42, d 4/1/22 in Plattsburgh (7-4/6)
3987. Havens, James m 3/20/08 Levina Jacobs, both of Troy (9-3/22)
3988. Havens, John m "a short time since" Acksy Burdick in Chazy (7-7/14/21)
3989. Havens, Jonathan N., Esq., congressman "for the District of Long and Staten Island", d 11/2/99 at his home on Shelter Island (9-11/5)
3990. Havens, Stephen Van Rensselaer m 6/26/23 Laura Towers, both of Plattsburgh, in P; Rev. Halsey (7-6/28)
3991. Haviland, Abel m 11/23/03 Hannah Hoag of Pawling (8-12/6)
3992. Haviland, Asahel of Quaker Hill in Pawling m 10/14/34 Phebe E. Preston of Dover; Rev. E. Perkins (8-10/22)
3993. Haviland, Caleb D. of Clinton (Dut. Co.) m 5/30/15 Susan Fort of Poughkeepsie; Rev. C. C. Cuyler (8-6/7)
3994. Haviland, Horace J. of Hyde Park m 9/22/30 Emily Silkreg of Red Hook in R H; Rev. Kittle (8-10/6)
3995. Haviland, Jacob, 50, farmer, of Washington (Dut. Co.) d 8/1/31 (8-8/10)
3996. Haviland, Willis m Susan Hart, dau of Philip, Esq., in Hartsville (Dut. Co.); Samuel Allen, Esq. All of H (8-5/14/34)
3997. Howes, John of Claverack m 8/7/13 Betsey Keenney (sic) of Hudson; Rev. Chester (6-8/10)
3998. Hawk, Conrad, 76, d "recently" in Pennsylvania ("he was the first man who drove a wagon over the Alleghenny Mountains") (3-4/27/15)
3999. Hawkins, Abigail, 39, wf of George, d in Plattsburgh (7-4/5/23)
4000. Hawkins, Barny (Dr.) m 2/22/27 Elizabeth Potter, both of Poughkeepsie; Rev. Dr. Reed (8-2/28)
4001. Hawkins, Benjamin, late of Ulster Co., d 8/14/13 in Herkimer (9-8/17)
4002. Hawkins, Benjamin (Col.), agent for Indian affairs in Virginia Creek country, d 6/6/16 "in the creek agency" (3-7/11)
4003. Hawkins, Hannah, 61, wf of Gaylord, d in Franklin (Dela. Co.) (6-8/3/13)
4004. Hawkins, Hannah, 53, relict of late Col. Samuel of NYC, d 1/7/32 in Buenos Ayres, South America (8-4/18)
4005. Hawkins, Hiram m 1/28/27 Mariah Mercellus, both of Troy; Rev. Howard (9-1/30)
4006. Hawkins, John m Polly Mooers, both of Constable, in C (7-11/27/13)
4007. Hawkins, Phebe, wid of Christopher formerly of Poughkeepsie, d 9/20/27 in Poughkeepsie (8-9/26)
4008. Hawkins, Rufus, merchant, 21, d 5/28/06 in Exeter (Ots, Co.) (surv by father, mother, brothers, and sisters) (funeral sermon by Rev. Daniel Nash) (3-6/5)
4009. Hawks, _____, wf of James, Esq., d 5/5/25 in Sherburne (3-5/9)
4010. Hawley, _____, 59, wf of Rev. Rufus, pastor of the Second Society of Farmington, CT, d 4/8/98 (3-4/26)

4011. Hawley, Elias, merchant, of Glens Falls m 1/22/30 Adeline Hawley, dau of
Martin, Esq., merchant, of Binghamton (1-2/3)
4012. Hawley, Henry m 10/24/11 Lucretia Barnes, both of Canaan, in C; Rev. Clark
(6-11/4)
4013. Hawley, Highland (Mr.), 42, d 11/2/32 in Keeseville (4 [Keeseville Herald]-
11/13)
4014. Hawley, J. Edwin (Dr.) m 9/14/29 Miranda Phillips, oldest dau of G. W.,
in Ithaca; Rev. Williston (1-9/22)
4015. Hawley, Lemuel, Esq. d 12/16/21 in Troy (9-12/18)
4016. Hawley, Lydia, 26, wf of Calvin and dau of Capt. Willard Eddy, d 5/25/25
in Richfield (3-6/6)
4017. Hawley, Philenia, 22, dau of late Francis, Esq., d 4/25/26 in Warren
(Herk. Co.) (3-5/8)
4018. Hawley, Stiles drowned 1/18/30 in the Kaskaakia River in Illinois (born
in CT and visited NY state as agent of the American Sunday School Union)
("In the winter" he left Springfield, IL for Macon Co. Later only his
horse was found.) (1-5/13)
4019. Hawley, William m 12/9/29 Arabella Elizabette Wheeler, dau of George A.,
Esq., in Bloomfield, Ontario Co.; Rev. U. M. Wheeler (1-12/23)
4020. Haws, J. H. Hobart m 11/10/30 Maria Louisa Thompson, dau of late George,
at Zion Church in NYC; Rev. Brichtnell (1-11/12)
4021. Haxton, Benjamin of Beekman m 3/26/28 Sarah Wolley, dau of William I., Esq.
of Pleasant Valley; Rev. Clark (8-4/2)
4022. Haxton, Washington, Esq. m 7/25/24 Sophia M. L. Taylor, both of NYC; Rev.
Dr. Reed (8-7/28)
4023. Haxtun, Jeremiah, 85, d 1/22/30 in Beekman (8-2/10)
4024. Hay, Martha, 19, consort of William of St. John, New Brunswick and dau of
Stephen Anders, Esq., d 10/5/22 in Troy, NY (9-10/8)
4025. Hay, Mary, 65, youngest dau of David, Esq. late of Fifeshire, Scotland,
d 9/19/24 in Poughkeepsie, NY (David arrived in this country "about
ninety years ago". He was son of Robert Hay of the noble fam of Hays
in Fifeshire. His mother was a descendant of the Earl of Murray,
Regent of Scotland during the minority of James the Sixth.) (8-10/6)
4026. Hay, Udney (Col.), 66, d 9/6/06 in Burlington, VT (9-9/23 and 6-9/30)
4027. Hayden, Hezekiah, 47, d 5/16/23 in Springfield (3-5/26)
4028. Hayden, Moses (Hon.), "a senator from the 8th district", d 2/13/30
(funeral from Eagle Tavern, Albany) (1-2/15)
4028a. Hayes, Don Augustine Iturbide S. S., s of R. Hayes, d 9/2/33 in Peru, NY
(4 [Keeseville Herald]-9/10)
4029. Hayes, James of Clinton m 2/21/24 Charity Cocks of Pleasant Valley; Tilley
Crouse, Esq. (8-3/3)
4030. Hayes, Joshua m 10/27/05 Harriot Hazard in Hudson; Rev. Sears (6-11/5)
4031. Haynes, Selden of Hudson m 4/16/28 Catharine Butler of Poughkeepsie;
Rev. E. Holmes (8-4/23)
4032. Hays, Chauncey of Prattsburgh (Steuben Co.) m 10/11/31 Cynthia C. Edwards,
dau of Alanson of Skaneateles, in S; Rev. Stockton (1-10/24)
4033. Hayt, Samuel, merchant, of Pleasant Valley m 9/12/22 Eliza Reed, dau of
Jesse of Washington (Dut. Co.); Rev. Clark (8-9/25)
4034. Hayt, Samuel Augustine of the firm of H. and S. Hayt, merchants, m 10/8/29
Catharine Ann Van Wyck; Rev. Dr. Cornelius D. Westbrook. All of
Fishkill (1-10/12)
4035. Hayt, Stephen, Esq., 74, d 9/17/34 in Patterson (lived there many years)
(8-10/1)
4036. Hayward, John, 32, d 9/2/23 in Troy (9-9/16)
4037. Haywood, Thomas "an aged inhabitant of Poughkeepsie" d 10/10/18 in P
(8-10/21)
4038. Hazard, John L. m 5/31/18 Hannah Crossman in Hudson; Rev. Pickering
(6-6/2)
4039. Hazard, Tiddeman d in Athens, NY (6-5/25/13)
4040. Hazard, William, 58, d 10/25/09 in Hudson (6-11/7)
4041. Hazen, Caleb (Col.), 56, d 3/31/06 at his home in Carmel (8-4/15)
4042. Hazen, Charles of Plattsburgh m 5/23/23 Polly Clark of Peru, NY in P;
Rev. Samuel Weaver (7-6/21)
4043. Hazen, Charles of the firm of Netterville and Hazen m 3/29/30 Eliza Monk,
youngest dau of late Christopher, in Albany; Rev. ___ (name blurred)
(1-3/31)

116

4044. Head, Isaac m Sally Head in Pembroke, NH (6-2/19/05)
4045. Headlock, Benjamin D. of Boston (state not given) m 3/27/11 Patty Lake
of Clinton (Dut. Co.), NY; Joshua Coffins, Esq. (8-4/3)
4046. Heady, Nathaniel D. m 11/26/31 Emeline Pullock, both of Union Vale, at
the Stone Church in Dover Plains; Thomas Hammond, Esq. (8-12/7)
4047. Healy, John m 10/1/28 Catharine Smith; Rev. Defreest. All of Troy
(9-10/3)
4048. Hearn, David G. (Capt.), 46, d 1/11/32 in Troy (influenza) (4 [Keeseville
Herald]-1/17)
4049. Heartt, Albert m 11/30/21 Susan Bayeux, both of Troy (9-12/11)
4050. Heartt, Albert P., merchant, m 11/11/27 Emily Fitch, dau of Capt. R. H.;
Rev. Tucker. All of Troy (9-11/30)
4051. Heartt, Ann Jane, 27, oldest dau of Benjamin of Troy, d 4/3/29 in Troy
(1-4/11)
4052. Heartt, Henry m 9/23/15 Love Brady, both of Watervliet, in W; Rev. Butler
(9-9/26)
4053. Heartt, Sarah, 3, dau of Jonas C., d 9/28/22 in Troy (9-10/1)
4054. Heath, Acel (Mr.), 33, d 11/4/21 in Greenwich (surv by wf and "several
children") (9-12/4)
4055. Heath, Jesse m 3/31/33 Hannah Allen in Peru, NY; E. Williams, Esq.
(4 [Keeseville Herald]-4/2)
4056. Heath, William m 1/12/15 Susan Henry in Columbiaville; Rev. Chester
(6-1/24)
4057. Heaton, Asahel m 12/25/16 Charlotte Wheeler, dau of Newcomb Wheeler; Rev.
John Culver (8-1/8/17)
4058. Hedden, Mary (Mrs.), 65, d 4/13/31 in Poughkeepsie (for many years member
of the Baptist Church and formerly of Newark, NJ) (8-4/27)
4059. Hedge, Joseph m 12/5/31 Harriet Mesick; Rev. Watkins. All of Albany
(1-12/8)
4060. Heermance, Jacob, Esq. of Rhinebeck m 9/5/31 Jane Hunter of NYC; Rev.
Beach (8-9/28)
4061. Heermance, John of Pleasant Valley m 2/1/28 Penelope Bartlett of Stanford
in S; Gilbert Thorne, Esq. (8-2/6)
4062. Heermance, Martin (Gen.), 58, d 7/31/24 in Rhinebeck (8-8/4)
4063. Heermance, Philip m 4/1/98 Polly McBride, both of Fishkill; Rev. Nicholas
Van Vranken (8-4/24)
4064. Heermance, Philip (Dr.) and his wife (not named) d (dates not given) in
Hudson (6-2/9/13)
4065. Hegeman, James, merchant, of Troy m 11/15/27 Lavina Ann Morgan, dau of
Elijah of Poughkeepsie; Rev. Richardson (8-11/21)
4066. Height, Silas E. of Washington (Dut. Co.) m 10/22/15 Rhoda Barritt of
Amenia (8-11/1/15)
4067. Heller, Matthias, merchant, m 4/16/33 Maria Rogers, dau of Jeremiah, in
Clintonville; Rev. Bates (4 [Keeseville Herald]-4/23)
4068. Helsop, John, about 30, only s of late John, Esq. of Geneva, NY, d in
Durham, England (1-2/8/30)
4069. Hemenway, Silas of Geneva m 7/27/29 Mary Ottly, dau of Capt. William of
Phelps, in P; Rev. P. M. Squier (1-8/3)
4070. Hempstead, Charles Y., 26, of the firm of Reed, Hempstead and Sturges of
NYC d 2/2/30 in Rochester (typhus) (1-2/13)
4071. Hempsted, Numa, 35, s of late Isaac, Esq., d 7/1/29 in Albany (funeral
from the home of his mother, 116 South Pearl St.) (1-7/3)
4072. Henchman, John m 6/19/34 Catharine Neill of NYC in NYC; Rev. Smith
(8-6/25)
4073. Hendershute, Michael m 8/4/98 Deborah Robinson, both of Poughkeepsie; Rev.
Brower (8-8/7)
4074. Henderson, John, 102, d 12/15/11 in Fishkill (fought in the battle of
Colloden in Scotland 4/17/1746; in the battle of Minden, Germany
8/14/1759; and in the taking of Quebec under Gen. Woll 4/28/1760.
After the latter battle he left the British army and had lived in the
Fishkill area "since".) (8-1/22/12)
4075. Henderson, John m 4/25/19 Dorethea Cole, both of Albia; Rev. Sommers
(9-5/4)
4076. Henderson, Maria T., 30, wf of Adam, d 10/28/34 in Poughkeepsie (8-11/5)

4077. Henderson, Matthew H., Rector-elect of Trinity Church in Newark, NJ m
Eliza H. McFarlane of the Island of St. Croix in Philadelphia, PA; Rev.
G. T. Bedell, D.D. (1-11/10/30)
4078. Henderson, Robert m 10/1/22 Mary Ann Niles, both of Troy; Rev. Dr.
Blatchfrod (9-10/8)
4079. Henderson, William, Esq., 56, of Hyde Park, for many years a merchant
of NYC, d 2/12/25 at the home of William A. Du__?__ in Albany
(8-2/16)
4080. Hendrick, John L., principal of Ithaca Academy, m 1/25/30 Sicily
McDonald, dau of D. McDonald of Albany, in Ithaca; Rev. William
Wisner (1-2/4)
4081. Hendricks, John m 10/1/23 Betsey Stoutenburgh, dau of late James, both of
Hyde Park; Rev. Clark (8-10/8)
4082. Hendrickson, George R. (Capt.), 28, s of John, d 4/16/30 in Albany
(funeral from his late home, 61 Division St.) (1-4/17)
4083. Hendrickson, Isaac, 21, s of Capt. Stephen of Poughkeepsie, d 7/26/99
on Long Island (consumption) (8-7/30)
4084. Hendrickson, Matthew of Albany m 6/11/29 Maria Hilton, only dau of
James of Bethlehem, in B; Rev.Holiday (1-6/12)
4085. Hendrickson, Stephen (Capt.), 63, "an old inhabitant" of Poughkeepsie,
d 3/5/14 (funeral attended by members of Solomon's Lodge) (deceased
had been a trustee of the Dutchess County Academy) (8-3/9)
4086. Hendrie, Robert C. S., Esq., one of the editors of the Orange County
Patriot,m 9/13/31 Mary C. Watkins in Goshen; Rev. Dr. Fisk. All of
Goshen (1-9/17)
4087. Henn, Bernhart, 48, d 1/9/25 in Cherry Valley (born in Albany; had been
a merchant sequentially in Ballston, Cooperstown, and Cherry Valley)
(3-1/17)
4088. Henry, David M., Esq. of Angelica (sheriff of Allegany Co.) m 12/1/31
(Mariah Hurlbut, dau of Daniel, Esq. of Avon, in A; Rev. Hart
(1-12/7)
4089. Henry, Francis, 3, s of Samuel, d 7/28/19 in Otsego. Also Priscilla, 17,
dau of Samuel, d 7/14. (3-8/23)
4090. Henry, John D. (Dr.) m 12/30/25 Elizabeth Case in Rochester (3-1/9/26)
4091. Henry, John V., Esq. of Albany m 4/27/19 _____ Wilkes, only dau of late
John Wilkes, Esq. of NYC; Rev. Stansbury (8-4/28)
4092. Henry, John V., Esq., 64, "a most distinguished lawyer", d 10/15/29 in
Albany (8-10/28)
4093. Henry, John V. m 9/13/31 Catharine Seaton in Amsterdam, NY; Rev. James V.
Henry (1-9/16)
4094. Henry, Joseph of Albany m 5/3/30 Harriet Alexander in Schenectady; Rev.
Van Vechten (1-5/4)
4095. Henry, Robert d 6/1/16 in Cooperstown (buried with Masonic honors)
(3-6/6)
4096. Henry, Rosetta (Miss), late of Utica, d 8/10/29 at the home of Col. C.
Snowden in Mount Pleasant (West. Co.) (1-8/28)
4097. Henry, Samuel of Otsego, NY m Lucy Averell of Pomfret, CT in P (3-11/12/21)
4098. Henry, William m 6/18/17 Mary Ann Stone, dau of Rev. William, in
Waterloo, NY (6-6/24)
4099. Henry, William from St. Johns, Lower Canada m 8/5/17 Caroline R. White
of Troy; Rev. Dr. Coe (9-8/12)
4100. Herick, James of Stanford (Dut. Co.) m 9/4/03 Abigal Castle of Amenia;
Rev. Barnet (8-9/27)
4101. Hermance, William, 3, d 8/24/22 in Troy (his parents are not named)
4102. Herick, Anna, 88, relict of Maj. Elijah (who had died 23 years earlier)
d 6/1/29 at her home in Duanesburgh (1-6/12)
4103. Herrick, Arthur, Esq., attorney, of Angelica d 5/9/31 in NYC (1-5/11)
4104. Herrick, Benjamin (Col.), 53, d 3/11/10 at his home in Amenia (8-3/21)
4105. Herrick, Caroline Matilda, 16, dau of S. H., Esq.,d 12/4/25 at her father's
home in Hyde Park. Also Maria, 20, another dau of S. H., Esq., d 1/10/26
(8-1/18/26)
4106. Herrick, Claudius (Rev.), 56, d 5/26/31 in New Haven, CT (founder of and
for 20 yrs supt. of the Seminary [for the educ. of females] in New
Haven) (1-6/3)
4107. Herrick, Elijah S. m 5/4/29 Abigail A. Morris, both of Milan; Rev. Clark
(8-5/13)

118

4108. Herrick, Ephraim, Jr. of Northeast m 11/6/15 Phebe Albertson, dau of
Capt. John of Clinton, Dut. Co.; Rev. Clark (8-11/15)
4109. Herrick, Hannah, 24, wf of Arthur, Esq. and dau of Gen. Samuel S.
Haight, d 4/4/29 in Angelica (1-4/18)
4110. Herrick, Jacob H., merchant, of NYC m 4/13/25 Julia Ann Lyon of Poughkeepsie;
Rev. Dr. Reed (8-4/20)
4111. Herrick, Matilda Caroline (Miss), 16, d 12/11/25 in Hyde Park (8-12/14)
4112. Herrick, Richard, 87, (a Rev. pensioner) d "suddenly in the road" in
Gloucester (state not given) (1-11/18/31)
4113. Herrick, Ruth, 19, late of Cooperstown, d 5/10/13 in Springfield (3-5/15)
4114. Herrick, Sally (Miss), 20, oldest dau of Maj. Benjamin of Amenia,
d 10/19/04 in Amenia (8-10/23)
4115. Herrick, Sally, wf of Conklin Herrick, d 1/4/27 in Northeast (8-1/17)
4116. Herrick, Samuel P. of Plattsburgh m 1/1/28 Minerva Hopkins, dau of Gen.
Samuel Herrick (sic) of Zanesville, OH (7-2/16)
4117. Herrin, George of White Creek m 2/17/24 Sena Jones of Cambridge; Rev.
Prime (9-3/2)
4118. Herring, S. C. of the firm of Gough and Herring of Albany, NY m 6/13/31
Mary A. Draper, dau of Simeon, Esq. of Brookfield, MA in B; Rev. Noyes
(1-6/23)
4119. Herrington, Joel, 21, of the firm of H. and J. Herrington d 1/23/30 in
Hoosick Falls (1-2/1)
4120. Herrington, Theophilus, late one of the assistant judges of the Supreme
Court of Vermont, d 11/21/13 "in Clarendon" (state not given - possibly
intended for Vermont) (7-12/4)
4121. Hester, Samuel W. of Newark, NJ m 11/9/34 Jane Van Anden of Poughkeepsie;
Rev. Dr. Reed (8-11/11)
4122. Hetherington, James, late of Derbyshire, England m 1/10/25 Rachel Sherman
of Cherry Valley in C. V.; Rev. Fitch (3-1/17)
4123. Heustis, James C. of Poughkeepsie m 1/28/29 Charlotte Loomis of Rhinebeck
in R; Rev. G. W. Bethune (8-2/11)
4124. Hewes, Joseph, 18, s of Daniel of Springfield (Ots. Co.), d 12/15/12 in
Cazenovia ("was a volunteer on his way home from Niagara")(3-1/16/13)
4125. Hewes, William, editor of the Patriot of Potsdam, NY m 6/23/30 Nancy Boden
in Cooperstown; Rev. F. T. Tiffany (1-6/24)
4126. Hewit, Nathaniel (Rev.) of Plattsburgh m Rebecca W. Hillhouse, dau of Hon.
James of New Haven, CT, in New Haven (7-10/26/16)
4127. Hewit, Richard (Maj.) (a Rev. veteran) d 9/3/25 in Milton (2-9/13)
4128. Hewitt, James m 12/24/26 Phebe Sheik, both of Clinton (Dut. Co.)
(8-1/17/27)
4129. Hewitt, Thomas, Jr., merchant, of NYC m 12/4/21 Eliza Pierce, dau of
Benjamin, merchant, of Troy; Rev. Dr. Coe (9-12/11)
4130. Hewlett, Benjamin m 10/20/31 Maria T. Mitchell, dau of late Dr. Charles,
in Great Neck (North Hempstead); Rev. James P. F. Clarke (1-10/24)
4131. Hewlett, Stephen D., Esq., 23, d 8/23/30 at his father's home in Cow Neck,
Long Island, NY (1-8/30)
4132. Hewson, Daniel m 9/5/20 Phebe Fitch of Cooperstown in C; Rev. John
Smith (3-9/11)
4133. Hewson, John W. of Schenectady m 2/1/29 Mrs. Gertrude G. Blake, dau of
late Isaac Truax of Albany, in Fort Plain; Rev. Van Olinda (1-2/14)
4134. Hewson, Robert B. d 9/25/25 in Albany (3-10/3)
4135. Hibbard, Thomas m "in August last" Amelia Fassett, both of Champlain, in
Champlain; Rev. Labaree (7-2/19/20)
4136. Hickock, Henry P. (Rev.) m 9/22/34 Maria Buell, dau of late Col. Ozias,
in Burlington, VT (7-9/27)
4137. Hickock, Lois, 9, dau of Daniel, d 5/2/31 in Beekmantown (Clinton Co.)
(4 [Keeseville Herald]-5/17)
4138. Hickock, Samuel S. m 8/31/31 Frances M. Myrick in Birmingham (state not
given); Rev. Lyman (double ceremony - see marr of Charles Adgate)
(4 Keeseville Herald]-9/6)
4139. Hickok, Elizabeth, 67, consort of Ezra of Lansingburgh, d 8/31/01 in L
(9-9/1)
4140. Hickok, Ezra, 70, d 4/23/07 in Lansingburgh (he was a long-term resident
there) (9-5/5)
4141. Hickok, Horatio m 12/2/02 Jane Dickinson, both of Lansingburgh; Rev. Coe
(9-12/7)

4142. Hickok, Nancy, 36, (formerly of Brooklyn), wife of Benjamin, d 3/1/28 in Troy, NY (9-3/11)
4143. Hickok, Zilphah, 49, wf of Capt. Samuel of Lansingburgh, d 1/18/03 (9-1/25)
4144. Hickox, Asa, Esq., 74, formerly of Victor, d 5/23/29 in Richmond ("the first white person that wintered in the country to the west of Utica") (1-6/16)
4145. Hickox, Henry, 14, s of Carlton of Brutus (Cay. Co.), d 6/2/29 in Catskill (had left home as an assistant on a canal boat and "was taken sick") (1-6/8)
4146. Hicks, _____ (Mr.), member of the state assembly from Brooklyn, d 3/25/08 in Albany (9-3/29)
4147. Hicks, Ann Eliza, about 16, dau of Judge Hicks, d 5/29/23 in Champlain (7-5/31)
4148. Hicks, Elias, 81, d 2/27/30 at his home in Jericho, L.I., NY (the noted preacher in the Society of Friends) (8-3/3)
4149. Hicks, Elizabeth, 24, wf of John, d 2/8/08 in Beekman (8-2/17)
4150. Hicks, Jemima, 78, consort of Elias, d 3/17/29 in Jericho, L.I., NY (was born in the same home in which she died; married to Elias 58 yrs; interred in the Friends burying ground in Jericho) (1-3/28)
4151. Hicks, Lydia, 51, relict of the late Thomas, d 4/25/14 in Hudson ("took an overdose of Stramonium [thorn apple] for a cure and was poisoned) (6-5/3)
4152. Hicks, Samuel (Judge), about 63, d 7/26/25 in Champlain (7-7/30)
4153. Hicks, Samuel, Jr. of Pleasant Valley m 9/17/32 Jerusha Underhill, dau of Stephen of Stanford (Dut. Co.); Samuel C. Allen, Esq. (8-9/19)
4154. Hicks, Timothy (Dr.) m 6/27/02 Arrayanchee Heermance, both of Fishkill; Rev. Van Vranken (8-7/6)
4155. Hiet, Stephen m 1/15/25 Jane Drake in Milton; Elihu Wing, Esq. (2-2/1)
4156. Hifle, _____ (Mr.), 28. See, possibly, Hiple, _____ (Mr.), 28 ...
4157. Higbie, _____, 2, child of Capt. Benjamin, d 10/10/12 in Troy (9-10/13)
4158. Higbie, Benjamin m 12/22/07 Mary Ann Earl, both of Troy; Rev. Butler (9-12/29)
4159. Higby, Emily, consort of William, d 2/9/17 (3-2/13)
4160. Higby, John, 89, a long-term resident of Ballston, d 10/16/21 in Ballston (2-10/17)
4161. Higgins, Amanda Malvina, dau of Cornelius of Albany, d 11/11/30 in Albany (funeral from her late home, 2 Liberty St.) (1-11/12)
4162. Higgins, Charles (Capt.) of Sodus m 8/11/29 Eliza Mumson of Schenectady (formerly of Stockbridge, MA); Rev. Mason (1-8/21)
4163. Higham, _____, child of Abraham, d in Hudson (6-5/13/06)
4164. Higham, Robert, architect and civil engineer, m 11/24/30 Elvira Geer, dau of Darius; Rev. Welch. All of Albany (1-11/26)
4165. Hildreth, Matthias B., Esq., Attorney General of NY State, m 3/13/08 Nancy Rust (dau of Amaziah, Esq.), both of Johnstown, in J; Rev. Hosack (9-3/29)
4166. Hildreth, Matthias B., Esq., Attorney General of NY State. d 7/11/24 in Johnstown, NY (7-7/24 and 3-7/25)
4167. Hildreth, Sarah, 73, relict of late Joshua, d 1/13/31 in Johnstown (1-1/15)
4168. Hill, Daniel m 12/31/12 Cornelia Seabury of Poughkeepsie; Rev. Cuyler (8-1/6/13)
4169. Hill, Ebenezer, editor of the Village Messenger, of Fayetteville, Tennessee, m 2/12/24 Mary Bryans of the same place (9-3/16)
4170. Hill, Henry of NYC m 7/30/21 Laura Porter, dau of Rev. Dr. Porter, in Catskill (3-8/6)
4171. Hill, Sarepta (Mrs.), 28, formerly of Ellington, CT, d 3/4/13 (consumption) (3-3/13)
4172. Hill, Thomas m 5/9/08 Elizabeth Titcomb, both of Albany (9-5/17)
4173. Hill, Wareham d 5/30/14 in Deposit (killed by a falling log near the Delaware River (surv by wf and 2 ch) (En route home from his funeral, a 20 mile trip, his mother was killed on her horse by a falling tree.) (6-6/21)
4173a. Hillequest, Casper of Poughkeepsie d 9/29/09 (8-104)

4174. Hillhouse, John G., Esq., about 50, d in Montville, CT (at time of his death, he was member-elect of the Gen'l. Assembly of Connecticut) (9-10/28)
4175. Hillhouse, Thomas m 10/8/12 Ann Ten Broeck, both of Troy; Rev. Coe (9-10/13)
4176. Hillyard, Daniel, Esq., 75, (a Rev. pensioner) d 11/20/34 in West Plattsburgh (had settled there permanently in 1798 and for many years served as Justice of the Peace) (he was father of 11 children, 10 of whom were still living at time of his death) (7-12/6)
4177. Hilton, James, about 24, "a stranger", d 5/24/05 in Hudson ("...he said he had a sister in Albany from whence he came last") (6-5/28)
4178. Hilton, Robert, Jr. of Root (Mont. Co.) m 2/26/29 Catharine Hilton, oldest dau of Richard of Bethlehem; Rev. Ira C. Boice (1-2/28)
4179. Hinckly, Abijah m 8/21/03 Alice Brown, both of Fishkill; Cyrus Benjamin, Esq. (8-8/30)
4180. Hind, John C., Esq., cashier of Levi McKeen's "Office of Discount and Deposit", m 6/3/17 Silonie Beebee of Kinderhook; Rev. Sickles (9-6/11)
4181. Hind, Mary, 43, wf of Thomas, d in Hudson (6-11/9/10)
4182. Hinds, John, 50, d 5/27/20 in Cooperstown (3-6/5)
4183. Hine, Harvey m 4/19/29 Sally Smith, both of Cairo, in C; Rev. Wyckoff (1-4/23)
4184. Hingston, Samuel, Jr., 24, youngest s of Samuel J., Esq., d 1/16/29 in Hinchinbrook (fell into a potash kettle of boiling salts)(1-2/14)
4185. Hinman, Anna, 53, d 1/25/06 in Hartwick ("left a family of 9 children") (3-1/30)-(Addendum: her husband was Joshua)
4186. Hinman, John m Sally Dodge, both of Hudson, in Claverack; Rev. Gephard (6-2/17/07)
4187. Hinman, William G., 28, late editor of the NY Evening Journal, d 12/18/29 in Catskill (1-12/25)
4188. Hinton, George L. (Rev.) of NYC m 6/4/29 Sarah C. West, dau of Reuben, Esq. of Onondaga, in O; Rev. Dr. Rudd (1-6/12)
4189. Hiple or Hifle, _____ (Mr.), 28, d 2/17/32 in Keeseville (consumption) (4 [Keeseville Herald]-2/21)
4190. Hiscox, G. C. of Petersburgh m 10/28/22 Harriet Crosby of Essex, the adopted dau of Amos Dexter, Esq., in Essex; S. C. Perry, Esq. (9-11/12)
4191. Hitchcock, _____, 74, m Hannah Moore, 74, in Woodstock, CT (9-12/13/14)
4192. Hitchcock, Enos (Rev.), D.D., 57, d 2/26/03 in Providence, RI (6-3/22)
4193. Hitchcock, James m 7/28/31 Eleanor Muneely, both of Gibbonsville; Rev. Sommers (9-8/7)
4194. Hitchcock, Jeremy of Genoa, NY m 12/3/30 Mrs. Parnel Pratt of Rensselaer-ville in R; Rev. Marcus Smith (1-12/6)
4195. Hitchcock, John F. of Queensbury m Adaline Moss, dau of Maj. J. Moss of Sandy Hill (Wash. Co.) in S. H.; Rev. Armstrong (9-9/12/15)
4196. Hix, Asa of Keeseville m 7/30/31 Sarah Carter in Chesterfield; Rev. Lyman (4 [Keeseville Herald]-8/2)
4197. Hoag, Ezra m 5/20/30 Roxana Culver, dau of Joshua, all of Pine Plains; Rev. Robert G. Armstrong (8-5/26)
4198. Hoag, Henry P. of Washington, Dut. Co. m 10/23/32 Helen Tapping, dau of late Hezekiah of Milan, in Poughkeepsie; Rev. Page (8-10/31)
4199. Hoag, Hulet m 9/10/15 Polly Ogden, both of Pittstown, in Troy; Archibald Bull, Esq. (9-9/19)
4200. Hoag, Isaac V. m 6/11/29 Maria G. Turner of Hyde Park; A. Raymond, Esq. (8-6/17)
4201. Hoag, James of the firm of Marshall, Hoag & Co. m 12/22/34 Charlotte Turner, dau of William; Rev. Dr. Reed. All of Poughkeepsie (8-12/24)
4202. Hoag, Peter of Washington, (Dut. Co.) m 11/18/09 Abigail Mott, dau of John of Beekman; John Titus, Esq. (8-11/22)
4203. Hobart, John Henry (Rev.), D.D., 55, Bishop of the Protestant Episcopal Church in the diocese of NYC, d 9/12/30 in Auburn (funeral from the Trinity Church in NYC where the deceased was rector) (1-9/15)
4204. Hobart, John Sloss (Hon.), (a Rev. patriot), Judge of the District Court of New York, d in NYC (6-2/19/05)
4205. Hobbie, Selah R., Esq., attorney, m 5/14/26 Julianne Root, dau of Gen. Erastus, in Delhi;Rev. Stephen Fenn (3-5/29)
4206. Hobby, _____, child of Caleb of the Manor of Livingston, died (date not given) ("burned to death by its clothes having taken fire") (6-9/9/06)

121

4207. Hobson, Darius (Col.) of the U.S. Army m Chloe Pi Mackwis "(or the Jumping Rabbit), a belle of the Chippasaw tribe", in Mountville, AL (8-12/9/29)
4208. Hochstraser, Jacob of Albany m 7/10/31 Louisa Brower of NYC in NYC; Rev. Clark (1-7/13)
4209. Hockley, Thomas, Esq. of the Branch Bank of the U.S. m 6/12/31 Betsey Warner, dau of Isaac, Esq., in Burlington, VT; Rev. Ingersoll (1-6/14 and 1-6/16)
4210. Hocum, Caterin (Mrs.), 42, lately from NYC, d in Hudson ("is said to have relations living in Williamstown, Mass.") (6-10/28/06)
4211. Hodge, James of Albany m 7/21/07 Mercy Morgan of Troy in T; Rev. Coe (9-7/28)
4212. Hodge, Philander, Esq. of the firm of Johnson, Hodge & Co. m 9/15/34 Eugenia Maria Barker, dau of Hon. P. A., in Buffalo; Rev. Shelton (8-10/1)
4213. Hodges, James, 31, d 2/4/13 in Peru, NY (7-2/12)
4214. Hodgkin, John m 12/24/26 Jane Donalson, both of Troy; Rev. Willis (9-1/5/27)
4215. Hodgkin, Thomas m 3/25/28 Adeline Penny, both of Troy; Rev. Willis (9-3/28)
4216. Hodgkinson, Frances of the New Theatre d in NYC (consumption) (9-10/11/13)
4217. Hodgkish, Joseph m 4/3/03 Elizabeth Farr, both of Amenia (8-4/26)
4218. Hoff, Sarah, 21, wf of Rev. B. Hoff and dau of Henry A. Livingston, Esq. of Poughkeepsie, d 9/13/18 in New Brunswick, NJ (8-9/23)
4219. Hoffman, _____, wf of Charles of Poughkeepsie, d 6/15/05 (8-6/18)
4220. Hoffman, Abraham, merchant, of Poughkeepsie m 5/10/98 Esther Thorn, dau of Dr. Stephen Thorn of New Hackensack(Dut. Co.) (8-5/15)
4221. Hoffman, Abraham (Capt.), 39, d 5/20/12 (8-5/27)
4222. Hoffman, Catharine, 68, relict of late Herman and sister of Mrs. Gertrude Hoffman of Poughkeepsie, d 5/4/33 in NYC (8-5/8)
4223. Hoffman, David Beekman of Red Hook d 4/13/28 on board the U.S. ship "Delaware" off the Island of Corsica (8-7/9)
4224. Hoffman, Derick Brinkerhoof m 10/15/34 Sarah Anne Manning; Rev. Dr. Reed (8-10/22)
4225. Hoffman, Edy, 82, relict of late Nicholas d 6/10/34 in Red Hook (8-6/18)
4226. Hoffman, Elias m 10/25/21 Hannah Phillips; Rev. Cuyler (8-10/31)
4227. Hoffman, Esther, consort of Abraham of Poughkeepsie, d 5/24/10 (8-5/30)
4228. Hoffman, Isaac, Esq. of Carmel m 4/23/18 Mary Sickles of Poughkeepsie; Rev. C. C. Cuyler (8-4/29)
4229. Hoffman, Jeremiah, Esq. of Claverack m 11/3/16 Julia Bushnell, dau of Capt. George of Hillsdale, in H (6-11/12)
4230. Hoffman, John L. m 4/28/31 Gertrude Van Derpool, both of Poughkeepsie; Rev. Dr. Cuyler (8-5/4)
4231. Hoffman, Martin (Capt.) d 11/25/97 at Mount Ross (in town of Pine Plains) (surv by wf and children) (8-12/12)
4232. Hoffman, Martin, Jr. of firm of Davis and Hoffman m 10/5/24 Julia Harrison, dau of Frederick of Poughkeepsie; Rev. Cuyler (8-10/6)
4233. Hoffman, Nicholas, Esq., 75, d 7/22/21 in Red Hook (8-8/1)
4234. Hoffman, Philip L. (b in NYC) d 7/18/29 in Key West, FL (8/24)
4235. Hoffman, Richard K. (Dr.) of U.S. Navy m 5/7/22 Jane Benson, dau of Robert, Esq. of NYC, in NYC; Rev. John Knox (8-5/22)
4236. Hoffman, Robert (Col.), farmer, of Poughkeepsie d 10/18/95 (buried in churchyard of Reformed Dutch Church, Poughkeepsie) (8-10/21)
4237. Hoffman, Robert, 57, d 8/31/27 in Poughkeepsie (surv by "a large family") (8-9/5)
4238. Hoffman, Samuel Anthony, 32, d 7/20/29 in Poughkeepsie (8-7/22)
4239. Hoffman, Sarah, wf of late Col. Robert of Poughkeepsie, d 10/31/95 (8-11/4)
4240. Hoffman, Van Wyck, 8, youngest s of Zachariah, m 7/19/22 in Red Hook (drowned while playing in a swollen freshet with some school mates) (8-7/24)
4241. Hogan, James of Newburgh m 11/27/14 Hannah Taylor of Troy (9-11/29)
4242. Hogeboom, Henry, Esq., attorney, of Hudson m 11/14/32 Jane Eliza Rivington, dau of James, Esq. of Poughkeepsie, in Hudson; Rev. William H. Thomas of Duanesburgh (8-11/21)

122

4243. Hogeboom, James (Dr.) of Castleton m 12/11/29 Helen Hogeboom, dau of
Tobias I. of Ghent, in G; Rev. J. Berger (1-12/19)
4244. Hogeboom, Jane (Miss), 37, oldest dau of Stephen, Esq., d 10/13/03 in
Claverack (pulmonary complaint) (6-10/18)
4245. Hogeboom, Jane, 19, oldest dau of Peter, d in Claverack (6-11/29/03)
4246. Hogeboom, Jane Mary, 11, dau of Peter, d 1/6/14 in Claverack (6-1/25)
4247. Hogeboom, Killian, Esq., formerly clerk of Columbia Co., drowned
8/18/11 in Claverack Creek (6-8/23)
4248. Hogeboom, Lawrence, Esq., 67, d 3/14/05 in Claverack (3-4/11)
4249. Hogeboom, Peter m AnnS. Hulbert, dau of Harry, in Ghent; Rev. Peter S.
Wynkoop. All of Ghent (1-4/1/31)
4250. Hogeboom, Sarah (Miss), 26, dau of John C., Esq., d 2/13/19 at the home
of Abraham A. Van Buren, Esq. (6-2/16)
4251. Hogeboom, Stephen, Esq., 69, d 4/2/14 at his home in Claverack (served in
both the state assembly and senate and had been a judge of the Columbia
Co. Court of Common Pleas) (6-4/19)
4252. Hoit, Charles, merchant, m 3/3/28 Temperance Parsons, dau of Jeremiah of
Beekmantown (Clinton Co.); Rev. Frederick Halsey (7-3/15)
4253. Holbrook, Chandler of NYC m 11/7/20 Mrs. D. H. Malcom of Hudson (late
of Philadelphia); Rev. Malcom (6-11/14)
4254. Holdridge, William of Orrville m 5/13/28 Eliza G. Willard of Troy; Rev.
howard (9-5/20)
4255. Holcomb, Lydia, wf of Dr. Dodorus H. Holcomb, d 10/3/39 in Westport
(4 [Keeseville Herald]-11/13)
4256. Holcomb, Silas A. of Elizabethtown m 10/12/32 Phebe Coolidge, dau of
Benjamin of Jay, in Peru, NY; A. Hayes, Esq. (4 [Keeseville Herald]-
10/14)
4257. Holden, David, 25, late of Granville, d 11/17/02 in Utica (9-11/30)
4258. Holden, Hezekiah S., 21, 2nd s of Daniel, Esq. of Johnstown, d 5/6/31
(consumption) (1-5/12)
4259. Holden, Oliver, Jr., merchant, of NYC m 3/14/22 Frances Sloan, dau of
Daniel, Esq. of Belleville, NJ, in B; Rev. Van Sanfort (8-3/27)
4260. Holden, Salmon m 7/3/19 Susan Allen, dau of Mrs. Simon Newcomb, in
Plattsburgh (7-7/10)
4261. Holden, Thomas (Gen.), 82, father of Oliver of Poughkeepsie, d 2/12/23 in
Warwick, RI (Deliverance Holden, the general's sister, d 2/3 in
Warwick, RI)(8-3/5)
4262. Holeman, Abigail, 31, consort of George, d in Hudson (6-7/24/04)
4263. Holeman, George m 10/3/04 Mary Ann Canady in Hudson (6-10/9)
4264. Holland, Susan, 52, consort of John, Esq. of Johnstown, d 7/20/31 in
Johnstown (1-7/30)
4265. Hollenback, Hannah, 61, wf of Henry, d in Hudson (6-11/1/08)
4266. Holley, Earl m 5/13/04 Phebe Stevens, both of Pawling (8-5/22)
4267. Holley, Elisha, Esq. of Livingston d at the home of E. O. Holley in
Hudson (6-12/8/18)
4268. Holley, Maria, 19, oldest dau of John M., Esq. of Salisbury, CT, d 12/4/20
at her father's home (6-12/19)
4269. Holliday, Gideon, Esq., 53, d 2/18/29 at his home in Duanesburgh (1-2/25)
4270. Hollis, Thomas m 9/20/21 Hannah Twogood, both of Pittstown (9-10/2)
4271. Hollister, David M., merchant, m 11/13/34 Rebecca Swift, dau of E. M.,
Esq.; Rev. A. Perkins. All of Dover (8-11/19)
4272. Hollister, Isaac, Jr. of Granville m 11/13/28 Martha De Wolf of Troy;
Rev. Beman (9-11/18)
4273. Hollister, Solomon, 75, d 7/24/22 in Ballston (2-8/6)
4274. Hollister, SolomonD., 44, of Ballston d 4/20/25 in B (2-4/26)
4275. Holman, Joseph George, Esq., 52, manager of the Charleston Theatre,
d 8/24/17 at the Watering Place, L. I., NY (6-9/2)
4276. Holman, Thomas (Dr.), 32, formerly of Cooperstown, NY, and for the past
few months a missionary in the Sandwich Islands (Hawaii), d in
Bridgeport, CT (3-3/6/26)
4277. Holme, John, Esq. m 10/20/31 Mrs. Ann B. Allen, dau of late Timothy Leonard,
at Trinity Church, Lansingburgh. All of Lansingburgh; Rev. P. L.
Whipple (1-10/27)
4278. Holmes, _____ (Mr.), late of Constable, NY d 2/20/13 in Plattsburgh
(7-2/26)

123

4279. Holmes, Alonzo m 7/3/25 Elizabeth Thompson at Salmon River (7-7/9)
4280. Holmes, Calvin m 7/18/19 Mary Kelso in Westford; Rev. George Colton. All of Westford (3-7/26)
4281. Holmes, Edwin (Rev.), pastor of the Reformed Dutch Church of Livingston (Dut. Co.), m 9/6/32 Sarah M. McClellan, dau of Dr. John of Livingston; Rev. Dr. Cuyler (8-9/12)
4282. Homes, Elias of Washington (Dut. Co.) m 9/23/24 Susan Wood of Pleasant Valley; Garret Adriance, Esq. (8-9/29)
4283. Holmes, Hiram of La Grange m 12/1/32 Maria Clarkson of Beekman; Rev. Buttolph (8-12/12)
4284. Holmes, Isaac m 5/15/04 Jemima Peters in Clinton (Dut. Co.); Rev. Clark (8-6/5)
4285. Holmes, Israel (Capt.) d 6/12/19 in Hudson (buried with Masonic honors) (6-6/15)
4286. Holmes, Jemima, about 50, consort of Isaac, Esq., d 2/22/34 in Pleasant Valley (8-2/26)
4287. Holmes, Joanna, wf of Obadiah of the firm of Bailey and Holmes and dau of Gen. John B. Van Wyck of Poughkeepsie, d 4/18/29 in NYC (8-4/22)
4288. Holmes, John m 12/5/21 Eliza Lockwood in Charlton; Rev. Sweetman (2-12/26)
4289. Holmes, John m 9/17/29 Sarah Hepinstall, both of Albany, in NYC; Rev. George Coles (1-9/21)
4290. Holmes, Joseph, 80, d in Surry, NH (9-8/1/15)
4291. Holmes, L. H. m 6/13/30 Caroline Perrot, dau of John, at St. George's Church in NYC; Rev. Todd (1-6/19)
4292. Holmes, Myron, merchant, of Sodus m 9/27/30 Eliza Hecox of Lyons in L (1-10/5)
4293. Holmes, O. of the firm of Holmes and Onderdonk m 12/29/12 Sarah Van Wyck, dau of Gen. John B., in Fishkill; Rev. Westbrook (8-1/6/13)
4294. Holmes, O. of the firm of Bailey and Holmes of NYC m 7/20/26 Joanna Van Wyck, dau of Gen. J. B. of Poughkeepsie; Rev. Cuyler (8-7/26)
4295. Holmes, Obediah, merchant, of NYC m 11/24/30 Jane Van Wyck, dau of Gen. John B. of Poughkeepsie; Rev. Dr. Cuyler (8-12/1)
4296. Holmes, Peleg, 76, "an early settler in this vicinity", d 7/21/31 in Palmyra (1-7/27)
4297. Holmes, Peter m 12/13/32 Sally Husted, both of Washington (Dut. Co.); Rev. Frederick Tuckerman (8-12/26)
4298. Holmes, Richard m 9/17/28 Phebe Martling; Rev. Beman. All of Troy (9-9/19)
4299. Holmes, Samuel m 10/24/28 Fanny Priest, both of Peterborough, NH, in Troy; Rev. Willis (double ceremony - see marr of Daniel Adams) (9-1028)
4300. Holmes, Susan, 36, consort of late Capt. Holmes, d 9/29/31 in Washington (Dut. Co.) (8-10/5)
4301. Holt, _____, 18, dau of Maj. Lester Holt, d 5/23/24 in Cherry Valley (3-5/31)
4302. Holt, Elijah, 64, of Buffalo d 9/26/26 in Cherry Valley (3-10/2)
4303. Holt, Jesse G., printer, m 2/4/09 Ann Catharine Dunn in Hudson; Rev. Wigton (6-2/7)
4304. Holt, Mary, 47, wf of Gen. Elijah, d 1/3/20 in Buffalo (3-1/24)
4305. Holt, William of Bermuda m 9/26/34 Jane Lyman in Burlington (state not given) (7-10/4)
4306. Holt, William A., 17, s of William J. of Montreal, Canada, d 12/2/11 in Chazy, NY (7-1/3/12)
4307. Holthuysen, J. C. of Pleasant Valley m 3/13/34 Susan S. Mitchell, dau of Stephen of Poughkeepsie; Rev. Dr. Reed (8-3/19)
4308. Holyoke, Edward Aug. (Dr.), 100, d 4/1/29 in Salem (1-4/6)
4309. Homans, James T. (Lt.) of the U.S. Navy m 9/1/29 Elizabeth Kay, dau of James Kay, Esq. of Albany; Rev. William B. Sprague (1-9/2)
4310. Homeston, Joseph of Washington (Dut. Co.) m 5/12/23 Abby Van Duzen of Amenia; Jesse Barlow, Esq. (8-5/21)
4311. Hommedieu, S. S. H., one of the proprietors of the Cincinnati Gazette, m Alma Hammond in Cincinnati (1-6/18/30)
4312. Hone, John, Jr., 37, of the firm of John Hone & Sons of NYC d 4/9/29 in Rome, Italy (1-6/10)
4313. Hone, John, Esq., 67, d 4/12/32 in NYC (8-4/18)
4314. Hooffman, Elizabeth, 39, wf of William, d in Claverack (6-9/26/09)

4315. Hoogeland, Eliza, 22, dau of Derrick, d 7/19/18 in Fishkill (8-7/29)
4316. Hooghkerk, Henry, 22, printer and late editor and publisher of the
      Canajoharie Telegraph, d 2/11/29 in Canajoharie (consumption) (1-2/17
      and 8-3/4)
4317. Hooker, Charlotte, 42, wf of Col. James, d 3/14/31 (1-3/15)
4318. Hooper, Judith (Mrs.) of Poughkeepsie d 4/29/04 (8-5/1)
4319. Hoornebeeck, Ludewick, Esq., 62, "late a member of the legislature",
      d 8/26/30 in Rochester, Ulster Co., NY (1-9/11)
4320. Hopkins, Asa Theodore (Rev.) of Albany m 2/4/29 Elizabeth Wisner, oldest
      dau of Asa of Ithaca, in I; Rev. Wisner (1-2/14)
4321. Hopkins, Boswell (Hon.), 73,(born in Amenia) d in Chazy (Clinton Co.)
      (8-9/23/29)
4322. Hopkins, Elias m 1/24/13 Nancy Paddock, both of Hudson; Rev. Chester
      (6-2/2)
4323. Hopkins, John S., formerly of Hudson, NY, d in Elizabethtown, NJ (6-3/2/12)
4324. Hopkins, Louisa H., 32, wf of Boyd Hopkins, d 11/7/33 in Plattsburgh
      (member of Methodist Episcopal Society) ("Printers in St. Lawreence
      Co., N.Y. and in St. Albans, Vt. are requested to notice the above")
      (7-11/9)
4325. Hopkins, Thomas S. d 11/13/28 in Poughkeepsie (was born in RI "but for
      many years a merchant of Poughkeepsie") (8-11/19)
4326. Hopkins, William, about 50, d 8/20/14 in Laurens (3-9/1)
4327. Hopoman, Anthony (surname blurred - may not be accurately copied therefore)
      of Pine Plains m 2/16/26 Sarah Barton, dau of Dr. Leonard Barton of
      Stanford (Dut. Co.); Rev. C. P. Wilson (8-2/22)
4328. Hopper, Abbey, 53, wf of Lambert Hopper, d 9/13/13 in Plattsburgh
      (7-9/18)
4329. Hopper, Jasper, Esq. of Albany m 10/4/00 Charlotte Newcomb, dau of
      Zaccheus, Esq. of Dutchess Co. (8-10/21)
4330. Hopper, John m 11/24/15 Sarah Seabury; Rev. Leonard. All of Poughkeepsie
      (8-11/29)
4331. Hopper, Matthew, printer, m 7/16/17 Mrs. Catharine Meloney, dau of late
      Michael B. Van Kleeck, deceased, of Poughkeepsie; Rev. C. C. Cuyler
      (8-7/23)
4332. Hoppin, George W. m Mary Philbrooks, dau of Capt. Philbrooks, in Providence,
      RI (6-1-/1/01)
4333. Hornbeck, Eleanor, 26, consort of Dr. Garett S. W. Hornbeck, d 10/29/07
      in Poughkeepsie (8-11/4)
4334. Horr, Anna, 30, wf of Capt. R. C., d 9/30/21 in Swanton, VT (7-10/6)
4335. Horr, Charlotte Amelia, 4 mo, dau of Ralph C., d 3/4/21 in Plattsburgh
      (7-3/10)
4336. Horr, R. C. (Capt.) m 5/9/22 Mary B. Angus in Plattsburgh; Rev. Halsey.
      All of Plattsburgh (7-5/11)
4337. Horsfull, Joseph m 7/29/30 Betsy Brooks, both of Poughkeepsie; Rev. Dr.
      Reed (8-8/4)
4338. Hortner, William m 5/7/22 Phebe Pooley, both of Fishkill; Rev. Barrett
      (8-5/29)
4339. Horton, Caleb, Esq., 60, d 12/12/28 in NYC (9-12/16/28)
4340. Horton, Hannah (Miss), 20, dau of Ebenezer, d 4/2/08 in Hebron, CT
      (3-4/16)
4341. Horton, Henry of Malone m 1/6/20 Delia Woodward, dau of Capt. William of
      Plattsburgh, in P; Rev. S. W. Whelpley (7-1/8)
4342. Horton, Hiram, Jr. m Adaline Wead in Malone (Could the original handwritten
      note-taker have intended the bride's surname to read Mead, one wonders)
      (7-2/2/22)
4343. Horton, Jacob m 8/6/23 Diana Storm, dau of Col. John, in Hopewell; Rev.
      De Witt. All of Fishkill (8-8/20)
4344. Horton, John Brinckerhoff, s of Coert, Esq. of Fishkill, d 3/27/29 "in the
      bloom of youth on The Island of St. Thomas in the West Indies" (1-5/7)
4345. Horton, Thomas m 3/3/03 Susannah Woolly, both of Beekmantown (perhaps
      intended for the town of Beekman in Dutchess Co.); Cornelius Williams,
      Esq. (8-3/15) (See Entry 4346 for a Beekman reference)
4346. Horton, Thomas m Phebe Conroe, both of Beekman (8-3/20/11)
4347. Hosack, Alexander E. (Dr.) m 12/17/29 Elizabeth M. Leger Hutchinson, dau
      of late Thomas Holland Hutchinson, Esq. of South Carolina, in NYC;
      Right Rev. Bishop Hobart (1-12/21)

4348. Hosack, Nathaniel P. of NYC m 9/21/31 Sophia H. Church, dau of Philip, Esq. of Angelica, in A; Rev. Thibow (1-10/1)
4349. Hosford, Elijah of late firm of E. & E. Hosford, printers and bookbinders, d 7/28/28 in Albany (9-8/1)
4350. Hosford, Elisha, of the former firm of E. & E. Hosford, printers and booksellers of Albany, d 11/15/30 in Hartford, CT (1-11/25)
4351. Hoskin, Matthew Marvin, 16, s of Shubael, d 1/26/09 in Loonenburgh (Athens, NY) (6-2/7)
4352. Hoskins, Shubael d in Hudson (6-2/9/13)
4353. Hosmer, Clarissa, 5 mo, only dau of Hezekiah L., Esq., d 1/4/14 in Hudson (6-1/11)
4354. Hosmer, Hezekiah L., 49, attorney and recorder of Hudson, d 6/9/14 in Hudson (member of Episcopal Church in Hudson) (buried with Masonic honors) (surv by wf and 2 inf sons)(6-6/14 and 8-6/22)
4355. Hosmer, John of Hudson, NY m 9/10/12 Eliza Pomeroy of Coventry, CT in C (6-9/28)
4356. Hosmer, Lucius d 8/31/30 in Bern, NY (had been married "but for a few months") (1-9/7)
4357. Hosworth, Elizabeth M. (Miss), 21, d 2/27/32 (had lived in Poughkeepsie about 4 yrs; was an assistant in Miss Bosworth's school; member of Reformed Dutch church, Poughkeepsie)(8-2/29)
4358. Hotchkin, James H. m 7/2/29 Nancy Elizabeth Jackson, dau of Dr. Z. S., in Prattsburgh; Rev. J. H. Hotchkin. All of Prattsburgh (1-7/13)
4359. Hotchkin, Seth of Amenia m 4/11/21 Abbey Hubbel of Kent, CT; Rev. Luman Birch (8-4/18)
4360. Hotchkiss, Leander of Matteawan m 9/29/27 Sarah Low of Manchester; Rev. C. C. Cuyler (8-10/3)
4361. Hotchkiss, Sarah, 24, wf of Carver Hotchkiss, d 10/2/31 in Windsor (Broome Co.) (1-10/11)
4362. Hough, Horatio G. (Dr.), 52, d 9/3/30 in Martinsburgh (Lewis Co.) (1-9/22)
4363. Houghtaling, Hannah, 67, d 12/6/31 (death place not given but the editor states that the deceased has "connexions" living in the western part of NY) (1-12/10)
4364. Houghton, Caroline (Mrs.), about 25, d "recently" in Champlain (7-1/8/13)
4365. Houghton, James of Troy m 1/28/06 Lydia Douglass of Wallingford, VT (9-2/11)
4366. Houghton, John m 12/27/21 Eliza Hawkins, both of Lansingburgh (9-1/1/22)
4367. House, John, merchant, of Waterford m 12/26/08 Abby Platt of Athens, NY in A; Rev. Prentice (6-1/10/09)
4368. Housinfratz, Peter, 96, d 1/28/29 in Onondaga (1-2/9)
4369. Housman, _____ (Mr.), a native of Poland and late a teacher of French at Fairfield Academy (Herkimer Co.),d 3/5/12 in Herkimer (born in a noble family; was educated in Petersburgh, Russia; left no will but $4000 in gold) (3-4/4)
4370. Houston, _____, brother of Ezra C., d "recently" (funeral from 42 Liberty St., Albany) (1-10/22/29)
4371. How, _____, wf of David of Ballston, d 8/13/24 (2-8/17)
4372. How, Ira m 8/21/17 Lucy Lathrop, both of Plattsburgh, in P (7-9/27)
4373. How, James C. (Rev.) of Springfield, NY m 9/6/26 Latitia Hamill, dau of Robert, Esq. of Norristown, PA, in N; Rev. Charles W. Nassau (3-10/2)
4374. How, James S. of Fishkill m 12/20/28 Eliza Ann Lee of Beekman; James Delong, Esq. (8-12/31)
4375. How, Luther J., Esq., attorney, m 9/21/29 Cornelia M. Parmely, both of White Creek (Wash. Co.), in White Creek; Rev. Fletcher (1-10/9)
4376. Howard, Eliza Ann (Miss), 22, dau of Samuel of Ravenna, OH, d 10/2/26 in Cleveland, OH (Samuel formerly of Sherburne[Chen. Co.], NY) (3-10/30)
4377. Howard, Hannah M., youngest dau of John of Milton (Sara. Co.) d 1/21/29 in NYC "where she was on a visit" (1-1/31)
4378. Howard, Henry m 7/20/06 Parloina Lossing, both of Beekman; Ebenezer Carey, Esq. (8-8/5)
4379. Howard, James m 9/18/23 Cynthia Crapo, both of Ballston, in B; Rev. R. Smith (2-9/23)
4380. Howard, Jesse (Dr.), 57, d 8/10/22 in Ballston (2-8/13)
4381. Howard, John V. m 2/28/25 Mary Wilde, both of Milton, in M; Rev. M. Plumb (2-3/22)

4382. Howard, Mary, 28, consort of Seth late of NYC, d 10/10/22 in New Orleans, LA (surv by husband and 2 small children) (8-11/27)
4383. Howard, Nathan m 3/18/20 Marietta Smith; Rev. Stanton. All of Hudson (6-3/21)
4384. Howard, Seth m Mary Stevens, dau of Rev. Thomas, in Louisville, KY. All formerly of Poughkeepsie, NY (8-11/5/17)
4385. Howard, William of White Creek m 3/19/20 Eliza Turby of Jackson; Solomon Dean, Esq. (9-4/11)
4386. Howden, Alexander m Margaret Wells, dau of Samuel, Esq. in Cambridge (Wash. Co.) (1-3/1/31)
4387. Howe, Artemas m Anna Parker in Decatur (3-5/1/20)
4388. Howe, Estes, 45, late recorder of Albany, d in Albany (3-1/2/26)
4389. Howe, Fanny, 32, wf of Artemas and dau of Dr. Timothy Parker of Decatur, d 5/4/19 in Westford (surv by hsband and children) (3-5/10)
4390. Howe, Jerome B. of Troy m 12/16/29 Catharine Budd, dau of Underhill Budd, Esq. of Schodack, in S; Rev. Hall (1-12/18)
4391. Howe, John, Esq., about 68, d 1/5/13 in Plattsburgh (7-1/8)
4392. Howe, Joseph m 11/29/47 Fanny Chambers, both of Troy; Rev. Martindale (9-12/7)
4393. Howe, Nehemiah of Plattsburgh, NY m 4/29/32 Pasiphae J. Kelsey of Salisbury, VT in S (7-5/5)
4394. Howe, Polly, wf of Capt. Epenetus, d 12/12/21 in Ballston (2-12/19)
4395. Howell, Silas W. d 9/29/05 in Albany (9-10/8)
4396. Howell, Stephen (Capt.), 85, d at Sag Harbor, L.I., NY (1-1/8/31)
4397. Howell, William (Capt.) of NYC d 8/19/22 in Saratoga Springs (apoplectic fit) (2-8/20)
4398. Howes, Lucinda, 47, wf of Dr. Thomas, d in Richfield (Ots. Co.) (1-8/7/29)
4399. Howland, Abraham of Washington (Dut. Co.) m 10/7/15 Mary Underhill, dau of Nathaniel of Clinton (Dut. Co.); Gideon Allen, Esq. (8-10/11)
4400. Howland, Gardiner G., Esq., merchant, of NYC m 7/7/29 Louisa Meredith, dau of J, Esq. of Baltimore, in B; Rev. Nevins (1-7/13)
4401. Howland, Humphrey m 11/20/03 Esther Sprague of Pawling (8-12/6)
4402. Howland, Jonathan m 12/22/03 Lynn Pearce, both of Pawling (8-1/10/04)
4403. Howland, Knowlton of Newton m 1/14/23 Susan Marshall of Saeatoga in S; Rev. Duryee (2-1/21)
4404. Howland, Lavina Ann, 16, dau of Benjamin, d 7/16/21 in Poughkeepsie (pulmonary disease) (8-7/18)
4405. Howland, Mahitable (consort of Capt. Joseph Howland of Poughkeepsie and formerly of New Bedford) d 4/30/23 (8-5/7)
4406. Howland, Samuel, 97, late of Washington Co., d 1/20/25 at the home of Peter Fish, Esq. in Northeast (8-1/26)
4407. Howland, Solomon m 12/31/33 Belinda Davis, both of Washington (Dut. Co.); Rev. S. Northrop (8-1/15/34)
4408. Howland, Zenas m 9/30/26 Sally Ann Lake; Rev. C. C. Cuyler (8-10/18)
4409. Hoxie, Christopher m 2/25/02 Mary Clark, dau of Nathaniel of NYC (7-3/9)
4410. Hoxie, Joshua B. m 12/29/11 Judah Carpenter, both of Stanford (Dut. Co.); William Bell, Esq. (8-1/15/12)
4411. Hoxie, Steohen H. m 7/24/27 Phebe Diliverge (sic); Gideon Cornell, Esq. All of Easton (perhaps Diliverge = De La Vergne) (9-7/31)
4412. Hoxie, Zervia, 34, wf of Christopher, d 5/17/01 in Hudson (Shortly before Zervia's death "her little daughter" died) (6-5/21)
4413. Hoyle, Pamelia, 31, wf of Maj. Robert of La C__?__, Lower canada d there 11/7/25 (interred in the cemetery in Champlain, NY "of which church she was a member") (7-11/19)
4414. Hoyle, Robert, Esq. m 10/1/21 Permelia Wright in Northampton, MA (7-10/13)
4415. Hoyle, William, Jr. of Poughkeepsie m 7/15/31 Henrietta Forgerson of Newburgh at St. George's Church in Newburgh; Rev. John Brown (8-7/20 and 1-7/22)
4416. Hoyt, David of the firm of E. Peek & Co. m 9/3/29 Adaline F. Mason, both of Rochester, in R; Rev. Comstock (1-9/9)
4417. Hoyt, Eli of Danbury, CT m Sophia Fish of Hudson, NY; Rev. Wigton 6-10/7/06)
4418. Hoyt, Gould, 67, d 7/2/03 in Norwalk, CT (8-7/19)
4419. Hoyt, Gould Reed20, s of Gould Hoyt of Albany, d 10/14/20 "on the canal near Utica" (consumption) (6-10/24)

127

4420. Hoyt, Henry m 11/2/29 Asenath Brown, dau of Edward; Rev. Reed. All of Albany (1-11/4)
4421. Hoyt, Joseph L. m 11/4/12 Hannah Fisher in NYC; Rev. Lyle (8-11/18)
4422. Hoyt, Lewis m Eliza Nichols in Plattsburgh (7-7/7/32)
4423. Hoyt, Stephen, 58, of Poughkeepsie, merchant, d 10/9/09 (8-10/18)
4424. Hoyt, Stephen, Esq. of Poughkeepsie, NY m 10/17/14 Esther Mary Raymond in Norwalk, CT; Rev. Judd (8-11/2)
4425. Hubbard, Christina (Mrs.), 68, d in Claverack (3-8/15/25)
4426. Hubbard, Elizabeth, 24, consort of Ruggles Hubbard, Esq., d 1/2/07 in Troy (9-1/6)
4427. Hubbard, Ezekiel (Deacon), 73, d 2/22/27 in Beekmantown (Clinton Co.) (7-3/3)
4428. Hubbard, George C. m 8/14/31 Mary Perry at the Presbyterian Church in Keeseville; Rev. Lyman (4 [Keeseville Herald]-8/16)
4429. Hubbard, Gideon R., innkeeper, d in Claverack (6-4/16/05)
4430. Hubbard, Giles H., Esq., about 24, graduate of Union College, sheriff of Schoharie Co., and editor of the Observer, d 12/14/20 at the courthouse in Schoharie (typhus) (surv by wf and one or more ch) (3-12/25 and 8-12/27)
4431. Hubbard, Harrison m 12/30/25 Eliza Gano in Westford; Rev. Caldwell, All of Westford (3-1/2/26)
4432. Hubbard, Harvey, s of Joseph of Cooperstown, d 12/19/15 in Harrisburg, PA (3-1/25/16)
4433. Hubbard, Harvey H. of Sheffield, MA m 6/22/17 Eliza Gale, dau of Col. Gale of Warsing (Ulster Co.) [Warsing probably intended for Wawarsing], in W (6-7/1)
4434. Hubbard, Jonas m Louisa Scripture in Mason, NH (8-7/16/28)
4435. Hubbard, Lucinda, 16, dau of Moses, d 11/26/04 in Claverack (6-12/4)
4436. Hubbard, Luman H. of Burlington, VT m 8/4/33 Louise Brigham of St. Albans, VT in S. A.; Rev. Marshal (7-8/10)
4437. Hubbard, Noah, brother of the senior editor of the Norwich (NY) Journal, d 4/20/31 in Salina on his way to Lockport (1-5/7)
4438. Hubbard, Ruggles, Esq. m 3/7/02 Elizabeth Livingston, both of Troy, in T; Rev. Coe (9-3/17)
4439. Hubbel, Lurianna, 23, consort of Lemuel, Jr. and dau of David Chapin of Richmond, MA, d 4/2/08 in Burlington (Ots. Co.), NY (surv by husband and 1 child) (3-4/9)
4440. Hubbell, Addison m 12/14/25 Nancy Green, both fo Middlefield, in M (3-12/26)
4441. Hubbell, Henderson, 23, s of Silas, Esq., d 3/6/31 in Champlain (7-3/22)
4442. Hubbell, Luther of Hudson m 10/9/08 Anna Slade, dau of William, lately of Hudson, in Athens, NY; Rev. Wigton (6-10/18)
4443. Hubbell, Nicholas m 5/17/20 Anna Rice, both of Middlefield, in M; Rev. George Colton of Westford (3-5/22)
4444. Hubbell, Peter, merchant, of Coxsackie m 9/11/30 Jane Prentiss, dau of Rev. Prentiss of Greenville, at Trinity Church in Athens, NY; Rev. J. Prentiss (1-9/18)
4445. Hubbell, Salmon, 75, (a Rev. soldier) d 3/11/30 in Bridgeport (8-3/24)
4446. Hubbell, Silas of Troy m 1/20/02 Sally Henderson of Bennington (state not given) in B (9-2/17)
4447. Hubbard, Henry m 1/17/19 Betsey Alrige in Plattsburgh (7-1/30)
4448. Hubble, Alfred m Mary Barker in Rochester; Rev. Dr. Comstock (9-12/16/28)
4449. Huddleston, George V., Esq., M.D., m 11/5/17 Eliza Dorlon, both of Speigletown, in S; Rev. Oglevie (9-11/11)
4450. Hudeu, Michael Gabriel, superintendent of the military stores of Albany, d 2/4/02 in Albany (buried with military and Masonic honors in the cemetery of the Episcopal Ch.) (3-2/11)
4451. Hudson, Daniel (Capt.), 73, d 8/31/23 in Troy (9-9/16)
4452. Hudson, Edward Henry, 17 mo, a foundling, d 3/1/10 in Hudson (This child had been maintained by the City ofHudson since it was found on the steps of a house Oct 24, 1808) (6-3/8)
4453. Hudson, Ephraim, Esq., 47, d 5/3/05 in Cherry Valley (3-5/9)
4454. Hudson, Ephraim, 15, s of late Judge Hudson of Cherry Valley, d 4/14/07 in Cooperstown (surv by his mother and sisters) (3-4/23)
4455. Hudson, Hannah, 62, relict of Ephraim, Esq., deceased, d 3/5/20 in Cherry Valley (3-3/13)

4456. Hudson, Jemima, 77, relict of late Daniel, d 7/17/27 in Troy (9-7/24)
4457. Hudson, Samuel of Exeter m 3/30/26 Freelove Bloss, dau of Manassah of
       Burlington (Ots. Co.), in B; A. Sheldon, Esq. (3-4/3)
4458. Hues, Joseph m 11/14/07 Desire Robbins, both of Troy, NY, in Wallingford,
       VT (9-11/17)
4459. Huestis, Martha Ann, dau of James and Charlotte, d 9/13/30 in Poughkeepsie
       (8-9/15)
4460. Huff, Cornelius of Oswego m 2/9/31 Abigail Haight of Rensselaerville in
       R; Judge J. B. Moore (1-2/14)
4461. Huff, Frances Martha, 4, d 11/4/22 in Troy (her parents not mentioned)
       (9-11/12)
4462. Hughes, David M., Esq. m 1/17/22 Maria T. Selkrig, both of Staatsburgh;
       Rev. Brown (8-1/23)
4463. Hughes, Fountain N., merchant, m 12/11/13 Eliza Rogers, both of Clinton;
       Rev. Cuyler (8-12/29)
4464. Hughes, James M. (Gen.), master in chancery, d 12/27/02 in NYC (8-1/4/03;
       6-1/11/03)
4465. Hughes, John R., 27, of Clinton (Dut. Co.) d 4/2/16 (8-4/10)
4466. Hughes, Morris (Dr.) d 12/23/30 in Milford (3-1/1/21)
4467. Hughs, Morris of Otsego m 11/8/07 Lucretia Potter of Hartwick; Rev. Conkey
       (3-11/21)
4468. Hughson, Benjamin (Dr.) m 3/9/25 Phebe Marshall; Rev. Clark. All of
       Pleasant Valley (8-3/16)
4469. Hughson, Christopher (Capt.) m 9/28/16 Phebe Van Bramer Van Voorhis,
       dau of William, Esq., all of Fishkill (8-10/2)
4470. Hughson, Cornelia Graham, wf of Jeremiah D., d 5/23/29 at the home of
       her grandfather, John Drake, Jr., Esq. (8-6/3)
4471. Hughson, Henry of Fishkill m 2/27/13 Eliza Thacker of Poughkeepsie; Rev.
       Reed (8-3/10)
4472. Hughson, Jeremiah D. of St. John's, New Brunswick m Cornelia Graham,
       dau of Alexander; Rev. Alonzo Welton (8-10/17/27)
4473. Hughson, John W., 20, late of Poughkeepsie and son of William, Esq. of
       Fishkill, d 7/10/17 in Savannah, NY (8-7/30)
4474. Hughson, Penelope, 54, consort of William of Fishkill, d 1/3/16 (8-1/10)
4475. Hughson, Stephen of Fishkill m 1/23/02 Phebe Frear, dau of Capt. Simeon,
       of Poughkeepsie; Rev. Brower (8-1/26)
4476. Hughson, Stephenson P. of Amenia m 10/2/19 Eliza Birch of Northeast in N;
       Rev. JohnButtolph)
4477. Hughson, William m 2/14/18 Maria Wright in Fishkill; Rev. Price. All of
       Fishkill (8-2/18)
4478. Huhn, Daniel m Julia AnnHochstrasser, dau of Paul, Esq. of Albany, in
       Philadelphia (state not given); Rev. Dr. Chambers (1-11/10/29)
4479. Hulbert, Edward, merchant, of Hudson m Martha Huntington, dau of Rev.
       Enoch of Middletown, CT, in M (6-7/2)
4480. Hulbert, John W. (Col.) d 10/19/31 in Auburn (1-10/25)
4481. Hulbert, Junius (Dr.), late of Catskill, NY, d 10/26/07 in Northfield, NH
       (6-11/10)
4482. Hulburt, ____, inf ch of Edward, d 8/14/14 in Hudson (6-8/16/14)
4483. Hulburt, Hannah Caroline, 23, wf of Col. John P., d 7/21/30 in Auburn
       (1-7/27)
4484. Hulett, ____ of Long Island m 5/25/97 Rebecca Woolley, dau of Joseph
       of Washington (Dut. Co.) (8-6/13)
4485. Hulin, Alexander (Rev.) of Saratoga m 5/16/27 Eliza Hart of Troy; Rev.
       Martindale (9-5/22)
4486. Hull, Elizabeth, 27, wf of Dr. Amos G., d 10/1/02 in New Hartford, NY
       (6-10/12)
4487. Hull, Gedeon (along with Samuel Pitcher, Robert Blum, ____ Wilcox,
       Jonathan Gladding, Dr. Ephraim Comstock, the widow of the late
       Josiah Gifford, three of her children, and a young woman who
       lived in this family) died between Sept. 15 and 22, 1797 in Providence,
       RI (yellow fever epidemic) (8-10/3)
4488. Hull, George m 9/5/05 Sally Barnard, both of Hudson; Rev. Gepherd
       (7-9/24)
4489. Hull, Henry of New Lebanon m Mary Ann Grant of Richmond, MA in Ballston
       Spa; Rev. William A. Clark (2-5/13/23)

4489. Hull, Henry, 69, of Stanford d in Mount Pleasant, OH (a lengthy account, blurred and faded, but with a discernible reference to "the Society of Friends") (8-108/34)
4490. Hull, Isaac (Capt.), late commander of the U.S. frigate "Constitution", m 1/2/13 Ann M. Hart of Saybrook, CT in Bloomingdale, NY (8-1/6)
4491. Hull, Lucy, 66, wf of Chester, d 7/4/29 in Lexington, Greene Co. (1-7/11)
4492. Hull, Lydia, 7, dau of Edward, d 2/21/34 in Stanford (8-3/12)
4493. Hull, Mary (Mrs.), 77, d 8/18/17 in Poughkeepsie (8-8/20)
4494. Hull, Robert of NYC m 5/20/32 Hannah Ann Janney, oldest dau of Joseph, Esq. of Alexandria, Dist. of Columbia, in Alexandria; Rev. Mann (8-6/13)
4495. Hull, Samuel, 17, s of Henry of Stanford, d 1/18/15 in Hudson (8-2/8/15)
4496. Hull, Silas m 10/29/16 Betsey Drake in Westford; Rev. George Colton. All of Westford (3-11/7)
4497. Hull, William of Milbury, MA, while waiting on a customer in the store of his brother, died "almost instantly" 8/7/29 (8-8/26)
4498. Hull, William of Buffalo m 6/5/32 Charlotte L. Clarke, dau of James B., Esq., in Brooklyn; Rev. James P. F. Clarke (8-6/13)
4499. Hultse, Ephraim, 51, d 12/22/26 in Sempronius (9-1/2/27)
4500. Humbert, Charles, youngest child of the editor of the Independent Republican, d 12/21/28 in Goshen (1-1/4/29)
4501. Humeston, James E., Esq. m 4/12/21 Betsey Perry of Amenia; Rev. Osborn (8-5/2)
4502. Humphrey, Daniel m 1/31/18 Caroline Van Deusen in Claverack; Rev. Sluyter (double ceremony - see marr of Richard Bogardus) (6-2/10)
4503. Humphrey, Frederick of Troy m 11/22/20 Ann Vanderwerken of Waterford; Rev. Dr. Coe (9-11/28)
4504. Humphrey, James d "recently" in Albany (funeral from his late home, 11 Washington St. (1-12/28/29)
4505. Humphrey, Thomas, a wealthy farmer, d 2/19/04 in Beekmantown (8-2/21)
4506. Humphreys, David (Gen.) d in New Haven (state not given) (8-3/4/18)
4507. Humphreys, Guy, 26, s of Hon. Reuben, Esq. of Onondaga, d 12/2/07 in Marcellus (6-12/15)
4508. Humphreys, Jacob of Beekman m 10/23/11 Martha Holden of Fishkill; Rev. Reed (8-10/30)
4509. Humphreys, Stern, 13, s of Hon. Reuben of Onondaga, d 8/31/06 in Onondaga (6-9/23)
4510. Humphry, Guy, merchant, m 2/13/06 Abigail Rice, dau of Samuel, Esq., in Marcellus. All of Marcellus (6-3/4)
4511. Hunn, John S., Esq., 64, cashier of the Bank of Newburgh, d 3/12/29 in Newburgh (1-3/13)
4512. Hunsden, Abel, 74, d 12/3/33 in Shreham, VT. Also, William Jones, 23, d in Shoreham (They were both thrown from their carriages in a collision caused by a runaway horse) (4 [Keeseville Herald]-1/6/34)
4513. Hunt, A. H. of the firm of Stocking and Hunt m 8/4/31 Sarah R. Welles, dau of John, in Utica; Rev. Aiken. All of Utica (1-8/12)
4514. Hunt, Alpheus M., merchant, m 3/24/08 Eliza Ann Barnard, dau of late Joseph, Jr.; Rev. Reuben Sears. All of Hudson (6-4/5)
4515. Hunt, David m 12/19/23 Betsey Burns, both of Schaghticoke, in S; David Tallmadge, Esq. (9-1/13/24)
4516. Hunt, Edward J. m 1/18/23 Sally Cowles, both of Poughkeepsie; A. Raymond, Esq. (8-1/22)
4517. Hunt, Ephraim, 46, d 10/16/05 in Albany (was a Rev. officer in the 4th Mass. Regiment and was a member of the Society of the Cincinnati) (interred in the Episcopal burying ground, Albany) (9-10/22)
4518. Hunt, Jonas of Beekman m 3/9/14 Hannah Margeson of Fishkill; Abraham D. Van Wyck, Esq. (8-3/16)
4519. Hunt, Joseph of Oswego m 5/16/31 AnnD. Morton, dau of Elihu of Elizabethtown, NJ; Rev. Long (1-5/19)
4520. Hunt, Philena, 66, a member of the Society of Friends, d 10/26/34 at the home of Hallock Thorne in Hamilton (Mad. Co.) (8-11/11)
4521. Hunt, S. W. (Lt.) m 6/11/18 Julia Ann Herrick in Plattsburgh; Rev. Halsey (7-6/20)
4522. Hunt, William m 7/27/29 Maria Lawson, dau of Benjamin, all of Poughkeepsie; Rev. Welton (8-7/29)

4523. Hunt, William, merchant, of Leedsville in Amenia m 9/14/31 Jane Bedel
Germond, dau of William, Esq. of Pleasant Valley, in P. V.; Rev. Aaron
Hunt (8-9/28)
4524. Hunter, Elijah m 8/23/21 Rachael Pullock, dau of Robert, all of Fishkill;
Rev. Price (8-8/29)
4525. Hunter, George, auctioneer, of NYC d 1/22/03 (8-2/1)
4526. Hunter, George, about 12, d 9/26/17 in Plattsburgh (7-10/4)
4527. Hunter, Hannah, 84, widow of Jonathan, d 9/19/34 in West Plattsburgh
(7-9/27)
4528. Hunter, Jonathan, 82, (a Rev. Soldier) d 3/21/34 in Plattsburgh (7-3/22)
4529. Hunter, Louiza, 6, dau of Edward, d 1/28/19 in Plattsburgh (7-1/30)
4530. Hunter, Nancy (Miss), 20, dau of Jonathan, d 11/10/15 in Plattsburgh
(7-11/18)
4531. Hunter, William Seton, s of M. H. of NYC, d 8/18/29 in Para, Brazil
(1-10/1)
4532. Hunting, Isaac, Esq., farmer, d 9/21/29 at his home in Stanford (8-9/23)
4533. Huntington, Abigal, 44, consort of Samuel, d 3/8/13 in Cooperstown
(3-3/13)
4534. Huntington, Ann, consort of Rev. Huntington and dau of Eleazer Dows,
d 10/3/22 in Charlton (2-10/15)
4535. Huntington, Anna (Mrs.), 66, d 1/28/16 in Hudson (6-2/6)
4536. Huntington, Benjamin, Esq. d 10/16/00 in Rome, NY (formerly of Connecticut
where he was a judge of the superior court and several times a
representative in the Congress under the old confederation") (9-10/28)
4537. Huntington, Chester m 7/7/04 Rachel Waring in Loonenburgh (Athens, NY);
Rev. Philip F. Mayer (6-8/7)
4538. Huntington, David (Rev.) m 5/6/24 Catharine Callaghan in Charlton; Rev.
Baldwin. All of C (2-5/11)
4539. Huntington, Elisha m 12/25/08 Lydia Paddock in Hudson (6-1/3/09)
4540. Huntington, Harriet, 47, d 10/13/19 in Charlotte "at the mouth of the
Genesee River. In 7 weeks Mr. Huntington has been deprived of four of
his family.": his wife on the 3rd; his dau Martha, 27, on the 25th;
Phoebe, 21, on the 29th of Aug.; and Harriet on the 13th of Nov. (all
died "of the fever that prevails on the shore of Lake Ontario")(7-11/13)
4541. Huntington, Jedediah (Gen.), 79, d in New London, CT ("the last but one
of the Major Generals of the Revolutionary Army") (8-10/21/18)
4542. Huntington, O. E. of the firm of Huntington and Dodge, NYC, m 6/10/30
Marianne Strong, dau of Joseph, Esq., in Norwich, CT; Rev. Dr. Strong
(1-6/19)
4543. Huntington, Sally, consort of Samuel, d 12/5/06 in Cooperstown (3-12/11)
4544. Huntington, Samuel G., Esq., attorney, of Waterford m 6/27/25 Janette
Cheever of Troy, in T; Rev. Beeman (2-7/5)
4545. Huntington, Simon (Deacon) d in Norwich (6-1/19/02)
4546. Huntley, George B., printer, m Mary Coles, dau of Benjamin, in NYC;
Rev. Dr. Milnor (double ceremony - see marr of John T. Huntley)
(3-7/2/21)
4547. Huntley, John T., printer, m Jerusha Coles, dau of Benjamin, in NYC; Rev.
Dr. Milnor (double ceremony - see marr of George B. Huntley) (3-7/2/21)
4548. Hurd, Benjamin D. m 6/3/19 Mary Campbell, dau of Archibald, Esq., in
Pawling; Rev. Candy. All of Pawling (8-6/16)
4549. Hurd, Eliza M., 28, wf of Nathaniel F., d 7/14/27 in Troy ("Printers in
New Hampshire and Massachusetts are requested to insert the above")
(9-7/17)
4550. Hurd, Eliza Montgomery, 28, wf of Nathaniel P., d 7/14/27 in Troy
"Printers in New Hampshire and Vermont are requested to publish the
above") (9-7/20) (Apparently the data in 4550 supercede those in
4549)
4551. Hurd, John of Pawling m 4/17/03 Abigail Stephens of Sheffield (state
not given - perhaps intended for Mass.) in Sheffield (8-4/26)
4552. Hurd, Judson, about 35, d 2/12/22 in Beekmantown (Clinton Co.) (consumption)
(7-2/16)
4553. Hurd, Owen Roberts, 33 mo, s of Gen. J(?). N. M. Hurd, d 9/22/29 in Albany
(1-9/25)
4554. Hurlburt, Aaron of Danbury, CT m 7/11/19 Laura L. Smith of Woodbury, CT
in W (3-8/16)

4555. Hurlburt, Frederick M. Of Utica m Sophia Dakin, dau of Samuel of New Hartford, in New Hartford; Rev. Adams (1-5/14/31)
4556. Hurlbut, Lemuel m 5/25/28 Lucretia Howard, both of Troy; Rev. Howard (9-5/27)
4557. Hurst, George W., about 35, of Albany d 2/23/31 at the Eagle Tavern in Elmira (surv by wf living in Albany; he had come to Elmira in very feeble health about 2 weeks prior to his death) (1-3/10)
4558. Huse, Elizabeth Sewall, inf dau of Rev. Huse, d 5/14/23 at Canadarago Spring (3-5/26)
4559. Huse, Nathaniel (Rev.), rector of St. Luke's Church in Richfield, m 6/6/22 Olive Beardsley, dau of Abadiah, Esq. of Richfield; Rev. Nash (3-6/17)
4560. Huson, John, Jr. m 1/6/31 Harriet Peck; John Boyden, Esq. All of Lorraine (1-1/22)
4561. Hussey, Thomas m 9/21/02 Patience Hazard, both of Hudson (6-9/28)
4562. Husted, James G. of Stanford (Dut. Co.) m 5/3/21 Elizabeth Harris of Northeast; Rev. Armstrong (8-5/16)
4563. Husted, Lewis m 10/9/24 Phebe Jackson; Isaac Sutherland, Esq. All of Stanford (8-10/13)
4564. Husted, Walter (Col.), 51, d 4/14/23 in Pine Plains (8-4/16)
4565. Hustis, Joseph of Southeast m 5/23/99 Sarah Leggett of Stanford (Dut. Co.) (8-6/4)
4566. Hutchings, Orville of New Lebanon m 8/2/31 Lavinia Woodbury of Albany; Rev. Dr. Ludlow (1-8/5)
4567. Hutchins, Ann, 61, d in Hudson (6-11/14/09)
4568. Hutchins, Baron Steuben m Mrs. Clifford in Hyde Park (8-7/21/24)
4569. Hutchins, Carver of Windsor, NY m 10/11/30 Sally Scott of Prospect (a suit was immediately filed against this pair for a breach of promise by a former swain of the bride) (8-11/17)
4570. Hutchins, Jacob m 2/4/03 Sybel Simoson(?), both of Clinton (Dut. Co.) (8-2/15)
4571. Hutchins, John Nathan, 81, d 7/8/82 (surv by his wf) (buried in Newburgh) (5-7/18)
4572. Hutchinson, Benjamin, 44, d 3/28/13 in Canaan (6-4/20)
4573. Hutton, Francis, about 30, of the firm of Taylor and Hutton d 10/5/30 in NYC (8-10/13)
4574. Huyck, John V. of the U.S. Army, late of Kingston, NY, d 2/20/29 in Washington City, Dist. of Columbia (8-3/14)
4575. Hyatt, Daniel, Esq. m Abigail Barton in Stanford; Jonathan Haight, Esq. All of Stanford (8-12/1/30)
4576. Hyatt, James W. B. m 2/15/23 Mary Taylor; Rev. Griffen (9-2/18)
4577. Hyde, Ezekiel, 33, d 2/10/05 in Wilkes Barre, PA (6-3/12)
4578. Hyde, Guy, 43, for many years a resident of Poughkeepsie, d 11/20/28 in NYC (8-11/26)
4579. Hyde, Harvey, 23, s of Isaac of Rensselaerville, d 3/24/29 in R (died on his birthday) (1-3/30)
4580. Hyde, James, Esq., 54, d 3/31/26 in Richfield (3-4/10)
4581. Hyde, James L. m 1/4/30 Cornelia Eggleston, both of Hyde Park, in H. P.; Rev. William Cahoon (8-1/13)
4582. Hyde, Jedediah (Capt.), 86, d 4/29/22 in Hyde Park (7-5/18)
4583. Hyde, Jedediah, Esq., 63, (a Rev. soldier) d in Burlington, VT "on his return from the legislature" (was a representative from Grand Isle, VT) (7-11/27/24)
4584. Hyde, John W., Esq., clerk of the common council, d 12/19/31 in Albany (1-12/20)
4585. Hyde, Jonathan of Middle Hero, Grand Isle, VT, m 3/15/18 Phebe Fillmore, dau of Capt. Septa Fillmore of Ghazy in C; Rev. A. Dunbar (7-3/21)
4586. Hyde, Roswell m Eunice Grey in Springfield; Rev. Putnam (3-2/3/23)
4587. Hyde, Samuel S., Esq. m 3/30/23 Mrs. Sally Maxon, both of Pittstown; James Mosher, Esq. (9-4/1)
4588. Hyde, William F. of the firm of W. F. and E. B. Hyde & Co. m 4/7/31 Jane Van ? kirk (perhaps intended for Buskirk), youngest dau of late Abraham, Esq., at Christ Church in NYC; Rev. Dr. Lyell (1-4/9)
4589. Hyzer, Eleanor, 70, wf of Michael T., formerly of Poughkeepsie, d 6/22/34 in Hyde Park (8-7/2/34)

4590. Iggett, John m 5/23/19 Catharine McCluspsy, both of Albany; Rev. Dr. Coe (9-5/25)
4591. Ingalls, Cyrus, merchant, of Peterboro', NH m 9/15/30 Mary Dakin, oldest dau of Samuel, Esq. of New Hartford, NY, in New Hartford; Rev. Adams (1-9/25)
4592. Ingalls, James, Esq. d 3/19/13 in Middlefield (3-3/20)
4593. Ingalls, Sarah, 70, relict of the late (blurred) (possibly given name James) d 1/27/31 in Middlefield (Otsego Co.) (1-2/7)
4594. Ingals, Charles F., Esq. m 10/22/18 Polly Rodgers, dau of Nathan, Esq., in Union Village; Elder Barber (9-10/27)
4595. Ingals, Erastus W. of Middlefield m 4/16/16 Fanny Goodsell, dau of Peter of Burlington, in B; Rev. Benedict (3-4/25)
4596. Ingals, Orrin, s of Stephen, d 6/26/14 in Middlefield (3-6/30)
4597. Ingersoll, Andrew m 11/6/02 Betsey Straight, both of Poughkeepsie; Rev. Van Vranken (8-11/16)
4598. Ingersoll, Mary, 3, dau of Capt. J. Ingersoll of the U.S. Army, d 2/9/21 in Troy (9-2/13)
4599. Ingraham, David m 12/26/33 Lucy Palmer; Rev. Cocran. All of Washington (Dut. Co.) (8-1/15/34)
4600. Ingraham, Duncan, Jr., Esq., 53, d 6/16/05 at his home in Poughkeepsie (8-6/18 and 6-6/25)
4601. Ingraham, Thomas S. m 11/3/23 Julia Ballis, dau of William, Esq.; Rev. Cyrus Silliman. All of Amenia (8-11/12)
4602. Innis, Ruth, dau of Capt. Aaron, d 6/1/34 in Poughkeepsie (8-6/11)
4603. Irish, Abigail, 81, consort of Charles of Newport, RI, d 11/23/16 in Hudson, NY (6-11/30)
4604. Irish, Joseph of Poughkeepsie m 11/11/30 Cornelia Ackert, dau of Jacob I. of Hyde Park (in Hyde Park?); John S. Van Wagner, Esq. (8-11/17)
4605. Irish, Montraville m 9/14/33 Louisa Reynolds; Thomas D. Gibson, Esq. (4 [Keeseville Herald]-10/30)
4606. Irons, Jeremiah, Sr., 85, d 7/4/96 in Bower's Patent (surv by numerous children) (3-7/7)
4607. Irons, Levi m 4/2/26 Laura Belknap, both of Burlington, in Hartwick; D. Kendal, Esq. (3-4/10)
4608. Irving, Gabriel F. m 4/9/31 Eliza Eckford, dau of Henry, Esq., in NYC; Rev. William Wure (1-4/13)
4609. Irving, Lewis G., merchant, of NYC m 6/16/23 Maria C. Hale, dau of Dr. M. Hale of the U.S. Army, in Plattsburgh; Rev. William S. Irving (7-6/21)
4610. Iverson, Alfred of Columbus m 4/7/31 Julia Frances Forsyth, oldest dau of Hon. John, near Augusta (1-5/6)
4611. Ives, Harriet (Miss), 20, of Tinmouth, VT, a student in the Albany Female Seminary, d 12/10/31 at the residence of Rev. Garfield in Albany (1-12/19)
4612. Ives, L. Silliman (Rev.), rector of Trinity Church in Philadelphia, PA, m 2/15/25 Rebecca Smith Hobart, dau of Right Rev. John H. Hobart, D.D., (Bishop of the state of NY), in NYC; Rev. Berrian (3-2/28)
4613. Jacacks, Samuel of Beekman m 1/24/24 Amanda Akin of Pawling in P (8-1/28)
4614. Jacket, Jonathan, youngest s of Chief Red Jacket, m 12/14/20 Yeeh-Ah-Weeh, a young woman from Cattaraugus, at the home of James Young near the Seneca Village; Rev. Stephen N. Rowan, Pres. of the NY Missionary Soc. (double ceremony - see marr of Thomas Armstrong) (9-1/2/21)
4615. Jackson, Alexander C., Esq. of the late firm of Jackson & McJimsey d 12/23/31 in NYC (His dau d 12/22; both died of scarlet fever) (1-12/30)
4616. Jackson, Amasa of NYC m 12/26/31 Jane E. Howell, dau of Nathaniel W., in Canandaigua; Rev. Eddy (1-12/31/31)
4617. Jackson, Ann Jane, consort of Hon. Joseph I. and dau of Hon. Henry Garrison of Phillipstown (Put. Co.), d 2/2/32 in Fishkill (8-2/8)
4618. Jackson, Edward Hunting, 7, s of Joseph I., d 7/14/32 in Fishkill (scarlet fever) (8-7/18)
4619. Jackson, Helen Maria Yates, 5, dau of Allen H., Esq. and gr-dau of Rev. W. Paige, d 12/15/31 in Gilboa (Schoharie Co.) (scalded) (1-12/29)
4620. Jackson, Increase, 77, farmer, d 4/13/28 at his home in Stanford (8-4/23)
4621. Jackson, Isaac W., Esq. of Union College m 8/26/29 Elizabeth Pomeroy, dau of Lemuel, Esq. of Pittsfield, MA, in P; Rev. Tappan (1-8/28)

4622. Jackson, Israel m 12/23/18 Esther Allen, dau of John, all of Peru, NY, in P; Lucius Elderkin, Esq. (7-12/26)
4623. Jackson, Joseph, 72, d 3/12/18 in Fishkill (8-3/18)
4624. Jackson, Joseph H., attorney, m 5/21/32 Helen M. Everitt, dau of Peter, Esq.; Rev. Dr. Reed (8-5/23)
4625. Jackson, Joseph I. of Fishkill m 10/25/08 Ann Jane Garrison, dau of Henry, Esq. of Phillipstown; Rev. Crane (8-11/2)
4626. Jackson, Joseph I. of Fishkill m 3/26/14 Mary B. Ingraham, dau of George of Amenia; Rev. Bangs (8-4/6)
4627. Jackson,Milly, 22, wf of Daniel and dau of Timothy Bedel, d 9/12/98 in Clinton (Dut. Co.) (8-9/18)
4628. Jackson, Peter (Rev.) m 10/22/29 Elizabeth Van Dyck, dau of Dr. L., all of Kinderhook, in Fulton (Oswego Co.); Rev. Colwell (1-11/4)
4629. Jackson, Richard B., Esq. of Stanford (Dut. Co.) m 11/6/19 Fanny German of Red Hook in R. H.;Rev. Kittle (8-11/17)
4630. Jackson, Richard B. m 7/2/24 Louisa Butts, both of Stanford (Dut. Co.); Rev. L. Birch (8-7/28)
4631. Jacob, Charles D. of Upper Red Hook m 12/10/29 Eliza Nelson of Hyde Park in H. P.; Rev. William Cahoon (8-12/16)
4632. Jacobs, Bethiah, 72, relict of ____ Jacobs of Hingham, MA d 1/19/08 in Hartwick, NY (surv by an only child, Ezekiel Jacobs, and 6 gr-ch) (funeral sermon by Elder Bostwick) (3-1/23/08)
4633. Jacobs, Leonard m 1/15/21 Peggy Thew (in Peru, NY?) (7-1/20)
4634. Jacobs, Mary, 56, wf of Nathaniel, Esq., formerly of Lansingburgh, d 10/21/15 at Schaghticoke Point (9-11/21)
4635. Jacocks, ____, wf of Thomas, d 3/20/30 (8-3/24)
4636. Jacocks, Abraham S. m 8/14/13 Susan Phillips; Rev. Cuyler (8-8/18)
4637. Jacocks, Gertrude, 25, wf of William, d 3/11/34 in Staatsburgh (consumption) (8-3/26)
4638. Jacocks, Isaac H., 36, formerly of Dutchess Co., NY, d 5/21/32 in Pittsford, VT (8-6/6)
4639. Jacocks, John m 1/2/12 Maria Phillips, both of Poughkeepsie; Rev. Cuyler (8-1/8)
4640. Jacocks, Mary, 34, wf of Nicholas, d 12/2/34 in New Paltz (8-12/10)
4641. Jacocks, Nicholas, formerly of Poughkeepsie, m 8/29/27 Mary Dakin of New Windsor (Orange Co.); Rev. Arbuckle (8-9/12)
4642. James, Daniel (Dr.) m Hetty Delevan, both of Albany, in A (Rev. Dr. Chester (3-6/16/23)
4643. James, Edward m 9/14/30 Ann Day, both of Albany; Rev. John Nott (1-9/15)
4644. James, Edward K., Esq. m 4/2/29 Louisa Matilda Livingston, both of Poughkeepsie; Rev. Dr. Cuyler (8-4/8)
4645. James, Edward K. m 3/21/29 Louisa Matilda Livingston of Poughkeepsie in P; Rev. Dr. Cuyler (1-4/10)
4646. James, Elizabeth, 11, dau of late Robert, d 7/12/30 in Albany (William James and Mrs. Stephen Lush, grandparents of the deceased, are mentioned) (funeral from the home of her father on North Pearl St.) (1-7/13)
4647. James, Francis,"an honest, industrious, and respectable man of color", d (in Troy?) (9-2/28/15)
4648. James, Gough m 8/24/31 Margaret H. McLaughlin, both of Albany, in NYC; Rev. Conroy (1-9/14)
4649. James, Richard, Esq., 45, formerly from the Island of Jamaica, d 1/3/23 at his home in Poughkeepsie (8-1/8)
4650. Jansen, John M. m Maria Louw, dau of Cornelius, Esq., in Kingston; Rev. King (bride and groom both of Shawangunk) (6-7/22/06)
4651. Jaques, Enos, 41, d 4/8/30 in Albany (funeral from 59 Beaver St.) (1-4/9)
4652. Jaques, Robert W. m 2/27/29 Eliza Gibson, both of Rhinebeck, in R; Rev. Fitch Reed (8-3/11)
4653. Jarvis, Augustus m 10/4/25 Julia Parsons; Rev. Willson (8-10/12)
4654. Jarvis, Horace m Julia AnnBetts in Coxsackie (6-10/7/06)
4655. Jarvis, Kent m 5/17/21 Uretta Williams in Fly Creek (Ots. Co.); Rev. Tiffany (3-5/21)
4656. Jarvis, Mary (wid) d in Cooperstown (3-12/27/04)
4657. Jarvis, Moses of NYC m 11/20/15 Mrs. Mary Bears of Troy; Rev. Coe (9-11/28)

4658. Jarvis, Nathaniel, Jr. of NYC m 9/3/31 Rebecca Dyckman Bussing, youngest dau of Aaron of Harlem, in H; Rev. Vermeule (1-9/12)
4659. Jarvis, Stephen m 9/26/31 Jenette Adams in Oak Hill; Rev. Norman H. Adams (1-10/3)
4660. Jarvis, William m 2/7/31 Lucinda Carter in Rensselaerville; Rev. Samuel Fuller. All of Rensselaerville (1-2/12 and 1-2/17)
4661. Jarvis, William B. of Poughkeepsie m 7/21/24 Sarah Lawson of Wappingers Creek in W. C.; Rev. Price (8-7/28)
4662. Jay, Peter, Esq. d 4/17/82 "at an advanced age" at his home in Pough- keepsie (had been for many years a merchant in NYC) (5-4/18)
4663. Jay, Sarah, 44, wf of John Jay, late gov. of NY and one of the daus of late Gov. Livingston, deceased, d 5/28/02 in Bedford (West. Co.) (6-6/8 and 8-6/8)
4664. Jaycox, Phebe, 70, wf of Joseph, d 10/8/32 in Chesterfield (member of Methodist Episcopal Ch.) (4 [Keeseville Herald]-10/16)
4665. Jeffers, Alburn m 4/14/21 Sarah Howard, both of Troy; Rev. Sommers (9-4/17)
4666. Jenkens, John m 4/31/18 Elizabeth Cobb; Rev. Luckey. All of Troy (9-5/5)
4667. Jenkins, Abisha m 8/22/02 Emma Finch in Hudson (6-8/24)
4668. Jenkins, Almira, dau of Barzilla, d 4/21/07 in Hudson (6-5/5)
4669. Jenkins, Charles, 65, d 8/30/08 in Hudson (6-8/9)
4670. Jenkins, Charles G., 27, s of late Lemuel, d 3/17/09 in Hudson (6-3/21)
4671. Jenkins, Clark m 10/3/27 Trena Beecher; Rev. C. P. Wilson. All of Amenia (8-10/10)
4672. Jenkins, Deborah (Mrs.), 64, d 6/3/05 in Hudson (6-6/11)
4673. Jenkins, Edgar of New Orleans, LA m 10/20/31 Mary Elizabeth Walworth, dau of Chancellor Walworth, in Albany; Rev. Dr. Sprague (1-10/21 and 8-10/26)
4674. Jenkins, Frederick, 4, s of Gardner Jenkins, d 12/7/20 in Hudson (6-12/12)
4675. Jenkins, Gardner m 8/31/09 Eunice Bingham, both of Hudson, in H; Rev. Sears (6-9/5)
4676. Jenkins, George Warner m Ann Relay in Hudson (6-11/6/04)
4677. Jenkins, Gertrude P., 28, wf of Lemuel, d 5/12/29 in Albany (funeral from her husband's home, 135 Washington St.) (1-5/14)
4678. Jenkins, Gilbert, 2, s of Gilbert, d 2/23/07 in Hudson (6-3/3)
4679. Jenkins, Gilbert, cashier of the Bank of Hudson, m Sally Worth, dau of S. Worth, Esq., in Hudson. All of Hudson (6-2/10/12)
4680. Jenkins, Hannah, 68, relict of the late Charles, d 6/27/18 (6-6/30)
4681. Jenkins, John F. of the firm of Robert Jenkins & Co. m 5/8/13 Eliza P--poon, both of Hudson; Rev. Chester (6-5/11)
4682. Jenkins, Lemuel d 5/22/17 in Hudson (buried with Masonic honors) (6-5/27)
4683. Jenkins, Marshal, 39, formerly clerk of Columbia Co., d 10/15/19 in Hudson (surv by 2 young ch) (6-10/26)
4684. Jenkins, Marshall, Jr., merchant, m 3/30/04 Sarah Jenkins, dau of Thomas, Esq., mayor of Hudson, in H (6-4/3)
4685. Jenkins, Mary, consort of Thomas, Esq., mayor of Hudson, d 12/23/01 in Hudson (6-12/24)
4686. Jenkins, Mary, wf of Gilbert, d 4/27/11 in Hudson (6-5/3)
4687. Jenkins, Polly, relict of the late Lemuel, d in Hudson (6-11/21/09)
4688. Jenkins, Prudence, 75, relict of John, formerly of Providence, d 4/30/03 in Hudson (6-5/3)
4689. Jenkins, Robert, Esq., 47, mayor of Hudson, d 11/11/19 "on his passage from New York (city) to this City (Hudson)" (he was struck by the boom of the sloop "John Hancock") (6-11/16) (See 4690)
4690. Jenkins, Robert, mayor of Hudson, d 11/10/19 on the sloop, "John Hancock" on his way from NYC to Hudson (apoplexy) (7-11/20) (See 4689)
4691. Jenkins, Robert H., merchant, of Albany m 1/23/30 Cornelia H. Jenkins, dau of Seth, Esq., in Columbiaville (Col. Co.); Rev. Stebbins (1-1/26)
4692. Jenkins, Sally, 26, wf of Marshal, Esq. and dau of late Thomas Jenkins, Esq., d 9/4/09 in Hudson (6-9/12)
4693. Jenkins, Sarah, sister of Robert Jenkins, Esq., d 11/9/19 in Hudson (6-11/23)
4694. Jenkins, Seth, Esq., 51, d 8/19/31 in Columbiaville (1-8/24)
4695. Jenkins, Susan (Miss), dau of John, formerly of Providence, RI, d 11/13/05 (in Hudson?) (funeral sermon by Rev. B. Judd) (6-11/19)

4696. Jenkins, Theodore H. of NYC m 6/5/31 Julia A. S. Livingston, dau of Robert S., Esq. of Red Hook, in R. H.; Rev. Sherwood (1-6/9?/31)
4697. Jenkins, Thomas, Esq., mayor of Hudson m 5/23/03 Margaret Hussey, wid of late Capt. Paul Hussey, of Hudson, in H (6-5/31)
4698. Jenkins, Thomas, Esq., 67, one of the first settlers and late mayor of Hudson, d 9/10/08 at the home of his son, Frederick, Esq. in NYC (his body placed on a packet for burial in Hudson, NY) (6-9/20 and 3-9/24)
4699. Jenkins, Valentine, 75, d "about the middle of June" in Poquague (Dut. Co.) (6-7/22)
4700. Jenkins, William, 35, late of Hudson, d 5/28/05 in Edgartown, Martha's Vineyard, MA (6-6/18)
4701. Jenkins, William m 3/9/31 Mary Ann Henry, oldest dau of late Dr. Henry of Geneva, in Utica; Rev. Elon Galusha (1-3/26)
4702. Jenks, Hervey (Rev.), 27, pastor of the Baptist Church of Hudson "for the past two years" d 7/15/14 (was publicly educated at the College in Rhode Island) (6-7/26)
4703. Jenks, Nathaniel m 12/26/07 Mary Toll (6-12/29)
4704. Jenne, John m 2/7/22 Mercy Bartlet, both of Charlton, in C; Rev. J. W. Platt (2-2/13)
4705. Jennings, _____, about 10, a son of Mrs. Lydia Jennings, drowned 6/23/05 "in Hudson's River" (6-6/25)
4706. Jenner, J. A. of St. Luke, Lower Canada, m 4/27/34 Harriet Caroline Porter, dau of late Dr. Porter of Montreal, Canada, in Champlain, NY; Rev. Kinney (7-5/10)
4707. Jenner, Samuel, about 56, d 4/15/25 in Plattsburgh (7-4/23)
4708. Jennings, Holly m Amy Fairchild in Franklin (8-1/10/04)
4709. Jennings, John (Rev.), pastor of the First Baptist Ch. in Beverly, MA, m 10/9/34 Susan C. Keyes of Salisbury, CT; Rev. Thomas Winter of Northeast (Put. Co.), NY (8-10/22)
4710. Jennings, Samuel m 9/11/23 AnnWakeman, both of Ballston, in Charlton; Rev. Smith (double ceremony - see marr of James Callahan)
4711. Jensen, Henry (Hon.) d 9/12/21 in Albany (a delegate to _?_ [page mutilated] from the counties of Ulster and Sullivan) (9-9/18)
4712. Jerome, Isaac, Esq., 36, d at his home 2 miles west of Geddes (Onon. Co.) (1-4/27/29)
4713. Jerome, Lucy, 23, consort of Rev. Amasa and dau of Lt. Gov. Treadwell, d in New Hartford, CT (6-10/23/04)
4714. Jersey, Henry d 2/21/13 in Plattsburgh (7-2/26)
4715. Jersey, Joseph d 9/1/19 in Plattsburgh (7-9/4)
4716. Jessup, Waterman, 8 mo, s of Benjamin, d 8/15/30 in Albany (funeral from 555 South Market St.) (1-8/16)
4717. Jewel, Richard W. m 6/27/22 Sarah Sheldon, both of Poughkeepsie; Rev. C. C. Cuyler (8-7/3)
4718. Jewell, John E. m 9/12/29 Sibble Van Vlack, both of Freedom; Isaac Holmes, Esq. (8-9/23)
4719. Jewell, Richard m 2/18/29 Maria Halstead, both of Fishkill Plains, in Poughkeepsie; Rev. Welton (8-2/25)
4720. Jewet, Jedediah m 5/24/29 Hannah Mosier, both of Union Vale, in U. V.; Rev. Arnold (8-5/28)
4721. Jewett, Simeon B., Esq. m 10/10/31 Nancy Cook, both of Clarkson (Monroe Co.), NY, in Montrose, PA; Rev. Samuel Marks (1-10/19)
4722. Jewett, Volkert D. d "recently" in Albany (funeral from his late home, 83 Maiden Lane) (1-6/30/30)
4723. Jewitt, N. H. of the firm of Ketcham and Jewitt m 4/13/24 Jane Hoffman, dau of late Abraham; Rev. Cuyler (8-4/16)
4724. Jewitt, William (Rev.) of Poughkeepsie m Jane Maria Stillwill of Woodstock; Rev. Bangs (8-4/23)
4725. Jillett, David m 11/10/18 Susanna Starr, dau of Salmon, Esq., in Butternuts (Ots. Co.); Rev. Wheeler. All of Butternuts (3-11/23)
4726. Jipson, Benjamin m 12/9/20 Hannah Whitmarsh, both of Gibbonsville; Rev. Sommers (9-1/16/21)
4727. Jobert, John of Montreal, Canada m 8/6/22 Sarah Norcross, dau of late Samuel, Esq. of Plattsburgh, in P; Rev. Frederick Halsey (7-8/10)
4728. Jobs, James (Deacon), 78, m 1/12/23 Mrs. Anna Young, about 60, in Ballston; Elder Jacob St. John (2-1/21)

4729. Johnes, Aaron P., merchant, of the firm of Marsh-Johnes & Co. of NYC
m 3/31/30 Lydia Denniston of Bloomingburgh (Orange Co.) in B (1-4/6)
4730. Johnson, _____ m Sally Folger (6-12/18/04)
4731. Johnson, _____, s of John C., d "recently" in Albany (funeral at the home
of his father-in-law, William Easton, corner Columbia and North Pearl
Sts.) (1-2/1/30)
4732. Johnson, Andrew m 12/26/07 Abigail Ellis in Milford; Rev. Dodge (3-1/2/08)
4733. Johnson, Augustus S., merchant, m 4/21/31 Sarah Ann Noyes, dau of George,
in Oriskany; Rev. Perry. All of Oriskany (1-4/28)
4734. Johnson, Barakiah (Lt.), 79, (a Rev. soldier) d 5/2/26 in Otsego (3-5/8)
4735. Johnson, Daniel, about 54, d "recently" in Champlain (7-1/8/13)
4736. Johnson, Daniel C. m 12/8/29 Ann Eliza Vanleuven; Rev. Ferris. All of
Albany (1-12/11)
4737. Johnson, Davis, bookseller, m 8/19/15 Catherine Everitt, dau of Richard,
all of Poughkeepsie; Rev. Reed (8-8/23)
4738. Johnson, Elener, 69, wf of Dole(?) Johnson, formerly of Worcester, MA,
d 8/23/12 in Chazy, NY (7-8/28)
4739. Johnson, Elijah m 2/3/25 Miranda Chamberlain (in Columbia, Herk. Co.?)
(3-2/14)
4740. Johnson, Hamblin, lately from Burlington, VT, d 11/1/12 in Plattsburgh,
NY (7-11/20)
4741. Johnson, Hannah (Mrs.), 81, d 11/24/34 in Poughkeepsie (funeral at the
Episcopal Ch.) (8-11/26)
4742. Johnson, Henry (Hon.) of Louisiana and late gov. of that state, m Miss
Elizabeth Key, dau of late Philip B., at the home of Mrs. Key
in Georgetown (state not given) (1-10/9/29)
4743. Johnson, Henry, 71, (a Rev. patriot) d in Madison Co., NY (1-1/1/30)
4744. Johnson, Isaac, 22, oldest s of Capt. Stephen W. of Lansingburgh, d 1/28/01
(9-2/3)
4745. Johnson, Jacob A. I., late of New Jersey, m 7/24/11 Lucretia Van Hoesen
of Hudson in H; Rev. Chester (6-8/2)
4746. Johnson, John of the firm of Johnson and Halsted, merchants, m 1/8/10
Abby B. Neil in NYC (8-1/10)
4747. Johnson, John, 52, d 5/4/29 in Albany (1-5/5)
4748. Johnson, John of Union Vale m 9/4/34 Anne(?) Northrop, dau of Samuel, Esq.
of Amenia, in A; Rev. Richard Wyman (8-9/10)
4749. Johnson, John C., 27, printer, d 9/12/30 in Albany (1-9/14)
4750. Johnson, Noahdiah, about 41, d recently in Kinderhook (was born in
Middletown, CT; his father, Elihu, moved from that town to Albany, NY
where he had a saddling business and where he died; Noahdiah had a sister
living in Oblong, Dutchess Co., NY and married to a "Mr. Wilcox" - this
info. furnished at the time of Noahdiah's death by Richard I. Goes of
Kinderhook) (8-11/30/08)
4751. Johnson, Parlay m 1/4/17 in Otsego (3-1/9)
4752. Johnson, Ralph, junior editor of the Norwich (NY) Journal, m Mary Randall
in Norwich (1-5/8/29)
4753. Johnson, Richard of Plattekill m 11/30/22 Laner Lester of New Paltz;
Rev. Ostrom (8-12/11)
4754. Johnson, Robert (or "the person calling himself that") d 1/5/07 in the
Albany gaol - committed for an attempt to rob the house of Mr. Pye on
the Albany road (R. J. died from a wound inflicted by Mr. Pye, "after
being himself shot thro' the body. Mr. Pye is said to be out of danger.")
(9-1/13)
4755. Johnson, Sally, 15, dau of Samuel of Poughkeepsie, d 3/4/05 (8-3/12)
4756. Johnson, Samuel, Jr., 25, d 9/2/25 in Otsego (3-9/5)
4757. Johnson, Samuel R. (Rev.) m 9/6/26 Elizabeth Johnston, 2nd dau of John,
Esq. of Hyde Park, at St. James Church in Hyde Park by Rev. William
L. Johnson, rector of St. Michael's Church in Trenton, NJ (8-9/13)
4758. Johnson, Seth (Lt.) of the U.S. Army m 3/16/20 Harriet Hubbel, dau of Levi,
in Hudson (6-3/21)
4759. Johnson, Simeon, formerly of Lansingburgh, NY, d 11/5/07 in Gonaives, St.
Domingo (9-1/19/08)
4760. Johnson, Stephen C., Esq., attorney, of Delhi m 1/6/31 Mary Ann Swift of
Franklin (Delaware Co.) in F; Rev. Daniel Waterbury (1-1/18)

137

4761. Johnson, Thomas A., Esq. m 5/7/30 Polly Birdsall, dau of Maurice, all of Greene (Chen. Co.), in G (1-6/15)
4762. Johnson, Timothy, about 12, d 9/23/04 in Cooperstown (suicide by hanging) (had lived in the home of Uriah Luce, Esq. about 6 weeks) (Timothy's father was killed about 4 years earlier in the fall of a tree, his mother died shortly thereafter, and a few years earlier his sister fell into a well and was drowned) (3-9-27)
4763. Johnson, William Kendal, 7 mo, only s of William and Lucy, d 8/29/23 in Troy (9-9/2)
4764. Johnson, William, Esq., 15, m Miss Mary Ann Miller, 37, formerly of Albany, in New Lebanon; Uriah Edwards, Esq. (8-6/21/26)
4765. Johnson, William, 61, d 1/22/29 at his home in Johnsonville (in Pittstown) (typhus fever) (1-1/31)
4766. Johnson, William Samuel, LL.D., 93, d 11/14/19 in Strafford, CT (7-12/4)
4767. Johnston, Charles, Esq., attorney, m 3/13/20 Eliza Bostwick, dau of Capt. Benjamin R., all of Pine Plains; Rev. Armstrong (8-3/15)
4768. Johnston, David, Esq., 84, d 1/7/09 in Washington (Dut. Co.) (8-1/25)
4769. Johnston, David I., 43, d 12/18/09 in Washington (Dut. Co.) (8-1/3/10)
4770. Johnston, Francis U. (Dr.) m 5/10/22 Mary Williamson of NYC in NYC; Rev. McVickar (8-5/22)
4771. Johnston, Jacob d 9/15/11 at his home in Washington (Dut. Co.) (8-9/18)
4772. Johnston, James, Esq. of Salisbury, CT m 8/30/18 Olive Jackson, formerly of Salisbury, CT, in Amenia, NY; Peter Fish, Esq. (8-9/9)
4773. Johnston, John m 1/25/17 Ada Ferris in Poughkeepsie; Rev. John Reed (8-1/29)
4774. Johnston, Magdalena, one of the daus of David, Esq. of Dutchess Co., d 3/15/03 (8-3/29)
4775. Johnston, Magdalene, 78, wf of David, Esq., d 8/20/06 at "Lithgo" (in town of Washington) (Dut. Co.) (8-9/2)
4776. Johnston, Peter of Beekman m 6/8/25 Polly Velie, dau of M. P. Velie of Pleasant Valley (8-6/15)
4777. Johnston, Robert, 49, of Poughkeepsie d 6/3/04 (8-6/5)
4778. Johnston, Robert of Clinton m 12/29/17 Phebe Doughty of Washington (Dut. Co.) (8-1/7/18)
4779. Jones, _____, a maniac for a considerable time past, d 9/14/23 in jail (had killed an aged woman and 2 small ch "at Mr. Dearin's in April last") (was not tried for that offense because the court believed it to have been committed under the influence of insanity) (8-9/17)
        Jones, Aaron P. See, possibly, Johnes, Aaron P.
4780. Jones, Abraham Pells, 6 mo, s of Nehemiah and Maria, d 12/18/34 in Poughkeepsie (8-12/24)
4781. Jones, Alfred m 9/8/32 Mary Burton; Thomas Hammond, Esq. (double ceremony - see marr of Oliver L. Orton) (8-9/19)
4782. Jones, Catharine Schuyler, wf of Hon. Samuel and dau of Philip I. Schuyler, Esq. late of Rhinebeck, d 11/20/29 in NYC (1-11/23 and 8-11/25)
4783. Jones, Cave (Rev.), 59, a chaplain in the U.S. Navy d 1/29/29 at the navy yard in Brooklyn (8-2/11)
4784. Jones, Danuel (Maj.), merchant, of Hartford, CT d 2/1/02 in H (9-2/17)
4785. Jones, Daniel, Esq., attorney, d 11/15/07 in Troy (consumption) (9-11/17)
4786. Jones, Ebenezer, Jr. of the firm of Jones, Shelding, and Jones of Troy m 11/16/07 Julia S. Backus of Albany in Albany; Rev. Dr. Romeyn (9-11/17)
4787. Jones, Ebenezer, Esq., 60, d 6/27/12 in Troy (9-6/30)
4788. Jones, Elijah B. (Dr.) d 6/2/32 in Plattsburgh (born in Jay; completed his studies with Dr. Mooers (sick with consumption he traveled to Florida in Nov., 1831) (member of Episcopal Church) (7-6/9)
4789. Jones, Hannah, consort of Richard l., merchant, formerly of Hartford, CT, d 5/18/00 in Granville (was on a tour to Troy, NY for her health from Leicester, VT "where they have for some time resided") (9-5/27)
4790. Jones, Horace, 48, d 3/30/28 in Troy (9-4/1)
4791. Jones, Jeremiah m 3/6/27 Sarah L. Malcomb, both of Albany; Rev. S. Martindale (9-3/9)
4792. Jones, John, merchant, of the firm of Jones and Cook m 1/27/17 Mary Hatch, dau of Dr. Erastus, in Richfield; Rev. Daniel Nash (3-1/30)
4793. Jones, John, Esq. m 2/9/23 Eunice Hatch, both of Richfield, in R; Rev. Hovey (3-2/17)

4794. Jones, John Coffin, Esq., 82, d 10/27/29 in Boston, MA (for many years a merchant there) (1-10/31)
4795. Jones, Joshua L., merchant. of Auburn m 11/14/28 Alvira V. Akin(?), dau of Albro Akin(?), esq., in Pawling; Rev. Benedict (8-11/26)
4796. Jones, La Fayette, 6, s of Pomeroy Jones, Esq., sergeant-at-arms of the state assembly, d 4/27/31 in Westmoreland (1-5/13)
4797. Jones, Margaret, 82, relict of late Thomas and mother of Mrs. De Witt Clinton, d 1/16/30 in NYC (1-1/21)
4798. Jones, Moses J. of Westford m 12/26/22 Brooksania Waters in Milford (3-12/30)
4799. Jones, Nehemiah m 2/26/29 Maria Boerum, dau of Jacob, all of Poughkeepsie; Rev. Dr. Cuyler (8-3/4)
4800. Jones, Nicholas m 6/22/15 Margaret Van Rensselaer, dau of Killian, Esq., in Hudson; Rev. Chester (6-6/27)
4801. Jones, Rebecca, 42, wf of Seth, d 5/17/07 in Hudson (6-5/26)
4802. Jones, Reuben (Dr.), 87, father of Dr. Reuben, Jr., d 1/7/33 in Keeseville (4 [Keeseville Herald]-1/15)
4803. Jones, Samuel, Jr., Esq. m 1/27/16 Catherine Schuyler, dau of Philip I., Esq., in Amenia; Rev. McMurray (8-2/21)
4804. Jones, Samuel, Esq., 85, d 11/25/19 in Queens County, NY (for many years a state senator and later its comptroller and "a distinguished jurist") (8-12/15)
4805. Jones, Samuel of Amenia, NY m 5/22/24 Margaret Forse of Livingston, NJ in L; Rev. Wilson (8-5/26)
4806. Jones, Seth, 45, d in Hudson (buried with Masonic honors) (6-8/9/08)
4807. Jones, Sidney of Brookville, Upper Canada m 8/12/29 Susan Isabella Ford, dau of Col. Ford, at the mansion of Col. David Ford near Ogdensburgh; Rev. Todd (1-8/24)
4808. Jones, William m 1/30/25 Polly Carpenter in Corinth; Rev. Dolphus Skinner (2-2/8)
4809. Jones, William m 1/10/32 Julia Ann Goucher in Jay; Rev. Pier (4 [Keeseville Herald]-2/7)
4810. Jones, William F. of Albany m 5/29/31 Hannah A. Peterson of Ghent in G; Rev. Wynkoop (1-6/2)
4811. Jordan, Ambrose L., Esq., attorney, of Cooperstown m 12/17/12 Cornelia Caroline Philips of Claverack; Rev. Gebherd (6-1/5/13)
4812. Jordan, Cornelius m 3/2/28 Catharine Nase, dau of John, all of Amenia; Rev. C. P. Wilson (8-3/12)
4813. Jordan, Nancy (Miss), 20, dau of Maj. William, d 11/7/08 in Hillsdale (6-11/29)
4814. Joslin, Benjamin (Dr.) of Union College m 12/30/26 Phebe Titus of Troy; Rev. Howard (9-1/5/27)
4815. Joslin, Thomas (Capt.), 25, s of Benjamin, d 2/23/27 in White Creek (9-3/6)
4816. Journey, _____, 80, m Mrs. Cole, 60, on Staten Island (6-7/13/02)
4817. Joy, William, 4, s of Levi, d 5/18/07 in Hudson (6-6/16)
4818. Joyce, Thomas m 4/14/23 Anna Boothe (8-4/30)
4819. Judah, Benjamin S., Esq. d (12/23?) in NYC (1-12/30/31)
4820. Judd, Bethel (Rev.), rector of Christ Church in Hudson, m Margaret Heron, dau of William, Esq. of Reading, CT, in R (6-5/17/03)
4821. Judd, Jonathan (Rev.) of Johnstown m 1/2/07 Abby Sergeant, dau of Rev. John of New Stockbridge (Oneida Co.), in N. S.; Rev. Amos G. Baldwin) (6-1/27)
4822. Juler, John of Hudson, NY m Dolly Freeman of Chatham, CT in C (6-9/26/09)
4823. June, Asa drowned prior to 8/4/19 in or near Catskill (returned to his flooded house to rescue his young daughter and was carried away by the current - this dau had been earlier safely removed unknown by her father) (this death announcement was copied from the Catskill Recorder dated 8/4) (7-8/21)
4824. Justice, Richard of Stanford (Dut. Co.) m 9/6/22 Deidema Williams of Clinton (Dut. Co.); John Wobley, Esq. (8-10/2)
4825. Justice, William H., 17, of Newbern, NC, a student at Geneva College, d 8/30/31 in Geneva (1-9/10)
4826. Kane, Archibald, merchant, late of the firm of James and Archibald Kane of Albany, NY, d in Port-au-Prince, St. Domingo (6-11/25/17)

139

4827. Kane, Elisha, merchant, of Albany m 12/12/93 Alida Van Rensselaer, dau of Maj. Gen. Van Rensselaer of Claverack (8-12/25)
4828. Kane, Hazielm 10/1/29 Mary Humphrey, dau of John, Esq.; Rev. Dr. Ludlow. All of Albany (1-10/3)
4829. Kane, John, Esq., 57, d 4/20/19 in NYC (8-4/28 and 7-5/8)
4830. Kay, Mungo, 43, editor of the Montreal Herald, d 9/6/18 in Montreal, Can. (8-9/23)
4831. Keane, Denis m 9/22/33 Mary Cummerford in Burlington, VT; Rev. J. O-Callaghan (7-10/5)
4832. Kearney, Robert, merchant, of NYC m 4/24/10 Ann L. Reade, dau of John, Esq. of Poughkeepsie, in NYC; Rev. Dr. Hobart (8-5/9)
4833. Keating, Ann, 60, wf of late John, merchant, of NYC, d 10/20/99 in Lansingburgh (9-10/29)
4834. Keaton, John, Jr., Esq. m Elzabeth S. Hopkinson, dau of Joseph, Esq., in Bordentown, NJ; Right Rev. Bishop White (3-6/7/24)
4835. Keeler, Ebenezer of Bangor m 10/1/12 Sally Coon of Plattsburgh; Rev. S. Rowley (7-10/9)
4836. Keeler, George, 9, s of Martin, d 6/3/29 in Kortright (1-6/10)
4837. Keeling, John, merchant, of Troy m 10/6/13 Abby Cornell of Rockaway, L.I., NY in Rockaway (9-10/12)
4838. Keeling, John, 45, merchant, of Amsterdam, NY d 6/12/31 in Troy (1-6/16)
4839. Keese, Oliver m 7/13/23 Mary Fisk, dau of Hon. Josiah, in Peru, NY; Rev. Halsey (7-7/19)
4840. Keese, William m 1/2/12 Lydia Hoag, both of Peru, NY in P (7-1/3)
4841. Keese, William Linn (Rev.) m 6/17/29 Mary M. Drake, dau of James, Esq., at St. John's Chapel, NYC; Right Rev. Bishop Hobart (1-6/20)
4842. Keith, Ansel, late of Troy, d 8/21/22 in NYC (yellow fever) (9-8/27)
4843. Kellogg, ____, 15 mo, dau of Timothy, d 10/25/12 in Hudson (6-10/26)
4844. Kellogg, Amelia, 38, wf of Aaron, Jr., d in Malta (Sara. Co.) (6-12/27/14)
4845. Kellogg, Andrew, 31, s of Stephen of Norwalk, CT, d 12/14/15 in Troy, NY ("the 3rd son [of 'Mr. Kellogg'] that has died in this village in 14 months." - the first, George, at age 11; the second, Nathan, at age 25)
4846. Kellogg, Ann Eliza, 32, consort of Day Otis Kellogg, Esq. of Troy, d 8/3/29 at the home of Hon. Charles Kellogg in Kelloggsville (Cay. Co.) (1-8/10)
4847. Kellogg, Cornelia, 26, wf of Augustus, Esq. of Utica d 11/6/31 at the home of her father in Utica (1-11/12)
4848. Kellogg, Day Otis, Esq., merchant, of Troy m 11/24/31 Mary A. Dimon of Fairfield, CT in F; Rev. Smith (1-12/1)
4849. Kellogg, Dolley, wf of Joseph and dau of Deacon Samuel A. Curtis of New Canaan (Col. Co.), d 11/27/19 in Franklin (Dela. Co.) (had moved to Franklin "in July last") (6-12/14)
4850. Kellogg, Dorastus of Baldwinsville (Onon. Co.) m 3/2/31 Sylvia Coon of Marcellus at the Baptist Church in Brockport (1-3/10)
4851. Kellogg, Ezekiel, 74, d 7/7/23 in Cooperstown (3-7/14)
4852. Kellogg, Nathan of the firm of J. A. and N. Kellogg, d 10/30/15 in Troy (9-10/31)
4853. Kellogg, Richard of Sharon m Betsey Swift of Amenia in A; Rev. Barnet (8-10/2/11)
4854. Kellogg, Robbins, Esq. of West Stockbridge, MA m 9/24/19 Evelina Dimon, oldest dau of Ebenezer, Esq. of Fairfield, CT, in F; Rev. Herst (6-10/12)
4855. Kellogg, Sally, 25, wf of Timothy (and dau of Dr. John Hulbert of Alford, MA) d 6/16/09 (6-6/20)
4856. Kellogg, Samuel, Esq., 63, (brother of Mrs. C. Campbell of Auburn, NY and of Daniel, Esq. of Skaneateles, NY) d 4/26/29 in Williamstown, MA (1-5/9)
4857. Kellogg, Stephen, Jr. of the firm of Bigelow and Kellogg (and formerly a merchant in Troy) m 1/1/23 Susan E. Bigelow, only dau of Asa, Esq. of Bristol (Ulster Co.) (9-1/7)
4858. Kellogg, Timothy, merchant, of Hudson m 8/25/08 Sally Hulbert, dau of John of Alford, MA, in Spencertown, NY (6-8/30)
4859. Kellogg, Timothy, merchant, of Hudson m 7/4/10 Betsey Millin of Athens, NY in A; Rev. Prentiss (6-7/13)
4860. Kellogg, Warren m 4/14/11 Abby Paine, both of Troy; Rev. Coe (9-4/16)
4861. Kells, Elizabeth (Mrs.), 71, d 2/17/16 in Claverack (6-2/27)

4862. Kells, John, 35, d 4/13/05 in Granger (6-4/16)
4863. Kells, John, 18,("lately of Livingston and brother of Betsey who was
       recently married to William Allen) m Mrs. Catharine Weaver, 40.
       (6-7/27/10)
4864. Kelly, Eliza (Mrs.) d 8/6/15 in Troy (9-8/15)
4865. Kelly, John d 1/4/99 in Albany (9-1/8)
4866. Kelly, Patrick, 32, d 10/1/06 (9-10/7)
4867. Kelsey, ____, wf of Jonas, d 2/17/11 in Poughkeepsie (8-2/27)
4868. Kelsey, Loretta, 25, wf of Richard, of Poughkeepsie d 1/9/02 (8-1/12)
4869. Kelsey, William, Esq., alderman of the 1st ward and formerly of NH,
       d 12/16/31 in Troy (1-12/22)
4870. Kelso, David m 9/3/23 Mary Prevost in Westford; Rev. Tiffany (3-9/8)
4871. Kelso, John, Jr. m 5/17/20 Almira Babcock in Westford; Rev. George Colton.
       All of Westford (3-5/22)
4872. Kelso, Marshal, 36, "for the last 5 years employed by Smith and Willard",
       d 2/4/30 (funeral at Welch's Coffee House, South Market St., Albany
       (1-2/5)
4873. Kelsy, Jonas d 12/29/17 in Poughkeepsie (8-12/31)
4874. Kemble, Mary Ann, wf of John C., Esq. (editor of the Troy Budget) and
       dau of Edward Whipple, Esq. of Hamilton, MA, d 8/2/31 in Troy (consumption)
       (1-8/5 and 4 [Keeseville Herald]-8/16)
4875. Kendall, Seth H. m 1/27/30 Anna Wemple, only dau of Andrew, Esq., in
       Minaville; Rev. Stevenson (1-1/30)
4876. Kendrick, Richard m 10/14/26 Phebe Bennet, both of Poughkeepsie; Rev. A.
       Pierce (8-10/18)
4877. Kenedy, Alexander of Argyle m Sally Ann Tise of Greenwich in G; Rev.
       Mars (9-11/6/21)
4878. Kennan, ____, 10 weeks, child of Isaac, d 2/3/23 in Plattsburgh (7-2/8)
4879. Kennedy, James (Dr.) of Montgomery Co. m Julia A. Lucas, dau of Isaac of
       NYC; Rev. Eli Baldwin (1-11/13/29)
4880. Kennedy, John, merchant, of Lansingburgh m Marcy Newell of Sturbridge,
       MA in S (probably a double ceremony - see marr of William L. Marcy)
       (9-10/13/12)
4881. Kenney, Charles C., 9, s of John, d 12/27/06 in Hudson (6-12/30)
4882. Kenney, John, 40, of Hudson d in Norwich, CT (6-7/11/09)
4883. Kent, Bloomer, merchant, m 11/28/31 Mary T. Gates, oldest dau of Joseph,
       in Franklin (Dela. Co.); Rev. Waterbury. All of Franklin (1-12/3)
4884. Kent, Henry m 10/7/24 Lodoiska Howe; Rev. Frederick Halsey. All of
       Plattsburgh (7-10/9)
4885. Kent, Horace L. of the firm of Baldwin, Ives & Co. of Richmond, VA
       m 8/10/30 Elizabeth Frances Baldwin, dau of Heman of NYC, in NYC;
       Rev. Dr. Spring (1-8/13)
4886. Kent, Isaac B. m 7/2/34 Cornelia Nichols in Plattsburgh; Rev. Halsey
       (7-7/5)
4887. Kent, John, Sr.,of the Theatre Royal, Drury Lane, and for many years a
       highly respected member of the N. Y. theatres, d 12/26/31 at Washington
       Hall, Albany (had had a severe illness for six weeks) (1-12/31)
4888. Kent, John W. m 10/1/25 Mercy Smith, both of Plattsburgh, in P; Rev.
       Duire of Essex (7-2/11)
4889. Kenyon, John of Albany m 8/9/29 Elizabeth C. Leonard of NYC in Saratoga
       (1-8/13)
4890. Kenyon, Martha, 51, wf of Wanton Kenyon, d 9/8/30 in Broadalbin
       (consumption) (1-9/13)
4891. Keown, James, 7, only s of Mrs. Frances B. Keown, d 11/5/29 in Albany
       (funeral from his mother's home, 66 Hudson St.) (1-1/7/30)
4892. Ker, Oliver L., Esq., clerk of the state assembly, d 10/21/96 in Albany
       (deceased was the only son of Rev. Nathan Ker, minister of the Presby-
       terian Church in Goshen. This clergyman's 2 daus died recently also)
       (3-11/10)
4893. Kerley, James (Col.) m 12/23/23 Sarah Ann Graves in Red Hook; Rev. Kittle
       (8-1/7/24)
4894. Kermit, Henry m 11/8/20 Hannah Crocheron, dau of Jacob formerly of NYC,
       at Fresh Kills, Staten Island, NY; Rev. Moore (8-11/15)
4895. Kern, Charles, 75, (a Rev. soldier "throughout the war") d 12/20/28 in
       Lenox (Mad. Co.) (1-1/3/29)

4896. Kerr, John of the firm of William and John Kerr m 11/30/31 Jane Ann Thomas, oldest dau of Capt. Thomas J. Thomas, in Albany; Rev. Lochead (1-12/2)
4897. Ketch, John m 1/9/25 Eliza Canfield, both of Poughkeepsie; Rev. Dr. Reed (8-1/12)
4898. Ketcham, Gilbert m 12/22/04 Aminta Baldwin, both of Poughkeepsie; Rev. Clarke (8-12/25)
4899. Ketcham, Isaac, formerly of Dutchess County, d 2/7/24 in Ithaca (8-3/3)
4900. Ketcham, Isaac H. m 12/4/28 Mrs. Gertrude Timerman, dau of Adam, in Manheim; Rev. I. S. Ketcham (9-12/19)
4901. Ketcham, Isaac S., formerly of Poughkeepsie, m 5/28/20 Sarah R. Sutphen, dau of John D., Esq. of New Brunswick, NJ; Rev. John Van Devoort (8-6/7)
4902. Ketcham, Israel of Poughkeepsie m 2/8/12 Alice Case, dau of late Rev. Wheeler Case of Pleasant Valley; Rev. Clark (8-2/12)
4903. Ketcham, John M., merchant, of Dover m 5/20/29 Eliza Ann Stevens, dau of Eben of Dover; Rev. Welton (8-5/28)
4904. Ketcham, Sarah, wf of David M. of Poughkeepsie, d 11/21/23 (8-11/26)
4905. Ketcham, Stephen m 5/27/28 Louisa Page, both of Pittstown; Rev. Webb of Lansingburgh (9-5/30)
4906. Ketchum, ____, a child of Maj. Ketchum, d 9/20/17 in Plattsburgh (7-9/27)
4907. Ketchum, Abijah, 70, (a Rev. soldier and an early settler in Peru, NY) d 5/6/25 in Peru (7-5/14)
4908. Ketchum, Hezekiah, merchant, of Troy, d 9/24/14 in Waterford (9-9/27)
4909. Ketchum, Joseph, merchant, of Waterford m 9/22/04 Maria Ten Broeck, dau of Maj. John C. of Hudson, in Troy; Rev. Coe (6-10/2)
4910. Ketchum, Nathaniel, 35, d 10/7/12 in Stillwater (9-10/20)
4911. Ketchum, Sidney m 1/28/21 Catharine Battey, dau of Robert of Peru, NY, in Peru; Rev. Halsey (7-2/3)
4912. Ketchum, Stephen (Capt.), 91, d 9/15/21 in Plattsburgh (7-9/29)
4913. Keyes, Chester, 24, merchant, s of Capt. Amasa of Hartford (state not given) d 8/30/02 "on his homeward passage from Trinidad." (6-10/12)
4914. Keyes, John, 88, d 4/13/24 at his home in Canajoharie (3-4/19)
4915. Keyes, William W. of Highgate, VT m 1/7/32 Eveline Drury of Beekmantown (Clinton Co.); Rev. Frederick Halsey (7-1/14)
4916. Keyser, Abraham A., editor of the Schoharie Republican, m 10/1/31 Elizabeth AnnTownsend, dau of late Job. E. of Newport, RI, at St. Paul's Church in Schoharie (1-10/8)
4917. Kidd, Charles m 1/27/25 Sophia Cook in Ballston Spa; Rev. Langworthy (2-2/1)
4918. Kidney, Gilbert K. m 7/26/24 Armenia Smith, both of Poughkeepsie; Rev. Clark (8-7/28)
4919. Kidney, Henry m 9/30/26 Silva Elwood, both of Poughkeepsie, in P; Rev. Cushman (8-10/11)
4920. Kidney, James m 3/28/18 Martha Gildersleeve (in Poughkeepsie?) (8-4/8)
4921. Kidney, John, 68, of Poughkeepsie d "recently" (8-12/6/03)
4922. Kidney, William H. m 10/14/26 Caroline Houghtaling; Rev. A. Pierce. All of Poughkeepsie (8-10/18)
4923. Kilborn, Theral d 2/16/06 in Troy (surv by wf and "several children") (9-2/18)
4924. Killey, Egbert B., junior editor of the Telegraph and Observer, m 8/27/29 Julia Ann Turner, dau of William; Rev. Dr. Reed. All of Poughkeepsie (8-9/2)
4925. Killey, Margaret, consort of Samuel, d 1/19/17 in Poughkeepsie (8-1/22)
4926. Killey, Samuel W. of Poughkeepsie m 11/12/17 "Mrs. Munger" of Fishkill in F (8-11/19)
4927. Killmore, Christopher m 12/22/10 Mrs. Elizabeth Bartlett; Rev. Chester. All of Hudson (6-12/28)
4928. Kilmore, Elizabeth, 35, d in Hudson (6-9/5/09)
4929. Kimbal, Sally, 39, wf of Nathaniel and dau of late Capt. James Bourke, d 4/21/19 in Hudson (6-4/27)
4930. Kimberly, Eliza, 49, wid of late Hazard Kimberly, d 6/30/27 in Troy (9-7/6)
4931. Kimberly, Hazzard, 51, d 6/2/27 in Troy (9-6/5)
4932. Kimberly, John R. of Troy m 11/3/28 Aurelia Aldrich of Rochester in R; Rev. James (9-11/11)

142

4933. King, ____, 8, s of John d in Hudson (6-5/21/05)
4934. King, Charles, Esq., editor of the American, m 10/10/26 Henrietta Low, dau of Nathaniel, Esq., in NYC; Rev. Dr. Wainwright (3-10/23)
4935. King, Charles A., 28(?), d 1/31/31 in NYC (1-2/4)
4936. King, Cornelius S. m 8/30/15 Sophia Phinney, both of Cooperstown, in C; Rev. Daniel Nash (3-9/7)
4937. King, Edward Esq., s of Hon. Rufus, m 5/15/16 Sarah Worthington, dau of Gov. Worthington of Ohio, in Chillicothe, OH (8-5/29)
4938. King, Frederick Gore (Dr.), 27, youngest s of late Rufus, d 4/23/29 in NYC (1-4/27)
4939. King, Joseph, 19, s of Isaac, d 11/10/13 in Hillsdale (6-11/16)
4940. King, Lydia (Miss), 22, dau of Fenner King of Cambridge (consumption) (funeral sermon by Rev. Friend Draper) (6-6/22 and 9-6/22)
4941. King, Mary, 49, wf of Hon. Rufus, d 6/9/19 in Jamaica, L.I., NY (3-6/14)
4942. King, Nathaniel (Col.) m 12/15/03 Otillia Meyen in Hamilton (Chen. Co.); Rev. Hosmer (6-2/7/04)
4943. King, Rebecca, 49, wf of John, Esq., d 9/30/29 in New Lebanon (deceased was dau of Peter W. Yates, Esq., formerly of Albany) (1-10/6)
4944. King, Roswell C., 26, formerly of Albany, NY, d 3/25/31 in New Orleans, LA (1-5/12)
4945. King, Rufus (Hon.), 72, d 4/30/27 at his home in NYC (8-5/2/27)
4946. King, Theodore F. (Dr.) of NYC m 5/20/29 Sarah Arnold, youngest dau of Col. Robert of Perth Amboy, NJ, in P. A.; Rev. J. Chapman (1-5/25)
4947. King, Vincent d 11/6/31 at his home on John St. near Ferry St. in Albany (1-11/17)
4948. Kingman, George G. m 12/1/31 Elizabeth Holly, dau of Myron, Esq., in Lyons; Rev. Hubbell (1-12/14)
4949. Kingsbury, Oliver m Charlotte Penfield, dau of D. Penfield, Esq., in Penfield, NY (6-12/23/11)
4950. Kingsland, Henry H. of Bellville, NJ m 6/6/24 Elizabeth V. D. L. Brinckerhoff, dau of John V. D. L. of Fishkill; Rev. Price (8-6/9)
4951. Kingsley, ____, 4 mo, child of Otigen A. Kingsley, d 9/16/19 (7-9/18)
Kingston, Samuel, Jr. See, possibly, Hingston, Samuel, Jr.
4952. Kinne, Stephen of Chenango Co. m 3/9/26 Amy Reed of Northeast; Rev. J. Buttolph (8-3/15)
4953. Kinney, Lemuel m 8/21/31 Mrs. Mary Gould in Washington (Dut. Co.); William G. Northrop, Esq. All of Washington (8-9/7)
4954. Kinney, Roswell, about 45, of Amenia d 8/28/21 when he fell from his oxen cart "and the wheel passed directly over his head: (8-9/5)
4955. Kinshimmer, Benjamin m 6/16/16 AnnPalmer, both of Poughkeepsie (8-6/19)
4956. Kinsley, Alonzo W. of Albany, NY d 11/15/29 in Savannah, GA (1-11/28)
4957. Kinsley, Cephas m 11/6/25 Lucinda New ____ (surname blurred), both of Chazy, in C; Rev. Stephen Kinsley (7-11/12)
4958. Kinsley, Hudson (Dr.) of NYC m 6/23/31 Frances Maria Elliot, dau of late "Dr. Elliot" of Goshen, in G; Rev. Dr. Fisk (1-6/27)
4959. Kinsley, Joseph W. of Beekmantown m 2/12/22 Amanda Phelps of Stanbridge, Lower Canada; Rev. Joel Byington (7-2/16)
4960. Kinsley, Stephen (Rev.), 73, (a Rev. War soldier) "recently Pastor of the Presbyterian Church in Beekmantown" (Clinton Co.), d 3/6/27 in Mooers ("at the time of death he was supplying the churches in Mooers") (7-3/10)
4961. Kinsley, Subina, 21, dau of Rev. Stephen, d 7/7/13 in Chazy (7-7/9)
4962. Kip, Henry, farmer, d 9/5/91 in Poughkeepsie (8-9/8)
4963. Kip, Jacob H. of Rhinebeck m 12/6/13 Anna Underhill of Washington (Dut. Co.) (8-12/8)
4964. Kip, James S., Esq., late sheriff of Oneida Co., d in Utica (6-5/23/15)
4965. Kip, James S., Esq., 64, d 8/27/31 at the home of his son-in-law, Theodore S. Gold, in Utica (deceased was an early settler there) (1-9/2)
4966. Kip, John B. m 4/24/26 Jane Eliza King, both of Rhinebeck, in R; Rev. David Packer (8-4/26)
4967. Kipp, Abraham d 11/9/16 in Poughkeepsie (8-11/13)
4968. Kipp, James m 8/15/30 Maria Phillips; Rev. Welton (8-8/18)
4969. Kipp, Ruluff of Schaghticoke m Sorchy (sic) Deyoe of Pittstown in P (9-8/26/06)

143

4970. Kirbey, _____ (Mrs.), 99, mother of Mrs. Samuel Davis, d 9/24/24 in Ballston (2-9/28)
4971. Kirby, Isaac F. m 11/23/30 Phebe Amelia Craig, dau of Hon. Hector; Rev. Arbuckle (1-11/26)
4972. Kirby, Jane Larned, 2, dau of Maj. R. M. Kirby of the U.S. Army, d at Fortress Monroe, Old Point Comfort, VA (1-8/11/29)
4973. Kirby, John (Lt.) of the U.S. Army m 12/31/15 Charlotte Buel of Troy in Troy; Rev. David Butler (9-1/2/16)
4974. Kirby, Seth, about 75, d 1/2/25 in Charlton (2-1/11)
4975. Kirby, William of Pawling m 3/21/34 Clarissa Baldwin of Poughkeepsie in P; Rev. Dr. Reed (8-4/2)
4976. Kirkland, Cornelia, wf of Charles P., Esq. and oldest dau of late John H. Lothrop of Utica, NY, d 7/20/31 at the home of Abraham Voorhes near New Brunswick, NJ (1-7/29)
4977. Kirkpatrick, William, Esq., superintendent of the salt springs, m 12/7/29 Nancy Dunscomb of Salina in S (1-12/25)
4978. Kissam, Benjamin (Dr.), about 44, d 7/13/03 in NYC (8-7/19)
4979. Kissam, Richard S. (Dr.) m 6/8/30 Julia Cooke, youngest dau of Oliver D., Esq., in Hartford, CT; Rev. Hawes (1-6/17)
4980. Kitridge, William C., Esq. of Fair Haven, VT m 10/3/27 Sarah M. Hatch, dau of Jonathan of Troy; Rev. Butler (9-10/9)
4981. Kittle, Andrew N. (Rev.) of Red Hook m 2/28/14 Eliza Gosman, dau of R. Gosman, Esq. of Kingston in K; Rev. Gosman (8-3/16 and 6-3/22)
4982. Kittle. Ann, 52, wf of Sybrant, d 5/19/30 in Albany (funeral from her late home, 43 Fox St.) (1-5/20)
4983. Kittle, Catharine, 2, dau of Daniel S., d 9/25/29 in Albany (1-9/30)
4984. Kittle, John, Jr. m Christiana Van Hoesen, dau of Abraham of Kinderhook, in K; Rev. Sickles (6-4/14/07)
4985. Kittle, Nicholas, 75, formerly of Kinderhook, d in Owego (1-4/18/31)
4986. Kive, Jacob of New Lebanon m 6/3/27 "widow Hannah Jenks of Westport";Rev. Howard (9-6/8)
4987. Klapp, Eugenia Stanhope (Mrs.), 42, wf of John, Esq., d 12/25/29 in Freedom (surv by husband "and several children") (8-12/30/29 and 8-1/27/30)
4988. Klapp, Harvey (Dr.), 42, d 1/28/32 in Philadelphia (state not given) (lived in Dutchess Co., NY for several years but moved to Philadelphia "more than twenty years since") (8-2/1)
4989. Kline, Philo m Harriet Swift in Amenia; Rev. Bronson (8-4/4/27)
4990. Klock, Isaac, 22, s of Capt. Peter, d 11/8/30 in Little Falls (1-11/16)
4991. Knap, Moses Hawley of NYC m 8/10/25 Caroline Reed of Amenia in A; Rev. C. P. Wilson (8-8/17)
4992. Knapp, Abel m 8/13/26 Maria Southwick in Mooers (7-9/2)
4993. Knapp, Abiah of Middlefield m 11/5/17 Hannah Cook of Westford in W; Rev. Colton (3-11/20)
4994. Knapp, Chauncey of Fishkill m 4/3/34 Mary A. Thorn, dau of Joseph of Poughkeepsie; A. Raymond, Esq. (8-4/9)
4995. Knapp. David Alexander Hamilton, 6, oldest s of David, Esq., attorney, d 12/26/09 in Hillsdale (6-1/4/10)
4996. Knapp, Gardner m 6/3/29 Almyra May, dau of Col. E. May; Rev. L. Lyons. All of Cortland (1-6/11)
4997. Knapp, Gilbert of Fishkill m 8/17/25 Anne Maria Dearin of Poughkeepsie; Rev. Cuyler (8-8/24)
4998. Knapp, Israel m 6/10/19 Emeline Fowler in Fishkill; Rev. Crane. All of Fishkill (8-6/16)
4999. Knapp, Sandford R. (Dr.) of NYC m 12/9/29 Mary Brown, dau of Stephen, Esq. of Peekskill, in P; Rev. Brondage of Brookfield, CT (1-12/28)
5000. Knapp, Sarah, 12, youngest dau of David, Esq. of Phillipstown, d 4/13/24 (8-4/21)
5001. Knapp, Tracy m Betsey Field in New Berlin; Rev. Wheeler (3-10/3/25)
5002. Knappin, Charles of Beekmantown (Clinton Co.) m 12/12/33 Mary Gilbert of Chazy in C; Rev. Foster (7-12/14)
5003. Kneeland, Charles m 4/30/29 Joanna Hone, dau of late Philip I., Esq., in NYC; Rev. Dr. Mathews (1-5/4)
5004. Kneeland, Solomon of Fishkill m 8/21/02 Betsey Kelsey, dau of Jonas of Poughkeepsie (8-8/24)

144

5005. Knevele, John W. m 6/15/26 Elizabeth Verplanck, 2nd dau of Daniel
       Cromelia Verplanck, Esq., at Mount Gulian; Rev. Thomas, rector of
       Trinity Church, Fishkill (8-6/21)
5006. Knickerbacker, ____, wf of Herman, Esq., d 3/27/14 in Schaghticoke
       (9-3/29)
5007. Knickerbacker, ____, wf of John, d 9/18/20 in Poughkeepsie (8-9/20)
5008. Knickerbacker, Abraham, Esq. of Schaghticoke m 6/5/28 Mary Ann Hale
       of Troy; Rev. Butler (9-6/6)
5009. Knickerbacker, Christina J. E., wf of Dr. Knickerbacker and dau of
       Nicholas Ten Broeck of Hudson, d 1/11/31 in Upper Red Hook (1-1/18)
5010. Knickerbacker, John, Esq. d 8/16/02 in Schaghticoke (9-8/25)
5011. Knickerbacker, John, 76, d 11/10/27 at his home in Schaghticoke (9-11/13)
5012. Knickerbacker, Milton G. m 3/10/30 Sylvia Dutcher of Amenia in A; Thomas
       Hammond, Esq. (8-3/24)
5013. Knickerbacker, Philip H. (Dr.) of Red Hook m 9/8/30 Christina J. C.
       Ten Broeck, dau of Nicholas, Esq. of Hudson, in H; Rev. Slytor
       (1-9/15)
5014. Knickerbocker, Cornelius m 10/7/04 Susannah Nash (or Nase?), both of
       Amenia; Rev. Wood (8-10/9)
5015. Knickerbocker, John, Jr. of Waterford, m Caroline Chester of Hartford, CT,
       in H (2-6/14/25)
5016. Kniffen, James m 6/23/05 Eliza Hazen, dau of Col. Caleb of Carmel, in C;
       Rev. Dodd (8-7/23)
5017. Knight, Abraham m 8/16/23 Martha Gray, both of Poughkeepsie; Rev.
       Babcock (8-8/27)
5018. Knight, Henry Walter m 12/29/30 Eliza Kent, both of Theatre Royal, in
       Montreal, Canada; Rev. Bethune (1-1/21/31)
5019. Knight, Rebecca, 30, wf of John and youngest dau of Valentine Jenkins
       of Dutchess Co., NY, d 8/15/04 in Stockport, PA (surv by husband
       and 2 ch) (6-9/11)
5020. Knower, Benjamin m 6/21/00 Sally Van Kleeck, oldest dau of late Capt.
       Lawrence of Poughkeepsie; Rev. C. Brouwer (8-6/24)
5021. Knowlton, Gideon A. (Rev.), 51, late of Cooperstown, d 8/15/10 in New
       Hartford (a Methodist preacher) (surv by wf "and several children")
       (3-9/1)
5022. Knowlton, Henry (Capt.) m 12/4/25 Arteminea Luce, dau of Uriah, in
       Otsego; Rev. Whitehead (3-12/12)
5023. Knowlton, Triphenia, 39, wf of Capt. Harry, d 2/13/25 in Otsego (3-2/21)
5024. Knox, Abraham m 1/23/06 Sally Reynolds, dau of Jonathan of Salem, in S;
       Rev. Ely (8-2/11)
5025. Knox, Anson of Blandford, MA m 9/12/27 Julia Melissa Thompson of
       Bethlehem, CT in Ameniaville, NY; Joel Brown, Esq. (8-9/19)
5026. Knox, John L. G., merchant, m 4/5/31 Mary Warren, oldest dau of Stephen,
       Esq., at St. Paul's Church in Troy; Rev. Butler. All of Troy (1-4/9)
5027. Knox, William d 4/4/32 in Poughkeepsie (8-4/11)
5028. Koon, Joseph (Dr.) m 9/21/31 Jane Osborn, dau of late Robert, in
       Schenectady; Rev. Proal. All of Schenectady (1-9/2())
5029. Kortz, Marx, 44, wf of John, Esq., d 12/15/20 in Hudson (6-12/19)
5030. Kouse, Matthew m 4/25/29 Cornelia Stewart, both of Bethlehem; Rev.
       Kissam (1-5/4)
5031. Kouse, Nelson m 11/5/27 Mary Ann Bage, both of Troy; Rev. Howard (9-11/13)
5032. Kunze, John C. (Rev.), D.D., minister of the German Lutheran Church in
       NYC, d 7/24/07 in NYC (funeral from his late residence, 100 Chatham St.
       (9-8/4 and 3-8/6)
5033. Labans, John m 8/23/28 Eunace Borzee; Jonathan Reed, Esq. of Pittstown
       (9-8/29)
5034. Lacey, Edgar M. of the U.S. Army m 5/21/31 Caroline Ann Boardman, dau of
       Maj. E. Boardman of the U.S. Army, at Fort Niagara; Rev. Thomas Green
       (1-6/4)
5035. Lacey, Gersham, "an old inhabitant of Ballston", d 6/14/25 in Ballston
       (2-6/14)
5036. Lacey, Hannah, 37, wf of Rev. Dr. Lacey, d 3/11/31 in Albany (funeral
       from the pastor's home on Lodge St. but the service was held at St.
       Peter's Church [Episcopal]) (1-3/14)

145

5037. Lacey, William B. (Rev. Dr.) m Elizabeth Hamilton Smith of Albany at
St. Peter's Church, Albany; Rev P. Alexis Proul, rector of St. George's
Church, Schenectady (8-8/1/32)
5038. Lacout, Samuel m Deborah Spriggs in Hanover, NH (9-6/16/02)
5039. Lacy, Catharine, 19, wf of Charles and only child of Samuel and
Magdalena Robinson, d 1/16/34 in Hyde Park (8-1/22)
5040. Lacy, Charles, formerly of Sharon, CT., m 12/25/30 Catharine Robinson of
Hyde Park, NY in H. P.; Rev. William Cahoone (8-1/5/31)
5041. Lacy, John T., Jr. m 5/7/29 Helen Valleau, youngest dau of late Theodore,
Esq. of NYC, in Buffalo; Rev. Kearney (1-5/13)
5042. Ladd, Aurelia (Miss), 18, of Burlington (Ots. Co.) d 11/15/15 in Cooperstown (3-11/16)
5043. Ladd, Elemuel m 9/10/16 Hannah Adams, dau of Amasa, Esq., all of Chazy
(7-9/14)
5044. Ladd James, keeper of the Albany Coffee House, d in Albany (9-8/29/15)
5045. Ladew, Thomas, 15, s of Stephen, d 9/9/31 in Albany (funeral from
21 Store Lane) (1-9/10)
5046. Ladue, Isaac, 32, d 9/8/30 at his home in Greenbush (1-9/11)
5047. Ladue, James (Lt. Col.), 39, d 1/29/28 at the home of his brother
(not named) in Greenbush (9-2/1)
5048. La Forge, Garret M. of the firm of Raynor and La Forge m 3/23/31
Catharine Martling, dau of Garret, Esq. of Castleton, Staten Island
in C; Rev. Dr. Van Pelt (1-3/29)
5049. La Grange, James m 11/18/15 Mary Shaw, both of Albany (9-11/21)
5050. Laidler, William (Lt.), 27, of the U.S. Infantry d 6/18/01 in Westminster,
VT (buried with Masonic and military honors) (6-7/2)
5051. Laidlow, James, about 45, d 2/13/10 in Poughkeepsie (born in Scotland)
("a very ingenious mechanic") (8-2/21)
5052. Lake, Edward C. m 12/10/29 Polly Goodrich; Amos Bryan, Esq. All of
Northeast (8-12/16)
5053. Lake, Peter C. of Washington (Dut. Co.) m 6/4/30 Elizabeth Carpenter of
Pleasant Valley in P. V.; Rev. Bronson (8-6/9)
5054. Lake, Selinda, wf of Henry, Jr. and dau of Vose Palmer, Esq., d 9/6/21 in
Plainfield (Ots. Co.) (3-9/17)
5055. Lake, Thomas of Kinderhook m 10/22/31 Emma Burdick of La Grange; Benoni
Pierce, Esq. (8-10/26)
5056. Lamb, Bouton m 2/12/24 Lydia Saburns; Seth Parsons, Esq. All of Hoosick
(9-2/24)
5057. Lamb, Ephraim L. of Pittstown m Nancy Smith, dau of Jared, Esq. of Norway,
NY in N; Rev. Jason Lathrop (9-2/26/22)
5058. Lamb, John (Gen.), 66, d 5/31/00 in NYC (9-6/10)
5059. Lamb, Mary, 35, wf of Anthony, d 5/24/31 in NYC (1-5/26)
5060. Lambert, Samuel of Lansingburgh m 7/11/02 Betsey Fitch of Windham, CT;
Rev. Coe (9-7/14)
5061. Lamoree, John m 9/14/24 Catharine Ostrom, dau of Col. Henry; Rev. Clark.
All of Pleasant Valley (8-9/29)
5062. Lamport, Freeborn S. m 4/27/30 Sarah M. A. Bull, dau of Archibald, Esq.;
Rev. Butler. All of Troy (1-5/4)
5063. Lamport, John m Peggy Cisson, both of Pittstown, in P; Rev. Wells
(9-1/13/07)
5064. Lancaster, Joseph, 60, m 5/23/06 Miss Hannah Corbin, 30, both of Beekman
(8-6/3)
5065. Lancaster, Joseph, Esq., 21, of East town m 2/24/14 Miss Elizabeth Everetts,
49, in Stanford (Dut. Co.) (8-3/9)
5066. Landers, John m Else Wadell of Poughkeepsie; Rev. Brouwer (8-10/5/96)
5067. Landon, Caty (Miss), 18, dau of Capt. Daniel of Schodack, d 11/7/05 at
the home of Rev. Butler in Troy (9-11/12)
5068. Landon, Charles d 11/15/33 in Peru, NY (4 [Keeseville Herald]-11/19)
5069. Landon, Jonathan, Esq., 72, d 11/4/14 in Pine Plains (8-11/23)
5070. Landon, Mary, 30, formerly of Salisbury, CT, wf of Gardner Landon,
d 8/27/28 in Troy (9-9/2)
5071. Landon, Norman, a merchant and a trustee of Otsego Academy, d 12/15/00 in
Cooperstown (consumption) (buried with Masonic honors) (funeral sermon
by Rev. Isaac Lewis) (3-12/18)
5072. Landon, Richard Montgomery (Capt.), 55, d 4/7/34 in NYC (8-4/16)

5073. Landson, Joel m 5/30/12 Deborah Selleck, both of Poughkeepsie; Rev. Clark (8-6/3)
5074. Lane, Aaron, 70, d 11/12/23 in Troy (had lived there a long time) (9-11/18)
5075. Lane, Aaron, 67, formerly of Troy, d 1/16/27 in Waterford (9-1/19)
5075a. Lane, Derick (Col.) of Troy m 7/14/05 Mrs. Angelica Van Rensselaer, wid of late John R. and dau of Col. Henry I. Van Rensselaer of Claverack, in C; Rev. Gephard (9-7/23)
5076. Lane, Derick (Col.), 76, (a Rev. soldier) d 3/19/31 in Troy (his military service is detailed in this release) (1-3/30)
5077. Lane, Jenny, wf of John, d recently in Champlain (7-1/8/13)
5078. Lane, John m 7/26/01 Hannah Hervey in Hudson (6-7/30)
5079. Lane, Mary, wf of Col. Derick Lane, d 12/12/02 in Troy (surv by her husband "and a large family of young children") (9-12/14)
5080. Lane, Matthew, merchant, m 5/31/31 Julia Maria Russell, dau of Joseph, Esq., in Troy; Rev. Tucker (1-6/3)
5081. Lane, Spencer m 7/20/16 Hesiah(?) Moss, both of Pawling; Albro Akin, Esq. (8-8/7)
5082. Langdon, Chauncey (Hon.), 66, d in Castleton, VT (1-8/14/30)
5083. Langworthy, Stillman S., 41(?), d 7/31/23 in Ballston Spa (2-8/5)
5084. Lansing, Abraham D. d 9/29/05 in Albany (10-10/8)
5085. Lansing, B. Bleecker, Esq. m 6/8/15 Sarah Breese, oldest dau of Arthur, Esq., all of Utica, in Utica (8-6/21)
5086. Lansing, Christopher Y., Esq. of Albany m 10/27/29 Caroline Thomas, dau of Dr. John of Poughkeepsie, in Duanesburgh; Rev. Thomas (1-10/30 and 8-11/4)
5087. Lansing, D. C. (Rev.) of Utica m 11/27/31 Susan Frances Van Ranst, dau of C. W.; Rev. Dr. Milnor (1-12/1)
5088. Lansing, Frederick, Esq. m 3/17/31 Catherine M. Alexander, both of Little Falls, in L. F. (1-3/21)
5089. Lansing, Gerrit G. (Col.), 70, (a Rev. officer) d 5/29/31 at his home in Oriskany (1-6/3)
5090. Lansing, Helena (Mrs.), 68, d 10/11/29 in Albany (her sons Peter and Jacob J. are mentioned) (funeral at her late home, 80 North Pearl St.) (1-10/13)
5091. Lansing, J. D., Esq. of Utica m 6/12/31 Jane Elizabeth Vanderheyden, only dau of Derick Y., late of Troy; Rev. McCollough of Lansingburgh (1-6/16)
5092. Lansing, Jacob A., Esq., 59, formerly of Lansingburgh, d 2/26/01 in Schaghticoke (interred in the family burying ground in Lansingburgh) (9-3/3)
5093. Lansing, Jacob L. of Lansingburgh m 7/10/02 Caty Vanderheyden, dau of Jacob D. of Troy, in Schaghticoke; Rev. Paige (9-7/14)
5094. Lansing, Jane A. d "recently" in Albany (Abraham Lansing is mentioned but his relationship, if any, not defined) (funeral from the home of Gerrit Y. Lansing on North Market St. in Albany) (1-11/5/30)
5095. Lansing, Jane Ann, oldest dau of Sanders, Esq. of Albany drowned 1/10/07 in the river about 10 miles below Albany (the horse-drawn sleigh, en route to Schodack, fell through the ice) (6-1/20)
5096. Lansing, Laura, 37, wf of Rev. D. C., d 3/6/31 in Utica (1-3/15)
5097. Lansing, Robert W., Esq. of Albany m 9/12/19 Elizabeth Hardy of Springfield in S; Rev. Andrew Oliver (3-9/30)
5098. Lapham, Solon, 58, m 7/25/13 Rachell Sherwood, 22, both of Stanford (Dut. Co.); Jahul Sacket, Esq. (8-7/28)
5099. Lapham, Solon of Stanford (Dut. Co.) d 2/16/32 (8-2/22)
5100. Larkin, Alonzo of Beekmantown (Clinton Co.) m 8/25/25 Margaret Reynolds of Plattsburgh (7-8/27)
5101. Larkin, Elisha, formerly of Richmond, RI, m 2/4/27 Hannah Adams of Stephentown, NY in S; C. Carr, Esq. (9-2/16)
5102. Larkin, Loyal of Plattsburgh m 12/26/21 Caroline Phelps of Barry (sic), VT in Beekmantown (Clinton Co,), NY (7-1/19/22)
5103. Larkins, Hiram m 2/24/20 Mary Marshall, both of Plattsburgh; Rev. Frederick Halsey (7-3/11)
5104. Larned, Simon (Col.), 63, d in Pittsfield (state not given) (7-12/6/17)

5105. Larretti, Elizabeth, 16, youngest dau of Joseph, Esq., deceased, died (date and place of death not stated) (9-12/19/28)
5106. Larson, John m 6/28/03 Nancy West, both of Poughkeepsie; Rev. Chase (8-6/28)
5107. Lasea, Bapiste (sic) I. d at the home of Elijah Ransom (killed in attempting to stop a runaway team drawing a cart which passed over him) (7-8/17/22)
5108. Lathrop, Ebenezer of Cherry Valley m 12/1/30 Almira K. Dodge, dau of late Noah, Esq. of Canajoharie; Rev. Wadsworth (1-12/16)
5109. Lathrop, John H., 59, cashier of the Ontario Branch Bank, d 6/10/29 in Utica (one of the earliest settlers there) (1-6/19)
5110. Lathrop, Joseph (Rev.), S.T.D., 89, d 12/31/30 in West Springfield, MA (3-1/15/31) (Notes indistinct: years could be 1820 and 1821)
5111. Lathrop, L. E. of Castleton, VT m 6/9/19 Maria Ludlow of Kinderhook, NY in Hudson; Rev. Stanton (6-6/15)
5112. La Touche, Joseph, late of Washington (Dist. of Columbia) m 5/19/25 Sarah Cook of Ballston Spa, NY in B. S.; Rev. E. P. Langworthy (2-5/24)
5113. Lattimore, James d 10/19/12 in Hudson (6-10/26)
5114. Lattin, Benjamin m 12/20/15 Hannah Thurston, dau of John M., Esq.; Rev. Leonard. All of Clinton (Dut. Co.) (8-12/27)
5115. Lattin, Hannah, 21, consort of Benjamin, Jr. and dau of John M. Thurston, Esq., d 8/10/17 in Clinton (Dut. Co.) (8-8/20)
5116. Lattin, John W. of Pleasant Valley m 9/2/29 Hannah Eliza Wilber, dau of Ellvanus of Hyde Park; Rev. Clark (8-9/9)
5117. Lattin, Joseph m 11/28/21 Mary Wright, dau of Elijah, all of Pleasant Valley; Rev.Clark (8-12/5)
5118. Lattin, William of Pleasant Valley m 12/24/28 Letty Wood, dau of Isaac of Hyde Park; Rev. Clark (8-12/31)
5119. Latting, Richard m 11/4/16 Sally Foster, dau of Paria, Esq., in Hillsdale; Rev. Ensign (6-11/19)
5120. Lauless, Jacob m 1/15/25 Sally Sleight; Tilly Crouse, Esq. All of Clinton (8-1/19)
5121. Laurence, William Beach, Esq. m Esther Rogers Gracie, dau of Archibald, Esq., at Grace Church, NYC; Rev. Wainright (3-5/28/21)
5122. Lavey, Catherine d 1/24/33 at the Poor House in Essex (consumption) (Catherine was from the town of Westport) (4 [Keeseville Herald]-1/29)
5123. Law, Prentis of the City Hotel, Montreal, Canada m 10/6/33 Irena Buck of Plattsburgh in West Plattsburgh; Rev. Sawyer of Essex (7-10/12)
5124. Lawrence, Betsey, dau of David, Esq., d 9/7/11 in Hudson (6-9/13)
5125. Lawrence, David, Esq., 66, "late Recorder and one of the first settlers of this city" [Hudson]), d 10/19/08 (6-10/25)
5126. Lawrence, Elizabeth (Miss), 27, dau of Stephen of Schoharie, d 8/22/29 (consumption) (1-8/28)
5127. Lawrence, Friend, merchant, of Albany m 6/1/31 Jane Lovett of Troy in T; Rev. Butler (1-6/4)
5128. Lawrence, Isaac of Newtown, L.I., NY m 7/28/29 Julia Anna Margaret Sturges, dau of Josiah of NYC, in NYC; Rev. Van Vleck (1-8/6)
5129. Lawrence, Joseph W., Jr. of Geneseo m 9/30/25 Susan North of Fly Creek; Rev. St. John (3-10/3)
5130. Lawrence, Nathaniel, Esq. (for 3 yrs Attorney General of NY) d 7/15/97 in Hempstead (3-8/3)
5131. Lawrence, Richard (Dr.), 37, d 7/25/04 in Newtown, L.I., NY (surv by wf and "a numerous train of relatives") (6-8/7)
5132. Lawrence, Robert m 12/11/08 Marsey Dodge, dau of Rev. Dr. Dodge, all of Clinton (Dut. Co.); Rev. Dr. Dodge (8-12/14)
5133. Lawrence, Robert of Fishkill Landing m 9/26/20 Jane Ann Schenck, dau of Abraham H., Esq. of Matteawan; Rev. C. D. Westbrook (8-10/4)
5134. Lawrence, Stephen V. m 1/18/27 Amanda Green, both of Berlin, NY; Rev. William Satterly (9-1/23)
5135. Lawrence, Thomas of Staten Island m Juliette Havens, dau of late Dr. Charles H. Havens, in Easthampton (1-5/7/30)
5136. Lawson, Helen (Miss), sister of James of NYC, d 8/25/31 "at Glasgow" (state or country not given - perhaps intended for Scotland - there is a Glasco village in Ulster Co., NY) (1-10/17)

5137. Lawson,Peter B. m 1/7/24 Maria Lawson, both of Poughkeepsie; Rev. C. C. Cuyler (8-1/14)
5138. Lawson, William, "nearly 100, d "a few days since" in Poughkeepsie (born in Dutchess County) (8-8/11/91)
5139. Lawton, _____, child of William, d in Hudson (6-6/1/10)
5140. Lawton, John, preceptor, m 9/14/06 Sally Davis, preceptress, of the Academy in Cambridge at C; Rev. E. H. Chapman (9-9/16)
5141. Lawton, Robert, 35, d 5/16/13 in Hudson (6-5/25)
5142. Lawton, Sarah (Mrs.), 50, formerly of Newport, RI, d 3/15/09 in Hudson, NY (6-3/21)
5143. Lawyer, Ruth, wf of John, Esq. and dau of Capt. Joseph Allen of Catskill, d in Schoharie (1-4/28/31)
5144. Lazell, Almon E. of Fishkill m 8/22/24 Nancy Whipple, dau of Amos of Poughkeepsie: Rev. Clark (8-8/25)
5145. Leach, DanielD.? "of the Albany Academy" m 3/17/31 Phebe T. Vanderlip, youngest dau of Elias; Rev. Green. All of Albany (1-3/19)
5146. Leach, G. Washington of NYC m 10/8/31 Martha Williams, dau of Josiah, Esq. of Poughkeepsie, in Pleasant Valley; Rev. Wile (8-10/12)
5147. Leach, Henry L. m 1/1/23 Phinetia Smith (7-1/4)
    Leak, James (Dr.). See Lear, James (Dr.).
5148. Leak, William C. m "a few days since" Martha Willey in Plattsburgh; Nathan Carver, Esq. (7-2/15/17)
5149. Leake, John, 81, father of John W., d 4/25/30 in Albany (funeral from the home of John W. on Herkimer St.) (1-4/26)
5150. Lear (or Leak?), James (Dr.), 28, d 2/22/31 in Stamford (1-3/10)
5151. Learned, George m 7/9/27 Emily Holbrook, both of Watervliet, in Gibbonsville; Rev. Howard (9-7/17)
5152. Le Breton, Edward A., 55, d 9/25/30 in Detroit, MI (born in England; member of Episcopal Ch.; one yr before his death, he arrived in Detroit where he enlarged and improved the Detroit Brewery - he had previously acquired a reputation as a brewer in Albany, NY) (1-10/7)
5153. Le Breton, John, 27, d 12/16/30 in Albany (funeral from his late home, 37 Division St.) (1-12/18)
5154. Le Conte John (Capt.) of the U.S. Engineers m Mary Ann Hampton, oldest dau of Jonathan H., Esq.,in NYC; Right Rev. Bishop Hobart (3-8/6/21)
5155. Le Count, Thomas of NYC m Sarah Wonderly of Poughkeepsie (above taken from the Philadelphia Union) (8-10/6/19)
5156. Ledyard, _____ (Dr.), health officer of the port of NY, d "at the Lazaretto" in NYC (6-9/6/03)
5157. Lee, _____, late wf of Samuel Lee, deceased, d 9/26/24 in Ballston (2-9/28)
5158. Lee, Ann H. of Georgetown, wid of Gen. Henry of the Rev. War, d 7/26/29 at Ravensworth, the home of W. F. Fitzhugh, "surrounded by her family and friends" (1-8/4/29)
5159. Lee, Caroline, 10, d 12/5/32 in Salisbury, CT (8-12/12)
5160. Lee, Edmund Per (Gen.), 69, d at his home in Amenia (8-4/24/22)
5161. Lee, Elias (Elder), 63, d 12/26/28 in Ballston Spa (a clergyman for 40yrs) (1-1/3/29)
5162. Lee, Hart of the firm of Lee and Woodward, druggists, m 3/2/30 Margaret M. B. Evertson, dau of late George B. formerly of Poughkeepsie, in Ithaca: Rev. Ralph Williston (1-3/19 and 1-3/24)
5163. Lee, James m 11/9/33 Jane Nelson, both of Peru, NY, in P; E. Williams, Esq. (4 (Keeseville Herald]-11/12 and 7-11/16)
5164. Lee, Margaret, relict of Elder Elias, d in Ballstown (7-11/16/33)
5165. Lee. Olive, wf of Rev. Chauncey and wid of late Alexander Spencer, Esq. of Dutchess Co., d 1/5/18 in Colebrook, CT (8-1/14)
5166. Lee, Orrin m 2/16/31 Polly Barkman in Rensselaerville; Judge Moore. All of Rensselaerville (1-2/23)
5167. Lee, Richard, Jr., proprietor of the Patriot and Family Medicines, d 4/3/06 in NYC (9-4/29)
5168. Lee, Robert of the U.S. Corps of Engineers m Mary A. R. Custiss (sic), only dau of G. W. P. Custiss, Esq. "at Arlington House"; Rev. Dr. Keith (1-7/11/31)
5169. Lee, Roger, 22, oldest s of Thomas of Union Vale, d 9/5/34 in Perinton (Monroe Co.) (8-9/24)

5170. Lee, Samuel m 10/14/26 Mrs. Clarissa Loire(?); Rev. C. C. Cuyler (8-10/18)
5171. Lee, Samuel, 44, late of Poughkeepsie, d 10/13/30 in Mount Pleasant, TN
       (8-11/13)
5172. Lee, William (Capt.) of Granville m 5/11/02 Sally Seymour of Stillwater
       in S (9-5/19)
5173. Leet, John, 76, d 12/28/22 in Stanford (Dut. Co.) (8-1/8/23)
5174. Leete, Harvey of Stanford (Dut. Co.) m 6/4/32 Elmira Sayre of Cairo
       (Greene Co.) in C; Rev. Buck of Cairo (8-7/4)
5175. Lefavre, Nathaniel of Lansingburgh m 6/13/03 Lucy Treadwell of Worcester,
       MA in W (9-6/21)
5176. Lefferts, John, Esq., 43, formerly a state senator, d in Flatbush
       (1-9/29/29)
5177. Leggert, James, Jr. m 3/24/05 Sophia Kittle, dau of late Capt. John of
       Kinderhook, in Claverack (6-4/2)
5178. Leggett, Abraham of the firm of A & J Leggett m 9/1/29 Sarah Lee, both of
       NYC, in NYC; Rev. F. H. Cone (1-9/7)
5179. Leisher, Jacob m Hester Stebbins; Rev R. G. Armstrong. All of Northeast
       (8-7/8/29)
5180. Lemur, Silas m 1/17/22 Miriam Tallmadge, both of Stanford (Dut. Co.);
       Isaac Sutherland, Esq. (8-1/30)
5181. Lent, Abraham m Matilda Rubottom, both of Easton, in Schaghticoke; Rev.
       Paige (9-9/8/02)
5182. Lent, Abraham m 10/21/29 Margaret Lake in Hyde Park; Rev. William Cahoon
       (8-10/28)
5183. Lent, Benjamin m 8/19/20 Margaret Warn, both of Troy; Rev. Sommers
       (9-8/29)
5184. Lent, Dennis, lately from Stillwater, d at the home of Lambert Bugert in
       Kinderhook (6-6/21/11)
5185. Lent, Phebe, 39, wf of James, d 3/11/23 in Otsego (3-3/24)
5186. Lent, William m 11/20/28 Mary Merchant, both of Lansingburgh; Rev. Howard
       (9-11/25)
5187. Leonard, _____ (Rev.) m Cynthia Babcock in Chatham; Rev. Porter (6-5/18/02)
5188. Leonard, Ephraim of Pittstown m 5/19/21 Elsa Hill of Grafton; James Moshier,
       Esq. (9-5/29)
5189. Leonard, Nathan (Pvt.), 17, (Capt. Clark's Co., 6th Infantry) d 7/17/16
       at the cantonment in Plattsburgh (his clothing caught fire while he
       was cleaning the hearth) (born in VT) (7-7/20)
5190. Leonard, Rhoda, 14, d 1/18/05 and Wesley Leonard, 13, d 1/28/05 in
       Spencertown (children of Daniel Leonard of Spencertown) (6-3/5)
5191. Leonard, Whitney A. of Troy m 4/18/32 Lucy Ann Soule of Poughkeepsie;
       Rev. Dr. Reed (8-5/2)
5192. Lerow, John (Lt.), 34, of Otsego d 10/4/24 in Orville (surv by wf and
       2 ch) (3-10/18)
5193. Le Roy, Anna Adelia, dau of Benjamin of Poughkeepsie, d 10/30/32 (8-10/31)
5194. Le Roy, Deborah (Mrs.), 76, d 11/12/00 in Poughkeepsie (8-11/18)
5195. Le Roy, James (Sgt.), 41st Regiment, U.S. Army, m 5/9/14 Asenah Tomkins
       of Claverack in Hudson (6-5/24)
5196. Leroy, John d 6/23/16 in Poughkeepsie (8-6/26)
5197. Leroy, John m 2/4/19 Gertrude Crofiser, both of Clinton (Dut. Co.);
       Rev. P. S. Wynkoop (8-2/10)
5198. Leroy, Levi m 11/2/25 Anna Maria Cropsey, both of Clinton (Dut. Co.);
       Rev. Clark (8-11/9)
5199. Le Roy, Martha, 60, relict of late Jacob, d 10/10/29 in NYC (1-10/14)
5200. Le Roy, Sarah Louisa, 22, wf of E. A., Esq., d 12/27/31 in NYC (1-12/28)
5201. Leslie, John of Hudson, NY m Sally Brooks of Chatham, CT in Chatham, CT
       (6-9/26/09)
5202. Leslie, Lavinia, 42, consort of John of Hudson, NY, d 8/13/08 in Middle
       Haddam, CT (6-8/30)
5203. Lester, _____ (Mrs.) d 3/15/18 (in Poughkeepsie?) (8-3/18)
5204. Lester, Nicholas m 3/10/19 Nancy Murray in Claverack; Rev. Gebhard
       (6-3/16)
5205. Lester, Peleg m 8/19/15 Clarissa Burges, both of Old Paltz; Rev. Lewis
       Leonard (8-8/23)
5206. Levans, Elhanan m 4/28/18 Sarah Leonard, both of Troy; Rev. Sommers
       (9-5/5)

150

5207. Leverse, Jacob m 5/5/07 Derica Vanderheyden, both of Brunswick; Rev. Coe (9-5/12)
5208. Levi, Henry m 2/8/12 Polly Roper; E. Hopkins, Esq. (8-2/12)
5209. Lewis, Abram m 2/8/24 Polly Ford, both of Ballston Spa, in B. S.; Thomas Palmer, Esq. (2-2/10)
5210. Lewis, Anne Mary, 76, consort of John and mother of Mr. A. G. Dauby, one of the editors of the Oneida Observer, d 2/8/31 in Whitestown (1-2/14)
5211. Lewis, Charles m 11/11/20 Jane F. Magennis, both of Fishkill; Rev. Westbrook (8-11/15)
5212. Lewis, Diana, consort of Sabin, Esq., d 11/28/28 in Poughkeepsie (8-12/10)
5213. Lewis, Elihu, 50, d 10/14/29 in Albany (funeral from his late home, 89 Washington St.)(1-10/15)
5214. Lewis, Erastus R. m 6/21/32 Catherine Eliza Adams; Rev. Dr. Reed. All of Poughkeepsie (8-6/27)
5215. Lewis, Isaac of Cooperstown m 11/20/23 Sarah Smith of Oaks Ville; Rev. Tiffany (3-11/24)
5216. Lewis, James, 82, d 3/5/27 in Plattsburgh (In the Rev. War "he fought side by side with the Rev. Mr. [Stephen] Kinsley") (had been a member of the Presby. Ch. in Plattsburgh) (7-3/10)
5217. Lewis, James, 47, d 3/8/31 in Poughkeepsie (8-3/9)
5218. Lewis, Leonard of Otsego m 9/11/21 Nancy Tunnicliff of Warren; Rev. Daniel Nash (double ceremony - see marr of George Tunnicliff) (3-9/17)
5219. Lewis, Leonard, 56, d 2/24/29 in Albany (1-2/25)
5220. Lewis, Leonard B., "one of our most aged citizens", d 8/22/25 in Poughkeepsie (8-8/24)
5221. Lewis, Olive, 28, dau of Maj. Elisha, d 1/2/33 at Port Kent (4 [Keeseville Herald]-1/15)
5222. Lewis, Phebe, 62, wf of Leonard, d 2/23/32 (8-2/29)
5223. Lewis, Peter (Mr.), age blurred, d 2/18/26 in Poughkeepsie (8-2/22)
5224. Lewis, Russel W. (Capt.) m 3/15/08 Mary Augusta Munn, both of Troy; Rev. Coe (9-3/22)
5225. Lewis, Sabin, Esq. m 2/17/29 Elizabeth Scott, both of Poughkeepsie; Rev. Dr. Reed (8-2/25)
5226. Lewis, Sally, dau of Jonathan, d 7/25/14 in Poughkeepsie (8-7/27)
5227. Lewis, Samuel A. m 1/2/30 Mary Ann Fuller; Rev. Dr. Sprague. All of Albany (1-1/7)
5228. Lewis, Sarah (Mrs.), 52, d 7/10/27 in Poughkeepsie (8-7/18)
5229. Lewis, Stewart, 53, d 4/16/29 in Albany (funeral from his late home, 76 State St.) (1-4/17)
5230. Lewis, Thomas, 29, d 5/30/17 in Poughkeepsie (8-6/4)
5231. L'Hommedieu, Ezra (Hon.), 77. d in Southold, Long Island, NY (6-10/7/11)
5232. Lightbourn, Eliza, consort of Joseph G., d 11/18/21 in Poughkeepsie (8-11/21)
5233. Limbrick, Thomas, 48, d 7/2/29 in Catskill (1-7/11)
5234. Lincklaen, John (Col.), the first settler in Cazenovia, d 2/9/22 at his home in Cazenovia (3-2/25)
5235. Lindley, _____ (Mr.) d in Brooklyn Heights while serving military duty there from Hudson (6-9/6/14)
5236. Lindley, Ebenezer m 10/16/13 Eliza Collins, both of Hudson, in H; Rev. Ezra Sampson (6-10/26)
5237. Lindsay, George F. (Lt.) of the U.S. Marine Corps m 12/5/23 Mary J. Smith, dau of late Col. Melancton of Plattsburgh, in P; Rev. Shelton (7-12/6 and 3-12/22)
5238. Linsay, John, 20, formerly of Milton, Ulster Co. and recently of Surinam, d 11/14/31 in Gloucester, MA (8-12/14)
5239. Lindsey, Aurelia, dau of Isaac late of Poughkeepsie, NY and consort of Charles, Esq. of Montgomery, NY, d in Litchfield, CT (8-8/10/14)
5240. Lines, _____ (Mr.), 22, recently from NYC, d 9/28/28 in Poughkeepsie (8-10/1)
5241. Lines, Horace m 6/28/34 Jane Ann Crouse in Hyde Park; William P. Williams, Esq. All of Hyde Park (8-7/16)
5242. Lines, William m 6/26/17 Hannah Marshall, dau of James; Rev. Clark. All Of Clinton (Dut. Co.) (8-7/2)
5243. Link, Peter of Sand Lake m 9/17/14 Elizabeth Hayner of Brunswick; Rev. Coe (9-9/27)

151

5244. Linn, _____ (Rev. Dr.) d 1/10/08 in Albany ("his remains were... deposited in the family vault of the Hon. Abraham Ten Broeck") (3-1/16)
5245. Linn, John Blair (Rev.) of NYC m 5/18/99 Betty Bailey, dau of Col. John of Poughkeepsie, in NYC; Rev. Dr. Linn (8-6/4)
5246. Linn, William (Rev. Dr.), 55, one of the ministers of the Reformed Dutch Church in NYC, d 1/8/19 in Albany (6-1/19; 9-1/19; and 8-1/20)
5247. Lintner, Mary, consort of Rev. George A. and dau of Joseph Waggoner, Esq. of Fort Plain, d 10/28/30 in Schoharie (1-11/16)
5248. Lion, Amos m 2/20/23 Margaret Scryver, dau of Capt. Peter A. of Hyde Park; Rev. Dr. Reed (8-2/26)
5249. Lippet, _____, 65, wf of Louden Lippet, d 2/21/26 in Hartwick (3-3/6)
5250. Lisle, Edmond m 9/15/26 Mary Hunt; Rev. C. C. Cuyler (8-10/18)
5251. Lisle, Samuel William Henry m 10/24/18 Ann Ritchie, both "of the medical department at Quebec", in Champlain, NY (7-10/31)
5252. Liswell, John, P. M. (perhaps Post Master?), d 12/27/30 in Caghnawaga (Fonda, NY) (1-1/1/31)
5253. Liswell, JohnT., merchant, of Caughnawaga (Fonda, NY) m 9/14/30 Catharine M. Yost, dau of William of Johnstown, in Kingston; Rev. A. C. Tredway (1-9/18)
5254. Little, George W. (Dr.) m 6/25/29 Delia A. Nash, oldest dau of Martin, Esq., late sheriff of Livingston Co., in Lima; Rev. Barnard (1-7/3)
5255. Little, Jonathan, merchant and long-term resident of NYC, d 12/19/26 in NYC (3-12/25)
5256. Little, Polly (Miss), 17, d 9/15/10 in Hudson (6-9/21)
5257. Livergood, John m 12/15/21 Irene Barry, both of Pittstown (9-1/1/22)
5258. Livingston, _____, 2 yrs old, 2nd s of Joel and Maria, d 5/24/16 ("after an uncommon season of anguish of four weeks and four days seldom ever witnessed resulting from a monstrously extensive scald") (7-6/1)
5259. Livingston, Alexander H., 30, son of late Alfred, d 9/16/34 in Poughkeepsie (dropsy) (8-9/24)
5260. Livingston, Anne, 31, wf of Brockholst Livingston, Esq., d 9/4/07 in Bloomingdale (9-9/22)
5261. Livingston, Anson, Esq. of NYC m 12/26/29 Anne Livingston, youngest dau of late Henry W.; Rev. Wackerhagen (1-1/130)
5262. Livingston, Brockholst, 65, d 3/18/23 in Washington (Dut. Co.) (7-4/5)
5263. Livingston, Brockholst, Esq. m Mirinda L. Peckham, dau of Peleg, Esq. of Cooperstown; Right Rev. Bishop Onderdonk (8-9/12/27)
5264. Livingston, Catharine, 73, wid of late Robert G., Esq., d 8/4/92 (her body to be removed to the family vault in NYC) (8-8/8)
5265. Livingston, Catharine, 40, wf of Brockholst, Esq., d in NYC (6-11/19/01)
5266. Livingston, Catharine, wid of late William Smith Livingston, Esq., formerly of NYC, d 9/29/23 in Rhinebeck (8-10/15)
5267. Livingston, Catharine G., 85, wid of late Gilbert, Esq., d 5/7/30 in Poughkeepsie (funeral sermon at the Presbyterian Church) (8-5/9 and 1-5/21)
5268. Livingston, Charles M. of the firm of Klapp and Livingston m 5/8/32 Martha King, dau of Aaron; Rev. Dr. Reed. All of Poughkeepsie (8-5/16)
5269. Livingston, Charles P. (Dr.) m 1/5/26 Eliza C. Brewer, both of Poughkeepsie; Rev. Dr. Reed (8-1/11)
5270. Livingston, Charlotte Emilia, 21, (wf of Francis A., Esq. and dau of Dr. Benjamin Kissam, late of NYC, deceased) d 12/19/20 in Rhinebeck (6-12/26)
5271. Livingston, Cornelia W., 11, dau of James S., Esq., d 9/22/11 at the Manor of Livingston (6-10/14)
5272. Livingston, Edward, Esq. m 6/2/05 Madame Marie Louisa Valentine Davezac Castra Moreau, wid of late Louis Moreau de Lassy, in New Orleans, LA; Rev. Dr. Walsh (9-7/16)
5273. Livingston, Edward P., Lt. Gov. of NY, m 6/13/32 Mary C. Broom, dau of William, Esq. of Hyde Park, in Albany; Rev. William B. Thomas, rector of Christ Church in Duanesburgh (8-6/20)
5274. Livingston, Elizabeth S., wf of Edward P., Esq. and oldest dau of late Chancellor Livingston, d 6/10/29 (1-6/13)
5275. Livingston, Emma, 21, consort of Francis A., d 12/19/20 in Rhinebeck (8-12/20)

5276. Livingston, Frances, 41, wf of Maj. Moncrief, d 5/9/14 in Hudson
(6-5/17)
5277. Livingston, Francis A., Esq. of Rhinebeck m 10/20/17 Emma C. Kissam of
NYC (in NYC?); Rev. Knox (8-10/29)
5278. Livingston, Francis A., Esq., 37, formerly district attorney of Dutchess
County and a member of the NY State Legislature, d 6/16/30 in Rhinebeck
(8-6/23)
5279. Livingston, Gilbert, Esq., 63, clerk of Dutchess Co., d 9/6/06 in
Poughkeepsie (6-9/23 and 9-9/23)
5280. Livingston, Hannah, 68, consort of Henry, Esq. of Poughkeepsie, d 5/21/93
(8-5/29)
5281. Livingston, Helen Catharine, 10 mo, dau of Peter R., d 2/1/14 at the Manor
of Livingston (6-2/15)
5282. Livingston, Henry, s of John, Esq. of Oak Hill m 12/28/16 Ann Eliza Van
Ness, dau of Hon. William W., in Claverack; Rev. John E. Gephard
(6-12/31/16 and 8-1/8/17)
5283. Livingston, Henry (Gen.) d 5/25/23 at his home "in the manor of Livingston"
(interred in the family vault in the village church) (deceased was born
1/19/1752) (9-6/10 and 8-6/18)
5284. Livingston, Henry, Esq., 79, (a Rev.soldier) d 2/29/28 at his home in
Poughkeepsie (formerly a judge in Dutchess Co.) (8-3/5)
5285. Livingston, Henry, Esq. d 11/21/28 in Claverack (had married the oldest
dau of late Judge William W. Van Ness "and inherited the princely estate
of the late Gen. Henry Livingston") (8-11/26)
5286. Livingston, Henry A. (Maj.) m 7/7/17 Frederica Sayers, dau of late James
of England, in Poughkeepsie; Rev. Reed (8-7/9)
5287. Livingston, Henry B. (Col.), 81, (a Rev. patriot) d 11/6/31 at his home
in Rhinebeck ("brother of the present Secretary of State") (1-11/17)
5288. Livingston, Henry G. (Maj.) of Red Hook m Ann Nutter, dau of Valentine
Nutter, bookseller, of NYC, in Rhinebeck (8-11/10/91)
5289. Livingston, Henry L., 23, s of Moncrief, Esq. of Livingston, d 11/14/19
(surv by wf and an inf ch) (6-11/16)
5290. Livingston, Henry W., Esq., 42, d 12/22/10 "in Linlithgow in the Manor
of Livingston"(b 6/12/1768; interred in the family vault in the Manor
Church; was formerly secretary to Governeur Morris, Esq., then
Ambassador to France; had been judge of the court of common pleas in
Columbia Co., NY; also had been a member of the NY state assembly
and a Congressman) (6-12/28/10 and 8-1/9/11)
5291. Livingston, Henry Welles, 35, d 10/26/13 in Hartford, CT (8-11/3)
5292. Livingston, Jacob, Esq. of Middleburgh m 6/26/21 Levantia White, dau of
Hon. Joseph of Cherry Valley, in C. V.; Rev. Tiffany (3-7/2)
5293. Livingston, James Howard, 31, of the firm of G. W. and L. H. Livingston
d 9/7/30 in NYC (1-9/9)
5294. Livingston, Johannah, 60, wf of Hon. Peter R. of the NY senate and sister
of late Chancellor Livingston, d 3/1/29 in Rhinebeck (1-3/5 and 1-4/20)
5295. Livingston, John A., Esq. m 4/30/32 Louisa R. Bradford, dau of late Rev.
Dr. Bradford, in Albany; Rev. Dr. Lacey (8-5/9)
5296. Livingston, John H. (Dr.), 78, Prof. of Didactic and Polemic Divinity at
the Theological Seminary of the Reformed Dutch Church and father of Col.
Henry A. of Poughkeepsie, d 1/20/25 in New Brunswick, NJ (8-1/26)
5297. Livingston, John M. P., 18, 2nd s of Gilbert R., Esq., d 8/8/03 at Red
Hook Landing (consumption) (6-8/23)
5298. Livingston, John W., 74, d 11/21/30 in Albany (1-11/25)
5299. Livingston, Judith (Mrs.), 73, d 8/31/08 in Poughkeepsie (8-9/7)
5300. Livingston, Margaret, 16, dau of Moncrief, d 1/28/08 (6-2/9)
5301. Livingston, Margaret, 72, relict of Hon. Peter, Esq., d 7/31/09 in Hudson
(6-8/8)
5302. Livingston, Margaret, 58, relict of Robert T., Esq., d 10/16/17 at the
Livingston Manor House (6-10/21)
5303. Livingston, Margaret, 73, relict of late Robert G. of Rhinebeck, d 12/15/24
in Poughkeepsie (8-12/22)
5304. Livingston, Margaret Maria, 34, wf of Robert L., Esq. of Clermont and
youngest dau of late Chancellor Livingston, d 3/9/18 in Clermont
(6-3/17 and 8-3/18)
5305. Livingston, Maria, about 16, dau of James, d 9/28/16 in Plattsburgh (7-9/28)

5306. Livingston, Mary Kierstead, 4, dau of James S., Esq., d 8/21/15 "at the Manor of Livingston"(6-8/29)
5307. Livingston, Morgan L. m 4/4/29 Catharine Manning, dau of late James, all of NYC; Rev. Dr. Matthews (1-4/7)
5308. Livingston, Peter R., Esq. m 10/15/05 Joanna Livingston at the home of Hon. Robert R. Livingston (in Clermont); Rev. Freeborn Garritson (8-10/22)
5309. Livingston, Robert G., Jr. of Ithaca m Cynthia Dodge of Whitesboro in W; Rev. Cornelius Brouwer (1-3/1/31)
5310. Livingston, Robert Gilbert, Esq. d 8/31/89 "at an advanced age" in Poughkeepsie (8-9/1)
5311. Livingston, Robert H., Esq., clerk of Dutchess Co., d in Poughkeepsie (3-9/20/04)
5312. Livingston, Robert James (Capt.) (a Rev. officer) d 4/12/27 in Rhinebeck (8-5/2)
5313. Livingston, Robert L., s of late Walter, m 7/10/98 Margaret Livingston, youngest dau of Hon. Chancellor Livingston, in Clermont (8-7/17)
5314. Livingston, Robert Le Roy, Esq. of Oak Hill in the town of Livingston (Col. Co.) m 6/22/11 AnnMaria Diggs, dau of late George, Esq. of Prince George's Co., MD, at Green Hill, MD; Rev. Dr. Carroll, Archbishop of Baltimore (6-7/12)
5315. Livingston, Robert R., Esq., 66, (for many yrs chancellor of NY and late American Minister to France), d 2/23/13 at his home in Clermont, NY (buried in the family vault) (6-3/2; 8-3/3; 3-3/6; and 9-3/9)
5316. Livingston, Robert Sayers, s of Col. Henry A., d 4/21/21 in Poughkeepsie (8-4/25)
5317. Livingston, Robert T. (Col.), 55, d 12/20/13 at the manor-house in the town of Livingston (6-12/28/13 and 3-1/8/14)
5318. Livingston, Sarah, 62, wf of Rev. Dr. Livingston, d 12/9/14 in New Brunswick, NJ (8-1/4/15)
5319. Livingston, Sarah Henrietta, dau of Col. Henry A. of Poughkeepsie, d 1/9/25 (8-1/12)
5320. Livingston, Sidney M. of Poughkeepsie m 10/10/29 Joanna M. Hetthuysen, dau of JohnS., merchant, of NYC, in NYC; Rev. Creighton (1-10/15 and 8-10/21)
5321. Livingston, Susan,/dau of late Robert H., Esq., formerly of Poughkeepsie, d 12/14/31 in Philadelphia (state not given) (1-12/20 and 8-12/21)
5322. Livingston, Theodore W., s of Philip H. of NYC, d in Montgomery, AL (1-11/12/31)
5323. Livingston, Thomas m 3/19/26 Margaret Lewis, both of Rhinebeck; Rev. Robert Scott (8-4/5)
5324. Livingston, Walter C., Esq. of Livingston Manor, NY m Mary Livingston Greenleaf, oldest dau of James, Esq., in Allentown, PA (3-7/26/24)
5325. Livingston, Walter H. (Dr.), 28, "post surgeon of the U.S. Army", d 4/5/22 in Troy (9-4/9 and 7-4/20)
5326. Lloyd, ____, wf of Andrew, d "recently" in Albany (funeral from the corner of Schuyler and Malcom Sts.) (1-9/20/31)
5327. Lloyd, Henry W., 28, formerly of NYG d 8/25/30 at the home of his father, Joseph, in Trenton, NY (1-9/2)
5328. Lloyd, James, Esq., 33, postmaster, d 2/28/24 in Plainfield (Ots. Co.) (3-3/8)
5329. Lloyd, Polly, 18, wf of James and dau of Daniel Coon, d 1/29/22 in Plainfield (Ots. Co.) (3-2/4)
5330. Lobdell, Ebenezer m 1/5/12 Sarah Brown, both of Beekman (8-1/15)
5331. Locherty, Ann, 30, wf of William, d 11/18/31 in Albany (dau of James Sickles of Albany) (funeral from 65 South Pearl St.) (1-11/19)
5332. Locke, JohnD. m 5/17/30 Julia A. Goff at Trinity Church in Geneva; Rev. Mason. All of Geneva (1-5/22)
5333. Lockwood, Edwin, Esq. of New Jersey m 8/21/34 Sary Ann Matholf; Rev. Dunbar (double ceremony - see marr of William Ferguson) (8-9/3)
5334. Lockwood, Harriet, 14, dau of Ezekiel, d 7/18/13 in Champlain (7-7/31)
5335. Lockwood, Jane, 44, wf of Millington Lockwood, d 5/21/30 in Albany (funeral from 292 North Market St.) (1-5/22)
5336. Lockwood, John of Champlain m 5/1/28 Margaret Lucretia Miller of Platts-burgh, dau of Eleazer, Esq., in Plattsburgh; Rev. Chase (7-5/3)

154

5337. Lockwood, Mary (Miss), 27, dau of Walter, d 8/21/25 in NYC (typhus) (8-8/31)
5338. Lockwood, Phebe (Mrs.), 82, d 3/11/34 at her home in La Grange (8-3/19)
5339. Lockwood, Sally, 42, consort of Ezekiel, Esq., d 9/6/17 in Champlain (consumption) (7-9/20)
5340. Lockwood, Solomon, 75, d 8/16/22 in Ballston Spa (2-8/20)
5341. Lockwood, Stephen of Stillwater m 1/13/27 Betsey Cropsey of Brunswick; Rev. Howard (9-1/23)
5342. Lockwood, Walter of the firm of Lockwood, Haggerty and Co., merchants, of NYC m 10/25/32 Hannah C. Hull, dau of John of Stanford (Dut. Co.), at the Friends Meeting house in Stanford (8-10/31)
5343. Long, E. R. (Lt.) of the U.S. Army m 11/10/30 "Miss Fitch" of Niagara, Upper Canada in N (1-12/3)
5344. Loomis, Andrew W., Esq. of New Lisbon. NY m 3/9/26 Martha M. Austin of Steubenville, OH in S; Rev. Lyman Potter (3-4/17)
5345. Loomis, Ann, 79, wf of George, d 2/14/31 in Albany (funeral from her former home, 9 Washington St.)(her son, George J. Loomis, is mentioned) (1-2/16)
5346. Loomis, Arphaxed, Esq. of Little Falls m 10/25/31 Ann P. Todd, dau of late Dr. Stephen, in Salisbury (Herk. Co.); Rev. Goodrich) (1-10/29)
5347. Loomis, Chauncey (Hon.) of Genesee Co. ("senator from the Western District") d 4/20/17 in Albany (7-4/26)
5348. Loomis, Eleazer, Jr., d 12/6/12 in Cleveland, OH (typhus) (3-1/9/12)
5349. Loomis, Eliza, 54, wf of Col. Lebbeus, d 7/3/23 in NYC (3-7/14)
5350. Loomis, Gustavus (Lt.) of the U.S. Corps of Artillery, m 7/4/17 Julia Ann Mix of NYC in Washington (Dut. Co.) (7-7/12)
5351. Loop, Jacob, 33, d 4/11/19 in Red Hook (8-4/14)
5352. Loop, Josiah m Catharine Osterhout, both of Rhinebeck; Rev. Romeyne (8-10/5/96)
5353. Lord, Abner R., 37, merchant, of NYC d 9/4/29 in NYC (1-9/7)
5354. Lord, Edwin, Esq. m 6/16/30 Jane Maria Stone, oldest dau of Asaph; Rev. Lunt. All of NYC (1-6/21)
5355. Lord, Russell (Capt.), 60, late of Troy, d 9/12/19 in Boston (state not given) (9-9/21)
5356. Lord, Ruth (Mrs.), 71, d 6/14/23 in Ballston (funeral sermon by Rev. Clark of Ballston Spa (2-6/17)
5357. Lord, Samuel, merchant, formerly of Troy, d 4/28 in Cambridge (9-5/7)
5358. Lordell, Nathan m 2/18/26 Phebe Canfield, both of Poughkeepsie; Rev. Cuyler (8-2/22)
5359. Losee, Francis of Beekman m 5/30/12 Sarah Germond, dau of Isaac of Washington (Dut. Co.); Rev. Clark (8-6/3)
5360. Losey, Abraham of Beekman m 6/27/22 Jane Black of Freedom; Rev. C. C. Cuyler (8-7/3)
5361. Losie, James of Washington (Dut. Co.) m 9/12/02 Mary Vail of Clinton (Dut. Co.); Rev. Clark (8-9/21)
5362. Lottridge, Thomas, about 60, d 12/10/02 in prison at Albany (had been confined there for "upwards of 15 years") (3-12/16)
5363. Love, John C. (Lt.) d 5/13/07 at the Marine barracks in Washington, Dist. of Columbia (suicide) (9-5/26)
5364. Love, Stephen, s of James of Washington (Dut. Co.) m 5/21/97 Amelia Pleas, dau of Morris, Esq. of Beekman (8-6/13)
5365. Lovejoy, _____, wf of Benjamin, d 8/8/12 in Chatham (6-8/17)
5366. Lovejoy, Daniel (Rev.), a Congregational minister, of Albion, Maine d 8/17/33 (suicide by hanging) (7-8/24)
5367. Lovell, Gertrude (Mrs.), 27, d 6/12/31 in Albany (her late father, John B. Visscher, is mentioned but not her husband) (funeral from 34 Columbia St.) (1-6/13)
5368. Lovell, Joseph, M.D., hospital surgeon, U.S. Army, m 9/16/17 Margaret Eliza Mansfield, dau of late Col. Samuel; Rev. Stanton (marriage place not given) (6-9/23)
5369. Loverin, Caleb A. m 8/31/34 Catherine Klein, both of Redford, in R; Rev. Turner (7-9/6)
5370. Low, Aaron, junior editor of the Telegraph and Observer, m 6/10/30 Mary C. Dean of Pleasant Valley; Rev. Wile (1-6/15 and 8-6/16)
5371. Low, Jacob m 12/7/05 Adrianna Mott; Rev. Brouwer (8-12/10)

5372. Low, Jacob of Poughkeepsie d about 2/5/24 near Manchester (state not given) (his frozen body was found in a field on 2/8/24 - "...it is supposed that he had frozen to death about Feb. 5") (8-2/11)
5373. Low, James (Dr.), 40, brother of David of Charlton, d 2/3/22 in Albany (buried in Charlton) (2-2/13)
5374. Low, John A., 48, d 4/16/28 in Poughkeepsie (consumption) (8-4/23)
5375. Low, Juliet, 30, wf of Dr. David, d 8/23/25 in Schenectady (2-9/6)
5376. Low, Peter m 7/4/22 Maria Ostrom, both of Poughkeepsie; Rev. Reed (8-7/10)
5377. Low, Reynold of Milford m 11/10/25 Susan Howard of Meredith (Dela. Co.); Elder Crane) (3-11/21)
5378. Low, Theodore m Sarah Bache Bleecker, dau of James, at St. John's Chapel in NYC; Right Rev. Bishop Hobart (1-6/25/29)
5379. Low, Walter m 12/31/23 Maria Wood; Gar ? Adriance, Esq. All of Pleasant Valley (8-1/7/24)
5380. Lowe, Michael (Capt.), 77, (a Rev. officer) d 9/3/19 in Washington, Dist. of Columbia (8-9/15)
5381. Lowe, Sarah, 89, wid of Nicholas, deceased, d 10/22/21 at Judge Beekman's in Sharon (3-11/5)
5382. Lown, Hans m 11/27/13 Gertrude Teal; Rev. Quitman (8-12/8)
5383. Loyster, John m 5/31/27 Mary Younie, dau of James late of London; Rev. M. W. Dwight (8-6/6)
5384. Luce, Edward m Rhoda Gunn in Westminster, VT (6-6/11/01)
5385. Luce, Hervey of Cooperstown m 12/7/18 Almira Griffin, dau of Samuel, Esq. of Middlefield in M; Rev. Smith (3-12/14)
5386. Luce, Nathan, 80, d 12/11/16 in Cooperstown ("an early settler in this county" [Otsego]) (3-12/12)
5387. Luce, Othniel, 56, d 3/13/18 in Middlefield (found dead in a field where he was drawing wood - coroner's verdict: "Visitation of Almighty God") (3-3/22)
5388. Luckey, James F. d 8/23/19 (8-8/25)
5389. Luckey, Samuel Jr. m 2/16/03 Polly Underhill, both of Poughkeepsie; Rev. Van Vranken (8-2/22)
5390. Luckey, Samuel, Esq. m 8/11/05 Hannah Tappen, dau of Teunis, Esq.; Rev. Brouwer. All of Poughkeepsie (8-8/13)
5391. Luckey, Thomas P. m 4/28/24 Jane Ann Hoffman, both of Poughkeepsie; Rev. C. C. Cuyler (8-5/5)
5392. Ludlow, Daniel, Esq., about 48, d 1/18/14 in Kinderhook (6-2/8)
5393. Ludlow, Henry G., formerly of Kinderhook, m 11/19/29 Abigail Woolsey Welles, dau of Dr. Noah, in NYC; Rev. Dr. Cox (1-11/24)
5394. Ludlow, James, inf s of William B., Esq., d 11/18/14 in Claverack (6-11/29)
5395. Ludlow, Mary, wf of Cornelius and dau of H. W. Boel of NYC, d 6/19/31 in NYC (1-6/28)
5396. Ludlow, Robert Henry m 3/24/31 Cornelia Le Roy, dau of late Jacob, Esq., in NYC; Rev. Dr. Wainwright (1-3/28)
5397. Ludlow, Samuel B., Esq. of Nassau, NY m 10/26/20 Nancy Douglass of Canaan in C; Rev. Azariah Clark (6-11/7)
5398. Ludlow, William H., "an aged resident of Claverack", d 3/14/03 in C (6-3/22)
5399. Luke, Abraham m 6/10/20 Mary E. Magou, both of Gibbonsville; Rev. Summers (9-6/20)
5400. Lunt, William P. (Rev.), pastor of the 2nd Unitarian Church of NYC, m 5/14/29 Ellen Hobart Hedge, dau of B. Hedge, Esq. of Plymouth, MA, in P; Rev. Dr. Kendall (1-5/28)
5401. Luse, Stephen, Esq., a long-term Albany resident, d in Albany (3-5/2/25)
5402. Lush, Richard, Esq. d 5/31/17 in Albany (3-6/5)
5403. Lusk, Chauncey, 29, attorney (late tutor in Williams College) d 10/23/03 in Lanesborough, MA (6-11/8)
5404. Lusk, Clarissa, 30, consort of Dr. Chester Lusk of Broome Co. and dau of Capt. Abraham Holdridge of Spencertown, d 10/11/10 in S (consumption) (6-10/26)
5405. Luther, Betsey (Mrs.), 47, d 10/25/21 in Providence (Sara. Co.) (her husband, not named, died many years earlier) (9-12/4)
5406. Luther, Caleb m 1/19/16 "Miss Fillmore", dau of Capt. Septa Fillmore, in Chazy (7-2/3)

5407. Luther, Caleb, Esq., 46, late sheriff of Clinton Co., d 10/20/28 in
       Plattsburgh (7-10/25)
5408. Luther, Fanny Vallonia, 18 mo, dau of Caleb, Esq., d 7/4/19 in Chazy
       (7-7/17)
5409. Luther, Gallatin Albert, 18 mo, and Walworth, 5 weeks, both sons of
       Caleb, Esq., d 8/2/23 in Plattsburgh (7-8/9)
5410. Luther, Martin (Deacon), 75, one of the first settlers in Otsego Co.,
       d 4/26/25 in Edmeston (3-5/9 and 3-5/16)
5411. Luyster, Anne (Mrs.), mother of Peter R. Maison, Esq. of Poughkeepsie,
       d 12/20/13 in Poughkeepsie (8-12/22)
5412. Luyster, Isaac of Washington, Dut. Co. m 3/7/12 Catherine Cole of
       Beekman; Mindert Velie, Esq. (8-3/11)
5413. Luyster, Matthew m 1/8/12 Jane Cornell, both of Fishkill; Rev. C. C.
       Cuyler (8-1/15)
5414. Lyde, Edward, Esq., "broker in Wall Street", d (12/23?) in NYC (1-12/30/31)
5415. Lyell, _____ (Rev. Dr.) m Elizabeth Bennett at Christ Church in NYC;
       Right Rev. Bishop Hobart (3-11/28/25)
5416. Lyle, Jane (Mrs.), 85, mother of Henry, Esq., d 11/5/21 in Red Hook
       (8-11/7)
5417. Lyle, P. V. A. (Mr.), 23, d 10/14/27 in Mobile, AL (8-11/7)
5418. Lyle, Thomas (Rev.) of NYC m Juliana Rhea in Trenton, NJ (3-1/27/23)
5419. Lyman, Almira C. Fish, wf of William of Montreal, Canada, d 7/17/34 in
       Burlington, VT (7-7/26)
5420. Lyman, Edwin, merchant, of Quebec, Canada m 6/3/29 Charlotte Macnider,
       youngest dau of John, Esq., in New Kilmarnock (near Quebec City); Rev.
       Dr. Harkness (1-6/15)
5421. Lyman, Elihu (Hon.), 44, member of Massachusetts senate and brother of
       late Joseph, Esq. of Cooperstown, NY, d 2/11/26 in Boston, MA (3-2/20)
5422. Lyman, George, merchant, m 10/16/20 Jane Bloom, both of Troy; Rev. Dr.
       Coe (9-10/24)
5423. Lyman, George, merchant, of Troy m 3/23/24 Mrs. Catharine Robinson of
       Bennington, VT in B; Rev. Absalom Peters (9-3/30)
5424. Lyman, Hicks, Esq. m 5/15/06 Rena Weatherwax, both of Schaghticoke, in S
       (9-5/20)
5425. Lyman, Lewis, merchant, of Montreal, Canada m 8/9/15 Mary P. Paine, dau
       of Amasa, Esq. of Troy (9-8/22)
5426. Lynch, Patt, merchant, m 10/30/12 Charlotte Gray, both of Bennington, VT,
       in Troy, NY; Rev. David Butler (9-11/3)
5427. Lynde, Cynthia R., 35, wf of Charles W., d 5/18/29 in Homer (1-5/28)
5428. Lynde, Elizabeth S., about 48, wid of late John of Plattsburgh, d 8/29/34
       in Plattsburgh (7-8/30)
5429. Lynde, John, first judge of common pleas, Clinton Co., d 8/21/31 in
       Plattsburgh (1-9/1)
5430. Lynde, Sarah (Mrs.), 75, mother of Charles W. and Dr. John of Homer,
       d 5/15/29 in Sherburne (Chen. Co.) (1-5/28)
5431. Lynde, Sarah Ann, about 4, dau of John, Esq., d 6/20/29 (1-7/4)
5432. Lynds, Charles L., merchant, of Syracuse m 9/27/30 S. Maria Ford, dau of
       Philip, Esq. of Troy, in T; Rev. Beman (1-9/29)
5433. Lynds, John, Esq., attorney, m 11/18/13 Elizabeth Stearns of Peru, NY
       in P (7-11/27)
5434. Lyon, Charles of Cherry Valley m 9/4/25 Caroline Stanard of Springfield
       in S; Rev. Fairchild (3-9/12)
5435. Lyon, Elenor, 60, (wf of Z. Lyon, formerly part owner of this newspaper,
       and mother of its present editor) d 9/15/13 in Royalton, VT (9-10/12)
5436. Lyon, Hezekiah W. m 12/22/23 Hannah Hughes in Cooperstown; Rev. Tiffany
       (3-12/29)
5437. Lyon, John W. m 8/7/13 Martha Jencks; Henry Vanderburgh, Esq. All of
       Clinton (8-8/18)
5438. Lyon, Martin, Esq. of Genoa m 6/22/31 Rachel Haight of Geneva in Geneva;
       Rev. M. P. Squier (1-7/2)
5439. Lyon, Mary, 44, formerly of Albany, d 12/12/30 in NYC (1-12/15)
5440. Lyon, Matthew (Col.), 76, formerly of Vermont, d 8/1/22 "at Spadre Bluff,
       Arkansas Terr." (2-10/15)
5441. Lyon, Sarah, 47, consort of Joseph of Hartwick, d 3/29/15 in H (3-4/6)
5442. Lyons, _____, wf of Samuel, d in Poughkeepsie (8-4/22/00)

157

5443. Lyvena, William m 5/20/28 Maria Prindle; Rev. Howard (9-5/27)
5444. McAllister, James of New Alexandria m 3/17/31 Mrs. Christian Ernest of
Greensburg, PA, "a disconsolate widow of four months and twenty-seven
days..."; Rev. Steck (1-3/24) - this notice copied by the Albany paper
from the Greensburg Gazette.
5445. McArdle, John, 50, d in Little Falls (killed by an explosion while
blasting rocks) (he had lost 7 sons accidentally, 5 through drowning)
(3-11/20/20)
5446. McArthur, Arthur d 6/5/11 in Hudson (6-6/7)
5447. McArthur, Daniel, printer, about 19, d 10/9/01 in NYC (6-10/22)
5448. McArthur, Duncan J. m 5/12/31 Elizabeth Walker, dau of James; Rev. Peter
Bullions. All of Albany (1-5/14)
5449. McAulay, John, merchant, of Newburgh m "last week" Caty Sloan of Poughkeepsie; Rev. Gray (8-4/5/92)
5450. McCall, Jane, 53, wf of Rev. Daniel and dau of Henry Scott, Esq. of
Milford, d 5/12/23 in Port Gibson (3-6/30)
5451. McCartney, William, Esq., 62, d 2/16/31 in Sparta (Liv. Co.) ("He was,
we believe, a native of Scotland but came to this country when very
young ... one of the earliest settlers in Genesee Country") (1-2/24)
5452. McCauley, Charles Stewart (Capt.) of the U.S. Navy m 10/25/31 Lilia
Elizabeth Dickens, oldest dau of Asbury, Esq. of the Treasury Dept.,
in Washington, Dist. of Columbia; Rev. Hawley (1-11/3)
5453. McCauley, Thomas (Deacon), 54, d in Seneca (1-3/1/31)
5454. McChain, James m 2/4/29 Julia Wisner, oldest dau of Rev. William, in
Ithaca; Rev. Wisner. All of Ithaca (double ceremony - see marr of
Rev. Asa Theodore Hopkins) (1-2/14)
5455. McChesney, Francis C. m 3/23/28 Eliza McChesney in Brunswick; Rev. Benson
(9-4/1)
5456. McChesney, Robert, Esq. m 1/27/99 Betsey Post, both of Troy; Rev. Coe
(9-2/5)
5457. McChestney, John K., 32, d in Albany (funeral from his late home, 8 Fox
St.) (1-6/27/29)
5458. McCleary, Daniel (Dr.), assemblyman-elect from Niagara Co., ("a republican")
d 1/2/16 in Clarence (3-1/25)
5459. McCleary, David, 22, late printer of the People's Press in Batavia, d in
Rupert, VT (1-3/1/31)
5460. McCloskey, James (Maj.) who accompanied the Winnebago Indians d "on his
return with the party" in Norwich, OH (1-1/13/29)
5461. McClure, Susanna, 29, wf of William, d 2/22/13 (born inDungannon,
Tyrone Co., Ireland) (9-3/2)
5462. McCollum, William George and John Richard, twin brothers, 23 mo, children
of Randal and Elizabeth, d 5/10/15 in Albany (both were placed in one
coffin in one grave) (6-5/23)
5463. McColly, William m 2/28/21 Electa Baker in Beekmantown (Clinton Co.);
Hallock Bromley, Esq. (7-3/24)
5464. McCombs, Elias C., 9, s of Capt. R. McCombs, d 10/29/05 at his father's
home near Augusta, GA (killed by the bite of a rattle snake) (8-11/26)
5465. McConihe, Thomas Jefferson, inf s of Isaac, Esq., d 8/23/27 in Troy
(9-8/24)
5466. McCord, Elizabeth, about 14, dau of David C., d 3/9/34 in La Grange
(consumption) (8-3/19)
5467. McCord, Hannah C., 38, wf of Rev. William I., d 2/20/34 in Poughkeepsie
(8-2/26)
5468. McCord, John of Beekman m 12/30/09 ___?___ Van Voorhis of Fishkill; Rev.
Cuyler (8-1/3/10)
McCord, William. See, possibly, Mecord, William.
5469. McCotter, Alexander of Plattsburgh m "a few days since" Hannah Grant of
Chazy in C (7-11/29/17)
5470. McCotter, James d 3/8/02 in Hudson (settled in Hudson "recently"
supposedly from Vermont) (6-3/16)
5471. McCoun, John, merchant, m 10/8/05 Maria Miller, both of Troy, in T; Rev.
Coe (9-10/15)
5472. McCoun, John d 8/6/12 in Troy (9-8/11)
5473. McCoun, John T., Jr., s of John, deceased, d 3/25/27 (9-3/30)
5474. McCoun, John T. m 9/9/28 Angelica R. D. Lane, dau of Col. Derrick Lane of
Troy; Rev. Mark Tucker (9-9/12)

158

5475. McCoun, Samuel, merchant, m Peggy Snow, both of Troy, in T (9-2/10/01)
5476. McCoy, Elizabeth (Miss) d by or before 9/9/13 when her body was found in
       the river in the town of Nottingham, NH ("one of the suspected
       perpetrators being arrested") (7-9/11)
5477. McCoy, Hannah (Mrs.), 86, d 12/10/29 in Albany (her son, John Bryan McCoy,
       is mentioned) (funeral at the home of Calvin Brown, 52 Hudson St.)
       (1-12/11)
5478. McCrachan, Joan, 60, wf of John, d 5/9/13 in Spencertown (6-5/25)
5479. McCracken, Samuel, 75, d 6/25/31 in Fort Ann (fatally injured in a fall
       from a wagon 6/21) (9-7/5)
5480. McCreedy, _____, 4 weeks, child of Jeremiah, d 3/7/21 in Plattsburgh
       (7-3/10)
5481. McCreedy, _____, 7 or 8 yrs old, s of James, d 2/1/27 (kicked by a horse)
       (7-2/3)
5482. McCreedy, Charles, about 70, d 3/28/13 in Plattsburgh (7-4/2)
5483. McCreedy, Jeremiah m 12/9/15 Silvia McCreedy, dau of Thomas (all of
       Plattsburgh), in Plattsburgh (7-2/3/16)
5484. McCreedy, John m 7/11/26 Caroline Rosevelt, dau of Solomon, in
       Beekmantown (Clinton Co.) (7-7/15)
5485. McCreedy, Phebe, about 60, wf of Charles M., d 3/7/13 in Plattsburgh
       (7-3/12)
5486. McCullen, Robert m 12/7/85 Eve De Camp of Troy (9-12/10)
5487. McCumber, Mary, consort of Solomon, Esq. and dau of Daniel Fobes,
       d 12/22/29 in Henderson (Jefferson Co.) (1-1/4/30)
5488. McCune, Harvey of Brattleboro, VT m 9/10/29 Catharine Ostrander, dau of
       John I., Esq. of Albany; Rev. Ferris (1-9/12)
5489. McCutchen, Alexander, 28, d 3/20/05 in Hudson (6-3/26)
5490. McDale, Hugh m 8/22/29 Hannah Tremble ("both belonging to the society
       of Shakers at Niskayuna, NY where they have lived about 20 years")
       in Whitesboro on board the boat "Oliver"; Uriah Stevens, Esq. (8-9/2)
5491. McDonald, Andrew, 16 or 18?, s of late Rev. D. McDonald, D.D., d 5/28/30
       in Geneva (1-6/12)
5492. McDonald, Daniel (Rev.), D.D., professor of languages in Geneva College,
       d 3/25/30 at his home near the village of Geneva (8-4/14)
5493. McDonald, James, about 30, d 10/9/06 in Gallatin (6-10/28)
5494. McDonald, James D. m 2/24/25 Elmira Darlan in Ballston Spa; Elder
       Thompson (2-3/15) In this same newspaper release are these two
       additional marriage reports: (1) Cyrus Whitcomb of Vermont m 2/27/25
       Mrs. Huldah Finch in Ballston Spa; Elder Thompson; and (2) Isaac
       Seely m 3/13/25 Emily P. Darlan in Ballston Spa; Elder Thompson
       (a mother and her two daughters married all within 17 days)
5495. McDonald, John, Esq. of the firm of C. and J. McDonald & Co. m 3/10/31
       Henrietta Maria Mallory, both of "Gananoque, Genesee Co.", at the
       home of Col. Stone in Gananoque; Rev. William Smart (1-3/24)
       (Note: Today there is a Gananoque, Prov. of Ontario, Canada but none,
       apparently, in NY)
5496. McDonald, John, Esq., 48, Pres. of the Bank of Pittsburgh, d 5/29/31 at
       the Exchange Hotel in Pittsburgh, PA (1-6/1)
5497. McDonald, Michael, 97, d 6/28/23 in Ballston ("In 1763 the deceased,
       with a brother, located themselves on the west bank of the Long or
       Ballston Lake on which spot the deceased continued until his death -
       they were the only white families in the town until 1770." (2-7/1)
5498. McDonald, S. (Lt.), 106, d at his home, "Isle of Tikes", NY ("left
       3 children under ten years of age"))1-2/10/31)
5499. McDonough, _____ (Commodore) d "in early December" (This sequence of
       persons listed in the funeral procession either from or to City Hall,
       NYC: detachment of State Artillery, marines of the U.S. Navy, pall
       bearers with casket, officers of the Navy, the Cincinnati Society,
       officers of the Army of the U.S., militia officers of the state,
       senators and representatives in Congress, U.S. Judges, Judges of
       NY state, etc. (7-12/10/25)
5500. McDonough, James of the firm of Butler, McDonough & Co. m 8/7/31 Eliza
       Cummins (dau of late George of Kilkenny, Ireland and sister of Rev. Dr.
       Cummins, formerly of Utica, NY) at St. John's Church in Utica; Rev.
       McCahill (1-8/12)

5501. McDonough, Lucy Ann, 34, consort of Commodore Thomas McDonough and dau
      of late Nathaniel Shaler, d 8/24/25 in Middletown (7-8/27)
5502. McDougall, Andrew d 2/25/19 at his plantation on the OOmulgee River near
      Fort Hawkins "having left to his friends in the neighborhood of Lake
      Champlain, NY an estate worth $10,000. Further particulars available
      in the office of the Albany Argus." (7-3/27)
5503. McDowell, John m 11/16/25 Letty Bregaw, both of Poughkeepsie; Rev. Dr.
      Reed (8-11/23)
5504. McDowell, Molly, 25, wf of A. McDowell, d 1/28/25 in Cooperstown
      (3-1/31)
5505. McDowell, Polly, wf of James R. A. McDowell, d 11/7/11 in Hudson (6-11/11)
5506. McElroy, James, merchant, of Ithaca m 5/15/31 Cordelia Richardson, dau of
      J., Esq. of New Hartford, in New Hartford; Rev. Skinner of Utica
      (1-5/22)
5507. McElroy, Robert m 4/18/22 June McCullom, both of Albany; Rev. Coe of Troy
      (9-4/30)
5508. McFaden, George S., 1 yr, s of George, d 3/23/14 in Plattsburgh (7-3/26)
5509. McFarlan, Henry, Esq., late of the firm of Blackwell & McFarlan, d 6/28/30
      while on a visit to his iron works in New Jersey (1-7/1)
5510. McFarlan, James of Troy m 1/8/29 Jane W. Anderson, dau of late Alex, in
      Brooklyn; Rev. James Otterson (1-1/15)
5511. McFarland, Asa, Esq., joint editor and proprietor of the New Hampshire
      Statesman, m Clarissa J. Chase, dau of late James, in Meredith
      (8-12/8/30)
5512. McFarlane, Nancy, 37, wf of Robert, d 2/25/30 in Albany (funeral from
      her husband's home, Westerlo St. near South Pearl St.) (1-2/26)
5513. McGinnes, Richard, Esq., 81, d 12/26/30 in Montreal, Canada (had lived
      there from the early part of the Amer. Rev. and was the oldest member
      of the Methodist Church in the provinces) (1-1/8/31)
5514. McGlashan, Alexander, 66, d 9/28/30 in Bethlehem (funeral at P. Clark's)
      (Alexander O. and James, sons of the deceased, are mentioned) (1-9/29)
5515. McGlashan, Alexander G. of Albany m 9/5/25 Louisa Bowne of Charlton in C;
      Rev. Baldwin (2-9/13)
5516. McGlashan, Daniel, Esq., 38, printer, d 4/13/30 in Albany (had been a city
      alderman and, at time of death, was one of the city judges) (1-4/14)
5517. McGlashan, James m 12/13/29 Mrs. Jane Maria Butler; Rev. Ludlow. All of
      Albany (1-12/15)
5518. McGlashan, James (Col.) of Cattaraugus Co. m 3/17/30 Sophia Foote of
      Albany; Rev. Dr. Sprague (1-3/18)
5519. McGlashan, Mary (Miss), 18, dau of Daniel, d 2/18/30 in Albany (funeral
      "from the upper part of Fox Street") (1-2/19)
5520. McGourkey, William G. m 11/14/31 Maria E. Wheldon; Rev. Campbell. All of
      Albany (1-11/16)
5521. McGown, Mary, 20, d 9/5/20 in Cherry Valley (consumption) (3-9/18)
5522. McHenry, Mary, 27, consort of Col. Daniel, sheriff of Allegany Co.,
      and only dau of Capt. Henry Magee, d 3/25/31 in Angelica (1-4/7 and
      1-4/9)
5523. McIlvane, Isaac (Rev.), pastor of the Presbyterian Church in Lansingburgh,
      m 5/12/29 Mary Ann Harrison, dau of Daniel, deceased, in Newark, NJ; Rev.
      William T. Hamilton (1-5/28)
5524. McIntosh, Delia B., wf of E. C. and dau of late Thomas Tisdall, Esq. of
      Hartford, CT, d 1/21/31 in Albany, NY (funeral from the late home of
      the deceased at 16 Liberty St. (1-1/24)
5525. McIntosh, James M. (Lt.) of the U.S. Navy m Lydia Wilson, youngest dau
      of late Abraham, Esq., merchant, of NYC, at Grace Church in NYC; Rev.
      Dr. Wainwright (1-4/30/29)
5526. McIntosh, Peter of Troy, merchant, m 6/5/05 Lucy Sloan, dau of Gen.
      Sloan, in Williamstown, MA; Rev. Swift (9-6/11)
5527. McJimsey, Robert m 9/16/29 Harriet Hoyt, both of NYC, in NYC; Rev.
      McJimsey (1-9/23)
5528. McKee, James m 10/26/27 Mary Alllen; Rev. Welton (8-10/31)
5529. McKeen, Helen, wf of Levi, Esq. of Poughkeepsie, d 12/3/20 in P (8-12/6)
5530. McKeen, John, 24, d 7/22/17 in Poughkeepsie (funeral from his late
      residence at Dr. Trivett's)(8-7/23)

5531. McKeen, Levi of Poughkeepsie m 6/10/23 Mary Prince(?), dau of Samuel of NYC (8-6/18)
5532. McKelvey, ____, child of Cornelius, d "recently" in Albany (funeral from the father's home, 24 Hamilton St.) (1-11/10/29)
5533. McKelvey, Cornelius, 43, a mechanic, d 8/23/30 in Poughkeepsie (surv by wf and 2 small ch) (funeral from his late home, corner Hamilton and Union Sts.) (1-8/24)
5534. McKenney, Aurora m 8/19/22 Hannah Graham; Rev. Cuyler (8-8/21)
5535. McKenney, Elizabeth, 80, relict of John, d 5/1/31 in Albany (her dau, Mrs. Jennet Cook, and William Cook [the latter presumably husband of Jennet] are mentioned) (funeral from the late home of the deceased, corner Steuben and North Pearl Sts.) (1-5/2)
5536. McKenney, Matthew, between 60 and 70, d in Orange County jail (had been in the Ulster and Orange Co. jail about 30 yrs for a single debt) (3-5/7/21)
5537. McKerchen, Duncan, one of the proprietors of the Advocate, m 5/29/30 Nancy Thomson, both of Albany, in Guilderland; Rev. Bullions (1-6/4)
5538. McKever, Charles, 76, d 9/26/24 in Galway, NY (2-10/12)
5539. McGibbon, Isaiah m 7/12/27 Betsey Zander, both of Troy; Rev. Howard (9-7/17)
5540. McKinney, Jacob S. m 2/9/31 Delia Herrick, both of Florida (Mont. Co.), in Schenectady; Rev. P. A. Proal (1-2/17)
5541. McKinney, James m 12/25/15 Amarilla Roberts, dau of Maj. John Roberts, 3rd, in Salmon River; R. H. Walworth, Esq. All of Plattsburgh (7-12/30)
5542. McKinnon, John of NYC m 10/13/31 Julia A. Wiltse of Fishkill Landing at F. L. (8-10/19)
5543. McKinson, John of NYC m 10/13/31 Julia A. Wilse, dau of Martin, Esq. of Fishkill Landing, at F. L.; Rev. William S. Heyer (1-10/17)
5544. McKinstry, Charles (Gen.), 64, d 12/30/18 in Hillsdale (6-1/5/19)
5545. McKinstry, Delia, 1 yr, dau of J. McKinstry, Jr., d 6/5/19 (6-6/29)
5546. McKinstry, Eliza, 38, wf of John, Jr., d 6/21/19 in Livingston (6-6/29)
5547. McKinstry, Henry, merchant, m 9/17/07 Julia Gardiner in Catskill; Rev. Porter (6-9/22)
5548. McKinstry, Robert of the firm of Hammond and McKinstry m 9/30/18 Sally Hammond, both of Hudson, in Claverack; Rev. Gebhard (6-10/20)
5549. McKinstry, William m 12/13/04 Rebecca Barnard, dau of Peter, in Hudson; Rev. Sears (6-12/18)
5550. McKinstry, William, 47, d 12/2/29 in Hudson (1-12/9)
5551. McKnight, John, 72, one of the first settlers in Charlton, d 10/3/22 in Charlton (2-10/15)
5552. McKowan, John, 30, d in Hudson (6-11/15/08)
5553. McKown, Absalom, son of William, d 8/17/31 in Guilderland (surv by wf and 10 ch) (1-8/27)
5554. McLean, Daniel m 8/21/28 Margaret Thompson, both of Poughkeepsie; Rev. Dr. Cuyler (8-8/27)
5555. McLean, Donald, a native of North Britain and an eminent druggist of that city, d 1/10/82 in NYC (5-1/31)
5556. McLean, Lois, 36 or 56?. wf of William, the printer and editor of the Cherry Valley Gazette, d 10/16/30 in C. V. (1-10/21)
5557. McLean, Maria, 30, wf of John, Jr., Esq. and oldest dau of Anthony I. Blanchard, Esq., d 3/26/27 in Salem, NY (7-4/7)
5558. McLean, William C., 28, brother of John C. of New Sweden, NY, d 5/17/31 in Greenwich (Wash. Co.) (4 [Keeseville Herald]-5/31)
5559. McLeod, ____, wf of Donald and mother of Duncan, d "recently" in Albany (funeral from her husband's home on Dean St.) (1-5/6/31)
5560. McLeod, Margery, 79, consort of Donald, d 5/4/31 (1-5/5)
5561. McManus, Robert m 12/13/29 Mrs. Catharine Leskin, both of Schenectady; Rev. Welch (1-12/18)
5562. McMartin, Peter, Esq., attorney, 17 (sic), s of Hon. McMartin of the senate, d 3/18/30 in NYC (1-3/25)
5563. McMason, Stephen, 90, m Amelia Simpson, 18, in New Orleans, LA (8-12/15/24)
5564. McMaster, Henrietta H., 26, wf of Truman J. and dau of Hon. Nathaniel Garrow, d 5/18/29 in Auburn (1-5/25)
5565. McMaster, William d 11/16/23 in Ballston (2-11/18)

161

5566. McMillen, Samuel, farmer, of Warwick, VT d "lately"(suicide by razor)
(about 20 yrs earlier had hanged himself but was then cut down by his
son and afterwards recovered) (6-8/31/02)
5567. McMullen, Andrew, Jr., 22, d 8/24/30 in Albany (funeral at the home of
his father, 417 South Market St.) (1-8/25)
5568. McMurry, Robert D. m 10/16/28 Caroline Truesdell; Rev Howard. All of
Troy (9-10/21)
5569. McNamee, John Lawrence, 4, oldest s of Lawrence, d 10/24/15 in Cooperstown
(3-11/2)
5570. McNaughton, James (Dr.) of Albany m 4/30/33 Caroline McIntyre, dau of
Archibald, Esq., in NYC; Rev. Dr. McAuly (8-5/8)
5571. McNeal, William, 57, late secretary of the National Insurance Co. of NYC,
d 1/15/34 at the home of his son-in-law, James Wiltse of Glenham, in
Fishkill (8-1/29)
5572. McNeil, Alexander of NYC d 8/18/03 in Hudson (6-8/23)
5573. McNight, William George from Green Castle, Island of Jamaica, d 10/11/30
at Montgomery Hall in Saratoga Springs, NY (1-10/14)
5574. McQuaid, Jacob m 4/14/22 Lucinda Herrington, both of Troy; Rev. Dr. Coe
(9-4/16)
5575. McQueen, William of NYC m 3/15/18 Hester Porter of Plattsburgh in P;
Rev. Halsey (7-3/21)
5576. McVail, Thomas m 2/9/26 Susan Ann Barlow in Freedom; Rev. Smith Arnold
(8-2/15)
5577. McVean, Duncan, 68, father of Charles, Esq. of Canajoharie, d 8/3/29 at
his home in Johnstown (1-8/18)
5578. McVean, John, 30, editor of the Canajoharie Telegraph, d 5/12/31 in C
(a teacher of the languages and science in Georgetown, Dist. of columbia,
and, later, "principal of a classical school" in Washington, Dist. of
Columbia) (buried in his birthplace, Johnstown, NY (1-5/20)
5579. McVickar, Anna, 20, oldest dau of John, d 3/8/31 in NYC (1-3/15)
5580. McVickar, John, Jr. of NYC m Eliza Bard, dau of Dr. Samuel of Hyde Park,
in H. P.; Rev. Dr. Beach (8-11/22/09)
5581. McWilliams, John of Milton m 12/5/21 Margery McDonald of Galway, NY in G;
Rev. Wilson (2-12/19)
5582. Mabbett, John, merchant, of Poughkeepsie m 3/12/14 Hannah Frink of Milton
(Sara. Co.); Rev. De Witt (8-3/16)
5583. Mabbett, Seneca of the firm of L & S Mabbett, merchants, of Albany
m 12/22/20 Maria Ketcham, dau of James, Esq. of Dover; Rev. L. Burch
(8-1/17/21)
5584. Macey, _____, ch of William R., d 1/6/09 in Hudson (6-1/10)
5585. Macey, Jared m Sarah Webb, dau of Job, at the Friends Meeting House in
Hudson (6-12/11/04)
5586. Mack, Daniel, 29, editor of the Chenango Republican, d 12/14/30 in Oxford
(1-12/25)
5587. Mack, Joel (Col.), 44, d 12/4/05 in Harpersfield (funeral sermon by Rev.
Stephen Fenn) (buried with military honors) (6-12/5)
5588. Mack, Stephen, Esq., editor of the American Farmer, d 4/16/14 in Owego
(3-4/23)
5589. Mackay, William, Jr. m 5/19/31 Caroline I. Canfield, dau of Judson, Esq.,
at St. George's Church in NYC (1-5/22)
5590. Mackay, William, Jr. m 5/21/31 Caroline E. Canfield, dau of Judson, Esq.
of NYC, at St. George's Church in NYC; Rev. Dr. Milnor (8-5/25)
5591. Mackey, John L. m 10/10/31 Rhoda Greatsinger; Rev. Cahoone. All of
Hyde Park (8-10/19)
5592. Macomb, Alexander, Esq., 67, formerly of NYC and father of Maj. Gen.
Macomb of the U.S. Army, d 1/19/31 at his home in Georgetown, Dist. of
Columbia (had been a member of the NY state legislature) (1-1/26)
5593. Macomb, Charles Marshall, 22, of the Artillery Corps d in Buffalo ("He fell
in an unfortunate encounter with Capt. John W. Gookin of the same corps."
(The deceased was born in NYC and was a younger brother of Maj. Gen.
Macomb) (9-1/31/15)
5594. Macomb, Julia Matilda (Miss), dau of Robert, Esq., d 7/20/30 "at
Kingsbridge (Yonkers) , the residence of her father." (1-7/23)
5595. Macomber, Archer, about 80, of Washington (Dut. Co.) d 5/30/32 in NYC
(8-6/6)

5596. Macy, Henry S. of Pleasant Valley m 1/2/34 Sarah Knox of Poughkeepsie; S. P. Dutton, Esq. (8-1/8)
5597. Macy, Reuben (Capt.), 67, d 6/10/10 in Hudson (6-6/22)
5598. Macy, Richard m Hannah Slade, dau of Capt. William, in Hudson; Rev. Wigton (6-2/5/05)
5599. Magee, John, member of Congress from NY state, m 2/23/31 Mrs. Arabella Snowden of Washington, Dist. of Columbia, in W; Rev. Hawley (1-3/3)
5600. Magenis, Arthur L., Esq. of St. Louis, MO m 2/22/31 Mary Macrea, dau of Col. Macrea of the U.S. Artillery at St. John's Chapel in NYC; Rev. Bishop Onderdonk (1-10/24)
5601. Main, James (Rev.) m 8/17/06 Anna Bly, both of Berlin, NY, in B (9-8/26)
5602. Malcolm, Amelia (Miss), dau of Dr. Henry formerly of Hudson, d 7/16/29 in Albany (funeral from the home of her brother-in-law, Frederick Porter, 69 Green St.) (1-7/18)
5603. Malcolm, Henry (Dr.), 76, (a Rev. War surgeon) d in the state of Penna. (in 1795 he was "appointed collector of Hudson" [NY] by Gen. Washington) (1-4/29/31)
5604. Malcolm, Joseph G., merchant, of Philadelphia (state not given) m 11/8/13 Angelica Malcolm, dau of Dr. Malcolm of Hudson, NY, in H (6-11/16)
5605. Malcolm, Rebecca, 45, wf of Dr. Henry, d in Hudson (6-3/15/10)
5606. Malcom, William (Brig. Gen.) d 9/1/91 in NYC (8-9/8)
5607. Malcomb, Charles, 67, d 12/30/31 in Albany (funeral from 54 Church St.) (his son, Charles, is mentioned) (1-12/31)
5608. Malcomb, Rensselaer, 17, d 5/31/30 in Albany (funeral from his late residence, 36 Lydius St.) (1-6/1)
5609. Mallery, Henry, 21, s of Capt. Samuel, d 6/18/24 in Hartwick (death resulted from an infected ax cut in his foot (3-6/28)
5610. Mallery, Isaac, 56, d 10/31/06 inHartwick (surv by wf and several ch) (born without feet and only one arm) (3-11/6)
5611. Mallery, Semantha (Miss), 21, dau of William, Esq., d 8/11/30 in Cortland (1-8/17)
5612. Mallett, Samuel, 76, d 8/18/24 in Stanford (Dut. Co.) (surv by wf and family - meembers not specified) ("The editors of the NY Commercial Advertiser, the Newburgh papers, and the Owego Gazette will confer a favor by copying the above...") (8-9/8)
5613. Mallory, James (Hon.), 43, d 2/21/27 in Troy ("Judge Mallory emigrated to this city [Troy] from the east a few years after its settlement"; served as Pres. of the Mechanic's Benevolent Association) (surv by his wf and children) (formerly a judge of the Rensselaer Co. courts and late senator from the 3rd District) (9-2/23 and 7-3/3)
5614. Mallory, Joel, merchant, m 4/11/22 Caroline Reeve, dau of John of Berlin, NY; Rev. Justus Hull (9-4/16)
5615. Mallory, John m 4/15/13 Betsey Parrot, both of Plattsburgh, in P (7-4/23)
5616. Mallory, Rollin C. (Hon.) of Vermont d 4/16/31 in Baltimore (state not given) (4 [Keeseville Herald]-4/26)
5617. Mambrut, Ezra m Hannah Morison, both of Claverack, in C; Rev. Gepherd (6-8/31/10)
5618. Man, Albon (Dr.), first judge of Franklin Co., d 9/14/20 in Constable (death resulted from a fall from a horse) (7-9/16)
5619. Manahan, George P., Esq., 24, a young Irish gentleman, d 11/26/25 in Champlain, NY (funeral sermon by Rev. Townsend) (7-12/3)
5620. Manchester, _____, wf of Thomas, d 11/14/04 in Hudson (6-11/20)
5621. Manchester, Abraham m 1/10/22 Hannah Duel in Providence, NY; Jonathan Delano, Esq. (2-1/16)
5622. Manchester, Isaac m 9/18/22 Jane Tupper, both of Troy; Rev. Griffin (9-10/8). See also 5624.
5623. Manchester, J. F., late of Providence, RI, d 9/25/20 in Augusta, GA (One of 25 persons attending a wedding reception; all persons became ill from poisoned food or drink; the bridegroom (not named) and five others had died "with still others not expected to survive") (J. F. Manchester was buried with Masonic honors) (8-10/18)
5624. Manchester, James m 9/18/22Jane Tupper, both of Troy; Rev. Griffin (9-9/24). See also 5622.
5625. Manchester, Jarvis m 10/1/25 Elizabeth Horton, both of Poughkeepsie; Rev. C. C. Cuyler (8-10/5)

5626. Manchester, Orry m 3/8/28 Harriet Glinn in Dover; Seneca Sole, Esq. All of Dover (8-3/19)
5627. Mann, Benjamin (Capt.), 93, (a Rev. patriot) d in Troy (1-12/13/31)
5628. Mann, David m 11/29/23 Adaline Morrison of Milton in Ballston Spa; Thomas Palmer, Esq. (2-12/2)
5629. Mann, Edward B. m 6/9/31 Mrs. Sarah Thorn, both of NYC, in NYC; Rev. A. McClay (1-6/13)
5630. Mann, George, 17, s of Jeremiah, d 11/7/22 in Milton (2-11/12)
5631. Mann, Jacob, 75, d 3/22/29 in Schoharie (formerly sheriff of Schoharie Co.) (died from taking saltpeter erroneously thinking it "a portion of salts") (1-3/28)
5632. Mann, Joel, 81, one of the first settlers in Milton, d 11/25/24 in Milton (2-12/7)
5633. Mann, Jonas, about 60, d 9/6/31 in Syracuse (he was "one of the oldest citizens of that village") (1-9/13)
5634. Mann, Lewis m 10/16/27 Mary Ann Phillips, both of Hyde Park; Rev. Vanderveer (8-10/24)
5635. Mann, Noah, formerly of Hudson, d 4/23/01 in Scipio (consumption) (6-8/20)
5636. Mann, Seth H. of Auburn m 9/6/30 Mary Holbrook, dau of Luther of Whitesboro, in W; Rev. Frost (1-9/17)
5637. Mann, Timothy of the firm of Silliman, Grant & Co. of Troy, NY m 11/26/28 Eliza Louisa Poinier, dau of J. Poinier, Esq. of Newark, NJ in N; Rev. T. Hamilton (9-12/2)
5638. Mann, Whiting (Capt.) m 3/4/06 Hannah Mann, both of Amenia, in A; Rev. Wood (8-3/25)
5639. Mann, William of England m 3/3/31 Eliza Murgatroyd, oldest dau of Cornelius of Hudson, in H; Rev. Whitcomb (1-3/15)
5640. Mannery, Enoch m 9/9/27 Eliza Pickelle, both of Troy; Rev. Howard (9-9/11)
5641. Manney, Elizabeth (Miss), 23, dau of John of Poughkeepsie, d 4/12/32 in Beekman (8-4/25)
5642. Manney, Henry W. of Poughkeepsie m 6/13/32 Helen Cornell of Beekman; Rev. Buttolph (8-6/27)
5643. Manney, Richard W. of Kingston m 9/30/24 Hannah Low of Poughkeepsie (8-10/6)
5644. Manney, Sophia, wf of Dr. Winans Manney, d 4/24/17 in Poughkeepsie (8-4/30)
5645. Manney, Wines of Poughkeepsie m 4/16/23 Mrs. Ellen Smith of Pleasant Valley; Rev. Cuyler (8-4/30)
5646. Manning, Aaron of Troy m 12/18/30 Harriet E. McCarty of Albany; Rev. Martin (1-12/20)
5647. Manning, Charles m 1/15/17 Maria Travis, both of Clinton; Rev. Lewis Leonard (8-1/22)
5648. Manning, Charles m 10/27/27 Lucretia Armstrong, both of Hyde Park, in H. P.; Rev. Hutchinson (8-10/31)
5649. Manning, Gerard m 11/12/29 Hannah Ann Sandford in Hyde Park; Rev. William Cahoon (8-11/18)
5650. Manning, Gilbert of Hyde Park m 9/30/24 Harriet Parmetier of Poughkeepsie; Rev. Babcock (8-10/6)
5651. Manning, John, 23, and Caleb Manning, Jr., 16, sons of Caleb of Pleasant Valley, d 9/16/25 (8-9/21)
5652. Manning, John B. m 10/19/28 Jane Ann Boerum, both of Poughkeepsie; Rev. Dr. Cuyler (8-11/4)
5653. Manning, Joseph m 4/15/23 Sally Atwater, both of Albany, in Troy; Rev. Griffen (9-4/29)
5654. Manning, Maria (Miss), dau of John, Esq. of Hemmingford, Lower Canada, d 1/1/13 in Chazy, NY (7-1/8)
5655. Manning, Mehitable, 39, wf of Charles of Clinton (Dut. Co.) d 3/19/02 (consumption) (surv by several children) (8-3/23)
5656. Manning, Mercy (Mrs.), 78, of Clinton (Dut. Co.) d "last week" (buried in the Reformed Dutch Church burial yard - town not given) (8-1/20/96)
5657. Manning, William of NYC m 8/7/26 Sarah Martin of Poughkeepsie; Rev. Cuyler (8-8/9)
5658. Manning, William H. of the firm of Clark and Manning, merchants, of Watertown m 6/21/31 Mary Ann Ford, dau of Hon. William D. of Sacketts Harbor, in S. H.; Rev. Gere of Brownville (1-7/2)

164

5659. Manny, Charles of Kinderhook m 3/28/23 Mary Morris of Poughkeepsie;
Rev. Dr. Reed (8-4/30)
5660. Mansfield, _____ (Col.), 52, d 2/5/10 in Hudson (buried with military and
Masonic honors) (6-2/8)
5661. Mansfield, Eliza, relict of late Col. Mansfield of NYC, d 11/27/20 in
Washington (state or District not given) (6-12/5)
5662. Manson, Margaret, 18, wf of Nathan, d 6/2/30 in Albany (funeral from
the home of her father, 35 Beaver St.) (1-6/3)
5663. Manson, Nathan, formerly of Oneida Co., m 9/29/29 Margaret Quackenbush
of Albany; Rev. Ferris (1-10/5)
5664. Manville, Jonas m 3/9/16 Mary Wheeler, both of Brunswick, in Troy; Rev.
Butler (9-3/12)
5665. Marble, John B. of Greenbush m 6/25/27 Catharine Haynor of Troy; Rev.
Howard (9-7/10)
5666. Marble, Nathaniel of Schaghticoke m 2/19/22 Adeline Bigelow of Troy; Rev.
Sommers (9-3/5)
5667. Marcy, Sarah, 4, only dau of Hon. William L., d 4/13/31 in Albany (funeral
from 132 State St.) (1-4/14)
5668. Marcy, William L., attorney, of Troy m Dolly Newell of Sturbridge, MA in
S (probably a double ceremony - see the marr of John Kennedy, merchant,
of Lansingburgh) (9-10/13/12)
5669. Marcy, William L., Esq., comptroller of NY State, m 4/29/24 Cornelia
Knower, dau of Benjamin, Esq., state treasurer, in Albany; Rev. Dr.
Chester (3-5/10 and 8-5/12)
5670. Markell, Henry, 39, late a Congressman, d 8/30/31 in Palatine, NY
(1-9/6)
5671. Markham, Anna (Mrs.), 48, d 4/19/11 in Jay (smallpox) ("The editor of
the American Mercury [Hartford, CT] is desired to insert the foregoing")
(7-5/10)
5672. Marks, Benoni H. m 7/1/24 Ann D. Garratt, dau of Maj. John, in Burlington
(Ots. Co.); Rev. Daniel Nash (3-7/12)
5673. Marr, William A. m 4/21/21 Catharine Rosecrants, both of Poughkeepsie;
Rev. C. C. Cuyler (8-4/25)
5674. Marriott, Henry, 48(?), d 3/12/27 in Poughkeepsie (8-3/14)
5675. Marselis, Gilbert, 30, d 5/27/27 in Troy (9-6/1)
5676. Marsh, Austin C. m 12/25/22 Zaida Case, both of Amenia; Rev. Wilson
(8-1/1/23)
5677. Marsh, Benjamin m 12/24/05 Catherine Philips, both of Troy; Rev. Coe
(9-1/7/06)
5678. Marsh, George, Esq., attorney, 35 or 85?, d 10/11/32 in Plattsburgh
(4 [Keeseville Herald]-10/14)
5679. Marsh, Harriet, 26, wf of George P., Esq. and dau of late Col. Ozias
Buel, d 8/16/33 in Burlington, VT (heart disease) (7-8/24)
5680. Marsh, John m 12/27/95 Roxana Shaw, dau of Joseph (all of Morris'
Patent, town of Unadilla) (3-12/31)
5681. Marsh, Joseph (Col.), 90, (a Rev. patriot) d "in the District of
Southwark," PA (7-12/23/26)
5682. Marsh, Matilda (Miss) d 5/1/93 in Poughkeepsie (8-5/8)
5683. Marsh, Samuel Wilder m 4/25/27 Temperance Catharine Havens in Plattsburgh;
Rev. Halsey (7-4/28)
5684. Marsh, Stewart C. of the firm of Marsh and Compton m 6/23/29 Amelia Martha
Bulkley, dau of John, Esq., in NYC; Rev. Snodgrass. All of NYC (1-6/25)
5685. Marsh, Sylvanus L. m 12/15/19 Sally Thorn, dau of William of Plattsburgh,
in P (7-12/18)
5686. Marshall, _____? (This is a mutilated segment of a death record reading
in its entirety: "last Saturday at the residence of his brother, Mr.
Elathon Marshall." [newspaper published Wednesday, May 9, 1830])
(8-5/9/30)
5687. Marshall, Bartlet m 9/30/23 Betsey Lattin, dau of Nathaniel, all of
Pleasant Valley; Rev. Clark (8-10/8)
5688. Marshall, Ellithan of Kinderhook m 1/8/27 Elizabeth Darrow of Poughkeepsie;
Rev. Cuyler (8-1/10)
5689. Marshall, Frederick W. of NYC m 6/11/29 Ann R. Tufts, dau of late William,
Esq. of Cambridge, MA; Rev. McMurray (1-6/15)
5690. Marshall, George, 4, s of George C. and Mary, d 10/22/34 in Poughkeepsie
(8-11/5)

5691. Marshall, George C. of Pleasant Valley m 1/16/27 Mary Balding of Poughkeepsie; Rev. Dr. Reed (8-1/17)
5692. Marshall, George W. of Clinton m 12/13/21 Catharine Pells, dau of John A. of Poughkeepsie; Rev. M. Wynkoop (8-12/19)
5693. Marshall, Henry, 75, d 2/7/24 in Hyde Park (8-2/11)
5694. Marshall, Henry S. m 12/5/16 Sarah Allen, dau of John I. (All of Clinton?) (8-12/11)
5695. Marshall, Hiram of Hyde Park m 9/17/30 Hannah E. Haight of Pleasant Valley; Rev. Cahoone (8-9/22)
5696. Marshall, Isaac m 12/24/34 Eliza A. Lawrence, dau of Robert, Esq.; Rev. William N. Sayre. All of Pleasant Valley (8-12/31)
5697. Marshall, J., late of Newcastle-upon-Tyne, England, m 10/19/34 H. Brownell, dau of A. Brownell, Esq. of Dutchess Co., NY; Rev. L. S. Rexford (8-10/29)
5698. Marshall, James d 4/18/15 in Clinton (Dut. Co.) ("an old inhabitant of that town") (8-4/26)
5699. Marshall, Jennet, 15 mo, dau of Paul, d 12/13/26 in Plattsburgh (7-12/16)
5700. Marshall, John m 11/2/17 Sally Ann Rosekrans, both of Albany (9-11/4)
5701. Marshall, John m 2/2/28 Caroline Williams, both of Washington (Dut. Co.); Rev. Rider (8-3/12)
5702. Marshall, John V., merchant, of Clinton (Dut. Co.) m 10/19/14 Sally _?_ of Fishkill; Rev. Jinks (8-11/2)
5703. Marshall, Lewis m 10/11/26 Sally Angevine, dau of Eli; Rev. Clark. All of Pleasant Valley (8-10/18)
5704. Marshall, Rebecka, dau of Paul, d 7/18/27 in Plattsburgh (7-7/21)
5705. Marshall, Stephen, editor of the Westchester Herald, m 3/22/20 Margaret Sherwood, dau of Maj. J. F., in Mount Pleasant (West. Co.); Rev. George Bourne (8-3/29)
5706. Marshall, Thomas Henry m 11/28/31 Sophia Fryer, both of Albany; Rev. Ferris (1-12/31)
5707. Marten, James B. of NYC m 8/20/28 Elizabeth Cronkrite of Freedom; Rev. Dr. Cuyler (8-8/27)
5708. Marten, Paul, merchant, m 9/22/29 Eliza Mason, dau of late Judge Mason of Poughkeepsie; Rev. Dr. Cuyler (8-9/23)
5709. Martin, Charles L. (Col.) of Martinsburg m 8/18/29 Theodosia Benham of Lowville (Lewis Co.) in L; Rev. I. Clinton (1-8/24)
5710. Martin, Elkanan (Mr.), 34, d 7/5/06 in Troy ("descended from a... family of Rehoboth,"MA (surv by wf and 5 ch) (9-7/8)
5711. Martin, Eliza C., 22, wf of Rev. Edward W. of Hampton and oldest dau of Rev. Charles Lee Hall, d 8/30/20 in New Lisbon (Ots. Co.) 9-10/19)
5712. Martin, Elizabeth, 45, wf of Andrew, d 6/25/18 in Hudson (6-6/30)
5713. Martin, Henry G. (Maj.), 50, d 11/12/22 at his home in Red Hook (8-11/20)
5714. Martin, Hiram m 1/7/21 Anginetta M. Webster, both of Amenia; Rev. Culver (8-2/7)
5715. Martin, James of Poughkeepsie m 11/27/34 Clarissa Tallmadge of Pleasant Valley; Rev. Buttolph (8-12/3)
5716. Martin, Jared W. of NYC m 11/4/26 Elizabeth Albertson of Poughkeepsie; Rev. Cushman (8-11/8)
5717. Martin, Michael S., Esq. of Red Hook m 11/2/16 Sally Benton, only dau of Dr. Orange Benton of Athens, NY, in A; Rev. Joseph Prentiss (6-11/5 and 8-11/13)
5718. Martin, Solomon d in Poughkeepsie (8-4/30/34)
5719. Martin, Truman m 2/15/16 Mary Coe; Rev. Bedell. All of Hudson (6-2/20)
5720. Martin, Walter (Hon.), 69, d 12/10/34 "at his mansion in Martinsburgh" (7-12/20)
5721. Marvin, Curtis B., merchant, of Hudson m Huldah Read of Reading, CT in R (6-6/18/05)
5722. Marvin, Francis m 12/7/26 Margaret Morey of Freedom; Rev. Cuyler (8-12/13)
5723. Marvin, Jared "and his wife" (not named) d "recently" in Champlain (7-1/8/13)
5724. Marvin, Jonathan m 12/18/14 Mary Seaver, both of Troy (9-12/20)
5725. Marvin, Jonathan D. (Dr.), late of Lyme, CT, m 12/31/11 Maria R. Bloom of Clinton (Dut. Co.), NY; Rev. Clark (8-1/8/12)
5726. Marvin, Joseph C. m 12/29/25 Eliza Crombie, dau of Col. William, in Otsego; Rev. John Smith (3-1/2/26)

5727. Marvin, Maria, wf of Dr. Jonathan D., d 6/11/14 in Clinton (Dut. Co.) (8-6/15)
5728. Marvin, Nathan d 7/3/06 in Exeter (Ots. Co.) (killed by the fall of a log from a log building) (funeral sermon by Rev. George Elliot of Canajoharie)(3-7/31)
5729. Marvin, Rowland m 2/26/20 Sally McForhn, dau of Daniel, all of Clinton (Dut. Co.); Rev. Clark (8-3/1)
5730. Marvin, Sabrina, 47, consort of David, d 4/25/24 at her home in Otsego (Fly Creek) (3-5/3)
5731. Marvin, Valentine, merchant, of Troy m 5/14/27 Phoebe Scudder, dau of Moses, Esq. of Huntington, L.I., NY in H; Rev. Brown (9-3/22)
5732. Marvin, William, 23, s of Abraham, d 5/9/19 in Cooperstown (3-5/17)
5733. Marvine, Edward F. (Maj.) of the firm of Gould and Marvine, merchants, of Delhi m 4/5/30 Frances J. Perry, dau of Charles B., Esq. of Hobart (Dela. Co.) in H; Rev. Hewlett R. Peters (1-4/12)
5734. Marvine, John C. m 11/12/15 Nancy B. Thatcher, both of Cooperstown, in C; Rev. Nash (3-11/16)
5735. Mason, Alvira, 24, wf of Milton S., d 6/16/21 in Amenia (surv by her husband and an infant child) (8-6/27)
5736. Mason, Darius, 35, s of Aaron, d 2/12/13 in Plattsburgh. Also in the same town: 2/18 Chloe, 51, Aaron's wf; 2/22 Lydia, 15, his dau; 3/18 John, 19, his son; 3/22 Thomas, 9, his son. (All died "of the prevailing epidemic") (7-4/2)
5736a. Mason, Eliakim m 12/28/17 Sally Broadwell in Plattsburgh; Rev. Halsey (7-1/3/18)
5737. Mason, George of Fort Ann m 1/18/27 Jane Gardiner of Troy; J. Martindale, Esq. (9-1/19)
5738. Mason, Henry M. (Rev.) of Salem, NJ m Adaline Hull, dau of late Gen. Hull of Cheshire, CT, at the home of H. Whittelsey, Esq. of Leeds (Greene Co.); Rev. Prentiss (1-12/13/30)
5739. Mason, Huldah, 34, wf of Ondley, d 3/20/13 in Peru, NY (7-4/2)
5740. Mason, James, 105, d "recently" in Greenbush (1-2/6/29)
5741. Mason, John M. (Rev.), D.D., 59, d 12/27/29 in NYC ("was for many years one of the most distinguished clergymen in the United States") (8-12/30)
5742. Mason, Joseph m 10/22/03 Elizabeth Dutcher, both of Poughkeepsie; Rev. Chase (8-10/25)
5743. Mason, Leonard, Esq. m 1/4/19 Helen E. Caldwell, niece of Hon. James Emott; Rev. Reed. All of Poughkeepsie (8-1/6)
5744. Mason, Milton S. m 11/4/23 Mary Ingraham, dau of Thomas, all of Amenia; Rev. Samuel Merwin (8-11/12)
5745. Mason, Ondley, 37, d 4/1/13 in Peru, NY (7-4/9)
5746. Mason, Stephen (Rev.) of Washington (Dut. Co.) m 5/1/23 Phebe S. Tallmadge, dau of late John, Esq. of Warren, CT, in W; Rev. Peter Starr (8-5/14 and 3-5/19)
5747. Mason, Thomas m 12/30/27 Sophia Webster, both of Troy; Rev. Willis (9-1/1/28)
5748. Massoneau, Catharine, 63, wf of Claudius G., d 4/3/32 in Red Hook (8-4/25)
5749. Masten, John B. m 3/15/27 Elizabeth Horton; Rev. C. C. Cuyler (8-3/28)
5750. Masters, John M., Esq., 55, d 12/28/19 when thrown from his wagon en route from Philadelphia to his home in Warwick Township, PA (8-1/19/20)
5751. Masters, Josiah (Hon.), 57, of Schaghticoke, NY d 6/30/22 in Fairfield, CT (late a Congressman and formerly a first judge of the court of common pleas of Rensselaer Co., NY) (9-7/9 and 3-7/15)
5752. Masters, Nicholas M., Esq. of Troy m 9/12/15 AnnT. Thomas, dau of John, Esq. of Sandy Hill (Wash. Co.), in S. H.; Rev. Armstrong (9-9/19)
5753. Mastin, Abraham of Poughkeepsie m 8/12/24 Mary Forman of Hyde Park; Rev. C. C. Cuyler (8-8/18)
5754. Mastin, Barnet of Clinton (Dut. Co.) m 11/6/17 Helen Ryan of Poughkeepsie; Rev. Reed (8-11/12)
5755. Mastin, Bernard d 8/26/17 in Poughkeepsie (8-8/27)
5756. Mastin, Silas m 1/1/25 Eliza Finch, both of Stanford; Rev. C. P. Wilson (8-1/12)
5757. Maston, Seril m 1/2/20 Sarah M. Porter in Kinderhook; Rev. Sickles (6-1/11)
5758. Mather, Charlotte Maria, wf of James O. and dau of L. Cruttenden, Esq., d 9/11/31 in Albany (funeral from the Eagle Tavern) (1-9/13)

5759. Mather, D. L. (Dr.), 24, s of Bethel Mather, Esq., d 6/5/31 in
Schaghticoke (pulmonary complaint) (1-6/17)
5760. Mather, D. W. of the firm of N. Monro and Co. of Jordan m 6/13/31 Caroline
M. Merriman, dau of C. J., Esq. of Elbridge, in E; Rev. T. Stow (1-7/2)
5761. Mather, Elias, merchant, m 2/18/29 Mrs. Cornelia Washburn; Rev. Ferris.
All of Albany (1-2/20)
5762. Mather, Helen, 4, oldest dau of William, d 12/5/28 in Troy (9-12/12/28)
5763. Mather, Russell m 1/9/16 Mary Graves in Cooperstown; Rev. John Smith
(3-1/18)
5764. Mather, Samuel, merchant, m 9/14/07 Catherine Livingston, both of Troy;
Rev. Dr. Nott (9-9/22)
5765. Mathers, Alfred P. m 8/17/23 Mrs. Salona Alcott in Laurens; John Blood,
Jr., Esq. (3-8/25)
5766. Matterson, Caleb m 11/30/26 Polly Crandall in Exeter; Elijah Babcock, Esq.
(3-12/4)
5767. Matterson, Reubin of Hoosick m 11/26/20 Sally Cronk of White Creek in W.C.;
Daniel Mosher, Esq. (9-12/12)
5768. Matteson, Abel, 2nd, of Burlington (Ots. Co.) m 2/9/26 Keziah Rudd, dau
of Joseph of Edmeston, in E; Elder J. C. Hulbert (3-2/13)
5769. Matteson, O. B., attorney, m 5/17/30 Mary Hurlburt, dau of Kellogg
Hurlburt; Rev. Aiken. All of Utica (1-5/21)
5770. Matthews, Frederick, Esq. d 6/4/30 in Albany (funeral from the home of Mrs.
Lockwood on North Pearl St. "with carriages waiting opposite the Capitol
Park") (1-6/5)
5771. Matthews, Jesse (Capt.) m Mrs. Susannah Peas in Hudson (6-12/18/04)
5772. Matthews, John m 8/21/23 Anna Maria Hoffman; Rev. Cuyler. All of
Poughkeepsie (8-8/27)
5773. Matthews, John of Albany m 10/24/29 Hester Gibson of Schenectady; Rev.
Goodsell (1-10/30)
5774. Matthews, Samuel d 7/19/20 and Mary Matthews, his wife, d 7/20. Both
died in Poughkeepsie. He b 9/25/1756 and she 12/15/1759; they were m
10/28/1783; she d of breast cancer. Three ch survive the parents. At
time of his death, Samuel was a ruling elder of the Reformed Dutch Church
in Poughkeepsie) (8-7/26)
5775. Matthewson, Bernard, farmer, of Stanford (Dut. Co.) d 9/26/23 at his home
in Stanford (8-10/1)
5776. Mattison, Asahel m 12/31/15 Mary Merriss (in Hartwick?) (3-1/11/16)
5777. Maulin, Moses m 9/26/20 Harriet Levans, both of Lansingburgh; Rev. Dr.
Coe (9-10/10)
5778. Maunsell, Elizabeth, 87, relict of late Lt. Gen. John of H. B. M.
(His British Majesty's?) service, d at her home in Harlaem Heights
(9-11/14/15)
5779. Maverick, Peter, 51, d 6/7/31 in NYC (1-6/10)
5780. Maverick, Samuel of NYC m 5/17/29 Clara Reynolds, oldest dau of Philip
of Johnstown, at St. John's Church in Johnstown; Rev. Whipple (1-5/22)
5781. Maxey, Jonathan (Dr.) d 6/4/20 at his home in South Carolina College
(had been for 16 yrs president of that institution and, earlier, had
been president of Union College in Schenectady, NY) (8-6/21)
5782. Maxon, _____ d 8/2/31 in Franklin, Dela. Co. (suicide by hanging) (1-8/15)
5783. Maxon, Steward, 18, d 1/5/24 in Troy (9-1/13)
5784. May, Charles (Lt.), 20, 6th Regiment, U.S. Infantry, a native of Vermont
"and a graduate of the Military Academy of July last", d 1/19/30 at
Jefferson Barracks, MO ("fell in a duel") (1-2/18)
5785. May, Theodore (Dr.) of Pittstown m 8/2/06 Nancy Stitt of Pittstown in P;
Rev. Fraelich (9-8/5)
5786. Maybee, _____ (Dr.) of Little Falls d 8/30/24 in Ballston Spa ("dropsy of
the chest") (2-8/31)
5787. Mayer, Philip F. (Rev.), pastor of Zion's Church in Loonenburg (Athens, NY),
m 5/24/04 Lucy W. Rodman; Rev. Jonathan Judd (6-5/29)
5788. Maynard, E. A., editor of the Oneida Observer, m 1/28/30 Wealthy Velona
Hart, in Utica; Rev. Dorr. All of Utica (1-2/1)
5789. Mayo, Asa of Troy, Ohio m 7/25/29 Amanda Fay of Warwick, MA in Albany,
NY; Rev. Bury (1-7/28)
5790. Maywood, Robert C. of NYC m 4/19/28 Mrs. Louisa Williams of Albany in Troy;
Rev. Willis (9-5/2)

5791. Mazeen, Ezekiel, 27,(great grandson of "the GREAT UNCAS", protector of the white settlers in the area), d 5/2/26 (interred "in the Royal burial place of the Mohegans in Norwich, Conn."). (The funeral was attended by Rev. William Palmer of the Baptist church. Mrs. Goddard, wf of Hon. Calvin, "served a collation" to the tribe at the funeral.) (3-5/15)
5792. Mead, Caroline, about 14, dau of Thaddeus, d 12/1/21 (9-12/4)
5793. Mead, Caroline Theresa, 3, youngest dau of George and Maria, d 6/24/29 in Poughkeepsie (8-7/2)
5794. Mead, George, merchant, of Poughkeepsie m 11/28/16 Maria Ann Spicer, dau of Francis, in NYC; Rev. C. C. Cuyler (8-12/4)
5795. Mead, Henry, 2, youngest s of George and Maria, d 8/8/30 in Poughkeepsie (8-8/11)
5796. Mead, Isaac, printer, of NYC, formerly of Poughkeepsie, m 11/2/16 Catharine Munn, dau of Rev. Benjamin of Percipany (sic), NJ in P (8-12/11)
5797. Mead, Joel of Pleasant Valley m 12/24/28 Mary Ann Boyce of NYC; Rev. Phebus (8-12/31)
5798. Mead, John K. m 2/28/27 Jane Amanda Sutherland, dau of Roger B., deceased, in Amenia; Rev. C. P. Wilson (8-3/21)
5799. Mead, Michael m 6/24/02 Elizabeth Van Tine, both of Pittstown, in P; Rev. Covell (9-6/30)
5800. Mead, Ralph of Galway m 2/21/22 Isabella Stewart of Amsterdam; Rev. Otterson (2-3/6)
5801. Mead, Samuel Henry, inf s of George and Maria, d 9/12/27 in Poughkeepsie (8-9/19)
5802. Mead, William, 25, d 11/10/18 in Poughkeepsie (member of Baptist Church) (8-11/18)
5803. Mechlar, Jobe(?), 40, d 6/2/07 in Spencertown (6-6/9)
5804. Mecord, William m Polly ___? of Clinton (Dut. Co.) (8-3/20/11)
5805. Medbury, Nathan (Capt.), Master of St. John's Lodge (Masonic order), d 3/15/22 in Greenfield (funeral sermon by Rev. William A. Clark; buried with Masonic honors) (2-3/20)
5806. Medbury, Nathaniel, Esq.,member of the state assembly from Chenango Co., d 2/2/13 in Albany (9-2/9)
5807. Meder, John and John McClenahan of Hudson, NY (the former master and the latter mate of the brig "Argo") d in New Orleans, LA "in the morning of life") (yellow fever) (6-9/21/19)
5808. Meeks, James C. of NYC m 5/17/30 Sarah Ann Harrison, dau of Frederick of Poughkeepsie, at Red Hook Landing; Rev. Kettell (1-5/25)
5809. Meier, John H. (Rev.), minister of the Reformed Dutch Church in Schenectady, d 9/11/06 in Albany (6-9/23)
5810. Meigs, Charles N. m 12/22/31 Phebe Parsons; Rev. Dr. Luckey. All of Albany (1-12/24)
5811. Meigs, Giles of Middletown, CT m 10/19/05 Macdala Yates of Albany, NY (9-10/22)
5812. Meigs, Return Jonathan (Col.) d 1/28/23 "at the Cherokee Agency" (3-3/3)
5813. Melendy, James m 3/9/27 Sylvia Bugbee, both of Troy; Rev. Willis (9-3/13)
5814. Melick, John (Capt.) of Lansingburgh m 4/30/03 Jennet Oliphant of Waterford in Ballston (9-5/3)
5815. Melius, Anthony m 2/29/20 Catherine Bogert in Hudson; John Raynor, Esq. All of H (6-3/7)
5816. Melius, William W. and Rufus, sons of S. W., d 9/15/19 in Livingston (6-9/21)
5817. Mellen, James, druggist, of Hudson m 9/29/16 Hannah Punderson of Red Hook in R. H. (6-10/1)
5818. Mellendey, Elias m 10/16/28 Maria Defriest. All of Troy (9-10/17)
5819. Melona, Julia Ann, 7, dau of David A., d 2/14/19 in Poughkeepsie (8-2/17)
5820. Melord, John m Eliza Ann Thorn, both of NYC, in NYC (9-1/2/27)
5821. Member, George S. m 7/20/15 AnnDepew, both of Poughkeepsie; Rev. C. C. Cuyler (8-8/2)
5822. Mercerau, Job T. (Capt.) of Union (Broome Co.) m 11/6/28 Harriet Wheeler, dau of Cyrus of Northeast; Rev. C. P. Wilson (8-11/12)
5823. Merchant, George, 73, d 8/14/30 in Albany (deceased a long-time resident there) (1-8/17)
5824. Merchant, Levi m 12/31/22 Roda Williams, both of Troy; Rev. Griffin (9-1/7/23)

5825. Meritt, Abraham d 6/14/25 at his home in Freedom (8-6/22)
5826. Merrick, Samuel m 9/12/02 Letty Weeks of Carmel; Barnabas Carver, Esq.
       (8-9/21)
5827. Merrill, Charles of Hudson, NY m 11/15/08 Anna Cramton, dau of Elon of
       Litchfield, CT, in L (6-11/29)
5828. Merrill, Lucas G., Esq., merchant, m Eunice Nichols of Gaines (Orleans Co.)
       in G; Rev. Bates (1-4/28/31)
5829. Merrill, Nathaniel, 28, formerly of Hartford, CT, d 3/1/20 in Cherry
       Valley, NY (6-3/28)
5830. Merrit, Edward B., 24, merchant, of Charlton (Sara Co.), formerly of
       Beekman (Dut. Co.) d 11/20/11 in Charlton ("interred in the burial ground
       of Waterford village")(8-12/4)
5831. Merritt, Abraham m 5/7/12 Delia Northrup, dau of William, all of Washington
       (Dut. Co.); William Thorne, Esq. (8-5/13)
5832. Merritt, Burton of Bridgewater m Constant Main, only dau of Rev. Dr. Main
       of Litchfield, in Bridgewater (3-1/31/25)
5833. Merritt, Charles m 6/28/27 Rebecca Banker, both of Troy; Dr. Howard
       (9-7/10)
5834. Merritt, Chittenden m 12/11/33 Lorinda B. Henman in Burlington, VT;
       Rev. J. E. Converse (7-12/14)
5835. Merritt, Daniel of Troy, 65, member of the Society of Friends, d 5/9/30
       in NYC (consumption) (his body brought to Albany on the steamboat
       "De Witt Clinton" "and thence to Troy in the "Matilda") (1-5/13)
5836. Merritt, E. C. of Benson, VT m 7/21/31 Caroline Remmington of Castleton,
       VT in Rochester, NY; Rev. Fillmore (1-7/29)
5837. Meserve, William m 8/16/01 Charity Hardwick, both of Hudson (6-8/20)
5838. Mesick, Jacob of Claverack m 10/10/06 Betsey Niece of Dover (Dut. Co.)
       in D (6-10/21)
5839. Mesick, John, Jr., 32, d 12/23/14 in Claverack (6-1/3/15)
5840. Mesick, Mary, 26, wf of Peter H., d 10/21/09 in Hudson (he was born in
       Hambleden, Hampshire, England) (6-10/24)
5841. Mesick, Peter H., 24, s of Henry I., d in Claverack (consumption)
       (6-12/7/10)
5842. Mesier, Abraham, 44, d 11/18/25 at Wappingers Falls (8-11/23)
5843. Mesier, Peter, Sr., 73, d 11/13/05 in NYC (8-11/19)
5844. Mesier, Peter, Esq. d 12/7/19 in NYC (for many years a resident there but
       for the last few months of Wappingers Creek (Dut. Co.) (8-12/15)
5845. Mesier, Peter J., 16, s of Matthew, Esq. of Dutchess Co., d 2/22/18 in
       NYC (graduated from Dutchess Academy; at time of death was a student
       at Columbia College (8-3/4)
5846. Mesier, Phebe (Miss), 48, dau of late Peter, d 4/19/32 at the home of
       Matthew Mesier, Esq. at Wappingers Creek (Dut. Co.) (8-4/25)
5847. Messeter, Mary, wf of Richard, d 10/3/23 in Poughkeepsie (8-10/8)
5848. Messier, Matthew of Fishkill m 8/24/00 Joanna Schenk, dau of Paul of
       Poughkeepsie; Rev. Brouwer (8-8/26)
5849. Metcalf, Chauncey m 8/10/23 Miranda Smith, dau of Jedediah, in Otsego;
       Rev. Tiffany (3-8/11)
5850. Metcalf, Elijah H., Esq., 43, d 9/14/21 in Cooperstown (3-9/17)
5851. Metcalf, Lois, 38, consort of Roger, d 11/9/15 in Cooperstown (3-11/9)
5852. Metcalf, Mary (Mrs.), 78, d 12/25/13 in Cooperstown (3-1/1/14)
5853. Metcalf, Orlando, attorney, of Canton, OH m 5/18/26 "Miss Knapp", dau of
       Charles, in New Berlin, NY (3-5/22)
5854. Metcalf, William, Esq., attorney, d 7/25/25 in Northumberland (surv by wf
       and 4 ch) (2-8/2)
5855. Meyers, William, 19, drowned 6/20/29 "above Hurl Gate" in the capsizing
       of a sail boat (1-6/24)
5856. Michael, Jeremiah m 8/2/02 Eliza Paddock in Pittstown; Lovett Head, Esq.
       All of Pittstown (9-8/18)
5857. Michel, William S., Esq., assistant Indian agent, m 7/14/18 "Jenney,
       oldest daughter of the celebrated Creek warrior, Gen. William McIntosh",
       at Thea-catch-kah near Fort Mitchell, Creek Nation (8-8/19)
5858. Middaugh, R. W. (Dr.) of Ithaca m Angeline B. Smith of Ulysses at the
       Reformed Dutch Church in Caroline (Tompkins Co.); Rev. Garrett
       Mandeville (1-6/28/30)
5859. Middlebrook, Jonathan, 22, s of Hezekiah, Jr., d 1/26/23 in Milton
       (2-1/28)

170

5860. Mildeberger, John, 34, d 1/29/07 in Hudson (6-2/17)
5861. Miles, Burrage, Jr., 26, youngest s of Maj. B. Miles, d 7/23/29 in
      Coventry (Chen. C.) (consumption) (1-8/3)
5862. Miles, John m 9/8/23 Olivia Vermiller; Rev. Barrett. All of Fishkill
      (8-9/24)
5863. Miles, Orison m 10/6/31 Semantia Peck in Jay; Rev. Orris Pier
      (4-[Keeseville Herald]-10/11)
5864. Miles, Thomas Y. m 10/10/27 Rebecca Ostrom, both of Troy; Rev. Martindale
      (9-10/12)
5865. Milford, William of the firm of Godfrey and Milford m 4/26/30 Miranda
      McKay in Geneva; Rev. J. F. McLaren. All of Geneva (1-5/3)
5866. Millard, Walter, Esq. of New Hamburgh m 11/13/34 Martha Bull, dau of
      William of NYC; Rev. William Parkinson (8-11/19)
5867. Millard, William m 3/9/23 Sarah Miter, both of Troy; Rev. Griffin (9-3/18)
5868. Milledoler, Susan, 45, wf fo Rev. Dr. Philip Milledoler, d in Haerlem, NY
      (9-8/29/15)
5870. Millee, David L., 8, only s of Thomas and Elizabeth, d 2/6/23 in Troy
      (9-2/9)
5871. Millen, John, 79, (a Rev. soldier) d 3/11/30 in Newark, NY (1-3/27)
5872. Miller, Abraham m 7/31/07 Lany Fonda, both of Brunswick;Rev. David
      Butler (9-8/4)
5873. Miller, Abraham m 1/1/32 Lucretia Miller in Plattsburgh; Rev. Frederick
      Halsey (7-1/14)
5874. Miller, Alexander, Esq. of Wallingford, VT m 9/16/07 Lucretia Robbins of
      Troy; Rev. Coe (9-9/22)
5875. Miller, Alfred of La Grange m 9/17/34 Cornelia Rogers, dau of late Dr.
      Rogers formerly of La Grange; Rev. Buttolph (8-9/24)
5876. Miller, Benjamin 7/4/11 Maria Smith, both of Gallatin, in Hudson; Rev.
      Chester (6-7/19)
5877. Miller, Charles W., 23, editor and proprietor of the Republican Advocate,
      d 11/21/31 in Batavia (1-12/10)
5878. Miller, David C. of Ballston, publisher of the Saratoga Advertiser,
      m 7/12/05 Lucy Gilbert of Stillwater (9-9/3)
5879. Miller, Elisha (Dr.), 42(?), of Ballstown d 3/9/12 in Cooperstown
      (3-3/14)
5880. Miller, Elizabeth (Mrs.), 67, d 4/24/29 (of burns) in Wilmington, Dela.
      (her clothes caught fire while she was staying at the LaFayette Hotel)
      (1-5/4)
5881. Miller, Epaphran A., merchant, of Rochester, NY m 4/28/29 Happelonia
      Vallette of Middlebury, VT m Rev. Prof. Hough (1-5/16)
5882. Miller, Henry Walter m 6/5/29 Christina Teal of Rhinebeck; Rev. W. J.
      Eyer (8-6/11)
5883. Miller, Jacob P. of Livingston m 1/2/17 Charlotte Simmons of Red Hook
      in Clermont; Rev. Wackerhagen (6-1/7)
5884. Miller, James, formerly of Cooperstown, m 3/19/26 Caroline Cramer of
      Holley (Orleans Co.) in H; Rev. John Bliss (3-4/3)
5885. Miller, James d. m 10/8/34 Elizabeth Balding; Henry Tallmadge, Esq.
      All of Stanford (Dut. Co.) (8-10/15)
5886. Miller, John (Dr.) of Fabius m 6/21/05 Phebe Adriance of Troy; Rev. Cob
      (9-6/25)
5887. Miller, John I. of Sand Lake m 2/24/16 Pamelia Filkins of Brunswick; Rev.
      Dr. Coe (9-2/27)
5888. Miller, Joseph m 7/9/29 Margaret Hancock in Poughkeepsie; Rev. Welton
      (8-7/15)
5889. Miller, Joseph R. M., Esq. of Cooperstown m 10/1/29 Harriet P. Roach of
      the Island of Barbadoes at St. __?__ 's Church in NYC; Right Rev. Bishop
      Hobart (1-10/6)
5890. Moeller, Julianna Margaret, 75, wf of Rev. Henry, d 7/12/24 in Hartwick
      (deceased was born in Germany; came to this country during the Rev. War
      with her former husband, Baron De Zetwitz (3-7/19)
5891. Miller, Loisa, 9 mo. dau of Conklin Miller, d in Hudson (6-10/12/13)
5892. Miller, Lucretia, 76, relict of Burnet Miller d 11/10/15 in Plattsburgh
      (7-11/11)
5893. Miller, Maria (Miss), dau of Dr. John, d 10/22/23 in Plattsburgh
      (7-10/25)

5894. Miller, Mary, inf dau of Rev. Frederick T., d 12/31/25 in Cooperstown (3-1/2/26)
5895. Miller, Matthias B. (Dr.), formerly of Dutchess Co., d in Savannah, GA (8-3/22/92)
5896. Miller, Morris S., 45, first judge of Oneida Co., d 11/16/24 in Utica (3-11/22)
5897. Miller, Nathan m 10/6/16 Hannah Barnes, dau of Jeremiah, in Plattsburgh; Nathan Carver, Esq. (7-10/12)
5898. Miller, Samuel m 6/8/04 Phebe Kidney, both of Poughkeepsie; Rev. Brower (8-6/12)
5899. Miller, Theodorus, 18, s of Gen. J. Miller of East Hampton, L.I. and brother of Jeremiah, Jr., Esq. of NYC, d 1/15/30 on the ship "Ajax" in the China Sea (1-4/26)
5900. Miller, Westen m 3/8/20 Sybill Berry; Rev. Price. All of Clinton (8-3/15)
5901. Miller, William (Rev.), pastor of the Asbury African Methodist Episcopal Church in NYC m 12/24/29 Harriet Judah of Charleston, SC in Philadelphia; Rev. Dr. Engles (1-1/12/30)
5902. Millies, John B. m 11/26/23 Harriet Lapham (8-12/3)
5903. Milliken, Sarah Ann (Miss), 18, d 7/18/30 in Schoharie (1-7/23)
5904. Millington, Jacob (Dr.), late of Herkimer Co., d 4/11/30 in St. Louis, MO (1-5/5)
5905. Millit, Daniel m 3/16/02 Mrs. Bashaba Gibbs, both of Pawling; George Casey, Esq. (8-3/23)
5906. Mills, Abraham m 3/17/16 Lydia Slater, both of Poughkeepsie; Rev. Lewis Leonard (8-3/27)
5907. Mills, Caspr M. m 11/28/29 Mary Hawkins, both of Poughkeepsie; Rev. Dr. Cuyler (8-12/2)
5908. Mills, Channing, 49, of the firm of Mills and Rider d 10/31/29 in Albany (funeral at his late home, 36 Dean St.) (1-11/2)
5909. Mills, Eleazer of Catskill m 9/21/29 Charity H. Bailey of Smithtown, L. I.; Rev. Greene (1-9/29)
5910. Mills, Henry m 5/24/06 Sally Van De Bogert, both of Poughkeepsie; Rev. Palmer (8-5-27)
5911. Mills, Ira, formerly of Lackawaxen, PA, drowned 4/20/29 in the Neversink River (1-4/30)
5912. Mills, John, Esq. formerly of Great Bealings, Suffolk, England, d 7/22/05 in Claverack, NY (surv by wf and children) (6-7/30)
5913. Mills, John m Polly Miller, dau of Stephen, in Claverack; Rev. Gebherd. All of Claverack (6-10/21/06)
5914. Mills, Mary Ann, 23, youngest dau of Bradley, Esq., d 2/27/29 in Kent, CT (1-3/17)
5915. Mills, Nathan m 6/5/19 Jane Ann Vail, both of Fishkill, in Poughkeepsie; Rev. Dr. Covil (8-6/9)
5916. Mills, Richard m Mrs. Ann Taylor in Batavia; T. Fitch, Esq. (9-12/19/28)
5917. Mills, Samuel m 11/27/14 Mary Damon in Burlington, VT (7-12/3)
5918. Mills, Seymour B., 19, s of Chauncey of Albany, d 9/20/29 in Albany (funeral from his father's home, 36 Dean St.) (1-9/22)
5919. Mills, Susan (Miss), dau of Capt. Roger of Canajoharie, d 1/8/08 at Cherry Valley (3-1/16)
5920. Mills, William (Dr.) of England, father of Mrs. Charles Belden and Mrs. George Belden of NYC, d 5/18/30 at the home of Ames Belden, Esq. in Carmel(The deceased had prescribed vaccine for the prevention of small pox "for some time before Dr. Jenner's publication." (1-5/22)
5921. Millus, Philo m 1/15/29 Adeline Knickerbacker in Pine Plains; Rev. C. P. Wilson (8-1/21)
5922. Minard, Isaac, 57, d 11/1/31 in NYC (1-11/3)
5923. Miner, Elisha of Pawling m 7/21/16 Amy Wright of Sherman (8-8/7)
5924. Minick, Jacob of Claverack m 10/18/06 Eliza Nase, dau of John of Dover, in D; Rev. Barnard (8-10/21)
5925. Minkler, Peter m 2/17/12 Betsey Gorsline in Hillsdale; Rev. Williams. All of H (6-3/23)
5926. Minor, John (Rev.), 65, d 7/5/08 in Southeast (8-7/20)
5927. Mitchel, Eustatia (Mrs.), 88, d 9/2/27 (8-9/5)
5928. Mitchel, James m 10/13/28 Eliza Munsey, both of Grafton, in Petersburgh; Jonathan Henning, Esq. (9-11/11)

5929. Mitchel, John J. m 5/23/21 Maria Groesbeck, both of Albany; Rev. Dr. Coe (9-5/29)
5930. Mitchell, ____ (Lt.) of the U.S. Army m 9/22/31 Louisa Trask Clark, dau of William A., Esq. of Cornwall,in C; Rev. M. Thomas (1-10/1)
5931. Mitchell, Benjamin d 11/24/32 in Union Vale ("an aged member of the Society of Friends") (8-11/28)
5932. Mitchell, Benjamin H. m 8/12/26 Maria Jane Barlow, dau of Elisha C., Esq. All of Freedom (8-8/16)
5933. Mitchell, Charles, Esq. (an attorney, a native of Conn., and s of "the hon. Judge Mitchell of Connecticut) d 6/11/31 in Baltimore, MD (1-6/17)
5934. Mitchell, Freelove, 75, d 5/7/27 at the home of (blurred) Barnes of Poughkeepsie (8-5/23)
5935. Mitchell, Hannah (Miss), 61, sister of late Thomas of Poughkeepsie, d 10/10-04 (8-10/30)
5936. Mitchell, Hugh, 101, d in Cherry Valley (born in Carrickfergus in Ireland; came to this country about 1764) (3-1/21/22)
5937. Mitchell, Isaac, 52, editor of the Northern Politician, d 11/26/12 (in Poughkeepsie?) (8-12/2)
5938. Mitchell, Margaret N., 50, d 11/8/29 in Poughkeepsie (surv by husband "and a numerous family") (8-11/11)
5939. Mitchell, Nelson m 1/12/30 Mary Ann McNary, both of Hyde Park, in H. P.; John S. Wagner, Esq. (8-1/20)
5940. Mitchell, Stephen, 68, (a Rev. patriot) d 11/21/34 at his home in Poughkeepsie (joined Methodist Church about 20 yrs before his death) (8-11/26)
5941. Mitchell, Thomas m 4/22/34 Ruth M. Tysen; Rev. Dr. Reed. All of Pough- keepsie (8-4/30)
5942. Mitchell, Thomas B., attorney, m 12/22/31 Helen Eliza Moyer, dau of John Henry Moyer, in Canajoharie; Rev. Wells (1-12/29)
5943. Mitchill, Freelove, 74, widow of Uriah, d 5/7/27 in Pleasant Valley (Dutchess Co.)
5944. Mix, (blurred) d "last week" at the home of Peter Vandenbergh in Hudson (The deceased, male, "said that he owned land at the westward and had left two watches in Hudson to be repaired.") (6-12/25/04)
5945. Mix, ____ , s of James, d "recently" in Albany (funeral from James' home "on Howard st. - first corner below the jail") (1-12/13/31)
5946. Mix, Dorothy, 52, wf of Rufus of Hartwick, d 3/26/14 in H (3-4/2)
5947. Mix, Ephraim d 4/6/13 in Hudson (6-4/13)
5948. Mixton, ____ , about 53, one of the chiefs of the Onondaga tribe of Indians, d "recently" in Onondaga (Onon. Co.).(He was "scarcely inferior to the celebrated Schenandoa in strength of mind and as possesssirg those qualities which adorn the human heart"; for more than 30 yrs a friend to the white people) (8-12/27/20)
5949. Mochrie, Edward of Albany m 4/13/18 Sally Mariah Cogswell of Troy in Waterford; Rev. Blatchford (9-4/21)
5950. Mofat, Anthony (Capt.) m 6/19/20 Julia Curtis, oldest dau of Abner, Esq., in NYC (8-6/20)
5951. Moffitt, Robert, senior proprietor of the Northern Budget, d 5/4/07 in Troy (9-5/5 and 6-5/12)--(He died at age 38)
5952. Moncieus, Jacob, merchant, of Albany m 4/3/06 Jane Ann Barber, dau of late Col. William of Poughkeepsie; Rev. Brouwer (8-4/8)
5953. Monell, Janett P., 15, dau of Hon. Robert of Greene, NY, d 10/31/31 in Great Bend, PA (1-11/12)
5954. Monell, Maria, 49, wf of Joseph D., Esq., d 2/24/31 in Hudson (1-3/7)
5955. Monfoort, Henry m 5/13/98 Deborah Phillips, both of Fishkill; Rev. Van Vranken (8-5/22)
5956. Monfoort, John m 11/30/11 Jane Monfoort, both of Fishkill; Rev. C. C. Cuyler (8-12/4)
5957. Monfoort, Peter B. m Maria Dubois in Fishkill (8-12/3/17)
5958. Monfort, Cornelius m 11/23/21 Sally Overacker, dau of Emanuel, Esq., in Freedom; Rev. Clark (8-11/28)
5959. Monfort, Cornelius, 19, d 12/17/23 in Poughkeepsie (8-12/24)
5960. Monfort, James, 58, d at his home in Fishkill (8-3/30/25)
5961. Monfort, Jeremiah V. K. m 12/3/28 Susan Patterson, both of Freedom; Rev. Dwight (8-12/10)

5962. Monroe, Amos of Troy m Jane C. Merrifield of Catskill in C (9-1/19/27)
5963. Monroe, James, Jr. of Virginia m Elizabeth Mary Douglass, dau of late
George, Esq. of NYC, in NYC; Rev. Whelpley (3-4/15/22)
5964. Montbrun, Deshons m 6/2/24 Mary Matilda Herrick in Plattsburg; Levi Platt,
Esq. All of Plattsburgh (7-6/5)
5965. Monteath, Walter N. (Lt.) of the U.S. Navy d 10/17/19 in Portsmouth, NH
(7-11/13)
5966. Monteith, Anna, wf of Rev. Walter, d 1/20/30 at the home of her father,
Abraham G. Lansing, in Watervliet (funeral from 368 North Market St.,
Albany)(1-1/22)
5967. Monteith, Walter (Rev.) of Schenectady m Anna Lansing, dau of Abraham G.,
Esq., in Albany; Rev. Dr. Chester (3-1/27/23)
5968. Montfoort, Theodorus, farmer, of Fishkill d 10/12/16 en route home from
Poughkeepsie when a load of boards fell on him in the upsetting of his
wagon (8-10/16)
5969. Monty, James, 58, (a Rev. soldier [Col. Hazen's Regiment] and a pensioner)
d 7/9/19 in Peru, NY (7-7/17)
5970. Mooers, Benjamin (Gen.) m 7/22/18 Mary Hughes, wid of late Gen. J. M.
Hughes of NYC, in Plattsburgh; Rev. Whelpley (7-7/25)
5971. Mooers, Benjamin H., merchant, of Plattsburgh m 2/17/14 Margaret P. Miller,
dau of Dr. John, in Plattsburgh (7-2/19/14)
5972. Mooers, Charles S. m 1/29/22 Julia A. Platt at the home of Hon. William
Bailey in Plattsburgh; Rev. S. W. Whelpley. All of Plattsburgh
(7-2/2)
5973. Mooers, John W. (Lt.) of U.S. Navy, s of Gen. Benjamin of Plattsburgh,
m 10/26/30 Lucy Miller, dau of late John S. of New London, CT, in
Brooklyn, NY; Rev. Levings (1-11/5)
5974. Mooers, Julia A., 25, wf of Charles S., d 7/5/24 at Cumberland Head near
Plattsburgh (7-7/10)
5975. Mooers, Moses H., about 57, d 3/8/13 in Champlain (7-3/12)
5976. Mooers, Susan, about 3, dau of Dr. Benjamin J., d 4/7/22 in Plattsburgh
(7-4/13)
5977. Mooklar, James, 47, d 5/3/08 in Hudson (6-5/10)
5978. Moon, _____, child of John, d in Hudson (6-5/18/10)
5979. Mooney, Hamilton m 9/3/16 Catharine M. Cane, both of Poughkeepsie; Rev.
John Reed (8-9/11)
5980. Moor, E. P., one of the editors of the Waterloo Observer, m 6/18/29
Elizabeth G. Sholes, oldest dau of John, Esq., in Waterloo; Rev.
A. D. Lane (1-6/29)
5981. Moore, _____, wid of Pliny, d "a few days since" in Champlain (7-5/7/25)
5982. Moore, _____, 89, consort of late Jonathan, d 4/16/26 in Butternuts
(Jonathan was a pioneer settler in B; he and his wf lived there 40 yrs;
he was buried in the Episcopal Church cemetery) (3-5/1)
5983. Moore, Allen R. (Hon.) of Champlain m 7/9/32 Eliza Woolley, dau of William
I., Esq. of Pleasant Valley, in P. V.; Rev. Wilde (8-7/11)
5984. Moore, Amasa, attorney, m 1/18/26 Charlotte Mooers, dau of Gen. Benjamin;
Rev. Halsey. All of Plattsburgh (7-1/21)
5985. Moore, Andrew of the firm of C. and A. Moore, merchants, of Red Hook
Landing m 12/29/12 Mary Bartholomew, oldest dau of Capt. Andrew, at
the home of the latter;Rev. Kittle (6-1/5/13)
5986. Moore, Andrew of Fort Ann m 5/10/27 Harriet Barney, dau of James of
Queensbury, in Q (8-5/16)
5987. Moore, Benjamin (Dr.), 57, of Champlain d 9/19/31 (this report copied
by the Albany editor from the Plattsburgh Republican) (1-10/14)
5988. Moore, Conrad, merchant, of Red Hook m 11/24/17 Dorothy Lewis of
Kinderhook in K; Rev. Sickles (8-12/3)
5989. Moore, Elmur Stockwell, 11 mo, s of Dana, d 7/26/29 in Watervliet
("Printers in Massachusetts are requested to insert this death")
(1-8/19)
5990. Moore, Esterbrooks m 5/14/31 Sarah Davis in Keeseville; Rev. S. Lyman
(4 [Keeseville Herald]-5/17)
5991. Moore, Hugh,"senior editor of this paper" m 12/2/33 Mary Jane Witherell,
dau of Elijah of Hinesburgh, VT, in H; Rev. Kent (7-12/7)
5992. Moore, Hugh, Esq., editor of the Burlington Sentinel, m 12/9/33 Mary
Jane Witherel, dau of Elijah, Esq. of Hinesburgh, VT, in H; Rev. Kent
(4 [Keeseville Herald]-12/10)

174

5993. Moore, Isaac m 3/17/25 Martha Heermance; Rev. Young. All of Poughkeepsie (8-3/23)
5994. Moore, John, 85, d 10/30/31 in Worcester, MA (7-11/12)
5995. Moore, Lewis m 5/2/32 Mary Mitchel, both of Plattsburgh; P. J. Roberts, Esq. (7-6/9)
5996. Moore, Martha, 25, wf of Isaac, d 7/19/30 (8-7/21)
5997. Moore, Mary, consort of Jacob of Plattsburgh, d 5/18/11 (typhus) (7-5/24)
5998. Moore, Mary, wf of Joshua, d 9/24/18 in Plattsburgh (7-10/3)
5999. Moore, Plato B. of Chatham m 11/28/29 Sarah Linda Davis, dau of Deacon Stephen of Austerlitz, in A; Rev. Joel Osborn (1-12/18)
6000. Moore, Pliny (Hon.) (Judge) d (date and place of death lacking) (born 4/14/1759 [the oldest son] in Sheffield, MA. Entered the army at age 17. During the French War [age 21] served in Army as a Lieut. Based on this service he received a land grant in the town of Champlain, NY and moved there with his fam. in 1789. Was first judge in Clinton Co. in 1805 and served in that capacity "till by law, his age disqualified him.") (7-8/31/22)
6001. Moore, Royal C. m Laura Whiteside in Cambridge (7-4/23/25)
6002. Moore, Sally, about 9, dau of Jacob, d 9/15/17 in Plattsburgh (7-9/20)
6003. Moore, Thomas J. (Dr.) m Ann Jones, dau of Jacob, Esq. of Jefferson (Scho. Co.); Rev. Stephen Fenn (1-3/7/31)
6004. Moores, Elizabeth, consort of Maj. Gen. Moores, d 1/22/18 in Plattsburgh (7-1/24)
6005. Moores, Frederick W., merchant, m 9/1/16 Harriet Hathaway; Rev. Bedell. All of Hudson (6-9/3)
6006. Moores, Naomi, 35, wf of Capt. Reuben, d in NYC (6-10/15/01)
6007. Moores, William m 4/29/11 Mary Bradley, both of Hudson (6-5/3)
6008. More, Andrew, merchant, of Fort Ann m 11/11/12 Sarah Oakley of Poughkeepsie; Rev. C. C. Cuyler (8-11/18)
6009. More, Peleg m 1/11/27 Maria Baltimore, both of Troy; Rev. Howard (see also the marriage of More Hardaway the same evening by the same pastor) (9-1/23)
6010. More, Reuben (Capt.) m 5/9/03 Hepza Huzzey, both of Hudson, in H (6-5/17)
6011. More, Samuel m 12/9/33 Jane Ann Sanders in Keeseville; Rev. J. C. Brisben (4 [Keeseville Herald]-12/10)
6012. Morehouse, Jay (Lt.) of Onondaga m 2/22/16 Mary Goodsell, dau of Peter, in Burlington (3-2/29) (Note: Burlington in Otsego Co.)
6013. Morehouse, William m 9/16/19 Mary Haskell; Rev. Sommers. All of Troy (9-9/21)
6014. Morel, John m 5/3/12 Elizabeth Ryphenburgh in Rhinebeck; Rev. Andrew N. Kittle (8-7/8)
6015. Morey, Charles R., 21, of Poughkeepsie d 9/3/27 in NYC (8-9/5)
6016. Morey, Peter, Esq. of Cazenovia m 5/5/31 Nancy Gorton, dau of late Rev. Hezekiah of Sempronius, at the home of Charles Brockway in Broadalbin; Rev. William Groom (1-5/12)
6017. Morey, Stephen m 10/11/20 Polly Husted of Stanford in S; Gilbert Thorne, Esq. (8-11/1)
6018. Morey, William of Amenia m 3/1/01 Sally Rogers of Poughkeepsie; Rev. (blurred) (8-3/3)
6019. Morford, John, papermaker, d 6/10/11 (in Troy?) (9-6/25)
6020. Morgan, _____ of Keeseville m Maria Grandy of Glens Falls (4[Keeseville Herald]-10/16/32)
6021. Morgan, Alfred m 7/25/24 Juliaet Loomis, both of Sherburne (Chen. Co.). in Utica; Rev. Aiken (3-8/2)
6022. Morgan, Daniel, (Gen.), 65, (a Rev. officer) d in Virginia (was awarded a Congrsssional medal "for his victory at the Cowpens over a superior force") (6-7/27/02)
6023. Morgan, David, silversmith, d 6/11/16 in Poughkeepsie (8-6/19)
6024. Morgan, Edwin B., merchant, m 9/23/29 Charlotte F. Wood, in Aurora; Rev. E. N. Nichols (1-10/6)
6025. Morgan, Elijah m 11/2/06 Nancy Smith, dau of William, all of Poughkeepsie; Rev. Scovill (8-11/4)
6026. Morgan, Elijah, 68, d 3/2/15 in Poughkeepsie (26 years a member of the Methodist Episcopal Church) (8-3/8)

6027. Morgan, George B., 28, d 4/9/31 in Poughkeepsie (8-4/13)
6028. Morgan, George B. m 8/4/31 Mary Ann Clow, both of Stuyvesant (Col. Co.),
       at the United States Hotel in Albany; Rev. Keyes (1-8/6)
6029. Morgan, Hatfield m 12/24/03 Hetty Arles, dau of Capt. Arles, all of
       Fishkill; Rev. Van Vranken (8-1/10/04)
6030. Morgan, Henry B. m 1/16/31 Sarah Valentine, both of Poughkeepsie; Rev.
       Perkins (8-1/19)
6031. Morgan, Jasper of Guilford (Chen. Co.) m 11/18/24 Hannah Cory of Coopers-
       town; Rev. Tiffany (1-11/22)
6032. Morgan, John B. m 1/25/26 Phebe Miller in Plattsburgh; Rev. Halsey. All
       of Plattsburgh (7-1/28)
6033. Morgan, Jonas, Esq. m 7/25/05 Mrs. Lucy Galpin, both of Lansingburgh, in
       Lansingburgh; Rev. Blatchford (3-7/2)
6034. Morgan, Joseph, merchant, of Poughkeepsie m 12/6/12 Nancy Fowler of
       Fishkill (8-12/16)
6035. Morgan, Peter B., 46, d 1/26/17 in Poughkeepsie (8-1/29)
6036. Morgan, Reuben m 11/22/34 Almira Palmateer; Rev. Dr. Reed. All of
       Poughkeepsie (8-11/26)
6037. Morgan, Sarah, 38, consort of Jonas, d 6/8/01 in Lansingburgh (9-6/16)
6038. Morgan, Sarah Jane, dau of Joseph of Poughkeepsie, d 12/2/32 (8-12/12)
6039. Morgan, Thomas of Prince Edward Co., Upper Canada m 7/18 Elizabeth Giles,
       dau of William of Fishkill, NY; Rev. S. Arnold (8-8/1)
6040. Morgan, Walter, merchant, m 8/9/04 Delia Darbyshire of Hartwick at Spring
       Hill; Rev. Isaac Lewis (3-8/23)
6041. Morgan, Walter, 48, a native of England, d 1/31/22 in Madison, NY (3-2/4)
6042. Morgan, William H., merchant m 2/14/22 Lucy Deming in Plattsburgh; Rev.
       Whelpley (7-2/16)
6043. Moriarty, Peter (Rev.), 55, d 6/4/14 in Hillsdale (an itinerant Methodist
       preacher "for upwards of 32 years") (6-6/14)
6044. Morrel, John of Albany m 6/22/99 Rebecca Bradt of Schaghticoke in S;
       Rev. Paige (9-7/2)
6045. Morrell, David, 16, of "Milford-ville" m 10/24/25 Widow Emma Brewer, 45,
       of Davenport in D; Daniel Babcock, Esq. (3-11/7)
6046. Morrell, George, Esq., attorney, of Cooperstown m Maria Webb, oldest dau
       of late Gen. Samuel B. of Claverack, in C; Rev. Gebhard (3-5/23/12)
6047. Morrell, Jacob m 10/11/34 Marinda Chappell in Plattsburgh; Rev. Marvin
       (7-10/18)
6048. Morrell, James Wright, Esq. of Oxford, England m 6/5/32 Mary Caroline
       Stewart of Quebec, Canada, dau of late Staff Surgeon William Stewart of
       Belfast, Ireland, in Champlain, NY; Rev. Ezra Kenny)
6049. Morris, Asahel (Dr.), 64, "one of the oldest physicians in the county",
       d 7/6/30 in Cambridge, Washington Co. (1-7/21)
6050. Morris, Augustus Frederick, Esq. m 12/10/23 Harriet Munro, dau of Peter J.,
       Esq., in Mamaroneck; Rev. De Lancey (3-12/22)
6051. Morris, Charles Valentine of Butternuts m 1/20/31 Eliza Moseley, dau of
       Elizur of Whitesboro, in W; Rev. Russel Wheeler (1-1/27)
6052. Morris, Edward H., s of Edmund of Puoghkeepsie, d 8/15/32 (cholera)
       (8-8/29)
6053. Morris, Elizabeth S., wf of Walter R. and youngest dau of Dr. Elias
       Willard, deceased, d 4/14/31 in Albany (funeral from the home of William
       C. Young, corner of Quackenbush and North Market Sts.) (1-4/16)
6054. Morris, Gouverneur, Esq. m 12/25/09 Ann Carey Randolph, dau of late Thomas,
       Esq. of Virginia; Rev. Wilkins (8-1/3/10)
6055. Morris, Gouverneur (Hon.), 64, d 11/2/16 in Morrisania (West. Co.) (6-11/12
       and 3-11/21)
6056. Morris, Henry, Esq. of Buffalo m 10/11/31 Mary Natalie Spencer, dau of
       Hon. John C., Esq., at St. John's Church in Canandaigua; Rev. Ravaud
       Kearney (1-10/15)
6057. Morris, Jacob of Butternuts m 3/1/30 Sophia Pringle, dau of John, Esq. of
       Richfield, in R; Rev. Daniel Nash (1-3/9)
6058. Morris, Jerome of NYC m 12/17/34 Eliza A. Free, dau of late John I. of
       Poughkeepsie; Rev. Van Vranken (8-12/31)
6059. Morris, Lewis (Col.), 70, oldest brother of George Jacob of Butternuts,
       d in Morrisania (West. Co.) (Col. Morris, a Rev. officer, was the oldest
       s of Gen. Lewis Morris) (3-11/29/24)

176

6060. Morris, Lewis Lee m 9/11/15 Hannah Winter, both of Butternuts, in B; Rev.
Russell Wheeler (3-9/14)
6061. Morris, Mary Walton, dau of James, Esq. late of Morrisania, d 12/8/30
at the home of Dr. Stevens in NYC (1-12/13)
6062. Morris, Richard L. of Morrisania m 10/15/29 Elizabeth S. Fish, dau of Col.
Nicholas, in NYC; Rev. Creighton (1-10/19)
6063. Morris, Robert, Esq., editor of the Pennsylvania Inquirer, m 11/10/31
Amanda Louisa Miller, dau of William of Philadelphia, PA, in Phila.;
Rev. Michael Hurley. All of Phila. (1-11/21)
6064. Morris, Valentine, late a commodore in the U.S. Navy, d 5/15/15 in
Westchester (6-5/30)
6065. Morrison, Condee m 4/18/08 Mary Warren Barry, both of Troy; Rev. D.
Butler (9-5/17)
6066. Morrison, James m 3/26/07 Sarah McChesney, both of Brunswick; Rev. Coe
(9-4/7)
6067. Morrison, John B. m 8/9/30 Ellen Greene; J. Holliday, Esq. All of Albany
(1-8/11)
6068. Morrison, Peter, merchant, of NYC m 3/20/06 Maria Hawkins late of Liverpool,
"Great Britain", in Claverack, NY; Rev. Bethel Judd (6-4/8)
6069. Morse, Abel (Dr.) of Otsego m 5/31/08 Mary Hatch of Burlington (Ots. Co.)
in B; Rev. Henry Chapman (3-6/4)
6070. Morse, Benjamin m 5/19/22 Polly Thorington; Elam Buel, Esq.. All of
Grafton. (double ceremony - see marr of Samuel Morse) (9-5/28)
6071. Morse, Benona (Mr.), 50, d 9/1/20 in Whitehall ("has left a numerous
family") (9-9/12)
6072. Morse, Cephas Austin, 22, s of Dr. Alexander, d 4/13/33 in Elizabethtown
(consumption) (4 [Keeseville Herald]-4/23)
6073. Morse, Elizabeth (Miss), 19, d 9/21/26 in Huntsville (Sara. Co.)
(3-10/23)
6074. Morse, Jacob m 1/1/14 Polly Smith, both of Clinton; Rev. Dr. Dodge
(8-1/12)
6075. Morse, Jedidiah (Rev.) D.D. and LL. D., 65, d 6/9/26 in New Haven, CT
(8-6/21)
6076. Morse, Mary, 26, dau of Thomas, d 8/30/26 in Peru, NY (7-1/8/27)
6077. Morse, Meriam, 38, consort of Timothy, Esq. of Burlington (Ots. Co.),
d 9/13/01 (3-10/8)
6078. Morse, Patience, 56, late consort of Daniel, d 5/19/09 in Otsego (3-6/3)
6079. Morse, Samuel m 5/19/22 Catharine Thorington; Elam Buel, Esq. All of
Grafton (double ceremony - see marr of Benjamin Morse) (9-5/28)
6080. Morton, _____, inf s of Seth, d 8/26/11 in Hudson (6-8/30)
6081. Morton, _____, 9 mo, s of Seth, d in Hudson (6-9/13/14)
6082. Morton, Charles S. of the U.S. Army m Henrietta Ellison, dau of late
Thomas of NYC, in NYC; Rev. Benjamin T. Onderdonk (1-3/8/30)
6083. Morton, Emmaline, 16 mo, dau of Seth, d in Hudson (6-6/1/10)
6084. Morton, Moses, 33, merchant, of Rochester d 6/20/30 in Rochester
(1-6/25)
6085. Morton, Seth, 22 mo, s of Seth, d 10/7/08 in Hudson (6-10/11)
6086. Morton, Seth, 9 mo, s of Seth, d in Hudson (6-8/31/13)
6087. Morton, Washington, Esq. of NYC d 5/3/10 in Paris, France (8-8/15)
6088. Morton, Whiting, 2, s of Seth, d 11/29/12 in Hudson (6-12/1)
6089. Morton, William B., 23, d in Hudson (6-11/22/14)
6090. Mosby, Robert, one of the editors of the Richmond Compiler, m Sarah Lynch,
2nd dau of James H., Esq., in Richmond, VA (1-3/10/30)
6091. Moseley, Edwin, 47, formerly of Westfield, MA, d 2/21/30 in Albany (surv
by wf and children) (1-3/2)
6092. Moseley, Joseph D., formerly of Albany, d 2/4/30 at the home of Col. N.
Howard in Stephentown (Renss. Co.) (1-2/8)
6093. Moseley, Lucilius H. m 3/12/26 Elizabeth Amerosia Lyon, both of Poughkeepsie; Rev. Dr. Reed (8-3/15)
6094. Mosely, Frederick C., 19, s of Gideon of Poughkeepsie, NY, d 8/10/20 in
Columbia, Maine (yellow fever) (8-10/4)
6095. Mosely, Joseph D. of New Lebanon m 6/23/29 Phebe N. Johnson of Stephentown (Renss. Co.) in S; Rev. Jones (1-7/3)
6096. Moses, Abraham of Saundersfield, MA m 1/23/28 Susan Rowland of Pittstown,
NY in P; Jonathan Reed, Esq. (9-1/29)

6097. Moses, David J. m 12/11/28 Amanda Ames, both of Watervliet, in Gibbons-
       ville; Rev. Howard (9-12/16)
6098. Moses, Hiram (Dr.) m 3/30/28 Abalina Worthington, dau of Maj. Gen. Worth-
       ington, in Petersburgh; John Henning, Esq. All of P (9-4/8)
6099. Moses, James m 7/10/24 Jane Jesse (sic) McKane, both of Hyde Park; Rev.
       Van Derveer (8-7/14)
6100. Mosher, David m 2/26/24 Mary Duel, both of Stanford (Dut. Co.), at the
       Friends Meeting House in Stanford (8-3/3)
6101. Mosher, David m 6/19/34 Mary Nobles, dau of Nathaniel, all of Washington
       (Dut. Co.); Samuel Allen, Esq. (8-6/25)
6102. Mosher, Eliphalet, 96, of the Society of Friends d in Washington (Dut. Co.)
       (3-6/23/23)
6103. Mosher, Ephraim, 96, a member of the Society of Friends, d 5/28/23 at his
       home in Washington (Dut. Co.) (had lived in Washington more than
       70 years) (8-6/11)
6104. Mosher, Isaac m 6/17/13 Leah Van Voknier, both of Stanford (Dut. Co.);
       Rev. Burch (8-6/23)
6105. Mosher, Jeremiah (Gen.), 77, (a Rev. officer) d in Lancaster, PA (1-4/2/30)
6106. Mosier, Mary (Miss), 17, d 7/29/22 in Ballston (2-8/6)
6107. Mott, Abraham of Hyde Park m 1/8/26 Magaret Marriott of Poughkeepsie; Rev.
       Dr. Reed (8-1/11)
6108. Mott, Ebenezer, Esq., 62, d 1/9/13 in Clinton (8-1/13)
6109. Mott, Ebenezer, 27, s of John Joslin Mott of Washington (Dut. Co.),
       d 2/14/27 (8-2/21)
6110. Mott, Jacob, 66, of Clinton d 12/17/13 (8-12/22)
6111. Mott, James, 81, a member of the Society of Friends, d 5/16/23 in NYC
       (8-5/21)
6112. Mott, Jane (Widow), 89, d in Hempstead, L. I. Her dau, Phebe Smith (wife
       of Zebulon),en route to visit her mother, "died on the road" (8-8/5/00)
6113. Mott, John of Troy m 9/18/22 Phoebe Paddock of Greenbush in G (9-10/8)
6114. Mott, John m 9/9/30 Maria Culver; Rev. Wile. All of Pleasant Valley
       (8-9/15)
6115. Mott, Joseph S. m 7/8/29 Mary Thorne, dau of Nicholas, Esq., formerly of
       Poughkeepsie "but now of Skaneateles", in S; Rev. Hollister (1-7/17 and
       8-7/22)
6116. Mott, Margaret, wife of Jeremiah of Cooperstown, d 6/21/04 (fell from her
       horse) (3-6/28)
6117. Mott, Stephen G. of Bridgewater m 3/7/21 Abigail Bowne at the Friends
       Meeting House in Butternuts (3-3/19)
6118. Mott, Thomas, house carpenter, d 7/31/00 in Poughkeepsie (8-8/5)
6119. Mott, William, "an aged inhsbitant of Beekman" (Dut. Co.), d 9/11/18 in
       Beekman (8-9/16)
6120. Mott, William H., merchant, m 5/20/29 Margaretta Buchan, youngest dau
       of late Robert, Esq. of NYC, at St. Luke's Church in NYC; Rev. Ives
       (1-5/25)
6121. Mount, Sexton, merchant, of Buffalo m Lucretia Reading, dau of Martin, Esq.
       late of Waterloo (Seneca Co.), in W (1-12/29/30)
6122. Mountfort, John (Maj.) of the U.S. Artillery m 6/23/29 Mary Matilda McNeil,
       dau of late Joseph of New Orleans, LA, in N. O.; Rev. James F. Hull
       (1-7/20 and 1-8/11)
6123. Mower, Peter A., Esq., 27, attorney, d at the home of Henry F. Penfield,
       Esq. in Canandaigua (consumption) (1-9/24/31)
6124. Muia(?), Abraham m 3/6/34 Hannah Hagadon of Stanford (Dut. Co.); James
       Humeston, Esq. (8-3/12)
6125. Muir, Ephraim, Jr., 7 mo, s of Ephraim, d 3/12/07 in Hudson (6-3/17)
6126. Mulford, _____ (Mrs.) d in Staatsburgh (8-3/17/13)
6127. Mulford, Ezekiel, 45, formerly of Staatsburgh, d 6/27/11 in Watervliet
       (8-7/10)
6128. Mulford, Hughes m 1/29/34 Phebe Golder; Rev. George Coles. All of
       Poughkeepsie (8-2/5)
6129. Mulford, Lemuel, 52, d 5/21/07 in Pittstown (a long-term resident there)
       (9-6/2)
6130. Mulford, Samuel, formerly a merchant of Poughkeepsie, d 9/14/19 in
       Hamilton, OH (8-11/10)

6131. Mulkins, James m 11/26/03 Betsey Covel, both of Beekman (8-12/13)
6132. Mumford, David, Esq., 64, for many years a merchant of NYC, d in Schenectady (3-3/3/23)
6133. Mumford, Gurdon S., Esq., formerly a mechanic in Albany, d 4/30/31 ("was one of Dr. Franklin's secretaries in France" during the Rev. War and a Congressman during Jefferson's administration) (1-5/4)
6134. Mumford, Samuel Jones, Esq. m 6/2/30 Caroline G. Astor in NYC; (1-6/5)
6135. Muncil, Eliakim S., 58, d 1/16/13 in Hartford, VT (In one year his entire family died - all of the "prevalent fever": Eliakim S., Jr., 27, 11/7/13; Daniel, 20, 11/26/13; Lucy Camp [wf of Jared Camp and dau of Eliakim, Sr.], 24, 12/22/13; and Hannah, wf of Eliakim, Sr., 52, 2/6/14) (6-4/12/14)
6136. Munn, Loisa (Mrs.), 22, d 1/26/13 in Troy (9-2/2)
6137. Munn, Sarah, 60, wf of Joseph, d 8/27/21 in Cooperstown (surv by husband and 2 daus) (3-9/3)
6138. Munson, Samuel S. of Windsor (Broome Co.) m 4/1/23 Phebe Ann Walker of Butternuts in B; Rev. Wheeler (3-4/1/23)
6139. Murdock, Carey, Esq. m 9/14/30 Catharine Dwight Parker, dau of Philip S., Esq.; Rev. Dr. Sprague. All of Albany (1-9/15)
6140. Murphey, Philip, a young man of Hudson, drowned 5/14/03 in the overturning of a small skiff on the Hudson River (6-5/17)
6141. Murphy, Debby C., 29 or 39?, consort of R. W., Esq., d 8/30/31 at Preston Hollow (1-9/8)
6142. Murphy, John (Capt.), 45, d 2/2/14 in Claverack (6-2/15)
6143. Murphy, Marinda, 31, wf of Ira, d 12/30/29 in Albany (funeral at 549 South Market St.) (1-1/1/30)
6144. Murray, Martha, 43, consort of Solomon, d 1/14/06 in Claverack (surv by husband and 7 children) (6-1/21)
6145. Murray, Thomas W. m 2/2/24 Sally Ann Skinner; Rev. Crandle (8-2/4)
6146. Murry, Malvina, 3, oldest dau of John of Newburgh, d 11/17/32 in Pough-keepsie (8-11/21)
6147. Mursick, Francis, 65, d in NYC ("born on the Island of Vayo near Venice") (9-1/2/27)
6148. Muser, John F., Jr. m 12/10/28 Jane Magee, both of NYC at St. George's Chapel in NYC; Rev. Milner (9-12/16)
6149. Musson, Ann, 16, wf of William of Butternuts, d 4/27/98 in Butternuts "in child-bed". (3-5/3)
6150. Musson, John of Unadilla m 12/11/23 Ann Elizabeth Burgess, dau of Dr. I. Burgess, in Butternuts; Rev. Garvin (3-12/22)
6151. Musson, William, 41, d 7/1/06 in Butternuts (b in Leicestershire, England but had lived "in America" 13 yrs) (3-7/10)
6152. Myers, Aaron of Peekskill m 12/4/22 June Myers of Poughkeepsie; Rev. Cuyler (8-12/11)
6153. Myers, Abraham, Esq. m 3/18/18 Elizabeth Cornell in Fishkill; Rev. Thomas De Witt (8-3/25)
6154. Myers, Abram m 9/5/31 Harriet Wendell, dau of Daniel T., in Gibbonsville; Rev. Stratton of Troy (1-9/8)
6155. Myers, Charles m 1/30/17 Catharine McCavy in Fishkill (8-2/5)
6156. Myers, Emiline (Miss), dau of Abraham I. of Fishkill, d 9/12/18 in Newburgh (8-9/16)
6157. Myers, Hazel, 45, d 2/3/09 in Hudson (6-2/7)
6158. Myers, Jacob of Red Hook m 7/5/34 Sarah Van Vredenburgh of Clinton (Dut. Co.); Rev. William J. Eyer (8-7/16)
6159. Myers, Jacob of Poughkeepsie m 7/28/34 Eliza Saumway Staats, dau of William, Esq. of Albany; Rev. Dr. Reed (8-7/30)
6160. Myers, Jane, 46, wf of Jacob, d 2/20/27 in Poughkeepsie (8-2/28)
6161. Myers, John, Sr. d 12/5/22 in Stillwater (member of Methodist Ch.) (2-12/10)
6162. Myers, John M. m 8/24/11 Hannah Yelverton, both of Poughkeepsie; Rev. Cuyler (8-8/28)
6163. Myers, Jonas, 60, d 2/21/07 at his farm in Northeast (8-3/3)
6164. Myers, Leonard of Fishkill m 12/3/34 Mary Velie, only dau of Dow Myers, in Poughkeepsie; Rev. Price (8-12/10)
6165. Myers, Mary, wf of Nathan, Esq., d 5/14/22 in Poughkeepsie (8-5/15)

6166. Myers, Mary, wf of Nathan, Esq., d 5/14/22 in Poughkeepsie (8-5/15)
6167. Myers, Mordecai (Capt.) of 13th Regiment of the U.S. Infantry m 1/22/14
       Charlotte Bailey, dau of William, Esq. of Plattsburgh, in P (7-1/29)
6168. Myers, Nathan (Col.) m 9/21/24 Mrs. Frances Brush, both of Poughkeepsie;
       Rev. Cuyler (8-9/22)
6169. Myers, Nathan (Col.) m 11/13/31 Sarah Hallock, both of Poughkeepsie; Rev
       Dr. Reed (8-11/16)
6170. Myers, Peter J. H., Esq., 45, president of the Whitehall Bank, d in White-
       hall (7-9/6/34)
6171. Myers, Robert R. (Capt.) m 6/20/18 Elizabeth Bennett, both of Hudson, in
       Northeast; Rev. Colver (6-6/23)
6172. Myers, Sarah, 15, dau of Nathan of Poughkeepsie, d 5/22/10 (8-5/30)
6173. Myers, William, Jr. m 9/4/19 Mary Esmond, both of Schaghticoke; Rev.
       Hooper Cumming (9-9/14)
6174. Mygatt, Ambrose m 3/6/34 Mary E. Clark, dau of Moses; Rev. T. Winter.
       All of Northeast (8-3/19)
6175. Mygatt, Thomas (Lt.) of Amenia m 9/5/08 Ann Waters of Poughkeepsie; Rev.
       Dr. Covel (8-9/7)
6176. Mygatt, Thomas, 30, d 3/21/14 in Amenia (8-3/30)
6177. Mykel, Peter m 6/10/21 Hannah Hayner, both of Brunswick (9-6/19)
6178. Naise, Margaret, wf of John, d 11/1/25 in Dover ("an affectionate mother")
       ("The editors of either of the Hudson papers is requested to give the
       above an insertion") (8-11/23)
6179. Nancrede, Joseph Gerard (Dr.) m Cornelia Truxton, dau of Commodore
       Truxton, in Philadelphia, PA; Right Rev. Bishop White (3-4/15/22)
6180. Nase, Elisha P., 15, s of John of Amenia, d in Amenia (8-6/6/10)
6181. Nase, Henry of Amenia, 43, d 10/16/29 in NYC (consumption) (8-11/4)
6182. Nase, Hervey m 12/23/07 Sally Swift, both of Amenia; Rev. Barnet (8-12/30)
6183. Nase, Philip I. of Amenia m 1/2/12 Sally Belden of Dover; Rev. Barnett
       (8-1/15)
6184. Nase, Rachael,74, wf of Philip of Amenia, d 1/17/02 (8-1/26), Same
       newspaper dated 2/9/02 - death date corrected to 12/7/01.
6185. Nase, William Henry of Amenia m 11/26/28 Emeline Tallmadge, dau of Thomas
       W. of Poughkeepsie; Rev. Dr. Cuyler (8-12/3)
6186. Nash, Daniel (Dr.) of Harpersfield m 6/16/24 Lavinia White in Windham
       (Greene Co.); Rev. Stimson (3-7/12)
6187. Nash, Edward P., 3, s of Rev. Daniel, d 8/19/19 in Exeter (3-8/23)
6188. Nash, Ezra, 31, d 5/17/24 in Cooperstown (b in Ballston Spa) (2-7/6)
6189. Nash,George C. of Lima m 11/18/30 Abigail H. James of Canaan in C; Rev.
       Taylor (1-12/20)
6190. Nash, Harry m 3/2/29 Rosilia Mancius Reuwee, both of Albany, in Watervliet;
       Rev. Bronk (1-3/27)
6191. Nash, Harvey, 22, d 7/9/29 in Albany (funeral from 22 Montgomery St.)
       (relatives, friends, and acquaintances "of Mrs. Catherine Mancius"
       are invited to the funeral) (1-7/10)
6192. Nash, Isaac, Esq. d 3/14/07 in Pittsfield (Ots. Co.) (surv by wf and
       several children) (buried with Masonic honers) (3-3/19)
6193. Nash, W. m 9/1/30 Lucy Green, dau of Byram, Esq., in Sodus (1-9/13)
6194. Nazro, Henry, merchant, m 3/18/15 Eliza Paine, dau of Amasa, Esq., all of
       Troy; Rev. Coe (9-3/21)
6195. Nazro, John P., merchant, of Utica, formerly of Troy, d 12/23/06 in Utica
       (9-1/13/07)
6196. Neels, Peter m 7/25/19 Pamelia Hunt, both of Hudson, in Claverack; Rev.
       Vedder (6-7/27)
6197. Neels, Peter m 3/6/24 Sibbe Ann Mills, both of Troy; Rev. Butler
       (9-3/16)
6198. Nefus, Gertrude (Mrs.), 97, d 12/8/22 in Poughkeepsie (lived until age 84
       "without God and without hope") (8-12/18)
6199. Neillson, Thomas, 17, drowned 9/23/22 by falling overboard from the sloop
       "Admiral" of Troy on her passage from NYC (Capt. Frasier and his crew
       "were unable to save him") (deceased was b in Liverpool, England)
       (9-10/8)
6200. Nelles, Abraham (Rev.), Indian missionary, m 5/10/31 Hannah Macklem "in
       Chippewa"; Rev. Larning (1-6/2)
6201. Nelson, _____ (Capt.) d 11/13/12 (killed in action "on the Niagara")
       (7-12/18)

6202. Nelson, (given name not stated) m 10/23/28 Rachel Cudgill of Fishkill; Rev. M. W. Dwight (8-11/26)
6203. Nelson, Alva m Laura Wells in Woodbury, VT (This entry includes a long statement of the tangled family relationships existing among the bride, groom, and the two witnesses "yet there was no blood relation between the bride and bridegroom") (8-12/24/28)
6204. Nelson, Jacob, 37 or 57, d 12/16/15 in Poughkeepsie (8-12/20)
6205. Nelson, Jacob of Cairo, NY m 1/1/24 Julia Smith of Hyde Park; Rev. Reed (8-1/7)
6206. Nelson, Jacob M. (Capt.), about 45, of Poughkeepsie d 3/3/34 (funeral at the Episcopal Church) (deceased is survived by his wife "and children") (8-3/5)
6207. Nelson, John Milton of Freedom m 2/15/22 Eliza Smith, dau of Granville Smith of Poughkeepsie in Hyde Park; Rev. Brown (8-2/20)
6208. Nelson, John P. of Newark, NY m 5/5/30 Cornelia Low of Poughkeepsie; Rev. D. Cuyler (8-5/12)
6209. Nelson, Joseph (Capt.), 25, of Poughkeepsie, formerly editor of the Political Barometer, d 11/3/12 in NYC (surv by wf and 3 small ch) (Capt. Nelson commanded the Artillery Company of Poughkeepsie stationed on Staten Island) (8-11/8)
6210. Nelson, Joseph of Somerstown (perhaps Somers in West. Co.?) m 2/6/25 Clarissa Hamlen of Beekman; Rev. Arnold of Freedom (8-2/23)
6211. Nelson, Nicholas m 11/28/16 Mrs. Hannah Ostrom, dau of Isaac Lomarce, all of Clinton (Dut. Co.) (8-12/11)
6212. Nelson, Richard, one of the proprietors of the Dutchess Observer, m 11/5/18 Mrs. Cornelia Adams; Rev. Leonard. All of Poughkeepsie (8-11/11)
6213. Nelson, Samuel of Poughkeepsie m 11/14/20 Christina Benner, dau of late Henry, Esq. of Red Hook; Rev. Kittle (8-11/22)
6214. Nelson, Samuel (Hon.), judge of the 6th Circuit District, m 4/7/25 Catharine Ann Russell, only dau of John, Esq., in Cooperstown; Rev. Tiffany (3-4/11)
6215. Nelson, Thomas of Poughkeepsie m 2/2/04 Mrs. Mary Delavan of Franklin in F; Rev. McNiece (8-2/7)
6216. Nelson, Thomas m 11/10/05 Jamima Smith, both of Poughkeepsie; Teunis Tappen, Esq. (8-11/12)
6217. Nelson, Thomas, Esq., "a very aged citizen", d 11/1/23 at his home in Poughkeepsie (8-11/5)
6218. Nelson, Thomas J. (Dr.) m 9/20/27 Mary Newcomb in Pleasant Valley; Rev. Dr. Reed (8-9/26)
6219. Nesmith, Mary Ann, 28, wf of John, Esq. of NYC and dau of Hon. Samuel Bell of NH, d 2/24/31 in St. Augustine, East Florida (consumption) (1-3/24)
6220. Neugent, John, 9 mo, s of John, d 2/24/07 in Hudson (6-3/3)
6221. Newberry, Freelove, 34, consort of Daniel, d 5/21/12 in Hudson (6-5/25)
6222. Newbold, George, Esq. of NYC m 7/27/29 Ann P. Fox, dau of late Samuel, Esq. of Philadelphia, PA, in Philadelphia; Right Rev. Bishop White (1-8/3)
6223. Newcomb, Christian, farmer, of Poughkeepsie d 7/25/20 (8-8/2)
6224. Newcomb, Elizabeth (Mrs.), 33, wf of Daniel, Esq., d 9/14/02 in Pittstown (9-9/15)
6225. Newcomb, Elizabeth, 76, wid of late Daniel of Hebron, CT, d 2/11/07 (6-2/17)
6226. Newcomb, Harvey of Poughkeepsie m 10/6/25 Maria Lewis, dau of Enoch of Pleasant Valley; Rev. Clark (8-10/12)
6227. Newcomb, Harvey, late editor of the Buffalo Patriot, m Alithea Wells, late of Auburn, NY, in New Albany, IN (1-6/18)
6228. Newcomb, Kezia (Miss), 16, d 2/20/22 in Chazy (7-4/6)
6229. Newcomb, Rachel, 44, wf of Thomas, d 4/27/12 in Clinton (Dut. Co.) (8-5/6)
6230. Newcomb, Simon m Eliphal Allen; Reuben H. Walworth, Esq. All of Plattsburgh (7-9/6/11)
6231. Newcomb, Zacheus (Dr.), "one of the oldest inhabitants of Pleasant Valley", d 8/30/31 at his home in Pleasant Valley (8-9/7)
6232. Newell, Abigal, 57, wf of Chauncey, d 2/7/24 in Otsego (3-2/16)

6233. Newell, John m 6/4/29 Mary Elizabeth Underhill, dau of P. B., Esq., all of Phelps, in Penn Yan; Rev. Eddy (1-6/22)
6234. Newell, Penelope, wf of Sirajah, d 8/23/15 in Cooperstown (3-8/31)
6235. Newell, Samuel (Deacon), 46, d "within a few days" in Champlain (7-1/8/13)
6236. Newell, Samuel (Rev.), American missionary, d "recently" in India. Also, "Mrs. Poor, wife of Rev. Mr. Poor, another of the missionaries", d "recently" (2-12/5/21)
6237. Newhouse, John m 9/14/28 Catherine Wilder; Rev. Samuel Merwin. All of Troy (9-9/16)
6238. Newhouse, Jonathan, Jr. m 11/2/14 Mary Morgan, both of Poughkeepsie; Rev. Cuyler (8-11/9)
6239. Newkirk, John, 28, d 1/5/10 in Clinton, Dut. Co. (surv by wf and 2 small ch) (8-1/17)
6240. Newlin, Thomas S. of Wilmington, DE m 4/22/30 Catharine Whitt(?), dau of Dr. Barton Whitt(?) in Fishkill; Rev. Dr. Westbrook (double ceremony - see marr of James Darrah) (8-5/12)
6241. Newman, Jesse m 4/21/03 Ruth Ann Crawford, dau of Job, Esq., all of Pawling; Stephen Hoyt, Esq. (8-4/26)
6242. Newman, Samuel m 1/1/20 Elizabeth Oothout; Rev. Chase (9-1/11)
6243. Newton, Mina (Miss), 18, d 3/4/26 in Otsego (3-3/13)
6244. Newton, Otis W., Esq. of Hamburgh m 5/22/29 Sophia A. Green, adopted dau of Henry Hill, Esq., in Aurora (Cay. Co.); Rev. Smith (1-6/11)
6245. Nicholas, John, Esq., 55, formerly a member of congress from Virginia and recently first judge ofNiagara Co., NY, d 12/31/19 in Geneva, NY (8-1/12/20)
6246. Nicholls, Joshua, Esq., first judge of the court of common pleas in Franklin Co., d "a few days since" in Chateaugay (7-4/6/16)
6247. Nichols, Ama (widow), 82, d 8/14/13 in Troy (9-8/17)
6248. Nichols, Caleb (Hon.) m 6/19/19 Permelia Green, dau of Joseph I., in Plattsburgh (7-6/26)
6249. Nichols, Charles d 2/22/17 in Plattsburgh (consumption) (7-3/8)
6250. Nichols, Charles L., 14, oldest s of Robert, merchant, of Trumbull, CT, d in T (Copied by the Poughkeepsie editor from the Farmer's Journal, Danbury, CT) ("The Poughkeepsie printers by publishing this death might convey the news to an unnatural mother") (8-12/23/00)
6251. Nichols, Cynthia, 15, dau of Capt. Philo, d 3/18/03 in Hudson (funeral from the Presbyterian Meeting House; funeral sermon by Rev. Sears) (6-3/22)
6252. Nichols, Elnathan m 7/2/22 Polly Kibby in Peru, NY; Elisha Button, Esq. All of Peru (7-7/6)
6253. Nichols, Henry, merchant, of Albany, NY m 5/31/31 Jane Wakeman of Saugatuck, CT in S; Rev. Davis (1-6/3)
6254. Nichols, Jenison B. m 2/10/13 Lucretia Conkey in Chazy (7-2/12)
6255. Nichols, Luke of Plattsburgh m 9/4/28 Mary Ann Wetherbee of Troy; Rev. Tucker (9-9/5)
6256. Nichols, Nicholas, 88, "an old inhabitant of Hudson", d 9/5/20 in Hudson (6-9/12)
6257. Nichols, Phebe, 58, consort of Caleb, Esq., d 10/24/16 (7-10/26)
6258. Nichols, Philo, 50, d in hudson (6-9/14/12)
6259. Nichols, Pierson, merchant, d 2/20/31 at his home in Montreal, Canada (surv by wf and inf child) (1-3/10)
6260. Nichols, Samuel, 83, d 8/14/06 in Hudson (6-8/19)
6261. Nichols, William, mechanic, d 9/29/23 in Poughkeepsie (8-10/1)
6262. Nicholson, James (Commodore), 68, d at his home near NYC (3-9/20/04)
6263. Nicholson, John, Esq., 47, d 5/27/21 in Albany ("Congressman" from Herkimer Co., NY) (3-6/4)
6264. Nickerson, Mercy (Mrs.), 67, of Clinton (Dut. Co.) d 12/21/01 (8-1/5/02)
6265. Nicol, William H., surgeon in U.S. Army and formerly of Poughkeepsie, d 3/5/31 at Jefferson Barracks, MO (8-4/6)
6266. Nicoll, William, merchant, of Sing Sing m 9/28/23 Mary Brinckerhoff, dau of John V. D. L., in Fishkill; Rev. Dewing (8-10/8)
6267. Nicols, William d 9/20/05 in Elizabethtown, NJ (yellow fever) (Personal papers revealed that he was of the firm of Perry G. and William Nicols of Fort Edward, NY and had left Albany on the sloop "Widow & Son" [Capt. Whipple] with a cargo of boards and planks which he sold to William Dayton & Co. of Elizabethtown, NJ) (9-10/8)

6268. Niel, William (Rev.) of Albany m 2/25/11 Frances King, dau of Gen. King of Ridgefield, CT, in R (3-3/9)
6269. Niell, Elizabeth, consort of Rev. William, late pastor of "the church in this place"(either Cooperstown or Albany, probably), d 11/14/09 in Albany (3-11/18)
6270. Niell, Samuel M., Esq. m 11/10/30 ___?___ Yates, dau of Hon. Joseph C., d in NYC; Rev. Ives. All of NYC (1-11/12)
6271. Niles, Eunice Galusha, 17, d 10/15/19 (in Troy?) (9-10/19)
6272. Niles, Gideon d 1/14/22 in Otsego (3-1/21)
6273. Niles, Hiram m Chloe Robinson, dau of Dr. Gain Robinson, in Palmyra; Rev. A. E. Campbell (1-3/10/31)
6274. Niles, Robert Duer, 22, s of H. Niles, editor of the Weekly Register, d 9/2/31 in Baltimore, MD (1-9/7)
6275. Niles, Zerviah, 9, youngest dau of Gideon, d 8/15/13 in Cooperstown (3-8/28)
6276. Nind, W. W. (Rev.) of the Methodist Episcopal Church m Mary Moore of Lowville in L; Rev. N. Salisbury (1-1/22/31)
6277. Nisbit, William (Rev.) of Geneva m 9/20/30 Ann Smith, dau of late Gerardus of NYC, in NYC; Rev. Dr. Kuypers (1-9/25)
6278. Nisbuhrt, Maria Ophelia, 5, dau of Henry, d 2/11/30 in Boston (death caused "by her clothes taking fire") (1-2/18)
6279. Niven, Robert S., bookbinder, d 10/28/23 in Poughkeepsie (8-10/29)
6280. Nixon, Elias of NYC m 2/25/12 Selina Hebard of Poughkeepsie; Rev. C. C. Cuyler (8-3/4)
6281. Nixon, John Greene, 5, s of James, d in Hudson (6-1/1/05)
6282. Noble, Aaron, 28, d 6/1/29 in Mobile, AL (born in Lansingburgh, NY) (1-7/15)
6283. Noble, Daniel (Hon.), 54, of Williamstown, MA d 11/29/30 in Portland (NY?) (1-12/1)
6284. Noble, Louisa, 20, oldest dau of Cyranus, Esq., d 7/15/29 in New Lisbon (Ots. Co.) (1-7/24)
6285. Noble, Lucy, 59, consort of Daniel, d 8/24/22 in Ballston (2-8/27)
6286. Noble, Stephen B., merchant, of Ballston Spa m 5/30/24 Sally Dunshie of Charlton in C; Rev. Kincade (2-6/1)
6287. Noble, Stephen C. (Capt.) of Lansingburgh m 11/16/22 Sally Rogers of Stillwater in S; Rev. Rogers (2-11/26)
6288. Noble, Walker m 12/9/13 Marcia P. Crossman, dau of Ebenezer, in Hudson; Rev. Chester (6-12/21)
6289. Nobles, James H. m 9/16/30 Maria Augusta Bundy, dau of Solomon, in Oxford; Rev. Abel. All of Oxford (1-10/5)
6290. Nodine, Dolly, 49, wf of Frederick, d 3/14/34 in Pine Plains (8-3/19)
6291. Noe, John, 24, late of Elizabethtown, NJ, d 1/12/29 in Little Falls, NY (while on a visit at the home of his uncle, Jacob Osborn) (1-1/22)
6292. Noonen, Timothy d 1/19/13 in Hudson (6-1/26)
6293. Noonin, John m 3/9/31 Margaret Schuyler, both of Troy, in Albany; C. H. Shear, Esq. (1-3/28)
6294. Norcut, Daniel m 10/7/20 Hannah Winslow, both of Troy; Rev. Sommers (9-10/10)
6295. Norman, John m Sally Finch in Hudson (6-5/13/06)
6296. Norman, Robert C., 28, d 5/27/30 in Hudson (1?-6/9)
6297. Norman, Sarah, inf dau of William E., d 2/4/14 in Hudson (6-2/15)
6298. Norman, William E., 51, bookseller, d 11/13/28 in Hudson, NY ("left a numerous family") (8-11/26)
6299. North, Cyrus, 32, d in Walton (Dela. Co.) (was blind from infancy) (3-9/19/25)
6300. North, John, 28, s of Gabriel, Esq. of Walton (Dela. Co.),d 10/5/30 in NYC (consumption) (1-10/7)
6301. North, Norris of Connecticut m 8/3/26 Mary Alger of Hartwick, NY in H; Rev. John H. Prentice (3-8/14)
6302. North, Oren m 9/1/31 Minerva Dayton in Cortland; Rev. John Keep (1-9/13)
6303. North, Robert (Capt.) "an aged inhabitant of Poughkeepsie" d 3/15/18 in Poughkeepsie (sailed a packet from Poughkeepsie to NYC for many years) (8-3/18)
6304. North, Sophia, dau of Lemuel, d 11/9/24 in Chazy (7-11/13)

6305. Northrop, Cyrus, Esq. of New Milford, CT m 2/5/34 Bulia (sic) M. Armstrong of Poughkeepsie at Maj. Hatch's Poughkeepsie Hotel; Rev. Dr. Reed (8-2/12)

6306. Northrop, Edward, 2, s of H. S., Esq., d 5/4/30 at the home of Mrs. Rogers in Poughkeepsie (scarlet fever) (8-5/12)

6307. Northrop, James B. m 4/10/23 Ann Maria Thorn, dau of John I., in Washington (Dut. Co.); Rev. Clark (8-4/16)

6308. Northrope, Edwin, late of Washington (Dut. Co.) m 5/27/29 Eliza Velis, dau of Hendrick of Pleasant Valley; Rev. Clark (8-6/4)

6309. Northrup, Daniel of Washington (Dut. Co.) m 11/3/13 Helen Sayres of Poughkeepsie; Rev. Reed (8-11/10)

6310. Northrup, Elon, merchant, of Washington (Dut. Co.) m 10/23/28 Mary Velie, dau of Hendrick of Pleasant Valley, in P. V.; Rev. P. C. Wilson (8-10/19)

6311. Northrup, Enos of Washington (Dut. Co.)m 3/16/19 Catharine Manney of Poughkeepsie; Rev. Cuyler (8-4/7)

6312. Northrup, Eunice, 35, wid of Enos, Esq., d 4/17/22 in Washington (Dut. Co.) (8-5/1)

6313. Northrup, Isaac Brooks, 6, s of H. S., Esq., formerly of Dutchess Co., d 2/8/34 in Ellenville (8-2/19)

6314. Northrup, John O. m 9/2/29 Charlotte Giddings; Rev. Maltby Gelston. All of Sharon, CT (8-9/16)

6315. Northrup, Nathan of Amenia m 8/3/02 Mrs Anna Haight of Stanford (Dut. Co.); Jeremiah Sherrell, Esq. (8-8/17)

6316. Northrup, Thompson of Lithgow m 9/7/30 Sarah Ann Purdy, dau of Francis, at Valley Grove in Fishkill; Rev. Hire (8-10/6)

6317. Northrup, William, 54, d 3/23/24 in Washington (Dut. Co.) (8-4/7)

6318. Norton, Daniel C., 12, s of Gideon of Lanesborough, MA, d 2/24/16 in Pittsfield, MA (fell under a load of wood drawn by an ox team) (3-3/7)

6319. Norton, Isaac, merchant, m Martha Carr, both of Cambridge in C; Rev. Peter D. Freileich (9-1/12/08)

6320. Norton, James (Hon.), late first judge of Steuben Co. "and since a judge of Yates County's court of common pleas",d 5/23/31 in Starkey (1-5/30)

6321. Norton, James Clinton, Esq. m Sarah Pearsall, dau of Thomas C., Esq., in NYC; Rev. Dr. Spring (3-8/6/21)

6322. Norton, John m 6/22/22 Mary Eliza Huestis; Rev. Smith. All of Poughkeepsie (8-6/26)

6323. Norton, Joseph Buel, Esq. drowned 11/16/31 in the Hudson River while "on his return to Bennington, VT in one of the night boats from New York (City) accompanied by his brother" ("an enterprising business man and member of the Baptist Church in Bennington, Vermont")(1-11/24)

6324. Norton, Mary, 16 mo, dau of John T., d 2/26/29 (1-2/27)

6325. Norton, Mary H., 27, wf of John T., Esq. of Albany, d 9/21/29 at the home of her father, Timothy Pitkin, in Farmington, CT (1-9/25)

6326. Norton, Nathaniel, Esq., 45, of Bloomfield (Ont. Co.) d 12/9/06 in NYC (buried in the family vault of John Kane "in the North Churchyard") (6-12/30)

6327. Norton, Seth m Charlotte Whiting, both of Hudson (6-5/11)

6328. Nott, Abraham (Hon.), 66, d 6/19/30 in Winnsborough, SC (1-7/5)

6329. Nott, Eliphalet (Rev.), president of Union College in Schenectady, m 8/3/07 Mrs. Getty Tibbits of Troy in T; Rev. Coe (9-8/4)

6330. Nott, Howard, Esq. (s of Dr. Nott, president of Union Col.) m 10/11/31 Margaretta Matilda Stewart, dau of J. M. Bowers, Esq., "at the Lakeland near Cooperstown"; Rev. Smith (1-10/19)

6331. Noxon, B. D., Esq., attorney, m 2/13/11 Sally Ann Van Kleeck, dau of Teunis of Poughkeepsie; Rev. Reed (8-2/27)

6332. Noxon, Bartholomew of Poughkeepsie m 12/27/09 Rachel Teller of Clinton; Rev. Cuyler (8-1/3/10)

6333. Noxon, Bartholomew, 48, d 2/1/13 in Poughkeepsie (8-2/3)

6334. Noxon, Benjamin of Beekmantown (perhaps intended for Beekman, Dutchess Co.) m 5/18/00 Eunice Howland of Pawling; Ebenezer Carey, Esq. (8-5/27)

6335. Noxon, Elizabeth, 35, wf of Bartholomew of Poughkeepsie, d 2/11/07 in Hudson (consumption) (6-2/17 and 8-3/25)

6336. Noxon, Esther, wf of Dr. Robert, d 11/20/00 (surv by husband and "several children") (funeral sermon by Rev. Chase at the Episcopal Church; burial in the churchyard cemetery) (8-11/25)

6337. Noyes, David Wainwright, 7, d 4/24/09 in Hudson (6-5/2)
6338. Noyes, John, Esq., 61, d 9/4/30 in Norwich (funeral sermon by Rev. Swan of the Baptist Church) (deceased had been a judge in Chenango Co. where he was an early settler - had moved into the town of Preston shortly after 1800) (1-9/11)
6339. Noyes, Mary Eliza, 26, wf of Enoch and dau of Earl P. Pease, d 11/21/29 in Albany (consumption) (1-11/24)
6340. Noyes, Nathan, Esq., 63, d 5/5/13 in Castleton (9-5/11)
6342. Noyes, Seth H., merchant of Hudson m Lucy Hosmer, dau of Hon. S. T. of Middletown, CT, in M; Rev. Huntington (6-9/27/08)
       Nugent, John. See, possibly, Neugent, John.
6343. Nugent, William W. (Dr.), formerly of Albany, NY m 5/20/29 Mary B. Minuse, dau of George of Milan Township, OH, in M. T.; Rev. C. P. Bronson (1-6/4)
6344. Nye, Ebenezer, Esq., 39, surrogate of Dutchess Co., d 9/29/24 in Poughkeepsie (8-10/6)
6345. Nye, Holland, ship's carpenter, of Poughkeepsie d 4/9/03 (killed "by the fall of a tree") (surv by wf and "a number of children") (8-4/12)
6346. Oakley, Elizabeth, 48, wf of Morris, d 9/2/30 in Albany (1-9/7)
6347. Oakley, George P. m Rebecca Wilkinson, dau of John, all of Beekmantown (probably intended for the town of Beekman in Dutchess Co.) (8-12/17/99)
6348. Oakley, Jackson of the firm of Oakley and Davis m 7/4/29 Abigail Logan in Newburgh; Rev. John Johnson. All of Newburgh (1-7/10 and 1-7/13)
6349. Oakley, Jerusha, 52, consort of Jesse, d 1/15/08 in Poughkeepsie (8-1/20)
6350. Oakley, Jesse, Esq. of Poughkeepsie m 11/19/08 Susan Lynsen Romayne, youngest sister of Dr. Romayne and of Rev. Romayne, both of NYC, in NYC; Rev. Romayne (8-11/30)
6351. Oakley, Jesse, Esq., 79, d 11/9/27 in Poughkeepsie (born on Long Island but lived in Dutchess Co. nearly 60 yrs and in Poughkeepsie more than 20 yrs) (8-11/14)
6352. Oakley, John, 91, brother of late Jesse of Poughkeepsie, d in Huntington, L. I., NY (8-4/22)
6353. Oakley, John C. of Clinton (Dut. Co.) m 2/29/12 Elizabeth Balding of Fishkill; Rev. C. C. Cuyler (8-3/11)
6354. Oakley, John W. m 12/30/09 Harriet Badger, both of Poughkeepsie; Rev. Cuyler (8-1/3/10)
6355. Oakley, Jonathan m 6/14/07 Sally Newcomb, dau of Obadiah; Rev. Hopkins (6-6/16)
6356. Oakley, Lydia, 42, wf of Thomas J., Esq., d 10/6/27 in Poughkeepsie (8-10/10)
6357. Oakley, Robert W., Esq., 28, d 8/28/32 in Poughkeepsie (8-8/29)
6358. Oakley, Samuel, merchant, of NYC m 11/24/34 Sally Davis of Poughkeepsie; Rev. Dr. Reed (8-11/26)
6359. Oakley, Susan, wid of late Jesse, d 7/28/34 in Poughkeepsie (8-7/30)
6360. Oakley, Thomas J. m 3/13/04 ___?___ Williams, dau of Robert, Esq.; Rev. Chase (8-3/20)
6361. Oakley, Thomas J. m 3/29/31 Matilda Caroline Cruger, dau of late Henry, Esq., in NYC; Right Rev. Bishop Onderdonk. All of NYC (1-4/1 and 8-4/6)
6362. O'Brien, Daniel A. of Philadelphia, PA m Rachel K. Van Voorhees of Dutchess Co., NY at Christ Church in NYC; Rev. Sneller (1-10/8/29)
6363. O'Brien, John, Esq. of Schoharie Co., NY, attorney, m 10/17/12 Clarissa Sanford of Great Barrington, MA in G.B.; Rev. Elijah Wheeler (6-11/2)
6364. O'Conner, Christianna (Mrs.), 74, d 1/27/29 in Oswego (member of Presbyterian Church there) (8-3/11)
6365. O'Connor, Cecilia (Miss), 43, d 5/18/29 at the Shaker Village in Watervliet (8-5/27)
6366. Odell, Abraham m 1/30/21 Catherine Dutcher; Rev. Clark. All of Clinton (Dut. Co.) (8-2/7)
6367. Odell, Azariah W. (Maj.), 33, an officer in the War of 1812 and late of the 23rd Regt., U. S. Infantry) d 7/5/22 at his home in Ballston Spa. (pulmonary complaint) (2-7/9)
6368. Odell, David, formerly of Ballston d 8/23/23 in Saratoga Springs ("In less than 14 months a father, son, and daughter have been consigned to the tomb." (2-8/26)

6369. Odell, Henry m 12/18/28 Delia Doty, both of Washington (Dut. Co.);
Thomas Hammond, Esq. (8-12/24)
6370. Odell, James m 12/8/13 Mary Dubois, dau of Koert, Esq.; Rev. Dr. Dodge.
All of Clinton (8-12/22)
6371. Odell, Samuel of Washington (Dut. Co.) m 12/17/17 Pamela Marshall of
Clinton (Dut. Co.), dau of John I.; Rev. Cuyler (8-12/24)
6372. Odell, Samuel, 29, d 9/22/23 in Ballston("Thus has a whole family been
consigned to the mansions of the dead in the space of about 14 months")
(2-9/23)
6373. Odell, Stephen S. of Union Vale m 12/25/34 Hannah Hunt of Dover; Rev. H.
Johnson (8-12/31)
6374. Odell, William G. d 2/17/34 in Poughkeepsie (8-2/19)
6375. Ogden, David A. (Hon.), late first judge of St. Lawrence Co., NY and
formerly of NYC, d 6/11/29 at the home of Meredith Ogden in Montreal,
Canada (1-6/22)
6376. Ogden, Elizabeth (Mrs.) d "recently" in Albany (funeral from the home of
Abraham Coverts on Van Schaick St.) (1-6/6/29)
6377. Ogden, Nicholas G. "of N.Y." m 9/13/31 Caroline Barker, dau of Marks
Barker, in Hudson (1-9/17)
6378. Ogilvie, James G. (Rev.) of NYC m 6/9/17 Elizabeth Wilson of Troy in T;
Rev. Wayland (6-6/24)
6379. Olcott, Horatio J., cashier of the Central Bank in Cherry Valley,
m 9/6/31 Harriet M. Leonard of Suffield, CT in S; Rev. Robinson
(1-9/13)
6380. Olcott, Michael, Esq., 53, Quartermaster General of the Connecticut
Militia, d 5/11/29 in Hartford, CT (1-5/21)
6381. Olcott, William, 4, s of John E., drowned 6/3/08 in Hudson (6-6/7)
6382. Olds, Frederick m 12/4/28 Sally Hill in Batavia; T. Fitch, Esq. (9-12/19)
6383. Olendorf, Arnold m Dorcas Low in Middlefield; Francis Henry, Esq.
(3-11/26/21)
6384. Olendorf, Catherine, 65, wf of Daniel, d 11/9/26 in Cooperstown (3-11/13)
6385. Olendorf, Garrit m 9/29/20 Eliza Platner; Rev. Tiffany. All of Cooperstown (3-10/2)
6386. Olin, Gideon (Hon.), 79, (a Rev. patriot) d in Shaftsbury, VT (one of the
founders of Vermont; was repeatedly Speaker of that state's assembly
and was twice elected to Congress)(3-3/3/23)
6387. Oliphant, Duncan, 74, d 4/1/22 in Ballston (2-5/8)
6388. Oliphant, John, 60, d 12/8/31 in Auburn (1-12/24)
6389. Oliver, Alfred m 11/9/20 Huldah Wormwood in Chazy (7-11/25)
6390. Oliver, Andrew F. (Dr.) of Penn Yan m 7/27/31 Mrs. Almira M. Gilbert of
Paris, NY in P; Rev. Southard (1-8/9)
6391. Oliver, Margaret, 36, wf of Dr. Andrew F., d 6/13/29 in Penn Yan (1-6/22)
6392. Oliver, William (a Rev. soldier and pensioner) d 11/12/31 in Salem
(1-11/18)
6393. Olmstead, Aaron, Esq., a state assemblyman from Columbia Co., d 1/26/13
in Albany (6-2/2 and 9-2/2)
6394. Olmsted, Aaron, Jr., 23, d 2/17/09 in Canaan (6-3/7)
6395. Olmsted, Alvah of Rush (Monroe Co.) m 5/5/31 Ann Bant, dau of Samuel,
Esq. of Broadalbin, in B; Rev. John R. Davis (1-5/12)
6396. Olmsted, Dennison, Esq., professor of natural philosophy in Yale College,
m 8/24/31 Julia Mason, sister of Rev. C. Mason of NYC; Rev. Cyrus
Mason (1-8/27)
6397. Olney, Ann P. (Mrs.), 74, of Hudson d 7/7/18 at the home of her grandson,
D. Malcolm, in Brooklyn (6-7/14)
6398. Olney, Joseph, 77, d 10/16/14 in Hudson (6-10/25)
6399. Onderdonk, Henry of Long Island m 2/7/95 Miss Sally Billings Van Kleeck
of Poughkeepsie; Rev. Speirin (8-2/11)
6400. Oppie, James W., Esq. of Fishkill m 11/1/31 Henrietta Maria Dyson Hunt,
dau of Maj. Benjamin of Newtown, L. I., NY, in Newtown; Rev. Shelton
(8-11/9)
6401. Orcutt, Eleazer m 12/31/23 Jane Giles, both of Troy; Rev. Howard
(9-1/13/24)
6402. O'Reilly, Alicia Ann (Mrs.), 44, mother of one of the editors of the
Rochester Daily Advertiser, d 7/27/29 in NYC (1-8/7)

6403. O'Reilly, Henry, editor of the Rochester Daily Advertiser, m 12/3/29 Marcia F. Brooks, dau of Gen. Micah, in East Bloomfield; Rev. Wheeler (1-12/12)
6404. Ormsby, Chloe, 36, wf of Gideon of Manchester, VT and step-dau of Rev. Daniel Barber of Claremont, NH, d 4/11/06 in Whitehall, VT (perhaps intended for Whitehall, NY?) (was taken sick on her way to Plattsburgh with her three small children) (surv by her husband, both her parents, and the children of previous mention here) (9-5/20)
6405. Ormsby, Leonard d in Albany (funeral from 9 Union St.) (1-3/3/31)
6406. Ormsby, Royal C., merchant, of NYC m 6/15/29 Sarah Ophelia Guion, dau of Abraham, Esq. of Rye Neck, in R. N.; Rev. J. M. Smith (1-6/19)
6407. Orne, William (Hon.), 63, president of the Essex Bank, d 10/28/15 in Salem (9-10/31)
6408. Orregon , V. of Mexico (presumably the country) m 11/15/31 Margaretta Hurry, dau of late Samuel of Philadelphia (state not given), at Christ's Church in NYC; Rev. Varela and "afterwards" by Rev. Berrian at St. John's Church (in NYC?) (1-11/18)
6409. Orton, Gerrit V. Z. of Winfield (Herk. Co.) m Rosamond Cook, dau of Philip, Esq. of Conhocton (Steuben Co.), in C (3-7/10/26)
6410. Orton, Oliver L. m 9/8/32 Ruth Burton, both of Dover; Thomas Hammond, Esq. (double ceremony - see marr of Alfred Jones) (8-9/19)
6411. Orton, Perez of Herk. Co. m 2/9/25 Eliza Storm, dau of Abraham G. of Poughkeepsie (8-2/23)
6412. Orton, Perez, 29, d 2/5/28 in Poughkeepsie (funeral at the home of A. G. Storm on Mill St.) (deceased was late of the firm of Orton and Luff of NYC (8-2/6)
6413. Orvis, Horatio m 6/16/25 Mrs. Harriet Bassett in Greenfield; Howell Gardner, Esq. (2-6/28)
6414. Osbern, Darwen m 1/11/26 Sally Hagerman, dau of John; Rev. M. Clark. All of Pleasant Valley (8-1/18)
6415. Osborn, B. W. m 2/1/29 Letitia Osborn King, dau of late William King, Jr. of NYC; Rev. Dr. De Witt (1-2/6)
6416. Osborn, Catharine Matilda, 1, youngest dau of William, d 6/27/31 in Albany (funeral from her father's home, 86 North Pearl St.) (1-6/28)
6417. Osborn, Cornelius (Dr.), 59, for many years a physician in Fishkill, d 8/23/82 in Fishkill (surv by wf and children) (5-8/29)
6418. Osborn, Elias, Esq., 66, d 8/20/30 in Erie (Erie Co.) (lived for many years in Delaware Co., NY and was a state assemblyman from that county) (in 1815 was an assemblyman representing the counties of Niagara, Chautauqua, and Cattaraugus) (1-9/1)
6419. Osborn, George H. m 9/16/29 Sarah Van Benschoten in Poughkeepsie; Rev. William Jewett (8-9/23)
6420. Osborn, John D. m 7/14/30 Emily La Vendee Vorce, both of Poughkeepsie; Rev. Dr. Cuyler (8-7/21)
6421. Osborn, John S., 59, d 10/20/29 in Stanford (Dut. Co.) (8-11/4)
6422. Osborn, Rebecca, 67, wid of late Daniel, d 7/12/26 (3-7/24)
6423. Osborne, _____ (Dr.) m 8/7/17 Jane Ann Platt in Constable (7-8/16)
6424. Osgood, Samuel, Esq., naval officer, d 8/12/13 in NYC (3-8/21)
6425. Osterout, Levi of Kingston m 8/12/29 Permelia Hoxie, dau of Wanton Hoxie, in Poughkeepsie; Rev. Welton (8-8/19)
6426. Ostrander, Harriett (Miss), 18, dau of Capt. William, d 11/15/30 in Albany (funeral from 652 North Market St.) (1-11/16)
6427. Ostrander, Henry m Mary Taylor, dau of Robert, all of Hudson, in Hudson (6-3/23/12)
6428. Ostrander, Henry S. m 1/13/20 Rachel Bradford, both of Plattsburgh, in P (7-1/22)
6429. Ostrander, Israel N. m 3/29/27 Clarissa Dustin; Rev. Halsey (7-3/31)
6430. Ostrander, Moses (Maj.), 50, d 1/4/14 in Cooperstown (3-1/8)
6431. Ostrander, Peter, merchant, of Hudson m 8/4/16 Caroline Livingston, oldest dau of Moncrief, Esq., at the home of the latter, Livingston Manor; Rev. Bedell (6-8/13)
6432. Ostrander, Peter M. m 5/24/23 Tamer Kirkham; Rev. Cuyler (8-5/28)
6433. Ostrander, Polly, 46, wf of Samuel, d 1/15/31 in Schenectady (1-1/19)
6434. Ostrander(?) (surname blurred), Sarah, youngest dau of John, d 3/22/28 at her father's home in Pleasant Valley (8-3/26)

6435. Ostrom, Catherine E., 17, dauof late Joshua, d 3/9/30 in Utica (1-3/2)
6436. Ostrom, Hendrick of Poughkeepsie d 4/29/22 (8-5/1)
6437. Ostrom, Isaac m 11/9/25 Mary Pells, dau of Zephaniah; Rev. Clark. All of
      Pleasant Valley (8-11/23)
6438. Ostrom, John, 82, of Poughkeepsie d "recently" (8-12/6/03)
6439. Ostrom, John C., merchant, of Clinton m 10/31/24 Eliza Hull of Rhinebeck
      in R; Rev. David Parker (8-11/10)
6440. Ostrom, John D., 60, d 12/23/14 in Clinton (Dut. Co.) (8-1/4/15)
6441. Ostrom, Sheperd m 5/26/12 Eliza Beadle, dau of John, Esq.; Rev. Clark.
      All of Clinton (Dut. Co.) (8-6/3)
6442. Ostrom, Zachariah m Hannah Lamoree; Rev. Clark (8-7/10/04)
6443. Ostrum, Jacobus of Poughkeepsie d 2/5/04 (8-2/7)
6444. Oswald, Elizabeth, wid of Col. Eleazer, d 9/18/97 in Philadelphia, PA
      (her son died a few days earlier) (yellow fever) (8-9/26)
6445. Otis, Jacob, d 10/6/31 in Truxton (killed in a bridge collapse while
      on his way home "from a visit at the house of one of his daughters")
      (1-10/20)
6446. Otis, Loring of Poughkeepsie m 9/1/30 Caroline Grimm of NYC; Rev. Dr.
      Cuyler (8-9/22)
6447. Ousely, William, attached to the British legation in Washington, D.C.
      m 3/27/28 Marcia Van Ness, dau of Gov. Van Ness of Vermont, in
      Washington, D.C. (9-4/8)
6448. Outcalt, William m Elizabeth Primer "in New Brunswick" (marriage place
      not further defined) (9-9/5/15)
6449. Outhout, Henry, Jr. of Watervliet m 12/18/14 Sarah Vanderheyden of Troy
      (9-12/20)
6450. Outhout, Volkert V. m 4/4/13 Fanny Millard, both of Watervliet; Rev. Coe
      (9-4/6)
6451. Overacker, Jacob, farmer, of Beekman d 3/7/14 (8-3/16)
6452. Overhiser, Conrad m 11/27/13 Mary Townsend, both of Beekman; Rev. Dewitt
      (8-12/8)
6453. Overocker, Baltus m 5/10/25 AnnThurston, both of Freedom; Rev. Clark
      (8-5/25)
6454. Overocker, Marvin of Freedom m 11/24/29 Sally Ann Bagsley of Pleasant
      Valley; Rev. Buttolph (8-12/2)
6455. Owen, _____, 67, consort of Daniel, d 3/14/25 in Beekmantown (Clinton Co.)
      member of Baptist Church) (7-3/19)
6456. Owen, Daniel of Scipio m 2/12/24 Maria Hasbrook, dau of Col. Benjamin of
      Fishkill; Rev. De Witt (8-3/3)
6457. Owen, Daniel (Deacon), 78, (a Rev. soldier) d 8/30/31 in Beekmantown
      (Clinton Co.) (1-9/12)
6458. Owen, James m 5/7/29 Sally Wood, both of Poughkeepsie; Rev. Welton
      (8-5/14)
6459. Owen, Joshua, 89, formerly of Dutchess Co., d 10/21 in Troy (8-11/10)
6460. P--ter, Mary (Miss), about 22, dau of Joseph and Mary, d 9/24/34 in Union
      Vale (8-10/1)
6461. Pace, Cyrus m 5/8/07 Evelina Whiteman, both of Rhinebeck, in R; Rev.
      Frederick Myer (8-5/10)
6462. Packard, Nathaniel R., merchant, m 4/21/14 Elizabeth Clery at Cherry
      Valley; Rev. Cooley. All of C. V. (3-4/23)
6463. Packer,John m 11/15/21 Alathea McAuley in Charlton; Rev. I. W. Platt
      (2-12/5)
6464. Packerd, Chester, 58, of Easton d 4/18/22 in Stillwater ("recently moved"
      from Wilmington, VT) (9-5/7)
6465. Paddock, _____, 4, child of Capt. Laban Paddock, d in Hudson (6-1/3/04)
6466. Paddock, Judah, about 18, s of Isaac of Southeast, d in Hudson (8-10/18/03)
6467. Paddock, Reuben (Capt.) m 9/1/04 Mary Nichols of NYC in NYC (6-9/11)
6468. Paddock, Stephen, Esq., 84, d 2/13/14 in Hudson (6-2/15)
6469. Paddock, William, 9 mo, s of Capt. Laban, d 7/12/09 in Hudson (6-7/18)
6470. Page, Benjamin (Lt.) of the U.S. Navy m 5/7/29 Eliza McEvers Livingston,
      dau of John R., in NYC; Rev. Ives (1-5/13)
      Page, Cyrus. See, possibly, Pace, Cyrus.
6471. Page, Elijah, 36, merchant, of the firm of McBain and Page d 8/16/22 in
      Ballston Spa (funeral at the Episcopal Church; funeral sermon by
      Rev. Ambler of Milton (2-8/20)

6472. Page, James N. m 12/8/24 Charlotte Potter, both of Sherman, CT; Rev. Maltby Gelston (8-12/22)
6473. Page, Jared, Esq., 59, father of Sherman Page, Esq. of Unadilla, d 10/23/15 in Chenango (Broome Co.) (3-11/12)
6474. Page, Jason of the firm of Wilder, Hastings & Co. m 6/17/29 Eliza G. Platt, dau of Ralph, Esq., in Albany; Rev. Dr. Upfold (1-6/19)
6475. Page, Sherman, Esq., attorney, m 7/13/06 Maria Crooker, both of Unadilla, in U; Rev. David Harrower (3-7/17)
6476. Paige, Eliza G., wf of Jason, d 9/11/31 at the home of Rev. Dr. Upfield in NYC (funeral from her late home on South Pearl St. in Albany) (Ralph Pratt, Esq., father of the deceased, is named) (1-9/13)
6477. Paige, Helen Maria, 31, wf of Hon. Joseph C. of Capitol Park, Albany, d 1/25/29 (1-1/27)
6478. Paine, Amasa (Hon.), 61, d 12/25/23 in Troy (9-12/30)
6479. Paine, Amasa (Lt.) of the U.S. Navy m Sarah Ann Burgess of Boston (state not given) in Providence, RI (7-5/10/34)
6480. Paine, Barnabas, Esq., 84, d 6/6/22 in Amenia (an early settler there) (8-6/26)
6481. Paine, Ephraim Thompson m 9/25/07 Catharine Livingston, both of Pough-keepsie; Rev. Buckley (8-10/7)
6482. Paine, Ephraim Thompson, Esq., attorney, formerly of Poughkeepsie, NY, d 8/12/13 in Springfield, TN (8-11/10)
6483. Paine, John, Esq. m 2/6/27 Eliza Ann Warren, dau of Esais, Esq., at St. Paul's Church in Troy. All of Troy (9-2/9)
6484. Painter, Abbey Victoria, 22, only child of Hon. Gamaliel, d 12/26/18 in Middlebury, VT (copied from the Middlebury Standard) (7-12/26?)
6485. Palmateer, Jacob m 10/14/29 Nancy H. Armstrong; Rev. Jewitt. All of Poughkeepsie (8-10/21)
6486. Palmatier, John m 7/15/32 Edy Maria Lockwood; Rev. Perkins. All of Poughkeepsie (8-7/18)
6487. Palmer, Abraham m 9/7/22 Polly Cornwall; Isaac Sutherland, Esq. All of Stanford (Dut. Co.) (8-9/18)
6488. Palmer, Amy, 47, wf of Capt. Joshua, d 4/23/09 in Canaan (consumption) (6-5/9)
6489. Palmer, Apame(?), 36, wf of John, d 2/28/30 in Poughkeepsie (8-3/3)
6490. Palmer, Barton m 12/25/21 Dorothy Nicols in Galway, NY; Rev. J. Mairs (2-1/9/22)
6491. Palmer, Benjamin, 83, d 2/12/11 in Stanford (surv by wf "and numerous family") (8-2/27)
6492. Palmer, Benjamin m 10/23/24 Emilia Beckwith in Stanford (Dut. Co.); Rev. Wilson (8-11/10)
6493. Palmer, Beriah, Esq., 71, (a Rev. Soldier) d 5/20/12 in Ballston (8-6/10)
6494. Palmer, C. G., senior editor of the Schenectady Whig, m 5/25/31 Clarine Amelia Colvard, dau of Asa, Esq. of Rensselaerville, in R; Rev. Fuller (1-5/28)
6495. Palmer, Daniel, late of the U.S. Army("one of the fortunate holders of the ticket which drew 25,000 dollars in the Medical Science Lottery...") m 4/24/17 Catherine Ostrom, dau of John H. of Poughkeepsie; Rev. C. C. Cuyler (8-4/30)
6496. Palmer, Daniel m 4/30/29 Euphemia Sutherland, dau of late Roger, all of Amenia; Rev. C. P. Wilson (8-5/6)
6497. Palmer, Ebenezer m Polly Sturges of NYC in Franklin (8-1/10/04)
6498. Palmer, Elihu, 41, of NYC d 3/31/06 in Philadelphia ("known as a moral and political lecturer") (9-4/15)
6499. Palmer, Ezekiel m 9/20/17 Phebe Heddy, both of Washington (Dut. Co.); Silas Waddle, Esq. (8-9/24)
6500. Plamer, Harvey, formerly of Orange Co., m 1/11/30 Maria Neilson of Pough-keepsie; Rev. Dr. Reed (8-1/20)
6501. Palmer, Henry H. m 1/2/23 Jane Manning; A. Raymond, Esq. All of Hyde Park (8-1/8)
6502. Palmer, Ichabod B., Esq., 69, d 11/12/07 in Butternuts (one of the earliest settlers in this region) (member of the Protestant Episcopal Church) (3-11/21)
6503. Palmer, James, Esq., late of the U.S. Army and son of Elias, Esq. of Stillwater d 5/28/19 at the cantonment in Greenbush (was an officer in the War of 1812) (7-6/19)

6504. Palmer, John m 1/18/10 Pama Parsons, both of Amenia; Rev. John Wood (8-1/31)
6505. Palmer, John, Esq. m 3/7/12 Charlotte Sailly, youngest dau of Peter, Esq., in Plattsburgh; Rev. Halsey (7-3/13)
6506. Palmer, John, 50, formerly of Dover, d 8/19/29 at the home of his brother, David (8-9/2)
6507. Palmer, John m 10/26/31 Euphemia Hendricks, both of Poughkeepsie, in Pine Plains; E. Taylor, Esq. (8-11/9)
6508. Palmer, John D. m 11/18/23 Betsey N. Palmer; Rev. Cuyler (8-11/26)
6509. Palmer, John G. m 11/3/17 Helen Bond, both of Pleasant Valley, in P. V.; Garret Adriance, Esq. (8-11/12)
6510. Palmer, John V., 38, formerly of Vermont, drowned 3/17/30 in Buffalo Creek "while attempting to cross on the ice" (1-4/2)
6511. Palmer, Marian, about 18 mo, dau of John, Esq., d 6/30/14 in Plattsburgh (7-7/2)
6512. Palmer, Mary, 37, consort of Thomas, Esq., d 6/20/23 in Ballston Spa (funeral at the Episcopal Church with the sermon by Rev. Clark) (2-6/24)
6513. Palmer, Peter, schoolmaster, formerly of Hudson, d 9/5/03 in NYC (6-9/20)
6514. Palmer, Thomas M., Esq. of Rhinebeck m 11/19/05 Louisa Charlotta Prevost, dau of Augustus, Esq. of Greenfield, in G; Rev. Budd (double ceremony - see marr of G. W. Prevost)
6515. Palmer, Thomas, Esq., attorney, m 9/15/23 Nancy Bradley in Ballston Spa; Rev. Clark. All of Ballston Spa (2-9/16)
6516. Palmer, Timothy of New Orleans, LA m 6/15/20 Mary Sheldon of Troy; Rev. Dr. Coe (9-6/20)
6517. Palmer, Vose, 64, d 7/28/26 in Plainfield, NY (3-8/7)
6518. Palmer, Washington, youngest s of Micha Palmer, d 11/25/09 - and the father, Micha (a member of the Masons), d 12/9/09 (both died in Pough-keepsie and were interred in the family burial ground there) (8-12/20)
6519. Palmer, William m 11/9/16 Rebecca Tompkins, both of Poughkeepsie, in Pleasant Valley (8-11/20)
6520. Palmer, William m 5/20/30 Emily Spinks, both of Peru, NY, in Peru; Rev. Heman Garlick (7-5/22)
6521. Palmer, William Frederick, 7, d 8/24/27 in Plattsburgh (7-8/25)
6522. Palmer, William K., about 14, d 12/30/23 in Plattsburgh (7-1/3/24)
6523. Pangburn, William m 4/16/29 Alicia Van Buren, both of Bethlehem; Rev. Kissam (1-4/20)
6524. Panon, Marius of Marseilles, France m 10/1/30 Charlotte De Wessenfels Ellery, dau of late Abraham Ellery, Esq. of New Orleans, LA in NYC; Rev. A. Verren (1-10/7)
6525. Pappan, _____ of Beekman m 1/23/22 Margaret Bogardus of Poughkeepsie; Rev. Price (8-2/6)
6526. Parce, _____, child of Perry Parce, d 2/10/22 (small pox) (7-2/16)
6527. Parce, Amos m 5/25/23 Laura McCarter, both of Beekmantown (Clinton Co.), in B; Hallock Brumley, Esq. (7-5/31)
6528. Pardee, W. J. (Col.) of the firm of Lansing and Pardee of Little Falls m 5/28/29 Laura E. S. Rodman, dau of late Daniel, Esq. of Albany, in Oxford (Chen. Co.); Rev. Wells (1-6/2)
6529. Pardy, Francis m "Miss Dominy", dau of William of Plattsburgh; Rev. Frederick Halsey (7-3/15).- Addendum: marriage date was 3/2/28.
6530. Pardy, Jane Ann, 32, wf of Francis, d 3/4/27 in Plattsburgh (7-3/10)
6531. Parent, John A. m 2/12/24 Catharine Deremer, both of Charlton, in C; Rev. Joseph Sweetman (2-2/17)
6532. Parents, Samuel T. m 4/22/29 Mary Ann Cassidy, both of Albany; Rev. Welch (1-5/1)
6533. Parish, John, about 31, d 3/13/27(in Plattsburgh?) (7-3/31)
6534. Park, Daniel of Amenia m 11/25/24 Sarah P. Benjamin in NYC; Rev. D. Lyell (3-12/6)
6535. Parker, Amasa J. (Hon.) of Delhi, NY m 8/27/34 Harriet Langdon Roberts, dau of Edmund of Portsmouth, NH, in P; Rev. Dr. Burroughs (8-9/3)
6536. Parker, Amos m 12/7/06 Betsey Aldridge, both of Hoosick, in H (9-12/16)
6537. Parker. Eleazer H., 44, d 1/29/14 in Standish, MA (hydrophobia from the bite of a wild cat) (8-3/9)
6538. Parker, Gardner of Pownal, VT m 6/24/07 Lydia Fowler of Brunswick, NY; Rev. Coe (9-6/30)

6539. Parker, George of Poughkeepsie d 3/20/11 (8-3/27)
6540. Parker, Janet Ann, 13, dau of William S., d 9/9/27 (9-9/11)
6541. Parker, Joseph B. m 7/27/04 Mary Spencer, dau of Thomas; Rev. Mayer.
       All of Loonenburgh (Athens, NY) (6-8/7)
6542. Parker, Lyman d 9/25/01 on Ferry Street in Albany (was shot 9/21 about
       midnight, it is believed, by a Timothy Parks whose house the deceased
       was then passing) (6-10/1)
6543. Parker, Mary, 41, wf of William S., d 1/30/22 in Troy (9-2/5)
6544. Parker, O. H., merchant, of Utica m 1/8/29 Ann Guiteau, dau of late
       Francis of Whitesboro, in Trenton, NY; Rev. Samuel C. Aiken (1- 1/23)
6545. Parker, Philip S., Esq., attorney, of Hudson m 8/21/03 Jennet Monell, dau
       of Dr. Monell of Claverack, in C (6-8/30)
6546. Parker, Philip S., Esq., 54, d 6/29/31 in Albany (funeral from his late
       home on State St.) (1-6/30)
6547. Parker, Richard of Long Branch, NJ m 6/24/30 Angelina Prentiss, dau of N.
       Prentiss, Esq. of NYC, in NYC; Rev. Heman Bangs (1-6/28)
6548. Parker, Sarah Anne, 28, wf of I. T. Parker "and sister of the senior
       editor of this paper" (his surname probably Moore or Stone -
       and if Stone then Roby G. Stone), d 4/13/34 in concord, NH (7-4/26)
6549. Parker, Sylvester m 3/30/17 Sally Thompson, both of Poughkeepsie; Rev.
       Reed (8-4/2)
6550. Parker, Thomas, 54, d 3/9/21 in Poughkeepsie (pulmonary complaint)
       (8-3/14)
6551. Parker, Thomas m 3/22/23 Elizabeth De Graff, both of Poughkeepsie; Rev.
       Dr. Reed (8-3/26)
6552. Parker, Thomas S., merchant, m Almira Holden, dau of Oliver, Esq; Rec. C.
       C. Cuyller. All of Poughkeepsie (8-4/30/28)
6553. Parkhurst, Curtis, M.D., of Lawrenceville, PA m 11/18/30 Jane A. Casson,
       oldest dau of Ambrose, Esq. of Syracuse; Rev. S. Porter of Jamesville
       (1-11/20)
6554. Parkhurst, Jabez, Esq. m "a few days since", Delia Man, dau of late Dr.
       Albon Man, in Constable (7-2/3/21)
6555. Parkhurst, Lemuel m 7/8/21 Mary Ann Roberts in Beekmantown(Clinton Co.);
       Rev. Stephen Kingsley (7-7/14)
6556. Parkinson, John, 82, d 3/12/29 in Poughkeepsie (8-3/18)
6557. Parkman, Chauncey d 4/3/14 in Hudson (6-4/5)
6558. Parkman, Frederick, 6 mo, s of Chauncey, d 12/11/12 in Hudson (6-12/15)
6559. Parkman, Mary, 34, consort of Chauncy, d in Hudson (6-9/21/12)
6560. Parkman, Mary Ann, 6, dau of Chauncey, d 3/2/12 in Hudson (6-3/9)
6561. Parkman, Thomas, 53, of Hudson d 1/25/13 in Albany (buried in Hudson)
       (6-2/2)
6562. Parks, Jonas of Durham m 2/24/31 Sabrina Ann Fish of Rensselaerville in
       R; Judge Moore (1-2/28)
6563. Parks, Phebe, 62, consort of Richard, d 10/2/23 in Pawling (8-10/22)
6564. Parmalee, John, 21, s of Joseph of Poughkeepsie, d 2/19/25 (8-2/23)
6565. Parmalee, Luman m 4/29/32 Jane Ann Lockwood; Rev. Thatcher. All of
       Poughkeepsie (8-5/2)
6566. Parmalee, Richard W. of the firm of Parmalee, Van Keuren & Co. m 4/4/32
       Sarah Adriance, both of Poughkeepsie; Rev. Dr. Reed (8-4/11). See 6568.
6567. Parmelee, Alvin m 7/9/26 Violette Hamilton in Springfield; Rev. Knapp
       (3-7/24)
6568. Parmelee, Richard W., merchant, m 3/9/34 Eliza Ann Adriance; Rev. Dr.
       Reed (8-3/12). See 6566.
6569. Parmentier, Andrew, 49, proprietor of the horticultural gardens in
       Brooklyn, d 11/27/30 in NYC (1-12/1)
6570. Parmentier, Charles of France m 10/2/26 Mary Ann Booth, dau of George of
       Poughkeepsie; Rev. Cushman (8-10/11)
6571. Parshall, Miner m 6/6/15 Experience Clark; Rev. John Smith. All of
       Cooperstown (3-6/15)
6572. Parsons, Abraham m 7/8/19 Fanny Woodworth, dau of Randal Woodworth, in
       Plattsburgh (7-7/10)
6573. Parsons, Achsah, 28, dau of Deacon Jabez Parsons, d 3/6/19 in Spencertown
       (consumption) (6-3/16)
6574. Parsons, Ambrose, 42, formerly of Poughkeepsie, d 9/6/25 in New Providence,
       NJ (8-9/14)

6575. Parsons, Anna (Mrs.), about 52, d 9/8/03 in Somers, CT (6-9/20)
6576. Parsons, Charles, Sr., about 45, d 2/9/23 in Plattsburgh (7-2/15)
6577. Parsons, Charles, about 8, s of Ansliem (sic), drowned 6/7/24 while
       swimming with other boys in the Saranac River (7-6/12)
6578. Parsons, Chester of Hudson, NY m 4/18/03 Phebe Turner of Hartford, CT in
       Hartford (6-4/26)
6579. Parsons, Clarissa, wf of Abraham, d 2/17/23 in Pine Plains (8-3/5)
6580. Parsons, Eliphaz (Mr.), 60, d 10/13/27 in Troy (9-10/16)
6581. Parsons, Frederick T., formerly of Poughkeepsie, m 5/24/26 Mehetable
       Turnbull of NYC in NYC; Rev. Chase (8-5/31)
6582. Parsons, Hester, about 32, wf of Charles, d 12/11/13 in Plattsburgh
       (surv by "five helpless children") ("The printer in burlington, Vermont
       is requested to give publicity to the foregoing for the information of
       friends") (7-12/18)
6582a. Parsons, Hial m 1/10/13 Patience Kenyon in Hoosick (9-1/26)
6583. Parsons, J. B. of the firm of Parsons and Baker, merchants, m 11/30/30
       Frances Lovell, adopted dau of C. H. Shear, Esq. (1-12/1)
6584. Parsons, Julia, 11, d 9/20/20 in Plattsburgh (7-9/23)
6585. Parsons, Maria Louisa, 2 yrs old, dau of Frederick and Mehetible,
       d 12/26/31 in NYC (scarlet fever) (8-12/28)
6586. Parsons, Miller m 9/4/28 "Miss Moore", both of Beekmantown (Clinton Co.);
       Rev. F. Halsey (7-9/6)
6587. Parsons, Nancy (Mrs.) d 10/26/15 in Plattsburgh ("at the bay of St. Amah")
       (7-11/11)
6588. Parsons, Peter of Franklin m Salome Pinny of West Windsor, CT in W.W.
       (6-11/2/02)
6589. Parsons, Peter, 54, d 11/11/04 in Somers, CT (6-12/4)
6590. Parsons, Phebe, 46, wid of Chester, d 11/6/28 in Poughkeepsie (8-11/12)
6591. Parsons, Ruth, 56, wf of Deacon Jabez, d 2/20/13 in Spencertown (6-3/2)
6592. Parsons, S., Jr., merchant, of Lockport m 8/11/29 Lucy Van Dake of
       Penfield (Monroe Co.) in P; Rev. Silas Parsons (1-8/18)
6593. Parsons, Seth, printer, m 10/21/13 Maria Ellis, both of Poughkeepsie;
       Rev. Cuyler) (8-10/27)
6594. Parsons, Stephen (Rev.), 71, d 1/7/20 in Lowville (was pastor of the
       Baptist Church) (3-2/21)
6595. Parsons, Sylvanus M., Esq., attorney, m 10/27/32 Eliza P. Bostwick in
       Burlington, VT; Rev. I. K. Converse (7-11/10)
6596. Parsons, William M. m 10/19/31 Sally Ann Pardy; Rev. Dr. Reed (8-10/26)
6597. Partridge, Pearl (Mr.) d 3/5/02 in Hudson (6-3/9)
6598. Passage, Maria (Mrs.), 96, d 8/30/30 in Duanesburg (1-9/2)
6599. Patchen, Hurbel of Richfield m Fanny Pardee of Warren in Springfield;
       Rev. Putnam (3-3/8/24)
6600. Patchin, Fregit (Gen.), 72, d 8/30/30 at his home in Blenheim (was
       confined in the Jersey Prison Ship during the Revolution and was once
       a prisoner in Quebec) (1-9/11)
6601. Paterson, John, Esq., 58, d 11/22/21 in Paterson (8-11/28)
6602. Paterson, Sarah, 92, relict of late Matthew, Esq., d 8/21/31 in Paterson
       (8-9/14)
6603. Patrick, Hiram m 3/30/25 Betsey Wilson in Butternuts. All of Butternuts
       (3-4/11)
6604. Patridge, Nathaniel m 3/28/24 Sarah Ann Gott in Hartwick; Rev. Potter
       (3-4/5)
6605. Patten, George m 3/1/12 Lucy Covel, dau of Rev. Zenas Covel. All of
       Poughkeepsie (8-3/4)
6606. Patten, John m 2/9/25 Margaret McRobie (3-2/14)
6607. Patten, Moses, Esq. m 11/18/19 Emma Colvard, dau of Philo, in Rensselaer-
       ville; Rev. Bronson (3-11/29)
6608. Patten, William m 10/31/20 Margaret McTavish in Cooperstown; Ambrose
       Clark, Esq. All of Pierstown (3-11/6)
6609. Patterson, Elizabeth, 13 mo, dau of Robert, d 10/24/09 in Hudson (6-11/7)
6610. Patterson, Elizabeth, wf of Elnathan, d 11/30/22 in Saratoga (surv by
       husband "and nine small children:) (2-12/17)
6611. Patterson, Elizabeth, 15 mo, dau of Elias, d 3/23/28 in Troy (9-3/28)
6612. Patterson, Ezra (Maj.), 67, d 8/24/29 in Pittsford (Monroe Co.) (1-9/8)
6613. Patterson, Harry, Esq. m 1/21/23 Lucy Russell, dau of Isaac of Petersburgh,
       in P (9-2/4)

6614. Patterson, John m 9/5/02 Hannah Fowler, both of Fishkill; Rev. Van Vranken (8-9/14)
6615. Patterson, Matthew, 84, d 2/18/17 at his home in Patterson (b in Scotland; came to America in 1756; fought in French and Indian War and in the Rev. War; was a New York legislator 12 yrs; for many years was a county judge) (8-2/26)
6616. Patterson, William (Hon.), one of the associate judges of the U.S. Supreme Court, d 9/9/06 at the mansion house of Stephen Van Rensselaer, Esq. in Albany (6-9/16 and 9-9/16)
6617. Paul, James, 80, d 6/23/30 in Adams, MA (1-7/7)
6618. Paul, James B., 33(?), formerly of Williamstown, MA, d 11/5/30 in Matilda, Upper Canada (1-11/29)
6619. Paul, Thomas (Rev.), 55, minister of the First African Church in Boston, Ma, d 4/13/31 in Boston (1-4/18)
6620. Paulding, John, one of the captors of Maj. Andre in the Rev. War, d 2/19/18 in Yorktown (West. Co.) (7-3/7)
6621. Paulding, John (Maj.), 87, d 12/31/19 in Staatsburgh (8-1/5/20)
6622. Pawling, Jacob m 2/28/22 Martha Russell, both of Hyde Park; Rev. Brown (8-3/6)
6623. Pawling, Levi, 30, d 10/22/21 in Ballston (had "dislocated his back-bone" in a fall from the frame of a barn) (2-10/31)
6624. Pawling, Levi d 4/13/22 in Ballston (2-5/8)
6625. Payne, _____, 32, consort of Dr. Lemuel C., d 12/23/21 in Broadalbin (2-12/26)
6626. Payne, Hiram of Albany m 1/15/15 Julia Ann Maria White, dau of C. White, merchant, of Troy; Rev. Coe (9-1/17)
6627. Payne, S. H., Esq. of Fort Covington m 7/2/27 Mary Shepherd of Peru, NY in P (7-7/21)
6628. Payne, William, Esq. m 5/6/13 Fanny Bartlett, both of Amenia; Rev. Hyde (8-5/19)
6629. Peabody, Oliver D. of Keeseville m 8/5/30 Helen Olmsted, dau of Jonas, Esq. of Northumberland (Sara. Co.), in N; Rev. Fonda (8-8/11 and 1-8/13)
6630. Peabody, Orra m 9/8/22 Matilda Loomis, both of Otsego, in O; Rev. John Smith (3-9/16)
6631. Peabody, Richard H., merchant, m 3/6/27 Eliza Pope, both of Keeseville, in K; Rev. Halsey (7-3/10)
6632. Peabody, Roswell (Capt.) d 10/2/13 in Cooperstown (typhus) (3-10/9
6633. Peak, Elizabeth, 31, wf of John, d 8/10/25 in Burlington (Ots. Co.) ("Editors in Boston and in New Hampshire generally are urged to insert the above")(3-8/15)
6634. Peale, James, Esq., 81, d 5/23/31 in Philadelphia, PA (was the first proprietor of the museum there and a distinguished painter) (1-5/30)
6635. Pearce, Thomas, 60, formerly of Scituate, RI, d in Hartford (Wash. Co.), NY (9-11/21/15)
6636. Pearsall, George m 2/5/31 Charity Palmer, both of Washington (Dut. Co.), in Washington; Rev. A. Bronson (8-2/23)
6637. Pearsall, Nathaniel of Nichols m 12/24/30 Maria Hayes of Unadilla; Rev. N. H. Adams (1-1/6/31)
6638. Pearsall, Thomas, Jr., 23, d 9/27/30 in La Grange (8-10/13)
6639. Pearson, George, merchant, m 12/21/08 Judith Van Vechten, oldest dau of Tunis T., Esq.; Rev. Bradford. All of albany (3-12/24)
6640. Pearson, Dimas, 25, consort of Samuel, d 10/7/06 in Hudson (6-10/14)
6641. Pease, Adriel m "lately" Maria H. Woodward, both of Hudson, in H; Rev. Cooper (6-12/14 and 6-12/21)
6642. Pease, Calvin m 10/21/18 Mary Wilson, both of Troy (9-10/27)
6643. Pease, Charles L. m 5/14/29 Ann Booth, both of Poughkeepsie; Rev. Welton (8-5/21)
6644. Pease, Chauncey D. of Cooperstown m 10/1424 Melinda Flint of Worcester in W; Rev. Caldwell (3-10/25)
6645. Pease, Hiram Coffin, 16, late of Hudson and son of Capt. Barzillai, d 12/18/16 in Stanford (Dela. Co.) (6-1/7/17)
6646. Pease, Leonard, 6, s of Capt. Barzillai, drowned 10/7/13 "from the steamboat wharf" in Hudson (6-10/12)
6647. Pease, Samuel, about 40, of Potsdam d 1/11/20 in Ogdensburgh (7-1/22)

6648. Peasely, Samuel of Peru, NY m Betsey Worth of Starksborough, VT in S
(4 [Keeseville Herald]-9/10/33 and 7-9/14)_(married at the Friends
Meeting House in Starksborough)
6649. Peck, Amelia, about 33, wf of Harmanus H. of Schenectady, d 1/10/31
(1-1/19)
6650. Peck, Chloe, 35 or 55?, wf of Everard, bookseller, d 12/5/30 in Rochester
(1-12/15 and 1-12/16)
6651. Peck, George, master ship-builder, of NYC d 9/26/99 in Poughkeepsie
(surv by wife "and a number of children") (8-10/1)
6652. Peck, Helen (Miss), 19, dau-in-law of Dr. Abel Catlin, d 5/27/22 in
Litchfield, CT (3-6/10)
6653. Peck, Jacob, 47, d 3/2/13 in Cooperstown (3-3/6)
6654. Peck, Jedidiah (Hon.), 73, d 8/15/21 at his home in Burlington (Ots. Co.)
(3-8/20 and 8-9/1) (Addendum: deceased was a Rev. patriot)
6655. Peck, John H., merchant, of the firm of J. and J. H. Peck m 11/14/33 Mary
Loomis, dau of Luther, Esq., in Burlington, VT; Rev. Ingersoll
(7-11/16)
6656. Peck, Phebe Maria, 28, wf of Samuel V., d 3/16/29 in NYC (surv by husband
and 5 young children) (8-3/25)
6657. Peck, Rheuamy, 54, consort of Ichabod, d 11/17/31 in Rensselaerville
(member of Episcopal Church "for a great number of years") (1-11/21)
6658. Peck, Samuel m 5/2/16 Mrs. Deborah Frear, both of Poughkeepsie; Rev.
Cuyler (8-5/15)
6659. Peck, Samuel V., late steward of the steamboat "New Philadelphia" and
formerly of Amenia, d 11/11/30 in Poughkeepsie (8-11/17)
6660. Peck, Seth, 50, d 9/8/29 at his home in Esperance (Schoharie Co.)
(1-9/19)
6661. Peckham, Amos m Maria Burgess at the Friends Meeting House in Bridgewater
(3-5/3/24)
6662. Peckham, George W., attorney, of Albany m Mary B. Watson, dau of Hon.
John of Southington, RI in Rensselaerville, NY; Rev. Dr. Fuller
(1-5/29/30)
6663. Peckham, Henry W. of Kinderhook m 10/1/29 Mary Ann Sanford, dau of
Austin of Coxsackie, in C; Rev. Searle (1-10/10)
6664. Peckham, Reuben, 36, d 10/4/04 in Hudson (6-10/9/04)
6665. Peebles, Joel (Lt.) of the U.S. Army m 4/28/14 Sally Ostrander (3-4/30)
6666. Peirce, Chancey, merchant, of Troy m 7/9/28 Eliza Hewitt of NYC in NYC
(9-7/18)
6667. Peirce, Jeremiah (Capt.), 62, of Troy d 2/8/06 in Troy (an early settler
in Troy village) (buried with Masonic honors) (9-2/11)
6668. Peirson, Patty, consort of Oliver of Cazenovia, d 4/13/06 (suicide -
her death resulted from her "discharging the contents of a loaded gun
in her breast") (6-5/13) (data copied from the Utica Patriot, 4/22/06)
6669. Pell, Constantine F., inf s of Alfred S., Esq., d 3/1/15 in Inwood
(8-3/8)
6670. Pell, Duncan C. of NYC m 5/15/34 Anna Clarke, dau of George, Esq. of
Hyde Park, in H. P.; Rev. F. J. Tiffany (8-5/21)
6671. Pell, William W. (Capt.) of the packet ship "Normandy" m Maria Antoinette
Varick, 2nd dau of John V. B. Varick, Esq. of Jersey City, NJ, in J. C.;
Rev. Lusk (8-5/14/34)
6672. Pellet, Elias, senior editor of the Anti-Masonic Telegraph, m Edith Ann
Pellett in Norwich (1-2/18/30)
6673. Pells, Abraham m 11/17/25 Phebe Holms,. dau of Joseph of Pleasant Valley;
Rev. Clark (8-11/23)
6674. Pells, Acca, dau of Abraham, d 5/6/09 in Poughkeepsie (8-5/10/09)
6675. Pells, Alfred S., 44, "formerly of New York", d 4/28/31 "on board the
ship 'Niagara' on her passage from Charleston (SC?) whither he had
gone for...his health") (1-5/5)
6676. Pells, Charles C., s of Abraham of Poughkeepsie, d 12/4/07 in Poughkeepsie
(8-12/9)
6677. Pells, Gerrit of Poughkeepsie m 9/20/32 Sarah Wilbur of Hyde Park; Rev.
Dr. cuyler (8-10/3)
6678. Pells, James F., 22, of Poughkeepsie ("Acting Surgeon's Mate") d about
11/3/22 on board the U.S. armed schooner, "Cyane" on the West India
station (8-12/4)

6679. Pells, Jane Ann, wf of Michael of Poughkeepsie, d 11/20/00 (interred in the Dutch Church cem.) (8-11/25)
6680. Pells, John m 4/2/03 Cornelia Boorom, both of Poughkeepsie; Rev. Bouwer (8-4/12)
6681. Pells, John, Jr. of La Grange m 12/22/30 Letitia Jewell of Fishkill; Rev. Buttolph (8-12/29)
6682. Pells, Mary (Miss), 18, d 2/26/01 in Poughkeepsie (8-3/3)
6683. Pells, Michael m 5/5/04 Polly Frear, both of Poughkeepsie (8-5/8)
6684. Pells, Peter of Poughkeepsie m 11/2/31 Ann Denman of Hyde Park; Rev. Dr. Cuyler (8-11/23)
6685. Pells, Peter of La Grange m 8/12/32 Ann Maria Briant of Fishkill; Rev. Sloth (8-8/22)
6686. Pells, Simon H. m 1/10/22 Parmela Van Wagoner, both of Rhinebeck; Rev. Parker (8-1/16)
6687. Pelton, Platt m 9/9/04 Phebe Snow, both of Southeast, in S; Rev. Jehu Minor (8-9/11)
6688. Pemberton, Ann, wf of Thomas L., d 12/26/31 in Albany(funeral from 92 North Pearl St.) (1-12/28)
6689. Pemberton, Ebn (sic) of Albany m Eunice Prentice, dau of Gideon of Augusta (Oneida Co.) in A; Rev. P. Brown (1-4/13/31)
6690. Pemberton, John m 5/5/29 Clarissa L. Henry; Rev. Ludlow. All of Albany (1-5/8)
6691. Pendleton, James M. (Dr.), brother of Hon. Edward H. of Hyde Park, d 1/16/32 in NYC (died of "influenza") (8-1/18)
6692. Pendleton, John Baird (possibly spelled "Bard") (Lt.), 35, (brother of Hon. E. H. of Hyde Park), 2nd Regiment, U.S. Infantry, d 2/2/30 in NYC (1-2/8 and 8-2/10)
6693. Pendleton, Susan, 58, wf of Nathaniel, Esq. of Clinton (Dut. Co.), d 1/15/16; Rev. Burch (8-1/17)
6694. Penfield, George, merchant, of Penfield (Monroe Co.) m 4/22/24 Jane Eliza Van Ness, dau of G. B., Esq. of Poughkeepsie; Rev. Cuyler (8-4/28)
6695. Penney, Joseph of Rochester m Margaret Sterling, dau of William, Esq. of NYC, in NYC; Rev. Whelpley (3-6/17/22)
6696. Penniman, _____, child of William C., d in Hudson (6-4/5/03)
6697. Penniman, Chiron who formerly lived near Cooperstown and kept a school part of the time, d about 11/20/15 in Claverack (suicide - found dead in a wood lot - had cut his throat with a razor "in a state of insanity" - according to the coroner's report) (9-12/5 and 3-12/7)
6698. Penniman, Mary, 29, consort of Obadiah, bookseller, d 9/19/05 in Troy (9-9/24)
6699. Penniman, Obadiah, 43, formerly a bookseller in Albany, d 9/13/20 in Troy (consumption) (3-9/15)
6700. Penniman, Sylvanus J., bookseller, m 10/11/05 Olive Fitch, both of Lansingburgh, in L (9-10/15)
6701. Penniman, William C. m 10/15/01 Lucinda Hamilton, dau of Dr. Joseph of Hudson (6-10/22)
6702. Penny, Edward m 12/27/21 Amanda Townsend, both of Pittstown (9-1/1/22)
6703. Penrose, William (Lt.) of the U.S. Army m Mary Huffman of Sacketts Harbor in S. H.; Rev. Snowden (1-1/7/30)
6704. Peom(?), James C., 41, d 1/15/31 (in Schenectady?) (1-1-19)
6705. Pepood, Daniel (Capt.), 65, d 11/12/20 in Stockbridge, MA (6-11/28)
6706. Pereins, John m 1/12/06 Almira Phelps, both of Troy; Rev. Coe (9-1/14)
6707. Perers, Abel, merchant, of Clinton (Dut. Co.) d 12/7/99 in Clinton (8-12/17)
6708. Periam, Joseph d 10/15/80 in Elizabethtown (probably in NJ) (5-10/19)
6709. Perin, Prudence, 27, wf of Ira, d 8/19/11 in Potsdam (7-9/6)
6710. Perine, John I. m 11/30/05 Jean Van Tile, both of Cambridge, in C; Rev. Chapman (9-1/7/06)
6711. Perkins, _____ (Dr.),"inventor of the metallic points", d "lately" in NYC (3-9/19/99)
6712. Perkins, Aaron (Rev.) m 5/27/15 Deborah Smith, both of Marlborough; Rev. Leonard (8-5/31)
6713. Perkins, Benjamin D. of the firm of Collins and Perkins, NYC, booksellers, d 10/20/10 at the country home of John Murray, Jr. (deceased was a member of the society of Friends) (8-10/24)

6714. Perkins, Bradley m 12/14/20 Sally Churchill, both of Clinton; Rev. L. Leonard (8-12/20)
6715. Perkins, Elisha, 28, of Hudson d 12/2/07 (consumption) (6-12/8)
6716. Perkins, Henry, M.D. d prior to December 6, 1830 in Oswego (On Dec 6 a resolution of respect to the deceased was signed at Oswego by A. H. Howland, M.D., chairman, and William G. Adkins, secretary, of the Medical Society with a copy sent to the wife and to the parents of the deceased) (1-12/14/30)
6717. Perkins, J. Newton, Esq. m 3/10/31 Elizabeth P. Bishop, oldest dau of Daniel L., in Ithaca: Rev. Mann (1-3/26)
6718. Perkins, Jehiel m 9/24/28 Alethea G. Northrop; Rev. C. P. Wilson. All of Washington (Dut. Co.) (8-10/1)
6719. Perkins, John, 62, d 11/1/12 in Burlington (Ots. Co.) (3-11/23)
6720. Perkins, John (Capt.) of the U.S. Army m Ann Eliza Croghan of Sacketts Harbor in S. H. (7-6/21/17)
6721. Perkins, Jonathan, late of Troy, d 8/21/22 in NYC (yellow fever)
6722. Perkins, Thomas Goodman, merchant, of Utica m 12/7/31 Ellen Sophia Clarke, dau of Dr. Peter of Montezuma, NY in M; Rev. Hubbard (1-12/20)
6723. Perlee, John S., s of Gen. Perlee of Amenia, m 5/30/18 Julia Ann Crosby, dau of Dr. Cyrenus of Poughkeepsie; Rev. C. C. Cuyler (8-6/10/18)
6724. Perry, George of Amenia m 6/3/19 Lois Belding of Washington (Dut. Co.) "after a pleasant courtship of seven years"; Rev. Birch (8-6/9)
6725. Perry, Isaac, 27, d 12/9/98 in Lansingburgh (9-12/11)
6726. Perry, Jonathan C. m 12/25/23 Phebe Dodge of Exeter in E (3-1/5/24)
6727. Perry, Martha Thorne, 2, dau of Eli, d 9/15/31 in Albany (funeral from her father's home on Schenectady Turnpike (1-9/17)
6728. Perry, Stephen H. d 10/2/25 in Poughkeepsie (8-10/5)
6729. Perry, Thomas, 66, d 9/16/18 in Amenia (8-9/30)
6730. Persall, William m 6/1/11 Ann Titus; Rev. Cuyler (8-6/5)
6731. Persons, Abraham m 4/19/17 Clarissa Trowbridge, both of Pine Plains, in P. P.; Rev. Vedder (8-4/23)
6732. Peters, _____, wf of David, d "recently" in Plattsburgh (7-1/8/13)
6733. Peters, Andrew, 20, s of John T. of Hartford, CT, d 10/29/29 at the home of Col. John Tighlman near Ceukeville, MD (had received his A.B. degree from Union College in July and had been admitted to Washington College) (1-11/12)
6734. Peters, David m 3/7/13 Sally Middleton in Plattsburgh (7-3/12)
6735. Peters, George m 12/28/15 Marietta Bolles; Rev. Ogilvie. All of Hudson (6-1/2/16)
6736. Peters, George m 11/27/17 Rachel Haywood, dau of Thomas, in Poughkeepsie (8-12/3)
6737. Peters, George P. (Maj.), 30, of the U.S. Army d 11/28/19 "of an inflammatory fever" at Fort Gadsden, East Florida (born in New Hampshire; enlisted in 1808 as a lieutenant - in this newspaper release his military experience is detailed) (7-1/15/20)
6738. Peters, Henry m 2/12/12 Sally Holmes, dau of Capt. William; Rev. John Clark. All of Clinton (Dut. co.) (8-2/26)
6739. Peters, Hulett of Pleasant Valley (Dut. Co.) m 9/3/22 Sarah Angeline Simmons "of Dunning Street" in D. S.; Dennis Marvin, Esq. (2-9/17)
6740. Peters, James m 3/6/07 Lydia Beebe, both of Cambridge, in C; Rev. R. H. Chapman (9-3/17)
6741. Peters, William of Troy m 3/25/24 Mrs. Permelia Sessions of Sand Lake in Troy; Rev. Butler (9-3/30)
6742. Peterson, William L. m 9/5/19 Anna Sruio(?), both of Albany, in A; Rev. Hooper Cumming (6-9/28)
6743. Petry, Frank of Quebec m 10/1/22 Catherine Maria Sim of Lansingburgh in Lansingburgh; Rev. Dr. Blatchford (9-10/8)
6744. Pettengil, Abigal, 24, wf of Rev. Amos, d 3/25/10 in Champlain (American Monitor of Plattsburgh-6/2)
6745. Pettis, Elizabeth (Widow), 73, d 5/4/05 (6-5/7)
6746. Pettit, Harvey m 11/14/32 Sarah Ann Hill, dau of Nathaniel of Poughkeepsie; Rev. Richardson (11-11/21)
6747. Pettit, Jacob of Freedom m 2/14/27 Hannah Johnston, dau of William of Clinton; Rev. Clark (8-2/21)
6748. Pettit, Joseph of Beekman m 2/24/20 Mary F. Mathewson, dau of Bernard, Esq. of Stanford (Dut. Co.); Rev. Clark (8-3/1)

6749. Phelps, Aaron M. m Florinda Russell in Hartwick (3-11/10/23)
6750. Phelps, Betsey, 43 (wf of Joshua and dau of Elias Peck, late of Colchester, CT) d 2/1/19 in Westford (3-3/8)
6751. Phelps, Charles S., merchant, of Staten Island, NY m 6/28/31 Harriet Butler, dau of Charles, Esq. of Poughkeepsie, in P; Rev. Dr. Cuyler (double ceremony - see marr of Lt. John C. Carter) (1-7/7)
6752. Phelps, George D. m 5/12/30 Frances H. F. Randolph, dau of John F., Esq., in NYC; Rev. Ives. All of NYC (2-5/14)
6753. Phelps, Henry, merchant, of the firm of Phelps and Buel of Albany m 9/16/29 Louise C. Lewis, dau of Luke, Esq., in Litchfield, CT; Rev. Hickock (1-9/21)
6754. Phelps, Isaac, Jr. (Lt.) of Granville, NY m 10/20/05 Nancy Mahar of Hartford, CT in Granville, NY; Rev. Nathaniel Hall (9-11/5)
6755. Phelps, Lucy (Miss), dau of Hon. John of Guilford, VT, d "recently" in Georgetown, D.C. (7-8/10/33)
6756. Phelps, William of Troy m Eliza Jackson of Pittstown in Schaghticoke; Rev. Paige (9-8/26/06)
6757. Philips, Darius m 10/24/05 Hannah Otis Strong, both of Union Village; Rev. Jonas Coe (9-10/29)
6758. Phillips, Isaac, 89, d 5/27/30 at his home in Nassau (fought in the French and Rev. Wars) (1-6/9)
6759. Philips, James m 7/1/19 Elizabeth Danker, both of Troy; Rev. Dr. Coe (9-7/6)
6760. Philips, Michael of Troy m 12/22/27 Anna McNames of Brunswick; Rev. Howard (9-1/128)
6761. Philips, Tolman m 10/12/28 Polley Muney, both of Grafton, in Peterborough; Jonas Henning, Esq. (9-11/11)
6762. Philips, William m 3/11/28 Rebecca Baldwin; Rev. Willis. All of Troy (9-3/14)
6763. Philips, William G. m 2/10/20 Caroline Fonda, dau of Capt. Abraham L., in Claverack; Rev. Sluyter (6-2/15)
6764. Phillips, Amanda, 41, wf of Col. Elijah, d 11/1/31 in Syracuse ("Mrs. Phillips was the granddaughter of the late Gen. Danforth of this county [Onondaga] and was the first white child born in it") (1-11/14)
6765. Phillips, Frederick, 72, d 5/10/29 at his home in Phillipstown (West. Co.) (1-5/14)
6766. Phillips, James (Rev.), 79, d 2/4/02 in Fishkill (8-2/9)
6767. Phillips, James of Cold Springs m 5/16/30 Angeline Smith; Rev. Welton (8-5/19)
6768. Phillips, Marquis De La Fayette m 4/5/17 Jane Pells, both of Poughkeepsie; Rev. C. C. Cuyler (8-4/9)
6769. Phillips, Mehitabel, 61, wf of John, d 3/9/26 in Cooperstown (3-3/13)
6770. Phillips, Sally Augusta, dau of David, d 9/21/10 in Poughkeepsie (8-9/26)
6771. Phillips, Tempa (Miss), 27, dau of John of Cooperstown, d 7/26/23 in Exeter (3-8/4)
6772. Phillo, Lyman m 11/2/29 Therese Barr, both of Albany, in NYC; Rev. George Cales (1-11/7)
6773. Phinney, Elihu, Esq., 58, d 7/12/13 ("was editor of this paper upwards of 18 years") (funeral sermon by Rev. John Smith) (buried with Masonic honors) (3-7/17)
6774. Phinney, Elihu of Cooperstown m 11/16/15 Nancy Whiting Tiffany of New Canaan (9-11/21)
      Phinney, Nathaniel. See, possibly, Finnay, Nathaniel.
6775. Phipps, Samuel of Albany m 5/13/20 Alcemena Hewson of Troy; Rev. Sommers (9-5/16)
6776. Phoebus, Thomas of NYC m Mabel Street, dau of Caleb of Catskill, in C; Rev. David Porter (6-12/27/03)
6777. Phoebus, W. (Rev. Dr.), 77, d 11/10/31 in NYC (1-11/12)
6778. Picken, James S. m 9/9/24 Polly Delong in Middlefield (3-9/13)
6779. Pier, Ethan m 11/14/11 Samantha Johnson of Oxford in O; Rev. Eli Hyde (3-11/23)
6780. Pier, George m 10/2/16 Melissa Williams, dau of Isaac, Esq. All of Cooperstown (3-10/10)
6781. Pier, Hiram m 2/3/25 Elvira Eddy in Fly Creek; Rev. Potter (3-2/7)
6782. Pier, John, oldest son of Abner, d 11/24/10 in Cooperstown (2-12/1)
6783. Pier, Marela (Mrs.), 54, d 12/6/21 in Norwalk, CT (7-12/29)

6784. Pier, Martha, 33, consort of Thomas, d 10/24/15 in Hartwick (3-11/2)
6785. Pier, Polly, dau of Abner, late deceased, d 12/31/10 in Cooperstown (typhus) (3-1/12/11)
6786. Pierce, Alfred H. m Esther Oatman, dau of Daniel, in Troy (7-9/21/33)
6787. Pierce, Ann (Miss), 43, d 1/26/02 in Litchfield, CT (6-2/23)
6788. Pierce, Azekam, 65, of Otego d 10/13/07 (member of Baptist Church "almost 50 years") (3-1031)
6789. Pirce, Chauncey, merchant, m 8/25/19 Eliza Bloom, both of Troy; Rev. Dr. Coe (9-8/31/19)
6790. Pierce, Deborah, consort of Capt. Marinus, d 3/13/18 in Poughkeepsie (8-3/18)
6791. Pierce, Eli (Dr.) m 4/28/23 Sarah Burgess, dau of William, Esq., in Butternuts; Rev. Russel Wheeler (3-5/5)
6792. Pierce, George, merchant, of the firm of Pierce and Howard m 7/10/30 Sophronia Leeland, dau of Lewis, in NYC; Rev. Dr. Phillips. All of NYC (8-7/28)
6793. Pierce, John W., merchant, m 2/13/34 Polina Worden, both of Kent (Putnam Co.), NY, in Hackensack, NY; Rev. C. L. Vancleff (8-2/26)
6794. Pierce, Lemuel m 11/22/06 Elizabeth Harris, both of Troy, in T; Rev. Coe (9-11/25)
6795. Pierce, Marinus of Poughkeepsie m 7/31/16 Deborah Reed, dau of Benjamin, Esq. of Marlborough (8-8/14)
6796. Pierce, Robert (Col.) m 6/7/29 Mrs. Marian Watts (she b in the north of Ireland) "in Peru, Union Village, Essex Co."; Joseph Everest, Esq. (1-6/16)
6797. Pierce, Ruby, 34, wf of Samuel, d 8/11/05 in Rochester, MA (9-9/3)
6798. Pierce, Samuel W., Esq., editor of the Ulster Palladium, m 10/2/31 Laura B. Hallock of New Paltz in N. P.; Rev. Beach (1-10/6 and 8-10/12)
6799. Pierrepont, William Constable of Ellisburgh (Jefferson Co.) m 6/2/30 Cornelia Avore Butler of Oxford, NY in Utica; Rev. Dorr (1-6/5)
6800. Pierson, Alanson m Rowena Fitch in Hartwick; Rev. John Smith (3-7/29/22)
6801. Pierson, Helen, wf of Isaac of NYC and dau of Major Fort of Poughkeepsie, d on her passage from New Orleans, LA where she had been for benefit of her health (8-5/17/20)
6802. Pierson, Henry L. m 12/23/30 Helen Maria Pierson, dau of Isaac, Esq.; Rev. Dr. Wainwright. All of NYC (1-12/28)
6803. Pilmore, Joseph (Rev.), D.D. (late rector of St. Paul's Church in Philadelphia, PA and formerly pastor of Christ church in NYC) d 7/31/25 in Philadelphia (8-8/3)
6804. Pinckney, Charles of Fishkill m 5/31/15 Catherine Dates of Poughkeepsie; Rev. Dr. C. C. Cuyler (8-6/7)
6805. Pine, _____, relict of John who lately died in Poughkeepsie, d "recently" in Poughkeepsie (8-1/28/18)
6806. Pine, Annanias m 12/1/21 Catharine See, both of Schenectady Co,, in Charlton; Jonathan Conde, Esq. (2-12/5)
6807. Pine, William d 6/2/22 in Freedom (8-1/8/23)
6808. Pinkham. Charles G. m 4/16/14 Catharine Ann Dewel of Hudson in H; Rev. Chester (6-4/26)
6809. Pinkham, Daniel, 71, d 4/25/06 in Hudson (6-5/6)
6810. Pinkham, Matthew of Hudson m 8/23/04 Hepzibeth Coffin of Chatham (6-8/28)
6811. Pinkney, Deborah, 33, wf of Dr. John, d 7/14/10 in Fishkill (8-7/25)
6812. Pitcher, Aaron m 9/9/20 Ann Ellis, both of Gibbonsville; Rev. Sommers (9-9/12)
6813. Pitcher, Eliza, 34, consort of John, Esq. and youngest dau of Maj. William Gamble of Washington Co., d 7/6/29 in Rockport, IN (1-8/10)
6814. Pitcher, Nathaniel (Gen.) of Sandy Hill (Wash. Co.) member of the late Congress, m 3/15/23 Anna B. Merritt of Freedom (Dut. Co.) in F (8-3/19 and 9-4/1)
6815. Pitkin, Elisha, Esq., 43. recorder of Hudson, NY, d 5/4/02 in Great Barrington, MA (6-5/11)
6816. Pitkin, Marvin of Hudson, NY m 2/10/02 Maria Budd, dau of Dr. John of Great Barrington, MA, in G. B.; Rev. Judson (6-2/16)
6817. Pitkin, Samuel (Dr.), for many years a physician in Ballston, d 3/27/23 in Saratoga Springs (2-4/1)
6818. Pitts, George B. m 2/2/23 Sally Ann Cook; Rev. Griffin (9-2/11)

6819. Place, Nehemiah of La Grange m 11/25/30 Cynthia Durland of Fishkill
(8-12/1)
6820. Platner, Peter m 1/29/24 Elvira Howe in Westford; Rev. Tiffany (3-2/2)
6821. Platner, Samuel of Hillsdale m 6/1/17 Betsey Noyes of Hudson; Rev.
Gephard (6-6/10)
6822. Platt, Ann (Mrs.), 83, wf of Capt. E. Platt, late of Kingsbury, d 1/6/25
in Ballston Spa (2-1/11)
6823. Platt, Caroline (Miss), 21, dau of Theodorus, d 8/8/18 in Plattsburgh
(7-8/15)
6824. Platt, Caroline, dau of Lt. Platt of the U.S. Navy, d 7/29/25 in
Plattsburgh (7-7/30)
6825. Platt, Charles (Judge), 80, d 5/29/24 in Plattsburgh (an early settler
there) (7-5/29)
6826. Platt, Charles T. (Lt.) of the U.S. Navy m 10/14/21 Eliza Ann Walworth
of Plattsburgh in P; Rev. Frederick Halsey (7-10/20 and 3-11/12)
6827. Platt, Charles Z., Esq., 46, late Treas. of NY, d 4/14/22 in Greenbush
(7-4/27)
6828. Platt, Daniel of Fishkill m 1/22/18 Phebe Adriance, dau of Abraham of
Poughkeepsie; Rev. De Witt (8-1/28)
6829. Platt, Daniel W., about 23, of the firm of E. and D. W. Platt of Troy,
d 10/26/23 (9-10/30)
6830. Platt, David, "about 19 or 20", son of Judge Platt, late of Dutchess Co.,
d 5/30/04 (consumption) (8-6/5/04)
6831. Platt, Eliphalet (Dr.) of Rhinebeck m 6/26/25 Mary Ann Dibblee of Pine
Plains; Rev. Vanderveer (8-7/13)
6832. Platt, George, Esq., merchant, d 9/9/18 in Montreal, Canada (8-9/23)
6833. Platt, Harvey D. of Fishkill m 11/5/34 Phebe Cary, dau of Dr. Egbert Cary
of Beekman; Rev. Barber (8-11/11)
6834. Platt, Henry of Sharon m 10/23/11 Sarah Dakin of Amenia; Rev. Allerton
(8-12/4) -(Perhaps Sharon is in Connecticut)
6835. Platt, Henry, merchant, of Plattsburgh m 1/1/17 Charlotte Elmore, dau of
Lott, Esq. of Peru, NY, in P (7-1/4)
6836. Platt, Henry L. of NYC m 9/2/29 Sarah Matilda Morey of Poughkeepsie in P;
Rev. Dr. Cuyler (8-9/9 and 1-9/14)
6837. Platt, Isaac C. of Clinton m Nancy Bristol, dau of Joel, Esq. of Clinton
in C (7-3/9/22) (Note: Since the town of Clinton in Clinton Co. was
not formed until 1845, presumably the town of Clinton of triple
reference above is the one in Dutchess Co., the county from which many
of the Platt family members migrated in the late 1700's and early 1800's)
6838. Platt, Isaac I. of Clinton (Dut. Co.) m 11/19/29 Angelina Balding or
Belding, dau of Isaac I. of Poughkeepsie; Rev. Dr. Reed (8-11/25 and
1-11/28)
6839. Platt, Isaac S., Esq., 35, late sheriff of Clinton Co., d 8/1/12 in
Plattsburgh (buried in Plattsburgh with Masonic honors) (7-8/7)
6840. Platt, James, Esq. m Susan K. Auchmoty in Utica; Rev. Aiken (1-3/10/31)
6841. Platt, James K. (Dr.) of NYC m 9/21/18 Elizabeth H. Henshaw, dau of
D. Henshaw of NYC, in Middlebury (state not given - try Vermont)
(7-10/24)
6842. Platt, James Kent, 33, M. D., a professor in the Institute of Surgery
at the University of Vermont, d 5/4/24 in Plattsburgh, NY (3-5/31)
6843. Platt, Jeremiah, Esq., 65, of Smithtown, L.I. d "in November" in Smithtown
(7-12/2/15)
6844. Platt, John, 35, d 9/11/17 in Fishkill (8-9/17)
6845. Platt, Jonas (Hon.), 64, late a judge of the State Supreme Court,
d 2/22/34 at his home in Peru, NY (7-3/1 and 8-3/5)
6846. Platt, Joseph, 56, d 11/7/27 at his home in Poughkeepsie (8-11/21)
6847. Platt, Maria N., 40, consort of Nathaniel C. and only dau of William Nase
of Amenia, d 4/25/31 in Plattsburgh (8-5/4)
6848. Platt, Mary, relict of late Judge Zephaniah, formerly of Dutchess Co., d
in Plattsburgh (8-11/22/09)
6849. Platt, N. Z. (Maj.) d 10/25/20 in Plattsburgh (7-10/28)
6850. Platt, Nathaniel (Capt.), 74, d 5/11/16 in Plattsburgh (7-5/11)
6851. Platt, Nathaniel of Plattsburgh m 2/22/27 Hannah Mooers of Champlain in
C; Rev. Joel Byington (7-3/3)

6852. Platt, Nathaniel C., merchant, of Plattsburgh m 5/14/14 Maria Nase, dau of William, Esq. of Amenia, in A (7-5/28/14)
6853. Platt, Phebe, 79, wf of late Capt. Nathaniel, d in Plattsburgh (7-10/18/23)
6854. Platt, Richard (Col.), 75, (a Rev. officer) d 3/3/30 in NYC (1-3/9)
6855. Platt, Stephen, 14, s of Maj. N. C., d 9/15/19 in Plattsburgh (7-9/18)
6856. Platt, Theodorus, Esq. m Julia Saillee, dau of Peter, Esq., member-elect of the next Congress, in Plattsburgh (bride and groom both of Plattsburgh at time of their marriage) (8-10/23/04)
6857. Platt, William, about 4 mo, s of Maj. N. Z., d 2/17/18 in Plattsburgh (7-2/21)
6858. Platt, William H. of Rhinebeck m 12/6/26 Sarah C. Stoutenburgh of Hyde Park in H. P.; Rev. F. H. Vanderveer (8-12/13)
6859. Platt, Zephaniah, 72, d 9/12/07 in Plattsburgh (b 5/27/1735; was for many years the first magistrate in Dutchess Co.) (8-10/7)
6860. Platt, Zephaniah T., about 25, s of Theodorus, deceased, d 12/12/13 in Plattsburgh (7-12/18)
6861. Plumb, _____, 2, child of David, d 3/1/07 "in consequence of a scald" (6-3/10)
6862. Plumb, Jared, 18 mo, only child of Jared, d in Hudson (6-9/14/13)
6863. Plumb, Mary, 16 mo, dau of Joseph, d 8/4/09 in Hudson (6-8/15)
6864. Plummer, Catharine Jane, 11, d 7/30/17 (8-8/20)
6865. Plummer, Joseph P. of Baltimore m 9/10/19 Lydia Husband of Washington (Dut. Co.); John Beadle, Esq. (8-9/15)
6866. Plummer, William of NYC m 5/25/08 Jane Dodge, dau of Henry of Poughkeepsie; Rev. Wayland (8-6/1)
6867. Plummer, William, lately of Poughkeepsie, d 6/4/25 in NYC (8-6/8)
6868. Pohel, Michael (b in Germany and for many years a soldier under the late Napoleon Bonaparte) d 3/12/22 in Ballston Spa., NY (2-3/13)
6869. Pollard, Polly (consort of Capt. Moses and dau of late Elisha Crosby of Shrewsbury, MA) d 12/23/02 in Hudson (6-12/28)
6870. Polock, Barnet m 2/8/16 Rachel Dubois, both of Brunswick; Rev. Dr. Coe (9-2/13)
6871. Pomeroy, Eleazer, Esq., 59, d in Coventry, CT (6-6/21/11)
6872. Pomeroy, Ellen, inf dau of George, d 9/5/19 in Cooperstown (3-9/13)
6873. Pomeroy, George m 5/16/03 Ann Cooper, only dau of Hon. William; Rev. Isaac Lewis. All of Cooperstown (3-5/19/03)
6874. Pomeroy, Paul m 4/6/15 Elizabeth Young, both of Troy; Rev. Coe (9-4/11)
6875. Pomeroy, Paul, 45, mechanic, d 3/11/28 in Troy (9-3/21)
6876. Pomeroy, Robert m Jane M. Atwater, dau of Hon. Moses, in Canandaigua; Rev. Barlow (3-7/2/21)
6877. Pomeroy, Thaddeus (Dr.) of Albany m 4/23/97 Eliza Sedgwick, oldest dau of Hon. Theodore, Esq., in Stockbridge (state not given); Rev. West (3-5/11)
6878. Pomeroy, Theodore (Dr.) of Utica m 11/1/26 Cornelia Voorhees of New Brunswick, NJ in N. B.; Rev. Dr. Hardenburgh (3-11/13)
6879. Poole, Silas of Peru, NY m 3/25/33 Mrs. Cynthia Stone in Chesterfield; Rev. Bates (4 [Keeseville Herald]-4/22)
6880. Pope, Gershom, d 3/22/10 in Burlington (Ots. Co.) (surv by wf and children) (3-4/7)
6881. Pope, Gershom of Oswegatchie (St. Law. Co.) m 2/24/16 Almira Miller, dau of John, in Cooperstown; Rev. Daniel Nash (3-2/29)
6882. Pope, Lothrop, Jr. of Keeseville m 1/23/33 Mary Ball of Northumberland (Sara. Co.) in N; Rev. Boyd (4 [Keeseville Herald]-1/29)
6883. Pope, Martin, Esq. d 4/13/31 in Keeseville (4 [Keeseville Herald]-4/19)
6884. Porter, Albert of Niagara Falls m 10/14/29 Julia Matthews, dau of Gen. V. Matthews of Rochester (1-11/2)
6885. Porter, Asahel S. m 8/7/23 Adeline Shaw in New Lisbon (3-8/11)
6886. Porter, Clarinda, consort of Asahel, Esq. of Greenfield (Sara. Co.), d in G (6-7/6/19)
6887. Porter, David S., publisher of the Utica Sentinel and Gazette, m 5/11/29 Charlotte Olmstead in Hartford, CT (1-5/14)
6888. Porter, Eliza H., 22, wf of John F., d 7/29/29 (in Albany?) (consumption) ("...papers in Rutland, Vermont are requested to copy the above") (mentioned is father of the deceased, Lemuel Sherwood of #7 Beaver St. [rear],and a "Mrs. Ira Porter", not further identified) (1-7/31)

6889. Porter, Granville m 1/18/27 Margaret Ann Dutcher, dau of David late of
       Freedom; Rev. Abner Morse (8-1/31)
6890. Porter, Ira, 48, formerly of Albany, d 3/31/23 at his home in Ballston
       (2-4/1)
6891. Porter, J. F. m 9/12/30 Mary Sherwood, both of Albany; Rev. Dr. Lacey
       (1-9/14)
6892. Porter, John, 5 mo, s of John F., d 4/26/29 in Albany (1-4/30)
6893. Porter, John (Master Commandant) of the U.S. Navy d in Watertown
       (1-11/7/31)
6894. Porter, Joshua (Dr.), 72, brother of Gen. Peter B., late Secretary of War,
       d 11/2/31 in Saratoga Springs (an early settler there and the first
       president of the village corporation) (1-11/4)
6895. Porter, Letitia P., 45, consort of Gen. P. B., d 7/27/31 at Black Rock
       (1-8/4)
6896. Porter, Samuel (Dr.), 67, "a skillful surgeon", d in Williamstown, MA
       (3-1/21/22)
6897. Post, Hezekiah C., s of Jotham, m 1/27/20 Ruth Gurney, dau of John, all
       of Stanford (Dut. Co.), at the Friends Meeting House in Stanford
       (8-2/23)
6898. Post, Jane Juliet, 19, dau of late J. J., Esq., d 11/6/31 in NYC
       (1-11/9)
6899. Post, Wright (Dr.), 62, d 6/14/29 at his home at Throg's Neck (on
       Westchester County's southern border) (8-6/25)
6900. Potter, ____, 8, s of Asa, Esq., d in Rhinebeck (6-2/5/05)
6901. Potter, Alonzo (Rev.), professor of mathematics and natural philosophy at
       Union College, m 4/14/23 Sarah Maria Nott, dau of Rev. Dr. Eliphalet
       Nott, at Union College in Schenectady (8-4/23)
6902. Potter, Ann, 16, oldest dau of Joseph of Freedom, d 9/2/26 at Miss
       Gibb's school in Hyde Park (8-9/6)
6903. Potter, Anthony m 12/3/08 Sarah Lockwood; Rev. Barcalo (8-12/7)
6904. Potter, Asa, Esq., 38, d 10/9/05 in Rhinebeck Flats (born in South Kingston,
       RI; had settled in NY state by 1787 (6-10/22)
6905. Potter, Asaph, 62, d 9/7/19 in Middlefield (3-9/13)
6906. Potter, Beekman, 17, s of Joseph and brother of the editor of this paper,
       d 4/1/12 in Beekman (8-4/8)
6907. Potter, Christopher, 79, d 7/23/22 in Greenfield (2-8/6)
6908. Potter, Dencey (widow), 63, d 5/1/34 in Poughkeepsie (8-5/7)
6909. Potter, Elizabeth, 35, consort of Rufus, d 9/20/15 (surv by husband and
       7 small children) (8-9/27)
6910. Potter, Evans, formerly of Otsego Co., d in Boston (Erie Co.), NY
       (3-9/12/25)
6911. Potter, Horatio (Rev.) m 9/7/27 Mary Jane Tomlinson, only dau of David,
       Esq. of Schenectady; Rev. Proal (8-9/19)
6912. Potter, Joel B., Esq., attorney, d 9/30/06 in Cherry Valley (typhus)
       (3-10/9)
6913. Potter, John, Esq. of Hoosick d "recently" (a wagon ran over him)
       (6-7/22/06)
6914. Potter, John of Utica m 2/25/29 Eliza Ann Talcott, dau of Capt. P. of
       Leyden (Lewis Co.) in Leyden (1-3/10)
6915. Potter, Joseph, 67, (a Rev. soldier) d 11/23/24 at his home in Freedom
       (born in Cranston, RI; lived in Dutchess Co., NY from 1792 until time
       of his death) (8-12/1)
6916. Potter, Maria, 46, consort of Sylvester of Beekman, d 8/11/08 (8-8/17)
6917. Potter, Mary, 50, wf of Asaph, d in Hartwick (consumption) (3-6/12/13)
6918. Potter, Mary, wf of Rufus of Poughkeepsie, d 1/23/27 (8-1/31)
6919. Potter, Mary Jane, 4, oldest dau of Rev. Horatio Potter, rector of St.
       Peter's Church in Albany, d 10/8/34 in Schenectady (8-10/15)
6920. Potter, Philo, 32, d 5/6/26 in Hartwick (3-5/15)
6921. Potter, Robert m 12/25/13 Sarah Pine, both of Beekman; Rev. Richardson
       (8-12/29)
6922. Potter, Rufus m 10/26/18 Mary Haywood in Poughkeepsie (8-10/28)
6923. Potter, Rufus of Poughkeepsie m 3/7/29 Susan Burlingham of Union Vale;
       John Klapp, Esq. (8-3/11)
6924. Potter, Russel m 1/17/13 Candace Goff; Rev. Chester (6-2/2)

6925. Potter, S. R., merchant, of Potter Hollow m 10/15/30 Eleanor Catharine Rightmyer, dau of Martin G., in Blenheim; Rev. W. Paige (1-11/6)
6926. Potter, Sheldon, formerly of Poughkeepsie, d 2/1/34 in Philadelphia, PA (deceased was "brother of the late editor of this paper but for the last 16 years a merchant in Philadelphia") (8-2/12)
6927. Potter, Stephen of Petersburgh m 8/13/11 Lauretty Carvin of NYC in Troy (9-8/20)
6928. Potter, Susan, wf of Rufus, d 2/16/34 in Poughkeepsie (8-2/19)
6929. Potter, Thomas, 42, d 7/31/13 at his home in Beekman (8-8/4)
6930. Potter, William T. (Rev.) m 6/9/30 Mrs. Henrietta R. Hamilton, both of New Haven, CT, at St. Paul's Chapel in New Haven; Rev. H. Croswell (1-6/19)
6931. Poucher, Hannah, 44, wf of Anthony, Esq., d 1/2/14 in Claverack (6-1/18)
6932. Powell, _____ (Dr.) m Amelia Cary, dau of late Col. Cary, in Springfield; Rev. Putnam (3-7/19/24)
6933. Powell, Abigail, 48, consort of John, d 7/25/09 in Hudson (6-8/1)
6934. Powell, Ann, 18, dau of John, d 12/25/07 in Hudson (6-12/29)
6935. Powell, John, 71, d 1/7/17 in Hudson (6-1/14)
6936. Powell, John H., Esq. of Philadelphia m 10/20/17 Julia Devereaux of NYC in NYC; Right Rev. Bishop Hobart (8-10/29)
6937. Powell, Sarah, 34, wf of John, d 12/20/01 in Hudson (6-12/24)
6938. Powell, Thomas, Jr., 23, youngest s of late Thomas of Schenectady, d 8/8/31 "at sea of an affection of the liver") (1-9/15)
6939. Powell, William of Schenectady, one of the proprietors of the western line of stages, d 9/19/20 between Albany and Schenectady (of an "apoplectic fit") (6-9/26)
6940. Powelson, Isaac V. of Troy m 10/13/20 Elizabeth Jessup of Stanford (sic), CT; Rev. Sommers (9-10/24)
6941. Power, Charlotte, 1 yr, dau of Isaacand Avis, d 5/15/12 in Hudson (6-5/25)
6942. Power, David of Amenia m 10/11/12 Sally Row of Hillsdale, dau of Garret, Esq. (8-11/4)
6943. Power, Eliza, 33, wf of Henry of Poughkeepsie, d 3/23/31 (8-3/30)
6944. Power, Henry m 9/25/19 Eliza Carman in Poughkeepsie; Rev. McJimpsey (8-9/29)
6945. Power, John m 9/15/11 Phebe Hussey(?), both of Hudson; Rev. Chester (6-10/14)
6946. Power, Luke m 10/6/11 Sally Lightbody, both of Hudson; Rev. Chester (6-10/14)
6947. Power, Nicholas, Jr. m 5/14/07 Catherine Sickles, both of Poughkeepsie; Rev. Brouwer (8-5/20)
6948. Power, Nicholas, former editor and proprietor of the Poughkeepsie Journal, d 9/21/11 in Poughkeepsie (8-9/25 and 6-10/7)
6949. Power, Nicholas, 42(?), d 4/15/25 in Poughkeepsie (8-4/20)
6950. Power, Phebe, 32, wf of Capt. John, d 6/7/20 in Hudson (6-6/13)
6951. Power, William (Dr.) of NYC m 9/8/29 Marianne Slane Doyle, oldest dau of Lawrence, Esq. of Halifax, Nova Scotia, in NYC (1-9/10)
6952. Power, William W. m 10/13/31 Julia McKinney, both of Albany; Rev. Lockhead (1-10/22)
6953. Powers, Gershom, Esq., 42, late a Congressman from Cayuga Co., d 6/26/31 in Auburn (was for several years a first judge of Cayuga Co.) (1-7/2 and 1-7/4)
6954. Powers, Isaac m 1/8/02 Rebecca Johnson in Hudson (6-1/12)
6955. Powers, James, Esq., attorney, m Nancy Day, dau of Stephen, Esq., in Catskill (6-1/5/08)
6956. Powers, Mary, 28, wf of Capt. John, d in Hudson (6-11/14/09)
6957. Powers, Mary Ann, 24, wf of _____ (name blurred), d in Plattsburgh (7-3/4/15)
6958. Powers, Rebecca, 32, consort of Isaac, d in Hudson (6-11/16/02)
6959. Powers, William, 13, s of Henry, merchant, of Plattsburgh, d 10/26/14 in Plattsburgh (7-10/29)
6960. Powers, William L., 22, d 7/13/34 in Burlington, VT (consumption) (7-7/26)
6961. Pratt, Annis, consort of Richard, d 7/28/22 in Burlington (Ots. Co.) (3-8/5)
6962. Pratt, David R. m 2/20/13 Christian Allen in Hillsdale; Rev. Somers. All of Hillsdale (6-3/2)

6963. Pratt, Esther, 64, wid of late Capt. Samuel and mother of Capt. Hiram, formerly from Windham County, VT, d 3/21/30 in Buffalo, NY (moved to Buffalo in 1804 and was one of the 12 members who formed the first church there in 1811) (1-4/2)
6964. Pratt, Heber W. of Lansingburgh m 9/2/15 Mary Gordon of Troy; Rev. Coe (9-9/12)
6965. Pratt, Ira m 3/2/07 Rebecca Turner, dau of James, in Bath. All of Bath (6-3/31)
6966. Pratt, Jeremiah of Burlington (Ots. Co.) m Sally Porter of New Lisbon; Rev. Henry Chapman (3-1/3/20)
6967. Pratt, Peter (Dr.) of NYC m 8/27/29 Jane Amanda Pratt, dau of Anson, Esq., in Chatham; Rev. Holmes (1-9/2)
6968. Pratt, Phineas M. of Boston m 10/31/30 Ann Eliza Callow of NYC in Hyde Park; Rev. P. P. Rouse of Brooklyn (8-11/17)
6969. Pratt, Richard of Burlington (Ots. Co.) m 9/9/24 Sarah Parsons of Paris (Oneida Co.) in P; Rev. Silas Parsons (3-9/30)
6970. Pratt, Zadoc (Col.) of Windham m 1/12/29 Abigail Watson of Rensselaerville; Rev. Smith (1-1/23)
6971. Preble, Edward (Commodore) d 8/25/07 in Portland (state not given) (6-9/8)
6972. Prentice, John H. of the firm of Packer, Prentice, and Co. m 3/8/31 Sarah Nichols Davis, dau of Nathaniel, Esq.; Rev. Dr. Sprague. All of Albany (1-3/10)
6973. Prentiss, George H., Esq., 28, s of Hon. Samuel, d 9/21/33 in Montpelier, VT (7-9/21/33)
6974. Prentiss, John H., editor of the Cooperstown Federalist, m 1/4/15 Catharine C. Morris, youngest dau of Gen. Jacob, in Butternuts (Ots. Co.); Rev. Russell Wheeler (6-1/24)
6975. Prentiss, William A., Esq. of Jericho, VT m 9/11/33 Eliza Sands in Keeseville, NY; Rev. Lyman (7-9/21)
6976. Prescott, ____, child of Charles, d 9/4/15 in Troy (9-9/5)
6977. Prescott, Alexander H., preceptor of the Academy in Plattsburgh m 9/25/21 Clarissa Smith of Champlain in C (7-9/29)
6978. Prescott, Alexander H., preceptor of Plattsburgh Academy, m 10/31/24 Lucinda P. Herrick; Rev. Whelpley. All of Plattsburgh (7-11/6)
6979. Prescott, Martha Ann, 4, dau of Charles d 9/30/31 in Keeseville (4 [Keeseville Herald]-10/11)
6980. Prescott, Ruth, 61, consort of Benjamin, Esq., d 1/20/21 in Cohoesville (9-1/30)
6981. Preston, Ebenezer m 11/29/32 Eliza McIntyre, both of Dover; Jesse Barlow, Esq. (8-12/12)
6982. Preston, John of Albany m 5/7/29 Phebe Ann Betts of Sand Lake in S. L.; Rev. Dr. Gregory (1-5/13)
6983. Preston, Maria, youngest dau of Asaph, d 11/30/28 in Albany (9-12/2)
6984. Preston, Samuel of Columbia (Chen. Co.) m 11/2/06 Electa Phelps of Troy; Rev. Isaac Webb (9-11/4)
6985. Prevost, Augustine (Maj.), 77, d 1/17/21 in Greenville (3-2/5)
6986. Prevost, G. W., Esq. of Locust Grove (Staatsburgh) m Eliza Maria Palmer of Rhinebeck; Rev. Budd (double ceremony - see marr of Thomas M. Palmer) (6-11/26/05)
6987. Price, Amy, wf of Halsted Price and dau of Israel Green of Plattsburgh, d 10/1/21 in NYC (typhus) (7-12/1)
6988. Price, David (Capt.) m 4/13/23 Polly Smith, both of Otsego, in Hartwick; Rev. Chapman (3-4/21)
6989. Price, John m 11/25/32 Mary O'Conner, both of Plattsburgh, in Corbao(?); Rev. Victor Dugas (7-12/1) (Corbao, probably Corbeau in town of Champlain)
6990. Price, Lydia, wf of David, d 11/29/21 (9-12/4)
6991. Price, William H., merchant, of Champlain m 10/16/20 Myraette Hitchcock, youngest dau of Dr. Hitchcock of Sandy Hill (Wash. Co.), in Chazy (7-10/28)
6992. Prichard, Elizabeth (Mrs.), about 84, d 12/17/17 in Plattsburgh (7-12/20)
6993. Priesac, Marquis m "lately" Catharine Livingston, youngest dau of Col. Robert G. late of Rhinebeck; Rev. Dr. Livingston (8-11/6/93)
6994. Priest, Frederick D. of NYC m 7/7/17 Eliza M. Brooks, dau of David, Esq. of Poughkeepsie; Rev. Reed (8-7/9) (wedding at Christ's Church)

6995. Prime, Edward, Esq. of NYC m 9/10/27 Mary Ann Bard, dau of William, Esq., in Hyde Park; Rev. Johnson (8-9/26)
6996. Prime, Frederick m 5/1/29 Mary R. Jay, dau of Peter, Esq., in NYC; Rev. William Richmond (1-5/5)
6997. Prince, Hannah Elizabeth, 11 mo, dau of Samuel, d 4/17/34 in Beekmantown (Clinton Co.) (whooping cough) (7-4/26)
6998. Prindle, Ermina, wf of Capt. Charles B., d 6/24/31 in Keeseville (funeral sermon by Rev. Lyman) (4 [Keeseville Herald]-6/28)
6999. Prindle, Mary Ann, 25, wf of Capt. Sherman Prindle and dau of Maj. Gilbert Bradley of Sunderland, VT, d 7/18/06 in Sandgate, VT (9-8/19)
7000. Prindle, William m 2/27/27 Julia Amanda Beecher (dau of Amos, deceased) in Sharon, CT; Rev. C. P. Wilson (8-3/21)
7001. Prindle, Z. m 1/31/16 Rachel Jones, dau of Daniel, all of Poughkeepsie; Rev. Weaver (7-2/3)
7002. Pringle, Homer m 3/2/26 Harriet Hatch in Richfield; Rev. Daniel Nash (3-3/13)
Pritchard. See also Prichard.
7003. Pritchard, Cornelia (Mrs.), 63, d 1/26/26 (in Poughkeepsie?) (8-2/1)
7004. Pritchard, James of Hyde Park m 5/1/22 Jane Ann Dates, dau of Abraham of Poughkeepsie; Rev. P. H. Wynkoop (8-5/8)
7005. Progue, Adam, 77, d 2/2728 (8-3/5)
7006. Proseus, John of Taughkanic m 2/1/17 Hannah Gilding of Claverack in Ancrum; Rev. Herman Vedder (6-2/11)
7007. Proudfit, Andrew, 64, d 5/7/22 in Argyle (long a resident of Argyle but formerly of Troy)(9-5/14)
7008. Proudfit, James (Rev.), 70, one of the ministers of the "associate congregation" of Salem, d 8/22/02 in Salem (died in his 50th year in the ministry) (9-11/3)
7009. Proudfit, John (Rev.) m 5/11/30 Abby H. Ralston, dau of Robert, Esq. of NYC, in Philadelphia, PA; Rev. Dr. Proudfit (1-5/22)
7010. Prout, William C. (Dr.) d 11/2/10 at the home of Hendrick Hagaman in Fishkill ("he was an indigent stranger" in that town at time of his death) (8-11/28)
7011. Prouty, Margaret M., 34(?), consort of Phineas and youngest dau of late Rev. Nicholas Van Vranken of Fishkill, d 9/12/30 in Geneva (1-9/18)
7012. Provost, Samuel (Right Rev.), bishop of the Protestant Episcopal Church in NYC, d in NYC (9-9/19/15)
Pruyn, Cornelius. See, possibly, Bruyn, Cornelius.
7013. Pruyn, John, 67, d 3/26/15 in Kinderhook (6-4/4)
7014. Pudney, Francis, 71, of Fishkill d 3/13/26 in F (8-3/15)
7015. Pudney, George W. m 5/10/32 Mary Anne Wilsie of Poughkeepsie; Rev. Dr. Reed (8-5/16)
7016. Pudney, Richard m 12/17/17 Jane Cooper, both of Poughkeepsie; Rev. Reed (8-12/24)
7017. Puffer, Charles D. of NYC m 10/18/31 Arminta D. Hasbrook of Fishkill in F; Rev. George H. Fisher (8-10/26)
7018. Pullen, John m 2/24/24 Permelia Pullen, both of Troy; Rev. Howard (9-3/2)
7019. Pulling, Daniel m 2/14/22 Phebe Frink in Providence, NY; H. Gardner, Esq. (double ceremony - see marr of Henry Shields) (2-3/27)
7020. Pulling, Zalmon m 3/10/22Mina Wheeler in Providence, NY; Joe Keeler, Esq. The marriages of Zalmon (the father), Daniel (his son), and Lucretia (his dau) are all reported separately in this newspaper dated 3/27/22 (2-3/27)
7021. Pultz, David m 1/20/22 Rosetta Rooke, both of Rhinebeck; Rev. Quitman (8-1/23)
7022. Pultz, William m 7/2/34 Margaret Steenburgh, both of Red. Hook; Rev. William J. Eyer (8-7/16)
7023. Pulver, Andries N., 32, d in Pine Plains (lock jaw) (8-6/22/31)
7024. Pulver, Fyler of Pine Plains m 2/28/28 Tammy Walling, dau of Elisha of Stanford (Dut. Co.); Rev. C. P. Wilson (8-3/12)
7025. Pulver, Henry of Pine Plains m 6/7/29 Jane Cook of Northeast; Rev. R. G. Armstrong (8-6/17)
7026. Pulver, Philip m Catharine Miller, dau of Samuel, in Claverack; Rev. Gebherd. All of C (6-10/28/06)

7027. Pumpelly, Charles, Jr., 25, merchant, s of Charles of Owego, d 2/10/30 in Owego (1-2/24)
7028. Pumpelly, Harmon m 11/16/30 Delphene Drake, dau of J. R., Esq.; Rev. Putnam. All of Owego (1-12/1)
7029. Punderson, Frank m 4/24/20 Caroline Marion Tallman, dau of Dr. John Tallman, mayor of Hudson, in H; Rev. Stebbins (6-4/25)
7030. Purdy, Anthony, 48, d in Syracuse (9-12/23/28)
7031. Purdy, Ezekiel B., 39, d 9/23/34 at Cold Spring (8-10/1)
7032. Purdy, John, merchant, m 6/14/15 Maria Flagler, dau of Solomon, all of Clinton; Rev. Clark (8-6/21)
7033. Purdy, Lovell of NYC m 6/19/29 Josephine Parfiate Cornet of Annet, dau of late Gen. Cornet, at the apartments of the American Consul in France; Right Rev. Bishop Luscom (1-8/27)
7034. Purdy, Monmouth of Poughkeepsie d 3/25/12 (8-4/1)
7035. Purdy, Stephen m 2/1/17 Ann Tubbs, both of Poughkeepsie; Rev. Jewitt (8-2/5)
7036. Purple, William D. (Dr.) of Chenango Co. m Julia Burnham of East Haddam, CT at St. Paul's Church in Albany; Rev. Kelsey (1-6/21/31)
7037. Putnam, Aaron (Rev.) of Springfield (Ots. Co.) m 8/31/22 Mary Elizabeth Hodgdon of Philadelphia, PA in Burlington, NJ; Rev. Welch (3-9/16)
7038. Putnam, Hamilton, merchant, m 4/20/31 Jane V. Cleaveland, dau of Gen. Erastus, in Madison; Rev. Pierce (bride and groom both of Madison) (1-4/29)
7039. Putnam, Jonathan of the state of Vermont m 2/1/32 Rebecca Rowell of Poughkeepsie in Pleasant Valley; Oliver D. Collins, Esq. (8-2/8)
7040. Putnam, Mary, 92, mother of Elisha and David of Albany, NY, d 1/30/30 in Chesterfield, NH (1-2/12)
7041. Quackenbush, Henry (Col.) d 2/4/13 in Albany (9-2/9)
7042. Quackenbush, Peter W., Esq. of Schoharie m 3/9/07 Fredrica Quitman of Rhinebeck in Schoharie; Rev. Quitman (8-2/25)
7043. Quirk, Thomas of NYC m 6/12/31 Elizabeth Charles of Albany in A; Rev. Campbell (1-7/15)
7044. Quitman, Frederick H. (Rev.) of Rhinebeck m 5/28/05 Mary M. Mayer in Athens, NY; Rev. Uhl (6-6/4)
7045. Quitman, Frederick Henry (Rev. Dr.), 72, pastor of the Evangelical Lutheran Congregation in Rhinebeck, d 6/26/32 in Rhinebeck (for many years was president of the Evangelical Lutheran Synod of the State of NY and "Senior of the Ministerium" at the time of his death (8-7/4)
7046. Quitman, Johanna Elizabeth Stueck, wf of Rev. Frederick H., d 2/24/04 in Rhinebeck (8-3/6)
7047. Rabine, Henry of Hudson drowned 10/13/01 (probably in or near Hudson, NY) (the deceased was subject to fits and "it is supposed that he fell from the cliff into the water taken by a seizure") (6-10/22)
7048. Rabineau, Henry of NYC m 6/18/29 Cornelia A. Jones, dau of Thomas F., Esq. of L. I. (1-6/20)
7049. Race, Isaac m 8/9/01 Catharine Bogardus in Hudson (double ceremony - see marr of Henry selleck) (6-8/13)
7050. Radcliff, David V. N., Esq. of Poughkeepsie m 5/7/34 Maria Graverart (niece of Robert Dunbar, Jr. and dau of late Isaac Graverart of Detroit, MI) in Albany; Rev. Dr. Ludlow (8-5/14)
7051. Radcliff, Jane V. N., oldest dau of William, Esq., d 7/1/22 in Rhinebeck (8-7/3)
7052. Radcliff, John m 10/24/98 Jane Van Ness, dau of Gen. David, all of Rhinebeck; Rev. Romeyn (8-10/30)
7053. Radcliff, John, 1 yr old, s of John, Esq., sheriff of Dutchess Co., d 3/22/16 in Red Hook (8-3/27)
7054. Radcliff, Margaret, 79, relict of Maj. William, d 5/4/34 at the home of John Radcliff in Rhinebeck (member of the church at Rhinebeck Flats for "upwards of 50 years") (8-5/14)
7055. Radcliff, Peter W., Esq. of Poughkeepsie m 10/4/00 Eliza Davenport, dau of Maj. Davenport of Stanford (sic), CT (8-10/7)
7056. Radcliff, William (Maj.), 76, d 9/13/13 in Rhinebeck (8-9/15)
7057. Radgley, George, Jr. m 12/20/15 Emma Seely; Rev. Clark (8-12/27)
7058. Rafferty, William (Rev.), D. D., 52, Pres. of St. John's College, Annapolis, MD, d 8/8/30 in Blooming Grove (Orange Co.), NY (deceased was formerly pastor of the Blooming Grove Presbyterian Church)(1-8/18)

7059. Rainey, _____ (Mr.) m "Mrs. Congden", both of Hyde Park, in H. P.; Rev. Brown (8-2/20/22)
7060. Ramsay, Nathaniel (Col.) (a Rev. officer) d 10/26/17 in Baltimore, MD (7-12/6)
7061. Ramsey, James, 62, d 12/11/05 in Hudson (6-12/17)
7062. Ramsey, William of Windham (Greene Co.) m 9/26/31 Jane Wands, dau of John, Jr. of Bethlehem; Rev. Fort (1-9/29)
7063. Ran, John W. m 8/19/12 Isabel Whorter, both of Hebron, in H; Rev. Dunham (9-8/25)
7064. Rand, Parnal, 48, wf of Silas, d in Hudson (6-1/21/06)
7065. Randal, Cyrus m 1/23/27 Louisa Winch in Plattsburgh; Rev. Halsey (7-1/29)
7066. Randall, Gershom of Bridgewater m Sally Rhodes of Paris, NY in P (3-1/31/25)
7067. Randall, Jacob (Capt.) m 12/6/20 Sally Ingraham, dau of George, Esq., all of Amenia; Rev. Washburn (8-12/20)
7068. Randall, Laura H., 30, oldest dau of Hon. William Wirt, d 12/17/33 at the home of her husband, Judge Randall, near Tallahasee, FL (8-1/8/34)
7069. Randall, Margaret, 40, wf of Henry, d 1/6/26 in Pittsfield (Ots. Co.) (3-1/16)
7070. Randall, Nathan, editor of the late Chenango Patriot, m 5/4/31 Catharine Monell, dau of Hon. Robert, in Greene (1-5/14)
7071. Randall, Nicholas P., Esq. m 2/14/23 Sibbil Dyer, dau of Edmund, Esq. of Rutland, VT, in Manlius, NY; Rev. Anthon of Utica (3-3/3)
7072. Randolph, Alonzo S. of Mississippi m 3/24/30 Phebe E. Vail of Troy in T; Rev. Butler (1-3/27)
7073. Randolph, Mary B., wf of Dr. Philip G. and sister of "Mrs. Eaton", d 10/21/31 in Washington, Dist. of columbia (1-10/27)
7074. Rankin, Robert G. of NYC m Laura Maria Wolcott of Litchfield, CT in L; Rev. Hickock (1-4/7/31)
7075. Rannay, William (Capt.), about 68, d 9/28/29 in Middlebury, CT (1-10/6)
7076. Ranous(?) (surname blurred), Moses m 10/16/28 Mary Ann Ellsworth, both of Pleasant Valley; Rev. Clark (8-10/29)
7077. Ransom, George m 5/5/25 Lydia Holly in Chazy; Rev. Joel Byington (7-5/14)
7078. Ransom, George m 7/13/26 Caroline Kingsley in Chazy (7-7/15)
7079. Ransom, Jared C. m Amanda Cook in Warren; Rev. Putnam (3-3/8/24)
7080. Ransom, Joshua, Esq., 87, (a Rev. patriot) d 10/25/29 at his home in Springfield (Ots. Co.) (1-11/6)
7081. Ransom, Louisa, 19, dau of Luther, d 8/24/22 in Chazy (7-8/31)
7082. Ransom, Rhoda (Mrs.), about 58, d 8/21/02 at Cumberland Head (near Plattsburgh) (deceased was wife of John Ransom, Esq., late assistant justice in the court of common pleas) (9-9/15)
7083. Ransom, William, 13 mo, s of Lewis, d 9/12/20 in Plattsburgh (7-9/16)
7084. Rantzinger, William P.,"purser in the navy",m Louisa F. Heyer in Washington (state not given) (9-10/31/15)
7085. Rapalje, Elizabeth, 54, wf of Jeromus Rapalje, d 1/2/19 in Hopewell (8-1/20)
7086. Rapalje, Isaac Van Wyck, 5, youngest s of Maj. Richard, d 12/7/09 in Fishkill (died "of the Hives") (8-12/20)
7087. Rapalje, Isaac Van Wyck, 11, s of Richard, Esq., d 7/31/24 in Fishkill (8-8/4)
7088. Rapalje, James m 3/28/18 Catharine Luckey (in Poughkeepsie?) (8-4/8)
7089. Rapalje, Jane Ann, 14, oldest dau of Richard, Esq., d 7/11/25 in Poughkeepsie (8-7/13)
7090. Rapalje, Richard m 11/15/20 "Miss Suthard", both of Fishkill; Rev. Westbrook (8-11/22)
7091. Rapalje, Richard, Esq., 61, d 9/2/25 in Fishkill (8-9/7)
7092. Rapalye, Archibald Currie, 14, s of late Richard, Esq., d 7/28/31 in Fishkill(had just returned home on vacation from Rutgers College) (8-8/3)
7093. Rathbone, David (Rev.), 60, formerly of Hoosick, d 8/2/23 in Lawrenceville (9-8/26)
7094. Rathbone, Jared L., 1 year old, s of Joel, d 8/23/31 in Albany (1-8/24)
7095. Rathbone, Joel (Col.) m 5/5/29 Emeline Munn; Rev. Weed. All of Albany (1-5/6) (Deceased was of the firm of Heermans, Rathbone & Co.)
7096. Rathbone, Justus H., Esq., attorney, m 5/24/26 Sarah E. Dwight, oldest dau of late Henry E., in Utica; Rev. S.C. Aiken (3-6/12)

7097. Rathbun, Daniel d 12/23/24 in Springfield (3-1/3/25)
7098. Rathbun, James, Esq. of the firm of Smith and Rathbun, Counsellors and Attornies at Law of Rhinebeck, m 5/19/19 Caroline Williams Hamilton of Athens, NY in A; Rev. Prentice (8-6/2)
7099. Rawdon, Freeman of the firm of Rawdon, Clarke and Co. of Albany, m 12/24/29 Mary R. Myers, dau of Col. Matthew, in Ogdensburgh; Rev. Smith (1-12/28)
7100. Ray, Benjamin, 67, d in Hudson (6-11/14/09)
7101. Ray, Caroline Perlina, dau of James of Brookfield, d 12/17/32 in Willsborough (4 [Keeseville Herald]-2/26/33)
7102. Ray, James H. of the firm of Warner, Prall and Ray, m 7/6/30 Margaretta M. Willett, only dau of Col. Marinus Willett, at Christ Church in NYC; Rev. Dr. Lyell (1-7/10)
7103. Raymond, ____, consort of James, d 8/16/07 in Troy (9-8/18)
7104. Raymond, Benjamin C., merchant, m 3/19/29 Lois P. Marther; Rev. Brown. All of Albany (1-3/23)
7105. Raymond, Clapp (sic), Esq., 65, d 5/16/31 in Poughkeepsie (an active Republican who was Clerk of Dutchess County in 1825) (8-5/18 and 1-5/26)
7106. Raymond, Francis m 11/14/33 Eliza Geror; Ahaz Hayes, Esq. All of Peru, NY (4 [Keeseville Herald]-11/19)
7107. Raymond, Henry of Detroit, MI m 8/31/29 Mary Alvord of Utica in Trinity Church, Utica; Rev. Dorr (1-9/4)
7108. Raymond, James m 7/21/11 Esther Allen, both of Troy (9-7/23)
7109. Raymond, John (Dr.), 65, d 9/19/29 in Kent (8-10/14)
7110. Raymond, Lemuel B., Esq. of Jordan (Onon. Co.) m 8/20/31 Lavantia E. Chase, dau of Hon. Seth of Worcester, in W; Rev. Tiffany (1-9/8)
7111. Raymond, Nathan, 81, one of the first settlers in Ballston, d 6/28/24 in B (2-7/6)
7112. Raymond, Nathaniel, 45, d 1/7/24 in Norwalk, CT (9-1/20)
7113. Raymond, Rebecca (Mrs.), 75, d 2/9/11 in Poughkeepsie (8-2/13)
7114. Raymond, Reliance, 42, wf of Alfred, Esq., d 4/10/31 in Poughkeepsie (8-4/13)
7115. Raymond, Sarah, 64, consort of Clapp Raymond, Esq., d 1/2/31 (8-1/5)
7116. Raymond, Sheldon C. D. m 9/30/20 Eliza Holden, both of Poughkeepsie; Rev. C. C. Cuyler (8-10/4)
7117. Raymond, Thaddeus m 1/16/19 Abigail Selick, both of Poughkeepsie; Rev. Lewis Leonard (8-1/20)
7118. Raymond, William, Jr. m 6/20/05 Polly Kellogg, both of Granville, in G; Rev. Hall (9-7/2)
7119. Read, ____, about 6, s of Benjamin, a blacksmith, d "lately" in Weathersfield, VT (his father accidentally struck his son on the temple "with a hot iron taken hastily out of the fire") (6-3/25/06)
7120. Read, John, 67, d 3/30/29 in NYC (1-4/6)
7121. Read, Susannah, 27, wf of Elijah, d 7/29/13 "at the Fourth-Town" (7-8/14)
7122. Reade, Catharine, 72, relict of the late John, Esq., d 2/26/29 in Poughkeepsie (8-3/4)
7123. Reade, John, Esq., 63, d 10/26/08 at his home in Poughkeepsie (funeral sermon by Rev. Bulkley at the Episcopal Church) (burial in the family vault in NYC)(8-11/2)
7124. Reade, Joseph, agent, 29 years, of the firm of Reade and Jacobson of Pough- keepsie, d 12/7/08 on the Island of Antigua (8-2/1/09)
7125. Reading, Samuel R. m 7/6/22 Alida Martin, both of Poughkeepsie; Rev. Cuyler (8-7/10)
7126. Record, Crandell m 9/24/28 Mary Terbush, both of Poughkeepsie; Rev. Dr. Reed (8-10/1)
7127. Record, John W. m 1/19/27 Cornelia Roberts, both of Poughkeepsie; Rev. Cushman (8-2/7)
7128. Rector, Henry m 11/4/15 Jane Ann Sickles (9-11/14)
* 7129. Redding, Maria, 39, consort of William, Esq. of Nassau, NY and oldest dau of Abel and Eunice Wright of New Lebanon, d 5/30/30 (surv by husband and "a numerous young family") (1-6/1)

* Descendants of William Redding, Esq. can probably claim ancestry through Richard Warren of the "Mayflower". Billie Redding Lewis in The Redding Family and Its Relatives (undated but early 1980's - author's address: 1104 Voncile St., Lake Wales, FL) claims for Moses[5] (William[4], Ebenezer[3], John[2], Thomas[1]) Redding and his second wife, Priscilla Rider, a total of eight children among whom are (this footnote continued at bottom of next page)

7130. Redfield, Lewis H., editor of the Onondaga Register, m Ann Maria Tredwell, dau of N. H. of Plattsburgh, in Clinton, NY (7-2/19/20)
7131. Redford, John, about 70, d 1/18/34 in Fishkill (8-1/22)
7132. Redington, Meriam, 58, consort of John, Esq., d 8/7/11 in Cobleskill (3-8/17)
7133. Rednor, William of Pittstown m 9/4/13 Sally Van Vechten of Schaghticoke (9-9/7)
7134. Reed, Abigail (Miss), about 15, d 12/16/18 in Plattsburgh (7-12/26)
7135. Reed, Almey of the firm of Judson and Reed of Coxsackie, m 9/7/31 Helen Van Dusen, dau of John of Livingston (Columbia Co.); Rev. Holmes (1-9/10)
7136. Reed, Daniel d 4/21/27 at the home of his father (not named) in Amenia (8-5/2)
7137. Reed, Ezra, Esq., 67, late of Hudson, d 8/4/07 in Coxsackie (6-8/11)
7138. Reed, Ezra, merchant, of NYC m 7/14/08 Eliza Thurston at the home of John Thurston, Esq. in Hudson; Rev. Prentiss (6-7/19)
7139. Reed, Ezra, 4, s of Rufus, d 10/12/18 in Hudson (6-10/20)
7140. Reed, Henry, 35, formerly of Cairo (Greene Co.) d 8/28/29 in NYC (1-9/5)
7141. Reed, James m 1/2/17 Eliza Hitchcock; Rev. Osborn. All of Amenia (8-1/8)
7142. Reed, Jesse m 1/22/26 Betsy Hurd; Rev. C. P. Reed. All of Amenia (8-1/25)
7143. Reed, John m 5/3/25 Maria Ostrom; Rev. Dr. Reed (8-5/11)
7144. Reed, John (Rev. Dr.) m 2/9/34 Elizabeth Parkinson at the Episcopal Church in Poughkeepsie; Rev. John Brown of Newburgh (8-2/12)
7145. Reed, Leonard m 1/30/24 Rachel Nase, dau of John; Rev. Wilson. All of Amenia (8-2/4)
7146. Reed, Luman, merchant, m 4/30/08 Polly Barker, dau of Eleazer, merchant, in Coxsackie; Rev. Henry Ostrander. All of Coxsackie (6-5/3)
7147. Reed, Nelson, 20, s of Isaac, d 9/15/17 in Hudson (6-9/23)
7148. Reed, Rufus A., formerly senior editor of the Cortland Chronicle, m 12/3/29 Lydia Ann Crosby, dau of Elisha, in Homer; Rev. A. Bennett. All of H. (1-12/10)
7149. Reed, Sally, 43, wf of Ketchel, d 5/21/30 in Lansingburgh (1-5/31)
7150. Reed, Sarah, 75, consort of late Ezra formerly of Hudson, d 4/15/18 in Coxsackie (6-4/21)
7151. Reed, Seth (Capt.) d 1/24/23 in Hartwick (3-1/27)
7152. Reed, Susan, 47, wf of Rev. Dr. Reed, rector of Christ's Church, d 8/21/32 in Poughkeepsie (8-8/22)
7153. Reed, Thomas C. of Poughkeepsie m 8/15/29 Eliza S. Duane, youngest dau of Hon. James C. of Schenectady, at St. George's Church in Schenectady; Rev. Dr. Reed (8-8/19 and 1-8/20)
7154. Reeder, Nathaniel m Mrs. Jane Crandle of New Paltz "it being her SEVENTH husband" (8-9/9/18)
7155. Reese, Ann, 13, of Ballston d 6/14/22 in B (2-6/18)
7156. Reese, George Bickham, Esq. of Philadelphia m 8/16/25 Margaret Mesier, dau of Matthew, Esq. of Fishkill; Rev. Thomas (8-8/24)
7157. Reese, Rush B., M. D., late professor of the Institutes of Medicine and Medicine Jurisprudence in Jefferson, College, d 10/9/31 in Philadelphia, PA (1-10/13)
7158. Reeve, John G., merchant, m 6/29/23 Anna Sweet; Benjamin Vars, Esq. All of Berlin, NY (9-7/15)
7159. Reeve, Tapping (Hon.), 79, formerly Chief Justice of the State of Conn., d 12/13/23 (8-12/24)
7160. Reeves, Sarah (Mrs.), 77, sister of Gen. Dunning of Ballston Spa, d 6/14/25 in Malta, NY (2-6/21)
7161. Reggles, Charles H. m 2/15/27 Gertrude Beekman, both of Kingston, in Fishkill; Rev. Westbrook (8-2/21)

(continuation of footnote found on the previous page)
William[6] Redding "b 31 May 1787; mar. Maria Wright" and Stephens[6] Redding "b. 27 Oct 1780; mar. Abigail (Gilman) Lapish." The Mayflower Index (1:592) traces the ancestry of "Steven Redding" (with father Moses and with wife Abigail Gilman), through his mother, Priscilla Rider, back to Richard Warren of the "Mayflower".

7162. Reid, Francis E. of "Clark's Ville" m 10/30/22 Pamelia Babcock of Westford in W (3-11/11)
7163. Reid, John (Maj.) of the U.S. Army ("aid of Gen. Jackson in his transaction against the Creeks and the British") d 1/18/16 at his father's home in Bedford, VA (9-2/13)
7164. Reilay, Marium, wf of Capt. John G., d 6/23/28 in Troy (9-6/24)
7165. Reilay, Volkert m 11/9/05 Hannah Snyder, both of Troy; Rev. Coe (9-11/12)
7166. Reillay, John G. m 19/3/19 Mariam Perkins, both of Albany, in A; Rev. Cummings (9-10/12)
7167. Reitzer, Asa m 8/4/98 Maria Cropsy, both of Poughkeepsie; Rev. Brower (8-8/7)
7168. Relay, Elizabeth, 71, wid of Lewis, d 10/5/99 in Clinton (8-10/15)
7169. Relay, Henry, 87, d 6/26/30 (8-6/30)
7170. Relay, Robert m 1/21/26 Margareta Harris, both of Poughkeepsie; Rev. Dr. Reed (8-1/25)
7171. Relay, Stephen Henry, 29(?), d 11/11/23 in NYC (8-11/26)
7172. Relyea, Lydia Anna, 23, wf of Simon and dau of William Davis, Esq. of Queenstown, Upper Canada, d 2/2/23 in Troy, NY (9-2/9)
7173. Remington, Roby (Miss), 122 yrs old (sic), d 9/5/20 in Cherry Valley (3-9/18)
7174. Remsen, Abraham Duryee m 12/17/23 Charlotte Storm, dau of Abraham; Rev. De Witt. All of Fishkill (8-12/24)
7175. Remsen, Edward of the firm of Balley and Remsen, merchants, of NYC m 4/18/26 Mary Van Wyck, dau of John B. of Poughkeepsie; Rev. Cuyler (8-4/26)
7176. Remsen, Edward of NYC m 4/11/32 Matilda White, dau of Dr. B. White, in Fishkill; Rev. Fisher (8-4/18)
7177. Remsen, Mary, wf of Edward of NYC and dau of John B. Van Wyck of Poughkeepsie, d 6/16/30 in NYC (8-6/23/30)
7178. Rephenback, Tunis, 103, "one of the surviving few who fought before the walls of Quebec at the fall of Wolfe", d in Sidney, NY (7-10/26/33)
7179. Requa, Gerrit, merchant, m 10/4/30 Margaret Chambers, dau of late David, all of Albany; Rev. Hugh Jolly (1-10/7)
7180. Reuwee, Wyman O., 27, formerly of Albany, d 6/2/31 in New Albany, IN (1-8/6)
7181. Rexford, Edward of Halfmoon m 6/3/24 Elizabeth Saunders of Ballston in B; Rev. R. Smith (2-6/15)
7182. Reynolds, Abraham, flour merchant of NYC, m 10/26/06 Sally Folger, dau of late Benjamin of Hudson, in H; Rev. Sears (6-10/28)
7183. Reynolds, Anna, dau of Allen, d 12/24/15 in Hudson (consumption) (6/1/2/16)
7184. Reynolds, Anna G., about 17, dau of Charles, deceased, d 4/16/22 (7-4/20)
7185. Reynolds, Cynthia, 26, consort of Marcus T., Esq. and dau of late Col. Benjamin Herrick of Amenia, d 11/25/20 in Amsterdam, NY (8-12/13)
7186. Reynolds, Isaac m 1/9/23 Sarah Ellison; Peter Fish, Esq. All of Amenia (8-1/15)
7187. Reynolds, John, 53, d 7/24/30 in Albany (1-7/27)
7188. Reynolds, Joseph m 1/12/19 Electa Garnsey, both of Amenia, in A; Rev. Lewis Leonard (8-1/20)
7189. Reynolds, Joseph m 3/1/28 Eliza McDonald, both of Freedom; Rev. Clark (8-3/12)
7190. Reynolds, Marcus T., Esq. of Amsterdam, NY m 1/28/14 Cynthia Herrick, dau of late Col. Benjamin of amenia, in A; Rev. Hyde (8-2/2)
7191. Reynolds, Philip, Jr., Esq., editor of the Johnstown Herald, m 3/31/31 Louisa Georgiana Richard, dau of Steohen of NYC, at St. John's Church in NYC; Rev. Dr. Berrian (1-4/1)
7192. Reynolds, Sarah, 51 or 31, wf of Jacob, d in Norwich, NY ("Printers in Providence, R. I. are requested to insert this.") (3-11/28/07)
7193. Reynolds, Seneca m 12/24/28 Helen Van Ness, dau of Cornelius, in Chatham; Rev. L. S. Rexford (1-1/3/29)
7194. Reynolds, Silas d 7/20/14 in Troy (9-7/26)
7195. Reynolds, William m 11/16/15 Mary Clancy, both of Hudson, in H; Rev. Rice (6-11/21)
7196. Rhind, Frederick of Troy m 10/14/15 Betsey Wilgus of Lansingburgh (9-10/31)
7197. Rhinelander, Philip, Esq. d 2/28/30 in NYC ("a member of the state convention for the revision of the constitution") (1-3/6)

7198. Rhoads, Philip of Marlborough m 3/10/21 Jane Ann Williams of New Paltz; Rev. Aaron Perkins (8-3/14)
7199. Rhodes, John, 18, "apprentice to the printing business in the office of the Constellation, d in Catskill (6-9/27/03)
7200. Rhinders, ____ (Mrs.), 91, d 5/19/20 in Poughkeepsie (8-5/24)
7201. (This entry repositioned)
7202. Rice, Ebenezer m 3/8/04 Frances Platt in Marcellus; Hon. Dan Bradley, Esq. (6-3/27)
7203. Rice, Ebenezer, S. m 2/15/20 Caroline White, both of Middlefield, in M; Rev. Andrew Oliver (3-2/28)
7204. Rice, Frances, 23, wf of Ebenezer, d 8/18/07 in Marcellus (6-9/8)
7205. Rice, H. P. (Mr.), 29, d 2/10/32 in Saratoga Springs (4 [Keeseville Herald]-2/21)
7206. Rice, Henry m 4/17/19 Harriet Barker in Middlefield; Elder Banjamin Sawin. All of M. (3-4/19)
7207. Rice, Jacob m 10/21/31 Mary Ann Smith in Poughkeepsie, both of Pleasant Valley; Rev. Welton (8-11/16)
7208. Rice, Joseph, Esq., attorney, m 1/27/25 Elisa Edson in Milford (3-1/31)
7209. Rice, Mary, 43, consort of Holden formerly of Middlefield, d 7/31/23 in Morrisville (3-8/18)
7210. Rice, Obed of Troy m 12/31/07 Sally Kinney of Greenbush in G (9-1/5/08)
7211. Rice, Olney m 5/22/22 Betsey Babcock in Westford; Rev. Garvin (3-5/27)
7212. Rice, Susan , 20, wf of Ebenezer, d in Marcellus (6-11/23/02)
7213. Rice, William, Esq., attorney, formerly of Ballston Spa., m 4/5/25 Rosalie M. Jackson of Charleston, SC in C (2-4/26)
7214. Rich, John T. of NYC m Julia Van Voorhis, youngest dau of   Maj. W. R. of Fishkill, in F; Rev. Dr. Westbrook (1-1/16/30)
7215. Richards, Albert m 2/1/27 Catharine S. Randal, dau of Enos; Rev. Martin-dale. All of Troy (9-2/6)
7216. Richards, Alpheus, 22, d 6/25/29 in Troy (1-6/27)
7217. Richards, Betsey, 29, wf of Col. Daniel, d 3/11/26 in Richfield (3-3/20)
7218. Richards, Caroline, 22, consort of Maj. Richards, d 10/17/26 in Richfield (3-10/23)
7219. Richards, Fanny (Mrs.), 32, d 9/22/23 in Cherry Valley (3-10/6)
7220. Richards, Gustavus U. of NYC m 7/31/33 Electra (sic) B. Wilder, dau of S. V. S. Wilder, Esq. of Bolton, NY in B; Rev. ?. W. Chickering (newspaper account contains details concerning unusual wedding festivities) (7-8/31)
7221. Richards, Henry of the firm of L. Richards and Sons of Troy, NY m Nancy Gilbert, 2nd dau of Daniel of Portland, ME, in P (1-9/9/30)
7222. Richards, James Sidney m 3/31/22 Mary Purdy; Rev. Halsey. All of Plattsburgh (7-4/6)
7223. Richards, John m 12/4/28 Ruth Turner, dau of James, in Riga; Rev. Halsey (9-12/16)
7224. Richards, Rufus, merchant, of Troy m 1/1/07 Rua Scofield of Stamford, CT in S (9-1/13)
7225. Richardson, A. L. (Lt.) of U.S. Army m 9/20/30 Sylvia R. Porter, dau of Chauncey, Esq., in Pittsford; Rev. Mahan (1-10/1)
7226. Richardson, Abel W. m 2/21/27 Patience Cole, both of West Troy; Rev. Howard (9-3/2)
7227. Richardson, Josephus of Halifax, VT m 10/7/20 Euphemia Anderson of Albia; Rev. Sommers (9-10/10)
7228. Richardson, Marvin of Brooklyn m 4/7/13 Sarah Morgan of Poughkeepsie; Rev. William Swazey (8-4/14)
7229. Richardson, Marvin D. of Brooklyn m 12/4/28 Sarah Johnson, only dau of Joseph of NYC; Rev. Richardson (8-12/10)
7230. Richardson, Sylvester m Caroline Mary Miles, dau of Capt. I. F., in Watertown; Rev. Morse (1-6/18/31)
7231. Richardson, William m 10/15/29 Nancy Alsop, both of England, in Albany; Calvin Pepper, Esq. (1-10/29)
7232. Richardson, William, 77, (a Rev. Soldier), father of Charles, Esq., the latter a member of the state assembly from Cortland Co., d 4/24/31 in Providence (Sara. Co.) (1-4/26)
7233. Richarson (sic), Peter, 20, d 2/3/03 in Germantown (Herk. Co.) (hydro-phobia from a dog bite) (8-3/1)

7234. Richert, David m Anna Merkel in Rhinebeck; Rev. Quitman (8-2/22/09)
7235. Richert, Jacob m 1/29/09 Catherine Risely in Rhinebeck; Rev. Quitman (8-2/22)
7236. Richie, Francis m 6/25/27 Eliza Barringer, both of Greenbush; Rev. Howard (9-7/10)
7237. Richmond, Silvanus, 47, d 3/21/14 in Hudson (6-3/29)
7238. Ricketson, Henry m 12/29/05 Polly Smith , both of Beekman, in B (8-1/7/06)
7239. Ricketson, Meribeth, 96, d 12/6/25 in Beekman (8-12/14)
7240. Ricketson, Walter L. of Beekman m 11/30/15 Nancy Strite of Clinton; Rev. Clark (8-12/6)
7241. Ricketts, Francis (Private), 20th Regiment, U.S. Infantry, d 3/11/14 ("one of the celebrated 'Circus Riders'") (7-3/19)
7242. Rider, Daniel, Jr. m 9/27/20 Lois Bedlow, both of Champlain, in Chazy; Rev. Byington (7-9/30)
7243. Rider, Duncan, son of William, d "some days since" in Poughkeepsie (8-11/13/98)
7244. Rider, Elizabeth, 42, wf of Stephen J., d 2/11/31 in Albany (1-2/14)
7245. Rider, Jacob d 12/23/19 near Littletown, PA (he informed his wife he must die; she helped him to bed and returning in about five minutes "found her husband a corpse") (8-1/12/20)
7246. Rider, Jesse D. m 2/28/28 Eustatia Heustis, both of Amenia; Rev. Rider (8-3/12)
7247. Rider, John, Esq. m 8/1/13 Mary Ann Tidd; Jehiel Sarkes, Esq. All of Stanford (Dut. Co.) (8-8/25)
7248. Rider, Margaret L., 3 mo, dau of Stephen J., d 12/9/30 in Albany (1-12/11)
7249. Rider, Samuel m 2/19/34 Melissa Miller, dau of Robert; Henry Tallmadge, Esq. All of Stanford (Dut. Co.) (8-2/26)
7250. Rider, Simeon d 5/9/12 in De Ruyter (buried with Masonic honors) (3-5/16)
7251. Rider, William of Poughkeepsie m 11/6/02 Harriet Webbers of Fishkill; Rev. Van Vranken (8-11/16)
7252. Ridgeby, Charles, 69, of Hampton, late gov. of Maryland, d 7/17/29 (death place not given) (1-7/22)
7253. Riggs, James W. of Freedom m 11/14/27 Mary Ann De Reimer of Poughkeepsie; Rev. C. C. Cuyler (8-11/21)
7254. Riggs, Stephen S., editor of the Schenectady Cabinet, m 11/24/31 Julia Hanmer (sic), dau of John B. Vedder of Schoharie, in S; Rev. Wiedman (1-12/2)
7255. Rikert, Henry m 3/26/29 Caroline Northrup, dau of late William of Washington (Dut. Co.); William Northrup, Esq. (8-4/8)
7256. Riley, John m 1/8/15 Elizabeth Van Lyngen, both of Troy (9-1/10)
7257. Riley, John H. of Washington, Dist of Columbia, m 6/17/21 Euphemia Butler, dau of Rev. Butler of Troy, at St. Paul's Church in Troy; Rev. David Butler (9-6/19)
7258. Riley, Lucy, 35, consort of Roger of Hudson, NY, d 7/20/01 in Berlin, CT (6-7/30)
7259. Riley, Sally G. (Miss), about 23, d 8/31/20 in Gibbonsville (9-9/5)
7260. Rinarts, Evert C. m 11/27/13 Elizabeth Elliston; Rev. Quitman (8-12/8)
7261. Rinck, Francis Anthony m 3/23/06 Mrs. Catharine Ricket, both of Poughkeepsie; Rev. Brouwer (8-3/25)
7262. Ring, Catharine, 29, wf of Peter, d 1/22/26 in Rhinebeck (8-2/1)
7263. Ring, Gouldsburn of Jay m Mary Emmons of Clintonville; E. Williams, Esq. (7-9/27/34)
7264. Ring, Lewis m 4/16/11 Elenor Dubois, dau of Koert, Esq., all of Clinton (Dut. Co.); Rev. Quitman (8-5/8)
7265. Ring, Peter m 9/20/20 Catharine Teal in Rhinebeck; Rev. William McMurray (8-9/27)
7266. Ripley, _____ (Maj. Gen.), lately of the U. S. Army, d "lately" in New Orleans, LA (yellow fever) (8-11/15/20)
7267. Ripley, John (Maj.), 47, of the firm of Ripley and Center, d 10/8/12 in NYC (6-10/12)
7268. Ripley, Nancy W., 15, dau of Ebenezer formerly of Cooperstown, d in Cherry Valley (3-6/25/21)
7269. Ripley, William, 17, only s of David, Esq. of Greenfield, MA, d 4/16/28 in Troy, NY (funeral from the home of Timothy Hall, Jr. on Ferry St.) (9-4/18)

7270. Ritchie, George, Jr., 28, printer, (formerly publisher of the Mohawk Sentinel) d 8/5/31 in Schenectady (1-8/11 and 4 [Keeseville Herald]-8/16)
7271. Ritchman, Silas of Fishkill m 10/10/31 Mrs. Catharine Quackenbush of Albany; Rev. Burch (1-10/12)
7272. Ritter, Frederick W. m 5/4/29 Angelica Gilbert Powers, oldest dau of Heman Powers, Esq., in Ithaca; Rev. Williston. All of Ithaca (1-5/11)
7273. Rivington, James (Col.) of Poughkeepsie d 5/1/34 at the home of his son-in-law, Henry Hogeboom, Esq. in Hudson (8-5/7)
7274. Roabson, John of Poughkeepsie m 3/2/11 Sarah Henderson of Fishkill; Rev. Reed (8-3/6)
7275. Robb, William, merchant, m Sally Benton in Catskill (6-6/15/02)
7276. Robbins, Amaris m 9/16/28 Julia Ann Burritt; Rev. Beman. All of Troy (9-9/19)
7277. Robbins, Joshua N., merchant, of Nassau, NY m 12/19/12 Sarah White of Troy; Rev. Wayland (9-12/22)
7278. Roberts, Alice, 55, wf of George, d 10/23/24 in Otsego (3-10/25)
7279. Roberts(?), Eli, 62, d 2/17/30 in Albany (funeral from his home, 124 State St.) (1-2/19)
7280. Roberts, George of Otsego m Mrs. Rhoda Wetmore of Westford in W; Rev. Spafford (3-11/7/25)
7281. Roberts, Hannah (Mrs.), 24, wf of Philo B., d 9/27/09 in Plattsburgh (7 [American Monitor]-10/14)
7282. Roberts, Harvey B., printer, formerly of Poughkeepsie, m Sarah Burr of Hartford, CT in H (8-1/8/17)
7283. Roberts, Hiram m 2/6/23 Sarah Kent; Rev. Frederick Halsey (7-2/15)
7284. Roberts, John d 6/9/16 at the home of Col. John Shaver ("Personal papers found upon him" indicated that he was a Pennsylvanian, had been a seaman in the U.S. Navy more than forty years, and had a pension certificate. He was discharged by Commodore Decatur from the "Guerrier".) (6-6/18)
7285. Roberts, Jonathan, 46, d 7/24/14 in Poughkeepsie (8-7/27)
7286. Roberts, Joseph (Dr.), 67, formerly of Hudson, d 6/4/15 in Owego (Broome Co.) (6-6/20)
7287. Roberts, Nathaniel P. m 1/25/24 Mariah Halsey in Plattsburgh; Rev. F. Halsey (7-1/31)
7288. Roberts, Owen M., Esq., step-son of Capt. Staats Morris of Lansingburgh and senior partner of the firm of Van Ryck, Prediger & Co., m Miss D. W. De Bockhorst of Batavia, Island of Java (3-7/14/23)
7289. Roberts, Peter J. of Plattsburgh m 2/28/19 Marial Bemis of Wethersfield, VT (7-3/13)
7290. Roberts, Polly, wf of Hiram, d 9/1/22 in Plattsburgh (7-9/21)
7291. Roberts, Polly, 55, wf of Maj. John, d 1/16/27 (7-1/22)
7292. Roberts, Ralph, about 20, d "a few days since" in NYC (had been a journeyman printer "for a considerable time" for the Northern Whig in Hudson) (6-7/30/16)
7293. Roberts, Rachel Antinette, 4, dau of Philip B., d 9/27/09 in Plattsburgh (7 [American Monitor]-10/14)
7294. Roberts, Walter B., 40, d 11/24/31 in Albany (funeral from his motehr's home, 124 State St.) (1-12/3)
7295. Roberts, William, Jr. of Queensbury (Wash. Co.), NY m 5/15/99 Betsey Gaylord of New Milford, CT in N. M. (9-6/2)
7296. Roberts, William m Sina Matteson, dau of David, in Hartwick; Rev. Bostwick (3-1/5/18)
7297. Robertson, Eliza Ann, 32, (wife of William, comedian) d "lately" in Hoboken, NJ (dropsy) (buried in Albany (1-5/9/31)
7298. Robertson, Jacob A. of NYC m 12/5/31 Helen Ackerman, dau of Jacobus, Esq. of La Grange, in L. G.; Rev. Dwight (8-12/7)
7299. Robertson, James of Broadalbin m 4/16/29 Eliza McNab of Gloversville in G; Rev. McLaren (1-4/20)
7300. Robertson, John m 7/3/27 Caroline Allen, both of Troy; Rev. Willis (9-7/6)
7301. Robertson, Thomas, 75, m 4/8/29 Esther McGill, 16, both of Cambridge, in Salem; Rev. Dr. Proudfit (1-5/6)

7302. Robertson, Thomas Esq. m 5/4/30 Elizabeth Teeter, 3rd dau of Jacob of Lansing, in L; Elder Sears (1-5/17)
7303. Robertson, Thomas m 10/8/31 Eliza Vandyke in Hyde Park; Rev. Cahoone. All of H. P. (8-10/19)
7304. Robie, John, 37, d 8/19/18 in Plattsburgh (7-8/22)
7305. Robins, Artimus of Easton m 2/9/02 Eve Toll, dau of Jesse, Esq. of Saratoga, in S; Rev. Paige (9-2/17)
7306. Robinson, Barbee m Louisa Shelland in Westford; Rev. Caldwell (3-1/5/24)
7307. Robinson, Clark of Albany, late of Palmyra, m 7/8/30 Delia Strong of Palmyra in P; Rev. A. E. Campbell (1-7/15)
7308. Robinson, Dan (Capt.), 85, d in Granville, MA (6-8/24/10)
7309. Robinson, Dennis, merchant, of Adams, MA d 11/21/07 (6-11/24)
7310. Robinson, Duncan m 11/5/18 Mary Van Voorhis, dau of Cornelius, Esq., all of Fishkill; Rev. Westbrook (8-11/11)
7311. Robinson, Edward m Eliza Kirkland in Clinton (Perhaps in Dut. Co.) (6-9/22/18)
7312. Robinson, Elizabeth, 33, wf of Samuel of Fishkill, d 10/17/04 (surv by husband and 5 ch) (8-10/23)
7313. Robinson, Elizabeth (Mrs.), 71, d in Hudson (6-2/22/10)
7314. Robinson, Erasmus D., merchant, of Binghamton m Mary Parmelia Smith of Troy in T; Rev. Hill (1-5/24/30)
7315. Robinson, George m 1/14/06 Elizabeth Fraser, both of Troy; Rev. Coe (9-1/21)
7316. Robinson, George W. of NYC d 2/10/28 at the home of his father (name of the latter not given) in Plainfield, CT (8-2/20)
7317. Robinson, Isaac m 9/25/31 Jane Maria Hunter, youngest dau of Gilbert, Esq., all of Fishkill; Rev. Wile of Pleasant Valley (8-10/5)
7318. Robinson, John, "an old inhabitant of Fishkill", d 11/24/11 (8-12/4)
7319. Robinson, John of Columbia m 10/10/32 Susan T. Haight of Pleasant Valley in P. V.; S. B. Dutton, Esq. (8-10/17)
7320. Robinson, John L., 35, d 3/8/31 (1-3/10)
7321. Robinson, Jonathan, 64, late a U. S. senator, d in Bennington, VT (7-11/20/19)
7322. Robinson, Jonathan E. d 4/27/31 in Bennington, VT (b in Vermont; a grad of Williams College; for many years served first as an attorney and later as a merchant in NYC; served also 3 yrs in NY state legislature) (1-5/2)
7323. Robinson, Joseph m 3/15/24 Adeline Phillips in Exeter; Rev. Duncan (3-3/22)
7324. Robinson, Rebecca, wf of Capt. Ziba, d 8/20/24 in Middlefield (3-8/23)
7325. Robinson, Samuel D., 28, d in Palmyra (1-8/31/29)
7326. Robinson, Sophia Jenkins, 4, youngest dau of James, d 4/11/29 in Albany (1-4/14)
7327. Robinson, William F., merchant, of Bennington, VT. m Juliette Staniford, dau of Daniel, Esq., in Burlington, VT (7-8/30/34)
7328. Robinson, John, Jr. m 7/24/03 Catharine Parter (sic), both of Fishkill; Rev. Van Vranken (8-8/2)
7329. Robison, John D. m 5/1/28 Sarah Forbus, both of Poughkeepsie, at Christ Church in P; Rev. Dr. Reed (8-5/7)
7330. Robison, Samuel, s of John, m Elizabeth Bush of Fishkill (8-2/3/96) Robson. See, possibly, Roabson.
7331. Roby, George m 2/5/28 Eliza Fearney, both of Poughkeepsie, in P; Rev. Hutchinson (8-2/6)
7332. Roby, Joseph of the firm of Benedict and Roby of Utica m 9/8/29 Margaret Breese, oldest dau of S. Sidney, in Sconondoa (Oneida Co.); Rev. Woodruff (1-9/18)
7333. Rochester, Amanda, 31, wf of Hon. William B., d 1/16/31 in Buffalo (1-1/24)
7334. Rochester, John W. m 8/12/24 Maria Phillips; Rev. C. C. Cuyler (8-8/18)
7335. Rochester, William B. of Buffalo m 4/9/32 Eliza Powers of Auburn in A (8-4/18)
7336. Rock, Andrew of Peru m 9/16/34 Mrs. Margaret Chavalier of Plattsburgh in P; Rev. Brinckerhoff (7-9/20)
7337. Rock, Christian of NYC m 5/15/00 Hannah Marquart of Rhinebeck; Rev. Quiman(?) (8-5/27)
7338. Rockaway, Chancey P. of Schodack m 12/23/26 Ruth Manning of Clinton; Rev. Clark (8-12/27)

213

7339. Rockwell, Eliza (Miss), 20, dau of John, d 4/1/23 in Otsego (Fly Creek) (3-4/7)
7340. Rockwell, Gould, merchant of the firm of G. and W. Rockwell, late of CT, d 8/22/07 in Troy (9-8/25)
7341. Rockwell, James Otis, 23, formerly of Manlius, NY and late editor of the Providence (R.I.) Patriot d 6/7/31 in Providence, RI (born in NY "where his parents reside") (1-6/13 and 1-6/21)
7342. Rockwell, John A., Esq., attorney, m Mary Watkinson, dau of Joseph, Esq., in Norwich, CT (1-10/22/31)
7343. Rodgers, Archibald, Esq. of NYC m 5/18/20 Anna P. Pendleton, dau of Nathaniel, Esq., in Hyde Park; Rev. Brown (8-5/24)
7344. Rodgers, James of Spencertown d "a few days since in the woods near his residence" (hanged himself) (9-9/21/19)
7345. Rodgers, Ravaud K. (Rev.), s of Dr. John B. of NYC, m 10/10/21 Caroline W. Thomas, dau of John S. of Sandy Hill (Wash. Co.), in S. H.; Rev. Dr. Coe of Troy (9-10/23 and 7-11/5)
7346. Rodman, Daniel, student of law in Albany, m 12/13/03 Eliza Jenkins of Hudson in H (6-1/17/04)
7347. Rodman, Daniel, Esq., 32, d 1/26/16 in Albany (9-2/13)
7348. Roe, Hiram, oldest s of Elihu, d 1/31/24 in Ballston (2-2/3)
7349. Roe, Joseph m Ann Lawrence, both of Fishkill; Rev. Barret (8-4/16)
7350. Roe, William, merchant, of Fishkill m 10/28/12 Abey Bradley of Gayhead; Rev. D. Crane (8-11/11)
7351. Roff, Elizabeth (Mrs.), 66, d 11/12/30 in Watervliet (1-11/27)
7352. Rogers, _____, about 4, drowned 8/13/01 near Catskill when struck by the boom and thrown overboard from the small sail boat of his father, William Rogers, Jr., who had attempted unsuccessfully to save his son (6-8/20)
7353. Rogers, _____ (Dr.), "Mrs. Bregan", and Philip Vanderbilt d "lately of the prevailing epidemic" in Fishkill (8-3/30/14)
7354. Rogers, Aaron, Esq. of New Orleans, LA m 1/19/10 Mrs. Susan McNew of Poughkeepsie, NY in Rhinebeck Flats; Rev. Jeremiah Romayn (8-2/7)
7355. Rogers, Armenia, 20, wf of Capt. Augustus, d 12/14/17 in Cooperstown (3-12/18)
7356. Rogers, Augustus (Capt.) of Cooperstown m 7/4/16 Armenia Mudge of Hartwick in H; Elder Bostwick (3-7/11)
7357. Rogers, Augustus (Lt. Col.) m 12/24/21 Eliza Boden in Cooperstown (3-12/31)
7358. Rogers, Bartlet (Mr.), 56, d 7/26/26 in Cooperstown ("cancerous tumor") (3-7/31)
7359. Rogers, Daniel, 39, d 10/16/04 in Hudson (6-10/23)
7360. Rogers, David m Emma Ann Allen, dau of Squire Allen, in Hudson (6-12/29/07)
7361. Rogers, David (Dr.), 87, (a surgeon in the Rev. War), formerly of Greenfield, CT, d 6/21/29 in Norwich, CT (1-6/29)
7362. Rogers, Elizabeth (Mrs.) of NYC, sister of Richard Davis of Poughkeepsie, d 10/17/03 in the home of Richard (8-10/25)
7363. Rogers, Elizabeth (Mrs.), 86, d 7/3/32 at her home near Poughkeepsie (8-7/18)
7364. Rogers, George W. of Vergennes, VT m Jane C. Emons, oldest dau of Adonijah, Esq. of Sandy Hill (Wash. Co.), NY, at S. H.; Rev. Seney (or Sevey) (1-8/8/31)
7365. Rogers, Harriot (Miss), 24, dau of Capt. Jeremiah, d "last week" in Clinton (Dut. Co.) (8-5/6/00)
7366. Rogers, Henry, Jr. m 8/27/34 Matilda Livingston, dau of John S., Esq., in Tivoli; Rev. Henry Anthon (8-9/7)
7367. Rogers, Hezekiah, Jr. m 12/13/95 Mary Cornwell in "Beekmantown" (probably intended for Beekman, Dut. Co.) (Beekmantown formed 1820)(8-12/16)
7368. Rogers, Hezekiah, Jr., 41, d 8/20/13 at his home in Beekman (8-8/25)
7369. Rogers, Ichabod of Hudson m 6/22/11 Eliza Cooper of Rhinebeck Flats in R. F.; Rev. Cuyler (6-7/5)
7370. Rogers, James of Poughkeepsie d 1/16/96 (buried in Reformed Dutch Church burial ground)
7371. Rogers, James of Clinton (Dut. Co.) m 6/16/14 Elizabeth Phoenix Platt of NYC in NYC; Rev. Milldoller (8-6/22)
7372. Rogers, Jeremiah, Esq. d 8/11/10 at his home in Clinton (Dut. Co.) ("an old inhabitant of this town") (8-8/15)
7373. Rogers, John, 39, d 9/16/05 in Hudson (consumption) (6-9/24)

7374. Rogers, John, merchant, d 1/17/16 at his home in Kinderhook (6-2/6)
7375. Rogers, John, Jr. of Pleasant Valley m 3/30/23 Harriet Ward of Poughkeepsie; Moses Armstrong, Esq. (8-4/2)
7376. Rogers, Jones, Lt. Commander of a Co. of Rangers (lately commanded by
James I. Stoutenburgh of Clinton) died (date and place lacking
in this newspaper account) (8-11/1/03)
7377. Rogers, Richard m 1/16/13 Sally Barton in Fishkill ("after a long and
tedious courtship of three days and three nights") (8-1/27)
7378. Rogers, Rufus m 11/16/25 Fanny Lock, both of Litchfield, in L; Rev. Giles
(3-11/28)
7379. Rogers, Theron m 2/14/22 Maria Preston in Westford; Rev. Benjamin Sawin
(3-2/18)
7380. Rogers, Thomas C., about 28, d 1/20/14 in Athens (6-1/25)
7381. Rogers, William (Rev.), D.D., 72, d in Philadelphia, PA (3-4/19/24)
7382. Rogers, William E. of Philadelphia, PA m 11/9/30 Harriet F. Ruggles,
dau of Oliver of NYC; Rev. Dr. Broadhead (1-11/13)
7383. Roggen, Edward of the firm of Roggen and Wood m 7/22/30 Elizabeth Van
Kleeck, dau of Richard, in Rochester; Rev. James. All of R. (1-7/28)
7384. Romain, Francis, 88, formerly of Pittstown, d 9/14/27 in Troy (9-9/25)
7385. Roman, Peter, 60, d in Maryland, NY (3-4/21/23)
7386. Romayne, James T. (Maj.), 28, of the U.S. Artillery, d 9/18/18 in NYC
(7-10/3)
7387. Rome, Henry 32, of NYC d 3/9/29 in Albany (1-3/11)
7388. Romer, Jacob M. m 10/31/21 Olive Gregory in Saratoga; Rev. R. Smith
(2-11/7)
7389. Romeyn, Eliza Rebecca, 7, oldest dau of Herman M., Esq. of Ulster Co.,
d 5/12/30 (1-5/14)
7390. Romeyn, Isaac F. m 2/24/12 Diantha Wilson; Rev. Cuyler (8-2/26)
7391. Romeyn, Jeremiah (Rev.), 49, one of the ministers and honorary professor
of Hebrew in the Reformed Dutch Church, d 7/17/18 in Woodstock (Ulster
Co.), NY (8-7/22 and 6-7/28)
7392. Romeyn, John B. (Rev.), D.D., 46, pastor of the Presbyterian Church,
d 2/22/25 in NYC (2-3/22)
7393. Romeyn, Rebecca, 11, youngest dau of Rev. Jeremiah, d 9/24/17 in Roxbury
(8-10/1)
7394. Romeyn, Susannah, wf of Rev. J. V. C. Romeyn and mother of Mrs. J. V. B.
Varrick of Poughkeepsie, d 4/22/26 in Hackensack, NJ (8-5/3)
7395. Romine, Benjamin m 12/15/99 Sally Frear, dau of Jacobus, all of Poughkeepsie; Rev. Brown (8-12/17)
7396. Roos?(surname blurred), Philip, druggist, of Canajoharie m 12/12/30
Elizabeth Loucks, oldest dau of Henry, Esq. of Palatine, NY, formerly
of Albany; Rev. Wells (1-12/29)
7397. Roosevelt, Edward, 34, d 6/9/32 in Poughkeepsie (8-6/13)
7398. Roosevelt, Jacobus, 52, merchant, lately of NYC, d 3/12/77 at the home of
Peter Heermans in Red Hook (5-5/15)
7399. Roosevelt, James I., Jr., Esq. of NYC m 5/30/31 Cornelia Van Ness (dau of
Hon. P. Van Ness, "Minister of the U.S. to the court of Madrid") at the
hotel of the American Minister in Paris, France (1-8/5)
7400. Roosevelt, Richard Varick of NYC m 4/22/23 Anna Maria Lyle, dau of Henry,
Esq. of Red Hook, in R. H.; Rev. A. N. Kittle (8-4/30 and 9-5/6)
7401. Roosevelt, Thomas, late of Baltimore, m 9/9/26 Maria Z. Flagler of
Pleasant Valley, NY; Rev. C. C. Cuyler (Baltimore, Maryland probably
intended above) (8-9/27)
7402. Root, Amos of Hartford, CT m 6/9/29 Orpha Stanton, dau of David, Esq. of
Westerlo, NY, in W; Rev. Woodbridge (1-6/17)
7403. Root, Charles (Midshipman), 19, oldest s of Hon. Erastus of Delhi, NY,
d 12/8/28 on board the U.S. frigate "Hudson" at Rio De Janeiro (died
of typhus less than 3 months after leaving his home) (1-2/11/29)
7404. Root, Elias of Cooperstown m 4/19/14 Nancy Sabin of Colchester, CT in
Cooperstown (3-4/23)
7405. Root, Erastus (Col.) of Delhi, NY m 10/4/06 Eliza Stockton, dau of C. W.
of Walton (Dela. Co.), in W (3-10/23)
7406. Root, Erastus (Dr.), 43, d 2/24/29 in Harpersfield (was a member of "the
local Lodge") (was born in Vermont; shortly after his arrival in NY
state his wife and 2 of his children died) (1-4/1)

7407. Root, James (Dr.), 41, s of Hon. Jesse, late Chief Justice of Connecticut, d 2/28/13 in Athens, NY (6-3/9)
7408. Root, James m 1/9/16 Philena Yeomans in Middlefield (3-1/18)
7409. Root, James of Northeast m 1/18/31 Phebe Brower of Poughkeepsie; Rev. Perkins (8-1/19)
7410. Root, Lyman of Albany m 9/19/07 Elizabeth Harwell of Watervliet; Rev. Coe (9-9/22)
7411. Root, Maria L., 29 (wf of Dr. Oliver S. and dau of Hon. Phineas Allen of Pittsfield, MA) d 10/20/31 at Rice Creek Springs, So. Carolina (1-11/17)
7412. Root, Mary, 19, d 12/1/13 in Cooperstown (3-12/4)
7413. Root, Reuben (Col.), 45, d 11/1/15 in Hartwick (3-11/2)
7414. Root, Silas m 2/24/03 Sally Wattles, both of Cooperstown (3-3/31)
7415. Root, William, Esq. of Albany m 8/24/06 Lucretia Star of Goshen, CT (9-9/16)
7416. Root, William H., Esq. of Ogdensburgh m Jane M. Haswell of Burlington, VT in B; Rev. G. G. Ingersoll (1-10/27/31)
7417. Roraback, Isaac, 47, d 5/15/12 in Red Hook (6-5/25)
7418. Roraback, Uriah m 10/19/08 Fanny Gridley in Hudson; Rev. Wigton (6-10/25)
7419. Rosa(?), V. V., merchant of Adams (Jeff. Co.) m 12/8/30 Caroline McKinstry of Rodman; Rev. Munro (1-12/13)
7420. Rose, Donald, 66, d 12/26/30 in Albany (cancer) (funeral from his late home, 73 Hudson St.) (1-12/28)
7421. Rose, John of Otsego m 2/15/24 Diana Robinsonof Exeter in E; Rev. Nash (3-3/1)
7422. Rose, John N. of Geneva m 5/26/29 Eliza Macomb, youngest dau of late John N. of NYC, in NYC; Rev. John A. Clark (1-5/27)
7423. Rose, Mary, wf of Gen. Rose and sister of Mr. Horace Allen of Albany, d 9/3/30 in Bridgehampton, L. I., NY (1-9/10)
7424. Roseboom, Henry M., Esq., 24, d 6/30/24 in Cherry Valley (3-7/5)
7425. Roseboom, John J., 54, d 3/15/29 in Cherry Valley (1-3/19)
7426. Roseboom, Robert (Hon.), 60, d 2/7/16 in Westford (3-2/15)
7427. Rosekrans, Benjamin of Lansingburgh m Esther Huntington, dau of Rev. Enoch of Middletown, CT, in M (6-11/5/05)
7428. Rosekrans, Depue, merchant, of Lansingburgh, NY m "a short time since" Sally Hubbard, dau of Nehemiah of Middletown, CT, in M (9-12/4/98)
7429. Rosekrans, Jonache, 85, widow of Capt. Henry late of Fishkill, d 2/10/03 in Beekman (Dut. Co.) (8-3/1)
7430. Rosevelt, Elizabeth, 39, wf of Solomon, Esq., d 2/27/20 in Chazy (survived by husband and 8 children) (7-3/11)
7431. Rosevelt, John I., Esq., 67, formerly a merchant in NYC, d 8/18/20 in Troy (9-8/22)
7432. Rosman, Edward W., 17, d 8/11/25 "at Lawrenceville (Chazy)" (hydrophobia) (bitten by a dog 5/26) ("Doctors Stephenson and Beckwith were called. Copious bleeding and the scull cap were administered thoroughly but in vain") (7-8/20)
7433. Rosman, George m 3/20/31 Samantha Hilliard in Plattsburgh; Tomas D. Gilson, Esq. All of Plattsburgh (7-3/29)
7434. Ross, Cynthia, 51, wf of Nathan, d 9/26/28 in Petersburgh (9-9/30)
7435. Ross, Daniel, Esq., 67, d 3/10/31 at the home of Gen. Henry H. Ross of Essex (one of the earliest settlers in Essex Co. having arrived there in 1783. Formerly sheriff of clinton Co. prior ot its division; first judge of Essex Co. immediately after its formation)(1-3/18)
7436. Ross, Duncan m 1/16/27 Sarah Cisco, both of Troy; J. Martindale, Esq. (9-1/19)
7437. Ross, Edward C. (Lt.), assistant professor of Mathamatics at the U.S. Military Academy,m 11/8/30 Anna De Witt Clinton, youngest dau of late Gen. James, in Newburgh; Rev. John Johnston (1-11/13 and 8-11/17)
7438. Ross, Elizabeth, 56 or 66?, wf of William, d 10/19/30 in Watervliet (1-11/17)
7439. Ross, Elizabeth R., 46, wf of Col. Theodorus, d 9/7/30 in Elizabethtown (1-9/14)
7440. Ross, Henry H., Esq. of Essex m 9/23/22 Susannah Blanchard, dau of Hon. Anthony I. of Salem, in S; Rev. Tomb (7-10/5)
7441. Ross, Howard Stephen, 15, died (date and place not given) (9-12/8/12)
7442. Ross, William, Esq., formerly of Newburgh, d 8/18/30 in NYC (1-8/26)

7443. Ross, William, 55, attorney, d 9/3/30 in Albany (buried in Newburgh) (1-9/7)
7444. Ross, William D. m 3/10/25 Mary Ann Gould, both of Essex, in E; Rev. Messer (7-4/2)
7445. Rosseter, Lucy, 49, consort of Maj. Samuel of Great Barrington, MA, d 9/20/16 in G. B. (6-10/1)
7446. Rosseter, Samuel (Maj.) of Great Barrington, MA m 2/18/17 Mrs. Abby Riley of Albany in A; Rev. Clowes (6-2/25)
7447. Rossman, John B. (Dr.) m 4/28/30 Elizabeth Fairbank, oldest dau of Thomas, Esq. of Schoharie Co., at the Hermitage in Livingston (1-5/13)
7448. Roswell, Elijah m 12/25/21 Almira Grace; Rev. Griffin (9-1/1/22)
7449. Roswell, William of Washington (Dut. Co.) m 6/12/30 Sarah Burnet of Pleasant Valley; Rev. Wile (8-6/30)
7450. Rouse, ____ (Mr.) of Athens, NY m 9/7/25 Paulina Vail of Freedom (8-9/28)
7451. Rouse, Abraham of Cairo, NY m 4/6/25 Jane Adaline Reynolds of Freedom; Rev. Clark (8-4/13)
7452. Rouse, John, 48, d 5/4/23 in Laurens (3-5/12)
7453. Rouse, Peter P. of Florida, NY m Eliza Scott, dau of late Dr. Moses Scott, in New Brunswick, NJ; Rev. Howe (3-6/17/22)
7454. Rouse, William (Col.) (a Rev. officer) d 6/16/29 in Charleston (1-6/29)
7455. Rousseau, A. J., merchant, m 1/1/23 Esther H. Richards; Rev. David Butler (9-1/7)
7456. Rousseau, Abraham of Troy m 11/24/31 Jane Ann Snyder of Albany; Rev. Lochead (1-11/29)
7457. Rousseau, John m 1/2/24 Elizabeth Gogswell, dau of Smith; Rev. Beman. All of Troy (9-1/6)
7458. Row, Morgan m 12/14/26 Lurana Gremond, both of Stanford (Dut. Co.); Rev. Birch (8-1/10/27)
7459. Rowley, David, merchant, of Poughkeepsie m 6/16/18 Sally Stuart of Milton (Dut. Co.) in Poughkeepsie (6-6/30)
7460. Rowley, James m 12/3/14 Sarah New, both of Claverack, in C; Rev. Gephard (6-12/13)
7461. Rowley, John, Esq., attorney, m 12/13/34 Mary Jane Mooney in Upper Red Hook; Rev. F. B. Thomson. All of Upper Red Hook (8-12/17)
7462. Rowlison, Carlton, 38, d 4/27/26 in Cooperstown (3-5/26)
7463. Rowlson, Harvey d 1/1/18 in Plattsburgh (7-1/3)
7464. Rowlston, John m 5/31/32 Malissa Moore, both of Plattsburgh, in P; Rev. Chase (7-6/9)
7465. Royce, Nancy C. Barnard, relict of late Dr. Thomas Royce of Monticello, NY, d 12/7/34 in Montpelier, VT (7-12/20)
7466. Royston, Thomas of Pleasant Valley m 4/10/22 Mary Bayliss of Germantown, PA; Rev. Reed (8-4/17)
7467. Rudd, Charles of the firm of Griffen and Rudd, booksellers, of NYC m 6/1/13 Sally Irish, dau of Capt. Charles of Hudson; Rev. Prentice (6-6/15)
7468. Rudd, Hilen, Esq., 27, d 12/6/19 in Poughkeepsie (typhus) (8-12/8 and 6-12/14)
7469. Rudd, Reuben B. m 2/22/13 Eliza Smith, both of Poughkeepsie; Rev. Cuyler (8-2/24)
7470. Rudd, Ruth, 71, wf of Bezaliel, d 7/10/30 in Northeast (8-8/4)
7471. Ruger, Alfred m 1/16/34 Sarah Hoffman of La Grange; Rev. William I. McCord (8-1/22)
7472. Ruggles, Amasa m Mary Parker, dau of Joseph, Esq., in Loonenburgh (Athens, NY). All of Loonenburgh (6-5/1/04)
7473. Ruggles, Azor of Canfield, OH m 9/25/32 Catharine Mary Adaline Mitchell, dau of Stephen of Poughkeepsie; Rev. Dr. Reed (8-10/3)
7474. Ruggles, Gertrude, wf of Charles H., Esq. of Kingston, d 11/22/28 in K (8-11/26)
7475. Ruggles, Herman, Esq., attorney, of NY m 8/26/13 Ellen McCoy of Coldenham (Orange Co.) in C (8-9/1)
7476. Ruggles, John m 10/10/27 Emily(?) Nichols, both of Essex, in Plattsburgh; Rev. Halsey (7-10/20)
7477. Ruggles, Joseph, 77, d 3/9/34 in Poughkeepsie (funeral from the home of Mrs. Noxon on Market St.) (8-3/12)

217

7478. Ruggles, Philo, Esq., attorney, 64, d 12/15/29 in NYC where he had
lived "in recent years" (born in Connecticut; moved to Poughkeepsie,
NY in 1814) (buried in Poughkeepsie) (8-12/23)
7479. Ruggles, Samuel R., attorney, late of Poughkeepsie, m 5/15/22 Mary Rosalie
Rathbone, dau of John, Esq. of NYC, in NYC; Right Rev. Bishop Hobart
(8-5/22 and 3-5/27)
7480. Rumsey, Delia Frances, 8, only dau of Levi, d 2/15/20 (in Troy?) (9-2/22)
7481. Rumsey, William (Col.), 46, d 7/3/20 at his home 4 mi east of Batavia
(formerly a state assemblyman) (buried with Masonic honors) (9-7/18)
7482. Rundal, Sally, 24, consort of Jacob and dau of George Ingraham, d 11/8/23
in Amenia (surv by husband and 5 small children) (8-11/12)
7483. Rundel, Hannah, 105, d 9/17/08 in Washington (Dut. Co.) (8-9/21)
7484. Rundle, Gerard m 11/16/09 Patty Palmer, both of Stanford (Dut. Co.);
John Thompson, Esq. (8-11/22)
7485. Rundle, Reuben, Jr. m 9/12/30 Charlotte King, both of Greenville (Greene
Co.), at Christ's Church in Greenville; Rev. Fuller
7486. Runkle, Christopher m 3/9/22 Ann Vandenburgh, both of Watervliet; Rev. Dr.
Coe (9-3/12/22)
7487. Runyan, Henry m 2/25/21 Polly, Reynolds in Richfield; Rev. Fairbanks
(3-3/19)
7488. Rush, Benjamin (Dr.) (a Rev. patriot) d 4/20/13 (in Philadelphia, PA?)
(7-4/30)
7489. Rush, Catharine, 110, d in Philadelphia (state not given) (7-5/31/17)
7490. Russel, Barnabas, 64, d 5/16/12 at his home in Easton (Wash. Co.) (member
of the Society of Friends) (8-5/20)
7491. Russel, Benjamin m 5/20/07 Martha Dayton in New Paltz; Rev. Porter (8-5/27)
7492. Russel, Gideon m 1/1/12 Mahetable St. John; Rev. Smith. All of Cooperstown
(3-1/4)
7493. Russel, Martin of Troy m 2/26/21 Eliza Choate of Lansingburgh; Rev. Sommers
(9-3/6)
7494. Russel, Avis (Miss), 24, dau of Capt. Benjamin, d 9/18/08 in Hudson
(6-9/27)
7495. Russell, Benjamin F., 22, d 2/28/31 in Albany (funeral from the home of
his father, Elihu, 49 Columbia St.) (1-3/2)
7496. Russell, Elihu, 8, s of Elihu, d 1/10/31 in Albany (funeral from
49 Columbia St.) (1-1/12)
7497. Russell, Isaac (Capt.) (a Rev. soldier) d 2/26/21 at his home in Staatsburgh (b in Sherburne, MA but had lived in Dutchess Co. for nearly
30 yrs) (8-2/28)
7498. Russell, Isaac F. of Staatsburgh m 6/28/21 Catherine Van Steenberg of
Rhinebeck; Rev. Dr. Quitman (8-7/4)
7499. Russell, Nathaniel m 4/29/20 Mary Young, both of Troy; Rev. Dr. Coe
(9-5/16)
7500. Russell, Rensselaer W., 22, only s of John, Esq., d 7/15/25 in Cooperstown
(3-7/25)
7501. Russell, Samuel (Lt.) of the U.S. Army m 3/10/22 Elizabeth Platt, dau of
late Maj. N.Z. of Plattsburgh, in P; Rev. Clapp (7-3/16)
7502. Rust, David m 6/2/24 Eliza Ann Gladd, dau of David, all of Poughkeepsie;
Rev. Babcock (8-6/9)
7503. Rust(?), James M., about 30, a native of Poughkeepsie, NY, d 11/23/30
in Macon, GA (1-12/15)
7504. Rust, Levi J. m 2/9/25 Almira Bates, youngest dau of Benjamin, in Amenia;
Rev. C. P. Willson (8-3/9)
7505. Rust, Nelson m 9/25/27 Eluthera Wetherbee, both of Troy; Rev. Tucker
(9-9/28)
7506. Rutenber, William m 4/17/25 Nancy Adams, both of Otsego; Rev. Smith
(3-4/25)
7507. Rutgers, Nicholas O. m 6/5/31 Eliza Hoffman, both of NYC, in Red Hook;
Rev. Sherwood (1-6/9?)
7508. Rutledge, Edward C. of the U.S. Navy m 6/16/29 Rebecca Motte Lowndes,
dau of late Hon. William, in Charleston (state not given but probably
S.C. since all three persons are defined as "of that city"); Rev. Dr.
Gadsden (1-7/1)
7509. Rutgers, James, 18, formerly of Poughkeepsie, d 6/27/24 in NYC (8-7/14)
7510. Rutzer, John, 44, formerly of Poughkeepsie, d 3/28/11 in NYC (8-4/3)

7511. Rutzer, Mary (Miss), 16, d 2/10/28 in Poughkeepsie (8-2/13)
7512. Ryan, John (Maj.) of Poughkeepsie d 3/8/12 (8-3/11)
7513. Ryan, Susan, 15, youngest dau of Maj. John, d 6/4/26 in Poughkeepsie (8-6/7)
7514. Ryer, Eliza, wf of Frederick and dau of William C. Smith formerly of Poughkeepsie, d 12/2/32 in NYC (8-12/12)
7515. Ryon, Cornelius m 2/5/34 Mary Dunn, both of Chesterfield, in Clintonville; Hon. E. Williams (4 [Keeseville Herald]-2/11)
7516. Sabin, Josiah of Niagara m Abigail Chapin of Otsego in O; Rev. Smith (3-4/25/25)
7517. Sabins, John S. m 12/2/26 Maria Overling, both of Freedom; Rev. Cuyler (8-12/13)
7518. Sacia(?), David F., Esq. of Canajoharie m 11/8/30 Angelica Matilda Marselis of Schenectady; Rev. Dr. Nott (1-11/12)
7519. Sacket, _____ (Judge) of Newburgh d 4/22/27 in Albany ("he died there on his way to Sacket's Harbor with the intention of becoming a resident of that place.") (9-4/27)
7520. Sacket, Samuel J. m Rosanna Case in Stanford (Dut. Co.); Rev. Wilson (8-2/7)
7521. Sackett, Daniel, merchant, of Troy m Sarah H. Pardee of Stephentown in S; Rev. Younglove (9-9/14/19)
7522. Sackett, James H. m 7/15/30 Jerusha Post, dau of William, Esq., at St. George's Chapel in NYC; Rev. Henderson (1-7/19)
7523. Sackett, Leonard of Stanford m 1/4/27 Ruth Gildersleeve, dau of Henry of Clinton (Dut. Co.); Isaac Sutherland, Esq. (8-1/10)
7524. Sackett, Rosanna, wf of Samuel, d 2/22/34 in Stanford (Dut. Co.) (8-3/12)
7525. Sackett, Theron of Stanford (Dut. Co.) m 12/17/25 Jerusha Smith of Clinton; Rev. Birch (8-12/28)
7526. Sackrider, Robert (Maj.) m 10/8/19 Permella White in Granville (7-10/9)
7527. Saffen, Thomas (Dr.), 43, d 7/14/10 in Beekman (8-7/25)
7528. Saffen, Thomas B. d 5/25/22 in Greenfield, NY (2-5/29)
7529. Safford, _____, inf child of Hiram, d 10/14/17 in Plattsburgh (7-10/18)
7530. Safford, Electa (Miss), about 29, dau of Capt. John of Cambridge, VT, d 2/2/21 in Plattsburgh (epilepsy) (at time of her death Electa was visiting her sister, "Mrs. Waterhouse", in Plattsburgh) (7-2/3)
7531. Safford, Hiram, 5, s of widow Anna, d 7/3/27 in Fairfax, VT (7-7/14)
7532. Safford, Lucy Marilla, about 18, dau of late Ozias of Plattsburg, d 4/10/27 in P (consumption) (7-4/14)
7533. Safford, Ozias d 2/22/27 in Plattsburgh (7-2/24)
7534. Sage, Norton m 12/27/27 Polly Chambers, both of Troy; Rev. Howard (9-1/1/28)
7535. Sagendorph, John H. m 12/20/12 Sally Gisselbergh, both of Claverack; Rev. Gebhard (6-12/22)
7536. Sailly, Amelia Louisa, 14, (dau "of the present Mrs. Bosworth and gr-dau of Peter Sailly, Esq. of Poughkeepsie", d 3/1/17 in Champlain ("of an enteritis") (7-3/8)
7537. Sailly, Peter, Esq., 71, d 3/16/26 in Plattsburgh (born in the Province of Loraine, France; migrated to this country in 1784 and settled on the shore of Lake Champlain where he remained until death) (Represented the northern district of NY in both the state and the federal legislatures; for past 18 yrs Collector of Customs, Champlain Dist.) (7-3/18)
7538. St. John, Harvey, merchant, of Canajoharie m 12/8/30 Ann Van Alstine, youngest dau of Nicholas of Canajoharie; Rev. D. Van Olinda (1-12/16)
7539. St. John, Horace, 27, d 3/27/25 in Ballston Spa (2-3/29)
7540. St. John, Noah, Jr. m 8/21/31 Eliza Lohnes(?), both of Bern; Judge Moore of Rensselaerville (1-8/24)
7541. Salisbury, Barnard m 8/22/24 Eliza Richmond in Westford; Rev. Pomeroy (3-8/30)
7542. Salisbury, Betsey, 16, d 10/31/09 in Hudson (6-11/7)
7543. Salisbury, H. A., Esq., proprietor of the Buffalo Patriot, m 9/6/29 Phoebe Osborne, dau of Elias, Esq., in Clarence, Erie Co.; Rev. Safford (1-9/19)
7544. Salisbury, Nancy, 42, wf of Smith H. Salisbury, editor of the Buffalo Republican, d 2/12/30 in Buffalo "in 46 hours after giving birth to a daughter and a son" (1-2/24)

7545. Salisbury, Smith H., editor of the Buffalo Republican, m 4/19/30 Flora
Case, oldest dau of Deacon Theophilus Humphrey of Sheldon, in S; Rev.
H. Wallace (1-4/27)
7546. Salmon, Eliphalet m 1/10/03 Tamer Lyon, both of Yorktown, in Westchester
(8-3/1)
7547. Salter, James D. H. of New Haven, CT m 9/25/34 Jane Van Vechten,
formerly of Fishkill, in NYC; Rev. Dr. Cox (8-10/1)
7548. Sammis, Henry of huntington, L. I. m 5/8/30 Hannah Philips of Albany in
NYC; Rev. McMurray (1-5/13)
7549. Sammons, Frederick m 12/23/30 Lorain H. Yost, dau of William, Esq., in
Johnstown; Rev. A. C. Treadway. All of Johnstown (1-12/31)
7550. Sampson, Charles, Esq., 27, late of Hudson, NY, d 1/5/16 at Port Oratava,
Island of Teneriffe "whither he went for...his health" (pulmonary
disease) (6-4/9)
7551. Sampson, Erra (Rev.), 76, d 12/13/23 in NYC (3-12/22 and 8-12/24)
7552. Sampson, Joseph, Esq. of NYC m 6/25/31 Adele Caroline Livingston, dau of
Col/ John W., at Lake Skaneateles; Rev. Brace (1-7/2)
7553. Sampson, Mary, 57, consort of Rev. Ezra of Hudson, d 6/1/12 (6-6/8)
7554. Sampson, Nancy, 57, wf of George, d 12/18/14 in Troy (consumption)
(9-12/20)
7555. Sanborn, Benjamin (Capt.) m 1/1/17 Sally P. Skinner, dau of Maj. Joseph,
at French Mills. All of F. M. (7-1/18)
7556. Sandford, John W., Esq., cashier of the Branch of the U.S. Bank at
Fayetteville, NC, m 6/30/30 Margaret Halliday, oldest dau of late Robert,
in Fayetteville, NC; Rev. W. G. H. Jones (1-7/10)
7557. Sandford, Lewis H., Esq. of Skaneateles m 6/4/29 Laura Porter, dau of late
Dr. Alanson Porter of Williamstown, MA, in Albany; Rev. Williams, pastor
of the 3rd Presbyterian Ch. (1-6/5)
7558. Sands, Eliza, 15, 2nd dau of Robert, d 7/29/02 in Rhinebeck (6-8/3 and
8-8/3)
7559. Sands, Griffen, 58, d 10/13/31 at his home near Sands Point, Long Island
(1-10/17)
7560. Sanford, Audustus (sic), merchant, m 11/20/28 Harriet Perlee, dau of Walter,
Esq., all of Amenia; Rev. C. P. Wilson (8-12/3)
7561. Sanford, Elisha of Northeast d 10/30/99 in Rome, NY (8-11/5)
7562. Sanford, Joseph (Rev.), 33, pastor of the 2nd Presbyterian Church in
Philadelphia, PA and formerly of Brooklyn, NY, d 12/25/31 in Philadelphia
(1-12/31)
7563. Sanford, William, proprietor of the Broad Street House, m Elizabeth Ann
Stammers, dau of Joseph from England, in Trinity Church, Utica; Rev.
Dorr (1-1/8/30)
7564. Sanger, Jedediah, 78, (a Lt. in the Rev. War) d 6/6/29 at his home in
New Hartford, NY (was one of the earliest settlers in Oneida Co.; in 1789
left New Hampshire in poverty; was first judge in Oneida Co, NY until
1810; for many years was an assemblyman and, later, a senator in NY)
(1-6/12)
7565. Sargeant, Ezra, 37, bookseller, of NYC d 6/27/12 in Hudson (consumption)
(surv by wf and 3 ch) (at time of death was en route "to visit some
friends in the mountains of Massachusetts...(to alleviate his disease")
(6-6/29)
7566. Sarles, Jesse m 8/27/29 Eliza Lang; Peter A. Scryver, Esq. All of Hyde
Park (8-9/2)
7567. Satterlee, Marcia Ann, about 17, d 7/1/22 in Middlebury, VT (7-7/6)
7568. Satterlee, Samuel, Jr., merchant, m 8/11/12 Joan Ketchum of Waterford
in W; Rev. D. Butler (9-8/18)
7569. Satterlee, V. W. R., cashier of the Bank of Plattsburgh, m 8/25/21
Cornelia Green (dau of Joseph I.), both of Plattsburgh, in P; Rev.
Frederick Halsey (7-9/1)
7570. Saunders, Theodore W. of Schenectady m 1/20/29 Margaret N. Sill, dau of
William N., Esq., in Bethlehem; Rev. Kissam (1-1/22)
7571. Savage, _____, 71, wf of James, Esq. of Plattsburgh, d 8/23/13 (7-9/4)
7572. Savage, Ezra d 11/4/22 in Milton (2-11/12)
7573. Savage, James, 86, d 6/3/24 in Plattsburgh (7-6/5)
7574. Savage, Joseph of Mnotreal, Canada m 5/18/29 Abby J. Lyman, dau of
Theodore of Amherst, MA, in A (1-5/25)
7575. Savage, Lewis m 12/31/20 Margaret Gocha in Plattsburgh (7-1/6/21)

7576. Savage, Thomas d 12/30/17 in Plattsburgh ("has left a family of 10 children") (7-1/3/18)
7577. Sawin, George, 98, d 4/7/26 at his home in Danube (Herk. Co.) (married at age 49; had 2 sons and 4 daus all of whom lived to become heads of families;"three of the sons are pastors of Baptist churches") (3-4/10)
7578. Sawyer, Christopher, 50, m 7/3/05 Eliza Weatherwax, 28, both of Schaghticoke, in S; Rev. Ketchum (9-7/16)
7579. Sawyer, George m 9/19?/33 Maria Howard in Peru; Rev. Lyman (7-9/21)
7580. Sawyer, Horace B. (Lt.) of the U.S. Navy m 10/30/33 Roxaiana Wardsworth of Burlington (state not given, perhaps VT) at St. Paul's Church in Burlington; Right Rev. J. H. Hopkins (7-11/2)
7581. Sawyer, James W. of NYC m 7/15/30 Margaret Caldwell, dau of John C., Esq. of Rochester, in R; Rev. James (1-7/20)
7582. Sax, Matthew, Esq. m 2/24/13 Polly Maria Lockwood in Champlain (7-3/5)
7583. Sax, Matthew, Esq. m 9/8/16 Betsey Graves, dau of Benjamin, Esq. of Champlain, in Chazy (7-9/14)
7584. Saxton, Thomas m 10/18/34 Agnes Horson(?); Rev. Dr. Reed. All of Poughkeepsie (8-10/22)
7585. Sayre, John m Helena Emott, dau of W., Esq., all of Poughkeepsie; Rev. Sayre (8-3/8/97)
7586. Sayre, Sarah, 42, consort of Nathan, formerly of Elizabethtown, NJ, d 8/16/08 in Hartwick, NY (3-8/20)
7587. Sayres, James E., 21, of Washington (Dut. Co.) d 4/24/22 (8-5/1)
7588. Savres, Josiah m 9/9/06 Sally Van Kleeck, dau of Peter B., all of Poughkeepsie; Rev. Buckley (8-11/11)
7589. Sayrs, John, 37 or 57, d 11/28/11 in Poughkeepsie (8-12/4)
7590. Schaeffer, Frederick G. (Rev. Dr.), 38, d 3/26/31 in NYC (late pastor of the Evangelical Lutheran Church of St. James, president of the synod in the NYC area and professor of German language and literature in Columbia College) (1-3/30)
7591. Schell, Christian, merchant, of Rhinebeck Flats d 3/19/25 in R. F. (8-3/23)
7592. Schell, Margaret (Mrs.), 80, mother of Christian, d 11/10/25 "at the home of her son, Peter Brown"(Peter perhaps son-in-law?), in Staatsburgh (8-11/23)
7593. Schenandoah, the Indian Chief, age 113, d at Oneida Castle (buried beside Rev. Kirkland) (3-3/28/16)
7594. Schenck, Abraham H., Esq., 56, 6/1/31 at his home in Matteawan (1-6/4 and 8-6/8)
7595. Schenck, Henry Livingston, 21, s of Paul, merchant, of Poughkeepsie d 9/3/07 (8-9/9)
7596. Schenck, John (Capt.), 31, s of Paul of Poughkeepsie, d 7/2/13 in Plattsburgh (7-7/9 and 8-7/28)
7597. Schenck, John m 5/21/16 Clarissa Kipp, dau of Maj. Andrew in Rhinebeck Flatts; Rev. William McMurray (8-5/22)
7598. Schenck, John (Hon.), 92, d 8/22/31 at his home in North Hempstead (1-9/9)
7599. Schenck, Paul, 77, d 11/14/17 in Poughkeepsie (8-11/19)
7600. Schenk, Abraham, Esq., late a senator from New York's middle district, d 11/11/00 at his farm in Fishkill (8-11/18)
7601. Schenk, Joanna, wf of Paul (he a merchant of Poughkeepsie), d 1/16/95 (surv by husband and 10 children) (8-1/21)
7602. Schermerhorn, Abraham V., Esq. of Schodack m 10/24/31 Sarah C. Doll of Kinderhook in Colchester (Dela. Co.); Rev. H. Jones (1-11/5)
7603. Schermerhorn, Bartholomew, Jr. of Rotterdam m 3/25/30 Margaret Swifts, dau of Gen. Jacob of Schenectady; Rev. Van Vechten (1-3/30)
7604. Schermerhorn, Catharine, wf of Maus, Esq., d 8/20/29 in Schenectady (1-8/31)
7605. Schermerhorn, Edward m 8/5/21 Phebe Wainwright, both of Dover; Seneca Soule, Esq. (8-8/8)
7606. Schermerhorn, Gertrude, 42, wf of Ryer, d 4/10/30 in Albany (funeral from her husband's home, 10 Orange St.) (1-4/12)
7607. Schermerhorn, Hendrick, 2nd, m Polly Hardick in Claverack (6-11/5/01)
7608. Schermerhorn, Jacob M., Esq. of Rochester m 10/26/31 Louisa A. Barbour in Homer; Rev. J. Keep (1-11/7)

7609. Schermerhorn, Peter V. D. V., Esq. m 3/21/30 Eliza Dockstader in Johnstown (Mont. Co.); Rev. Van Horne. All of Johnstown (1-4/10)
7610. Schermerhorn, Simon I. (Dr.), about 30, oldest s of John S., d 2/6/30 in Schenectady ("pleurisy") (1-2/12)
7611. Schmidt, Peter, 51, formerly a merchant in NYC, of the firm of Muhlenburgh and Schmidt, d 7/18/31 in Philadelphia (PA?) (1-7/22)
7612. Schoonmaker(?), Essex(?) (Maj.) [name blurred], 68, d 6/18/26 (a Rev. soldier who was taken prisoner at Fort Montgomery) (8-6/21)
7613. Schoonmaker, David (Capt.), 61, d 2/15/13 in Red Hook(surv by wf and children) (8-2/24)
7614. Schoonmaker, Jane, 16, youngest dau of Maj. Henry, d 10/7/12 in Poughkeepsie (8-10/14)
7615. Schoonmaker, Margaret, 25, dau of Egbert, d 6/10/19 in Catskill (6-6/15)
7616. Schouten, Jeremiah m 9/26/18 Elizabeth Henderson, dau of Samuel; Rev. De Witt. All of Fishkill (8-9/30)
7617. Schram, Delia Adaline, nearly 2, only child of William and Sarah, d 10/23/34 in Poughkeepsie (8-10/29)
7618. Schriver, _____, inf s of Abraham, d 8/6/11 in Hudson (6-8/16)
7619. Schriver, _____, 3, s of Abraham, d in Hudson (6-8/23/11)
7620. Schriver, Sally (Mrs.), about 20, d 4/22/19 in Manchesterville (8-4/28)
7621. Schryver, Albert of Hyde Park m 2/24/30 Eleanor Fitch ? of Poughkeepsie; Rev. Dr. Cuyler (8-3/3)
7622. Schryver, Gilbert m 12/30/15 Sally Cornwell; Rev. Cuyler. All of Poughkeepsie (8-1/3/16)
7623. Schryver, Gilbert L. m 9/5/22 Mrs. Sarah Mastin; Rev. Clark (8-9/11)
7624. Schryver, Jacob, Esq. m 2/5/95 Mrs. Stoutenburgh, both of Clinton (Dut. Co.); Rev. Marsh (8-2/11)
7625. Schryver, Jacob of Clinton d 1/28/14 (8-2/2)
7626. Schultz, John F. m 11/15/13 Elizabeth Ackert in Rhinebeck; Rev. McMurray (8-12/8)
7627. Schultzs, Benjamin m 1/16/13 Catherine Ackert in Rhinebeck; Rev. Quitman (8-2/3)
7628. Schureman, John (Rev. Dr.), 39, (professor of ecclesiastical history in the Theological College in New Brunswick, NJ and formerly one of the ministers of the Reformed Church in NYC) d 5/15/18 (8-5/27)
7629. Schuyler, Catharine, consort of Hon. Philip, Esq. of Albany, d 3/7/03 in Easton (3-3/24)
7630. Schuyler, Christiana (Miss), 20, d 9/13/23 in Poughkeepsie (pulmonary complaint) (8-9/17)
7631. Schuyler, Henry, 41, d 9/26/12 in Troy (9-9/29)
7632. Schuyler, John, Esq. of Watervliet m 10/23/19 Maria McCoun of Troy; Rev. Dr. Coe (9-10/26)
7633. Schuyler, John A., Esq. of New Barbadoes Neck, NJ m 8/10/06 Catharine Van Rensselaer of Claverack, dau of late Gen. Robert, deceased, at the home of Jeremiah Van Rensselaer, Esq. in Utica (6-8/26)
7634. Schuyler, Peter, Jr. m 2/8/31 Maria Weidman in Bern, NY; Rev. J. H. Van Wagenen (1-2/17)
7635. Schuyler, Philip (Maj. Gen.), 70, d 11/25/04 or, possibly, 11/18/04 (interred with military honors in the family vault of Abraham Ten Broeck)
7636. Schuyler, Philip I. of Troy m "Miss Carpenter" of Washington (Dut. Co.) in W. (2/10/01)
7637. Schuyler, Queden P. of Ithaca m Maria H. Ten Broeck, dau of Nicholas, in Hudson; Rev. William Chester (1-9/29/29)
7638. Scoatenburgh(?), John L. (Capt.) of Clinton (Dut. Co.) d 11/22/93 in NYC (interred in family burying ground in Clinton, Dutchess Co.) (8-12/4)
7639. Scoby, David d 7/26/27 in Chester, NJ (surv by wf and 2 ch) (8-8/8)
7640. Scofield, Isaac M., 24, d 1/29/23 at his father's home in Phillipstown (8-2/5)
7641. Scofield, Jane (Miss), 21, dau of Lebbeus of Fishkill, d 4/16/24 (8-4/21)
7642. Scofield, Miles, 63, a native of Stamford, CT but for many years a resident of Phillipstown, NY, d 12/9/24 (8-12/15)
7643. Scofield, Philander H., 26, formerly of Danbury, CT, d 12/26/34 at the home of his brother, S. Scofield (in Poughkeepsie?) (8-12/31)
7644. Scofield, Stephen of the firm of Coffin and Scofield m 3/29/28 Deborah Bailey; Rev. Richardson. All of Poughkeepsie (8-4/2)

7645. Scollard, James D., Esq. of Springfield (Ots. Co.) m 10/1/29 Eliza Lewis of Albany; Rev. Dr. Sprague (1-10/9)
7646. Scot, William, merchant, m 5/5/18 Sally Myers, formerly of Poughkeepsie, in York, Upper Canada (8-7/15)
7647. Scott, Alexander m 11/10/25 Eliza Stochan, both of Pleasant Valley; Rev. Clark (8-11/23)
7648. Scott, Charles M. m 12/18/33 Sabrina A. Fisk, dau of Solomon, Esq., in Chazy; Rev. S. D. Ferguson (7-12/28)
7649. Scott, Daniel L. of Clermont m 12/4/31 Mary Ann Jones of NYC in Upper Red Hook; J. Rowley, Esq. (8-12/14)
7650. Scott, Frederick m 8/27/28 Ruby Squires; Rev. Mervin. All of Troy (9-9/12)
7651. Scott, George m 8/12/29 Ann Pratt; Rev. Mathias. All of Albany (1-8/14)
7652. Scott, Orren (Col.) of NYC m 8/29/33 Sarah Minerva Beach of Hinesburgh, VT in H (7-9/14)
7653. Scott, Orrin (Col.) of NYC m 8/29/33 Else Minerva Beach of Hindsburgh in H.; John Wheelock, Esq. (4 [Keeseville Herald]-9/10)
7654. Scott, Simeon m 9/11/19 Elizabeth Cooper, both of Troy; Rev. Dr. Coe (9-9/14)
7655. Scott, William m 11/17/30 Louisa C. Hoyt, only dau of James J., Esq., in NYC; Rev. Dr. Milnor. All of NYC (1-11/20)
7656. Scovel, Jonah, 80, (a Rev. patriot) d 4/2/31 in Albany (funeral from his late home, 650 So. Market St.) (1-4/3)
7657. Scovel, Mary Loisa, 7, dau of Hezekiah, d 2/24/29 in Albany (funeral from the parents' home, 96 State St.) (1-2/26)
7658. Scovel, Nelson, merchant, m 9/30/29 Alice Rusk, both of Albany; Rev. Weed (1-10/2)
7659. Scovill, H. W. (Col.) of Augusta, GA m 9/26/31 Mrs. Maria Ann Richardson of Montreal, Canada, dau of Hon. Matthew Sax of Chazy, NY (1-10/6)
7660. Scoville, Enos d 8/10/32 in Poughkeepsie (cholera) (8-8/15)
7661. Scribner, Alfred m 10/2/21 Fanny Wright, both of Ballston, in B; Rev. Brackett (2-10/17)
7662. Scribner, Dennis m 10/5/11 Eliza Copman, both of Poughkeepsie; Rev. C. C. Cuyler (8-10/9)
7663. Scribner, Jeremiah m "a short time since" Eleanor Banker, dau of John, in Plattsburgh; Rev. Halsey (7-1/6/21)
7664. Scribner, Levi, 65, d 12/21/18 in Plattsburgh (7-12/26)
7665. Scribner, Sally (Miss), about 22, dau of Levi, d 11/1/18 in Plattsburgh (7-11/7)
7666. Scriver, John m 1/13/20 "Miss Bartlet"; Rev. P. S. Wynkoop. All of Clinton (Dut. Co.) (8-1/19)
7667. Scriver, John m 1/1/34 Melinda Hatch in Odletown, Lower Canada; Rev. Booth (7-1/4)
7668. Scriver, John P. m 1/24/07 Julianna Hoyt, both of Troy; Rev. Coe (9-2/3)
7669. Scriver, Robert m 10/27/31 Eunice Skinner in Hyde Park; Rev. William Cahoon. All of Hyde Park (8-11/2)
7670. Scrugham, William W., merchant, m 12/3/30 Mary Stone, both of NYC; Rev. Dr. Milner (1-12/13)
7671. Scudder, John, proprietor of the American Museum, d 8/7/21 in NYC (8-8/15)
7672. Seabury, Isaac m 8/11/16 Frances Fitchet, both of Poughkeepsie; Rev. Dr. Covel (8-8/14)
7673. Seabury, John m Jane Pells, both of Poughkeepsie; Rev. Reed (8-9/6/20)
7674. Seafford, Benoni, Esq., attorney, of Delaware Co. m 11/4/30 Sarah Jane Swart, dau of Peter, Jr., Esq., in Middleburgh; Rev. Garretson (1-11/16)
7675. Seaman, James m 9/22/07 Bernice Noyse, both of Schodack; Rev. Coe (9-9/29)
7676. Seaman, James (Dr.) m Amelia Ketcham, dau of Rev. Joel late of Troy, in NYC; Rev. Ross (9-7/9/22)
7677. Seaman, John Bond of NYC m 9/8/30 Catharine Amelia Lawson of Cedar Grove (Fishkill Landing) in C. G.; Rev. J. Brown (1-9/13)
7678. Seaman, Nathaniel N. m 12/10/25 Catharine Finen, both of Poughkeepsie; Rev. C. C. Cuyler (8-12/28)
7679. Seaman, Robert m 1/19/26 Eliza Van Wagner, dau of Jacob; Rev. Clark. All of Pleasant Valley (8-2/1)

7680. Seamans, Robert of Fishkill m 10/21/30 Malvina German of Union Vale; Rev.
       Nathaniel Robinson of Putnam Co. (8-10/27)
7681. Searl, Sarah, consort of Comfort, d 6/14/19 in Charlton (9-7/6)
7682. Searle, Jane, 68, relict of George of Cambridge, d 4/18/23 in Rochester
       (9-4/22)
7683. Sears, _____, 14, s of Christian, d in Hudson (6-3/12/05)
7684. Sears, Elizabeth, 7, oldest dau of William, d 8/3/22 in Ballston (2-8/6)
7685. Sears, Isaac (Dr.), 45, d 2/8/24 in Stillwater (surv by wf and several
       young children) (2-2/10)
7686. Sears, Judah (Mr.), 38, d 2/8/11 in Hudson (6-2/15)
7687. Sears, Levi of Groton (Tompkins Co.) m 1/15/22 Peninah Curtis of Ballston
       in B; Rev. Reuben Smith (double ceremony - see marr of Daniel Tippet)
       (2-1/16)
7688. Sears, Oliver L. of Albany m 11/1/21 Fanny Field of Troy; Rev. Sommers
       (9-11/13)
7689. Sears, Peninah, 33, consort of Levi,formerly of Ballston, d 10/30/22 in
       Locke (Tompkins Co.) (she is the second wf of Levi to die within
       three years) (2-11/22)
7690. Sears, Thomas (Capt.), 58, d 4/28/04 in Southeast (was a Masonic member
       27 yrs) (funeral sermon by Rev. John Minor) (8-5/8)
7691. Sebring, Isaac d 2/24/30 at his home in Fishkill (8-3/3)
7692. Secor, Elijah, merchant, of NYC m 12/8/10 Maria Heermance of Poughkeepsie;
       Rev. Reed (8-12/12)
7693. Sedam, Cornelius m 11/26/14 Deborah Marble, both of Troy; Rev. Coe
       (9-11/29)
7694. Sedgwick, Pamela, 54, consort of Hon. Theodore, Esq., d in Stockbridge,
       MA (9-10/13/07)
7695. Seelding, Rufus J., 23, (s of Thomas, merchant, of NYC) d 4/3/30 in
       Greenbush (1-4/5)
7696. Seeley, James, s of Sylvanus, d 10/7/08 in Hudson (6-10/11)
7697. Seely, Isaac, bridegroom. See marr record of James D. McDonald dated
       2/24/15
7698. Seely, Jehiel m 11/7/13 Betsey Williams in Athens, NY; Rev. Prentice
       (6-11/16)
7699. Seely, Nehemiah, 65, of Ballston d 6/12/22 in Ballston (2-6/18)
7700. Seely, Polly, 9, dau of Joseph, d 11/10/18 in Plattsburgh (The editor of
       the Republican Farmer of Bridgeport, Conn. is requested to publish this
       for the information of the connections in Norwalk.") (7-11/21)
7701. Seely, William, Esq., 45, m 2/1/27 Sarah Austin, 15, dau of Rufus, Esq.;
       Isaac Sutherland, Esq. All of Stanford (8-2/14)
7702. Seelye, Abigail, 30, wf of Seth of Lansingburgh, d 7/8/00 in Newfield, CT
       (surv by husband and 2 ch) (9-7/29)
7703. Seelye, Desire, 24, wf of Lewis, d 11/30/98 in Lansingburgh (9-12/4)
7704. Seelye, Seth of Lansingburgh m "a short time since" "Miss Hickock" of
       Danbury, CT in D (9-2/17/02)
7705. Seelve, William Henry, 14, only s of Isaac, Esq., d 3/24/22 in Cherry
       Valley (3-4/1)
7706. Seerritt(?), Peter, 31, d 8/19/31 in Albany (funeral from his late home,
       corner No. Pearl and Van Schaick Sts.) (1-8/20)
7707. Selden, Samuel Lee m 7/28/31 Susan M. Ward, dau of Levi, Jr., Esq., in
       Rochester; Rev. Penney. All of R (1-8/3)
7708. Seley, Henry K. of Sherman, CT m 12/4/27 Lyda (sic) Maria Lucas, 3rd dau
       of Joseph of White Creek, in W. C.; Rev. Prindle (9-12/14)
7709. Seley, John (Dr.), 47, d 5/24/29 in Canton (St. Law. Co.) (1-6/2)
7710. Selkerk, Alexander m 10/12/31 Lemira Wilber; Rev. Campbell. All of Albany
       (1-10/14)
7711. Selkrig, Loring, formerly of Poughkeepsie and a shoemaker, d 2/17/26 in
       Buffalo ("killed in a scuffle with one of his comrades") (8-2/22)
7712. Selkrigg, Loring m 9/15/10 Jemima Vassar, both of Poughkeepsie; Rev. Weylard
       (8-10/3)
7713. Sellars, Lewis T. (Capt.) of NYC m 7/14/29 Elizabeth B. Henry of Utica
       in U; Rev. Elon Galusha (1-7/25)
7714. Selleck, Columbus m 10/9/34 Eliza Brown; Rev. Thomas Winter. All of
       Northeast (8-10/22)
7715. Selleck, Frederick, 20, oldest s of Capt. Stephen, d 9/10/05 (9-9/17)

7716. Selleck, Henry m 8/9/01 Hannah Bogardus in Hudson (double ceremony - see Isaac Race) (6-8/13)
7717. Sellon, John (Rev.) d 3/2/30 in Albany ("pulmonary disease") (funeral from the home of L. Crottenden on Park Place) (1-3/4)
7718. Selvidge, Robert m 6/11/18 Eliza Frear, both of Poughkeepsie; Rev. L. Leonard (8-6/24)
7719. Seney, Robert (Rev.) of Poughkeepsie (formerly of NYC) m 5/18/24 Jane A. Ingraham, dau of George of Amenia; Rev. Silliman (8-5/26)
7720. Sentell, Edward W, m 2/11/30 Deborah Harvey, both of Geneva, at Trinity Church in Geneva; Rev. Mason (1-2/20)
7721. Server, Robert m 8/13/29 Mary Ann Buckbee, dau of John, all of Albany; Rev. Lacy (1-8/18)
7722. Seward, Isaac B., 16, d 10/4/32 in Fishkill (8-10/10)
7723. Seward, Philander (Capt.) of Fishkill m 1/18/26 Susan Monfort of Beekman; Rev. Dewitt (8-1/25)
7724. Seward, Porter m 12/25/22 Martha Barney in Worcester (3-1/6/23)
7725. Seward, Sarah, widow of Rev. William of Killingworth, CT, d 11/24/03 in Hudson (6-11/29)
7726. Seward, William, Esq., "an aged farmer", d 7/18/22 at his home in Hackensack (Prob. in NY - in Dut. Co.) (8-7/24)
7727. Sexton, Levi d "recently" in Albany (funeral from his late home, 9 Daniel St.) (1-1/23/3))
7728. Seymour, Charles, merchant, m Catharine Perkins, dau of Rev. Dr. Perkins of West Hartford (prob. in Conn.) (6-1/3/04)
7729. Seymour, Ebenezer (Rev.) of Milton m 8/9/31 Mary Hoe, dau of Robert, Esq. of NYC in NYC; Rev. Rowland (1-8/13)
7730. Seymour, Gurdon I., printer, of Savannah, GA m Catharine Costigen in NYC (6-1/3/04)
7731. Seymour, Hart of Hartwick m 9/14/26 Mercy North of Fly Creek in F. C.; Rev. Prentice (3-10/2)
7732. Seymour, Hiram of Plattsburgh, NY m 9/12/11 Tanzar Murray of Williston, VT in W. (7-9/13)
7733. Seymour, Hope, 45, widow of late Major Horace, formerly of Lansingburgh, d 9/15/06 in NYC (9-9/23)
7734. Seymour, Horace (a Rev. officer), late of Lansingburgh, NY but a native of Hartford, CT, d 12/14/99 (interred in the burial yard of the new Brick Church) (surv by a wf and 3 ch) (9-12/17)
7735. Seymour, Israel m 1/11/24 Lucinda Pearce, both of Troy; Rev. Howard (9-1/13)
7736. Seymour, Sally, 63, wf of Stephen, d 4/4/22 in Otsego (3-4/8)
7737. Seymour, Timothy m 8/30/29 Elizabeth Bradt, both of Albany, in Troy; Rev. Tucker (1-9/1)
7738. Seymour, William of Newburgh m 8/19/15 Jane Ann Maison, dau of Peter R., Esq. of Poughkeepsie; Rev. Reed (8-8/23)
7739. Seymour, Zachariah, Esq., 63, president of Utica Branch Bank in Canandaigua, d 7/2/22 (7-7/27)
7740. Shaff, James, victualer of Fulton Market, weighing 63 lbs., m Matilda Castine of the same weight, both of NYC; Rev. Kniles (8-7/1/29)
7741. Shales, Minor, Jr. m Mary Sheldon in Burlington (Ots. Co.) (3-11/24/23)
7742. Shankland, Henry B. m Sarah Ann Rosencrans in NYC (3-7/1/22)
7743. Shankland, Peter V. of the firm of Shankland and Corning m 9/22/25 Susan Lagrange, dau of James, Esq., in Albany; Rev. Ferris. All of Albany (3-10/3)
7744. Shankland, Rachel, 51, wid of late Thomas, Esq., d 10/21/26 in Cooperstown (3-10/23)
7745. Sharp, Abraham, merchant, m 2/21/21 Helen C. Pitcher, dau of Capt. John, all of Red Hook; Rev. Kittle (8-3/7)
7746. Sharp, Abraham m 5/8/29 Helen C. Kip, both of Upper Red Hook; Rev. Kittle (8-5/14)
7747. Sharp, George of Greenbush m 12/22/05 Maria Young of Troy (9-12/24)
7748. Sharp, Nicholas of Greenbush d "last week" in Troy (the kick of a horse fractured his skull) (9-1/5/13)
7749. Sharpe, Jacob m 10/29/02 Sally Ranny, both of Claverack (6-11/2)
7750. Sharpe, Peter, merchant, of the firm of Numan and Sharpe m 4/26/31 Emily Babcock, dau of Oliver, deceased, in Troy; Rev. David Butler. All of Troy (1-4/28)

7751. Sharpsteen, Richard m 3/6/34 Jane Haight, both of Stanford (Dut. Co.); James Humeston, Esq. (8-3/12)
7752. Sharts, John, printer, m 8/10/20 Polly Schermerhorn in Hudson; Rev. Howard Malcom (6-8/22)
7753. Shattuck, Solomon m 8/30/16 H. Folger (in Hudson?) (6-9/3)
7754. Shaw, Angus of Montreal, Canada (formerly a partner of the North West Co.) d 7/26/32 in New Brunswick, NJ (having arrived there only a day or two before his death) (had a "pulmonary affection") (8-8/1)
7755. Shaw, Charles A., merchant, m 5/10/17 Sophia Deyo, both of Kinderhook, in Claverack; Rev. Gebhart (6-5/20)
7756. Shaw, Henry m Jemima Quick, dau of Gerardus, both of Rhinebeck; Rev. Hebard (8-5/29/04)
7757. Shaw, James, merchant, about 36, d 5/28/29 in Herkimer (1-6/5)
7758. Shaw, John m 11/2/99 Nabby Draper, both of Lansingburgh; Rev. Coe (9-11/5)
7759. Shaw, Leander m 3/16/33 Pamela Larrabee, both of Peru, NY; Ezra Williams, Esq. (4 [Keeseville Herald]-3/19)
7760. Shaw, Lucy Cornelia, about 2, dau of Rev. John B., d 8/4/32 in Plattsburgh (7-8/11)
7761. Shaw, Samuel, Esq., 47, a justice of the peace for the County of Otsego, d 1/3/01 in Butternuts (3-1/15)
7762. Shean, Frederick of Pleasant Valley m 1/18/32 Emma Hadgley of Clinton (Dut. Co.); Rev. E. Price of Fishkill (8-1/25)
7763. Shear, Catherine (Miss), 26, dau of Israel, d 4/24/16 in Beekman (8-5/8)
7764. Shear, George m 12/24/29 Sarah McLean, both of Poughkeepsie; Rev. D. Cuyler (8-12/30)
7765. Shearer, Daniel of Albany m 2/7/27 Lucy Nobles of Troy; Rev. Howard (9-2/13)
7766. Shearer, John L. of Albany, 31 or 81?, d in Greenwich (Wash. Co.) (1-8/23/31)
7767. Shearer, William m 5/23/25 Margaret Barr of Vermont; Rev. McCabe (2-5/31)
7768. Shearman, David m 9/21/34 Naomi Edson, both of Chesterfield; E. Williams, Esq. (7-9/27)
7769. Shearman, Frederick, about 28-30, a shoemaker, d 9/7/29 in Cayuga (was apprenticed in Johnstown and carried on his business in Mayfield, both towns in Montgomery Co.) ("The residence of his friends is not known.") (1-10/5)
7770. Shears, Zachariah, 67, d 3/16/14 in Sheffield (8-4/6)
7771. Shelden, Ambrose m 1/27/30 Mary Ann Lasell at St. Paul's Church in Troy; Rev. Butler. All of Troy (1-2/1)
7772. Shelden, Arunah C., about 8, s of Arunah, d 1/29/27 in Plattsburgh (whooping cough) (7-2/10)
7773. Shelden, Julia Ann, 23, d 10/14/19 (in Troy?) (9-10/19)
7774. Sheldon, _____, 41, consort of Col. Artemas, d 3/16/26 in Burlington (Ots. Co.) (3-3/20)
7775. Sheldon, D. S., merchant, m Eliizabeth Egleston, dau of David S., Esq., at Port Kent; Rev. Lyman (4 [Keeseville Herald]-9/13/31)
7776. Sheldon, Daniel m 9/14/19 Martha Van Cott; Rev. Sommers (9-9/21)
7778. Sheldon, Hannah (Mrs.), 76, d 9/14/30 in Albany (funeral from the home of her son-in-law, Lyman Chapin of 31 Green St) (1-9/16)
7779. Sheldon, Henry m 10/12/14 Sarah Ann Winchell, both of Amenia; Enos Hopkins, Esq. (8-10/19)
7780. Sheldon, Jacob m 11/26/23 Polly Pulver; Rev. Armstrong (8-12/3)
7781. Sheldon, Job, 74, (a Rev. soldier) d 4/1/32 at the home of his son, William B. in Poughkeepsie, NY (born in Cranston, RI in Jan 1758; received 2 badges of honor "under the hand of Washington for wartime services; after the War lived first in Providence, RI, later in Litch-field Co., CT, and still later until a few months before his death in Warren Co., NY) (8-4/18)
7782. Shelters, Emily S., 3, dau of Henry of NYC, d 3/18/29 (funeral from the home of James Clark, corner State and South Market Streets in Albany) (1-3/19)
7783. Shepard, Charles E., merchant, m Catharine AnnCuyler, dau of Glen, Esq., in Aurora; Rev. Seth Smith (2-3/15/31)
7784. Shepard, Fitch, maerchant, m 7/10/28 Delia Maria Dennis, only dau of late Paul, Esq. of Cambridge at Schaghticoke Point; Rev. T. Fletcher (9-7/15)

7785. Shepard, Joshua, about 50, merchant, d 9/12/29 in Dansville (1-9/22)
7786. Shepard, William, 62, (a Rev. soldier) oldest s of late Gen. William, d in Canandaigua (born in Westfield, MA) (3-8/4/23)
7787. Shephard, Jere. m 3/16/24 Laura Curtiss in Exeter; Rev. Duncan (3-3/22)
7788. Shephard, Leonard m 12/15/29 Susannah Gould; Rev. Welch (1-12/18)
7789. Shepherd, Eliza, 16, d in Buffalo (9-1/2/27)
7790. Shepherd, George m Ann E. King, both of NYC; Rev. W. W. Phillips (8-7/23/28)
7791. Shepherd, Henritetta, 21, wf of John of Northampton (MA?) d 7/24/06 at the home of her father, Judge Tryon, in New Lebanon, NY (funeral sermon by Rev. allen of Pittsfield, MA)(6-8/19)
7792. Shepherd, John H. of NYC m 8/3/16 Elizabeth S. Mills, dau of late John, Esq. of Claverack, in C; Rev. Gephart (6-8/13)
7793. Shepherd, Theodorus, Esq., 28, attorney, of Argyle d 7/17/30 in Salem (consumption) (1-7/23)
7794. Sherburne, _____ (Mr.) d 1/31/13 in Troy (9-2/2/13)
7795. Sherburne, John, 73, judge of the U.S. District Court, d in Portsmouth, NH (was "aid-de-camp to Gen. Whipple" in the Rev. War) (1-8/14/30)
7796. Sherman, _____, wf of Ezra, d 9/13/18 in Poughkeepsie (8-9/9)
7797. Sherman, A. N., publisher of the Albanian, m 5/21/30 Fanny Slawson; Rev. Green. All of Albany (1-5/25)
7798. Sherman, Adam, formerly of Troy, m 6/12/23 Eleanor Smith of White Creek; Rev. Tinkham (9-7/1)
7799. Sherman, Ansel of Connecticut m 12/30/24 Wealthy Gurnsey of Northeast; Rev. C. P. Wilson (8-1/12/25)
7800. Sherman, Constant m 9/26/16 Amelia Doubleday, dau of Maj. Seth; Rev. John Smith. All of Cooperstown (3-10/10)
7801. Sherman, Dana of Massachusetts m 5/13/30 Eliza Tate, formerly of NYC, in Albany; Rev. Dr. Ludlow (1-5/17)
7802. Sherman, Darius m 12/25/28 Almira Tabor, dau of Thomas, in Dutchess Co.; Rev. Bronson. All of Dover (8-12/31/28 and 1-1/3/29)
7803. Sherman, Deborah (Mrs.) of Pawling d 3/21/04 (8-4/3)
7804. Sherman, Israel, 37, of the firm of Michael S. Van Der Cook and Co., merchants, of Pittstown, NY, d 9/5/07 in Newport, RI (9-9/22)
7805. Sherman, Lemuel Hawley of Newtown, CT m 4/26/13 Brittania McManus of Troy in T; Rev. David Butler (9-5/4)
7806. Sherman, Maria (Miss), 16, dau of Uriel, d 1/24/23 in Stanford (Dut. Co.) (consumption) (8-1/29)
7807. Sherman, Martha (widow), 100, formerly of Dartmouth, MA, d 11/18/21 in Peru, NY (7-12/1)
7808. Sherman, Richard H. m 2/5/28 Sally Essigh, both of Dover, in D; Rev. C. P. Wilson (8-2/13)
7809. Sherman, Samuel, 65, formerly of Otsego, d 12/16/25 in Milo (3-1/2/26)
7810. Sherman, Sarah, 89, relict of James, d in New Haven, CT (6-2/23/02)
7811. Sherman, Shadrach, 41, of Dover d 12/5/12 (surv by wf and "a large family of children") (8-12/16)
7812. Sherman, Walter, merchant, m 8/30/34 Cornelia Allerton, dau of Samuel W., Esq., at Ashland in Amenia; Rev. Taylor (8-9/3)
7813. Sherman, William E. (Capt.) of Philadelphia (state not given) m Sally Dillingham, dau of Maj. Nathan of Lee, MA, in L (6-3/19)
7814. Sherrill, Sanford m 9/5/28 Elvira Everest, both of Peru/NRev. F. Halsey (7-9/6)
7815. Sherwood, Aaron m 12/2/26 Maria, dau of Peter Youmans; Rev. Peery. All of Milan (8-12/13)
7816. Sherwood, Jehial m 9/15/00 Mary Russel, both of Southeast, in S; Rev. Jehu Miner (8-9/16)
7817. Sherwood, Jeremiah, 65, formerly of Geneva and brother of Isaac, Esq. of Skaneateles, d 7/25/30 in Bath (1-8/3)
7818. Sherwood, Jonathan (Dr.), 48, d 4/15/29 at his home in Turin (Lewis Co.) (1-4/27)
7819. Sherwood, Juliet A., 20, dau of Hon. Samuel, d 7/29/23 in Delhi, NY (3-8/11)
7820. Shields, Henry m 2/14/22 Lucretia Pulling in Providence, NY; J. Keeler, Esq. (2-3/27)

7821. Shields, Janet (Miss), 28, d 1/28/31 in Albany (funeral from 22 Van
        Schaick St., this perhaps the home address of the person identified
        as "her uncle, Adam Smith") (1-1/29)
7822. Shiffer, Henry, 45, d 6/18/20 in Claverack (consumption) (6-6/27)
7823. Shiffer, Joseph D., 35, leather merchant of Albany, d 9/14/30 (consumption)
        (surv by children) (funeral from the Franklin House) (1-9/15)
7824. Shipherd, Bazaleel of Peru, NY d 1/23/14 (7-1/29)
7825. Shipherd, Theodorus, Esq., 28, attorney, of Argyle d 7/17/30 at the home
        of Rev. Dr. Proudfit in Salem (1-8/10)
7826. Shipley, Robert m 2/11/21 Mary Eckert, both of Pleasant Valley; Rev.
        John Clark (8-3/7)
7827. Shipley, William of Pleasant Valley (Dut. Co.) m 12/28/02 Phebe Comstock,
        dau of Thomas of Hudson, at the Friend's Meeting House (6-2/1/03)
7828. Shipman, David, 84, d 2/27) (3-3/6)
7829. Shipman, Horace m 12/7/25 Abby Ann Williams in Otsego; Rev. Tiffany
        (3-12/12)
7830. Shipman, Michael, 46, d 5/25/23 in Otsego (3-6/2)
7831. Shirts, Christian P. m 2/9/15 Betsey Backus "of Dutchess" in Ancram; Rev.
        Rea (6-2/21)
7832. Shirts, Joseph of Livingston m 8/10/16 Lana Van Deusen of Great Barrington,
        MA in G. B.; Rev. Beyley (6-8/20)
7833. Shirts, Margaret, 22, wf of Joseph, d 3/27/15 in Livingston (6-4/11)
7834. Shoemaker, Jane, 42, wf of John M., d 8/14/19 (6-8/24)
7835. Sholes, Abel m 4/18/16 Lucy Chaney; Rev. John Smith. All of Cooperstown
        (3-4/25)
7836. Shook, Edward of the firm of Traver and Shook, merchants, of Upper Red
        Hook m 12/15/28 Catharine Lyle, dau of Henry, Esq. of Upper Red Hook,
        at the home of Jacob in Catskill; Rev. Dr. Porter (9-12/23 and 8-12/24)
7837. Short, John "OL" m Clarissa Grom-on (third last letter missing in surname),
        both of Hartwick, in H (3-2/28/20)
7838. Shove, Daniel of Middlesex, NY was killed "lately" by the fall of a
        tree (6-5/13/06)
7839. Shove, Tabor of New Lisbon m Polly Marvin in Milford (3-3/19/21)
7840. Shufeldt, George A., Esq. of Red Hook m 6/15/17 Mary Wilson, dau of
        Hon. William of Clermont, at the Reformed Dutch Church in Red Hook; Rev.
        Kittle (8-6/18)
7841. Shufelt, George A., Esq. of Red Hook m 6/15/17 Mary Wilson, dau of Hon.
        William of Clermont, in Red. Hook; Rev. Kittle (6-6/24)
7842. Shufelt, Peter, about 40, a bachelor, d 6/8/04 in Freehold (struck by
        a falling tree) (3-6/28)
7843. Shultz, Christian Otto m 2/25/14 Maria Kip, dau of Jacobus, in Rhinebeck;
        Rev. Quitman (8-3/9)
7844. Shultz, Frederick B. of Clinton m 9/12/22 Melissa Watermyre, dau of David
        of Stanford (Dut. Co.); Rev. Clark (8-9/25)
7845. Shultz, Jacob, 78, of Rhinebeck d 11/24/30 (8-12/1)
7846. Shumate, _____ (Dr.) "of the Army" d 9/1/13 at Fort George the result of
        a duel between him and Lieut. Smith of the 16th Regiment (copied
        from the Buffalo Gazette) (7-9/18)
7847. Shurtleff, J. B., editor of the Tioga County Gazette, m 5/11/31 Elizabeth
        C. Taylor, dau of Gen. W. Taylor, in Wheeler; Rev. Daniel Higgins
        (1-5/22)
7848. Sibley, John, Jr. m 5/17/18 Amelia Crandal in Middlefield; Elder Benjamin
        Sawin. All of Middlefield (3-5/25)
7849. Sibley, John m 10/13/27 Hannah Hayner, both of Brunswick; Rev. Howard
        (9-10/16)
7850. Sickels, Mary (Mrs.), 89, d 5/27/29 in Albany (1-5/3)
7851. Sickels, Thomas of Catskill m 4/12/07 Margaret Poulton of Athens, NY in
        Hudson; Rev. Wigton (6-4/14)
7852. Sickler, Ann, 36, dau of Peter, d 1/13/32 in Beekman (8-1/25)
7853. Sickles, Catharine d 5/15/17 in Poughkeepsie (8-5/21)
7854. Sickles, Eliza (Miss), 25, dau of James, d 12/21/29 in Albany (funeral
        from the home of her father, 24 Quay St.)(1-12/22)
7855. Sickles, Helen, dau of James, d 11/25/31 in Albany (funeral from 24 Quay
        St.) (1-11/26)
7856. Sickles, Stephen I. of Troy m 12/26/21 Mary Cooper of Albany in A; Rev.
        Meyer (9-1/122)

7857. Signor, Joel m 8/30/32 Mary Ann Smith in Keeseville; Ahaz Hayes, Esq. (4 [Keeseville Herald]-9/4)
7858. Silby, William m 8/24/06 Abigail Robbins in Hudson; Rev. Wigton (6-9/16)
7859. Sill, Elisha, merchant, of the firm of Tuttle and Sill m 10/27/31 Delight Coffeen, dau of Henry H., Esq., in Watertown; Rev. G. S. Boardman (1-11/7)
7860. Sill, Francis Nichol of Bethlehem m 10/23/30 Edwardanna L. Scheffelin of NYC; Rev. Dr. Coe(or Cox) (1-10/27)
7861. Sill, Helen T., 69, consort of Deacon Andrew, d 3/24/24 in Burlington (Ots. Co.) (3-4/12)
7862. Sill, Henry, merchant, m 7/29/18 Abigail Dimock in Burlington (Ots. Co.); Rev. Nash. All of B (3-8/10)
7863. Sill, Henry E. m Lucy B. Bliss, dau of Dr. Bliss, in Black Rock; Rev. Kearney (1-1/31/29)
7864. Sill, Richard E., 22, formerly of the Geauga Gazette, d 10/27/27 in Buffalo, NY (1-11/9)
7865. Sill, Theodore, Esq., attorney, m Eliza Mann, dau of late Dr. John Milton, in Whitesborough (Oneida Co.) (6-10/5/10)
7866. Sill, William E., Esq. of Geneva m 9/13/31 Juliann Hopkins, dau of Samuel M., Esq. of Albany; Rev. Dr. Sprague (1-9/15)
7867. Silsby, Thomas m 9/20/31 Fanny Germain, both of Albany; Rev. Luckey (1-9/23)
7868. Silvey, Jeremiah m 10/14/23 Maria Loomis, adopted dau of Elijah Birge, in Greenwich; Rev. J. D. Fonda (9-11/4)
7869. Sim, James m 4/24/23 Margaret Van Valkenburgh; Rev. Griffen (9-4/29)
7870. Sim, Margaret (Mrs.), 91, d 10/31/21 in Lansingburgh (9-11/6)
7871. Sim, William T. m 3/1/25 Eliza A. Stone, both of Lansingburgh; Rev. Griffen (9-3/4)
7872. Simington, Thomas killed 2/28/03 in Fishkill (by an axe swung by William Conklin in a drunken quarrel) (8-3/8)
7873. Simmons, Charles W. (Col.) m 8/9/29 Eliza C. Dewey in New Berlin (Chenango Co.); Rev. Andrews (1-8/27)
7874. Simmons, Isaac m 6/5/07 Sally Sprague, both of Poughkeepsie; Rev. Coville (8-8/26)
7875. Simmons, Isaac, optician, of Northeast m 1/29/13 Maria Van Keuren of Rhinebeck; Rev. Quitman (8-2/3)
7876. Simmons, Jason m 1/29/23 Rebecca Upham in Nassau, NY (9-2/4)
7877. Simmons, Peter J. m 9/25/28 Anna Renouf; Elam Buel, Esq. All of Troy (9-9/30)
7878. Simmons, Thomas m 10/24/02 Sally Baily, both of Hudson (6-11/2)
7879. Simonds, Joseph, Esq., 30, attorney, of Paris, NY d 6/7/07 in Palatine, NY (consumption) (3-7/2)
7880. Simons, George, 23, formerly of Ballston Spa, d 12/6/24 in NYC (small pox) (1-12/21)
7881. Simons, John of Neskauna (possibly intended for Niskayuna of today?) m 10/19/05 Jane Simons of Troy; Rev. Jonas Coe (9-10/22)
7882. Simpson, James m 1/21/02 Caty Simmons of Clinton (Dut. Co.); Rev. Dr. Dodge (8-2/2)
7883. Simpson, Robert m 12/31/17 Betsey Green; Rev. Clark. All of Clinton (8-1/7/18)
7884. Sims, Peter, about 80, d 5/27/19 in Lansingburgh (9-6/1)
7885. Sinnott, Edward Dimick, Jr., inf s of E. D. and Maria of West Troy, d 12/11/31 (1-12/14)
7886. Sinsebah, Moses m 6/22/34 Anne Eliza Dawson, both of Fishkill; Ward M. Gately, Esq. (8-7/16)
7887. Sisson, Isaac, 22, d 4/27/29 in Washington (Dut. Co.) (8-5/7)
7888. Sizer, Henry H., cashier of the Bank of Michigan, m 9/8/30 Mary E. Whiting at the home of Joel Northrop, Esq. of Utica, NY; Rev. S. C. Aiken) (1-9/17)
7889. Sizer, Josephus B. of Middlefield m 1/30/15 Edna Hyslep of Hartwick in H; Rev. Henry Chapman (3-2/9)
7890. Skeel, Thomas m 8/28/28 Sally Hayner in Brunswick; Rev. Samuel Merwin (9-9/16)
7891. Skerritt, John, 68, d 3/18/29 (funeral from his late home, 23 No. Pearl St.) (1-3/18)

229

7892. Sketchley, Thomas, Jr. of Poughkeepsie m Margaret Armstrong, "lately from Ireland", in NYC (8-8/3/02)
7893. Skidmore, Harmon, 33, of the firm of Skidmore and Howard d 9/6/29 in Perry (1-9/22)
7894. Skidmore, Joseph, about 30, d 1/13/34 in Poughkeepsie (8-1/15)
7895. Skidmore, Russell J., 25, s of Luther M., d 10/1/24 in Butternuts (3-10/11)
7896. Skiff, Deborah (Miss), 18, d 10/25/01 in Hudson (6-10/29)
7897. Skillman, John B., merchant, m 1/31/25 Sarah Ann Stewart, dau of Alexander, Esq., in NYC (3-2/7)
7898. Skinner, ____, wf of Stephen, d 12/12/30 in Poughkeepsie (8-12/15)
7899. Skinner, A. A. of Painesville, OH m 7/3/29 Theodosia S. Meeker, dau of John, Esq. of Tully, NY, on board the packet boat "Niagara" of Utica; Rev. Mahan (1-7/8)
7900. Skinner, Henry (Dr.), 33, late a surgeon in the U.S. Army, d 6/23/19 in Eddyville, KY (died of a "pulmonary complaint contracted on the Canadian frontiers") (7-8/21)
7901. Skinner, Henry P. m Mary Burke 12/27/07 (6-12/29)
7902. Skinner, John B., attorney, m 10/27/30 Catharine Stoddard, only dau of Richard M., Esq., in Le Roy; Rev. G. Crawford (1-11/2)
7903. Skinner, John B. L., Esq. of Plattsburgh m Julia Lowry, dau of Heman, Esq. of Burlington (prob. in Vermont), in B; Rev. Dr. Chapman (4 [Keeseville Herald]-12/13/31)
7904. Skinner, Nelson m 10/21/29 Sarah Ann Pullock, both of Poughkeepsie; Rev. Dr. Reed (8-1-/28)
7905. Skinner, Peter R. m 1/28/18 Clasena Thompson, dau of Judah, in Chatham; Rev. Pickering (6-2/3)
7906. Skinner, Phebe, 26, wf of St. J. B. L. Skinner and oldest dau of Gen. Benjamin Mooers, d 4/25/27 in Plattsburgh (7-4/28)
7907. Skinner, Roger (Hon.), judge of the U.S. court for the northern district of NY, d 8/19/25 in Albany (2-8/23; 8-8/24; and 3-8/29)
7908. Skinner, St. John B. L., Esq. m 9/16/21 Phebe Maria Mooers (dau of Gen. Mooers), both of Plattsburgh; Rev. Frederick Halsey (7-9/22)
7909. Skinner, St. John B. L., Esq., attorney, of Plattsburgh m 11/9/31 Julia Lowry, dau of Hon. Heman also of Plattsburgh, in Burlington, VT; Rev. Dr. Chapman (1-12/13)
7910. Skinner, Stephen, Jr., 39, d 5/3/33 in Poughkeepsie (8-5/8)
7911. Skinner, Tamer, 25, consort of Warren, d 8/18/19 in Poughkeepsie (8-8/25)
7912. Skinner, Warren m 12/22/16 Tamer Gunn, both of Poughkeepsie; Rev. Reed (8-12/25)
7913. Skinner, Warren (Capt.) m 2/7/32 Ann R. Ketcham, both of Poughkeepsie; Rev. Dr. Cuyler (8-2/8)
7914. Skuman, William m 12/8/21 Rachael Rehern (9-12/11)
7915. Skutt, Joseph I. m 8/2/16 Martha Carrigan;Rev. Lewis Leonard. All of Poughkeepsie (8-8/7)
7916. Slade, Philip (Rev.), 67, for nearly 40 yrs pastor of the Baptist Church in Swanzey (state not given), d "recently" in Swanzey (9-9/19/28)
7917. Slaight, G., merchant, of NYC m 9/15/30 Sarah Green of La Grange; Rev. Buttolph (8-9/22)
7918. Slater, ____ (Rev.) d 4/20/31 in Jay (was pastor of the Presbyterian Ch. in Jay) (4[Keeseville, Herald]-4/26)
7919. Slater, Elizabeth, 60, consort of late James, d 12/9/28 in Poughkeepsie (8-12/17)
7920. Slater, George W. m 1/12/32 Harriet Trumbull in Jay; Rev. Pier. All of Jay (4 [Keeseville Herald]- 1/17)
7921. Slater, Henry of Burlington, VT m 4/22/21 Eliza Weaver of Peru, NY in P; Rev. Heman Garlick (7-5/12)
7922. Slater, James, 64, d 11/8/28 in Poughkeepsie (born in Lynn, England but for many yrs a resident of Poughkeepsie, NY)(8-11/12)
7923. Slater, James, 1 yr, s of Dr. James E., d 7/13/31 in Marlborough (Ulster Co.) (8-7/20)
7924. Slater, James E. (Dr.), formerly of Poughkeepsie, m 10/11/27 Caroline Fowler, dau of late Caleb of Newburgh; Rev. Ostrom (8-10/17)
7925. Slater, Thomas of Fishkill m 11/12/29 Elizabeth Baker of Poughkeepsie; Rev. Dr. Reed (8-11/18)

7926. Slee, Samuel m 7/9/12 Isabel Nuby, both of Poughkeepsie; Rev. Reed (8-7/15)
7927. Sleght, Henry of Beekman m 12/26/12 Freelove Potter of Poughkeepsie; Rev. Cuyler (8-12/30)
7928. Sleght, Henry, 83, farmer, d 8/19/24 at his home in Clinton (Dut. Co.) (removed from Long Island to Dutchess Co. "56 years ago" and upon arrival lived in Clinton continuously until he died) (8-8/25)
7929. Sleight, Jacob T. m 10/16/29 Mary E. Stoutenburgh, dau of Isaac, in Hyde Park; Rev. William Cahoone (8-10/21)
7930. Sleight, James E., 22, s of Col. James, d 8/17/25 in Freedom ("death was occasioned by drinking cold water imprudently") (8-8/24)
7931. Sleight, Martin of Clinton (Dut. Co.) m 1/29/17 Accuh Williams of Washington (Dut. Co.), dau of John Smith Herrick, Esq. (8-2/19)
7932. Sleight, Morris (Capt.) m 2/5/19 Hannah Gibbs; Rev. P. S. Wynkoop. All of Hyde Park (8-2/10)
7933. Sleight, Peter B. of Freedom m 10/3/27 Sarah K. Barnes, dau of David of Poughkeepsie; Rev. C. C. Cuyler (8-10/10)
7934. Sleight, Peter R. of La Grange m 12/18/32 Catharine S. Barnes, dau of David of Poughkeepsie; Rev. B. F. Wile (8-12/26)
7935. Sleight, Sarah E., wf of Peter R. and dau of David Barnes, d 10/20/29)
7936. Slingerland, _____ of Halfmoon m Hannah Douglas of Schaghticoke; Rev. Close (9-3/15/03)
7937. Slingerland, Abraham m 1/20/22 Thankful Kinney in Broadalbin; Elder Joslin. All of Broadalbin (2-2/20)
7938. Sloan, Altye (Mrs.), 60, d in Poughkeepsie (8-4/22/00)
7939. Sloan, George m 11/24/02 Sally Nash, youngest dau of Azor, Esq., in Butternuts (3-12/9)
7940. Sloan, William of Hudson m 5/4/18 Elizabeth Shears of Albany in A; Rev. Chester (6-5/12)
7941. Slocum, David m 6/13/07 Catherine Lee, both of Dover, in D (8-6/24)
7942. Slocum, Giles, Jr., 29, d 8/25/15 in Claverack (6-8/29)
7943. Slocum, Job, 76, of Dover d 2/3/15 (8-2/15)
7944. Slocum, John m 3/20/14 Sally Collins (6-3/29)
7945. Sloo, Thomas (a Rev. soldier) d 5/17/29 in Shawneetown, IL (born in NY in 1758) (1-6/25)
7946. Slosson, William, Esq. of NYC m 2/18/06 Mrs. Catharine Bellin of Pough-keepsie; Rev. Breuwer (8-2/25)
7947. Slosson, William, Esq., 52, of NYC, formerly of Poughkeepsie, d 4/21/32 in Augusta, GA (had gone to Augusta for his health) (8-5/2)
7948. Smalley, Henry of NYC m 9/15/20 Mrs. Elizabeth Wiltsie of Poughkeepsie; Rev. Reed (8-9/20)
7949. Smead, Henry D., printer, of Bath, NY m Mary B. Smith of Utica in U (1-2/19/31)
7950. Smead, R. C. (Lt.) of the U.S. Army m 12/9/29 Sarah Matilda Radcliff, dau of John, Esq., in Rhinebeck; Rev. G. W. Bethune (1-12/11 and 8-12/16)
7951. Smith, _____, wf of James, d 2/6/13 in Plattsburgh (7-2/12)
7952. Smith, _____, 1 yr, child of Capt. Sidney Smith, d in Plattsburgh (7-8/4/21)
7953. Smith, _____ (Dr.) of Monkton, VT m 5/5/24 Ursula Winchell, dau of Martin of Plattsburgh, NY, in P; Rev. Halsey (7-5/8)
7954. Smith, _____ston m 5/30/24 Mary Beckwith, dau of Dr. Baruc Beckwith, in Beekmantown (Clinton C.) (7-6/26)
7955. Smith, Aaron of Loonenburgh (Athens, NY) m 12/9/04 Zadya Hamilton, dau of Dr. Joseph, in Claverack (6-12/18)
7956. Smith, Aaron,(Capt.) d 5/21/24 in Champlain (death the result of a fall from a horse (7-6/5)
7957. Smith, Abraham m 12/8/30 Jane Robinson, both of Fishkill, in Hyde Park; Rev. Dwight (8-12/22)
7958. Smith, Albert G. of the firm of E. F. Smith & Co. of Rochester, NY m 5/12/30 Julia A. Burrows of Groton, CT in G (1-6/1)
7959. Smith, Alexander, Jr. m 10/3/01 Harriet Geary in Hudson (6-10/8)
7960. Smith, Alexander m Sally Macy, both of Hudson, in H (6-12/2/06)
7961. Smith, Alexander d 6/5/12 in Hudson (6-6/8)
7962. Smith, Ambrose m 9/10/17 Polly Mead, both of Amenia; Rev. Burch (8-9/17)
7963. Smith, Ann (Mrs.), 71, d 2/9/29 in albany (funeral from her former home on Lodge St. two doors south of Pine St.) (1-2/10)

7964. Smith, Archibald, Esq., attorney, m 10/23/17 Cornelia Heermance, dau of
Gen. Martin Heermance, in Rhinebeck; Rev. McMurray. All of Rhinebeck
(6-10/28 and 8-10/29)
7965. Smith, Aruna D. m 5/21/04 Polly Lansing, both of Poughkeepsie; Rev.
Chase (8-5/22)
7966. Smith, Aruna D., a schoolmaster, d 9/19/05 in Poughkeepsie (8-9/24)
7967. Smith, Asa m 2/3/22 Betsey Rose in Oaksville; Rev. Daniel Nash (3-2/11)
7968. Smith, Benjamin, first lieutenant of the frigate "Chesapeake", d 10/14/07
on board that ship (9-10/27)
7969. Smith, Benjamin H. m 3/17/33 Mary Signor, both of Peru, NY; Ezra Williams,
Esq. (4 [Keeseville Herald]-3/19)
7970. Smith, Benjamin P. of Hudson, NY m 7/30/11 Theoda Smith of New London, CT
in N. L. (6-8/16)
7971. Smith, Burrage of Rochester, one of the participants in the Morgan
abduction, d in New Orleans, LA (yellow fever) (1-10/10)
7972. Smith, C. H. of Pine Plains m 10/8/34 Mary Best of Milan; Rev. William
N. Sayre (8-10/15)
7973. Smith, Calvin, 27, d 8/17/22 in Charlton (2-8/20)
7974. Smith, Charles (Lt.), 31, 1st Regiment, U.S. Army, d 1/30/00 in Trenton,NJ
(3-2/20)
7975. Smith, Charles, Jr. of Rochester m 6/13/31 Catharine H. Colt, youngest
dau of late Joseph of Palmyra, at Zion's church in P; Rev. Hickox
(1-6/20)
7976. Smith, Clarissa, 36, wf of Dr. E. A. Smith, d in Huntington, VT (7-9/27/34)
7977. Smith, Cornelia, wf of Melancton, Esq. and dau of Dr. Gardner Jones of
NYC, d 9/18/10 in Plattsburgh (8-10/10)
7978. Smith, Daniel m 4/8/08 Eunice Brown in Exeter (Ots. Co.) (3-4/16)
7979. Smith, Daniel m 4/20/29 Maria Kimmey, both of Bethlehem; Rev. Kissam
(1-4/23)
7980. Smith, Daniel H. m 1/22/02 Mrs. Hephziba Pinkham in Hudson (6-1/26)
7981. Smith, Daniel M. of Sharon m Sally Fitch of Amenia; Rev. Woolsey
(8-10/21/12)
7982. Smith, David m 8/2/18 Phebe McCreedy, dau of Thomas, in Plattsburgh; Rev.
Frederick Halsey (7-8/8)
7983. Smith, Edward of Rhinebeck m 5/27/29 Sarah Ann Lee, dau of Samuel of
Poughkeepsie; Rev. Dr. Cuyler (8-6/24 and 1-6/26)
7984. Smith, Edwin, Esq. of Butternuts (Ots. Co.), NY m Phoeba Robinson of the
Banlieue of Quebec, Canada, in Q; Rev. Dr. Harkness (1-5/11/29)
7985. Smith, Eli m 6/29/29 Cynthia Fitch, dau of Hon. Asahel, all of Scipio,
in S; Elias Manchester, Esq. (1-7/3 and 1-7/7)
7986. Smith, Elihu, about 52, d 10/2/23 in Champlain (7-10/11)
7987. Smith, Elisha Lord, 18, s of Capt. Aaron, d 3/8/25 in Champlain ("Editors
of newspapers in the city of New York will confer a favor by publishing
...") (7-3/19)
7988. Smith, Elizabeth, 63, consort of Stephen, d 3/30/10 in Hartwick (surv by
husband and children) (3-4/7)
7989. Smith, Elizabeth, about 6, dau of Melancton Smith, d 5/20/12 in Plattsburgh (7-6/5)
7990. Smith, Elizabeth, 42, relict of Willison(?) D.(?) _____ (his name blurred)
d 2/1/26 (8-2/15)
7991. Smith, Ensign m 9/11/22 Eliza Thorn, dau of Amos; Rev. Clark. All of
Pleasant Valley (8-9/25)
7992. Smith, Ezra (Capt.), 37, d 5/17/12 in Hudson (6-5/25)
7993. Smith, George m 11/25/15 Betsy Conger, both of Watervliet (9-11/28)
7994. Smith, Gilbert (Dr.) m 6/2/99 Helen De Witt, both of Clinton (Dut. Co.);
Rev. Quitman (8-6/11)
7995. Smith, Hannah, 25, wf of Jabez, d 12/15/22 in Ballston Spa (2-12/17)
7996. Smith, Harvey m "a short time since" Eleanor Sanburn in Plattsburgh;
Rev. Frederick Halsey (7-3/24/21)
7997. Smith, Henry m 11/1/28 Harriet Wright, both of Troy, in T; Rev. Willis
(9-11/7)
7998. Smith, Hezekiah m 7/14/22 Polly Patterson, both of Edinburgh (Sara. Co.)
in Northampton (2-7/30)
7999. Smith, Hiram of Chautauqua m 5/30/27 Electa Mead of Amenia in A; Rev. C.
Wilson (8-6/6)

232

8000. Smith, Horace m 2/17/20 Orchestra Stephens, dau of Josiah, in Cooperstown. All of C (3-2/21)
8001. Smith, Horace, 24, late of Bostom, MA, d 10/14/29 in Albany, NY (1-10/16)
8002. Smith, Howell, Esq., 30, d 8/27/07 in Granville (6-9/29)
8003. Smith, Isaac, 17, m 2/9/23 Sophronia Beardsley, 15, both of Richfield, in
R (3-2/24)
8004. Smith, Isaac, Esq. (Judge), "an extensive farmer", d 7/10/25 at his home
in Washington (Dut. Co.) (8-7/13)
8005. Smith, Isaac V. of Albany m 9/28/29 Frances E. Ward, dau of James, Esq.
of Hartford, CT, in H (1-10/1)
8006. Smith, James of Butternuts m 11/2/17 Anna Bolkcom, dau of Dr. J. of New
Lisbon, in N. L. (3-11/13)
8007. Smith, James m 1/6/20 Harriet Hill, both of Troy (9-1/11)
8008. Smith, James m 3/25/27 Minerva Jones in Plattsburgh; Rev. Halsey (7-3/31)
8009. Smith, James Scott, Esq., attorney, d 12/26/10 in Haverstraw (8-1/9/11)
8010. Smith, James W. (Maj.), 27, late of the 44th Brigade, NYS Infantry,
d 2/28/31 in Brooklyn (1-3/7)
8011. Smith, Jehiel m 3/4/30 Maria M. Hustis in Poughkeepsie; Rev. Welton
(8-3/10)
8012. Smith, Jeremiah, clockmaker, of NYC d 9/22/99 in Poughkeepsie (8-9/24)
8013. Smith, Job A., editor of the Elmira Gazette, m 11/20/29 Susan Fulton of
Orange Co. in Elmira; Rev. Barton (1-12/9)
8014. Smith, Joel, 79, (a Rev. soldier) d 6/3/29 in Evans Mills (Jeff. Co.)
(In Rev. War a Conn. volunteer who fought in the Boston area, on Long
Island, and at White Plains, NY) (1-6/19)
8015. Smith, John of NYC m 7/22/00 Sally Van Kleeck, oldest dau of late Col.
Leonard of Poughkeepsie; Rev. Chase (8-7/29/00 (8-7/29)
8016. Smith, John m 5/29/03 Peggy Dusenbury, both of Poughkeepsie; Rev. Brouwer
(8-5/31)
8017. Smith, John, 38, under-sheriff of Dutchess Co. and quaretermaster in Col.
Sleight's Regiment of Milita, d 2/15/04 in Poughkeepsie (consumption)
(8-2/28)
8018. Smith, John, merchant, m 2/6/10 Gertrude Deal, dau of Henry (6-2/8)
8019. Smith, John (Rev.) of Cooperstown m 9/15/12 Polly Laird of Chanceford
Township, York Co., PA; Rev. Samuel Martin (3-10/3)
8020. Smith, John m 3/4/15 Catherine Wolf; Rev. Coe (9-3/14)
8021. Smith, John, Jr. m 6/4/17 Polly Parck in Plattsburgh; Rev. Kinsley (7-6/7)
8022. Smith, John m 4/25/20 Dotha Wilbur, both of White Creek, in Cambridge;
Daniel Moshier, Esq. (9-5/16)
8023. Smith, John (Rev. Dr., 65) principal and professor of the Theology
Seminary, d in Bangor, ME (1-5/10/31)
8024. Smith, John B. (Rev.), minister of Pine street Church in Philadelphia, PA
and late president of Union College (Schenectady, NY), d 8/23/99 in
Philadelphia (9-9/3 and 3-9/5)
8025. Smith, John B. m 8/27/29 Elizabeth Gilbert, dau of Joseph, all of White
Creek, NY, in W. C.; Rev. Foster of South Carolina
8026. Smith, John W. of Salina m 5/5/31 Elizabeth Sabin, dau of William H., Esq.
of Onondaga Hollow, in O. H.; Rev. Fairchild (1-5/14)
8027. Smith, Joseph N. (Dr.), 44, d 4/23/29 (in NYC?) (1-4/27)
8028. Smith, Joshua m 12/24/15 Lucy Gale, dau of Abraham, in Beekmantown (north)
(Clinton Co.); R. H. Walworth, Esq. All of Plattsburgh (double
ceremony - see Oliver Culver) (7-12/30)
8029. Smith, Josiah (Hon.), 62, late Congressman for Plymouth District, d in
Hanover, NH (small pox contracted in NYC while he was en route home
from Congress) (9-5/3/03)
8030. Smith, Juliana M. P., 3, dau of P. L., Esq., d 3/4/29 in NYC (1-3/8)
8031. Smith, Keziah, about 11, dau of James, d 3/28/12 in Plattsburgh (7-4/3)
8032. Smith, Laura (formerly "Miss Raymond"), 20, wf of William, d 9/19/30 in
NYC (1-9/22)
8033. Smith, Lewis, Esq., 43, late sheriff of Onondaga Co., d 9/7/29 in
Skaneateles (1-9/14)
8034. Smith, Lucretia, 58, mother of Capt. Ezra Smith, d 5/18/12 in Hudson
(6-5/25)
8035. Smith, Luke of Wilmington m Sirissa Bloyd of Peru, NY in Wilmington; Elder
J. Bradley (7-3/29/31)

8036. Smith, M. (Mr.), 79, d 5/12/29 in Utica; also (same day?) his grandchildren, Elizabeth H. and William H. Moore of NYC "after a few
hours illness" (1-6/3)
8037. Smith, Margaret, 68, consort of late Judge Melancton of NYC, d at the home
of her son, Capt. Sidney Smith of the U.S. Navy (7-5/15/19)
8038. Smith, Margaret, 7, dau of Charles Smith, d 12/30/30 in Albany (funeral
at the home of her grandfather, Isaac D. Fryer of North Market St.)
(6-1/1/31)
8039. Smith, Maria (Miss), 16, dau of Nathaniel of NYC, d 4/30/30 in Poughkeepsie
(had come to Poughkeepsie "a few weeks ago" for her health) (8-5/5)
8040. Smith, Melancton, Esq., merchant, of NYC d 7/29/98 in NYC (formerly judge
of court of common pleas in Dutchess Co. and formerly sheriff of this
same co.) (8-8/7)
8041. Smith, Melancton m 5/4/16 Ann Green in Plattsburgh; Rev. Hewit (7-5/11)
8042. Smith, Melancton (Col.), 38, s of Judge Melancton Smith, d 8/28/18 in
Plattsburgh (served in the defense of Plattsburgh in the War of 1812)
(8-9/9)
8043. Smith, Milo of Laurens m 7/28/22 Betsey Crandal of Middlefield in Laurens
(3-8/5)
8044. Smith, Minerva, 30, wf of Rev. Reuben, d 1/19/24 in Ballston (2-1/27)
8045. Smith, Morgan I. (Capt.) of Delaware Co. m 2/15/26 Maria Pells, dau of
John E. of Poughkeepsie; Rev. Cuyler (8-2/22)
8046. Smith, N. (Dr.) of Burlington (Ots. Co.) m 1/25/10 Diadamia H. Cushman
of Exeter in E (3-1/27)
8047. Smith, Nathan (Capt.), 32, s of Anning Smith, Esq., d 9/30/98 in New
Marlborough (Ulster co.) (surv by wf and 4 ch) (8-10/16)
8048. Smith, Nehemiah d 6/23/11 in Troy (killed in a dive for a swim from a
boat when his head struck bottom and he "injured the pith of the
neck bone") (9-6/25)
8049. Smith, P. Sken. (Gen.) of Oxford m 5/15/26 Anne V. B. Prentiss, dau of Rev.
Joseph of Catskill, at St. Luke's Church in Catskill (3-5/29)
8050. Smith, Phebe, 62, consort of Alexander, d 11/2/15 in Chatham (6-11/7)
8051. Smith, Phebe, 24, dau of late Judge Isaac Smith, d 1/6/32 at the home of
her brother-in-law, the Hon. N. P. Tallmadge (8-1/11)
8052. Smith, Phineas m 2/19/26 Nancy Ferris in Northeast; Rev. R. G. Armstrong
(8-3/22)
8053. Smith, Platt, Esq. d 11/4/98 at his home in Amenia (member of the state
assembly from Dutchess Co.) (8-11/13)
8054. Smith, Platt m 3/6/34 Betsey Brown, dau of Noah; Rev. T. Winter. All of
Northeast (8-3/9)
8055. Smith, R. G. m 12/2/29 Susan M. Tompkins, dau of late Daniel D., in NYC;
Rev. Creighton. All of NYC (1-12/5)
8056. Smith, Reuben (Rev.) of Ballston m 4/28/25 Elizabeth Porter of Hadley, MA
in Ballston Spa, NY; Rev. H. A. Wood of Amsterdam, NY (2-5/3)
8057. Smith, Roswell m 2/3/15 Nancy Purdy, both of Troy, in T; Rev. David
Butler (9-2/7)
8058. Smith, Royal m 6/21/20 Eunice Howland, both of Dartmouth, MA, in Hudson,
NY; Edward C. Thurston, Esq. (6-6/27)
8059. Smith, Rufus, 26, of the firm of Woodcock, Smith and Co. d 11/26/18 in
Leicester, MA (typhus) (6-1/19/19)
8060. Smith, Rufus of Clinton (Dut. Co.) m 12/4/28 Elizabeth Thorne of Washington
(Dut. Co.); Isaac Sutherland, Esq. (8-12/10)
8061. Smith, Samuel, 53, d 9/2/13 in Essex, VT (7-9/18)
8062. Smith, Samuel m 7/1/29 Deborah Dubois, both of Poughkeepsie, in P; Rev.
Welton (8-7/8)
8063. Smith, Samuel of Poughkeepsie m 11/25/32 Mrs. Juliana Van Bramer of
Fishkill; Rev Dr. Cuyler (8-11/28)
8064. Smith, Sarah, wf of Capt. John and dau of Mrs. Jane Van Kleeck of
Poughkeepsie, d 10/16/03 (consumption) (8-10/18)
8065. Smith, Seth (Deacon), 94, d 7/7/29 in Norway (Herk. Co.) (born in Suffield,
CT; an officer in the French and Indian War; fought at Bunker Hill,
Trenton, Monmouth, and White Plains in the Rev. War) (1-7/18)
8066. Smith, Sidney (Capt.) of the U.S. Navy m 8/18/16 Phebe Bailey, dau of
William, Esq., in Plattsburgh; Rev. Hewit (7-8/24)

8067. Smith, Stephen H. of Clinton (Dut. Co.) m Lydia S. Vail, dau of Solomon of Stanford (Dut. Co.) at the Friends Meeting house in Stanford (8-10/31/32)
8068. Smith, Sukey, 35, wf of Matthew, d in Hudson (6-10/15/01)
8069. Smith, Susan, 24, wf of Isaac, d 6/22/27 in Plattsburgh (7-7/21)
8070. Smith, Thomas m 2/15/16 Abigail Brightman in Beekmantown (Clinton Co.) (7-2/24)
8071. Smith, Thomas Jr. m 12/24/21 Maria Noble in Ballston Spa; Rev. William A. Clark. All of Ballston (2-12/26)
8072. Smith, Thomas H., 17, s of Samuel, late of Dartmouth, MA d 7/9/19 in Plattsburgh (consumption) (7-7/17)
8073. Smith, Timothy Tredwell, "professor of moral philosophy and logick in Union College", d in Schenectady (6-11/8/03)
8074. Smith, Truman, about 23, "belonging to the State Prison Guard under Capt. Daniel Baldwin", d 3/16/11 ("Printers at Albany, Utica, Cooperstown, and Oxford are requested to insert the above for the benefit of the relatives of the deceased") (3-3/30)
8075. Smith, Vivius W., one of the editors of the Onondaga Standard, m Clarissa Caroline Earll, only dau of Hon. J. Earll, Jr., in Onondaga; Rev. Beardsley (1-3/1/31)
8076. Smith, William of Newburgh m 9/17/25 Maria Phillips of Poughkeepsie in Pleasant Valley; Garret Adriance, Esq. (8-9/21)
8077. Smith, William (Col.) m 6/4/29 Emily Whallon, dau of Hon. Reuben, in Essex (Essex Co.); Rev. Taylor (1-6/16)
8078. Smith, William m 5/10/31 Mary Ann Raymond in NYC; Rev. Edward Mitchell. All of NYC (1-6/4)
8079. Smith, William A. of NYC, s of Arthur of Red Hook, m 6/11/23 Eleanor Ferris, oldest dau of Solomon, Esq. of New Paltz; Rev. Bork (8-6/18)
8080. Smith, William C. of Stanford (Dut. Co.) m 10/2/34 Caroline Walling, only dau of William of Washington (Dut. Co.); Rev. Wiles (8-10/8)
8081. Smith, William H., merchant, of NYC m 4/30/28 Charlotte Young of Troy in Troy; Rev. Cyrus Mason of NYC (9-5/2)
8082. Smith, William M. of Sharon, CT m 2/19/09 Helen Maria Livingston, dau of Gilbert R. of Red Hook, in R. H.; Rev. Andrew N. Kittle (6-3/7)
8083. Smith, William S. (Col.), late a congressman from NY, d 6/10/16 at his home in Madison Co., NY (8-6/19)
8084. Smith, William S., 6, only s of Granville Smith of Poughkeepsie, d 6/3/21 in P (8-6/13)
8085. Smith, William T. m 6/6/27 Lucy Pierce, dau of Benjamin, merchant; Rev. Butler. All of Troy (9-6/8)
8086. Smitheson, _____, wf of Francis d 8/1/29 in Porter. On that date her infant child (not named) also died. Her husband, Francis, d 8/2/29. All three were buried in the same grave (this family had migrated from Howder near York in Yorkshire, England) (8-8/26)
8087. Smyth, Charles of Albany m 10/8/29 Cornelia A. Strong of NYC in NYC; Rev. Dr. Knox (1-10/12)
8088. Snedekor, Elias D. (Dr.), 22, d 3/2/13 in Schodack (surv by wf) (9-3/9)
8089. Snediker, Elias D. of Schodack m 11/8/12 Elizabeth Nazro of Troy; Rev. Wlaillon (9-11/10)
8090. Snell, Leister m 8/21/28 Phebe Ann Weatherwax in Schaghticoke; John M. File, Esq. All of S (9-8/29)
8091. Snider, Henry of Guilderland m 5/3/28 Elenor Smith of Troy; Rev. Howard (9-5/20)
8092. Snodgrass, William D. (Rev.) of NYC m Charlotte H. Moderwell in Lancaster, PA; Rev. Dr. Ely of Philadelphia (3-12/22/23)
8093. Snow, Philo m 12/16/28 Pamelia Gregory in Troy; Rev. Bell. All of Troy (9-12/19)
8094. Snowden, A. H., merchant, formerly of Nashville, TN m 3/16/31 L. A. Bogardus, dau of Gen. Robert; Rev. George Uphold. All of NYC (1-3/21)
8095. Snyder, David m 11/15/21 Lorene Wheeler of Brunswick; Rev. Butler (9-12/11)
8096. Snyder, Henry m 7/24/24 Harriet Hanson of Cherry Valley in C. V.; Rev. Caldwell of Westford (3-8/2)
8097. Snyder, John W., 47, d 9/17/10 in Claverack (6-9/21)
8098. Sockridge(?), Robert, about 30, d 9/8/26 in Granville (7-9/16)

8099. Soernberger, George A. m 12/20/28 Cornelia Livingston Wheeler, dau of
Thomas N., all of Northeast; Rev. Armstrong (8-1/21/99)
8100. Sofield, (sic), John of NYC m 8/3/22 Juliana Grant of Poughkeepsie; Rev.
Cuyler (8-8/7)
8101. Solomon, Charlotte (Mrs.), 50, d 12/15/27 in Plattsburgh (7-12/29)
8102. Somaradyck, Sarah, 17, dau of Mrs. Cornelia, d 10/25/34 in Poughkeepsie
(8-10/29)
8103. Somerby, John Frazier, about 30, d in Hudson (born in Newburyport, MA)
d in Hudson (6-5/4/13)
8104. Somerindike, George W., merchant, of NYC m 2/3/14 Cornelia Van Kleeck,
dau of Tunis of Poughkeepsie; Rev. Cuyler (8-2/9)
8105. Somers, Charles G. m 2/17/17 Sarah Skelding in Troy; Rev. Wayland
(6-2/25)
8106. Son, Francisco was executed 3/28/06 in NYC "pursuant to his sentence")
(6-4/8)
8107. Soper, Cornelius m 6/18/30 Elizabeth Wood; Peter A. Schryver, Esq. All
of Hyde Park (8-6/23)
8108. Soper, David of Ballston m 5/21/23 Ellen Larow of Milton in M; Rev. Clay
(2-6/10)
8109. Soper, Dorastus m 10/7/22 Lucy Boorn, both of Plattsburgh, in P; John
? ___ de, Esq. (surname blurred) (7-10/12)
8110. Soper, Walter of New Paltz m 10/21/30 Sophia Traver of Hyde Park; Rev.
Dr. Cuyler (8-10/27)
8111. Sornborger, Jeremiah, 34, m 4/13/17 Harriet Hamblin, 16, both of Amenia;
Rev. Buttolph (8-4/23)
8112. Souls, John, about 38, d "recently" in Champlain (7-1/8/13)
8113. South, _____ m 1/3/22 Elizabeth Deremer, both of Charlton, in C; Rev. I.
W. Platt (2-1/9)
8114. Southard, Jacob of Fishkill m 4/22/29 Almira Bennett, dau of Peter W. of
Poughkeepsie in P; Rev. Welton (8-4/29)
8115. Southerland, John of Otsego m 10/4/24 Lucinda P. Hyde, dau of Ira, in
Richfield; James Hyde, Esq. (3-10/11)
8116. Southerland, Talmadge (Dr.) of Rensselaerville m 5/5/14 Mary Post, dau of
Ezra, Esq. of Durham (Greene Co.) in D; Rev. Williston (6-5/17)
8117. Southwick, Adna H. m 2/8/27 Mary Reynolds, dau of James of Poughkeepsie;
Rev. Cuyler (8-2/14)
8118. Southwick, Catherine, a member of the Society of Friends and wf of
Edward, d 2/15/13 in Troy (surv by husband and several small children)
(8-2/24)
8119. Southwick, Daniel, merchant, m 1/12/18 Frances Paine, dau of Amasa S.;
Rev. Dr. Coe. All of Troy (9-1/20)
8120. Southwick, Henry m 7/10/14 Hannah Winans, both of Poughkeepsie, at Flagler's
Hotel in Pleasant Valley; John Beadle, Esq. (8-7/13)
8121. Southwick, Richard C. m 8/23/31 Elizabeth R. Bevier, dau of Dr. Benjamin
R., in Wawarsing; Rev. M. Switz. All of Wawarsing (8-8/31 and 1-9/2)
8122. Southwick, Robert B. of Poughkeepsie m 10/11/24 Julia Ann Adee, dau of
David of NYC; Rev. Rufus Babcock (8-10/13). Rob't. d 2/2/28 (8-2/6)
8123. Southwick, Stephen m 10/18/32 Adaline Brewster, dau of Gilbert; Rev. Dr.
Reed (8-10/24)
8124. Southwick, William H., 23, d 2/1/18 (in Poughkeepsie?) (consumption)
(8-2/4)
8125. Southwick, Zadock, 58, formerly of Poughkeepsie, d 10/22/23 at his home
in Wawarsing (8-10/29)
8126. Southworth, James M. m 6/20/13 Ruth Mosher, both of Dover (8-7/28)
8127. Southworth, Richmond, 30, formerly of Rhode Island, d 3/31/31 in Clinton
(Oneida Co.), NY ("Editors of Eastern papers are requested to publish
the above.") (1-5/13)
8128. Souza, Joseph Imanuel, a native of Portugal but for many years a resident
of Lansingburgh, NY, d 7/5/06 in Lansingburgh (his funeral service "in
the Masonic order") (9-7/8)
8129. Soverhill, James M. m 9/1/31 Phebe Crawford in Geneva; Rev. B. Mattison.
All of Geneva (1-9/10)
8130. Sower, Sevina, 72, wid of late Ulrick, d 4/14/12 in Claverack (6-4/20)
8131. Sower, Ulrick, age 110-120, a native of Germany, d 8/8/10 in Claverack
(surv by wf, children, and grandchildren) (6-8/17)

8132. Spafford, John (Col.) (a Rev. soldier), father of Dr. Spafford d 4/24/23
in Lowville (Lewis Co.) (Dr. Spafford is author of the Gazetteer of NY)
(Col. Spafford was born in Conn. but settled early as a proprietor in
Tinmouth, VT) (9-5/13)
8133. Spalding, Azel, Esq. of Montpelier, VT m 7/14/34 Maria Theresa Wainwright,
dau of John, in Middlebury, VT; Rev. T. A. Merrill (7-7/26)
8134. Spalding, Erastus, a former resdient of Rochester, d 7/16/30 on a canal
boat near Schenectady en route to his home in Lockport (1-7/31)
8135. Sparks, Jared of Boston m 10/16/32 Frances Allen, dau of William, Esq.
of Hyde Park, in H. P.; Rev. Johnson (8-10/24)
8136. Sparrow, Erastus, merchant, of the firm of Sparrow and Webb m 10/25/15
Mary Ann Griffin, dau of Maj. Joseph; Rev. Smith. All of Cooperstown
(3-10/26)
8137. Spaulding, Asa, 46, d "recently" in "Merimac, Ms." (probably intended for
Merrimac, Mass.); two days later his mother, 85, and 2 of his children
died (a son age 17 and a dau age 15) (9-5/16/15)
8138. Spaulding, Levi (Capt.), 89, (fought in French War and was an officer in
the Rev. War) d 4/1/25 in Plainfield (Ots. Co.) (3-4/11)
8139. Spears, Elihu d 2/5/23 in Milton (2-2/11)
8140. Spears, Ira m 2/12/24 Ann Case; Seth Parsons, Esq. All of Hoosick (9-2/24)
8141. Speed, Robert Goodhue Harper, Esq., 23, attorney, d 11/19/29 in Ithaca
(was "recently" admitted to the bar of this state) (1-11/26)
8142. Speirs, James, Jr., 22, d 3/4/24 in Ballston (2-3/16)
8143. Speirs, Joseph of Ballston m 2/27/23 Eleanor McDermid of Milton in M; Rev.
James Mairs (2-3/4)
8144. Spencer, Ackery m 3/30/28 Nancy Lewis, both of Petersburgh, in P; Rev.
Satterlee (9-4/8)
8145. Spencer, Alexander, Esq., state assemblyman from Dutchess County,
d 3/19/02 in Albany (9-3/24)
8146. Spencer, Ambrose (Hon.), one of the justices of the Supreme Court, m Mrs.
Mary Norton, oldest dau of Maj. Gen. James Clinton, in NYC; Rev. Dr.
McKnight (6-12/22 and 9-12/22)
8147. Spencer, Ambrose, Jr., "aid to Gen. Brown", d "lately" of the wounds he
received in the battle of Niagara Falls (9-8/16/14)
8148. Spencer, Austin m Sally Root in Otsego; Rev. Smith (3-2/14/25)
8149. Spencer, Charles Edward, 8 mo, youngest s of Philip, Jr., Esq., d 1/4/11
in Poughkeepsie (8-1/9)
8150. Spencer, George B., merchant, of Albany m Charlotte Hoxie, dau of
Christopher of Hudson, in H (6-5/9/09)
8151. Spencer, Hamilton, Esq. (a native of Utica, NY and a graduate of
Hamilton College near there) d "recently" at the home of Gen. Isaac
Townsend "in the Plains, Baton Rouge", LA (1-10/7/31)
8152. Spencer, Harriet, dau of Philip, Jr., Esq, d 2/25/97 in Northeast
(8-3/8)
8153. Spencer, Harriet F., 15, dau of Henry, d 5/27/30 in Albany (funeral from
593 Market, St. at the corner of Bass St.) (1-5/28)
8154. Spencer, James M (Lt.) of the 2nd Regiment of Artillery, U.S. Army,
d 8/16/29 in Shieldsborough, Bay of St. Louis, MO (1-9/29)
8155. Spencer, Laura, 39, wf of Hon. Ambrose, d 5/18/07 in Albany (9-5/26 and
6-6/9)
8156. Spencer, Mary, 35, wf of Judge Spencer and oldest dau of Gen. James
Clinton, d 9/4/08 in Albany (6-9/20)
8157. Spencer, Nancy, 14, oldest dau of Ethan of Elbridge, drowned 5/14/31 at
the outlet of the Skaneateles Lake near the village of Jordan (1-5/30)
8158. Spencer, Philip, Esq., formerly of Dutchess Co., NY and brother of Hon.
Judge Spencer, d 10/15/17 at Bayou Bouff near Alexandria, LA (typhus)
(surv by wf and several children "in a land of strangers") (8-12/31)
8159. Spencer, Samuel of Poughkeepsie m 7/21/17 Mrs. Anna Noxon of Clinton; Rev.
Clark (8-7/3))
8160. Sperry, Anson J. (Gen.), 40, d 2/14/30 in Plattsburgh (1-2/25)
8161. Sperry, Gilead, Esq. m 5/9/12 Catharine Marsh, both of Plattsburgh, in P;
Rev. Halsey (7-5/15)
8162. Spicer, _____, 17 mo, child of Tobias, d 8/31/15 in Troy (9-9/5)
8163. Spicer, John of Hoosick m 12/7/06 Polly Thompson of Pittstown in P
(9-12/16)

8164. Spicer, William d 10/15/29 in Columbus (Chenango Co.) (suicide) (1-10/24)
8165. Spooner, William, 63, d in Milo (1-8/31/29)
8166. Spotts, S. (Maj.), late of the U.S. Army, m 10/14/29 Harriet Clitherall, dau of Dr. G. C. of the U.S. Army, in Smithville, NC (1-10/28)
8167. Sprague, Henry, 22, oldest s of William, Esq. of Cooperstown, d 10/31/15 in Hartwick (surv by wf and 1 child) (3-11/9)
8168. Sprague, Hezekiah B. m 12/31/23 "Miss Percy Newton" in "Oaks-ville" (Otsego); Rev. Smith (3-1/5/24)
8169. Sprague, J. S. (Dr.) of Carlisle m 9/1/25 Prudence Noble of Richfield in R; Rev. Tredway (3-9/5)
8170. Sprague, Joseph, 70, d 3/14/09 in Cooperstown (3-4/1)
8171. Sprague, Mary Day, 6, dau of Maj. Joseph, d 10/25/15 (in Hartwick?) (3-11/2)
8172. Sprague, Phillis, 69, d 7/10/14 in Cooperstown (3-7/14)
8173. Sprague, Rachel Ann, 12, dau of Maj. Joseph, d 6/27/19 in Hartwick ("Printers in Buffalo are requested to insert the above") (3-7/5)
8174. Sprague, William, 2nd, m 8/19/06 Polly Thompson in Hartford, NY; Lyman Hall, Esq. (9-9/2)
8175. Sprague, William, age 45-50, d 12/13/30 (at the home of A. W. Stark, 529 South Market, St., Albany) ("supposed to be an inhabitant of Maine, penniless and in want) (1-12/14)
8176. Springer, Jacob m 12/29/24 Hannah Daveau in Warren. All of Warren (3-1/17/25)
8177. Squiers, Lemuel (Dr.) m 9/13/20 Mary Tucker in Cooperstown; Rev. Tiffany. All of Cooperstown (3-9/18)
8178. Squires, Amson(?), about 19, of Champlain drowned 5/23/12 in the Saranac River in the town of Plattsburgh (in attempting to break up a log jam) (7-5/29)
8179. Squires, Justus, 70, (a Rev. soldier) d 5/23/29 in Lexington (Greene Co.) (1-6/8)
8180. Staats, Ann, 81, relict of Barent I., d 4/14/29 in Bethlehem (1-4/28)
8181. Staats, Anna, 82, wid of Henry, d 2/25/29 in Albany (funeral from her late home at 2 South Pearl St.) (1-22/8)
8182. Staats, Anna, 81, wid of late William, d 6/3/29 (funeral from her late home at 195 Market St., Albany) (1-6/4)
8183. Staats, B. P. (Dr.) m Caroline Porter, dau of G. W., Esq., in Albany (7-9/21/33)
8184. Staats, Jeramiah F., about 4, s of Barent P., d 10/21/31 in Buffalo (1-10/24)
8185. Staats, John L. (Dr.) m 9/8/29 Susan Knapp, wid of late John L., deceased; Rev. Welch. All of albany (1-9/17)
8186. Staats, John Y. d "recently" in Albany (funeral from the home of his brother, William W., at 195 North Market St.) (1-4/23/30)
8187. Staats, Maria A. Winne, 25, wf of Barent P., d 5/9/30 (pulmonary disease) (1-5/11)
8188. Staats, Maria Knowlton, 24, wf of Philip, d 2/9/30 in Greenbush (funeral from the home of her father, Manassah Knowlton) (1-2/11)
8189. Stacy, L. C. Thomas, Esq., 48, d in St. Louis (MO?) (was educated at Hanover College and at time of his death was Secretary of the Iroquois Nation (7-4/23/13)
8190. Stafford, Benjamin m 8/16/27 Deborah Dominy, dau of William; St. John B. I. Skinner, Esq. (7-8/18)
8191. Stafford, Catharine, about 30, dau of Rufus, d 1/27/26 in Plattsburgh (7-1/28)
8192. Stafford, Elizabeth (Miss), about 20, d 1/11/24 in Plattsburgh (7-1/24)
8193. Stafford, Horatio Gates m Hannah Bristol in Canaan (6-6/11/01)
8194. Stafford, James Romeyn, Esq. of Lockport m 6/20/31 Carolina Augusta Cook, dau of late Samuel of Schenectady, in Jersey City, NJ; Rev. B. C. Taylor of Bergen, NJ (1-6/22)
8195. Stafford, Luther m 8/30/32 Ruth Thew in Peru, NY (4 [Keeseville Herald]-9/4)
8196. Stafford, Rowland, 75, d 6/9/19 in Plattsburgh (7-6/19)
8197. Stafford, Sally, about 30, wf of Benjamin, d 1/3/25 in Plattsburgh (7-1/8)

8198. Stafford, Spencer, Jr. of the firm of Spencer, Stafford & Co., merchant, of Utica m Sarah Eames of New Hartford in N. H.; Rev. Shaw (3-7/2/21)
8199. Stafford, William of Kinderhook m 4/16/32 Catharine Matilda Hughson, dau of Stephen of Poughkeepsie; Rev. Dr. Cuyler (8-4/18)
8200. Stagg, John, Jr., Esq., sheriff of New York City and County d 8/29/03 in NYC (6-9/6)
8201. Stalker, Duncan (Rev.) of North Argyle (Wash. Co.) m 11/8/31 Agnes Strachan, late of Swinton, Berwickshire, Scotland, in NYC; Rev. Stark (1-11/12)
8202. Standish, Matthew M., merchant, m 9/2/18 Catharine P. Miller, dau of Dr. John (all of Plattsburgh) in Plattsburgh; Rev. Frederick Halsey (7-9/5)
8203. Standish, Zachariah (Dr.), 40, surgeon of the Hillsdale regiment of militia, d in Spencertown (buried with Masonic honors) (surv by wf and 4 ch) (6-1/10/04)
8204. Standring, Emma (Mrs.), 58, d 7/10/29 in Johnstown (Mont. Co.) (consumption) (1-7/18)
8205. Staniford, Thomas (Lt.) of the U.S. Army m 12/8/16 Mrs. Jane Patterson of Plattsburgh; Rev. John Staniford (7-12/14)
8206. Stanley, Lydia, relict of late Hon. Rufus, Esq., d in Catskill (6-12/24/01)
8207. Stanley, Rufus (Hon.), 33, one of the judges of the Greene County Court of Common Pleas, d 10/6/01 in Catskill (6-10/22)
8208. Stanter, Robert H., 29, d 12/23/28 in NYC (9-12/23)
8209. Stanton, David m 5/16/31 Mary Lewis; Rev. Jewett. All of Poughkeepsie (8-6/1)
8210. Stanton, E. Lodowick (Col.), 81, (a Rev. patriot and father of G. W. of Albany) d 3/16/29 in Lebanon, NY (buried in Pittsfield, MA beside his wf and 2 sons) (1-3/19)
8211. Stanton, William, Jr. m 7/15/31 Eliza Field, dau of Joseph, Esq. of Rochester, at St. Luke's Church in Rochester; Rev. H. J. Whitehouse (1-8/9)
8212. Stanwix, John m 4/21/10 Sarah Newby, dau of Robert, in Poughkeepsie; Rev. Cuyler (8-5/16)
8213. Stanwix, Newby, 9, only s of John of Poughkeepsie, d 10/11/20 in P (8-10/18)
8214. Staples, Dorcas, 42, wf of Abraham and a member of the Society of Friends, d 1/7/13 in Troy (9-1/12)
8215. Staples, Stephen M. L., Esq., surveyor general of the state of Chichuachua in Mexico, m Elizabeth P. Lewis, dau of late Hon. Lathrop Lewis, in Gorham, ME (1-10/24/31)
8216. Star, Robert, 26, s of Daniel of Ballston, d 9/9/21 in the state of Virginia (2-10/31)
8217. Stark, James, "90½", a member of the party which destroyed the tea in Boston, d in Jay, NY (born in New London, CT; fought in the French War in 1758 after which he moved to Boston, MA) (1-1/24/31)
8218. Starkie, Luther m 9/13/33 Melinda Johnson; Thomas D. Gibson, Esq. (4 [Keeseville Herald]-10/30)
8219. Starks, Ira of Peru, NY d "a few days since" in Quebec, Canada ("His remains have been brought home for interment") (surv by a wf and 2 ch) (7-12/25/19)
8220. Starkweather, Jane, inf dau of Samuel, Esq., d 9/16/25 in Cooperstown (3-9/19)
8221. Starr, Caleb of Danbury, CT m 12/6/02 Huldah Booth of "Hudson-district", NY (6-12/7)
8222. Starr, D. L. (Dr.) of Poughkeepsie m 12/20/33 Lydia Jane Pelton, dau of Hon. P. Pelton of Monticello (Sullivan Co.), in M; Rev. Nathan Rice (8-1/22/34)
8223. Starr, Elisha, one of the publishers of the Le Roy Gazette, m 10/1/29 Sarah E. Hosmer, dau of A., in Le Roy; Rev. Beardsley. All of Le Roy (1-10/10)
8224. Starr, Ezra (Capt.), an old resident of Milton, d 7/23/25 in M. (consumption) (fuenral sermon by Rev. Eber Tucker (2-7/26)
8225. Starr, George, 19, oldest s of R. Starr, d 7/28/31 in Albany (funeral from 124 South Pearl St.) (1-7/29)
8226. Starr, George, about 14, oldest s of Richard of Albany, d 7/29/31 in Chatham (severely injured in an accident) [data continued next pg.]

8226 continued - ("To Mr. Rider, and his family in particular [who cared for this injured person, 7/24-29], no thanks can be commensurate") (1-7/30)
8227. Starr, Jesse H., about 26, d 6/26/14 (3-6/30)
8228. Starr, John m Sophia Baker, both of Hudson (6-5/9/09)
8229. Starr, Maria A., dau of David of Newburgh, d 2/11/34 "in Pearl Street, N.Y." (scarlet fever) (8-12/17)
8230. Starr, Olive, 55, wf of Ira, d 5/26/26 in Middlefield (3-6/5)
8231. Starr, Peter (Rev.), 84, father of Chandler Starr of Albany, d 7/17/29 in Warren, CT in the 58th year of his ministry (1-7/21)
8232. Starr, Samuel, Esq. of Troy m 10/31/07 Lydia S. Burr of New Haven, CT in N. H.; Rev. Hubbard (9-11/10)
8233. Starr, Samuel, 64, d 8/31/30 in Albany (funeral from his late home, 42 Washington St.) (1-9/1)
8234. Starr, Sarah (Miss), 27, dau of Jonah, d 11/6/22 in Milton (2-11/12)
8235. Starr, Seth, formerly of Milton, m 4/24/23 Lucy Bacon of Ballston in B; Rev. Joseph Sweetman (2-5/6)
8236. Staughton, William (Rev.), D.D., m Anna C. Peale, dau of James, in Philadelphia (1-9/2/29)
8237. Stayner, Richard M. m 12/19/29 Sarah Colwell in Poughkeepsie; Rev. Welton (8-12/23)
8238. Stead, Henry (Rev.), senior minister of the Methodist Episcopal Church in NYC, m 9/9/26 Mrs. Hetty Hart of Fishkill in F; Rev. S. Lockey (8-9/13)
8239. Stearns, Adeline, 2, dau of L. S., d 8/19/33 in Plattsburgh (7-8/24)
8240. Stearns, Lemuel m 11/22/17 Parny Rawson, both of Pittstown; John Stitt, Esq. (9-2/24/18)
8241. Stebbins, Harlow B. (Lt.), about 23, of the 29th U. S. Infantry d 11/25/13 in Plattsburgh ("interred with the honors of War") (7-11/27 and 6-12/21)
8242. Stebbins, Mary, 34, wf of Benjamin, d 4/22/11 in Albany (8-5/3)
8243. Stebbins, Mary Bates, 8 mo, "daughter of the editor of this paper", d 5/26 (6-6/1)
8244. Steel, Hezekiah m 8/3/06 Avis Barnard in Hudson; Rev. Sears (6-8/5)
8245. Steele, George A., printer, formerly of Poughkeepsie, m 11/6/17 Charity Rutan of NYC in NYC (8-11/12)
8246. Steele, Henry, 15, s of late Daniel, d 7/2/31 in Williamstown, MA (1-7/6)
8247. Steele, John R. of Salem, NY m Eliza Holloway of NYC in NYC; Rev. W. Philips (3-7/15/22)
8248. Steele, Joseph (Rev.) of Castleton, VT m 10/31/30 Julia A. Bacon, dau of Reuben, Esq. of Great Barrington, MA, in G. B. (1-11/9)
8249. Steele, Richard (Dr.) of Durham, NH m Caroline Vernam, dau of Stephen, Esq. of Mechanicville, NY, in albany; Rev. Welch (1-12/11/30)
8250. Steele, Roderick C. of Woodbury, CT m 9/21/29 Julia S. Perry, dau of Charles, Esq. of Hobart (Dela. Co.), in H; Rev. Hewett R Peters (1-10/2)
8251. Steenbarch, Elias m 10/15/08 Sally Kidney, dau of Robert J., all of Poughkeepsie; Rev. Brouwer (8-10/19)
8252. Steere, Phoebe, wf of James of Hartwick, d 1/16/16 in Hartwick (consumption) (3-1/25)
8253. Stephens, John, Jr. m 1/5/15 Polly De La Mater, both of Sand Lake; Rev. Coe (9-1/10/15)
8254. Stephens, Mary Ann (Miss), 19, dau of H. R., Esq. of Carmel, d 6/22/32 in Poughkeepsie (fell from a horse) (8-6/27)
8255. Stephens, Moses M., 37, oldest s of Archibald, Esq., d 11/2/29 at his home in Stephensville in the town of Coeymans (surv by wf and 3 ch) (1-11/18)
8256. Stephens, Samuel m 7/21/19 Polly Hambleton (7-7/24)
8257. Sterling,Mary, 36, wf of David, d in Hudson (6-8/3/12)
8258. Sternbergh, Jacob, m 1/25/31 Charlotte Ann Ball; Rev. Dr. Ludlow. All of Albany (1-1/27)
8259. Sterrett, Benjamin, Esq. of the firm of Barr, Auchincloss & Co. of NYC m 6/2/30 Jane Keyse, dau of J. F., Esq. of Cincinnati, OH, in C (1-6/28)
8260. Stetson, John S. m 4/27/26 Eliza Robinson, both of New Lisbon; Rev. Seth Gregory (3-5/1)
8261. Stetson, Lemuel, Esq., attorney, of Keeseville m 2/24/31 Helen Hascall, dau of late Ralph of Essex, in Plattsburgh; Rev. Creagh(1-3/10)

8262. Stevens, _____, wf of George M. of 130 State St., Albany, d about 1/12/29 (1-1/15)
8263. Stevens, Byam Kerby m 4/6/30 Frances Gallatin, only dau of Hon. Albert, in NYC; Rev. Dr. Wainwright (1-4/9)
8264. Stevens, Darius (Rev.), 28, of the Methodist Episcopal Church d 4/16/23 in Peru, NY (7-4/19)
8265. Stevens, Ebenezer m 6/5/03 Betsy Cushion, both of Pawling; Rev. Gibson (8-6/14)
8266. Stevens, Ebenezer m 7/3/27 Polly Worthington, both of Grafton; Rev. Howard (9-7/10)
8267. Stevens, Frederick H. m 4/11/19 Abbey Eliza Sears, dau of Nathan, in Hudson; Rev. Sampson (6-4/20)
8268. Stevens, Herman m 12/30/28 Lucy Belding, dau of Taber, Esq. of Amenia; Rev. Winter (8-1/28/29)
8269. Stevens, Hestor I., Esq. m 9/6/29 Charlotte Sedgwick in Rochester; Rev. Dr. Comstock (1-9/11)
8270. Stevens, John of NYC m 11/16/28 Frances Mosely, dau of Gideon of Poughkeepsie; Rev. Dr. Reed (8-11/19)
8271. Stevens, Levi m 1/4/13 Rebecca Herrick, dau of Dr. Elijah (7-1/8)
8272. Stevens, Nancy, 22, consort of Henry ("to whom she had been married but a few weeks") d 1/15/11 in Cooperstown (typhus) (She, a dau of Abner Pier, was the fifth member of that family to have died within 8 weeks, with a sixth "in a very dangerous situation from the same disease" - see the marr of Ebenezer Wilbur for another Pier reference) (3-1/19)
8273. Stevens, Nancy, 29, wf of George, d 1/12/29 in Albany (1-1/14)
8274. Stevens, Patience (Mrs.), formerly of Plainfield, CT, d 8/30/13 at the home of William Pierce, her son-in-law, in Troy (9-8/31)
8275. Stevens, Ralph, oldest s of Stephen of Poughkeepsie, d 12/13/93 (8-12/18)
8276. Stevens, Richard m 2/24/21 Frances Biggs, both of Poughkeepsie; Rev. Leonard (8-3/7)
8277. Stevens, Samuel of NYC m 8/23/18 Lorenda Delong of Troy; Rev. Butler (9-9/1)
8278. Stevens, Samuel (Capt.), 28, drowned 5/29/29 "near the falls" in Swanton, VT (1-6/11)
8279. Stevens, William, inf s of G. M. Stevens, d "recently" in Albany (funeral from his parents home, 130 "State St. continued")(1-4/7/29)
8280. Stevenson, Frances McK (Miss), 17, d 7/22/05 in Troy (9-7/30)
8281. Stevenson, James (Rev.), pastor of the Reformed Dutch Church of Florida (Mont. Co.), m 8/3/30 Jane Hubbard, dau of Teunis of Minaville, in M; Rev. P. P. Rouse (1-8/12)
8282. Stevenson, Miles (Dr.) m 5/2/19 Theodosia Goldsmith, dau of Thomas, all of Chazy, in C (7-5/15)
8283. Stevenson, Polly (Miss), 14, d 5/16/11 in Plattsburgh (7-5/24)
8284. Stevenson, Seymour m Lucretia Wheeler in Plattsburgh; John Lynde, Esq. (7-9/21/22)
8285. Stevenson, William, 62, d in Kinderhook (was born near Beverly, Yorkshire, England (6-7/19/14)
8286. Steward, John, Esq., 82, (a Rev. soldier) d 8/12/29 in Goshen (for many years a judge of the inferior court) (1-8/18)
8287. Stewart, Archibald, 56, merchant, of Poughkeepsie d 8/5/04 (8-8/7)
8288. Stewart, Bradley d in Warren (3-1/3/25)
8289. Stewart, Catharine, 11, oldest dau of Alvan, d 4/4/30 in Cherry Valley (his second dau who died within a few days, both of scarlet fever) (1-4/13)
8290. Stewart, Charles (Capt.) of Albany m Mary Ann Southwick, dau of late H.C., in NYC; Rev. McLeod (3-5/27)
8291. Stewart, Harriet, wf of Rev. C. S. of the U.S. Navy, d 9/6/30 in Cooperstown (1-9/11)
8292. Stewart, James, D.D., m 10/8/25 Maria Onderdonk Cushman, dau of "Minerva Cushman, Esq." of Exeter (Ots. Co.) at St. Luke"s Church in NYC; Rev. Upfold (3-10/17)
8293. Stewart, James of Fishkill, NY m 5/12/34 Salome P. Young of Windham, CT in W; Rev. Corson (8-5/21)
8294. Stewart, John, merchant, m 7/6/02 Eliza Dickinson, both of Lansingburgh; Rev. Butler (9-7/7)

8295. Stewart, Joram N. m 11/5/26 Martha Caunon in Poughkeepsie; Rev. Charles Walker (8-11/8)
8296. Stewart, Joseph m 1/5/05 "Miss Harris Simpson", both of Cooperstown; Rev. Daniel Webster (3-1/10)
8297. Stewart, Levi m 4/28/25 Eliza Northrop, both of Sherman, CT; Rev. Maltby Gelston (8-5/11)
8298. Stewart, Ruth, 27, wf of Rev. James W. Stewart (preceptor of Washington Academy) and dau of Gideon Gifford of Argyle, d 12/11/31 in Salem (Washington Co.) (1-12/17)
8299. Stickle, John J. m 1/18/27 Pamilla Pudvo(?) in Plattsburgh; Peter Weaver (7-1/27)
8300. Stickles, Edward m 9/19/33 Bridget Kane in Peru, NY; Rev. Lyman (7-9/21)
8301. Stiles, Ezra m 1/24/21 Harriet Roeblee(?) in Chazy (7-2/3)
8302. Stiles, Reuben m 7/24/22 Mrs. Boin(?), both of Chazy, in C (7-8/10)
8303. Stillman, Lawrence A. of NYC m 5/17/30 Maria Malcomb of Albany; Rev. Welch (1-5/19)
8304. Stillman, Sarah, 21, consort of Dr. Willētt Stillman, d 7/3/30 in Durhamville (in the town of Verona) (1-7/19)
8305. Stillman, Willet (Elder), 49, d 11/17/26 in Plainfield (3-11/27)
8306. Stillman, Willett (Dr.) m 9/18/31 Amelia Sykes, dau of Col. Solomon, in Durhamville (Verona); Rev. Benjamin Newcomb (1-9/22)
8307. Stillwell, John B. m 11/14/33 Caroline Lamora___(?) in Burlington, VT; John Bates, Esq. (7-12/14)
8308. Stilwell, Leban of Freedom m 11/3/24 Julia Bell of Poughkeepsie (8-11/10)
8309. Stirling, _____, 34, wf of David, d 11/7/04 in Hudson (6-11/13)
8310. Stirling, David m 1/9/05 Mariam Kelly of Hudson in Claverack; Rev. Judd (6-1/15)
8311. Stockholm, Andrew, Esq., brother of Col. Aaron of Fishkill, d 4/11/19 in NYC (8-4/14)
8312. Stockholm, Derick B., Esq. m 2/23/15 Maria Rouse, both of Poughkeepsie; Rev. Cuyler (8-3/1)
8313. Stockholm, John C. of Fishkill m 10/15/17 Eliza Underhill, dau of Gilbert of East Chester, in NYC; Rev. Mervin (8-10/22)
8314. Stocking, _____, wf of Austin, d 12/4/29 in Hudson (1-12/9)
8315. Stocking, Austin m 12/20/10 Eliza Mann; Rev. Chester. All of Hudson (6-12/28)
8316. Stocking, James M. of Morristown (St. Law. Co.) m 5/4/31 Catherine Metcalf, dau of Elijah H., Esq. of Cooperstown, in C; Rev. F. T. Tiffany (1-5/12)
8317. Stocking, Froman, 12, s of Samuel, d 10/13/09 in Hudson (6-10/17)
8318. Stockwell, David m 7/22/19 Cornelia Dopp, both of Plattsburgh (7-7/24)
8319. Stockwell, Dorothy (widow), 77, formerly of Norwich, CT, d 1/26/16 in Troy, NY (9-1/30)
8320. Stockwell, Ezra William, youngest s of Henry Stockwell, bookseller, of Troy, d 4/21/18 in Troy (9-4/28)
8321. Stockwell, Henry, bookseller, 44, d 1/15/24 (consumption) (9-1/20)
8322. Stodard, Jeduthan m 1/7/15 Margaretta H. C. Herod (9-1/10)
8323. Stoddard, Abel and his dau (not named) d 9/8/19 in Hillsdale (killed by lightning in the house in which they lived alone) (9-9/21)
8324. Stoddard, Charlotte, 35, wf of Dr. Israel late of Whitehall, NY, d 8/10/20 in Blakely, AL (9-9/12)
8325. Stoddard, Eliza, 16, dau of Ashbel, d 4/17/13 in Hudson (6-4/20)
8326. Stoddard, Heley m 5/21/26 Betsey Bates, oldest dau of Benjamin; Rev. C. P. Wilson. All of Washington (Dut. Co.) (8-5/31)
8327. Stoddard, Isaac, Jr., 20, m 7/27/19 Bartana Isbel, 12, both of Cambridge, in C; Daniel Mosher, Jr., Esq. (9-8/3)
8328. Stoddard, John (Dr.) of Bedford m 2/18/11 Lavina Stone; Rev. Felch (8-3/6)
8329. Stone, Elizabeth, 35, wf of Isaac, d 11/6/05 in Troy (9-11/12)
8330. Stone, George B. m 8/29/24 Mercy Loomis, dau of Israel, in Otsego; Rev. Smith (3-9/6)
8331. Stone, Heber, 45, for many years a resident of Albany, d 9/3/31 in Esperance (1-9/7)
8332. Stone, Lorren, 20, m 5/24/25 Sally Ann Foster, 15; Rev. Nott (2-5/31)
8333. Stone, Steven, 23, of Sodus (s of Rev. William and brother of one of the editors of the Commercial Advertiser) d 3/27/30 in Sodus (1-4/12)

8334. Storer, Catherine (Mrs.), 54, d 11/1/05 in Troy (9-11/5)
8335. Storm, Charles of the firm of J. M. and J. T. Storm & Co. of NYC m 3/23/31 Catharine Vincent, dau of late Leonard of Poughkeepsie, in P; Rev. Dr. Cuyler (8-3/30 and 1-4/1)
8336. Storm, Charles G. m 10/21/29 Mary Adriance, dau of Isaac R., in Fishkill (8-11/4)
8337. Storm, Jacob T., 21, s of Thomas I. of Fishkill, d 7/21/22 in NYC (8-7/24)
8338. Storm, John A. of Poughkeepsie m 2/11/24 Catharine Adriance, dau of Isaac R. of Hopewell, in H; Rev. De Witt (8-2/18)
8339. Storm, John C. m 5/28/19 Mary Ann Boerman of Fishkill; Rev. Thomas De Witt (8-6/2)
8340. Storm, Mary, 56 or 36, wf of Abraham of Poughkeepsie, d 12/7/16 (8-12/25)
8341. Storm, Richard of Claverack m 1/28/09 Christina Fonda of Poughkeepsie; Rev. C. C. Cuyler (8-2/1)
8342. Storm, Stephen, 80, d 8/9/29 in Claverack (1-8/26)
8343. Storm, Thomas G., 59, d 2/26/30 at his home in Fishkill (8-3/3)
8344. Storm, William m 11/16/20 Elizabeth Boernum, niece of Mrs. Duryee, all of Fishkill; Rev. Thomas Jewett (8-11/22)
8345. Storrs, Amariah m 12/2/04 Mary Ann Gunn, dau of John, in Hudson (6-12/11)
8346. Storrs, Amariah (Mr.), 46, d 11/28/18 in Hudson (6-12/1)
8347. Storrs, Bele, formerly of Burlington, VT, d 4/29/13 in Plattsburgh, NY (consumption) (7-4/30)
8348. Storrs, Eelcta S., 28, dau of Col. Seth of Plattsburgh, d at Mount Zion, GA (7-11/1/17)
8349. Storrs, Sarah, consort of Nathan and dau of Hon. Tomothy Dwight, deceased, d 3/7/05 in Northampton, MA (6-4/2)
8350. Storrs, William L., 27, d 3/27/31 in Burlington, VT (7-3/29)
8351. Story, Jedediah, 15, d 7/1/25 in Cooperstown (3-7/4)
8352. Stote, Jonathan m 6/24/17 Julia Bennett, both of Hudson; Rev. Sampson (6-7/1)
8353. Stotes, Washburn of Upper Canada m 3/2/20 Sarah Reynolds of Plattsburgh (7-3/11)
8354. Stott, _____, infant child of Robert, d in Hudson (6-12/12/20)
8355. Stoughton, Livy m 12/15/05 Chloe Ellis in Troy; Rev. Butler (9-12/17)
8356. Stoughton, Thomas P. m Elizabeth Thompson; Rev. Dr. Knox (8-10/29/34)
8357. Stoutenburgh, Catharine, 75, wf of John, Esq. of Clinton, d 8/27/05 (cholera) (8-9/10)
8358. Stoutenburgh, Catharine Mary, 3, dau of Tobias, Esq. of Johnstown, d 10/31/31 in J (1-11/3)
8359. Stoutenburgh, Jacob m 2/1/21 Hester Travis, both of Clinton; Rev. Leonard (8-2/7)
8360. Stoutenburgh, Jacobus, over 80, d in Clinton (Dut. Co.) (8-2/9/02)
8361. Stoutenburgh, John, s of Capt. Tobias W., m 12/10/23 Polly Vanwagoner, all of Hyde Park; Rev. Cuyler) (8-12/17)
8362. Stoutenburgh, John I. m 10/14/19 Mary Albertson, both of Clinton; Rev. Wynkoop (8-11/3)
8363. Stoutenburgh, Mary, 66, wf of Benjamin, d 2/18/28 in Clinton (8-3/12)
8364. Stoutenburgh, Peter I., 16, m 3/25/04 Polly Briggs, 14, only dau of John, both of Clinton; Ahab Arnold, Esq. (8-4/3/04)
8365. Stoutenburgh, T. A., Esq. of Johnstown m 1/4/30 Emily Maverick, oldest dau of Peter of NYC in NYC; Rev. Eastburn (1-1/14)
8366. Stoutenburgh, Tobias, Jr. of Clinton m 4/27/16 Betsey Fraver of Northeast in Rhinebeck; George Lambert, Jr., Esq. (8-5/15)
8367. Stoutenburgh, Tobias of Hyde Park m 10/20/30 Maria Albertson of Pleasant Valley in P. V.; Rev. Cahoon (8-11/3)
8368. Stoutenburgh, Tobias L. m 11/28/12 Esther Rogers, both of Clinton; Rev. Cuyler (8-12/2)
8369. Stoutenburgh, William m 11/9/20 Maria Degraff, dau of Evert, all of Clinton; Rev. Clark (8-11/15)
8370. Stoutenburgh, William J. m 1/22/29 Caroline Allen of Clinton; Rev. F. H. Vandeveer (8-1/28)
8371. Stow, Gardner, Esq. of Keeseville m 6/7/31 Sophia Patrick of Windsor in W (4 [Keeseville Herald]-6/21)
8372. Stow, Prudence, 62, wf of Daniel, d 4/26/13 in Chatham (6-5/4)

243

8373. Stow, William S., Esq. m 9/12/25 Maria Augusta De Zeng, both of Bainbridge, in Geneva (3-10/3)
8374. Stowel, ____, inf s of James, d 7/19/26 in Cooperstown (3-7/24)
8375. Stowel, William, 63, d 2/27/22 in Otsego (3-3/4)
8376. Stowell, Samuel m 12/25/22 Sarah Smith, both of Brunswick; Rev. Griffin (9-1/7/23)
8377. Stowell, Susan, 24, consort of James, d 7/6/15 in Hartwick (3-7/13)
8378. Strachan, David R., one of the printers of the St. Lawrence Gazette, m 8/13/17 Hester Frazer, both of Ogdensburgh, in O (7-9/13)
8379. Straight, Job, 45, m 10/31/19 Abigail Brownell, 13, in Laurens (3-11/15)
8380. Straight, Job, 22, m 10/31/19 Abigail Brownell, 16, in Laurens; Oliver Myers, Esq. (ages as earlier noted "were misrepresented by some evil-minded and mischievous person") (3-11/29)
8381. Stranahan, Ferrand (Col.), 48, d 10/22/26 in Cooperstown (3-10/30)
8382. Stranahan, Sarah S., wf of Col. Farrand Stranahan, d 1/26/24 in Coopers-town (3-2/2)
8383. Stratton, ____, 18 mo, child of Seth, d 10/7/03 (her nightgown caught fire) (6-10/18)
8384. Stratton, Daniel, 19, s of Joel, d 11/17/02 in Hudson ("seized with sciatica; in July 1791 [and] at different periods endured a dislocation of most of the joints of his body") (6-12/7)
8385. Stratton, Esther, 74, consort of John, d 4/12/19 in Plattsburgh (consumption) (7-4/17)
8386. Stratton, Hannah (Miss), 20, dau of Latham Stratton of Poughkeepsie, d 11/18/20 (8-11/22)
8387. Stratton, Hannah, 31, dau of David formerly of Esopus, d in Greenfield, at the home of her uncle, Howell Gardiner, Esq. (9-12/19/28)
8388. Stratton, N. M., formerly of Poughkeepsie, m 10/6/30 Mary Oatman, dau of Daniel, Esq., all of Troy, in T; Rev. Butler (8-10/13)
8389. Stratton, Robert M. m 6/23/24 Jane Wilson, dau of James, in NYC (bride and groom both of NYC earlier but recently of Poughkeepsie (8-6/30)
8390. Stratton, Uriel, 28, d 2/27/03 in Hudson (6-3/1)
8391. Strawbridge, John Taylor, 16, s of John "of this vicinity" (Albany, NY), drowned 7/10/29 near Newtown, Bucks Co., PA (1-7/30)
8392. Street, Benjamin of Connecticut m 10/24/04 Nancy Johnston of Poughkeepsie; Rev. Dr. Kuensie (8-11/6)
8393. Street, Randal, Esq. m Cornelia Billings in Poughkeepsie (6-6/29/02)
8394. Streight, Justus of Stanford (Dut. Co.) m 11/22/29 Phebe Farrington, dau of Timothy of Pleasant Valley; Oliver D. Collins, Esq. (8-12/2)
8395. Stringham, Samuel of Amenia m 12/25/11 Susannah Chamberlain of Sharon, CT; Rev. Perry (8-1/8/12)
8396. Strong, Adonijah of Salisbury, CT m 10/26/24 Mary Ann Myers, dau of Col. Nathan of Poughkeepsie; Rev. Cuyler (8-11/10)
8397. Strong, D. (Col.) of the Western Army d in Wilkinsonville (state not given) (6-10/22/01)
8398. Strong, David of Warren m 1/31/26 Eunice Pickett of Sherman, CT; Rev. Maltby Gelston (8-2/22)
8399. Strong, Edward A. m 10/5/31 Marianne Clay, dau of late Ralph of Savannah, GA, in NYC; Rev. Manton Eastburn (1-10/7)
8400. Strong, Eleazer, Jr., 41, d 7/26/23 in Ballston ("was found dead lying near the brink of a brook to which it is supposed he went to drink") (2-7/29)
8401. Strong, Hepsibah (Miss), 67, d in Lebanon, CT (through an injury when she was 19 she has been unable to walk) (3-11/4/22)
8402. Strong, Isaac, 2, s of Robert, d 12/30/31 in Albany (funeral from the father's home, corner Pearl and Lydius Sts.) (1-12/31)
8403. Strong, John M., s of Rev. Dr. Strong, drowned in Hartford, CT (6-9/30/06)
8404. Strong, Nathan (Rev. Dr.), 68, pastor of 1st Ecclesiastical Church in Hartford, CT, d 12/25/16 in Hartford (6-1/7/17)
8405. Strong, Pascal N. of the Dutch Church in NYC d 5/7/25 in St. Croix (probably the St. Croix [aka Sancroyd and other similar spellings] found on early maps within the northern bounds of the present town of Hoosick in Rensselaer Co.) (3-5/9)
8406. Strong, William L., Esq. of Burlington, VT m 8/4/34 Jane L. C. Hunt, oldest dau of Luther B., at the Episcopal Church in St. Albans, VT; Rev. Hard (7-8/9)

8407. Stroud, William D. of Peru, NY m 1/22/32 Laura Ann Lee of Wilmington in W (4 [Keeseville Herald]-2/7)
8408. Stryker, Peter M., merchant, of Broome (Schoharie Co.) m 9/18/31 Catharine Maria Hardenburgh, dau of Col. Lewis of Roxbury, in R; Rev. Dr. Paige (1-10/1)
8409. Sturges, _____, wf of John G. of Poughkeepsie, d 12/5/31 (8-12/7)
8410. Sturges, Isaac M. of CT m 8/15/16 Catharine Ann Van Buskirk, dau of Abraham Jr., Esq. of Athens, NY at Trinity Church in Athens; Rev. Joseph Prentice (6-8/20)
8411. Sturges, John G. m 4/5/32 Frances Vanderburgh, both of Poughkeepsie; Rev. Welton (8-4/11)
8412. Sturges, Joseph m 10/12/00 Olive Foster, both of Lansingburgh; Rev. Coe (9-10/14)
8413. Sturges, Olive, 22, wf of Joseph of Lansingburgh, d 7/24/02 (9-7/28)
8414. Sturges, Rachel (Mrs.), 89, d 6/25/17 at the home of Samuel Jarvis in Amenia (8-7/2)
8415. Sturges, Rufus m 10/19/06 Polly Brayton, both of Pittstown, in P; Rev. Ensign (9-11/4)
8416. Sturgis, John of the firm of Sturgis and Perkins m 5/14/29 Mary Regina Morton, dau of late Washington Morton, Esq., in NYC; Rev. Ware (1-5/18)
8417. Sturtevant, Henry, 17, s of Cornelius, Jr., printer, d 9/6/12 in Hudson (6-9/14)
8418. Sudam, Ann, consort of John, Esq. and only dau of Col. Tallmadge of Poughkeepsie, d 1/15/09 (John Sudam, Esq. is of Kingston) (8-1/25)
8419. Sullivan, James, Esq., 26, attorney, s of Hon. William of Boston, d 9/13/29 in Dorchester (both places, presumably, in Mass.) (1-9/16)
8420. Sullivan, Timothy (Capt.) d 3/13/25 in Beekmantown (Clinton Co.) (funeral attended by members of the Clinton Lodge [prob. of the Masonic order] of which he was a meember)(7-3/19)
8421. Sully, Delarson m 1/1/23 Anna Bucknum; Rev. John Perry. All of Stanford (Dut. Co.) (8-1/8)
8422. Sumner, Ebenezer of Edinburgh (Sara. Co.) m 7/14/22 Zilpha Neuvil of Northampton (Mont. Co. then but later in Fulton C.) in N (2-7/30)
8423. Sunderland, Emily, dau of William of Plattsburgh, d 5/16/24 (7-6/4)
8424. Sunderland, William, about 50, d 4/25/26 in Plattsburgh (7-4/29)
8425. Sutherland, Jacob, Esq. m 9/18/11 Frances Lansing, dau of Hon. John, Jr., all of Albany; Rev. John M. Bradford (8-9/25)
8426. Sutherland, Luther, 26, d 1/14/30 at Mr. Adams' boarding house, 34 Dean St., Albany (surv by wf (1-1/18)
8427. Sutherland, Polly, dau of Solomon, deceased, d "last week" at the home of Ezra Thompson in Stanford (8-10/18/03)
8428. Sutherland, Solomon, Esq., 38, d 9/12/02 "at his farm house" in Pough-keepsie (consumption) (buried in the family cemetery in Stanford (Dut. Co.) (had been state senator for the middle district) (8-9/14; 9-9/15; and 6-9/21)
8429. Sutherland, Walter, 28, s of Col. Josiah, d 6/30/21 in Stanford (8-7/4)
8430. Sutten, Aaron of Somers m 11/22/32 Anna Haight of Washington (Dut. Co.) at the Friends Meeting House in Washington (8-11/28)
8431. Sutton, Gilbert, 35, d 9/6/27 at the home of Thomas Andrews in Union Vale ("hit his head on a tree while riding a runaway horse while in company with a son of Thomas") (8-9/12)
8432. Suydam, Abraham of NYC m 4/21/30 Julia W. Olcott of Brooklyn in B; Rev. P. P. Rouse (1-4/26)
8433. Suydam, John, Esq. of Kingston m 5/30/04 Ann Tallmadge of Poughkeepsie; Rev. Gano (8-6/5)
8434. Suydam, Richard of NYC m 2/28/28 Elizabeth German of Troy; Rev. Howard (9-3/4)
8435. Swaide, John of Freedom m 10/9/23 Hannah Johnson of Beekman; Rev. Willson (8-10/12)
8436. Swain, _____, ch of Thomas, d in Hudson (6-9/27/08)
8437. Swain, Gideon m Sally Doolittle, both of Hudson, in H; Rev. Wigton (6-3/8/08)
8438. Swain, Hepsibach, 33, wf of Capt. Isaiah, d in Hudson (6-10/15/01)
8439. Swain, Isaiah (Capt.), 43, d 2/27/09 in Hudson (6-3/7)

8440. Swain, James P. m 9/8/30 Mary Araminta Mercein, dau of Thomas R., Esq.;
Rev. Robert McCartee. All of NYC (1-9/13)
8441. Swain, Martha H., 34, wf of Robert, d 1/3/30 in Albany (funeral from
the home of her husband opposite the Roman Catholic Church on Chapel
St.) (1-1/5)
8442. Swain, Robert m 10/13/31 Helen Coffee; Rev. Smith. All of Albany
(1-10/22)
8443. Swain, Stephen, 76, d 11/28/03 in Hudson (6-12/13)
8444. Swan, Andrew, late of Fifeshire, Scotland, d 7/18/34 in Plattsburgh
(7-7/26)
8445. Swan, Elisha, about 60, d 12/4/23 in Milton (2-12/9)
8446. Swan, H. R. of Albany m 1/4/30 Mary Mell of Utica in U; Rev. Aiken
(2-1/9)
8447. Swan, John H., 51, d 10/21/29 in Albany (funeral from his late home,
10 South Pearl St.) (1-1022)
8448. Swan, Joseph m 11/15/27 Waity Slade; Clark Baker, Esq. All of Hoosick
(9-11/23)
8449. Swan, L. B., merchant, of Rochester m 4/21/31 Elizabeth Wells of Utica;
Rev. S. C. Aiken (1-4/28)
8450. Swan, Lemuel S., merchant, of Milton m 2/22/25 Rachel J. D. Pulsifer of
New Hampshire in N.H.; Rev. Cloyes (2-3/22)
8451. Swart, Cornelius, 89, d 2/19/17 in Red Hook (a long-time resident there)
(surv by ch, gr.ch., and great gr.ch. "to the 4th genreation, more
than 100 in number")(8-3/5)
8452. Swart, Edward, 19, youngest s of late Thomas, d 10/25/31 in Upper Red
Hook (8-11/2)
8453. Swart, Peter (Judge), 77, d 11/5/29 (in Schoharie, the town?) (1-11/6)
8454. Swartout, John of Albia m Widow Catharine Masters of Sand Lake in Troy;
Rev. Howard (9-12/16/28)
8455. Swartwout, Altie, 82, wf of Gen. Jacobus of Fishkill, d 3/20/22 (8-3/27)
8456. Swartwout, Isaac, 62, d 3/10/34 in Fishkill (8-3/19)
8457. Swartwout, James m 7/5/32 Almyre Case; Daniel H. Schultz, Esq. All of
Clinton (Dut. Co.) (8-7/11)
8458. Swartwout, Johannis, 88, of Poughkeepsie d "recently" (8-12/6/03)
8459. Sweatland, Sibyl, wf of Joseph, d 5/27/14 in Cooperstown (3-6/1)
8460. Sweeney, Edward m 8/17/08 Eliza Andrus in Hudson; Rev. Sears (6-8/9)
8461. Sweet, Isabella, 16, ("the only remaining child of Thomas Sweet, Esq.
of Poughkeepsie...") d 11/25/31 in NYC (scarlet fever) (two younger
sisters of Isabella, their names not given, had died"within the past
three months") (8-11/30 and 1-12/2)
8462. Sweet, Jonathan, Esq., 54, d 2/28/28 in Stephentown (consumption)
(9-3/14)
8463. Sweet, Katharine (widow), 78, d 11/19/24 at her home in Stanford (Dut. Co.)
(smallpox) (See also the death of Marie Sweet this date) (8-12/15)
8464. Sweet, Marie, 18, wf of Lewis, d 11/19/24 in the same house where Katharine
Sweet died (which see) on that same day (smallpox) ("Editors of Utica
papers are requested to give this an insertion")(8-12/15)
8465. Sweet, Stephen m 9/14/11 Louisa Northrup, both of Washington (Dut. Co.);
William Thorne, Esq. (8-9/25)
8466. Sweet, Thomas, Esq. of Poughkeepsie m 10/16/22 Margaret Ann Cheeseman of
NYC; Rev. Cuyler (8-10/23)
8467. Sweetland, William, Esq., attorney, m Mrs. Elizabeth De Lord, widow of
late Judge De Lord, in Plattsburgh; Rev. Moses Chase (1-7/4/29)
8468. Swetland, ____, wf of "Mr. Swetland",d 4/6/21 in Plattsburgh (7-4/7)
8469. Swetland, William, Esq., attorney, of Plattsburgh m 11/19/11 Henrietta
Julia Kirtland of Granville in G (7-12/13)
8470. Swift, Charles H. (Dr.) of Peru, NY m Celia Morgan of Burlington (VT?)
in B; "Rev. President Marsh") (4 [Keeseville Herald]-7/19/31)
8471. Swift, Henry m 7/23/07 Rebecca Warner, dau of Thomas of Poughkeepsie; Rev.
Buckley (8-8/5)
8472. Swift, Isaac, a native of England, drowned 7/25/17 when the horse he was
riding (owned by A. S. Pell, Esq.) plunged into the Hudson River
(included in this news item is a lengthy description of the proper
way to swim a horse across a river) (8-8/13)
8473. Swift, James F., U. S. civil engineer, m 1/2/30 Maria Farquhar, dau of
Jephson, in NYC; Rev. George Upfold (1-1/7)

8474. Swift, James Foster, 24, U.S. civil engineer and son of Gen. G. Joseph, d 3/18/30 in Washington, Dist. of Columbia (1-3/24)
8475. Swift, John, 20, s of Capt. John of Hudson, NY, presumably died "last January" when a ship commanded by "Capt. Holbrook" and homeward bound from the "Northwest coast of America" was lost "in the gulph stream" (6-12/7/02)
8476. Swift, John (Brig. Gen.) (a Rev. officer) d 7/12/14 in battle near Fort George (interred "on the American side of the Niagara") (3-7/28)
8477. Swift, Maria, 27, consort of Thomas and dau of Thomas Barlow, Esq., d 5/2/20 in Amenia (consumption) (8-5/31)
8478. Swift, Thomas of Amenia m 10/10/24 Emma L. Grant, dau of James, Esq. of Dover; Rev. C. P. Willson (8-10/13)
8479. Swift, Thomas Delano, 16, s of Gen. J. G., d 9/2/29 in Geneva (1-9/5)
8480. Swords,Francis D., merchant, of Fishkill Plains m 8/17/24 Phebe Myers of Harlem in Newburgh; Rev. Joseph McCarroll (8-8/25)
8481. Sylvester, Peter (Hon.), 73, d 10/21/08 in Kinderhook (6-11/8)
8482. Symonds, Lydia, 25, d 5/11/28 in Rindge, NH (consumption) ("Editors in Vermont, New Hampshire, and Massachusetts are requested to give the above an insertion.") (9-6/13)
8483. Taber, Harvey m 9/29/33 Nancy Blackman, both of Peru, NY, in P; Ahaz Hayes, Esq. (4 [Keeseville Herald]-10/1 and 7-10/5)
8484. Tabor, Joseph m Rachel Austin, both of Beekman; E. Cary, Esq. (8-8/14/04)
8485. Tabor, Thomas, 62, of Dover Plains d 6/13/30 (8-6/16)
8486. Taft, _____, wf of David, d 2/27/23 in Richfield (3-3/24)
8487. Taft, Nathaniel, 47, formerly a merchant in Troy, NY, d "in August last at Pittsburgh" (PA?) (9-10/9/21)
8488. Taggart, Moses, Esq. of Batavia m 7/13/29 Fanny E. Henshaw of Aurora (Erie Co.) in A; Rev. William Wallace Smith (1-8/3)
8489. Talborn, Solomon, 42, d 4/26/13 at the French Mills in Constable (deceased was a Chief and Brig. Gen. of the Iroquois Nation) (7-5/21)
8490. Tallmadge, Ann, 72, (wf of late Col. James and dau of David Sutherland of Stanford) d 7/14/27 in Poughkeepsie (8-7/18)
8491. Tallmadge, Charles, 6, oldest s of Mrs. Ann Tallmadge, d 2/16/31 in Albany ("Friends and relatives of Israel Smith and of his daughter Mrs. Tallmadge are requested to attend his funeral from the home of Israel Smith on North Market Street.") (1-2/17)
8492. Tallmadge, David B., Esq. m 1/28/23 Mary Jenkins, dau of Thomas, all of Hudson, in H; Rev. Reed (8-2/5)
8493. Tallmadge, Edward, 7 mo, s of Col. James, Jr. of Poughkeepsie, d 6/15/13 (8-6/16)
8494. Tallmadge, Franklin Sutherland, 3, youngest s of late George Clinton Tallmadge, d 4/10/34 in NYC (8-4/23)
8495. Tallmadge, Frederick Augustus, Esq. of NYC m 5/22/15 Eliza Canfield, dau of Judson, Esq. of Poughkeepsie; Rev. Reed (8-5/24)
8496. Talimadge, Henry (Capt.) of Varna (Tompkins Co.) m 10/10/31 Mary R. Warring of Marcellus in M; Rev. Rundell (1-10/18)
8497. Tallmadge, James, Jr., Esq. m 1/21/10 Laura Tallmadge of Warren, CT in W; Rev. Peter Starr (8-1/31)
8498. Tallmadge, James (Col.), 77, (a Rev. officer) d 12/21/21 at his mansion house in Poughkeepsie (interred in the Baptist burying ground) (born in Sharon, CT 9/5/1744 and settled early as a farmer in Dutchess Co.) (8-12/26)
8499. Tallmadge, James Edward, 4, s of Gen. Tallmadge, d 6/17/24 in Poughkeepsie (8-6/23)
8500. Tallmadge, Joel, 77, (a Rev. soldier), father of Hon. N. P. of the U.S. Senate, d 1/26/34 in Candor (Tioga Co.) (8-2/12)
8501. Tallmadge, John, Esq., father of "Mrs. Gen. Tallmadge" of Poughkeepsie, d 2/24/23 in Warren, CT (8-3/12)
8502. Tallmadge, John James, 7, s of Hon. James, Jr. of Poughkeepsie, d 1/19/19 in Warren, CT (8-1/27)
8503. Tallmadge, John S., Esq. (brother of "Mrs. Gen. James Tallmadge" and late first judge of Wayne Co.) d 10/17/25 in Lyons (8-10/26)
8504. Tallmadge, Jonathan m 1/26/32 Ester Ann Suby(?); Isaac Sutherland, Esq. All of Stanford (8-2/8)
8505. Tallmadge, Laura, 45, wf of Gen. James, d 2/21/34 in NYC (8-2/26)

8506. Tallmadge, Louisa, 13 mo, dau of Hon. Nathaniel P., d 8/6/30 in Poughkeepsie (8-8/11 and 1-8/13)
8507. Tallmadge, Mary, 41, consort of Hon. Benjamin, Esq., d in Litchfield,
CT (6-6/18/05)
8508. Tallmadge, Matthias B., Esq., state senator from Herkimer, NY,m "lately"
Elizabeth Clinton, dau of his Excellency Gov. Clinton, in Albany; Rev.
Nott (8-11/1 and 3-11/10)
8509. Tallmadge, Matthias B., 45, late U.S. District Judge for the northern
district of NY, d 10/8/19 at his father's home in Poughkeepsie
(pulmonary complaint) (8-10/13 and 9-11/2)
8510. Tallmadge, Nathaniel P., Esq. of Poughkeepsie m 11/27/22 Abby L. Smith,
dau of Isaac, Esq. of Lithgow, in L; Rev. Dr. Reed (8-12/4)
8511. Tallmadge, Sutherland, 1 yr, "fourth and last son" of Gen. James,
d 7/13/24 in Poughkeepsie (8-7/21)
8512. Tallman, Maria, 28, wf of James, d 1/1/29 in NYC (1-1/4)
8513. Tallman, Solomon of Washington (Dut. Co.) m 1/25/29 Jane Ann Newton of
Union Vale; George Hammond, Esq. (8-2/4)
8514. Tallman, Timothy m 12/20/17 Maria Dobbs; Rev. Sommers. All of Troy
(9-12/23)
8515. Talmage, Ann Amanda, wf of William, d 8/21/30 in NYC (1-8/25)
8516. Talmage, Josiah, 53, d 8/23/02 in Schaghticoke (funeral sermon by Rev.
Paige) (buried with Masonic honors) (surv by widow and "a large family
of children") (9-8/25)
8517. Talmage, Josiah m 6/19/03 Ann Dunnings, both of Beekmantown (this is
probably intended for Beekman, Dut. Co.); Rev. Clark (8-6/28)
8518. Talman, Cornelia D., 4, dau of Dr. John, d 4/29/08 in Hudson (6-5/3)
8519. Talman, George Washington, s of Dr. John, d 2/2/15 in Hudson (6-2/7)
8520. Talman, James m 3/17/16 Dorcas Weaver, both of Newport, RI, in Troy, NY;
Rev. D. Butler (9-3/19)
8521. Talman, John T., cashier of the Bank of Monroe in Rochester, m Mary
E. Fitz Hugh, dau of Col. William, in Hampton (Liv. Co.); Rev. Croes(?)
(1-6/2/31)
8522. Tanner, Amos m 4/30/14 Catharine Rynders of Fishkill; Rev. Cuyler (8-5/4)
8523. Tanner, Anna (Widow), 32, d 8/24/25 in Otsego (3-8/29)
8524. Tanner, Cornelius m 3/6/34 Cynthia Velie, both of La Grange; Rev.
Buttolph (8-3/12)
8525. Tanner, Martin H. of Freedom m 1/31/28 Jane Hageman of Poughkeepsie; Rev
C. C. Cuyler (8-2/6)
8526. Tanner, Reuben P., 1 yr, s of Martin H., d 7/11/30 in Poughkeepsie
(8-7/14/30)
8527. Tanner, Thomas (Capt.) (a Rev. officer) d 1/18/18 in Cooperstown (3-1/19)
8528. Tanner, Zeba m 3/17/25 Lucy Chapman in Otsego; Rev. Smith (3-3/21)
8529. Tappen, Caroline, dau of Mrs. Elizabeth, d 10/2/22 in Poughkeepsie
(8-10/9)
8530. Tappen, Elizabeth, 80, widow of late Dr. Peter, d 5/26/29 in Poughkeepsie (8-5/27)
8531. Tappen, John, Esq., "for seventeen years past editor of the Western
Plebeian", d in Kingston (8-4/27/31)
    Tarpenning. See also Teerpenning.
8532. Tarpenning, Jane (Miss), 26, d 12/5/27 in Poughkeepsie (8-12/12)
8533. Tater, Frederick, "upwards of 50", d 3/13/21 in Troy (9-3/20)
8534. Tator, Lewis of Lysander m 8/29/29 Pamelia Chandler of Saratoga Co. in
Weedsport (Cayuga Co.); Rev. Joseph Baker (1-9/15)
8535. Taylor, _____ (Dr.) m Phebe Latting in Hillsdale (6-10/8/01)
8536. Taylor, _____, 15 mo, child of Peter, d in Hudson (6-9/20/08)
8537. Taylor, _____, 3 mo, s of Elisha, d 10/28/15 in Cooperstown (3-11/2)
8538. Taylor, _____ (Mrs.), 72, wf of "Judge Taylor" d 12/19/24 in Charlton
(2-12/21)
8539. Taylor, _____, ventriloquist, comedian, and a stranger, d 2/22/26 in
Cooperstown ("... had recently taken lodgings at the Hotel of Messrs.
White and Kelly") (born in England; surv by "four motherless daughters
in England") interred in the Episcopal burying ground in Cooperstown
(3-2/27)
8540. Taylor, Charles, 6, s of Nathan, drowned 6/21/18 in Peru, NY (7-7/4)
8541. Taylor, David m 12/30/21 Mrs. Mary Lewis, both of Troy (9-1/1/22)

8542. Taylor, Elias M., merchant, of Poughkeepsie m 6/25/23 Mary E. Knapp, dau of Charles, Esq. of Stamford. CT., in S; Rev. Smith (8-7/2)
8543. Taylor, Elizabeth, 26, wf of Charles J., d 10/1/29 (funeral from her husband's home, 39 Maiden Lane, Albany) (1-10/3)
8544. Taylor, Francis W., Esq. of Poughkeepsie m 9/23/19 Sarah L. Beekman, dau of late Richard L. of NYC, in NYC; Rev. Dr. Cooper (8-9/29)
8545. Taylor, Francis W., Esq., 31, s of George of Poughkeepsie, d 10/4/29 in NYC (8-10/7)
8546. Taylor, George (Capt.), 77, d 7/4/31 in NYC (buried in Catskill, his former residence place)(1-7/11)
8547. Taylor, Henry (Lt.) of the U.S. Army m 10/5/18 Lucy Hempsted of Albany in Waterford (7-11/28)
8548. Taylor, James m 6/6/31 Eliza Cosgraves, both of Albany; Rev. Dr. Luckey (1-6/7)
8549. Taylor, James Edwin, 22, oldest s of William, Esq. of Charlton, d 4/10/30 at the home of his uncle, Maj. E. Taylor in Cherry Valley (2-4/16)
8550. Taylor, Jane E. (Miss), dau of William formerly of Pine Plains, d 6/12/31 in Plymouth, MA (8-6/22)
8551. Taylor, John (Col.), 49, professor of languages at Union College, d 11/5/01 in Schenectady (9-11/18 and 6-11/19)
8552. Taylor, John, long-term merchant of NYC, d in NYC (yellow fever) (8-9/20/03)
8553. Taylor, John, 80, father of Hon. John W. of Ballston Spa., d 5/3/29 (probably in Albany) (1-5/7)
8554. Taylor, John, Esq., formerly of NY state, "a clerk in the general post office department", d 6/3/29 in Hagerstown, MD "whither he had gone for his health" (1-6/12)
8555. Taylor, John, Esq., 35, merchant, d 3/6/31 in Canajoharie (1-3/15)
8556. Taylor, John B. d 3/3/27 in Troy (9-3/6)
8557. Taylor, Joseph m 11/29/27 Eliza Byrom Lindley; Rev. Beman. All of Troy (9-11/30)
8558. Taylor, Laura, inf dau of Peter, d in Hudson (6-12/12/20)
8559. Taylor, Mahlon of Troy d 4/26/99 in Troy (funeral sermon by Rev. Roe) (buried with Masonic honors "with brethren in attendance from Lansingburgh, Waterford, and Albany"(9-4/30)
8560. Taylor, Robert Burns, attorney, m 12/18/32 Susan A. Burritt, dau of Josiah, Esq.; Rev. Dr. Reed. All of Poughkeepsie (8-12/19)
8561. Taylor, Sally, 24, wf of Erastus and dau of Thomas Truesdell of Hillsdale (Col. Co.) d 5/17/10 in Seneca (Ont. Co.) (6-6/15)
8562. Taylor, Samuel of Albany m 2/14/14 Amelia J. Beecher of Goshen in Troy; Rev. Howard (9-2/17)
8563. Taylor, Saul m 10/22/15 Rachel McLean in Hudson (6-10/31)
8564. Taylor, William of Fishkill m "lately" Sally Kelly of Poughkeepsie (8-3/11)
8566. Taylor, William m 10/1/32 Mrs. Amanda Deuel in Peru, NY; N. Rice, Esq. (4 [Keeseville Herald]-10/16)
8567. Teal, William A. m 9/5/22 Catharine Cole; Rev. Cuyler (8-9/11)
8568. Teall, Horace (Dr.) of Geneva m Susan Ann Hall, dau of Judge Hall of Wayne (Steuben Co.), in W; Rev. Johnson (1-6/22/30)
8569. Teasor, Francis m 6/15/21 Tamar Eagelsen, both of Troy (9-6/19)
8570. Teel, Elizabeth, late wife of Joseph of Rhinebeck, d 4/6/11 (8-4/17 and 8-5/8)
Teerpenning. See also Tarpenning.
8571. Teerpenning, George W. m 11/24/27 Hester Cay Kendall, both of Deer Park, Orange Co.; Rev. C. C. Elting (8-12/5)
8572. Teft, L. S. (Dr.) m 5/14/23 Hetty M. Carrington (2-5/20)
8573. Tell, Thomas m 6/3/04 Elizabeth Vantine, both of Fishkill, in Poughkeepsie; Rev. Palmer (8-6/5)
8574. Teller?, Charles W. m 6/15/26 Caroline M. Thompson, both of Fishkill; Rev. Thomas (8-6/21)
8575. Teller, Edward m 11/3/34 Rachael Egbert in Matteawan; Rev. R. Van Kleeck. All of Matteawan (8-11/11)
8576. Teller, Henry R., 63, (a Rev. soldier) d 2/28/29 in Sch3nectady (1-3/7)
8577. Teller, Henry S. of Fishkill Landing m 5/15/16 Catharine Storm, dau of Col. John of Hopewell, in H; Rev. De Witt (8-5/22)
8578. Teller, William J., Esq., 40, surrogate of Schenectady Co., d in Schenectady (9-8/1/15)

249

8579. Temple, Elizabeth, 27, consort of William, Jr., d 10/25/16 in Middlefield (3-10/31)
8580. Temple, Joseph (Capt.), 78, d 11/22/25 in Middlefield (3-11/28)
8581. Templer, William, Esq., 55, d 4/3/29 in Princetown (Schenectady Co.) (1-4/4)
8582. Ten Broeck, Anthony A., 21, d in Claverack (he had just completed his medical studies) (6-3/22/14)
8583. Ten Broeck, Christina, 55, wf of Anthony, d 1/2/17 in Claverack (6-1/7 and 6-1/28)
8584. Ten Broeck, Dirck W., 24, s of Samuel I., Esq., d 4/29/17 in Hudson (6-5/13)
8585. Ten Broeck, Hannah (Mrs.), 83, d 7/17/92 at the home of Myndert Van Kleeck where she had lived many years (8-7/19)
8586. Ten Broeck, John V. R., Esq. of Red Hook m 8/1/20 Emeline P. Parker, dau of Rev. D. Parker of NYC, in NYC; Rev. Dr. Romeyn (6-8/15)
8587. Ten Broeck, Peter B., formerly of Claverack, d 5/26/07 in Niagara (7-6/16)
8588. Ten Brouck, ___?___ m 11/7/21 Ann Benner, dau of late Henry, Esq., in Upper Red Hook; Rev. Kittle (8-11/14)
8589. Ten Eyck, Abraham (Col.), about 60, d 3/14/13 in Troy (was one of its early settlers) (9-3/16)
8590. Ten Eyck, Abraham C. d "recently" (funeral at the home of his father, Jacob H. in Whitehall (1-5/21/30)
8591. Ten Eyck, Jacob A. of Schodack m 10/23/13 Sally Van Alstyne of Hudson; Rev. Chester (6-11/9)
8592. Ten Eyck, Jeremiah V. R., Esq., 36, formerly of Albany, d 7/21/29 in Detroit, MI (was formerly a merchant in Detroit but more recently until death he had been register of probate and clerk of Wayne Coounty [MI] court) (1-7/31)
8593. Ten Eyck, Magdelena, dau of Conrad A., d recently (funeral from the home of Conrad's father-in-law, Jacob Ten Eyck in Bethlehem) (1-12/30)
8594. Ten Eyck, Maria, 28, wf of Harman Hoffman Ten Eyck and only dau of William Beekman, Esq., d 12/31/24 in Sharon (3-1/17)
8595. Ten Eyck, Sarah, 52, consort of late Col. Abraham of Kingston, d 5/6/19 in K (9-5/18)
8596. Terbel, Jason d 1/22/14 in Plattsburgh (7-1/22)
8597. Ter Bush, Cornelius, merchant, of Poughkeepsie d 3/22/92 (8-3/29)
8598. Terrill, Thomas (Capt.), 58, d 1/21/05 in Canaan, NY ("Printers of the Connecticut Courant are requested to notice the above death in their paper") (6-2/19)
8599. Terry, George, 35, merchant, of Rochester, NY, formerly of Hartford, CT, d 6/29/30 in NYC "while on a business visit there" (1-7/1)
8600. Tew, John E. of Otsego m Mary Washburn in Norwich, CT (3-3/10/23)
8601. Thacher, Charles, youngest child of late Gen. N. F. Buck, d 2/27/31 in Schenectady (1-3/1)
8602. Thacker, _____ (Rev. Dr.) of Onondaga Hollow m Sarah E. Morrell in NYC (9-12/23/28)
8603. Thacker, John, 21, late of Poughkeepsie, d 8/10/17 in NYC (smallpox) ("a mother is thus bereft of an only son") (8-8/20)
8604. Thane, Ann McKinstry, 19, dau of Dr. Samuel, d 5/19/19 in Greene River Village, Hudson, NY (6-6/1)
8605. Thayer, _____, wf of Edward, d "recently" in Albany (funeral from her husband's home, east side of Washington Square) (1-3/19/31)
8606. Thayer, Amasa, Esq. m 1/29/24 Elvira Howe in Westford; Rev. Tiffany (3-2/2)
8607. Thayer, Amasa, Esq., attorney, of Middlefield m 7/15/24 Waity Smith of Westford in W; Rev. Caldwell (3-7/19)
8608. Thayer, Benjamin, 35, d 9/25/29 in Albany (funeral from his late home, 553 South Market St. (1-9/26)
8609. Thayer, Jonathan, 102, d in Middletown (state not given) (8-12/21/02)
8610. Thayer, Thomas, s of Ezra, d "recently" (funeral from his parents' home, "on the Schenectady turnpike") (1-2/6/29)
8611. Thayer, William m 1/3/18 Abigail Stone in Cooperstown (3-1/5)
8612. Thew, Gilbert, Jr. d 5/27/17 in Peru, NY (7-5/31)
8613. Thew, John m 1/14/21 "Miss Coxe" of Chesterfield in Peru, NY (7-1/20)
8614. Thomas, Alanson of Washington (Dut. Co.) m 8/19/24 Elsey V. Marshall, dau of James of Clinton (Dut. Co.); Rev. Clark (8-8/25)

8615. Thomas, B. W., merchant, of Utica m 7/19/30 Mrs. Ann Willard of Albany;
Rev. Kirk (1-7/20)
8616. Thomas, Calvin, about 30, d 1/12/17 in Middlefield (consumption) (3-1/16)
8617. Thomas, Daniel, 71, of Ballston d 4/22/25 in Milton (2-4/26)
8618. Thomas, Daniel V. (Dr.) m 5/23/25 Eliza Green, both of Richfield, in R;
Rev. Clark (3-5/30)
8619. Thomas, Elizabeth, wf of John of Poughkeepsie, d 10/24/95 (8-10/28)
8620. Thomas, Henry m 6/24/19 Hannah Mayo in Burlington, VT; Rev. S. Clark
(7-7/10)
8621. Thomas, Irish, painter, d 4/8/31 in Worcester, MA (reportedly the oldest
printer living in the U.S. then) (4 [Keeseville Herald]-4/19)
8622. Thomas, Isaiah, Jr., 44, bookseller, d 6/25/19 in Boston, MA (7-7/17)
8623. Thomas, Job m 6/25/07 Penelope Hull, dau of Tiddeman, at the Friends
Meeting House in Hudson (6-6/3))
8624. Thomas, John (Dr.) of Poughkeepsie m 6/14/97 Gitty Fonda at the home of
Col. Barber in Poughkeepsie (8-6/20)
8625. Thomas, John,(Dr.), 60, d 10/21/18 in Poughkeepsie (in the Rev. War
entered the army at age 17 as a surgeon's mate and before age 19 was
promoted to surgeon; settled in Poughkeepsie at the end of the war)
(8-1028)
8626. Thomas, John m 7/8/27 Susan Maxon in Berlin, NY; C. P. Vary, Esq. All of
Berlin (9-7/17)
8627. Thomas, John, "a young man lately from Vernon, Oneida County", d 9/9/29
in Buffalo (1-9/12)
8628. Thomas, John H. m 6/16/22 Sarah G. Russell of Troy; Rev. Griffen (9-6/18)
8629. Thomas, John Hanson, 35, d 5/2/15 in Frederickstown (6-5/23)
8630. Thomas, Leonard, 40, d 2/27/20 in Chazy (7-3/11)
8632. Thomas, Martin, 9, s of Dr. Joseph S., drowned 5/15/30 at Bluff Point,
3 miles south of Plattsburgh (7-5/22)
8633. Thomas, Patty, 19, consort of William, d 2/26/06 in Chatham (6-3/4)
8634. Thomas, Samuel of Cazenovia m 10/4/14 Mary Crosby Benjamin, dau of Cyrus,
Esq., merchant, of Fishkill; Rev. Pine (8-10/19)
8635. Thomas, William, 4, s of Dr. William, d 3/25/32 in Poughkeepsie (8-3/28)
8636. Thomas, William B. (Rev.), rector of Christ's Church in Duanesburgh,
m 11/22/30 Jane P. Livingston, dau of late Judge Henry, in Poughkeepsie;
Rev. Dr. Reed (1-11/27)
8637. Thompson, Alexander, 63, d 1/25/12 in Hillsdale (6-2/3)
8638. Thompson, Asa m 10/1/29 Mary Bartlett of Hillsdale in H; Rev. Burch
(8-10/14)
8639. Thompson, Caleb, an aged farmer of Stanford (Dut. Co.), d 1/12/23 in
Stanford (8-1/22)
8640. Thompson, Ebenezer (Hon.), 65, d in Durham, NH (6-8/31/02)
8641. Thompson, Edward, 24, nephew of John A. Thompson, Esq. of Catskill,
d 2/25/31 in NYC (1-3/1)
8642. Thompson, Edward G. m 7/19/30 Mary Kellogg, dau of J. W., Esq., at
Flatbush, Long Island, NY; Rev. Strong (1-7/22)
8643. Thompson, Edward P. m 11/11/29 Cynthia Thorn, dau of Gilbert, Esq. of
Stanford; Rev. Armstrong (8-11/25)
8644. Thompson, Egbert m 12/14/03 Catherine Dibblee, dau of Ebenezer; Rev. Judd.
All of Dutchess County (6-12/27)
8645. Thompson, Eli C. m 7/28/15 Almira Washburn, both of Poughkeepsie; Rev.
Lewis Leonard (8-8/2)
8646. Thompson, Eneas, "almost 89", father of late Judge Thompson, d 6/16/06 at
his home in Pittstown (was foreman of the first grand jury that sat in
this state "after the commencement of the revolution") (9-6/24)
8647. Thompson, Ezra, Jr., Esq. m 1/5/12 Rebecca Fort, both of Poughkeepsie;
Rev. Cuyler (8-1/8)
8648. Thompson, George m 1/3/13 Susan Grace, both of Troy (9-1/5)
8649. Thompson, Gideon, Sr., 75, m 9/5/04 Miss Anna West, 69, late of Rhode
Island, in Pawling; Rev. Dythick (8-9/18)
8650. Thompson, Gilbert I. m Arietta L. Tompkins, dau of Daniel D., on Staten
Island, NY (7-7/18/18)
8651. Thompson, Henry, merchant, of Troy m 8/23/25 Ruby Clark of Plattsburgh;
Rev. Halsey (7-8/27)

8652. Thompson, Israel (Hon.), Esq., 63, (a Rev. soldier) d 11/25/05 in Pittstown (a former state legislator and a judge in the court of common
pleas) (9-12/3)
8653. Thompson, J. W., Esq., attorney, m Mary Bishop, oldest dau of late Isaac,
in Granville (7-8/10/33)
8654. Thompson, Jacob m 1/1/16 Susanna Wheeler, both of Brunswick; Rev. D.
Butler (9-1/9)
8655. Thompson, James, Esq. of Rhinebeck d 8/21/25 in NYC (8-8/24)
8656. Thompson, James (Hon.) of Saratoga Co. m 10/5/31 Mary Stansbury, dau of
Daniel, Esq. of NYC, in NYC; Rev. Dr. Phillips (1-10/10)
8657. Thompson, John m 3/15/21 Harriet Roberts, dau of Benjamin, in Mooers
(7-3/24)
8658. Thompson, John of Poughkeepsie m 2/8/28 Electa Ferris of New Paltz in N.P.;
Rev. Basset (8-2/13)
8659. Thompson, John m 12/8/30 Content Scoby; Rev. Jewett. All of Poughkeepsie (8-12/22)
8660. Thompson, John, Esq. of Poughkeepsie m 4/23/34 Mary Smith, dau of late
Isaac of Lithgow, in L; Rev. George B. Andrews (8-4/30)
8661. Thompson, John (Capt.) of Stanford (Dut. Co.) m 10/16/34 Ann A. Vanderburgh, dau of G. L. of Beekman, in B; Rev. Barber (8-10/22)
8662. Thompson, John C., one of the assistant justices of the supreme court of
Vermont, d 6/27/31 at his home in Burlington, VT (1-7/6)
8663. Thompson, John L., merchant, of Troy, NY m 8/17/29 Mary Perkins Thompson,
dau of Dr. Isaac of New London, CT, in N. L.: Rev. Judd (1-8/20)
8664. Thompson, Maria, consort of Samuel of Lockport, d in L (1-8/22/29)
8665. Thompson, Morris m 3/2/26 Ann Haskins in Washington (Dut. Co.); Rev.
R. G. Armstrong (8-3/22)
8666. Thompson, Nathan m 7/2/20 Almyra McIntyre, both of Plattsburgh, in P;
Elder John Spaulding of Beekmantown (Clinton Co.) (7-7/8)
8667. Thompson, Nahum m 3/13/25 Betsey Elliot, both of Decatur, in Maryland, NY;
Rev. Pomeroy (3-3/28)
8668. Thompson, Rachael, dau of Ezra, Esq. of Poughkeepsie, d 9/2/22 at the home
of her father (9-9/10)
8669. Thompson, Rhoda, consort of Hon. James, Esq., d 1/17/25 in Milton
(pulmonary complaint) (2-1/25)
8670. Thompson, Sarah Augusta, consort of William, Jr. and sister of Messrs.
J. H. and Walter Cunningham of Poughkeepsie, d 4/3/17 in Goshen
(8-4/9)
8671. Thompson, Thomas, 91, d in CT (has left 15 ch, 77 gr ch, 167 gr-gr ch,
"and 20 in the 5th generation) (8-12/21/02)
8672. Thompson, Thomas, 80, d 10/24/23 in Moreau (2-11/11)
8673. Thompson, Thomas m 8/17/24 Lan ? Franklin in Plattsburgh; Rev. Whelpley
(9-8/21)
8674. Thompson, Thomas L., merchant, of Schenectady m 6/4/32 Helen Elizabeth
Coolidge, dau of late Daniel, Esq., formerly of Poughkeepsie; Rev. Dr.
Perrine (8-6/6)
8675. Thompson, William, Jr. of Goshen m 11/26/08 Augusta Cunningham, dau of
Garwood H. of Poughkeepsie; Rev. Bulkley (8-11/30)
8676. Thompson, William (Rev.), rector of Christs's Church in Rye (West. Co.),
d 8/26/30 in Rye (8-9/1)
8677. Thompson, Thomas d in Catskill (6-6/25/05)
8678. Thorn, Clarissa, wf of Thomas, d 5/3/22 in Plattsburgh (7-5/11)
8679. Thorn, Elizabeth, relict of Dr. Stephen, d 6/22/05 "at an advanced age"
(8-6/25)
8680. Thorn, Gilbert m 1/15/08 Hannah Lewis in Amenia; Rev. Broadhead (8-1/20)
8681. Thorn, Platt d 8/19/25 Betsey Platts in Plattsburgh; Rev. Halsey (7-8/27)
8682. Thorn, Samuel, farmer, of Fishkill d 4/2/20 (8-4/5)
8683. Thorn, Stephen (Dr.), physician and farmer, d in Hackensack (in the town
of Fishkill), NY (8-10/28/95)
8684. Thorn, Stephen (Col.) d 3/20/13 in Granville (a former state senator of NY
and one of the managers of the Union College lottery) (9-3/30 and 7/4/2)
8685. Thorn, Susan (Miss), about 18, d 8/29/32 in Washington (Dut. Co.) (8-9/5)
8686. Thorn, Thomas m 12/31/22 Mary Ann Fordham (7-1/4/23)
8687. Thorn, Van Rensselaer m 6/11/31 Ann Case, both of Pine Plains; Daniel
Sherwood, Esq. (8-6/29)

8688. Thorn, William, 99, d 3/6/92 at the home of Joseph Thorn in Washington (Dut. Co.) ("Printers in Albany and Goshen are requested to print this")
8689. Thorne, Benjamin, 65, d 4/1/19 at his home in Milan (Dut. Co.) (8-4/7)
8690. Thorne, Edwin, 15, only s of William, d 3/5/25 in Pleasant Valley (8-3/9)
8691. Thorne, Frances Abigail, about 2, dau of Gilbert, Esq., d 3/20/23 in Stanford (Dut. Co.) (8-3/26)
8692. Thorne, John of Milan (Dut. Co.) m 9/28/20 Mary Weeks of Oyster Bay (Queens Co.), L.I. at the Friends Meeting house in Matinecock, L.I., NY (8-10/4)
8693. Thorne, Lewis m 5/13/34 Abbey Miller; Elder Luman Birch. All of Stanford (Dut. Co.) (8-5/14)
8694. Thorne, Nicholas, formerly of Poughkeepsie, d 1/5/32 in Skaneateles (8-1/18)
8695. Thornton, Cyrus m 10/20/05 Sally Briggs, both of Hartwick; Elder Bostwick (3-10/24)
8696. Thorp, Frances Mary, 7, oldest dau of Aaron, d 9/25/30 in Albany (1-9/29)
8697. Thorp, John, 53, of Butternuts d 9/29/98 in Butternuts (3-10/4)
8698. Thorp, John m 9/26/04 Mary Skidmon (sic) of Newton, CT in Butternuts, NY; Rev. Kirby (3-10/4)
8699. Thresher, Ebenezer of Providence, RI m 9/13/27 Elizabeth Fenner of Poughkeepsie, NY in NYC; Rev. Fenner (8-9/19)
8700. Throop, Benjamin, Jr., merchant, of Hudson m 3/28/07 Lavinia Smith of Athens in A; Rev. Judd (6-3/31)
8701. Throop, Evelina, 37, consort of Enos T., d 6/29/34 in NYC (buried in Auburn, NY) (8-7/2)
8702. Throop, George B., Esq. of Auburn m Frances M. Hunt, dau of Montgomery Hunt, Esq. of Utica, at Trinity Church in Utica; Rev. Anthon (3-4/17)
8703. Throop, Richard Henry, 6, only child of Benjamin, Jr. formerly of Hudson, d 5/15/14 in Montreal, Canada (6-5/31)
8704. Thurber, Abner G. of Delhi m 11/7/23 Lucy Dunham of Middlefield in M; Rev. John Smith (3-11/10)
8705. Thurber, Caleb B. m 1/1/22 Maria Dennend (3-1/14)
8706. Thurber, Edward E., merchant, of Troy of the firm of Smith and Thurber m 9/8/29 Judith Ann Spoor of Coxsackie in C; Rev. Searles (1-9/12)
8707. Thurber, Henry Albert, 3, s of Capt. Ezra, drowned 5/7/17 in Champlain (wandered off and fell from a wharf near his parents' home) (7-5/17)
8708. Thurber, Horace K. (Dr.) m 10/13/25 Millicent Penfield, both of Harpersfield, in Meredith (Dela. Co.); Rev. Fisher (3-10/17)
8709. Thurber, Ira A. of Utica m 2/28/22 Huldah Clark, dau of Abel of Otsego, in O; Rev. Tiffany (3-3/4)
8710. Thurber, Isaiah, 51, d 3/15/13 in Cooperstown (3-3/20)
8711. Thurber, John, about 48, d "recently" in Champlain (7-1/8/13)
8712. Thurber, Polly (Mrs.), 53, d 1/31/20 in Cooperstown (3-2/7)
8713. Thurston, _____, 51, consort of John M., d 5/27/12 (8-6/3)
8714. Thurston, Abill (Mr.), 21, d 2/26/13 (3-3/6)
8715. Thurston, Edward (Capt.), 79, d 11/24/19 (surv by "numerous offspring") (3-11/29)
8716. Thurston, Edward C., s of late John of Hudson, m 1/15/12 Eliza Van Vreden Burgh, dau of late William of Red Hook; Rev. Prentice (6-1/20)
8717. Thurston, Eliza Elenor, 11 mo, dau of Edward C. of Vermont, d in Hudson, NY (6-2/15/14)
8718. Thurston, Elizabeth (Mrs.) d 8/19/15 at her home in Hudson (6-8/29)
8719. Thurston, Frances Sampson, inf dau of Edward C., d 1/4/20 in Hudson (6-1/11)
8720. Thurston, Ira, 22, d 8/9/13 in Cooperstown (3-8/14)
8721. Thurston, Isaac m 1/31/17 Rebecca Rosecrantz in Fishkill (8-2/5)
8722. Thurston, John, Esq., 68, "one of the first settlers in Hudson", d 1/6/09 at his home near Hudson (6-1/10)
8723. Thurston, Lewis M., 23,[of the firm of Proud and Thurston, merchants of Baltimore (MD?) and son of John, merchant, of NYC] d 2/15/03 in Philadelphia, PA (funeral from the home of John Reynell Coats in Philadelphia) (interred in the Friends Burial Ground) (6-3/8)
8724. Thurston, Maria (Miss), 24, d 8/9/26 in Springfield, NY (3-8/21)
8725. Thurston, Mary Jane, 23, consort of Thomas G. and dau of John Stoddard of Albany, NY, d 2/24/29 in Louisville, KY (1-3/17)

8726. Thurston, Robert I., merchant, of NYC d 7/21/06 (6-7/29)
8727. Thurston, Samuel M. of Clinton m 2/18/13 Hannah Ackerman, dau of Capt. Casparus Ackerman of Coeymans; Rev. Hotchkins (8-2/24)
8728. Thurston, Samuel T. m 1/3/16 Ruth Roe, both of Fishkill; Rev. Crane (8-1/10)
8729. Thurston, Thankful, 63, consort of Edward, d 9/14/13 in Cooperstown (typhus) (3-9/25)
8730. Tibbits, Benjamin of NYC m 4/21/29 Elizabeth Bleecker, dau of John R., Esq. of Albany; Rev. Dr. Ludlow (1-4/23)
8731. Tibbitts, Benjamin, merchant, of Troy d 9/13/02 at Fort Miller (Wash. Co.) (On his return from Canada "caught the fever usually prevalent on the lakes at this season of the year") (9-9/15)
8732. Tice, Isaac, merchant, m 3/21/31 Maria Jacocks, both of Poughkeepsie; Rev. Dr. Cuyler (8-3/30)
8733. Tice, Rensselaer m 12/6/27 Jane Ham, both of Troy; Rev. Howard (9-12/11)
8734. Tice, Tabitha, 39, consort of Capt. Isaac, d 6/10/30 in Poughkeepsie (consumption) (surv by her husband) (8-6/23)
8735. Tichnor, Charles m 8/31/21 Ann Perry of Poughkeepsie; Rev. Smith (8-9/5)
8736. Tidor, John of Milan m 1/16/34 Lydia Caroline Traver of Rhinebeck; Rev. William J. Eyer (8-1/22)
8737. Tiffany, F. T. (Rev.) of Cooperstown m 9/11/22 Hetty Eliza Moore, dau of Maj. Benjamin Moore of Claverack, at Christ's Episcopal Church in Hudson; Rev. Stebbins (3-9/16 and 9-9/17)
8738. Tiffany, Hiram of Prattsburgh m Nancy S. Demming of Phelps in P; Rev. H. P. Strong (1-1/16/30)
8739. Tiffany, Isaiah of Utica m 5/4/26 Mary Metcalf, dau of Judge Metcalf, in Cooperstown; Rev. Tiffany (3-5/8)
8740. Tiffany, John L., 20, d 11/21/30 at the home of Harmanus Bouck, Esq. in Schoharie (consumption) (1-11/24)
8741. Tiffany, William, 25, d 11/28/15 in Cooperstown (3-12/7)
8742. Tilden, Esther, 73, wf of Col. Daniel formerly of Lebanon, CT, d in Warren (Herk. Co.), NY (3-6/11/21)
8743. Tilden, Isaiah m 10/7/21 Mary Williams in Warren (3-10/15)
8744. Tillinghast, Nicholas, merchant, formerly of Troy, d in Northumberland, NY "a few minutes after he had set out ..." (9-9/30/06)
8745. Tillman, Charity (Mrs.), 77, formerly of Albany, d in Sandy Hill (Wash. Co.) (1-3/10/31)
8746. Tillman, Lewis T., Esq. of Troy m Maria C. Radcliff (dau of Hon. Jacob, formerly Judge of the supreme Court of this state and late mayor of NYC) at St. Paul's Church in Troy; Rev. Butler (9-11/13/27)
8747. Tillotson, Edward Howard (midshipman in the U.S. Navy and youngest son of Thomas, Esq. of Rhinebeck) d 1/6/13 in Rome, NY en route home from Sacketts Harbor "which place he left on account of an indisposition" (6-1/19)
8748. Tillotson, Margaret, wf of Thomas, Esq. of Rhinebeck, d 3/19/23 (8-3/26)
8749. Tillotson, Thomas, Esq., 80, d 5/6/32 at his home in Rhinebeck (8-5/9)
8750. Tillson, Elizabeth, 41, consort of Cephas, d 3/11/22 in Butternuts (printers in Conn. are asked to insert this notice) (3-3/25)
8751. Tinckom, William of Fly Creek m 7/21/25 Lydia Smith of Hartwick in H; Elder Bostwick (3-7/25)
8752. Tinkham, Samuel (Dr.) d 9/30/04 in Owego (6-10/23)
8753. Tinkham, Susan (Mrs.), 24, late of Hudson, d 12/14/16 in Wiscasset (state not given) (6-12/31)
8754. Tinslar, B. R. (Dr.) of the U.S. Navy m 4/6/30 Jane Catalina Van Benthuysen, dau of late John, Esq., in Poughkeepsie; Rev. Dr. Reed (8-4/7 and 1-4/9)
8755. Tippet, Daniel m 1/15/22 Laura Picket, both of Ballston, in B; Rev. Reuben Smith (double ceremony - see marr of Levi Sears) (2-1/16/22)
8756. Tipple, David of Hudson m 8/2/09 Elizabeth Mesick of Claverack in C; Rev. Gephard (6-9/5)
8757. Titcomb, William, "a victim of quackery" d in Newburyport (state not given) (A person had recommended a "ground sweat" [to relieve rheumatism] whereby the victim was partially buried in heated earth ...) (9-2/10/01)
8758. Titus, Anstiss, 48, wf of Platt Titus, d 7/22/29 in Troy (1-7/25)
8759. Titus, David of Manchester m 2/11/26 Jane Ann Copeman of Freedom; Rev. Babcock (8-2/15)

8760. Titus, Henry, 89, father of Hon. Peter S., a state assemblyman from NYC, d 4/9/29 in NYC (1-4/11)
8761. Titus, James m 5/4/25 Eliza Nott, both of Ballston, in B; Rev. R. Smith (2-5/10)
8762. Titus, Jeremy of Cooperstown m 11/3/16 Jerusha Temple, dau of Capt. Joseph of Middlefield, in M; Rev. John Smith (3-11/7)
8763. Titus, John, Esq. of Washington (Dut. Co.) m 7/19/06 Elizabeth Vincent of Beekman (Dut. Co.); Ebenezer Haight, Esq. (8-8/5)
8764. Titus, Platt, keeper of the Troy House, d 3/4/33 in Troy (4 [Keeseville Herald]-3/12)
8765. Titus, Richard m 7/24/03 Nancy Parker, both of Clinton; Rev. Dodge (8-8/2)
8766. Tobey, _____, 39, wf of Cornelius, d 8/16/03 in Loonenburgh (Athens, NY) (6-8/23)
8767. Tobey, Charles E., "late a captain in the U.S. Army and aid to the late Gen. Pike, d in NYC (suicide - "threw himself from a fourth story window") (9-8/29/15)
8768. Tobey, Nathaniel, 33, d 12/4/21 in Ballston Spa (funeral from the Episc. Ch.; funeral sermon by Rev. Reuben Smith) (2-12/5)
8769. Tobey, Seth, 69, d 7/20/16 in Hudson (6-7/23)
8770. Tobey, Silas m 1/1/07 Elizabeth Hardick in hudson; Rev. Wigton (6-1/6)
8771. Toby, _____ (Capt.) of the U.S. Infantry m 3/19/13 Mrs. Eliza C. Platt in Plattsburgh (7-3/26)
8772. Toby, Cornelius m 9/5/04 Susan Webb in Hudson (6-9/11)
8773. Toby, Joshua, 41, d 2/22/14 in Hudson (was born in Sandwich, MA but had lived in Hudson nearly 20 years) (funeral sermon by Rev. Chester of the Presbyterian Ch.) (surv by wf and 4 ch.) (served as alderman in Hudson for several yrs) (6-3/1)
8774. Toby, Lucy Ann, 11, oldest dau of late Alderman Toby, d 9/4/14 in Hudson (6-9/6)
8775. Todd, Benjamin, 27, d 8/9/14 in Cooperstown (3-8/11)
8776. Todd, Bethel of Otsego m 5/23/22 Elizabeth Maria Hull of Butternuts in B; Rev. Wheeler (3-5/27)
8777. Todd, Carlton, 33, d 5/8/29 in Fredonia (1-5/15)
8778. Todd, John R., merchant, formerly of Poughkeepsie, m 8/28/97 Clarissa Harlow Chesebrough of Albany; Rev. Johnson (8-8/29)
8779. Todd, John W. m 1/6/20 Martha Manning; Rev. P. S. Wynkoop. All of Clinton (8-1/19)
8780. Todd, Oliver m 10/4/21 Eliza Cornell; Rev. C. C. Cuyler (the bride and groom may have both been residents of Freedom, NY at time of their marr.) (8-10/10)
8781. Todd, Walker m 8/28/11 Sally Ann Smith, both of Poughkeepsie; Rev. Reed (8-9/5)
8782. Todd, William, formerly of NYC, d 4/30/30 in Washington (state not given) (1-5/5)
8783. Toffy, Akin m 11/24/03 Ann Akin, dau of James of Pawling (8-12/6)
8784. Toffy(?), Hulet m 1/28/03 Martha Scofield, both of Pawling; Job Crawford, Esq. (8-3/1)
8785. Toll, Philip R. m Nancy De Graff, both of Schenectady, in S (8-1/15/17)
8786. Tolley, _____, wf of William, Esq., d 6/27/18 in Athens, NY (6-6/30)
8787. Tomlinson, David (Dr.) of Rhinebeck m 2/6/10 Cornelia Adams of Litchfield, CT in Rhinebeck; Rev. Frederick H. Quitman (8-2/21)
8788. Tomlinson, Gideon, Esq. m 11/1/06 Barbary McManus, both of Troy, in Lansingburgh; Rev. Blatchford (9-11/4)
8789. Tompkins, _____ (Judge), father of the vice pres. of the U.S., d 5/22/23 at his home in Westchester County, NY (9-6/10)
8790. Tompkins, Benson of NYC m 5/21/29 Esther Culver of Hyde Park; Rev. Dr. Reed (8-5/27)
8791. Tompkins, Caleb G. of Hyde Park m Harriet Travis of Pleasant Valley; Rev. Perkins (8-12/25/22)
8792. Tompkins, Daniel D. of the U.S. Army m 2/11/22 Mary P. Peirce, dau of William of Troy; Rev. Dr. Coe (9-2/19)
8793. Tompkins, Daniel D., 50, late vice pres. of the U.S. and for many years gov. of NY, d 6/11/25 at his home on Staten Island (funeral service at St. Mark's Church in NYC)(interment in the family vault in Westchester) (3-6/20 and 7-6/25)

8794. Tompkins, Eleazer, Esq., 55, late of Paris (Oneida Co.) d 8/16/24 in Maryland, NY (3-8/23)
8795. Tompkins, Elias m 3/12/29 Susan Velie, dau of Minard B.; Rev. Vandeveer (8-3/25)
*8796. Tompkins, Elijah, brother of the Gov. of NY, d in Greenburgh (West. Co.)
*8797. Tompkins, Frances Adelaide, 19 mo, youngest child of Lt. D. D. Tompkins of Old Point Comfort, VA, d 9/30/29 in Troy, NY (1-10/3)
8798. Tompkins, George of Clinton m 2/5/22 Hannah Ostrom, dau of Daniel, Esq. of Pleasant Valley; Rev. Clark (8-2/13)
8799. Tompkins, Hannah, relict of late Daniel D., d 2/18/29 in NYC (1-2/25)
8800. Tompkins, Jacob S. m 8/12/32 in Hyde Park (8-8/15)
8801. Tompkins, John m 11/25/15 Sally F. Hopkins, both of Poughkeepsie; Rev. Smith (8-12/6)
8802. Tompkins, John m 1/28/19 Sarah Van Keuren, both of Poughkeepsie; Rev. Cuyler (8-2/3)
8803. Tompkins, Jonathan G. (Hon.), 86, father of his excellency Daniel D. Tompkins, vice pres. of U.S., d 5/22/23 in Scarsdale, NY (8-5/28; 3-6/2; and 7-6/7)
8804. Tompkins, Joshua m 1/23/30 Maria Osborn, both of Poughkeepsie; Rev. Dr. Cuyler (8-1/27)
8805. Tompkins, Peter of Freedom m 7/30/22 Mrs. Maria Balding of Poughkeepsie; Rev. Cuyler (8-8/7)
8806. Tompkins, Peter S. of Hyde Park m 11/12/34 Jane Delamater of Hurley; Rev. D. Van Olinda of New Paltz (8-11/19/34)
8807. Tompkins, Sarah, 71, wf of Hon. Jonathan Griffen Tompkins and mother of the gov. of NY, d in Scarsdale (West. Co.) (3-5/12)
8808. Tooker, James H. m 8/25/31 Cornelia A. R. Clark, dau of late Rev. Orin Clark, in Seneca; Rev. John A. Clark (1-9/3)
8809. Toppan, Charles of NYC m 7/17/26 Laura Ann Noxon of Poughkeepsie; Rev. Dr. Reed ((8-7/19)
8810. Topping, George m Prudence Cheney, dau of Abbel Cheney, in Hudson; Rev. Sears (6-1/6/07)
8811. Torrey, _____, 7 weeks old, child of Abner, d 8/20/21 in Plattsburgh. Also, another child of Abner, Cornelia, 2 yrs, d 8/27 in Plattsburgh, the residence place of their father (7-9/1)
8812. Tounsend, Stephen, late of NYC, m 6/29/05 at the Friends Meeting House, Avis Peckham, dau of Samuel of Little Nine Partners, in L. N. P. (8-7/9)
8813. Tourtellot, S. K. of Hammondsport m 11/22/31 Eleanor McClure, dau of Gen. George of Bath, in B; Rev. Platt (1-12/13)
8814. Town, Ira S. of Montpelier, VT m 6/4/34 Frances M. Witherell, dau of Elijah Esq., in Hinesburgh, VT; Rev. Kent (7-6/7)
8815. Towner, James m 12/11/03 Polly Akin, both of Franklin (8-1/10/04)
8816. Towner, John of Franklin m 12/25/03 Jane Haviland of Pawling (8-1/10/04)
8817. Towner, Theron of Goshen, CT m Sophronia Roberts of Owego, NY in O; Rev. May (6-2/20)
8818. Townley, Niel, about 47, d 4/15/29 in Bloomingburgh (Sullivan Co.) (8-4/22)
8819. Townsend, Anna P., 25, wf of Charles W. of Flushing and dau of late Benjamin Prince, d 8/15/29 (1-8/19)
8820. Townsend, Anne Eliza, 28, wf of Rev. M. Townsend and dau of Dr. Oliver Davidson formerly of Plattsburgh, d 4/19/34 in Clarenceville, Lower Canada (consumption) (7-4/26)
8821. Townsend, Elijah, "an aged farmer" d 4/3/24 in Freedom (8-4/7)
8822. Townsend, Elizabeth, 78, widow of Samuel, d 3/6/31 at her late home in North Hempstead, L.I. (1-3/10)
8823. Townsend, Hervey m 4/7/31 Harriet Vail, dau of James, at St. Paul's Church in Troy; Rev. Butler (1-4/11)
8824. Townsend, Isaac, 41, lifelong resident of Southeast, d 9/11/03 (surv by wf and 10 ch) (8-9/27)
8825. Townsend, Jackson of Freedom m 11/29/21 Catharine Velie of Pleasant Valley (8-12/5)
8826. Townsend, John Robison, 26, s of Isaiah, d 6/28/31 in Albany (funeral from the home of his father, corner State and Eagle Sts.) (1-6/29)
8827. Townsend, Samuel m 1/30/03 Sally Longwall, both of Carmel (8-3/1)
* 8796a Tompkins, Elizabeth, 44, wf of Nehemiah, d 8/13/21 in Po'keepsie (surv by husband and several children) (8-8/15)

256

8828. Townsend, Samuel m 1/1/18 Eliza Velie, dau of Minard, Esq., all of Beekman (8-1/7)
8829. Townsend, Sarah, 74, wf of John formerly of Norwich, L.I., NY, d 3/3/34 in Hyde Park, NY (8-3/12)
8830. Townsend, Thomas, 71, of Frederickstown d 3/16/02 (8-3/30)
8831. Townsend, Timothy, 89, m 2/5/27 Miss Mary Olmstead, 69, in Canaan (8-2/28)
8832. Townsend(?), Vincent(?) [name blurred], one of the first settlers in (town blurred) died (date blurred) (7-3/19/25)
8833. Tracy, _____, only son of John, Esq. of Oxford, drowned 12/31/29 (fell through the ice) (1-1/4/30)
8834. Tracy, Albert H., Esq. m Harriet Norton, dau of Ebenezer, Esq., in Buffalo; Rev. Crawford (3-11/21/25)
8835. Tracy, Avery m 1/1/25 Aurelia T. Loomis in Buffalo (3-1/17)
8836. Tracy, Gardiner, editor of the Lansingburgh Gazette, m Catharine Lansing, dau of Cornelius, Esq., in Lansingburgh (6-2/19)
8837. Tracy, Henry S. m 1/7/30 Hannah Luce, both of Albany (1-1/14)
8838. Tracy, Jedediah, merchant, of Troy m 1/30/06 Sally Hubbel of Lansingburgh in L (9-2/11)
8839. Tracy, Jesse m Sally Crandal, both of Troy, in T; Rev. Howard (9-5/9/28)
8840. Tracy, Uriah (Hon.) of the U.S. Senate from Conn. d 7/19/07 (9-7/28)
8841. Tracy, William G., 60, d 4/15/30 in Whitesborough (was an early settler there) (1-4/23)
8842. Tracy, William H. N., 8 mo, s of Lemuel, d 11/6/32 in Keeseville (4 [Keeseville Herald]-11/13)
8843. Traver(?), Garret m 1/3/04 Margaret Cookingham, dau of Michael, all of Clinton (Dut. Co.); Rev. Quitman (8-1/17)
8844. Traver, John m 1/13/20 Ann Traver; Rev. P.S. Wynkoop. All of Clinton (8-1/19)
8845. Traver, John P. of Rhinebeck m 7/3/03 Caty Melhealm of Northeast; Rev. Quitman (8-7/19)
8846. Traver, Myner m 11/1/32 Emeline Frost; Daniel H. Schultz, Esq. All of Clinton (8-11/14)
8847. Traver, Robert m 6/22/22 Elizabeth Barnes, both of Clinton; Rev. Quitman (8-6/26)
8848. Traver, William of Rhinebeck m 3/29/28 Hannah Eighmy of Milan; Rev. Wm. J. Eyer (8-4/2)
8849. Traver, William of Hyde Park m 11/17/29 Mary Budd, dau of James of Pleasant Valley; Rev. William Cahoone (8-11/25)
8850. Travers, Henry m 11/9/15 Catharine Van Valkenberg; Rev. G. T. Bedell (6-11/21)
8851. Traverse, Gabriel of Waterford m 9/19/27 Susan D. Winne of Brunswick; Rev. Beman (9-9/21)
8852. Travis, James m 11/13/34 Jane Floutenburgh; Rev. Buttolph. All of La Grange (8-12/3)
8853. Travis, Martin D. m 11/22/34 Anna Mosher, dau of Amos; Henry Tallmadge, Esq. All of Stanford (Dut. Co.) (8-11/26)
8854. Treadway, Alfred (Dr.) of Dover m 10/10/07 Catharine Hart of Washington (Dut. Co.); Ebenezer Haight, Esq. (8-10/21)
8855. Treadwell, Amanda Fuller, 21, wf of J. Treadwell of Cooperstown, d 6/15/15 (my notes not clear: possibly his name is J. Treadwell Fuller) (3-6/22)
8856. Treat, Joseph, Esq., 63(?), d 11/12/27 in East Hartford (state not given) (9-12/7)
8857. Treat, Rachel, 2nd dau of Richard, Esq. of Albany, d 8/11/19 at the home of Hon. W. W. Van Ness in Claverack (buried in Albany) (6-8/17)
8858. Tredwell, Betsey (Miss), about 52, dau of Hon. Thomas, d 6/19/22 at Bay St. Amaugh (Clinton Co.) (7-6/22)
8859. Tredwell, Thomas (Hon.), 88, (a Rev. patriot) d 12/30/31 at his home in Beekmantown (he was the last survivor of the convention which framed the Constitution of NY in 1777) (graduated from Princetown [sic] College; lived in Suffolk Co., NY at outbreak of Rev.; fled with his family to Conn.; British took over his farm; moved to Beekman, NY area in 1792; state senator from there) (7-1/14)
8860. Tremain, Augustus Porter of Ancram m 11/11/30 Amanda Collin, dau of David, Esq. of Hillsdale, in H; Rev. Woodbridge (1-11/17)
8861. Trenor, James, about 45, for many years a clerk in the office of the Secretary of State, d 10/18/31 in Albany (1-10/19 and 1-10/20)

8862. Trimble, John H., 34, s of Richard of Newburgh, d 5/22/29 ("lost in a gale of wind at sea" from the packet ship "Birmingham" 1-6/12)
8863. Tripp, _____ (Lt.) of the U.S. Navy, commander of the brig "Vixen", died at sea ("had signalized himself in the Tripolitan war") (3-9/1/10)(see 8869.)
8864. Tripp, George of Washington (Dut. Co.) m 6/26/13 Emma Haviland of Pawling; Rev. Foss (8-7/7)
8865. Tripp, Isaac of Washington (Dut. Co.) m 11/16/25 Amanda Arnold, dau of David, Esq.; Rev. J. Fosse (8-11/30)
8866. Tripp, Job (Dr.), 74, d 9/16/23 in Berlin, NY (thrown from a wagon and fatally injured) (9-9/23)
8867. Tripp, Lot (Dr.), 53, member of the Society of Friends, d in NYC (administered medical aid "principally to the poor and friendless") (6-3/5)
8868. Tripp, Susan, 7, of Dutchess County d 5/13/31 in NYC (very large - weighed 227 lbs. several months prior to her death (8-5/18 and 1-5/22)
8869. Trippe, _____ (Lt.) of the U.S. Navy died "at sea on his passage from the Havanna to New Orleans" (was in command of the brig "Vixen" at the time of his death (9-8/28/10). See also 8863.
8870. Trively(?), Oliver m 5/11/30 Caroline Leighton in Poughkeepsie; Rev. Welton (8-5/19)
8871. Trivett, Elias (Dr.) m 11/16/11 Lucy Slater, both of Poughkeepsie; Rev. Reed (8-11/20)
8872. Trivett, James, 52, formerly of Poughkeepsie, d 7/25/21 in NYC (8-8/1)
8873. Trobridge, Charles m 12/29/27 Betsy Ann Vanvolkingburgh, both of Troy; Rev. Howard (9-1/1/28)
8874. Tronson, Robert Gilbert Livingston, merchant, m 2/11/17 Eliza Davis, youngest dau of Isaac, all of Rhinebeck Flatts, in R. F.; Rev. McMurray (8-2/19)
8875. Trotter, _____ (Gen.) (a Rev. officer) d "recently" in Albany (funeral from the St. Andrew Society)(after the Rev. War he engaged in the mercantile trade in Albany and subsequently captained a sloop sailing between Albany and NYC)(1-12/13)
8876. Trotter, Sarah Ten Eyck, 40, wf of John and dau of late Dr. Elias Willard, d 10/22/30 in Albany (consumption) (funeral from the home of her husband, 224 North Market St.) (1-10/23)
8877. Trowbridge, Alexander m 1/24/26 Sally Clark, dau of Douglas, Esq. of Northeast; Rev. C. P. Wilson of Amenia (8-2/1)
8878. Trowbridge, Augustus m 4/8/13 Lucy Birce, dau of Austin Birce, in Claverack; Rev. Chester (6-4/13)
8879. Trowbridge, James of Plattsburgh m Cornelia Rogers of Vergennes, VT in V (7-11/5/14)
8880. Trowbridge, John m 9/18/04 Nancy Folger in Hudson; Rev. Sears (6-9/25)
8881. Trowbridge, John, formerly of Hudson, NY, d in Savannah (state not given) (6-10/7/17)
8882. Truax, Major (Major his given name) m 9/4/25 Julia Ann Penny, both of Schenectady, in Ballston Spa; Rev. Babcock (2-9/6)
8883. Truesdell, _____, child of Capt. P. Truesdell, d in Troy (9-2/13/16)
8884. Truesdell, Ichabod, 77, d 5/25/10 in Plattsburgh (fought in both the French and the Rev. Wars) (7 [American Monitor]-6/2)
8885. Truman, Alexander m 5/12/31 Hannah Maria Low, both of Poughkeepsie; Rev. Dr. Cuyler (8-5/18)
8886. Truxton, Thomas (Commodore), 67, d 5/5/22 in Philadelphia (state not given) (8-5/22)
8887. Tryon, John, Esq., 50, d 9/13/07 in New Lebanon (6-9/29)
8888. Tubbs, Erastus of Cummington, MA m 2/19/29 Ann E. Smith of Bethlehem, NY; Rev. Kissam (1-2/25)
8889. Tubbs, Hannah of Cooperstown, dau of Samuel, Esq., d 8/29/00 (consumption) (3-9/4)
8890. Tucker, Catharine, wf of Richard J., d in NYC (9-1/2/27)
8891. Tucker, Luther, editor of the Rochester (NY) Republican, m Mary Sparhawk, dau of E., Esq., in Rochester, VT (7-10/26/33)
8892. Tucker, Lyman H. of Greenwich m 4/24/31 Puella Tice of Northumberland in N; Rev. Robert Washburn (1-4/28)
8893. Tucker, Mark (Rev.) of Stillwater m 2/18/18 Harriet Lord of Troy; Rev. Dr. Coe (9-2/24)
8894. Tull, William m 10/7/21 Minerva Carter, both of Greenwich; Rev. Lewis (9-10/23)

8895. Tullar, Martin (Rev.), pastor of the Congregational Church in Royalton, VT, d 10/1/13 in R (9-10/12)
8896. Tullidge, _____ (Mrs.), 46, wf of Benjamin of Albany, d 8/16/31 (surv by husband and children) (1-8/22)
8897. Tundy, Daniel of Ancram m 1/30/32 Mary Mitchell of Washington (Dut. Co.); Isaac Sutherland, Esq. (8-2/8)
8898. Tunicliff, Cornelius C., 36, d in Richfield (3-10/11/24)
8899. Tunnicliff, George of Warren m 9/11/21 Harriet Cary of Springfield, dau of late Col. Cary; Rev. Daniel Nash (double ceremony - see marr of Leonard Lewis) (3-9/17)
8900. Turbush, Henry m 5/15/22 Eliza Tillman, both of Poughkeepsie; Rev. C. C. Cuyler (8-5/22)
8901. Turnbull, Andrew E. m 7/9/34 Hannah Turner in NYC; Rev. C. G. Sommers (8-7/16)
8902. Turner, Charles Henry m 10/13/27 Elizabeth M. Winne, both of Troy; Rev. Martindale (9-10/19)
8903. Turner, Christiana, widow of John, merchant, d 6/2/01 in NYC (6-6/11)
8904. Turner, Coonrad m 10/23/20 Phoebe Ketch; Rev. Leonard (8-10/25)
8905. Turner, Cornelius W., manufacturer, of the firm of Turner and Burtch of Pine Plains m 10/11/34 Eliza Ann Young, dau of Daniel of Stanford; Henry Tallmadge, Esq. (8-10/15)
8906. Turner, Edward, A. M., professor of mathematics and natural philosophy in Middlebury Col., m Sophrona Storrs, dau of Col. Seth, in Middlebury, VT (1-9/14/29)
8907. Turner, Elias of Lansingburgh m 12/30/26 Betsey Wood of Cambridge; Rev. Howard (9-1/5/27)
8908. Turner, Elisha R. m 4/20/28 Juliann Hydorn, both of Troy; Rev. Willis (9-4/25)
8909. Turner, Francis of France m 8/12/30 Maria C. Wooster, dau of late Col. T. Wooster, all of NYC, in Poughkeepsie; Rev. Dr. Reed (8-8/18 and 1-8/21)
8910. Turner, James m 4/16/18 Sarah Case, both of Milan (8-4/29)
8911. Turner, John m 1/17/30 Helena Martin, dau of Abraham; Rev. Marvin. All of Troy (1-1/19)
8912. Turner, John E. m 9/16/34 Sarah M. Stoutenburgh in Hyde Park; Rev. Van Vranken (8-9/24)
8913. Turner, Jonathan m Mercy Smith, both of Plattsburgh, in P; Rev. Halsey (7-10/20)
8914. Turner, Peter, surgeon's mate in the Regiment of Flying Artillery, d 11/5/12 "at this post" (probably the one at Plattsburgh) (7-11/13)
8915. Turner, William m 5/8/08 Clarissa Parsons, both of Poughkeepsie; Rev. Buckley (8-5/11)
8916. Tuthill, Daniel H., Esq., late surrogate of Orange Co., d in St. Augustine, East Florida "where he had gone for ... his health" (1-12/24/31)
8917. Tuthill Greene M., Esq., clerk of Tioga Co., m 10/4/31 Elsie Decker of Newburgh in N; Rev. Joseph McCarroll (1-10/19)
8918. Tuthill, Horace of Goshen m 10/8/29 Mary Duzenberre of Wallkill, dau of Maj. Stephen, in Newburgh; Rev. McJimpsey (1-10/19)
8919. Tuttle, _____ (Col.) "of the regular army" d "lately" at Fort George (9-8/17/13)
8920. Tuttle, Abby, dau of Merrit and Sally of Duanesburg, d 11/8/31 in Albany (funeral from the home of John Wilson, 150 Washington St.) (1-11/9)
8921. Tuttle, Gershom, about 25, formerly a proprietor of the Gospel Advocate, d 2/23/29 in Westmoreland (1-3/8)
8922. Tuttle, Nathaniel m 6/27/19 Anna Guy, both of Westford, in W; Elder Benjamin Sawin (3-7/5)
8923. Twining, Alexander C. of New Haven, CT m 3/9/29 Harriet A. Kinsley of West Point, NY in W.P.; Rev. Sutherland Douglass of Rochester (1-3/10)
8924. Twiss, Benjamin of Montreal m 8/18/24 Almira Dewey of Champlain in C (7-8/21)
8925. Tyler, Harvey H. m 4/26/20 Perses Mills in Westford; Rev. George Colton. All of Westford (3-5/1)
8926. Tyler, Isaac Hughes, Esq. d 11/25/29 in Baton Rouge, LA (yellow fever) (had been married for only three days to Elizabeth Gurley, dau of Hon. H. H. Gurley of Baton Rouge)(1-12/5)

259

8927. Tyler, Moses m 4/16/22 Abigail Lent, both of Troy; Rev. Coe (9-4/30)
(9-4/30)
8928. Tyler, Orrin, merchant, of Onondaga, NY m Nancy Bliss, dau of Isaac, in
Hartford (CT?); Rev. Hawes (1-5/21/29)
8929. Tyler, Royal, Esq. (Hon.), 66, d 8/16/26 in Brattleboro, VT (born in
Boston, MA; shortly after the Rev, War he moved to Vermont where he
served as Chief Justice of the Supreme Court) ((surv by wf and "a numerous
family of children") (7-9/9)
8930. Tyler, William Augustus m 1/19/06 Mary Knowles, both of Troy; Rev. Coe?
(9-1/21)
8931. Tysen, George W. of the firm of Tysen andPhelps m 6/1/31 Caristiana A.
Jackson, dau of Alexander C., Esq., in NYC; Rev. Dr. Matthews. All
of NYC (1-6/4)
8932. Ufford, Sarah (widow), 74, d 11/28/26 in Fairfax, VT (7-12/23)
8933. Uhl, Eleanor, 29, wf of H_? , d 3/10/34 in Hyde Park (8-3/26)
8934. Uhl, Frederick m Jane Ann Hutchins, both of Poughkeepsie; Rev. William
Cahoon (8-1/6/30)
8935. Uhl, John m 11/12/14 Mary Bartley, both of Clinton (Dut. Co.); Rev.
Leonard (8-11/16)
8936. Uhle, John, 40, d 4/25/08 in Staatsburgh (8-4/27)
8937. Ule, Henry m 9/2/24 Anna Maria Ruger; Rev. Clark. All of Pleasant Valley
(8-9/8)
8939. Ulshoeffer, Jacob, 35, d 1/24/31 in NYC (1-1/27)
8940. Ulshoeffer, Michael, Esq. m Mary Ann Gracie, dau of late Archibald, in NYC
(3-1/20/23)
8941. Umphry, Henry m 8/5/27 Tanner Welch, both of Beekman; Stoddard Judd, Esq.
(8-8/15)
8942. Underhill, Abraham m 3/3/08 Mary Raymer, both of Troy; Rev. Coe (9-3/8)
8943. Underwood, _____ (widow) d 9/12/05 (9-9/17)
8944. Upham, Susan Abigal, 4, d 8/29/17 in Troy. Also, Ruth Marinda Upham,
19 mo, d 9/1/17 in Troy (their parents not named) (9-9/9)
8945. Upton, George (Dr.) m 8/27/34 Eliza Vermilya, both of La Grange, in
Washington Hollow; James Humeston, Esq. (8-9/17)
8946. Upton, Henry H. m 12/16/30 Area(?) Ann Haight in Stanford (Dut. Co.);
Elisha Welling, Esq. All of Stanford (8-12/22)
8947. Upton, Paul, Jr. m 1/25/04 Anna Carman, dau of Lott, all of Stanford (Dut.
Co.) at Creek Meeting House of Friends in Nine Partners (Dut. Co.)
(6-2/7)
8948. Upton, Robert m 4/30/28 Mary Valentine, both of Troy; Rev. Houghtaling
(9-5/9)
8949. Urst, Mosher of Newburgh m 1/9/23 Mary Hughes of Fishkill; Theodorus
Anuin (could this be intended for Annin?), Esq. (8-1/15)
8950. Utley, Ralph (Capt.) m Sally Huntington, both of Hudson, in H (6-2/10/12)
8951. Vail, Aaron m 1/24/28 Demaris Underwood at the Friends Meeting House in
Stanford (Dut. Co.). All of S (8-1/30)
8952. Vail, Abraham m 6/18/25 Mrs. Mary Hasbrook, both of Fishkill; Rev. Dr.
Reed (8-6/22)
8953. Vail, B. C., merchant, of Troy m 12/7/30 Eliza Ann Archer of NYC in NYC;
Rev. Snodgrass (1-12/30)
8954. Vail, Eliza, consort of Henry, d 2/5/15 in Troy (9-2/7)
8955. Vail, George, merchant, of Troy m 10/7/13 Jane Thomas, dau of Gen. David
of Salem, in Salem (Wash. D.C.); Rev. Dr. Proudfit (9-10/12 and 7-10/19)
8956. Vail, Henry of Stanford (Dut. Co.) m 10/23/32 Jane Ann Thorne of NYC in
NYC; Walter Bowne, Esq. (8-10/31)
8957. Vail, Ira (Dr.) m 1/28/19 Pamela Flagler, dau of Solomon; Rev. Clark.
All of Clinton (8-2/3)
8958. Vail, Isaac (Col.), 61, d 8/7/08 in Fishkill (members of "St. Simon's
and St. Jude's Lodge" attended the funeral) (8-8/17)
8959. Vail, Isaac m 1/15/18 Eliza Hughson, both of Fishkill (8-1/21)
8960. Vail, Isaac, a farmer of Freedom,d 3/29/22 at his home in Freedom. Rebecca
Vail, his widow, d 4/21 (8-4/24)
8961. Vail, Michael of Clinton m 3/16/11 Polly Germond of Washington (Dut. Co.)
(8-3/20)
8962. Vail, Moses d 6/20/17 at his home in Beekman (8-6/25)
8963. Vail, Reed, 46, d 5/18/27 in Staatsburgh (8-6/6)

8964. Vail, Reynolds m 2/11/23 Susan C. Bennet; John Klapp, Esq. All of Freedom (8-3/12)
8965. Vail, Thomas d 3/31/13 at his home in Beekman (8-4/7)
8966. Vail, Thomas (Lt.), 30, d 9/9/15 in Troy (9-9/12)
8967. Vail, Townsend M., merchant m 5/31/31 Martha Maria Card, dau of Joseph, Esq.; Rev. Tucker. All of Troy (1-6/3)
8968. Vail, William m 10/5/25 Lavina Wiley, dau of Jacob; Rev. Clark. All of Pleasant Valley (8-10/12)
8969. Vale(?), Rebekah (Mrs.), 27, d 2/6/26 in Poughkeepsie ("a tender mother, a faithful wife, and an affectionate sister") (8-2/15)   (8-8/2)
8970. Valentine, Adelaide, 9 mo, dau of Isaac, merchant, of Poughkeepsie, d 7/27/20/
8971. Valentine, Adelaide Eliza, 2, dau of late Isaac, d 3/20/23 (in Poughkeepsie?) (8-3/26)
8972. Valentine, Elias, 28, engraver and copper plate printer, d 5/1/23 in NYC (8-5/14)
8973. Valentine, Jacob m Lydia ? ne in Charlton; Rev. Sweetman (2-8/26/23)
8974. Valentine, James, 80, d 5/24/07 in Poughkeepsie (8-5/27)
8975. Valentine, John m 9/6/27 Catharine Wing, both of Hyde Park; Rev. Clark (8-9/12)
8976. Valentine, Matthew, 29, late of Poughkeepsie, d 8/24/21 in Fishkill (8-8/29)
8977. Van Aernam, Jacob m 6/25/31 Isabella Scrafford, oldest dau of Adam, in Guilderland; Rev. Crounse (1-6/29)
8978. Van Alen, Evert of Greenbush m 8/9/01 Deriah Knickerbacker, dau of John, Jr., Esq. of Schaghticoke; Rev. Page (9-8/11)
8979. Van Alen. James L. m 8/16/04 Lidia Wyncoop, widow of late John C., Esq. and dau of Judge Sylvester, d 8/16/04 in Kinderhook; Rev. Sickles (6-8/28)
8980. Van Alen, John E., Esq., recently a Congressman, d 2/28/07 in Greenbush (9-3/3)
8981. Van Alen, John I. m Maria Vosburgh in Kinderhook; Rev. Livingston (6-4/13/12)
8982. Van Alen, Lucas I. of Bruyn-Right (sic) m 1/16/15 Elizabeth Van Derpoel of Chatham in Kinderhook; Rev. Sickles (6-2/14)
8983. Van Alen, Peter L. (Capt.) of Kinderhook drowned 9/9/06 when his wagon was upset as he attempted to ford the creek called Major Abraham's Kill ("He has left a very large family") (6-9/16)
8984. Van Allen, Lawrence, 82, d 9/29/09 in Kinderhook (6-10/10)
8985. Van Allen, Peter, 72, d at his home in Red Hook (one of the early settlers in that region (8-1/2/22)
8986. Van Alstyne, Abraham of Kinderhook d "recently" in Greenbush (a wagon ran over him (6-7/22/06)
8987. Van Alstyne, John I. of Schodack m Polly Ashley of Hudson in H (6-1/18/11)
8988. Van Alstyne, Lawrence, 39, d 5/7/06 in Amenia (surv by wife and 3 ch) (8-5/13)
8989. Van Alstyne, Martin, merchant, m 2/11/29 Rebecca Dyre; Rev. Kirk. All of Albany (1-2/13)
8990. Van Alstyne, Samuel of Amenia m 12/9/20 Penelope Wyatt of Stanford; Noah Ingersol, Esq. (8-12/20)
8991. Vanamay, James S., about 28, formerly of Pittstown, d 3/23/28 in Carroll (Chaut. Co.) (surv by wf and small children) (("his relatives" resided at time of his death in Pittstown) (9-4/8)
8992. Van Anden, Abram, 57, d 10/8/30 in Poughkeepsie (8-10/13)
8993. Van Anden, James m 3/3/27 Jane Flagler in Poughkeepsie; Rev. Welton (8-3/7)
8994. Van Antwerp, Ahasuerus (sic) m 7/5/21 Hannah Potter; Rev. McCabe. All of Milton (8-7/8)
8995. Van Antwerp, Isaac Ver Plank, Esq. m 7/27/30 Jane Maria Yates, dau of John, Esq.; Rev. Dr. Lacy. All of Albany (1-7/29)
8996. Van Antwerp, Lewis, 57, d 12/11/28 in Schaghticoke (9-12/19)
8997. Van Antwerp, William, 30, son of Daniel L., Esq., d 4/22/29 in Albany (funeral from his late home on Washington St. near the western hay scales) (1-4/24)
8998. Van Benschoten, Caroline, 74, widow of late col. Elias, d 6/6/25 (3-6/13)
8999. Van Benschouten, Peter, farmer, of Fishkill d 4/25/05 ("Lung indisposition") (8-4/30)

9000. Van Benschouten, Tunis of Poughkeepsie d 6/12/27 (8-6/20)
9001. Van Benthuysen, Anna, 71, relict of late Abram, d 8/29/34 in Red Hook (8-9/3)
9002. Van Benthuysen, John, Esq., 52, clerk of Dutchess County, d 10/6/19 in Poughkeepsie (8-10/13 and 9-11/2)
9003. Van Bergen, Anthony of Coxsackie, NY m 4/19/06 Clarine Peck of Lyme, CT in Troy, NY; Rev. Jonas Coe (9-4/22)
9004. Van Bergen, Hannah, 41, wf of Peter, d in Hudson (6-10/15/01)
9005. Van Bergen, Peter A., Esq., a senatorof the middle district and one of the judges of Greene Co., d in Greene County (3-9/20)
9006. Van Brackle, James, 9 mo, s of James, d 7/27/19 in Troy (9-8/3)
9007. Van Bramer, Peter, 35, d 11/13/19 in Hudson (was employed at the factory of Robert Jenkins & Co. in Columbiaville) (fell overboard and was crushed between two boats at the Hudson dock) (surv by wf and 9 ch) (6-11/16)
9008. Van Bunschooten, Matthew, Esq., 83, d 1/23/25 at his home in Fishkill (8-1/26)
9009. Van Bunschoten, Ann (Mrs.), 92, of Fishkill d "recently" (8-12/6)
9010. Van Bunschoten, Elias E. m 7/12/98 Polly Dubois of NYC in Poughkeepsie; Rev. Brower (8-7/17)
9011. Van Bunschoten, Jacob, 79, d 5/5/30 at his home in Fishkill (8-5/9 and 1-5/21)
9012. Van Bunschoten, John E., son of Col. Van Bunschoten of Poughkeepsie, m 1/21/96 Rachel Sackett of Horse Neck (West. Co.) (1/27)
9013. Van Bunschoten, Richard m 12/21/26 Catharine Taylor, both of Freedom; Rev. Clark (8-12/27)
9014. Van Buren, Abraham A., Esq. m 5/8/16 Catharine Hogeboom, dau of John C. of Claverack, at the home of the latter; Rev. Sickels (6-5/14)
9015. Van Buren, Hannah, 35, wf of Hon. Martin, d 2/5/19 in Albany (3-2/15)
9016. Van Buskirk, Charles Andrew m 4/6/30 Eliza Parker, oldest dau of late Capt. B. Parker, in NYC; Rev. Spencer Cone(?) (1-4/12)
9016a. Van Buskirk, John M., about 42, d in Plattsburgh (7-10/12/22)
9017. Van Buskirk, Lawrence m 2/5/10 Maria Provost in Athens; Rev. Prentice (6-2/8)
9018. Van Buskirk, Morris S. of Lansingburgh m 9/22/31 Catharine Knickerbacker, dau of Hon. Heman of Schaghticoke, in S; Rev. A. A. Marcelus (1-9/23 and 1-10/12)
9019. Van, C---e (surname blurred), Abraham m 5/17/26 Sally Converse in Plattsburgh (7-5/20)
9020. Van Cleve, E. J., editor of the Lansingburgh Gazette, m 4/6/30 Orpha Ives, dau of Chauncy, Esq. in Lansingburgh; Rev. Whipple. All of Lansingburgh; Rev. Whipple.   (1-4/24)
9021. Van Courtlandt, Philip (Gen.), 82, ("a Revolutionary hero"), d 11/5/31 "at his seat om the North River" (was elected Congressman from NY in 1793 and retired in 1809) (1-11/11)
9022. Vandenbergh, Garrett, 86, d 4/25/28 in Schodack (9-4/29)
9023. Vandenbergh, Mary, 10 mo, dau of John, d 12/18/31 in Albany (1-12/20)
9024. Vandenbergh, Wilhelmus m Susan Colegrove, dau of late Andrew, Esq., in Worcester; Elder Beaman (3-4/21/23)
9025. Van Denburgh, Garret, 59, d 12/9/27 in Troy (9-12/14)
9026. Vandenburgh, Gilbert m 9/15/31 Sarah Maria Thayer; Rev. Meyer. All of Albany (1-9/17)
9027. Van Denburgh, Henry m 8/28/06 Cynthia Dakin, dau of Paul; Rev. Wigton. All of Hudson (6-9/2)
9028. Vandenburgh, James, 58, d 3/8/28 in Troy (9-3/11)
9029. Vandenburgh, Matthias, 76, d 11/9/27 at his home in Greenbush (9-11/13)
9030. Vandenburgh, Rhoda (Miss), about 23, d 5/22/29 in Beekman (consumption) (8-5/27)
9031. Vanderbilt, Ares, 72, of Fishkill d 3/5/08 (8-3/9)
9032. Vanderbilt, Joseph m Sally Olcott; Rev. Wigton. All of Hudson (6-6/16)
9033. Vanderbilt, Mary, widow of Aves, d 2/4/27 in Freedom (8-2/21)
9034. Vanderbilt, Mary, 71, widow of late John, Esq., d 8/31/30 in Flatbush, L.I., NY (1-9/7)
9035. Vanderbilt, Peter m 9/22/02 Mary Everitt, both of Fishkill; Rev. Van Vranken (8-10/12)

9036. Vanderbilt, Sally, 19, wf of Joseph, d 4/5/08 in Hudson (6-4/12)
9037. Van Derbilt, Sarah, 49, consort of Aaron, d 12/16/31 in NYC (1-12/22)
9038. Vanderburgh, _____ (Mrs.), wf of John of Poughkeepsie, d "at a very
       advanced age" (8-7/13/96)
9039. Vanderburgh, _____, wf of Henry, Esq., d "lately" in Clinton (8-12/13/20)
9040. Vanderburgh, Henry, Esq. of Poughkeepsie d "last week" (formerly a judge
       of the Dutchess County Court of Common Pleas) (8-4/5/92)
9041. Vanderburgh, Henry, Esq. m 3/27/23 Mrs. Abigail Seaman in Pleasant
       Valley; Rev. Clark (8-4/2)
9042. Vanderburgh, Henry m 11/27/28 Sarah Miller, both of Manchester; Rev. Dr.
       Cuyler (8-12/3/28)
9043. Vanderburgh, James of Beekmantown (Beekman, Dut. Co.) d 4/4/94 (funeral
       sermon by George H. Speirin(?), "a Masonic Brother"; C. D. Colden
       delivered a eulogy) (members of several Masonic lodges in Dutchess
       Co. attended this funeral service) (8-4/9)
9044. Van Derburgh, Jasper m 4/23/07 Jennett Leavenworth; Rev. Sears. All of
       Hudson (6-4/28)
9045. Vanderburgh, John of Poughkeepsie d "at an advanced age" (8-3/11/00)
9046. Vanderburgh, John m 12/29/05 Sally Leroy, both of Poughkeepsie; Rev.
       Clark (8-1/7/06)
9047. Vanderburgh, Richard, printer, formerly of Poughkeepsie, d 6/23/06 near
       St. Anthony's Church in Montgomery (Orange Co.) (8-7/8)
9048. Vanderburgh, Richard m 9/24/14 Maria Stanton, both of Poughkeepsie; Rev.
       Covel (8-10/5)
9049. Vanderburgh, Richard H. m 9/3/30 Maria Davis, dau of Charles; Rev. Jewett
       8-10/13)
9050. Vanderburgh, William, s of late Col. James, d 4/30/00 in Beekman (surv
       by wf and 1 ch) (buried with Masonic honors) (8-5/6)
9051. Van Dercook, Gilbert m 6/29/20 Ruth Perry, both of Pittstown; Rev. Dr.
       Coe (9-7/11)
9052. Vander Cook, Mahettabel, 31, consort of Maj. Michael S., d 6/19/06 in
       Pittstown (9-6/24)
9053. Van Der Cook, Sally, 34, consort of Michael S., Esq. and oldest dau of
       Gen. Gilbert Eddy, d 4/4/23 in Pittstown (9-4/8)
9054. Vander Cook, Simon (Capt.), 81, (a Rev. patriot) d in Pittstown (1-12/18/29)
9055. Vander Cook, William Henry, 23, oldest s of Gilbert of Pittstown,
       d 11/26/28 in Troy (9-12/2)
9056. Vanderheyden, J. D. E., Esq. of Troy m 5/16/31 Catherine Gaston, dau of
       John, Esq. of Lansingburgh, in Troy; Rev. Dr. D. C. Lansing (1-5/19)
9057. Vander Heyden, Jacob L. of Troy d in Troy (9-8/25/01)
9058. Vanderhoff, Abraham m 1/24/02 Caty Tremper, both of Rhinebeck (8-2/2)
9059. Vanderhoff, Abraham (Col.), formerly of Rhinebeck, d in NYC (8-2/15/32)
9060. Vanderpool, Abraham V., Esq. of Kinderhook m 5/26/18 Harriet Goodwin,
       dau of Joseph, in Hudson; Rev. Jacob Sickels (6-6/2)
9061. Vanderveer, Ferdinand H. (Rev.) of Hyde Park, NY m 5/11/26 Mary V.
       Gildersleeve, dau of Rev. Cyrus of Wilkes Barre, PA (8-5/24)
9062. Vandervoort, Cornelius, 38, d 7/22/22 in Beekmantown (Clinton Co.)
       (7-8/3)
9063. Van Deusen, Abraham, 63, d 9/21/19 in Claverack (6-9/28)
9064. Van Deusen, Gertrude, wf of Abraham, d 7/30/18 in Claverack (6-8/11)
9065. Van Deusen, James, 85 or 35?, d 6/7/20 in the Manor of Livingston
       (6-6/13)
9066. Van Deusen, James P. (of the firm of Hayes and Van Deusen) m Annis
       Hathaway, dau of late Robert, in Claverack (bride and groom both of
       Hudson); Rev. Gebhard (6-3/8/08)
9067. Van Deusen, John, Esq. of Livingston m 3/3/14 Maria Elting, dau of
       Peter of Hudson in H; Rev. Chester (6-3/15)
9068. Van Deusen, Lenah, 30, consort of John, merchant, of the village of
       Johnstown (in town of Livingston) d 1/11/13 (6-1/19)
9069. Van Deusen, Robert A. m Catherine Tremper in Claverack; Rev. Gephard
       (6-11/28/09)
9070. Vandewater, Herman d 7/30/16 in Poughkeepsie (printers in Hudson are
       requested to insert the above) (8-8/7)
9071. Van De Water, William m 1/23/17 Lavina Ward, dau of John I., in Po'keepsie;
       Rev. Jewitt (8-1/29)

9072. Van Duran, Silas m 10/20/34 Hannah Sowle, both of Dover; Rev. A. Perkins
(8-10/22)
9073. Van Dusen, John of Livingston, merchant, m 6/17/17 Ann Maria Whitbeck of
Red Hook in R. H.; Rev. K (name blurred) (8-7/16)
9074. Van Dusen, John T. m 11/22/20 Ester Woodruff, both of Claverack, in C;
Rev. Gephard (6-12/26)
9075. Van Duyn, James m 10/8/23 Catherine Hansen, both of Freedom; Rev.
Willson (8-10/22)
9076. Van Dyck, Francis, 16, s of Abraham, d 11/22/31 in Coxsackie (1-12/2)
9077. Van Dyck, Lawrence, Jr., Esq., senior editor of the Greene County
Advertiser, m 7/8/31 Clarissa Van Schaick of Kinderhook; Rev. Jacob
Sickles (1-7/16)
9078. Van Dyck, Stephen H. (Dr.), s of Dr. Henry L. of Kinderhook, d 6/12/30 in
Hallowell, Upper Canada (1-6/26)
9079. Van Dyke, Catharine, 38, wf of Lawrence, Jr., d 2/2/29 in Kinderhook
(1-2/14)
9080. Van Eck, Christopher m 11/26/25 Catherine Winslow, both of Poughkeepsie;
Rev. Pearce (8-11/30)
9081. Van Etten, William m 2/24/03 Polly Williams, both of Clinton (Dut. Co.);
Rev. Dodge (8-3/8)
9082. Van Gaseburgh, Alida (Miss), 54, of Amsterdam (for many years a resident
in the family of Rev. J. H. Livingston, late pastor of the Reformed
Dutch Church in NYC) d 7/25/32 in NYC (8-8/1)
9083. Van Hoesen, Abigail, 26, consort of Leonard, d 3/11/08 in Hudson
(6-3/15)
9084. Van Hoesen, Elizabeth, 66, d 3/16/14 in Nassau, NY (6-4/19)
9085. Van Hoesen, George A., 31, d 3/31/14 in Kinderhook (6-4/5)
9086. Van Hoesen, Leonard of Hudson m 7/1/07 Abigail Field of Peekskill; Rev.
Silas Constant (6-7/14)
9087. Van Hoesen, Maria, "nearly 80", relict of late Peter, d 10/21/07 in Hudson
(6-10/27)
9088. Van Horne, Augustus of NY (City?) m 8/18/03 Margaret Livingston, dau of
Col. Robert G., deceased; Rev. Chase (8-8/30)
9089. Van Horne, David, Esq., late State Adjutant General, d 5/12/01 in NYC
(buried with military honors) (9-5/19 and 3-5/28)
9090. Van Horne, Richard, Esq., 53, d 3/12/23 at his home in Danube (Herk. Co.)
(frequently had been a state assemblyman and was a delegate to the
late State Convention) (3-3/24)
9091. Van Housen, Sanford of Johnstown m Ann Maria Liswell, oldest dau of
John, Esq., of Caughnawaga, in C; Rev. Albert Amerman (1-7/24/29)
9092. Van Hovenbergh, Rudolph (Capt.), 56, d 3/16/08 in Kinderhook (6-4/5)
9093. Van Huren, T. Jork of Waterford m 1/12/22 Mrs. Elenor Fero of Troy
(9-1/15)
9094. Van Huyck, John (Col.), late of the U.S. Army and of the State of NY,
d 2/20/29 in Washington, Dist. of Columbia (1-2/27)
9095. Van Ingen, H. S. of Albany m 10/18/30 Catharine Elizabeth Hook, oldest
dau of J. C., Esq. of White Lake (Sullivan Co.) in W L; Rev. Edward
K. Fowler (1-10/22)
9096. Van Keuren, Benjamin (Rev.), pastor of the Reformed Dutch Church in
Esopus, m 10/29/27 Mary ann Forrest, dau of Robert of Poughkeepsie;
Rev. C. C. Cuyler (8-10/31)
9097. Van Keuren, Cornelius C. of Kinderhook m 10/16/08 Elizabeth Van Hoesen
of Philipstown in New Lebanon; Rev. Morse (6-10/25)
9098. Van Keuren, John, merchant, of the firm of Parmelee, Van Keuren & Co.
m 9/28/31 Jane Ann Carman in Poughkeepsie; Rev. Dr. Reed. All of
Poughkeepsie (1-9/30)
9099. Van Kleeck, Charity, 57, consort of Peter B. of Poughkeepsie, d 11/2/07
(printers in Hudson, NY and at Stockbridge, MA are requested to publish
this notice) (8-11/4)
9100. Van Kleeck, Cornelia, 59, d 2/12/10 at the home of her brother, Rev. Dr.
Livingston, in NYC (8-2/21)
9101. Van Kleeck, Edgar, late of Poughkeepsie, m 10/11/27 Nancy Graham of Fishkill in F; Rev. Price (8-10/17)
9102. Van Kleeck, George, merchant, m 3/16/26 Mary Eliza Tallmadge of Poughkeepsie;
Rev. C. C. Cuyler (8-3/22)

9103. Van Kleeck, Irene, 55, widow of late Tunis, d 12/1/31 (8-12/7)
9103a. Van Kleeck, Jacobus, 79, d 11/17/04 (8-11/17)
9104. Van Kleeck, John, Esq., 66, late of Poughkeepsie, d 11/6/07 in Fishkill
       (8-11/11)
9104a. Van Kleeck, Leonard m 7/18/07 Betsey Phillips, both of Poughkeepsie; Rev.
       Brouwer (8-7/22)
9105. Van Kleeck, Matthew of Fishkill m 7/16/12 Phebe Dimond of Poughkeepsie;
       Rev. Cuyler (8-7/22)
9106. Van Kleeck, Peter V. m 11/9/24 Hetty Tynders; Rev. Babcock (8-11/17)
9107. Van Kleeck, Polly (Mrs.), 86, widow of late John, Esq., d 4/13/24 at the
       home of Stephen Thorn in Freedom (8-4/14)
9108. Van Kleeck, Robert R. (Rev.) m 6/9/34 Margaret S. Teller, dau of Isaac
       Depeyster Teller, at Fishkill Landing; Rt. Rev. R. T. Onderdonk, D.D.
       (8-6/18)
9109. Van Kleeck, Tallmadge, 9, only s of George, d 9/29/27 (8-10/10)
9110. Van Kleeck, Tallmadge, 4, s of George, d 10/13/32 in Poughkeepsie (8-10/17)
9111. Van Kleeck, Tunis, 58, d 9/1/31 in Poughkeepsie (was born in Poughkeepsie
       and was engaged in business there for nearly 30 yrs.) (8-9/7)
9112. Van Kuren, Robert m 10/15/21 Julia Odell; Rev. Cuyler (8-10/31)
9113. Van Loan, M. D., merchant, of NYC m 10/27/30 Julia A. Thomson of Catskill
       at St. Luke's Church in Catskill; Rev. Joseph Prentiss (1-11/3)
9114. Van Loon, Jacob m 2/19/04 Mrs. Catherine De Groot; Rev. Mayer. All of
       Loonenburgh (Athens, NY) (6-3/6)
9115. Van Loon, John J. of Millville m 4/22/29 Anna Maria Hoes of Coxsackie in
       Kinderhook; Rev. J. Berger (1-5/2)
9116. Van Ness, _____, widow of late Judge William P., d 9/7/29 in NYC (8-9/9
       and 1-9/10)
9117. Van Ness, Cornelia, relict of late Gen. David, formerly of Dutchess Co.,
       d 8/13/29 in Troy (8-8/19)
9118. Van Ness, Cornelia, 78, relict of late George, d 8/13/29 in Troy (1-8/29)
9119. Van Ness, David (Gen.), 74, formerly of Dutchess Co., d 10/4/18 in Troy
       (9-10/6 and 8-10/7)
9120. Van Ness, Garret B., Esq. of Red Hook m 4/18/98 Sarah Tappen, dau of late
       Peter, Esq. of Poughkeepsie; Rev. Brouwer (8-4/24)
9121. Van Ness, Garret B., Esq., 32, attorney, of Poughkeepsie d 10/7/06 in
       Poughkeepsie (8-10/14 and 6-10/21)
9122. Van Ness, Gertrude, 96, d 1/10/04 in Claverack (6-1/17)
9123. Van Ness, Harriet, 23, (consort of Jacob, Esq., attorney, of Red Hook and
       dau of Ebenezer Dibblee, Esq. of Pine Plains) d 9/18/13 in Red Hook
       (surv by husband and a dau "but a few hours old") (6-9/21 and 8-9/22)
9124. Van Ness, Jacob, Esq., attorney, of Red Hook m 1/2/11 Harriet Dibblee,
       dau of Ebenezer of Pine Plains, in P P; Rev. Veeder (8-1/9)
9125. Van Ness, Jacob, Esq., clerk of Dutchess Co., m 11/28/25 "Mrs. Stevenson",
       dau of Ebenezer Dibblee of Pine Plains, in P. P. (8-12/7)
9126. Van Ness, John, 78, d in Chatham (6-3/30/02)
9127. Van Ness, John, Esq. of Schodack m 9/11/05 Widow Van Schaack in Kinderhook;
       Rev. Sickles (6-9/24)
9128. Van Ness, John, Esq., 49, formerly of NY State, d 11/16/25 in"Demarara"
       (8-1/11/26)
9129. Van Ness, John P., Congressman "from this district", m 5/6/02 Marcia Burns,
       "a lady celebrated for the splendor of her fortune & c", in Washington,
       Dist. of Columbia (6-5/25)
9130. Van Ness, Peter, Esq, (Hon.), late judge of the court of common pleas
       of Columbia Co., d in Kinderhook (6-12/25/04)
9131. Van Ness, Theron R., merchant, of Poughkeepsie d 8/6/32 ("a young man")
       (8-8/8)
9132. Van Ness, William m Mary Smith in Ballston Spa; Elder Elias Lee. All of
       Ballston Spa (2-11/25/23)
9133. Van Ness, William Cantine, oldest son of late William W. of NY, d 7/17/28
       in Warren (Trumbull Co.), Ohio (8-8/13)
9134. Van Ness, William P. (Hon.) d suddenly 9/12/26 in the home of J. O.
       Hoffman, Esq. (for the past 14 yrs U.S. District Judge for the southern
       district of NY) (8-9/13)
9135. Van Ness, William W., for many years a judge of the NY State Supreme Court,
       d 2/28/23 in Charleston, SC (8-3/12 and 9-3/18)

9136. Van Norwich, Philip m 12/23/10 Dinah Delemater; Rev. Chester. All of Hudson (6-12/28)
9137. Vanornam, Levi m 1/14/26 Harriet Bridges in Peru, NY; Nathan Taylor, Esq. All of Peru (7-2/18)
9138. Van Pelt, Alexander of Brunswick m 8/29/22 Eliza Maria Andres, dau of Stephen, Esq. of Troy, at the Methodist Episcopal Church; Rev. Griffin (9-9/3)
9139. Van Pelt, Anthony, age 126 yrs, d in Greene Co., NC (During Rev. War was over-age for military service) (8-5/12/30)
9140. Van Pelt, Isaiah m 12/27/23 Elizabeth Wilson in Brunswick; Rev. Griffin (9-1/6/24)
9141. Van Rensselaer, Catharine, wf of John I., d 9/30/07 in Greenbush (9-10/13)
9142. Van Rensselaer, Harry, 32, s of Killian, Esq. of Hudson, d in Albany (interred in the family vault in Claverack) (6-3/30/13)
9143. Van Rensselaer, Henry I. (Col.), 72, d 3/22/14 (in Hudson?) (6-3/29)
9144. Van Rensselaer, Henry K. (Gen.), 72, d 9/9/16 in Albany (3-9/19)
9145. Van Rensselaer, Henry P. of Claverack m Jane Fort of Hoosick; Rev. Dunlap (6-11/1/14)
9146. Van Rensselaer, Jeremiah, Esq., 60, d 1/29/29 in Canandaigua (1-2/5)
9147. Van Rensselaer, Jeremiah H., 37, d 8/4/15 in Claverack (6-8/15)
9148. Van Rensselaer, John (Col.), late of Lansingburgh and a Rev. officer, d 6/23/02 at the Glass House "near Albany" (9-7/7)
9149. Van Rensselaer, Margaret (consort of Hon. Stephen, Lt. Gov. of NY) d 3/14/01 in the Manor House in Watervliet (9-3/17)
9150. Van Rensselaer, Margaret, 66, wf of Killian K., d 4/21/30 in Albany (funeral from her husband's home, 116 State St.) (1-4/23)
9151. This entry repositioned.
9152. Van Rensselaer, Maria (age blurred), relict of Col. Philip of Cherry Hill (now in the south end of Albany, then in Bethlehem) d 12/20/30 (1-12/22)
9153. Van Rensselaer, Philip (Hon.), 58, d 9/27/24 in Albany (3-10/4)
9154. Van Rensselaer, Philip S. (Hon.), 58, d 10/2/24 in Albany (2-10/5)
9155. Van Rensselaer, Pierre de Peyster, 4, only child of Jacob Rutsen (and Cornelia) Van Rensselaer, d 6/1/02 in Claverack (smallpox) (6-6/15)
9156. Van Rensselaer, Robert, 61, d 9/12/02 in Claverack (6-9/14)
9157. Van Rensselaer, Stephen, Esq., late Lt. Gov. of NY, m 5/17/02 Cornelia Paterson, dau of Hon. William, Esq. (he one of the judges of the U.S. Supreme Court) in New Brunswick, NJ (8-5/25 and 9-5/26)
9158. Van Rensselaer, Stephen, Jr., Esq., son of Stephen Van Rensselaer, Esq. of Albany, m 1/2/17 Harriet Elizabeth Bayard, youngest dau of William, Esq. of NYC; Right Rev. Bishop Hobart (8-1/8)
9159. Van Schaack, Cornelius, Esq. m 3/28/04 Clarisa Deming in Kinderhook (6-4/3)
9160. Van Schaack, Elizabeth, consort of Peter, Esq., d 1/22/13 in Kinderhook (6-2/2)
9161. Van Schaack, Jane, 73, wf of Henry, Esq., d 5/14/15 in Kinderhook (6-5/30)
9162. Van Schaack, John, 20, a graduate of Union College and s of Peter, Esq. of Kinderhook, d 5/18/11 in Kinderhook (interred in the family burying ground) (6-5/24)
9163. Van Schack, Cornelius, Esq., 40, d 4/28/17 in Kinderhook (6-5/6)
9164. Van Schaick, 78, relict of Gen. Gozen, d 1/15/29 (1-1/16)
9165. Van Schaick, _____, child of John, d "recently" in Albany (funeral from John's home, 42 Union St.) (1-4/30/30)
9166. Van Schaick, David, Esq. m 10/5/30 Catharine Sickles, dau of Rev. Jacob, all of Kinderhook, in K (1-10/8)
9167. Van Schaick, Gerrard, 37, d 7/28/30 on Van Schaick's Island opposite Lansingburgh (1-7/31)
9168. Van Schaick, Henry, Esq., 33, formerly of Lansingburgh, d 10/14/29 in L (1-10/15)
9169. Van Schaick, Nicholas, merchant, m 9/2/30 Jane Van Wie, dau of Benjamin; Rev. Ferris. All of Albany (1-9/3)
9170. Van Schayck, Clarissa, 20, consort of Capt. William, d 1/29/07 (6-2/17)
9171. Van Schoonhoven, _____, inf child of John, d "recently" in Albany (Funeral from John's home, 71 Market St.) (1-10/15/31)

9172. Van Schoonhoven, Gerrit, 29, d 6/6/31 in Albany (his father, James, and his brothers, John and Henry, are named) (funeral from 71 North Market St.) (1-6/7)
9173. Van Schoonnover, William H., Esq. of Troy m 9/1/34 Margaret S. Brinkerhoff, dau of Stephen I., Esq. of NYC, in Lithgow; Rev. George B. Andrews (8-9/10)
9174. Van Slyck, Henry, Esq. of Hudson d in Claverack (6-6/7/11)
9175. Van Slyck, Jesse M., alderman and merchant, m 1/13/31 Maria Eliza Teller, dau of John W., in Schenectady; Rev. Coles Carpenter. All of Schenectady (1-1/20)
9176. Van Slyke, Daniel, Esq., 32, late resident engineer and superintendent of the Chesapeake and Ohio Canal, d 12/4/31 at his home in Orville (Onon. Co.), NY (consumption) (1-12/17)
9177. Van Steenburgh, Benjamin m 8/28/30 Mrs. Jane Lorillard, both of Rhinebeck; Rev. Dr. Cuyler (8-9/1)
9178. Van Steenburgh, John m 5/25/26 Margaret Van Keuren, both of Rhinebeck, in R; Rev. William Mink (8-5/31)
9179. Van Syth, Henry, 80, m Susan Lewis, 50 or 30?, step-dau of Caesar Carr, oysterman, in NYC. All of NYC (8-11/27/16)
9180. Van Tassel, David R. m 12/23/26 Catharine Overlin, both of Poughkeepsie, in P; Rev. Welton (8-12/27)
9181. Van Tassell, Nathaniel m 11/14/26 Phebe Carpenter, both of Northeast; Rev. Clark (8-11/22)
9182. Vantine, Albro m 3/20/34 Hannah Way in Fishkill; Rev. Fisher. All of F (8-3/26)
9183. Van Tyne, John of Chazy m 2/25/19 Lucretia Leek of Plattsburgh; Rev. Frederick Halsey (7-2/27)
9184. Van Valen, Gideon, 77, d 5/11/20 in Poughkeepsie (8-5/24)
9185. Van Valin, Abigail, widow of late Gideon, d 7/13/24 "at an advanced age" in Freedom (8-7/21)
9186. Van Valin, Abraham of La Grange m 1/20/31 Catharine Dubois of Poughkeepsie; Rev. Dr. Cuyler (8-1/26)
9187. Van Valin, Jeremiah m 10/19/15 Mary Meddle; Rev. Leonard (8-10/25)
9188. Van Valkenburgh, Daniel (Rev.), late of Manheim, m 7/26/30 Mary Weber, dau of Michael, in Richfield (Otsego Co.); Rev. Snyder (1-8/4)
9189. Van Valkenburgh, Harmon (Dr.) of Fulton (Oswego Co.) m 8/18/29 Catharine Pruyn of Kinderhook in K; Rev. Jacob Sickles (1-8/22)
9190. Van Valkenburgh, Henry m 8/27/06 Anna Van Valkenburgh, dau of Barney, all of Kinderhook, in Claverack; Rev. Gebhard (6-9/2)
9191. Van Valkenburgh, Jacob m 1/20/29 Cornelia Caroline Race (in Catskill?); Rev. Wyckoff (2-2/14)
9192. Van Valkenburgh, James m 8/30/05 Anna Van Cott, both of Troy, in T (9-9/3)
9193. Van Valkenburgh, John, inf s of Capt. John C., d 8/12/22 in Poughkeepsie (8-8/14)
9194. Van Valkenburgh, John C. m 2/3/31 Sarah Good, both of Poughkeepsie; Rev. Dr. Cuyler (8-2/9)
9195. Van Valkenburgh, Sarah, wf of John C., d 5/3/28 (8-5/7)
9196. Van Valkenburgh, Sarah, consort of John, d 7/1/34 in Poughkeepsie (8-7/16)
9197. Van Vechten, Catharine, 55, wf of Abraham, d 9/10/20 in Albany (3-9/25)
9198. Van Vechten, Catharine, 59, d 7/21/30 in Schuylerville ("she has left a large family...") (1-7/26)
9199. Van Vechten, Elizabeth (Mrs.), 77, d 12/1/31 in Albany (funeral from her late home, corner North Market St. and Maiden Lane (1-12/3)
9200. Van Vechten, Gerritt W. m 1/16/23 Martha Thorn in Saratoga; Rev. Duryee (2-1/28)
9201. Van Vechten, Samuel (Rev.) of Bloomingburgh (Sullivan Co.) m 9/7/24 Louisa Van Wyck, dau of Gen. Abraham, in Fishkill; Rev. Van Vechten of Schenectady (8-9/15)
9202. Van Vechten, William of Schaghticoke m 12/7/28 Elizabeth Van Allen, dau of Evert of Bloomingdale (Renss. Co.) in B; Rev. Dumont (9-12/9)
9203. Van Vlack, Abram m 6/4/31 Phebe Devine, both of Pleasant Valley; Rev. Welton (8-6/8)
9204. Van Vlack, Elizabeth, 83, wf of John H. formerly of Fishkill, d 10/2/30 in Poughkeepsie (8-10/6)

267

9205. Van Vleck, Abraham, 39, supervisor of Kinderhook, d 1/2/14 in K (6-1/18)
9206. Van Vleck, Abraham of Hurley m 4/20/26 Margaret Myer, dau of P. T. B. Myer of Poughkeepsie (8-4/26)
9207. Van Vleck, Abraham P. m 10/26/15 Ruhama Preston in Canaan; Rev. Clark (6-11/7)
9208. Van Vleck, Catharine (Miss), 34, dau of Peter, d 1/22/29 in Kinderhook (1-1/30)
9209. Van Vleck, John P. of Kinderhook m 3/25/30 Mary Baldwin, dau of Benjamin of Millville (Columbia Co.),in M; Rev. J. Sickles (1-4/6)
9210. Van Vleet, Jacob m 12/29/31 Catharine Wooden, both of Hyde Park, in H. P.; Rev. William Cahoone (8-1/5/31)
9211. Van Vliet, Ethalinda, inf dau of Benjamin C., d 7/29/32 in Poughkeepsie (8-8/1)
9212. Van Vliet, Rachel (Miss), 21, dau of C. Van Vliet, d 3/15/10 (in Pough- keepsie?) (8-3/21)
9213. Van Vliet, Benjamin C. m 12/7/30 Sally Ann Dakin, dau of E. K.; Rev. Dr. Reed. All of Poughkeepsie (8-12/8)
9214. Van Vliet, Hannah (Mrs.), 86, d 3/5/34 at Fishkill Landing (8-3/12)
9215. Van Vliet, Henry H. of the firm of Van Vliet and Sullivan, merchants, of Poughkeepsie m 1/20/20 Jane Harris, dau of Capt. Joseph; Rev. Cuyler (8-1/26)
9216. Van Vliet, John m 10/20/27 Maria Cox, both of Hyde Park; Rev. Vanderveer (8-10/24)
9217. Van Vliet, John, Jr. m 4/11/32 Hannah Bogardus, dau of Isaac, all of Fishkill Landing, at F. L.; Rev. Hyer (8-5/2)
9218. Van Vliet, Maria Evertson (wf of Col. John[?] and dau of John[name blurred] Esq. of Pleasant Valley) d 3/4/27 in Hyde Park (8-3/28)
9219. Van Vliet, Maria Smith, inf ch of H. H., d 12/2/31 in NYC (8-12/7)
9220. Van Volkenburgh, James of NYC m 9/10/27 Mary E. Church of Troy; Rev. Howard (9-9/14)
9221. Van Volkenburgh, Lambert J. m 12/25/28 Elizabeth Vosburgh, dau of Col. Samuel, in Kinderhook; Rev. J. Sickles (1-1/3/29)
9222. Van Volkenburgh, Peter, 68, d 4/28/07 in Kinderhook (6-5/5/07)
9223. Van Voorhees, Henry m 12/29/25 Amanda Lamson, both of Fishkill; Rev. Thomas (8-1/11/26)
9224. Van Voorhes, Jacob, merchant, of Catskill m 2/2/13 Esther Dibblee, dau of Ebenezer of Pine Plains, in P. P.; Rev. Hyde (6-2/9)
9225. Van Voorhes, John of Decatur m Elvira Leach of Westford in W; Rev. Caldwell (3-12/6/24)
9226. Van Vorhies, Jacob m 9/7/25 Nancy Jones, both of Fishkill; Rev. Clark (8-9/28)
9227. Van Vorst, Helen (Mrs.), 48, d 1/10/31 (in Schenectady?) (1-1/19)
9228. Van Vorst, Philip, 84, (a Rev. officer lieutenant) d 4/11/30 in Schenectady (1-4/12)
9229. Van Vranken, Nicholas (Rev.), minister of the Reformed Dutch Church of Fishkill, New Hackensack, and Hopewell, d 5/20/04 (8-5/22)
9230. Van Vranken, Nicholas, s of late Rev. Nicholas of Fishkill,d 8/9/05 at the home of Maus(?) Van Vranken, Esq. in Schenectady (8-8/27)
9231. Van Vreedenburgh, Isaac m 5/23/25 Maria Rikert, both of Rhinebeck; Rev. Dr. Reed (8-5/25)
9232. Van Wagener, _____, merchant, of NYC m 3/21/08 Mary Wheeler, dau of Dr. William, in Red. Hook; Rev. Tittle (8-3/30)
9233. Van Wagener, David H. m 1/8/24 Ann Maria Van Keuren, both of Poughkeepsie; Rev. C. C. Cuyler (8-1/14)
9234. Van Wagener, John m 2/16/03 Betsey Youngs; Lemuel Conklin, Esq. All of Clinton (Dut. Co.)
9235. Van Waggoner, Evert m 5/30/32 Sally Humphrey, dau of John of Pleasant Valley; Rev. John Clark (8-6/6)
9236. Van Waggoner, Jacob m 10/2/07 Margaret Bond, both of Clinton; Rev. Brouwer (8-11/4)
9237. Van Waggoner, John N., 46, d 7/22/27 in Pleasant Valley (8-8/1)
9238. Van Wagner, Alexander m 9/28/34 Maria Harris; Rev. G. Coles. All of Poughkeepsie (8-10/1)
9239. Van Wagner, Gilbert of Pleasant Valley m 9/1/30 Lydia Knox of Poughkeepsie; Rev. Wile (8-9/15)

9240. Van Wagner, John S. of Hyde Park m 12/17/22 Eleanor M. Dunham of Poughkeepsie; Alfred Raymond, Esq. (8-12/25)
9241. Van Wagoner, Eli m 10/15/28 Nancy Van Wagoner, dau of Benjamin; Rev. Clark.
All of Pleasant Valley (8-10/29)
9242. Van Wagoner, Isaac of Pleasant Valley m 9/25/32 Sarah Ann Vincent, dau of
James of La Grange; Rev. Buttolph (8-10/3)
9243. Van Wagoner, John D. of Rhinebeck m 6/29/31 Susan Smith, dau of Maurice
of Hyde Park; Rev. Perkins (8-7/6)
9244. Van Wagoner, Nicholas m 12/9/09 Cornelia Prechard, both of Clinton; Rev.
Clark (8-12/20)
9245. Van Wart, Henry, Jr. of Birmingham, England m 8/18/30 Susan Clark Storrow,
oldest dau of Thomas W., Esq. of NYC, at "the Hotel of His Excellency
William C. Rives, Minister of the U.S., near the Court of France"; Rev
H. H. Luscombe, deputy chaplain of the British Embassy (1-10/23)
9246. Van Wyck, Alfred of Poughkeepsie m Charlotte Veitz, dau of Henry, Esq.
of Becket, MA, in B; Rev. Lelilles (8-6/16 and 1-6/18)
9247. Van Wyck, Barbara(?), 76, consort of Richard, Esq., d 8/16/07 in Fishkill
(8-8/26)
9248. Van Wyck, Catharine (Miss), 19, dau of Gen. John B., d 3/3/22 (8-3/6)
9249. Van Wyck, Charles m 4/18/27 Eliza Rugar; Rev. Clark. All of Pleasant
Valley (8-4/25)
9250. Van Wyck, Cornelius, 18, s of Isaac, Esq., d 2/14/04 in Fishkill
(8-2/21)
9251. Van Wyck, Cornelius, Esq., 73, d 12/9/32 at his home near Fishkill
(8-12/12)
9252. Van Wyck, Elizabeth, 43, wf of Col. Richard C., d 5/29/31 in Fishkill
(8-6/8)
9253. Van Wyck, Hannah, 68, wf of Theodorus R., d 8/31/34 in Fishkill (8-9/10)
9254. Van Wyck, Henry of Fishkill m 4/24/33 Ann Lee, dau of Judge Lee of
Yorktown, in Phillipstown; Rev. S. Van Vechten (8-5/8)
9255. Van Wyck, Isaac, Esq., 55, of Fishkill (a Rev. soldier) d 8/28/11 at the
home of Zacharius Hoffman in Red Hook (8-9/4 and 8-9/11)
9256. Van Wyck, Isaac (of the firm of Isaac C. Van Wyck and Co. and son of
Cornelius C., Esq.) m 12/10/14 Hannah Van Voorhis, dau of Maj. William
R.; Rev. Westbrook. All of Fishkill (8-12/14)
9257. Van Wyck, Isaac I. m 6/2/14 Amelia M. Jackson, dau of Joseph, all of
Fishkill; Rev. De Witt (8-6/8)
9258. Van Wyck, Jacob G., 35, d 9/4/28 at his home in Fishkill (8-101)
9259. Van Wyck, James m 11/12/34 Cornelia Van Wyck, both of Fishkill; Rev. George
H. Fisher (8-11/19)
9260. Van Wyck, John (Col.) of Fishkill m 9/29/98 Susan Schenk, dau of Paul,
merchant, of Poughkeepsie; Rev. Breuer (8-10/2)
9261. Van Wyck, John C. of the firm of Isaac C. Van Wyck and Co. m 4/7/14
Delia Griffin, dau of Jacob, deceased; Rev. Westbrook. All of Fishkill
(8-4/13)
9262. Van Wyck, Maria, 15, dau of Isaac, Esq., d 10/7/05 in Fishkill (surv by
her father, brothers, and sisters [none named]) (8-10/22)
9263. Van Wyck, Peter Esq. of the firm of Prall and Van Wyck of NYC m 12/14/12
Sarah Stewart Wickham, dau of Dr. Thomas, deceased, of Blooming Grove,
SC, at the home of Edward Huntting in Fishkill, NY (8-12/16)
9264. Van Wyck, Richard, merchant, m 3/9/11 Betsey Thorn, dau of Dr. James, all
of Fishkill; Rev. Barculo (8-3/20)
9265. Van Wyck, Richard T., 36, d 4/13/26 at his home in Fishkill (8-4/19)
9266. Van Wyck, Sarah, 44, consort of Theodorus W., Esq., d 12/4/08 in
Fishkill (8-12/28)
9267, Van Wyck, Theodorus, Esq. d 2/11/23 in Fishkill (8-2/19)
9268. Van Wyck, Theodorus C. (Dr.) m 9/5/20 Elizabeth Maison, dau of Peter R.
Esq. of Poughkeepsie; Rev. Reed (8-9/6)
9269. Van Wyck, William, Esq., 65, of Fishkill d 11/24/93 at the home of Judge
Platt in Poughkeepsie "while on a visit in this town" (8-11/27)
9270. Van Zandt, Edward, s of Wynant, Esq. of Flushing, L.I., m 5/22/29 Lydia
Bradford Collins, youngest dau of Gen. C. Collins, Lt. Gov. of RI, in
Newport, RI; Rev. Wheaton (1-5/29)
9271. Van Zandt, Sarah (Mrs.), 84, d 12/13/30 in Albany (funeral from the
home of her son, J. R. at 430 South Market Street) (1-12/14)

9272. Varian, Michael, butcher, late of Poughkeepsie, drowned 9/7/04 while crossing the river at Catskill in a small boat ("was run over by the sloop 'Montgomery', Capt. Hathaway, of Hudson") (8-10/23)
9273. Varick, Benjamin V. m 6/18/31 Jane Tooker, dau of late Charles, Esq., at the Middle Dutch Church in NYC; Rev. Dr. De Witt (1-6/20)
9274. Varick, John H. of Poughkeepsie m 9/4/32 Susan Storm, dau of Jacob, in Stormville (Dut. Co.); Rev. Cahoon (8-9/12)
9275. Varick, Richard A. (Dr.) m 11/19/28 Eliza Harris, youngest dau of Capt. Joseph of Poughkeepsie; Rev. Dr. Cuyler (8-11/26)
9276. Varrick, Theodore Romeyn, 1, youngest child of J. V. B. Varrick, d 1/1/22 in Poughkeepsie (8-1/2)
9276a. Vary, Richard G. m 9/27/21 Dorcas Haviland, both of Washington (Dut. Co.); Smith Herrick, Esq. (8-10/10)
9277. Vassar, Mary Elizabeth Atkinson, 11, youngest dau of James, d 4/30/34 in Poughkeepsie (8-5/14)
9278. Vassar, Matthew of Poughkeepsie m 3/7/13 Catherine Valentine of Fishkill; Rev. Leonard (8-3/10)
9279. Vassar, Thomas m 12/31/03 Hannah Ellison, both of Poughkeepsie; Rev. Brouwer (8-1/3/04)
9280. Vassar, William m 11/17/31 Mary Hageman, dau of Adrian, all of Poughkeepsie; Rev. Dr. Cuyler (8-11/23)
9281. Vaughan, Alanson H. m 1/1/28 Epsyby Bean in Saranac (7-1/19)
9282. Vaughan, Benjamin, Esq. m 2/19/14 Mrs. Mary Reynolds, consort of Charles Reynolds, deceased, in Plattsburgh (7-2/26)
9283. Vaughan, Benjamin, Jr. m 2/15/27 Hannah Comstock in Plattsburgh (7-2/24)
9284. Vaughan, Daniel B. (Col.), about 44, d 5/10/26 in Saranac (7-5/13)
9285. Vaughan, Nathan(?) m 10/10/27 Sally Baker, both of Plattsburgh, in P. (7-10/2))
9286. Vaughan, Russell, 42, of Willsboro d 10/27/21 in Plattsburgh (7-11/5)
9287. Vaughan, Silvina, wf of Benjamin, d recently in Plattsburgh (7-1/8/13)
9288. Veazie, Charles m 3/2/19 Mary Ann Titus, dau of Platt Titus; Rev. Sommers. All of Troy (9-3/9)
9289. Velie, Barnet m 10/19/05 Jane McCord, both of Fishkill; Rev. Brouwer (8-10/22)
9290. Velie, Cornelius d 3/7/13 in Poughkeepsie (8-3/10)
9291. Velie, Cornelius Ivin of Michigan Territory m 9/18/26 Sally Birch, dau of Charles of Pleasant Valley, NY; Garret Adriance, Esq. (8-9/27)
9292. Velie, Harry of Pleasant Valley m 1/22/24 Susan Herrick, dau of Stephen of Hyde Park; Rev. Clark (8-1/28)
9293. Velie, Henry W., inf s of George P., d 3/7/29 in Pleasant Valley (8-3/18)
9294. Velie, Isaac of Freedom m 11/26/21 Parmelia Wheeler of Poughkeepsie; Rev Wynkoop (8-11/28)
Velie, Maria Ann. See, possibly, Felie, Maria Ann.
9295. Velie, Minard of Pleasant Valley m 7/10/28 Abigail Allen of Washington (Dut. Co.); Rev. Clark (8-7/23)
9296. Velie, Minard M., merchant, of Poughkeepsie m 9/30/34 Ann Elizabeth Brown, dau of late Cornelius of Peekskill, at the home of Mr. E. M. Delavergne in La Grange; Rev. Van Kleef (8-10/8)
9297. Velie, William m 1/16/22 Sally Allen, dau of Nicholas, in Pleasant Valley; Rev. Quitman(?) (8-1/23)
9298. Veltman, Hiram of the firm of Veltman and Falls, merchants, of Newburgh, m 4/18/30 Elizabeth M. Butler, youngest dau of Charles of Poughkeepsie, in P; Rev.Dr. Cuyler (8-5/9 and 1-5/21)
9299. Vemont, John P. (Capt.) m 7/7/96 Mary Brooks, both of Poughkeepsie (8-7/13)
9300. Vemont, John Peichot, formerly of Poughkeepsie, d 12/8/10 in Kingston, Island of Jamaica (8-2/13/11)
9301. Vemont, Mary (Mrs.) d 4/2/12 in Poughkeepsie (8-4/8)
9302. Vemont, Sarah, wf of Capt. John P.of Poughkeepsie, d 11/21/95 (8-11/25)
9303. Vernam, Cramer, merchant, m 1/24/30 Eliza Farnam, dau of Joel, in Mechanicville. All of M; Rev. Cheever of Waterford (1-1/30)
9304. Vernon, George, 32, "brother-in-law of the celebrated Miss Clara Fisher and formerly a manager of the Albany Theatre", d 6/13/30 in Albany (1-6/15)
9305. Vernor, Charles, inf s of John T., d "recently" in Albany (funeral from his father's home on Fayette St. (1-7/13/30)

9306. Verplanck, Anna Sophia, 30, dau of late Gillian, d 9/14/19 at the home of
William Allen, Esq. in Fishkill (8-9/22)
9307. Ver Planck, Daniel C. (Hon.) d 3/29/34 in Fishkill (formerly a Congressman
and a Dutchess County judge) (8-4/2)
9308. Verplanck, Johnson, Esq., one of the editors of the NY American, m 6/27/23
Louisa Augusta Governeur in NYC; Rev. McVickar (8-7/2 and 3-7/14)
9309. Verplanck, Johnson, 41, d 7/8/29 at his home near Belleville (1-7/13)
9310. Verplanck, Philip A., Esq. m 11/20/28 Adaline Eliza Verplanck, dau of
late Philip of Verplanck's Point, in NYC; Rev. Phillips (8-11/26)
9311. Verplanck, Samuel, Esq., 84, d 1/27/20 at the home of the Hon. Daniel
Verplanck in Fishkill (8-2/2)
9312. Verren, Antoine (Rev.), rector of the French Church du St. Esprit,
m 10/18/30 Anna Maria Hammersley, dau of Thomas, Esq,, at St. John's
Chapel in NYC; Rev. Benjamin T. Onderdonk, D.D., Bishop-elect of the
diocese of NY (1-10/20)
9313. Ver Valen, Isaac H. of Fishkill m 1/4/21 Diana Vail of Clinton; Rev. C.C.
Cuyler (8-1/10)
9314. Ver Valen, James m 11/23/08 Sarah Velie, both of Fishkill; Rev. Dr. Covel
(8-11/30)
9315. Ver Valin, Gideon, Jr. of Fishkill m "lately" Polly Deen of Claverack
in C (8-4/8/00)
9316. Vethake, Frederick Albert, 58, (born in Westphalia, Germany) d 4/2/10 in
Poughkeepsie, NY (funeral from his late home in the Dutchess Academy
(8-4/4)
9317. Vibbard, Timothy, 46, d 8/31/23 in Galway (2-9/2)
9318. Vicher, Garrit A. m 6/11/20 Eliza Stephens, both of Albany; Rev. Sommers
(9-6/20)
9319. Viele, Christopher Columbus, 18, s of Jacob S., late of Columbia Co.,
d 8/24/23 in Wolcott (Wayne Co.) (2-9/2)
9320. Vile, John, 97, d 2/24/25 in Middlefield (3-2/28)
9321. Viele, Ludowiceus, merchant, m 7/1/29 Caroline E. Hunt, dau of Hiram,
Esq., all of Pittstown; Rev. Tucker of Troy (1-7/4)
9322. Viele, Philip, Esq., attorney, m 6/4/28 Catharine G. Brinkerhoff, dau of
late Isaac, in Troy; Rev. Tucker. All of Troy (9-6/6)
9323. Villers, _____ (Mr.), recently from NYC, d 9/3/03 in Loonenburgh
(Athens, NY) (6-9/6)   7/31/14
9324. Vincent, Addi M. of Hillsdale m/Lavinia M. Somers of Sharon, CT in S; Rev.
Perry (6-8/30)
9325. Vincent, Alpheus, "notorious for his crimes" d "in the state prison"
(6-6/1/02)
9326. Vincent Ambrose L., 29, d 7/23/12 in Hillsdale (6-8/3)
9327. Vincent, Gilbert m 2/28/02 Rebecca Justus in Beekman (8-3/2)
9328. Vincent, John (Capt.), 95, an Indian, d in Parkerstown, VT. In 1755 he
commanded the Canawogga tribe "then opposed to these colonies and the
provinces." (Was early educated by a Roman Catholic priest in the
French language. He bequeathed his French Bible to the Rev. Heman
Ball.) (6-8/3/10)
9329. Vincent, Jonathan, 70, d 7/12/24 in Washington (Dut. Co.) (8-7/14)
9330. Vincent, Leonard of Poughkeepsie m 5/30/11 Mary Flagler of Beekman; Rev.
Cuyler (8-6/5)
9331. Vincent, Levi,merchant, of Verbank m 3/22/27 Mary Vail, dau of late Moses
of Freedom; Rev. Clark (8-3/28)
9332. Vincent, Michael, 87, d 8/6/08 at his home in Beekman ("The printers in
Hudson and Catskill will confer a favor...by inserting the above...")
(8-8/10)
9333. Vincent, Ruth, wf of Michael (he a farmer of Beekman) d 4/4/94 (8-4/9)
9334. Vine, George of Princetown (Schen. Co.) m 10/8/29 Elizabeth Fryer of
Albany; Rev. Weed (1-10/10)
9335. Vinton, D. H. (Lt.) of the U. S. Army m 7/14/29 Pamela Brown, dau of late
Maj. Gen. Jacob Brown, in Brownville (Jeff. Co.), NY; Rev. W. L. Keese
(1-7/20)
9336. Visscher, James d 6/24/31 in Albany (funeral from his mother's home,
81 North Market St.) (1-6/24)
9337. Visscher, Nanning (Maj.), 49, d 12/12/21 in Greenbush (2-12/26)
9338. Volk, Thomas m 12/31/28 Sarah M. Myers; Rev. Williams. All of Albany
(1-1/3/29)

9339. Voorhes, James C. of Saugerties m 6/11/25 Eliza Tarpenning of Poughkeepsie; Rev. C. C. Cuyler (8-6/15)
9340. Vosburgh, Abraham R. (Capt.) m 11/6/23 Abigail Crawford in Charlton. All of C (2-11/18)
9341. Vosburgh, Garret of Kinderhook Landing m 2/27/02 Sally Van Allstyne, dau of Col. Abraham I. of Chatham, in Kinderhook; Rev. Sickles (6-3/9)
9342. Vosburgh, Jacob m 3/6/14 Sarah Salisbury in Kinderhook; Rev. Chester (6-3/15)
9343. Vosburgh, John A., 72, d in Kinderhook (6-11/28/09)
9344. Vosburgh, Thomas m 12/30/21 Alida Miller, both of Charlton (2-1/9/22)
9345. Vredenburgh, Edward R. of the firm of Lundy and Vredenburgh of Auburn m 10/3/30 Ann Scott of Geneva in G; Rev. Mason (1-10/11)
9346. Vredenburgh, John m 5/21/29 Eliza Sherwood, dau of William, all of Amenia; Rev. C. P. Wilson (8-5/27)
9347. Vredenburgh, Matthias d 9/25/82 in Red Hook (surv by wf, 4 ch, and "an aged father") (5-10/3)
9348. Vroman, Lawrence, Esq. of Schenectady m 12/9/17 Susanna Wendell of Greenbush in Troy; Rev. Dr. Coe (9-12/16)
9349. Vrooman, Peter, 22, d 9/6/30 in Schenectady (1-9/10)
9350. Vrooman, Peter I. d 5/26/01 in Schoharie (whereabouts of his only son, Cornelius, is not known) (3-6/11 and repeated 3-6/25)
9351. Wackerhagen, Augustus (Rev.) of Schoharie m 9/5/06 Mary A. Meyer in Rhinebeck; Rev. Frederick H. Quitman (8-9/9 and 6-9/16)
9352. Waddle, William m 6/28/27 Mariah Bentley, both of Troy; Rev. Howard (9-7/10)
9353. Wadsworth, Amos, merchant, of Farmington, CT m 5/30/22 Amanda Mann of Amenia; Rev. C. P. Willson (8-6/5)
9354. Wadsworth, Cornelia (Miss), 18, 2nd dau of James, Esq., d 3/28/31 in Geneseo (1-4/11 and 8-4/20)
9355. Wadsworth, George M. of Lansingburgh m 4/5/20 Annes Sherman of Troy; Rev. Sommers (9-5/16)
9356. Wadsworth, Jeremiah, 60, d 4/30/04 in Hartford (state not given) (for many years a Congressman from NY) (6-5/29)
9357. Wadsworth, John, Esq., merchant, of NYC m Caroline A. Masi, dau of Francis, Esq. of Washington, Dist. of Columbia (1-6/1/29)
9358. Wadsworth, Jonathan m 5/22/29 Mary Valentine, both of Poughkeepsie; Rev. Dr. Reed (8-5/28)
9359. Wadsworth, Joseph m 1/2/30 Emma Williams, dau of Thomas, all of Poughkeepsie; Rev. Dr. Reed (8-1/6)
9360. Wadsworth, Warren E. of Pittstown m Nancy Slade, dau of Joseph of Hoosick, in H; Rev. Keach (9-1/29/28)
9361. Wagar, Michael m 7/26/27 Pamala M. Egleston, both of Troy; Rev. Howard (9-7/31)
9362. Wagoner, William m 5/27/29 Helena Vroman; Rev. Kissam. All of Bethlehem (1-5/30)
9363. Waine, John, 18, s of John, d 2/7/24 in Middlefield (3-2/16)
9364. Wainright, _____, wf of Alfred, d 4/1/22 (in Plattsburgh?) (7-4/6)
9365. Wainwright, Alfred T. m 12/28/30 Maria Ellen Marney, both of Poughkeepsie; Rev. Dr. Cuyler (1-1/5)
9366. Wainwright, Ransom, 20, oldest s of Jonathan, d 3/20/31 in Middlebury, VT (lung complaint) (7-3/29)
9367. Wainwright, William of Great Barrington, MA m 8/30/01 Mary Leonard of Sunderland, MA in Great Barrington (6-9/10)
9368. Wait, Esther (Mrs.), 72, d 1/15/27 in Plattsburgh (lived there 45 yrs) (7-1/22)
9369. Wait, Henry m 1/1/24 Maria Baker, both of Easton, in Schaghticoke ; David Tallmadge, Esq. (9-1/13)
9370. Wait, Polly, 39, consort of Daniel and dau of Capt. John Coggsdell of Whitehall, d 10/26/24 in Beekmantown (7-11/6)
9371. Wait, Roswell of the firm of Griffin and Wait d 11/14/29 in Plattsburgh (1-11/28)
9372. Wakelee, Abel, s of Isaac of Weston, CT, d 12/14/24 in Milton, NY (typhus) (funeral sermon by Rev. McCabe) (buried with Masonic honors) ("Printers in Connecticut are requested to notice this.") (2-12/21)

9373. Wakely, David m 2/21/18 Phebe Hasbrouk, both of Poughkeepsie, in Washington (Dut. Co.); Samuel Thurston, Esq. (8-3/4)
9374. Wakeman, Lloyd, 65, d 8/16/25 at his home in Ballston (cholera) (2-8/23)
9375. Wakeman, Sarah, wf of Burr Wakeman of NYC and dau of Lloyd Wakeman of Ballston, d 12/6/24 in NYC (2-12/14)
9376. Walbridge, Henry S., Esq. of Ithaca m 1/25/28 Susan H. Dana, dau of Eleazer, Esq. of Owego, in O; Rev. Putnam (1-1/8/29)
9377. Walby, Ralph m 4/15/24 Mary Ann Ingalls in Middlefield; Rev. Smith (3-4/19)
9378. Walby, William, 58, d 12/15/25 in Otsego (3-12/26)
9379. Waldo, Charles (Dr.) of Mansfield, CT m 2/9/03 Betsey Besley, dau of William of Fishkill; Rev. Clark (8-2/15)
9380. Waldo, David R., 37, d 10/16/15 in Hudson (deceased was of the firm of Plumb, Waldo, Morton & Co.) (6-10/17)
9381. Waldo, Nathan, 58, d 10/22/25 in Milford (3-10/31)
9382. Waldo, Ozias d 11/3/07 in Cherry Valley (typhus) (surv by wf and several young ch) (3-11/7)
9383. Waldo, Samuel (Rev.), 61, of Poughkeepsie d 9/16/93 (surv by wf and children) (8-9/18)
9384. Waldron, Evert, 94, d 1/20/29 in Halfmoon (Sara Co.) (had never called a physician or taken any medicine) (surv by three brothers: Cornelius, Gerrit, and William , one living in each of the following: Bethlehem, Waterford, and Halfmoon) (1-2/28)
9385. Waldron, Henry d "recently" in Albany (funeral from his late home, 23 Steuben St.) (1-7/14/29)
9386. Waldron, John C., merchant, m 3/26/29 Roxanna Haskell, both of Albany, in A; Rev. Kissam (1-3/28)
9387. Waldron, Joseph J., merchant, m 4/26/27 Julia Ann Belden, dau of William T., all of Poughkeepsie, in Christ Church, Poughkeepsie; Rev. Dr. Reed (8-5/2)
9388. Waldron, Peter of Fishkill m 2/21/96 "Miss Swartwout, dau of Gen. Swartwout also of Fishkill"(8-3/2)
9389. Waldron, Platt B., 6 mo, s of Joseph J. and Julia, d 8/26/34 in Pough- keepsie (8-9/3)
9390. Waldron, Tunis of Schaghticoke m 2/18/22 Mary Ann Storey of Albany; Rev. Sommers (9-3/5)
9391. Walker, Caleb m 2/9/20 Esther Darrow, both of Chatham, in Austerlitz; Rev. Summers (6-2/15)
9392. Walker, Edward, Esq., 62, d in Lenox, MA (6-7/2/01)
9393. Walker, Edward M., 33, d 2/19/31 in St. Augustine, FL "whither he had gone for...his health") (1-3/15)
9394. Walker, Hiram (Dr.) of Clinton (Dut. Co.) d "about ten days ago" (8-6/8/02)
9395. Walker, John, member of state assembly from Clinton Co., d "recently" (8-1/18/32)
9396. Walker, John B., s of Capt. Enos, d 6/26/32 in Beekmantown (7-7/7)
9397. Walker, Joseph (formerly a member of the Society of Shakers in Lebanon, NY) m 2/8/27 Lucy Harrington of Berlin, NY in B; Benjamin Vars, Esq. (9-2/27)
9398. Walker, Lemuel m 11/10/25 Polly Delong in Beekmantown; Rev. Halsey (7-11/19)
9399. Walker, Mary, 6, dau of Lt. B. Walker of the U.S. Army, d 9/22/31 in Concord, NH (1-9/28)
9400. Walker, Phineas m 10/27/16 Maria Williams in Claverack; Rev. John G. Gebbard. All of Claverack (6-11/5)
9401. Walker, Ruby, 36, wf of Joseph, d 2/2/30 in Albany (funeral from 228 South Pearl St.) (1-2/3)
9402. Walker, Samuel G. of Utica m 1/4/26 Waty Eldred of Milford in M; Rev. Fellows (3-1/16)
9403. Walker, Stephen, Jr. m 3/20/22 Sally Rudd of Hudson in Butternuts; Rev. Russel Wheeler (3-3/25)
9404. Walker, Sylvester late of Cooperstown, m 11/7/16 Lucy Howard of New Berlin in N B; Rev. John Smith (3-11/14)
9405. Walker, Thomas R., Esq., attorney, m 5/19/29 Sarah Anne Breese, dau of late Arthur, Esq., in Utica; Rev. Samuel C. Aiken (1-5/28)
9406. Walker, William m 12/21/24 Sarah Ingalls in Middlefield; Rev. John Smith (3-12/27)

273

9407. Wallace, Jesse, 20, d 4/1/07 in Troy (surv by his father "and other relatives") (9-4/7)
9408. Wallace, John, 102, d 3/19/12 in North Salem (West. Co.) (8-4/1)
9409. Wallace, John, 82, d in NYC at the home of his son, James D. (9-12/16/28)
9409a Wallworth, James C. (Capt.) of Argyle m Helen Sill of Burlington (Ots. Co.) in B; Rev. John Lord (3-7/25/12)
9410. Walradt, Joseph, farmer, d 10/5/31 in Canajoharie (suicide by hanging - "mental derangement occasioned by the resolution of the consistatory of the seceding Reformed Dutch Church of this town [Canajoharie] of which consistatory he was a member excluding from their communion adhering free masons") (1-10/11)
9411. Walsh, Alexander, merchant, of Lansingburgh m 11/7/15 Ann Vanwyck, dau of Theodorus W., Esq. of Fishkill Hook, in Fishkill (9-11/21)
9412. Walsh, Dudley, for many years a merchant of Albany, d 5/26/16 in Albany (8-5/29 and 3-6/6)
9413. Walsh, John S. m 4/27/31 Laura Spencer Townsend, dau of John; Rev. Dr. Sprague. All of Albany (1-4/28)
9414. Walter, Elizabeth W., 9, dau of Joel of New Haven, CT, d 5/11/31 at the home of her grandfather, William Leavenworth in Albany, NY (funeral from her grandfather's home near "the lower end of South Pearl St.) (1-5/13)
9415. Walter, George, 22, formerly of Poughkeepsie, d 8/16/17 in Richmond, VA (8-8/27)
9416. Walter, Henry, 38, d 1/6/14 in Red Hook (surv by wf and "a large and infant family") (8-1/12)
9417. Walter, Nathan m 8/23/17 Rebecca Burlingame; Silas Waddle, Esq. All of Washington (Dut. Co.) (8-8/27)
9418. Waltermyer, Michael, 52, d 6/2/13 in Claverack (6-6/8)
9419. Walters, Aaron m 11/10/31 Miss Orpha Bliss Griswold, both of Plattsburgh; Rev. Halsey (7-11/12)
9420. Walters, Henry m 10/19/31 Betsey Vanderwarker in Keeseville; John Fitzgerald, Esq. (4 [Keeseville Herald]-10/25)
9421. Walton, E. (Gen), editor of the Vermont Watchman, d in Montpelier, VT (3-9/12/25)
9422. Walton, H. N. of Oswego m 6/17/29 Elizabeth H. Mather, dau of Samuel of Middletown, CT, in M; Rev. Crane (1-6/25)
9423. Walton, Samuel d 11/14/07 (9-11/17)
9424. Walton, Sarah S., inf dau of Joseph, Esq., d 7/2/22 in Cooperstown (3-7/8)
9425. Walworth, Hiram m 12/31/27 Delia A. Griffin, oldest dau of Jonathan, Esq., in Plattsburgh; Rev. Moses Chase (7-1/5/28)
9426. Walworth, James C. (Capt.), merchant, of Argyle m 7/20/12 Helena Sill, dau of Deacon Isaac of Burlington, VT, in B; Rev. John Lord (9-8/4)
9427. Walworth, John (Maj.) of the U.S. Army m 12/31/14 Catherine Bailey of Plattsburgh in P (7-1/7/15)
9428. Walworth, Sarah, wf of Capt. John of the 6th U. S. Infantry and only child of Col. Simonds, d 2/8/13 in Plattsburgh (7-2/12)
9429. Wands, James B. m 7/8/30 Ellen Russell; Rev. Holliday. All of Bethlehem (1-7/10)
9430. Wanzer, Elihu m 12/23/28 Tamma Hobby, dau of C. K., all of Northeast; Rev. Armstrong (8-1/21/29)
9431. Ward, Daniel, 81, of Clinton (Dut. Co.) d 12/8/09 (8-12/20)
9432. Ward, Griffin of Washington (Dut. Co.) m 3/1/27 Sally Maria Olmsted, dau of Benjamin G. of Sharon, CT, in Amenia, NY; Rev. C. P. Wilson (8-3/21)
9433. Ward, Harriet B., 19, wf of Levi A. and dau of William Barton, Esq. formerly of Hartford, CT, d 5/27/30 in Rochester, NY (1-6/21)
9434. Ward, Hiram, 26, d 3/25/29 in Brutus, Cayuga Co. (received his B.A. degree from Union College, Schenectady, in 1828) (1-5/7)
9435. Ward, Jacob m 1/21/23 Joannah Coles, both of Pleasant Valley; A. Raymond, Esq. (8-1/22)
9436. Ward, John m 10/23/26 Mary Holmes, both of Poughkeepsie (8-11/1)
9437. Ward,Jonathan (Dr.) d 9/13/13 in Poughkeepsie (8-9/15)
9438. Ward, Joseph d in Sharon (NY or CT - not clear) (6-7/1/06)
9439. Ward, Mary Anna, 26, wf of Col. William H., d 1/9/31 in Rochester (1-1/24)
9440. Ward, Owen I. of Pleasant Valley m 9/14/20 Harriet Pinckney, dau of Dr. P. Ward, formerly of Fishkill, in Hampton (Orange Co.); Rev. Ostrom (8-9/20)

9441. Ward, Richard, 1 yr, s of Robert R., d 7/12/13 in Cooperstown (3-7/17)
9442. Ward, Stephen, Esq., 68, d 12/8/97 in East Chester (Westchester Co.) (8-12/19)
9443. Wardell, Elizabeth (Mrs.) 80(?), d 6/1/21 in Poughkeepsie (8-6/6)
9444. Wardell, John, 47, d 1/24/19 in Poughkeepsie (8-1/27)
9445. Warden, Ethan A. (Capt.) m Abigal Ann Kellogg, dau of Hon. Charles, in Kelloggsville, Cayuga Co.; Rev. Gregory (1-3/1/31)
9446. Wardsworth, Jared m 1/24/27 Katurah Rodgers, both of Troy; Rev. Howard (9-1/30)
9447. Wardwell, Stephen m 11/19/29 Eliza Snediker; Rev. Buttolph. All of Freedom (8-11/25)
9448. Ware, George W. of Keeseville m 10/29/32 Amanda M. Rand of Townshend, VT in T; Rev. Brown (4 [Keeseville Herald]-11/13)
9449. Warford, John (Rev.) of Salem d in S (6-6/1/02)
9450. Warford, Lawrence, about 4, s of John, Esq., d 8/29/22 in Plattsburgh (7-8/31)
9451. Warner, _____, child of Willard, d 10/26/15 in Troy (9-10/31)
9452. Warner, Annis, 46, wf of Dr. Walt Warner, d 9/4/33 in Chazy (7-9/14)
9453. Warner, Betsey, 33, wf of Jason, Esq., formerly of Norwich, CT, d 9/21/16 in Canaan, NY (6-10/1)
9454. Warner, David of Fishkill m 3/22/29 Sarah Hornbeck of Poughkeepsie; Rev. Richardson (8-3/25)
9455. Warner, Effingham m 4/27/31 Anne B. Summerfield, youngest dau of late William, at St. Stephen's in NYC; Rev. Francis I. Hawks (1-4/29)
9456. Warner, Elijah of Genesee m 4/25/04 Sally Ball, dau of Maj. Jonathan of Claverack (6-5/8)
9457. Warner, Eliza C., 32(?), relict of late Henry and dau of John Whiting of Canaan, NY, d 8/10/31 at the home of her brother, Dr. J. L. Whiting, in Detroit, MI (1-9/3)
9458. Warner, George Washington, Esq., 30, s of Jason, Esq. of Canaan, NY d in Maclarin, Georgia (1-10/7/29)
9459. Warner, Isaac, 28, d 2/18/16 in Poughkeepsie (8-2/21)
9460. Warner, J. R. (Capt.), merchant, of Utica m 10/22/29 Rebecca Washburn of Albany in A; Rev. Ferris (1-10/23)
9461. Warner, John,(age blurred), d 10/30/16 in Poughkeepsie (8-11/6)
9462. Warner, Laura, 37, wf of Zacharia, d 12/15/25 in Burlington (Ots. Co.) (3-12/26)
9463. Warner, Nancy, 23, wf of Roger late of Weathersfield, CT, d 10/14/07 in Troy, NY (9-10/20)
9464. Warner, Olive (Mrs.) d 6/27/23 in Ballston (apoplexy) (2-7/1)
9465. Warner, Olivia Ann, 14, d 8/25/22 in Ballston (2-9/3)
9466. Warner, Rebekah (Mrs.), 90, d 3/11/12 in Canaan (had lived a widow 36 years, had 238 descendants of whom 211 outlived her) (6-3/23)
9467. Warner, Reuben m 2/10/02 Peggy Green, both of Clinton (Dut. Co.) (8-2/23)
9468. Warner, Richard, about 78, of Poughkeepsie d 6/14/02 (8-6/22)
9469. Warren, _____, 9 mo, a child of Esaias (sic) Warren, Esq., d 4/5/15 in Troy (9-4/11)
9470. Warren, Darius, 69, d 8/20/29 in Otsego (an early settler there) (1-8/27)
9471. Warren, Eliakim, 78, d 9/4/24 in Troy (3-9/13)
9472. Warren, Esaias (sic), late mayor of Troy, d 4/19/29 in Troy (1-4/23)
9473. Warren, Eunice, 50, wf of Parker Warren, d 9/13/19 in Beekmantown (7-9/18)
9474. Warren, George B. of Troy m 12/15/23 Mary M. Bowers, oldest dau of John M., Esq.; Rev. John Smith (3-12/22)
9475. Warren, John S. of Poughkeepsie m 7/9/17 Sally Brewster, oldest dau of Absalam, Esq., in Fishkill; Rev. Crane. All of Phillipstown (Put. Co.) (8-7/30)
9476. Warren, Julius m 10/21/23 Abigail Cook of Sherburne in Cooperstown; Rev. Smith (3-11/24)
9477. Warren, Nathan, merchant, m 4/24/08 Mary Bouton, both of Troy; Rev. Butler (9-4/26)
9478. Warren, William (Capt.), 79, (a Rev. "hero"), d 7/29/31 in Worcester, MA (commanded a company at Bunker Hill where he was wounded) (1-8/11)
9479. Washburn, Bashtheba (Mrs.), 86, late of Hartford, CT, d 7/25/28 in Troy (9-8/1)
9480. Washburn, Daniel of Lockport, NY d 12/4/29 in Georgetown, Dist. of Columbia (1-12/12)

9481. Washburn, Silas, 56, d 8/28/25 in Freedom (surv by wf and children) (8-8/31)
9482. Wasthorn(?), Darius(?) (name blurred) d 2/5/26 at his home in Beekman (8-2/15)
9483. Waterhouse, _____, 30, wf of Cyrus, d 4/30/25 in Plattsburgh (7-5/7)
9484. Waterman, _____, about 15 mo, s of Maj. Barnabas, d 6/8/19 in Hudson (6-6/15)
9485. Waterman, _____, 1 yr, s of Gen. T. G., d 8/31/29 in Binghamton (1-9/2)
9486. Waterman, Sally, 30, wf of Barnabas, d 9/5/09 in Hudson (6-9/12)
9487. Waterman, Simeon, 81, d 4/21/22 in Otsego (3-4/29)
9488. Waterman, William W., about 4, s of Gen. T. G., d 8/28/29 in Binghamton (1-9/8)
9489. Watermire, John m 6/26/29 Jane Swartwout, dau of Samuel, all of Clinton; Isaac Sutherland, Esq. (8-7/2)
9490. Waterous, Ambrose m 11/24/15 Sarah Grimshaw; Rev. Leonard (8-11/29)
9491. Waters, Daniel m 1/16/23 Eunice Fitch in Cooperstown (3-1/20)
9492. Watrous, Louisa, 47, wf of John R., Esq., d 2/15/23 in Colchester, CT (3-3/3)
9493. Watson, Aaron m 10/28/21 Nancy Green; Rev. Cuyler (8-10/31)
9494. Watson, Ebenezer, 80, a Rev. patriot, d 8/18/30 in Penfield. Also Anna, 79, died the same day (both were born in Gorham, ME) (1-9/1)
9495. Watson, Frances S., 20, wf of Winslow C. of Plattsburgh, NY, d 4/26/29 at the home of her father, the Hon. Richard Skinner of Manchester, VT (1-5/14)
9496. Watson, James, Esq., 55, d 5/15/06 in NYC (had held several state and federal offices - details not given) (9-5/27 and 6-6/3)
9497. Watson, John, Esq., 55, d 5/14/06 in NYC (8-5/20)
9498. Watson, Malborne, Esq. of Durham m 9/14/31 Mary Hickok of Greenville (Greene Co.) in G; Rev. Hervey (1-9/29)
9499. Watson, Winslow C., attorney, of Plattsburgh, NY m 4/28/28 Frances B. Skinner, dau of Chief Justice Skinner late gov. of VT, in Manchester, VT (7-5/24)
9500. Watt, Alexander m 12/7/27 Agnes Duncan; Rev. Beman. All of Troy (9-12/11)
9501. Wattles, Jehiel, 24, formerly of Cooperstown, d 10/25/26 in Springfield (3-11/6)
9502. Wattles, Nsthaniel, Esq., state assemblyman from Delaware Co., d 1/5/98 in Albany (8-1/16)
9503. Watts, Charles of Nova Scotia m 10/31/30 Mary Jones of Albany; Rev. Mathias (1-11/1)
9504. Watts, John (Dr.) of Albany, physician and pres. of the College of Physicians and Surgeons, d before 2/4/31 in NYC (1-2/8)
9505. Watts, Robert, Jr., Esq. of NYC m 7/7/11 Matilda Ridley at Oak Hill, home of John Livingston, Esq.; Rev. Chester (6-7/12)
9506. Watts, Robert J., s of John, Esq., d 2/9/30 in NYC (1-2/16)
9507. Way, Martha Jane, 18 mo, dau of James B., d 9/20/30 in Poughkeepsie (8-9/29)
9508. Way, Thomas m 10/16/22 Sally Ann Corrington in Troy; Rev. Griffin (9-10/22)
9509. Wayne, C. W., Esq., attorney, of Plattsburgh m 5/19/31 Sarah F. Skinner, dau of late Hon. Richard of Manchester, VT, in M (1-6/2)
9510. Wead, Stephen of Hopkinton m Lucinda Amsden in Malone (7-2/2/22)
9511. Weatherwax, Abraham m 1/26/13 Hannah Magee; Rev. Quitman (8-2/3)
9512. Weatherwax, Margaret, 59, consort of Andrew G. formerly of Pittstown and "the mother of a large family", d 11/21/30 in Little Falls (1-11/29)
9513. Weaver, Henry m Margaret Ruby in Albany (6-10/26/02)
9514. Weaver, John m 11/13/32 Elenora Linton; Rev. Dr. Reed. All of Poughkeepsie (8-11/21)
9515. Weaver, Julia, 22, dau of Gen. John, d 2/20/31 in Deerfield (Oneida Co.) (1-3/1)
9516. Weaver, Priscilla (Mrs.), 72, d 2/28/13 (3-3/6)
9517. Weaver, William m 11/9/31 Catharine Belinda Cuyler, dau of Tobias V., all of Albany, in Brooklyn; Rev. John C. Green (1-11/15)
9518. Webb, Amelia Barclay, 14 mo, dau of James Watson Webb, d 10/11/30 in NYC (1-10/16)
9519. Webb, Catharine, 36, wf of Gen. Samuel B., d 10/14/05 in Claverack (6-10/22)

9520. Webb, Charles, a preacher of the Society of Friends, d in Newburgh
(8-1/26/31)
9521. Webb, Frances De Lord, about 20, wf of Henry L., d 3/15/31 in Albany
(7-3/22). See also #9522 below.
9522. Webb. Frances H., wf of H. L., Esq., died (date and place not given).
(The paper of reference below (#7) copied her obit from the Albany
Journal and Telegraph thus: "Immediately after her marriage (she)
visited Europe in company with her husband and passed some time in
France of which her father was a native") (surv by her husband, her
mother, and an only child - an infant [name of latter not given])
(7-3/29/31). See also 9521 above.
9523. Webb, Harriet E., 18, wf of Capt. S. H. Webb of the U.S. Army, d 8/14/24
in Detroit, MI (3-8/30)
9524. Webb, James Watson (Lt.) of the 3rd Regiment, U.S. Infantry, m 7/1/23
Helen Lispenard Stewart, dau of Alexander L., Esq., in NYC; Rev.
Parkinson (3-7/14)
9525. Webb, Rebecca, 87, consort of late Derick Webb, d 9?/31/24 in Plattsburgh
(7-10/23)
9526. Webb, S. H. (Capt.) of the 3rd U.S. Infantry m 5/4/23 Harriet E. Baker,
dau of Maj. D. Baker of the U.S. Army "at the post of Saguana"
(3-6/2)
9527. Webb, Samuel B. (Gen.), 51, d 12/3/07 in Claverack (6-12/8)
9528. Webb, Stephen H. (Capt.) of the U.S. Army m Mary J. Stewart, dau of A. L.,
Esq., in NYC; Rev. Parkinson (3-2/27)
9529. Webb, Thomas Smith (Col.), formerly of Providence (RI?) and past master
of the Grand Lodge of Rhode Island, d 7/6/19 in Cleveland, OH (8-7/28)
9530. Webb, Walter W. of Williamsburgh, VA m 3/8/31 Julia Frances Converse, dau
of John, Esq., in Troy; Rev. Butler (1-3/11)
9531. Webster, Benjamin m 3/30/26 Minerva Bissell, youngest dau of Elisha; Rev.
Wilson. All of Northeast (8-4/12)
9532. Webster, Daniel (Hon.) of Boston m 12/12/29 Caroline Le Roy, youngest dau
of Herman, Esq. of NYC; Rev. Dr. Wainwright (1-12/16)
9533. Webster, George, one of the editors of the Albany Gazette, m "a short
time since" Rachel Bush of Sheffield, MA (9-3/19/99)
9534. Webster, George, 60, bookseller and one of the editors of the Albany
Gazette and Daily Advertiser, d 2/21/23 in Albany (He was of the firm
of C.R. and G. Webster) ("He has left a large family") (2-2/25; 3-3/3;
and 8-3/5)
9536. Webster, Grace, wf of Hon. Daniel Webster, Congressman from Mass., died
(date and death place not given) (surv by husband and 3 ch) (buried in
Boston, MA) (9-1/29/28)
9537. Webster, James Oliver, 23, s of Dr. J., d 5/4/30 in Fort Plain (1-5/11)
9538. Webster, Jonathan L. d 1/1/18 in Plattsburgh (7-1/3)
9539. Webster, Lyman m 1/25/16 Sarah Gifford; Rev. Ogilvie. All of Hudson
(6-1/30)
9540. Webster, Noah, Esq., 91, d 11/9/13 in Hartford, CT (3-11/27)
9541. Webster, Sarah, 7, oldest dau of Chauncey, d 10/5/30 in Albany (funeral
at Chapel Street, foot of Pine St.) (1-10/6)
9542. Webster, Thomas m 5/10/21 Content Branch, both of West Point; Rev. Somers
(9-6/19)
9543. Webster, William, a native of Ireland, d 2/3/21 in Westford (killed in a
fall while carrying a heavy log on his shoulder) (surv by a wf and 6 ch)
(3-2/12)
9544. Weed, Anna, 52, wf of Elijah, d 10/15/23 in Hyde Park (8-10/22)
9545. Weed, Anson M., 24, late senior editor of the Livingston Register,
d 2/2/31 in Avon (1-2/19)
9546. Weed, Charles W. of the firm of Rhoads and Weed m 6/9/31 Mary Ann Howell;
Rev. John M. Krebs. All of NYC (1-6/13)
9547. Weed, Hart m 2/9/04 Roxana Crosby in Southeast; Rev. Minor (8-2/21)
9548. Weed, K. m Fanny Hathaway, both of Jay, in Clintonville; E. Williams, Esq.
(7-3/29/31)
9549. Weed, Thurlow, printer, of Albany m 4/26/18 Katherine Ostrander of Cooperstown; Rev. John Smith (3-4/27)
9550. Weekes, Albert m 5/27/30 J. Shaw; Rev. Wile. All of Pleasant Valley
(8-6/2)

9551. Weekes, Henry and __?__ Ackerley were executed 4/21/81 in Poughkeepsie "pursuant to the sentence of a court-martial" (5-4/26)
9552. Weekes, Joseph, merchant, of NYC m 11/2/31 Isabella A. Grand Lax, dau of late Thomas Lax of Flushing, in F; Rev. Lewis (1-11/7)
9553. Weeks, ____, wf of Daniel, d 3/31/26 in Poughkeepsie (8-4/5)
9554. Weeks, Benjamin of Montgomery (Orange Co.) m 9/23/28 Hannah Van Vliet of Fishkill in F; Rev. Hyer (8-10/8)
9555. Weeks, Carlisle T. m Eliza Ann Mead, both of NYC, in NYC (9-12/23/28)
9556. Weeks, George U., merchant, of Peekskill m 1/18/26 Almira Jenckes of Georgia in Poughkeepsie; Rev. Dr. Reed (8-1/25)
9557. Weeks, Isaac d 7/31/14 in Poughkeepsie (8-8/3)
9558. Weeks, Jacob, Esq., attorney, m 1/3/22 Helen Billings in Poughkeepsie; Rev. Reed (8-1/9)
9559. Weeks, Jacob, about 69, d 8/11/22 in Troy (9-8/13)
9560. Weeks, Julia Hall, 26, wf of Robert D., d in NYC (9-12/19/28)
9561. Weeks, William R. (Rev.) of Plattsburgh m 12/14/11 Hannah Randell, dau of John of the town of Colonie, in Albany; Rev. Neill (7-1/31/12)
9562. Weever, Palen m 1/9/08 Josete Crahan, both of Troy; Rev. Coe (9-1/12)
9563. Welch, ____, s of William, d "recently" (funeral from the "Connecticut Coffee House") (location of Coffee House not given - perhaps in Albany, publication place of this death notice) (1-2/13/29). See 9566.
9564. Welch, ____, child of William, d "recently" in Albany (1-4/24/30)
9565. Welch, John, Jr., 16, s of John, Esq. of Litchfield, CT, d 3/11/15 in Albany (9-3/21)
9566. Welch, Margaret (Mrs.), 59, d 6/8/30 in Albany (her son William is mentioned; funeral from the Connecticut Coffee House, South Market St.) (1-6/9). See 9563.
9567. Weld, Joseph, Jr., 36, d 9/20/23 (9-9/23)
9568. Welland, John (Hon.) of Salem m 5/14/29 Elizabeth C. Smith, a teacher at the Troy Female Seminary; Rev. Merwin (1-5/15)
9569. Welles, Benjamin, Esq., sheriff of Steuben Co., d 4/19/13 in Steuben (8-7/28)
9570. Welling, Smith m 10/16/22 Sally Lawrence, dau of Richard; Rev. Clark. All of Pleasant Valley (8-10/23)
9571. Welling, Thomas, Jr. m 11/30/14 Sally Forman, both of Clinton; Rev. John Clark (8-12/7)
9572. Wellman, Ira, 30, d 4/13/23 in Milford ("in a fit of apoplexy") (3-4/21)
9573. Wells, Archibald (Sgt.) d 12/23/12 at the 6th Regiment cantonment near Plattsburgh (born in Conn. but a resident of Hudson, NY "for some time previous to his enlistment") (6-2/2/13)
9574. Wells, Arnold m 5/25/28 Maria Van Curen, both of Lansingburgh, in Troy; Rev. Willis (9-6/3)
9575. Wells, Eliphalet m 5/11/20 Nancy Gardner in White Creek; Rev. Lewis (9-5/30)
9576. Wells, Frances Cora, 15 mo, dau of Philander, d 8/11/27 in Troy (9-8/14)
9577. Wells, Henry m 10/1/17 Sabre Marsh, dau of Joseph C., all of Plattsburgh (7-10/11)
9578. Wells, John of Plattsburgh m 1/19/17 Peggy Mills of Champlain in C; Rev. Byington (7-1/25)
9579. Wells, John D., M.D., 31, late professor of Anatomy in Baltimore and Berkshire Medical Colleges, d in Boston, MA (1-8/10/30)
9580. Wells, John P., inf s of Philander, d 11/24/28 in Troy (9-11/25)
9581. Wells, Noah B., merchant, m 1/4/19 Almira M. Pomeroy in St. Albans, VT; Rev. Strong (9-1/19)
9582. Wells, Philander A. of Pittsfield, MA m 2/26/27 Sally W. Daniels of Lansingburgh; Rev. Howard (9-3/2)
9583. Wells, Ransford (Rev.) of Canajoharie m 4/20/31 Joanna Hardenburgh, dau of Jacob R., Esq. of NYC, in NYC; Rev. Dr. Jacob Broadhead (1-4/28)
9584. Wells, Ransom of Alburg, VT m 9/12/21 Harriet Travis of Plattsburgh, NY; Rev. Frederick Halsey (7-9/22)
9585. Wells, Richard I., Esq., attorney, m 10/1/19 Ann Maria Olcott, dau of Josiah of hudson (6-10/5)
9586. Wells, William, 28, d 1/31/11 in Milford (Ots. Co.) (surv by wf and 4 small ch) (3-2/9)

9587. Welton, John Alonzo, inf s of Rev. Welton, pastor of the Presbyterian Ch. in Poughkeepsie, d 8/3/30 ("In the space of a few months this family has been bereft of three...children (8-8/4)

9588. Welton, Shubael, 70, (a Rev. soldier) father of Rev. Welton of Poughkeepsie, d 3/6/31 in Rochester (8-3/23)

9589. Welton, Virginia L., oldest and only remaining child of Rev. A. Welton, d 3/26/30 in Poughkeepsie (two of his children had died within a five week period - these not identified by name in this report) (8-3/31 and 1-4/2)

9590. Wemet, Joseph d before 8/9/22 (his body was found in the river near Chazy village) (coroner's verdict: accidental drowning) (7-8/17)

9591. Wemple, E. L. m 9/27/29 Ann Hanna, both of Albany, in Lansingburgh; Rev. McIlvaine (1-10/3)

9592. Wendall, Anne (possibly Abbe) (Miss), about 18, recently of Schenectady, d 3/20/30 in Albany (1-3/22)

9593. Wendell, John, merchant, m 10/19/30 Ruth Ann Shaw, both of Albany; Rev. Welch (1-10/21)

9594. Wendell, Mary (widow), 77, d 3/14/31 in Albany (funeral from her late home at 59 Hamilton St. (1-3/16)

9595. Wendell, Samuel, 33, formerly of Albany, NY, d 5/26/29 in New Orleans, LA (yellow fever) (1-6/25)

9596. Wendell, Sarah, 58, d 4/20/30 in Albany (funeral from her late home, 112 State St.) (1-4/21)

9597. Wentworth, Sanford, about 21, s of Reuben of Sudbury, d 6/12/25 when the family dwelling huse was struck by lightning (a younger brother of Sanford, about 14, was severely injured) (7-6/25)

9598. Werden, Jerusha, 27, consort of Elias, was killed by lightning 7/17/08 (6-7/19)

9599. Werth, John J. d 1/31/32 in Poughkeepsie "where he has resided for the past five or six months" (was born in Westphalia, Germany, "but for the greater part of the last 20 years a resident of Richmond, Virginia") (funeral at the home of the Misses Schoonmaker on Main Street) (8-2/1)

9600. West, Benjamin, a native of Dover (Dut. Co.) "in a state of mental derangement killed himself (7/3/17) by diving into the shallow Fallkill near Poughkeepsie " (this verdict reached at the coroner's inquest)

9601. West, David m 12/20/07 Rebecca Clark, dau of Daniel, in Hudson; Rev. Sears (6-12/22)

9602. West, Isaac m 1/3/04 Charlotte Traver, dau of Jacob P., all of Clinton (Dut. Co.); Rev. Dodge (8-1/17)

9603. West, John of Syracuse m 7/1/29 Prudence Martindale of Cazenovia in Onondaga; Rev. Cloud (1-7/14)

9604. West, Richard m 12/27/28 Hannah Waldron; Rev. Beman. All of Troy (9-1/1/28)

9605. Westbrook, Cornelius D. (Rev.) m 1/24/07 Hannah Van Wyck, dau of Isaac, Esq., in Fishkill; Rev. George Barcalo (6-2/17 and 8-2/25)

9606. Westbrook, Cornelius D. (Rev.) of Fishkill m 1/26/19 Sarah Beekman of Kingston in K; Rev. De Witt (8-2/3)

9607. Westbrook, Frederick (Gen.), 73, (a Rev. soldier) d 12/6/27 at the home of his son, Rev. Cornelius D. (8-12/12)

9608. Westbrook, Hannah, 29, consort of Rev. Cornelius, d 2/23/17 in Fishkill (8-2/26)

9609. Westcoat, James R. of the firm of Westcoat and La Farge(?) m 8/24/31 Maria B. White in NYC; Rev. Cyrus Mason. All of NYC (1-8/27)

9610. Westcott, Davis m 12/22/17 Anna Chapman, oldest dau of Zenas, in Cooperstown (3-12/29)

9611. Westerlow, Rensselaer, Esq. m 5/6/05 "Miss Lansing", dau of Hon. John, Chancellor of NY; Rev. Bassett (6-5/21)

9612. Westervelt, Casparus, "an aged inhabitant of Poughkeepsie" d 5/7/21 (8-5/9)

9613. Westervelt, Cornelius C. m 1/23/12 Rebecca Yerry; Rev. C. C. Cuyler. All of Poughkeepsie (8-2/5)

9614. Westervelt, Edward m 4/7/31 Eliza Tidd in Hyde Park; Rev. Welton (8-4/13)

9615. Westervelt, Elias m 10/31/07 Ruth Jacocks, both of Poughkeepsie; Rev. Brouwer (8-11/4)

9616. Westervelt, James, Jr. m 9/22/29 Harriet Frear, dau of Jacobus; Rev. Dr. Cuyler (8-9/23)

9617. Westervelt, Joseph, 77, a long-term resident of Poughkeepsie, d 2/19 (8-2/23)
9618. Westervelt, Peter m 3/29/14 Hannah Lennington, both of Poughkeepsie; Rev. Cuyler (8-4/6)
9619. Westervelt, Ralph A. (Rev.), 46, pastor of the Reformed Dutch Church in Wynantskill, d 4/12/23 in Greenbush (surv by wf and children) (9-4/22)
9620. Westfall, Simon B. d 8/25/07 in Rhinebeck (8-9/9)
9621. Westfall, William of Rhinebeck m 1/22/18 Peggy Hicks, dau of Elias of Clermont (8-1/28)
9622. Weston, Isaac Newton, s of Dr. Isaac, m 1/5/31 Mary Ann McConnell, dau of Isaac, Esq., in Lorraine (1-1/22)
9623. Weston, Levi M., merchant, of Poughkeepsie m 8/21/28 Esther Maria Knapp of Washington (Dut. Co.) in W; Rev. Clark (8-8/27)
9624. Weston, Mary, 2, only dau of Levi, formerly of Poughkeepsie, d 5/19/34 at Bull's Bridge, CT (8-6/4)
9625. Wetherly, Timothy m 11/1/01 Abigail Clark, dau of Capt. George, in Hudson (6-11/5)
9626. Wetmore, Alphonso (Lt.), 23rd Regiment, U.S. Infantry, m 9/5/13 Mary Smith of Canajoharie in C; Rev. Elliot (3-9/11)
9627. Wetmore, Chester m 7/12/21 Mary Dumot in Westford; Elder Sawin (3-7/23)
9628. Wetmore, Edmund A., Esq. m 6/3/29 Mary A. Lothrop, dau of John H., Esq., in Utica; Rev. Aiken (1-6/12)
9629. Wetmore, William H. of NYC m 10/24/21 Sarah Ann Brinckerhoff of Fishkill in F.; Rev. Westbrook (8-10/31)
9630. Wetsel, Martin m 7/5/30 Maria Depue, both of Catskill; Rev. Dr. Cuyler (8-7/21)
9631. Whalen, _____ (Mrs.), mother of Ezekiel, d 11/5/22 in Milton (2-11/12)
9632. Whallon, Samuel m 1/26/06 Eliza Williams, both of Troy; Rev. Coe (9-1/28)
9633. Wharry, David Miller (Dr.) m 11/10/34 Margaret Bates, dau of Bernard, Esq.; Rev. Vandeveer. All of Shawungunk (Ulster co.) (8-11/19)
9634. Wheaton, Homer, Esq. of Syracuse m 6/23/30 Louisa Smith, dau of late Isaac, Esq. of Lithgow (Dut. Co.), in Poughkeepsie; Rev. Dr. Reed (1-6/25 and 8-6/30)
9635. Wheeler, Almon, Esq., attorney, of Malone m 11/9/13 Eliza Woodward of Plattsburgh in P; Rev. William R. Weeks (7-11/20)
9636. Wheeler, Almon, Esq., 32, attorney and late postmaster of Malone, d 1/5/27 in M ("interred in the new burying ground with Masonic honors") (7-1/13)
9637. Wheeler, Calus m 12/18/28 Mary Ann Weaver in Troy; Rev. Tucker. All of T (9-12/26)
9638. Wheeler, Ebenezer (Maj.), 43, d 2/28/13 in Hancock (Dela. Co.) (6-4/6)
9639. Wheeler, Elizur (Dr.) d 5/5/15 in Windham (hydrophobia - bitten by a wolf) (3-5/18)
9640. Wheeler, George, Esq., attorney, of Troy m Mary Ann McNeil in Whitehall; Rev. A. Fleming (7-7/26/34)
9641. Wheeler, Henry of Poughkeepsie m 9/23/29 Mrs. Rhoda Holmes of Pleasant Valley; Rev. Clark (8-9/30)
9642. Wheeler, Ira m Lucerne Murdock in Hartford; Elder Bostwick. All of H (3-4/1/09)
9643. Wheeler, James, Esq. of Orange Co. m 12/1/29 Cornelia Van Emburgh Hunn, dau of late John S., Esq. of Newburgh; Rev. Dr. De Witt (1-12/5)
9644. Wheeler, John m 10/12/31 Mary Ann Whitney in Poughkeepsie; Rev. Dr. Reed (8-10/26)
9645. Wheeler, John W., Esq. of Red Hook m 12/24/27 Sarah R. R. Warren, dau of John G., Esq. of NYC, in NYC (8-12/26)
9646. Wheeler, Jonathan E. of Northeast m 11/10/32 Hepzibah M. Vincent of Union Vale; Rev. Buttolph (8-11/28)
9647. Wheeler, Lemuel (Dr.) d 8/31/01 in Salisbury, CT (6-9/3)
9648. Wheeler, Mary, 46, wf of Henry d 8/7/27 in Poughkeepsie (8-8/15)
9649. Wheeler, Philip m 12/30/23 Roxana M. Shepherd, both of Troy; Rev. Butler (9-1/13/24)
9650. Wheeler, Ralph of the firm of Bessac and Wheeler m 8/10/31 Elizabeth Gaul in Hudson; Rev. Chester (1-8/24)
9651. Wheeler, Walter D. m 5/11/29 Sally Ann Bond in Poughkeepsie; Rev. Welton (8-5/14)
9652. Wheeler, Wilhelmina, relict of late dr. William of Red Hook, d 1/23/13 in Albany (8-2/3)

280

9653. Wheeler, William (Dr.), 56, d 4/14/10 at his home in Red Hook (surv by wf and children) (6-4/19)
9654. Wheeler, William of Ballston m 3/5/22 Eliza Davenport of Charlton in C; Rev. Platt (2-3/20)
9655. Wheeler, William W. of Pleasant Valley m 11/29/17 Jane Gildersleeve of Poughkeepsie (8-12/3)
9656. Wheeler, Zebediah m 2/28/19 Mrs. Sabrah Hickok of Milton, VT (7-3/6)
9657. Wheelock, Burress (Rev.) of Boston m Fanny W. Richards, only dau of Dr. J. Richards of Hillsdale, in H; Rev. Quilting (1-7/21)
9658. Wheelock, Elizabeth, 34, wf of Phineas, d 7/26/24 in Plattsburgh (7-8/7)
9659. Whelpley, Philip M. (Rev.), 30, pastor of the First Presbyterian Society in NYC, d 7/17/24 at Schooley's Mountain (3-7/26)
9660. Whelpley, Samuel W. (Rev.) of Plattsburgh, NY m Susan R. Angus of Perth Amboy. NJ in Brooklyn, NY; Rev. P. M. Whelpley (7-6/20)
9661. Whipple, _____, consort of Barnet of Cooperstown, d 3/21/96 in Cooperstown (3-3/24)
9662. Whipple, Abraham (Commodore), 85, a native of Rhode Island, d 6/27/19 in Marietta, Ohio ("He fired the first shot on the water , June 25, 1775, at the outbreak of the Rev. War.") (8-7/7)
9663. Whipple, Benajah, 43, d 2/27/13 in Cooperstown (surv by wf and several children) (3-3/6)
9664. Whipple, Daniel S. m 12/24/12 Susan Barker, both of Troy; Rev. Coe (9-1/5/13)
9665. Whipple, Ezra (Capt.) (a Rev. officer), father of Barnum of Albany, d 11/20/29 in Sunderland, VT (father of 21 children) (1-11/28)
9666. Whipple, James d 3/16/14 in Cooperstown (3-3/19)
9667. Whipple, Job m 2/16/25 Lydia Robinson, both of Cambridge, in Easton; Simeon Dennis, Esq. (9-3/4)
9668. Whipple, Seth m 2/7/21 Euncice Metcalf in Otsego; Rev. Gary (3-2/12)
9669. Whippy, George S. m 7/17/19 Sarah C. West, both of Hudson, in Claverack; Rev. Gephard (6-7/20)
9670. Whistler, George W. (Lt.) of the U.S. Army m 11/3/31 Anna Matilda McNiel, dau of late Dr. Daniel of North Carolina, in NYC; Rev. L. P. Bayard (1-11/7)
9671. Whistler, John (Maj.) of the U.S. Army d 9/2/29 in Belfontaine, Missouri (1-9/29)
9672. Whitaker, _____, 14, s of Ezra of Adams, MA, d "lately" (in taking a horse to water had fastened the halter to his wrist and when the horse bolted the boy's head struck a rock) (6-3/25/06)
9673. Whitaker, James Henry, 20 mo, s of Walter of Troy, d 10/10/19 (9-10/12)
9674. Whitaker, Mariah Adelaide, 25, wf of Walter, Esq. of Troy, d 9/18/20 on a visit at her father's home near NYC (9-9/26)
9675. Whitaker, Oliver, 47, d 8/31/20 in Hudson (6-9/5)
9676. Whitcher, Joseph, about 24, d 5/18/11 in Plattsburgh (smallpox) (7-5/24)
9677. Whitcomb, Cyrus, bridegroom. See marr record of James D. McDonald dated 2/24/1815.
9678. White, _____, s of John G., d "recently" in Albany (funeral from his father's home, 27 Chapel St.) (1-5/14/31)
9679. White, Alfred, merchant, of Waterford m 10/17/02 Mrs. Margaret Jones of Stillwater; Rev. Paige (9-10/27)
9680. White, Betsey, wf of John and dau of John Wood of Lansingburgh, d 10/23/00 in NYC (9-9/30)
9681. White, Calvin, 23, late of Hudson, NY, d 4/29/09 in Coventry, CT (6-5/9)
9682. White, Caroline F. (Miss), 15, dau of Elijah, Esq., d 6/25/29 in Plattsburgh (1-7/4)
9683. White, Cynthia W., about 16, d at the home of her father, Hon. H. L. White, near Knoxville, NY (1-2/20/29)
9684. White, Devillo (Dr.) m 12?9/24 Caroline Pratt in Sherburne; Rev. Manning (3-12/13)
9685. White, George (Dr.), 24, formerly of Hebron, CT, d 10/16/12 in Lansingburgh, NY (6-10/19)
9686. White, Henry Kirk, 1 yr, only s of Jesse P., d 2/11/31 in Albany (funeral from 53 Hudson St.) (1-2/14)
9687. White, Hiram m 10/23/25 Abigail Barns in Maryland, NY (3-11/7)

9688. White, Hugh, 80, d 4/16/12 in Whitestown (Moved in 1784 from Middletown, Ct. to Sedaghquate [now Whitesborough village], NY. Judge White moved to the westward of the German settlements along the Mohawk. (8-6/10)

9689. White, Ira A. (Capt.) of Tyrone m Phidelia Johnson, dau of Calvin, Esq. of Columbia (Herk. Co.) in C; Rev. Hovey (1-3/1/31)

9690. White, Isaac of Washington (Dut. Co.) m 3/16/11 Mary Cline of Beekman (8-3/20)

9691. White, James m 6/6/30 Jane Quackenbush; Rev. White. All of Albany (1-6/9)

9692. White, James, Esq., 38, d 7/4/30 in Glens Falls (1-7/24)

9693. White, James d "recently" in Albany (funeral from his late home, 55 Church St.) "His brothers" are mentioned but not in number or by name) (1-6/23/31)

9694. White, James T., 19, s of James of Cooperstown, drowned 8/11/19 at Chicago on Lake Michigan (3-9/27)

9695. White, Joseph of Catskill m 9/2/20 Eliza Lester of Troy; Rev. Dr. Coe (9-9/5)

9696. White, Lawrence, 54, d 5/3/29 in Auburn (1-5/9)

9697. White, Loyal W., 22, d 8/24/29 in Sparta (Liv. Co.) (born in Mount Holly, VT) (1-9/8)

9698. White, Philip, 46, d 1/1/15 in Claverack (6-1-10)

9699. White, Rufus m 9/25/34 Helen B. Lillie, dau of James, Esq., in Pine Plains; Rev. William N. Sayre (8-10/8)

9700. White, Solomon, 52, d 9/30/15 in Hudson (6-10/3)

9701. White, William m 1/1/16 Almira Story (in Hartwick?) (3-1/11)

9702. White, William of Newburgh m 3/2/21 Elizabeth Green of Poughkeepsie; Rev. Leonard (8-3/7)

9703. White, William W., merchant, m 9/25/22 Mary Green, dau of William. all of Poughkeepsie; Rev. Cuyler (8-10/2)

9704. Whitehead, Jesse m 4/25/22 Sophia Candy, both late of England, at Christ's Church in Poughkeepsie; Rev. Reed (8-5/1)

9705. Whiteley, Hiram R., 24, d 1/30/31 in Dover (Newspapers in the Utica and Cayuga Co. areas are requested to insert this notice) (8-2/9)

9706. Whitely, Dorus m 3/12/29 Hannah Bondish; Rev. Job Foss. All of Dover (8-3/25)

9707. Whitely, Joseph O. of Dover m 10/15/28 Jane Ann Ross, dau of William of Mentz (Cay. Co.); Rev. Rudd (8-10/29)

9708. Whiteside, James, Esq., 45, a distinguished agriculturist, d 12/24/31 in Cambridge, NY (1-12/29)

9709. Whitfield, Richard (Capt.), 21, m Mary Almand, 95, in Hampton; Rev. Richard Gilliam. All of Hampton (3-4/17/26)

9710. Whitford, Samuel (Capt.) m 10/28/26 Sophia Clarke of Plainfield; Rev. Maxon (3-11/6)

9711. Whitiker, Judith (Miss), 21, d 10/28/19 in Plattsburgh (7-10/30)

9712. Whiting, Bowen, Esq. of Geneva m Nancy McKinstry at the home of Gen. Charles McKinstry in Hillsdale (6-9/15/18)

9713. Whiting, Charles of the firm of John Rogers & Co. m 8/11/11 Margaret Rogers in Kinderhook; Rev. John Sickles. All of Kinderhook (6-8/16)

9714. Whiting, Harriet C., 31, wf of Dr. John L., d 5/10/29 in Detroit, MI (deceased is dau of Dr. John Tallman of Hudson, NY) (1-6/1)

9715. Whiting, James Abner, 17, s of Gen. Charles, d 12/15/29 in Kinderhook (consumption) (1-12/19)

9716. Whiting, Lydia (consort of John, Esq. and dau of Christopher Leffingwell, Esq. of Norwich, CT) d 3/6/09 in Canaan, NY (surv by husband and 6 ch) (3-4/8)

9717. Whiting, Martha, 42, consort of Spencer, d 7/17/20 in Hudson (6-8/1)

9718. Whiting, Samuel, one of the editors of the Albany Sentinel, m Fanny Leffingwell, dau of Christopher, Esq. of Norwich, CT, in N (9-11/30/02)

9719. Whiting, Sarah, 49, wf of Willaim, d 4/30/09 in Hudson (6-5/2)

9720. Whiting, Thomas F. m 6/28/27 Rosalinda Nettleton; Rev. C. P. Wilson (8-7/4)

9721. Whiting, William B., Esq., 65, d 10/18/96 in Canaan (3-12/8)

9722. Whiting, William H., 23, engraver, d 5/30/13 in Hudson (surv by wf to whom he had been married but a short time) (6-6/8)

9723. Whiting, William H., 28, d 9/14/22 in Troy (9-9/17)

9724. Whitlock, Adams, 81, d 9/6/07 in Hudson (Printers in Danbury, Conn. are asked to insert the above) (6-9/8)

9725. Whitlock, Elizabeth, 46, wf of Thomas, d 3/22/12 in Hudson (consumption) (6-3/30)
9726. Whitlock, Samuel, 70, m 2/17/03 "Mrs. Clark", 30, both of Hebron in H. (9-3/15)
9727. Whitlock, Thomas, Jr., 20, s of Thomas of Hudson, d 10/3/18 in Hudson (6-10/13)
9728. Whitmore, William of Ballston Spa. m 9/18/25 Sally Soals of Taghconick (Columbia Co.) in Ballston Spa; Rev. E. P. Langworthy (2-9/20)
9729. Whitney, ____, s of Selleck Whitney, d "recently" in Albany (funeral from Selleck's home. 46 Division St.) (1-10/22/31)
9730. Whitney, A. G., Esq. of Detroit, Mich. Terr. m 4/3/20 Anne Eliza Tallman, dau of Dr. John Tallman, mayor of Hudson, NY, in H; Rev. Stebbins (6-4/4)
9731. Whitney, Benjamin m Rachel M. Spooner in Hudson; Rev. Sears. All of Hudson (6-12/2/06)
9732. Whitney, Elisha M. of the firm of Butler and Whitney of Poughkeepsie m 8/18/31 Helen Forman, dau of Judge Forman of Syracuse, in S; Rev. Dyer (8-8/24 and 1-8/26)
9733. Whitney, George L., publisher of the Detroit Journal, m 1/25/31 Lucinda B. Williams, dau of Dr. William A., in Canandaigua; Rev. A. D. Eddy (1-1/27)
9734. Whitney, Porter, 20, d in Pittsfield, MA (smallpox) (6-7/2/01)
9735. Whittet, John of Binghamton m 11/29/34 Letty Van Kleeck of Fishkill in Newburgh; Alexander C. Mulliner, Esq. (8-12/10)
9736. Wickes, Daniel m Eve Winne, both of Schaghticoke, in S; Rev. Paige (9-2/1/03)
9737. Wickes, Elizabeth, wf of Capt. Silas formerly of Hyde Park, d 12/4/30 in Starkey (Yates Co.) (8-12/15)
9738. Wickes, Jonas m 10/28/06 Sally Betts, both of Troy, in T; Rev. Coe (9-11/4)
9739. Wicoff, I. W. (Rev.) m 11/1/31 Jane Kyes in NYC; Rev. Dr. Phillips. All of Catskill (1-11/5)
9740. Wier, John, merchant, of Hudson m 6/26/09 Martha Crawford, dau of Hayes Crawford of Coeymans, in New Scotland; Rev. Hallidy (6-7/11)
9741. Wigg, William m 4/24/24 Margaret Ann Manning; Rev. Vandaveer. All of Hyde Park (8-4/28)
9742. Wiggins, James m 6/24/19 Eleanor Smith, dau of James; Rev. Clark. All of Pleasant Valley (8-6/30)
9743. Wiggins, Ruth (Mrs.), about 90, mother of Jacob and Nathaniel, d "a few days since" in Duanesburgh (1-6/12/29)
9744. Wigram, John S. m Ann Witbeck in Watervliet; Rev. John Bassett (6-3/17/07)
9745. Wigton, Elias, 1, s of William, d 4/8/07 in Hudson (6-4/14)
9746. Wigton, Elizabeth, consort of Samuel, d 8/4/13 (in Albany or in Hudson - not clear which is intended) (6-8/31)
9747. Wigton, Samuel m 8/21/13 Mrs. Maria Skinner (both of Albany or of Hudson - not clear which is intended) (6-8/31)
9748. Wigton, Samuel, 61, d 1/30/29 at his home, 13 Hamilton St., Albany (1-1/31)
9749. Wilber, Job m Robe Potter, both of Easton, in E (9-3/15/03)
9750. Wilber, Joel m 11/10/30 Truelove Merritt, dau of William, in Hyde Park; John S. Van Wagner, Esq. All of Hyde Park (8-11/17)
9751. Wilber, John m Sarah Bragg, both of Easton, in E (9-3/15/03)
9752. Wilber, John C. m 5/14/23 Pame Germond, dau of Isaac; Rev. Price. All of Washington (Dut. Co.) (8-6/4)
9753. Wilber, Smith of Clinton (Dut. Co.) m 11/19/03 Ann Hewit of Beekman (8-11/22)
9754. Wilbour, Ebenezer m 2/7/11 Nama Pier, both of Cooperstown (3-2/9)
9755. Wilbur, Cynthia, 43, consort of James, d 7/26/18 in Middlefield (surv by husband and 10 ch) (3-7/27)
9756. Wilbur, Edward G. m Loisa Phelps, oldest dau of Winthrop, Esq., in Chatham; Rev. Hall (1-1/16/30)
9757. Wilbur, Eleanor Francis (sic), 13, only dau of Curtis, d 6/19/30 in Troy (1-7/5)
9758. Wilbur, Ephraim of Red Hook m 11/30/23 Eliza Ellison of Northeast; Peter Fish, Esq. (8-12/3)
9759. Wilbur, George, 5, s of Gideon, died (date and place not given) (died from the cave-in of a gravel bank in which he was playing) (9-9/24/05)
9760. Wilbur, George m 9/20/24 Gitty Stevenson in Richfield; James Hyde, Esq. (3-9/27)

9761. Wilbur, Hiram, printer, of Hudson m 5/23/19 Hannah Haviland, only dau of Benjamin of Athens, in A; Rev. Prentice (6-5/25 and 9-6/8)
9762. Wilbur, Louisa Emeline, 7, oldest dau of Hiram, Esq., editor of the Hudson Gazette, d 5/14/30 in Hudson (1-5/25)
9763. Wilbur, Samuel S. of Chatham m 12/23/04 Hannah Fitch, dau of Capt. Cyprian of Canaan, in C (6-1/1/05)
9764. Wilbur, Solomon, Jr., one of the publishers of the Troy Gazette, m 8/30/05 Rhoda Martindale of Lenox, MA in L (6-9/3)
9765. Wicocke, Samuel H. of Plattsburgh, NY, editor of the Scribbler, m 8/22/25 Ann Lewis late of South Lambeth near London, England, in Rouse's Point, NY (a previous secret marriage between the parties had taken place in 1821 in Montreal, Canada) (7-8/27)
9766. Wilcox, Columbus of Ballston m 8/25/25 Jane Andrews of NYC in NYC (2-8/30)
9767. Wilcox, Elias, 71, farmer, d 1/20/10 at his home in Dover (8-2/14)
9768. Wilcox, Elias, formerly of Dutchess Co., NY m 3/7/25 Mary Babcock, dau of Hon. Judge John W. Babcock of Massachusetts, in Harpersfield, NY; Rev. Fenn (8-3/9)
9769. Wilcox, Sarah, 65, wf of Gen. Sylvanus and dau of late Deacon Robert Johnson of West Stockbridge, MA, d 7/1/30 in Glen (Montgomery Co.) (1-7/7)
9770. Wilcoxson, Julius m 7/7/19 Maria Goes in Kinderhook; Rev. Sickels. All of K (6-7/13)
9771. Wilde, Jacob of Fishkill m 6/3/15 Mary Bogardus of Poughkeepsie (8-6/7)
9772. Wiley, Clark of Dutchess Co. m 9?/25/34 Ann Marian Bedell, oldest dau of Capt. William of Staten Island, in NYC (8-10/1)
9773. Wiley, John of Clinton m 2/6/22 Sally Allen, dau of William, Esq. of Pleasant Valley; Rev. Clark (8-2/13)
9774. Wiley, John W. m 9/25/34 Susan Dubois; Rev. Richardson. All of Pough-keepsie (8-10/1)
9775. Wiley, Squire of Clinton (Dut. Co.) m 7/1/29 Hester Allen, dau of William of Pleasant Valley, in P V; Rev. C. P. Wilson (8-7/8)
9776. Wilkes, Thomas S. (Rev.) m 9/15/29 Julia Penniman, dau of S. J., Esq. of Greenbush, in G; Rev. Weed (1-9/17)
9777. Wilkins, Gouverneur Morris, Esq. m 6/2/30 Catharine Van Rensselaer, dau of Hon. Stephen; Rev. Dr. Ludlow (1-6/4)
9778. Wilkinson, Content (Widow), 91, d 5/6/34 in Union Vale (8-5/14)
9779. Wilkinson, George m 8/4/31 Sophia Cary, dau of Dr. Egbert Cary; Rev. Buttolph. All of Beekman (8-8/17)
9780. Wilkinson, Gilbert m 7/2/27 Velina Oakley, dau of Jesse, Esq.; Rev. Cuyler (8-7/4)
9781. Wilkinson, James m 10/25/11 Sally Copeman; John Flint, Esq. All of Amenia (8-11/13)
9782. Wilkinson, Jemima, 66, d 7/1/19 in Penn Yan, NY (she was called "the Universal Friend") (died of dropsy) ("Her mansion stands on a barren heath...some distance from the settlements.") (8-7/28)
9783. Wilkinson, John, Jr. m 3/5/34 Mary Holden; Rev. Buttolph. All of Union Vale (8-3/12)
9784. Wilkinson, Livingston, 22, youngest s of John late of Beekman, deceased, d 12/27/09 at St. John (inflammation of the lungs) (8-1/17/10)
9785. Wilkinson, Rhoda, about 22, wf of George, d 1/13/30 in Union Vale (8-1/20). See also entry 9786.
9786. Wilkinson, Rhoda, 23, consort of Joseph, Esq., d 1/13/30 at her home in Union Vale (surv by husband and 2 ch.) (8-1/27). Apparently this entry is a correction and addendum to the release shown in entry 9785.
9787. Wilkinson, Robert (a Rev. soldier) d 1/15/10 in Stanford (8-1/24)
9788. Wilkinson, William, 40, d 5/24/04 (surv by wf and 6 daus) (8-5/29)
9789. Willard, _____, child of John of North Market Street, Albany, d "recently" in Albany (1-9/11/29)
9790. Willard, Elizabeth, 59, wf of Timothy, d 9/11/16 in Elizabethtown (7-10/5)
9791. Willard, Horace of Catskill m 6/22/06 Susan Kemper, dau of John of Hudson, in H; Rev. Sears (6-7/1)
9792. Willard, Horace K. (Dr.), formerly of Catskill, m 10/26/31 Harriet E. Merwin, dau of Col. A. Merwin, in Bloom Ville (Dela. Co.); Rev. J. M. Tappan (1-11/5)

9793. Willard, John of Albany m 4/7/13 Mary Ann Jenkins in Hudson; Rev. Chester (6-4/13)
9794. Willard, John D., Esq. of Troy m Laura Barnes of Berlin, CT (1-11/25/29)
9795. Willard, Martha, 86, consort of Deacon David, d 12/14/05 in Hartwick (3-12/26)
9796. Willard, William T. m 7/10/27 Lucretia Paine, dau of Amasa, Esq.; Rev. Butler (9-7/13)
9797. Willcox, Franklin m Polly Brown in Paris, NY (3-1/31/25)
9798. Willet, Polly, widow, d "some weeks since" in Chazy (surv by several small ch) (7-1/8/13)
9799. Willet, Marinus (Col.), 90, d 8/22/30 in NYC (1-8/25)
9800. Willett, Mary, 23, d 8/22/31 (consumption) (1-8/24)
9801. Willets, Eliza, 14, dau of Jacob, d in Washington (Dut. Co.) (8-12/7/31)
9802. Willey, Abijah, a soldier in Capt. J. Brook's Co., 3rd Regiment, U.S. Artillery, formerly of Neversink (Sullivan Co.), d 3/19/14 at the artillery cantonment in Plattsburgh (surv by wf "and a numerous family") ("In order that his heirs may apply for the benefits...the editors of the Albany Argus and Plebeian are requested to insert this...") (7-3/26)
9803. Willey, Elisha F. (Rev.) m 11/2/15 Susan Brown in Albany (9-11/14)
9804. Williams, ____, consort of William, d 6/11/14 in Poughkeepsie (8-6/15)
9805. Williams, ____, inf s of Dr. Williams, d 9/12/23 in Troy (9-9/16)
9806. Williams, A. D. m 8/23/29 Julia Ann Hayes at St. Matthews Church in Unadilla; Rev. Norman H. Adams (double ceremony - see the marr of Peter J. Betts) (1-9/29)
9807. Williams, Abby, consort of Hon. Judge Williams of Poughkeepsie, d 11/18/09 at her father's home in Newark, NJ where she had gone for a visit (8-11/22)
9808. Williams, Albert A., Esq., attorney, m 6/9/29 Sarah Ann Gedney of NYC in NYC; Right Rev. Bishop Hobart (1-6/10)
9809. Williams, Andrew m 2/25/23 Marietta Metcalf in Otsego; Rev. Tiffany (3-3/31)
9810. Williams, Ann, 27, wf of Andrew of Albany, d 6/18/31 in Worcester, Ots. Co. (1-6/22)
9811. Williams, Bille (sic) (Capt.), 41, d 4/16/25 in Hartwick (3-4/18)
9812. Williams, Charles of the firm of Clark and Williams m 12/8/30 Catharine Elizabeth Bogert, dau of James, Jr., Esq.; Rev. Dr. Browslee. All of NYC (1-12/13)
9813. Williams, Chester m 9/19/19 Fanny Henry, both of Hudson (6-9/21)
9814. Williams, Christopher, house carpenter, of Cranston, RI d 12/2/05 in Hudson, NY (6-12/10)
9815. Williams, Clarisa Elisa, 14, d 8/13/19 in Spencertown (6-8/24)
9816. Williams, Cornelius (Dr.) m 1/21/21 Catalina Van Ness; Rev. Dr. Coe. All of Troy (9-1/30)
9817. Williams, Daniel W. m 10/17/18 Frances Murdock Pells, both of Clinton (Dut. Co.) (8-10/21) (Marriage official: Rev. Cuyler)
9818. Williams, David m 1/1/32 Catharine Rigeley, both of Clinton (Dut. Co.), in C; Daniel H. Schultz, Esq. (8-1/11)
9819. Williams, Elias W. (Dr.) of the firm of Schuyler and Williams d 9/25/28 in Claverack (9-9/30)
9820. Williams, Eliphalet, 45, d 6/7/17 (surv by wf, numerous children, brothers, and sisters) (3-6/12)
9821. Williams, Emma Josephine, dau of William, d 7/29/31 in Poughkeepsie (8-8/3)
9822. Williams, Ephraim, 36, d 7/29/03 in Hudson (6-8/2)
9823. Williams, George Ashley, 18, s of William, Esq. and a senior at Williams College, d 8/18/29 in Salem (Wash. Co.), NY (1-8/22)
9824. Williams, Grosvenor E., 19, oldest s of Elisha, Esq., d 9/30/19 in Hudson (typhus) (6-10/5 and 8-10/13)
9825. Williams, Hannah (Miss), oldest dau of Capt. Bille (sic) of Hartwick, d 9/18/05 (had taught school "the past summer" in Cooperstown) (3-9/26)
9826. Williams, Henrietta, consort of Andrew and dau of late Tracy Metcalf, d 7/15/26 in Otsego (3-7/24)
9827. Williams, Henry of Beekman m 10/17/19 Eliza Traver; Rev. Wynkoop (8-11/3)
9828. Williams, Henry of Westford m 2/16/26 Rebecca Tilton of Worcester in W; Rev. Cole (3-2/27)

285

9829. Williams, Henry m 9/17/29 Sarah Oliver; Rev. J. J. Matthias. All of Albany (1-9/19)
9830. Williams, Horace m 12/29/11 Rhoda Wilkinson, both of Canaan, in C; Rev. Plamer (6-2/10/12)
9831. Williams, Isaac of Gallatin m 3/26/14 Laura Roe of Amenia; Rev. Allerton (8-4/13)
9832. Williams, Isaac, "an aged citizen", d 12/1/14 in Cooperstown (3-12/18)
9833. Williams, Israel m 2/3/25 Betsey Getman in Columbia (Herk. Co.) (3-2/14)
9834. Williams, James m 1/6/27 Winne Martin in Plattsburgh; Rev. Quinlan (7-1/8)
9835. Williams, James A. m 3/19/21 Deborah Weaver of Poughkeepsie; Rev. Leonard (8-3/21)
9836. Williams, Jerusha, 75, relict of Col. Ebenezer formerly of Pomfret, CT, d 9/23/05 in Hudson (funeral at the home of Elisha Williams, upper end of Warren St.) (6-9/24)
9837. Williams, John, Jr., about 50, of Cooperstown d 10/11/04 in a fall from a wagon (buried in Pierstown, "the place of his late residence") (3-10/18)
9838. Williams, John (Gen.), 53, d 7/22/06 in Salem, NY (born in England but came to this country when young; was a member of the state legislature first and later a Congressman) (9-8/5 and 6-8/12)
9839. Williams, John of Poughkeepsie m 3/19/11 Joanna Waring of Southeast; Peter R. Malson, Esq. (8-3/27)
9840. Williams, John m 10/7/13 Sophia Stephens, both of Cooperstown (3-10/23)
9841. Williams, John, Jr. of Hyde Park m 12/24/21 Mary Doty of Clinton; Rev. M. Wynkoop (8-12/26)
9842. Williams, John m 3/17/28 Elizabeth Patterson, both of Troy; Rev. S. Martindale (9-3/21)
9843. Williams, Judah (Capt.), 65, d 3/4/07 in Utica (9-3/24)
9844. Williams, Lucia, 23, wf of Silas, merchant, of Columbus, OH, d 4/20/19 in Columbus(Lucia, dau of William Garratt, Esq. of Otsego Co.) (3-5/17)
9845. Williams, Lucretia, 13 mo, dau of Col. Russell Williams, d 8/13/20 in Cooperstown (3-8/21)
9846. Williams, Lucy, 20, wf of William, Esq., late cashier of the Bank of Niagara, d 8/31/29 in Buffalo (1-9/5)
9847. Williams, Margaret, about 60, wf of Joseph H. of Middlesex(?) (a side reference is made to Penn Yan in my notes), d 9/14/31 (suicide by hanging) ("She had been partially deranged for some time") (1-9/26)
9848. Williams, Margaret Elizabeth, inf dau of Ezra, Esq., d 3/8/25 in Westford (3-3/21)
9849. Williams, Mary, 59, wf of Thomas, d 9/1/04 in Hudson (6-9/11)
9850. Williams, Mary, 47, consort of Gen. John R., d 1/18/30 in Detroit, MI (consumption) (surv by husband and 9 ch) (1-2/5)
9851. Williams, Olive, dau of Thomas, d 6/30/25 in Champlain (7-7/9)
9852. Williams, P. m 1/18/23 Margaret Harris; Rev. Griffin (9-1/21)
9853. Williams, Rensselaer, merchant, of Cooperstown d 12/13/01 in Trenton, NJ (consumption) (surv by 2 sisters) (3-12/31)
9854. Williams, Robert, Esq. m 11/20/10 Mrs. Sanford of Southeast in S; Rev. Hibbard (8-11/28)
9855. Williams, Robert, Esq., 49, d 3/5/13 in Poughkeepsie (8-3/10)
9856. Williams, Samuel (Rev.), LL. D. died (date not given) in Rutland, VT (formerly Hollis Professor of Mathematics and Natural Philosophy at Harvard; member of the Meteorological Society in Germany, of the Philosophical Society in Philadelphia, and of the Academy of Arts and Sciences in Massachusetts) (6-1/28/17)
9857. Williams, Samuel m 9/15/18 Lucinda Ray, dau of Nathaniel; Rev. Tucker. All of Schaghticoke (9-9/22)
9858. Williams, Sherman m Emma Stevens in Otsego; Rev. Tiffany (3-3/28/25)
9859. Williams, Silas of the firm of R. & S. Williams of Cooperstown m 10/13/17 Lucia Garratt, dau of William, Esq. of Garrattsville, in G (3-10/16)
9860. Williams, Simon, 57, d 10/25/27 in New Euctrecht (New Utrecht), Long Island (7-11/17)
9861. Williams, Solomon, 38, of the firm of Williams and Whiting, booksellers, d 10/8/10 in NYC (6-10/12)

9862. Williams, Sophia, 47, wf of John, Esq., d in Wethersfield, CT (deceased is a sister of "Mrs. Ames, relict of the Hon. Fisher Ames", and the youngest dau of the late Hon. John Worthington of Springfield, MA) (6-5/18/13)
9863. Williams, Sophia, 23, consort of John, d 5/22/20 in Cooperstown (3-5/29)
9864. Williams, Sophia W., 40, wf of Col. William, d 11/19/31 in Utica (1-11/21)
9865. Williams, Thomas, Jr., 35, d 5/25/05 in Hudson (6-5/28)
9866. Williams, William, Esq., 76, "an old...inhabitant of Poughkeepsie", d 7/31/17 at the home of his son-in-law, Zephaniah Pells (8-8/6)
9867. Williams, William E., Esq. m 3/2/31 Mary Ann Friday, dau of Abraham, Esq. of Albany; Rev. Welch (1-3/21)
9868. Williams, William F. of Poughkeepsie m 5/17/29 Susan Wright of Fishkill; Rev. Dr. Cuyler (8-5/20)
9869. Williams, William W., 61, d 1/19/30 in Albany (a "Mr. D. McGlashan" is mentioned either as a close friend or as a relative of the deceased) (funeral from 83 Beaver St.) (1-1/21)
9870. Williamson, _____ (Mrs.), "a widow lady from New York (City) who was on a visit to her relatives", d 9/1/20 in Poughkeepsie (death resulted through her taking in error a dose of salt peter instead of "salts") (8-9/6)
9871. Williamson, Ezra, 17, s of Capt. Griffen Williamson d 10/2/25 in Poughkeepsie (8-10/5)
9872. Willis, Anson of Poughkeepsie m 2/17/25 Jane Ketcham, dau of Job of NYC; Rev. Nathan Bangs (8-2/23)
9873. Willis, George of Cornwall, CT m 9/18/28 Liphena Anson, dau of Job, deceased, of Northeast, NY, in Northeast; Rev. C. P. Wilson (8-10/8)
9874. Willis, Thomas, Esq., attorney, of Albany ("who lately took passage to Havanna for...his health") d the fourth day after leaving the port of Albany (1-2/4/31)
9875. Willis, William H. of the firm of Willis & Bros. m 7/14/30 Lydia Waring, dau of William, all of NYC, at the Friends Meeting House on Henry St., NYC (1-7/19)
9876. Willoughby, Elijah, formerly of Poughkeepsie, d 9/15/29 in NYC (8-9/23)
9877. Willson, Samuel M. m 3/18/24 Louiza Duncan, both of Troy; Rev. N. Bigelow (9-3/23)
9878. Willson, William of NYC m 10/15/12 Ann McComb in Claverack; Rev. Chester (6-10/19)
9879. Wilmerding, Henry A., merchant, m 5/28/30 Nancy B. Clute, dau of Julius, Esq., in Moscow (Liv. Co.); Rev. Walker (1-6/7)
9880. Wilmoth, Nathan of Ira, VT m 6/22/02 Lucy Guild of Lansingburgh, NY; Rev Coe (9-6/23)
9881. Wilsey, David m 12/26/33 Harriet Downs in Washington (Dut. Co.); Rev. Cocran (8-1/15/34)
9882. Wilson, _____, 9, s of Samuel, d 7/28/07 in a fall from a wagon 7/27 (9-7/28)
9883. Wilson, Alexander, Esq., attorney, m Mary Livingston, dau of late Peter R., Esq. of the manor of Livingston, in Albany; Rev. Romeyn (6-5/14/05)
9884. Wilson, Benjamin M. of Troy m 5/14/29 Hannah Budd of Greenville (Greene Co.) in G; Rev. Thompson (1-5/23)
9885. Wilson, Caleb W. (Rev.) of Amenia m 1/20/22 Sarah W. Fare of Livingston, NJ in L; Rev. A. Eliott (8-2/6)
9886. Wilson, David, 45, m 8/17/27 Mary Ann Shepherd, 13, in Jamesville; Black Prince, Esq. (8-9/12)
9887. Wilson, Ebenezer, Jr., Esq. m 1/31/02 Polly Moulton, both of Troy, in Waterford; Rev. Close (9-2/17)
9888. Wilson, Henry m 4/27/06 Nancy Sickles, both of Troy; Rev. Coe (9-4/29)
9889. Wilson, Hiram, Esq. of Northeast m 2/12/24 Eliza Reynolds, dau of Dr. Israel of Pine Plains; Rev. Clark (8-3/3)
9890. Wilson, James m 1/28/15 Nancy Stanton, both of Poughkeepsie; Rev. L. Leonard (8-2/1)
9891. Wilson, James, 23, s of John, d 2/16/24 in Ballston (2-2/24)
9892. Wilson, James L. (Capt.) m Margaret Jane Humphreys, dau of late Capt. Humphreys, all of NYC, in Bordeaux (state or country not given) (1-6/2/30)
9893. Wilson, John Lawson, 20, s of James formerly of Poughkeepsie, d 7/7/32 in NYC (8-7/11)

9894. Wilson, Justice (Mr.) m Ann Duncan, both of Stanford (Dut. Co.) in S (8-6/24/00)
9895. Wilson, Marvin m 8/13/23 Nancy Hubbell in Middlefield; Elder Sawin (3-8/18)
9896. Wilson, Nathaniel, Jr., 23, printer, s of Dr. N. Wilson of Mendon, d 9/20/30 in Rochester (1-9/25)
9897. Wilson, Polly d 5/29/17 in Plattsburgh (7-5/31)
9898. Wilson, Samuel of Hyde Park m 1/23/22 Jane Purdy of Sommerstown (West. Co.) [probably the present-day town of Somers] in Sommerstown; Rev. Shaw (8-2/6)
9899. Wilson, Samuel d "recently" in Albany (funeral from the home of his brother, John, at 126 Washington St.)(1-8/30/30)
9900. Wilson, Solomon, Jr., one of the publishers of the Troy Gazette, m 7/30/05 Rhoda Martindale of Lenox, MA in L (9-8/13)
9901. Wilson, Theron m 1/15/29 Lydia Louisa Collins, oldest dau of Capt. James, in Northeast; Rev. C. P. Wilson (8-1/21)
9902. Wilson, Walter m 3/8/15 Catharine Davison, both of Beekman; Rev. Smith (8-3/15)
9903. Wilson, William, 25, of Lansingburgh d 7/13/11 on his passage to Long Island, NY where he was going for his health (9-7/23)
9904. Wilson, William m 12/31/11 Aurelia Osborn, both of Cooperstown; Rev. Nash (3-1/4/12)
9905. Wilson, William H. of Columbia County, NY m 3/18/29 Anne Hulme, oldest dau of Thomas, Esq. of Philadelphia (state not given), in P; Rev. Furniss (1-3/25)
9906. Wilson, William Y m 3/14/28 Lydia Partrick (sic); Rev. Beman. All of Troy (9-3/21)
9907. Wiltse, James W. of Fishkill m 5/8/30 Elizabeth W. McNeal, dau of William of NYC, in NYC; Rev. F. C. Schaeffer (8-5/12 and 1-5/13)
9908. Wiltse, John C., Esq., farmer, d 10/28/20 at his home in Beekman (8-11/1)
9909. Wiltsie, Cornelius, "an aged inhabitant of Poughkeepsie" d 5/6/21 (8-5/9)
9910. Wiltsie, Hendrick d 6/14/24 at his home in Poughkeepsie (was a member of the Reformed Dutch Church in Poughkeepsie)(8-6/16)
9911. Wiltsie, Isaac A., Esq. of Westerlo (Albany Co.) m 4/15/24 Mary Matthews of Poughkeepsie; Rev. Cuyler (8-4/28)
9912. Wiltsie, Jane, widow of late John, d 8/26/22 in Poughkeepsie (8-8/28)
9913. Wiltsie, John, 74, of Poughkeepsie d 8/13/22 (8-8/14)
9914. Winans, _____, wf of James, Jr., d 9/8/02 in Saugerties (8-9/14)
9915. Winans, Aletia, 84, wf of Girardus, d 10/10/19 in Northeast (8-11/10)
9916. Winans, Catherine (wf of Capt. John formerly of Poughkeepsie and oldest dau of Capt. John Stewart, for many years a shipmaster out of NYC) d1/29/25 in Ticonderoga (8-2/16)
9917. Winans, James of Poughkeepsie d in Albany (8-8/30/03)
9918. Winans, James J., 62, formerly of Poughkeepsie, NY, d 9/14/30 at Basin Harbor, VT (8-9/29)
9919. Winans, Johannah (Mrs.), 87, d 8/10/32 at the home of James Reynolds in Poughkeepsie (8-8/15)
9920. Winans, John of Watervliet m 2/16/07 Mary Carpenter of Troy (9-2/24)
9921. Winans, John (Capt.), 63, well known in Poughkeepsie and on Lake Champlain as a ship carpenter, d 6/5/27 in Poughkeepsie (8-6/20)
9922. Winans, William m 6/6/22 Elizabeth Thomas; Rev. R. G. Armstrong. All of Northeast (8-6/12)
9923. Winch, Lydia (Mrs.), 57, d 6/19/27 in Plattsburgh (7-6/23)
9924. Winchell, James (Rev.), pastor of the First Baptist church in Boston, MA, m 6/28/14 Tammy Thompson, dau of Ezra, Jr. of Poughkeepsie, NY; Rev. Leonard (8-6/29)
9925. Winchell, James M. (Rev.), A. M., 28, a native of Dutchess County, NY and lately pastor of the First Baptist Church of Boston, MA, d in Boston (surv by wf, 3 small children, and his "aged father") (8-3/1/20)
9926. Winchell, Philo M., Esq. of Northeast, member of the state assembly from Dutchess County, m 9/6/30 Mrs. Hester Ladd of Albany in A; Rev. Welch (1-9/9 and 8-9/15)
9927. Winchester, David m 10/16/23 Harriet Andrus, both of Amenia; Rev. Willson (8-10/22)

9928. Winchester, Henry L. m 2/3/27 Gitty Ham, both of Troy; Rev. Howard
       (9-2/6)
9929. Windsor, Amos of Laurens m 4/21/25 Esther Pattengill, only dau of Capt.
       Lemuel of Laurens, in New Lisbon; Elder Gregory (3-5/2)
9930. Winegar, Oliver d 12/1/14 in Cooperstown (3-12/8)
9931. Wing, ____, child of Dr. J. A. Wing, d "recently" in Albany (funeral
       service at the doctor's home "on Public Square") (1-2/28/31)
9932. Wing, Daniel W. of Port Edward (perhaps intended for Fort Edward)
       m 8/18/25 Almira Higby of Cooperstown in Glen's Falls; Rev. John Clark
       (2-8/23)
9933. Wing, David (Hon.), 40, d in Montpelier, VT (6-10/7/06)
9934. Wing, Jacob, merchant, m 2/23/32 Ann Maria Cornwell, both of Poughkeepsie,
       at the Friends Meeting House in Poughkeepsie (8-2/29)
9935. Wing, Theodorus of Clinton (Dut. Co.) m 1/18/16 Hannah Carpenter of
       Stanford; Rev. McMurray (8-1/24)
9936. Wing, William Walker, s of Capt. James of Stanford (Dut. Co.), m Martha
       Ann Haight, dau of Dr. Nathaniel of Rensselaerville, in R; J. Moore,
       Esq. (8-6/9/30)
9937. Wingate, Moses m 2/18/24 Maria Hayward, both of Troy; Rev. Howard
       (9-2/24)
9938. Winne, Daniel D., merchant, m 5/12/29 Mary Ann Wormer in Albany; Rev.
       Ferris. All of Albany (1-5/16)
9939. Winne, Henry m 1/22/06 Jane Blane, both of Watervliet; Rev. Coe (9-1/28)
9940. Winne, John W. m 2/18/30 Sarah Diamond, dau of William S.; Rev. Ferris.
       All of Albany (1-2/24)
9941. Winne, Kilian, "an old inhabitant of Albany", d 9/12/29 in Cazenovia
       (1-9/16)
9942. Winne, Myndert, 25, s of late Daniel T., Esq., d in Albany (consumption)
       ("The relatives...of Myndert, deceased,...are invited to attend his
       funeral" from the home of his mother, the widow of the late Daniel
       T. Wayne, Esq. at 282 North Market St.)
9943. Winne, N. V. (Dr.) m 2/25/29 Rachel V. S. Bleecker, dau of G. V., Esq.
       of Albany; Rev. Kissam (1-2/27)
9944. Winne, Philip m 12/22/21 Roxana Roberson, both of Brunswick (9-1/1/22)
9945. Winne, Robert of Troy m 12/18/19 Harriet Van Vechten of Schaghticoke; Rev.
       Dr. Coe (9-12/21)
9946. Winne, Robert R. of Troy m 12/21/22 Elizabeth Winne of Brunswick in B;
       Rev. Griffin (9-12/24)
9947. Winne, Sarah, 24, wf of John W. and dau of William M. Diamond, d 11/1/30
       in Albany (funeral from 91 Lydius St.) (1-11/3)
9948. Winney, Moses m 12/20/17 Maria Lansing; Rev. Luckey. All of Troy
       (9-12/23)
9949. Winslow, Richard H. of the firm of Morgan and Winslow m 12/10/29 Rachael
       Ann Robertson, dau of Archibald, Esq., all of NYC, in NYC; Rev. Dr.
       Brownlie (1-12/15)
9950. Winslow, Robert m 2/3/28 Mary Mosher, both of Poughkeepsie; Rev.
       Richardson (8-2/6)
9951. Winslow, Thomas, hatter, (an employee of Teunis Van Kleeck) of Pough-
       keepsie d 12/2/16 (fractured his skull in a fall from the second story
       of the shop) (surv by wf and several small children) (8-12/11)
9952. Winsor, Amos, Esq., 77, d 8/17/19 in Hartwick (3-8/23)
9953. Winst, Tommy (an Indian) m 10/20/25 Hannah Gilbert, dau of John of
       Brothertown, in Augusta (3-11/14)
9954. Wintringham, Hannah, 81, wf of John, d 9/2/24 in Washington (Dut. Co.)
       (born in Yorkshire, England) (8-9/15)
9955. Wisner, Charles of Poughkeepsie d 9/25/34 at the home of his brother in
       Utica (8-10/1)
9956. Wisner, James m 12/13/21 Eleanor Marshall, both of Hyde Park; Rev. Clark
       (8-12/19)
9957. Wisner, Nancy, 54, wf of Col. Moses, d 11/20/31 in Springport (Cay. Co.).
       Their son, Harrison, 14, died the same day. (1-12/5)
9958. Wisner, Pollydore B., Esq. d 7/13/14 in East Bloomfield (3-7/28)
9959. Wiswall, John, 69, d 3/16/04 in Hudson (6-3/20)
9960. Wiswall, Lemuel, 6 mo, s of Capt. Samuel, d 5/23/09 in Hudson (6-5/30)
9961. Wiswall, Polly, 29, wf of Capt. Samuel, d 8/18/10 in Albany (buried in
       Hudson) (6-8/24)

9962. Wiswell, William J. (Capt.) m 7/11/26 Sarah M. Kidney, dau of Richard, Esq. of NYC, in NYC; Rev. Dubois (8-7/19)
9963. Witbeck, Andries(Col.), 81, d 5/27/02 in Kinderhook (6-6/8)
9964. Witherell, John of Plattsburgh m 3/5/12 Clara Averill, dau of Noble Averill of Granville, in G. (7-3/13)
9965. Withington, Samuel m 10/8/20 Mahala Williams, both of Troy; Rev. Sommers (9-10/10)
9966. Wolcott, Alexander, 39, Indian agent in Chicago, IL, d 11/23/30 (born in Connecticut) (1-12/16)
9967. Wolcott, Betsey, consort of Oliver, Esq., d in Litchfield, CT (9-10/15/05)
9968. Wolcott, Horace B., 22, of Utica, s of late Dr. Wolcott, d 7/18/29 in Cherry Valley (1-7/23)
9969. Wolcott, S. W. m 2/5/34 A. Thurber, dau of Gen. Ezra, at Rouse's Point; Rev. Chace of Plattsburgh (7-2/15)
9970. Wolford, William of Schoharie m Betsey Marselus of Knox in K (1-1/25/30)
9971. Wolsey, Mary (Mrs.), formerly of Albany, d 12/1/29 in Gorham (Ont. Co.) (1-12/14)
9972. Wood, _____, wf of Abel of Poughkeepsie, d 3/22/05 in Poughkeepsie (8-3/19)
9973. Wood, (possibly intended for Weed),Abraham m 5/30/04 Deborah Lattin; Rev Clark (8-6/5)
9974. Wood, Ann Elizabeth, 7, oldest dau of Augustus, d 4/4/28 in the state of Georgia (near Milledgeville?) (the family was en route to their future residence "in Coweta Co. - far into the unpeopled wilderness of the West") (death the result of the child's fall from a wagon) (9-4/15)
9975. Wood, Calvin d 3/9/14 in Pleasant Valley (8-3/23)
9976. Wood, Digby m 9/8/32 Sarah Bottomly, both of Poughkeepsie; Rev. Dr. Cuyler (8-9/12)
9977. Wood, Elias of Greenfield m 9/15/25 Jane Forbes of Wilton in W; Elder S. M. Plumb (2-9/20)
9978. Wood, Elijah m Betsy Aylsworth in Canaan; Rev. Clark (6-2/9/13)
9979. Wood, G. W. (Rev.) of the Troy Conference m 8/13/34 Juliet C. Ketchum, dau of B., Esq. of Peru; Rev. T. Seymour (7-8/30)
9980. Wood, George H. m 5/14/29 Deborah AnnDill, dau of late Robert, Esq., at St. Peter's Church, Auburn; Rev. Dr. Rudd (double ceremony - see marr of John B. Dill) (1-5/25)
9981. Wood, Gulielma, 38, wf of Charles, d 10/15/29 in Poughkeepsie (8-10/21)
9982. Wood, H. P. T. of the U.S. Navy, Philadelphia, m 2/28/31 Edna M. Walworth, dau of Thomas P. of NYC, in NYC; Rev. Elihu W. Baldwin (1-3/10)
9983. Wood, Humphrey m 1/19/12 Maria De Cantillon, both of Clinton; Rev. Brower (8-2/5)
9984. Wood, James, 85, d 7/9/05 in Schaghticoke (had lived there 37 yrs) (9-7/16)
9985. Wood, Jonathan K. m 4/17/17 Betsey Balch; Rev. Halsey. All of Plattsburgh (7-4/19)
9986. Wood, Joseph, 76, d 7/16/30 in Greenfield (Sara. Co.) (1-7/31)
9987. Wood, Joseph M. (Dr.) of Auburn, NY m 5/15/32 Adeline Van Rensselaer Van Kleeck, dau of L. L. Van Kleeck, Esq., in Washington, Dist. of Columbia; Rev. Dr. Laurie (8-5/23)
9988. Wood, Mary, 87, wid of Abraham, d 4/29/31 in Pleasant Valley (8-5/11)
9989. Wood, Nicholas m 4/2/34 Frances H. Adriance; Rev. Dr. Reed. All of Pough-keepsie (8-4/16)
9990. Wood, Robert Crooke, surgeon in U.S. Army, m Ann M. Taylor, dau of Col. Zachary, in (town name blurred), Mississippi (1-11/12/29)
9991. Wood, Samuel, 3rd, of Springfield m 9/26/13 Elsey Holcomb of Otsego, late of New Durham; Elder Hulbert (3-10/2)
9992. Wood, Samuel G. m 8/5/27 Margaret Quackenbush, both of Troy; Rev. Howard (9-8/7)
9993. Wood, Silas (Hon.) m Elizabeth Smith, dau of late Josiah, in Huntington, Long Island, NY (1-1/1/30)
9994. Wood, Timothy m 2/27/18 Betsey Martin, both of Fishkill, in Poughkeepsie; Rev. Reed (8-3/4)
9995. Wood, William of Clinton (Dut. Co.) m 10/19/23 Hannah Houtalen of Pleasant Valley; Rev. Dr. Reed (8-10/22)
9996. Woodard, Benjamin of Troy m 8/2/19 "Miss Russell" of Petersburgh in P; Rev. Butler (9-8/10)

9997. Woodard, Benjamin of Hebron m 12/26/22 Mary D. Babcock of Easton (9-1/21/23)
9998. Woodbridge, Enoch (Hon.), late Chief Justice of the state of Vermont,
d in Vergennes, VT (6-5/14/05)
9999. Woodbridge, H. H., attorney, m Maria Louisa Rosekrans at Arbor Hill in
Delhi, NY; Rev. E. K. Maxwell (1-5/25/30)
10000. Woodburn, Lewis of the firm of S. Mabbett & Co. of Albany, NY m 9/7/29
Frances S. Young, oldest dau of Rev. James Young of New Haven, CT in
New Haven (1-9/10)
10001. Woodbury, Lucius (Dr.), about 35,("formerly of New Hampshire, recently
from the City of Mexico, and at the time of his death on his way to
Philadelphia") d 9/12/29 in Buffalo, NY (1-9/19)
10002. Woodbury, William, Esq., about 58, d 8/2/29 in Lisle (Broome Co.)
(formerly sheriff and for several years clerk of Broome Co.) (1-9/2)
10003. Woodhouse, John m 2/16/04 Mary Hutchinson, both lately from England,
in Hudson, NY; Rev. Sears (8-2/21)
10004. Woodhouse, Lemuel, 72, d 3/5/25 in Otsego (3-3/14)
10005. Woodhouse, Melissant, 28, consort of Joseph, d 10/8/14 in Cooperstown
(3-10/13)
10006. Woodhouse, William m 12/30/05 Sally Tanner, both of Cooperstown (3-1/2/06)
10007. Woodin, Laura Ann, wf of David G., d 9/30/31 in Kinderhook (deceased is
dau of Isaac Ford, Esq. of Austerlitz, NY) (1-10/8)
10008. Woodland, Isaac, 34, "a man of color", d 5/21/30 in Poughkeepsie
(deceased was "a local preacher of the African Methodist Church at
Baltimore"; had lived in Poughkeepsie nearly a year and had taught in
the African school there) (8-5/26)
10009. Woodruff, E. P. of the firm of E. P. and A. Woodruff, merchants m 8/9/31
Mary Clarkson Crolius, dau of Clarkson Crolius, Esq., in NYC; Rev. Dr.
Kuypers. All of NYC (1-8/12)
10010. Woodruff, Hannah, about 18, and Charity, about 4, daus of Elias, d 3/30/13
in Plattsburgh (7-4/2)
10011. Woodruff, John m 1/3/34 Ann Moore, dau of Samuel, in Plattsburgh; Rev. J.
Howland Colt (7-1/25)
10012. Woodruff, John of Lower Canada m 2/9/34 Adaline Mayo of Peru, NY in P;
Ahaz Hayes, Esq. (4 [Keeseville Herald]-2/11)
10013. Woodruff, Nathaniel T. of Utica m 1/28/28 Mary Eliza Craft of Troy;
Rev. Butler (9-1/29)
10014. Woods, Dennis m 11/10/04 Lydia McKildo, both of NYC (8-11/20)
10015. Woods, James W., 78, d 12/6/30 in Greenbush (funeral from his late home
in the village of Bath) (1-12/14)
10016. Woodward, ___?___, d recently in Troy (page mutilated, sex of the deceased
not known, therefore) (9-9/18/21)
10017. Woodward, Benedict of New Lebanon m 1/14/23 Zulyma Potter of Nassau, NY
in Nassau; Rev. Peirce (9-1/21)
10018. Woodward, Hannah, 53, consort of Dr. Benjamin of Troy, d 9/12/18 in Troy
(9-9/22)
10019. Woodward, Sylvester, attorney, d in Franklinton, OH ("a young man of
merit...") (6-7/22/17)
10020. Woodward, Theophilus m 12/5/19 Polly Wait in Plattsburgh; Rev. Joel
Byington. All of Chazy (7-12/11)
10021. Woodward, William Shepherd, 21, merchant, of Plattsburgh d 7/12/17
(consumption) (7-7/19)
10022. Woodworth, Betsey, about 26, oldest dau of Asahel, d 10/5/16 in Claverack
(pulmonary complaint) (6-10/22)
10023. Woodworth, Hannah, wf of Randal Woodworth, d 4/7/19 in Plattsburgh
(7-4/10)
10024. Woodworth, John, Esq., 36, d in Schodack ("died of a quick consumption")
(9-6/13/28)
10025. Woodworth, Lucy, 31, wf of John, Esq., d 10/11/27 in Troy (9-10/12)
10026. Woodworth, Nancy, wf of John, Esq. of Troy, d 11/7/02 in Troy (9-11/9)
10027. Woodworth, Nancy (Miss), 23, d 4/9/17 in Claverack (6-4/15)
10028. Woodworth, Randal m 6/27/19 Jane Atwood in Plattsburgh (7-7/3)
10029. Wool, James, 80, m "a short time since" Mrs. Peggy Roberts, 50, both of
Schaghticoke, in S (9-3/15/03)
10030. Wooley, George W., merchant, of Poughkeepsie m 11/10/31 Mary H. Todd, dau
of Hon. Walker Todd, Esq. of Carmel,in C; Rev. Dr. Reed (1-11/14 and
8-11/16)

10031. Wooley, Miles T. (Rev.) m 6/26/06 Susanna Mowry of Cazenovia in C; Hon.
Judge Yeau (3-7/31)
10032. Woolley, Isaac m 10/28/24 Ann M. Gregory, both of Washington (Dut. Co.);
Rev. Wilson (8-11/10)
10033. Woolsey, John of NYC m 12/13/25 Mary Baily, dau of Maj. John of Hyde Park;
Rev. John Clark (8-12/21)
10034. Woolsey, John, merchant, of NYC m 9/26/31 Maria Engle, dau of James, Esq.
of Brooklyn, in B; Rev. Green (1-9/30)
10035. Woolsey, Melancton Lloyd (Gen.), 62, d 6/29/19 in Trenton, NY, 14 miles
from Utica (was en route from Plattsburgh, his home, on a visit to his
son, Commodore Woolsey of Sacketts Harbor, NY) (In 1776 left Long
Island when that area was invaded and enlisted in the army where he
became a field officer before age 23) (surv by wf and 7 ch) (8-7/7;
3-7/12; and 7-7/17)
10036. Woolsey, Melancthon T., Esq. (Capt.) of the U.S. Navy m 11/3/17 Susan C.
Tredwell at Christ's Church in Poughkeepsie; Rev. Reed (8-11/5)
10037. Woolsey, Noah, Esq., 70, of Marlborough m 2/21/21 Miss Phebe Thomson, 50,
of Stanford (Dut. Co.) in S; Rev. Armstrong (8-3/14)
10038. Woolsey, William Cecil m 3/31/29 Catharine Rebecca Bailey, youngest dau
of late Gen. Theodorus, all of NYC; Rev. Dr. Phillips (1-4/7)
10039. Woolson, Charles Jarvis of Keene, NH m 4/26/30 Hannah Cooper Pomeroy,
dau of George, Esq. of Cooperstown, in C; Rev. Tiffany (1-5/3)
10040. Wooster, Henry, Esq., 43, sheriff of Cattaraugus Co., d 9/21/31 in
Ellicottville (1-10/3)
10041. Worcester, Samuel (Rev.), D.D., 50, of Salem, MA d 6/7/21 at Brainard
"in the Cherokee nation" (8-7/8)
10042. Wordell, Joseph of Washington m 1/8/24 Henrietta Maria Wheeler, dau of
Col. Anthony Wheeler of Northeast, in Northeast; Rev. Osborn (2-2/4)
10043. Worden, Pamela, consort of Robert, d 2/11/06 in Cooperstown (3-2/20)
10044. Wordon, Ebenezer m 9/28/31 Elizabeth Churchill in Manchester (a village
on the Poughkeepsie-La Grange town line); Rev. Welton (8-10/5)
10045. Workman, Margaret Manson, wf of Benjamin, editor of the Canadian Courant,
d 7/14/29 in Montreal, Canada (1-7/22)
10046. Worth, Abigail, 33, wf of Capt. Thomas, d 6/28/01 in Hudson (6-7/2)
10047. Worth, Anna, 65, wf of Thomas, d 4/22/09 in Hudson (6-5/2)
10048. Worth, Gorham A., Esq., cashier of the Bank of Hudson, m 11/8/10 Lydia
Dakin, dau of Paul; Rev. Chester. All of Hudson (6-11/16)
10049. Worth, William E. m 8/5/27 Fanny Curtis, both of Lansingburgh; Rev.
Howard (9-8/7)
10050. Worthington, Daniel d 6/6/16 in Plattsburgh (consumption) (7-6/8)
10051. Worthington, Denison, merchant, m 12/24/29 Martha Searing; Rev. Dr.
Sprague. All of Albany (1-12/28)
10052. Worthington, Erastus, Esq., 70, postmaster, (formerly of Colchester, CT)
d 1/8/31 in Brooklyn, NY (1-1/10)
10053. Worthington, John, s of Hon. George of Montpelier, VT, m 11/4/30 Catherine
Ann Bassett, dau of Benoni of Albany, in NYC (1-11/8)
10054. Worthington, Jonathan m 11/30/28 Lovilla Debois in Pittstown; Rev. Howe
(9-12/16)
10055. Wortley, William of the American Hotel in Hudson (successor to Mr.
Butler) m 8/22/30 Susannah Re_?_ (surname blurred) also of Hudson
at St. Paul's Church in Albany; Rev. Keese (1-8/24)
10056. Wotkyns, Alfred (Dr.) of Troy m 5/16/27 Mary Augusta Williams of NYC
at St. Paul's Church (in Troy?); Rev. Butler (9-5/22)
10057. Wright, Abraham of Pleasant Valley m 12/3/23 Jane Allen, dau of Joseph,
Esq. of Poughkeepsie; Rev. Clark (8-12/10)
10058. Wright, Alfred m 9/2/30 Louisa Barber in Sennett; Rev. Mills (1-9/11)
10059. Wright, Chauncey L. of Albany m Lucia Griswold of Lyons in L; Rev. L.
Hubbell (1-3/10/31)
10060. Wright, Dan of Maryland (Ots. Co.) m 7/10/20 Ruby Fellows of Stephentown
in S; Rev. Daniel Brayton (3-7/24)
10061. Wright, Daniel, Esq. m 8/29/29 Ann Van Kleef at the Eagle Tavern in
Albany; Rev. David Brown (1-9/2)
10062. Wright, Daniel S. m 2/20/18 Minerva Church, both of Troy; Rev. Sommers
(9-2/24)
10063. Wright, Erskine, 21 or 14?, wf of James, editor of the Herald, d 5/17/29
at Sandy Hill (Wash. Co.) (1-5/23)

10064. Wright, Isaac of Northeast m 3/25/15 Christian Waldruff of Ancram; Rev. John Colver (6-4/18)
10065. Wright, James, editor of the Sandy Hill Herald, m 3/14/30 Charity B. Baker, dau of late Hon. John, in Sandy Hill; Rev. Rodgers (1-4/1)
10066. Wright, Jesse m 6/5/03 Magdalen Kipp, both of Fishkill; Joseph Harris, Esq. (8-6/7)
10067. Wright, John Crafts, one of the publishers of the Troy Gazette, m 8/22/05 Mary Buel Collier of Litchfield, CT in L; Rev. Champion (9-9/3 and 6-9/24)
10068. Wright, Josiah, merchant, of Syracuse, NY m 12/8/31 Celia Bliss of Springfield, MA in Syracuse; Rev. J. W. Adams (1-12/17 and 1-12/26)
10069. Wright, Lyman m 9/1/22 Sally Smith, both of Mooers, in M; Isaac Fitch, Esq. (7-9/28)
10070. Wright, Mary (Miss) d 5/31/13 at the home of Philip Heartt near Troy (9-6/8)
10071. Wright, Roswell m 2/22/27 Sally McKlusky, both of Albany; Rev. Howard (9-3/2)
10072. Wright, Roswell, Esq., 44, d 6/16/30 at his home in Unadilla (1-7/5)
10073. Wright, Sereno, editor of the Weekly Wanderer, m Fanny Carpenter in Randolph, VT (6-12/27/03)
10074. Wright, Silas, Jr. (Hon.) "senator in congress", m Clarissa Moody in Canton, NY (7-9/21/33)
10075. Wright, Walter m 2/10/02 Rebecca Chace; Rev. Clark (8-2/23).
        Wyckoff. See also Wicoff.
10076. Wyckoff, Edward, about 40, d 9/21/20 in Conhocton (poisoned from the sting of bees as he took honey from a tree) (9-10/19)
10077. Wyckoff, Hendrick (Col.) of the firm of Smith & Wyckoff d 10/21/89 in New Lotts, Long Island, NY (8-10/27)
10078. Wylie, Richard (Capt.), commander at Fort Jay, m 11/25/07 Maria Jane Ann Crook, step-dau of William Kettleras, Esq., in NYC; Rev. Bishop Moore (8-12/9)
10079. Wyman, Jacob B. of Albany m 2/21/29 Magdelin Hallenbeck of Bethlehem; Rev. Kissam (1-2/25)
10080. Wyman, Luther B. m 5/12/29 Cecelia Augusta Warren, both of Troy, in T; Rev. Whittemore (1-5/16)
10081. Wynkoop, Augustus, merchant, of NYC m Ann Maria Sylvester, dau of Judge Sylvester of Kinderhook, in K (3-2/13/08)
10082. Wynkoop, Evert, 87, d 4/23/30 in Saugerties (1-4/26)
10083. Yanney, Elizabeth, 74, relict of late Henry, d 7/16/30 in Johnstown (Mont. Co.) (1-7/22)
10084. Yates, John A. (Prof.) of Union College m 9/17/29 Henrietta Maria Cobb, dau of late Henry, Esq. of Albany, in Chittenengo (Madison Co.); Rev. Dr. Yates (1-9/29)
10085. Yates, John B., Esq. of NYC m 10/17/20 Mary E. Skelding of Troy; Rev. Sommers (9-10/24)
10086. Yates, John G., s of Maj. Gen. Yates of Brunswick, m 1/22/20 Catharine Ciperlie of Brunswick; Rev. Sommers (9-2/8)
10087. Yates, Rachel, 83, relict of Richard, deceased, d 1/16/30 in Greenbush (1-1/21)
10088. Yates, Robert, Esq., late Chief Justice of the State Supreme Court, d 9/8/01 in Albany (9-9/15 and 3-9/24)
10089. Yates, Sarah, 21, wf of Nicholas, d 9/2/31 in Schenectady (1-9/8)
10090. Yates, Stephen of Oppenheim m 4/22/30 Gertrude Schermerhorn, dau of John S., Esq. of Schoharie, in S; Rev. Weidman (1-4/24)
10091. Yelverton, _____ (Mrs.), 83, d 7/5/20 in Poughkeepsie (8-7/12)
10092. Young, Andrew, 27, lately one of the teachers in Dutchess Academy, d 11/3/14 (8-11/9)
10093. Young, Andrew M. m 9/21/11 Laura Delavan, both of Poughkeepsie; Rev. Cuyler (8-9/25)
10094. Young, Charles C., Esq. of NYC m 4/17/33 Charlotte Huntington, dau of George, Esq., in Rome, NY; Rev. Gillet (4 [Keeseville Herald]-4/30)
10095. Young, Curtiss of Smyrna m 5/12/25 Lucy Lincoln in Sherburne; Rev. Sprague (3-5/23)
10096. Young, George d 11/6/14 in Troy (9-11/8)
10097. Young, Henry m 8/5/17 Mary L. Hyde, both of NYC, in NYC; Rev. Spring (9-8/12)

10098. Young, Henry of Charleston (Mont. Co.) m 3/21/24 Julia Ann Faulkner of
       Middlefield in M; N. Brewer, Esq. (3-3/29)
10099. Young, James C., 24, d 3/28/26 in Middlefield (3-5/1)
10100. Young, John, 60, d 3/10/07 in Norwich, CT (9-3/24)
10101. Young, John T. (Dr.) m 2/26/23 Harriet Greene of Otego in O (3-3/3)
10102. Young, Mary, wf of Col. Samuel, d 8/22/25 in Ballston (1-8/23 and 3-8/29)
10103. Young, Monroe m 4/26/27 Nancy Marshall in Plattsburgh (7-4/28)
10104. Young, Thomas, 69, father of Col. Samuel, d 7/22/22 in Ballston (2-8/6)
10105. Young, William, 27, one of the proprietors of the Weekly Visitor,
       d 9/15/05 in NYC (6-10/8)
10106. Young, William "formerly teacher of the Lancasterian school in this
       village" (Plattsburgh) m "a short time since" Prudence Averill of
       Plattsburgh in Kent, CT (7-11/7/18)
10107. Younglove, Mary, 3, only dau of late Rev. John of Brunswick, d 9/15/28
       in Brunswick (9-9/23)
10108. Younglove, Moses (Dr.) d 1/31/29 in Hudson "at a very advanced age"
       (1-2/4)
10109. Youngs, David m 1/19/12 Electa Hubbard, both of Northeast; E. Hopkins,
       Esq. (8-2/26)
10110. Youngs, Joseph, 45, d 6/22/06 "at the poor house" in Hudson (6-6/24)
10111. Zeilley, George S., merchant, m 6/9/31 Sarah Ruby, dau of Robert of
       Albany, at Palatine Bridge; Rev. Ketchum (1-6/14)
10112. Zoeller, Daniel, merchant, m 4/25/30 Henrietta Maria Miller, dau of Dr.
       John C., in Sharon; Rev. Philip Wieting. All of Sharon (1-4/29)

APPENDIX

MARRIAGE OFFICIALS

Name; religious affiliation (if applicable and given); residence town; date
span of ceremonies performed; number of ceremonies performed.

Abel, ___ (Rev.); Oxford; 1831; 1
Abercrombie, ___ (Rev. Dr.); Philadelphia, PA?; 1831; 1
Adams, ___ (Rev.); New Hartford?; 1830; 1
Adams, Ezra, Esq.; Milford; 1821 and 1830; 2
Adams, J. W. (Rev.); Syracuse; 1831 and 1833; 2
Adams, Norman H. (Rev.); St. Matthew's Church; Unadilla; 1829-31; 6
Addoms, John T. (Rev.); Plattsburgh; 1821; 1
Addoms, S., Esq.; South Hero, VT?; 1832; 1
Adriance, Garret, Esq.; Pleasant Valley; 1817-25; 5
Aiken, Albro, Esq.; Pawling?; 1816; 1
Aiken, Samuel C. (Rev.); Utica; 1824-31; 15
Alerton, ___ (Rev.); Northeast?; 1812; 1
Alexander, ___ (Rev.); Trenton, NJ?; 1831; 1
Allen, ___ (Rev.); Amenia?; 1811; 1
Allen, Gideon, Esq.; Clinton (Dut. Co.)?; 1815; 1
Allen, Samuel C., Esq.; Dutchess County; 1832-34; 5
Allen, T. G. (Rev.); Philadelphia, PA?; 1834; 1
Allerton, ___ (Rev.); Amenia?; 1811-14; 3
Ambler, ___ (Rev.); Milton; 1823; 1
Amerman, Albert (Rev.); Caugnawaga (Fonda)?; 1829; 1
Amy, Samuel (Rev.); Sand Lake; 1828; 1
Andrews, ___ (Rev.); Amenia; 1832; 1
Andrews, ___ (Rev.); New Berlin (Chen. Co.); 1829; 1
Andrews, Edward (Rev.); Norwich; 1829; 1
Andrews, George B. (Rev.); Lithgow; 1834; 2
Anson, ___ (Rev.); Ballston?; 1825; 1
Anthon ___ (Rev.); Trinity Church; Utica; 1822-23; 3
Anthon, Henry (rev.); Tivoli?; 1834; 1
Anuin, Theodorus, Esq.; Fishkill?; 1823; 1
Arbuckle, ___ (Rev.); Albany?; 1830; 1
Arbuckle, ___ (Rev.); New Windsor?; 1827; 1
Armstrong, ___ (Rev.); Sandy Hill (Wash. Co.); 1815; 2
Armstrong, Moses, Esq.; Poughkeepsie; 1823 and 1824; 2
Armstrong, Robert G. (Rev.); Dutchess County; 1820-34; 25
Arnold, ___ (Rev.); Freedom; 1825; 1
Arnold, ___ (Rev.); Poughkeepsie; 1822; 1
Arnold, Ahab, Esq.; Clinton (Dut. Co.); 1804; 1
Arnold, Smith (Rev.); Fishkill; 1825-30; 7
Arthur, Richard D.. Esq.; Ticonderoga; 1831; 1
Axtell, D. C. (Rev.); Clinton (Oneida Co.); 1830; 1
Babcock, ___ (Rev.); Ballston Spa; 1825-29; 4
Babcock, ___ (Rev.); Poughkeepsie; 1823-26; 10
Babcock, Daniel, Esq.; Davenport; 1825; 1
Babcock, Elijah, Esq.; Exeter; 1826; 1
Babcock, Rufus (Rev.); New York City?; 1824; 1
Baiety, ___ (Rev.); New Utrecht?; 1823; 1
Bailey, ___ (Rev.); Pittsfield, MA?; 1825; 1
Baker, ___ (Rev.); Greenbush; 1806; 1
Baker, Clark, Esq.; Pittstown-Hoosick area; 1823-27; 3
Baker, Joseph (Rev.); Weedsport; 1829; 1
Baker, Lucas. Esq.; Beekman?; 1834; 1
Baldwin, ___ (Rev.); Charlton; 1824 and 1825; 2
Baldwin, ___ (Rev.); Poughkeepsie?; 1798-99; 2
Baldwin, Amos G. (Rev.); New Stockbridge (Oneida Co.); undated; 1
Baldwin, Elihu W. (Rev.); New York City; 1829-31; 3
Bangs, ___ (Rev.); Amenia; 1814; 1

Bangs, ___ (Rev.); Woodstock?; undated; 1
Bangs, Heman (Rev.); New York City; 1830; 1
Bangs, Nathan (Rev.); New York City; 1825; 1
Barber, ___ (Rev.); Beekman; 1834; 3
Barber, Edward (Elder); Greenwich (Wash. Co.); 1812-18; 3
Barculo, George (Rev.); Dutchess County; 1806-11; 6
Barker, Samuel A., Esq.; Beekman; 1803 and 1807; 2
Barlow, ___ (Rev.); Canandaigua; 1821; 1
Barlow, ___ (Rev.); Syracuse; 1827; 1
Barlow, Jesse, Esq.; Dutchess County; 1823 and 1832; 2
Barlow, Milton, Esq.; Dutchess County; 1819; 1
Barnard, ___ (Rev.); Dover?; 1806; 1
Barnard, ___ (Rev.); Lima; 1829; 1
Barnes, Dan (Rev.); Exeter?; 1822; 1
Barnet, John (Rev.); Amenia; 1803-12; 5
Barrett, ___ (Rev.); Fishkill; 1805-23; 5
Barton, ___ (Rev.); Elmira?; 1829; 1
Barton, Joel, Esq.; Stanford (Dut. Co.); 1819; 1
Barton, Leonard, Esq.; Stanford (Dut. Co.); 1812; 1
Basset, ___ (Rev.); New Paltz; 1828; 1
Bassett, John (Rev.); Watervliet?; 1807; 1
Bates, ___ (Rev.); Chesterfield?; 1831-33; 4
Bates, John, Esq.; Burlington, VT?; 1833
Bayard, L. P. (Rev.); New York City?; 1831; 1
Beach, ___ (Rev. Dr.); Hyde Park?; 1809; 1
Beach, ___ (Rev.); New York City?; 1831; 1
Beach, Horace, Esq.; Peru-Keeseville area; 1821-31; 3
Beadle, John, Esq.; Pleasant Valley?; 1814-19; 2
Beaman, ___ (Elder); Worcester?; 1823; 1
Beardsley, ___ (Rev.); Le Roy; 1829; 1
Beardsley, ___ (Rev.); Onondaga?; 1831; 1
Beckwith, ___ (Rev.); Le Roy?; 1831; 1
Bedell, Gregory T. (Rev.); Hudson; 1815-18; 5
Bedell, G. T. (Rev.); Philadelphia, PA?; 1830;1
Bell, ___ (Rev.); Troy; 1828; 1
Bell, William, Esq.; Stanford (Dut. Co.); 1808 and 1811; 2
Beman, ___ (Rev.); Troy; 1823-31; 25
Benedict, ___ (Rev.); Burlington (Ots. Co.); 1816;1
Benedict, ___ (Rev.); Pawling?; 1828; 1
Benedict, ___ (Rev.); Rhinebeck?; 1829; 1
Benedict, E. (Rev.); Lewis (Essex Co.)?; 1832;1
Benedict, G. (Rev.); Ridgebury, CT?; 1829; 1
Benedict, Joel T. (Rev.); Chatham; 1817; 1
Benjamin, Cyrus, Esq.; Beekman-Fishkill area; 1803; 2
Bennett, A. (Rev.); Homer; 1829; 1
Bennett, Alva (Rev.); St. John's Church; Johnstown; 1829; 1
Benson, ___ (Rev.); Brunswick; 1828; 1
Bently, ___ (Rev.); Middle Haddam, CT; 1829; 1
Berger, J. (Rev.); Ghent-Claverack-Kinderhook area; 1829-31; 3
Berrian, W. (Rev. Dr.); St. John's Church; New York City; 1825-31; 8
Bethune, ___ (Rev.); Montreal, Canada; 1831; 1
Bethune, G. W. (Rev.); 1828-29; 3
Beyley, ___ (Rev.); Great Barrington, MA?; 1816; 1
Bibbens, ___ (Rev.); Geddes?; 1829; 1
Bigelow, Noah (Rev.); Lansingburgh; 1823-24; 2
Birch/Burch, Luman (Rev.); Stanford (Dut. Co.); 1812-34; 15
Birge, James, Jr., Esq.?; Westford; 1824; 1
Blakesley, E. (Rev.); Palmyra?; 1831; 1
Blatchford, ___ (Rev. Dr.); Lansingburgh?; 1805-27; 9
Bliss, John (Rev.); Holley?; 1826; 1
Blodget, ___ (Rev.); Hoosick Falls?; 1833; 1
Blood, John, Jr., Esq.; Laurens; 1823; 2
Boardman, George S. (Rev.); Watertown; 1830-34; 4
Bogardus, ___ (Rev.); Schenectady; 1809; 1
Bogart, D. S. (Rev.); New York City; 1829; 1

Bogue, ___ (Rev.); Butternuts; 1822; 1
Bogue, ___ (Rev.); Canaan?; 1803; 1
Boice, Ira C. (Rev.); Bethlehem; 1829; 1
Bois, ___ (Rev.); Albany?; 1829; 1
Booth, ___ (Rev.); Odletown, Lower Canada; 1834; 1
Bork, ___ (Rev.); New Paltz?; 1823; 1
Bostwick, ___ (Elder); Hartwick; 1805-25; 9
Bostwick, William (Rev.); Methodist Church; Bath; 1829; 1
Bourne, George (Rev.); Mount Pleasant (West. Co.); 1820; 1
Bowen, ___ (Rev.); Milford?; 1820; 1
Bowne, Walter, Esq.; New York City?; 1832; 1
Boyd, ___ (Rev.); Northumberland?; 1833; 1
Boyden, John, Esq.; Lorraine; 1831; 1
Brace, ___ (Rev.); Lake Skaneateles?; 1831; 1
Brackett, ___ (Rev.); Ballston; 1821; 1
Bradford, John M. (Rev.); Bath; 1805; 1
Bradford, John M. (Rev.); Albany; 1808 and 1811; 2
Bradley, Dan, Esq.; Marcellus?; 1804; 1
Bradley, J. (Elder); Wilmington?; 1831; 1
Brayton, ___ (Rev.); Washington (Dut. Co.)?; 1821; 1
Brayton, Daniel (Rev.); Stephentown?; 1820; 1
Breuwer, ___ (Rev.); Poughkeepsie?; 1798 and 1806; 2
Brewer, N., Esq.; Middlefield; 1824; 1
Brichtnell, ___ (Rev.); Zion Church; New York City; 1830; 1
Brienthall, Thomas (Rev.); New York City; 1829; 2
Briggs, Avery (Rev.); Hudson?; 1818-19; 3
Brimmer, Martin, Esq.; Genesee, undated; 1
Brinckerhoff, ___ (Rev.); Plattsburgh?; 1834; 1
Brisben, J. C. (Rev.); Keeseville; 1833; 1
Broadhead, ___ (Rev.); Amenia; 1808; 1
Broadhead, Jacob (Rev. Dr.); New York City; 1829-31; 3
Broadwell, Noah, Esq.; Plattsburgh; 1812; 1
Bromley, ___ (Elder); Plattsburgh area?; 1823; 1
Bromley, Hallock, Esq.; Beekmantown (Clinton Co.)?; 1821; 1
Brondage, ___ (Rev.); Brookfield, CT; 1829; 1
Bronk, ___ (Rev.); Watervliet; 1829; 1
Bronson, ___ (Rev.); Rensselaerville; 1819; 1
Bronson, Asahel (Rev.); Dutchess County; 1827-31; 15
Bronson, C. P. (Rev.); Milan Township, Ohio; 1829; 1
Brouner, Jacob H. (Rev.); New York City; 1829; 1
Brouwer, ___ (Rev.); Poughkeepsie; 1795-1826; 30
Brouwer, Cornelius (Rev.); Whitesboro; 1831; 1
Brown, ___ (Rev.); Huntington, L.I.; 1827; 1
Brown, ___ (Rev.); Hyde Park; 1820-22; 7
Brown, ___ (Rev.); Poughkeepsie; 1799; 1
Brown, ___ (Rev.); Townshend, VT?; 1832; 1
Brown, David (Rev.); Albany; 1829; 2
Brown, Joel, Esq.; Amenia; 1827; 1
Brown, John; Fishkill; 1815; 1
Brown, John (Rev.), St. George's Church; Newburgh?; 1830-31; 3
Brown, John (Rev.); Poughkeepsie; 1834; 1
Brown, P. (Rev.); Augusta; 1831; 1
Brownell, ___ (Right Rev. Bishop); Christ Church, Sharon, CT?; 1823; 1
Brownlie, ___ (Rev. Dr.); Middle Brick Church; New York City; 1823-31; 1
Bruce, ___ (Rev.); Phelps?; 1831; 1
Bruce, ___ (Rev.); Skaneateles; 1831; 1
Brumley, Halloch, Esq.; Beekmantown (Clinton Co.); 1822 and 1833; 2
Bryan, Amos, Esq.; Northeast; 1829; 1
Bryant, ___ (Rev.); Keeseville; 1831; 1
Buck, ___ (Rev.); Cairo, NY; 1832; 1
Buckley, ___ (Rev.); Poughkeepsie; 1806-08; 6
Budd, ___ (Rev.); Greenfield?; 1805; 1
Budd, ___ (Rev.); Staatsburgh?; 1805; 1
Buel, Elam, Esq.; Grafton-Troy area; 1822 and 1828; 2
Bulkley, ___ (Rev.); Poughkeepsie; 1808; 1

Bull, ___ (Rev.); Groveland; 1830; 1
Bull, Archibald, Esq.; Troy; 1815; 1
Bullions, Alexander (Rev.); Cambridge-Jackson area; 1823; 2
Bullions, P. (Rev.); Argyle?; 1823 and 1830; 2
Bullions, Peter (Rev.); Albany-Guiderland area; 1830 and 1831; 2
Bullock, ___ (Rev.); Stanford (Dut. Co.); 1802; 1
Burch, ___ (Rev.); Albany; 1831; 2
Burch, ___ (Rev.); Hillsdale; 1829; 1
Burroughs, ___ (Rev. Dr.); Portsmouth, NH?; 1834; 1
Bury, ___ (Rev.); Albany; 1829; 1
Bury, ___ (Rev.); Detroit, MI; 1830; 1
Bush, ___ (Rev.); Berkshire (Tioga Co.); 1829; 1
Butler, ___ (Rev.); Schenectady?; 1818; 1
Butler, David (Rev.); St. Paul's Church; Tory; 1802-31; 62
Buttolph, John (Rev.); La Grange; 1817-34; 25
Button, Elisha, Esq.; Peru; 1822; 1
Byer, William J. (Rev.); Rhinebeck?; 1827; 1
Byington, Joel (Rev.); Chazy; 1817-32; 12
Cady, A. D. (Rev.); Canandaigua?; 1829; 1
Cahoone, William (Rev.); Hyde Park; 1829-32; 20
Caldwell, ___ (Rev.); Westford; 1824-25; 7
Campbell, ___ (Rev.); Albany; 1830-31; 7
Campbell, A. E. (Rev.); Macedon-Palmyra area; 1829-31; 3
Campbell, Alfred E. (Rev.); Worcester; 1824; 1
Candy, ___ (Rev.); Pawling; 1819; 1
Carey, Ebenezer, Esq.; Beekman; 1800-10; 4
Carle, John (Rev.); Perryville; 1831; 1
Carle, John H. (Rev.); Halseyville; 1829; 1
Carpenter, Coles (Rev.); Schenectady; 1831; 1
Carr, C., Esq.; Stephentown; 1827; 1
Carroll ___ (Rev. Dr.); Baltimore, MD; 1803 and 1811; 2
Carroll, ___ (Rev.); Brooklyn; 1830; 1
Carroll, ___ (Right Rev. Bishop); Carrollton; 1801; 1
Carter, John (Rev.); Hudson; 1815; 1
Carver, Barnabas, Esq.; Carmel?; 1802; 1
Carver, Nathan, Esq.; Plattsburgh; 1816; 1
Case, Wheeler (Rev.); Poughkeepsie; 1783; 1
Casey, George, Esq.; Pawling?; 1802; 1
Castle, ___ (Rev.); Lockport; 1829; 1
Chamberlin, ___ (Rev.); Keeseville; 1831; 1
Champion, ___ (Rev.); Litchfield, CT?; 1805; 1
Chapman, ___ (Rev. Dr.); Burlington, VT?; 1831; 2
Chapman, E. H. (Rev.); Cambridge; 1805-07; 3 (Initials possibly R. H.)
Chapman, Henry (Rev.); 1808-23; 6
Chapman, Henry (Rev.); Otsego Co.; 1823; 2
Chapman, J. (Rev.); Perth Amboy, NJ; 1820 and 1829; 2
Chase, ___ (Rev.); New York City; 1826; 1
Chase, ___ (Rev.); Poughkeepsie; 1800-04; 9
Chase, ___ (Rev.); Troy; 1820; 1
Chase, Moses (Rev.); 1827-34; 7
Cheever, ___ (Rev.); Waterford; 1830; 1
Cheney, ___ (Rev.); Middlebury, VT?; 1820; 1
Chester, ___ (Rev. Dr.); Albany; 1818-24; 5
Chester, William (Rev.); Galway; 1822; 1
Chester, William (Rev.); 1810-31; 32
Chevers, M. L. (Rev.); Hampton; 1831; 1
Chickering, _. W. (Rev.); Bolton?; 1833; 1
Christie, J. J. (Rev.); Warwick?; 1830; 1
Churchill, ___ (Rev.); Canaan-New Lebanon area; 1814 and 1828; 2
Clancy, ___ (Rev.); Kingsborough; 1825; 1
Clapp, ___ (Rev.); Plattsburgh; 1822; 1
Clapp, John, Esq.; Freedom?; 1822; 1
Clark, ___ (Rev.); Lockport?; 1831; 1
Clark, ___ (Rev.); Mount Pleasant (West. Co.); undated; 1
Clark, ___ (Rev.); Richfield?; 1825; 1

Clark, ___ (Rev.); Waterford; 1831; 1
Clark, Ambrose, Esq.; Pierstown; 1820; 1
Clark, Azariah (Rev.); Canaan; 1811-15; 3
Clark, Daniel A. (Rev.); Bennington, VT?; 1828; 1
Clark, Henry (Rev.); Baptist Church; Brookfield?; 1821; 1
Clark, John (rev.); Glens Falls; 1825; 1
Clark, John (Rev.); Pleasant Valley; 1802-32; 127
Clark, John A. (Rev.); Christ Church; Geneva, NY; 1816-31; 3
Clark, John A. (Rev. Dr.); New York City; 1819 and 1829; 2
Clark, S. (Rev.); Burlington, VT?; 1819; 1
Clark, Theodorius (Rev.); Chatham; 1823; 1
Clark, William A. (Rev.); Ballston Spa; 1821-23; 6
Clark, William A. (Rev.); NYC?; 1829
Clarke, ___ (Rev.); Locust Grove, L.I.; 1839; 1
Clarke, James P. F. (Rev.); Great Neck?; 1831
Clarke, James P. F. (Rev.); Brooklyn; 1832
Clay, ___ (Rev.); Milton?; 1832; 1
Clayton, J. A. (Rev.); Moreau?; 1830; 1
Cleef, C. L. (Rev.); Hackensack, NY?; 1834; 1
Clinton, I. (Rev.); Lowville?; 1829; 1
Close, ___ (Rev.); Waterford-Lansingburgh-Schaghticoke area; 3
Cloud, ___ (Rev.); Cazenovia?; 1829; 1
Cloud, ___ (Rev.); Geddes?; 1829; 1
Cloves, ___ (Rev.); New Hampshire?; 1825; 1
Clowes, ___ (Rev.); Albany?; 1817; 1
Cob, ___ (Rev.); Troy?; 1805; 1
Cobel, ___ (Rev.); Granger? (Columbia Co.)?; 1801; 1
Cocran, ___ (Rev.); Washington (Dut. Co.); 1833; 2
Coe, ___ (Rev.); Bloomfield?; 1831; 1
Coe, ___ (Rev.); New Hartford?; 1818; 1
Coe, ___ (Rev.); New York City; 1811; 1
Coe, ___ (Rev. Dr.); New York City; 1830; 1
Coe, Jonas (Rev.); Troy; 1799-1828; 130
Coffins, Joshua, Esq.; Clinton (Dut. Co.); 1811; 1
Coit, J. Howland (Rev.); Rector, Trinity Church; Plattsburgh; undated; 1
Cole, ___ (Rev.); Worcester; 1826; 2
Coles, George (Rev.); New York City; 1829; 2
Coles, George (Rev.); Poughkeepsie; 1834; 4
Collins, Oliver D., Esq.; Pleasant Valley; 1829-32; 3
Collins, Patrick B., Esq.; Newburgh?; 1822; 1
Colt, J. Howland (Rev.); Plattsburgh?; 1834; 1
Colton, George (Rev.); Westford; 1816-20; 6
Colver, ___ (Re.); Hudson; 1818; 1
Colver, ___ (Rev.); Northeast?; 1818; 1
Colver, John (Rev.); Ancram; 1815; 1
Colwell, ___ (Rev.); Fulton?; 1829; 1
Comstock, ___ (Rev. Dr.); Rochester; 1828-29; 3
Conde, Jonathan, Esq.; Charlton?; 1821; 1
Cone, ___ (Rev.); Edmeston?; 1825; 1
Cone, F. H. (Rev.); New York City; 1829; 1
Cone, Spencer (Rev.); New York City?; 1830
Conkey, ___ (Rev.); Hartwick?; 1807; 1
Conklin, Lemuel, Esq. Clinton (Dut. Co.); 1803; 2
Conroy, ___ (Rev.); New York City; 1831; 1
Constant, Silas (Rev.); Peekskill?; 1807; 1
Converse, I. K. (Rev.); Burlington, VT?; 1832; 1
Converse, J. E. (Rev.); Burlington, VT; 1833; 1
Converse, K. (Rev.); Burlington, VT?; 1834; 1
Cook, Michael S. V. D., Esq.; Pittstown; 1807; 1
Cook, Silas, Esq.; Marietta, Ohio; 1830; 1
Cooley, ___ (Rev.); Cherry Valley; 1814; 2
Coon, ___ (Rev.); Brookfield; 1826; 1
Cooper, ___ (Rev.); Hudson; 1806-10; 4
Cooper, ___ (Rev. Dr.); New York City; 1819; 1
Cornell, Gideon, Esq.; Easton; 1827; 1

299

Corning, A. (Rev.); Lafayette; 1831; 2
Cornwall, John (Rev.); Pleasant Valley; 1807; 2
Corson, ___ (Rev.); Windham, CT?; 1834; 1
Covel, ___ (Rev. Dr.); Bedford, CT?; 1817; 1
Covel, ___ (Rev. Dr.); Poughkeepsie; 1807-19; 15
Covell, ___ (Rev.); Pittstown?; 1802; 1
Covil, ___ (Rev.); Brooklyn?; 1829; 1
Cowan, ___ (Rev.); Cherry Valley; 1831; 1
Cox, ___ (Rev. Dr.); New York City; 1829-34; 4
Crandle, ___ (Rev.); Dutchess Co.; 1824; 1
Crane, ___ (Rev.); Fishkill area; 1808-20; 5
Crane, ___ (Elder); Meredith; 1825; 1
Crane, ___ (Rev.); Middletown, CT; 1829; 1
Crane, ___ (Elder); Milford (Ots. Co.)?; undated; 1
Crane, D. (Rev.); Gayhead?; 1812; 1
Crawford, ___ (Rev.); Buffalo?; 1825; 1
Crawford, G. (Rev.); Le Roy; 1830; 1
Crawford, Job, Esq. Pawling?; 1803; 2
Creagh, ___ (Rev.); Plattsburgh?; 1831; 1
Creighton, ___ (Rev.); NYC; 1829; 3
Crocker, ___ (Rev. Dr.); Providence?; 1830; 1
Croes, ___ (Rev.); Hampton (Liv. Co.); 1831; 1
Crookson, ___ (Rev.); Middletown, CT?; 1829; 1
Crosby, ___ (Rev.); Mount Pleasant?; 1829; 1
Croswell, H. (Rev.); New Haven, CT?; 1830; 1
Crounse, ___ (Rev.); Guilderland; 1831; 1
Crouse, Tilley, Esq.; Clinton (Dut. Co.); 1823-26; 8
Culver, John (Rev.); Amenia-Poughkeepsie area; 1816 and 1821; 2
Cumming, Hooper (Rev.); Albany and Schaghticoke; 1819; 4
Cummings, Simeon (Hon.); Batavia?; 1830; 1
Curey, W. F. (Rev.); Lockport?; 1831; 1
Cushman, ___ (Rev.); Poughkeepsie; 1826-27; 5
Cutler, ___ (Rev.); Prince William, VA?; 1831; 1
Cuyler, C. C. (Rev. Dr.); Poughkeepsie; 1809-32; 227
Dagg, John L. (Rev.); Philadelphia, PA?; 1829; 1
Dagget, ___ (Rev.); Patterson?; 1813; 1
David, ___ (Rev.); Troy; 1813; 1
Davis, ___ (Rev.); Saugatuck, CT?; 1831; 1
Davis, John R. (Rev.); Broadalbin?; 1831; 1
Dean, Solomon, Esq.; Jackson?; 1820; 1
Dechant, J. W. (Rev.); Philadelphia (state not given); 1826; 1
De Freest, ___ (Rev.); Troy; 1827 and 1828; 2
Delancey, ___ (Rev.); Mamaroneck?; 1823; 1
Delancey, ___ (Rev. Dr.); Philadelphia, PA; 1829; 1
Delano, Jonathan, Esq.; Providence?; 1822; 1
De Long, James, Esq.; Beekman; 1806 and 1828; 2
Dennis, Simeon, Esq.; Easton?; 1825; 1
Dewey, ___ (Rev.); New Bedford, MA?; 1831; 1
Dewing, ___ (Rev.); Fishkill; 1823; 1
De Witt, ___ (Rev.) Greenbush; 1816; 1
De Witt, ___ (Rev.); Milton?; 1814; 1
De Witt, Thomas (Rev.); Fishkill; 1805-26; 28
De Witt, Thomas (Rev. Dr.); 1829-31; 3
Dickinson, Baxter (Rev.); Newark, NJ?; 1831; 1
Dillaway, ___ (Rev.); Adamsville (Wash. Co.)?; 1831; 1
Dodd, ___ (Rev.); Carmel area; 1804-09; 4
Dodge, ___ (Rev.); Milford?; 1807; 1
Dodge, ___ (Rev.); Southeast; 1799; 1
Dodge, D. (Rev. Dr.); Clinton (Dut. Co.); 1802-14; 9
Donaldson, Asa (Rev.); Guilford?; 1830; 1
Donalson, ___ (Rev.); Exeter?; 1818; 1
Dorr, ___ (Rev.); Waterford; 1823; 1
Dorr, Benjamin (Rev.); Trinity Church; Utica; 1829-31; 6
Douglass, Sutherland (Rev.); Rochester; 1829; 1
Draper, Samuel (Rev.); White Creek; 1823; 1
Dubois, ___ (Rev.); New York City; 1826 and 1831; 2

Dugas, Victor (Rev.); Champlain?; undated; 1
Duire, ___ (Rev.); Essex; 1825; 1
Dunbar, ___ (Rev.); New York City; 1834; 2
Dunbar, A. (Rev.); Chazy; 1818; 1
Duncan, ___ (Rev.); Baltimore, MD; 1829; 1
Duncan, ___ (Rev.); Exeter; 1824; 3
Dunham, ___ (Rev.); Hebron?; 1812; 1
Dunlap, ___ (Rev.); Hoosick?; 1814; 1
Dunlap, John (Rev.); Constantia; 1817; 1
Duryee, Philip (Rev.) Saratoga-Schuylerville area; 1823; 4
Dutton, S. B. (or S. P.), Esq.; Poughkeepsie; 1832 and 1834; 2
Dwight, M. W. (Rev.); La Grange; 1827-32; 16
Dwyer, J. H. (Rev.); Essex?; 1828; 1
Dyer, P. (Rev.); Syracuse; 1830-31; 3
Dythick, ___ (Rev.); Pawling; 1804; 1
Eastburn, Manton (Rev.); New York City; 1830-31; 3
Eaton, ___ (Rev.); Buffalo?; 1830; 1
Eddy, A. D. (Rev.); Penn Yan-Canandaigua area; 1829-31; 5
Edwards, Uriah, Esq.; New Lebanon?; 1826; 1
Elderkin, Lucius, Esq.; Peru, NY; 1818; 1
Eli, ___ (Rev.); Carmel; 1834; 1
Elliot, George (Rev.); Canajoharie; 1806 and 1813; 2
Elliot, Joseph (Rev.); Batavia?; 1829; 1
Elliott, A. (Rev.); Livingston, NJ?; 1822; 1
Elliott, Andrew (Rev.); New Milford; 1811; 1
Ellison, Thomas (Rev.); Albany; 1801; 1
Elting, C. C. (Rev.); Deer Park; 1827; 1
Ely, ___ (Rev. Dr.); Philadelphia, PA?; 1823; 1
Ely, ___ (Rev.); Salem; 1806; 2
Engles, ___ (Rev. Dr.); Philadelphia, PA; 1829; 1
Ensign, ___ (Rev.); Hillsdale?; 1816; 1
Ensign, ___ (Rev.); Pittstown?; 1806; 1
Ernst, John Frederick (Rev.); Cooperstown; 1802; 1
Everest, Joseph, Esq.; Union Village; 1829; 1
Eyer, William J. (Rev.); Red Hook-Rhinebeck area; 1827-34; 8
F___, Job (Rev.); Dover?; 1826; 1
Fairbanks, ___ (Rev.); Richfield?; 1821; 1
Fairchild, ___ (Rev.); Onondaga Hollow; 1831; 1
Fairchild, ___ (Rev.); Springfield?; 1825; 1
Fairchild, Edward (Rev.); Milford; 1826; 1
Fairchild, Jesse, Esq.; Cambridge; 1807; 1
Felch, ___ (Rev.); Dutchess Co.?); 1811; 1
Fellows, ___ (Rev.); Milford; 1826; 1
Fenn, Stephen (Rev.); Jefferson-Harpersfield-Delhi area; 1805-31; 4
Fenner, ___ (Rev.); New York City; 1827; 1
Ferguson, S. D. (Rev.); Plattsburgh-Chazy area; 1833-34; 2
Ferris, ___ (Rev.); Albany; 1825-31; 14
File, John M., Esq.; Schaghticoke; 1828; 1
Fillmore, ___ (Rev.); Rochester; 1831; 1
Filmore, ___ (Rev.); Alexandria; 1828; 1
Finkum, Daniel (Rev.); White Creek?; 1820; 1
Finney, Charles G. (Rev.); Rochester; 1831; 1
Fish, ___ (Rev.); Goshen; 1823; 1
Fish, Peter, Esq.; Amenia; 1818-23; 2
Fisher, ___ (Rev.); Meredith (Dela. Co.); 1825; 1
Fisher, George H. (Rev.); Fishkill; 1831-34; 6
Fisher, Samuel (Rev.); Paterson, NY; 1831; 1
Fisk, ___ (Rev. Dr.); 1831; 2
Fitch, ___ (Rev.); Cherry Valley; 1822 and 1825; 2
Fitch, Isaac, Esq.; Mooers; 1822; 1
Fitch, T., Esq.; Batavia; 1828; 2
Fitzgerald, John, Esq.; Keeseville; 1831; 1
Flemming, A, (Rev.); Whitehall; 1833-34; 3
Fletcher, T. (Rev.); Schaghticoke-White Creek area; 1828-29; 2
Flint, ___ (Rev.); Bridgewater; 1816; 1

301

Flint, ___ (Rev. Dr.); Hartford, CT?; 1821; 1
Flint, John, Esq.; Amenia; 1811; 1
Fonda, J. D. (Rev.); Northumberland-Greenwich area; 1823 and 1830; 2
Force, Stephen, Esq.; Union Vale; 1829; 1
Fort, ___ (Rev.); Bethlehem?; 1831; 1
Foss, Job (Rev.); Dover; 1813-29; 5 (possibly in Sand Lake in 1819)
Foster, ___ (Rev.); Chazy; 1833; 1
Foster, ___ (Rev.); South Carolina; 1829; 1
Fowler, ___ (Prof.); Middlebury, VT; 1830; 1
Fowler, Edward K. (Rev.); Sullivan County; 1830-32; 3
Fox, ___ (Rev.); Glens Falls; 1832; 1
Freilich, Peter D. (Rev.); Cambridge-Pittstown area; 1806 and 1808; 2
Frost, ___ (Rev.); Whitesboro or Auburn?; 1830; 1
Fuller, ___ (Rev.); Christ's Church; Greenville; 1830; 1
Fuller, ___ (Rev.); Rochester, VT?; 1834; 1
Fuller, Samuel (Rev.); Rensselaerville; 1830-31; 4
Fulton, ___ (Rev.); Sherburne; 1825; 1
Furniss, ___ (Rev.); Philadelphia (state not given); 1829; 1
Gadsden, Christopher (Rev.); Charleston, S. C.; 1829 and 1834; 2
Galusha, Elon (Rev.); Utica; 1829 and 1831; 2
Gano, ___ Rev.); Poughkeepsie area; 1801 and 1804; 2
Gano, ___ (Rev. Dr.); Providence, RI?; 1818; 1
Gardner, ___ (Rev. Dr.); New York City; 1829: 1
Gardner, Howell, Esq.; Greenfield-Providence area; 1822 and 1825; 2
Garlick, Heman, Rev.); Peru, NY; 1815-33; 7
Garretson, ___ (Rev.); Middleburgh; 1830; 1
Garritson, Freeborn (Rev.); Clermont; 1805; 1
Garvin, ___ (Rev.); Westford-Butternuts area; 1822 and 1823; 2
Gary, ___ (Rev.); Otsego; 1821; 1
Gately, Ward M., Esq.; Fishkill; 1834; 1
Gault, John, Esq.; Cherry Valley; 1820; 1
Gebhard, John G. (Rev.); Claverack; 1803-21; 34
Geissenheimer, S., Jr. (Rev.); St. Matthew's Church; New York City; 1829; 2
Gelston, Maltby (Rev.); Sherman, CT; 1824-29; 4
Gere, ___ (Rev.); Brownville; 1831; 1
Gibson, ___ (Rev.); Pawling; 1803; 1
Gibson, Thomas B., Esq.; Keeseville; 1833; 3
Gilbert, ___ (Rev.); Syracuse; 1831
Giles, Charles (Rev.); Hartwick; 1817 and 1825; 2
Giles, ___ (Rev.); Litchfield; 1825; 1
Gillet, ___ (Rev.); Rome, NY; 1829 and 1833; 2
Gilliam, Richard (Rev.); Hampton; 1826; 1
Gilson, Thomas D., Esq.; Plattsburgh area; 1831 and 1833; 2
Gooden, ___ (Rev.); Sand Lake; 1827; 1
Goodrich, ___ (Rev.); New Hartford; 1831; 1
Goodrich, ___ (Rev.); Salisbury; 1831; 1
Goodsell, ___ (Rev.); Schenectady; 1829; 2
Goodyear, ___ (Rev.); Litchfield?; 1830; 1
Gosman, ___ (Rev.); Kingston; 1814; 1
Gosman, ___ (Rev.); Rhinebeck; 1826; 1
Gray, ___ (Rev.); Poughkeepsie; 1792-93; 3
Green, Caleb (Rev.); Lansingburgh; 1802; 1
Green, John C. (Rev.); Albany; 1829-31; 6
Green, John C. (Rev.); Brooklyn; 1831; 2
Green, Thomas (Rev.); Niagara; 1829-31; 3
Greene, ___ (Rev.); Smithtown, L.I; 1829; 1
Gregory, ___ (Rev.); Kelloggsville (Cayuga Co.); 1831; 1
Gregory, ___ (Elder); New Lisbon; 1825; 1
Gregory, Justus (Rev.); Sand Lake; 1829; 2
Gregory, Seth (Rev.); New Lisbon; 1826; 1
Griffin, ___ (Rev.); Schenectady; 1821; 1
Griffin, ___ (Rev.); Troy; 1821-25; 30
Griswold, E. (Rev.); South Hadley, MA?; 1829; 1
Groom, William (Rev.); Broadalbin; 1822-31; 3
Gunn, ___ (Rev.); Bloomingdale; 1827; 1

302

Haight, Ebenezer, Esq.; Washington (Dut. Co.); 1806-07; 3
Haight, Jonathan, Esq.; Stanford (Dut. Co.); 1830; 1
Hall, ___ (Rev.); Chatham; 1830; 1
Hall, ___ (Rev.); Schodack; 1829; 1
Hall, Lyman (Rev.); Hartford, NY; 1806 and 1807; 2
Hall, Nathaniel (Rev.); Granville; 1803-05; 4
Halliday, ___ (Rev.); New Scotland; 1809; 1
Halsey, ___ (Rev.); Riga; 1828; 1
Halsey, Frederick (Rev.); Plattsburgh; 1811-32; 74
Hamilton, William T. (Rev.); Newark, NJ; 1828 and 1829; 2
Hammond, George, Esq.; Union Vale; 1829; 1
Hammond, Thomas, Esq.; Dover Plains; 1826-32; 7
Hard, ___ (Rev.); Episcopal Church; St. Albans, VT; 1832 and 1834; 2
Hardenburgh, (Rev. Dr.); New Brunswick, NJ; 1826; 1
Hardenburgh, ___ (Rev.); Rhinebeck; 1830 and 1834; 2
Harkness, ___ (Rev. Dr.); Banlieue and New Kilmarnock, Quebec, Canada; 1829; 2
Harrington, ___ (Rev.); Fort Ann, NY; 1811; 1
Harris, Joseph, Esq.; Fishkill; 1803; 1
Harris, William (Rev.); Little Bloomingdale; 1814; 1
Harrower, David (Rev.); Unadilla?; 1806; 1
Hart, ___ (Rev.); Avon?; 1831; 1
Hart, P. A. (Rev.); New York City?; 1829; 1
Hart, William H. (Rev.); Walden; 1831; 1
Hawes, ___ (Rev.); Hartford, CT; 1829-30; 3
Hawes, ___ (Rev.); Lyme, CT; 1831; 1
Hawks, Francis I. (possibly Francis L.) (Rev.); St. Stephens Church; New York
    City; 1831; 3
Hawley, ___ (Rev.); Washington, Dist. of Columbia?; 1819-31; 3
Hawley, Henry A., Esq.; Essex; 1821; 1
Hay, ___ (Rev.); "New Ark" (perhaps intended for Newark, NY); 1823; 1
Hayes, Ahab, Esq.; Peru, NY; 1832-34; 6
Hazelius, ___ (Rev.); Cooperstown-Middlefield-Hartwick area; 1821-29; 4
Hebard, ___ (Rev.); Rhinebeck; 1804; 1
Hebard, Daniel, Esq.; Poughkeepsie; 1811; 1
Henderson, ___ (Rev.); New York City; 1830; 1
Henning, John, Esq.; Petersburgh; 1828; 1
Henning, Jonas, Esq.; Petersburgh; 1828; 1
Henning, Jonathan, Esq.; Petersburgh; 1828; 1
Henry, Francis, Esq.; Middlefield; 1821; 1
Henry, James V. (Rev.); Amsterdam, NY; 1831; 1
Henshaw, ___ (Rev.); Brooklyn; 1816; 1
Hernet,)___ (Rev.); Amenia; 1803; 1
Herrick, Smith, Esq.; Washington (Dut. Co.); 1821; 1
Hervey, ___ (Rev.); Greenville; 1831; 1
Hewit, ___ (Rev.); Plattsburgh; 1816; 3
Hewlet, ___ (Rev.); Plattsburgh; 1816; 1
Heyer, William S. (Rev.); Fishkill Landing; 1831; 1
Hibbard, ___ (Rev.); Southeast; 1810; 1
Hickock, ___ (Rev.); Litchfield, CT; 1829 and 1831; 2
Hickox, ___ (Rev.); Palmyra; 1831; 1
Hide, Samuel S., Esq.; Pittstown; 1824; 1
Higgins, Daniel (Rev.); Wheeler; 1831; 1
Higgins, David (Rev.); Cayuga; 1807; 1
Hill, ___ (Rev.); Troy; 1830; 2
Hire, ___ (Rev.); Fishkill; 1830; 1
Hitchcock, B. (Rev.); Essex; 1833; 1
Hobart, ___ (Rev. Dr.); Poughkeepsie; 1810; 1
Hobart, John H. (Right Rev. Bishop of N. Y. State) (ceremonies in NYC [Christ's
    Church and St. John's Church], Hudson [Christ's Church], Newburgh [St.
    George's Church], and Red Hook [St. Paul's Church]);1816-29; 18
Hogarth, Richard, Esq.; Seneca; 1821; 1
Holley, ___ (Rev.); Boston, MA; 1817; 1
Holliday, ___ (Rev.); Bethlehem; 1829-30; 3
Holliday, J., Esq.; Albany; 1830; 1
Hollister, ___ (Rev.); Skaneateles; 1829; 2

Holmes, E. (Rev.); Livingston (Columbia Co.); 1829-31; 3
Holmes, Isaac, Esq.; Freedom; 1829; 1
Hopkins, ___ (Rev.); Hudson; 1807; 2
Hopkins, Asa Theodore (Rev.); Ithaca; 1829; 1
Hopkins, D. C. (Rev.); Weedsport; 1831; 1
Hopkins, Enos, Esq.; Amenia area; 1812-14; 3
Hopkins, J. H. (Right Rev.); St. Paul's Church; Burlington, VT; 1833; 1
Hopkins, Josiah (Rev.); Auburn; 1831; 1
Horr, B. W. (Rev.); Norton, MA?; 1827; 1
Hosack, ___ (Rev. Dr.); 1828-30; 4
Hosmer, ___ (Rev.); Hamilton (Chenango Co.); 1803; 1
Hotchkins, ___ (Rev.); Coeymans?; 1813; 1
Hough, ___ (Rev. Prof.); Middlebury, VT; 1829; 1
Hough, J. S. (Rev.); Weedsport; 1829; 1
Houghtaling, ___ (Rev.); Troy; 1828; 1
Hovey, ___ (Rev.); Columbia (Herk. Co.); 1831; 1
Hovey, ___ (Rev.); Richfield; 1823; 1
Hovey, ___ (Rev.); Winfield; 1824; 1
Howard, ___ (Rev.); Gibbonsville; 1827-28; 5
Howard, ___ (Rev.); New Lebanon or Westport?; 1827; 1
Howard, ___ (Rev.); Worthington, MA; 1828; 1
Howard, Leland (Rev.); Troy; 1814-29; 59
Howe, ___ (Rev.); New Brunswick, NJ; 1822; 1
Howe, ___ (Rev.); Pittstown; 1828; 1
Hoyt, Stephen, Esq.; Pawling; 1803
Hubbard, ___ (Rev.); Montezuma?; 1831; 1
Hubbard, ___ (Rev.); New Haven, CT; 1807; 1
Hubbell, L. (Rev.); Geneva; 1829; 1
Hubbell, L. (Rev.); Lyons; 1831; 2
Hulbert, J. C. (Elder); Otsego County; 1813-26; 3
Hull, James F. (Rev.); New Orleans, LA; 1829; 1
Hull, Justus (Rev.); Berlin, NY; 1822 and 1824; 2
Humeston, James, Esq.; Dutchess County; 1834; 2
Hunt, Aaron (Rev.); Pleasant Valley; 1831; 1
Hunt, Oliver W. (Rev.); Flemington, NJ; 1805; 1
Hunter, Eli S. (Rev.); Middlebury; 1830; 1
Huntington, ___ (Rev.); Middletown, CT; 1808; 1
Hurley, Michael (Rev.); Philadelphia, PA; 1831; 1
Huse, ___ (Rev.); Hartwick-Otsego-Richfield area; 1822-23; 4
Hutchinson, W. (Rev.); Amenia area; 1827-32; 4
Hyde, ___ (Rev.); Amenia area; 1813-14; 3
Hyde, Eli (Rev.); Oxford; 1811; 1
Hyde, James, Esq.; Richfield; 1824; 2
Hyde, James, Jr., Esq.; Cooperstown; 1823; 1
Hyer, ___ (Rev.); Fishkill; 1828 and 1832; 2
Ingersoll, G. G. (Rev.); Burlington, VT; 1831-34; 5
Ingersoll, Noah, Esq.; Stanford (Dut. Co.); 1820; 1
Irvine, ___ (Rev.); Hebron?; 1831; 1
Irving, William S. (Rev.); Plattsburgh; 1823; 1
Ives, ___ (Rev.); New York City; 1829-30; 4
Ives, ___ (Rev. Bishop); New York City; 1831; 1
James, ___ (Rev.); Rochester; 1828-30; 5
Jenks, ___ (Rev.); Washington (Dut. Co.); 1814; 1
Jewett, John, Esq.; Dover-Amenia area; 1808-15; 3
Jewett, Thomas (Rev.); Fishkill; 1820; 1
Jewett, William (Rev.); 1816-32; 11
Jinks, ___ (Rev.); Fishkill; 1814; 1
Johns, ___ (Rev.); state of Georgia; 1831; 1
Johnson, ___ (Rev.); Albany; 1797; 1
Johnson, ___ (Rev.); Beekman; 1806; 1
Johnson, ___ (Rev.); Pawling; 1820 and 1825; 2
Johnson, ___ (Rev.); Potsdam; 1816; 1
Johnson, ___ (Rev.); Wayne (Steuben Co.); 1830; 1
Johnson, H. (Rev.); Dover; 1834; 1
Johnson, John (Rev.); Newburgh; 1822-30; 3

Johnson, John B. (Rev.); Albany; 1801; 1
Johnson, Nehemiah (Elder); Pawling; 1834; 1
Johnson, William (Rev.); Auburn; 1829; 1
Johnson, William (Rev.); Hyde Park; 1827 and 1832; 2
Johnson, William L.; Rector, St. Michael's Church; Trenton, NJ; 1826; 1
Johnston, John (Rev.); New York City; 1828; 1
Jolly, Hugh (Rev.); Albany; 1830; 1
Jones, ___ (Rev.); Rochester; 1830; 1
Jones, ___ (Rev.); Stephentown; 1829; 1
Jones, H. (Rev.); Colchester (Dela. Co.); 1831; 1
Jones, W. G. H. (Rev.); Fayetteville, NC; 1830; 1
Joslin, ___ (Elder); Broadalbin; 1822; 1
Judd, ___ (Rev.); Dutchess County; 1803; 1
Judd, ___ (Rev.); Hudson; 1803-06; 3
Judd, ___ (Rev.); New London, CT; 1829; 1
Judd, ___ (Rev.); Norwalk, CT; 1814; 1
Judd, Bethel (Rev.); Claverack-Kinderhook area; 1805-07; 4
Judd, Jonathan (Rev.); Athens, NY; 1804 and 1807; 2
Judd, Stoddard, Esq.; Beekman; 1823-27; 3
Judd, W. (Rev.); Salisbury (Herk. Co.); 1830; 1
Judson, ___)Rev.); Great Barrington, MA; 1802; 1
Keach, ___ (Rev.); Hoosick; 1828; 2
Kearney, ___ (Rev.); Buffalo-Black Rock area; 1829; 2
Kerney, Ravaud (Rev.); St. John's Church; Canandaigua; 1831 and 1832; 2
Keeler, Joe, Esq.; Providence, NY; 1822; 2
Keep, ___ (Rev.); Ithaca; 1830; 1
Keep, J. (Rev.); Rochester; 1831; 1
Keep, John (Rev.); Cortland; 1831; 1
Keese, ___ (Rev.); Albany; 1830; 1
Keese, W. L. (Rev.); Brownville (Jeff. Co.); 1829; 1
Kelsey, ___ (Rev.); St. Paul's Church; Albany; 1831; 1
Kemp, ___ (Rt. Rev. Bishop); Baltimore, MD; 1815; 1
Kendal, D., Esq.; Hartwick; 1826; 1
Kendall, ___ (Rev. Dr.); Plymouth, MA; 1829; 1
Kennedy, ___ (Rev.); Whitehall; 1830; 1
Kenney, Ezra (Rev.); Champlain; 1834; 2
Kent, ___ (Rev.); Hinesburgh, VT; 1833-34; 2
Ketcham, I. S. (Rev.); Manheim; 1828; 1
Ketchum, ___ (Rev.); Palatine Bridge; 1831; 1
Ketchum, ___ (Rev.); East Canada Creek; 1831; 1
Ketchum, ___ (Rev.); Schaghticoke; 1805; 1
Keys, ___ (Rev.); Albany; 1830 and 1831; 2
Kincade, ___ (Rev.); Charlton; 1824; 1
Kinet, ___ (Rev.); Pittstown; 1828; 1
King, ___ (Rev.); Kingston; 1806; 1
King, ___ (Rev.); Laurens; 1829; 2
Kingsley, Stephen (Rev.); Beekmantown (Clinton Co.); 1821; 2
Kinney, ___ (Rev.); Champlain; 1834; 1
Kinsley, ___ (Rev.); Plattsburgh; 1817; 1
Kinsley, Stephen (Rev.); Chazy; 1825; 1
Kirby, ___ (Rev.); Butternuts; 1804; 1
Kirk, E. N. (Rev.); Albany; 1829-31; 5
Kissam, ___ (Rev.); Bethlehem; 1829; 11
Kittle, Andrew N. (Rev.); Reformed Dutch Church; Red Hook; 1807-30; 22
Klapp. John, Esq.; Freedom; 1823-29; 5
Knapp, ___ (Rev.); Springfield; 1826; 1
Knight, ___ (Rev.); New Berlin; 1812; 1
Kniles, ___ (Rev.); New York City; 1829; 1
Knox, John (Rev. Dr.); New York City; 1817-34; 6
Krebs, John M. (Rev.); New York City; 1831; 1
Kuensie, ___ (Rev. Dr.); Poughkeepsie; 1804; 1
Kuypers, ___ (Rev. Dr.); New York City; 1805-31; 5
Labagh, ___ (Rev.); Catskill; 1801; 1
Labaree, ___ (Rev.); Champlain; 1820-24
Lacey, William B. (Rev.); Pittsfield (state not given); 1816; 1

Lacey, W. B. (Rev. Dr.); Albany; 1821-32; 10
Lake, ___ (Elder); Kortright; 1813; 1
Lambert, George, Jr., Esq.; Rhinebeck; 1816; 1
Lampson, ___ (Rev.); Dedham, MA; 1830; 1
Lane, A. D. (Rev.); Phelps-Waterloo area; 1829; 2
Langworthy, E. P. (Rev.); Ballston Spa; 1825; 3
Lansing, D. (Rev. Dr.); Troy; 1831; 1
Lansing, Saunders; Fort Edward?; 1823; 1
Larning, ___ (Rev.); Chippewa (state not given); 1831; 1
Lascombe, Henry H. (Rev.); Paris, France; 1830; 1
Lathrop, Jason (Rev.); Norway, NY; 1822; 1
Laurie; ___ (Rev. Dr.); Washington, Dist. of Columbia; 1832; 1
Lee, Elias (Elder); Ballston-Saratoga area; 1807-25; 5
Legett, ___ (Rev.); Peekskill; 1829; 1
Lelilles, ___ (Rev.); Becket, MA; undated; 1
Lennebacker, Philip (Rev.); Gibbonsville; 1831; 1
Leonard, Lewis (Rev.); Poughkeepsie; 1813-21; 41
Lessis, ___ (Rev.); Albany; 1828; 1
Lester, James, Esq.; Ancram; 1815; 1
Levine, ___ (Rev. Dr.); New York City; 1832; 1
Levings, ___ (Rev.); Brooklyn; 1830; 1
Lewis, ___ (Rev.); Flushing; 1831; 1
Lewis, ___ (Rev.); White Creek-Greenwich area; 1820 and 1821; 2
Lewis, Isaac (Rev.); Cooperstown area; 1803-04; 3
Linn, ___ (Rev. Dr.); Albany; 1806 and 1807; 2
Linn, ___ (Rev. Dr.); New York City; 1799 and 1807; 2
Livingston, ___ (Rev. Dr.); Dutchess County; 1793; 1
Livingston, ___ (Rev.); Kinderhook; 1812; 1
Lockey, S. (Rev.); Fishkill; 1826; 1
Lockhead, ___ (Rev.); Albany; 1831; 3
Lockwood, ___ (Rev.); Binghamton; 1827 and 1829; 2
Long, ___ (Rev.); Elizabethtown, NJ; 1831; 1
Loomis, ___ (Rev.); Hudson; 1829; 1
Lord, John (Rev.); Burlington, Otsego Co.; 1812; 2
Lossing, ___ (Rev.); Poughkeepsie (Rev.); 1
Low, ___ (Rev.); Amenia; 1834; 1
Lucas, ___ (Rev.); Litchfield, CT; 1831; 1
Luckey, ___ (Rev.); Troy; 1817-18; 3
Luckey (Rev. Dr.); Albany; 1831; 5
Ludd, ___ (Rev. Dr.); St. Peter's Church; Auburn; 1826; 1
Ludlow, ___ (Rev. Dr.); Albany; 1828-34; 17
Lunt, ___ (Rev.); NYC; 1830; 1
Luscom, ___ (Right Rev. Bishop); France?; 1829; 1
Luscombe, H. H. (Rev.); London or Birmingham, England; 1830; 1
Lusk, ___ (Rev.); Jersey City, NJ; 1834; 1
Lyell, D. (Rev. Dr.); Christ's Church; New York City; 1824-31; 5
Lyle, ___ (Rev.); New York City; 1812; 1
Lyman, S. (Rev.); Presbyterian Church; Keeseville; 1831-34; 12
Lunde, John, Esq.; Plattsburgh; 1822; 1
Lyons, L. (Rev.); Cortland; 1829; 2
McAuly, ___ (Rev. Dr.); New York City; 1833; 1
McCabe, ___ (Rev.); Milton; 1821; 1
McCabe, ___ (Rev.); state of Vermont; 1825; 1
McCahill, ___ (Rev.); St. John's Church; Utica; undated; 1
McCarroll, Joseph (Rev.); Newburgh; 1824-31; 3
McCartee, Bobert (Rev.); New York City; 1830 and 1831; 2
McClane, ___ (Rev.); New York City; 1831; 1
McClay, Archibald (Rev.); New York City; 1830-31; 3
McCollough, ___ (Rev.); Troy; 1831; 1
McCord, William I. (Rev.); La Grange; 1834; 1
NcCullom, ___ (Rev.); Washington; Dist. of Columbia; 1834; 1
McElroy, ___ (Rev. Dr.); New York City; 1831; 1
McGilligan, ___ (Rev.); Troy; 1827; 1
McIlvaine, ___ (Rev.); Lansingburgh; 1829; 3
McJimpsey, ___ (Rev.); Newburgh; 1829; 1

McJimpsey, ___ (Rev.); Poughkeepsie; 1819; 1
McJimsey, ___ (Rev.); New York City; 1829; 1
McKnight, ___ (Rev. Dr.); New York City; undated; 1
McLaren, ___ (Rev.); Gloversville; 1829; 1
McLaren, J. F. (Rev.); Geneva; 1830; 1
McLeod, ___ (Rev.); New York City; undated; 1
McManus, William, Esq.; Troy-Greenbush-Brunswick area; 1806-07; 3
McMurray, William (Rev. Dr.); New York City; 1821-31; 4
McMurray, William (Rev.); Rhinebeck area; 1812-20; 9
McNiece, ___ (Rev.); Franklin; 1804; 1
McVickar, ___ (Rev.); New York City; 1822 and 1823; 2
Mahan, Asa (Rev.); Pittsford area; 1829-31; 4
Mairs, J. (Rev.); Galway-Providence area; 1821 and 1824; 2
Malcom, Howard (Rev.); Hudson; 1820; 2
Malson, Peter R., Esq.; Southeast; 1811; 1
Manchester, Elias, Esq.; Scipio; 1829; 1
Mandeville, Garrett; Reformed Dutch Church; Caroline, NY; 1830; 1
Manly, Ira (Rev.); Essex; 1819; 1
Mann, ___ (Rev.); Alexandria (Dist. of Columbia)?; 1832; 1
Mann, ___ (Rev.); Ithaca; 1831; 1
Manning, ___ (Rev.); Sherburne; 1824; 1
Marcelus, A. A. (Rev.); Schaghticoke; 1831; 1
Mariarty, Peter (Rev.); Beekman; 1803; 2
Marks, ___ (Rev.); Binghamton; 1830; 1
Marks, Samuel (Rev.); Montrose, PA; 1831; 1
Marrs, ___ (Rev.); "Glen's Ville"; 1823; 1
Mars, ___ (Rev.); Greenwich; 1821; 1
Marseillus, ___ (Rev.); Poughkeepsie; 1826; 1
Marsh, ___ (Rev. President); Burlington, VT; 1831; 1
Marsh, ___ (Rev.); Clinton (Dut. Co.); 1795; 1
Marshal, ___ (Rev.); St. Albans, VT; 1833; 1
Martin, ___ (Rev.); Albany; 1830; 1
Martin, Samuel (Rev.); Chanceford Township, York Co., PA; 1812; 1
Martindale, J., Esq.; Troy; 1827; 2
Martindale, S. (Rev.); Troy; 1827-28; 10
Marvin, ___ (Rev.); Plattsburgh; 1834; 1
Marvin, ___ (Rev.); Troy; 1830; 1
Marvin, Dennis, Esq.; Dunning Street, Ballston Spa; 1822; 1
Mason, ___ (Rev. Dr.); Trinity Church; Geneva; 1830; 4
Mason, ___ (Rev.); Schenectady; 1829; 1
Mason, Cyrus (Rev.); New York City; 1828-31; 3
Mason, Erskin (Rev.); New York City; 1831; 1
Matthews, ___ (Rev. Dr.); Albany; 1831; 1
Matthews, ___ (Rev. Dr.); New York City; 1829 and 1831; 2
Matthias, J. J. (Rev.); Albany; 1829-30; 4
Mattison, B. (Rev.); Geneva; 1831; 1
Maxon, ___ (Rev.); Brookfield; 1826; 1
Maxon, ___ (Rev.); Plainfield; 1826; 1
Maxwell, E. K. or E. R. (Rev.); Delhi; 1826-30; 3
May, ___ (Rev.); Hoosick; 1827; 1
Mayer, ___ (Rev.); Albany; 1830; 1
Mayer, Philip F. (Rev.); Loonenburgh (Athens), NY; 1804; 2
Merrill, T. A. (Rev.); Middlebury, VT; 1819-34; 2
Mervin, ___ (Rev.); New York City; 1817; 1
Merwin, ___ (Rev.); New Haven (state not given); 1828; 1
Merwin, Samuel (Rev.); Amenia; 1823; 1
Merwin, Samuel (Rev.); Troy; 1828-29; 7
Messenger, ___ (Rev.); Fairfield; 1830; 1
Messer, ___ (Rev.); Essex; 1825; 1
Metcalf, Elijah H., Esq.; Burlington (Otsego Co.); 1808; 1
Meyer, ___ (Rev.); Albany; 1821 and 1831; 2
Milldollar, ___ (Rev.); New York City; 1814; 1
Miller, ___ (Rev. Dr.); Albany area (possibly Boght); 1805; 1
Miller, ___ (Rev.Dr.); New York City; 1806; 1
Miller, ___ (Rev.); Sag Harbor; 1830; 1

Miller, Alpha (Rev.); Bridgewater; 1823; 1
Millerton, ___ (Rev.); "Tockhomack"; 1811; 1
Mills, ___ (Rev.); Sennett; 1830; 1
Milner/Milnor, ___ (Rev. Dr.); St James and St. George's Churches; New York
    City; 1821-31; 7
Miner/Minor, Jehu (Rev.); Southeast; 1800 and 1804; 2
Mink, William (Rev.); Rhinebeck; 1826; 1
Mitchell, Edward (Rev.); New York City; 1831; 1
Monger, Sheldon, Esq.; Southeast; 1805; 1
Monteith, ___ (Rev.); New York City; 1827; 1
Monteith; ___ (Rev.); Schenectady; 1820; 1
Moore, ___ (Right Rev. Bishop); Richmond, VA; 1830; 1
Moore, ___ (Rev.); Staten Island; 1820; 1
Moore, Bishop (Rev.); New York City; 1807; 1
Moore, J. B. (Judge); Rensselaerville; 1830-31; 7
Morris, ___ (Rev.); Glen; 1829; 1
Morse, ___ (Rev.); Canaan-Hillsdale-New Lebanon area; 1808-13; 3
Morse, ___ (Rev.); Watertown; 1831; 1
Morse, Abner (Rev.); Freedom; 1827; 1
Mosher, Daniel, Jr., Esq.; Cambridge-White Creek area; 1819-20; 3
Mosher, James, Esq.; Grafton-Pittstown area; 1821-23; 3
Mott, Ebenezer, Esq.; Amenia; 1803; 1
Mott, James, Esq.; ?, 1822; 1
Mulliner, Alexander C., Esq.; Newburgh; 1834; 1
Munro, ___ (Rev.); Rodman; 1830; 1
Myer, Frederick, Esq.; Rhinebeck; 1807; 1
Myer, John S., Esq.; Poughkeepsie; 1827; 1
Myers, Oliver, Esq.; Cooperstown; 1826; 1
Nash, Daniel (Rev.); Otsego County; 1804-30; 25
Nassau, Charles W. (Rev.) Norristown, PA; 1826; 1
Neill, ___ (Rev.) Albany; 1811; 1
Nevins, ___ (Rev.); Baltimore, MD?; 1829; 1
Nevins, ___ (Rev.); Washington (Dut. Co.); 1831; 1
Newcomb, Benjamin (Rev.); Verona; 1831; 1
Nichols, E. N. (Rev.); Aurora; 1829; 1
Northrop, S. (Rev.); Washington (Dut. Co.); 1833; 1
Northrop/Northrup, William G., Esq.; Washington (Dut. Co.); 1829 and 1831; 2
Norton, Heman (Rev.); ; Reading, PA; 1830; 1
Nott, ___ (Rev.); Ballston-Broadalbin area; 1824 and 1825; 2
Nott, ___ (Rev. Dr.); Schenectady; 1830; 1
Nott, ___ (Rev. Dr.); Troy; 1807; 1
Nott, ___ (Rev. Dr.); Watervliet; 1831; 1
Nott, John (rev.); Albany; 1830; 2
Nott, Samuel (Rev.); Galway; 1824-25; 4
Noyes, ___ (Rev.); Brookfield, MA; 1831; 1
Ogilvie, ___ (Rev.); Hudson; 1815 and 1816; 2
Ogilvie, ___ (Rev.); Troy-Speigletown area; 1817; 2
Oliver, Andrew (rev.); Springfield-Middlefield area; 1819-26; 3
Onderdonk, Benjamin T. (Right Rev. Bishop); St. John's Church; New York City;
    1827-34; 12
Orton, Samuel (Rev.); Westfield; 1831; 1
Osborn, ___ (Rev.); Amenia; 1817 and 1821; 2
Osborn, ___ (Rev.); Northeast; 1824; 1
Osborn, Joel; Austerlitz and Spencertown; 1829 and 1831; 2
Osborn, John, Esq.; Stanford (Dut. Co.); 1813; 1
Osgood, Artemos, Esq.; Troy; 1819; 1
Ostrander, ___ (Rev.); Greenbush; 1831; 2
Ostrander, Edward, Esq.; Schaghticoke; 1803; 1
Ostrander, Henry (Rev.); Coxsackie; 1804 and 1808; 2
Ostrander, Henry (Rev.); Ulster County; 1834; 1
Ostrom, ___ (Rev.); Hampton (Orange Co.); 1820; 1
Ostrom, ___ (Rev.); Newburgh; 1827; 1
Ostrom, ___ (Rev.); New Paltz; 1822 and 1825; 2
Otterson, ___ (Rev.); Amsterdam, NY; 1822; 1
Otterson, James (Rev.); Brooklyn; 1829; 1

Paddock, ___ (Rev.); Cooperstown; 1818; 1
Page, ___ (Rev.); Poughkeepsie; 1832; 1
Paige, ___ (Rev. Dr.); Roxbury; 1831; 1
Paige, ___ (Rev.); Schaghticoke-Saratoga area; 1799-1806; 10
Paige, W.)Rev.); Blenheim; 1830; 1
Palfrey, ___ (Rev.); Boston (state not given); 1830; 1
Palmer, ___ (Rev.); Poughkeepsie; 1804 and 1806; 2
Palmer, Joshua, Esq.; Mooers; 1827; 1
Palmer, Sylvanus (Rev.); Canaan; 1811; 2
Palmer, Thomas, Esq.;Ballston Spa; 1823-25; 3
Paquin, J. P. (Rev.); Lacoule, Lower Canada; 1826; 1
Parker, Daniel (Rev.); Rhinebeck; 1822; 1
Parker, David (Rev.); Rhinebeck; 1821-26; 3
Perker, Joel (Rev.); Brooklyn; 1831; 1
Parkinson, Wm. (Rev.); New York City; 1823-34; 4
Parmelee, Asahel (Rev.); Malone; 1819 and 1833; 2
Parsons, Seth, Esq.; Hoosick; 1824; 2
Parsons, Silas (Rev.); Paris, NY; 1824; 1
Parsons, Silas (Rev.); Penfield; 1829; 1
Patten/Patton, ___ (Rev.); New York City; 1828; 2
Pearce, Isaac (Rev.); Trenton, NY; 1831; 1
Peck, ___ (Rev.); Ulysses; 1829; 1
Peirce, ___ (Rev.); Nassau, NY; 1823; 1
Pell, ___ (Rev.); Beekman; 1831; 2
Penney, Joseph (Rev.); Rochester; 1831; 3
Pepper, Calvin, Esq.; Albany; 1829; 1.
Perkins, A. (Rev.); Poughkeepsie area; 1822-34; 11
Perkins, Aaron (Rev.); New Paltz; 1821; 1
Perrine, ___ (Rev. Dr.); Poughkeepsie; 1832; 1
Perry, ___ (Rev.); Oriskany; 1831; 1
Perry, ___ (Rev.); Salisbury-Sharon-Kent area, CT; 1811-22; 4
Perry, John (Rev.); Milan-Stanford area; 1823 and 1826; 2
Perry, S. C., Esq.; Essex; 1822; 1
Persons, S., Esq.; Hoosick; 1824; 1
Peters, Absolom (Rev.); Bennington, VT; 1824; 1
Peters,Hewett (Rev.); Hobart (Dela. Co.); 1829 and 1830; 2
Phebus, ___ (Rev.); New York City; 1828; 1
Phelps, Eliakim (Rev.); Geneva; 1830; 1
Phillips, ___ (Poughkeepsie); 1806; 3
Phillips, W. W. (Rev. Dr.); New York City; 1822-31; 6
Phinny, ___ (Rev.); Coldenham; 1818; 1
Pickering, ___ (Rev.); Hudson-Chatham area; 1818; 3
Pier, Orris (Rev.); Jay; 1831 and 1832; 2
Pierce, ___ (Rev.); Madison; 1831; 1
Pierce, A. (Rev.); Poughkeepsie area; 1825-27; 5
Pierce, Benoni, Esq.; La Grange; 1831; 1
Pine, ___ (Rev.); Fishkill; 1814; 1
Platt, ___ (Rev.); Bath; 1831; 1
Platt, I. W. (Rev.); Charlton; 1821-22; 4
Platt, Levi, Esq.; Plattsburgh; 1824; 1
Plumb, M. (Rev.); Milton; 1825; 1
Plumb, S. M. (Elder); Wilton; 1825; 1
  Pomeroy, ___ (Rev.); Palmyra; 1825; 1
Pomeroy, ___ (Rev.); Westford-Maryland area of New York; 1824 and 1825; 2
Porter, David (Rev. Dr.); Catskill; 1803-29; 6
Porter, ___ (Rev.); Chatham; 1802; 1
Porter, ___ (Rev.); New Paltz; 1807; 1
Porter, S. (Rev.); Jamesville; 1830; 1
Potter, ___ (Rev.); St. Paul's Church; Boston, MA?; 1827; 1
Potter, Job (Rev.); Hartwick-Fly Creek area; 1824-9; 3
Potter, Lyman (Rev.); Steubenville, Ohio; 1826; 1
Potts, J. (Rev.); Morristown, NJ; 1830; 1
Power, ___ (Rev. Dr.); St. Peter's Church; New York City; 1829; 2
Prentice, ___ (Rev.); Hudson-Red Hook area; 1808-17; 5
Prentice, John H. (Rev.); Hartwick-Fly Creek area; 1826; 2

Prentice, Joseph (Rev.); Trinity Church, Athens and St. Luke's Church, Hudson;
    1808-1830; 16
Preston, ___ (Rev.); Athens, NY; 1825; 1
Price, Eliphalet (Rev.); Fishkill area; 1813-34; 22
Priestly, ___ (Dr.); Saratoga; 1828; 1
Prime, ___ (Rev.); Cambridge; 1824; 1
Prince, Black, Esq.; Jamesville; 1827; 1
Prindle, ___ (Rev.); White Creek; 1827; 1
Proal, P. Alexis (Rev.); St. George's Church; Schenectady; 1822-32; 5
Proudfit, ___ (Rev. Dr.); Philadelphia, PA?; 1830; 1
Proudfit, ___ (Rev. Dr.); Salem (Wash. Co.); 1813 and 1829; 2
Putnam, ___ (Rev.); Danby; 1830; 1
Putnam, ___ (Rev.); Owego; 1828 and 1830; 2
Putnam, ___ (Rev.); Springfield; 1822-24; 5
Putnam, Aaron (Rev.); Warren (Herk. Co.); 1824 and 1826; 2
Quarter, ___ (Rev.); New York City; 1830; 1
Quilting; ___ (Rev.); Hillsdale; undated; 1
Quinlan, ___ (Rev.); Plattsburgh; 1826 and 1827; 2
Quinn, ___ (Rev.); Hyde Park; 1834; 1
Quitman, ___ (Rev.); Schoharie; 1807; 1
Quitman, Frederick H. (Rev.); Rhinebeck; 1799-1822; 20
Raftery, James Francis (Rev.); Keeseville; 1833; 1
Raymond, Alfred, Esq.; Hyde Park-Poughkeepsie area; 1822-34; 7
Raynor, John, Esq.; Hudson; 1820; 1
Rea, ___ (Rev.); Ancram; 1815; 1
Reed, ___ (Rev. Dr.); Albany; 1834; 1
Reed, ___ (Rev.); Coldenham; 1818; 1
Reed, ___ (Rev.); Germantown, PA?; 1822; 1
Reed, ___ (Rev.); Hudson; 1822; 1
Reed, ___ (Rev.); Lisbon, CT?; 1813; 1
Reed, ___ (Rev.); Madison; 1809; 1
Reed, ___ (Rev. Dr.); New York City; 1814-27; 3
Reed, ___ (Rev. Dr.; St. George's Church; Schenectady; 1829; 1
Reed, C. P. (Rev.); Amenia; 1826; 1
Reed, Fitch (Rev.); Rhinebeck; 1829; 1
Reed, John (Rev. Dr.); Christ;s Church; Poughkeepsie; 1810-34; 134
Reed, Jonathan, Esq.; Pittstown; 1828; 4
Reichter, John W., Esq.; Gallatin; 1811; 1
Rexford, ___ (Rev.); Burlington (Otsego Co.); 1826; 1
Rexford, ___ (Norwich; 1831; 1
Rexford, L. S. (Rev.); Chatham; 1828; 1
Rexford, L. S. (Rev.); Dutchess County?; 1829; 1
Rice, ___ (Rev.); Hudson; 1815; 1
Rice, N., Esq.; Peru, NY; 1832; 2
Rice, Nathan (Rev.); Monticello, NY; 1834; 1
Richards, ___ (Rev. Dr.); Auburn; 1830; 1
Richardson, ___ (Rev.); Beekman; 1813; 1
Richardson, ___ (Rev.); Poughkeepsie; 1827-34; 14
Richmond, William (Rev.); New York City; 1829; 1
Rider, ___ (Rev.); Dutchess County (Amenia?); 1821-28; 4
Rider, Stephen (Rev.); Philadelphia (state not given); 1831; 1
Riggs, ___ (Rev.); Caroline (Tompkins Co.); 1829; 1
Robards, William, Esq.; Queensbury; 1815; 1
Roberts, P. J., Esq.; Plattsburgh; 1832; 1
Robertson, ___ (Rev.); Beekman; 1830; 1
Robinson, ___ (Rev.); Suffield, CT; 1831; 1
Robinson, George, Esq.; Burlington, VT; 1832; 1
Robinson, Nathaniel (Rev.); Putnam County; 1830; 1
Roe, ___ (Rev.); Albany; 1806; 1
Roe, ___ (Rev.); Lansingburgh; 1803; 1
Roe, Norman, Esq.; Scriba; 1831; 1
Rodgers, ___ (Rev. Dr.); New York City; 1806; 1
Rodgers, ___ (Rev.); Sandy Hill (Wash. Co.); 1830; 1
Rogers, ___ (Rev.); Stillwater; 1822; 1
Romeyn, ___ (Rev. Dr.); Albany; 1805 and 1807; 2

Romeyn, ___ (Rev. Dr.); New York City; 1808-20; 3
Romeyn, ___ (Rev.); "Twot Dale"; 1798; 1
Romeyn, James (Rev.); Nassau, NY; 1822; 1
Romeyn, Jeremiah (Rev.); Rhinebeck; 1796-1810; 4
Ross, ___ (Rev.); New York City; 1822
Ross, ___ (Rev.); Troy; 1821; 1
Rouse, P. P. (Rev.); Brooklyn?; 1830; 1
Rouse, P. P. (Rev.); Hyde Park?; 1830; 1
Rouse, P. P. (Rev.); Minaville?; 1830; 1
Rowan, Stephen N. (Rev. and President of the N. Y. Missionary Society); "near
    the Seneca Village"; 1820; 2
Rowland, ___ (Rev.); New York City; 1831; 1
Rowley, J., Esq.; Upper Red Hook; 1831; 1
Rowley, S. (Rev.); Plattsburgh; 1812; 1
Rudd, ___ (Rev. Dr.); St. Peter's Church; Auburn; 1829-31; 6
Rudd, ___ (Rev.); Mentz (Cayuga Co.); 1828; 1
Rudd, ___ (Rev.); Prattsburgh; 1831; 1
Rundell, ___ (Rev.); Marcellus; 1831; 1
Ryland, ___ (Rev.); Washington, Dist. of Columbia; 1829; 1
Sacket, Jehiel, Esq.; Stanford (Dut. Co.); 1813-14; 4
Safford, ___ (Rev.); Clarence (Erie Co.); 1829; 1
St. John, ___ (Rev.); Fly Creek; 1825; 1
St. John, Jacob (Rev.); Ballston and Greenfield; 1823; 2
Salisbury, N. (Rev.); Lowville; 1831; 1
Sampson, Ezra (Rev.); Catskill; 1801; 2
Sampson, Ezra (Rev.); Hudson; 1801-20; 6
Sandford, P. P. (Rev.); La Grange; 1831; 1
Sarkes, Jehiel, Esq.; Stanford (Dut. Co.); 1813; 1
Satterlee, William (Rev.); Berlin-Petersburgh area; 1820-28; 6
Sawin, Benjamin (Elder); Middlefield-Westford area; 1816-23; 9
Sawin, George (Elder); Warren; 1826; 2
Sawin, John (Elder); Middlefield; 1820; 1
Sawyer, ___ (Rev.); Essex; 1833; 1
Sayre, ___ (Rev.); Poughkeepsie; 1797; 1
Sayre, William N. (Rev.); Pine Plains area (Dutchess Co.); 1834; 5
Schaeffer, F. E. (Rev.); New York City; 1829-30; 3
Schroeder, ___ (Rev.); New York City; 1829; 1
Schryver, Peter A., Esq.; Hyde Park; 1829-30; 2
Schultz, Daniel H., Esq.; Clinton (Dut. Co.); 1831-32; 6
Schultz, John F.; Clinton (Dut. Co.); 1815; 1
Scott, Robert; Rhinebeck; 1826; 1
Scovill, ___ (Rev.); Poughkeepsie; 1806; 1
Searle, Addison (Rev.); St. Paul's Church; Buffalo?; 1829; 2
Searles, ___ (Rev.); Coxsackie; 1829; 2
Sears, ___ (Prof.); Hamilton; 1831; 1
Sears, ___ (Elder); Lansing; 1830; 1
Sears, Reuben (Rev.); Hudson; 1803-09; 17
Seedgrass, ___ (Rev. Dr.); New York City; 1830; 1
Seger, John (Rev.); Burlington County, NJ; 1830; 1
Seney, ___ (Rev.); Poughkeepsie; 1824; 1
Seney, ___ (Rev.); Sandy Hill (Wash. Co.); 1831; 3
Seymour, Truman (Rev,); Keeseville and Peru, NY; 1834; 2
Shaw, ___ (Rev.); New Hartford; 1821; 1
Shaw, ___ (Rev.); Somerstown (perhaps intended for Somers, NY); 1822; 1
Shear, C. H., Esq.; Albany; 1830 and 1831; 2
Sheldon, Artemas, Esq.; Burlington (Otsego Co.); 1825-26; 3
Shelton, ___ (Rev.); Buffalo; 1834; 1
Shelton, ___ (Rev.); Newtown, L.I.; 1831; 1
Shelton, ___ (Rev.); Plattsburgh; 1823; 1
Shelton, ___ (Rev.); Ransom Grove (Erie Co.); 1830; 1
Shepherd, Samuel (Rev.); Lenox, MA; 1828; 1
Sherrell, Jeremiah, Esq.; Stanford (Dut. Co.); 1802; 1
Sherrill, Isaac, Esq.; Stanford (Dut. Co.); 1817; 1
Sherwood, Daniel, Esq.; Pine Plains; 1831; 1
Sherwood, ___ (Rev.); Red Hook; 1831; 2

311

Sickles, Jacob (Rev.); Kinderhook; 1802-31; 20
Sickles, John (Rev.); Kinderhook; 1811; 1
Silliman, Cyrus (Rev.); Amenia area; 1823-24; 3
Simmons, ___ (Elder); Mayfield; 1822; 1
Skinner, ___ (Rev.); Utica; 1831; 1
Skinner, Dolphus; Corinth; 1825; 1
Skinner, St. John B. L., Esq.; Plattsburgh; 1821-32; 4
Sloth, ___ (Rev.); Fishkill; 1832; 1
Sluyter, ___ (Rev.); Claverack; 1818-31; 7
Smart, William (Rev.); Gananoque (state not given - possibly intended for
   Gananoque, Ontario, Canada); 1831; 1
Smith, ___ (Rev.); Beekman; 1815; 1
Smith, ___ (Rev.); Fairfield, CT?; 1831; 1
Smith, ___ (Rev.); Lockport; 1830; 1
Smith, ___ (Rev.(; New York City; 1834; 1
Smith, ___ (Rev.); Ogdensburgh; 1829; 1
Smith, ___ (Rev.); Poughkeepsie; 1815-22; 5
Smith, ___ (Rev.); Rensselaerville; 1829; 1
Smith, ___ (Rev.); Schenectady; 1797; 1
Smith, ___ (Rev.); Stamford, CT?; 1823; 1
Smith, Charles (Rev.); Albany; 1830-31; 3
Smith, D. (Rev.); Bath; 1831; 1
Smith, J. M. (Rev.); Rye Neck; 1829; 1
Smith, James M. (Rev.); Williamsville; 1830; 1
Smith, John (Rev.); Cooperstown; 1812-31; 53
Smith, Lucius (Rev.); St. James Church; Batavia; 1829-31; 3
Smith, Marcus (Rev.); Rensselaerville; 1830; 1
Smith, Reuben (Rev.); Episcopal Church; Ballston Spa; 1821-25; 22
Smith, T. R. (Rev.); Richland (Oswego Co.); 1829; 1
Smith, William, Esq.; Westport; 1832; 3
Smith, William Wallace; Aurora (Erie Co.); 1829; 2
Sneller, ___ (Rev.); Christ Church; New York City; 1829; 1
Snodgrass, ___ (Rev. Dr.); New York City; 1829-31; 3
Snowden, ___ (Rev.); Sackets Harbor; 1830; 1
Snyder, ___ (Rev.); Richfield; 1830; 1
Snyder, Henry (Rev.); Herkimer; 1829; 1
Sole, Seneca, Esq.; Seneca; 1828; 1
Sommers, ___ (Rev.); Albany; 1820-22; 3
Sommers, ___ (Rev.); Gibbonsville; 1820-31; 7
Sommers, ___ (Rev.); Hillsdale-Austerlitz area; 1813-20; 5
Sommers, ___ (Rev.); Sandy Hill (Wash. Co.); 1819; 1
Sommers, ___ (Rev.); Troy; 1817-22; 29
Sommers, ___ (Rev.); West Point; 1821; 1
Sommers, C. G. (Rev.); New York City; 1829 and 1834; 2
Soul, ___ (Rev.); Milford; 1824; 1
Soule, Seneca. Esq.; Dover?; 1821; 1
Southard, ___ (Rev.); Paris, NY; 1831; 1
Spafford, ___ (Rev.); Westford; 1825; 1
Spaulding, John (Elder); Beekmantown (Clinton Co.); 1820; 1
Spier, John, Esq.; Coventry, CT; 1807; 1
Spierin, ___ (Rev.); Poughkeepsie; 1793 and 1795; 2
Spencer, E. M. (Rev.); Lodi; 1829; 1
Spoore, ___ (Rev.); Broome; 1829; 1
Sprague, ___ (Rev.); Sherburne; 1825; 1
Sprague, William B. (Rev.); Albany; 1829-31; 14
Spring, ___ (Rev. Dr.); New York City; 1817-31; 4
Squier, M. P. (Rev.); ?, 1831; 1
Squier, P. M. (Rev.); Phelps; 1829; 1
Stacy, Nathaniel (Rev.); Pierstown; 1815; 1
Staniford, John (Rev.); Plattsburgh; 1
Stanley, Frederick, Esq.; New Hartford, NY; 1816; 1
Stansbury, Arthur J. (Rev.); NYC; 1819; 2
Stanton, ___ (Rev.); Hudson; 1817-20; 5
Stark, ___ (Rev.); New York City; 1831; 1
Starr, Peter (Rev.); Warren, CT; 1810 and 1823; 2

Stead, Henry (Rev.); Rensselaerville; 1829; 1
Stebbins, Cyrus (Rev.); Christ's Episcopal Church; Hudson; 1820-30; 5
Stebbins, ____ (Rev.); Troy; 1830; 1
Steck, ____ (Rev.); Greensburg, PA; 1831; 1
Stetson, L., Esq.; Peru, NY; 1834; 1
Stevenson, ____ (Rev.); Minaville; 1830; 1
Stewart, ____ (Rev.); Cooperstown; 1822; 1
Stewart, ____ (Elder); Greenville; 1814; 1
Stillman, Cyrus (Rev.); Fallsburgh; 1834; 1
Stimson, ____ (Rev.); Windham; 1824; 1
Stimson, Henry B. (Rev.); Reformed Dutch Church; Schoharie; 1829; 1
Stitt, John, Esq.; Pittstown; 1818; 1
Stockton, ____ (Rev.); ?; 1831; 1
Stone, ____ (Rev.); New Lisbon; 1826; 1
Stone, ____ (Rev.); Warren; 1825; 1
Stow, T. (Rev.); Elbridge; 1831; 1
Stratton, ____ (Rev.); Canfield, Ohio; 1830; 1
Stratton, ____ (Rev.); New York City; 1834; 1
Stratton, ____ (Rev.); Troy; 1831; 1
Strong, ____ (Rev.); Colchester, CT; 1831; 1
Strong, ____ (Rev.); Flatbush, L.I.; 1830; 1
Strong, ____ (Rev.); Geneva; 1829; 1
Strong, ____ (Rev. Dr.); Norwich, CT; 1814 and 1830; 2
Strong, ____ (Rev.); St. Albans, VT; 1819; 1
Strong, H. P. (Rev.); Phelps; 1830 and 1831; 2
Strong, Paschal N. (Rev.); Corresponding Secretary of the N.Y. Missionary
    Society; 1820; 1
Sturges, ____ (Rev.); Stuyvesant; 1829; 1
Sullivan, ____ (Rev.); Keene, NH; 1829; 1
Sutherland, Isaac, Esq.; Stanford (Dut. Co.); 1822-32; 21
Swan, ____ (Rev.); Warren; 1824; 1
Swazey, William (Rev.); Poughkeepsie; 1813; 1
Sweetman, Joseph (Rev.); Charlton; 1821-24; 6
Swift, ____ (Rev.); Williamstown, MA; 1805; 1
Switz, M. (Rev.); Wawarsing-Napanoch area; 1831 and 1834; 2
Tallmadge, David, Esq.; Schaghticoke; 1823-24; 3
Tallmadge, Henry, Esq.; Stanford (Dut. Co.); 1834; 8
Tappan, ____ (Rev.); Pittsfield, MA; 1829 and 1831; 2
Tappan, J. M. (Rev.); Bloom Ville (Dela. Co.); 1831; 1
Tappen, Teunis, Esq.; Poughkeepsie; 1805; 1
Taylor, ____ (Rev.); Amenia; 1834; 1
Taylor, ____ (Rev.); Burlington (Otsego Co.); 1817; 1
Taylor, ____ (Rev.); Canaan; 1830; 1
Taylor, ____ (Rev.); Essex; 1829; 1
Taylor, ____ (Rev. Dr.); New Haven, CT; 1831; 1
Taylor, B. C. (Rev.); Bergen, NJ; 1831; 1
Taylor, Benjamin C. (Rev.); Albany; 1830; 1
Taylor, E., Esq.; Pine Plains; 1831; 1
Taylor, Hutchins (Rev.); Canaan Center; 1830; 1
Taylor, Nathan, Esq.; Peru, NY; 1826; 2
Thatcher, ____ (Rev.); Poughkeepsie; 1832; 1
Thibow, ____ (Rev.); Angelica; 1831; 1
Thomas, ____ (Rev.); Petersburgh; 1827; 1
Thomas, M. (Rev.); Cornwall; 1831; 1
Thomas, William B. (Rev.); Albany; undated; 1
Thomas, William B. (Rev.); Rector, Trinity Church; Fishkill; 1824-26; 6
Thomas, William B. (Rev.); Rector, Christ Church; Duanesburgh; 1832; 1
Thompson, ____ (Elder); Ballston Spa; 1825; 2
Thompson, ____ (Rev.); Greenville; 1829; 1
Thompson, Jesse, Esq.; Amenia; 1899; 2
Thompson, Joel, Esq.; Sherburne; 1807; 1
Thompson, John, Esq.; Stanford (Dut. Co.); 1809 and 1812; 2
Thomson, F. B. (Rev.); Upper Red Hook; 1834; 1
Thorn, Stephen, Esq.; Clinton-Milan area of Dutchess County; 1822 and 1827; 2
Thorne, Gilbert, Esq.; Stanford (Dut. Co.); 1820 and 1828; 2

313

Thorne, William, Esq.; Washington (Dut. Co.); 1811 and 1812; 2
Thurston, Edward C., Esq.; Hudson; 1820; 1
Thurston, John M., Esq.; Clinton (Dut. Co.); 1817; 1
Thurston, Samuel, Esq.; Washington (Dut. Co.); 1818; 1
Tiffany, F. J. (Rev.); Hyde Park; 1834; 1
Tiffany, F. T. (Rev.); Christ Church; Cooperstown; 1820-31; 32
Tinkham, ___ (Rev.); Shaftsbury, VT?; 1822; 1
Tinkham, ___ (Rev.); White Creek; 1823; 1
Tinney, F. Y. (Rev.); Claverack?; 1830; 1
Tittle, ___ (Rev.); Red Hook?; 1808; 1
Titus, John, Esq.; Beekman; 1809; 1
Todd, ___ (Rev.); St. George's Church; New York City; 1830; 1
Todd, ___ (Rev.); Ogdensburgh; 1829; 2
Toll, ___ (Rev.); Milford?; 1809; 1
Tomb, ___ (Rev.); Salem?; 1822; 1
Tomlinson, B., Esq.; Ticonderoga; 1830; 1
Tooker, ___; Benton; 1830; 1
Townsend, ___ (Rev.); Phelps or Palmyra?; undated; 1
Treadway, ___ (Rev.); New Hartford; 1829; 1
Treadway, ___ (Rev.); Richfield; 1825; 1
Treadway, A. C. (Rev.); Johnstown; 1830; 1
Treadway, A. C. (Rev.); Kingston?; 1830; 1
Treadwell, ___ (Lt. Gov.); New Hartford, CT; 1804; 1
Tresdall, Joseph (Rev.); Franklin?; 1803; 1
Tripp, Howard, Esq.; Washington (Dut. Co.); 1831; 2
Tucker, ___ (Rev.); Schaghticoke; 1818; 1
Tucker, Eber (Rev.); Milton; 1825; 1
Tucker, Mark (Rev.); Troy; 1827-31; 17
Tuckerman, Frederick (Rev.); Washington (Dut. Co.); 1832; 1
Turner, ___ (Rev.); Redford?; 1834; 1
Tuttle, ___ (Rev.); Meredith?; 1831; 1
Uhl, ___ (Rev.); Albany; 1805; 1
Upfold, ___ (Rev. Dr.); Albany; 1829; 1
Upfold, ___ (Rev.); Exeter; 1825; 1
Upfold, ___ (Rev.); New York City; 1829; 1
Upfold, George (Rev.); New York City; 1830-31; 3
Upham, ___ (Rev.); St. Thomas Church; New York City; undated; 1
Van Buren, ___ (Rev.); Schodack; 1816 and 1819; 2
Vancleff, C. L. (Rev.); Hackensack, NY; 1834; 1
Vanderbergh, Henry, Esq.; Clinton (Dut. Co.); 1813; 1
Vanderveer, F. H. (Rev.); Hyde Park and vicinity; 1824-29; 8
Vanderveer, ___ (Rev.); Shawungunk; 1834; 1
Vanderwarker, ___ (rev.); Jay; 1836; 1
Van Devoort, John (Rev.); New Brunswick, NJ?; 1820; 1
Van Horne, ___ (Rev.); Johnstown; 1830; 1
Van Kleeck, R. (Rev.); Fishkill; 1834; 1
Van Kleef, ___ (Rev.); La Grange?; 1834; 1
Van Olinda, D. (Rev.) Fort Plain-Palatine-Canajoharie area; 1829-30; 3
Van Olinda, D. (Rev.); New Paltz; 1834; 1
Van Pelt, ___ (Rev. Dr.); Castleton, Staten Island; 1831; 1
Van Sanfort, ___ (Rev.); Belleville, NJ; 1822; 1
Van Vechten, ___ (Rev.); Schenectady; 1830; 2
Van Vechten, S. (Rev.); Phillipstown; 1833; 1
Van Vechten, Samuel A. (Rev.); Poughkeepsie; 1834; 1
Van Vleck, ___ (Rev.); New York City; 1829; 1
Van Vliet, Levi, Esq.; Clinton; 1831; 1
Van Vranken, ___ (Rev.); Fishkill-Hyde Park-Poughkeepsie area; 1827-34; 3
Van Vranken, Nicholas (Rev.); Fishkill; 1794-1804; 16
Van Wagenen, J. H. (Rev.); Bern?; 1831; 1
Van Wagner, John S., Esq.; Hyde Park; 1830-31; 5
Van Wagoner, ___ (Rev.); Bern; 1829; 1
Van Wyck, Abraham D., Esq.; Fishkill; 1814; 2
Varela, ___ (Rev.); Christ Church; New York City; 1831; 1
Vars, Benjamin, Esq.; Berlin, NY; 1823 and 1827; 2
Vary, Calvin P., Esq.; Berlin, NY; 1827 and 1828; 2

Vedder, H. (Rev.); Livingston; 1808-13; 3
Vedder, Herman (Rev.); Claverack; 1817 and 1819; 2
Veeder, ___ (Rev.); Pine Plains; 1811 and 1817; 2
Velie, Mindert, Esq.; Poughkeepsie and Washington (Dut. Co.); 1812 and 1813; 2
Vermeule, ___ (Rev.); Harlem; 1831; 1
Verren, A. (Rev.); New York City?; 1830; 1
Vincent, Leonard, Esq.; Dover; 1832; 1
Wachenhagen, Augustus (Rev.); Schoharie?; 1808; 1
Wackerhagen, Augustus (Rev.); Claverack-Clermont-Red Hook area; 1817-30; 5
Waddle, Solas, Esq.; Washington (Dut. Co.); 1817; 2
Wadsworth, ___ (Rev.); Warren; 1825; 2
Wadsworth; ___ (Rev.); Canajoharie; 1830; 1
Wagner, John S., Esq.; Hyde Park; 1830; 1
Wainwright, ___ (Rev. Dr.); Grace Church, New York City; 1821-31; 11
Walker, ___ (Rev.); Moscow (Livingston Co.); 1830; 1
Walker, Charles (Rev.); Poughkeepsie; 1826; 1
Walker, J. (Rev.); Greenbush; 1834; 1
Wallace, H. (Rev.); Sheldon?; 1830; 1
Walsh, ___ (Rev. Dr.); New Orleans, LA; 1805; 1
Walters, ___ (Rev.); Canaan; 1811; 1
Walworth, Reuben H., Esq.; Plattsburgh; 1811-15; 6
Ware, ___ (Rev.); New York City?; 1829; 1
Warren, ___ (Rev.); Waterbury, VT; 1833; 1
Wartrous, John (Rev.); New Concord (Columbia Co.); 1803; 1
Washburn, ___ (Rev.); Amenia; 1820; 1
Washburn, Robert (Rev.); Northumberland; 1831; 1
Waterbury, Daniel (Rev.); Franklin (Dela. Co.); 1831; 3
Waterman J. P. (Rev.); Brooklyn Heights; 1831; 1
Waters, John (Rev.); Chatham area; 1808-13; 3
Watkins, ___ (Rev.); Albany; 18#1; 1
Wayland, ___ (Rev.); Poughkeepsie; 1808-11; 3
Wayland, ___ (Rev.); Troy; 1812-17; 3
Weaver, ___ (Rev.); Poughkeepsie; 1816; 1
Weaver, Peter (Rev.); Plattsburgh; 1827; 1
Weaver, Samuel (Rev.); Peru, NY; 1823; 1
Webb, Isaac (Rev.); Troy; 1806 and 1828; 2
Webster, Daniel (Rev.); Cooperstown; 1805; 1
Weed, ___ (Rev.); Albany; 1823-29; 7
Weed, H. R. (Rev.); Pittstown; 1830; 1
Weeks, William R. (Rev.); Plattsburgh; 1812 and 1813; 2
Weidman, ___ (Rev.); Schoharie?; 1830; 1
Welch; ___ (Rev.); Burlington, NJ; 1822; 1
Welch, ___ (Rev.); Schenectady; 1829; 1
Welch, B. T. (Rev.); Albany; 1829-31; 18
Welling, Elisha, Esq.; Stanford (Dut. Co.); 1822; 1
Wells, ___ (Rev.); Oxford (Chenango Co.); 1829; 1
Wells, ___ (Rev.); Pittstown; 1807; 1
Wells, Ransford; (Rev.); Platine, NY; 1830; 2
Welton, ___ (Rev.); Hyde Park; 1814; 1
Welton, Alonzo (Rev.); Presbyterian Church; Poughkeepsie; 1826-32; 43
West, ___ (Rev.); Stockbridge, MA; 1797 and 1804; 2
Westbrook, Cornelius D. (Rev.); Fishkill; 1810-30; 18
Westcott, Isaac (Rev.); Stillwater; undated; 1
Westfall, ___ (Rev.); Rochester (Ulster Co.); 1829; 1
Whaling, Francis (Rev.); Saratoga?; 1828; 1
Wheaton, ___ (Rev.); Newport, RI; 1829 and 1830; 2
Wheeler, ___ (Rev.); East Bloomfield; 1829; 1
Wheeler, ___ (Rev.); New Berlin; 1825; 1
Wheeler, Elijah (Rev.); Great Barrington, MA; 1812; 1
Wheeler, Russell (Rev.); Zion Church; Butternuts; 1815-23; 10
Wheeler, Russell (Rev.); Whitesboro; 1831; 1
Wheelock, John, Esq.; Hindsburgh, VT; 1833; 1
Whelpley, Philip M. (Rev.); First Presbyterian Society; New York City; 1819-24; 5
Whelpley, S. W. (Rev.); Plattsburgh; 1818-25; 11
Whetmore, ___ (Rev.); North Guilford, CT; 1829; 1

Whipple, ___ (Rev.); Johnstown; 1829; 2
Whipple, ___ (Rev.); Salisbury (Herk. Co.); 1824; 1
Whipple, P. L. (Rev.); Lansingburgh; 1830 and 1831; 2
Whitcomb, ___ (Rev.); Hudson; 1831; 1
White, ___ (Rev.); Albany; 1830; 1
White, ___ (Right Rev. Bishop); Bordentown, NJ?; 1824; 1
White, ___ (Right Rev. Bishop); Philadelphia, PA; 1822-29; 3
White, Seneca (Rev.); Bath, Maine?; 1831; 1
Whitehead, ___ (Rev.); Otsego; 1825; 1
Whitehead, Charles (Rev.); Stormville (Dut. Co.); 1832; 1
Whitehouse, H. J. (Rev.); St. Luke's Church; Rochester; 1830 and 1831; 2
Whiting, ___ (Rev.); Batavia; 1830; 1
Whittemore, ___ (Rev.); Troy; 1829; 2
Wiedman, ___ (Rev.); Schoharie; 1831; 1
Wier, ___ (Elder); Hartwick; 1813; 1
Wieting, Philip (Rev.); Sharon; 1830; 1
Wigton, ___ (Rev.); Hudson; 1806-09; 12
Wilcox, Abner, Esq.; Richfield; 1817; 1
Wilcox, Abner, Esq.; Stanford (Dut. Co.); 1822; 1
Wilde, P. F. (Rev.); Pleasant Valley; 1832 and 1834; 2
Wilder, ___ (Rev.); Pleasant Valley; 1830; 1
Wile, B. F. (Rev.); Pleasant Valley; 11
Wilkins, ___ (Rev.); state of Virginia; 1809; 1
Williams, ___ (Rev.); Albany; 1829; 2
Williams, ___ (Rev.); Fairfield, CT; 1813; 1
Williams, ___ (Rev.); Hillsdale; 1806 and 1812; 2
Williams, ___ (Rev.); Knox; 1830; 1
Williams, ___ (Rev.); Poughkeepsie; 1806; 1
Williams, Cornelius, Esq.; Beekman (Dut. Co.); 1803; 1
Williams, Ezra, Esq.; Peru, NY area; 1831-34; 14
Williams, John (Rev.); New York City?; 1818; 1
Williams, William D., Esq.; Beekman; 1804; 1
Williams, William P. (title not given); Hyde Park; 1834; 1
Willis, ___ (Rev.); Troy; 1826-28; 15
Williston, ___ (Rev.); Durham; 1814; 1
Williston, Ralph (Rev.); Ithaca; 1829-30; 3
Wilson, ___ (Rev.); Galway; 1821; 1
Wilson, ___ (Rev.); Livingston, NJ; 1824; 1
Wilson, C. P. (Rev.); Amenia; 1822-29; 65
Wing, Elihu, Esq.; Milton; 1825; 1
Winter, Thomas (Rev.); Northeast; 1826-34; 9
Wisner, William (Rev.); Ithaca; 1820-29; 3
Wlailon, ___ (Rev.); Troy; 1812; 1
Wood, H. A. (Rev.); Amsterdam, NY; 1825-33; 3
Wood, John (Rev.); Dutchess County (Amenia area?); 1803-10; 4
Woodbridge, Timothy (Rev.); Hillsdale; 1829 and 1830; 2
Woodbridge, ___ (Rev.); Westerlo, NY; 1829; 1
Woodle, Silas, Esq.; Washington (Dut. Co.)?; 1812; 1
Woodruff, ___ (Rev.); Sconondoa (Oneida Co.); 1829; 1
Woodruff, Hezekiah (Rev.); Aurora (Cayuga Co.); 1807; 1
Woolsey, ___ (Rev.); Amenia; 1812; 1
Wright, ___ (Elder); Maryland, NY; 1824; 1
Wure, William (Rev.); New York City; 1831; 1
Wyckoff, ___ (Rev.); Catskill-Cairo area; 1829-30; 3
Wyman, Richard (Rev.); Amenia; 1834; 1
Wynkoop, M. (Rev.); Poughkeepsie; 1821; 3
Wynkoop, Peter S. (Rev.); Hyde Park and vicinity; 1817-22; 15
Wynkoop, Peter S. (Rev.) Ghent; 1831; 2
Yale, Calvin (Rev.); Charlotte, VT; 1831; 1
Yates, ___ (Rev. Dr.); Chittenengo; 1829; 1
Yates, ___ (Rev. Dr.); Schenectady; 1821; 1
Yeau, ___ (Judge); Cazenovia; 1806; 1
Young, ___ (Rev.); Poughkeepsie; 1825; 2
Younglove, ___ (Rev.); Stephentown and Pittstown; 1819 and 1821

Armstrong, Margaret 7892
*Armstrong, Maria P. 2363
*Armstrong, Matthew 271
Armstrong, Moses 263
Armstrong, Nancy H. 6485
Armstrong, Robert 266
Armstrong, Sally 2616
Armstrong, Thomas 4614
Arnett, Mary N. 3587
Arnold, Ahab 291
Arnold, Amanda 8865
Arnold, Benjamin 282
Arnold, David 8865
Arnold, Jacob 289
Arnold, Joseph 272, 284
Arnold, Levi 286
Arnold, Lydia H. 3252
Arnold, Mary Ann 2847
Arnold, Robert 4946
Arnold, Rodney 280
Arnold, Sarah 4946
Arnold, Smith 281
Arthur, Elizabeth 1655
Ashley, Polly 8987
Ashworth, Alice 3883
Asite, Bashaba 2795
Astor, Caroline C. 6134
Atherton, Mary 1095
Atwater, Caleb 305
Atwater, Jane M. 6876
Atwater, Moses 6876
Atwater, Sally 5653
Atwood, Eliza 121
Auchincloss, ___ (Mr.) 8259
Auchmoty, Susan K. 6840
Austin, Alanson 3766
Austin, Diadamia 3766
Austin, Martha M. 5344
Austin, Rachel 8484
Austin, Rufus 7701
Austin, Sarah 7701
Austin, Seth 308
Averell, Lucy 4097
Averill, C. K. 315
Averill, Clara 9964
Averill, J. K. (Mr.) 314
Averill, Lovicy B. 1382
Averill, Nathan 313, 320
Averill, Noble 9964
Averill, Prudence 10106
Averill, William 319
Avery, John H. 323
Axtell, ___ (male) 327
Axtell, Henry 329
Aylsworth, Asahel 331
Aylsworth, Betsey 9978
Babbet, James 335
Babcock, Almira 4871
Babcock, Betsey 7211
Babcock, Christopher 348
Babcock, Cynthia 5187
Babcock, Emily 7750
Babcock, Frederick 342
Babcock, Gardner 337
Babcock, John W. 9768
Babcock, Mary 9768
Babcock, Mary D. 9997
Babcock, Oliver 7750
Babcock, Pamelia 7162
Bache, Margaret Hartman 2671
Backus, Betsey 7831
Backus, Electus 3277
Backus, Flora 3277
Backus, Julia S. 4786
Bacon, Ann 1951
Bacon, Benjamin 362
Bacon, Julia A. 8248
Bacon, Lucy 8235
Bacon, Reuben 8248
* Armstrong, Mary 126

Bacon, William C. 360
Baden, Rachel 3407
Badger, Harriet 6354
Badgley, Eliza 1236
Badgley, Joseph 368
Badge, Mary Ann 5031
Bagsley, Sally Ann 6454
Bailey, ___ (Gen.) 386, 388
Bailey, ___ (Judge) 392
Bailey, ___ (Mr.) 4287, 7175
Bailey, Betty 5245
Bailey, Catharine Rebecca
  10038
Bailey, Catherine 9427
Bailey, Cena 3612
Bailey, Charity H. 5909
Bailey, Charlotte 6167
Bailey, Deborah 7644
Bailey, Elizabeth 2125
Bailey, Esther 24
Bailey, John 369, 375, 5245
Bailey, Phebe 8066
Bailey, Rowland 383
Bailey, Sarah 370
Bailey, Sarah C. 3807
Bailey, Theodorus 385, 10038
Bailey, William 5972, 6167,
  8066
Baily, John 10033
Baily, Mary 1048, 10033
Baily, Sally 7878
Bain, ___ (Mr.) 3640
Bain, Elizabeth 3232
Bain, Margaret 1434
Bain, Peter 1434
Baker, ___ (Mr.) 6583
Baker, Abigail 62
Baker, Betsey 2654
Baker, Charity B. 10065
Baker, D. (Maj.) 9526)
Baker, Daniel 403
Baker, Eddy 399
Baker, Electa 5463
Baker, Elizabeth 7925
Baker, Erastus 728, 2654
Baker, Frances 728
Baker, George 397, 426
Baker, Hannah 716
Baker, Harriet E. 9526
Baker, Jane Anne 2079
Baker, Jemima K. 407
Baker, John 10065
Baker, Lydia M. 2603, 3262
Baker, Maria 9369
Baker, Mary 1231
Baker, Nehemiah 420
Baker, Ozias 403
Baker, Patty 1750
Baker, Rebecca S. 393
Baker, Ruth 1033
Baker, Sally 9285
Baker, Samuel 409
Baker, Solomon 428
Baker, Sophia 8228
Baker, Sylvia 426
Baker, Valentine 400, 421, 424
Balch, Betsey 9985
Balding, Angelina 6838
Balding, Elizabeth 5885, 6353
Balding, Isaac I. 6838
Blading, Maria 8805
Balding, Mary 5691
Balding, Sarah 2741
Baldwin, ___ (Mr.) 4885
Baldwin, Aminta 4898
Baldwin, Benjamin 9209
Baldwin, Charles 435
Baldwin, Clarissa 4975
Baldwin, Daniel 8074

Baldwin, Ebenezer 434
Baldwin, Eliza 1897
Baldwin, Elizabeth Frances 4885
Baldwin, Fanny 756
Baldwin, Heman 4885
Baldwin, Joseph 443
Baldwin, Mary 440, 9209
Baldwin, Rebecca 6762
Baldwin, Squire, 1897
Balie, Ann M. 3790
Balie, William 3790
Balis, Ann M. 3790
Balis, William 3790
Ball, Charles 771
Ball, Charlotte Ann 8258
Ball, Heman 9328
Ball, Jonathan 9456
Ball, Mary 6882
Ball, Sally 9456
Ballentine, Eliza 1596
Ballis, Julia 4601
Ballis, William 4601
Baltimore, Maria 6009
Bancroft, Evolinah 452
Banker, Eleanor 7663
Banker, John 457, 7663
Banker, Nancy 3295
Banker, Rebecca 5833
Banks, Laura 2697
Bant, Anna 6395
Bant, Samuel 6395
Barber, ___ (Col.) 8624
Barber, Amos 464
Barber, Daniel 6404
Barber, Jacob 471
Barber, Jane Anna 5952
Barber, Laura 1577
Barber, Louisa 10058
Barber, Patience 3682
Barber, William 5952
Barbour, Louisa A. 7608
Bard, Eliza 5580
Bard, John 476
Bard, Mary Ann 6995
Bard, Samuel 475, 477, 5580
Bard, William 6995
Bardwell, Armylla 2088
Bargy, Peter 479
Baringer, Patty 3112
Barker, Caleb 486
Barker, Caroline 6377
Berker, Deborah 1344
Barker, Eleazer 7146
Barker, Eugehia Maria 4212
Barker, Harriet 7206
Barker, Helen Maria 2355
Barker, Jacob 471
Barker, Lydia 3390
Barker, Mark 2796
Barker, Marks 6377
Barker, Mary 4448
Barker, P. A. (Mr.) 4212
Barker, Polly 7146
Barker, Robert 471
Barker, Samuel A. 488
Barker, Samuel Augustus 483
Barker, Sarah 2796
Barker, Susan 9664
Barkman, Polly 5166
Barlow, Elisha C. 5932
Barlow, Lemuel 494
Barlow, Maria Jane 5932
Barlow, Myra 1800
Barlow, Susan Ann 5576
Barlow, Thomas 1800, 8477
Barnard, Avis 8244
Barnard, D. D. (Hon.) 507
Barnard, Eliza Ann 4514
Barnard, Enoch 503

318

Barnard, John 505
Barnard, Joseph 504
Barnard, Joseph, Jr. 4514
Barnard, Peter 5549
Barnard, Rebecca 5549
Barnard, Sally 4488
Barnard, Ursula 3422
Barnes, ___ (Mr.) 1545, 5934
Barnes, Catharine S. 7934
Barnes, David 510, 7933, 7934, 7935
Barnes, Elizabeth 8847
Barnes, Hannah 5897
Barnes, Mary 409
Barnes, Jeremiah 515, 516, 5897
Barnes, John 509
Barnes, Laura 9794
Barnes, Lucretia 4012
Barnes, Maria 2846
Barnes, Sarah K. 7933
Barney, Catherine 2118
Barney, Harriet 5986
Barney, Henrietta 766
Barney, James 5986
Barney, Martha 7724
Barnham, Caleb 524
Barns, Abigail 9687
Barns, Catharine 3540
Barns, Mahala 2668
Barns, Richard 525
Barr, ___ (Mr.) 8259
Barr, Margaret 7767
Barr, Therese 6772
Barrell, Mary Ann 45
Barret, Abraham 3806
Barret, Amelia 3806
Barringer, Eliza 7236
Barritt, Rhoda 4066
Barron, Fidelia 2248
Barry, Irene 5257
Barry, Mary Warren 6065
Bartholomew, Andrew 541, 542
Bartholomew, Eliza 363
Bartlet, ___ (Miss) 7666
Bartlet, Mercy 4704
Bartlett, Elizabeth 4927
Bartlett, Fanny 6628
Bartlett, J. B. (Dr.) 552
Bartlett, Lois 1369
Bartlett, Mary 8638
Bartlett, Penelope 4061
Bartley, Margaret 31
Bartley, Mary 8935
Barton, ___ (Mrs.) 475
Barton, Abigail 4575
Barton, Benjamin 454
Barton, Eliza 2457
Barton, Leonard 4327
Barton, Maria 954
Barton, Phebe 101
Barton, Phebe R. 1638
Barton, Roger 562
Barton, Ruth 895
Barton, Sally 7377
Barton, Sarah 4327
Barton, William 9433
Bassett, ___ (Rev. Dr.) 567
Bassett, Benoni 10053
Bassett, Catherine Ann 10053
Bassett, Harriet 6413
Bassett, John 567
Bates, Almira 7504
Bates, Benjamin 7504, 8326
Bates, Bernard 9633
Bates, Betsey 8326
Bates, Harriet 2488
Bates, John 572

Bates, Margaret 9633
Bates, Nancy 3097
Bates, Rachel 1143
Bates, Sarah 3308
Battel, Joseph 579
Battey, Catharine 4911
Battey, Robert 4911
Baxter, Ann 583
Baxter, Jotham 583
Bay, John 586
Bayard, Harriet Elizabeth 9158
Bayard, William 9158
Bayeux, Henry B. 588
Bayeux, Susan 4049
Bayliss, Mary 7466
Beach, Else Minerva 7653
Beach, Sarah Minerva 7652
Beadle, Daniel W. 596, 597
Beadle, Elisha 3146
Beadle, Eliza 6441
Beadle, John 6441
Beadle, Mary 3146
Beadle, Sally 2430
Beadle, Timothy 601, 602, 2430
Beal, Lewis 605
Beal, Permela 605
Bean, Epsyby 9281
Bearding, Abigail 1213
Beardsley, Abadiah 4559
Beardsley, Amos 614
Beardsley, Jabez 616
Beardsley, Obadiah 622
Beardsley, Olive 4559
Beardsley, Sophronia 8003
Beare, William H. 623
Bears, Mary 4657
Becker, cornelia 3085
Becker, William 631
Beckwith, ___ (Dr.) 7432
Beckwith, ___ (Miss) 2142
Beckwith, Baruc 7954
Beckwith, Emilia 6492
Beckwith, Mary 7954
Becraft, Mehitable 34
Bedel, Remma 1782
Bedel, Timothy 4627
Bedell Ann Marian 9772
Bedell, T. (Rev.) 6410
Bedell, William 9772
Bedford, john 644
Bedlow, Lois 7242
Beebe, Emmeline 2947
Beebe, Hosea 648
Beebe, Levi 2947
Beebe, Lydia 6740
Beebe, Rebecca 1627
Beebe, Sarah 191
Beebee, Salonee 4180
Beecher, Amelia J. 8562
Beecher, Amos 7000
Beecher, Julia Amanda 7000
Beecher, Mary Eliza 3063
Beecher, Trena 4671
Beekman, ___ (Judge)
Beekman, Gertrude 7161
Beekman, John P. 653
Beekman, Richard L. 8544
Beekman, Sarah 9606
Beekman, Sarah L. 8544
Beekman, Stephen D. 655
Beekman, William 8594
Belden, Ames 5920
Belden, Charles (Mrs.) 5920
Belden, Ebenezer 660
Belden, Eliza 196
Belden, George (Mrs.) 5920
Belden, John 661
Belden, Joseph 196

Belden, Julia Ann 9387
Belden, Sally 6183
Belden, William T. 663, 664, 668, 9387
Belding, Angelina 6838
Belding, Isaac I. 6838
Belding, Lois 6724
Belding, Lucy 8268
Belding, Silas 671
Belding, Taber 8268
Belknap, Laura 4607
Bell, David 679
Bell, Julia 8308
Bell, Samuel 6219
Bell, Sarah 2831
Bell, William 678
Bellin, Catharine (Mrs.) 7946
Bellows, Maria 1554
Bellows, Martha Jennet 3523
Beman, Samuel 683
Bement, William 685
Bemington, Hannah (Mrs.) 1835
Bemis, Marial 7289
Ben, Tine (Miss) 1744
Benedict, ___ (Mr.) 7332
Benedict, James 700
Benedict, Lewis 699
Benedict, Mary 47
Benedict, Trowbridge 696
Benham, Theodosia 5709
Benjamin, Caleb 708
Benjamin, Cyrus 8634
Benjamin, Eliza 3257
Benjamin, Harriet 3950
Benjamin, J. (Capt.) 706
Benjamin, Joseph 3257
Benjamin, Mary Crosby 8634
Benjamin, Sarah P. 6534
Benner, Ann 8588
Benner, Christina 6213
Benner, Henry 6213, 8588
Bennet, Phebe 4876
Bennet, R. O. K. (Mr.) 713
Bennet, Rebecca 3218
Bennet, Susan C. 8964
Bennet, Thomas 3218
Bennett, Almira 8114
Bennett, Charlotte 1607
Bennett, Cynthia Maria 301
Bennett, Elizabeth 5415, 6171
Bennett, Julia 8352
Bennett, Mary 1864
Bennett, Nathaniel 2258
Bennett, Peter W. 8114
Bennett, Polly 724
Bennitt, Increase (Capt.) 726
Benson, Frederick 2654
Benson, Jane 4235
Benson, Robert 4235
Bentley, Mariah 9352
Bentley, Richard W. 734
Benton, Adeline 651
Benton, Joel 651
Benton, Orange 5717
Benton, Sally 5717, 7275
Berault, Emily 1915
Berault, John M. 1915
Bergh, Sarah S. 845
Bergh, Tunis 845
Berrien, J. McPheron (Mr.)2782
Berrien, John M. 745
Berrien, Margaret L. M. 2782
Berry, Charles 1373
Berry, Maria 40
Berry, Sybill 5900
Besley, Mary 9379
Besley, William 9379
Bessac, ___ (Mr.) 9650

Best, Mary 7972
Betts, Azuba Ann 2375
Betts, Burwell 758
Betts, Julia Ann 4654
Betts, Peter J. 9806
Betts, Phebe Ann 6982
Betts, Sally 9738
Betts, Samuel 2657
Betts, Susan 2657
Bevier, Benjamin R. 8121
Bevier, Elizabeth R. 8121
Bevier, Philip 1220
Bevier, Sarah 1220
Beyeaux, Eliza 3538
Beyeaux, Sally 2398
Beyeaux, Thomas 2398
Bicknell, Emily 2716
Bidelman, Catherine 2892
Bidelman, Valentine 2892
Bigelow, Adeline 5666
Bigelow, Asa 4857
Bigelow, Ellen 1356
Bigelow, Mary Ann 1264
Bigelow, Susan E. 4857
Biggs, Frances 8276
Bignall, John 769
Billings, Cornelia 8393
Billings, Helen 9558
Billings, Jabez S. 778
Billings, Perez 773
Bingham, Caleb 786
Bingham, Chester 787
Bingham, Eunice 4675
Bingham, Fanny 785
Bingham, Flavel 784
Birce, Austin 8878
Birce, Lucy 8878
Birch, Charles 9291
Birch, Eliza 4476
Birch, Sally 9291
Bird, J. (Mr.) 794
Bird, John 793
Bird, Julia 1166
Bird, Moore 1166
Birdsall, Deborah 2951
Birdsall, Maurice 796, 4761
Birdsall, Polly 4761
Birdwell, Calrissa 2445
Birge, Elijah 7868
Birge, Hansy 3417
Birge, Harriet 674
Bishop, ___ (Mr.) 1496
Bishop, Daniel L. 6717
Bishop, David 799
Bishop, Elizabeth P. 6717
Bishop, Hannah 3121
Bishop, Isaac 8653
Bishop, Mary 8653
Bissell, Elisha 9531
Bissell, Minerva 9531
Black, Jane 5360
Black, Sally 325
Blackman, Nancy 8483
Blackwell, ___ (Mr.) 5509
Blackwood, ___ (Mr.) 1122
Blague, P. (Miss) 3126
Blair, Abby 813
Blair, Mary 3548
Blake, Gertrude G. 4133
Blakeslee, Amaziah 820
Blanchard, Anthony I. 5557, 7440
Blanchard, John 822
Blanchard ,Susannah 7440
Blane, Jane 9939
Bleecker, Barent 827
Bleecker, Elizabeth 8730
Bleecker, G. V. (Mr.) 9943
Bleecker, G. V. S. (Mr.) 826

Bleecker, James 829, 5378
Bleecker, John 832, 835
Bleecker, John H. 833
Bleecker, John R. 834, 8730
Bleecker, Nicholas 828
Bleecker, Rachel V. S. 9943
Bleecker, Sarah Bache 5378
Blin, Diana 534
Bliss, ___ (Dr.) 7863
Bliss, Celia 10068
Bliss, Isaac 8928
Bliss, James C. 842
Bliss, Nancy 8928
Bliss, William M. 839
Blood, Caroline 798
Bloodgood, Margaret E. 3789
Bloom, ___ (Judge) 3943
Bloom, Eliza 6789
Bloom, George 853, 859
Bloom, Jane 5422
Bloom. John M. 861
Bloom, Jonathan 860, 862
Bloom, Maria R. 5725
Bloom. Phebe 3943
Bloomfield, John W. 595
Bloss, Freelove 4457
Bloss, Manassah 4457
Blossom, Elisha 540
Blossom, Eliza 867
Blossom, Mary Tyler 540
Blossom, William 867
Bloyd, Sirissa 8035
Blum, Robert 4487
Bly, Anna 5601
Boardman, ___ (Capt.) 871
Boardman, ___ (Mr.) 54
Boardman, Caroline Ann 5034
Boardman, E. (Capt.) 875
Boardman, E. (Maj.) 5034
Boardman, Elisha 869
Boardman, Eliza C. 1753
Boardman, Elizabeth B. 3739
Boardman, H. (Mr.) 874
Boardman, William 3739
Bockus, Mary 3712
Boden, Eliza 7357
Boden, Nancy 4125
Boel, H. W. 5395
Boerman, Mary Ann 8339
Boernum, Elizabeth 8344
Boerum, Jacob 882, 885, 2256, 4799
Boerum, Jane Ann 5652
Boerum, Maria 4799
Boerum, Sarah Ann 2256
Bogardus, Catharine 7049
Bogardus, Hannah 7716, 9217
Bogardus, Isaac 9217
Bogardus, L. A. (Miss) 8094
Bogardus, Margaret 6525
Bogardus, Mary 9771
Bogardus, Nicholas 898
Bogardus, Richard 4502
Bogardus, Robert 8094
Bogardus, William W. 888
Bogert, Abigail Anna 1712
Bogert, Adeline 599
Bogert, Catherine 5815
Bogert, Catherine Elizabeth 9812
Bogert, E. (Mr.) 899
Bogert, James, Jr. 599, 1712, 9812
Bogert, Rezina 1684
Bogert, Susan 1848
Boggs, William 902
Boice, Rhoda 613
Boin, ___ (Mrs.) 8302
Bolkcom, Anna 8006

Bolkcom, J. (Dr.) 8006
Bolles, John R. 907
Bolles, Marietta 6735
Bolles, Richard 906
Bolsaubin, Louisa Antoinette 3148
Bolsaubin, Vincent 3148
Bolton, ___ (Rev.) 910
Bomford, George 912
Bonaparte, Napoleon 6868
Bond, Helen 6509
Bond, Margaret 9236
Bond, Nancy L. 915
Bond, Sally Ann 9651
Bond, Sarah R. 2977
Bond, William M. 2977
Bondish, Hannah 9706
Bondecou, Clarissa 2611
Booge, Ebenezer 920
Boorn, Lucy 8109
Boorom, Cornelia 6680
Booth, Ann 6643
Booth, George 927, 929, 6570
Booth, Hezekiah 925
Booth, Huldah 8221
Booth, James 3702
Booth, Mary Ann 6570
Booth, Mary Minerva 3702
Boothe, Anna 4818
Boothe, John 2752
Boothe, Laura 2752
Boothe, Lydia 2207
Borden, Eliza 1847
Borzee, Eunace 5033
Bostwick, ___ (Elder) 3775
Bostwick, Benjamin R. 4767
Bostwick, Betsy 1524
Bostwick, Eliza 4767
Bostwick, Eliza P. 6595
Bostwick, Philura 1820
Bostwick, R. W. (Mr.) 939
Bostwick, Solomon 936
Bostwick, William 1820
Bosworth, ___ (Miss) 4357
Bosworth, ___ (Mrs.) 7536
Bosworth, David 945
Bosworth, Jabish 944
Bosworth, James 948
Bosworth, Josiah 947
Botsford, Alice 1121
Botsford, Caleb 949
Botsford, Vine (Capt.) 1121
Bottomly, Sarah 9976
Bouck, Harmanus 951, 8740
Bourke, James 4929
Bouton, Esther 1447
Bouton, Mary 9477
Bouton, Nathan 959
Bowen, Saphronia 2802
Bower, ___ (Mr.) 4606
Bowers, J. M. (Mr.) 6330
Bowers, John 9474
Bowers, Maria 1087
Bowers, Mary M. 9474
Bowles, William 967
Bowman, Horace 3097
Bowman, Joseph 970
Bowman, Nathaniel 969, 971
Bowne, Abigail 6117
Bowne, Louisa 5515
Boyce, Mary Ann 5797
Boyd, James 986
Boynton, Jedediah 995
Brace, Arvilla 2072
Brackett, James 1517
Brackett, Mary Elizabeth 1517
Bradford, ___ (Rev. Dr.) 5295
Bradford, George W. 1001
Bradford, Hannah 635
Bradford, Louisa R. 5295

Bradford, Maria 844
Bradford, Perez 1004
Bradford, Rachel 6428
Bradhead, ___ (Dr.) 878
Bradley, Abey (Miss) 7350
Bradley, Daniel 1010
Bradley, Eliza 2794
Bradley, Gilbert 6999
Bradley, Helen 1005
Bradley, Mary 6007
Bradley, Nancy 6515
Bradt, elizabeth 7737
Bradt, Rebecca 6044
Brady, Love 4052
Bragaw, Ann 3227
Bragg, Fanny 2859
Bragg, Sarah 9751
Braim, Mary 2899
Brainard, Edwin 1036
Bramin, Ruth 2851
Branch, Content 9542
Brandt, Philip 1022
Brantley, Mary Ann 1980
Brantley, W. T. (Rev.) 1980
Braverse, Susan 2923
Brayan, Elizabeth White 1692
Brayan, William 1692
Brayton, Polly 8415
Breakenridge, Eliza A. M. S. 1571
Breakenridge, James 1571
Breck, Moses 1030
Breese, Arthur 1032, 5085, 9405
Breese, Margaret 7332
Breese, S. Sidney 7332
Breese, Sarah 5085
Breese, Sarah Ann 9405
Bregan, ___ (Mrs.) 7353
Bregaw, Letty 5503
Brett, ___ (Mr.) 1565
Brewer, Eliza C. 5269
Brewer, Emma 6045
Brewer, Halsey 1015
Brewster, Absalam 9475
Brewster, Adaline 8123
Brewster, Gilbert 8123
Brewster, Sally 9475
Breyman, Rachel 1271
Briant, Ann Maria 6685
Bridge, Thomas Atwood 9, 1048A
Bridges, ___ (Mr.) 3413
Bridges, Harriet 9137
Bridges, Lucy B. 2252
Briggs, Cynthia 2827
Briggs, Jane 1252
Briggs, John 8364
Briggs, Margaret 3710
Briggs, Polly 8364
Briggs, Sally 8695
Brigham, Louise 4436
Brightman, Abigail 8070
Brigs, Jerusha 197
Brigs, Noah 197
Brill, Polly 95
Brinckerhoff, Abraham 1071
Brinckerhoff, Elizabeth V. D. L. 4950
Brinckerhoff, John 924
Brinckerhoff, John V. D. L. 4950, 6266
Brinckerhoff, Mary 924, 6266
Brinckerhoff, Sarah Ann 9629
Brinckerhoff, Tunis 1075
Brinckerhoof, Stephen I. 1077
Brinker, Timothy 1078
Brinkerhoff, Catharine G. 9322
Brinkerhoff, H. R. (Gen.) 1081
Brinkerhoff, Isaac 1082, 9322

Brinkerhoff, Margaret S. 9173
Brinkerhoff, Mary 2020
Brinkerhoff, Stephen I. 9173
Brisben, James 1083
Bristol, Hannah 8093
Bristol, Joel 6837
Bristol, Nancy 6837
Bristow, John 1088
Broadhead, Thomas 2683
Broadwell, Aaron 2199
Broadwell, Jane 441
Broadwell, Noah 1098
Broadwell, Sally 5736a
Broadwell, Sibra 2199
Broas, Sarah Ann 953
Broas, Smith 1101
Brockway, Charles 6016
Brockway, Lathrop 1111
Brockway, Levi 1108
Brockway, Reed 919, 1106
Brockway, Semanthe 919
Brodhead, G. (Miss) 2682
Brodhead, Thomas 2682
Bromley, Daniel 1115
Bromley, Daniel W. 1114
Bromley, Mary B. 1114
Bronson, ___ (Mr.) 2122
Brook, J. (Capt.) 9802
Brooks, Betsy 4337
Brooks, David 1126, 6994
Brooks, Eliza M. 6994
Brooks, Gertrude Margaret 3434
Brooks, Marcia F. 6403
Brooks, Mary 9299
Brooks, Micah 6403
Brooks, Sally 5201
Broom, Mary C. 5273
Broom, William 5273
Brower, Louisa 4208
Brower, Phebe 7409
Brower, William 1140
Brown, ___ ("Brown Bros. & Co.") 1170
Brown, ___ (Gen.) 8147
Brown, ___ (Miss) 1783
Brown, ___ (Widow) 1173
Brown, Alice 4179
Brown, Almira 3858
Brown, Ann Elizabeth 9296
Brown, Asenath 4420
Brown, Betsey 8054
Brown, Calvin 5477
Brown, Charles 1165
Brown, Charles Bruckden 1182
Brown, Christopher B. 1145
Brown, Cornelius 9296
Brown, David 1154
Brown, Edmund 1184
Brown, Edward 4420
Brown, Elisha 3724
Brown, Eliza 7714
Brown, Eliza T. 2478
Brown, Eunice 7978
Brown, Francis 1157
Brown, Grace C. 903
Brown, Harriet 55
Brown, Henry 1158, 1167
Brown, Henry C. 537
Brown, Isabella 1167
Brown, Jackson 2478
Brown, Jacob 9335
Brown, Jonas 1181
Brown, Joseph 1149, 1172
Brown, Lucinda 1489
Brown, M., Jr. (Dr.) 3745
Brown, Mary 4999
Brown, Mary Ann 3745
Brown, Mary W. 537
Brown, Mildred Ann Perkins 3724

Brown, Nancy 334
Brown, Nehemiah, Jr. 1189
Brown, Noah 8054
Brown, Pamela 9335
Brown, Peggy 1420
Brown, Peter 1420, 7592
Brown, Polly 9797
Brown, Ruah 755
Brown, S. (Maj.) 55
Brown, Sarah 5330
Brown, Sophronia 780
Brown, Stephen 4999
Brown, Stephen C. 1159
Brown, Susan 9803
Brownejohn, Samuel 1198
Brownell, A. (Mr.) 5697
Brownell, Aaron 1200, 2155
Brownell, Abigail 8379, 8380
Brownell, Eunice 2155
Brugiere, Charles 1208
Brumley, Hallock 1210, 1211
Brush, ___ (Gen.) 1218
Brush, Emily 3286
Brush, Frances 6168
Brush, Jesse G. 1216
Brush, Platt 1215
Bryan, Amos, 3649
Bryan, James 1223
Bryans, Mary 4169
Bryant, Amos 1228
Bryant, Lydia 2015
Buchan, Margaretta 6120
Buchan, Robert 6120
Buck, B. (Mr.) 455, 1235
Buck, Belina (Mr.) 420, 1230, 1234
Buck, Bilinia (Mr.) 422
Buck, HulDah 634
Buck, Irene 5123
Buck, Maria 422, 455
Buck, N. F. (Gen.) 8601
Buck, Nancy 3172
Buckley, Lucinda 75
Buckley, Martha Ann 271
Buckley, William 271
Buckly, Abigal 2515
Bucknum, Anna 8421
Budd, Catharine 4390
Budd, Hannah 9884
Budd, James 8849
Budd, John 6816
Budd, Maria 6816
Budd, Mary 8849
Budd, Sarah 432
Budd, Susan 704
Budd, U. (Mr.) 704
Budd, Underhill 4390
Buel, ___ (Mr.) 6753
Buel, A. P. (Miss) 1309
Buel, Charlotte 4973
Buel, David 1251
Buel, Elam 1247
Buel, Jesse 1246
Buel, Ozias 5679
Buel, William 1250
Buell, Maria 4136
Buell, Ozias 4136
Buckbee, John 7721
Buckbee, Mary Ann 7721
Bugbee, Betsey 1834
Bugbee, Ezra 1216
Bugbee, Orpha M. 1131
Bugbee, Phebe 1531
Bugbee, Sylvia 5813
Bugbey, Abel 1258
Bugert, Lambert 5184
Bull, Charlotte 795
Bull, William 5866
Bullock, Rachael 4524

Caswell, John 1542
Catlin, Abel 6652
Catlin, Asa 1549
Caunon, Martha 8295
Cavanaugh, John H. 1391
Cedar, Helenor 3852
Center, ___ (Mr.) 3505, 7267
Center, Abby P. 3328
Center, Robert 1557, 1558, 3328, 3332
Chace, Eliza 410
Chace, Rebecca 10075
Chamberlain, Miranda 4739
Chamberlain, Rebecca 125
Chamberlain, Susannah 8395
Chamberlin, Colbert 1566
Chambers, David 7179
Chambers, Fanny 4392
Chambers, Margaret 7179
Chambers, Polly 7534
Champlin, John T. 1574
Chandler, Pamelia 8534
Chane, Susan 2233
Chaney, Lucy 7835
Chapin, Abigail 7516
Chapin, David 4439
Chapin, Enoch 1580
Chapin, Gad 1579
Chapin, Lorinda 347
Chapin, Lydia Ann 1757
Chapin, Lyman 7778
Chapin, Mary A. 1580
Chapman, ___ (Rev.) 3155
Chapman, Ann Maria 3231
Chapman, Anna 9610
Chapman, Lucy 8528
Chapman, Zenas 9610
Chappell, Elizabeth 2556
Chappell, Marinda 6047
Charles, Elizabeth 7043
Charles, George 1591
Charlott, Nancy 3681
Charlott, Sally 3537
Chase, ___ (Rev.) 2312, 3164
Chase, Caroline 450
Chase, Clarissa J. 5511
Chase, James 5511
Chase, Joanna 247
Chase, Lavantia E. 7110
Chase, Maria (Mr.) 450
Chase, Perris 1146
Chase, Seth 7110
Chase, Sylvia 2146
Chatfield, Polly Maria 3237
Chatman, Clarissa 2036
Chauncey, Commodore 1604
Chavalier, Margaret 7336
Cheever, Janette 4544
Cheeseman, Margaret Ann 8466
Cheles, John 1610
Cheney, Abbel 8810
Cheney, Prudence 8810
Chesebrough, Clarissa Harlow 8778
Chester, ___ (Rev.) 8773
Chester, Caroline 5015
Chever, W. D. (Mr.) 1616
Chichester, Harriet 2985
Child, Sally 205
Childs, Caleb, Jr. 1617
Childs, David W. 1620
Childs, Edmund B. 1617
Chittenden, Minerva 1312
Chittendon, George 11
Choat, Lois 1177
Choate, Eliza 7493
Choate, Francis 1628
Christian, Jane 1316
Christie, Paulina 2593

Church, John B. 1639
Church, Mary E. 9220
Church, Minerva 10062
Church, Philanda 1433
Church, Philip 4348
Church, Sophia H. 4348
Churchill, Edward 3635
Churchill, Eliza 3214
Churchill, Elizabeth 10044
Churchill, Ezekiel 1648
Churchill, Martha 3635
Churchill, Sally 6714
Ciperlie, Catharine 10086
Cisco, Sarah 7436
Cisson, Peggy 5063
Clancy, Elizabeth 1715
Clancy, Mary 7195
Clancy, William 1715
Clapp, Jesse I. 1654
Clapp, Ruth 3171
Clapper, ___ (Mr.) 1140
Clapper, Peter 1140
Clarge, George 1656
Clark, ___ (Mrs.) 9726
Clark, ___ (Mr.) 5658, 9812
Clark, ___ (Rev.) 383, 5336, 6512
Clark, Abel 1668, 1675, 8709
Clark, Abigail 2531, 9625
Clark, Alexander 1663
Clark, Allen 1669
Clark, Almira 239
Clark, Asahel 1664
Clark, Benedict, 1666
Clark, Caroline 519
Clark, Catharine M. 15
Clark, Cornelia A. R. 8808
Clark, Cyrus 1657
Clark, Daniel 9601
Clark, Douglas 519, 8877
Clark, Experience 6571
Clark, George 1656, 9625
Clark, George T. 1705
Clark, Henry 1689
Clark, Henry, Jr. 1686
Clark, Huldah 8709
Clark, James 1698, 7782
Clark, Jane 1011
Clark, Jerome 1662
Clark, John 1687, 1702
Clark, Julia 2042
Clark, Lester 1660
Clark, Louisa Trask 5930
Clark, Lucy 1686
Clark, Margaret 1465
Clark, Maria 1179
Clark, Mary 3721, 3884, 4409
Clark, Mary Ann 1933
Clark, Mary E. 6174
Clark, Miranda 3564
Clark, Moses 6174
Clark, Nathaniel 4409
Clark, Orin (Rev.) 8808
Clark, P. (Mr.) 5514
Clark, Polly 1722, 4042
Clark, Rachel Aurelia 1702
Clark, Rebecca 9601
Clark, Ruby 8651
Clark, Ruthetta 3831
Clark, Sally 8877
Clark, Susan 771
Clark, Thomas S. 1685
Clark, William 3884
Clark, William A. 5805, 5930
Clarke, ___ (Mr.) 7099
Clarke, Almira Brooks 3413
Clarke, Anna 6670
Clarke, Charlotte L. 4498
Clarke, Ellen Sophia 6722

Clarke, G. (Mr.) 1733
Clarke, George 1734, 6670
Clarke, James B. 4498
Clarke, Peter (Dr.) 6722
Clarke, Sophia 9710
Clarkson, Maria 4283
Clary, Sally 1799
Clary, Samuel 1799
Clay, Marianne 8399
Clay, Ralph 8399
Cleaveland, Erastus 7038
Cleaveland, Jane V. 7038
Clement, Sarah 182
Clendener, P. (Mr.) 1752
Clendening, John 1261
Clendening, Margaret 1261
Clero, Laurent 1754
Clery, Elizabeth 6462
Clifford, ___ (Mrs.) 4568
Cline, Margaret 224
Cline, Mary 9690
Clinton, ___ (Gov.) 1765, 8508
Clinton, Anna Dewitt 7437
Clinton, De Witt (Mrs.) 4797
Clinton, Elizabeth 8508
Clinton, George 655, 3393
Clinton, James 7437, 8146, 8156
Clinton, John 1766
Clitherall, G. C. (Dr.) 8166
Clitherall, Harriet 8166
Clough, Anne 2082
Clow, Mary Ann 6028
Clowes, Thomas 1770, 1771
Cluett, Elizabeth 2933
Cluett, Garret 2933
Clute, Alenda 1775
Clute, Julius 9879
Clute, Nancy B. 9879
Clyde, Joseph 1779
Coates, Emily 2800
Coates, Ezra 223
Coats, Azubah 3460
Cobb, Elizabeth 4666
Cobb, Freeman 3916
Cobb, Hannah 2749
Cobb, Henrietta Maria 10084
Cochran, ___ (Mrs.) 539
Cochran, E. (Miss) 128
Cochrane, Walter 1785
Cocks, Charity 4029
Coe, ___ (Rev. Dr.) 1789, 1791
Coe, Benjamin 1794
Coe, Eliza M. 1170
Coe, Jane 2577
Coe, Jonas 1170
Coe, Mary 5719
Coe, William 1788, 1790
Coffee, Helen 8442
Coffeen, Delight 7859
Coffeen, Henry H. 7859
Coffin, ___ (Mr.) 2454, 7644
Coffin, Adeline R. 1735
Coffin, Alexander J. 1802
Coffin, Gideon 1744
Coffin, Gorham 1804
Coffin, Hepzibeth 6810
Coffin, Ralph 1735
Coffin, Sally 470
Coffin, Salmon 1797
Coffrin, Elizabeth 1265
Coggsdell, John 9370
Coggswell, Smith 1809
Cogswell, Elizabeth 7457
Cogswell, Polly 3285
Cogswell, Sally Mariah 5949
Cogswell, Smith 7457
Cogswell, Thomas 1810
Colby, Rebecca 3846
Colden, ___ (Judge) 2289

Crane, John 2098
Crane, Joseph 2091
Crane, Marilla 814
Crane, Rufus 427
Crapo, Cynthia 4379
Crapo, Sally 656
Crapsey, Mary 2317
Crary, ___ (Col.) 2105, 2106
Crary, Anne Caroline 3954
Crary, John 2103
Crawford, Abigail 9340
Crawford, Ammi 2110
Crawford, Eleanor 2296
Crawford, George 2111
Crawford, Hayes 9740
Crawford, Job 2114, 6241
Crawford, Martha 9740
Crawford, Phebe 8129
Crawford, Ruth Ann 6241
Crippen, Mary 1520
Crippen, Silas 1520
Criscy, Nancy 3532
Crocheron, Hannah 4894
Crocheron, Jacob 4894
Crofiser, Gertrude 5197
Crofit, Lucy G. 3981
Croghan, Ann Eliza 6720
Crolius, Clarkson 10009
Crolius, Mary Clarkson 10009
Crombie, Eliza 5726
Crombie, William 5726
Cronk, Sally 5767
Cronkite, ___ 3396
Cronkrite, Elizabeth 5707
Crook, Catharine 2135
Crook, James 2134
Crook, Maria Jane Ann 10078
Crook, Samuel W. 2135
Crooke, John 3874
Crooker, Maria 6475
Crooks, John 705
Crooks, Margaretta L. 705
Cropser, Charity 1526
Cropsey, Ann Maria 5198
Cropsey, Betsey 5341
Cropsie, Sarah 3312
Cropsy, Maria 7167
Crosby, Cyrenus 6723
Crosby, Elisha 6869, 7148
Crosby, Harriet 4190
Crosby, Julia Ann 6723
Crosby, Lydia Ann 7148
Crosby, Roxana 9547
Cross, Edward 2140
Cross, Julian Ann (Miss) 965
Cross, Maria 288
Cross, Sophia Ann 367
Crossman, Ebenezer 6288
Crossman, Hannah 4038
Crossman, Marcia P. 6288
Croswell, caleb 2152
Croswell, Georgiana 2009
Croswell, Harry 2154
Croswell, Mackay 2147
Crottenden, L. (Mr.) 7717
Crouse, Jane Ann 5241
Crowley, Maria Josephine 1238
Crowninshield, B. W. (Mr.) 2158
Cruger, Caharine 477
Cruger, Daniel 2160, 3139
Cruger, Eliza M. 3139
Cruger, Henry 6361
Cruger, Matilda Caroline 6361
Cruger, Nicholas 477
Cruttenden, L. (Mr.) 1155, 5758
Cruttenden, Mary B. 1155
Cudgill, Rachel 6202

Culver, Esther 8790
Culver, Francis 2167
Culver, James 2168
Culver, Maria 6114
Culver, Oliver 8029
Cummerford, Mary 4831
Cummins, ___ (Rev. Dr.) 5500
Cummins, Eliza 5500
Cummins, George 5500
Cunningham, Augusta 8675
Cunningham, Catharine 1391
Cunningham, Garwood H. 8675
Cunningham, J. H. (Mr.) 8670
Cunningham, Mahitable 574
Cunningham, Mary 1740
Cunningham, Walter 2186, 8670
Cure, Elias 2191
Curliss, Betsey 2875
Curtis, Abner 5940
Curtis, Fanny 10049
Curtis, Julia 5940
Curtiss Julia Frances 2369
Curtis, Peninah 7687
Curtis, Samuel 2204
Curtis, Samuel A. 4849
Curtis, Z. (Mr.) 2369
Curtiss, Erastus 2208
Curtiss, Laura 7787
Cushion, Betsy 8265
Cushman, Calvin 2215
Cushman, David 2212
Cushman, Diadamia H. 8046
Cushman, Maria Onderdonk 8292
Cushman, Minerva 8292
Cushman, Ralph 2215
Custiss, G. W. P. 5168
Custiss, Mary A. R. 5168
Cutler, Maria Eliza 3187
Cuyler, ___ (Rev. Dr.) 2020, 2230, 2231, 2402
Cuyler, C. C. (Rev.) 2227
Cuyler, Catharine Ann 7783
Cuyler, Catharine Belinda 9517
Cuyler, Cornelius 2229
Cuyler, Cornelius C. (Rev.) 2229
Cuyler, Eleanor 6
Cuyler, Glen 7783
Cuyler, Henry, Jr. 2223
Cuyler, Jane 1094
Cuyler, John C. 3317
Cuyler, Tobias B. 2225
Cuyler, TobiaS V. 9517
Dakin, Cynthia 9027
Dakin, E. K. (Mr.) 9213
Dakin, Ebenezer K. 2234, 2236
Dakin, Lydia 10048
Dakin, Mary 4591, 4641
Dakin, Paul 9027, 10048
Dakin, Sally Ann 9213
Dakin, Samuel 4555, 4591
Dakin, Sarah 6834
Dakin, Sophia 4555
dal Ponte, Frances 211
dal Ponte, Lorenzo 211
Damon, Mary 5917
Dana, Eleazer 9376
Dana, Susan H. 9376
Danforth, ___ (Gen.) 6764
Daniels, Eliza M. 496
Daniels, Mary Ann 3972
Daniels, Sally W. 9582
Danker, Elizabeth 6759
Darbyshire, Delia 6040
Darbyshire, Emma 1645
Darlan, Elmira 5494
Darlan, Emily P. 5494
Darling, Emeline 446
Darling, Hannah 1946

Darling, Rowena 2807
Darrah, James 6240
Darrow, Elizabeth 5688

darrow, Esther 9391
Darrow, Prudence 1708
Dater, Abraham 2269
Dater, Mary 3497
Dates, Abraham 7004
Dates, Catherine 6804
Dates, Jane 2974
Dates, Jane Ann 7004
Daton, Jacob 2274
Dauby, A. G. (Mr.) 5210
Dauchy, H. B. (Mr.) 2276
Daveau, Hannah 8176
Davenport, ___ (Maj.) 7055
Davenport, Eliza 7055, 9654
Davenport, Mary Ann 1206
Davidson, John 2283
Davidson, Oliver 8820
Davies, Charlotte 2737
Davies, John I. 2284
Davies, Thomas L. 2287
Davies, William 1327, 2285, 2286, 2737
Davis, ___ (Mr.) 809, 4232, 6348
Davis, Belinda 4407
Davis, Caroline 1924
Davis, Charles 9049
Davis, Eliza 1706, 8874
Davis, Elizabeth 2190
Davis, Freelove 1196
Davis, Henry 2190, 2293
Davis, Hester 2163
Davis, Isaac 8874
Davis, Jacob 1718
Davis, James 2292
Davis, Jerusha 2428
Davis, John 2315
Davis, John H. 2309
Davis, Maria 9049
Davis, Martha 3400
Davis, Nathaniel 6972
Davis, Patience B. 2247
Davis, Rebecca 1718
Davis, Richard 1924, 2312, 7362
Davis, Sally 1732, 6358, 5140
Davis, Samuel (Mrs.) 4970
Davis, Sarah 5990
Davis, Sarah Linda 5999
Davis, Sarah Nichols 6972
Davis, Stephen 5999
Davis, Temperance 3054
Davis, Thomas 2303
Davis, William 7172
Davison, Catharine 9902
Davoue, Frederick 622
Davoue, Mary Egbert 622
Dawson, Ann Eliza 7886
Day, Amos 2335
Day, Ann 4643
Day, Electa 3788
Day, Julia 3329
Day, Margaret 994
Day, Nancy 6955
Day, Rodman G. 2336
Day, Stephen 3329, 3788, 6955
Dayton, Hezekiah 2346
Dayton, Martha 7491
Dayton, Minerva 6302
Dayton, Robert 2343, 2347
Dayton, William 6267
Deal, Gertrude 8018
Deal, Henry 8018
Dean, Caroline Newcomb 2689
Dean, Charles B. 2351

Dean, Evelina 3023
Dean, Gilbert 2689
Dean, Israel 2350
Dean, John 2357
Dean, Mary C. 5370
De Angelis, Paschel C. L. 2361
Dearin, ___ (Mr.) 4779
Dearin, Ann Maria 4997
De Bockhorst, D. W. (Miss)7288
Se Bresson, Charles Joseph 2368
De Camp, Catherine 1811
De Camp, Eve 5486
Decamp, Sally 1248
De Cantillon, Maria D. 9983
De Cantillon, Richard 2370
Decatur, ___ (Commodore) 7284
Decker, Elsie 8917
Dederick, Hannah 2376
Dederick, William 2376
Deen, Polly 9315
De Forest, Abel 2382
De Forest, Samuel 2381
De Freest, Cornelia 2386
De Freest, Jacob F. 2388
De Freest, Peter 2383
De Freest, Susan 2387
Defriest, Maria 5818
De Graff, Anne 1999
De Graff, Eleanor 2224
De Graff, Elizabeth 6551
De Graff, Evert 8369
De Graff, Isaac 2224, 2403
De Graff, John I. 2402, 2403
Degraff, Maria 8369
De Graff, Nancy 8785
De Groot, Catherine 9114
de la Fayette, Marquis 1985
Delamater, Jane 8806
De La Mater, Polly 8253
Delano, Stephen 2421
de Lavan, Cordelia 43
Delavan, Daniel 2426
Delavan, Edward C. 2424, 2425
Delavan, Laura 10093
Delavan, Mary 6215
De La Vergne, Ann 425
De La Vergne, Catharine 2571
Delavergne, E. M. (Mr.) 9296
De La Vergne, Isaac 425
De La Vergne, John 425
De La Vergne, La Grange 2571
de La Vergne, Phebe 4411
Delemater, Dinah 9136
Delevan, Hetty 4642
De Long, Catharine 3439
De Long, Hannah 2136
Delong, Helen 873
Delong, Lorenda 8277
Delong, Malona 3044
Delong, Polly 6778, 9398
De Lord, ___ (Judge) 8467
De Lord, Elizabeth 8467
Delphene, J. R. (Mr.) 7028
Demcrest, Emeline 2093
Demerest, Eleanor 3386
Deming, Clarisa 9159
Deming, Elizabeth 591
Deming, Howard 591
Deming, John 2448
Demming, John C. 2446
Deming, Lucy 6042
Deming, Semantha B. 2255
Deming, William B. 2443
Demming, Nancy S. 8738
Demott, Betsey 1409
Deniston, Archibald 2267
Deniston, Sarah M. 2267
Denman, Ann 6684

Dennend, Maria 8705
Dennis, Amy Mary 765
Dennis, Catharine 2619
Dennis, Delia Maria 7784
Dennis, Paul 7784
Denniston, Lydia 4729
Denny, John 4
Denslow, Susan 3057
Denton, Joel, Jr. 2462
De Pew, Ann 5821
De Peyster, Eliza M. C. 3767
Depeyster, George 2706
Depeyster, Georgianna 2706
De Peyster, James W. 3767
Depue, Maria 9630
Derby, E. H. (Gen.) 1548
Derby, Elizabeth F. 2820
Derby, Lucy Ann 1548
De Reimer, Mary Ann 7253
Deremer, Catharine 6531
Deremer, Elizabeth 8113
De Riemer, Peter 2473
Deuel, Amanda 8566
Deuel, Jonathan 2480
Deuel, Stephen 2482
Deveaux,Andrew 2485
Devereaux, Julia 6936
Devine, Mary Ann 2874
Devine, Phebe 9203
Devine, William 2874
Dewel, Benjamin 2489
Dewel, Catharine Ann 6808
Dewey, Almira 8924
Dewey, David 2532
Dewey, Eliphalet 2495
Dewey, Eliza C. 7873
Dewey, Olive 2532
Dewey, Royal 2491
De Witt, ___ (Col.) 2500
De Witt, E. (Mr.) 2506
De Witt, Helen 7994
De Witt, John 2501
De Witt, Peter 2504
De Wolf, Martha 4272
Dexter, Amos 4190
Dexter, Andrew 2509
Dexter, John B. 2511
Dexter, Samuel 2508
Deyo, Maria 3915
Deyo, Sophia 7755
Deyoe, Sorchy 4969
De Zeng, Maria Augusta 8373
De Zetwitz, ___ (Baron) 5890
Diamond, Sarah 9940
Diamond, William M. 9947
Diamond, William S. 9940
Dibble, ___ (Mr.) 939
Dibble, Sarah A. 547
Dibblee, Catherine 8644
Dibblee, Ebenezer 2528, 8644,
    9123, 9124, 9125, 9224
Diblee, Esther 9224
Dibblee, Harriet 9124
Dibblee, Henry 2525
Dibblee, Mary Ann 6831
Dickens, Asbury 5452
Dickens, Lila Elizabeth 5452
Dickerson, Charlotte 1197
Dickinson, Eliza 8294
Dickinson, Jane 4141
Dickinson, Louisa 1624
Dickinson, Sally 1323
Dickinson, Tertullus 1323
Diell, ___ (Mr.) 2720
Diell, John 2538
Digert, Catharine 2540
Digert, O. (Mrs.) 2540
Digert, Warner 2540

Diggs, Ann Maria 5314
Diggs, George 5314
Diliverge, Phebe 4411
Dill, Deborah Ann 9980
Dill, Robert 9980
Dilling ham, Nathan 7813
Dillingham, Rebeckah 2496
Dillingham, Sally 7813
Dimock, Abigail 7862
Dimock, Timothy 2543
Dimon, Ebenezer 4854
Dimon, evelina 4854
Dimon, Mary A. 4848
Dimond, Nancy 1500
Dimond, Phebe 9105
Dinge, Mabe 2544
Disbrow, Elias 2545
Dix, Catharine A. 904
Dix, J. G. 2548
Dix, John A. 904
Dix, P. (Mr.) 2547, 2548
Dobbs, Maria 8514
Dockstader, Eliza 7609
Dodge, ___ (Mr.) 4542
Dodge, ___ (Rev. Dr.) 5132
Dodge, Almira K. 5108
Dodge, Cynthia 5309
Dodge, Deborah 3591
Dodge, Elijah 2559
Dodge, Henry 2570, 3591, 6866
Dodge, Jane 6866
Dodge, Joseph 3796
Dodge, Marsey 5132
Dodge, Mary 1786
Dodge, Newel 2569
Dodge, Noah 5108
Dodge, Phebe 6726
Dodge, Rebecca 3796
Dodge, Richard 2557
Dodge, Sally 4186
dodge, Samuel 2561
Dodge, William 1786
Dogherty, Bethiah 1050
Dole, Delia Maria 3944
Dole, James 2572, 2575, 3934,
    3944
Dole, Lewis 2573
Doll, Sarah C. 7602
Dominy, ___ (Miss) 6529
Dominy, Ann 3083
Dominy, Deborah 8190
Dominy, william 6529, 8190
Donalson, Jane 4214
Donalsson, Gitty 3454
Donnelly, John M. 2585
Donnelly, Sarah 1113
Doolittle, Calvin 2587, 2588
Doolittle, Sally 8437
Dopp, Cornelia 8318
Doris, Mary Ann 1970
Dorland, Philip 2592
Dorlon, Cornelia F. 3170
Dorlon, Eliza 4449
Dorr, Catharine V. S. 1778
Dorr, Jonathan 984
Dorr, Mary 984
Dorr, Russell 1778
Dorset, Cleory 3614
Doty, Delia 6369
Doty, Elias 2602
Doty, Joseph W. 2603
Doty, L. (Dr.) 3180
Doty, Mary 9841
Doubleday, Abner 2608
Doubleday, Amelia 7800
Doubleday, Seth 7800
Doud, ___ (Mr.) 3676
Dougherty, Adelaide 1824

Dougherty, W. W. (Mr.) 1824
Doughty, ___ (Mr.) 2776
Doughty, Amelia 113
Doughty, Cornell, 3609
Doughty, Deborah 3659
Doughty, Eveline 762
Doughty, Jane Eliza 3609
Doughty, Joseph 2613, 2614, 2618, 2620
Doughty, June 3350
Doughty, Meribeth 1065
Doughty, Phebe 4778
Doughty, Polly 1562
Doughty, Sally 203
Doughty, Samuel 3659
Doughty, Thomas 3350
Douglas, ___ 2724
Douglas, Hannah 7936
Douglas, Nancy 2623
Douglass, Alanson 2627
Douglass, Elizabeth Mary 5963
Douglass, George 5963
Douglass, Lydia 4365
Douglass, Nancy 5397
Douglass, Thomas 2625
Dow, Ruth 3041
Dowe, Alice 3905
Dones, John 2636
Downie, Mary 2639
Downs, Harriet 9881
Downs, James 2645
Downs, Sophia 3258
Dows, Eleazer 4534
Dox, Gerrit L. 2649
Doyle, Lawrence 6951
Doyle, Maryanne Sloane 6951
Drake, Betsey 4496
Drake, Charles H. 728
Drake, Delphene 7028
Drake, James 4841
Drake, Jane 4155
Drake, John 2655
Drake, John, Jr. 2364, 3534, 4470
Drake, Lucy 2364
Drake, Mary M. 4841
Drake, S. (Dr.) 2659
Drake, William 2653
Draper, Friend 4941
Draper, John C. 2660, 3531
Draper, Mary A. 4118
Draper, Nabby 7758
Draper, Simeon 4118
Drury, Eveline 4915
Du___, William A. (Rev.) 4079
Duane, Eliza S. 7153
Duane, James C. 7153
Du Bois, ___ (Gen.) 2676
Du Bois, Betsey 380
Dubois, Catharine 9186
Dubois, Christian 380, 2678
Dubois, Deborah 8062
Dubois, elenor 7264
Dubois, Elisha 1394
Dubois, Eliza 1894
Dubois, Koert 1894, 2695, 6370, 7264
Dubois, Maria 5957
Dubois, Mary 6370
Dubois, Polly 9010
Dubois, Rachel 6870
Dubois, Rebecca 1839
Dubois, Susan 9774
Duel, Hannah 5621
Duel, Mary 6100
Duer, ___ (Judge) 2701
Duke, Rachel 775
Dumbleton, Elizabeth 2888
Dumot, Mary 9627

Duncan, Agnes 9500
Duncan, Ann 9894
Duncan, Louiza 9877
Dundee, ___ (Mr.) 1561
Dunham, Amy 1423
Dunham, Eleanor M. 9240
Dunham, Guy 2711
Dunham, Lucy 8704
Dunlap, ___ (Rev.) 3155
Dunlap, Eliza 1180
Dunn, Ann Catharine 4303
Dunn, Christopher 2723
Dunn, Edward 2726
Dunn, Jane N. 3551
Dunn, Mary 7515
Dunn, Richard 2726
Dunning, ___ (Gen.) 7160
Dunning, John (Gen.) 2728
Dunnings, Ann 8517
Dunscomb, Nancy 4977
Dunshie, Sally 6286
Durand, Jane J. 3296
Durand, M. F. (Col.) 3296
Durkee, ___ (Widow) 778
Durkee, Mary 1498, 2828
Durland, Cynthia 6819
Durming, Minerva 294
Duryee, ___ (Mrs.) 8344
Dusch, Evelina 2679
Dusch, John 2679
Dusenberry, Caroline 114
Dusenberry, Richard 114
Dusenbury, Peggy 8016
Dustin, Clarissa 6429
Dutcher, Catherine 6366
Dutcher, David 2745, 6889
Dutcher, Elizabeth 5742
Dutcher, John W. 2747
Dutcher, Margaret Ann 6889
Dutcher, Maria 3640
Dutcher, Sylvia 5012
Duton, George W. 2753
Duzenberre, Mary 8918
Duzenberre, Stephen 8918
Dwelley, Caroline 1156
Dwight, ___ (Mr.) 2760
Dwight, Henry E/ 7096
Dwight, Sarah E. 7096
Dwight, Timothy 2760, 8349
Dyckman, William 2762
Dyer, Edmund 7071
Dyer, John 1295
Dyer, Martha 3026
Dyer, Sally 1295
Dyer, Sibbil 7071
Dyre, Rebecca 8989
Eagelsen, Tamar 8569
Eager, Catharine 3012
Eames, Julia Ann 3238
Eames, Sarah 8198
Earl, John 2767
Earl, Laura M. 2041
Earl, Mary Ann 1092, 4158
Earles, Catharine 1543
Earll, Clarissa Caroline 8075
Earll, J., Jr. 8075
Eastburn, James 2771
Easton, Elizabeth 3000
Easton, William 4731
Eaton, ___ (Mrs.) 7073
Eaton, ___ (Rev.) 2775
Eaton, Amos 2779
Eaton, Thurzy 963
Eaton, William 2777
Eckert, Mary 7826
Eckford, ___ (Miss) 2411
Eckford, Eloza 4608
Eckford, Henry 2411, 4608
Eddy, Elizabeth 1288

Eddy, Elvira 6781
Eddy, Gilbert 9053, 9055
Eddy, Mary 2499
Eddy, Sally 1947
Eddy, Tisdale 1288
Eddy, Willard 2787, 4016
Edgerton, Bela 2793
Edmonds, ___ (Gen.) 2798
Edmonds, Ann 3363
Edson, Dean 2801
Edson, Elisa 7208
Edson, Naomi 7768
Edson, Oliver 2803
Edwards, ___ (Ensign) 2988
Edwards, ___ (Mr.) 2814
Edwards, Alanson 4032
Edwards, Cynthia C. 4032
Edwards, Ogden 2811
Edwards, Rebecca T. 2198
Edwards, William 2198
Egbert, Rachael 8575
Eggleston, Cornelia 4581
Eggleston, Loretta 1028
Eggleston, Mary Ann 492
Egleston, David 7774
Egleston, Elizabeth 7775
Egleston, Pamela M. 9361
Eighmy, Hannah 8848
Eights, Abraham 2821
Elderkin, Eunice 2211
Elderkin, Rodolphus 2211
Eldred, Waty 9402
Eldridge, Armina 340
Elkins, Abigale 3608
Ellery, Abraham 6524
Ellery, Charlotte Se Wessenfels 6524
Elliot, ___ (Dr.) 4958
Elliot, Andrew 2822
Elliot, Betsey 8667
Elliot, Elthera 3145
Elliot, Frances Maria 4958
Elliot, William 2833
Ellis, Abigail 4732
Ellis, Ann 6812
Ellis, Chloe 8355
Ellis, Elizabeth 2189
Ellis, Lucy 26
Ellis, Maria 6593
Ellison, Eliza 9758
Ellison, Hannah 9279
Ellison, Henrietta 6082
Ellison, Sarah 7186
Ellison, Thomas 6082
Elliston, Elizabeth 7260
Ellsworth, Mary Ann 7076
Elmendorf, Edmund 2854
Elmendorf, Jacob C. 2853
Elmendorph, Cornelius 2855
Elmore, Charlotte 6835
Elmore, Lott 6835
Elmore, Selencia 3524
Elsbury, Harriet 3967
Elting, Henry 2867
Elting, Maria 9067
Elting, Peter 9067
Elwood, Silva 4919
Ely, Horace 1720
Ely, Sarah E. 1720
Emery, Susan 2484
Emmerson, Eliza 2582
Emmons, Asa 2880
Emmons, Mary 7263
Emons, Adonijah 7364
Emons, Jane C. 7364
Emott, Belinda 2299
Emott, Helena 7585
Emott, James 2105, 2299, 2882, 2884, 5743

Emott, William 2883
Enders, Catharine B. 3375
Engle, James 10034
Engle, Maria 10034
Eno, Stephen 2886
Ensign, Susan 1777
Ensworth, Jedediah 2890
Ernest, Christian (Mrs.) 5444
Ernst, John F. 1659, 2894
Ernst, Mary Elizabeth 1659
Erwin, Elizabeth 3432
Erwin, John 3432
Esmond, Mary 6173
Esselstyne, Christina 770
Essigh, Sally 7808
Evans, Mary 3525
Everest, Elvira 7814
Everest, James 2905
Everett, Jesse 2907
Everetts, Elizabeth 5065
Everitt, Catherine 4737
Everitt, Deborah 3888
Everitt, Helen M. 4624
Everitt, Hester 1736
Everitt, John 2915, 2918
Everitt, Mary 9035
Everitt, Peter 4624
Everitt, Richard 2912, 2919, 4737
Everson, George B. 2924
Everson, Jacob 2925, 2926
Everst, Emily 2714
Everton, Mariah 823
Evertson, Cornelia 3812
Evertson, G. B. (Mr.) 3812
Evertson, George B. 5162
Evertson, John 2931
Evertson, Magdelene 13, 3800
Evertson, Margaret M. B. 5162
Ewing, Charles 3597
Ewing, Emily 3597
Eycleshimer, Betsey 1349
Fairbank, Elizabeth 7447
Fairbank, Thomas 7447
Fairchild, Amy 4708
Fairchild, Eunice 234
Fairchild, Mary Susan 54
Fairchild, Nancy 3577
Fairchild, William 2944
Fairlee, James 2946
Fairman, Sarah 1546
Falconer, Catharine 1781
Falls, ___ (Mr.) 9298
Fanning, Abigail 1816
Fanning, Hiram 2954, 2956
Fanning, Robert B. 2958, 2960
Fare, Sarah W. 9885
Farlin, Dudley 2964
Farling, Andrew 2965
Farnam, Eliza 9303
Farnam, Joel 9303
Farquhar, Jephson 8473
Farquhar, Maria 8473
Farr, Elizabeth 4217
Farrington, Elizabeth 1930
Farrington, Mary W. 206
Farrington, Phebe 8394
Farrington, Timothy 1746, 8394
Farrington, Welthy 1746
Fasset, Amos J. 2976
Fassett, Amelia 4135
Faulkner, Julia Ann 10098
Fay, amanda 5789
Fay, Jonas 1400
Fay, Mary J. 1400
Fearney, Eliza 7331
Feeter, William 2983
Felie, Joseph 2984
Fellers, Andrew 3764

Fellers, Margaret 3764
Fellows, Jane A. 1681
Fellows, Joshua 2987
Fellows, Ruby 10060
Fenner, Elizabeth 8699
Ferguson, Robert 3047
Ferguson, William 5333
Fero, Elenor 9093
Ferris, Ada 4773
Ferris, Caroline 3128
Ferris, Eleanor 8079
Ferris, Electa 8658
Ferris, Hannah 3516
Ferris, Jacob 1822
Ferris, Nancy 8052
Ferris, Priscilla 3901
Ferris, Sarah 237
Ferris, Solomon 237, 3006, 3010, 8079
Fidler, Robert 3013
Field, Abigail 9086
Field, Betsey 5001
Field, Catharine 1103
Field, Eliza 8211
Field, Elizabeth 364
Field, Fanny 7688
Field, John 3019
Field, Joseph 8211
Field, Joseph C. 3017
Field, S. Kellogg (mr.) 3016
Fields, Harriet 3603
Fields, John 3603
Fields, Philipina 1492
Filken, Sally 3656
Filkins, Eliza 3284
Filkins, Pamelia 5887
Fillmore, ___ (Miss) 3031, 5406
Fillmore, Cleora 1588
Fillmore, Lavius 3029
Fillmore, Nathaniel 3031
Fillmore, Phebe 4585
Fillmore, Septa (Capt.) 5406
Finch, Eliza 5756
Finch, Emma 4667
Finch, Hannah 1974
Finch, Huldah 5494
Finch, Sally 6295
Finck, Ann 3311
Finck, J. C. (Mr.) 3311
Finen, Catharine 7678
Fish, Elizabeth S. 6062
Fish, Nicholas 6062
Fish, Peter 4406
Fish, Sabrina Ann 6562
Fisher, Clara 9304
Fisher, E. R. (Miss) 2547
Fisher, Gertrude 1575
Fisher, Hannah 4420
Fisher, Jerome 3001
Fisher, John N. 3042
Fisher, Laura 3368
Fisher, Luretta 3001
Fisher, Mary Ann 546
Fisher, Paul 2547
Fisher, Rufus 3045
Fisher, Sophia 4417
Fisher, Thomas 3043
Fisher, William 1575
Fisk, Betsey 1916
Fisk, Josiah 4839
Fisk, Mary 4839
Fisk, Sabrina A. 7648
Fisk, Solomon 7648
Fitch, ___ (Miss) 5343
Fitch, A. (Mr.) 547
Fitch, Anjinette 2778
Fitch, Asahel 7985
Fitch, Betsey 5060

Fitch, Cynthia 7985
Fitch, Cyprian 9763
Fitch, Eleanor 7621
Fitch, Eliza 2494
Fitch, Emily 4050
Fitch, Eunice 9491
Fitch, Hannah 1037, 9763
Fitch, John 2220
Fitch, Mary 3096
Fitch, Olive 6700
Fitch, Phebe 4132
Fitch, R. H. (Capt.) 4050
Fitch, Rowena 6800
Fitch, Sally 2220, 7981
Fitchet, Frances 7672
Fitz Hugh, Mary E. 8521
Fitzhugh, W. F. 5158
Fitz Hugh, William 8521
Flagg, Loucy 1254
Flagler, Henry 3074
Flagler, Jsne 8993
Flagler, Maria 7032
Flagler, Maria Z. 7401
Flagler, Mary 9330
Flagler, Pamela 8957
Flagler, Solomon 1462, 3075, 7032, 8957
Flagler, Tamer 1462
Flagler, Thomas 3069
Flanders, Mahettable 1170
Flint, Melinda 6644
Flint, Moses H. 3081
Floutenburgh, Jane 8852
Fobes, Clarissa L. 1222
Fobes, Daniel 5487
Folger, Abraham 3099
Folger, Benjamin 7182
Folger, Benjamin F. 3091
Folger, Deborah 3094
Folger, Eunice 975
Folger, H. (Miss)7753
Folger, Judith 216
Folger, Nancy 8880
Folger, Phebe 1978
Folger, Reuben C. 975
Folger, Sally 4730, 7182
Follett, F. M. (Mr.) 3101
Follett, Oran 3102
Follett, Susan 3101
Fonda, Abraham L. 6763
Fonda, Caroline 6763
Fonda, Christina 8341
Fonda, Gitty 8624
Fonda, James H. 3115
Fonda, John L. 3108
Fonda, Lany 5872
Fontaine, Alice Virginia 256
Fontaine, Carter 256
Foot, Celestia 3933
Foot, Elisha 1691
Foot, Lyman 3119
Foot, Sarah M. 1691
Foote, Elisha 3127, 3129
Foote, Justin 2288
Foote, Maria 2288
Foote, Sophia 5518
Forbes, Elisha 3132
Forbes, Jane 9977
Forbes, Sally 3698
Forbus, John 3135, 3136
Forbus, Sarah 7329
Ford, David 4807
Ford, Harriet P. 1726
Ford, Ira 1685, 1726
Ford, Isaac 10007
Ford, Mary Ann 5658
Ford, Philip 5432
Ford, Polly 5209
Ford, S. Maria 5432

328

Giddings, Adelia 2751
Giddings, Buel 2751
Giddings, Charlotte 6314
Giddings, Mary 2961
Gidley, Maria 3932
Giffoed, Abigail 2038
Gifford, Gideon 8298
Gifford, Humphry 3419
Gifford, John 3425
Gifford, Josiah 4487
Gifford, Mary 3803
Gifford, Sarah 9539
Gilbert, Almira M. 6390
Gilbert, Asahel 3428
Gilbert, Daniel 7221
Gilbert, Elizabeth 8025
Gilbert, Hannah 9953
Gilbert, John 9953
Gilbert, Joseph 8025
Gilbert, Lucy 5878
Gilbert, Martha E. 1419
Gilbert, Mary 5002
Gilbert, Nancy 7221
Gilchrist, Daniel 3437
Gilchrist, William 3438
Gildersleeve, Cyrus 9061
Gildersleeve, Henry 7523
Gildersleeve, Jane 9655
Gildersleeve, Martha 4920
Gildersleeve, Mary V. 9061
Gildersleeve, Ruth 7523
Gilding, Hannah 7006
Giles, Elizabeth 6039
Giles, Jane 6401
Giles, Maria 1340
Giles, William 6039
Gill, ___ (Mr.) 3238
Gill, Bennington 3444, 3446
Gillespie, Susan 3161
Gillet, Stephen 1666
Gilliland, Anna 2046
Gilliland, Betsey 1329
Gilliland, David 2046
Gilliland, William 3451
Gillingham, Matthias 3453
Gillingham, Moses 3453
Gillispie, Harriet 2669
Gilman, Abigail 7129
Gilman, Cynthia 3165
Gilmore, Robert 2938
Gilmore, Sarah Ann 2938
Gilson, Elizabeth 3459
Gilson, Thomas D. 3459
Gird, Mary E. 1237
Gisselbergh, Sally 7535
Gitty, John 3053
Given, James 3462
Gladd, David 7502
Gladd, Eliza Ann 7502
Gladding, Jonathan 4487
Gladding, William 3465
Glen, Sally 39
Glentworth, Harriet S. 1478
Glentworth, P. F. (Dr.) 1478
Glinn, Harriet 5626
Glower, Benjamin 3471
Glover, Elizabeth 3665
Glover, James 3470
Gloysford, ___ (Mr.) 3404
Gocha, Margaret 7575
Goddard, ___ (Mrs.) 5791
Goddard, Calvin 5791
Godfrey, ___ (Mr.) 5865
Godfrey, Phebe 1151
Goelet, Thomas B. 3473
Goes, Isaac 3475
Goes, Maria 9770
Goes, Richard I. 4750

Goes, Richard J. 3476
Goewey, Jacob 3477
Goff, Candace 6924
Goff, Julia A. 5332
Gold, Benjamin R. 952
Gold, Harriet R. 952
Gold, Theodore S. 4965
Golder, Phebe 6128
Goldsmith, Theodosia 8282
Goldsmith, Thomas 3484, 8282
Good, Sarah 9194
Good, William 3486
Goodale, R. (Dr.) 3488
Goodell, Richard 1308
Goodell, Sophia E. 1308
Goodman, Julia 23
Goodman, Simeon 23
Goodman, Titus, Jr. 3492
Goodrich, Chauncy 3493
Goodrich, Lucretia 438
Goodrich, Polly 5052
Goodsell, Fanny 4595
Goodsell, Lewis 3501
Goodsell, Mary 6012
Goodsell, Peter 104, 3502,
    4595, 6012
Goodwin, ___ (Mr.) 3506
Goodwin, Harriet 9060
Goodwin, Joseph 9060
Goodwin, Samuel 3507
Gookin, George W. 5593
Gordon, Louisa 201
Gordon, Mary 6964
Gordon, William 3510
Gordon, William I. 3511
Gorsline, Betsey 5925
Gorton, Eluzai 1467
Gorton, Hezekiah 6016
Gorton, Nancy 6016
Gorton, William 3517
Gosman, Eliza 4981
Gosman, Joanne B. 2969
Gosman, Jonathan B. 2969
Gosman, R. (Mr.) 4981
Gott, Nathaniel 3521
Gott, Sarah Ann 6604
Goucher, Julia Ann 4809
Gough, ___ (Mr.) 4118
Gould, ___ (Mr.) 3524, 5733
Gould, Abraham 3522
Gould, David 2634
Gould, James 3526
Gould, Mary 4953
Gould, Mary Ann 7444
Gould, Mary Anne 566
Gould, Sally 2634
Gould, Susannah 7788
Gould, W. (Mr.) 3523
Goulder, Ellen 1907
Goundry, George 3528
Gourgas, Henrietta C. C. 2550
Gourlay, James 1408, 3841
Governeur, Louisa Augusta 9308
Grace, Almira 7448
Grace, Angelina 1965
Grace, Etna Maria 2043
Grace, Susan 8648
Gracie, Archibald 5121,8940
Gracie, Esther Rogers 5121
Gracie, Mary Ann 8940
Gracie, Robert 3533
Graham, Adah 3550
Graham, Adam 3536
Graham, Alexander 3534, 4472
Graham, Cornelia 4472
Graham, Hannah 5534
Graham, James M. 3546
Graham, Joseph 3543

Graham, Nancy 9101
Grandy, Maria 6020
Granger, Betsey 1257
Granger, Harvey 3552
Granger, Phebe Eliza 2472
Grant, Emma L. 8478
Grant, Hannah 5469
Grant, James 3567, 8478
Grant, Juliana 8100
Grant, Mary Ann 4489
Grant, Nancy 1649
Graverart, Maria 7050
Graves, Benjamin 3575, 3578,
    7583
Graves, Betsey 1109, 7583
Graves, Calvin 3573
Graves, Ezra 3582
Graves, Hannah 1330
Graves, Mary 5763
Graves, Mary Ann 1646
Graves, Recompense 3581
Graves, Sarah Ann 4893
Gray, ___ (Mr.) 3037
Gray, Charlotte 5426
Gray, Martha 5017
Gray, William 3589
Greatsinger, Rhoda 5591
Green, Amanda 5134
Green, Amelia 883
Green, Ann 1939, 8041
Green, Betsey 7883
Green, Byram 6193
Green, Charlotte 1798
Green, Cornelia 7569
Green, Deborah 2906
Green, Eliza 8618
Green, Elizabeth 9702
Green, Elizabeth (Mrs.) 1676
Green, Esther 2451
Green, Israel 6978
Green, Jane Eliza 1232
Green, John 3606
Green, Joseph I. 3596, 6248,
    7569
Green, Lucretia 3810
Green, Lucy 6193
Green, Maria (Mrs.) 1317
Green, Mary 3455, 3592, 9703
Green, Mary Ann 2120
Green, Nancy 4440, 9493
Green, Oliver 3592
Green, Peggy 9467
Green, Permelia 6248
Green, Sarah 7917
Green, Sophia A. 6244
Green, Thomas 3590
Green, William 883, 3613, 9703
Greenbrech, John 3621
Greene, ___ (Gen.) 3622
Greene, Ellen 6067
Greene, Harriet 10101
Greene, Joseph H. 3626
Greenleaf, James 5324
Greenleaf, Mary Livingston 5324
Greenman, Josiah 3631
Gregory, Abraham V. P. 3175
Gregory, Eliza Ann 3379
Gregory, Jane 670
Gregory, Julia F. 3175
Gregory, Louisa 662
Gregory, Olive 7388
Gregory, Parmelia 8093
Gregory, Stephen 3636
Gremond, Lurana 7458
Grenell, Olive 8
Grey, Eunice 4586
Gridley, Fanny 7418
Gridley, Noah 3650

330

Grieve, Walter 3652
Griffen, ___ (Mr.) 7467
Griffin, ___ (Mr.) 9371
Griffin, Almira 5385
Griffin, Delia 9261
Griffin, Delia A. 9425
Griffin, Elizabeth 1977, 3421
Griffin, Gratis 2712
Griffin, Jacob 9261
Griffin, Jonathan 9425
Griffin, Joseph 8136
Griffin, Mary Ann 8136
Griffin, Samuel 2712, 5385
Griffith, Margaret 3668
Griffith, Nijah 3670
Griggs, Marcia 1190
Griggs, William C. 3674
Grimm, Caroline 6446
Grimshaw, Ann 1130
Grimshaw, Sarah 9490
Griswold, ___ (Miss) 1100
Griswold, Amos 3683
Griswold, Chester 3678
Griswold, H. M. 3680
Griswold, Lucy 10059
Griswold, Orpha Bliss 9419
Griswold, Sarah 1122
Griswould, Ann 521
Groesbeck, Cornelius W. 3688
Groesbeck, David W. 3689
Groesbeck, Gerrit I. 3692
Groesbeck, John 3687
Groesbeck, Maria 5929
Groesbeck, William 3690
Grom-on, Clarissa 7837
Grosvenor, Marcia 14
Grosvenor, Seth 3697
Grosvenor, Thomas P. 3697
Gudcomb, Phidelia B. 1016
Guernsey, James R. 2422
Guernsey, Melinda 358
Guernsey, Peter B. 3703
Guernsey, Sarah C. 2422
Guest, Edward 3704
Guild, Lucy 9880
Guion, Abraham 6406
Guion, Sarah Ophelia 6406
Guiteau, Ann 6544
Guiteau, Francis 3708, 6544
Gulnac, Jacob 3711
Gunn, John 3717, 8345
Gunn, Joseph 3716
Gunn, Mary Ann 8345
Gunn, Rhoda 5384
Gunn, Tamer 7912
Gurley, Elizabeth 8926
Gurley, H. H. (Hon.) 8926
Gurney, John 6897
Gurney, Ruth 6897
Gurnsey, Wealthy 7799
Guthrie, Joseph 3723
Guy, Anna 8922
Hackett, Allen 3725
Hadgley, Emma 7762
Hadley, Samuel W. 3726
Hagadon, Hannah 6124
Hagadon, Harriet 3728
Hagadon, John 3728
Hagadorn, Jacob 3730
Hagadorn, Peter 3729
Hagaman, Elizabeth 3210
Hagaman, Hendrick 7010
Hageman, adrian 9280
Hageman, Eliza D. (Mrs.) 3738
Hageman, Jane 8525
Hageman, John 3737
Hageman, Mary 9280
Hagerman, Diana 2392

Hagerman, John 2392, 6414
Hagerman, Sally 6414
Haggerty, ___ (Mr.) 5342
Haight, Abigail 4460
Haight, Anna 6315, 8430
Haight, Anny 1350
Haight, Area Ann 8946
Haight, Ebenezer
Haight, Hannah E. 5695
Haight, Jacob 3761
Haight, Jane 7751
Haight, Julia Ann 2070
Haight, Martha Ann 9936
Haight, Nathaniel 9936
Haight, Rachel 5438
Haight, Robert 3740
Haight, Samuel 2070
Haight, Samuel S. 3756, 4109
Haight, Susan T. 7319
Haight, Thomas 3741
Haile, W. F. (Mr.) 3763
Haines, Elias 2263
Haines, Mary Ogden 2263
Hale, Daniel 3769
Hale, George 1418
Hale, Hannah 555
Hale, M. (Dr.) 4609
Hale, Maria C. 4609
Hale, Mary ann 5008
Hale, Sophia 1418
Halenbake, Isaac B. 1140
Halenbake, Isaac Rue 1140
Hall, ___ (Judge) 8568
Hall, Ann 2517
Hall, Charles Lee 5711
Hall, Chloe 377
Hall, Easther (Mrs.) 1272
Hall, Emmeline 809
Hall, Eveline 3951
Hall, Green (Mr.) 809
Hall, Israel B. 3786
Hall, John 2517, 3777, 3951
Hall, Lois 3518
Hall, Susan Ann 8568
Hall, Thomas 3775
Hall, Timothy, Jr. 7269
Hallenbeck, Christina 3799
Hallenbeck, Lawrence 3797, 3798
Hallenbeck, Magdelin 10079
Hallett, Polly 2827
Halliday, Margaret 7556
Halliday, Robert 7556
Hallock, Israel 3804
Hallock, James 3802
Hallock, Laura B. 6798
Hallock, Sarah 6169
Halsey, Eliza 695
Halsey, Frederick 3817, 3818, 3819
Halsey, Gains 3820
Halsey, Hannah H. 1881
Halsey, Harriet 2117
Halsey, Mariah 7287
Halsey, N. (Mr.) 1881
Halsey, T. I. (Mr.) 2117
Halstead, Maria 4719
Halstead, Reuben 3823
Halsted, ___ (Mr.) 4746
Ham, Abbey 1997
Ham, Gitty 9928
Ham, Jane 8733
Ham, Margaret 3833
Hambleton, Allicia 1315
Hambleton, Polly 8256
Hamblin, Harriet 8111
Hamill, Letitia 4373
Hamill, Robert 4373
Hamilton, ___ (Dr.) 1826

Hamilton, Caroline Williams 7098
Hamilton, Eliza 1825
Hamilton, Henrietta R. 6930
Hamilton, Isaac 3841
Hamilton, Joseph 1825, 3839, 6701, 7955
Hamilton, Lucinda 6701
Hamilton, Maria 1826
Hamilton, Sarah 3055
Hamilton, Violette 6567
Hamilton, Zadya 7955
Hamlen, Clarissa 6210
Hamlin, Aroxey 3571
Hamlin, Julia 2277
Hamlin, Martha M. 349
Hammersley, Anna Maria 9312
Hammersley, Thomas 9312
Hammond, ___ (Mr.) 5548
Hammond, Abner 751
Hammond, Alma 4311
Hammond, Charlotte 3641
Hammond, Jabez D. 3854
Hammond, Jonathan 3916
Hammond, Maritta 751
Hammond, Sally 5548
Hampton, James B. 3855
Hampton, Jonathan H. 5154
Hampton, Mary Ann 5154
Hampton, Zalmon 3855
Hancock, Margaret 5888
Hands, James 18
Handy, Elizabeth 2707
Handy, William 2707
Haner, Philip 3860
Hanmer, Julia 7254
Hanna, Ann 9591
Hansen, Catharine 3184
Hansen, Catherine 9075
Hansen, Deborah 3185
Hanson, Harriet 8096
Hanson, Mary Jane 3701
Hard, Peter N. 3869
Hardaway, More 6009
Hardeck, Peter F. 3873
Hardenbrook, Rebecca 1995
Hardenbrook, William A. 1995
Hardenburgh, Catharine Maria 8408
Hardenburgh, Cornelius 3874
Hardenburgh, Jacob R. 9583
Hardenburgh, Joanna 9583
Hardenburgh, Lewis 8408
Hardick, Elizabeth 8770
Hardick, Polly 7607
Hardick, Charity 5837
Hardy, Elizabeth 5097
Hare, David 3878
Harman, Ruth 2115
Harmon, E. D. (Dr.) 3894
Harnum, Elizabeth 1940
Harper, James 3896
Harrington, Lucy 9397
Harrington, Martha A. 1642
Harris, ___ (Capt.) 1928
Harris, Ann 3381
Harris, Ann Maria 1485
Harris, Asa 3904
Harris, Charles 2374
Harris, Edward 3914
Harris, Eliza
Harris, Elizabeth 4562, 6794
Harris, Elizabeth Pearl 2374
Harris, Eunis 1302
Harris, Ezekiel 3906
Harris, Helen 3224
Harris, Jane 9215
Harris, Joseph 9215, 9275

Harris, Margaret 9852
Harris, Margareta 7170
Harris, Maria 514, 9238
Harris, William 1485
Harrison, Daniel 5523
Harrison, Frederick 3920, 4232, 5808
Harrison, Julia 4232
Harrison, Mary Ann 5523
Harrison, Sarah Ann 5808
Harrison, William H. 3926
Hart, ___ (Mr.) 3884
Hart, Ann M. 4490
Hart, Catharine 8854
Hart, Charlotte 2173
Hart, Elisha 3940
Hart, Eliza 4485
Hart, Hetty (Mrs.) 8238
Hart, Philip 116, 3996
Hart, Richard 3934
Hart, Richard P. 3942
Hart, Susan 3996
Hart, Wealthy Velona 5788
Harvey, Deborah 7720
Harvey, James 3952
Harwell, Elizabeth 7410
Harwood, Electa 3122
Hasbrook, Arminta D. 7017
Hasbrook,Benjamin 3957, 6456
Hasbrook, Catharine 2674
Hasbrook, Jane 565
Hasbrook, Maria 6456
Hasbrook, Mary 8952
Hasbrook, Tunis 565, 2674
Hasbrouck, Phebe 9373
Hasbroyck, Sarah S. 1677
Hascall, Helen 8261
Hascall, Ralph 3960, 8261
Haskell, Abigail 3964
Haskell, Mary 6013
Haskell, Roger 3965
Haskell, Roxanna 9386
Haskell, Zebulon 3964
Haskins, Ann 8665
Haskins, Azariah 991
Haskins, Clarissa 991
Haskins, Martha 3826
Hastings, ___ (Mr.) 6474
Haswell, Jane M. 7416
Haswell, Sarah 3625
Hatch, ___ (Maj.) 6305
Hatch, A. (Maj.) 3957
Hatch, Dorus 3974
Hatch, Erastus 4792
Hatch, Eunice 4793
Hatch, Harriet 7002
Hatch, Lucy 3561
Hatch, Mary 3955, 4792, 6069
Hatch, Melinda 7667
Hatch, Sally 1152
Hatch, Samuel 3971
Hatch, Sarah M. 4980
Hatfield, Edmund 2378
Hatfield, Jennett R. 2378
Hsthaway, ___ (Capt.)
Hathaway, Annis 9066
Hathaway, Baley (Capt.) 3977
Hathaway, Chloe 2897
Hathaway, Fanny 9548
Hathaway, Harriet 6005
Hathaway, John 645
Hathaway, Nichplas 3983
Hathaway, Phebe 654
Hathaway, Robert 9066
Hathaway, Sally 209
Havemeyer, Charlotte 2904, 2937
Haven, Margaret 3984
Havens, Charles H. 5135

Havens, Juliette 5135
Havens, Temperance Catharine 5683
Haviland, Benjamin 9761
Haviland, Dorcas 9276a
Haviland, Emma 8864
Haviland, Hannah 9761
Haviland, Jane 8816
Hawk, Rufus 4010
Hawkins, Christopher 4007
Hawkins, Eliza 4366
Hawkins, Gaylord 4003
Hawkins, George 3999
Hawkins, Maria 6068
Hawkins, Mary 5907
Hawkins, Mary C. 914
Hawkins, Samuel 914, 4004
Hawks, James 4009
Hawley, Adeline 4011
Hawley, Calvin 4016
Hawley, Francis 4017
Hawley, Martin 4011
Hawskins, Laurina 2049
Hawven, Anna 610
Haxton, Benjamin 1994, 3201
Haxton, Louiza 1994
Hay, Mary 3520, 4025
Hay, Robert 4025
Hay, William 4024
Hayden, David, Jr. 2777
Hayes, ___ (Mr.) 9066
Hayes, Julia Ann 9806
Hayes, Maria 6637
Hayes, R. (Mr.) 4028a
Hayner, Elizabeth 5243
Hayner, Hannah 6177, 7849
Hayner, Sally 7890
Haynor, Catharine 5665
Hays, Abby 1582
Hays, Stephen 1582
Hayt, H. (Mr.) 4034
Hayward, Maria 9937
Haywood, Mary 6922
Haywood, Rachel 6736
Haywood, Thomas 6736
Hazard, Harriet 4030
Hazard, Patience 4561
Hazen, Caleb 5016
Hazen, Eliza 5016
Head, Sally 4044
Heart, ___ (Mr.) 1144
Heartt, Benjamin 4051
Heartt, Philip 10070
Heath, Polina 1682
Hebard, Selina 6280
Hecox, Eliza 4292
Hedden, Tamer 1301
Heddy, Phebe 6499
Hedge, B. (Mr.) 5400
Hedge, Ellen Hobart 5400
Hedges, Mary C. 3045
Hedges, William 3045
Heermance, Andrew G. 3834
Heermance, Arrayanchee 4154
Heermance, Cornelia 7964
Heermance, G. (Miss) 3834
Heermance, Maria 7692
Heermance, Martha 5993
Heermance, Martin 7964
Heermans, ___ (Mr.) 7095
Heermans, Peter 7398
Heermans, Sally 680
Helsop, John 4068
Hemferman, Rebecca 269
Hempsted, Isaac 4071
Hempsted, Lucy 8547
Henderson, Adam 4076
Henderson, Elizabeth 7616
Henderson, Sally 4446

Henderson, Samuel 7616
Henderson, Sarah 7274
Hendricks, Euphemia 6507
Hendrickson, John 4082
Hendrickson, Stephen 4083
Henman, Lorinda B. 5834
Henry, Clarissa L. 6690
Henry, Elizabeth B. 7713
Henry, Fanny 9813
Henry, Harriet Eliza 2810
Henry, Henry 4701
Henry, Henry B. 2216
Henry, Mary 2216
Henry, Mary Ann 4701
Henry, Priscilla 4089
Henry, Samuel 4089
Henry. Susan 4056
Henry, William 2810
Hensdel, Phebe 1193
Henshaw, D. 6841
Henshaw, Elizabeth H. 6841
Henshaw, Fanny E. 8488
Hepburn, Harriet Jane 498
Hepinstall, Sarah 4289
Herick, Elijah 4102
Hermans, Phebe Ann 265
Herod, Margaretta H. C. 8322
Heron, Levi 1570
Heron, Margaret 4820
Heron, William 4820
Herrick, Arthur 4109
Herrick, Benjamin 4114, 7185, 7190
Herrick, Conklin 4115
Herrick Cynthia 7190
Herrick, Delia 5540
Herrick, Elijah 8271
Herrick, John Smith 7931
Herrick, Julia Ann 4521
Herrick, Lucinda P. 6978
Herrick, Maria 4105
Herrick, Martha Matilda 5964
Herrick, Minerva 4116
Herrick, Rebecca 8271
Herrick, S. H. (Mr.) 4105
Herrick, Stephen 9292
Herrick, Susan 9292
Herrington, Eleanor 1045
Herrington, H. (Mr.) 4119
Herrington, Lucinda 5574
Hervey, Hannah 5078
Hesley, James 1359
Hesley, Sally 1359
Heszelton, Sarah 3887
Hethuysen, Joanna M. 5320
Hethuyson, John S. 5320
Heustis, Eustatia 7246
Hewes, Daniel 4124
Hewit, Ann 9753
Hewitt, Eliza 6666
Hewitt, Mary Ann 1902
Hewitt, Phebe 3482
Hewitt, Thomas 1902
Hewlett, Phebe 1060
Hewlett, Samuel 1060
Hewson, Alcemena 6775
Hewson, Margaret 3457
Hewson, Thomas 3457
Heyer, Louisa F. 7084
Hickock, ___ (Miss) 7704
Hickock, Daniel 4137
Hickock, Ezra 4139
Hickock, Samuel S. 83
Hickok, Benjamin 4142
Hickok, Mary 9498
Hickok, Sabra 9656
Hickok, Samuel 4143
Hickox, Carlton 4145
Hicks, ___ (Judge) 4147

Hicks, Catharine 1745
Hicks, Elias 4150, 9621
Hicks, John 4149
Hicks, Mary A. 1368
Hicks, Oliver A. 1368
Hicks, Peggy 9621
Higbie, Benjamin 4157
Higby, ___ (Miss) 2826
Higby, Almira 9932
Higby, Lucy 2945
Higby, Sarah Ann 2824
Higby, William 4159
Higgins, Cornelius 4161
Higham, Abraham 4163
Highdecker, Maria 3038
Hildreth, Catharine Mary 849
Hildreth, Joshua 4167
Hildreth, Matthias 849
Hildreth, Milison 2339
Hill, Alma 3686
Hill, Deborah Brown 1725
Hill, Elizabeth R. 3594
Hill, Elsa 5188
Hill, Harriet 8007
Hill, Henry 6244
Hill, Nathaniel 6746
Hill, Sally 6382
Hill, Sarah Ann 6746
Hillequist, Mary 1118
Hillhouse, Harriet 1244
Hillhouse, James 4126
Hillhouse, John G. 1244
Hillhouse, Rebecca W. 4126
Hilliard, Semantha 7433
Hillson, Mary 1205
Hilton, Catharine 4178
Hilton, James 4084
Hilton, Maria 4084
Hilton, Richard 4178
Hinckley, Sarah 413
Hind, Thomas 4181
Hines, Lydia P. 3922
Hingston, Samuel J. 4184
Hinman, Ann 2323
Hinman, Joshua 4185
Hirst, Hannah 1006
Hiscox, Roxsina 1882
Hitchcock, ___ (Dr.) 6991
Hitchcock, Eliza 962, 7141
Hitchcock, Harriet C. 2468, 2475
Hitchcock, Myraette 6991
Hitchcock, Rachel 1896
Hitchcock, Sarah Newcomb 218
Hoag, Hannah 3991
Hoag, Joshua 4197
Hoag, Lydia 4840
Hoag, Thomas 2336
Hobart, ___ (Right Rev. Bishop) 3881
Hobart, Elizabeth Catherine 3881
Hobart, John H. (Rev.) 4612
Hobart, Rebecca Smith 4612
Hobby, Caleb 4206
Hobby, Tamma 9430
Hobes, Catherine 2291
Hochstrasser, Julia Ann 4478
Hochstrasser, Paul 4478
Hodgdon, Mary Elizabeth 7037
Hodgeman, Lydia 1059
Hodgkins, Lucy 2735
Hodgkins, William 2735
Hoe, Mary 7729
Hoe, Robert 7729
Hoes, Anna Maria 9115
Hoff, B. (Rev.) 4218
Hoffman, Abraham 4227, 4723

Hoffman, Anna Maria 5772
Hoffman, Catherine 258
Hoffman, Caty 1071
Hoffman, Charles 4219
Hoffman, Eliza 7507
Hoffman, Eliza G. 802
Hoffman, Euphemia 343
Hoffman, Gertrude 4222
Hoffman, Herman 2638, 4222
Hoffman, J. O. (Mr.) 9134
Hoffman, Jane 4723
Hoffman, Jane Ann 5391
Hoffman, Maria Gertrude 2638
Hoffman, Nicholas 4225
Hoffman, Robert 1071, 4239
Hoffman, Sarah 7471
Hoffman, Zachariah 2867, 4240
Hoffman, Zacharius 9255
Hogeboom, Catharine 9014
Hogeboom, Helen 4243
Hogeboom, Henry 7273
Hogeboom, John C. 4250, 9014
Hogeboom, Peter 4245, 4246
Hogeboom, Stephen 4244
Hogeboom, Tobias I. 4243
Holbridge, Lucy 1089
Holbrook, ___ (Capt.) 8475
Holloway, Eliza 8247
Holbrook, Emily 5151
Holbrook, Luther 5636
Holbrook, Mary 5636
Holcomb, Dodorus H. (Dr.) 4255
Holcomb, Elsey 9991
Holden, Almira 6552
Holden, Deliverance 4261
Holden, Eliza 7116
Holden, Fanny 1214
Holden, Martha 4508
Holden, Mary 9783
Holden, Oliver 4261, 6552
Holden, Robert 350
Holdridge, Abraham 5404
Holeman, George 4262
Holland, John 426$
Hollenbeck, Henry 4265
Holley, Clarissa G. 624
Holley, E. O. 4267
Holley, John M. 4268
Holley, Myron 624
Holliday, ___ (Mrs.) 2139
Holly, Elizabeth 31, 4948
Holly, Lydia 7077
Holly, Myron 31, 4948
Holmes, ___ (Capt.) 4300
Holmes, ___ (Mr.) 378
Holmes, Abadiah 4287
Holmes, Betsey 49
Holmes, Cornelia 1127
Holmes, Eldad 1127
Holmes, Harriet 684
*Homes, Isaac 4286
Holmes, Joseph 6673
Holmes, Mary 9436
Holmes, Miranda 3445
Holmes, Polly 658
Holmes, Rhoda 9641
Holmes, Sally 6738
Holmes, Samuel 49
Holmes, William 6738
Holms, Phebe 6673
Holt, Elijah 4304
Holt, Lester 4301
*Holt, William J. 4306
*Homes, Susan 557
Hone, Joanna 5003
Hone, Philip I. 5003
Honeywood, St. John 1427
*Homes, Isaac unintentionally misplaced

Honeywood, Sally 1427
Hooffman, William 4314
Hoogeland, Derrick 4315
Hooghkerk, Henry 4316
Hook, Catharine Elizabeth 9095
Hook, J. C. (Mr.) 9095
Hooker, James 4317
Hopkins, Boyd 4324
Hopkins, Enos 1163
Hopkins, Hannah 1163, 2094
Hopkins, Julian 7866
Hopkins, Minerva 4116
Hopkins, Phebe 230
Hopkins, Sally F. 8801
Hopkins, Samuel 7866
Hopkinson, Elizabeth S. 4834
Hopper, Lambert 4328
Hornbeck, Garett S. W. 4333
Hornbeck, Sarah 9454
Horr, R. C. (Capt.) 4334
Horr, Ralph C. 4335
Horson, Agnes 7584
Horton, Amy 634A
Horton, Coert 4344
Horton, Ebenezer 4340
Horton, Elizabeth 5625, 5749
Horton, Mary N. 2341
Hosack, ___ (Dr.) 388
Hosford, E. (Mr.) 4349, 4350
Hosmer, A. (Mr.) 8223
Hosmer, Hezekiah L. 4353
Hosmer, Lucy 6342
Hosmer, Maria 3374
Hosmer, Prosper 3374
Hosmer, S. T. (Mr.) 6342
Hosmer, Sarah E. 8223
Hoskin, Shubael 4351
Hotchkiss, ___ (Mr.) 3793
Hotchkiss, Carver 4361
Houghtaling, Caroline 4922
Houston, Ezra C. 4370
Houtalen, Hannah 9995
How, David 4371
How, Mary Y. 3382
Howard, ___ (Mr.) 6792, 7893
Howard, Betsey Amelia 3945
Howard, John 4377
Howard, Juliette A. 3025
Howard, Lucy 9404
Howard, Maria 7579
Howard, N. (Col.) 6092
Howard, Sally 115, 2379
Howard, Samuel 4376
Howard, Sarah 4665
Howard, Sarah Ann 3583
Howard, Seth 4382
Howard, Susan 5377
Howard, William 3945
Howden, Samuel 4386
Howe, Artemas 4389
Howe, Elvira 6820, 8606
Howe, Epenetus 4395
Howe, Lodoiska 4884
Howe, Louise 1611
Howell, Jane E. 4616
Howell, Mary Ann 9546
Howell, Nathaniel W. 4616
Howes, Thomas 4398
Howland, A. H. (Dr.) 6716
Howland, Eunice 6334, 8058
Howland, Eveline J. 2025
Howland, James 2025
Howland, Joseph 4405
Howland, Olivia 899
Howland, Reuben 899
Hoxie, Charlotte 8150
Hoxie, Christopher 4412, 8150
Hoxie. Elizabeth 2420

Hoxie, John 2420
Hoxie, Permelia 6425
Hoxie, Wanton 6425
Hoyle, Robert 4413
Hoyt, ___ (Mr.) 2980
Hoyt, Gould 4419
Hoyt, Harriet 5527
Hoyt, James J. 7655
Hoyt, Julianna 7668
Hoyt, Louisa C. 7655
Hubbard, Electa 10109
Hubbard, Jane 8281
Hubbard, Joseph 4432
Hubbard, Lucretia 3572
Hubbard, Moses 4435
Hubbard, Nehemiah 7428
Hubbard, Ruggles 4426
Hubbard, Sally 7428
Hubbard, Tunis 8281
Hubbel, Harriet 4758
Hubbel, Lemuel, Jr. 4439
Hubbel, Levi 4758
Hubbel, Sally 8838
Hubbell, Abbey 4359
Hubbell, Nancy 9895
Hubbell, Silas 4441
Huddleston, Hester 717
Hudson, ___ (Judge) 2314, 4454
Hudson, Daniel 4456
Hudson, Elizabeth 2314
Hudson, Ephraim 4455
Huestis, Charlotte 4459
Huestis, James 4459
Huestis, Mary Eliza 6322
Huffman, Mary 6703
Hughes, Hannah 5436
Hughes, J. M. (Gen.) 5970
Hughes, Mary 8949
Hughes, Mary 5970
Hughson, Antoinette 2429
Hughson, Catharine Matilda 8199
Hughson, Eliza 8959
Hughson, Jeremiah D. 4470
Hughson, Maria 2769
Hughson, Martha 3022
Hughson, Nancy 2467
Hughson, Stephen 2429, 8199
Hughson, William 2769, 4473, 4474
Hulbert, Ann S. 42$9
Hulbert, Caroline A. 2172
Hulbert, Harry 4249
Hulbert, John 4855, 4858
Hulbert, John W. 2172
Hulburt, Sally 4858
Hulburt, Edward 4482
Hulburt, John P. 4483
Hulette, Elizabeth 415
Hull, ___ (Gen.) 5738
Hull, Amos G. 4486
Hull, Edward 4492
Hull, Eliza 6439
Hull, Elizabeth Maria 8776
Hull, Hannah C. 5342
Hull, Henry 4495
Hull, Jabez 4497
Hull, John 5342
Hull, Penelope 978, 8623
Hull, Tiddeman 8623
Hullen, ___ (Mr.) 3891
Hulme, Anne 9905
Hulme, Thomas 9905
Humphrey, Adelaide Josephine 3872
Humphrey, Daniel 894
Humphrey, Humphrey, Gideon 3872
Humphrey, John 4828, 9235

Humphrey, John 4828
Humphrey, Sally 9235
Humphrey, Theophilus 7545
Humphreys, ___ (Capt.) 9892
Humphreys, Margaret Jane 9892
Humphreys, Reuben 4507, 4509
Humphry, Dorcas 3207
Hunn, Cornelia Van Emburgh 9643
Hunn, John S. 9643
Hunt, Benjamin 6400
Hunt, Betsy 3472
Hunt, Caroline E. 9321
Hunt, Eve 3601
Hunt, Frances M. 8702
Hunt, Hannah 6373
Hunt, Henrietta Maria Dyson 6400
Hunt, Hiram 9321
Hunt, Jane L. C. 8406
Hunt, Luther B. 8406
Hunt, Mary 5250
Hunt, Montgomery 8702
Hunt, Pamela 6196
Hunter, ___ (Mrs.) 1136
Hunter, Edward 4529
Hunter, Gilbert 7317
Hunter, Jane 4060
Hunter, Jane Maria 7317
Hunter, Jonathan 4527, 4530
Hunter, M. H. (Mr.) 4531
Hunter, Matilda 749
Hunter, Robert 1136
Hunting, Sarah M. 3655
Huntington, Charlotte 10094
Huntington, Enoch 4479, 7427
Huntington, Esther 7427
Huntinton, Frances 1245, 1514
Huntington, George 10094
Huntington, Harriet 4540
Huntington, Martha 4479, 4540
Huntington, Phebe 4540
Huntington, Sally 8950
Huntington, Samuel 4533, 4543
Huntley, Calvin 3779
Huntley, Caroline 3779
Huntley, George B. 4547
Huntley, John T. 4546
Huntting, Edward 9263
Hurd, Betsy 7142
Hurd, J. N. M. (Gen.) 4553
Hurd, Jonas 73
Hurd, Lavina 73
Hurd, Nathaniel F. 4549
Hurd, Nathaniel P. 4550
Hurlburt, Kellogg 5769
Hurlburt, Mary 5769
Hurlbut, Daniel 4088
Hurlbut, Mariah 4088
Hurry, Margaretta 6408
Hurry, Samuel 6408
Husband, Lydia 6865
Huse, ___ (Rev.) 4558
Hussey, Margaret 4697
Hussey, Paul 4697
Hussey, Phebe 6945
Husted, Catharine 2358
Husted, Polly 6017
Husted, Sally 4297
Hustis, Maria M. 8011
Hutchins, Jane Ann 8934
Hutchinson, Elizabeth M. Leger 4347
Hutchinson, Lorinda 212
Hutchinson, Mary 10003
Hutchinson, Thomas Holland 4347
Huzzey, Hepza 6010

Hyde, ___ (Mr.) 3838
Hyde, Clarinda H. 151
Hyde, E. B. (Mr.) 4588
Hyde, Ira 8115
Hyde, Isaac 4579
Hyde, Lucinda P. 8115
Hyde, Mary L. 10097
Hyde, Samuel 151
Hydorn, Juliann 8908
Hyslep, Edna 7889
Hyzer, Michael T. 4589
Ingals, Erastus W. 104
Ingals, Fanny 104
Ingalls, James 4593
Ingalls, Mary Ann 9377
Ingalls, Sarah 9406
Ingersoll, J. (Capt.) 4598
Ingersoll, Jonathan 184
Ingersoll, Sally 184
Ingraham, George 4626, 7067, 7482, 7719
Ingaham, Jane A. 7719
Ingraham, Mary 5744
Ingraham, Mary B. 4626
Ingraham, Sally 7067
Ingraham, Thomas 5744
Innis, Aaron 4602
Inslee, Betsey 1313
Inslee, Joseph 1313
Irish, Charles 4603, 7467
Irish, Elsey 3882
Irish, Sally 7467
Isbel, Bartana 8327
Ives, ___ (Mr.) 4885
Ives, Ann G. 1310
Ives, Charity 513
Ives, Chauncy 9020
Ives, Orpha 9020
Jacket, Jonathan 26
Jacket, Rebecca 126
Jackson, ___ (Col.) 3821
Jackson, ___ (Gen.) 7163
Jackson, Alexander C. 8931
Jackson, Allen H. 4619
Jackson, Amasa 3558
Jackson, Amelia M. 9257
Jackson, Christiana A. 8931
Jackson, Daniel 4627
Jackson, Eliza 6756
Jackson, Emily 737
Jackson, Harriet 3558
Jackson, John J. 2249
Jackson, Joseph 9257
Jackson, Joseph I. 4617, 4618
Jackson, Lydia 345
Jackson, Nancy Elizabeth 4358
Jackson, Olive 4772
Jackson, Phebe 4563
Jackson, Rosalie M. 7213
Jackson, Sarah D. 3821
Jackson, Sophia 1858
Jackson, Ursula 1178
Jacobs, ___ (Mr.) 4632
Jacobs, Catherine E. 1674
Jacobs, Ezekiel 4632
Jacobs, Levina 3987
Jacobs, Nathaniel 4634
Jacobs, Susannah 2896
Jacobson, ___ (Mr.) 7124
Jacocks, Hannah 1393
Jacocks, Maria 8732
Jacocks, Ruth 9615
Jacocks, Thomas 4635
Jacocks, William 4637
James, Abigail H. 6189
James, Mary 1541
James, Robert 4646
Jan ?___, Lucinda 2555
Janney, Hannah Ann 4494

334

Janney, Joseph 4494
Jaques, Frances D. 857
Jaques, Harriet 2477
Jarvis, Elizabeth B. 25
Jarvis, John 25
Jarvis, Samuel 8414
Jay, ___ (Gov.) 462
Jay, John 4663
Jay, Maria 462
Jay, Mary R. 6996
Jay, Peter 6996
Jaycox, Joseph 4664
Jefferson, Thomas 3087, 6133
Jenckes, Almiia 9556
Jencks, Martha 5437
Jenison, Rebecca 1267
Jenkins, Barzilla 4668
Jenkins, Benjamin 1556
Jenkins, Charles 4680
Jenkins, Eliza 7346
Jenkins, Eliza P. 2512
Jenkins, Eunice 1556
Jenkins, Frederick 4698
Jenkins, Gardner 4674
Jenkins, Gilbert 4678, 4686
Jenkins, Henrietta 2237
Jenkins, Ira 868
Jenkins, John 4688, 4695
Jenkins, Lemuel 4670, 4677, 4687
Jenkins, Lemuel W. 2511
Jenkins, Lydia 3760
Jenkins, Marshal 4692
Jenkins, Mary 8492
Jenkins, Mary Ann 9793
Jenkins, Robert 4681, 4693, 9007
Jenkins, Sally 788
Jenkins, Sarah 487, 4684
Jenkins, Seth 4691
Jenkins, Thomas 487, 3760, 4684, 4685, 4692, 8492
Jenkins, Valentine 5019
Jenks, Emeline Cordelia 3544
Jenks, Hannah 4986
Jenks, Nathaniel 3544
Jenner, ___ (Dr.) 5920
Jennings, Lucy 1411
Jennings, Lydia 4705
Jennings, Samuel 1411
Jerome. Amasa 4713
Jervis, Susan Maria 595
Jessup, Benjamin 4716
Jessup, Elizabeth 6940
Jewell, Letitia 6681
Johnson, ___ (Mr.) 4212
Johnson, Ann 2952
Johnson, Calvin 9689
Johnson, Dole 4738
Johnson, Elihu 4750
Johnson, Hannah 8435
Johnson, Harriet Emeline Jane 3283
Johnson, Jesse 2720
Johnson, John 2458
Johnson, John C. 4731
Johnson, Joseph 3283, 7229
Johnson, Lucy 4763
Johnson, Melinda 8218
Johnson, Noahdiah 4750
Johnson, Patty 1319
Johnson, Phebe 6095
Johnson, Phidelia 9689
Johnson, Polly 3865
Johnson, Rebecca 6954
Johnson, Robert 9769
Johnson, Samuel 4755
Johnson, Sarah 7229
Johnson, Semantha 6779

Johnson, Stephen W. 4744
Johnson, Walter 3865
Johnson, William 4763
Johnston, David 5, 173, 4774
Johnston, Elizabeth 4757
Johnston, Hannah 6747
Johnston, John 4757
Johnston, Mary 173
Johnston, Nancy 2102, 8392
Johnston, William 2102, 6747
Jones, ___ (Mr.) 4786
Jones, Alfred 6410
Jones, Ann 2028, 6003
Jones, Betsey 2554
Jones, Caroline 236
Jones, Catharine 1761
Jones, Cornelia A. 7048
Jones, Daniel 7001
Jones, Eliza Bianca 2519
Jones, Endina 2132
Jones, Frances Ann 2162
Jones, Gardner 7977
Jones, Jacob 6003
Jones, Joshua 2162
Jones, Margaret 9679
Jones, Maria 4780
Jones, Marion 461
Jones, Mary 9503
Jones, Mary Ann 1273, 7649
Jones, Minerva 8008
Jones, Nancy 9226
Jones, Nathan 236
Jones, Nehemiah 4780
Jones, Polly 3742
Jones, Pomeroy 4796
Jones, Rachel 7001
Jones, Reuben, Jr. 4802
Jones, Richard I. 4789
Jones, Samuel 4782
Jones, Sena (Miss) 4117
Jones, Seth 2554, 4801
Jones, Thomas 1761, 4797
Jones, Thomas F. 7048
Jones, William 1273, 4512
Joslin, ___ (Mr.) 197
Joslin, Benjamin 4815
Jordan, William 4813
Joy, Levi 4817
Judah, Harriet 5901
Judd, Lydia Ann 3271
Judson, ___ (Mr.) 7135
Justus, Rebecca 9327
Kane, Archibald 4826
Kane, Bridget 8300
Kane, Elias 3408
Kane, James 4826
Kane, John 6326
Kane, Mary 3408
Kay, Elizabeth 4309
Kay, James 4309
Kerney, William 1373
Keating, John 4833
Keeler, Martin 4836
Keeling, Helen 1814
Keenney, Betsey 3997
Kellogg, ___ (Mr.) 4857
Kellogg, A. (Mr.) 199
Kellogg, Aaron, Jr. 4844
Kellogg, Abigal Ann 9445
Kellogg, Amelia Ann 199
Kellogg, Augustus 4847
Kellogg, Charles 4846, 9445
Kellogg, Day Otis 4846
Kellogg, Eliza 1640
Kellogg, George 4845
Kellogg, J. A. (Mr.) 4852
Kellogg, J. W. (Mr.) 8642
Kellogg, Jacob 2152
Kellogg, Joseph 4849

Kellogg, Mary 8642
Kellogg, N. (Mr.) 4852
Kellogg, Nathan 4845
Kellogg, Polly 7118
Kellogg, Stephen 4845
Kellogg, Timothy 4843, 4855
Kells, Betsey 189, 4863
Kelly, ___ (Mr.) 8539
Kelly, Mariam 8310
Kelly, Sally 8564
Kelsey, Betsey 5004
Kelsey, Helen 3113
Kelsey, Jonas 2563, 4867, 5004
Kelsey, Pasiphae J. 4393
Kelsey, Richard 4868
Kelsey, Susan 2563
Kelso, Mary 4280
Kemble, John C. 4874
Kemper, John 9791
Kemper, Susan 9791
Kendall, Hester Cay 8571
Kenman, Isaac 4878
Kennedy, John 5668
Kenney, John 4881
Kent, Eliza 5018
Kent, Elizabeth 2081
Kent, Sarah 7283
Kenyon, Patience 6582a
Kenyon, Sarah Ann 1017
Kenyon, Wanton 4890
Keous, ___ (Mr.) 1262
Keown, Frances 4891
Ker, Nathan 4892
Kerr, John 4896
Kerr, William 4896
Ketch, Phoebe 8904
Ketcham, ___ 4723
Ketcham, Amelia 7676
Ketcham, Ann R. 7913
Ketcham, Catharine S. 3747
Ketcham, Daniel 2242
Ketcham, David M. 4904
Ketcham, Israel 3220
Ketcham, James 5583
Ketcham, Jane 3220, 9872
Ketcham, Job 9872
Ketcham, Joel 7676
Ketcham, Maria 5583
Ketcham, Mary Ann 1560
Ketchum, ___ (Rev.) 4906
Ketchum, B. (Mr.) 9979
Ketchum, Joan 7568
Ketchum, Juliet C. 9979
Ketchum, Phebe 2792
Ketchum, Susan 580
Kettleras, William 10078
Key, ___ (Mrs.) 4742
Key, Elizabeth 4742
Key, Philip B. 4742
Keyes, Amasa 4913
Keyes, Susan C. 4709
Keyse, J. F. (Mr.) 8259
Keyse, Jane 8259
Keyser, Samuel 990
Keyser, Sophia E. 990
Kibby, Polly 6252
Kidney, Elizabeth 1773
Kidney, Helen 2684
Kidney, Jonathan 1140, 1773
Kidney, Margaret 2621
Kidney, Phebe 5898
Kidney, Richard 9962
Kidney, Robert J. 8251
Kidney, Sally 8251
Kidney, Sarah M. 9962
Kidney, William 1140
Killey, Samuel 4925
Kimbal, Nathaniel 4929
Kimberly, Hazard 4930

Kimmey, Maria 7979
King, ___ (Gen.) 6268
King, Aaron 5268
King, Ann E. 7790
King, Charlotte 7485
King, Eliza Caroline 1451
King, Fenner 4940
King, Frances 6268
King, Henry 1451
King, Isaac 4939
King, Jane Eliza 4966
King, John 4933
King, John 4943
King, Letitia Osborn 6415
King, Martha 5268
King, Mary Ann 1904
King, Nathaniel 4934
King, Rufus 4937, 4938, 4941
King, William 1904
King, William, Jr. 6415
Kingman, Mary 3141
Kingman, Mary Ann 2294
Kingsley, Caroline 7078
Kingsley, Otigen A. 4951
Kinney, Sally 7210
Kinney, Thankful I. 7937
Kinsley, Stephen 4960, 5216
Kip, Betsey 3443
Kip, Helen C. 7746
Kip, Jacobus 7843
Kip, Maria 7843
Kipp, Andrew 7597
Kipp, Clarissa 7597
Kipp, Magdalen 10066
Kirby, R. M. (Maj.) 4972
Kirk, Andrew 541
Kirkham, Tamer 6432
Kirkland, ___ (Rev.) 7593
Kirkland, Charles P. 4976
Kirkland, Eliza 7311
Kirkpatrick, Mary 502
Kirtland, Ann B. 3773
Kirtland, Henrietta Julia 8469
Kirtland, John 3773
Kissam, Benjamin 5270
Kissam, Emma C. 5277
Kittle, Ann Mariah 1314
Kittle, Catharine 3371
Kittle, Daniel S. 4983
Kittle, John 5177
Kittle, S. (Capt.) 1314
Kittle, Sophia 5177
Kittle, Sybrant 4982
Klapp, ___ (Mr.) 5268
Klapp, Isaac B. 89
Klapp, Maria 245
Klapp, Mary 89
Klein, Catherine 5369
Klock, Peter 4990
Knapp, ___ (Miss) 5853
Knapp, Charles 5853, 8542
Knapp, Colbey (Dr.) 2665
Knapp, David 4995, 5000
Knapp, Esther Maria 9623
Knapp, John L. 8185
Knapp, Lucy 2665
Knapp, Mary E. 8542
Knapp, Pamelia 520
Knapp, Susan 8185
Knappen, Olive Alvira 968
Knickerbacker, ___ (Dr.) 5009
Knickerbacker, Catharine 9018
Knickerbacker, Deriah 8978
Knickerbacker, Heman 9018
Knickerbacker, Herman 5006
Knickerbacker, John 5007
Knickerbacker, John, Jr. 8978
Knight, John 5019
Knower, Benjamin 5669

Knower, Cornelia 5669
Knowles, Mary 8930
Knowlton, Harry 5023
Knowlton, Manassah 8188
Knox, Lydia 9239
Knox, Sarah 5596
Koon, Maria 3755
Kortz, John 5029
Kronk, Susan 1553
Kyes, Jane 9739
Lacy, Charles 5039
Lacy, Eliza 2605
Ladd, Hester (Mrs.) 9926
Ladew, Stephen 5045
La Farge ___ (Mr.) 9609
Lagrange, James 7743
Lagrange, Susan 7743
Laight, Maria 2389
Laird, Polly 8019
Lake, Harriet 2705
Lake, Henry, Jr. 5054
Lake, Margaret 5182
Lake, Patty 4045
Lake, Sally Ann 4408
Lamb, Anthony 5059
Lamb, Eliza 2586
Lamb, Emeline F. 120
Lambert, George 1963
Lambert, Lucy Ann 1963
Lamora, Caroline 8307
Lamoree, Hannah 6442
Lamoree, Phebe 177
Lamoree, Timothy 177
Lamport, Harriette R. 3680
Lamson, Amanda 9223
Lanard, Ruth 3637
Landon, Daniel (Capt.) 5067
Landon, Gardner 5070
Lane, Angelina R. D. 5474
Lane, Derick (Col.) 5079
Lane, Derrick 5474
Lane, John 5077
Lane, Sarah 59
Lang, Eliza 7566
Lang, John 3914
Langworthy, ___ (Mr.) 129
Lansing, ___ (Miss) 9611
Lansing, ___ (Mr.) 3177, 6528
Lansing, Abraham G. 5967
Lansing, Anna 5967
Lansing, Catharine 8836
Lansing, Cornelius 142, 8836
Lansing, Eliza 142
Lansing, Elizabeth 64
Lansing, Frances 8425
Lansing, Garrett P. 2407
Lansing, Gerrit Y. 5094
Lansing, Jacob J. 5090
Lansing, John 9611
Lansing, John, Jr. 8425
Lansing, Maria 9948
Lansing, Peter 5090
Lansing, Polly 7965
Lansing, Richard 64
Lansing, Sally Maria 2407
Lansing, Sanders 5095
Lapham, Harriet 5902
Lapham, Hannah 3752
Lapham, Malinda 1361
Lapham, Solon 1361
Lapish, Abigail 7129
Larow, Ellen 8108
Larrabee, Pamela 7759
Larretti, Joseph 5105
Lasell, Ann 7771
Lasell, Lydia 3335
Lathrop, Charles 3808
Lathrop, Fanny Leffingwell 3808

Lathrop, Lucy 4372
Lathrop, Mary P. 2447
Lattin, Benjamin, Jr. 5115
Lattin, Betsey 5687
Lattin, Deborah 9973
Lattin, Nathaniel 5687
Lattin, Sally 2690
Latting, Phebe 8535
Law, Jane Ann 558
Lawless, Sarah 1038
Lawrence, Ann 7349
Lawrence, Betsey 3348
Lawrence, Bigelow 304. 305
Lawrence, David 5124
Lawrence, Diana 304
Lawrence, Eliza A. 5696
Lawrence, Maria Louisa 1035
Lawrence, Richard 9570
Lawrence, Robert 5696
Lawrence, Sally 9570
Lawrence, Stephen 5126
Lawrence, Thomas 1035
Lawson, Benjamin 4522
Lawson, Catharine Amelia 7677
Lawson, James 5136
Lawson, Maria 4522, 5137
Lawson, Sarah 4661
Lawson, Sarah Ellen 1102
Lawton, William 5139
Lawyer, John 5143
Lax, Isabella A. Grand 9552
Lax, Thomas 9552
Lay, ___ (Dr.) 2208
Lay, ___ John 328
Lay, Juliet 328
Leach, Elvira 9225
Leake, John W. 5149
Learned, ___ (Col.) 3365
Leavenworth, Jennet 9044
Leavenworth, William 9414
Le Bar, ___ (Miss) 210
Lee, ___ (Judge) 9254
Lee, Ann 9254
Lee, Catherine 7941
Lee, Chauncey 5165
Lee, Daniel 2644
Lee, Elias 5164
Lee, Eliza 482
Lee, Eliza Ann 4374
Lee, Francis 1693
Lee, Harriet E. 3615
Lee, Henry (Gen.) 5158
Lee, Jane 1795
Lee, Laura Ann 8$07
Lee, Mary 1693, 2978
Lee, Nancy 2644
Lee, Samuel 2978, 5157, 7983
Lee, Sarah 5178
Lee, Sarah Ann 7983
Lee, Sarah B. 2373
Lee, Thomas 5169
Leech, Mary Ann 1055
Leek, Lucretia 9183
Leeland, Lewis 6792
Leeland, Sophronia 6792
Leet, Clarinda 1352
Leet, Frances M. 3512
Leet, Martin 3512
Leffingwell, Christopher 9716, 9718
Leffingwell, Fanny 9718
Leggett, Sarah 4565
Leighton, Caroline 8870
Lennington, Hannah 9618
Lent, ___ (Mr.) 896
Lent, Abigail 8927
Lent, James 5185
Leonard, Daniel 5190
Leonard, Elizabeth C. 4889

336

Leonard, Harriet M. 6379
Leonard, Mary 9367
Leonard, Sarah 5206
Leonard, Timothy 4277
Leonard, Wesley 5190
Leroy, Amelia 1412
Le Roy, Benjamin 5193
Le Roy, Caroline 9532
Le Roy, Cornelia 5396
Le Roy, E. A. (Mr.) 5200
Le Roy, Herman 9532
Le Roy, Jacob 5199, 5396
Leroy, Mary Ann 3662
Leroy, Sally 9046
Leskin, Catharine 5562
Leslie, John 5202
Lester, Eliza 9695
Lester, Eliza Jane 1488
Lester, Laner 4753
Levans, Harriet 5777
Lewis, Amanda 451
Lewis, Ann 9765
Lewis, Billie Redding 7129
Lewis, D. W. (Mr.) 3700
Lewis, Dorothy 5988
Lewis, Elisha 5221
Lewis, Eliza 7645
Lewis, Elizabeth P. 8215
Lewis, Enoch 6226
Lewis, Hannah 8680
Lewis, Isaac 5071
Lewis, John 5210
Lewis, Jonathan 5226
Lewis, Lathrop 8215
Lewis, Leonard 5222
Lewis, Louise C. 6753
Lewis, Luke 6753
Lewis, Margaret 5323
Lewis, Maria 6226
Lewis, Mary 8209
Lewis, Mary (Mrs.) 8541
Lewis, Matilda 3186
Lewis, Nancy 8144
Lewis, Sabin 5212
Lewis, Sophia Matilda 2806
Lewis, Susan 9179
Lewis, Z. (Mr.) 2806
Lieber, ___ (Mr.) 1407
Lightbody, Sally 6946
Lightbourn. Joseph G. 5232
Likes, Gitty 3867
Lillie, Helen B. 9699
Lillie, James 9699
Lincoln, Lucy 10095
Lindley, Eliza Byrom 8557
Lindsey, Charles 5239
Lindsey, Isaac 5239
Linsenbigler, Elizabeth 2785
Lintner, George A. 5247
Linton, Elnora 9514
Lippet, Louden 5249
Liswell, Ann Maria 9091
Liswell, John 9091
Little, Betsy R. 500
Livingston, ___ (Gov.) 4663
Livingston, ___ (Mr.) 788
Livingston, ___ (Rev.) 5318
Livingston, ___ (Rev. Dr.) 9100
Livingston, Adele Caroline 7552
Livingston, Alfred 5259
Livingston, Ann 488
Livingston, Anne 5261
Livingston, Brockholst 5260, 5265
Livingston, Caroline 6431
Livingston, Catharine 6481, 6993
Livingston, Catharine Ann 2412
Livingston, Catherine 5764

Livingston, Caty 1034
Livingston, Chancellor 5274, 5294, 5304, 5313
Livingston, Cornelia 2523
Livingston, Edward P. 5274
Livingston, Eliza McEvers 6470
Livingston, Elizabeth 988, 4438
Livingston, Francis A. 5270, 5275
Livingston, G. W. (Mr.) 5293
Livingston, Gilbert 5267
Livingston, Gilbert R. 1917, 5297, 8082
Livingston, Gitty 2222
Livingston, Helen Maria 8082
Livingston, Henry 5280, 5285, 8636
Livingston, Henry, Jr. 1034
Livingston, Henry A. 3251, 4218, 5296, 5316, 5319
Livingston, Henry Gilbert 507
Livingston, Henry W. 5261
Livingston, J. H. (Rev.) 9082
Livingston, James 3815, 5305, 5306
Livingston, James S. 5271
Livingston, Jane P. 8636
Livingston, Joanna 5308
Livingston, Joel 5258
Livingston, John 5282, 9505
Livingston, John R. 2126, 2127, 6470
Livingston, John S. 7366
Livingston, John W. 2412, 7552
Livingston,Julia A. S. 4696
Livingston, L. H. (Mr.) 5293
Livingston, Levina 2127
Livingston, Louisa Matilda 4644, 4645
Livingston, Margaret 2113, 5313, 9088
Livingston, Maria 3815, 5258
Livingston, Mary 2124, 9883
Livingston, Mary I. Wilson 2112
Livingston, Matilda 7366
Livingston, Moncrief 5289, 5300, 6431
Livingston, Peter 5301
Livingston, Peter R. 2112, 5281, 5294, 9883
Livinston, Philip H. 5322
Livingston, Robert G. 5264, 5303, 6993, 9088
Livingston, Robert H. 5321
Livingston, Robert L. 5304
Livingston, Robert N. 988
Livingston, Robert R. 5308
Livingston, Robert S. 4696
Livingston, Robert T. 2124, 5302
Livingston, Serena 2126
Livingston, Susan Maria 1917
Livingston, Walter 2222, 5313
Livingston, Walter T. 2113
Livingston, William Smith 5266
Lloyd, James 5329
Lloyd, Joseph 5327
Lobdell, ___ (Mr.) 3311
Locherty, William 5331
Lock, Fanny 7378
Lockwood, ___ (Mrs.) 5770
Lockwood, ___ (Mr.) 481
Lockwood, Edwin 3002
Lockwood, Edy Maria 6486
Lockwood, Eliza 4288

Lockwood, Ezekiel 5334, 5339
Lockwood, Jane Ann 6565
Lockwood, Millington 5335
Lockwood, Polly Maria 7582
Lockwood, Sarah 6903
Lockwood, Walter 5337
Lockyear, Mary Ann 1764
Logan, Abigail 6348
Lohnes, Eliza 7540
Loire, Clarissa 5170
Lomarce, Isaac 6211
Longwall, Sally 8827
Loomis, Aurelia T. 8835
Loomis, Charlotte 4123
Loomis, Fidelia 3508
Loomis, Gamaliel 3508
Loomis, George 5345
Loomis, George J. 5345
Loomis, Israel 8330
Loomis, Juliaet 6021
Loomis, Libbeus 5349
Loomis, Luther 6655
Loomis, Malina 3292
Loomis, Maria 7868
Loomis, Mary 6655
Loomis, Matilda 6630
Loomis, Mercy 8330
Loomis, Sarina A. 1665
Loomis, Thaddeus 3292
Loop, Anna 1378
Loop La Fayette (Miss) 964
Lord, ___ (Maj.) 85
Lord, Harriet 8893
Lord, Louisa 1341
Lord, Nancy 85
Lorillard, Jane 9177
Losee, Ann 715
Losee, Carmella 2083
Losee, Clarissa 1392
Lossing, Catharine 3272
Lossing, Parloina 4378
Lothrop, John H. 4976, 9628
Lothrop, Mary A. 9628
Loucks, Elizabeth 7396
Loucks, Henry 7396
Louw, Cornelius 4650
Louw, Maria 4650
Lovake, Olive 1857
Lovell, Frances 6583
Lovett, Jane 5127
Low, Adriannah 2435
Low, Cornelia 6208
Low, David 5373, 5375
Low, Dorcas 6383
Low, Hannah 5643
Low, Hannah Maria 8885
Low, Henrietta 4934
Low, Jane 3632
Low, Jane Maria 2838
Low, John A. 2435, 3632
Low, Maria 2077
Low, Rebecca 3555
Low, Sally 2408
Low, Sarah 4360
Low, Thankful 522
Lowe, Nicholas 5381
Lowndes, Rebecca Motte 7508
Lowndes, William 7508
Lowry, Heman 7903, 7909
Lowry, Julia 7903, 7909
Lucas, Isaac 4879
Lucas, Joseph 7708
Lucas, Julia A. 4879
Lucas, Lyda Maria 7708
Luce, Arteminea 5022
Luce, Hannah 8837
Luce, Uriah 4762, 5022
Luckey, Catharine 7088
Luckey, Jane 2365

Luckey, Rachel 2656
Ludlow, Cornelius 5395
Ludlow, Frances Elizabeth 1174
Ludlow, Maria 5111
Ludlow, Robert 1174
Ludlow, William B. 5394
Ludlum, Julia Frances 3959
Luff, ___ (Mr.) 6412
Lummis, Elizabeth E. 2834
Lummis, William N. 2834
Lundy, ___ (Mr.) 9345
Lush, Mary 1002
Lush, Stephen 1002, 4646
Lusk, Chester 5404
Lusk, Mary A. 346
Lusk, William 346
Luther, Caleb 5408, 5409
Luther, Walworth 5409
Luyster, Arietta Maria 2914
Lyle, Anna Maria 7400
Lyle, Catharine 7836
Lyle, Henry 5416, 7400, 7836
Lyle, Jacob 7836
Lyman, ___ (Rev.) 6998
Lyman, Abby J. 7574
Lyman, Jane 4305
Lyman, Joseph 5421
Lyman, Theodore 7574
Lyman, William 5419
Lynch, James H. 6090
Lynch, Sarah 6090
Lynde, Charles W. 5427, 5430
Lynde, Charlotte 1513
Lynde, John 5428, 5430, 5431
Lynde, Jonathan 1513
Lyon, Joseph 5441
Lyon, Julia Ann 4110
Lyon, Tamer 7546
Lyon, Z. (Mr.) 5435
Lyons, Samuel 5442
McArthur, Euphemia 714
McArthur, John 714
McAuley, Alathea 6463
McBain, ___ (Mr.) 6471
McBride, Polly 4063
McCabe, ___ (Rev.) 9372
McCabe, Margaret 2726
McCall, Daniel 5450
McCammon, Elizabeth 2894
McCammon, John 2894
McCartar, Catharine 2440
McCarter, Laura 6527
McCArty, Harriet E. 5646
McCavy, Catharine 6155
McChesney, Eliza 5455
McChesney, Eve 17
McChesney, Rachel 754
McChesney, Sarah 6066
McClellan, Mary 1270
McClellan, Sarah M. 4281
McClelland, Mary 2766
McClenahan, John 5807
McClure, Eleanor 8813
McClure, George 8813
McClure, William 5461
McCluspsy, Catharine 4590
McCollum, Elizabeth 5462
McCollum, Randal 5462
McComb, Ann 9878
McCombs, R. (Capt.) 5464
McConnell, Isaac 9622
McConnell, Mary Ann 9622
McCord, David C. 5466
McCord, Jane 9289
McCord, William I. 5467
McCoun, John 5473
McCoun, Maria 7632
McCoy, Ellen 7475
McCoy, John Bryan 5477

McCrachan, John 5478
McCradle, Eliza 570
McCready, Jane 2574
McCreedy, Charles M. 5485
McCreedy, James 5481
McCreedy, Jeremiah 5480
McCreedy, Phebe 7982
McCreedy, Silvia 5483
McCreedy, Thomas 5483, 7982
McCullom, June 5507
McCumber, Solomon 5487
McDermid, Eleanor 8143
McDonald, C. (Mr.) 5495
McDonald, D. (Rev.) 5491
McDonald, Eliza 7189
McDonald, Elizabeth 3034
McDonald, James D. 7697, 9677
McDonald, Jane Maria 1679
McDonald, Margery 5581
McDonald, Sicily (Miss) 4080
McDonald, William 1679
McDonough, Thomas 5501
McDowell, A. (Mr.) 5504
McDowell, James R. A. 5501
McFaden, George 5508
McFarland, Ann 584
McFarland, Sally 3024
McFarlane, Eliza H. 4077
McFarlane, Robert 5512
McForhn, Daniel 5729
McForhn, Sally 5729
McGill, Esther Salem 29
McGlashan, Alexander O. 5514
McGlashan, D. 9869
McGlashan, Daniel 5519
McGlashan, James 5514
McGlashin, ___ (Capt.) 3864
McHarg, Alexander 3774
McHenry, Daniel 5522
McIntosh, Jenney 5857
McIntosh, William 5857
McIntyre, Almyra 8666
McIntyre, Archibald 5570
McIntyre, Caroline 5570
McIntyre, Eliza 5491
McJimsey, ___ (Mr.) 4615
McKane, Jane Jesse 6099
McKay, Miranda 5865
McKeen, Joseph 2963
McKeen, Levi 4180, 5529
McKelvey, Cornelius 5532
McKenny, John 5535
McKildo, Lydia 10014
McKinnen, Sarah W. 1031
McKinney, Julia 6952
McKinstry, Caroline 7419
McKinstry, Charles 9712
McKinstry, J., Jr. 5545
McKinstry, John 5546
McKinstry, Nancy 9712
McKlusky, Sally 10071
McKnight, Eleanor 1027
McKnight, John 1027
McKown, William 5553
McLaughlin, Margaret H. 4648
McLean, Jane Ann 517
McLean, John 5557
McLean, John C. 5558
McLean, Rachel 8563
McLean, Sarah 7764
McLean, William 5556
McLeod, Donald 5559, 5560
McLeod, Duncan 5559
McManus, Barbary 8788
McManus, Brittania 7805
McMartin, ___ (Hon.) 5562
McMaster, Truman J. 5564
McMurray, William (Rev.) 7597
McNab, Eliza 7299

McNamee, James 1675
McNamee, Lawrence 5569
McNames, Anna 6760
McNary, Mary Ann 5939
McNeal, Elizabeth W. 9907
McNeal, William 9907
McNeil, Joseph 6122
McNeil, Mary ann 9640
McNeil, Mary Matilda 6122
McNew, Susan 7354
McNiel, Anna Matilda 9670
McNiel, Daniel 9670
McNitt, ___ (Capt.) 2219
McQueen, Martha 3020
McRobie, Margaret 6606
McTavish, Margaret 6608
McVean, Charles 5577
McVickar, John 5579
Mabbett, L. (Mr.) 5583
Macey, William R. 5584
Mack, Electa 1838
Mack, Stephen 1477
Mackay, Elizabeth 2259
Macklem, Hannah 6200
Mackoll, Margaret 1289
Mackwis, Chloe Pi 4207
Macnider, Charlotte 5420
Macnider, John 5420
Macomb, ___ (Maj. Gen.) 5592, 5593
Macomb, Eliza 7422
Macomb, John N. 7422
Macomb, Robert 5594
Macrea, ___ (Col.) 5600
Macrea, Mary 5600
Macumber, Susan H. 615
Macy, Sally 7960
Madough, Betty 411
Magee, Hannah 9511
Magee, Henry 5522
Magee, Jane 6148
Magennis, Jane F. 5211
Magou, Mary E. 5399
Mahar, Nancy 6754
Main, ___ (Rev. Dr.) 5832
Main, Constant 5832
Maison, Caroline 2696
Maison, Elizabeth 9268
Maison, Jane Ann 7738
Maison, Peter R. 5411, 7738, 9268
Malcolm, ___ (Dr.) 5604
Malcolm, Angelica 5604
Malcolm, Ann B. 3843
Malcolm, Charles, Jr. 5607
Malcolm, D. (Mr.) 6397
Malcolm, Henry 5602, 5605
Malcom, D. H. (Mrs.) 4253
Malcomb, Maria 8303
Malcomb, Sarah L. 4791
Mallery, Samuel 5609
Mallery, William 5611
Mallery, Henrietta Maria 5495
Man, Albon 6554
Man, DElia 6554
Manchester, Thomas 5620
Mancius, Catherine 6191
Mancius, Jacob 1135
Mandell, Ephraim 442
Mandell, Polly 442
Manley, Anne 2332
Manly, Ann 3248
Mann, Amanda 9353
Mann, Eliza 7865, 8315
Mann, Hannah 5638
Mann, Jeremiah 5630
Mann, Maria 3816
Mann, Sarah I. 1328
Manney, Catharine 6311

338

Manney, Elida 2461
Manney, Eliza 2153
Manney, John 5641
Manney, Winans 5644
Manning, Caleb 5651
Manning, Caleb, Jr. 5651
Manning, Catharine 5307
Manning, Charles 5655
Manning, James 5307
Manning , James 6501
Manning, John 5654
Manning, Margaret Ann 9741
Manning, Maria 2710
Manning, Martha 8779
Manning, Ruth 7338
Manning, Sarah Ann 4224
Manny, Rhoda 2878
Mansfield, ___ (Col.) 5661
Mansfield, Margaret Eliza 5368
Mansfield, Samuel 5368
Manson, Nathan 5662
Maps, Jerusha 3007
Marble, Deborah 7693
Marbury, Ellen 1508
Marbury, William 1508
Marcaud, Esther 3166
Marcy, William L. 4880, 5667
Margeson, Hannah 4518
Marney, Maria Ellen 9365
Marquart, Hannah 7337
Marriot, Margaret 6107
Marselis, Angelica Matilda 7518
Marselus, Betsey 9970
Marsh, ___ (Mr.) 4729
Marsh, Catharine 8161
Marsh, Clarissa 2740
Marsh, George P. 5679
Marsh, Joseph C. 149, 9577
Marsh, Lydia 149
Marsh, Sabre 9577
Marsh, Susan Elizabeth 837
Marshall, ___ (Mr.) 2122
Marshall, Anthony 3404
Marshall, Catharine 3404, 3830
Marshall, Elathon 5686
Marshall, Eleanor 9956
Marshall, Elsey V. 8614
Marshall, George C. 5690
Marshall, Hannah 5242
Marshall, James 3850, 5242, 8614
Marshall, John I. 6371
Marshall, Mary 5103, 5690
Marshall, Nancy 10103
Marshall, Pamela 6371
Marshall, Paul 5699, 5704
Marshall, Phebe 4468
Marshall, Susan 4403
Marshall, Thankful 456
Marther, Lois P. 7104
Martin, Abraham 8911
Martin, Alida 7125
Martin, Andrew 5712
Martin, Betsey 9994
Martin, Edward W. 5711
Martin, ElizabetH 2941
Martin, Helena 8911
Martin, Mary 2348
Martin, Sarah 3620, 5657
Martin, Winne 9834
Martindale, Prudence 9603
Martindale, Rhoda 9764, 9900
Martling, Catharine 5048
Martling, Phebe 4298
Marvin, ___ 3642
Marvin, Abraham 5732
Marvin, David 5730

Marvin, Jonathan D. 5727
Marvin, Laura 3576
Marvin, Polly 7839
Masi, Caroline A. 9357
Masi, Francis 9357
Mason, ___ (Judge) 5708
Mason, Aaron 5736
Mason, Adaline F. 4416
Mason, C. (Rev.) 6396
Mason, Chloe 5736
Mason, Eliza 5708
Mason, John 5736
Mason, Julia 6396
Mason, Lydia 5736
Mason, Milton S. 5735
Masoneau, Catharine 5748
Masters, Catharine 8454
Mastin, Sarah 7623
Mather, Bethel 5759
Mather, Elizabeth H. 9422
Mather, Fanny 937
Mather, James O. 5758
Mather, Samuel 9422
Mather, William 5762
Mathewson, Bernard 6748
Mathewson, Mary F. 6748
Matholf, James 3002
Matholf, Sary Ann 5333
Matholf, Susan 3002
Matteson, David 7296
Matteson, Nancy 1229
Matteson, Sina (Miss) 7296
Matthews, Julia 6884
Matthews, Mary 9911
Matthews, Mary 5774
Matthews, V. (Gen.) 6884
Maunsell, John 5778
Maverick, Emily 8365
Maverick, Peter 8365
Maverick, Rebecca Martha 3911
Maverick, Samuel 3911
Maxfield, Sally 2176
Maxim, Trena 2601
Maxon, Sally 4587
Maxon, Susan 8626
Maxwell, ___ (Mrs.) 1404
Maxwell, Armenia 124
May, Almyra 4996
May, E. (Col.) 4996
Mayer, Mary M. 7044
Mayo, Adeline 10012
Mayo, Hannah 8620
Meacham, Horace 2302
Meacham, Mary Ann 2302
Mead, Adeline 4342
Mead, Electa 7999
Mead, Eliza Ann 9555
Mead, George 5793, 5795, 5801
Mead, Maria 5793, 5795, 5801
Mead, Nancy 703
Mead, Polly 7962
Mead, Rhoda 2349
Mead, Thaddeus 5792
Meadon, Mary ann 1772
Meddaugh, Helen Elmira 2680
Meddle, Mary 9187
Meed, Solomon 2530
Meeker, John 7899
Meeker, Theodosia S. 7899
Melhealm, Caty 8845
Melius, Rufus 5816
Mell, Mary 8446
Melona, David A. 5819
Meloney, Catharine 4331
Membert, Nancy 2385
Mercin, Mary Araminta 8440
Mercein, Thomas R. 8440
Mercellus, Mariah 4005

Mercer, Patience 2056
Merchant, Mary 1873, 5186
Meredith, J. 4400
Meredith, Louisa 4400
Merkel, Anna 7234
Merkel, Eliza 2615
Merkel, George 2615
Merrifield, Jane C. 5962
Merrill, ___ (Mr.) 3916
Merrill, Caroline 2164
Merrill, Flavia 2943
Merrill, Nathaniel 2164
Merriman, Caroline M. 5760
Merriss, Mary 5776
Merritt, Angelina 1475
Merritt, Anna B. 6814
Merritt, Elizabeth 3253
Merritt, Truelove 9750
Merritt, William 9750
Merwin, A. (Col.) 9792
Merwin, Harriet 9792
Mesick, Elizabeth 8756
Mesick, Harriet 4059
Mesick, Henry I. 5841
Mesick, Peter H. 5840
Mesier, Margaret 7156
Mesier, Matthew 5845, 5846, 7156
Mesier, Peter 5846
Messeter, Richard 5847
Metcalf, ___ (Judge) 8739
Metcalf, Arunah (Mr.) 2205, 2208
Metcalf, Catherine 8316
Metcalf, Elijah H. 8316
Metcalf, Eunice 9668
Metcalf, Marietta 9809
Metcalf, Mary 2205, 8739
Metcalf, Roger 5851
Metcalf, Tracy 9826
Meyen, Otilla 4942
Meyer, Mary A. 9351
Middlebrook, Hezekiah, Jr. 5859
Middleton, Sally 6734
Mider, Martha 2732
Miles, ___ (Mrs.) 3912
Miles, B. (Maj.) 5861
Miles, Caroline Mary 7230
Miles, I. F. (Capt.) 7230
Millard, Fanny 6450
Milledoler, Philip 5868
Millee, Elizabeth 5870
Millee, Thomas 5870
Miller, Abbey 8693
Miller, Alida 9345
Miller, Almira 6881
Miller, Amanda Louisa 6063
Miller, Burnet 5892
Miller, Catharine 742, 2483, 7026
Miller, Catharine P. 8202
Miller, Conklin 5891
Miller, Eleazer 5336
Miller, Frederick T. 5894
Miller, Hannah 3921
Miller, Henrietta Maria 10112
Miller, J. (Gen.) 5899
Miller, Jeremiah, Jr. 5899
Miller, John 5893, 5971, 6881, 8202
Miller, John C. 10112
Miller, John J. 742
Miller, John S. 5973
Miller, Lucretia 5873
Miller, Lucy 5973
Miller, Margaret Lucretia 5336
Miller, Margaret P. 5971

Miller, Maria 5471
Miller, Mary Ann 2406, 4764
Miller, Melissa 7249
Miller, Peggy 3409
Miller, Phebe 6032
Miller, Robert 7249
Miller, Samuel 7026
Miller, Sarah 9042
Miller, Tina 3169
Miller, William 6063
Millin, Betsey 4859
Mills, Bradley 5914
Mills, Chauncey 5918
Mills, Eliza Julia Ann 2004
Mills, Elizabeth S. 77792
Mills, John 2004, 7792
Mills, Mary 2959
Mills, Mary Ann Julia 2008
Mills, Peggy 9578
Mills, Perses 8925
Mills, Roger 5919
Mills, Sibbe Ann 6197
Mills, Stephen 5913
Mills, Susan 863
Milton, John 7865
Minor, John (Rev.) 7690
Minuse, George 6343
Minuse, Mary B. 6343
Mitchel, Mary 5995
Mitchell, ___ (Judge) 5933
Mitchell, Charles 4130
Mitchell, Maria T. 4130
Mitchell, Mary 8897
Mitchell, Catharine Mary
  Adaline 7473
Mitchell, Minott 579
Mitchell, Stephen 4307, 7473
Mitchell, Susan S. 4307
Mitchell, Thomas 5935
Mitchell, Uriah 5943
Miter, Sarah 5867
Mix, James 5945
Mix, Julia Ann 5250
Mix, Rufus 5946
Moderwell, Charlotte H. 8092
Moncrief, ___ (Maj.) 5276
Monell, ___ (Dr.) 6545
Monell, Catharine 7070
Monell, James 750
Monell, Jenett 750
Monell, Jennet 6545
Monell, Joseph D. 5954
Monell, Robert 5953, 7070
Monfoort, Jane 5956
Monfort, Susan 7723
Monk, Christopher 4043
Monk, Eliza 4043
Monro, N. (Mr.) 5760
Monroe, James (Pres.) 3530
Monroe, Maria Hester 3530
Montross, Elizabeth 1053
Monteith, Walter 5966
Moeller, Henry 5890
Moody, Clarissa 10074
Mooers, ___ (Dr.) 4788
Mooers, ___ (Gen.) 7908
Mooers, A. (Miss) 3456
Mooers, Benjamin 3456, 5973,
  5984, 7906
Mooers, Benjamin J. 5976
Mooers, Charlotte 5984
Mooers, Hannah 6851
Mooers, Phebe Maria 7908
Mooers, Polly 4006
Moon, John 5978
Mooney, Mary Jane 7461
Moor, Charlott 1644
Moor, Joel F. 321
Moor, Susannah 321

Moore, ___ (Judge) 1068
Moore, ___ (Miss) 6586
Moore, ___ (Mr.) 6548
Moore, Ann 10011
Moore, Anna Maria 3938
Moore, Benjamin 3938, 8737
Moore, C. (Mr.) 5985
Moore, Dana 5989
Moore, Elizabeth H. 8036
Moore, Hannah 4191
Moore, Hetty Eliza 8737
Moore, Isaac 5996
Moore, Jacob 5997, 6002
Moore, Jonathan 5982
Moore, Joshua 5998
Moore, Julia 2675
Moroe, Malissa 7464
Moore, Matilda L. 1068
Moore, Mary 6276
Moore, Olive 723
Moore, Sally 1427
Moore, Samuel 10011
Moore, William 2675
Moore, William H. 8036
Moores, ___ (Maj. Gen.) 6004
Moores, Reuben 6006
More, Peleg 3871
Moreau, Louis de Lassy 5272
Moreau, Marie Louisa Valentine
  5272
Morey, Margaret 5722
Morey, Mary 2909
Morey, Sarah Matilda 6836
Morgan, ___ (Mr.) 7971, 9949
Morgan, Adeline 2964
Morgan, Celia 8470
Morgan, Celia M. 3611
Morgan, Elias 1812
Morgan, Elijah 4065
Morgan, Fanny 2715
Morgan, Harriet Eliza 1867
Morgan, Jonas 6037
Morgan, Joseph 6038
Morgan, Lavina Ann 4065
Morgan, Lucinda 3908
Moogan, Mary 6238
Morgan, Mary Ann 1812
Morgan, Mercy 4211
Morgan, Peter B. 1867
Morgan, Sarah 7228
Morgan, Sarah M. 1372
Morgan, William 3908
Morison, Hannah 5617
Morrell, Sarah E. 8602
Morris, ___ (Gen.) 1988
Morris, ___ (Mr.) 5680
Morris, Abigail A. 4107
Morris, Anna (Mrs.) 848
Morris, Catharine C. 6974
Morris, Edmund 6052
Morris, Frances S. 1125
Morris, George Jacob 6059
Morris, Governeur 5290
Morris, Jacob 6974
Morris, James 6061
Morris, Julia 1383
Morris, Lewis 6059
Morris, Mary 5659
Morris, Mary Ann 1990
Morris, Robert 3959
Morris, Staats 7288
Morris, Walter R. 6053
Morrison, Adaline 5628
Morrison, Malcom 57
Morrison, Susan 57
Morse, Alexander 6072
Morse, Ann Eliza 2764
Morse, Benjamin 6079
Morse, Cornelia 1699

Morse, Daniel 6078
Morse, Thomas 6076
Morse, Timothy 6077
Morse, William 2764
Morton, ___ (Mr.) 9380
Morton, Ann D. 4519
Morton, Elihu 4519
Morton, Mary Regina 8416
Morton, Michael 2603
Morton, Perez 2509
Morton, Seth 6080, 6081, 6083,
  6085, 6086, 6088
Morton, Washington 8416
Moseley, Eliza 6051
Moseley, Elizur 6051
Mosely, Charlotte 3059
Mosely, Frances 8270
Mosely, Gordon 6094, 8270
Moses, ___ (Capt.) 1047
Mosher, Amos 8853
Mosher, Anna 8853
Mosher, Eliza 1057
Mosher, Isaac 1057
Mosher, Mary 9950
Mosher, Ruth 8126
Mosier, Hannah 4720
Moss, Adaline 4195
Moss, Hesiah 5081
Moss, J. (Rev.) 4195
Mott, Abigail 4202
Mott, Adrianna 5371
Mott, Elizabeth B. 1044
Mott, Jeremiah 6116
Mott, John 4202
Mott, John Joslin 6109
Mott, Maria 1913
Mott, Samuel 1044
Mott, Susan 158
Moulton, Abigail 3677
Moulton, Betsey 2442
Moulton, Frances E. 2629
Moulton, H. (Mr.) 2629
Moulton, Polly 9887
Mowry, Susanna 10031
Moyer, Helen Eliza 5942
Moyer, John Henry 5942
Mudge, ___ (Mr.) 938
Mudge, Armenia 7356
Muhlenburgh, ___ (Mr.) 7611
Muir, Ephraim 6125
Mulford, Almira 3813
Mullany, ___ (Mr.) 2124
Mulliner, Polly 1386
Mulliner, Susan 1547
Mumford, John P. 842
Mumson, Eliza 4162
Muncil, Daniel 6135
Myncil, Eliakim S., Jr. 6135
Muncil, Hannah 6135
Muncil, Lucy 6135
Muneely, Eleanor 4193
Muney, Polley 6761
Munger, ___ (Mrs.) 4926
Munger, Cynthia 2635
Munn, Benjamin 5796
Munn, Catharine 5796
Munn, Emeline 7095
Munn, Joseph 6137
Munn, Mary Augusta 5224
Munn, Sarah T. 2026
Munn, Stephen 2026
Munro, Harriet 6050
Munro, Peter J. 6050
Munsey, Eliza 5928
Murdock, Lucerne 9642
Murdock, Samuel 2319
Murfey, Maria 300
Murgatroyd, Cornelius 5639
Murgatroyd, Eliza 5639

340

Murphy, Ira 6143
Murphy, R. W. (Mr.) 6141
Murray, John, Jr. 6713
Murray, Eliza 851
Murray, Maria Wey 2869
Murray, Nancy 5204
Murray, Solomon 6144
Murray, Tanzar 7732
Murray, Thusday 437
Murry, John 6146
Musson, William 6149
Myer, Margaret 9206
Myer, P. T. B. (Mr.) 9206
Myers, Abraham I. 306, 6156
Myers, Catharine 3076
Myers, Helen 2183
Myers, June 6152
Myers, Mary Ann 8396
Myers, Mary R. 7099
Myers, Matthew 7099
Myers, Nathan 6165, 6166,
  6172, 8396
Myers, Phebe 8480
Myers, Sally 7646
Myers, Samuel 3076
Myers, Sarah M. 9338
Myrick, Caroline 83
Myrick, Eliza 3750
Myrick, Frances M. 4136
Myrick, Lucy 241
Myrick, Samuel 241
Nagus, Jane 1586
Naise, John 6178
Nase, Catharine 4812
Nase, Eliza 5924
Nase, John 4812, 5924, 6180,
  7145
Nase, Maria 6852
Nase, Philip 6184
Nase, Rachel 7145
Nase, Susannah 5014
Nase, William 6841, 6852
Nash, Azor 7939
Nash, Daniel 1988, 2005, 6187
Nash, Delia A. 5254
Nash, Martin 5254
Nash, Sally 7939
Nash, Susannah 5014
Nazro, Elizabeth 8089
Neafus, Julia Ann 3900
Neil, Abby B. 4746
Neill, Catharine 4072
Neilson, Lydia 1637
Neilson, Maria 6500
Neilson, William 3533
Nelson, ___ (Mrs.) 2400
Nelson, Dorinda H. 293
Nelson, Eliza 4631
Nelson, Hannah 3647
Nelson, Jane 5163
Nelson, Jane A. 3557
Nelson, William 293
Nesmith, John 6219
Netterville ___ (Mr.) 4043
Nettleton, Rosalinda 9720
Neugent, John 6220
Neuvil, Zilpha 8422
New ?_, Lucinda 4957
New, Sarah 7460
Newberry, Daniel 6221
Newbold, Martha Clementine
  1389
Newby, Robert 8212
Newby, Sarah 8212
Newcomb, Charlotte 4329
Newcomb, Christian 159
Newcomb, Daniel 6224, 6225
Newcomb, Eliza 159

Newcomb, Margaret G. 1900
Newcomb, Mary 6218
Newcomb, Obadiah 6355
Newcomb, Sally 6355
Newcomb, Simon 4260
Newcomb, Thomas 6229
Newcomb, Zaccheus 4329
Newcomb, Zacheus 1900
Newell, Chauncey 6232
Newell, Dolly 5668
Newell, Louisa A. 3183
Newell, Marcy 4880
Newell, Sirajah 6234
Newlin, Thomas S. 2264
Newman, Hanry 3037
Newman, Martha 3037
Newton, Jane Ann 8513
Newton, Percy 8168
Nichols, Caleb 6257
Nichols, Catharine 1929
Nichols, Cornelia 4886
Nichols, Eliza 4422
Nichols, Emily 7476
Nichols, Eunice 5828
Nichols, Mary 6467
Nichols, Philo 6251
Nichols, Robert 6250
Nichols, William 1929
Nicols, Dorothy 6490
Nicols, Perry G. 6267
Niece, Betsey 5838
Niell, William 6269
Niels, Harriet 1815
Niels, Mary Ann 4078
Nile, Martha T. 3162
Niles, Gideon 6275
Niles, H. (Mr.) 6274
Nisburht, Henry 6278
Nixon, James 1804, 6281
Nixson, Elizabeth S. 1141
Nixson, W. E. (Mr.) 1141
Noble, Alnathan 2804
Noble, Cyranus 6284
Noble, Daniel 6285
Noble, Eliza 3863
Noble, Maria 8071
Noble, Mary ann 757
Noble, Prudence 8169
Noble, Sally 2804
Nobles, Lucy 7765
Nobles, Mary 6101
Nobles, Nathaniel 6101
Nodine, Frederick 6290
Noel, Elizabeth 1358
Noel, Joseph 1358
Norcross, Samuel 4727
Noocross, Sarah 4727
Norman, William E. 6297
North, Gabriel 6300
North, Lemuel 6304
North, Mercy 7731
North, Susan 5129
Northrop, Alethea G. 6718
Northrop, Anne 4748
Northrop, Eliza 8297
Northrop, H. S. (Mr.) 6306
Northrop, Harriet A. 669
Northrop, Joel 1345, 7888
Northrop, Laura 2513
Northrop, Samuel 4748
Northrup, Caroline 7255
Northrup, Cornelia Ann 666
Northrup, Delia 5831
Northrup, Enos 6312
Northrup, Louisa 8465
Northrup, William 666, 5831,
  7255
Norton, Ebenezer 8834
Norton, Elizabeth S. 3671

Norton, Gideon 6318
Norton, Harriet 8834
Morton, Heman 3671
Norton, John T. 6324, 6325
Norton, Mary (Mrs.) 8146
Nostrand, ___ (Mr.) 2025
Nott, ___ (Dr.) 6330
Nott, Eliphalet 6901
Nott, Eliza 8761
Nott, Eliza Bruen 1927
Nott, Samuel 1927
Nott, Sarah Maria 6901
Noxon, ___ (Mrs.) 7477
Noxon, Anna (Mrs.) 8159
Noxon, Bartholomew 6335
Noxon, Cynthia 1870
Noxon, Laura Ann 8809
Noxon, Robert 940, 6336
Noyes, Betsey 6821
Noyes, Enos 6339
Noyes, George 4733
Noyes, Nathan 1551
Noyes, Sally 1551
Noyes, Sarah Ann 4733
Noyes, Bernice 7675
Nuby, Isabel 7926
Numam, ___ (Mr.) 7750
Numan, Laura 1491
Numand, Sarah 3200
Nutter, Ann 5288
Nutter, Valentine 5288
Nye, Hannah 3405
Oakey, Eliza 3941
Oakley, Jesse 6349, 6352, 6359,
  9780
Oakley, John W. 3562
Oakley, Mary 3562
Oakley, Morris 6346
Oakley, Patty 876
Oakley, Sarah 6008
Oakley, Thomas 6356
Oakley, Velina 9780
Oathout, Mary 3946
Oatman, Daniel 6786, 8388
Oatman, Esther 6786
Oatman, Mary 8388
Obear, Abigail P. 2589
Obear, Oliver 2589
O'Conner, Mary 6989
Odell, ___ (Maj.) 1139
Odell, Alice 1139
Odell, Julia 9112
Odin, Esther K. 2595
Odin, John 2595
Ogden, Benjamin 2757
Ogden, Eliza Ann 2757
Ogden, Gertrude, Gertrude
  Waddington 3928
Ogden, Polly 4199
Olcott, Ann Maria 9585
Olcott, John E. 6381
Olcott, Josiah 9585
Olcott, Julia W. 8432
Olcott, Lydia 84
Olcott, Phineas 84
Olcott, Sally 9032
Oldiman, Roxy 367@
Olds, Almira 150
Olds, Horace 150
Olendorf, Daniel 6384
Oliphant, Jennet 5814
Oliver, Andrew F. 6391

Oliver, Pamelia 3658
Oliver, Rebecca 753
Oliver, Sally 2175
Oliver, Sarah 9829
Olmstead, Charlotte 6887
Olmstead, Mary 8831

Olmstead, Sylvia 330
Olmsted, Benjamin G. 9431
Olmsted, Halen 6629
Olmsted, Jonas 6629
Olmsted, Nathaniel 331
Olmsted, Sally Maria 9431
Onderdonk, ___ (Mr.) 4293
Onderdonk, Sally 3051
Oothout, Elizabeth 6242
Orendorff, Katharine 3568
Ormsby, Gideon 6404
Orton, Clarissa 465
Orton, Oliver L. 4781
Osborn, Aurelia 9904
Osborn, Caroline 324
Osborn, Daniel 6422
Osborn, Elnathan 499
Osborn, Jacob 6291
Osborn, Jane 5028
Osborn, Lorinda 499
Osborn, Maria 8804
Osborn, Robert 5028
Osborn, William 6416
Osborne, Elias 7543
Osborne, Phoebe 7543
Osburn, Eliza 2597
Osburn Sally 657
Osterhout, Catharine 5352
Ostrander, Catharine 5488
Ostrander, Cornelia 722
Ostrander, John 6434
    ---   ---
Ostrander, John I. 5488
Ostrander, Katherine 9549
Ostrander, Sally 6665
Ostrander, Samuel 6433
Ostrander, William 6426
Ostrom, Catharine 5061
Ostrom, Catherine 6495
Ostrom, Daniel 3441, 8798
Ostrom, Dency 3441
Ostrom, Hannah 6211, 8798
Ostrom, Henry 5061
Ostrom, John H. 2169, 6495
Ostrom, Joshua 6435
Ostrom, Maria 5376, 7143
Ostrom, Mary I. 2170
Ostrom, Pamela 2169
Ostrom, Rebecca 5864
Oswald, Eleazer 6444
Otis, J. A. (Mr.) 3182
Otis, Mabell 544
Otis, Mary Ann 549
Otis, Perez 544
Ottly, Mary 4069
Ottly, William 4069
Overacker, Anna 2598
Overacker, Emanuel 5958
Overacker, Sally 5958
Overlin, Catharine 9180
Overling, Maria 7517
Overrocker, Hannah 3913
Owen, Daniel 6455
Owen, Jane 406
P--poon, Eliza 4681
P--ter, Joseph 6460
P--ter, Mary 6460
Packer, ___ (Mr.) 6972
Paddock, Eliza 5856
Paddock, Isaac 6466
Paddock, Laban 6465, 6469
Paddock, Lydia 4539
Paddock, Nancy 4322
Paddock, Phoebe 6113
Page, Louisa 4905
Page, Maria C. 1169
Page, Sherman 6473
Paige, ___ (Rev.) 8516
Paige, Jason 6476

Paige, Joseph C. 6477
Paige, W. (Rev.) 4619
Pain, ___ (Mrs.) 1703
Pain, John 1703
Paine, Abby 4860
Paine, Amasa 5425, 6194, 9796
Paine, Amasa S. 8119
Paine, Barnabas 733
Paine, Chloe 270
Paine, Eliza 6194
Paine, Frances 8119
Paine, Lucretia 9796
Paine, Mary P. 5425
Painter, Gamaliel 6484
Palen, Eliza 3781
Palen, Matilda 2681
Palen, Peter G. 3781
Palmateer, Almira 6036
Palmer, Ann 2356, 4955
Palmer, Betsey N. 6508
Palmer, Charity 6636
Palmer, David 6506
Palmer, Elias 6503
Palmer, Eliza Maria 6986
Palmer, John 6489, 6511
Palmer, Joshua 6488
Palmer, Lucy 4599
Palmer, Mahala 2320
Palmer, Micha 6518
Palmer, Nancy 3605
Palmer, Patty 7484
Palmer, Thomas 6512
Palmer, Vose 5054
Palmer, William (Rev.) 5791
Parce, Perry 6526
Parck, Polly 2201, 8021
Pardee, Ann E. 2122
Pardee, Fanny 6599
Pardee, Lucy Ann 3645
Pardee, Luther 2122
Pardee, Sally Maria 3648
Pardee, Sarah Ann 3646
Pardee, Sarah H. 7521
Pardee, Stephen 3644, 3645,
   3648
Pardy, Francis 6530
Pardy, Sally Ann 6596
Parin, William 1373
Parker, Anna 4387
Parker, B. (Capt.) 9016
Parker, Catharine Dwight 6139
Parker, D. (Rev.) 8586
Parker, Eliza 9016
Parker, Emeline 960
Psrker, Emeline P. 8586
Parker, I. T. (Mr.) 6548
Parker, Joseph 7472
Parker, Lydia 356
Parker, Mary 7472
Parker, Nancy 8765
Parker, Olive 1667
Parker, Philip S. 6139
Parker, Timothy 4389
Parker, William S. 6540, 6543
Parkinson, Elizabeth 7144
Parkman, Chauncey 6558, 6559,
   6560
Parks, Ann Augusta 1355
Parks, David 545
Parks, Lydia 545
Parks, Richard 6563
Parks, Thomas 6542
Parmalee, Joseph 6564
Parmele, Frances Caroline 1827
Parmelee, ___ (Mr.) 1410, 9098
Parmelee, Catherine 1410
Parmelee, Joseph 1410
Parmely, Cornelia M. 4375
Parmetier, Harriet 5650

Parrot, Betsey 5615
Parsons, Abraham 6579
Parsons, Ann Maria 824, 3759
Parsons, Ansliem 6577
Parsons, Charles 6582
Parsons, Chester 6590
Parsons, Clarissa 8915
Parsons, Frederick 6585
Parsons, Jabez 6573, 6591
Parsons, Jeremiah 4252
Parsons, Julia 4653
Parsons, Mary Sullivan 2534
Parsons, Mehetible 6586
Parsons, Pama (Miss) 6504
Parsons, Phebe 512, 5810
Parsons, Sarah 6969
Parsons, Temperance 4252
Parter, Catharine 7328
Partrick, Lydia 9906
Paterson, Cornelia 9157
Paterson, Matthew 6602
Paterson, William 9157
Patrick, Sophia 8371
Pattengill, Esther 9929
Pattengill, Lemuel 9929
Patterson, Elias 6611
Patterson, Elizabeth 913, 9842
Patterson, Elnathan 6610
Patterson, Harriet 573
Patterson, Jane 8205
Patterson, Polly 7998
Patterson, Robert 6609
Patterson, Susan 5961
Patterson, William 913
Pawling, Margaret 2866
Payne, Lemuel C. 6625
Peak, John 6633
Peale, Anna C. 8236
Peale, James 8236
Pearce, Abby 1530
Pearce, Chloe C. 1325
Pearce, Dutee J. 1530
Pearce, Lucinda 7735
Pearce, Lynn 4402
Pearsall, Sarah 6321
Pearsall, Thomas C. 6321
Pearson, Samuel 6640
Peas, Susannah (Mrs.) 5771
Pease, Almira 2688
Pease, Barzillai 6645, 6646
Pease, Earl P. 6339
Pease, Pamelia 1120
Pease, Sally 2770
Peck, ___ (Judge) 3440
Peck, Clarine 9003
Peck, Elias 6750
Peck, Emeline 3440
Peck, Everard 6650
Peck, Harmanus H. 6649
Peck, Harriet 4560
Peck, Ichabod 6657
Peck, Isabel 3720
Peck, J. 6655
Peck, Maria 484
Peck, Nathaniel 484
Peck, Samuel V. 6656
Peck, Smantia 5863
Peckham, Avis 8812
Peckham, Betsy 283
Peckham, Henrietta L. 1861
Peckham, Mirinda L. 5263
Peckham, Peleg 5263
Peckham, Samuel 8812
Peirce, Lorain 2300
Peirce, Mary P. 8792
Peirce, William 8792
Peirson, Oliver 6668
Pell, A. S. (Mr.) 8472
Pell, Alfred S. 6669

Pellett, Edith Ann 6672
Pells, Abraham 6674, 6676
Pells, Catharine 5692
Pells, Frances Murdock 9817
Pells, Jane 6768
Pells, John A. 3907, 5692
Pells, John E. 8045
Pells, Margaret 3907
Pells, Maria 8045
Pells, Mary 6437
Pells, Zephaniah 6437, 9866
Pelton, Lydia Jane 8222
Pelton, P. (Mr.) 8222
Pendleton, Anna P. 7343
Pendleton, E. H. (Hon.) 6692
Pendleton, Edward H. 6691
Pendleton, Nathaniel 6693, 7343
Penfield, Charlotte 4949
Penfield, D. (Mr.) 4949
Penfield, Daniel 2811
Penfield, Henry F. 6123
Penfield, Millicent 8708
Penniman, Julia 9776
Penniman, Nancy 1957
Penniman, Obadiah 6698
Penniman, S. J. (Mr.) 9776
Penniman, William C. 6696
Pennoyer, Alethea (Mrs.) 1576
Pennoyer, Betsey 37
Pennoyer, John C. 1576
Pennoyer, Jonathan 37
Penny, Adeline 4215
Penny, Julia Ann 8882
Pepperell, ___ (Gen.) 592
Perin, Ira 6709
Perkins, ___ (Mr.) 8416
Perkins, ___ (Rev. Dr.) 7728
Perkins, Catharine 7728
Perkins, Eliza Green 2551
Perkins, Mariam 7166
Perlee, ___ (Gen.) 6723
Perlee, Harriet 7560
Perlee, Walter 7560
Perrot, Caroline 4291
Perrot, John 4291
Perry, Ann 8735
Perry, Betsey 4501
Perry, Charles 8250
Perry, Charles B. 5733
Perry, Eli 6727
Perry, Frances J. 5733
Perry, Julia S. 8250
Perry, Lydia 130
Perry, Mary 4428
Perry, Philena 3173
Perry, Ruth 9051
Peters, David 6732
Peters, Jemima 4284
Peters, John T. 6733
Peters, Sally 643
Peterson, Hannah A. 4810
Pettengill, Amos (Rev.) 6744
Pettice, Eliza 3358
Phelps, ___ (Mr.) 8931
Phelps, Elmira 6706
Phelps, Amanda 4959
Phelps, Caroline 5102
Phelps, Charles S. 1509
Phelps, Darius 2950
Phelps, Electa 6984
Phelps, Elizabeth S. 1509
Phelps, John 6755
Phelps, Joshua 6750
Phelps, Loisa 9756
Phelps, Lucinda 2950
Phelps, Mary 2148
Phelps, R. B. (Mr.) 1509
Phelps, Winthrop 9756

Philbrooks, ___ (Capt.) 4332
Philbrooks, Mary 4332
Philip, Alberta 933
Philips, Betsy 1695
Philips, Catherine 5677
Philips, Cornelia Caroline 4811
Philips, Hannah 7548
Phillips, Adeline 7323
Phillips, Betsey 9104a
Phillips, David 6770
Phillips, Deborah
Phillips, Elijah 6764
Phillips, G. W. (Mr.) 4014
Phillips, Hannah 4226
Phillips, Jane 3910
Phillips, John 6769, 6771
Phillips, Maria 4639, 4968, 7334, 8076
Phillips, Mary Ann 5634
Phillips, Meyry 2641
Phillips, Miranda 4014
Phillips, Susan 4636
Philo, Delia 3629
Phinney, Betsey 3722
Phinney, Jabez 3722
Phinney, Sophia 4936
Pickelle, Eliza 5640
Picket, Laura 8755
Pickett, Eunice 8398
Pier, Abner 246, 6782, 6785 8272
Pier, Clarissa 3966
Pier, Nama 9754
Pier, Thomas 6784
Pierce, Benjamin 4129, 8085
Pierce, Eliza 4129
Pierce, Lucy 8085
Pierce, Marinus 6790
Pierce, Rebecca 3628
Pierce, Samuel 6797
Pierce, William 8274
Pierson, Helen Maria 6802
Pierson, Isaac 6801, 6802
Pike, ___ (Gen.) 8767
Pinckney, Harriet 9440
Pinckney, P. (Dr.) 9440
Pine, ___ (Capt.) 2581
Pine, Amy 3114
Pine, John 6805
Pine, Mary 1606
Pine, Nancy 2133
Pine, Pamelia 865
Pine, Samuel 3114
Pine, Sarah 6921
Pinkham, Hephziba 7980
Pinkney, ___ (Dr.) 6811
Pinney, Lucinda 3616
Pinny, Salome 6588
Pitcher, Ann Maria 2852
Pitcher, Helen C. 7745
Pitcher, John 6813, 7745
Pitkin, Timothy 6325
Place, Sarah 2667
Plant, David 1626
Plant, Lucy M. 1626
Platner, Eliza 6385
Platner, Eva 3570
Platner, Mary 1042
Platt, ___ (Judge) 1069, 6830, 9269
Platt, ___ (Lieut.) 6824
Platt, Abby 4367
Platt, Abigail G. 3563
Platt, Ann T. 3123
Platt, Betsey 3617, 3485
Platt, Catherine 3033
Platt, Charles 3819

Platt, Deborah 627
Platt, E. (Capt.) 6822
Platt, E. (Mr.) 6829
Platt, Eliza C. 8771
Platt, Eliza G. 6474
Platt, Elizabeth 317, 7501
Platt, Elizabeth Phoenix 7371
Platt, Frances 7202
Platt, Harriet E. 1041
Platt, Isaac 3123
Platt, Jane Ann 6423
Platt, Julia A. 5972
Platt, Levi 1428
Platt, Maria 1069, 1401
Platt, Mary L. 1428
Platt, N. Z. (Maj.) 6857, 7501
Platt, Nathaniel 6853
Platt, Nathaniel C. 6847
Platt, Ralph 6474
Platt, Sarah Ann 390
Platt, Stephen J. 1074
Platt, Theodorus 1401, 3607 6823, 6860
Platt, Zephaniah 3485, 6848
Platts, Betsey 8681
Pleas, Amelia 5364
Pleas, Morris 5364
Plue, Catharine 3709
Plumb, ___ (Mr.) 9380
Plumb, Anna Maria 3049
Plumb, David 6861
Plumb, Jared 6862
Plumb, Joseph 6863
Poinier, Eliza Louisa 5637
Polhemus, Sally 2145
Pollard, Moses 6869
Polmantier, Catharine 881
Polter, Mary 381
Pomeroy, Almira M. 9581
Pomeroy, Eliza 4355
Pomeroy, Elizabeth 4621
Pomeroy, George 6872, 10039
Pomeroy, Hannah Cooper 10039
Pomeroy, Lemuel 2490, 4621
Pomeroy, Olivia 2490
Pond, Temperance 2666
Pooley, Phebe 4338
Poor, ___ (Mrs.) 6236
Poor, ___ (Rev.) 6236
Pope, Eliza 6631
Pope, Rebeckah 1088
Pope, Thomas 1088
Popham, ___ (Maj.) 1370
Porter, ___ (Dr.) 2730, 4706
Porter, ___ (Rev.) 3770
Porter, ___ (Rev. Dr.) 4170
Porter, Alanson 7557
Porter, Asahel 6886
Porter, Caroline 8183
Porter, Chauncey 7225
Porter, Elizabeth 8056
Porter, Frederick 5602
Porter, G. W. (Mr.) 8183
Porter, Harriet Caroline 4706
Porter, Hester 5575
Porter, Ira (Mrs.) 6888
Porter, John 6888
Porter, John F. 6892
Porter, Laura 4170, 7557
Porter, Mary Ann 2730
Porter, P. B. (Gen.) 6895
Porter, Peter B. 6894
Porter, Rebecca 2354
Porter, Sally 6966
Porter, Sarah M. 5757
Porter, Sylvia R. 7225
Post, Betsey 5456
Post, Elizabeth 3639

Redding, William 7129
Redington, John 7132
Reed, ___ (Mr.) 4070
Reed, ___ (Rev. Dr.) 821, 7152
Reed, Amy 4952
Reed, Benjamin 6795
Reed, Betsey 741
Reed, Caroline 4991
Reed, Deborah 6795
Reed, Eliza 4033
Reed, Ezra 741, 2527, 7150
Reed, Huldah 2327
Reed, Isaac 7147
Reed, Jane C. E. 2325
Reed, Jesse 4033
Reed, Ketchel 7149
Reed, Rufus 7139
Reeve, Caroline 5614
Reeve, John 1025, 5614
Reeve, Lenchy 1025
Rehern, Rachael 7914
Reid, Minerva 569
Reid, William 569
Reilay, John G. 7164
Relay, Ann 4676
Relay, Lewis 7168
Relyea, Simon 7172
Remington, susan 2432
Remmington, Caroline 5836
Remsen, Edward 7177
Renouf, Anna 7877
Resler, Sarah 2729
Reuwee, Rosilia Mancius 6190
Reynolds, ___ (Miss) 1096
Reynolds, Allen 7183
Reynolds, Charles 7184, 9282
Reynolds, Clara 5780
Reynolds, Eliza 9889
Reynolds, Elizabeth 2920
Reynolds, G. (Mr.) 310
Reynolds, Hannah 3138
Reynolds, Israel 9889
Reynolds, Jacob 7192
Reynolds, James 8117, 9919
Reynolds, Adaline 7451
Reynolds, John F. 3598
Reynolds, Jonathan 1212, 5024
Reynolds, Joshua 2768
Reynolds, Louisa 4605
Reynolds, Marcus T, 7185
Reynolds, Margaret 5100
Reynolds, Maria 310
Reynolds, Mary 8117
Reynolds, Mary (Mrs.) 9282
Reynolds, Phebe 3598
Reynolds, Philip 2920, 5780
Reynolds, Polly 1212, 7487
Reynolds, Reuben 1096
Reynolds, Sally 5024
Reynolds, Sarah 8353
Reynolds, Zadock 1212
Rhea, Juliana 5418
Rhoads, ___ (Mr.) 9546
Rhodes, Julia 2887
Rhodes, Polly T. 922
Rhodes, Rosannah 3593
Rhodes, Sally 7066
Rice, Abigail 4510
Rice, Ann G. 1431
Rice, Anna 4443
Rice, Ebenezer 7204, 7212
Rice, Holden 7209
Rice, Samuel 4510
Richard, Louisa Georgiana 7291
Richard, Stephen 7191
Richards, ___ (Maj.) 7218
Richards, Daniel 7217
Richards, Esther H. 7455

Richards, Fanny W. 9657
Richards, J. (Dr.) 9657
Richards, L. (Mr.) 7221
Richards, Mary Elizabeth 1224
Richards, Rufus 1224
Richardson, Catharine 2084
Richardson, Charles 7232
Richardson, Cordelia 5506
Richardson, J. (Mr.) 5506
Richardson, Maria Ann 7659
Richmond, Betsey 33
Richmond, Eliza 7541
Richmond, Harriet 2980
Richmond, Samuel N. 2980
Richy, Clarissa 1199
Ricket, Catharine 7261
Rider, ___ (Mr.) 3884, 5908, 8226
Rider, Priscilla 7129
Rider, Stephen J. 7244, 7248
Rider, William 7243
Ridley, Matilda 9505
Rigeley, Catharine 9818
Rightmyer, Eleanor Catharine 6925
Rightmyer, Martin C. 6925
Rikert, Maria 9231
Riley, Abby 7446
Riley, Roger 7258
Rinaus, Linah 690
Rinds, Mary 242
Ring, Peter 7262
Ripley, David 7269
Ripley, Ebenezer 7268
Risely, Catherine 7235
Ritchie, Ann 5251
Rives, William C. 9245
Rivington, James 9, 4242
Rivington, Jane Eliza 4242
Rivington, Sarah 9
Roach, Harriet P. 5889
Robbins, Abigail 7858
Robbins, Desire 4458
Robbins, Lucretia 5874
Roberson, Roxana 9944
Roberts, Amarilla 5541
Roberts, Ann 3490
Roberts, Areta 485
Roberts, Benjamin 8657
Roberts, Cornelia 7127
Roberts, Deborah 801
Roberts, Edmund 6535
Roberts, Elizabeth 3226
Roberts, George 7278
Roberts, Harriet 8657
Roberts, Harriet Langdon 6535
Roberts, Hiram 7290
Roberts, Isabella 1625
Roberts, John 5541, 7291
Roberts, Margaret 3715
Roberts, Mary 2270
Roberts, Mary Ann 6555
Roberts, Peggy 10029
Roberts, Philip B. 7293
Roberts, Philo B. 7281
Roberts, Sally 3143
Roberts, Sophronia 8817
Robertson, ___ (Mr.) 2776
Robertson, Archibald 9949
Robertson, Helen 2123
Robertson, James 2123
Robertson, Rachael Ann 9949
Robertson, William 7297
Robinson, Ann Maria 2975
Robinson, Catharine 5040, 5423
Robinson, Chloe 6273
Robinson, Deborah 4073
Robinson, Diana 7421

Robinson, Eliza 8260
Robinson, Gain 6273
Robinson, James 7326
Robinson, Jane 7957
Robinson, Lydia 9667
Robinson, Magdalena 5039
Robinson, Mary Ann 1090
Robinson, Phoeba 7984
Robinson, Sabina 1622
Robinson, Samuel 5039, 7312
Robinson, Ziba 7324
Robison, John 7330
Roblee, Harriet 2253
Rochester, William B. 7333
Rockwell, John 7339
Rockwell, Mary 1201
Rockwell, W. (Mr.) 7340
Rodgers, John B. 7345
Rodgers, Katurah 9446
Rodgers, Nathan 4594
Rodgers, Polly 4594
Rodman, Daniel 6528
Rodman, Laura E. S. 6528
Rodman, Lucy W. 5787
Roe, ___ (Rev.) 8559
Roe, Elihu 7348
Roe, Helen 2465
Roe, Laura 9831
Roe, Ruth 8728
Roeblee, Harriet 8301
Roff, Margaret Maria 2823
Rogers, ___ (Dr.) 5875
Rogers, ___ (Mrs.) 6306
Rogers, ___ (Mr.) 590
Rogers, Alice 2338
Rogers, Augustus 7355
Rogers, Cornelia 5875, 8879
Rogers, Eliza 4463
Rogers, Esther 8368
Rogers, Hannah 3814
Rogers, Jeremiah 4067, 7365
Rogers, John 9713
Rogers, Margaret 9713
Rogers, Maria 4067
Rogers, Martha 3436
Rogers, Mary 1738
Rogers, Sally 6018, 6287
Rogers, William, Jr. 7352
Romain, Benjamin 783
Romain, Catharine 783
Romayne, Susan Lynsen 6350
Romeyn, Herman M. 7389
Romeyn, J. V. C. (Rev.) 7394
Romeyn, Jeremiah 7393
Rooke, Rosetta 7021
Root, Erastus 4205, 7403
Root, Jesse 7407
Root, Julianne 4205
Root, Oliver S. 7411
Root, Sally 8148
Roper, Polly 5208
Rose, ___ (Gen.) 7423
Rose, Betsey 7967
Rose, Elmira 568
Rose, Harriet 531
Roseburgh, James 444
Roseburgh, Margaret 444
Rosecrants, Catharine 5673
Rosecrantz, Rebecca 8721
Rosekrans, Henry 7429
Rosekrans, Maria Louisa 9999
Rosekrans, Marshall 5700
Rosencrans, Sarah Ann 7742
Rosevelt, C. C. (Mr.) 2935
Rosevelt, Caroline 5484
Rosevelt, Elizar 2935
Rosevelt, Solomon 5484, 7430
Ross, Henry H. 7435

Ross, Jane Ann 9707
Ross, Mary McLean 1380
Ross, Nathan 7434
Ross, Stephen 1926
Ross, Theodorus 7439
Ross, William 1380, 7438, 9707
Rosseter, Samuel 7445
Rouse, Elizabeth 3478
Rouse, Maria 8312
Row, Andrus 2260
Row, Bas_ ? (Mr.) 291
Row, Garret 6942
Row, Harriet 2260
Row, Mary 291
Row, Sally 6942
Rowe, Carolyn V. 1353
Rowell, Rebecca 7039
Rowell, Soproma 1417
Rowland, Sally 858
Rowland, Susan 6096
Royce, Sally 2463
Royce, Thomas 7465
Rubottom, Matilda 5181
Ruby, Margaret 9513
Ruby, Robert 10111
Ruby, Sarah 10111
Rudd, Bezaliel 7470
Rudd, Joseph 5768
Rudd, Keziah 5768
Rudd, Olivia 1893
Rudd, Sally 9403
Rude, Elizabeth 1448
Rude, Nathan 1448
Rugar, Eliza 9249
Ruger, Maria 8937
Ruggles, Charles H. 7474
Ruggles, Harriet F. 7382
Ruggles, Oliver 7382
Rumsey, Levi 7480
Rundal, Jacob 7482
Rusk, Alice 7658
Russel, Benjamin 7494
Russel, Mary 7816
Russell, ___ (Miss) 9996
Russell, Ann 2261
Russell, Catharine Ann 6214
Russell, Eli 1460
Russell, Elihu 7495, 7496
Russell, Ellen 9429
Russell, Florinda 6749
Russell, Harriet 1460
Russell, Isaac 1672, 6613
Russell, Jane A. M. 316
Russell, John 6214, 7500
Russell, Joseph 5080
Russell, Julia Maria 5080
Russell, Lucy 6613
Russell, Maria 1672
Russell, Martha 6622
Russell, Sally 1051
Russell, Sarah G. 8628
Russell, Thomas 2261
Rust, Amaziah 4165
Rust, Nancy 4165
Rutan, Charity 8245
Ryan, Helen 5754
Ryan, John 7513
Ryer, Frederick 7514
Rykert, Catharine 1972
Rynders, Catharine 8522
Ryphenburgh, Elizabeth 6014
Rysdorph, Jane A. 1385
Sabin, Elizabeth 8026
Sabin, Nancy 7404
Sabin, William H. 8026
Sackett, Minerva 1522
Sackett, Rachel 9012
Sackett, Samuel 7524

Safford, Anna 7531
Safford, Hiram 7529
Safford, John 7530
Safford, Ozias 7532
Sage, Roda 3870
Sagges, Mary 3515
Saillee, Julia 6856
Saillee, Peter 6856
Sailly, Charlotte 6505
Sailly, Eleanor 993
Sailly, Peter 993, 6505, 7536
St. John, ___ (Widow) 2209
St. John, Harriet 16
St. John, Henrietta 3783
St. John, Mahetable 7492
Salisbury, Sarah 9342
Salisbury, Smith H. 7544
Salisbury, Susan 1921
Sampson, ___ (Mr.) 3718
Sampson, Clarissa 578
Sampson, Ezra 35, 7553
Sampson, Frances 3098
Sampson, George 7554
Sampson, Mary 35
Sanborn, Mary 1944
Sanburn, Eleanor 7996
Sanders, Jane Ann 6011
Sandford, Hannah Ann 5649
Sands, Benjamin 481
Sands, Eliza 6975
Sands, Griffith 204
Sands, Mary Eliza 204
Sands, Rachel W. 481
Sands, Robert 7558
Sands, Sarah 2865
Sanford, ___ (Mrs.) 9854
Sanford, Amy 3090
Sanford, Ann 1869
Sanford, Austin 6663
Sanford, Clarissa 6363
Sanford, Mary Ann 6663
Sanford, Phebe 2700
Sanford, William 1869
Sanger, ___ (Judge) 3238
Sanger, Sarah 192
Satterlee, Edward R. 743
Satterlee, Frances L. 743
Saultz, Catharine M. E. 274
Saultz, John F. 274
Saunders, Elizabeth 7181
Saunders, Phebe 1982
Savage, James 7571
Savage, Jazette 1632
Savage, Margaret 3228
Sax, Matthew 7659
Sayers, Frederica 5286
Sayers, James 5286
Sayre, Elmira 5174
Sayre, Nathan 7586
Sayres, Helen 6309
Sayrs, Selia 1351
Scheffelin, Edwardanna L.
   (Miss) 7860
Schell, Christian 7592
Schell, Emily 2986
Schell, Jane Ann 3447
Schell, William 3447
Schenck, Abraham H. 5133
Schenck, Jane Ann 5133
Schenck, Paul 7595, 7596,
   9260
Schenck, William C. 2005
Schenk, Joanna 5848
Schenk, Paul 5848, 7601
Schenk, Susan 9260
Schermerhorn, Gertrude 10090
Schermerhorn, John S. 7610,
   10090

Schermerhorn, Maus 7604
Schermerhorn, Polly 7752
Schermerhorn, Ryer 7606
Schoonmaker, ___ (Miss) 9599
Schoonmaker, Egbert 7615
Schoonmaker, Henry 884, 7614
Schoonmaker, Sally 884
Schram, Sarah 7617
Schram, William 7617
Schriver, Abraham 7618, 7619
Schriver, Peter 621
Schriver, Sally 621
Schruyver, Rachel 2876
Schryver Dorotha 118
Schryver, Martha 2156
Schryver, Mary Ann 414
Schryver, Peter A. 414, 2156
Schultz, Anna 2202
Schuyler, ___ (Mr.) 9819
Schuyler, Arent 2159
Schuyler, Catherine 4803
Schuyler, Margaret 6293
Schuyler, Mary M. 2159
Schuyler, Philip 1639, 7629
Schuyler, Philip I. 4782, 4803
Scoby, Content 8659
Scofield, Lebbeus 7641
Scofield, Martha 8784
Scofield, Rua 7224
Scofield, S. (Mr.) 7643
Scott, ___ (Mr.) 752
Scott, Ann 9345
Scott, Elizabeth 5225
Scott, Henry 5450
Scott, Moses 7453
Scott, Sally 4569
Scovel, Hezekiah 7657
Scrafford, Adam 8977
Scrafford, Charles 1297
Scrafford, Isabella 8977
Scribner, Elizabeth 1281
Scribner, Levi 7665
Scripture, Louisa 4434
Scryver, Margaret 5248
Scryver, Peter A. 5248
Scudder, Moses 5731
Scudder, Phoebe 5731
Seabury, Cornelia 4168
Seabury, Sarah 4330
Seaman, ___ (Mr.) 1322, 3632
Seaman, Abigail 9041
Seaman, David 2128
Seaman, Elizabeth H. 2128
Seaman, William 623
Searing, Martha 10051
Searl, Comfort 7681
Searle, George 7682
Sears, Christian 7683
Sears, Eliza 7453, 8267
Sears, Levi 7689
Sears, Nathan 8267
Sears, William 7684
Seaton, Catharine 4093
Seaver, Maria 50
Seaver, Mary 5724
Seaward, Sylvia 2765
Sebring, Isaac 3535
Sebring, Margaret 3535
Seckel, Maria H. 3748
Sedgwick, Charlotte 8269
Sedgwick, Eliza 6877
Sedgwick, Theodore 6877, 7694
See, Catharine 6806
Seelding, Thomas 7695
Seeley, Sylvanus 7696
Seely, Emma 7057
Seely, Isaac 5494
Seely, Joseph 7700

Seelye, Isaac 7705
Seelye, Lewis 7703
Seelye, Seth 7702
Segar, Lydia 2699
Selden, Harriet 3302
Selick, Abigail 7117
Selkrig, Maria T. 4462
Selkrig, Mary S. 3326
Selleck, Deborah 5073
Selleck, Emeline 789
Selleck, Henry 7049
Selleck, Stephen 7715
Sellick, Harriet 1589
Sergeant, A. (Col.) 2360
Sergeant, Abby 4821
Sergeant, Caroline 3514
Sergeant, Eliza Ophelia 2360
Sergeant, James 3514
Sergeant, John 4821
Sessions, Permelia 6741
Severance, C. (Mr.) 1948
Severance, Elizabeth M. 1948
Seward, Electa 2564
Seward, William 2564, 7725
Seymour, Daniel 3151
Seymour, Harriet Eliza 147
Seymour, Horace 7733
Seymour, Jane Maria 636
Seymour, Martha 3937
Seymour, Milton 7729
Seymour, Moses 636
Seymour, Sally 3151, 5172
Seymour, Stephen 7736
Shaler, Nathaniel 5501
Shankland, Pamila 3327
Shankland, Thomas 7744
Sharp, Catharine 13, 2672
Sharpe, Maria F. 2444
Shaver, John 7284
Shaw, Adeline 6885
Shaw, Helen 2818
Shaw, J. (Miss) 9550
Shaw, John B. 7760
Shaw, Joseph 5680
Shaw, Mary 5049
Shaw, Noah 604
Shaw, Polly 1597
Shaw, Roxana 5680
Shaw, Ruth Ann 9593
Shaw, Sally 604
Shear, C. H. (Mr.) 6583
Shear, Christian H. 3523
Shear, Elizabeth 889
Shear, Israel 7763
Shears, Elizabeth 7940
Shedden, Jane Agnes 1987
Sheik, Phebe 4128
Shelden, Arunah (Mr.) 7772
Shelding, ___ (Mr.) 4786
Sheldon, Aaron 180
Sheldon, Artemas 7774
Sheldon, Lucinda A. 180
Sheldon, Mary 6516, 7741
Sheldon, Sarah 4717
Sheldon, William B. 7781
Shelland, Louisa 7306
Shelters, Henry 7782
Shepard, Harriet F. 2750
Shepard, Noah 2750
Shepard, William 7786
Sheperd, Jane 831
Sheperd, Thomas 831
Shepherd, ___ (Miss) 1422
Shepherd, Eliza 3780
Shepherd, John 7791
Shepherd, Mary 6627
Shepherd, Mary Ann 9886
Shepherd, Roxana M. 9649

Sherman, Annes 9355
--- ---
Sherman, Ezra 7796
Sherman, James 7810
Sherman, Josiah 579
Sherman, Laura 559
Sherman, Rachel 4122
Sherman, Uriel 7806
Sherman, William 559
Sherrill, Emeline 2610
Sherrill, Esther 1397
Sherrill, Jacob 1397
Sherrill, Nathaniel 2610
Sherwood, Eliza 9346
Sherwood, Isaac 7817
Sherwood, J. F. (Maj.) 5705
Sherwood, Lemuel 6888
Sherwood, Margaret 5705
Sherwood, Mary 2161, 6891
Sherwood, Rachell 5098
Sherwood, S. (Mr.) 914
Sherwood, Samuel 7819
Sherwood, William 9346
Shields, Henry 7019
Shirts, Joseph 7833
Shoemaker, John M. 7834
Sholes, Elizabeth G. 5980
Sholes, John 5980
Shove, Cordelia 980
Shrimpton, Sally 2321
Shultz, Ann 3857
Shultz, Jacob 3857
Shultz, Rebecca 3963
Shute, Nelly 1889
Shute, Sally 633
Sickler, Peter 7852
Sickles, Catharine 9166
Sickles, Catharine Jane 3137
Sickles, Catherine 6947
Sickles, Jacob 9166
Sickles, James 3137, 5331, 7854
7855
Sickles, Jane Ann 7128
Sickles, Mary 4228
Sickles, Mary Ann 3822
Sickles, Nancy 9888
Signor, Mary 7969
Silkreg, Emily 3994
Sill, Andrew 7861
Sill, Helen 9409a
Sill, Helena 9426
Sill, Isaac 9426
Sill, Margaret N. 7570
Sill, William N. 7570
Silliman, ___ (Mr.) 5637
Silliman, Benjamin 1643
Silliman, Maria Turnbull 1643
Sim, Catherine Maria 6743
Simmons, Abraham 3607
Simmons, Caty 7882
Simmons, Charlotte 5883
Simmons, Elizabeth 3607
Simmons, Hannah 3919
Simmons, Julia 3809
Simmons, Sarah Angeline 6739
Simonds, ___ (Col.) 9428
Simons, J. Dewar 155
Simons, Jane 7881
Simons, Mary M. 155
Simoson, Sybel 4570
Simpson, Amelia 5562
Simpson, Harris (Miss) 8296
Sincebox, Margaret 2090
Sinclair, Eliza Sands 1919
Sinclair, William J. 1919
Sinnott, E. D. (Mr.) 7885
Sinnott, Maria 7885
Sizer, Henry H. 1345

Skelding, Mary E. 10085
Skelding, Sarah 8105
Skidmon, Mary 8698
Skidmore, Luther M. 7895
Skidmore, Maria 1195
Skidmore, Walter 1195
Skilbern, Joseph 3891
Skilbern, Maria 3891
Skinner, ___ (Chief Justice) 9499
Skinner, Chloe M. 2849
Skinner, Eliza 2809
Skinner, Eunice 7669
Skinner, Frances B. 9499
Skinner, Joseph 1105, 7555
Skinner, Maria 9747
Skinner, Phebe B. 1105
Skinner, Richard 9495, 9509
Skinner, St. John J. B. L. 7906
Skinner, Sally Ann 6145
Skinner, Sally P. 7555
Skinner, Sarah F. 9509
Skinner, Stephen 7898
Skinner, Warren 7911
Slack, R. W. (Miss) 3299
Slade, Anna 4442
Slade, Hannah 5598
Slade, Joseph 9360
Slade, Nancy 9360
Slade, Waity 8448
Slade, William 4442, 5598
Slason, Charlotte 3560
Slater, Eliza 628
Slater, James 7919
Slater, James E. 7923
Slater, Lucy 8871
Slater, Lydia 5906
Slawson, Fanny 7797
Slawson, Mary 311
Slecht, James 3414
Slecht, Harriet 3414
Sleight, Belinda 800
Sleight, Elizabeth 3569
Sleight, Harriet 2391
Sleight, James 7930
Sleight, James S. 3569
Sleight, Peter R. 7935
Sleight, Rosetta 2157
Sleight, Sally 5120
Sloan, ___ (Gen.) 5526
Sloan, Chloe 1581
Sloan, Daniel 4259
Sloan, Frances 4259
Sloan, Lucy 5526
Sluiterman, Ellen Margaret 2910
Smalley, Elizabeth 3192
Smith, ___ (Gov.) 2288
Smith, ___ (Judge) 3939
Smith, ___ (Lieut.) 7846
Smith, ___ (Mr.) 4872, 7098, 8706, 10077
Smith, Aaron 7987
Smith, Abby L. 8510
Smith, Adam 7821
Smith, Alexander 8050
Smith, Almira 67
Smith, Angeline 6767
Smith, Angeline B. 5858
Smith, Ann 6277
Smith, Ann E. 8888
Smith, Anning 8047
Smith, Armenia 4918
Smith, Arthur 1630, 8079
Smith, Catharine 719, 4047
Smith, Charles 8038
Smith, Charlotte 2057

Smith, Clarissa 2034, 6977
Smith, Deborah 6712
Smith, E. A. (Dr.) 7976
Smith, E. F. (Mr.) 7958
Smith, Eleanor 641, 7798, 9742
Smith, Elenor 8091
Smith, Eliza 779, 6207, 7469
Smith, Elizabeth 560, 1694, 9993
Smith, Elizabeth C. 9568
Smith, Elizabeth Hamilton 5037
Smith, Ella (Mr.) 536
Smith, Ellen 5645
Smith, Ezra 8034
Smith, Gerardus 6277
Smith, Granville 8084
Smith, Hannah 1441, 1563
Smith, Harriet 2548
Smith, Isaac 921, 1074, 1077, 8051, 8069, 8510, 8660, 9634
Smith, Israel 8491
Smith, J. H. (Mr.) 3939
Smith, Jabez 7995
Smith, Jacob 2872
Smith, James 8031, 9742
Smith, Jamima 6216
Smith, Jedediah 5849
Smith, Jerusha 7525
Smith, John 6773, 8064
Smith, John Augustine 1432
Smith, Josiah 9993
Smith, Julia 6205
Smith, Laura L. 4554
Smith, Lavinia 8700
Smith, Louisa 536, 9634
Smith, Lydia 8751
Smith, Maria 5876
Smith, Marietta 4383
Smith, Martha 1209
Smith, Mary 8660, 9132, 9626
Smith, Mary Ann 7207, 7857
Smith, Mary B. 7949
Smith, Mary J. 5237
Smith, Mary Parmelia 7314
Smith, Matthew 8068
Smith, Maurice 9243
Smith, Melancton 5237, 7977, 7989, 8037, 8042
Smith, Mercy 4888, 8913
Smith, Miranda 5849
Smith, Manson 1062
Smith, Nancy 5057, 6025
Smith, Nathaniel 351, 2219, 8039
Smith, Olivia Bicknell 351
Smith, P. L. (Mr.) 8030
Smith, Peggy 2748
Smith, Peter 1785
Smith, Phebe 264, 6112
Smith, Polly 6074, 6988, 7238
Smith, Rebecca 2872
Smith, Reuben 8044
Smith, Sally 1630, 2310, 4183, 10069
Smith, Sally Ann 8781
Smith, Samuel 8072
Smith, Sarah 1062, 1168, 5215, 8376
Smith, Sarah P. 1432
Smith, Sidney 7952, 8037
Smith, Stephen 641, 7988
Smith, Susan 9243
Smith, Susanna 1348
Smith, Tamer Ann 2864
Smith, Theoda 7970
Smith, Waity 8607
Smith, William 1694, 6025, 7990, 8032

Smith, William C. 264, 7514
Smith, Wright 1348
Smith, Zebulon 6112
Smitheson, Francis 8086
Smyth, Charles 2979
Snedecer, Catharine 2297
Snedeker, Hannah 3209
Snedeker, Sarah B. 3829
Snediker, Eliza 9447
Snow, Catharine 2474
Snow, Peggy 5475
Snow, Phebe 6687
Snowden, Arabella 5599
Snowden, C. (Col.) 4096
Snyder, Bythena 3420
Snyder, Hannah 7165
Snyder, Jane Ann 7456
Soals, Sally 9728
Somaradyck, Cornelia 8102
Somendyke, Sarah Ann 309
Somers, Lavinia M. 9324
Sormberger, John S. 3433
Sormberger, Lucetta 3433
Soul, Polly 2228
Soule, Lucy Ann 5191
Southwick, ___ (Mr.) 2972
Southwick, Edward 8118
Southwick, H. C. (Mr.) 8290
Southwick, Lydia 866
Southwick, Maria 4992
Southwick, Mary ann 8290
Southwick, Sarah 1840
Southwick, Sarah S. 3263
Southwick, Wilmarth 3263
Southwick, Zadoc 866
Sower, Ulrich 8130
Sowle, Hannah 9072
Spafford, ___ (Dr.) 404, 8132
Spafford, Martha H. 404
Spalding, Matilda 2281
Sparhawk, E. (Mr.) 8891
Sparhawk, Mary 8891
Sparks, Eliza 3046
Sparks, Samuel 3046
Speary, Ophelia 629
Spencer, ___ (Judge) 8156, 8158
Spencer, ___ (Mr.) 8198
Spencer, Alexander 5165
Spencer, Ambrose 8155
Spencer, Ethan 8157
Spencer, Henry 8153
Spencer, John C. 1762, 6056
Spencer, Laura Catharine 1762
Spencer, Mary 6541
Spencer, Mary Natalie 6056
Spencer, Philip, Jr. 8149, 8152
Spencer, Susan 1534
Spencer, Thomas 6541
Sperry, Rhoda 3130
Spicer, Francis 5794
Spicer, Maria Ann 5794
Spicer, Tobias 8162
Spinks, Emily 6520
Spooner, Rachel M. 9731
Spoor, Judith Ann 8706
Sprague, Esther 4401
Sprague, Fanny 675
Sprague, Joseph 8171, 8173
Sprague, Lucy 2213
Sprague, Sally 7874
Sprague, William 8167
Spriggs, Deborah 5038
Spring, Amanda 2327
Squires, Angeline 357
Squires, B. (Miss) 3066
Squires, Lewis 357

Squires, Ruby 7650
Sruio, Anna 6742
Staats, Barent I. 8180
Staats, Barent P. 8184, 8187
Staats, Eliza Saumway 6159
Staats, Henry 8181
Staats, Nancy 3452
Staats, Philip 8188
Staats, William 6159, 8182
Staats, William W. 8186
Stacy, Elizabeth 214
Stacy, Isaac 214
Stafford, Benjamin 8197
Stafford, Harriet 3640
Stafford, Rufus 8191
Stafford, Spencer 3640
Stammers, Elizabeth Ann 7563
Stammers, Joseph 7563
Stanard, Caroline 5434
Stanhope, John 4987
Staniford, Daniel 7327
Staniford, Juliette 7327
Stanley, Lucretia S. 3700
Stanley, Rufus 8206
Stansbury, Daniel 8656
Stansbury, Mary 8656
Stanton, David 7402
Stanton, Esther 1612
Stanton, G. W. (Mr.) 3793, 8210
Stanton, Maria 9048
Stanton, Nancy 9890
Stanton, Orpha 7402
Stanton, Phineas 1612
Stanwix, John 8213
Staples, Abraham 8214
Staples, Dorothy 2238
Staples, Mary M. 2971
Star, Daniel 8216
Star, Lucretia 7415
Starbuck, ___ (Mr.) 3719
Stark, A. W. (Mr.) 8175
Starks, Eleanor 3279
Starks, Stephen 3279
Starkweather, Maria 812
Starkweather, Samuel 8220
Starr, Chandler 8231
Starr, Clarissa 1164
Starr, David 8229
Starr, Ira 8230
Starr, Jane 1443
Starr, Jonah 8234
Starr, Marsha 2815
Starr, Packard 1443
Starr, R. (Mr.) 8225
Starr, Rachael 1595
Starr, Richard 8226
Starr, Salmon 4725
Starr, Sarah 135
Starr, Susanna 4725
Stearns, Elizabeth 5433
Stearns, L. S. 8239
Stebbins, Almira 2431
Stebbins, Benjamin 8242
Stebbins, Eliza 2266
Stebbins, Hester 5179
Steele, Daniel 8246
Steele, Eliza 672
Steenburgh, Margaret 7022
Steere, James 8252
Stephens, Abigail 4551
Stephens, Archibald 8255
Stephens, Betsey 1458
Stephens, Ebenezer 2434
Stephens, Eliza 2791, 9318
Stephens, H. R. (Mr.) 8254
Stephens, Josiah 1458, 8000
Stephens, Orchestra 8000
Stephens, Sally 51

Stephens, Sophia 9840
Stephens, Theresa 2434
Stephenson, ___ (Dr.) 7432
Stephenson, John 3300
Sterling, David 8257
Sterling, Jerusha 2558
Sterling, Margaret 6695
Sterling, William 6695
Stevens, ___ (Dr.) 6061
Stevens, Eben 4903
Stevens, Eliza Ann 4903
Stevens, Eliza S. 466
Stevens, Emma 9858
Stevens, G. M. (Mr.) 8279
Stevens, George 8273
Stevens, George M. 8262
Stevens, Henry 8272
Stevens, Mary 4384
Stevens, Phebe 4266
Stevens, Stephen 8275
Stevens, Thomas 4384
Stevenson, ___ (Mrs.) 9125
Stevenson, Eliza 3303
Stevenson, Gitty 9760
Steward, Polly 1932
Stewart, ___ (Mr.) 2871
Stewart, A. L. (Mr.) 9528
Stewart, Alexander L. 9524
Stewart, Alvan 8289
Stewart, C. S. (Rev.) 8291
Stewart, Cornelia 5030
Stewart, Eliza 935, 1363
Stewart, Helen, Lispenard 9524
Stewart, Henry 1363
Stewart, Isabella 5800
Stewart, James W. 8298
Stewart, John 9916
Stewart, Laura Abigail 3369
Stewart, Margaretta Matilda 6330
Stewart, Mary Caroline 6048
Stewart, Mary J. 9528
Stewart, Molly 694
Stewart, Sarah Ann 7897
Stewart, Solomon W. 3369
Stewart, William 6048
Stickles, Lydia 3835
Stickles, Polly 2245
Stillman, Willett 8#04
Stirling, David 8309
Stit, Margaret 1426
Stit, Polly Noxon 1426
Stitt, Nancy 5785
Stochan, Eliza 7647
Stockholm, aaron 8311
Stocking, Austin 8314
Stocking, Samuel 8317
Stockton, C. W. (Mr.) 7405
Stockton, Eliza 7405
Stockwell, Elizabeth C. 2243
Stockwell, Henry 8330
Stoddard, Ashbel 8325
Stoddard, Catharine 7902
Stoddard, Israel 8324
Stoddard, John 8725
Stone, ___ (Col.) 5495
Stone, Abigail 8611
Stone, Amanda 1908
Stone, Asaph 5354
Stone, Cynthia 6879
Stone, Eliza A. 7871
Stone, Hannah 3695
Stone, Isaac 8329
Stone, Jane Maria 5354
Stone, John 1216
Stone, Lavina 8328
Stone, Mary 7670
Stone, Mary Ann 4098
Stone, Nathaniel 1908

Stone, Roby J. 6548
Stone, William 2219, 4098,
  8333
Storer, Mary 3028
Storey, Mary Ann 9390
Storm, A. G. (Mr.) 6412
Storm, Abraham 7174, 8340
Storm, Abraham G. 6411
Storm, Catharine 8577
Storm, Charlotte 7174
Storm, Diana 4343
Storm, Eliza 6411
Storm, J. M. (Mr.) 8335
Storm, J. T. 8335
Storm, Jacob 1403, 9274
Storm, John 4343, 8577
Storm, John 4343
Storm, Sarah Ann 1403
Storm, Susan 9274
Storm, Thomas I. 8337
Storms, Lucretia 3359
Storrow, Susan Clark 9245
Storrow, Thomas W. 9245
Storrs, ___ (Col.) 1388
Storrs, Amariah 2001
Storrs, Delia 1388
Storrs, Mary 2001
Storrs, Nathan 8349
Storrs, Seth 8348, 8906
Storrs, Sophrona 8906
Story, Almira 9701
*Stott, Robert 8354
*Stoutenburg, Betsey 4081
Stoutenburg, ___ (Mrs.)
  7624
Stoutenburgh, Benjamin 8363
Stoutenburgh, Isaac 7929
Stoutenburgh, James 4081
Stoutenburgh, James I. 7376
Stoutenburgh, John 8357
Stoutenburgh, Mary V. 7929
Stoutenburgh, Sarah C. 6858
Stoutenburgh, Sarah M. 8912
Stoutenburgh. Tobias 8358,
  8361
*Stoughton, Lucy 1634
Stow, Daniel 8372
Stow, Mary 3850
Stowel, ___ (Mr.) 1659
Stowel, James 8374
Stowell, James 8377
Strachan, Agnes 8201
Straight, Betsey 4597
Stranahan, Farrand 8382
Strang, Maria 535
Stratton, David 8387
Stratton, Joel 8384
Stratton, John 8385
Stratton, Latham 8386
Stratton, Seth 8383
Strawbridge, John 8391
Street, Caleb 6776
Street, Fanny 646
Street, Mabel 6776
Striker, ___ (Mrs.) 166
Strite, Nancy 7240
Strong, ___ (Rev. Dr.) 8403
Strong, Cornelia A. 8087
Strong, Delia 7307
Strong, Hannah Otis 6757
Strong, Joseph 4542
Strong, Lydia 1651
Strong, Marianne 4542
Strong, Robert 8402
Stuart, Sally 7459
Sturges, ___ (Mr.) 4070
Sturges, Isabella Busher 808
Sturges, John G. 8409
*Stoughton, Lucy unintentionally misplaced

Sturges, Joseph 8413
Sturges, Josiah 5128
Sturges, Julia Anna Margaret
  5128
Sturges, Polly 6497
Sturges, Sally 1276
Sturtevant, Cornelius, Jr. 8417
Suby, Ester, Ann 8504
Suckley, George 3355
Sudam, John 8418
Sullivan, ___ (Mr.) 9215
Sullivan, William 8419
Summerfield, Anne B. 9455
Summerfield, William 9455
Sumner, Naomy 3062
Sunderland, William 8423
Sutherd, ___ (Miss) 7090
Sutherland, Ann 2622
Sutherland, David 8490
Sutherland, Euphemia 6496
Sutherland, Jane Amanda 5798
Sutherland, Josiah 8429
Sutherland, Polly 2590
Sutherland, Roger 6496
Sutherland, Roger B. 5798
Sutherland, Solomon 2622, 8427
Sutphen, John D. 4901
Sutphen, Sarah R. 4901
Swackhammer, Susan Margaret
  2493
Swain, Calven H. 1481
Swain, Cynthia M. 1481
Swain, Isaiah 8438
Swain, Robert 8441
Swain, Thomas 8436
Swan, ___ (Rev.) 6338
Swan, Mary B. 278
Swan, Sarah Jane 2221
Swan, William 2221
Swart, Peter, Jr. 7674
Swart, Sarah Jane 7674
Swart, Thomas 8452
Swartwout, ___ (Gen.) 9388
Swartwout, ___ (Miss) 9388
Swartwout, Benardus 2972
Swartwout, Catharine 2130
Swartwout, Cornelia 2019
Swartwout, Elizabeth 1602
Swartwout, Jacobus 8455
Swartwout, Jane 9489
Swartwout, John B. 1602,
  2130, 2767
Swartwout, Julia Ann 480
Swartwout, Robert 480
Swartwout, Sally Ann 2972
Swartwout, Samuel 9489
Sweatland, Joseph 8459
Sweet, Anna 7158
Sweet, Katharine 8464
Sweet, Lewis 8464
Sweet, Marie 8463
Sweet, Thomas 8461
Swetland, ___ (Mr.) 8468
Swift, Betsey 4853
Swift, Cynthia 122
Swift, E. M. 4271
Swift, Eliza 550
Swift, Harriet 4989
Swift, Harriot 134
Swift, J. G. (Gen.) 8479
Swift, John 122, 134, 8475
Swift, Joseph 8474
Swift, Mary Ann 4760
Swift, Rebecca 4271
Swift, Sally 6182
Swift, Thomas 8477
Swifts, Jacob 7603
Swifts, Margaret 7603

349

Tidd, Eliza 9614
Tidd, Mary Ann 7247
Tidd, William 1869
Tiffany, Martha 233
Tiffany, Nancy Whiting 6774
Tighlman, John 6733
Tilden, Daniel 8742
Tillman, Eliza 8900
Tillotson, Thomas 8747, 8748
Tillson, Cephas 8750
Tilton, Rebecca 9828
Timberlake, J. (Mr.) 2778
Timberlake, Margaret 2778
Timerman, Adam 4900
Timerman, Gertrude 4900
Tippet, Daniel 7687
Tisdall, Thomas 5524
Tise, Sally Ann 4877
Titcomb, Elizabeth 4172
Titus, Ann 6730
Titus, Lydia H. 2642
Titus, Mary Ann 9288
Titus, Peter S. 8760
Titus, Phebe 4814
Titus, Platt 8758, 9288
Titus, Sarah 200
Tobey, Cornelius 8766
Tobey, Eveline Maria 3931
Tobey, Nathaniel 3931
Toby, ___ (Mr.) 8774
Todd, Ann P. 5346
Todd, Harriet 1934
Todd, Lucinda 3157
Todd, Mary 2087
Todd, Mary H. 10030
Todd, Sally 1497
Todd, Samuel 3157
Todd, Stephen 5346
Todd, Walker 10030
Toll, Eve 7305
Toll, Jesse 7305
Toll, Mary 4703
Tolley, William 8786
Tomkins, Asenah 5195
Tomlinson, David 6911
Tomlinson, Eliza 3973
Tomlinson, Mary Jane 6911
Tompkins, ___ (Gov.) 8796, 8807
Tompkins, Arietta L. 8650
Tompkins, D. D. (Lieut.) 8797
Tompkins, Daniel D. 8055, 8650, 8799, 8803
Tompkins, Eliza 730, 2397
Tompkins, Frances 127
Tompkins, Jane Ann 423
Tompkins, Jonathan Griffen 8807
Tompkins, Lavena 2470
Tompkins, Mary 1116
Tompkins, Michael 730
Tompkins, Nehemiah 8796a
Tompkins, Rebecca 6519
Tompkins, Sally 561
Tompkins, Susan M. 8055
Tooker, Charles 9273
Tooker, Jane 9273
Topping, Henry 2217
Topping, Louisa 2217
Topping, Sarah Jane 590
Torrey, Abner 8811
Torrey, Cornelia 8811
Towers, Laura 3990
Townsend, ___ (Rev.) 5619
Townsend, Amanda 6702
Townsend, Charles W. 8819
Townsend, Ebenezer 3507
Townsend, Elizabeth Ann 4916
Townsend, Helen Ann 3333

Townsend, Isaac 8151
Townsend, Isaiah 8826
Townsend, Job E. 4916
Townsend, John 8829, 9413
Townsend, Laura Spencer 9413
Townsend, M. (Rev.) 8820
Townsend, Mary 6452
Townsend, Samuel 8822
Tracy, Abigail 2329
Tracy, John 8833
Tracy, Lemuel 8842
Trall, Laura 3357
Traver, ___ (Mr.) 7836
Traver, Ann 8844
Traver, Charlotte 1, 9602
Traver, Eliza 9827
Traver, Jacob P. 1, 9602
Traver, Jane 2193
Traver, Julia Ann 2051
Traver, Lydia Caroline 8736
Traver, Sophia 8110
Traverse, Susannah 816
Travis, Harriet 8791, 9584
Travis, Hester 8359
Travis, Maria 5647
Treadwell, J. (Mr.) 8855
Treadwell, Lucretia 1523
Treadwell, Lucy 5175
Treat, Richard 8857
Tredwell, Ann Maria 7130
Tredwell, N. H. (Mr.) 7130
Tredwell, Susan C. 10036
Tredwell, Thomas 8858
Tremble, Hannah 5490
Tremper, Catherine 9069
Trickey, Harriet 818
Trimble, Richard 8862
Tripp, Charity 3836
Tripp, Phebe Ann 917
Trivett, ___ (Dr.) 5530
Trivett, Sophia Ann 896
Trotter, John 8876
Trowbridge, Catharine W. 3642
Trowbridge, Clarissa 6731
Trowbridge, Henry 3642
Trowbridge, Polly 2345
Truax, Isaac 4133
Truesdell, Caroline 5568
Truesdell, P. (Capt.) 8883
Truesdell, Thomas 8561
Trumbull, Harriet 7920
Truxton, ___ (Commodore) 6179
Truxton, Cornelia 6179
Tryon, ___ (Judge) 7791
Tubbs, Ann 7035
Tubbs, Samuel 8889
Tucker, Harriet 1304
Tucker, Mary 8177
Tucker, Richard J. 8890
Tufts, Ann R. 5689
Tufts, William 5689
Tullidge, Benjamin 8896
Tunnicliff, George 5218
Tunnicliff, Nancy 5218
Tunnicliff, Persis Narina 2101
Tupper, Jane 5622, 5624
Turby, Eliza 4385
Turnbull, Mehetable 6581
Turner, ___ (Mr.) 1348
Turner, Charlotte 61, 4201
Turner, Hannah 8901
Turner, James 6965, 7223
Turner, John 8903
Turner, Julia Ann 4924
Turner, Maria G. 4200
Turner, Phebe 6578
Turner, Rebecca 6965

Turner, Ruth 7223
Turner, Sarah 1119
Turner, William 4201, 4924
Turney, Abel 1495
Turney, Ellen 1495
Turrill, Marcy E. 285
Tuttle, ___ (Mr.) 7859
Tuttle, Laura 2086
Tuttle, Merrit 8920
Tuttle, Sally 8920
Twogood, Hannah 4270
Twogood, William 2603
Tynders, Hetty 9106
Tysen, Ruth M. 5941
Uhl, Frederick 3449
Uhl, Margaret 3449
Underhill, Anna 4963
Underhill, Eliza 8313
Underhill, Gilbert 8313
Underhill, Jerusha 4153
Underhill, Mary 4399
Underhill, Mary Elizabeth 6233
Underhill, Nathaniel 4399
Underhill, P. B. (Mr.) 6233
Underhill, Phebe 3539
Underhill, Polly 5389
Underhill, Stephen 4153
Underwood, Demaris 8951
Underwood, Mary 2455
Underwood, Weeden 2455
Upfield, ___ (Rev.) 6476
Upham, Rebecca 7876
Upham, Ruth Marinda 8944
Vail, Diana 9313
Vail, Elizabeth 3969
Vail, Harriet 8823
Vail, Henry 8954
Vail, James 8823
Vail, Jane Ann 5915
Vail, Levinah 3805
Vail, Martha Louisa 589
Vail, Lydia S. 8067
Vail, Mary 3958, 5361, 9331
Vail, Moses 9331
Vail, Paulina 7450
Vail, Phebe 3341
Vail, Phebe E. 7072
Vail, Rebecca 8960
Vail, Solomon 8067
Valentine, Catherine 9278
Valentine, Isaac 1161, 8970, 8971
Valentine, Mary 1161, 8948, 9358
Valentine, Sarah 1375, 6030
Valleau, Helen 5041
Valleau, Theodore 5041
Vallette, Happelonia 5881
Van ___kirk, Abraham 4588
Van ___kirk, Jane 4588
Van Allen, Elizabeth 9202
Van Allen, Evert 9202
Van Allstyne, Abraham I. 9341
Van Allstyne, Sally 9341
Van Alstine, Ann 7538
Vanalstine, Ellen Matilda 1636
Van Alstine, Nicholas 7538
Vanalstine, Tanica 2384
Van Alstyne, Sally 8591
Van Anden, Jane 4121
Van Antwerp, Daniel 8997
Van Aps, Jane 1012
Van Arnum, Eleanor 1275
Vanarnum, Elizabeth 3352
Van Benschoten, ___ (Col.) 2676
Van Benschoten, ___ (Miss) 2676
Van Benschoten, Elias 8998

351

Van Benschoten, Jacob 1889
Van Benschoten, Malvina 1833
Van Benschoten, Sarah 296, 6419
Van Benthuysen, Abram 9001
Van Benthuysen, Ann 429
Van Benthuysen, Cornelia 830
Van Benthuysen, Jane Catalina 8754
Van Benthuysen, John 830, 8754
Van Bergen, Peter 9004
Van Brackle, James 9006
Van Bramer, Juliana 8063
Van Bunschoten, ___ (Col.) 9012
Van Bunschoten, Catharine 821
Van Bunschoten, Jemimah 3610
Van Buren, Abraham A. 4250
Van Buren, Albertine 840
Van Buren, Alicia 6523
Van Buren, Lydia Ann 1886
Van Buren, Martin 9015
Van Buskirk, Abraham 4588
Van Buskirk, Abraham, Jr. 8410
Van Buskirk, Catharine Ann 8410
Van Buskirk, Jane 4588
Van C---e, Abraham 9019
Van Cott, Anna 9192
Van Cott, Catharine 3866
Van Cott, Martha 7776
Van Curen, Maria 9574
Van Dake, Lucy 6592
Van De Bogert, Sally 5910
Vandeburgh, Catherine 2755
Vandenburgh, Peter 5944
Vandenburgh, John 9023
Vandenburgh, Ann 7486
Van Derbilt, Aaron 9037
Vanderbilt, Aves 9033
Vanderbilt, John 9034
Vanderbilt, Joseph 9036
Vanderbilt, Philip 7353
Vanderburgh, Ann A, 8661
Vanderburgh, Frances 8411
Vanderburgh, G. L. (Mr.) 8661
Vanderburgh, Henry 3073, 9039
Vanderburgh, James 9050
Vanderburgh, John 9038
Vanderburgh, Maria 3073
Vander Cook, Michael S. 7802,
  9052, 9053
Vanderheyden, Caty 5093
Vanderheyden, Derica 5207
Vanderheyden, Derick Y. 5091
Vanderheyden, Jacob D. 5093
Vanderheyden, Jane Elizabeth
  5091
Van Derheyden, Nancy 3202
Vanderheyden, Sarah 6449
Vanderheyden, Tinby 63
Vanderlip, Elias 5145
Vanderlip, Phebe T. 5145
Van Derpoel, Elizabeth 8982
Van derpool, Gertrude 4230
Vanderwarker, Betsey 9420
Vanderwater, Elizabeth 2746
Vanderwerken, Ann 4503
Van Deusen, ___ (Mr.) 3405
Van Deusen, Abraham 9064
Van Deusen, Caroline 4502
Van Deusen, Christina 2857
Van Deusen, Gertrude 894
Van Deusen, John 9068
Van Deusen, Lana 7832
Van Deusen, Polly 2856
Van Duerson, Caty 1837
Van Duerson, William 1837
Van Dusen, Helen 7135
Van Dusen, John 7135
Van Duzen, Abby 4310
Van Dyck, Abraham 9076

Van Dyck, Elizabeth 4628
Van Dyck, Henry L. 9078
Van Dyck, L. (Dr.) 4628
Vandyke, Eliza 7303
Van Dyke, Lawrence, Jr. 9079
Van Dyne, Hannah Maria 2273
Van Evert, Mary Ann 1899
Van Every, Eliza 2280
Van Hoesen, Abraham 4984
Van Hoesen, Charity 2898
Van Hoesen, Christiana 4984
Van Hoesen, Elizabeth 9097
Vanhoesen, Hannah 2966
Van Hoesen, Leonard 9083
Van Hoesen. Lucretia 4745
Van Hoesen, Peter 9087
Van Hoesen, Sally 2035
Van Keuren, ___ (Mr.) 1410,
  6566
Van Keuren, Ann Maria 9233
Van Keuren, Margaret 9178
Van Keuren, Maria 7875
Van Keuren, Sarah 8802
Van Kleeck, Adeline Van
  Rensselaer 9987
Van Kleeck, Catherine 973
Van Kleeck, Cornelia 8104
Van Kleeck, Eliza 2047
Van Kleeck, Elizabeth 7383
Van Kleeck, George 9109,
  9110
Van Kleeck, Jane 8064
Van Kleeck, John 9107
Van Kleeck, L. L. (Mr.) 9987
Van Kleeck, Lawrence 5020
Van Kleeck, Leonard 8015
Van Kleeck, Letty 9735
Van Kleeck, Louisa 593
Van Kleeck, Michael B. 4331
Van Kleeck, Myndert 8585
Van Kleeck, Penelope 1971
Van Kleeck, Peter B. 7588,
  9099
Van Kleeck, Richard 7383
Van Kleeck, Sally 5020,
  7588, 8015
Van Kleeck, Sally Ann 6331
Van Kleeck, Sally Billings
  6399
Van Kleeck, Teunis 593,
  6331, 9951
Van Kleeck, Tunis 8104, 9103
Van Kleef, Ann 10061
Vanleuven, Ann Eliza 4736
Van Loan, Maria 3092
Van Lyngen, Elizabeth 7256
Van Ness, ___ (Gov.) 6447
Vsn Ness, Anne 2734
Van Ness, Catalina 9816
Van Ness, Catherine 3559
Van Ness, Cornelia 7193,
  7399
Van Ness, David 2734, 7052,
  9117
Vsn Ness, G. B. (Mr.) 6694
Van Ness, George 9118
Van Ness, Gertrude 3718
Van Ness, Helen 7193
Van Ness, Jscob 9123
Van Ness, Jane 7052
Van Ness, Jane Eliza 6694
Van Ness, Marcia 6447
Van Ness, P. (Mr.) 7399
Van, Ness, W. W. (Mr.) 8857
Van Ness, William P. 9116
Van Ness, William W. 3559,
  5285, 9133
Van O'Linda, P. (Dr.) 1436

Vanorder, Mary 460
Van Ranst, C. W. (Mr.) 5087
Van Ranst, Lucretia 3871
Van Ranst, Susan Frances 5087
Van Rensselaer, ___ (Maj.Gen.
  4827
Van Rensselaer, Alida 4827
Van Rensselaer, Angelica 5075a
Van Rensselaer, Catharine
  9141, 9777
Van Rensselaer, Catherine
  7633
Van Rensselaer, Cornelia 9155
Van Rensselaer, J. 9141
Van Rensselaer, Jeremiah 7633
Van Rensselaer, John I. 9141
Van Rensselaer, Killian 9142
Van Rensselaer, Killian K.
  9150
Van Rensselaer, Margaret 4800
Van Rensselaer, Philip 9152
Van Rensselaer, Robert 7633
Van Rensselaer, Stephen 6616,
  9149, 9158, 9777
Van Ryck, ___ (Mr.) 7288
Van Schaack, ___ (Widow) 9127
Van Schaack, Elizabeth 9160
Van Schaack, Peter 9160, 9162
Van Schack, Henry 9161
Van Schaick, Clarissa 9077
Van Schaick, Gozen 9164
Van Schaick, John 9165
Van Schaik, Elizabeth 3242
Van Schaik, Peter 3242
Van Schayck, William 9170
Van Schoonhoven, Henry 9172
Van Schoonhoven, James 9172
Van Schoonhoven, John 9171,
  9172
Van Solingen, Jane Maria 642
Van Steenberg, Catherine 7498
Van Tile, Jean 6710
Van Tine, Elizabeth 5799
Vantine, Elizabeth 8573
Van Valen, Helen 864
Van Valin, Gideon 9185
Van Valkenberg, Catharine
  8850
Van Valkenburgh, _?_ 1387
Van Valkenburgh, Anna 9190
Van Valkenburgh, Barney 9190
Van Valkenburgh, Catherine
  1362
Van Valkenburgh, John 9196
Van Valkenburgh, John C.
  9193, 9195
Van Valkenburgh, Margaret
  7869
Van Vechten, Abraham 9197
Van Vechten, Harriet 9945
Van Vechten, Jane 7547
Van Vechten, Judith 6639
Van Vechten, Sally 7133
Van Vechten, Tunis T. 6639
Van Vlack, John H. 9204
Van Vlack, Sibble 4718
Van Vleck, Christina 3072
Van Vleck, Peter 9208
Van Vliet, Benjamin C. 9211
Van Vliet, C. (Mr.) 9212
Van Vliet, Clara M. 1544
Van Vliet, Cornelius 1544
Van Vliet, Cornelius, Jr.
  1544
Van Vliet, Gitty 2845
Van Vliet, H. H. (Mr.) 9219
Van Vliet, Hannah 9554
Van Vliet. Helen 1019

Van Vliet, John 9218
Van Voknier, Leah 6104
Vanvolkingburgh, Betsy Ann 8873
Van Voorhees, Rachel K. 6362
Van Voorhis, _?_ 5468
Van Voorhis, Cornelius 7310
Van Voorhis, Hannah 9256
Van Voorhis, Julia 7214
Van Voorhis, Maria 28
Van Voorhis, Mary 7310
Van Voorhis, Phebe Van Bramer 4469
Van Voorhis, Stephen 1985
Van Voorhis, W. R. (Maj.) 7214
Van Voorhis, William 4469
Van Voorhis, William R. 9256
Van Vranken, Nicholas 7011, 9230
Van Vrankin, Catherine 1076
Van Vreden Burgh, Eliza 8716
Van Vredenburgh, Sarah 6158
Van Vreden Burgh, William 8716
Van Wagenen, Sarah 2085
Van Wagner, Eliza 7679
Van Wagner, Jacob 7679
Van Wagoner, Benjamin 9241
Van Wagoner, John 2599
Van Wagoner, Nancy 9241
Van Wagoner, Parmela 6686
Vanwagoner, Polly 8361
Van Wagoner, Sarah 2599
Van Wie, Benjamin 9169
Van Wie, Jane 9169
Vanwyck, Ann 9411
Van Wyck, Catharine Ann 4034
Van Wyck, Cornelia 9259
Van Wyck, Cornelius C. 760, 9256
Van Wyck, Hannah 9605
Van Wyck, Isaac 9250, 9262, 9605
Van Wyck, Isaac C. 9256, 9261
Van Wyck, J. B. (Gen.) 4294
Van Wyck, Jane 4295
Van Wyck, Joanna 4294
Van Wyck, John B. 4287, 4293, 4295, 7175, 7177, 9248
Van Wyck, Louisa 9201
Van Wyck, Margaret C. 760
Van Wyck, Mary 7175
van Wyck, Richard 9247
Van Wyck, Richard C. 9252
Van Wyck, Sarah 4293
Van Wyck, Theodorus R. 9253
Van Wyck, Theodorus W. 9266, 9411
Van Zandt, Benjamin 649
Van Zandt, Cornelia 2333
Van Zandt, J. R. (Mr.) 9271
Van Zandt, Maria 202, 649
Varick, John V. B. 6671
Varick, Maria Antoinette 6671
Varrick, J. V. B. (Mrs.) 7394
Varrick, J. V. B. (Mr.) 9276
Vassar, James 249, 302, 930 9277
Vassar, Jemima 7712
Vassar, Maria 930
Vassar, Sophia 249
Vaughan, Benjamin B. 9287
Vaughan, Deborah R. 1759
Vedder, John B. 7254
Vedder, Julia 7254
Veitz, Charlotte 9246
Veitz, Henry 9246
Veley, Abigail 718
Velie, Catharine 8825
Velie, Cynthia 8524
Velie, Eliza 8828

Velie, George P. 9293
Velie, Hendrick 6310
Velie, Mary 6164, 6310
Velie, Minard 8828
Velie, Minard B. 8795
Velie, Polly 4776
Velie, Sarah 9314
Velie, Susan 8795
Velis, Eliza 6308
Velis, Hendrick 6308
Veltman, ___ (Mr.) 2951
Vemont, John P. 9302
Vermiller, Olivia 5862
Vermillion, Elizabeth 777
Vermilya, Eliza 8945
Vernam, Caroline 8249
Vernam, Stephen 8249
Vernor, John T. 9305
Verplanck, Adeline Eliza 9310
Verplanck, Daniel 9311
Verplanck, Elizabeth 5005
Verplanck, Gillian 9306
Verplanck, Philip 9310
Viele, Jacob S. 9319
Vincent, Catharine 8335
Vincent, Elizabeth 8763
Vincent, Hepzibah M. 9646
Vincent, James 9242
Vincent, Leonard 8335
Vincent, Michael 9333
Vincent, Sarah Jane 9242
Visscher, Gazena Catherine 2394
Visscher, Herman 2394
Visscher, John B. 5367
Voorhees, Cornelia 6878
Voorhees, Ralph 1117
Voorhees, Sarah Ann 1117
Voorhes, Abraham 4976
Vorce, Emily La Vendee 6420
Vosburgh, Eddy (Miss) 1716
Vosburgh, Elizabeth 9221
Vosburgh, Maria 8981
Vosburgh, Samuel 9221
Vroman, Helen 9362
Vrooman, Cornelius 9350
Wackenhagen, ___ (Rev. Dr.) 1081
Wackenhagen, Caroline 1091
Waddington, Thomas 3928
Wadell, Else 5066
Wadsworth, Harriet 1067
Wadsworth, James 1067, 9354
Wadsworth, Jane 1023
Wadsworth, Joseph 1023
Wagar, Catharine 609
Waggoner, Joseph 5247
Waine, John 9363
Wainright, Alfred 9364
Wainwright, Ann Maria 3270
Wainwright, John 8133
Wainwright, Jonathan 9366
Wainwright, Maria Theresa 8133
Wainwright, Phebe 7605
Wait, Daniel 9370
Wait, Polly 10020
Wait, Sally 2567
Wakelee, Isaac 9372
Wakeman, Ann 4710
Wakeman, Burr 9375
Wakeman, Jane 6253
Wakeman, Lloyd 9375
Wakeman, Mary 1242
Wakeman, Nancy 3491
Waldimall, _?_ 747
Waldron, Cornelius 9384
Waldron, Gerrit 9384
Waldron, Hannah 9604

Waldron, Joseph J. 9389
Waldron, Julia 9389
Waldron, William 9384
Waldruff, Christian 10064
Waldry, Sarah 379
Walker, B. (Lieut.) 9399
Walker, Benjamin 1872
Walker, Eliza 1872
Walker, Elizabeth 5448
Walker, Elizabeth Donly 900
Walker, Enos 9396
Walker, James 5448
Walker, Joseph 9401
Walker, Mary Ann 1000
Walker, Phebe Ann 6138
Walker, Richard L. 900
Walker, Sarah A. 275
Wallace, James D. 9409
Wallace, Sally 1601
Walley, Garret 2539
Walley, Mary 2359
Walling, Caroline 8080
Walling, Elisha 7024
Walling, Tammy 7024
Walling, William
Wallis, ___ (Rev.) 2481
Walsh, Dudley 2505
Walsh, Sarah 2505
Waltenmire, Michael 3370
Waltenmire, Polly 3370
Walter, Joel 9414
Walter, Sarah Ann 2449
Walter, William 2449
Walton, Joseph 9424
Walworth, Ann 2584
Walworth, Edna M. 9982
Walworth, Eliza Ann 6826
Walworth, John 9428
Walworth, Mary Elizabeth 4673
Walworth, Thomas 9982
Walworth, Thomas P. 9982
Wands, Jane 7062
Wands, John 7062
Ward, Frances E. 8005
Ward, Harriet 7375
Ward, I. 131
Ward, James 8005
Ward, Jane B. 3065
Ward, John 1853
Ward, John I. 9071
Ward, Joshua 2, 3065, 3288, 3289
Ward, Juliana 3542
Ward, Lavina 9071
Ward, Levi 7707
Ward, Levi, Jr. 1670
Ward, Levi A. 9433
Ward, Mehetibel E. 1670
Ward, Pamelia 2, 3289
Ward, Permelia 1525
Ward, Rebecca 528
Ward, Robbrt R. 9441
Ward, Sally 1853
Ward, Susan 131
Ward, Susan M. 7707
Ward, William H. 9439
Warden, Mary Ann 2541
Wardsworth, Roxaiana 7580
Warford, John 9450
Waring, Joanna 9839
Waring, Lydia 9875
Waring, Rachel 4537
Waring, William 9875
Warn, Margaret 5183
Warne, Elbert P. 3008
Warne, Mary D. 3008
Warner, Betsey 4209
Warner, Elias 2121
Warner, Henry 9457

Warner, Isaac 4209
Warner, Jason 9453, 9458
Warner, Lucretia 3776
Warner, Mary W. 2121
Warner, Rebecca 3579, 8471
Warner, Roger 9463
Warner, Thomas 8471
Warner, Walt 9452
Warner, Willard9451
Warner, Zacharia 9462
Warren, Ann 1343
Warren, Cecelia Augusta 10080
Warren, Cynthia 594
Warren, Eliza Ann 6483
Warren, Esaias 9469
Warren, Esais (Mr.) 6483
Warren, John G. 9645
Warren, Lydia 3268
Warren, Maria 3892
Warren, Mary 5026
Warren, Parker 9473
Warren, Richard 7129
Warren, Sarah R. R. 9645
Warren, Stephen 5026
Warring, Mary R. 8496
Washbon, Mary Ann 810
Washbon, Zebah 810
Washburn, Almira 8645
Washburn, Cornelia 5761
Washburn, Hepzibah 3545
Washburn, Mary 3418, 8600
Washburn, Noah 3545
Washburn, Rebecca 9460
Waterbury, Rhoda 2268
Waterhouse, ___ (Mrs.) 7530
Waterhouse, Cyrus 9483
Waterman, Barnabas 9484, 9486
Waterman, T. G. (Gen.) 9485,
    9488
Watermire, David 7844
Watermyre, Melissa 7844
Waters, Ann 6175
Waters, Brooksania 4798
Waters, Charlotte 1532
Waters, Elizabeth H. 3354
Waters, Francis H. 3354
Watkins, Mary C. 4086
Watkinson, Joseph 7342
Watkinson, Mary 7342
Watrous, John R. 9492
Watson, Abigail 6970
Watson, Anna 9494
Watson, John 6662
Watson, Mary B. 6662
Watson, Winslow C. 9495
Wattles, Sally 7414
Watts, John 9506
Watts, Marian 6796
Way, Elizabeth 20
Way, Hannah 9182
Way, James B. 9507
Wayne, Daniel T. (Mrs.) 9942
Wead, Adaline 4342
Weatherwax, Andrew G. 9512
Weatherwax, Eliza 7578
Weatherwax, Phebe Ann 8090
Weatherwax, Rena 5424
Weaver, Catharine 4863
Weaver, Deborah 9835
Weaver, Dorcas 8520
Weaver, Eliza 7921
Weaver, Jacob 2219
Weaver, John 9515
Weaver, Mary Ann 9637
Weaver, Sally 2116
Weaver, Sarah 3448
Webb, ___ (Mr.) 8136
Webb, Derick 9525
Webb, Eliza 3282

Webb, Henry L. 9521
Webb, James Watson 9518
Webb, Jane H. 312
Webb, Job 5585
Webb, John 2507
Webb, Maria 6046
Webb, Mary 3240
Webb, N. 2508
Webb, Naphthah 2507
Webb, S. H. (Capt.) 9523
Webb, Samuel B. 312, 6046, 9519
Webb, Sarah 5585
Webb, Susan 8772
Webbers, Harriet 7251
Weber, Mary 9188
Weber, Michael 9188
Webster, ___ (Mr.) 3238
Webster, Anginetta M. 5714
Webster, C. R. (Mr.) 9534
Webster, Chauncey 9541
Webster, D. (Hon.) 836
Webster, Daniel 9536
Webster, J. (Dr.) 9537
Webster, Phila 1, 136, 1339
Webster, Sophia 5747
Webster, Visa 1339
Weed, Abraham 9973
Weed, Elijah 9544
Weeks, Daniel 9553
Weeks, Delilah 2624
Weeks, Letty 5826
Weeks, Mary 1444, 8692
Weeks, Robert D. 9560
Weeks, Rosanna 1923
Weidman, Maria 7634
Welch, ___ (Mr.) 4872
Welch, John 9565
Welch, Phebe 3504
Welch, Tanner 8941
Welch, William 9563, 9564, 9566
Weld, Harriet 2031
Weld, Joseph 2031
Welles, Abigail Woolsey 5393
Welles, John 4513
Welles, Noah 5393
Welles, Sarah R. 4513
Wells, Alithea 6227
Wells, Elizabeth 8449
Wells, Laura 6203
Wells, Philander 9576, 9580
Welton, ___ (Rev.) 2396, 3225,
    9587, 9588
Welton, A. (Rev.) 9586
Wemple, ___ (Mr.) 1731
Wemple, Andrew 4875
Wemple, Anna 4875
Wendell, Daniel T. 6154
Wendell, Harriet 6154
Wendell, Susanna 9348
Wentworth, Reuben 9597
Werden. Elias 9598
Wescott, Elizabeth 1955
West, Anna 8649
West, John 3794
West, Lucy 3794
West, Nancy 5106
West, Reuben 4188
West, Sarah C. 4188, 9669
Westbrook, Cornelius 9608
Westbrook, Cornelius D. 9607
Westervelt, Daniel 2438
Westervelt, Jane 2438
Westervelt, Lavina 3204
Westervelt, Rebecca 2053
Weston, Adaline 3968
Weston, Ephraim 3968
Weston, Isaac 9622
Weston, Levi 9624
Weston, Roswell 2964

Wetherbee, Eluthera 7505
Wetherbee, Mary Ann 6255
Wetmore, Rhoda 7280
Whale, Julian E. W. (Miss) 217
Whale, Thomas 217
Whalen, Ezekiel 9631
Whallon, Emily 8077
Whallon, Reuben 8077
Wheaton, John 958
Wheaton, Polly 958
Wheeler, Ann 2487
Wheeler, Anthony 10042
Wheeler, Arabella Elizabette
    4019
Wheeler, Charlotte 4057
Wheeler, Cornelia Livingston
    8099
Wheeler, Cyrus 5822
Wheeler, Elizabeth 3021
Wheeler, George A. 4019
Wheeler, Harriet 5822
Wheeler, Henrietta Maria 10042
Wheeler, Henry 9648
Wheeler, Lorene Brunwick 21
Wheeler,Lucretia 8284
Wheeler, Mary 5664, 9232
Wheeler, Mina 7020
Wheeler, Newcomb 4057
Wheeler, Parmelia 9294
Wheeler, Sarah 1587
Wheeler, Sarah R. 3746
Wheeler, Susanna 8654
Wheeler, Thomas N. 8099
Wheeler, William 9232, 9652
Wheelock, Phineas 9658
Wheldon, Maria E. 5520
Whelpley, Samuel W. 392
Whipple, ___ (Capt.) 6267
Whipple, ___ (Gen.) 7795
Whipple, Amos 5144
Whipple, Ann 292
Whipple, Barnet 9661
Whipple, Barnum 9665
Whipple, Edward 4874
Whipple, Elsie 3223
Whipple, Malachi 292
Whipple, Nancy 5144
Whipple, Olive 847
Whissler, ___ (Maj.) 1751
Whissler, Eliza 1751
Whit, Helena 2264
Whitaker, Ezra 9672
Whitaker, Walter 9673, 9674
Whitbeck, Ann Maria 9073
Whitcomb, Cyrus 5494
Whitcomb, Esther 1600
White, ___ (Mr.) 8539
White, B. (Dr.) 7176
White, C. (Mr.) 6626
White, Caroline 7203
White, Caroline R. 4099
White, Daniel 784
White, Elijah 9682
White, Emmeline 501
White, Frances 3578
White, H. L. (Mr.) 9683
White, James 9694
White, Jesse P. 9686
White, John 9680
White, John G. 9678
White, Joseph 5292
White, Julia SnnMaria 6626
White, Lavinia 6186
White, Lavantia 5292
White, Maria B. 9609
White, Martha 3429
White, Matilda 7176
White, Permella 7526
White, Polly 1192

354

White, Sally 2279
White, Samuel 501
White, Sarah 7277
Whiteman, Evelina 6461
Whiteside, Laura 6001
Whitford, Sally Ann 2210
Whiting, ___ (Mr.) 9861
Whiting, Charles 9715
Whiting, Charlotte 6327
Whiting, Harriet R. 1345
Whiting, J. L. (Dr.) 9457
Whiting, John 1268, 9457, 9716
Whiting, John L. 9714
Whiting, Mary E. 7888
Whiting, Sarah 1268
Whiting, Spencer 9717
Whiting, William 9719
Whitlock, Thomas 9725, 9727
Whitmarsh, Hannah 4726
Whitmore, Joseph 1036
Whitmore, Louisa 1036
Whitmore, Lucy 1015, 1036
Whitney, Abigail 1063
Whitney, Charlotte E. 1661
Whitney, Eliza 453
Whitney, Esther A. 372
Whitney, Mary Ann 9644
Whitney, Nathan 1063
Whitney, Selleck 9729
Whitt, Barton 6240
Whitt, Catharine 6240
Whittelsey, H. (Mr.) 5738
Whittemore, Elmira 2835
Whittemore, Samuel 2835
Whittlesey, Elisha 1851
Whittlesey, Harriet 1851
Whorter, Isabel 7063
Wickes, Frances 825
Wickes, Rebecca 511
Wickes, Silas 511, 9737
Wickham, Sarah Stewart 9263
Wickham, Thomas (Dr.) 9263
Wickoff, Sarah 3040
Wigg, Jane Ann 3181
Wiggins, Jacob 9743
Wiggins, Nathaniel 9743
Wigton, Samuel 9746
Wigton, William 9745
Wilber, Becca 725
Wilber, Ellvanus 5116
Wilber, Freelove 153
Wilber, Hannah Eliza 5116
Wilber, Lemira 7710
Wilbur, Charlotte 29
Wilbur, Curtis 9757
Wilbur, Dotha 8022
Wilbur, Ebenezer 8272
Wilbur, Gideon 9759
Wilbur, Hiram 9762
Wilbur, James 2395, 9755
Wilbur, Sarah 6677
Wilcox, ? 4487
Wilcox, ___ (Mr.) 4750
Wilcox, Almira 2313
Wilcox, Julia Ann 2298
Wilcox, Polly 1294
Wilcox, Silvester 2298
Wilcox, Sylvanus 9769
Wilde, Mary 4381
Wilder, ___ (Mr.) 6474
Wilder, Catherine 6237
Wilder, Electra B. 7220
Wilder, S. V. S. (Mr.) 7220
Wiley, Cornelia T. 195
Wiley, Jacob 8968
Wiley, Lavina 8968
Wilgus, Betsey 7196
Wilkes, ___ (Miss) 4091

Wilkes, John 4091
Wilkin, Betsy 1528
Wilkin, James W. 1528
Wilkinson, ___ (Gen.) 3469
Wilkinson, George 9785
Wilkinson, John 2617, 6347, 9784
Wilkinson, Joseph 9786
Wilkinson, Maria 2836
Wilkinson, Mary 2617
Wilkinson, Rebecca 6347
Wilkinson, Rhoda 9830
Willard, ___ (Mr.) 4872
Willard, Ann (Mrs.) 8615
Willard, David 9795
Willard, Elias 6053, 8876
Willard, Eliza G. 4254
Willard, John 9789
Willard, Timothy 9790
Willcox, Ann 384
Willets, Jacob 9801
Willett, Margaretta M. 7102
Willett, Marinus 7102
Willey, Martha 5148
Williams, ___ (Dr.) 9805
Williams, ___ (Judge) 2901, 9807
Williams, ___ (Miss) 6360
Williams, A. D. (Mr.) 757
Williams, Abbey 841
Williams, Abby Ann 7829
Williams, Accuh 7931
Williams, Andrew 9810, 9826
Williams, Betsey 7698
Williams, Bille 9825
Williams, Caroline 2307, 5701
Williams, Deidema 4824
Williams, E. (Mr.) 14
Williams, Ebenezer 9836
Williams, Elisha 9824, 9836
Williams, Eliza 9632
Williams, Emma 9359
Williams, Eunice 2607
Williams, Ezra 9848
Williams, Isaac 6780
Williams, Jane Ann 7198
Williams, John 9862
Williams, John R. 9850
Williams, Joseph H. 9847
Williams, Josiah 2307, 5146
Williams, Louisa 5790
Williams, Lucinda B. 9733
Williams, Lucy 1700
Williams, Mahala 9965
Williams, Maranda 3499
Williams, Maria 9400
Williams, Martha 5146
Williams, Mary 8743
Williams, Mary Augusta 10056
Williams, Melissa 6780
Williams, Mercy 1690
Williams, Polly 9081
Williams, R. (Mr.) 9859
Williams, Robert 6360
Williams, Roda 5824
Williams, Russell 9845
Williams, Sarah M. 619
Williams, Silas 9844
Williams, Thomas 9359, 9849, 9851
Williams, Uretta 4655
Williams, William 9804, 9821, 9823, 9846, 9864
Williams, William A. 9733
Williamson, ? 3760
Williamson, Caroline C. 105
Williamson, Griffin 3259, 9871
Williamson, Mary 3259, 4770

Willmarth, Sarah 2089
Wilmarth, Ann Mercy 2861
Wilse, Martin 5543
Wilsey, Eve 3395
Wilsie, Mary Anne 7015
Wilson, ___ (Judge) 2526
Wilson, ___ (Mrs.) 2108
Wilson, ___ (Mr.) 3675
Wilson, Abraham 5525
Wilson, Alexander 2108
Wilson, Betsey 133, 6603
Wilson, Catharine 1502
Wilson, Diantha 7390
Wilson, E., Jr. 2007
Wilson, Elizabeth 879, 6378, 9140
Wilson, Frances 2526
Wilson, Henrietta 564
Wilson, James 1502, 8389, 9893
Wilson, Jane 8389
Wilson, John 8920, 9891, 9899
Wilson, Lydia 2822, 5525
Wilson, Mary 6642, 7840, 7841
Wilson, Mary E. 1565
Wilson, Mary M. 2007
Wilson, N. (Dr.) 9896
Wilson, Samuel 9882
Wilson, William 1565, 7840, 7841
Wiltse, Elsey 893
Wiltse, James 5571
Wiltse, Julia A. 5542, 5543
Wiltsie, Elizabeth 7948
Wiltsie, John 9912
Winans, Girardus 9915
Winans, Hannah 8120
Winans, James, Jr. 9914
Winans, John 9916
Winch, Louisa 7065
Winch, Nancy 3880
Winch, Nathaniel 3879
Winch, Susan 3879
Winchel, Zilpha 139
Winchell, Aaron E. 2524
Winchell, Caroline 1711
Winchell, Charlotte I. 2524
Winchell, Martin 7953
Winchell, Mary 3948
Winchell, Philo M. 1142, 1711, 3948
Winchell, Sally 1142
Winchell, Sarah Ann 7779
Winchell, Ursula 7953
Winchester, Harriet M. 2565
Winegar, Conrad 1566
Wing, Catharine 8975
Wing, J. A. (Dr.) 9931
Wing, James 9936
Wing, Maria 2606
Wingate, Joseph F. 2109
Wingate, Virginia Ann 2109
Winn, Eliza 2841
Winn, Timothy 2841
Winne, Daniel T. 9942
Winne, Elizabeth 9946
Winne, Elizabeth M. 8902
Winne, Eve 9736
Winne, Hannah 2743
Winne, Hetty Ann 58
Winne, John W. 9947
Winne, Susan D. 8851
Winne, Susanna 3389
Winslow, Catherine 2469, 9080
Winslow, Eliza 3047
Winslow, Hannah 6294
Winslow, Mary 2673
Winsor, Mary 1052
Winter, Hannah 6060

Wintringham, Eliza 3691
Wintringham, John 3691, 9954
Wirehouse, Mary 3762
Wires, Susan 571
Wirt, Elizabeth Gamble 3483
Wirt, William 3483, 7068
Wisner, Asa 4320
Wisner, Elizabeth 4320
Wisner, Harrison 9957
Wisner, Julia 5454
Wisner, Moses 9957
Wiswall, Samuel 9960, 9961
Witbeck, Ann 9744
Witbeck, Christina 1455
Witherel, Elijah 5992
Witherel, Mary Jane 5992
Witherell, Elijah 5991, 8814
Witherell, Frances M. 8814
Witherell, Mary Jane 5991
Wolcott, ___ (Dr.) 9968
Wolcott, Laura Maria 7074
Wolcott, Oliver 9967
Wolden, Jacob T. 1959
Wolden, Sophia Ferris 1959
Wolf, Catherine 8020
Wolf, Elizabeth 2637
Wolfe, ___ (Gen.) 7178
Wolley, Sarah 4021
Wonderly, Sarah 5155
Wood, ___ (Mr.) 2532, 7383
Wood, Abel 9972
Wood, Abraham 9988
Wood, Aminta K. 3109
Wood, Augustus 9974
Wood, Betsey 8907
Wood, Charles 9981
Wood, Charlotte F. 6024
Wood, Comfort 1906
Wood, Elizabeth 8107
Wood, Enos 3916
Wood, Eunice 2454
Wood, George H. 2541
Wood, Isaac 1906, 5118
Wood, James 2454
Wood, Jemima 1018
Wood, John 9680
Wood, John A. 3109
Wood, Leah 2401
Wood, Letty 5118
Wood, Maria 5379
Wood, Sally 6458
Wood, Susan 4282
Wood. Willis 3916
Woodbury, Lavinia 4566
Woodcock, ___ (Mr.) 8059
Woodcock, Cornelia 3004
Woodcock, David 3004
Wooden, Catharine 9210
Woodhouse, Joseph 10005
Woodin, David G. 10007
Woodruff, ___ (Rev.) 1480
Woodruff, A. (Mr.) 10009
Woodruff, Cahrity 10010
Woodruff, Elias 512, 10010
Woodruff, Ester 9074
Woods, Abel (Rev.) 2062
Woods, Sarah J. 2062
Woodward, ___ (Mr.) 5162
Woodward, Benjamin 10018
Woodward, Delia 4341
Woodward, Eliza 9635
Woodward, Eliza Ann 575
Woodward, Maria H. 6641
Woodward, William 4341
Woodworth, Almira S. 2628
Woodworth, Asahel 10022
Woodworth, Fanny 6572
Woodworth, John 10025, 10026
Woodworth, Randal 6572, 10023

Woodworth, William 2628
Woolbridge, Louisa 1901
Woolley, Eliza 5983
Woolley, Joseph 4484
Woolley, Rebecca 4484
Woolley, Susan H. 3260
Woolley, Susannah 4345
Woolley, William I. 4021, 5983
Woolsey, Hester 2452
Woolsey, Melancton L. 932
Woolsey, Rebecca 932
Wooster, Maria C. 8909
Wooster, T. (Col.) 8909
Worden, Adeline 419
Worden, Diantha 3458
Worden, Eliza 3027
Worden, Phebe 3005
Worden, Polina 6793
Worden, Robert 10043
Workman, Benjamin 10045
Wormer, Mary Ann 9938
Wormwood, Huldah 6389
Worth, Betsey 6648
Worth, S. 4679
Worth, Sally 4679
Worth, Thomas 10046, 10047
Worthington, ___ (Gov.) 4937
Worthington, Abalina 6098
Worthington, George 10053
Worthington, John 9862, 9863
Worthington, Polly 8266
Worthington, Sarah 4937
Wray, Catherine 3480
Wright, Abel 7129
Wright, Amy 5923
Wright, Elijah 5117
Wright, Eunice 7129
Wright, Fanny 7661
Wright, Gilbert 2366
Wright, Harriet 7997
Wright, Jane 2366
Wright, Maria 4477, 7129
Wright, Mary 5117
Wright, Permelia 4414
Wright, Susan 9868
Wy--, Jennet 1954
Wyatt, Penelope 8990
Wyckoff, Cynthia 2342
Wyncoop, John C. 8979
Wyncoop, Lydia 8979
Wynkoop, ___ (Mr.) 885
Yanney, Henry 10083
Yates, ___ (Maj. Gen.) 10086
Yates, Ann 2433
Yates, J. (Miss) 6270
Yates, Jane Maria 8995
Yates, John 2423, 2433, 8995
Yates, Joseph C. 6270
Yates, Macdala 5811
Yates, Nicholas 10089
Yates, Peter W. 4943
Yates, Polly 2423
Yates, Richard 10087
Yeeh-Ah-Weeh (Miss) 4614
Yelverton, Frances Belinda 2631
Yelverton, Hannah 6162
Yeomans, Philena 7408
Yerry, Catharine 1014
Yerry, Rebecca 9613
Yoe, Charles 3772
Yoe, Jane Amelia 3772
Yost, Catharine M. 5253
Yost, Lorain H. 7549
Yost, William 5253, 7549
Youmans, Maria 7815
Youmans, Peter 7815
Young, Anna 4728
Young, Charlotte 8081
Young, Daniel 8905

Young, Eliza Ann 8905
Young, Elizabeth 6874
Young, Frances S. 10000
Young, James 269, 4614, 10000
Young, Maria 7747
Young, Mary 7499
Young, Salome P. 8293
Young, Samuel 10102, 10104
Young, William C. 6053
Younglove, John 10107
Youngs, Betsey 9234
Younie, James 5383
Younie, Mary 5383
Zander, Betsey 5539
Zieglar, Mary Wilhelmine 532

356

www.ingramcontent.com/pod-product-compliance
Lightning Source LLC
Chambersburg PA
CBHW070546270326
41926CB00013B/2217